YOU'RE THE JUDGE!

How To Understand Sports, Torts & Courts

by JOHN M. FOTIADES

E&N
EDGEWORTH & NORTH BOOKS
WORCESTER, MASSACHUSETTS

(hardcover) ISBN 0-926-565-00-1
(pbk) ISBN 0-926-565-01-x

Although the author and publisher have made every effort to insure the accuracy and completeness of information contained in this book, we assume no responsibility for errors, inaccuracies, omisssions and any inconsistencies herein. Any slights of people or organizations are unintentional. Readers should use their own judgment for application to their individual needs.

Library of Congress Cataloging in Publication Data

Fotiades, John M., 1946-
You're the judge!

Includes index.
1. Sports--Law and legislation--United States--Popular Works. 2. Liability for sports accidents--United States--Popular works. I. Title.
KF3989.Z9F67 1989 346.7303'22 89-1430
ISBN 0-926565-00-1 347.306322
ISBN 0-926565-01-X

Published by Edgeworth & North Books
Post Office Box 812
West Side Station
Worcester, Massachusetts 01602-0812
(508) 799-9860

Printed and Bound in the United States of America

DEDICATION

In loving memory of my mother, Marion.
Also to my father, Michael, with love and admiration.

IN APPRECIATION

Thanks to my wife Valla Dana, for her many hours of assistance in the research and completion of *You're The Judge!*

Thanks to Tom and Marilyn Ross and Clyde McVicar for their invaluable help with this book.

Thanks to New England School of Law and the University of Miami School of Law for the use of their libraries, and; to Richard Gibson at Nova Law School for his assistance.

Special thanks to Alex Gazonas who took my art work and illustrations and, with his unique touch, gave them life, and; to Jim Canada for his imaginative help in the book's design.

CONTENTS

ABOUT THIS BOOK 1

1 CHARIOTS & COMPLAINTS!. 7

Chariots & Complaints! traces the history of sports—as a means for man to feed and protect himself and his possessions—and the law—rules to be followed for an orderly society. This chapter explains how people's rights and the law developed, and further details both their influences on sports. Do you know how a court or a jury decides a legal dispute that comes before it?

2 AMATEURS & ELIGIBILITY 17

Amateurs & Eligibility spells out amateurs' rights and responsibilities regarding their eligibility to participate in amateur sports for their school or in other competitions. These rights and responsibilities govern both the athletes' and the schools' conduct, covering areas from recruiting and the granting of scholarships to grades, conduct and awards. What is "redshirting"? Do amateur athletes have to be well-groomed?

3 DUE PROCESS & EQUAL PROTECTION 47

Due Process & Equal Protection goes into the effect that the Fourteenth Amendment to the Constitution, and its requirements, has on the enforcement of rules and regulations by amateur athletic organizations. A sample Complaint highlights the issues that are examined. Can student-athletes be deprived of the right to an education or the right to participate in sports without the opportunity for a fair and impartial hearing? Should all athletes be treated alike?

4 DISCRIMINATION 63

Discrimination discusses attempts to discriminate or differentiate in favor or against athletes or others in sports on the basis of prejudice because of the race, sex, color or disability of the person. Are girls physiologically inferior to boys? Should girls be permitted to participate in contact sports (football) on the same team as, or against, boys?

5 ATHLETES & INJURIES 79

Athletes & Injuries discusses and comments on personal injuries to professional and amateur athletes which are caused by intentional misconduct **(assault and battery),** or by non-intentional misconduct **(negligence).** Injuries to amateur athletes may occur while they are participating for a school or other organized team, or while just playing around. There are defenses to the charges of assault and battery or negligence. In addition, this chapter covers injuries at work and those caused by extraordinary risks or conditions "not fit for play." Do injured athletes assume the risk of injury or are they guilty of contributing to their injury when they are aware of the dangers of the sport in which they are participating? Are parents responsible for the conduct of their children?

ABOUT THIS BOOK

You're The Judge! — How To Understand Sports, Torts & Courts is an indispensable book for anyone with an interest in sports, either as a participant, spectator, parent, teacher, coach, or in any of the many other ways that people are involved with sports. In easy to understand language, this book will help you interpret sports and the laws, rules and regulations that control and affect them. These same laws will apply to many similar situations that occur in everyday life.

In recent years, the law and judicial scrutiny by the courts have emerged to play a major role in controlling the affairs of sports and its activities.

Sports, with their games and contests, have been moving from the playing fields and sports arenas to a very different arena. This one is comprised not of bases, end zones and baskets, but of judges, juries and lawyers; of "Hear Ye! Hear Ye!" instead of the National Anthem; of lawsuits and damages instead of cheering and booing, and; of guilt or innocence instead of victory or defeat. Today, the issues aren't tickets, programs, snackbars or replays—but instead, complaints, legal defenses and legal decisions.

In a court of law, the stakes are higher and the play is very real. The law—decisions of courts, regulations and rules established to make it easier for us to live with one another—has been increasingly applied to sports activities in order to determine one's rights and duties. Additionally, the law determines whether or not there has been a violation of these rights or duties which caused injury to another.

You're The Judge! can be easily read, understood and enjoyed by all. It contains law for the layman, law which is not technical, but explanatory and informational. *You're The Judge!* has over 1,000 pieces of art and cartoons. This is not an attempt to make light of the seriousness of some of the cases described here, but to point out the humor in some situations.

Over 1,000 cases, each with a set of facts followed by a decision where **YOU'RE THE JUDGE!**, are presented so you can understand how the law affects sports and how to protect yourself and others. For example:

> FACTS: While attending a baseball game, you were hit in the head and injured by an errant baseball.
>
> Manny, the leftfielder for the Tiajuana Tacos, mad at having dropped a fly ball, admitted, "I threw the ball into the stands." Did you assume the risk of such an injury? Could you recover damages against Manny or his team? **YOU'RE THE JUDGE!**
>
> DECISION: Had the ball slipped, there would be no recovery. You would have assumed the risk of such an injury as being an injury common to the game of baseball. However, Manny intentionally threw the ball into the stands. His team was liable for your injury.

Occasionally, the legal decision is omitted. This may be because the case was either hypothetical to illustrate a legal point, or because there was no decision. Such cases will stimulate thought and allow you the fun of deciding the ruling or verdict on your own.

Many of the names of the plaintiffs or defendants in lawsuits have been changed to protect their privacy. The goal of the book is not to glorify or vilify athletes or others involved in sports, but to point out how the laws, rules and regulations concerning sports affect you and everyone else in everyday life.

Because of the nature of this unique reference work, you will find the same sports discussed and explored throughout all of its pages. The same legal terms and the same or similar case histories may appear more than once because they apply to and serve as examples for different situations.

In reading the case histories the reader may feel that the masculine image was overused. The simple fact is that many of the case histories involved males. Real names—when not actually used—were merely substituted with ones of the same sex and seemingly similar ethnic origins. No slights to either females or ethnic groups were intended in the choice of names and gender.

You're The Judge! begins with the history of sports and law, and shows how a legal controversy proceeds: from an injury, to a complaint, and then to a decision or settlement.

Each chapter generally concludes with an *Odds & Ends* section where miscellaneous or non-serious, comical situations are discussed, followed by a brief closing comment. Occasionally, a summary or further discussion of an important issue is presented.

How did sports and law begin? Do you know what a personal injury is? Who would be liable if you were injured by an errant ball or "slipped bat?" Who would be liable if a seat or a protective barrier was defective and, as a result, you were injured? Do you assume the risk of injury in certain situations? Can a participant be liable for an injury? What about his team, the operator of a facility, a manufacturer of sports equipment, a teacher, coach, school, city, or a property owner? If you are injured during a lunchtime game at work, is your employer liable?

Do you know what a "redshirt" is? Do you know how an athlete's eligibility is determined or can be affected by outside activities, such as by accepting gifts or money, or by transferring to another school? What's a nuisance? Libel? Slander? Is discrimination permitted in sports? What's a conspiracy or monopoly? Who decides what unsportsmanlike conduct is? How are "wars" between leagues settled? Are you entitled to privacy? Are athletes entitled to equal protection? Can you waive your rights to recover damages for any injury you received? Can you be denied admission to a sports event even if you have a ticket?

FACTS: You left your car at a parking lot while attending a baseball game; it was stolen. You left your tennis racket at a repair shop and it was destroyed in a fire. Who would be liable?

DECISION: **YOU'RE THE JUDGE!**

You're The Judge! answers all of these questions and many, many more concerning any involvement in sports by participants, spectators and others. Many of these situations concern the small guy or fan, the one who is hit by a ball, injured at an autorace, hurt in a high school game or practice, or injured in a pick-up game.

Sports, both amateur and professional, have become big business. Because of television and masses of spectators, professional athletes (after successful collegiate careers) now command and receive lucrative contracts.

This increased financial stake for players, as well as for schools, teams, leagues, cities and others, has provided an increased concern about decisions affecting these parties. Therefore, when misfortune occurs, those aggrieved will more likely resort to the courts. In turn, this has led to significant changes both in the law as it affects sports and in how amateur and professional sports are conducted and played.

This book covers laws, rules and regulations as they affect participation in any sport. And it covers other than participants—such as spectators, parents, schools, cities, manufacturers, promoters, officials, operators of sports facilities, doctors, the media, owners, teams, coaches, instructors, landowners and many others involved with sports.

You're The Judge! does not have to be read from front to back, although you can. It is meant to serve as a sort of encyclopedia of sports and law where you can read about those topics that presently interest you most. It is a vast storehouse of information that can be referred to as needed or desired. As topics come up from reading the sports page or a magazine, from watching TV, or from participating in or watching a sport, you can then find that topic and read about it.

These days you almost have to be a lawyer to interpret the sports page. Instead of just reading about the home team's chances for the upcoming season, or of nostalgic stories about teams or players past, you now read of contract negotiations, strikes, law suits, arbitration awards.

FACTS: Why is understanding the law and rules and regulations concerning sports so important? **YOU'RE THE JUDGE!**

DECISION: Because it affects the lives, occupations, safety and enjoyment of almost everyone, whether or not you or your children or friends participate in or just watch sports.

Sports and its legal implications affect everyone: from the ticket taker to the sports facility construction workers, from the athletes to those who benefit from their contributions. Those who support teams by buying tickets, cities and schools who take part in and benefit from the revenue that sports generates, manufacturers who make sports equipment, and those responsible for protecting participants and spectators from injury are also affected. So are those who promote, officiate and control sports events, those who care for the injured, those who set up rules and regulate participation in and admittance to sports events, and those who interpret and enforce such rules, regulations and the law as they relate to sports.

Many legal and other important words and terms (in bold) are defined and discussed as they appear. To locate these, see the page reference in *Words & Terms* or the *Index*. These words and terms and others used generally throughout *You're The Judge!* are defined in *Words & Terms*. Every attempt has been made to present information and terms in a way which will be clearly understood. If a term requiring defining appears elsewhere in another chapter, such as negligence or the defense of assumption of the risk, then the term is again discussed and illustrated. There is no need to refer elsewhere.

FACTS: What law applies to sports? Is it different from other law? What is the law's purpose? **YOU'RE THE JUDGE!**

DECISION: The law that applies to sports is the same everyday law that is applied to other similar situations. The same law applies to personal injuries whether it involves someone in an auto accident or fight or to an athlete or spectator hit by a participant.

Law consists of the entire body of principals that govern conduct and the observance of which can be enforced in court. The purpose of the law is to provide order, stability and justice—to inform everyone of their rights and duties concerning the interaction between themselves and others—and to change as the needs and values of society change.

Although the principles upon which all laws are founded are the same, laws may vary from state to state depending on a particular state's needs. Federal laws will be the same no matter where applied.

However, even where it may appear that the facts are the same or quite similar, a different decision may be reached for a number of reasons. For example, a jury, court or other tribunal (such as an arbitrator) may interpret or weigh evidence or facts differently, or the witnesses or presentation of the facts or evidence may sway others to reach a different verdict. And one state or locale may find certain behavior more or less tolerable than another.

Any decision or information given in *You're The Judge!* is not intended to be a substitute for proper legal or other advice. This book does not, nor can it, guarantee similar results, for the reasons stated above. It is suggested that you use the book as an informational guide only; then seek out competent legal or other advice as necessary.

ENJOY!

1

CHARIOTS & COMPLAINTS!

WHAT'S IT ABOUT?

Chariots & Complaints! traces the history of sports—as a means for man to feed and protect himself and his possessions—and the law—rules to be followed for an orderly society.

This chapter explains how people's rights and these laws developed, and further details both their influences on sports. Do you know how a court or a jury decides a legal dispute that comes before it?

1500 B.C.

Pre-Historic News

UGH!

Long before the Olympic Games, **sports**—from the Latin word desport meaning to carry away, or a diversion or amusement—began as a religious cult and in preparation for life. Its roots were in man's desire to protect himself and his tribe, crops, cattle and territory.

For self-defense, man learned to "run and jump, to project spears by hand and later by bow, and also to defend himself by what is now called wrestling, judo or boxing." New sports evolved, not from this early training, but from the basic need for existence and not as a diversion or a pastime.

Most importantly though, sports began as a "rite to ensure productive crops by the return of the rains, sun and favorable winds."

Competing groups represented the earth and the heavens. And as no one would dare cheat or challenge the gods, referees were unnecessary.

When, in Egypt and Mesopotamia, self-preservation ceased to be man's constant preoccupation, sports became more of an avocation.

SPORTS & LAW

The Olympic Games, which began in 776 B.C., were governed by special laws—sets of rules to be followed as a means to an orderly society—subject to penalties meant to preserve peace and guard the honor of the Games.

Athletes and trainers swore by Zeus to "obey the rules and compete fairly." And as Zeus was a terrible and avenging God, competitors generally obeyed. If they did not, penalties consisting of exclusion from the Games, fines and flogging were imposed. Judges' power was nearly absolute. Whipbearers kept order amongst the spectators and peddlers.

FACTS: The Olympia Women's Club decided that they wanted to attend and compete in the Olympic Games. Several women wanted to compete in the foot races. Was this permitted? **YOU'RE THE JUDGE!**

DECISION: Most women, at least until late in the pre-Christian era, were not only prohibited from competing, but under penalty of death, were prohibited from even attending the Olympics!

Footraces were the first events at the Olympics. Later boxing, chariot and horse races, wrestling and other events were added.

FACTS: The year was 706 B.C. You were at the Olympics, at the stadium in the sacred city of Olympia, Greece, built in honor of the Greek God, Zeus. You went to see the foot and chariot races and other sporting events.

You explained what happened next, "It was a beautiful day... but not for long. As the first chariots and their warriors, with all their metal gleaming in the bright sun, passed in front of the viewing stands, there was a thunderous crash. Chariot parts flew through the air, striking me and breaking my nose." What were your rights? Could you recover damages for your injury?

DECISION: **YOU'RE THE JUDGE!**

Boxing, the most brutal of the sports, was ferocious. Blood was encouraged by the spectators. Death was a certain risk to the boxers!

FACTS: Igor and "Max the Ax" squared off for the Mediterranean Boxing Championship.

The referee explained what happened, "In the third round, Igor went down from a hard right. Max was the winner. But as Igor attempted to regain his feet, Max again began to pummel the defenseless Igor. Max killed him." Did Igor assume the risk of such an injury? Could Igor's family recover damages from Max? **YOU'RE THE JUDGE!**

DECISION: There was no right to sue for injuries, let alone recover damages. When death came to one of the participants, the offender—although not jailed—was required by law to make amends to the bereaved family by the payment of "blood money."

Although the world relied on the Code of Hammurabi and, from 1200 B.C., the Ten Commandments, these laws dealt mostly with criminal matters. They did not allow for the obtaining of relief or

monetary damages for personal injuries.

In 450 B.C., the Romans published The Twelve Tables, a set of moral principles and practices. However, their influence did not reach the Olympic Games.

By 146 B.C., when Greece was conquered by the Romans, the Olympic Games no longer bore any meaningful relationship to the values that athletics had represented to the ancient Greeks.

Hellenic News

Summer 144 B.C.

BLOOD & BRUTALITY!

"Events were staged to satisfy the crowd's thirst for blood and brutality. Athletes were not chosen from amongst native-born sons of proven virtue. But instead, gladiators were criminals, or slaves from conquered lands. Their reward for fighting and winning was freedom, but only if they pleased the crowd with bravery and skill.

The Games consisted of contests between unarmed combatants and also with unfed lions. Friends and brothers fought to the death, only to be spared if the tyrant saw fit to withhold the arbitrary gesture of 'thumbs down!'

The Olympic Games and gladiator contests ended as Christianity was establishing itself in Rome. For centuries to come, sports was looked upon as a symbol of religious decay."

Around 560 A.D., all laws were brought together into a Body of Civil Laws. The most complete collection of laws to that time, this had an enormous influence on the development of law. As the Roman Empire gradually fell apart, much of the Roman law became the canon law of the Catholic Church.

The English began developing their own legal system after the invasion by the Normans in 1066. They won their basic rights in the Magna Charta from King John in 1215, and for the rest of their rights, a system began to develop which would later become the foundation for modern American law.

Common Law & The Jury

FACTS: Long before the English, the Greeks tried legal cases before citizens whom we now call a jury. These juries, together with early courts and occasionally from acts of Parliament, began to make what was called common law. What is a jury? What was the common law? **YOU'RE THE JUDGE!**

DECISION: A **jury** is a "group of people selected to hear evidence and decide the matter before them." **Common law** was law developed from "custom, tradition, decisions by judges and juries and from acts of Parliament."

By the 14th century, underground popularity for sports spread This was so, even against laws (especially in England) created to make the playing of certain sports illegal. People began to see sports as a "way to fill leisure time and obtain some measure of importance."

Although at this time, participation in sports was frowned upon, laws pertaining to the playing of sports were now beginning to emerge. These laws, combined with the emerging common law, now gave an injured participant or spectator at least an opportunity to seek damages for injuries or other wrongs.

FACTS: Shawn was injured during a boxing match. He complained, "My opponent, Jake, attacked me from behind before the fight started." Although no one, as yet, had thought of suing to recover for such injuries, suppose Shawn sued, alleging that Jake intentionally violated the rules. "Could I recover?" asked Shawn. **YOU'RE THE JUDGE!**

DECISION: Although Shawn may have been permitted to bring an action, there was not, as yet, any law permitting recovery.

The common law developed in England would become the single most important root of the American legal system. It would become two different kinds of law: **case law**—that law based on earlier court decisions (precedents), and; **statutory law**—that law which comes from written acts of federal, state, or local legislation.

Puritans in early Massachusetts sought to limit participation in sports by the colonists. Again, religion played a major role. The Sabbath was strictly enforced and religious conformity was fostered. Laws passed in the 1600's were designed to "ensure obedience, prevent drinking, gambling and other conduct which would weaken the morals of society." Sports were promoted to fulfill military training needs.

Do you know what "blue laws" are?

FACTS: The Puritans sought to control sports by the enactment of Sunday **"blue laws"**—laws regulating religious and personal conduct. The colonists wanted to "play baseball on Sunday afternoons, our only day off from work." Were they allowed to play? **YOU'RE THE JUDGE!**

DECISION: The blue laws specified which sports were legal, and that any such sports were to be played without disturbing other people or their property.

Playing areas, out of the general public's way, had not yet been well defined. Certain sports, such as baseball, were prohibited in public. Later, when the blue laws were amended, recreation, as well as baseball, was allowed in municipal parks on Sunday.

In 1776, with the advent of the Declaration of Independence, an entirely new legal system had to be developed. This led to the U .S. Constitution in 1789, which—along with its amendments (Bill of Rights) and state constitutions—became the principal source of individual rights. Certain other basic rights were derived from the old English common law.

From this new constitution evolved the basic rights of the opportunity for an aggrieved person to be heard, and the right to a jury trial.

Should I Sue?

Into the 1960's, if participants received injuries from competing in sports, they just didn't sue. It wasn't the thing to do.

But, as people became more conscious of their rights, and as the courts began to hand down decisions in favor of those injured, attitudes changed.

FACTS: Tommy was injured by a "late hit" during a high school football game. He sued, charging, "I wouldn't have been hurt if the tackle was proper."

The opposing player and school defended, "Tommy assumed the risk of injury from conduct which was part of the game of football." Could Tommy recover for his injury? **YOU'RE THE JUDGE!**

DECISION: Although Tommy assumed the risk of injury from ordinary risks of the game, such as a proper tackle, he did not assume the risk of injury from an intentional "late hit," as was encouraged by the opposing coach to intimidate players. Tommy could recover damages for his injury.

The awareness that negligent conduct might lead to liability brought about dramatic changes in sports, such as improved safety in equipment, supervision, facilities and medical care, and in laws protecting participants, spectators and the public from negligent conduct.

FACTS: After being injured by that flying chariot wheel, you left the stadium and saw a healer. He said, "You'll always have pain and a scar from your injury."

Suppose that the present judicial system was in place back in 706 B.C., what would have been the **procedure**—process for enforcing rights and seeking redress—for seeking damages for your injury?

DECISION: **YOU'RE THE JUDGE!**

Plan of Attack

Arbitration—process where a dispute is submitted to an impartial party for resolution—will not be used. You will seek relief through the court, leaving open the possibility of a **settlement**—agreement settling the matter without the further need for a decision by the court.

Depending on the type of action, parties involved, amount in dispute, and other matters, you might file a complaint in either a federal, state or local court.

To help in explaining the civil process, assume that Greece was a state in this country and present-day law ruled.

Complaint & Summons

You filed a **complaint**—document setting forth the facts on which you base your claim for relief. You named Yani (the driver of the chariot), Mikali (the owner of the chariot and sponsor of the race), and Greco (the manufacturer of the chariot), as **defendants**—persons against whom your complaint is brought. You, as the complaining party bringing the action, are the **plaintiff.**

FACTS: In part, your complaint alleged, "Each of the defendants—Yani, Mikali, and Greco—breached their duty to insure my safety. As a result of their breaches, I was injured. What court should I file my complaint in? " **YOU'RE THE JUDGE!**

DECISION: The **small claims court**—which handles claims below a specified monetary limit and where, generally, a lawyer is not needed—is out as your claim will exceed its limit. If the defendants were residents of states different from the one in which you lived, **diversity of citizenship** would exist and you might bring this action in the federal court.

However, assuming all of the defendants lived in your state, then the **jurisdiction**—power of the court to hear and adjudicate your claim—will be in the state court. The **venue**—geographical place where you filed the complaint—will be the county where you live.

Your complaint was served on the defendants—Yani, Mikali, and Greco—by way of a **summons**—written order requiring the defendants to answer the complaint against them.

Answer & Defenses

The defendants all filed an **answer**—document answering a complaint, and containing any denial and listing any defenses.

They contended, "You were never injured. But, if you were, we're not negligent."—**general denial.** "You assumed the risk of,

and contributed to, your injury by attending the Games and sitting in a seat too close to the track."—**specific denial.**

Mikali alleged, "I didn't know of Yani's reckless driving."

"We were not negligent in making the chariot," Greco added.

If you had violated the **Statute of Limitations**—statute limiting the time in which an action must be brought—or had unreasonably delayed filing the complaint to the detriment of a defendant—**laches,** then the defendants might have asserted either of these as a defense.

Also, the defendants could make motions regarding the correctness of the complaint, jurisdiction, or possibly for a more definite statement or explanation of your complaint. They might also include in their answer any **counterclaims**—claims that they might have against you. Possibly, you owed one of them money. What next?

Discovery!

FACTS: How would you go about discovering and obtaining evidence to use in presenting your case to the court—**discovery? YOU'RE THE JUDGE!**

DECISION: Discovery may consist of **depositions**—testimony of a witness recorded outside of the court for use at trial.

You may want to ask Yani questions such as, "Is that how you always drive?"; to Mikali, "Were you aware of Yani's reputation as a driver?" or; to Greco, "Did you know of the ease with which the chariot would fall apart?"

You might want to have an engineer inspect the chariot or the stadium racecourse.

Some of these **interrogatories** could be taken at the trial, but it simplifies the trial and lessens the time needed—as well as takes out any element of suprise—when answers have been obtained before trial and there is an opportunity to check into the validity of any information given.

To discover your injuries, the defendants could request that you submit to a medical examination. You will also have a report from your own doctor.

Trial

If a settlement cannot be reached then a trial, which may be some time in coming, will follow.

Voir dire—the method by which a jury is selected—is conducted after a case has been called and the parties are present and ready to proceed.

The right to a jury trial is guaranteed by the Constitution but may be waived, thus allowing the court—through the judge—to make a decision based upon the facts of the case.

FACTS: Because you brought the action, it is your job, through your attorney, to persuade the court of the merits of your case. You bear the burden of proof. How convincing does your evidence have to be for you to recover? **YOU'RE THE JUDGE!**

DECISION: It is your duty in a civil case (as opposed to a criminal case) to establish the truth of your claim by a clear "preponderance of the credible evidence"—that is, by presenting evidence having a more convincing effect on the jury than does the defendant's.

Your attorney makes his **opening statement** to the court—telling of your injuries and that he will prove that the defendants are all guilty of **negligence**—a breach of their duty to care for your safety—which breach caused your injury and damages.

The defendants (each with their own attorney) present their opening statements. They all deny any negligence and tell what their evidence will later prove.

Each side now presents its case to the court. You go first. Your attorney calls his witnesses—fellow spectators who witnessed the accident, your doctor, the engineer, and you. The engineer presents the physical evidence showing how the chariot wheel was defectively manufactured. Can your witnesses be cross-examined?

FACTS: The defendants' attorneys may **cross-examine**—ask questions of your witnesses—after they testify. What may they question your witnesses about? **YOU'RE THE JUDGE!**

DECISION: They must restrict their questions to the coverage of the original testimony by your witnesses.

Next, the defendants present their cases, calling their own doctor, engineer and themselves. They attempt to refute your testimony and show they are not negligent. You also have the opportunity to cross-examine their witnesses.

Now, assuming that there is no **rebuttal**—reexamination of your witnesses in an attempt to refute their testimony—or that any motions for summary judgment without further evidence, mistrial or dismissal of the case have been denied, then, you are ready for your **closing statement.**

Your attorney summarizes to the court what he feels he has proved and then asks the court "to find for us in an amount that you feel is just and necessary."

Of course, the defendants tell the jury "The plaintiffs have not proven their case and, therefore, should not recover any damages."

Burden of Proof

The court then instructs the jury on: what the law is regarding negligence; the **burden of proof**—your duty to prove those facts necessary to win a judgment by a clear preponderance of the credible evidence; and the rules to be followed in deciding the case.

The jury then deliberates until it has reached a **verdict**—decision by court or jury of issues—and finds for a party on each issue submitted to them by the court.

The losing party may, with certain restrictions, appeal any decision. Any appeal will extend the time necessary to complete the procedure from the filing of a complaint to a final decision.

ODDS & ENDS....

You versus Yani, Mikali & Greco - Could You Recover?

FACTS: Your complaint alleged in part:

"While I was attending the chariot races, the defendant, Yani, negligently drove and crashed his chariot, causing me severe and permanent injuries.

The owner of the chariot, Mikali, was negligent in that he was aware of Yani's propensity for reckless driving, but made no effort to prevent such driving.

Greco was negligent in the manufacturing of the chariot. Had he taken proper precautions, the wheel would not have come off and injured me."

The complaint also alleged that Greco had been notified of several other crashes of his defective chariots.

The stadium had no wire screening to protect spectators from flying debris. Could you recover damages for your injuries? **YOU'RE THE JUDGE!**

DECISION: "The defendants are all negligent," the court held. "They breached their duty to insure your safety: Yani by driving recklessly, Mikali by fostering such reckless driving (and further by not constructing proper screening to protect the spectators), and Greco by manufacturing defective chariots."

The defendants' breaches caused your injuries and damages. That is, you would not have received the injuries but for their negligence. You were awarded damages for your pain and suffering, medical expenses and lost pay from missing work due to the injuries.

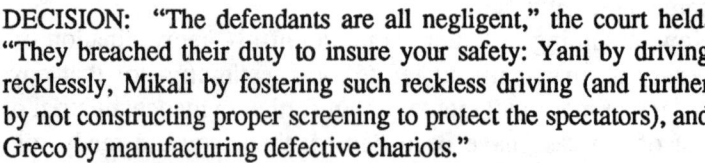

You now have a basic understanding of how a legal dispute or controversy winds its way through the legal system.

2

AMATEURS & ELIGIBILITY

WHAT'S IT ABOUT?

Amateurs & Eligibility spells out amateurs' rights and responsibilities regarding their eligibility to participate in amateur sports for their school or in other competitions.

These rights and responsibilities govern both the athletes' and the schools' conduct, covering areas from recruiting and the granting of scholarships to grades, conduct and awards. What is "redshirting?" Do amateur athletes have to be well-groomed?

Podunk University
1211 University Drive
Justice, Georgia 22220
Member NCAA

Dear Student-Athletes:

Congratulations! You've been accepted to Podunk University, home of the "Fighting Wabaws."

As recent changes in the law have made amateur sports increasingly subject to judicial scrutiny, it is important that you become aware of your rights and responsibilities.

In the past, amateur sports were more recreational in nature. Now, due to television and the increased attraction by spectators and participants, amateur sports have become "big business." Although amateur sports and money are not supposed to mix, money does have a definite effect upon your future and your rights.

If you are successful in athletics, prosperity may lie ahead in pro sports, however slim the chance. Thus, you have a significant financial stake in the decisions and events affecting your eligibility.

Therefore, in order to protect your rights, you should be aware of amateur status and eligibility. For more information, refer to your college's manual or to the rules of your high school athletic association.

Best of Luck,

President, Podunk University

WHAT IS AN AMATEUR?

The International Olympic Committee (IOC) states that an athlete, to be an **amateur**—"must pursue athletic activity as an 'avocation' (hobby), not as a 'vocation' (occupation), and must engage in sports solely for the educational, physical, mental, and social benefits obtained." Simply put, the athlete must compete for fun, not for pay.

FACTS: Jim Thorpe competed in the 1912 Olympic Games, winning gold medals in the pentathlon and decathlon events. Two years earlier he had competed, for pay, in a semi-pro baseball league. Should Thorpe have been ruled a professional and "stripped " of his medals? **YOU'RE THE JUDGE!**

DECISION: Thorpe was stripped of his medals for having competed while a professional.

In 1985, the IOC restored Thorpe's medals to his family. This was due, in part, to the fading distinction—in the eligibility rules for Olympic athletes—between an amateur and a professional.

Professionals are now allowed to compete in some Olympic competitions.

This could signal the end of the rule holding that an athlete is ineligible to take part in amateur sports "if he enters into a contract or agreement to compete as a professional athlete."

Some amateur athletes, including Olympic hopefuls, may now receive funds for traveling, training and living expenses, as well as for product endorsements. Some of the funds are placed in trust until the athletes no longer compete as amateurs.

The National Collegiate Athletic Association (NCAA) definition of an amateur differs from that of the IOC in several respects.

The NCAA permits athletes to compete professionally in one sport and yet retain their amateur status in others.

This change would have allowed Thorpe to compete as a professional in baseball, but still retain his amateur status in track and field.

FACTS: Al and Babe were professional baseball players while attending Sports U. (where they wanted to play tennis and golf). Could they compete with or against amateurs? **YOU'RE THE JUDGE!**

DECISION: These professional student-athletes can compete with or against amateurs in both intercollegiate tennis and golf, but not in baseball.

None of these definitions of an amateur, however, are binding upon the courts in deciding cases relating to amateur athletics.

THE NCAA

The National Collegiate Athletic Association (NCAA), a voluntary organization of almost all major colleges and universities, was formed in 1906 to regulate and supervise collegiate athletics in the U.S.

The most powerful of the associations regulating college athletics, the NCAA is divided into three divisions (based in part upon the school's or its athletic facility's size). All divisions are subject to NCAA rules and regulations governing education and athletics in their division.

The rules cover admittance requirements, academic standing and recruiting and eligibility. They also provide for enforcement and sanctions.

FACTS: "I was improperly recruited to attend Ames U," confessed Joe. Could Joe, the school, or both be penalized? If so, what penalties? **YOU'RE THE JUDGE!**

DECISION: The rules apply to schools as well as to athletes. Sanctions to the athlete may be temporary or permanent ineligibility. Sanctions to the school may be: probation, loss of television appearances, forfeit of television or post-season proceeds or a loss of scholarships.

In addition, any school (on probation for violations in a sport) which is found guilty of additional violations in that sport within five years will be given the **"death penalty"**—they may have to drop that sport for a minimum of two years.

Ames U. was prohibited from giving football scholarships and playing football for one year. In addition, they could only play road games during the second year, and were banned from post-season play for two years.

LET'S HAVE A CONFERENCE

Although collegiate conferences, such as the Athletic College Conference (ACC) or Big Ten, generally have rules and regulations that are the same as, or similar to, those of the NCAA to which they belong, such rules may differ.

FACTS: Bubba Jackson, a star collegiate football player, accepted an airplane ride from a pro football team interested in drafting him. According to his college conference's rules, this made Jackson a professional. He was declared ineligible to compete for the school's baseball team.

The NCAA permits a college athlete to be a pro in one sport

while competing as an amateur in another. Could Jackson continue to play for the college baseball team? **YOU'RE THE JUDGE!**

DECISION: No. A student-athlete must abide by his school's conference rules as well as those of the NCAA. Jackson could not play on the college baseball team.

SCHOLARSHIPS

Typically, student-athletes receive **financial aid**—school funds such as scholarships, grants, loans or on-campus work—over which the school has some determining authority.

Scholarships are awarded on a one-year basis and are renewable for up to four years. Renewal is not automatic, but is based upon athletic and educational performance. Exceptions relate to academic awards and some loans. Prospective student-athletes may be denied an athletic scholarship unless they meet certain minimum academic standards.

Generally, the amount of financial aid a student-athlete may receive without jeopardizing his eligibility is based upon the total amount necessary for tuition and fees, room and board and required books and materials.

Student-athletes are prohibited from receiving financial aid other than from the school (boosters), if it is related to athletic ability or participation. This prohibition does not apply to any earnings as a pro in a sport other than the athlete's college sport.

FACTS: "I was offered money from a local booster club to help pay expenses for attending and playing football for Aztec U," admitted E.Z. Smith. "The help was offered because of my athletic ability." If E.Z. accepted the money, would it jeopardize his eligibility as a student-athlete? **YOU'RE THE JUDGE!**

DECISION: Yes. This would be aid based upon athletic ability other than from the school. E.Z. would be ineligible to compete as an amateur.

A major difference exists between the IOC and the NCAA regarding financial aid.

FACTS: Bob received financial aid from his college in return for playing football. If he became ineligible or left the sport for personal reasons, the aid could be cancelled.

Bob quit the football team and asked, "If I decide to prepare for the shotput for the upcoming Olympics, will I have an eligibility problem? " **YOU'RE THE JUDGE!**

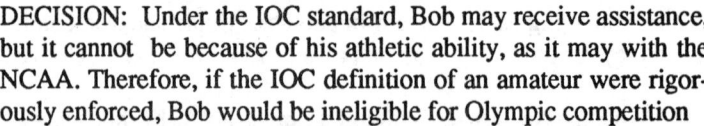

DECISION: Under the IOC standard, Bob may receive assistance, but it cannot be because of his athletic ability, as it may with the NCAA. Therefore, if the IOC definition of an amateur were rigorously enforced, Bob would be ineligible for Olympic competition

Therefore, even though the IOC now allows certain professionals to compete in some Olympic sports, an aspiring Olympic athlete should insure that his financial aid arrangement is structured to resemble an educational grant, with receipt dependent upon fulfillment of scholastic obligations, not athletic ability.

Could the way athletic scholarships are viewed by the courts present a problem?

FACTS: A prospective college basketball player, "Hoops," was awarded an athletic scholarship. It was withdrawn, however, when the college learned that his high school grade point average was miscalculated, thus making him ineligible for the scholarship under NCAA rules.

Another high school athlete, Marston, was also awarded a college athletic scholarship. It too, was revoked after Marston—who originally did not participate because of low grades—raised his grades but then did not report for football.

Hoops and Marston sued their colleges. "We would like to keep the scholarships," they declared. "Receiving them was not contingent on our being able to play basketball or football. Can we keep our scholarships?" **YOU'RE THE JUDGE!**

DECISION: The courts treated the relationship between the athletes and their schools as contracts (agreements)—the schools would award the scholarships if the athletes played. Because the athletes could not live up to their agreements to play, they were denied the scholarships.

If the scholarship is treated as a contract—where the athlete must participate in return for the consideration of the scholarship—then the athlete may be considered to be playing the sport as a vocation (occupation) rather than as an avocation (hobby), thus jeopardizing amateur status!

FACTS: Tony and Dan received scholarships to attend Quinsigamond U. The scholarships were contingent upon the athletes' athletic performance for the school's football team.

A new tax ruling held that the total amount of the scholarships, including room and board, must be considered income for tax purposes. Will this make Tony and Dan pros for receiving money to play football? Will they lose their amateur status?

DECISION: **YOU'RE THE JUDGE!**

If the courts treated these arrangements as educational grants, the grant would be viewed as a gift, under the condition that the athlete maintain eligibility, but without the risk of loss of amateur status.

YOU'RE THE JUDGE!

FACTS: The players and coaches of the Correcto University badminton team did not file disclosure affidavits listing all financial aid and benefits received—from the school or others—and also listing anything promised to them. Were the players and the school declared ineligible for the NCAA championships? **YOU'RE THE JUDGE!**

DECISION: Yes, both were declared ineligible. The affidavits help the NCAA make sure that schools comply with financial aid rules. Individual athletes or a team will lose their eligibility if they or their head coach fail to complete the affidavits.

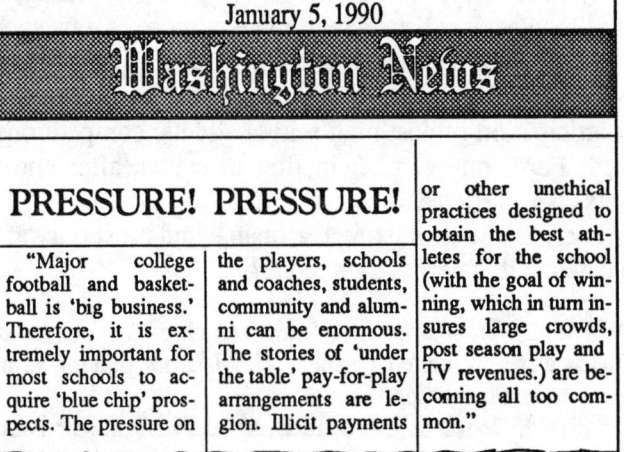

January 5, 1990

Washington News

PRESSURE! PRESSURE!

"Major college football and basketball is 'big business.' Therefore, it is extremely important for most schools to acquire 'blue chip' prospects. The pressure on the players, schools and coaches, students, community and alumni can be enormous. The stories of 'under the table' pay-for-play arrangements are legion. Illicit payments or other unethical practices designed to obtain the best athletes for the school (with the goal of winning, which in turn insures large crowds, post season play and TV revenues.) are becoming all too common."

The acceptance of prohibited benefits by college athletes has led to frequent instances of a loss of eligibility to participate for the athlete and suspension for the school.

YOU'RE THE JUDGE!

FACTS: Davis was thrown off his college football team for accepting money from boosters. As he no longer was eligible to play amateur football, could Davis immediately play as a pro? **YOU'RE THE JUDGE!**

DECISION: The National Football League's (NFL)"Red Grange Rule" prohibited Davis from playing both collegiate and pro football in the same season.

One case is somewhat different from the normal situation. This is where an athlete or prospective player accepts aid in the form of money or otherwise.

FACTS: "Skates," while playing "amateur" hockey in Canada, accepted compensation for three years while in high school, and also for two years between high school and college. Was he ineligible to play in college? **YOU'RE THE JUDGE!**

DECISION: Skates was ineligible. Compensation for the two years between high school and college was not in connection with his obtaining an education. This may mean that had he not accepted the pay for the intervening two years, he would have been eligible, as the other three years pay was in conjunction with his obtaining an education.

NON-APPROVED CAMPS

Rules denying eligibility to athletes participating in events not approved by their school (summer camps or clinics) will generally be upheld as long as they have a legitimate purpose. A few such purposes include: preventing undesirable consequences (exploiting the athlete) or promoting academics and equal opportunity for all athletes. Thus, participation in post high school athletic competitions must be approved. Furthermore, participation in events after enrollment in college is also restricted.

However, the rules must be reasonable and must only affect those whose conduct it is necessary to control.

FACTS: To prevent athletes from receiving pay for playing, all athletes were prohibited by their schools from playing in all-star games, unless given permission.

Jorn said, "Without approval, I played in an all-star basketball game to raise money for charity."

Ray played in an all-star baseball game, attended summer camp where baseball clinics were held and played in a summer basketball league. Were Jorn and Ray still eligible to play as amateurs? **YOU'RE THE JUDGE!**

DECISION: Jorn would probably still be eligible as it may be unreasonable to prevent him from playing in a charity event. Ray would lose his eligibility if he had not been approved to participate in his activities.

FACTS: Tom was a member of his school's hockey team. A school rule read: Students may not "participate in hockey during the off-season, attend non-approved camps or clinics or participate on independent hockey teams."

Tom wanted to play on such a team. He contended, "The rule is unreasonable. It denies me my constitutional right to equal protection—that is, to be treated like the others who will be permitted to play." Was the rule unreasonable? **YOU'RE THE JUDGE!**

DECISION: The rule was not unreasonable. Tom could become a member of an approved hockey team, or he could attend an approved camp or clinic.

FACTS: Several parents challenged a rule suspending varsity athletes for attending "special" summer camps. They claimed, "The rule's objective of fostering interschool competitions as an aid in the preparation for life, interferes with our authority in child rearing, family choice, private life and right to send our children to camp." Could the parents send their children to camp? **YOU'RE THE JUDGE!**

DECISION: No. The rule was reasonable. It did not interfere with parents sending their children to camps giving an over-all activity program, but only restricted attendance at those camps specializing in football or basketball.

The purpose of the rule was to control over-zealous parents, teachers and coaches and to achieve competitive balance with those who could not attend and to avoid undue pressure on the students.

HOW LONG MAY I PLAY?

To prevent schools from retaining athletes until they are either needed, or have matured athletically, certain rules restricting the time within which an athlete is eligible to compete (generally to four years in high school) exist. The object of such rules is to prevent **"redshirting"**—the intentional retention or keeping back of athletes.

Such rules may only apply to students who want excess eligibility in order to continue participating athletically.

FACTS: John passed the eighth grade. But because his parents felt their son was not ready for the ninth grade, he was forced to repeat the eighth.

After competing for the school football team in the ninth-eleventh grades, John was declared ineligible. He wanted to play, and asked the the court to "allow me." What was the court's decision? What if John had failed the eighth grade? What if he had dropped out of school to help his family overcome a desperate financial problem? **YOU'RE THE JUDGE!**

DECISION: A rule providing that a student repeating a grade which he has passed loses his fourth year of eligibility in high school would be upheld.

However, if John had failed the eighth grade, he then would not lose his fourth year of eligibility. But John could not compete the first semester after failing. This "forced" time off would allow him time to study. And if John had dropped out of school to help his family, the rule probably would not be applied to deny his competing after four years.

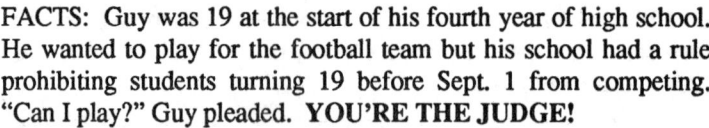

FACTS: Guy was 19 at the start of his fourth year of high school. He wanted to play for the football team but his school had a rule prohibiting students turning 19 before Sept. 1 from competing. "Can I play?" Guy pleaded. **YOU'RE THE JUDGE!**

DECISION: No. As long as such a rule has a legitimate purpose related to the school's interest in assuring fair competition and minimizing the risk of having its high school athletes compete against older, more skilled athletes, it will be enforced.

Maturity may also be considered in deciding eligibility. Some states have eligibility standards which allow students with "advanced, or slower, rates of maturity" to compete at team levels best suited to their stage of maturity. This allows certain students to play above or below their age group. It may also extend their period of eligibility.

REDSHIRTING & HARDSHIP

Redshirting—the intentional retention or keeping back of athletes—is a practice also used by most colleges. The NCAA allows this practice under what is called the "five-year rule." This may be done solely to allow an athlete to continue to compete for the school.

FACTS: Andy was a promising freshman quarterback, but the team already had Peter, a potential All-American. Could Andy be redshirted for his freshman year—making it possible for him to spend his first year on scholarship without playing—and then, still have four years eligibility remaining? **YOU'RE THE JUDGE!**

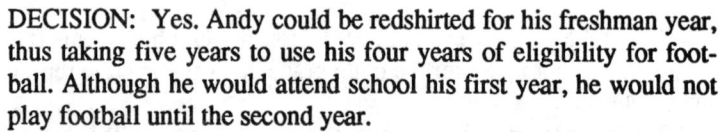

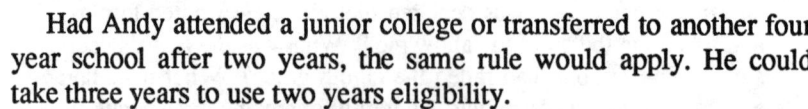

DECISION: Yes. Andy could be redshirted for his freshman year, thus taking five years to use his four years of eligibility for football. Although he would attend school his first year, he would not play football until the second year.

Had Andy attended a junior college or transferred to another four year school after two years, the same rule would apply. He could take three years to use two years eligibility.

A student-athlete may be granted an additional year of eligibility for reasons of hardship (unless the athlete had been redshirted), such as an incapacity resulting from an injury or illness. The injury or illness, as long as it occurs after the athlete has reported for team practice, does not have to result from athletics. It could, for instance, happen while the athlete was working or while just walking across campus.

FACTS: "I broke my toe," moaned Frank. He was injured in the sixth football game of an eleven game schedule.

"I fractured my ankle," groaned Tom. He was injured in the fifth game of a twenty-seven game basketball schedule.

Both would not play for the remainder of that season. Could either of them ask for a hardship ruling, and thereby retain that year of eligibility? **YOU'RE THE JUDGE!**

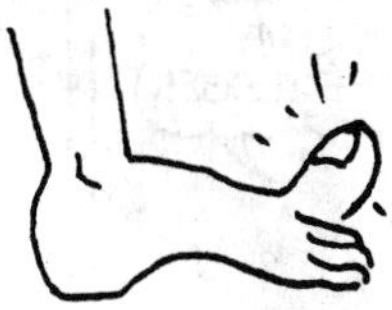

DECISION: If Frank or Tom had not played in more than 20% of their teams games (including scrimmages with outside competition), or had not played in more than two events, whichever figure was greater, and the injury or illness occurred in the first half of the season, then hardship would apply.

The sixth game would leave five remaining. Therefore, Frank's injury occurred in the second half of the season. He could not be granted hardship.

Tom's injury occurred in the first half of the season and he had not played in 20% of his teams games (20% of twenty-seven games equals the sixth game). Tom could apply for hardship to save that year's eligibility.

"BONA FIDE" TRANSFERS

Students transferring between high schools or colleges are subject to rules generally requiring that residency requirements and grades be considered. These rules are designed to discourage ill-advised transfers and prevent improper recruiting.

The NCAA requires that a student-athlete maintain certain minimum grades for eligibility. In addition, student-athletes may be required to attend the school that they are transferring to for up to one year before becoming eligible to participate in intercollegiate sports competition for that school.

FACTS: "My school was placed on probation," objected Lou.

Bill complained, "My school did not have a football team." Both transferred to Sports U. Will they have to sit out a year if they want to play football there? **YOU'RE THE JUDGE!**

DECISION: There are exceptions to the one-year residency rule. One applies to college students transferring from schools placed on probation. These students may be eligible immediately.

In addition, students transferring from a school which has dropped the sport (or never sponsored it to begin with) generally do not have to sit out a year before being allowed to participate.

Athletes attending a college which is not an NCAA member will not be governed by NCAA rules.

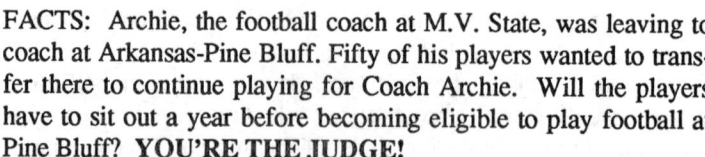

FACTS: Archie, the football coach at M.V. State, was leaving to coach at Arkansas-Pine Bluff. Fifty of his players wanted to transfer there to continue playing for Coach Archie. Will the players have to sit out a year before becoming eligible to play football at Pine Bluff? **YOU'RE THE JUDGE!**

DECISION: Pine Bluff is a member of the National Association of Intercollegiate Athletics (NAIA), which permits transferees to become eligible to play immediately.

High school transfers are also subject to the one-year transfer rule. Generally, unless a transfer is due to the student-athlete's parents making a **bona fide**—good faith—move from one school district to another—or for some other "unavoidable circumstance" (health, compelling personal reason, work)—such a student will be required to sit out one year before being allowed to participate.

FACTS: A high school football player, Walter, said dejectedly, "After having married, I was required to transfer due to a rule prohibiting attendance by married students. After transferring, my parents moved into our new apartment." Was this a bona fide move, which would enable Walter to play football without waiting a year? **YOU'RE THE JUDGE!**

DECISION: The high school association declared that the parents move was not a bona fide or good faith move and declared Walter ineligible. This was unfortunate in that Walter had no choice but to transfer.

Most often, unless a student's transfer is to a legitimate guardian (not to a relative's or friend's home with the intention of circumventing the transfer rule), eligibility will be denied. But, where the move is necessary, eligibility will not be denied.

FACTS: John moved with his family from Vermont to Texas. His father was transferred in his job.

Although John had played basketball in high school in Vermont, he was not recruited to play in Texas. "When I enrolled in school, I was declared ineligible to play ball because of the one-year transfer rule," muttered John. "Could I play immediately without sitting out a year?" **YOU'RE THE JUDGE!**

DECISION: Yes. The rule's purpose was to prevent recruiting, not to unfairly deprive John and his family of important rights—the right to travel and the right to privacy in family matters.

Warren moved to Indiana to live with his brother, who was appointed Warren's legal guardian. The move was due to "demoralizing and detrimental conditions" existing Warren's home and school environment in Florida (friends and teammates involved with drugs and ten sisters living in a two bedroom home). He was declared ineligible to participate in sports for one year. When Warren brought suit, the court held, "Although the school's objective in preventing recruitment and 'school jumping' was a proper concern, Warren's move was because of unavoidable circumstances." Warren could participate immediately.

If a school district has such a rule, would it have be applied to all of the schools in that district?

FACTS: Seven students, after graduating from a Lutheran parochial school wanted to attend the only Lutheran high school available to them.

One of them explained what happened, "Upon transferring to this school in another district, we were declared ineligible to participate athletically for one year. Unless we are allowed to transfer and retain our athletic eligibility, we will be denied the right granted others— to participate." Could the students retain their eligibility after transferring? **YOU'RE THE JUDGE!**

DECISION: Yes. Because some schools were exempted from its coverage, the rule was found unconstitutional. To be found constitutional, the rule would have to apply to all schools in the district.

FACTS: Susan said, "After finishing the ninth grade, I transferred to another school but was declared ineligible to compete in interscholastic athletics for one year."

Susan and her parents felt, "The decision to transfer had nothing to do with athletics; Susan was not recruited. She only wanted to attend a school that would better prepare her for college." Susan wanted to play field hockey. Could she? **YOU'RE THE JUDGE!**

DECISION: The transfer rule carries out the state's interest in protecting students from recruiting. The students were aware of the rule. Only in a situation in which the student has no control, such as a family work transfer, will the rule be waived.

Everyone has a fundamental right to freedom of travel. If a transfer rule attempts to restrict that right, the rule—to be upheld—must be supported by a compelling interest (such as to prevent improper recruiting).

AM I STILL ELIGIBLE?

Between the completion of high school, and while in college, a student-athlete must be concerned with eligibility rules. Student-

athletes must sign (under penalty of loss of eligibility), a statement submitting information related to eligibility, recruiting, financial aid, amateur status and gambling.

FACTS: Charles said, "Prior to enrolling at Aztec U., I signed a contract with an agent, obtained a loan which did not have to be paid back, received benefits and services due to my athletic ability and not available to other students, received excessive expenses for reporting to and visiting the Zumbas pro volleyball team and signed a pro contract to play for pay with the Zumbas." Did any of these activities affect Charles' eligibility when he enrolled at Aztec U.? **YOU'RE THE JUDGE!**

DECISION: All of the activities were in violation of NCAA rules. Charles was not eligible to participate in athletics at Aztec U.

FACTS: Bob, Susan, and Cheryl participated, respectively, in track and field, golf and tennis competitions. They received expenses based upon how they finished. Depending on how well they did, expenses may have exceeded the actual and necessary expenses allowed. Was this permitted? **YOU'RE THE JUDGE!**

DECISION: No. Receiving such expenses would be considered taking pay for participation. That is not permitted.

FACTS: Edgar attended Gonzo U. He explained what happened. "A local booster club outside the school, and an agent, liked my athletic ability. They paid my expenses for attendance. Did this affect my eligibility?" **YOU'RE THE JUDGE!**

DECISION: Yes. Financial assistance, based upon athletic ability, paid by an outside source, is not permitted. Edgar lost his eligibility to participate.

FACTS: All of the members of the Wilder U. football team received tickets to home games. Some of the guys decided to sell the tickets.

The price printed on the ticket was $10. John sold his for $5; Bob sold his for $15. Sam sold his for $10, while Gabe traded his for a free round of golf. Was the eligibility of any of these players jeopardized? **YOU'RE THE JUDGE!**

DECISION: Yes. They all used their athletic skill for pay and have received extra benefits not available to the general student body.

FACTS: Wearrite Sports Co. donated equipment to Aqua U. athletes and then publicized that fact in their ads in the local newspaper. Was the eligibility of the athletes jeopardized? **YOU'RE THE JUDGE!**

DECISION: No, provided the students names or pictures were not used, either in the ads or on any equipment or other commercial items, such as T-shirts or posters.

The students would forfeit their eligibility only if their names and/or pictures were used with their permission.

FACTS: Judson, a football player at All-American U., signed autographs at a prep rally held at the local mall. Did this jeopardize Judson's eligibility? **YOU'RE THE JUDGE!**

DECISION: Yes. An athlete cannot use his name for any commercial business. According to NCAA rules, by signing the autographs, Judson became a pro! He forfeited his remaining eligibility.

A student-athlete, or the athlete's parents, cannot accept any gift or "extra benefit" of value from an agent, company or team unless the same is offered to all of the students at that school.

FACTS: Vinnie, a star athlete at Aqua U, listed what he was offered from local businesses. "I was offered, free of charge: movie tickets, dinners, use of rental cars, sports equipment and legal and medical services at a reduced cost." Could Vinnie accept any of these without jeopardizing his eligibility? **YOU'RE THE JUDGE!**

DECISION: Unless these same products and services were available to the general student body under the same conditions, Vinnie could not accept any of them without jeopardizing his eligibility.

FACTS: Two hockey players received room, board, book and other expenses while playing as prep players in Canadian amateur hockey. They were declared ineligible to compete in college hockey in the U.S. due to receiving this assistance. Did the court require the school to declare them eligible? **YOU'RE THE JUDGE!**

DECISION: "Conditions were much different in Canada than in the U.S. The athletes were required to play for teams often a considerable distance from home, but received no more assistance than would players in the U.S. In order to not deprive these athletes of the opportunity to play, they were allowed to accept such assistance and still maintain eligibility for collegiate play in the U.S."

RECRUITING BY SCHOOLS

The NCAA provides rules concerning the recruiting of prospective student-athletes—athletes who have not enrolled in a college and have not exhausted their high school eligibility, but who have been contacted by a college. Contact for recruiting, with certain limitations, may be by providing transportation to the college, entertaining the athlete or his family, or by telephone contact or visits to the athlete or his family.

The rules also allow for physical exams of prospective student-athletes, reimbursement of expenses and the exchange of financial aid information. All of these areas are strictly covered by rules intended to insure proper recruiting.

FACTS: Alan stated, "I was given financial aid by a college. A booster club gave me cash, a car, clothes and special discounts. Also, they bought my football tickets for a higher price than printed on the ticket." Did this jeopardize Alan's eligibility to participate in athletics for his college? **YOU'RE THE JUDGE!**

DECISION: Yes. The rules do not permit financial aid, such as: improper inducements, cash, promises of work, special discounts, use of autos or clothing. Alan was declared ineligible to participate.

Also, NCAA rules do not permit: contacts (other than as allowed—whether with the athlete or his school), certain publicity and press conferences, nor do they allow certain entertainment of the athlete, his family or friends.

RECRUITING BY PROS

The NCAA has specific rules that apply to amateur eligibility for athletes who are considering competing as professionals.

FACTS: "I was paid to play pro football for the Wreckers, but I'd still like to play on my college baseball team," said Joe.

Before enrolling in Charles College, Joe tried out with the Wreckers, received expenses for the tryout and was employed to give instructions. Was Joe still eligible to play baseball for his college? **YOU'RE THE JUDGE!**

DECISION: Joe could take pay in one sport and still be eligible in another. He could retain his eligibility as long as the try-out was not against another team and as long as he only received necessary expenses. However, Joe could not try out during school.

Joe's school's or conference's rules may differ.

Joe would not be eligible for baseball if he had taken or accepted a promise of pay for baseball, had negotiated or entered into a contract to play pro baseball, had requested to be placed on the pro baseball draft list, or if he had received any salary, expenses (not permitted) or other financial assistance based upon his athletic ability or participation.

FACTS: Joe agreed to be represented by an agent, Herman. Also, Joe was paid to promote and to allow his name and picture to be used for an ad for "Joe's Fly-Fast Tennis Shoes." Was Joe's eligibility jeopardized? **YOU'RE THE JUDGE!**

DECISION: Yes. Joe could not agree to be represented by an agent for baseball and still be eligible to compete as an amateur in other sports unless such representation was for only that one sport. If Joe agreed to be represented generally, he would be ineligible in all sports.

Joe forfeited his eligibility in all sports by accepting pay and for allowing his name and picture to be used commercially.

FACTS: Shelton, while attending State U. signed a pro contract with the American Basketball Association (ABA). Despite a void—no good—contract, the school declared him ineligible to participate.

Shelton argued, "The contract was unenforceable because I was induced by fraud and was pressured. The school should let me play." Should Shelton have been allowed to play? **YOU'RE THE JUDGE!**

DECISION: The court held, "The rule requiring ineligibility was reasonable in attempting to preserve amateurism in college athletics. Furthermore, the school would have no way of knowing whether or not the contract was void. If they allowed this, then anyone could sign a contract, then allege that the contract was unenforceable and play in college while having the option of entering the pros at any time."

All participants in Division I, NCAA basketball tournaments are required to sign an affidavit stating that they have not signed with an agent, nor will they during a tournament.

This action allows the NCAA to not just penalize the athlete's school, but to pursue the player and his agent for any damages which the school might suffer (fine for playing an ineligible player).

NCAA schools have counseling panels to give student-athletes information about careers, schools, representation, determination of worth and rules. These panels may not accompany an athlete in meeting with a pro team, nor may their assistance result in a contract.

Lee News December 12, 1978

AMATEUR SPORT'S ACT

"In the 1972 Olympics, because of improper medications, missed starting times, improper conduct and officiating, medals were lost or forfeited by U.S. Olympic Team athletes. The U.S. Olympic Committee was charged with having inadequate authority, insufficient experience and a great reluctance to change—selecting committee members without consideration to merit."

Out of all the controversy brought about by these problems, the Amateur Sport's Act of 1978 was born. Its goal is to promote, develop and support physical fitness, safety and participation in U.S. amateur athletics, and to resolve disputes and coordinate athletic activity by U.S. amateurs.

LETTER OF INTENT

Prospective college student-athletes may sign a National Letter of Intent to attend a certain college. Generally, this signing takes place during recruiting.

FACTS: "Switch," after signing a letter of intent to attend and play volleyball for G.U., decided to transfer to another school.

Could he do so without a loss of eligibility? **YOU'RE THE JUDGE!**

DECISION: The letter committed Switch to attending and participating for G.U. After the letter was signed, only G.U. was permitted to have contact with him. Switch may be faced with up to two years of ineligibility should he transfer to another school.

Exceptions would be where his school was either placed on probation, or dropped that sport and students then transferred. In such situations, the students would not lose their eligibility.

For a National Letter of Intent to be official, the signature of a parent or legal guardian, or whomever is looking after the student's best interests at that time, is required (unless the student has reached the age of eighteen or other legal age).

REPORT CARDS & CREDITS

The primary objective of schools should be the encouragement and support of scholastic, not athletic, achievement.

FACTS: A state rule barred public school students from extracurricular activities for six weeks if they failed any course. This was called the "no-pass, no-play rule."

Affected students sued their schools, arguing, "The rule discriminated against us by not allowing us to play, but allowing others to." Should the students who failed a course have been allowed to play before the six weeks were up? **YOU'RE THE JUDGE!**

DECISION: The court held, "No. Grade maintenance rules, designed to insure academic achievement, which may prevent participation by those unable to perform academically—either before acceptance to, or while attending, college—will generally be upheld."

Admissions to college are governed by rules requiring a certain grade point average and fulfillment of a specified number of credits. These rules are intended to insure that only academically qualified student-athletes become eligible to participate in sports. This will prevent athletes, thought to have little or no chance of academic success, from attending.

FACTS: Barbara was declared ineligible to participate in intercollegiate athletics. Her high school, in computing her grade point average, excluded her mark in physical education. Without that mark, her grade point average fell below the average required for participation. Should the school have included the physical education mark? **YOU'RE THE JUDGE!**

DECISION: "The policy of the NCAA not to interfere with a high school clearly furthers the objective of admitting and allowing to participate individuals who will be students first and athletes second," said the court.

Barbara will have to improve her grades before she will be eligible to participate.

Students must meet the NCAA's "satisfactory progress" guidelines to remain eligible to participate in intercollegiate sports.

These rules must be reasonable and must only affect those unable to maintain academic requirements. Thus, where students were not allowed to participate even after maintaining suitable grades, the rule was held unenforceable. The students were allowed to participate.

Other decisions based on similar facts did not allow students to participate.

FACTS: Five high school basketball players were recruited to play in college. The college was warned that the players did not qualify under the NCAA's grade point average rule. The athletes were nonetheless granted scholarships and continued to play.

When the NCAA declared both the athletes and their college ineligible to participate in post-season play, the school asked a court to decide if the students could play. How did the court decide? **YOU'RE THE JUDGE!**

DECISION: The court decided, "The NCAA's rule requiring athletes to possess and maintain a certain grade point average was a reasonable rule, intended to insure academically prepared students before allowing them to participate in athletics. Neither the school nor the athletes could participate in post-season play."

The courts felt that if they allowed these students to participate, then schools would recruit academically unqualified .

In order to become eligible, the students would have to "sit out" until they improved their grades.

FACTS: Ben played for the TriCity College football team. After attending summer school, he was told by TriCity, "These credits will allow you to remain eligible for the football team." But Ben was then declared ineligible when the school decided not to accept the credits.

"The school lied to me. Because I didn't have a chance to impress the scouts, I was not drafted in a higher round," Ben complained. Was the school responsible? **YOU'RE THE JUDGE!**

DECISION: If TriCity knew that the summer course would not help Ben retain his eligibility, and failed to warn him of this, then they would be liable for any loss in potential earnings.

However, if Ben knew that the summer course was not acceptable, then the school would not be liable.

In any event, there is no way of knowing how Ben would have performed had he played. It might well be too speculative to determine what his damages, if any, would have been.

PERSONAL CONDUCT

Podunk University
1211 University Drive
Justice, Georgia 33323

Dear Parents, Student-Athletes & Concerned Citizens:

There have been many recent court decisions involving the conduct, grooming and marriage of student-athletes. Further decisions concerning sanctions, expulsions and awards in amateur sports are also noteworthy.

Issues, which in the past were not subject to judicial scrutiny, now are. The law is playing an increasingly major role in controlling the affairs of amateur sports.

As eligibility may be jeopardized, it is in your best interest that you become familiar with these issues and decisions.

Furthermore, these issues have (and will continue to have) an effect on student and community opinion and morale in amateur sports.

Thanking you for your attention,

School Board 12, State Athletic
Conference and Podunk U., member of NCAA

A COACH'S AUTHORITY

A coach has the most frequent and direct contact between an athlete and his school. While a coach may be granted broad authority to control an athlete's athletic life, this control must be reasonable.

Such authority includes the power to establish and maintain health and training rules, direct and conduct practices, issue instructions during practice and games and impose penalties for violations.

Can a coach control an athlete's private life?

FACTS: Zephyr High and its football coach adopted several rules. All players had to be dressed properly, according to standards set by the school, and had to "hustle" during practices.

The coach determined that Bob and Gary "did not hustle during the last practice, and they dressed improperly during the school vacation." Could the coach impose a penalty? **YOU'RE THE JUDGE!**

DECISION: If the school and coach had authority to adopt these rules, the hustling rule probably would be upheld as being necessary to prepare the team for competition. However, the rule would have to be reasonable.

The dress code might be necessary while the students were in school or traveling to athletic events, but would not be upheld for a violation taking place outside of school during an athlete's private life.

One court was asked to rule on whether or not a coach's authority extended to allowing a radio receiver in a quarterback's helmet. The court said, "No." The coach was suspended, the school's victory forfeited and the school was fined.

FREEDOM OF EXPRESSION

Two cases involving the limits of the school or coach's authority had to do with armbands.

In the first case, students who wore armbands to school in protest of the Vietnam war were expelled for violating a school policy.

The court held that this action deprived the students of their First Amendment right to freedom of expression. There was no evidence that the wearing of the armbands would cause a disruption. The second case had a different result.

FACTS: Coach Jones instituted a rule prohibiting "the players participating in demonstrations or protests."

A group of players informed the coach, "In protest of the policies of our opponent and their church, we intend to wear armbands to the next game." When the athletes did so, they were dismissed.

The school reasoned, "It was our intention to protect an invasion of the rights of others (fans) by avoiding a hostile expression by the athletes." Was the school's reasoning in dismissing the players proper? **YOU'RE THE JUDGE!**

DECISION: No. This was not enough to allow the school to dismiss the players. The school had to show that the wearing of the armbands would potentially cause disruption. Nevertheless, the students were not allowed to wear the armbands during the game.

A coach has authority to control his players as long as any rules are reasonable and do not affect a player's rights of freedom of expression or conduct. If these rights are affected, then—to enforce the rule—the school must show that any violation of the rule will cause disruption or otherwise substantially affect the operation of the school.

BENCHED!

FACTS: Two football players at Red U. were "benched" for missing practice. Xavier was benched for one game, Lora for five. Before the benchings, should they have been given an opportunity for hearings to determine if the penalties were warranted and proper? **YOU'RE THE JUDGE!**

DECISION: Lora should been given a hearing for such a severe penalty. Xavier's discipline was short. It did not require a hearing.

As the length of any disciplinary action increases, so too does the need for a fair and impartial hearing, with representation, to determine if the penalty is justified and proper.

HAVE YOU BEEN BEHAVING?

Good conduct rules—rules requiring appropriate conduct under penalty of sanctions—are often adopted by schools.

Generally, such rules will be upheld so long as they "notify the athletes of the conduct expected of them, and are related to a legitimate, athletics-concerned objective."

FACTS: Brenton High School had a rule providing:

"Anyone discovered using alcohol, drugs or tobacco will be expelled from athletic competition."

Five of the school's athletes were expelled for being at a party where there was drinking. However, they had the right to appeal and to due process—a fair and impartial hearing with representation. Should the athletes have been expelled? **YOU'RE THE JUDGE!**

DECISION: The court stated, "Seeking to deter athletes from using liquor was a legitimate and reasonable goal." The students were also afforded due process. They all had adequate notice of the rule and had admitted guilt. The purpose of such rules is to protect the health and welfare of the athletes.

Other similar cases have produced different results. In one, an athlete lost eligibility for violating a "beer rule"—providing for suspension for possession, consumption, or transportation of alcohol or drugs. The athlete was stopped, during the off-season, in a car containing beer. He brought suit to enjoin enforcement of the rule.

"The rule was unenforceable," ruled the court. The rule was too broad in that it presumed guilt for merely being present in the car.

Rules prohibiting smoking on school grounds generally have been upheld where students were aware of the rule, warned of the penalty, afforded due process, and where the school had acted in good faith and in the best interests of the school and its students.

What if the students were not aware of another's violation of such a rule?

FACTS: West High School had a rule, "Anyone using or transporting drugs, alcohol or tobacco, in the presence of another, will be suspended." Was this rule too broad? Might it discipline someone not intended to be disciplined? **YOU'RE THE JUDGE!**

DECISION: The rule would probably be considered too broad. An athlete might be in the presence of someone carrying drugs, but without being aware of it. To expect one athlete to be responsible for others' violations would be stretching what otherwise may be a valid and enforceable rule.

In addition, the rule would not cover the situations where a drug was bought "over the counter" and had no effect on an athlete's ability to perform, or was taken under the direction of a physician.

Generally, subjecting an athlete to blood, urine or saliva testing for drugs will be in violation of the Fourth Amendment's prohibition against unreasonable search and seizure, as well as against the Fifth Amendment's privilege against self-incrimination. Such tests may also be an invasion of the athlete's privacy.

FACTS: Sharon, after failing a drug test, was declared ineligible to participate in the NCAA diving championships. He challenged the NCAA test as an invasion of her privacy. Did the court allow Sharon to participate? **YOU'RE THE JUDGE!**

DECISION: Yes. The court concluded, "The NCAA's drug testing as an eligibility rule was too broad. It did not show evidence that drugs would enhance performance. The test was ruled an invasion of privacy.

However, other courts have held that the testing was not an invasion of privacy of student-athletes' rights. Athletes, amateur and professional, continue to be asked to submit to such tests as are thought necessary to detect the use of banned drugs—which such athletes are prohibited from using. A player refusing to submit to such testing generally may be banned from participating.

For fighting in an NCAA college basketball game, a player will be ejected for that game. For a second offense, the player will be suspended for one additional game. But for a third offense, the penalty is suspension for the remainder of the season.

MARRIAGE & GROOMING

FACTS: A state high school association rule read:

"MARRIED STUDENTS SHALL NOT BE PERMITTED TO PARTICIPATE IN ANY SPORTS."

Rule 203 D.F. S. School Board

This rule was adopted in an attempt to exclude married students not only from athletics, but also from extracurricular activities. Did the rule discriminate against married students? Could it be enforced? **YOU'RE THE JUDGE!**

DECISION: Even though the rule did not prohibit unmarried athletes from participating, no discrimination was found. The rule could be enforced.

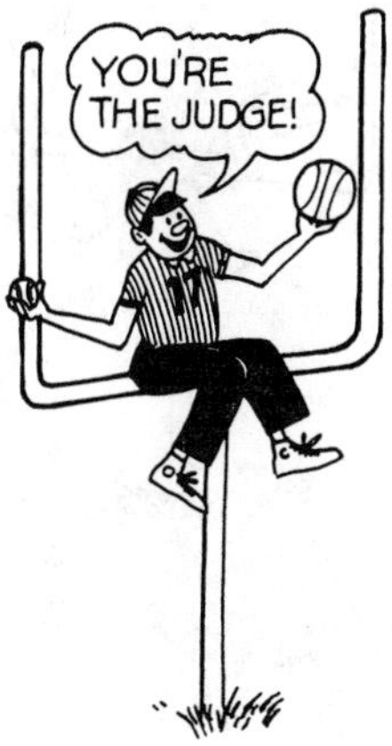

Such exclusionary rules have generally been upheld by the courts. Reasons given have been that married students have responsibilities, financial obligations and an essential need for an education greater than that of other students. In addition, married athletes influence other athletes. The married athletes may be held in some esteem and their actions often emulated by other students. Furthermore, approval of participation by married athletes might indicate that the school condones teenage marriages.

Do you think that married athletes should be prohibited from participating in sports?

FACTS: Harold, a married student, hoped, "By playing football, I might get a college scholarship."

A school district rule prevented married students from participating in athletics.

Harold felt that he was being discriminated against and should be allowed to participate as were unmarried students. Should he have been permitted to play?

DECISION: **YOU'RE THE JUDGE!**

FACTS: John was married and an excellent baseball player. "I want to play in the pros," he said. Several colleges were interested in granting him a scholarship. John's high school board prohibited married students from participating in athletics.

John argued, "I am being deprived of the fundamental right of marital privacy." Should John have been allowed to play? **YOU'RE THE JUDGE!**

DECISION: Both school boards were enjoined from enforcing marriage exclusion rules. Both athletes were permitted to participate.

LONG HAIR & EARRINGS!

Rules attempting to regulate the length and style of hair worn by athletes have also come under attack.

Reasons given by public school boards have been: interest in teaching hygiene, instilling discipline, compelling uniformity, and enhancing school and community spirit.

If a rule prescribing length or style of hair applies to all students and is a reasonable means of furthering a concern in the appearance and health of its students, then the rule will probably be upheld. Otherwise, it will not be enforceable.

FACTS: Members of a high school tennis team were dismissed by their coach because of a violation of a grooming code regulating the length of hair and sideburns. The code only applied to athletes. "The length of our hair did not affect our playing ability," said the players.

Another coach attempted to enforce a hair code during the off-season. Were the grooming codes enforceable? **YOU'RE THE JUDGE!**

DECISION: The courts held, "The rules were violations of the athletes' fundamental rights to determine their own hair style and personal appearance." There was no compelling necessity for the rules.

May a school prohibit students from wearing earrings while attending class?

FACTS: Kevin and Andy, members of their high school football team, bragged, "We wore earrings to class."

Their school district banned them from wearing earrings while attending classes. The district reasoned, "Earrings might indicate youth gang activity." Was such a ban enforceable? **YOU'RE THE JUDGE!**

DECISION: The court found that the school district had the right to enforce the ban as necessary to ensure the safety and welfare of the school's students.

Private Schools

Constitutional requirements do not apply to wholly private schools. Therefore, if a private school adopts a grooming code, it may be upheld. This is because the Constitution only applies to schools where the state is involved with its activity. States generally are involved with public (not private) schools. Therefore, rights granted by the Constitution, such as equal protection, due process (right to hearing and representation), and protection of fundamental rights (personal grooming and marriage privacy) do not apply to wholly private schools.

FIRST PRIZE IS....

The NCAA permits personalized awards that do not exceed specified amounts. The awards must be approved by the school and the school's conference.

FACTS: The coach of the champion "Fighting Tiger" football team asked, "May the players be given TV's for awards?" **YOU'RE THE JUDGE!**

DECISION: Awards that cannot be personalized, such as gift certificates, televisions, appliances or club memberships, and which may exceed a specified amount, may not be awarded.

Student-athletes enrolled in NCAA member schools or high schools, who accept unapproved awards for a sport, jeopardize their eligibility—not only for that sport—but for all sports.

FACTS: The Polar Bears, a high school football team, had an outstanding year and was honored by the community. Team members were awarded lettered jackets and a book of religious testimonials by famous athletes. The price of the jackets was within the limits allowed of acceptable awards, but the book was not. When the team found this out, they returned the books. Should the school have been placed on probation? **YOU'RE THE JUDGE!**

DECISION: Even though the team returned the books, the school was still placed on probation for three years!

Generally though, medals, letters, trophies, and other awards not exceeding a nominal value may be accepted.

The interest is in preserving amateur status and preventing "pro athletes" from competing in high school sports. A rule declaring that any student who receives an award of more than a nominal value is considered to be a professional is reasonable. Otherwise, athletes could be paid simply by giving them awards, which they could exchange for money.

Can a grammar school student-athlete be considered a pro?

FACTS: Andy won the 60-meter dash in a grammar school track competition and was given a candy bar as a prize. Did such an award jeopardize Andy's eligibility? **YOU'RE THE JUDGE!**

DECISION: Although the prize was of nominal value, officials claimed that the prize made Andy a professional. He was banned from further competition

These cases point out the need to be aware of which awards are acceptable without jeopardizing the eligibility of either the athlete or the school.

ODDS & ENDS....

It's A Tie?

FACTS: Georgia's high school athletic association adopted a curfew calling for weeknight basketball games to end by 9:00 P.M., even if there was time on the clock, and even if the game was tied. If a player was fouled at 9:00 P.M., could he take the free throws? **YOU'RE THE JUDGE!**

DECISION: The controversial rule was rescinded.

Speaking Out!

FACTS: Jan, an instructor at G. U., alleged, "My right to free speech was violated when I was fired for 'speaking out' against the school's policy of academic favoritism and preferential treatment for student-athletes in an attempt to keep them eligible."

Testimony revealed that academic standards were lowered for some athletes while others were promoted without meeting grade requirements.

If Jan's dismissal was in retaliation for her speaking out against these practices, could she recover back pay and other damages? **YOU'RE THE JUDGE!**

DECISION: A jury found that Jan's "...right to free speech, as guaranteed by the First Amendment, was violated." She was awarded back pay and damages, including punitive damages.

Are We Pros?

FACTS: Eric, a high school senior, won a sports car in a field-goal kicking competition after a random drawing at a pro football game.

"Stick," also a high school senior, won money by throwing in a three quarter court length basket after a random drawing at a pro basketball game.

If either kept their prize, would they be ineligible to compete in college? **YOU'RE THE JUDGE!**

DECISION: "Accepting the car or money would make Eric and Stick pros and thus ineligible to compete at any NCAA school." However, they may compete at a smaller college division school.

All amateur athletes desiring to compete in organized amateur sports should fully understand their rights and responsibilities concerning elegibility.

3

DUE PROCESS & EQUAL PROTECTION

WHAT'S IT ABOUT?

Due Process & Equal Protection goes into the effect that the Fourteenth Amendment to the Constitution, and its requirements, has on the enforcement of rules and regulations by amateur athletic organizations A sample Complaint highlights the issues that are examined. Can student-athletes be deprived of the right to an education or the right to participate in sports without the opportunity for a fair and impartial hearing? Should all athletes be treated alike?

John & Susan, plaintiffs
v.
Z. University, defendant

4th Circuit, Essex County, RI

COMPLAINT

The plaintiffs, John & Susan, allege as follows:

1. that they were student-athletes on athletic scholarships at ZU; John a member of the football team, Susan a member of the tennis team;
2. that, due to alleged violations, their scholarships and team memberships were terminated;
3. that certain of their rights were violated, namely:
   a. rules were applied discriminatorily, treating them differently than others similarly situated, a violation of the **Equal Protection Clause;**
   b. they have been deprived of the right to develop athletically, thus greatly diminishing their potential worth, and lessening their chances of becoming pros;
   c. that their scholarships were terminated without **Due Process**—the opportunity for a fair and impartial hearing with representation;
   d. that as a result of the termination of their scholarships, plaintiffs will not be able to continue work towards a degree, and;
   e. that the defendant "exploited" plaintiffs, using their athletic skills without regard to educational needs and desires, and dismissing them when they were no longer needed in advancing the athletic pursuits of ZU;
4. that as a result of ZU's actions, John & Susan have suffered, and will continue to suffer, immediate and irreparable harm and economic loss;

WHEREFORE, John & Susan ask:
1. that ZU be enjoined from terminating their scholarships and team memberships;
2. that they be given a hearing and opportunity to defend themselves, and;
3 that they be awarded damages in an amount that the court deems necessary and appropriate for injuries suffered and to be suffered.

IMPROPER ACTS

The enforcement of rules and regulations by amateur athletic organizations consists of the investigation of alleged improper acts and, if necessary or required, a fair and impartial hearing. Such proceedings to determine violations, if any, must be conducted within the organization's power and authority.

FACTS: For fighting in a game, Ally and Ben were suspended for five games. This was their first violation of the "no fighting" rule. The rule provided for a two game suspension, but the school decided to "set an example" in an attempt to prevent further fighting. Was the discipline fair? Should Ally and Ben have been given an opportunity to defend themselves? **YOU'RE THE JUDGE!**

DECISION: The discipline was improper. Furthermore, the severity of the sanction required minimum due process—a fair and impartial hearing with representation.

RULE-MAKING BY PRIVATE SCHOOLS

The essential difference between public and private schools is the extent of state involvement in their activities.

Schools, public or private, which are affected with **state action**—state involvement in providing "public" education, such as public schools—are bound by the requirements of the Constitution (due process and equal protection).

If a private school is not affected with state action, then they are only bound by their given authority.

A private group of people or associations, combined to achieve a common goal, is usually considered voluntary. Such membership is a privilege rather than a right. Thus, a private association may adopt rules and conditions for eligibility that will not be subject to constitutional requirements, as long as they are not in conflict with state or federal laws.

FACTS: John was a student-athlete at T.R.U., a private school not affected with "state action." His eligibility and athletic scholarship were terminated for fighting and destroying school hockey equipment. In addition, there was a question about his transfer from another college. "What are my rights and the school's duties?" asked John. **YOU'RE THE JUDGE!**

DECISION: If John's scholarship was viewed as an implied contract—a scholarship in return for athletic participation—then the court would look to see if both parties had lived up to the agreement.

The court would consider the student-athlete's inferior "take-it-or-leave-it" position.

Although John's eligibility and schooling may be terminated for fighting and destroying equipment, he may not be declared ineligible for any of the following reasons: because he transferred from a junior college, had taken the last year off, had transferred from a school without a hockey team or one on probation, or had not previously competed in hockey.

When a court decides to interfere in a school's affairs, it attempts to strike a balance; both between the interests of the parties (and similarly situated persons), and the potential harm to the parties (and whether the court can grant meaningful relief).

If John had the potential for becoming a professional hockey player, would the courts look more closely at any attempt to terminate his eligibility?

Loss of an education or eligibility, where a student-athlete may have the potential for a professional career, requires that courts scrutinize the actions of the association to determine if its rules and their objectives are reasonable. They may not assume that students have only "privileges" and no rights relating to sports activities.

THE CONSTITUTION REQUIRES....

Rule-making by associations that are "affected" with "state action," whether public or private, is governed by the Fourteenth Amendment to the Constitution. It requires that:

> **"No state shall ... deprive any person of life, liberty, or property, without due process of law; nor deny to any person ... the equal protection of the laws."**

If a student-athlete is declared ineligible due to a rule's violation, due process may be required—that is, the opportunity for a fair and impartial hearing with representation. The court will decide what process is due.

Cases where the Fourteenth Amendment is not an issue, or where it has already been resolved, will be decided by state or common law, or by the school's rules.

Must a student-athlete whose eligibility has been terminated be given due process?

> FACTS: John's school explained, "Without giving any reason, John missed seven games. We declared him ineligible and took away his athletic scholarship to Sun Tan U." Should John have been given a hearing before being declared ineligible? **YOU'RE THE JUDGE!**

DECISION: The loss of eligibility for missing practice, although a severe sanction, did not require a hearing. The rule clearly provided for ineligibility, unless a reason were given and a hearing was requested within thirty days. John did neither, even after being notified of his rights.

In a case like this, a sanction will generally be upheld as long as it is reasonably related to the rule violated and to the severity of the offending conduct.

State Action

"No *state* shall ... deprive any person of life, liberty, or property, without due process of law; nor deny to any person ... the equal protection of the laws."

Student-athletes wishing to claim their right to due process or equal protection must show that the NCAA (or whatever association or conference governs their school) is involved in state action, meaning state involvement in providing "public" education.

Several cases have held that regulation of college athletes by the NCAA did not involve state action as it was not an activity "traditionally reserved exclusively to the state."

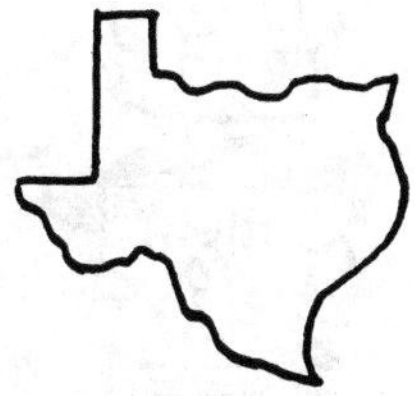

FACTS: Coach "K," the football coach at U.N.V.L., was ordered suspended by the NCAA for two years for alleged rules violations. The state court ruled that the coach had not been given his due process rights during the NCAA's investigation. The NCAA appealed. Did the NCAA have to give the coach a fair and impartial hearing during its investigation before imposing any sanctions? **YOU'RE THE JUDGE!**

DECISION: No. The Supreme Court held that the NCAA is not a state entity bound by the Constitution, but that it acted as a private entity, an agent of its member schools. It did not have to give the coach a hearing.

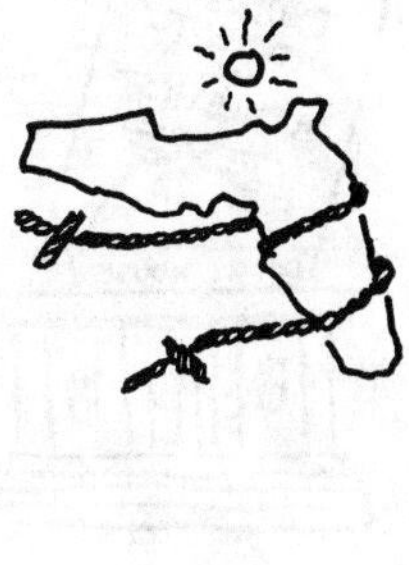

Although this case may discourage lawsuits involving alleged violations of due process, it is generally thought that the NCAA, high school athletic associations and college conferences are all "affected" with state action.

FACTS: The state government authorized, encouraged and delegated its authority to associations, schools and conferences to carry out the state's duties to provide education, including athletics.

The schools received public funds. Also, the state, allowed the use of publicly owned facilities for athletic events. Were such actions by the state considered state action? **YOU'RE THE JUDGE!**

DECISION: Yes. All of the affected associations, schools, and conferences will be governed by the U.S. Constitution.

Will a court interfere where a private association treated a student-athlete unfairly?

Courts may intervene in the affairs of private associations—at least where the plaintiff can show substantial injury resulting from the association's actions. Such intervention would not be based on constitutional grounds, but might be based on grounds of equality or fairness.

Give Me Liberty....

"No state shall ... deprive any person of life, *liberty,* or property, without due process of law; nor deny to any person ... the equal protection of the laws."

What is liberty? The most obvious meaning of liberty would be freedom from bodily restraint. But liberty also includes the freedom to be educated and the freedom of opportunity.

FACTS: A football player at a major university, Mark, asked, "Does liberty include the freedom to keep an athletic scholarship that could ensure me an opportunity for an education or an opportunity to expose my athletic ability that might lead to a pro career?"

DECISION: **YOU'RE THE JUDGE!**

It's My Property!

"No state shall ... deprive any person of life, liberty, or *property,* without due process of law; nor deny to any person ... the equal protection of the laws."

After showing state action, a plaintiff or student-athlete, alleging an improper loss of eligibility, must show that he has a right to participate.

May property be defined here, not as land or an object, but as a right to participate?

High School

Courts have generally found that a high school student-athlete does not have a **property interest**—a right to participate—in athletics.

FACTS: Chico was suspended without a hearing for slugging a teammate. "The suspension of my right to participate will injure my chances of becoming a pro. I have a property right to an education. Sports is a part of that!" argued Chico. Did Chico have a right to participate in athletics that required a hearing when suspended? **YOU'RE THE JUDGE!**

DECISION: No. Although Chico may have had a property right in the whole educational system, he did not have a property interest in each separate part, such as athletics.

High school athletes are not pursuing careers, have not yet sufficiently developed, and the opportunities for their exposure are minimal.

But there are cases holding that high school athletes have a separate property interest in athletics that can be protected.

One court commented, "If classes such as physical education are a required part of a student's curriculum, then athletic participation should be given the same protection. If one were declared ineligible from a required course, such as physical education, due process would apply. It, therefore, should also apply to sports participation."

College

Participation in collegiate athletics may be quite different.

FACTS: For fighting in a college basketball game, Alonzo—without a hearing—was declared ineligible. He challenged the dismissal. "Shouldn't I have been given a fair and impartial hearing?" he asked. **YOU'RE THE JUDGE!**

DECISION: The court held that the right to participate in athletics was a valuable right that could not be denied without due process. The chance to display their athletic prowess in college stadiums and arenas may be worth more in economic terms than the chance to get a college education.

Despite some language of a few courts to the contrary, college athletes do have a constitutionally protected property right to participate in sports. This right entitles them to participate and to given due process safeguards to ensure that their interest in participation is properly protected.

There's No Process Like Due Process!

"No state shall ... deprive any person of life, liberty, or property, without *due process* of law; nor deny to any person ... the equal protection of the laws."

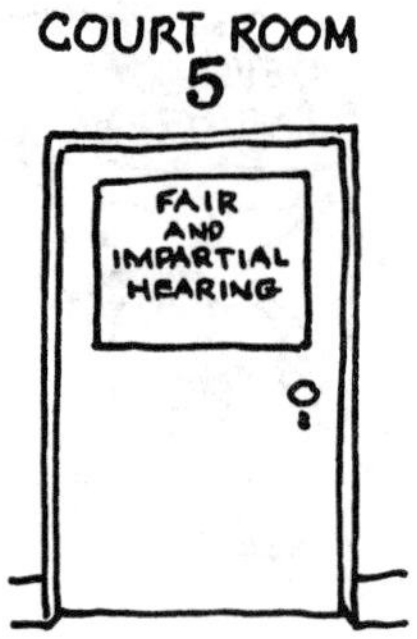

FACTS: As a result of a violation of a transfer rule, Susan was informed by her school, "You are ineligible to participate in golf for one year."

Susan was denied the opportunity to show that the rule did not apply to her because she had already sat out a year. Should she have been allowed to participate? **YOU'RE THE JUDGE!**

DECISION: Susan had already sat out a year before transferring. An earlier hearing would have revealed that fact and she then would have been allowed to participate.

Due process would require: notice of the proceedings to declare her ineligible; the opportunity to prepare, to have representation and to obtain discovery—the information that the action is based on and who furnished such information—and; the opportunity to be heard—a fair and impartial hearing.

How Much Process Is Due?

If an attempt to convince a court that a protectible interest has been deprived is unsuccessful, then no due process is available. If, however, a liberty or property interest is involved, the court must then decide what protection the plaintiff should be given.

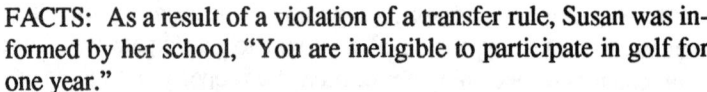

FACTS: For "goofing around," Jerry was benched for one game. Sara was declared ineligible for one year after being accused of "cheating in a golf match." Who was entitled to more "protection" from their loss of eligibility? **YOU'RE THE JUDGE!**

DECISION: The length, severity and reason for ineligibility required that Sara be given much more substantial protection, such as a hearing.

Generally, as the length and severity of any potential loss becomes greater, required safeguards become more necessary to fulfill the requirements of due process.

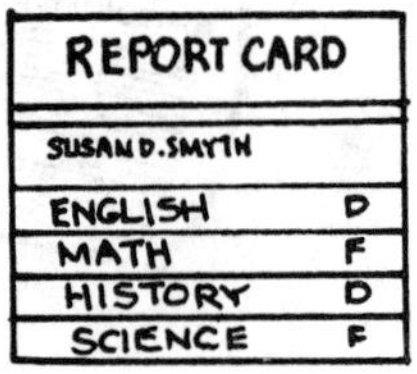

FACTS: Because of poor grades, Susan was declared ineligible to participate in athletics for one semester; at which time she would be reinstated provided she improved her grades. She complained, "The rule is unfair." What process was Susan due?

Suppose Susan decided to challenge the procedure used to calculate her grades, or felt that there was personal bias by one of her professors? Or what if she maintained her low grades were punishment for allegedly stealing a book and that she was declared ineligible for three years? What process would be due now? **YOU'RE THE JUDGE!**

DECISION: The first situation would only require modest procedural safeguards. But when Susan challenged the method for calculating her grades, the personal bias, and the charge of stealing—it became much more important for her to have a fair and impartial hearing with representation.

If a court found a school's tribunal to be fair and impartial, then the right to representation would be diminished.

Equal Protection

"No state shall ... deprive any person of life, liberty, or property, without due process of law; nor deny to any person ... the *equal protection* of the laws."

As with the due process clause, the equal protection clause requires state action; it does not apply to any action of wholly private associations.

The equal protection clause prohibits discrimination in either laws or their administration. It is intended to insure that "all persons similarly situated shall receive no different or greater penalty. They shall be treated alike."

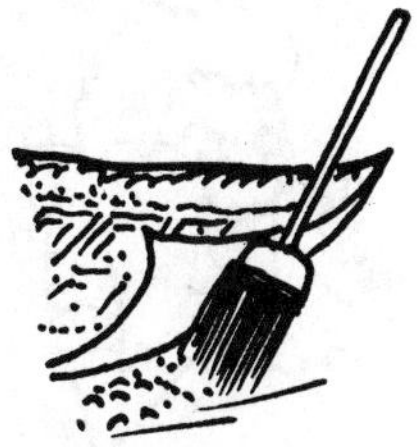

It strikes down overly-broad rules that sweep or catch into their nets individuals who are not intended to, or should not, be included within the reaches of these rules.

FACTS: A transfer rule read, "Any transfer athlete shall sit out one season in their sport." The rule was intended to prevent improper recruiting.

Bob transferred to Eastern U. from Western U. He did not play football at Western. He further took a year off before transferring. Bob was declared "ineligible to play football for one year from the transfer." "Shouldn't I be allowed to play immediately?" asked Bob. **YOU'RE THE JUDGE!**

DECISION: Yes. The rule was intended to prevent improper recruiting. As Bob was not recruited, did not play at Western, and sat out a year—declaring him ineligible would be a violation of the equal protection clause as "sweeping" too broadly by including him in the class of athletes intended to be covered by the rule.

There are two tests that may be applied in determining whether a rule is a violation of the equal protection clause.

The first is the **rational basis test.** This was what Bob's case was decided upon. It requires, "The rule or classification must be reasonable, not arbitrary, so that all persons similarly situated are treated alike."

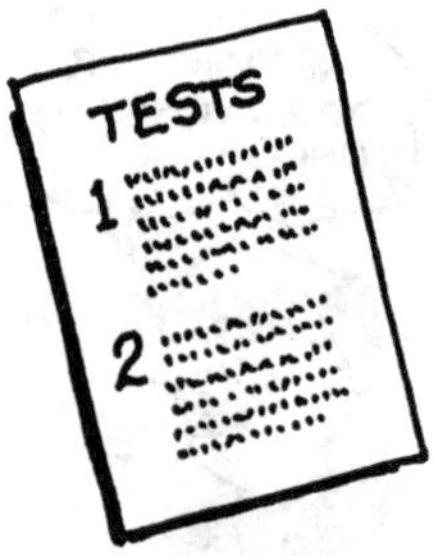

The second is called the **strict scrutiny test.** It requires, "Where a 'suspect class' (race, sex, color) or 'fundamental interest' (marriage, interstate travel) is involved, the rule will be unconstitutional unless there is a compelling interest to be protected or promoted."

FACTS: Susan transferred to Tutten High from out of state. She wanted to try out for the boys' golf team (there was no girls' team), but was denied because, "Girls are not allowed to play on boys' teams."

Also, she was declared "ineligible to participate in any sport for one year due to the transfer rule." Susan did not play golf at her previous school. She transferred because her father was transferred from his job. Should Susan have been permitted to try out? **YOU'RE THE JUDGE!**

DECISION: The refusal of a tryout was based on sex. The transfer rule discriminated against interstate travel for a valid reason (work transfer). Both were subject to the strict scrutiny test. Neither served to promote any compelling reason for their discrimination. Susan was denied equal protection. She was permitted to try out for the boys' golf team.

Some schools reason: "Boys are bigger and stronger than girls." Are these compelling enough reasons to deny equal protection?

FACTS: What if there had been a girls' golf team or what if Susan had wanted to participate on the boys' football team? Would your decision be any different? **YOU'RE THE JUDGE!**

DECISION: The school's reasons for not allowing Susan to play on the boys' golf or football teams were, "There is a girls' team for golf, and football is too rough for girls." They cited the differences in size, strength and ability, and the chance to compete against others of the same sex and abilities.

A court might well feel these are "compelling enough reasons" to deny Susan's claim of denial of equal protection.

Due process and equal protection by the laws can only be demanded where there is a "protectible interest"—such as the right to interstate travel. A court may nevertheless deny a claim where due process has already been given or equal protection of the laws has not been denied.

PUBLIC REGULATION OF SPORTS

Most states have athletic commissions which regulate specific sports. If self-regulation has failed or the interests of those involved requires review, public regulation may be necessary.

Generally, the sports requiring public regulation are: horse, dog and automobile racing, boxing and wrestling.

Athletic Commissions

An **athletic commission**—a group of appointed officials—attempts to prevent abuses that may be a part of a sport and promote and protect the interests of the public in having sportsmanlike conduct. A commission, created by law, becomes—in effect—an agent of the state, subject to judicial review.

FACTS: Some of these sports, particularly boxing and horse racing, have attracted gamblers, criminals and "fixing" of results. In addition to establishing rules and regulations, what may commissions do to help insure proper conduct? **YOU'RE THE JUDGE!**

DECISION: To insure proper conduct, the commission will issue licenses and provide rules, regulations and enforcement.

Do You Have A License?

With certain exceptions, anyone desiring to take part in one of the sports requiring regulation will be required to obtain an appropriate license. This requirement includes participants, referees, owners, trainers and sponsors. What will the applicants be questioned about?

Applicants must submit information regarding their conduct, training, character, physical and financial condition, and past activities.

Numerous courts have concluded, "A commission's authority may be broad and exclusive. Their decisions concerning rules will not be overturned unless there is a clear abuse of authority. A commission may only reject a license for good and reasonable cause."

FACTS: Because of his conviction for refusing to be inducted into the armed services, Ali was denied a boxing license. Was the boxing commission's action reasonable? **YOU'RE THE JUDGE!**

DECISION: No. The court observed, "Many others had been issued licenses before and after being convicted of crimes." These facts were overwhelming proof that the commission's denial of Ali's application for a boxing license was unlawful, arbitrary, unreasonable, and a violation of the equal protection clause, guaranteeing the same treatment received by others similarly situated. The commission was enjoined from denying Ali a license.

Courts have also held that denial of a license application may require due process—notice, hearing, and the opportunity for the applicant to answer and defend any charges used as a basis for its denial.

The Rules Are....

The authority to make and enforce rules and regulations is included in the law creating the commission.

Whether a court will review any enforcement of a commission rule will depend upon whether the claimant is attacking the rule itself or whether he is challenging the interpretation of the rule.

FACTS: Vinnie was denied a promoter's license for boxing. He alleged, "The rule requiring promoters to be licensed was invalid. If it did apply to me, I was exempted from needing a license because I only promote fights for charitable purposes for local fairs." Should Vinnie have been exempted from the license rule? What authority did the court have? **YOU'RE THE JUDGE!**

DECISION: The court could decide if the rule was within the boxing commission's power, whether it was issued pursuant to the proper procedure and if it was reasonable. The court can substitute its judgment for that of the commission in interpreting the rule. However, the court will not question the boxing commission's decision on the facts.

The rule was not invalid, but Vinnie could be exempted from the license requirement because he only promoted fights for charitable purposes.

Conduct & Character

A state has an interest in determining whether an applicant possesses the necessary character and fitness for certain professions. The types of conduct and character considered for a license will, in part, depend upon what profession the applicant desires to enter.

Rules must be reasonable and must only affect those persons whose conduct it is necessary to control.

FACTS: Al and Manuel were convicted of stealing. Will such action affect their applications for a promoter's or jockey's license? **YOU'RE THE JUDGE!**

DECISION: Al, convicted of stealing, may be denied a license to promote. However, this fact may have little bearing on Manuel becoming a jockey—at least not enough to deny his application.

EXPLOITATION

JANUARY 6, 1986

Winston News

I'VE BEEN EXPLOITED!

Colleges and universities have been accused of: recruiting athletes lacking the intellectual skills necessary to succeed academically, forging and altering transcripts, giving credits and grades not warranted by academic performance, channeling the athletes into meaningless courses, and, failing to provide the education promised to athletes.

FACTS: Curtis, a former collegiate basketball star, sued the colleges he attended, and the coaches and officials. Curtis was recruited, and transferred, from a school for slow learners to a regular school where he did not receive the special attention he needed. He was "passed" through school without passing work and induced into attending college. Yet, he could not read or write well enough to fill out the application! (The coach filled it out!) Cheating and other improper acts were used to maintain his eligibility.

Curtis was taunted and insulted mercilessly. He had a mental breakdown, requiring constant medical attention. Was this exploitation of Curtis' athletic abilities to the detriment of his educational needs? Could Curtis recover damages?

DECISION: **YOU'RE THE JUDGE!**

Some former student-athletes have charged that colleges and universities exploited them by using them for their athletic ability—with no concern for their educational advancement—and later discarding them when they no longer could help the school athletically. These student-athletes alleged that such exploitation was done solely to advance the interests of the school.

FACTS: Eight basketball players sued their college for "depriving us of a legitimate education." They claimed, "We wasted our careers on courses designed only to keep us eligible for basketball. There was fraud and misrepresentation on the part of the school. We were denied access to adequate counseling." Were these students exploited for their athletic ability?

DECISION: **YOU'RE THE JUDGE!**

FACTS: Several football players at Big Time U. were advised by their academic advisor, "Certain summer courses will be accepted for credits needed to retain your eligibility next season."

After being declared ineligible, the students alleged, "We were exploited for our athletic abilities to the detriment of an education." Was this exploitation?

DECISION: **YOU'RE THE JUDGE!**

Whose fault is it for the system's failure to provide students with an education? Is the university obligated to provide an education to a scholarship athlete?

Each case has to be treated separately, but maybe the reasoning lies in the court's handling of a case where a basketball star was declared ineligible by his school because he had "not met academic standards." The player took the school to court to win reinstatement. The judge commented:

Orevill News

"...athletes... are given little incentive to be scholars and few care how they perform academically. The talented student-athlete is led to perceive athletic programs as farm teams for pro sports leagues. It may well be that a good academic program for the athlete is made virtually impossible by the demands of sports at the college level. If this situation causes harm to the university, it is because the schools have fostered it, and the school, rather than the individual, should suffer the consequences.

New academic standards have to be strictly enforced. Admission requirements have to be tightened. Proof must be required that shows real and substantial progress towards a degree."

ODDS & ENDS....

Old Age!

When is an athlete too old to participate?

FACTS: John, 27, said, "I went from playing high school basketball to working in the coal mines of Pennsylvania, playing only city basketball during those years. When I wanted to play college basketball, I was declared ineligible. Should I have been eligible?" **YOU'RE THE JUDGE!**

DECISION: An NCAA rule reads, Participating in "...any organized competition after an athlete is age 20 will count against his college eligibility."

This prevents older, more experienced players from dominating. It also promotes equality in competition and discourages students from delaying entrance to college in order to develop their skills. Each year of such competition counts as one year of college eligibility. Had John played fewer than four years of city basketball he would have had eligibility remaining.

Sweatpants?

May student-athletes wear clothing, other than their "standard" uniform, while playing in competition?

FACTS: Lisa, a member of her college basketball team, wore a scarf and sweatpants while playing. This was in conflict with dress code rules prohibiting the wearing of such articles of clothing. "I wore the scarf and sweatpants for religious reasons." explained Lisa. Should Lisa have been prohibited from playing? **YOU'RE THE JUDGE!**

DECISION: Because her religion prohibited showing physical beauty, Lisa was granted an exception to the dress code rules. She could wear the clothing and continue to participate.

The rights to due process (the opportunity for a fair and impartial hearing), and equal protection (intended to insure that all persons similarly situated shall be treated alike), will apply to numerous situations in everyday life, not just those involving the right and opportunity to an education and the right to participate in sports.

For example, where a suspect class (race, sex, color) or fundamental interests (marriage, interstate travel) is involved, any law or rule will be unconstitutional unless there is a compelling interest to be protected or promoted, such as the protection and safety of those affected.

4

DISCRIMINATION

WHAT'S IT ABOUT?

Discrimination discusses attempts to discriminate or differentiate in favor or against athletes or others in sports on the basis of prejudice "because" of the race, sex, color or disability of the person.

Are girls physiologically inferior to boys? Should girls be permitted to participate in contact sports (football) on the same team as, or against, boys?

SEX DISCRIMINATION

FACTS: Sally wanted to try out for the boys' basketball and tennis teams at All-Am High. The school had a girls' basketball team, but not a girls' tennis team.

As other schools in the area did not have girls' basketball teams, All- Am's girls' team only played a few games against local pick-up teams. The boys' basketball team played mostly other small, local schools. Before transferring to All-Am after her family moved, Sally was a star basketball player for North High's girls' team.

Jack wanted to try out for the girls' volleyball team. There was no boys' team.

The eligibility rules for the school's sports program were pinned to the bulletin board outside the athletic office. One rule in particular read:

ELIGIBILITY RULES

"Girls shall not be permitted to participate in athletic games against boys, either as a member of a boys' team or as a member of the girls' team playing against a boys' team. Girls' teams shall not accept male members."

When Sally found out that the State High School Association was responsible for the rule, she asked for an explanation. She received a letter which read, in part:

> "The separation of males and females in athletic competition is necessary to achieve equitable competition.
>
> Due to their physiological superiority, males outperform females. This superiority makes it necessary to separate the two in order to prevent psychological injuries to females, and to allow for the development of female athletic programs.
>
> Furthermore, the separation of males and females in sports is a 'tradition'...."

"Those rules are nothing more than old prejudices and myths," complained Sally. "I'm being discriminated against because of my sex. Can I enjoin the school from enforcing the eligibility rule?" she asked. Should Jack have been allowed to try out for the girls' volleyball team?

DECISION: **YOU'RE THE JUDGE!**

A number of our nation's documents and laws prohibit discrimination. The most important are the Constitution, the Equal Rights Amendment (ERA) and Title IX.

EQUAL PROTECTION

The Fourteenth Amendment to the Constitution provides:

"No state shall ... deny to any person ... the equal protection of the laws."

This is called the Equal Protection Clause. It prohibits laws or rules that are either discriminatory, or are applied in a discriminatory manner.

Where a state is sufficiently involved, by either conducting, encouraging, authorizing, administering, or participating in private conduct (such as by delegating its duty to provide an education), to a school or athletic association, then the Equal Protection Clause applies to the rule or conduct of the private association. This is called **state action**. It must exist. The Equal Protection Clause does not apply to actions of wholly private schools or associations.

Any rule, and its purpose, must be fair and reasonable. All persons similarly situated must be treated alike.

Must eligibility to play be based on ability and not on a student-athlete's sex?

FACTS: Cynthia and Peggy wanted to try out for the boys' tennis team at their high school.

Antoinette wanted to try out for the boys' skiing and cross-country running teams.

All of the girls' high schools had rules "prohibiting mixed athletic teams. Males are physiologically superior to females." Further, such rules were necessary for the development of female athletic programs, of which there were none. Did the rules discriminate against girls? **YOU'RE THE JUDGE!**

DECISION: Yes. In both cases, the court found that "the rules discriminated against the girls solely because of their sex. Such rules are arbitrary, unreasonable, and in violation of the Equal Protection Clause." Separating males and females is not necessary to achieve equitable competition. Eligibility to play must be based upon ability, regardless of sex.

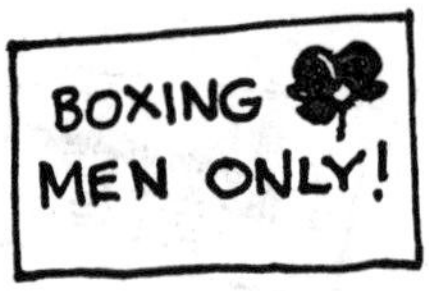

If the court determines that a rule is based on a "suspect" classification (sex, color, race), then such a rule is unconstitutional unless there is a "compelling" reason for it.

FACTS: Natalie wanted to enter a men's boxing tournament. A "MEN ONLY" rule denied women permission to enter boxing competitions. "I want to be treated like the boys and allowed to box," grumbled Natalie. "Can't I box?" **YOU'RE THE JUDGE!**

DECISION: The court found that the "MEN ONLY" rule did not violate the Equal Protection Clause because the Boxing Federation was an entirely private organization not involved in "state action." Even if there had been state action, the law permitted gender classification in contact sports.

The Equal Protection Clause has led many schools to accept girls on boys' teams, especially in non-contact sports.

The challenges to the segregation of the sexes in sports arose in two main types of situations: girls who wanted to play on boys' teams where there were no girls' teams, and where outstanding female athletes wanted to play on boys' teams (even where there was a separate girls' team) because the male team better suited their athletic ability.

But girls were not always allowed to play on the boys' teams!

FACTS: As there was no girls' team, Maria wanted to try out for the boys' high school track team.

Sandra Lynn, an outstanding swimmer, wanted to try out for the boys' team. There was a girls' swim team.

The Athletic Conference's rule forbids girls on boys' teams, reasoning that the rule reflected "custom and tradition." Also, the rule was intended "to prevent psychological damage to both males and females." Did the rule discriminate against girls? **YOU'RE THE JUDGE!**

DECISION: The court found no discrimination. "Boys will get no thrill from defeating girls. The challenge to win, and the glory of achievement would become nullified. Athletic competition should build character in our youth. We do not need that kind of character (born of constant defeat) in our girls, the women of tomorrow."

Courts began to recognize the absurdity of this position.

JoBeth qualified for the boys' high school golf team, there being no girls' team. She was not permitted to play due to a rule "prohibiting male and female students from competing on the same team or against each other." The court decided, "The rule denied girls the opportunity to participate with boys in non-contact sports solely because of sex. JoBeth must be judged solely on her ability." The court also noted that had there been a separate team for the girls, then there would be no discrimination in prohibiting JoBeth from participating on the boys' team.

FACTS: Tammie and Carolyn wanted to participate on the boys' high school cross country teams. There was no girls' teams. Although they were qualified, a school rule denied them the opportunity to participate. Should they have been allowed to participate on the boys' teams? **YOU'RE THE JUDGE!**

DECISION: Yes. "The rule discriminated against the girls by not treating them in the same manner as the boys, that is, to judge them on ability, and not prohibit their participation solely because of their sex," held the court.

These suits were, in part, responsible for a number of states passing laws requiring that girls be allowed to compete for positions on boys' teams in non-contact sports where there was no girls' team.

What if a girl wanted to try out for a boys' team even where there was a girls' team?

FACTS: Maria and some of her girlfriends wanted to play little league baseball. They were qualified, but were prohibited from playing because of a rule prohibiting girls "because of physical differences between the sexes. Girls were more likely to be injured in the game, which is played with a hard ball, than boys."

The girls charged, "We're being treated differently than the boys. That's a violation of the Equal Protection Clause." Was it? **YOU'RE THE JUDGE!**

DECISION: Yes. Girls of this age group were not subject to a greater hazard of injury, while playing baseball, than boys of the same age group. Medical evidence showed that girls of ages 8 to 12 are at least as strong as their male peers, with no less reaction time. They can compete safely and as successfully as boys in the game.

The little league had to allow girls to play, if they were capable.

This decision became part of state law. Congress then revised the Little League's charter to permit girls to play, and deleted that passage which said the purpose of little league was to instill manhood. Sportsmanship became the goal.

Athletic Segregation At Any Age?

Brenda, 12, and Nichole, 13, were permitted to play on their school's boys' football teams. The courts decided that they should not be denied the opportunity to play unless they lacked the required physical ability.

However, other high school girls have been ruled ineligible to play football because "they were more likely to get hurt than boys."

One doctor testified, "Whether you like it or not, God made women the weaker sex." Under similar reasoning, girls have also been prohibited from playing on boys' hockey teams, but not on boys' baseball teams.

FACTS: Jo Ann, 17, wanted to play on the boys' high school baseball team. There was no girls' team. At first, after cutting her hair, she was allowed. Later, she was informed, "You cannot participate. Baseball is a contact sport and you would be subject to an unreasonable risk of harm."

Jo Ann alleged, "I was being denied the right to play because of my sex." Could Jo Ann enjoin the school from preventing her from playing? **YOU'RE THE JUDGE!**

DECISION: Yes. Jo Ann was denied the right to play solely because of her sex. She had the physical ability to play.

When Susan and Nina, both 16, were denied the opportunity to try out for the boys' baseball and soccer teams at their high school, the court found discrimination and ordered the schools to either drop the sports, establish girls' teams, or allow the girls to try out.

Separate Seasons

FACTS: Classical High School established separate seasons of play for male and female athletic teams in order to allocate limited facilities and to maximize participation by both sexes.

Several girls argued, "Because the weather and competition was better for tennis in the spring, we were not being treated like the boys. The rule discriminated against us." Did it? **YOU'RE THE JUDGE!**

DECISION: No discrimination was found. Neither season was so substantially better than the other that equal protection of the laws was denied the girls.

EQUAL RIGHTS AMENDMENT (ERA)

Sex discrimination in sports has also been litigated under state Equal Rights Amendments. A typical state ERA provides:

"Equality of rights and responsibility ... shall not be denied or taken away ... on account of sex."

FACTS: Commerce High School's sports eligibility rule read: "Girls shall not compete or practice against boys in any athletic contest." Did the rule violate an ERA prohibition against sex discrimination? **YOU'RE THE JUDGE!**

DECISION: The court found that the rule violated both the ERA and the Equal Protection Clause. "The notion that girls—as a whole—are weaker, more injury prone and less skilled, cannot justify such a rule."

Even where there are separate teams for boys and girls, the most talented girls should have the opportunity to play at that level of competition which their ability warrants.

Every student is guaranteed, and should have, an individual determination of qualification to play on school sports teams. Especially where, concerning girls, the school provides no corresponding girls' team. Girls can be protected from physical injury by appropriate equipment.

Discrimination Against Boys!

The Equal Protection Clause and Equal Rights Amendment have also allowed boys to play on girls' athletic teams, at least where there was no corresponding boys' team.

FACTS: The Massachusetts ERA required that any classification by sex must serve a compelling purpose. A high school athletic association rule read: "To protect the welfare and safety of all students participating in athletics, no boy may play on a girls' team, but a girl may play on a boys' team if that sport is not offered for the girl."

Several high schools that permitted boys to play on girls' teams in volleyball, softball, swimming, tennis, and basketball, where there were no boy's teams, challenged the rule.

One school—with only a few boys—could not field teams exclusively for boys. Could the boys play on the girls' teams? **YOU'RE THE JUDGE!**

DECISION: The court ruled, "Yes. Any rule which classifies by sex alone is subject to close examination." The problem of boys playing on the girl's team was marginal. Where the problem becomes more acute as by girl's sports being overrun by boys, it can be met by measures less offensive and less sweeping than a complete sex barrier.

Although one state prohibited boys from playing on a girls' field hockey team for safety reasons, a Massachusetts high school (David Hale Fanning) allowed the boys to play on the girls' field hockey team. "To show their dedication to the sport, the boys wore blue plaid kilts while playing!"

DISCRIMINATION IN EDUCATION

Title IX of the Educational Amendments Act provides:

"No person ... shall, on the basis of sex, be excluded from participation in, be denied the benefit of, or be subject to discrimination under any education program or activity receiving federal financial assistance."

Title IX was intended to eliminate inequalities and discrimination in sports by requiring equal funding for both men's and women's programs, encouraging athletic participation by females, and increasing the number of sports offered to women. The goal is to elevate women's competition.

FACTS: Football U. wanted to spend more on its men's football program than on the women's intramural touch football program. Would such unequal spending violate Title IX? **YOU'RE THE JUDGE!**

DECISION: Title IX permits nonequivalent spending in certain spectator sports, such as football, provided that the difference results from nondiscriminatory factors. In the case of football, equipment, injuries and needed facilities and their maintenance make football expensive. Therefore, schools are justified in spending more on this traditionally male sport.

Contact Sports

Title IX regulations make a crucial distinction between contact and non-contact sports. In the case of contact sports, such as basketball, football, wrestling, and ice hockey, a school may operate single-sex, "separate-but-equal" teams.

FACTS: "I wanted to play for the boys' basketball team," declared Karen. She was not permitted. She had been given the opportunity to play on the girls' basketball team, but refused to try out. The girls' team and their schedule were top-rated. Was this discrimination? **YOU'RE THE JUDGE!**

DECISION: No. The equality of the teams and her voluntary refusal to try out for the girl's team lessened her claim of injury.

The rationale seems to be that in rough sports, it isn't reasonable to expect boys and girls to compete equally. Therefore, a school does not have to let a girl try out. Her only recourse would be to gather enough girls and start their own team. The school would be obligated to support them as long as girls were limited in that sport and there was sufficient interest, ability and a reasonable expectation of competition. Would this be true for all schools?

FACTS: Susan wanted to play on the boys' high school baseball team. There was no girls' team. She had the required ability.

Sherry wanted to play basketball and football, but there were no girls' teams in those sports at her high school. Should Susan and Sherry have been permitted to play on the boys' teams? **YOU'RE THE JUDGE!**

DECISION: Yes. The court held that there was no specific prohibition on girls playing on boys' teams in a contact sport. Girls must be allowed to try out for the boys' team, even if it was the football team. They must be judged on ability and not discriminated against because of their sex.

Would the decision have been different had the girls wanted to play on college football and basketball teams where the boys are bigger and stronger, and the game rougher?

Non-Contact Sports

In non-contact sports, schools can offer separate teams for sports such as tennis, golf, swimming and track. If there are teams for boys and girls in all these sports, there generally will be no problems. The exception is where there is no girls' team, or where one of the girls possesses unique ability.

FACTS: "I want to try out for the boys' track team. There is no girl's track team," said Tammie.

Helena, the state's 100 yard dash champion, wanted to run for the boys' track team even though there was a girls' track team. Would they be allowed the try-out? **YOU'RE THE JUDGE!**

DECISION: The court held that the girls must be permitted to try out for the boy's track team. The same would hold true for tennis, swimming, or golf.

Until Congress intervened in 1988—where a school's athletic program did not receive federal assistance—Title IX could not be used to prohibit discrimination in the school's selection process for that team or in providing unequal funding for women's and men's sports programs. Now, regardless of whether or not a school's athletic program receives federal assistance, if a public or private school receives federal assistance, equal funding for both women's and men's athletic programs is required with no discrimination (football is an exception).

SEX DISCRIMINATION ON THE JOB

Claims for wages, based upon sex discrimination, have had mixed success.

Where coaching duties are substantially similar, coaches of girls' and boys' sports must receive pay on an equal basis without regard to the coach's sex or the students coached. Laws prohibiting such discrimination may also require other equal terms and conditions of employment concerning hiring and assignment.

FACTS: Melissa, a sportswriter, sued the commissioner of baseball, stated, "He ordered all major league baseball teams to take a 'unified stand' against the admission of women sportswriters into major league clubhouses. Because of that order, I was excluded from the Blue Sox clubhouse. Did they discriminate against me?" **YOU'RE THE JUDGE!**

DECISION: Other pro sports admitted women sportswriters to their locker rooms. Adequate steps could be taken to ensure the necessary privacy of the players. The custom of refusing to allow female reporters into the locker room was discrimination. Such discrimination violated Melissa's right to equal protection (to be treated as male reporters were treated), and unreasonably interfered with her right to pursue her profession. The Blue Sox were enjoined from refusing her admission to the locker room area.

To accommodate all reporters, professional teams set aside a room where the players would go to be interviewed. Thereby, they could still retain their privacy.

DISABILITY

"No otherwise qualified handicapped individual ... shall, solely by reason of a handicap, be excluded from participation in, be denied benefits of, or be subject to discrimination...." in athletics.

This is the Rehabilitation Act. As in Title IX, it covers any athletic program or activity receiving federal financial assistance.

Handicapped athletes have been prevented from participating where a school would be forced to make substantial modifications to accommodate a handicapped athlete, or where the public school system acted pursuant to its **loco parentis** (acting as parents) powers to protect the well-being of students not old enough to weigh the risks involved and make a mature, informed decision.

What if there is no substantial risk of serious injury related to the handicap?

FACTS: "Tank," with an artificial leg below his left knee, wanted to run the 40 yard low hurdles for his school's track team. The school said, "No." Could Tank participate? **YOU'RE THE JUDGE!**

DECISION: In ruling "Yes." the court commented, "No athlete should be denied the opportunity to participate solely because of a handicap. Hard work and dedication can and have overcome enormous odds."

Disabilities alleged by professional athletes are not covered by the Rehabilitation Act.

FACTS: Pierre, a pro hockey player, was barred from playing when it was discovered that he was blind in one eye.

Charlie, a jockey, was denied a jockey's license because of blindness in one eye. Although both athletes had performed satisfactorily in the past, they were ruled medically unfit to continue playing. Were Pierre and Charlie discriminated against? Should they have been allowed to participate?

DECISION: **YOU'RE THE JUDGE!**

A Massachusetts little league faced the loss of their charter unless they banned three teams of physically and mentally handicapped players from competing.

FACTS: The little league organization felt that the handicapped children should not compete since they were not covered by insurance and, also, because they were not coached by professionals, but by volunteers. Would such a ban be discrimination?

DECISION: **YOU'RE THE JUDGE!**

RACE OR COLOR - CIVIL RIGHTS ACT OF 1964

"All persons shall be entitled to the full and equal enjoyment ... of any place of public accommodation ... without discrimination or segregation on the grounds of race, color...."

This is to eliminate "the inconvenience, unfairness and humiliation of racial discrimination."

A place of public accommodation may be a sports arena, bowling alley, golf course, YWCA, health club, skating rink, public or private swimming area open to the public or any other place of entertainment open to the general public.

FACTS: Lake Nixon Amusement Club had recreation facilities including: swimming, boating, dancing, miniature golf and a snack bar. It advertised in a magazine and on the radio. Whites who patronized the club were routinely furnished "membership cards" for a small fee.

Blacks were denied admission. They alleged that they were being discriminated against solely because of their race. They asked the court for an injunction prohibiting the club from denying them admission. Was this a violation of the Civil Rights Act? **YOU'RE THE JUDGE!**

DECISION: Yes. The court held that Lake Nixon was not a private club. It was "open in general to all of the public who are members of the white race." The club, in violation of the Civil Rights Act, discriminated against Blacks. It was enjoined from continuing the practice.

The Civil Rights Act applies whether patrons are spectators or participating in a sport or other activity.

Therefore, where membership to an athletic program or team was denied solely due to race, the Civil Rights Act was used to prohibit such discrimination. And where a school refused to promote a coach, solely because of his race, the court found racial discrimination and ordered that he either be promoted or compensated as if he were.

Are public golf courses covered by the Civil Rights Act?

FACTS: An ordinance made it unlawful for Black people to use parks owned and maintained by the city for use of white people, and unlawful for white people to frequent or use any park maintained by the city for the use and benefit of Black persons.

Holmes argued, "Me and other Black citizens couldn't use the golf courses run by the city. They did that because of our race and color. It was discrimination." Did the ordinance discriminate against Blacks? **YOU'RE THE JUDGE!**

DECISION: Yes. The court held that segregation of public facilities could not be justified. The city was enjoined from refusing to allow Holmes to play golf on any golf course that it ran.

Justice Douglas of the U.S. Supreme Court, in addressing the problems of discrimination, declared: "Segregation of Negroes... is a relic of slavery. It is a badge of second-class citizenship. It is a denial of a privilege... of national citizenship and of the equal protection guaranteed by the Constitution...."

PRIVATE CLUBS

Private clubs that discriminate against females and racial minorities, and whose goal is to "permit exclusive membership to gather together away from public view," have become very controversial for condoning such "impermissible snobbery."

Now, a growing number of cities have passed ordinances requiring many men-only or whites-only clubs to accept women and minority members.

FACTS: John, Tom and Andy joined the Lago Lake Club, a pri-

vate golf and tennis club that prohibited women and certain minorities from becoming members.

Their wives (who also wanted to join the club but were refused membership) protested, "The club is discriminating against us!"

State's Attorney Warren filed a discrimination suit against the club, arguing, "The club's tax breaks, lease of city property at a reduced rate and the IRS's allowance of membership-costs as a business deduction all make the club 'public.' The public is paying for those savings."

Furthermore, Warren explained, "When a club provides a place where business is transacted, then the club must not discriminate. As are other businesses, it must be open to all who desire membership."

The husbands pleaded, "The Constitution guarantees us the right of free association, to associate or not with whomever we please." Should the club be allowed to continue prohibiting women and minorities as members?

DECISION: **YOU'RE THE JUDGE!**

ODDS & ENDS....

Ladies' Night!

FACTS: Bruce and his wife went to a Supersonic's basketball game. It was "Ladies' Night." Bruce requested to pay the same admission price (a 50% discount) for himself as that paid by female spectators.

"The ticket seller refused to allow this," said Bruce. Was Bruce discriminated against? **YOU'RE THE JUDGE!**

DECISION: The Court concluded that "Ladies Night" ticket prices constituted sex discrimination. Men could not be charged more than ladies. The injustice would be easily recognized if it arose concerning race. It would be inconceivable to have a "Blacks' Night" or a "Whites' Night" or a "Filipinos' Night."! The Court suggested a "Spouses' Night" as a way to promote the ladies' attendance.

Similarly, discrimination was found where other professional teams held a "Ladies' Day" with discount prices for women only.

Weight For Me!

FACTS: "I wanted to march in the school band!" cried Peggy.

Sue wanted to play basketball. They were both told that they could not participate because they were overweight. Their school imposed the weight restrictions for performance and to avoid heckling by the fans. "Were we discriminated against?" asked the girls. Will it depend upon how overweight they were? **YOU'RE THE JUDGE!**

DECISION: There were no such restrictions applying to boys. This was sex discrimination in violation of the equal protection clause. Even if the restriction applied to boys, discrimination might still be found where it could be shown that a loss of weight might be injurious to health, or that the extra weight would not affect performance.

The prohibitions of discrimination in the Constitution, Equal Rights Amendment, Title IX and The Civil Rights Act apply equally to all, not just athletes.

5

ATHLETES & INJURIES

WHAT'S IT ABOUT?

Athletes & Injuries discusses and comments on personal injuries to professional and amateur athletes which are caused by intentional misconduct (assault and battery), or by non-intentional misconduct (negligence). Injuries to amateur athletes may occur while they are participating for a school or other organized team, or while just playing around. There are defenses to the charges of assault and battery or negligence.

In addition, this chapter covers injuries at work and those caused by extraordinary risks or conditions "not fit for play."

Do injured athletes assume the risk of injury or are they guilty of contributing to their injury when they are aware of the dangers of the sport in which they are participating? Are parents responsible for the conduct of their children?

PERSONAL INJURIES

"They were playing soccer." said John. "Bob intentionally kicked Gil, fracturing his jaw!"

"I didn't mean it. I was only trying to tackle him. It was an accident," cried Gil.

This is a case of personal injury–someone was hurt. It can happen in any sport. It doesn't matter if you're a pro, an amateur in school, or just playing around.

If you're hurt, you can claim damages for your injury. But there are defenses. Anyone you sue might claim that you contributed to your injury by participating, or that you assumed the risk of getting hurt. You have to prove that they were at fault.

FREE seminar!
Learn all about personal injuries and YOUR RIGHTS...

ASSAULT & BATTERY

FACTS: Some neighborhood boys were playing soccer. John explained what happened, "Tempers were growing short when Gil was on the ground, wreathing in pain. Just moments before, he and Bob were eye to eye. I think Bob threatened Gil."

Gil was taken to the hospital and treated for a fractured jaw. After finding out he might have a permanent speech defect, Gil filed a complaint charging Bob with negligently causing his injuries. In addition, Bob might be charged with assault and battery. Was Bob guilty of assault and battery? Was Bob's conduct negligent?

DECISION: **YOU'RE THE JUDGE!**

Although most cases involving injuries to participants during sporting events are based on **negligence** (an unintentional act), some may be the result of **assault and battery** (an intentional act).

For Bob to be found guilty of a **tort**—a civil wrong committed against an individual—certain things have to be proven.

What if Bob had threatened Gil with harm? Gil was a better player and maybe Bob hoped to intimidate him. If Gil was aware of Bob's conduct, and was also reasonably apprehensive, fearing that Bob intended to immediately cause him injury by contact (hitting him), then Bob would be liable for **assault** upon Gil.

Would it still be an assault if Bob pushed someone else onto Gil?

FACTS: "Bob committed harmful and offensive contact, intending to hurt me. That's a **battery!**" charged Gil.

"I didn't hit you, Harry fell on you," Bob yelled.

Sam said, "Bob knocked Gil down and then pushed Harry, who fell on Gil."

If Bob intended to push Harry onto Gil, was Bob still liable for battery on Gil, even though he didn't directly hit Gil? **YOU'RE THE JUDGE!**!

DECISION: Yes, Bob would be liable. He would not have to touch Gil if he intended to hurt him, but could do so indirectly by, pushing someone into Gil, hitting him with an object or touching something Gil was holding.

DEFENSES TO ASSAULT & BATTERY

Bob insisted, "Gil gave his **consent** to the contact. He challenged me, 'You wanna fight, come on, let's go!'"

Gil denied this, contending that he "only consented to reasonable contact within the rules of soccer."

Next, Bob claimed **self-defense.** "After Gil hit me first, I defended myself, only using enough force to prevent Gil from harming me. If anyone else was hurt, I'm not liable for those injuries either. I didn't intend to hurt them."

Lastly, Bob argued, "Gil was beating up on Harry and Tom, so in **defense of others,** I used that force that they could have used to defend themselves."

Boston Times SPORTS September 12, 1987

BATTER STRUCK OUT!

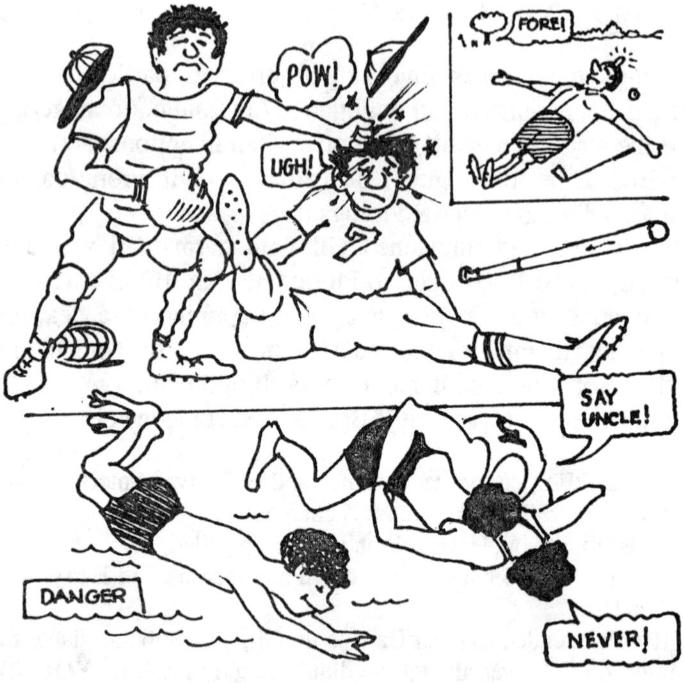
POW!
UGH!
FORE!
SAY UNCLE!
DANGER
NEVER!

In a semi-pro baseball game last month, Lyle, the Lookouts' shortstop, had his jaw fractured. He was the batter when Earl, the Vols' catcher, struck him on the jaw. Was Earl liable? Yesterday, after listening to testimony, the court reached a decision.

Lyle explained in court what had happened, "I was up once before and Lane threw me curve balls outside. So the next time up, after the catcher gave his sign, I stepped up to try to hit the pitch before it broke. The ball almost hit me."

The pitcher then shouted, "Nobody does that to me. If you do it again I'll stick it in your ear!"

Lyle continued, "Well, I stepped forward and was hit. I knew that he was throwing at me. So, I started to throw the bat towards him, but held up and dropped it. That's all I remember."

Then, Earl, without any warning, struck Lyle with his fist, fracturing Lyle's jaw. Was Earl's team liable for the act of its player—vicarious liability?

The court found that, "Although Earl may have been personally liable for the injury to Lyle, the team was not. Earl was not performing his job when he hit Lyle. The team had no knowledge of any such previous conduct."

BURDEN OF PROOF

How convincing would the evidence have to be to prove assault and battery?

In a civil case involving negligence, the **plaintiff**—party bringing an action—has the **burden of proof.** He must prove to the judge or jury that the defendant is guilty by a mere majority of the clear and convincing evidence.

However, in a criminal case, such as one charging assault and battery, the prosecuting attorney must prove that the defendant is guilty beyond all reasonable doubt before there can be a conviction.

In other words, if the jury is more than 50% sure that the evidence shows that Bob was guilty, then they must return a verdict in Gil's favor and against Bob.

FACTS: Bill Smith threw a punch while tackling Jay Jones during a football game. After the pile-up, he punched Jones again, causing a severe eye laceration.

Jim Kirby, during a basketball game, struck Wally Shaw in the face with his fist, causing lacerations and broken teeth.

Hank Lovel, a softball coach, beat an opposing coach with a bat.

When assault and battery charges were brought against Smith, Kirby and Lovel, they defended by stating, "They gave their consent to the contact. We acted in self-defense, only using enough force necessary to stop them from hurting us." Were the defendants guilty of assault and battery? **YOU'RE THE JUDGE!**

DECISION: Yes. The acts of Smith, Kirby and Lovel were intentional acts of misconduct—assault and battery.

Would the courts use a different approach for a pro game, knowing that professional players play for their livelihood, that the game is rougher, and that fighting may be more a part of the game, and therefore accepted?

ASSAULT & BATTERY IN PRO SPORTS

Northfield News June 24

VIOLENCE ON THE FIELD!

Injuries in professional sports, where there is fault, may be due to either intentional or negligent conduct. Those that are intentional—assault and battery—are often referred to as acts of violence.

"As far back as 70 A.D., spectators at the games in Pompeii broke into wild sword fights. Centuries later many people were killed in riots set off by chariot racing."

Soccer matches have turned into mayhem and many other acts of violence have taken place between fans, and even between players. Is there a connection between spectator violence and violence on the field?

Pressure from teammates, coaches and fans may encourage athletes to take part in "generally accepted" violence during a game. Violence may be looked upon as a legitimate "part of the game." Leagues may accept and condone the use of violence while the media exploits it.

The fear of being labeled for not "performing," or of being waived, cut or traded helps to carry on this "macho code," leading to violence and injury.

Winning becomes the sole criteria for success. Violence has its part in determining that success... or lack of.

To review, the elements for cases involving intentional torts—assault and battery—that cause personal injury are: intentional, impermissible, and harmful or offensive contact to a person or something in his control. The defenses available to a defendant are consent, self-defense and defense of others.

Assault and battery may occur in numerous situations involving different sports.

Hockey

FACTS: The Town Crier newspaper reported, "There was a scramble in front of the hockey net. Danny, an NHL pro hockey player, in attempting to clear the puck away, hit Walt in the face with his stick. Walt, reacting quickly, swung his stick like a baseball bat, striking Danny on the bridge of his nose."

Injury to Danny: broken nose, concussion, facial lacerations. Danny sued Walt and the owner of Walt's team, alleging assault and battery and negligence. Did Danny assume the risk of such an injury? **YOU'RE THE JUDGE!**

DECISION: Judgment was for the plaintiff, Danny. Walt's conduct was intentional, impermissible and harmful, to which Danny did not consent. Danny only consented to that contact reasonably expected to be part of the game. Nor was the contact in self-defense. In addition to actual damages, Danny was awarded **punitive damages**—intended to serve as a deterrent to the defendant and others in preventing such conduct in the future.

Hockey may well produce the most violence. Insufficient suspensions for violent conduct and the general lack of enforcement of its rules by the NHL, have been severely criticized. Brawls have led to criminal actions. The fans expect violence; the teams and leagues condone it.

FACTS: Jay, an announcer, told of another fight in the NHL. "Matty and Brown pursued the puck behind the net. A skirmish developed. Brown struck Matty in the face with his glove. Matty retaliated by striking Brown in the stomach with his stick. After a penalty was called, a stick fight broke out. It was unclear who struck the first blow. Matty was struck near the shoulder and Brown was struck with a blow that resulted in a fractured skull."

Criminal assault charges were brought against both players by the district attorney. Both claimed that they were "acting in self-defense," and that the other player had "consented" to the injury by voluntarily playing hockey. Did the players consent to their injuries? **YOU'RE THE JUDGE!**

DECISION: The court concluded, "No athlete should be presumed to accept malicious, unprovoked, or overly violent attack." Nevertheless, both players were acquitted—found not guilty.
The court felt Matty consented to being struck by the glove because that was a common practice in hockey and not likely to result in serious injury. The court also felt that Brown's action was in self-defense and reasonable under the circumstances. No civil complaints for damages for personal injuries were ever filed.

Could a hockey stick be considered a deadly weapon when used to injure a player?

FACTS: Jacques and Pierre were assessed penalties after Jacques attacked Pierre. Upon serving out the penalties and leaving the penalty box, another fight broke out. Jacques allegedly assaulted Pierre from behind, striking him with his hockey stick and pummeling him with his fists. Jacques was charged with aggravated assault with a deadly weapon, a criminal charge. Was this aggravated assault? **YOU'RE THE JUDGE!**

DECISION: The jury could not agree upon a verdict (**hung jury**) and a **mistrial**—no decision—was declared. Unless the criminal charges were dropped, there would be a re-trial. No civil charges were filed.

Soccer

Soccer can also be a violent sport. Although play may be even rougher in the stands, leading to riots (especially after unfavorable officials' decisions), play on the field may lead to injuries for the players.

FACTS: A soccer player, Mario, was "dribbling" the ball toward his opponent's goal. When an opponent appeared in his path, Mario kicked the ball away. The opponent then jumped in the air and struck Mario in the stomach with his knee, rupturing Mario's intestines. When Mario died the next day, manslaughter charges were brought. Was this an assault and battery? **YOU'RE THE JUDGE!**

DECISION: In a criminal action, the court remarked, "If the defendant was acting within the rules, not motivated by any malicious motive which he knew could result in injury, then there was no crime. If he acted outside of the rules, intending to cause harm, was indifferent and reckless, the act would be unlawful."

The court concluded that, "There was not enough evidence to show that harm was intended." The accused player was acquitted.

What is the standard of proof in a criminal action? What must the plaintiff prove to the court?

In a criminal action, the jury must find, after hearing the evidence, that there was intent and "guilt beyond a reasonable doubt." That is much more difficult to prove than in a civil action, where the standard of proof is "by a mere majority of the clear and convincing evidence."

FACTS: Mario's wife brought suit for the death of her husband. Could she prevail in a civil action for damages?

DECISION: **YOU'RE THE JUDGE!**

Baseball

Baseball has perhaps the most lethal weapon in all of sports, the "beanball." This occurs when the ball is intentionally thrown at a batter's head. An umpire has the power—within certain guidelines (warning)—to eject a pitcher for intentionally throwing toward or at a batter. This may be a deterrent. However, it has not put an end to the beanball.

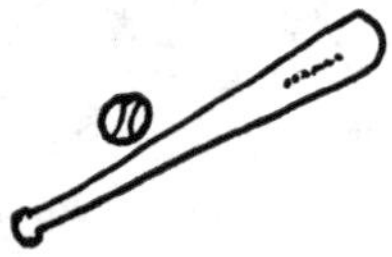

FACTS: Sam, a pro baseball player, was at bat and was hit by a pitch. When Sam threw his bat at the pitcher, he was struck by the catcher, Bob. Sam's jaw was fractured. He sued Bob and Bob's club for his injury.

Bob claimed assumption of the risk and self-defense of others as defenses. Bob pleaded, "I was defending the pitcher from being assaulted." "Was Bob liable for my injuries?" asked Sam. **YOU'RE THE JUDGE!**

DECISION: Yes. As the batter, Sam, made no further attempt to injure the pitcher. The pitcher was not in imminent (immediate) danger. Therefore, Bob did not have to defend Sam. Bob's act was intended to cause harm and did.

The court held that, "The club was not liable." reasoning that the assault was not performed within the **scope of employment**—Bob was not doing things normally permitted as part of his job. The club had no **vicarious liability**—liability for another's negligent acts.

How far can a player go in claiming that he was acting in self-defense when injuring another player?

FACTS: Another catcher, Gluefingers, in throwing the ball back to the pitcher, hit the batter—who happened to be the opposing pitcher. The batter hit the catcher over the head with his bat causing serious injuries. Was the batter acting in self-defense? **YOU'RE THE JUDGE!**

DECISION: There was no self-defense. Hitting the batter was unintentional and caused no damages. The defendant batter was suspended and fined; the suit was settled out of court. Gluefingers received money damages.

Basketball

In an attempt to keep things in order on the court, there have been many fights in pro basketball. Penalties for fighting may include fines and suspension, but they are not mandatory.

May an injured player recover damages against the team of the player who injured him?

FACTS: Adam and John got into a fight. Rudy, not involved in the fight, was struck in the face by Adam as he came toward the two. Rudy suffered fractures of the face and skull, a concussion, severe lacerations, a loss of teeth and a separated jaw.

As one witness testified, "The punch sounded like a watermelon being dropped on a cement floor!"

Rudy sued Adam's team, alleging vicarious liability–team liability for its players' actions. "The team was responsible for Adam's acts." Was the team liable for Adam's conduct? **YOU'RE THE JUDGE!**

DECISION: Yes. The jury found that Adam acted as an employee of his team. The team had failed to train him adequately so as to avoid such violence. Knowing his "dangerous" tendencies, the club did nothing to prevent the violence which occurred. The acts were a battery and reckless disregard for the safety of another person. In addition to actual damages, punitive damages were awarded. The case was settled before appeal.

Football

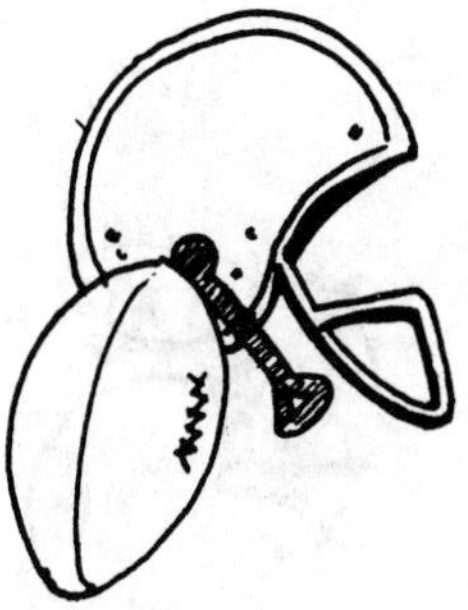

Football, like hockey, is an aggressive and, sometimes, violent sport. Rules have been changed in an attempt to lessen excessive violence. But physical contact and intimidation remain part of the game.

FACTS: After attempting to block Jim, Hank remained on one knee watching the play. The facts given to the court explained what happened next. Jim, acting out of anger and frustration but without specific intent to injure, struck the back of Hank's head and neck with his right forearm.

It was discovered that Hank had a serious neck injury. In addition to having pain and suffering, he felt that his career had been shortened. Hank sued Jim and Jim's team under vicarious liability. Who was liable? **YOU'RE THE JUDGE!**

DECISION: The court held, "Tort principles are not suspended simply because an injury takes place during a game, even a professional game." The court looked to reckless conduct as the measure for liability. A settlement was reached between Hank and Jim's team.

NEGLIGENCE

The most frequent allegation and claim for relief when a participant is injured will be, "Someone was negligent. Their conduct, or lack of conduct, fell below that expected of an ordinary and responsible person in similar circumstances."

FACTS: If Jones, Shaw and the battered coach–all assaulted and battered–each brought separate actions to recover damages for their injuries, could a jury find the defendants negligent for their conduct? **YOU'RE THE JUDGE!**

DECISION: The defendants' conduct was below that expected of them. They breached their duty to care for the plaintiff's safety. They were negligent and, therefore, liable for damages.

The elements of **negligence** are: a **duty** owed to the plaintiff by the defendant (such as to play by the rules to insure everyone's safety), a **breach of** that **duty** by the defendant (the **injury** would not have happened **"but for"** the act of the defendant), and an injury resulting in **damages.**

The defenses that may be used by a defendant are: **contributory negligence**—the plaintiff contributed to his injuries by participating, **comparative negligence**—where a plaintiff's own negligence may reduce any amount that he recovers for injuries, and **assumption of the risk**—the plaintiff assumed the risk of injury from a known danger.

FACTS: The teams had warmed up for the state championship football game. The Fighting Wabaws won the toss.

Paul received the kickoff for the Polar Bears and headed up the field. In a sea of bodies, crunching and groaning, the play came to an end. The players unpiled; all except Paul.

X-rays revealed that Paul had a sprained neck. It could have been much worse.

"It could get worse when he gets older. Paul should no longer play football," the doctor warned his parents.

Paul missed work, incurred medical expenses and will always have pain and suffering from the injury. He brought an action against Billy, the player who tackled him, and Ray, the opposing coach. Who was at fault? Do you have enough evidence to decide if there was fault?

DECISION: **YOU'RE THE JUDGE!**

Paul must show by a majority of the clear and convincing evidence that one, or both, of the defendants was guilty of negligence (an unintentional tort—a breach of a duty of care) that caused his injury and damages.

Duty Of Care

Coach Ray had a duty to teach his players the proper way to tackle. Billy had a duty to tackle in the proper manner.

Their **duty of care** was to act as reasonable people would act under the same circumstances, considering the potential harm, and considering the precautions that were available. That is the duty owed by an adult. Billy, participating in an adult activity, is treated as an adult.

If Billy was a minor, would he have the same duty? A minor may be held to a lesser duty of care.

Breach Of Duty

FACTS: Paul accused Billy, "You breached your duty of care by tackling with your head."

Paul further charged, "Coach Ray taught Billy and his teammates to use their heads and helmets to tackle, or at the least, he did not discourage the practice." Would such conduct be negligent? **YOU'RE THE JUDGE!**

DECISION: Tackling, by using one's head, was a violation of safety rules and therefore, negligent. The coach had a duty to protect Paul from unreasonable risks of injury, such as that caused by head tackling.

"But For...."

Paul contended, "Billy's and Coach Ray's breach of duty was the **proximate cause** of my injury and damage. That is, 'but for' their actions, I would not have been hurt."

In other words, had Coach Ray taught the proper way to tackle, and had Billy tackled properly, Paul would not have been injured.

Injury & Damages

Paul must prove his injury and show damages. These may be **special damages**—all medical related costs and loss of earnings (real or potential), or **general damages**—pain and suffering and loss of enjoyment of life.

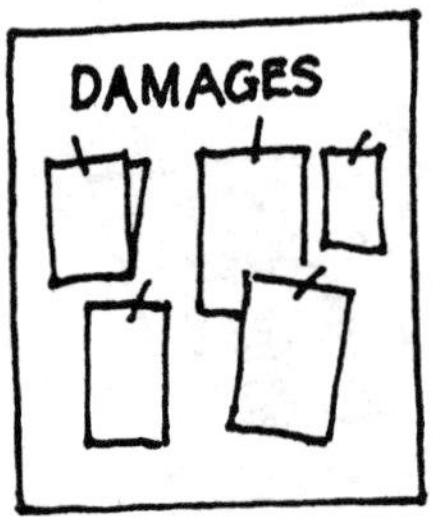

Paul can't recover **punitive damages**—damages which are meant to punish and penalize the defendant—unless he shows that one or both of the defendants were grossly negligent and acted with **malice**—recklessness or evil intent.

DEFENSES TO NEGLIGENCE

What defenses may the defendants claim against the action by Paul to recover damages for his injury?

The defendants claimed **contributory negligence.** "Paul was aware of the danger and risk involved. He contributed to his injury by playing and by lowering his own head."

FACTS: Tom was injured during a pick-up football game. "I stepped in a hole in the field," he said. Tom had played there many times before and was well aware of the condition of the field. Did he assume the risk of injury? Was he guilty of contributory negligence? **YOU'RE THE JUDGE!**

DECISION: Tom cannot recover for his injury. He assumed the risk of, and contributed to, his injury by playing there. He violated a duty to protect himself.

In addition, the defendants argued, "Paul had the **last clear chance** to avoid the injury, didn't, and he should be guilty of contributory negligence, preventing any right to recover."

The defendants also felt that **assumption of the risk** should prevent Paul from recovering any damages. "Paul knew the risk of being injured existed and was common to the game. He voluntarily proceeded anyway."

FACTS: Paul said, "I only assumed the ordinary risks of the game. I did not contribute to the injury. Furthermore, I didn't assume extraordinary risks, such as from head tackling. Nor did I assume the risk of injury from such an unforseeable violation of the rules. Can I recover for my injury?"

DECISION: **YOU'RE THE JUDGE!**

Billy and Coach Ray thought that because Paul lowered his own head, that Paul's **comparative negligence** should be compared with theirs. If they were found guilty, any recovery by Paul should be reduced because of his own negligence.

If an injury is from an unavoidable **pure accident**—unforseeable or could not be prevented by reasonable caution—it may be unavoidable and not actionable. Assumption of the risk will be a valid defense.

FACTS: One baseball player was injured when a ball curved around a screen. Another was injured when a ball bounced off a wall and into the dugout. This had never happened before.

A football player who was run out of bounds lamented, "I was so mad, I ran far past the sideline and was hurt when I tripped over a tree stump in a lot next to the field." Did the players assume the risk of such injuries? **YOU'RE THE JUDGE!**

DECISION: If an injury is unforseeable (pure accident), or could not be prevented by reasonable caution, it may then be unavoidable. Both players assumed such risks and could not recover damages.

Assumption of the risk or contributory negligence may arise where a participant is clearly aware of the risk or danger involved and, yet, voluntarily proceeds to encounter that danger.

FACTS: Tom played for the Aztec U. basketball team. He explained, "I know that it gets rough under the hoop, so I decided to play rough myself. While trying to grab a rebound, my nose was broken by someone's elbow." "Did I assume the risk of injury? Was I guilty of contributory negligence? " asked Tom. **YOU'RE THE JUDGE!**

DECISION: Tom assumed the risk of injury and—by knowing of the danger, but continuing the rough play—he was also guilty of contributory negligence.

Where a player receives injuries from accidents that are a result of normal or reasonable conduct, there will be no liability.

FACTS: Robert, while playing in a pick-up football game, injured his knee. He charged, "There was no preparation for the game, no equipment and inadequate supervision. They piled on me. Also, I was encouraged at too early an age, 15, to play." Did Robert assume the risk of injury? **YOU'RE THE JUDGE!**

DECISION: Robert assumed the risk of injury from the normal and reasonable conduct of the game. There was negligence for no preparation and equipment, but that didn't cause the injury, nor did being encouraged to play at too early an age. Robert was aware of the danger.

As long as play is in pursuit of the normal and accepted goals of the game, then any injuries arising from contact may be considered as from ordinary risks of the game.

But what if a player, whether intentionally or not, pursues the game in a way which creates a risk that it is not a normal and expected risk of participating in that game?

FACTS: A softball player, Lucky, was injured when a runner, Spikes, "rounded second, ran out of the base path and intentionally dove head first into me, injuring my knee."

"Was that a normal or ordinary risk of the game?" questioned Lucky. **YOU'RE THE JUDGE!**

DECISION: Ordinary risks are assumed, but not where another acts intentionally and in violation of the rules. This was a breach of Spike's duty to care for Lucky's safety.

What if the injured was a voluntary participant, such as a ball boy?

FACTS: A basketball coach, Ishy, was injured. "I slipped on the floor and fractured my ankle." he groaned.

A ball boy, Wally, while at a baseball game, was hit and injured by a foul ball.

A caddy, Bobby, was struck by an errant golf shot which broke his wrist. He had gone ahead of the players to watch where the balls landed. Could any of the three recover for their injuries? **YOU'RE THE JUDGE!**

DECISION: No. Voluntary participants and others, who in some way are involved in a sports activity, assume all the ordinary risks of that sport, so long as the activity is played in good faith and the injury is not the result of intentional misconduct.

Where accidents are so many that a game is too dangerous to continue without change (such as where accidents on an auto racetrack were numerous and continuous), assumption of the risk may not be a valid defense.

Also, where risks are created by the negligence of third persons—such as medical personnel, a referee or a coach—assumption of the risk may not be a valid defense.

FACTS: A hockey player, Francis, sued his team for breach of its duty to care for his safety. "I was ordered to play while I had a separated shoulder. The team knew about my injury," said Francis. A check by an opposing player then left him with permanent injuries to his spinal cord. Were his team and coach liable for the injury? **YOU'RE THE JUDGE!**

DECISION: Yes. Francis' club was vicariously liable for the coach' negligence. In addition to actual damages, punitive damages were assessed against the team for conduct "such as to merit condemnation."

In determining if there is liability by a defendant, courts use a two-step process. If the first duty, owed by the defendant to the plaintiff is violated, the plaintiff should recover. However, if the plaintiff has violated the second duty—that of using reasonable care to protect himself—this will prevent any recovery for damages for a resulting injury.

REVIEW! REVIEW!

There are two general rules concerning injuries to participants in sports activities.

First, the owner or operator of a sports or public amusement facility is not an insurer of a participant's safety.

The owner or operator is bound to exercise "ordinary and reasonable" care for the safety and protection of his patrons; that is, the care which an ordinary, prudent, careful and cautious person would have exercised under the same or similar circumstances.

Second, athletes assume all ordinary and inherent risks of an activity, but do not assume extraordinary risks, unless they know of and voluntarily assume them.

Defenses that owners or operators may assert in defense of charges of negligence against them will be assumption of the risk, and contributory or comparative negligence.

Negligence resulting in injuries to athletes may occur in many different sports, activities and situations.

BOXING

Where there are no laws prohibiting boxing, courts have held that a person who engaged in, and consented to, a boxing or "prize" fight, generally cannot recover from an opponent for injuries he suffers. Assumption of the risk and consent to the contact will be valid defenses.

If there is a law making boxing unlawful, then participants can file complaints against each other for assault. Here, consent will not excuse any act resulting in injury.

BOWLING

Bowling premises are to be kept in a reasonably safe condition. There is a duty to warn of dangerous conditions of which the proprietor is or should be aware.

Does a proprietor of bowling premises have a duty to inspect the premises for defects which can cause injuries?

The proprietor must inspect the premises at reasonable intervals and correct any dangerous conditions within a reasonable time, or warn patrons.

A bowler assumes the ordinary risks of bowling and may be contributorily negligent if aware of an unsafe condition, but still exposes oneself to it.

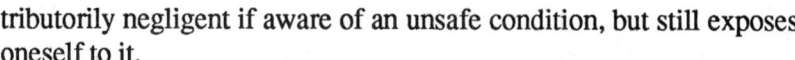

FACTS: One bowler was called to the control stand, another went to the bathroom before returning to bowl. Both unknowingly picked up liquid on their shoes. They were injured when they both slipped and fell on the approach. Who was liable, the bowlers or the proprietor? **YOU'RE THE JUDGE!**

DECISION: The proprietor would be liable where he knew or should have known by reasonable inspection that the premises were unsafe.

But where it could not be proven how long the substance was there, and the bowler knew that there were drinks in the area, the proprietor will not be liable for any resulting injury.

Where it is alleged that there was a substance present, the plaintiff must also prove that the injury was as a result of the substance and not due to some other cause, such as worn shoes or the condition of the bowler (drunk). But if the worn shoes, rented from the proprietor, caused an injury, the proprietor may be responsible for not properly inspecting and replacing them.

If an injury is the result of a "faulty" approach, of which the bowler was not aware, liability will be based on either a failure to discover the defect, or on a failure to correct it.

Who would be liable where a bowler selected a house ball and was injured when it "stuck" in her hand?

FACTS: Mary selected a house ball and began to warm up for the bowling league.

"When her fingers stuck in the ball, she slipped to the floor, injuring her hip," explained Sue. Mary alleged negligence on the part of the proprietor for not inspecting the ball. "Was the proprietor at fault? **YOU'RE THE JUDGE!**

DECISION: No. Although the proprietor has a duty to inspect for defects and unsafe conditions, it would be burdensome to require the constant checking all of the balls. Of course, if the proprietor knew of the condition, but didn't correct it, and the bowler could not know of the consequences until actually using the ball, the proprietor may be liable.

ROLLER & ICE SKATING

The owner or operator of a skating rink does not insure a patron's safety. However, he must exercise reasonable and ordinary care. This duty includes inspecting the premises and maintaining them in a reasonably safe condition.

Participants must exercise reasonable care for their own safety, and they assume the ordinary risks and dangers of the sport.

FACTS: Several skaters were injured when they tripped over holes and soft spots on the ice. They were "fooling around" when injured. Was the proprietor liable for these injuries? **YOU'RE THE JUDGE!**

DECISION: No, unless the proprietor had enough time to discover the defects, and either knew or should have been aware of them.

Negligence has been found where skaters unknowingly skated into a pile of litter and ice scrapings and were injured, and were cut from glass doors that were too close to the rink.

Negligence was not found where a skater was injured while skating in an off-limits area (an entrance) or where a skater tripped over a railing necessary for the protection of patrons to separate the rink from the walkway.

Does a proprietor have a duty to furnish safe equipment?

FACTS: A proprietor furnished skates which were loose, falling apart, or otherwise defective. The skaters were either not aware of the defects, or were encouraged to use the skates nonetheless. Who would be liable for any resulting injuries? **YOU'RE THE JUDGE!**

DECISION: Some risks may be ordinary ones, such as a broken shoelace. For these, the skater assumes the risk, as he also will when using equipment improperly. Otherwise, the proprietor may be negligent if he furnishes equipment which he either knew, or by reasonable inspection should have known, was defective and such equipment causes an injury.

Does a proprietor have a duty to protect patrons where he either knew or should have known that another's conduct might cause injury?

A proprietor may be liable for improper supervision which results in an injury if he allows rowdy conduct: skaters going too fast or into an area reserved for less experienced skaters, too many skaters on the rink, or allowing known "rowdies". on the ice.

An operator may not be liable where an injury occurs from an ordinary risk of the sport (unintentional bumping), or if a skater participated in unpermitted activity.

FACTS: "John and Jack, weaving in and out, were skating too fast. They crashed into Susan, injuring both her and Jack," noticed Tony.

The proprietor was not aware of this "sudden" breach of the rules. Who was liable for the injuries? **YOU'RE THE JUDGE!**

DECISION: Jack assumed the risk of and contributed to his own injury. Both John and Jack were liable for Susan's injury. This was not an ordinary risk of the sport.

SWIMMING & WATER SKIING

The duties imposed upon operators of premises used for swimming or water skiing, and the responsibility of participants and others, depends upon whether the facilities are regarded to be public or private.

Public Facilities

Operators of facilities open to the general public are bound to use ordinary and reasonable care for the safety of the public. This includes the duty to provide and exercise proper supervision. These duties may be affected by laws and the age of a child.

Will greater care be required for younger children?

FACTS: Greg, 12, drowned at a public pool in the neighborhood park. There was no lifeguard on duty when the incident occurred (2:00 P.M.). Was the operator of the pool liable? **YOU'RE THE JUDGE!**

DECISION: Yes. The operator had a duty to provide a lifeguard, especially where younger children used the pool.

If a drowning occurs due to either the non-presence or inattentiveness of a lifeguard, liability will be found.

However, if a lifeguard would not have been able to save a swimmer, or the swimmer placed himself in a position of danger (such as jumping or swimming into water known to be too deep, especially after being warned), there may be no liability by the operator the facility.

Unexplained drownings also may not impose liability, unless the drowning occurred at a crowded pool where there was an insufficient number of lifeguards, or they were inattentive.

Negligence may also be found where there was a delay in a rescue, or where it was improperly attempted, or with improper rescue equipment.

What if a swimmer was injured during "horseplay?"

FACTS: "Johnnie jumped into the water, struck his head on the bottom and was then cut by broken glass. Frankie was pushed in on top of Johnnie and Bob jumped on top of them," testified Sherry. All were injured. Was the operator liable for these injuries? **YOU'RE THE JUDGE!**

DECISION: If Johnnie jumped into the shallow water after he knew, or should have known, its depth, there will be no liability by the operator. The operator should have known of the glass by inspection. He was negligent.

If there was a lifeguard on duty to warn of the danger from horseplay, and the warning was not heeded or if the injury happened suddenly, there will be no liability to the operator. There would be liability if a lifeguard was not present, was inattentive, or did not try to prevent such conduct. That would be improper supervision.

Patrons are held to assume the ordinary risks of the sport. If an accident was either unavoidable, or if the patron contributed to his injury, assumption of the risk and contributory negligence will be valid defenses.

Private Facilities

A patron at a private swimming facility must exercise ordinary care for his own safety. If he either knew, or should have known, of a danger, but proceeded anyway to place himself in danger, he may be held to have assumed the risk of venturing into water too deep and contributed to any injury.

Private operators (such as a hotel, resort or private club) of premises used for swimming have a duty to use ordinary and reasonable care for the safety of patrons.

FACTS: Bill injured his neck diving into a pool unmarked for depths; Joe cut himself on glass in the pool; Mary was injured when other kids piled on top of her after coming down the water slide; Jeremy was injured when bumped into by some kids fooling around in the bathhouse. What were the operator's duties? **YOU'RE THE JUDGE!**

DECISION: The operator has a duty to: mark the varying depths of the water, keep it clear of dangerous substances, warn of unsafe conditions, provide adequate and attentive supervision where required, and properly control the patrons and maintain the premises. These duties extend to the bathhouse or shower rooms.

Water Skiing

Operators of premises used for water skiing must exercise reasonable and ordinary care to maintain the premises in a reasonably safe condition. Water skiers and others involved assume the normal risks of water skiing. If they place themselves in a perilous or dangerous condition, they may be guilty of contributory negligence.

FACTS: Henry was injured while water skiing. "I was forced to dive to the side to avoid a swimmer!" he testified.

Kirk was also injured while water skiing when he hit a rock in shallow water fifty feet from shore. There was no notice of the shallow depth, and Kirk did not know of it. What were the operator's duties? **YOU'RE THE JUDGE!**

DECISION: The operator of the premises should provide a separate area for both swimmers and water skiers. This area should be clearly marked and a proper warning, either oral or by sign should be given. Shallow water should be properly marked where it would not be apparent, and notice should be given as to the acceptable speed limit in such an area.

What duty does the operator of a boat used for water skiing or in the area of swimmers have?

The operator of a towing, or other, boat has the same duty of due care for the safety of those using the water. He may be responsible for a sudden start without warning or before the skier is ready or for not providing a necessary lookout and signals.

FACTS: Sue charged, "I was getting ready to be towed. Without warning, the driver intentionally accelerated the boat, injuring me!"

Leona, sunbathing on a float, drowned after she was knocked off the float by a tow rope. The water skier attempted to flip the rope over her as he passed between her and the shore. Did Sue or Leona assume such risks? **YOU'RE THE JUDGE!**

DECISION: No. These were not ordinary risks inherent to using the water. The conduct of the drivers was in reckless disregard for the girls' safety. In addition to actual damages, punitive damages were awarded—to punish the drivers and water skier.

A water skier may be guilty of contributory negligence when aware of the danger involved, such as an inexperienced driver, shallow water or the speed of the boat.

An operator of another boat in the area may be liable for failure to exercise ordinary care, such as when coming too close to a waterskier, going too fast, or being inattentive (thereby causing an injury).

Boating Laws

Laws governing the use of boats may have a provision prohibiting operating a boat:

"...in a reckless or negligent manner so as to endanger the life, limb, or property of any person...."

"Reckless or negligent manner" prohibits: excessive speed, overloading, improper—or a lack of—safety equipment, improper passing, operating under the influence, "buzzing" of other boats or persons, using dangerous waters, standing in the boat, and generally failing to take proper precautions on approach of bad weather or other situations involving risk of safety.

SKIING, SNOWMOBILES....

An operator of premises used for winter skiing and other activities is not an insurer of a participant's safety. However, the operator must exercise ordinary and reasonable care in maintaining the premises and in giving proper and adequate warning of possible dangers.

Participants are held to assume the ordinary risks and dangers involved in such activities.

An operator may be held liable where he breaches his duty of care, such as by permitting snowmobiles in the same area as skiers, failing to properly inspect and maintain the premises, or where proper and adequate warnings of dangers are not given.

FACTS: A novice skier, Holly, fell and became entangled in brush concealed by loose snow. She was rendered a permanent quadriplegic. She sued the operator at the ski resort for failure to provide a safe place to ski. Was the operator liable? **YOU'RE THE JUDGE!**

DECISION: The operator was found liable for Holly's injury. This was a breach of the operator's duty to provide and maintain premises safe for their intended use.

However, where the risk is obvious, assumption of the risk may be a valid defense.

FACTS: A skier, Walter, struck a utility pole, which allegedly was not properly padded, and was injured. A state statute read: "The skier accepts the dangers that are inherent in skiing." in reference to obvious dangers. "Did I assume the risk of injury?" asked Walter. **YOU'RE THE JUDGE!**

DECISION: This case established assumption of the risk as a defense. The skier was, or should have been, aware of the obvious danger. Walter assumed the risk of injury.

Unless an operator is negligent in providing supervision, the operator may not be liable for injuries occurring as a result of collisions between skiers. The operator may be liable where different areas are necessary, but not set out for different levels of skill.

As between two skiers, they both assume the ordinary and inherent dangers of the sport. But they will not assume extraordinary dangers, such as where a more experienced skier "cut off" one less experienced, or where the general rules of the slope (right-of-way) were not obeyed and injury resulted.

Competitors may assume ordinary risks within their control. Therefore, where a ski-jumper was blown out of position by the wind, he assumed the risk of injury.

What if, to mark off a course, an operator used improper equipment which resulted in an injury?

FACTS: Several skiers were injured when they collided with poles used to mark off a racecourse. There were other thinner, less dangerous poles available. Was the operator liable for the injuries? **YOU'RE THE JUDGE!**

DECISION: The operator was liable for using improper poles. The injuries would not have happened but for the negligence of the operator.

Foresight and caution in guarding against dangers involving chair lifts are also required of the operator. This generally will involve proper maintenance and supervision.

A skier must exercise care for his own safety, both in the use of chair lifts and on the slopes.

Does an operator have a duty to inquire of the experience of those renting his equipment?

FACTS: Novice renters of skis and snowmobile equipment said, "We were injured when we went out of control. We did not know how to use the ill-fitted equipment." They sued the operators, alleging a neglect of a duty to give proper instructions for using the equipment. Was the operator liable? **YOU'RE THE JUDGE!**

DECISION: Yes. When an operator rents out equipment to be used in skiing, snowmobiling or other winter activities, he has a duty to insure that it is fit for its intended use and that the user is given proper instructions. Through inquiry, the operator should have known that the skiers were novices.

As to the use of snowmobiles, skimobiles, sleds and toboggans used in racing or otherwise, care must be taken to: inspect the area to be used, give adequate warnings to participants and spectators, use barriers where necessary, and, to properly mark off-limit areas.

An operator will not be an insurer of a participant's or other's safety. Participants and others must use proper precautions for their own safety and will assume the ordinary risks involved.

GOLF

What is the duty of the operator of a golf course?

The operator of a golf course has a duty to exercise reasonable care for the safety of others, both in the supervision of play, and in maintaining the premises and equipment under her control in a safe condition.

However, she is not an insurer of a patron's safety. Golfers will assume the risks of injury from the ordinary and usual hazards inherent in the game. She will not assume liability from extraordinary risks brought about by others.

Who would be liable where an operator employs a starter or ranger to help in supervising play, and an injury results?

FACTS: At the instruction of the starter to "Go ahead." Ray and John teed off. They both struck and injured players in the same and adjacent fairways. Who was liable for the injuries? **YOU'RE THE JUDGE!**

DECISION: If a golfer "tees off" at the instruction of a starter, liability by the starter can be established where the injured player was on the same hole, in front of the golfer teeing off and not yet out of range.

If Ray and John were aware that a player was within their range on the hole they were playing and, nevertheless, teed off and injured that player, the golfer and the operator may share liability.

If the injury occurs to one in an adjacent area, the golfer teeing off may be liable if a warning is not given, if required and which may have prevented the injury.

The operator of a golf course has a duty to maintain the golf course and surrounding premises.

Who would be liable where a golfer did not know of an incorrect yardage and therefore, in hitting the ball, used "too much club," injuring another golfer?

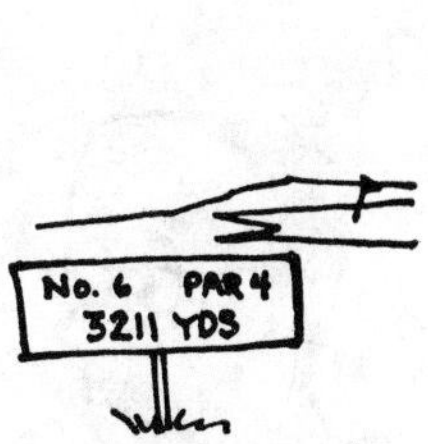

FACTS: Ivan was teeing off on the eighth hole at Orchard Country Club. Not having played there before, he checked the card — 315 yards. When the group in front of him reached the green, Ivan teed off. His drive struck Joe, who was pulling the pin out of the hole.

After the accident, Ivan said disbelievingly, "I just can't understand how I could hit a ball that far." In fact, the hole was only

225 yards long. Joe sued Ivan for striking him, and the golf course for incorrectly stating the yardage. Who was liable for Joe's injury? **YOU'RE THE JUDGE!**

DECISION: The club was found liable for Joe's injury. The manager of the golf course, in a conversation with Ivan's wife, admitted, "Two years ago, we moved the green forward. We got a lot of cards left here. When we print them up again, we'll probably change them."

Where screens or fencing, designed for the safety of players, are not properly maintained, liability may be established if an injury is a result of such negligent maintenance.

An operator has a duty to exercise due care in maintaining equipment, ensuring that it is fit for its intended use. Therefore, if the brakes on a cart are not properly inspected and an injury results, the operator may be liable.

FACTS: Rental golf clubs were not inspected. A reasonable inspection would have revealed a loose or broken clubhead. As a result, Guy was injured when his partner swung a club and the head flew off, striking him. "Who was liable, the proprietor?" asked Guy. **YOU'RE THE JUDGE!**

DECISION: Yes, particularly where the danger was not apparent to the user. A renter of equipment has the right to assume that the equipment is fit for the use intended.

If a golfer yells "Fore!" after hitting an errant shot, is he relieved of liability for any resulting injury?

FACTS: Paul hit a golfer in another fairway with an errant shot. He saw the other player when he hit the ball. Was Paul liable? What if he yelled "Fore"? **YOU'RE THE JUDGE!**

DECISION: Paul had a duty to give a timely and adequate warning to the other player. If he did so, he would not be liable. The other player would have assumed the risk as one ordinary to the game. The exception might be where Paul intended the ball to start in the direction of the other golfer, hoping to "draw" or "fade" the ball. Here, he will be held to have at least waited until the other player was out of range.

In holding that an injured golfer assumed the risk of injury from an errant golf shot, one judge stated, "Generally, it is well known that a slight deviation of the club head may send the ball in a most unexpected direction. To hold that a golfer is negligent merely because his ball did not go in a straight and intended line would be to impose a greater duty of care than the creator endowed him with faculties to carry out."

What if a golfer is "waived on" by a golfer up ahead and he then hits that golfer?

FACTS: John, 36, teed off after he was waived on by the players ahead of him.

His ball struck Mike, 24, one of the players who waived him on. Did Mike assume the risk of such an injury? **YOU'RE THE JUDGE!**

DECISION: Mike assumed the risk of injury after waiving John through. He was also guilty of contributory negligence.

What if Mike was only 10 years old? Who would be liable then?

Where a player up ahead is very young and not mindful of the danger involved, an older, more experienced golfer may assume the responsibility and liability.

Who would be liable for injuries from a reckless swing or a caroming ball?

FACTS: Barney, frustrated over hitting two balls into the woods, took a reckless swing. His club "flew" twenty feet and struck his partner, Tim, in the face. "I didn't assume the risk of such an injury, did I?" asked Tim. **YOU'RE THE JUDGE!**

DECISION: No. Barney breached his "duty to exercise reasonable care in controlling his golf club." He was liable for Tim's injury.

FACTS: Andy's ball caromed off a tree, injuring a golfer in another fairway. Was Andy guilty of negligence? **YOU'RE THE JUDGE!**

DECISION: Their was no liability. Such a result could not reasonably be anticipated.

Where a caddie or groundskeeper voluntarily went "up ahead," or worked in an area known to be within the range of errant golf shots and was injured, assumption of the risk will prevent any recovery.

This will not be the case where a golfer was aware of the presence of others, but did not give a timely or adequate warning which could have prevented the injury.

Generally, the operator of a driving range will be responsible for properly supervising "play"—ensuring that golfers are hitting from and to a permitted area.

FACTS: The operator of a driving range hired several young junior high school boys to "shag" balls from the range. He told the golfers to hit "away" from the boys.

An errant shot struck one of the boys, Stevie, who then sued the golfer and the operator. Who was liable? **YOU'RE THE JUDGE!**

DECISION: The operator had the duty to protect the boys by whatever means were necessary, including stopping golfers from practicing until the boys were done. Any golfer, although encouraged to continue, may share such liability.

"RACK 'EM UP"

The operator of premises used for pool or billiards is not an insurer of a patron's safety. However, he must exercise reasonable care in supervising and in keeping the premises and equipment reasonably safe for its intended use.

FACTS: A patron at a pool hall was injured when a fight spread to the area he was playing in. The operator yelled, "Break it up!" but it was too late. The operator had ample notice and time.

Another injury resulted from flying splinters, where there was no advance notice of the disturbance. Were the operators liable for these injuries? **YOU'RE THE JUDGE!**

DECISION: The first operator was negligent and liable for the injuries. The second operator did not have notice. He was not liable, although the patron causing the injury may have been.

JOGGING, CYCLES, SKATES....

The general duty owed to pedestrians, "joggers," cyclists and others is one of reasonable care and maintenance of public ways. However, those in charge of such ways are not insurers of pedestrian's and other's safety. Generally, pedestrians and others will assume the ordinary and inherent risks involved in using or traveling a public way. They will not assume extraordinary risks or dangers.

Pedestrians, cyclists, joggers, skateboarders, and rollerskaters, while using public ways, are subject to and shall: obey traffic signals, use sidewalks, use that side of the roadway facing traffic where there is no sidewalk, yield and be yielded the right of way—depending on the circumstances—and cross only in marked walkways and in a proper manner.

FACTS: John and Valla were out for a walk. They decided to walk in the street instead of on the sidewalk. When crossing the street, they didn't use the marked crossing area.

Kevin, out for a jog, ran through a red light.

Jimmy rode his bike with the flow of the traffic where there was no sidewalk. He also rode at night without using reflectors. Were any of these practices prohibited? **YOU'RE THE JUDGE!**

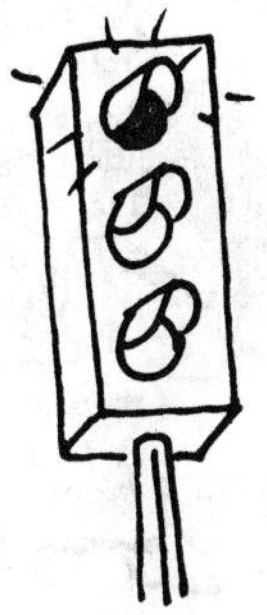

DECISION: All of the practices were prohibited. John and Valla are required to use the proper areas set off for walking and crossing the street.

Jimmy is required to have reflectors on his bike when riding at night.

Kevin was given a $17 citation by a police officer, but the judge reduced the fine to $7 when he discovered that he could run a faster mile than Kevin. "He saved $10 for being slower than me," chuckled the judge.

Where private property or public ways are "set aside" for pedestrians for walking, jogging or for marathons, is a higher degree of care required to maintain the way?

FACTS: "I was hurt when I fell after my bike hit a hole in the bike path. I never saw the hole," muttered Henry. Did Henry assume the risk of his injury? **YOU'RE THE JUDGE!**

DECISION: The town was liable. They had notice of and opportunity to attend to the hole or other defects not readily apparent to users. However, the town could not be sued. Sovereign immunity—which may apply to some towns—prevented any recovery.

Runners in a race, such as a marathon, may generally assume that the course is in the condition required for its intended use. A runner will assume the risks and dangers ordinarily inherent in running, such as from other runners, or cars (if not in a race).

Motorcyclists have the same rights and duties as those of the driver of any other vehicle.

Does a bicyclist have those same rights and duties?

Yes. Therefore, a cycle may only carry that number of people that it is equipped to carry while being ridden: it cannot be attached to a vehicle, it must be kept to the right except when passing, making a turn or to avoid an accident; one hand must be on the handlebars at all times, and pedestrians must be given the right-of-way on a sidewalk.

What about using radio headsets?

FACTS: Tom and Maria, with their radio headsets turned on, went out for a bicycle ride. They raced down the sidewalk past all of the stores on Main Street. Right behind them on skateboards were Jorni and "T.J." "Were we doing anything wrong?" they asked. **YOU'RE THE JUDGE!**

DECISION: Yes. All persons operating a bicycle or skateboard shall not ride on a sidewalk within a business district, or where otherwise prohibited.

Bicyclists, motorcyclists, rollerskaters and joggers may be prohibited from wearing radio headsets as this gear could restrict the necessary ability to hear.

TENNIS

The operator of a tennis facility, in supervising and in maintaining the premises, will be held to exercise reasonable care for the safety of others.

However, an operator is not an insurer of the participant's safety. Participants and others will assume the ordinary and inherent risks of the game, but not extraordinary ones.

FACTS: Andy, in disgust at his play, threw his racket. It hit Tom and broke his nose! Who was liable for Tom's injury? **YOU'RE THE JUDGE!**

DECISION: The injury was not from an ordinary risk of the game. Andy was liable for the injury.

Where an operator had forewarning and notice of improper conduct, he will be liable for injury caused by improper supervision.

FACTS: John was injured when he was struck in the eye with a tennis ball. He claimed, "Peter intentionally tried to hit Hank in the face after he screamed 'Eat this!' But the ball hit me instead."

Peter and Hank had been screaming at each other for some time before the injury to John. Who was liable? **YOU'RE THE JUDGE!**

DECISION: John assumed normal risks, not extraordinary ones. Peter and the proprietor, for allowing the improper conduct to continue, shared liability.

GYMNASTICS

Is supervision required where a proprietor has a trampoline on the premises?

At Sarge's Trampoline Center, a notice read, "Patrons use the trampoline at your own risk."

A patron, Paul, 18, was injured while jumping on the trampoline. Could he recover damages?

Paul assumed the risk of injury. The trampoline was not in a defective condition and the danger was obvious. Furthermore, in this situation, supervision was not required. If Paul was only ten years old (or the trampoline was at a school), would supervision then be required?

HUNTING

The basic rule for hunters is that a hunter "must not pull the trigger without ample assurance that he is shooting only at game."

Therefore, where a hunter shot at something which turned out to be a man picking berries, the hunter was liable for negligence. He breached his duty to exercise reasonable care for the safety of others. A hunter must handle his gun with extraordinary care.

FACTS: Johnson left the safety off of his gun. The gun discharged when he fell from a wobbly duck blind. A companion was hit in the leg. Did the injured hunter assume the risk of injury? **YOU'RE THE JUDGE!**

DECISION: No. Johnson, who must handle his weapon with extraordinary care, was found negligent. He was liable for the injury.

No liability was found for an injury resulting from a hunter firing in a direction where any experienced bird hunter would not be without having given warning of his changed position.

PICNICS

FACTS: Henderson chided his friends at a picnic, "You can't throw me in the lake!" In the roughhousing which followed, he was severely injured when someone fell on top of him. Who was liable? Could he recover for his injury? **YOU'RE THE JUDGE!**

DECISION: No. Recovery was denied. It was reasonably foreseeable that injury might occur during the horseplay. Henderson assumed that risk. Furthermore, he was guilty of contributing to his own injury.

Had Henderson not invited or consented to the contact, then there would be liability for "unconsented contact."

Also, if someone had consented to contact, but the contact was beyond that normally expected, liability may also attach. This would be especially so where the injured, after first consenting, later retracted that consent ("Cut it out!") and was injured.

CAMPS

Generally, in part due to the age of the participants, there will be a greater than normal duty to use reasonable care in supervising most activities at camps. Some degree of risk will be assumed, but not excessive or unpermitted force, nor injury from extraordinary hazards.

YOU'RE THE JUDGE!

FACTS: Jan sobbed, "I dove off the platform as I had many times the previous year. I cut my head on a rock." Was the operator of the camp liable for the injury? **YOU'RE THE JUDGE!**

DECISION: Yes. The platform had been moved during the winter. This created an extraordinary hazard for which the operator was liable. He should have inspected the premises beforehand.

Operators of camps must also maintain the premises in a satisfactory condition, considering its intended use. Premises may include the water, trails, general play areas and any housing accommodations.

GO-CARTS

FACTS: John and Robby were injured when their go-carts collided and tires, stacked up to prevent the cars from leaving the track, fell on them.

Jennifer was injured when her brakes wouldn't function after she hit a puddle. Their parents asked, "Can we recover damages?" **YOU'RE THE JUDGE!**

RACE TRACK

DECISION: John and Robby assumed the ordinary and inherent risks of the sport, such as an unintentional collision or falling tires after a collision.

Jennifer could recover damages. She did not assume extraordinary risks, such as oil or water on the track, where there was notice and opportunity for the operator to correct such a danger.

An operator has a duty to properly supervise such an activity and to maintain the premises in a safe condition.

FISHING

Does a weather bureau have a duty to properly forecast oncoming inclement weather?

One court ruled that they did. The court held a weather bureau liable for the drowning deaths of three fishermen. They drowned when a sudden and violent storm struck.

Will one fisherman be liable for "hooking" another?

FACTS: Gary, in his excitement to get his pole in the water, paid no attention to Lou, who was baiting his hook. "I didn't see him," said Gary. Gary "hooked" Lou in the mouth. Did Lou assume the risk of such an injury? **YOU'RE THE JUDGE!**

DECISION: No. Gary owed Lou a duty of reasonable care for his safety. By casting with indifference as to where Lou was, Gary was liable.

AUTO RACETRACK

The owner, promoter or operator of an auto racetrack may be liable for an injury to a participant where there was negligence in the construction or maintenance of the racetrack, when the owner or operator knew, or should have known, of the defect.

FACTS: "Cannonball" Jones was injured in an auto race when his car skidded off the track and hit a retaining wall.

"Cannonball was injured during the first lap. The oil from a previous accident had not been cleaned up as required," explained an attendant. Was the owner or operator of the track liable for Cannonball's injury?

DECISION: **YOU'RE THE JUDGE!**

There will be no liability where negligence was not the proximate (but for) cause of any injury. Therefore, where an auto racer's car went out of control, due either to unavoidable circumstances or the driver's neglect, the driver was held to have contributed to, and assumed the risk of, such an injury.

It is a a common practice in racing to "ride" the bumper of a car in front. Injuries arising from such conduct are accepted as normal risks of the sport.

Pit crew members are treated, in most instances, as a driver is, with the same rights and responsibilities.

THEY'RE AT THE GATE!

FACTS: A jockey, Gene, sued the racetrack operator for injuries received when the horse he was riding "bolted through a removable railing." The railing was at the location where horses were accustomed to leaving the track. Gene contended, "The railing should have been painted a different color than the rest of the infield fence." Was the track operator liable for my injuries? asked Gene. **YOU'RE THE JUDGE!**

DECISION: The court ruled, "The track operator did not maintain the race track in good condition. It violated a safety regulation by providing inadequate and unsafe fencing around the track infield."

Gene's injuries would not have occurred "but for" the negligence of the racetrack. Horses are color blind and can only distinguish between black and white. All other colors appear gray. Therefore, because the railing, through which the horse bolted, was

not painted white, it may have visually blended with the gray infield. Coincidentally, that was the location where the horses were accustomed to leaving the track.

Injuries received by jockeys when "cut off" are generally assumed risks, due in part to the sometimes uncontrollable nature of a horse. To recover, a jockey would have to show reckless, wanton or intentional conduct (malice) by another jockey.

The defense of assumption of the risk will be a deterrent to most actions for damages for injuries to professionals. Professionals are acutely aware of the dangers and risks inherent in their sports. They will not be able to pass along that responsibility to others except in those situations where an injury was as a result of the negligence or intentional misconduct of others.

WORKMEN'S COMPENSATION

May an athlete, injured while performing duties for his team, recover damages against his own team for an injury?

FACTS: Ellis, a pro football player for the Pushovers, injured his knee during a football game. He sued an opposing player for making an improper tackle. He also sued his own coach and team. "They played me while I was injured," charged Ellis. Could Ellis recover damages from his team? **YOU'RE THE JUDGE!**

DECISION: No. Where workmen's compensation applied, Ellis' only remedy against his own team (not an opponent's) was provided by workmen's compensation. Ellis could not sue his coach. He could sue an opposing team or player, as they would not be his employer.

When an athlete is injured while performing a duty for his employer, relief may be available under **workmen's compensation statutes.**

These statutes provide that employees, with certain exceptions, "may receive compensation for injuries which are related to their employment."

In effect, each side (the team and the players) gives up rights in return for others. The employer gives up any defenses he may have in return for limited liability. The employee gives up the right to bring an action in negligence against the employer (but not against others) and, in return, receives limited compensation for any injuries.

Injured parties must prove they are employees and their injuries resulted from work (or activities related to work) and under the employer's control and direction.

Professional Athletes

YOU'RE THE JUDGE!

FACTS: Al, a pro baseball player, broke his ankle sliding into third base.

Pat, a pro football player, was injured while driving from his home to a game.

Carlo, a pro basketball player, slipped and broke his hip while doing team promotional work at a local mall. Were any of these athletes covered by workmen's compensation? **YOU'RE THE JUDGE!**

DECISION: Al and Carlo, performing duties for their teams, were covered. Pat was on his way to a game, and not yet covered.

Are all professional athletes covered by workmen's compensation?

Professional athletes may be excluded from workmen's compensation coverage because participation in pro sports is "highly dangerous." Additionally, professional team athletes generally receive their salaries for the remainder of the year under their contracts.

In addition, some states—although covering athletes under workmen's compensation—have denied benefits where the injury was not an "accidental" injury, even though occurring as a result of a legitimate physical contact.

FACTS: "Killer" McGee, a linebacker for the Devils, injured his shoulder making a vicious tackle.

The team doctor, on orders from the owner, told Killer, "Your shoulder is fine, you can play." when, in fact, it was not. Killer permanently injured the shoulder during the next game. Was the team owner liable for Killer's injury? Could Killer recover workmen's compensation? **YOU'RE THE JUDGE!**

DECISION: An employer may be liable for aggravating injuries where an employer—or the employer's agent—fraudulently conceal the existence of injury to the player, who then is injured further by playing, not knowing of the injury. The team's owner was liable.

Had the employer been found not liable, Killer could recover workmen's compensation benefits.

YOU'RE FINE!

FACTS: What if Killer, while traveling to the next game, injured the shoulder when he slipped and fell in the airport. Could he recover workmen's compensation? **YOU'RE THE JUDGE!**

DECISION: Injuries occurring while traveling with the team between games are covered. Killer was engaged in activities related to his work for his employer.

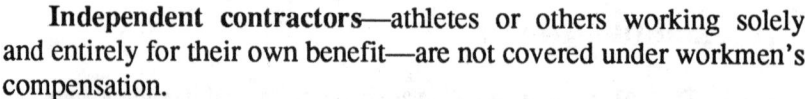

Independent contractors—athletes or others working solely and entirely for their own benefit—are not covered under workmen's compensation.

Jockeys may, or may not, be considered employees, depending upon any agreement with an owner of a track or horse.

Other athletes, such as pro tennis players or golfers, will only be covered by any applicable workmen's compensation statutes if they are working for an employer, under the employer's control and for the employer's benefit, and while engaged in the employer's employ and not playing for part of a purse, where they keep anything that they earn.

FACTS: A pro golfer, Ian, represented a golf club. He worked there on occasion, but mainly went out on the tour fending solely for himself. While playing in a tournament, he slipped and injured his back. Was he covered by workmen's compensation?

If he was injured while not on tour, but while working for the employer at the club, would he then be covered? **YOU'RE THE JUDGE!**

DECISION: Ian would not be covered while playing entirely for himself. But while working at the club, he would be covered and could receive workmen's compensation benefits.

University & College Athletes

As a general rule, a college or university athlete will not be considered an employee because of the receipt of an athletic scholarship. However, where the performance of athletic services is required for the scholarship, the athlete will be an employee for purposes of workmen's compensation coverage.

FACTS: An athlete, Sam Vanderly, was killed in a plane crash returning from an away game for his college football team.

His family claimed, "Sam's scholarship and rent money, received from the school, was payment for his playing football. He was an employee of the school." Could his family recover workmen's compensation benefits? **YOU'RE THE JUDGE!**

DECISION: Yes. The court held, "The scholarship and rent money received by Vanderly were payment for his football activities. Therefore, he was an employee and his family could recover workmen's compensation benefits."

However, in most instances, receiving a scholarship will not be dependent upon an athlete performing athletically. He can receive the scholarship even if he no longer participates in the sport for which he was granted a scholarship. In these situations, if the athlete is injured while participating in athletics, he will not be able to collect workmen's compensation benefits.

FACTS: Clark Reddon, while playing football for Indian St. on an athletic scholarship, was injured during practice. The injury left him a quadriplegic. Could he recover workmen's compensation benefits? **YOU'RE THE JUDGE!**

DECISION: The court found, "Reddon was not an employee of the college. He could not recover benefits."

The court considered the student's financial aid arrangement, which included the NCAA bylaw that sports was viewed as part of the educational system and that taking pay was prohibited, subject to a loss of eligibility. Furthermore, Reddon did not report the scholarship as income.

Athletic Activities On The Job

Employer sponsored or sanctioned athletic activities may range from pick-up games (played mostly during lunch breaks) to athletic teams. Whether these athletes will be covered under workmen's compensation statutes for injuries received during these activities will depend upon whether the athletes are employees and, if so, whether their activities were related to work, for the employers' benefit and under their control.

As a general rule, an employee's activities may be considered within the course of employment when the activities occur on the employer's premises and during work hours.

FACTS: While at work, Warren, attempting to catch a pass during a lunch hour touch football game, was injured when his hand went through a glass window. The game was on the employer's premises. Warren filed a claim for workmen's compensation benefits. "Can I recover?" he asked. **YOU'RE THE JUDGE!**

DECISION: Yes. "The injury was within the course of employment. The accident happened during lunch hour and on the employer's premises. Warren could recover benefits," ruled the court.

An employee's activities will also be within the course of his employment when an employer requires participation or is responsible for organizing activities, such as softball games and golf tournaments. And this is especially so where an employer provides transportation to the activities, or has them on his premises.

Compensation may be denied where an activity takes place outside of an employer's premises, not during working hours, not under his control or encouragement, and where employees furnished their own transportation.

FACTS: "Eagle" Parr painfully explained, "It was my day off. While at a driving range provided by my boss, I was struck on the head by a golf club." Could Eagle claim workmen's compensation benefits for his injury? **YOU'RE THE JUDGE!**

DECISION: "The accident was not incurred in the course of employment. Additionally, it was not a required part of his employment to enjoy recreation on his day off—the employer did not require his presence there and received no benefit." commented the court.

EQUIPMENT

Injury to a participant in a sports activity may arise out of the misuse of equipment.

FACTS: "John was injured when Pierre intentionally swung his hockey stick!" said a teammate.

In a baseball game, an on deck batter was injured when struck by a baseball bat which slipped from the batter's hands. Were Pierre and the batter liable for the injuries they caused? **YOU'RE THE JUDGE!**

DECISION: Pierre was liable. He intentionally, and without regard for the safety of others, caused John's injury.

The batter was not liable. Such a risk will be assumed as one ordinary to the game.

GREAT DANGER!

What if a participant continues to encounter an unreasonably great risk. Would that be contributory negligence? Will he be able to recover damages for any resulting injury?

FACTS: Wayne was injured during a fight in a hockey game with an opposing player, Niko. Niko screamed, "Wayne was guilty of contributory negligence. He can't recover damages." Can he? **YOU'RE THE JUDGE!**

DECISION: No. Courts use a two step process. If the first duty, owed by the defendant to the plaintiff, is violated, the plaintiff should recover. However, if the plaintiff has violated the second duty, that to ensure one's own safety, that will prevent recovery.

As a general rule, voluntary participants, including coaches, bat and ball boys, caddies, and others involved in sports contests, assume all of the ordinary and inherent risks of that sport, so long as the activity is played in good faith and the injury is not the result of intentional misconduct.

HIDDEN DANGER!

If any dangers common to a particular sport are hidden, unobserved or so serious as to require safety precautions, the general rule of assumption of the risk for injuries received during voluntary participation in that sport may not apply as a valid defense.

Such may be the case where there are holes in a ball field, or where the danger of a ride at an amusement park cannot be observed, and—in either case—a participant, unaware of the defect, is injured.

Will assumption of the risk be a valid defense where accidents have been so many that a game or activity is too dangerous to continue without change?

FACTS: Before high school basketball practice, the boys played "Mexican basketball," a brutal game in which fouls were not called.

The bumper cars at an amusement park consistently went too fast, causing injuries to many riders.

In a "paddle" football contest, paddles were lined up at the 50 yard line, with freshmen and sophomores at opposing goal lines. The goal was to get the paddles back to your end zone. There were no rules. Were these games too dangerous to continue without change? If participants were injured playing these games, could they recover damages for their injuries against their schools or the amusement park?

DECISION: **YOU'RE THE JUDGE!**

FACTS: The "Slasher," known for crushing his roller derby opponents into the railings, was seriously injured. "A weak guardrail gave way, and I crashed to the floor," he related.

Randy was hospitalized when, during a skydiving competition, "I landed in the target circle and was severely stung by a colony of red ants!"

"Big Pappa" crashed his drag racer into a briar patch after completing the quarter mile. The stopping area was too short.

Were the dangers in these sports hidden, unobserved or serious enough to warrant safety precautions for the participants? Did the participants assume the risk of such injuries, or were the operators or supervisors of the events liable?

DECISION: **YOU'RE THE JUDGE!**

PRESSURE! PRESSURE!

Volition (voluntary exercise of free will) of a participant to assume a risk of injury from participation in a sports activity may be overcome in extreme situations where there has been undue pressure.

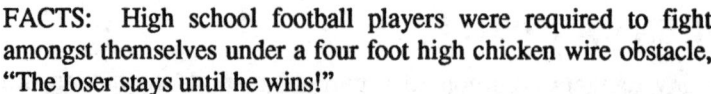

FACTS: High school football players were required to fight amongst themselves under a four foot high chicken wire obstacle, "The loser stays until he wins!"

Another high school football player was injured during a practice session in a game of "jungle football"—a rough version of touch football, played without equipment.

"You can't play without participating in these practices," warned the coaches. Did these players voluntarily assume the risk of injury? **YOU'RE THE JUDGE!**

DECISION: No. Volition may be robbed by the disciplinary authority of a coach, or by pressure to play from fellow players and schoolmates.

The courts held, "The players did not play voluntarily. They did not assume the risk of injury from negligent or reckless conduct by other participants or coaches. The risks involved were not ones ordinarily inherent to the game of football.

FACTS: John, a star football player for Emerson High, had not yet recovered from an ankle injury. His personal doctor recommended that he not play, "Any play before you're fully healed could jeopardize your future in football."

John's coach cautioned, "You must play if we are to win the play-offs. Don't forget, your play could get you college scholarship offers. And your teammates are depending on you."

John played, seriously reinjuring his ankle. John then sued the coach and school for "pressuring" him into playing. John asked, "Can I recover against the coach and school for negligence?" **YOU'RE THE JUDGE!**

DECISION: Yes. John's volition was robbed by the "pressure and disciplinary authority" of the coach. He did not voluntarily assume the risk of injury. He could recover from the school and its coach.

GOOD FAITH COMPETITION?

Where other than good faith competition is involved, or risks are not ordinary and part of the sport, participants will not assume the risk of injury.

What if conduct is negligent, but unintentional?

FACTS: Two high school teams squared off in a soccer match. Julian, a goaltender, received a pass in the penalty area, and then crouched, hugging the ball to his chest. Bill, an opposing forward, unintentionally kicked Julian in the head, causing a fractured skull and permanent brain damage.

A safety rule prohibited any contact with the goalie in the penalty area. Could Julian recover for his injury? **YOU'RE THE JUDGE!**

DECISION: The court ruled for Julian, remarking, "Players have a duty to refrain from conduct forbidden by safety rules which are included to protect players from serious injury. Players assume the normal risks of the game, but do not assume the risk of unintentional, but negligent, conduct."

Conduct, in violation of a safety rule, if either deliberate, willful, or with reckless disregard for another's safety (malice) may be negligent.

FACTS: Barry, a second baseman on his high school baseball team, received a fractured jaw when a baserunner—who had been on first base—ran into him full speed in an attempt to prevent a double play. Did Barry assume the risk of such an injury? **YOU'RE THE JUDGE!**

DECISION: No. Although Barry assumed ordinary risks (such as being spiked), he did not assume the risk of injury from unexpected and unsportsmanlike conduct. Testimony revealed, "The runner ran five feet from the base and hit Barry under the chin with his arm." The runner breached his duty to play in a sportsmanlike manner.

POOR JUDGMENT!

FACTS: Mary, a little league player, was injured when she was struck by lightning. Her parents sued, contending, "The game should have been stopped earlier when it was obvious that the storm was worsening." "Isn't the coach responsible for not stopping the game?" they asked.

DECISION: **YOU'RE THE JUDGE!**

NOT FIT FOR PLAY!

The most important risk that will not be assumed by participants will be any risk created by a breach of duty by owners or operators of sports facilities.

FACTS: Playing on a baseball field for the first time, Johnson stepped in a hole in the base path and was injured. He sued, claiming, "They neglected their duty to keep the field safe."

The defendant, operator of the field, maintained, "Johnson didn't use reasonable care for his own safety. He should have seen the hole." Did Johnson assume the risk of injury? **YOU'RE THE JUDGE!**

DECISION: The holes were hidden from view by grass. By knowingly maintaining the holes on the base path which players had to use, the defendant breached his duty to maintain the premises in a reasonably safe condition.

ARE PARENTS RESPONSIBLE?

Under common law, parents are not responsible for the acts of their children. But many states have passed laws which may impose potential limited liability on parents for the acts of their children.

Where such laws exist, parents are generally held responsible until a child reaches age 18, but may not be responsible if the child is under a certain age (varies from 7-13).

The kinds of torts committed by children for which their parents may be responsible are intentional or malicious acts.

FACTS: While playing in a football game, Wade, 13, received permanent injuries when he was beaten up by Jason, 14. Wade had not consented to the contact. Jason had been in many fights before. Were Jason's parents liable for Wade's injuries? **YOU'RE THE JUDGE!**

DECISION: In finding Jason's parents liable, the court stated, "The better rule is that parents be held to a requirement of reasonable care concerning their child's conduct when it might lead to serious injury."

When will parents be responsible for their child's conduct? Parents will be responsible for their child's conduct if:

- they are aware that their child has a "vicious propensity" to commit acts injuring others and fail to restrain and control him, or;
- they are present when a fight takes place and do nothing to stop it (if they had the time and opportunity), or;
- they—in any other way—direct, consent or approve of their child's conduct, or;
- the child is acting as his parent's agent in committing the act (this may apply if the child were on an errand for his parents).

FOSTER PARENTS

Although not related through blood or legal ties, foster parents raise their foster children and give other parental care. Are they responsible for their foster child's conduct?

FACTS: Jennifer and Jeff, foster parents, were sued when their foster child, Eddie, beat up an opposing player during a high school football game. "Are we liable for Eddie's conduct?" they asked. **YOU'RE THE JUDGE!!**

DECISION: Where foster parents are found to be "agents of the state," that is, acting for or on behalf of the state, they will not be held responsible for the acts of their foster child.

However, this immunity from liability may not extend to where the foster parents have willfully neglected or improperly supervised their foster children.

ODDS & ENDS....

FACTS: "Stash The Masher," a local wrestling favorite, sued his opponent, "Bimp The Wimp," for injuries Stash received during their wrestling match.

Stash claimed, "Bimp went outside of our 'choreographed' script where no one was supposed to be trying to hurt each other. We were supposed to be 'faking' it. I didn't know that Bimp would be really trying."

Bimp defended that Stash assumed the risk of injury from such a "dangerous" sport. Further, that he contributed to his own injury by competing. Did Stash assume the risk of such an injury, or was Bimp guilty of negligence by not following the choreographed script?

DECISION: **YOU'RE THE JUDGE!**

Robert, after finishing football practice, was hungry. So, when the walk-in section of a local fast food restaurant was closed, he drove his bicycle up to the drive-through lane.

He was told, "The drive-through lane is only for cars."

"It's unfair!" griped Robert. There was no mention of no bicycles on the drive-through's sign.

Because bicyclists are subject to the same laws as vehicles where Robert lives, he felt that he should have been served. Should he have? The police thought otherwise.

The most frequent allegation and claim for relief when a participant is injured will be, "Someone was negligent. Their conduct, or lack of conduct, fell below that expected of an ordinary and responsible person in similar circumstances."

There are two general rules concerning injuries to participants in sports activities.

First, the owner or operator of a sports or public amusement facility is not an insurer of a participant's safety.

The owner or operator is bound to exercise "ordinary and reasonable" care for the safety and protection of his patrons; that is, the care which an ordinary, prudent, careful and cautious person would have exercised under the same or similar circumstances.

Second, athletes assume all ordinary and inherent risks of an activity, but do not assume extraordinary risks, unless they know of and voluntarily assume them.

Defenses that owners or operators may assert in defense of charges of negligence against them will be assumption of the risk, and contributory or comparative negligence.

6

DID I WAIVE MY RIGHTS?

WHAT'S IT ABOUT?

Did I Waive My Rights? details attempts by those controlling some sports activities, such as an amusement park, auto racing, skiing and golf, to limit their liability for injuries to participants by having them accept or sign a waiver or otherwise surrender their right to recover damages for an injury.

Are waivers effective? Are they effective if signed by a minor, a minor's parents, or by another for a participant? What happens if a waiver isn't signed?

WAIVER

It was the summer. You gleefully declared, "I'm going to do all of the things that I've never done before: enter an auto race, play golf, go rollerskating, scuba dive, go to the amusement park and join a health club!"

Several of the sponsors or operators of these activities wanted you to sign or accept a waiver. This would relieve them from any liability for any injuries to you.

Therefore, to participate in some of these activities, they told you, "Sign this waiver!"

WAIVER

I hereby release the operator or owner from any duty to care for my protection and safety and from all liability for any injuries that I may receive while participating. I assume full responsibility for any injuries to me, promise not to hold anyone else liable, and will not sue for any such injuries. I HAVE READ, UNDERSTAND, AND VOLUNTARILY AGREE TO THIS WAIVER OF LIABILITY.

________________________ Date ____________

FACTS: Some of these activities did not require a waiver to be signed, but included it on the back of the admission ticket. What would happen if you signed this waiver, or used a ticket with such a waiver on it, and were then injured? Would the waiver prevent you from recovering damages for any injuries?

DECISION: **YOU'RE THE JUDGE!**

A **waiver** or release—which may be inferred from one's conduct—is a voluntary surrender of a right (right to recover damages for an injury) with both knowledge of its existence and an intention to surrender it.

What effect does a waiver have on an injured participant who accepted a waiver?

A waiver alters ordinary negligence principles that would otherwise apply—that is, that one should be responsible for his negligent acts that cause injuries to others.

FACTS: Tony played for his company's softball team, Astra Tools. Right before the league championship game, the company's owner told the players, "Sign this waiver or you can't play!" They all signed.

Tony told how he was injured. "I ran into the fence attempting to catch a foul flyball. I broke my foot." "Can I seek recovery of damages or workmen's compensation benefits?" asked Tony. **YOU'RE THE JUDGE!**

DECISION: Yes. A waiver or release must be voluntary. If it comes out of a relationship with unequal bargaining power, such as between an employer and employee, then such a waiver is invalid.

In addition, for a waiver to prevent liability for an injury to a participant, the participant must have had actual (knew) or constructive (should have known) knowledge of the waiver or release.

FACTS: Vic signed an agreement before competing in a football tryout. It contained a waiver. Vic could have read it before signing, or kept a copy and taken time to read the waiver after signing. But before competing he did neither. When injured, he sued the promoter of the tryout. "Did I have knowledge of the waiver?" asked Vic. **YOU'RE THE JUDGE!**

DECISION: Vic knew or should have known of the waiver. He had both the time and opportunity to read the waiver before participating in the tryout.

Furthermore, it must be shown that a participant had the intention to sign and thereby waive any right to a claim for injuries.

What if a participant intended to sign an agreement, but didn't know that a waiver or release was included?

FACTS: When several semi-pro basketball players showed up for a summer clinic, they were asked to sign, as in the past, an attendance sheet. Only this year, a waiver clause had been added to the back of the sheet.

Emil signed without seeing the waiver. Stan, before signing, asked about the waiver. The director of the clinic replied, "Just a requirement, go ahead."

When Emil and Stan were injured and sued, the director defended, "They signed the waiver." Did Emil and Stan intend to release the director of any liability? **YOU'RE THE JUDGE!**

DECISION: No. Ignorance negates the waiver, as does consent given under mistake or misapprehension of fact.

For any waiver or release to be valid, it may be necessary to support it with consideration. That is, each party must give up something—such as the right to enter or participate—in return for admission or pay.

Therefore, when Rick, a participant, was issued a free pass to compete in a "Beat The Goalie" contest and was injured, the waiver on the pass did not release the operator from liability for his negligence in allowing Rick to play without proper equipment. Because the pass was free, the operator gave no consideration.

Auto Racing

FACTS: An auto racer explained, "I was hurt when a wheel from another automobile struck me while I was working in the pit area."

Another racer was injured when a car went out of control after hitting a piece of a fender on the track after an accident. The racers, who had signed waivers to obtain their racing licenses, sued. Could they recover damages for their injuries? **YOU'RE THE JUDGE!**

DECISION: No. The court held, "An agreement between the racers and the promoter—providing that the racers, in consideration for obtaining a racing license, would release the promoter from all liability due to his negligence—would be upheld."

Would such a waiver be upheld if it was contrary to safety regulations?

A waiver will not be enforced—where it is against public policy—because it renders safety requirements, prescribed by law, ineffective.

One court held that a stock car racer, McCarthy, could recover despite a signed waiver. He was injured when his car burst into flames. The sponsor failed to inspect the car, which did not comply with safety regulations.

Other courts have also questioned waiver agreements.

FACTS: Adamson, a stock car driver, was rendered a quadriplegic following an accident. The announcer told what happened. "His car swerved off the course, crashed through a guardrail and struck a utility pole."

Rescue personnel, attempting to put out the fire, sprayed Adamson with chemicals, resulting in brain damage. He sued the track owner and race promoter for inadequate and improperly trained rescue personnel.

The defendants produced a waiver which Adamson had signed, releasing them from liability. Did the waiver release the owner and sponsor from liability? **YOU'RE THE JUDGE!**

DECISION: No. Waivers containing very broad release clauses will only prevent claims within the understanding of the parties. The improper rescue operations were not within the agreement.

Moreover, waivers will not be enforceable where injuries are the result of intentional or reckless misconduct (such as where a track owner did not fill barrels with sand, as necessary to slow down out of control cars, and thus protect pit crew workers).

How Old Are You?

Is a waiver or release valid if it is signed by a minor? And what if the minor lied about his age?

FACTS: A waiver was signed by a minor, Kirk, who was then injured when his car turned over in a demolition derby. He knew what he was signing, but misrepresented his age. "I'm twenty-one," he lied.

When he sued the track owner for his injuries, the owner defended by producing the signed waiver. "Can I still recover?" asked Kirk. **YOU'RE THE JUDGE!**

DECISION: When Kirk, a minor, reaches majority (18-21), he may disaffirm the waiver, thereby creating liability for the track owner. This would be so even if Kirk misrepresented his age in signing the waiver.

Toboggans & Snowmobiles

Nor did the waiver (by itself), signed by a minor, Marie, release an operator from liability when the toboggan sled, in which Marie was riding as a paying customer, tipped over and she was injured. Although she disaffirmed the waiver upon reaching majority, the operator was found not negligent.

Another participant, Jenkins, signed and kept a copy of a "Notice To Patrons," which he knew included a release of liability for the owner of the toboggan ride. He was bound by the release and could not recover for injuries.

What if a participant signed a paper which contained a release, but didn't get a copy?

FACTS: A participant, Johnson, signed a receipt which contained a similar waiver. He swore, "I didn't get a copy!" When he was injured due to the owner's negligence and sued, the owner of the snowmobile ride produced the signed waiver. Did the waiver prevent Johnson from recovering damages for his injury? **YOU'RE THE JUDGE!**

DECISION: The waiver did not relieve the owner from liability for Johnson's injury. The participant had no actual (knew) or constructive (should have known) knowledge that the receipt contained a release.

Parents

Parents cannot sign away the rights of a minor. If parents sign a form releasing a school, coach or any other party from liability for any negligence for injuries to their child, the form is either illegal or may be disaffirmed by the minor upon his reaching majority.

FACTS: Lanny's father said, "I was required to sign a waiver so that Lanny could attend football summer camp." When he was injured and sued, the camp defended with the waiver. Did the waiver prevent Lanny from recovering? **YOU'RE THE JUDGE!**

DECISION: The court found, "It is doubtful that a parent could waive a child's right for damages from an injury due to the negligence of the camp." There also was unequal bargaining power between the boys and the camp.

Even if the father could waive any right to recover by his child, the waiver relieving the camp of liability would be frowned upon by the public.

Skiing, Horses & Scuba Diving

FACTS: A ski jumper, Garretson, was injured when blown out of position, allegedly due to adverse weather conditions. As he had done for previous competitions, Garretson read and signed an "Entry Blank" releasing the sponsors of the competition from any liability for injuries to participants. Could he recover for his injury? **YOU'RE THE JUDGE!**

DECISION: No. Garretson voluntarily signed the waiver with both knowledge of its release and an intent to give up the right to recover.

A like decision was reached after a rider, Peter, was injured after he knowingly signed a waiver upon renting a horse. Hewitt, a scuba diver who hit his head on a rock and drowned (after signing a waiver from "inherent or ordinary dangers") was similarly denied.

Would your answer be different if it was known that a participant was inexperienced?

A waiver signed by another equestrian, Palmquist, did not release the riding academy, from where he rented a horse, of liability. The academy "knew of Palmquist's inexperience and yet gave him a dangerous horse, from which he was thrown and injured." That was gross negligence.

Hidden Waivers

Golf

FACTS: Marvin sued for an injury to his shoulder. He was thrown out of a moving golf cart. "The cart tipped over when the brakes stuck," said Marvin. He had signed a receipt which contained a waiver on the back. Can I still recover?" asked Marvin. **YOU'RE THE JUDGE!**

DECISION: The "not liable" clause was "hidden" in the receipt. It was void as against public policy. It would be unconscionable to allow the lessor to exclude himself from liability by the use of an agreement which "tends to injure the public," commented the court.

Health Club

Another court had the same problem where a waiver on a health club membership form was buried in fine print on the back of a form which the plaintiff had signed.

But at gyms, where one woman slipped near the pool and another in the shower room on a smooth spot, and they sued for negligent maintenance, the courts held that their membership contracts excused the gyms from liability. "The language was clear. Their applications were voluntary and they had time to read them and, they agreed to the terms."

Amusements & Beach Clubs

Any agreement between a patron and an amusement operator, which exempts an operator from liability, must be fairly and honestly negotiated and understandingly entered into. If it is, then it will be valid.

However, such agreements will be closely scrutinized and strictly interpreted against the operator.

> FACTS: Two patrons, Jones and O'Connell, were thrown from their horses and injured, allegedly due to the negligence of Wally World management.
>
> The waiver, which they knowingly signed, read in part:
>
> I AGREE TO ASSUME THE RISKS INHERENT IN HORSEBACK RIDING. I WAIVE ALL CLAIMS THAT I MAY HAVE AGAINST WALLY WORLD FOR INJURIES RECEIVED WHILE HORSEBACK RIDING.

> Jones and O'Connell wanted to recover damages for their injuries. Could they? **YOU'RE THE JUDGE!**
>
> DECISION: The court found that the waiver did not prevent them from suing for the park's negligence, as the language in the release did not indicate the intent to release the park for its own negligence.

A similar decision was reached where a swimming club member was injured when he fell off the gangplank leading to a dock. The court held that the words: "WAIVE CLAIM FOR ANY PERSONAL INJURY" was not sufficiently clear or explicit to relieve the club from liability for its own negligence.

Waiver Signed For Patron

A waiver read that an applicant to a beach club, Michaels, would "waive all claims for injury occurring in the use of the club." A friend had signed it for him. Would this prevent Michaels from recovering for an injury caused by the club?

The waiver did not release the club from liability for its own negligence. Even if the waiver were valid, it would not bind Michaels as he did not sign it, and the friend who did was not his agent—one authorized to act for another.

Unsigned Waivers On Tickets

Unsigned waivers, as sometimes appear on the back of admission tickets, generally will not release an operator from liability for injuries which are due to the operator's negligence.

FACTS: A waiver on the back side of a rollerskating rink admission ticket stated that patrons "assume the risk of any injury." The tickets were collected immediately at the door.

When O'Brien, who had skated at that rink many times, was injured and sued, the operator defended with the waiver on the ticket. Did the waiver relieve the operator of liability? **YOU'RE THE JUDGE!**

DECISION: No. The warning was not properly brought to O'Brien's attention. Otherwise, it may have been effective to relieve the operators of liability for their negligence in causing O'Brien's fall and injury.

Even if O'Brien had read it, she could not be held to have understood the implications of the waiver.

Similar decisions resulted where waivers on tickets and on signs, such as at an amusement park's roller coaster ride, were not properly brought to the attention of patrons.

ODDS & ENDS....

FACTS: You decided to try riding "Boltin' Benny," the mechanical bull at a local country nightclub. After you had had a few too many, you signed this waiver:

> **WAIVER**
> I, an aspiring cowboy, assume the risk of any injuries that I may receive while attempting to ride the mechanical bull. I release the operator from any claims for injuries and of any liability for negligence on his part.
>
> Signature——————————Date ————

You got on "Boltin Benny." After success at a slow pace, you bellowed to the operator, "Turn 'er all the way up!!" He did, and you fell. You got back on and were again thrown.You bounced off the mats and crashed into the wall. Result: separated shoulder and broken ankle.

When you sued, the club defended, "He signed this waiver!" Would the waiver prevent you from recovering for your injuries? **YOU'RE THE JUDGE!**

DECISION: You could not be held to have understood the implications of such a waiver, especially in your condition, which the operator knew or should have known of.

The club was negligent for allowing you to ride while in such condition, and, furthermore, for not providing proper protection for your safety—the bull was too close to the wall.

It is important to remember that to effectively waive any right you may have to recover damages for an injury received as a participant in a sports activity, you must know of and voluntarily surrender that right.

7

CITIES & SCHOOLS - IT'S THEIR DUTY!

WHAT'S IT ABOUT?

Cities & Schools—It's Their Duty! outlines a school's or municipality's (city or town) duty to exercise reasonable care for the safety of those either under their control or using their facilities, such as ballfields or swimming pools.

But there are defenses to allegations, such as for negligent supervision or improper instructions. One of those defenses, sovereign immunity, originated out of the belief "The King can do no wrong." Can he?

School District & City Board
4545 Eastern Ave.
Essexshire, MA 68743

Dear athletes, students, parents & others:

Sports activities and sports related injuries occur most often on the fields and in the gyms and at other facilities of cities, towns & schools.

In the interest of having everyone understand who may be responsible for these injuries, and in the hopes of minimizing or eliminating them, we would like you to read the following material. It discusses the rights and duties of schools and municipalities (cities and towns) and of the athletes, who come under the school's or municipalities' control or guidance, or anyone using their athletic facilities.

Yours truly,

School District & City of Essexshire

YOU HAVE A DUTY TO....

FACTS: Several roller and ice skating participants were injured at city and school owned skating rinks. The injuries were due to: accidents, defective barricades and equipment, and, as one skater put it, "There was no supervision. Everyone just raced around and knocked me over." What were the city's and school's duties? Did they neglect these duties?

DECISION: **YOU'RE THE JUDGE!**

Schools and municipalities (cities and towns) have a duty to exercise ordinary and reasonable care for the protection and safety of those either under their control or using their facilities. They must provide proper supervision where necessary, insure that facilities are safe and correct any defects which are known or, by inspection, should be known of. This is particularly important as regarding hidden hazards or defects.

There can be no liability for a school or municipality unless all of the elements of negligence are present.

What must a plaintiff show in order to succeed on a charge of **negligence** against a school or municipality?

A plaintiff must show: a duty owed by the school or municipality, a breach of that duty which was the cause of an injury, and damages. That is, that the injury would not have occurred but for the school's or municipality's conduct or lack of conduct.

FACTS: Bauer was injured during a soccer game on a town field. "I stepped in a hole that was hidden by uncut grass. I didn't see it," he complained.

Williams was injured at the town swimming pool by a group engaged in "roughhousing." "I wasn't involved," he moaned.

Did the town have a duty to inspect and correct the field? Did they have a duty to provide supervision at its pool?

DECISION: **YOU'RE THE JUDGE!**

For school sponsored sports activities taking place on municipal property, the school has the primary duty to provide instruction and supervision. Both the school and the municipality in control of the property have a duty to ensure that the property is free from any hazards or defects.

A school's or municipality's duty to those to whom they owe a duty is to protect them from unreasonable risks of injury that are foreseeable and that can be reduced by proper care.

Should consideration be given to the type of activity or the age of the participants?

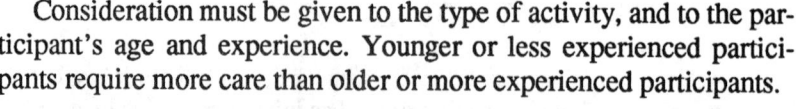

Consideration must be given to the type of activity, and to the participant's age and experience. Younger or less experienced participants require more care than older or more experienced participants.

FACTS: Johnny, 8, was injured when, "Some kids jumped in the town pool and landed on me." This conduct had been going on for some time without any warning from the authorities.

Jason, 18, was injured during a "pile-up" in a rough football game with the town's rival. Could either of the boys recover damages for their injury? **YOU'RE THE JUDGE!**

DECISION: The court held, "The town's breach of its duty to provide proper supervision was the cause of Johnny's injury. The age of the children demanded stricter supervision."

Jason was older and playing a more inherently dangerous sport. He "assumed the risk of, and, by playing, contributed to, such an unintentional injury."

General supervision is required where participants are engaged in activities which are not usually dangerous, such as soccer or baseball.

Specific supervision is required where activities are unusually dangerous, or where the activity is not familiar, such as football or gymnastics.

For activities taking place at, or under the control, of a school, a participant may assume that proper instruction, supervision, equipment and facilities will be given.

However, for sports activities taking place at a municipal facility, most of the activities (with the exception of swimming pools and municipally run park's programs—which demand the same duty as that expected of a school) will not be supervised.

In these instances, will participants have a duty to protect themselves?

Where there is no required supervision, participants have more of a duty to exercise ordinary and reasonable care for their own protection and safety than do those participating in a supervised activity.

FACTS: Hogan explained, "I was hurt when I was tackled in a pick-up football game at the town field. We had no equipment." Did the town have a duty to provide equipment and supervision? **YOU'RE THE JUDGE!**

DECISION: No. As the game was not under the control of the town, the town had no duty to provide equipment or supervision. Hogan assumed the risk of and contributed to his injury by playing.

Participants assume all of the ordinary and common risks in a sport. A school or municipality does not insure a participant's safety.

They may only be held liable for their own negligent acts, or for those committed by one for whom they are responsible, such as a teacher, coach or instructor.

DEFENSE! DEFENSE!

A school or municipality may (in addition to the **Statute of Limitations**—which bars any action not brought within a specified period of time) have certain legal defenses available which may prevent a participant from bringing a suit or from recovering damages in part or fully.

Immunity For The King!

"The King can do no wrong." It was thought in England, in the 1700's, that the king or sovereign could do no wrong. Therefore, as the courts received their powers from the sovereign, they did not have the power to hold the ruler liable.

Are schools or municipalities **agents** (one appointed to act for another) of the sovereign? This idea of **sovereign immunity** was adopted in this country and eventually was extended to include as immune from liability, municipalities and schools, both as agents of the sovereign.

Others saw immunity as a "convenience to the people, who, when carrying out their governmental powers, should use school or municipal funds solely for those purposes." Therefore, they should not be sued.

Did this mean that a school or municipality could not be found liable for an injury even where they were negligent?

FACTS: School officials used unslaked lime to line a football field. Johnson sighed, "I had my face pushed into the lime, causing a permanent loss of sight in one eye and severely damaging the other." Johnson sued the school for not protecting his safety. Was the school negligent? Could Johnson recover damages? **YOU'RE THE JUDGE!**

DECISION:: The immunity doctrine acted as a complete defense to Johnson's suit. Even though the school may have been negligent, he could not recover.

Because of such harsh results from the immunity doctrine, states began to chip away at it, thus making municipalities and public schools liable to those injured because of the municipality's or school's negligence.

Could a coach or other person responsible for an injury be held liable?

Even where a school or municipality was immune from liability, an individual supervisor, teacher, instructor or coach involved could be subject to liability.

FACTS: Several football players on a town sponsored team were injured when their coach instructed them to participate in tackling drills without equipment. "Was the coach responsible?" asked the players. **YOU'RE THE JUDGE!**

DECISION: Yes. The town was protected by sovereign immunity. But the coach, due to the improper instruction and supervision, was liable for the injuries.

Save-harmless

Where an injured plaintiff may be prevented from bringing an action against the school, he could sue the teacher or coach personally.

"Save-harmless" statutes may be used to grant immunity from liability by indemnifying school personnel (teachers and coaches) for judgments rendered against them.

FACTS: Richardson, a little league baseball player, "misjudged a fly ball and was struck in the face and injured." His parents sued the coach and his assistant—another parent—alleging that they were negligent in instructing Richardson how to play. Could Johnnie recover damages for his injury? **YOU'RE THE JUDGE!**

DECISION: Yes. Although an out of court settlement was reached, later legislation—save-harmless statutes—now offers some protection for coaches, parents and others associated with civic sports programs. Had Richardson been older, he may have been held to have assumed the risk of such an injury as one ordinary or common to the game.

Charitable Immunity

Charitable immunity, which may apply to charitable organizations, such as the Little League, YMCA, YWCA, and other nonprofit organizations, provides a shield of protection from liability similar to that of sovereign immunity. The theory here was that since funds were for charitable purposes, they should not be diverted for other uses, such as to pay damages for injuries to participants.

This doctrine also came under criticism and therefore, has been widely rejected. Those engaged in charitable activities are not, for that reason alone, immune from liability.

FACTS: Sarah was injured during a little league baseball game. "I tried to slide into home and crashed head first into the catcher."

she explained. She sued, alleging that the coach "did not properly instruct me how to slide. He never said I couldn't make head first slides." The little league claimed the defense of charitable immunity. Did this defense relieve the league or coach of potential liability? **YOU'RE THE JUDGE!**

DECISION: No. Charitable immunity did not protect the league or the coach.

Assumption Of The Risk

Assumption of the risk will apply as a defense if a participant knew of the risk or danger as one ordinary to the sport, but then proceeded voluntarily to assume that risk.

What if a participant is required to participate, such as in a gym class? Is that voluntary participation?

Assumption of the risk is less likely to be used in defending against an injury from a physical education class. This is because students are required to participate, and therefore there may be no voluntariness of assuming any risk. But, not always.

FACTS: Hanson, during a gym class, was instructed in the proper method to jump over the horse. He was also told, "It's dangerous. You shouldn't try if you don't think you can do it."

Hanson attempted the jump, was injured, and then sued the school for negligence. Although it was a mandatory class, the school claimed, "Hanson assumed the risk of injury."

"Whose fault was it?" asked Hanson. **YOU'RE THE JUDGE!**

DECISION: Although the class was mandatory, Hanson was given the option of not participating. In trying the jump, Hanson assumed the risk of injury and, therefore, relieved the school of any liability.

When considering whether a participant understood and appreciated a risk, consideration must be given to his age and experience, and to the nature of the activity. However, if the injury is the result of another's negligence, there can be no assumption of the risk.

FACTS: Susan, 12, was injured when the go-cart she was driving at a city owned facility crashed. She said, "I went through the retaining barrier into a wall." Had the retaining barrier been properly installed, it would have prevented Susan from hitting the wall. Was the city negligent? **YOU'RE THE JUDGE!**

DECISION: Susan only assumed the risk of the ordinary and inherent dangers of the sport, not of the city's negligence.

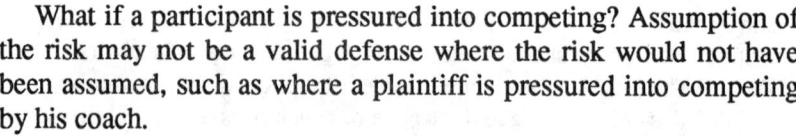

What if a participant is pressured into competing? Assumption of the risk may not be a valid defense where the risk would not have been assumed, such as where a plaintiff is pressured into competing by his coach.

FACTS: "Tank" tried out for the school wrestling team. He was warned by the coach of the risk of injury, but nevertheless, agreed to try out.

Similarly, John was warned when trying out for the football team. When both were injured during the normal play of the sport, they sued the school.

"Pig," nicknamed for his enormous appetite and size, had never wrestled. Although skeptical about trying out for the wrestling team, he was talked into doing so by the coach. He was injured during his first practice. Were any of these participants pressured into competing? **YOU'RE THE JUDGE!**

DECISION: Tank and John assumed the risk of injury; their consent was voluntary. Pig's consent was by undue pressure. He may recover for his injury, the others may not.

Contributory & Comparative Negligence

Participants in sports activities are held to a duty of exercising ordinary and reasonable care for their own protection and safety. That is, that care which an ordinary or reasonable person would exercise in the same or similar circumstances. Participants may be guilty of **contibutory negligence** where they are aware of a risk or danger, but proceed anyway and are then injured.

The question becomes, "Did the participant have sufficient knowledge, awareness and appreciation of the danger?"

Many school-related injuries involve minors. The standard of care to which the minors are held is that of an ordinary and reasonable child (of the same age and capacity) to appreciate and avoid danger in the same—or similar—circumstances.

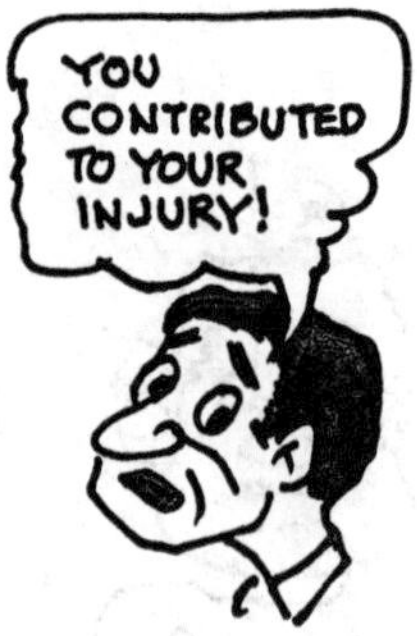

FACTS: Jimmy, 14, and Frankie, 15, asked their school's physical education teacher if they could try boxing. He said, "Sure, put the gloves on and give it a go!"

Frankie, much the bigger of the two, hurt Jimmy. Jimmy sued the coach and the school, alleging improper instructions and no supervision. The school defended, "He contributed to his injury by participating. He can't recover." Could he?

DECISION: **YOU'RE THE JUDGE!**

May a participant who contributed to his injury still recover?

Some states have **comparative negligence**—where any recovery by a plaintiff may be reduced by the amount of his own negligence. Or the plaintiff can recover for that amount of the defendant's negligence. Comparative negligence statutes vary from state to state. In some, if the plaintiff's negligence is equal, to or exceeds, the defendant's, there can be no recovery. In others, any negligence on the part of the plaintiff will completely bar recovery.

FACTS: Kenny and Stan were injured in school football games. They sued their schools, which were not protected by sovereign immunity.

Both were guilty of contributory negligence, but Kenny's school was in a state with comparative negligence. The school was found to be 40% at fault and Kenny 60% at fault. Could either Stan or Kenny recover for their injuries? **YOU'RE THE JUDGE!**

DECISION: Because Stan was guilty of contributory negligence, he could not recover.

In some states, Kenny could not recover because his degree of fault exceeded the school's. In such a state which reduces Kenny's award by the amount of his own negligence, he would have to be less than 50% at fault to recover.

In other states, Kenny would recover, but only the 40% that the school was found to be at fault; or, if the school were 60% at fault and Kenny 40%, Kenny could recover the difference, which would be 20% of the total negligence award.

In the following discussion, assume that there is no immunity from liability for a municipality or school for any negligence which causes an injury to a participant.

MUNICIPAL LIABILITY

Municipalities (cities and towns) have a duty to exercise ordinary and reasonable care for the protection and safety of those using their facilities.

It may be sufficient to charge a municipality with negligence where the municipality had an opportunity to discover unsafe conditions by inspection (or had knowledge of these conditions, or allowed a lack of supervision) and injuries followed.

FACTS: Lou and Richie were injured when they fell after hitting pot holes on the town's paved bicycle trail. Richie said, "I knew that the path was in need of repair, but Lou didn't." The holes had washed out after a heavy rain a few weeks earlier. Could the town be charged with negligence? **YOU'RE THE JUDGE!**

DECISION: Lou knew of the danger; he assumed the risk. As to

YOU'RE THE JUDGE!

Richie's injury, the town had an opportunity to discover the danger. They could be charged with negligence.

A municipality also has a duty to warn the public of any lack of supervision or of a defective condition at one of its facilities. This could be done by posting a warning.

What if the warning is removed? If a warning is removed, the municipality may still be charged where an inspection would have revealed the missing warning.

Will a warning protect a municipality from liability where further action is necessary?

FACTS: A large hole had been left on a municipal ballfield with a sign warning: DO NOT USE THIS FIELD. Several grammar school children were playing kick ball when one of them fell into the hole and was injured. Was the municipality negligent for not taking further precautions? **YOU'RE THE JUDGE!**

DECISION: The failure to either fill in the hole or take other more necessary precautions to protect children was negligence. The children's age negated any contributory negligence or assumption of the risk.

Ballfields

Participants using municipal ballfields have a right to assume that those facilities will be free from any hazards or defects, and that necessary warnings will be posted alerting them to any hidden dangers.

Participants assume ordinary and inherent risks, such as from running into fences or bleachers. In addition, participants may assume risks inherent in playing a particular game on a specific field.

YOU'RE THE JUDGE!

FACTS: Jerry was injured chasing a foul pop-up in a pick-up softball game. "I tripped over the curbing of a surrounding track and sidewalk and then fell over the concrete bench near the field," he testified. Jerry, who had played on this field many times before without injury, sued the city, complaining that the field was negligently designed and constructed. Was the city liable for Jerry's injuries? **YOU'RE THE JUDGE!**

DECISION: No. Although the field was not in the condition that could reasonably be expected, Jerry had played on the field before and was aware and had knowledge of the condition. He assumed the risk of, and contributed to, his injury.

Unless it had posted a conspicuous sign warning of the dangerous condition, the city may have been held liable even if Jerry not played on the field before.

FACTS: Hank, running out for a pass in a pick-up touch football game, fell and broke his ankle. "My foot got caught in a hole hidden by long grass. And I cut myself on a broken bottle." Hank sued the town which owned the field. Was the town liable for Hank's injuries? **YOU'RE THE JUDGE!**

DECISION: If the hole was open and obvious, Hank would have assumed the risk of injury. But where the hole was hidden because of the failure of the town to either cut the grass or fix the hole, the town was liable. Hank had no knowledge or appreciation of the danger.

As to the cut, Hank was held to have contributed to his injury by playing on the field without making at least a visual inspection, which would have revealed the broken bottle.

Similarly, where a town did not warn of a defective fence surrounding their facility, they were held liable when a player unintentionally ran into the fence, which then collapsed, injuring him. Here, even an adequate warning may not have been enough. The town should have either fixed the fence or prohibited use of the field until the fence was fixed.

What if the player had noticed the defective fence before playing there?

Even if the player had noticed the fence's condition, temporary forgetfulness while in the heat of the game, might have excused him from assuming any risk of injury. It would be up to a judge or jury to decide if the player had forgotten.

If a city or town furnishes equipment, it must be in proper condition. Liability may attach where any equipment has a hidden or unknown defect. However, liability will not attach where a player knew of the defect.

Will a potentially dangerous game broaden a municipality's duty of care?

FACTS: A town issued gear to the neighborhood boys for a football game. Because of a cracked helmet, one of the boys was injured and sued the town. Did the town have a responsibility to issue proper equipment, or provide either instruction, supervision, or both? **YOU'RE THE JUDGE!**

DECISION: The town would not only be responsible for issuing equipment in the proper condition, but may also have a duty to instruct or warn the boys of the dangers, and to provide supervision to ensure their protection and safety.

Swimming

A municipality has a duty to exercise ordinary or reasonable care for the protection and safety of those using municipal swimming facilities. This duty includes giving proper warnings concerning the use of a facility and known hidden hazards (as well as the inspecting and cleaning up of all foreign substances on the grounds and in and around any protective barriers.)

This duty extends to bathhouse and changing areas. There is also a duty to have required safety equipment in proper condition.

FACTS: John, while walking next to a city owned and supervised pool, slipped and fell into the pool. Jay held out the safety hook, "It fell apart." he said. John went under. Attempts to resuscitate him were unsuccessful. John's family sued the city "for negligently operating its swimming pool." Was the city negligent? **YOU'RE THE JUDGE!**

DECISION: Yes. The city breached its duty to provide proper safety equipment. This breach was the cause of John's death.

A city's duty to keep its swimming facilities in proper condition may not extend to unsupervised, unimproved public property. Such might be the case where a city was either not aware of a water's use or had posted warnings.

FACTS: Keith drowned when, at a local pond, he jumped out of a tree and landed on a rock along the bank. His family sued the city for "not preventing the kids from using the pond." They asked, "Was the city liable?" **YOU'RE THE JUDGE!**

DECISIONS: Keith contributed to and also assumed the risk of such an injury. He knew, or should have known, of the condition. The city is not an insurer of a user's safety. Nor can it guarantee, or be held liable for, the safety of all users.

A municipality's duty to care for the safety of its users may extend to other situations which could result in injuries (such as by having inattentive, or an insufficient number of, lifeguards).

What if a lifeguard uses improper life-saving techniques or none at all in attempting a rescue?

FACTS: Will, a lifeguard at a city-owned swimming facility, was giving instructions in life-saving techniques. Susan, a beginning swimmer, ventured into the deep end, but started thrashing about when she realized where she was. She drowned. Efforts to revive her were unsuccessful.

The city claimed that the lifeguard was giving necessary instruction to other swimmers. "He could not be held liable to protect everyone in the pool at every moment. Susan assumed the risk of drowning." Was the city liable for Susan's death? **YOU'RE THE JUDGE!**

DECISION: Yes. Although the city may not have been negligent where an injury was the result of an unexplained tragedy (no one's fault), this tragedy happened because the lifeguard was improperly supervising the pool. Had he been observant as required, Susan would have been under the water for a much shorter time and, in the view of medical opinion, saved.

If facilities are off-limits, then there is a duty to provide adequate safeguards, such as a barrier and posting as such. This duty extends to periodically inspecting the area to ensure that the barrier is intact.

FACTS: Several kids were using the diving board at the city pool. Frank hit the bottom, severely spraining his neck. Upon inspection, it was found that, although the marking on the side of the pool showed the depth to be 8 feet; the actual depth was 6 1/2 feet.

Testimony was given, "Had the pool been 8 feet deep, it is unlikely that the injury would have occurred." Frank sued the city for not warning him of the depth of the water. Did Frank assume the risk of such injury? **YOU'RE THE JUDGE!**

DECISION: No. Although had Frank known of the shallower water, he may have assumed the risk, it was not evident that the water was shallower than marked. The city was held liable.

Basketball, Tennis & Rinks

Any defective conditions in basketball or tennis courts, or a skating rink—such as holes, cracks, broken supports or unmended fences—will most likely be open and obvious. Therefore, assumption of the risk will bar recovery for such conditions, even if there is no warning. Is supervision necessary at such facilities?

FACTS: The neighborhood kids were playing a three-on-three basketball game at an outdoor court. "J.D. and Slammer collided while going for a loose ball," explained another player.

J.D. was injured and sued the city. Was the city liable for not providing supervision? **YOU'RE THE JUDGE!**

DECISION: No. The court held, "J.D. assumed the risk of injury. Even if the city had provided supervision, it could not be shown that such supervision would have prevented injury from an ordinary and inherent risk of the game."

If, however, supervision was given and a supervisor knew (or should have known) of rough play that could lead to injury, then a city may be held to have been on notice of such potential injury and could be found responsible for not taking proper safety measures.

Golf

As it is well known that injury may result from an errant golf shot, assumption of the risk is a widely used and successful defense to actions alleging negligence for such an injury.

For a hazard, other than a normal hazard on a golf course, there may exist a duty to warn by an appropriate sign or barrier and to make periodic inspections.

Who is liable for injuries to passersby from errantly struck golf balls?

FACTS: Moe, Larry and Curly were injured while driving their cars on the road next to the city owned, Highlands Golf Course.

Moe was struck by a ball that went through a hole in the fence; Larry was hit by a ball which sailed over the fence; Curly was hit by a ball where there was no fence.

Moe and Larry were aware of the course and its danger, Curly was not. He insisted, "I never drove on that road before." Was the city liable for the injuries? **YOU'RE THE JUDGE!**

DECISION: Larry assumed the risk of being struck by an occasional errant ball, but would not assume the risk if the city was aware, or should have been aware, of this being more than a common occurrence.

Moe and Curly did not assume the risk of injury due to the city's negligence in not repairing the fence, or in not constructing one where it was needed to protect the public.

Racing

Where a participant or an observer of either unauthorized or prohibited drag racing of cars on public streets is injured, contributory negligence and assumption of the risk will generally be successful defenses.

What if a city knew or should have known of such conduct, but did nothing to prevent it?

FACTS: Robinson, using a city park, was injured when he was struck by a vehicle which was drag racing on an adjacent street. The city was aware of the prohibited racing, but found it difficult to control. Was the city liable for Robinson's injury? **YOU'RE THE JUDGE!**

DECISION: The city was not liable. A city has a duty to maintain its streets in a reasonably safe condition. However, where a city makes an acceptable effort to prevent such racing, recovery for any resulting injury may be barred, at least as against the city.

Trampoline

An 11-year-old, Marie, while bouncing on a trampoline at a city park, lost her balance, fell, and fractured her jaw on a metal pipe near the trampoline.

When she sued the city, the court held, "At the least, there should have been instructions, adequate warning and properly placed equipment." The city-run trampoline center failed to exercise reasonable care. But, what if Marie were older?

FACTS: Daniel, 35, and college educated, was injured using a trampoline at a city gym. Signs were posted telling patrons to: ASK FOR INSTRUCTIONS, IF NEEDED. Warnings were also given. Did Daniel assume the risk of injury? **YOU'RE THE JUDGE!**

DECISION: Daniel assumed the risk of his injury from using the trampoline. He was old enough to understand the warning and the risk of using the trampoline.

SCHOOL LIABILITY

School authorities owe to those who participate for a school or on school property, the duty to exercise ordinary and reasonable care for their protection and safety.

Schools, however, are not insurers of safety. They will only be liable for injuries where they or their agents, such as a teacher or coach, fail to meet the required duty.

Do students have a duty to protect themselves? Students have a duty to exercise reasonable care for their own protection and safety. They will assume the risks and dangers ordinarily inherent in a game or sport including a risk of injury from an unforseeable accident for which no amount of precaution, except elimination of the activity, could prevent injury.

FACTS: Mitch failed to complete a simple exercise, a jumping jack, and was injured. A baseball bat slipped from the coach's hands and injured Guy. Mary was hurt during a kickball game. The only explanation for this injury was the presence of many participants.

Sue was injured during basketball practice. It was later discovered that she had very weak ankles which could not support jumping. Could any of these participants recover from the coaches or schools for their injuries? **YOU'RE THE JUDGE!**

DECISION: All of the injuries were the result of unforseeable accidents. They all assumed the risk of such injuries.

Students may also be held to have assumed the risk of, or contributed to, their injury where they are aware of—and appreciate—the risk or danger, but choose to proceed anyway.

FACTS: Hank's nose was broken during a boxing match. Bill hurt his back rebounding during a rough, but fair, basketball game. Judy, with a qualified spotter, was injured attempting a difficult gymnastics maneuver which she had done before. Could any of these student-athletes recover for their injuries against the school? **YOU'RE THE JUDGE!**

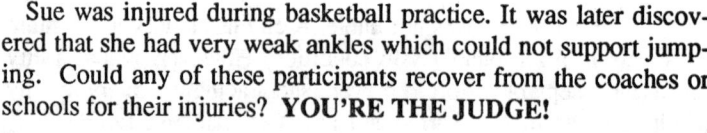

DECISION: Hank, Bill and Judy had consented to subject themselves to the known dangers and risks. Therefore, they contributed to, and assumed the risk of, injury from their participation.

Should consideration be given to: the type or manner of consent given, the nature of the activity, and the age and experience of the student?

FACTS: Jeff, 16, in his first try-out for the school's football team, was instructed, "In this drill, you must attempt, without blockers, to run through five tacklers."

Susan, 15, in her first try-out for the school gymnastics team, was instructed, "You have to execute five consecutive tuck-and-rolls." Both were then injured. Was either's consent informed? Was it voluntary? Were they pressured? Who was liable?

DECISION: **YOU'RE THE JUDGE!**

Respondeat Superior!

In states which have waived sovereign immunity, schools may—under the rule of **respondeat superior**—be held liable for the negligent acts of their teachers and coaches.

This rule provides, "A school is liable for injury caused by employees of the school, acting within their duties, if such conduct would allow a complaint against the employee, as an individual, apart from the school."

FACTS: Junior, a coach at Emerald High, negligently instructed football players during tackling drills. When several of the players were injured while using the improper tackling techniques, they sued the school. Was the school liable for the acts of their coach? **YOU'RE THE JUDGE!**

DECISION: The school was held liable under the rule of respondeat superior.

A SCHOOL'S DUTY MAY EXTEND TO THESE OBLIGATIONS:

Greater New England High School Athletic Association
4141 Fairfax Ave.
Greendale, MA 34341

- ☐ Equipment
- ☐ Training
- ☐ Facilities
- ☐ Medical Attention
- ☐ Competition
- ☐ Physical Condition of Participants
- ☐ Instructions
- ☐ Supervision
- ☐ Coach Or Instructor
- ☐ Discipline & Rules
- ☐ Transportation

Equipment — Was the equipment suitable, in proper condition and provided, where necessary, to ensure the safety of participants?

FACTS: During a floor hockey game, Warren was struck in the head by the puck. "He wasn't wearing a helmet," said the coach.

Another player, Evan, was seriously injured when a hockey puck hit between gaps in the helmet he was wearing. Was the school liable for the injuries? **YOU'RE THE JUDGE!**

DECISION: The court found that requiring the students to play without proper protective equipment was negligent.

Any equipment furnished must be proper. Another high school athlete, Wilfred, participating in the high jump, was injured when he fell in a landing pit consisting of vinyl bags filled with foam rubber. The school was found negligent for supplying improper equipment and facilities.

But where a pole-vaulter, Walt, fell backwards into the wooden boxes used to support the vaulting bar, recovery for his injuries was denied. The court commented that "the usefulness of the boxes outweighed the risk of injury."

Can a violation of safety standards that results in injury, lead to liability for negligence?

FACTS: Howard, 15, was injured while participating in a high school summer football practice. The practice was supervised by two coaches. The team, without protective equipment, was engaged in a game of "jungle football." Howard was struck in the eye, resulting in blindness. He sued the school for providing neither proper equipment nor supervision. Was the school liable? **YOU'RE THE JUDGE!**

DECISION: Yes. The practice sessions were in violation of safety standards, which required both proper equipment and proper supervision.

Courts have found other school districts liable for carelessly and negligently allowing players to wear ill-fitting, inadequate equipment (cracked helmet) and, furthermore, for refusing to furnish proper equipment upon request.

Instructions — Were instructions given adequately and propely, including any warnings necessary to ensure the safety of participants?

FACTS: Gardner, 11, injured his shoulder. He said, "I was attempting to perform a headstand. There were no instructions."

Felicia, a 17 year-old high school student, broke her wrist when she was instructed to try an exercise known as "jumping the buck." She told the instructor, "I don't want to, I have weak wrists." But nevertheless, she was instructed to try the exercise.

Landers injured his back attempting a backward somersault during gym class. The teacher was aware that Landers was overweight, untrained and fearful, but instructed him to "work on the maneuver on your own." He collided with another student who was also instructed to do the same exercise on the same mat.

Another student, James, was instructed to execute a somersault. In so doing, he was injured. He had done them many times before without injury. Were the schools negligent for not providing proper instructions? **YOU'RE THE JUDGE!**

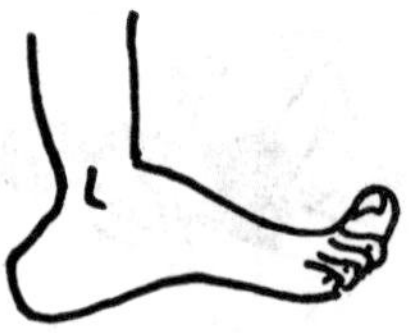

DECISION: James assumed the risk of, and contributed to, his injury. The courts found the other schools negligent and liable for the injuries. They either gave improper instructions or no instructions where they were required.

Negligence has also been found where inadequate instructions on using the trampoline, rings and springboard all resulted in injuries to students.

Similarly, negligence for improper instructions was found where students were injured after being instructed to try tumbling exercises in stocking feet and slipped, or where students were instructed to play in bare feet, and their bare feet stuck to the floor, causing them to fall.

Participants will assume the risk of injury from an unforseeable accident, where there is no negligence in instructions or in providing equipment or supervision. Can participants also be guilty of contributory negligence?

FACTS: Ed Sowers ran into a javelin during an outdoor physical education class. He had been ordered, "Stay on the track!" but forgot and was running on the grass when the accident happened. Should the school have taken other precautions? **YOU'RE THE JUDGE!**

DECISION: No. The instructions were adequate. Sowers, not wearing his glasses, was unable to see the javelin. His own negligence was the cause of his injury.

Can participants be guilty of assuming the risk of, or contributing to, their injuries where they are not aware of the dangers that face them?

FACTS: "We started to box. We wanted to see who would get the best of it, so we went right at it as hard as we could. In the second round we started just as bad as ever and I got hit in the temple. I became dizzy and staggered." testified Hector.

Neither Hector nor his opponent had received proper training. Hector received serious injuries to his head, which required draining hemorrhaging blood. The supervising teacher sat in the bleachers, watching and gave no instructions or warning.

Darrow, 10, suffered injuries when he ran into another player while playing line soccer at school. He had never received instructions on what to do if two players arrived at the ball simultaneously, and was never warned of the dangers of the game. Did Hector and Darrow assume the risks of such injuries? **YOU'RE THE JUDGE!**

DECISION: No. Teachers must exercise reasonable care to prevent injuries, including giving warnings and instructions, before allowing participation in a dangerous activity. The plaintiffs could not assume risks that they were not aware of.

A similar result was reached where students, trying out for their high school football team, were urged to lift weights by the coach. They were not given proper instructions, nor were they warned of the risk of injury. Varon, 15, fell while lifting a 250-pound weight, resulting in paraplegia.

In baseball, are proper instructions and a warning necessary when teaching participants how to slide?

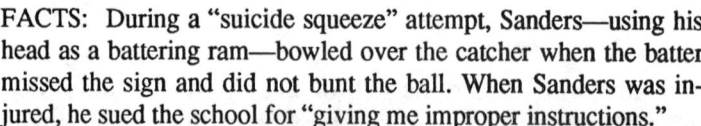

FACTS: During a "suicide squeeze" attempt, Sanders—using his head as a battering ram—bowled over the catcher when the batter missed the sign and did not bunt the ball. When Sanders was injured, he sued the school for "giving me improper instructions."

In a previous incident, Sanders had used his body in a slide into third base. The coach shouted, "Nice play!" Did such a statement mean that the coach approved of the head first slide? Was there negligence in not providing proper instructions or a warning of the risk of injury from such a slide?

DECISION: **YOU'RE THE JUDGE!**

Are instructions and a warning of the risk of injury always required? What if a participant was experienced and already knew, or should have known of the dangers of that sport?

FACTS: Handel, a high school freshman football player weighing 140 pounds, said, "I broke my neck carrying the ball." He sued the school district for not providing proper or sufficient instructions and warning and for furnishing him with defective equipment.

Handel described what happened, "I saw the Hale players in front of me and I knew I couldn't go any farther so I put my head down and just ran into 'em. That's when I heard my neck snap."

Handel had received instruction in carrying the ball, but alleged that the hazards and risks of the game had never been explained. Was the school liable? **YOU'RE THE JUDGE!**

DECISION: No. Handel had played football for the two previous years; he was not inexperienced. The coaches gave adequate, standard instructions; practices were held without negligently omitting any details. Handel assumed the risk of, and, by playing, contributed to, such an injury.

But where it is found that coaches either did not give proper instructions and warnings, or gave instructions that were either incomplete or for improper techniques—such as by suggesting or condoning fighting—then liability may be found where injury results.

Training — Was training adequate, proper and of the amount necessary to ensure the safety of participants?

FACTS: A 200-pound student, Govel, 18, was injured while performing an exercise called the "elephant." The exercise consisted of executing a somersault in midair from a springboard over parallel bars. While in the air, his foot struck the bars and he fell to the bare floor. Was the instructor negligent for instructing an untrained student to try such an exercise? **YOU'RE THE JUDGE!**

DECISION: The instructor was negligent. The exercise should only have been attempted by highly skilled pupils. Furthermore, the instructor was negligent for failing to have mats in the proper places.

What if a training program is too rigorous and an injury results?

FACTS: Sampson was injured during weight training. Although 6'2" and 250 pounds, he had never lifted weights before. He was instructed to perform numerous exercises and was injured after one hour of lifting. Sampson alleged that the injury occurred because of physical fatigue, brought about by too rigorous a training program for a beginner. Who was liable for the injury?

DECISION: **YOU'RE THE JUDGE!**

Another student was injured while voluntarily umpiring a baseball game. Instead of wearing the usual umpire equipment, he stood behind a portable backstop. A foul ball came back against the netting, striking him in the eye. He couldn't recover for his injury. The court found, "He was aware of the danger and risk of such an injury."

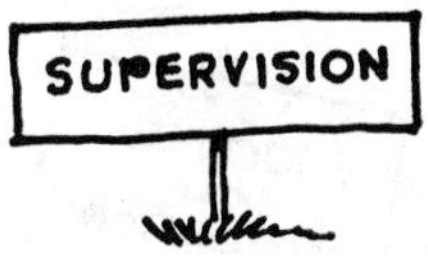

Supervision — Was proper supervision provided to prevent participants from confronting unreasonable risks of injury? Was consideration given to the size and strength of the participants?

FACTS: Morry, 15, was participating in wrestling for the first time. He practiced with the wrestling team for about six weeks. Then, during a wrestling match, broke his neck and severed his spinal cord.

The coach, a former wrestler, had only one season of previous coaching experience. Morry was required to wrestle two matches with boys heavier than he was.

Was the school liable for negligent instruction and supervision? **YOU'RE THE JUDGE!**

DECISION: Morry did not receive proper instruction or supervision. He was not taught the proper way to escape from the hold responsible for the injury. The coach was also negligent for improperly delegating "the important function of refereeing" to another student.

While the referee (an agent working for one of the schools) had his attention diverted from the wrestling match as he was fixing the mats, Stephens' spinal cord was severed by his opponent's illegal full-nelson.

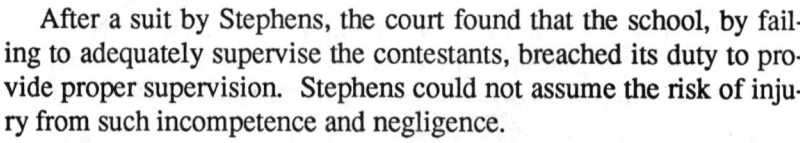

After a suit by Stephens, the court found that the school, by failing to adequately supervise the contestants, breached its duty to provide proper supervision. Stephens could not assume the risk of injury from such incompetence and negligence.

What if there are too many participants to supervise, or too small a playing area and injury results? In these cases, similar decisions were reached where injuries resulted.

FACTS: Many basketball players were allowed to participate in a gym class. One student, Richy, was struck by a player on an opposing team when a third player on an adjacent court ran onto the court where Richy was playing, pushing the opposing player into him. Was this proper supervision? **YOU'RE THE JUDGE!**

DECISION: The court held that there was a failure to provide sufficient supervision. With proper supervision, the injury would not have occurred.

Negligence may also be found where a supervisor fails to provide an experienced and competent person to supervise.

FACTS: Kirk, a school football player, tore a ligament in his knee while being tested for leg strength by an untrained student. Was the school liable for the injury? **YOU'RE THE JUDGE!**

DECISION: The school was held liable for providing improper supervision.

Another school district was found liable for the death of a student who was accidently struck in the head by a golf club.

The court reasoned, "Death would not have occurred had the supervisor not rearranged the mats so that the golfers were in violation of the teaching procedure."

The student wasn't familiar with the game, hadn't attended the class where instruction was provided, and none was provided prior to the accident.

But where Judy, 18, and Henrietta, 17, were injured "fooling around" on the trampoline and horizontal bars after class, and the teacher had warned the students, "Do not use the equipment!" the students' education and prior experience in using the equipment was considered. The court found that the participants were aware of, and appreciated, the risk involved. They were liable for their injuries.

Who would be liable for an injury where no amount of supervision could have prevented it?

FACTS: Karl died from a head injury he received when he bumped heads with another player. He was trying for a rebound in a basketball game at the school gym. His family sued the school, alleging, "Improper supervision caused the injury."

Wright was hit in the eye and injured by a tennis ball thrown by one student for another to hit. The coach was in his office. Were the schools liable? **YOU'RE THE JUDGE!**

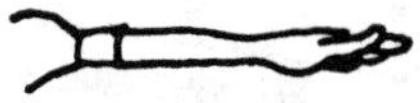

DECISION: The bumping of heads during a basketball game, or being hit by an unintentionally thrown ball, are hazards of those games which participants assume. The accidents were unforseeable. Even if supervision had been present, the likelihood of the accident occurring would have been the same.

Would fault be found if unsupervised games were often rough and had resulted in previous injuries?

FACTS: Red was injured while being blocked during a school touch football game.

Vinnie was injured when, during a high school football practice, "An opponent tackled me, using his arm as a battering ram."

Dirk was injured when "the players started horsing around and playing very rough." These practice games were all unsupervised. Did the schools exercise reasonable care for the players' protection and safety? **YOU'RE THE JUDGE!**

DECISION: If proper supervision would not have prevented an injury, then there will be no liability. Red was blocked in the proper manner. The lack of supervision was not the cause of the injury.

As to Vinnie's injury, the presence of proper supervision may have prevented the injury. If the coach knew, or should have known, that any improper technique might be used in playing the game when he wasn't present—then the school could be guilty of negligence for not providing proper supervision.

As to Dirk's injury, the coach was negligent. It could be expected that proper supervision would have prevented such an injury.

Similarly, a lack of supervision was found where a 16-year-old student fell and died from a fractured skull after "slap boxing" outside the school gym during gym class.

The teacher responsible for supervision was "sitting with his back to the office window." Testimony showed the teacher would have stopped the fight had he seen it, and that the students would not have been fighting had he been present.

Can a school be held responsible for not supervising spectators?

FACTS: During a high school softball game, spectators moved toward the field and took over the players' benches. A third baseman, Domino, while attempting to catch a foul ball, tripped over a spectator, fell over a bench, and broke his leg. Was the school negligent for not providing proper supervision? **YOU'RE THE JUDGE!**

DECISION: School supervisors were held liable for the injury. Negligence was for allowing the spectators to congregate close to the base line, where they pushed the bench into a dangerous position obscuring it from the view of any player.

Physical Condition Of Participants — Was there proper concern for the physical condition of the participants?

Reasonable steps must be taken to minimize the possibility of injury, particularly where any participant may not be physically able to perform, either due to an injury or otherwise generally unfit.

One student, Lowe, was required to participate in gym exercises over her protest, "I don't want to, I'm hurt." When she was injured, the school was found negligent for improperly requiring her participation.

FACTS: A student, Ann, was injured after she was instructed, "Work on your own." She was attempting a backward somersault during physical education class. The teacher was aware that Ann was overweight, untrained and fearful. Did the teacher have the proper concern for Ann's safety? **YOU'RE THE JUDGE!**

DECISION: No. The injury was the result of negligence in instructing Ann to work on the maneuver on her own. She was unfit to participate.

Similar decisions have been reached where students were too weak to perform and injury resulted when they were forced to attempt an exercise.

FACTS: Chris, 17, was injured attempting a diving somersault over two persons kneeling on the floor. The instructor was watching. Proper performance of this feat depends upon a participant's agility and strength. This was not tested. Did Chris assume the risk of such an injury? **YOU'RE THE JUDGE!**

DECISION: The court ruled, "The school was negligent for improper supervision. The instructor should have had knowledge of Chris' capabilities prior to allowing her to attempt such a feat."

Would it be proper concern for a participant's safety where the participant is "persuaded" to play while injured?

FACTS: Lowell, 17, a high school football player, charged, "I was injured during practice. Two weeks later I was persuaded by the coach to play. He knew that I hadn't recovered from my injury." Lowell was injured further, necessitating a back operation. Was the coach negligent? **YOU'RE THE JUDGE!**

DECISION: The court held that the coach knew or should have known that Lowell had not recovered from his previous injury and that further serious injury was likely to result. The coach persuaded Lowell to play while injured. That was a violation of the coach's duty to exercise reasonable care for the safety of the player.

However, where an exercise such as a sit-up did not require any more than a minimum of strength, and a student—appearing able to perform—willingly attempted it and was injured, the student was held to have contributed to his injury by attempting the exercise.

Facilities — Did the school fulfill its duty to provide safe, suitable and adequate facilities in the proper condition?

Where a student was tackled and had his face pushed into unslaked lime used to mark the sidelines, or; where a school knew or should have known of holes in the field, or; where sharp metal sideline markers were used, or; where a barrier surrounding a field was falling down; (and players' injuries resulted from all of these conditions) negligence by the schools may be found for their not maintaining the facilities in the conditions necessary for the protection and safety of the participants.

Numerous other situations have been found to be violations of the duty to provide safe facilities.

FACTS: Students were forced to play on a street marked off next to their school. One student was struck by a car.

Other students were injured when forced to play on an outdoor court where there were holes, slick spots and broken glass.

Also, where a school was aware, or should have been aware, that glass in a door adjacent to the gym was not safety glass and that a wall was too close to the basket, participants—not aware of these safety hazards—were injured. Were the schools negligent in not providing proper facilities? **YOU'RE THE JUDGE!**

DECISION: The court found the schools negligent for "not providing proper and suitable facilities" and, for, violating their duty to exercise due care for the students' protection and safety.

Schools have also been found negligent, where injuries resulted, in maintaining facilities when: there was no proper padding of poles or supports, floors were too slippery, or mats did not stay in place.

If an injury was caused by an open and obvious condition, or one not dangerous, will an injured participant assume such risks as part of the game?

FACTS: In a softball game during gym class, Walter fell into a ditch while chasing a foul fly quite a distance from the field. "I saw the ditch while warming up, but forgot about it." he grumbled. Did Walter assume the risk of such an injury? **YOU'RE THE JUDGE!**

DECISION: The facility was not inherently dangerous. Walter assumed the risk of such an injury.

FACTS: Martin sustained a back injury when he slipped and fell going in for a lay-up during a basketball game. Water had condensed on the floor and had been mopped up prior to the game. Fans helped, and heaters were used in an attempt to dry it. Did the school breach its duty to take reasonable care to protect the players? **YOU'RE THE JUDGE!**

DECISION: No. Since none of the coaches or referees responsible for approving the playing conditions considered the floor's condition serious enough to even discuss canceling the game, the school did not act unreasonably.

Coach Or Instructor — Did the school fulfill its duty to exercise due care in the selection of coaches and instructors, considering their qualifications and ability, especially where the activity was a potentially dangerous one?

FACTS: Bill Rosel drowned during a required swimming class. He had remained unnoticed on the bottom of the pool for five or six minutes.

The complaint filed by Rosel's parents charged, "The school was negligent in allowing student assistants to supervise a beginners class without having experience and training sufficient to protect the swimmers." The assistants had certification for lifesaving, but not for water safety instruction. Was the school liable for the injury? **YOU'RE THE JUDGE!**

DECISION: Yes. The court held that the school was negligent in the selection of the instructors.

An activity, otherwise safe, may become potentially dangerous because of the nature of the activity or due to large numbers of participants where there is unqualified supervision.

FACTS: A school placed a janitor in charge of a gym class during lunch hour. Alex, 12, was injured during a tumbling maneuver in which the janitor participated.

Another school, after dismissing the football coach, temporarily placed a teacher in charge of practices. A player was injured while performing improper tackling and blocking drills. Did either school breach its duty to provide qualified coaching? **YOU'RE THE JUDGE!**

DECISION: The courts held that the schools were negligent and had breached their duty to carefully select and obtain suitable coaching for students, especially where safety was involved.

What if the instructions were improper, but the player knew the proper technique?

Where a coach gives improper instructions, a player may be held to have assumed the risk of, or contributed to, any injury if he knew that following the improper instructions might result in injury. This would be especially so where a participant was not forced into using such improper instructions.

Furthermore, if an injury is the result of an accident, an accepted risk of the game and no one's fault, such as where a bat slipped from a coach's hands, there will be no liability. Assumption of the risk will apply.

Medical Attention — Did the school fulfill its duty to provide proper medical attention to ensure the protection and safety of the participants?

This duty may include providing medical assistance where immediate attention is necessary (such as in lifesaving techniques) or may require that a player be monitored while awaiting trained medical assistance better able to handle more difficult situations

Where a coach or assistant attempts to provide medical assistance, it should be provided with the care required to prevent further injury. Furthermore, it should only be given within their training and experience in handling such emergencies.

FACTS: Walsh was injured during a high school football scrimmage. When he couldn't get up, the coach suspected a neck injury. After finding that the player could still move his fingers and toes, the coach allowed Walsh to be taken from the field without the aid of a stretcher. When Walsh reached the sidelines, he had no movement in his hands or feet.

Undisputed expert testimony indicated that additional spinal damage took place after the tackle, due to his being moved. Was this proper medical attention? **YOU'RE THE JUDGE!**

DECISION: No. The coach was negligent for not only removing Walsh from the field, but for not waiting for a doctor.

The death of another high school football player resulted from heatstroke suffered during football practice. He was placed in a shower of room temperature water, covered with a blanket and given an ammonia capsule.

Expert testimony indicated, "Every effort should have been made to stop the player's accumulation of heat. Room temperature water and a blanket increased his accumulation of heat." The coaches "were negligent in denying the boy medical assistance and in applying an ill-chosen first aid."

A school will assume liability where it allows a student to participate, knowing that further injury is more likely. It will not be liable where an injury is due to a previous or hidden injury (unknown to the school) or properly not thought serious enough to limit or prohibit participation.

Discipline & Rules — Did the school fulfill its duty to make and establish rules for the maintenance of discipline?

This may be especially important in physical education classes where large numbers of students may be present.

May an instructor discipline students? An instructor may discipline a student as long as it is not excessive or too physically punishing.

Punishment drills or other excessive forms of discipline may be negligent where they exceed that discipline reasonably expected as part of the game, or where the discipline breaches the duty to exercise reasonable care for the player's protection and safety.

FACTS: Robert was put through a series of punishment drills for damaging a door in the dorm.

The punishment came after a two-hour football practice and lasted for 90 minutes. Robert became completely disoriented. He was found dead in his room, the cause of death acute dehydration. His family sued, alleging improper training and discipline. Was the school negligent? **YOU'RE THE JUDGE!**

DECISION: The suit was settled for the family. Reportedly, one of the terms of the settlement was an agreement that the school would not subject players to such drills in the future.

Another coach, displeased with a seventh grader's blocking, grabbed him by the face mask and knocked him to the ground. The player received a severely sprained neck. When a suit by the player against the school followed, the court held that the coach was negligent. He could use reasonable force necessary for discipline, but could not use physical violence.

As long as rules are reasonable, are known by the players, and have as their purpose the aiding in and providing for orderly and safe play, they will be upheld. However, where they are not enforced (or improperly enforced), liability for negligence may attach where such a violation of a rule was the cause of an injury.

Competition — Did the school use reasonable care in selecting competition, taking into consideration the nature of the sport and the age and experience of the participants?

FACTS: During a high school football game, Barret, 17, was killed in a collision with a twenty-year-old player. A rule prohibited players over nineteen from playing. The deceased player's family sued the school for negligence for allowing improper competition. Was this negligence? **YOU'RE THE JUDGE!**

DECISION: The court held that the rule was not for the safety of the players, but to encourage students desiring to compete to complete their education before reaching the age of twenty. Therefore, the violation of the rule was not the cause of the injury. Recovery was denied.

If the reason for the rule was to prevent older and potentially more experienced and bigger players from playing, would the result have been different?

Where participants are engaged in a contact sport, size and experience should be a concern.

FACTS: Jackson High started a new football program. They scheduled the state's top-rated team, the Worcester Maulers.

Many of the players were doubtful of their ability to compete. "That team is so much more experienced, bigger and physical!" the players complained.

The coach replied, "It'll be rough, but you need the experience." When several of the much smaller and less experienced Jackson High players were injured, they sued the school. The players asked, "Did the school use due care in selecting our competition?" Was the school liable for the injuries?

DECISION: **YOU'RE THE JUDGE!**

Where an injury is the result of unforseeable contact, or an accident, there may no liability. Therefore, where a student in a gym class was injured when run into by an older, much heavier student in a game of tag, there could be no recovery of damages.

Transportation — Did the school provide safe and timely transportation, exercising the highest degree of care for the protection and safety of the students?

There may be no duty where either sovereign immunity exists (unless the driver may be sued individually) or where the school has properly delegated its duty to transport the students to an independent contractor (such as a local bus company).

The transportation of student-athletes involves a greater than normal incidence of hazardous situations. Negligence may arise where the school employs an improper driver and injury results.

FACTS: A high school football coach directed one of his players, "Speedy," to drive the others home after practice, knowing that he was reckless and that he had an unsafe vehicle. After Speedy crashed, while driving too fast, the injured students sued the school for not providing safe transportation. Was the school liable for the injuries? **YOU'RE THE JUDGE!**

DECISION: Directing an unqualified, unauthorized or unsafe driver to transport students or allowing their transport in a known unsafe vehicle is negligence, even if the coach drives (unless qualified or authorized to do so).

Similarly, recovery was allowed where one vehicle was overloaded and injury resulted when the vehicle couldn't stop due to the overloading. It was also allowed where a passenger fell out of an overloaded vehicle.

Liability may also attach where a vehicle transporting student-athletes starts moving before all students are either in (or have exited from) or have gotten out of the vehicle's path, and injury results.

Other potential negligence may involve a violation of laws (i.e. speeding and allowing underage or non-licensed people to drive). Neglecting dangerous driving conditions or for allowing passengers to distract and affect the driver's ability to safely transport them are a few more examples.

FACTS: While on the team bus, headed for an away football game, several players, as usual, got very boisterous and began roughhousing. One player was knocked into the driver, who then crashed the bus into a pole. Several players received minor injuries. They sued the school for not providing safe transportation. Was the school liable for providing safe transportation? Did the players contribute to their injuries? May any of them recover damages for their injuries?

DECISION: **YOU'RE THE JUDGE!**

ODDS & ENDS....

FACTS: John, Ray, Charles and Edward were playing golf at the municipal golf course. They teed up their balls for the 18th hole in complete darkness.

After "teeing off," John and Ray began running down the fairway, golf bags over their shoulders, in a hurry to see where their drives ended up.

John fell in a fairway trap; Ray ran into a stalled electric golf cart. Charles and Edward drove into a hole dug to repair the watering and electrical systems. Edward, in his attempt to get out touched a "live" wire.

All were injured and sued the city. "The city maintained the golf course in a faulty condition. It neglected its duty to exercise reasonable care for our protection and safety." they alleged.

The city claimed that the golfers assumed the risk of, and contributed to, their injuries by playing in the dark. Could any of the golfers recover for their injuries? **YOU'RE THE JUDGE!**

DECISION: John could not recover. He assumed the risk of falling into the trap, a normal hazard of the sport.

Ray could recover, although his recovery might be eliminated or reduced for comparative negligence. The city was negligent in allowing the "dead" cart to remain on the course. But Ray was partially guilty of contributing to his injury by running in the dark, knowing that there may be hazards or other dangers.

Charles and Edward could recover if it could be shown that there were no warning signs, ropes or other evidence of an open and obvious danger.

Even if Edward and Charles assume the risk of falling into the hole, the city was found negligent for leaving a live wire exposed.

"The King can do no wrong" is not the prevailing belief that it once was. Nowadays, schools and municipalities are much more diligent in their duty to exercise reasonable care for the safety of those either using their facilities or under their control.

For activities taking place at, or under the control, of a school, a participant may assume that proper instruction, supervision, equipment and facilities will be given.

However, for sports activities taking place at a municipal facility, most of the activities (with the exception of swimming pools and mu-

nicipally run park's programs—which demand the same duty as that expected of a school) will not be supervised.

In these instances, will participants have a duty to protect themselves?

Where there is no required supervision, participants have more of a duty to exercise ordinary and reasonable care for their own protection and safety than do those participating in a supervised activity.

Participants assume all of the ordinary and common risks in a sport. A school or municipality does not insure a participant's safety. They may only be held liable for their own negligent acts, or for those committed by one for whom they are responsible, such as a teacher, coach or instructor.

8

PRODUCTS GUARANTEED SAFE

WHAT'S IT ABOUT?

Products Guaranteed Safe delves into **product liability**—the liability of a manufacturer or seller of a product (such as a football helmet) for an injury caused by their product.

Can a participant who is injured by a product be prevented from recovering damages where the advice "Buyer beware!" was not heeded?

PRODUCT LIABILITY

FACTS: The TELEGRAM, a local newspaper, reported, "Last month, the following players were injured while participating in sports in the Stowe area: Johnson, when his football helmet cracked; James, when he caught and broke several fingers in a metal basketball net; Anders, when he tripped over and was stabbed by the football side-line marker; Turner, when he crashed through a shatterproof glass partition; Hanks, when Bob's new golf club came apart and struck him, and; 'Killer', when—during a boxing match,—the ropes gave way and he fell out of the ring."

Were the manufacturers of any of these products liable for defects in designing or manufacturing them? Did any of the participants assume the risk of, or contribute to, their injuries? **YOU'RE THE JUDGE!**

DECISION: Your answer will depend upon several factors: Did the players know of the defects? Were the dangers hidden? Was a warning necessary? The answers to these questions and other factors (such as age, experience, coaching and instruction) will help decide who was liable.

Product liability—the liability of a manufacturer or seller of a product for injury caused by a defect in that product—has undergone considerable change.

In early times, when **caveat emptor**—buyer beware—applied, a buyer was held to have assumed all risks of injury for any defects in a product!

FACTS: Mr. and Mrs. Johnson bought a new sportscar. While out for a ride, "The brakes failed and we crashed into Mason's barn. We hurt our backs," complained Mrs. Johnson.

Tommy got a new toy racing car for his birthday. When he accidentally dropped it, the glass window broke and cut him. Were the manufacturers of the sportscar and toy liable for the injuries? **YOU'RE THE JUDGE!**

DECISION: Caveat emptor prevented any recovery. Mr. and Mrs. Johnson and Tommy assumed all risks of such injuries!

Because, in many cases, caveat emptor treated consumers unfairly, it was replaced by shifting to the manufacturer and seller of a product the burden to use reasonable care to make certain that the products they made and sold did not harm purchasers.

In addition, manufacturers and sellers are now required to test for and warn against any hidden dangers. However, the manufacturer or seller does not insure the purchaser's safety.

What if the purchaser doesn't take care of the product he buys, or doesn't follow instructions and is then injured? Will the manufacturer be liable?

A manufacturer will not be held liable for injuries caused by improper use of any of its products as a result of failure to follow properly given instructions. Product tampering, improper maintenance or the predictable deterioration of a product at the end of its useful life are also valid defenses for a manufacturer in cases of product liability.

FACTS: John was using his new shovel to dig out rocks for his backyard putting green. "The handle splintered and gashed my arm!" he complained.

David got a new chemistry set for making the all-star softball team. He failed to follow instructions. "I mixed the wrong chemicals and was burned," he confessed

Rusty altered the engine on his new dirt bike and was injured when he crashed it. "The throttle stuck and I couldn't stop," he said.

Sarah never maintained the filter on her sport-fishing tank, causing the pump to malfunction, thereby killing her fish.

Jake was injured when his three year-old baseball bat splintered and cut his hand and arm. Were the manufacturers of any of these products liable for any of the injuries?

DECISION: **YOU'RE THE JUDGE!**

MANUFACTURER'S LIABILITY

Negligence

A manufacturer has a duty to use reasonable care, including inspections and warnings, to ensure the safety of those who may use their products. The breach of that duty, which results in an injury and damages, is **negligence.**

FACTS: Jackson broke his hand when, "My new bike rack snapped shut on my hand!"

The manufacturer used a clip which hadn't been tested properly; it couldn't hold back the spring.

Sandy, after being warned by Jackson, was injured while putting her books in the same rack. Was the manufacturer negligent? **YOU'RE THE JUDGE!**

DECISION: As to Jackson, the manufacturer was negligent for not using reasonable care in manufacturing or testing the rack.

Sandy was guilty of **contributory negligence** and assumption of the risk. Her lack of care for her own protection and safety contributed to the injury. Furthermore, having actual knowledge and appreciation of a danger—and then voluntarily assuming that danger—is **assumption of the risk.**

Strict Liability

Strict Liability—absolute liability regardless of any fault or improper care by the user—will apply if a potentially dangerous, defectively manufactured product causes an injury. Because of the unreasonably dangerous nature of such a product, there is an absolute duty to make it safe.

FACTS: Tommie, 14, and Susan, 7, were killed when they crashed their three-wheeled, all-terrain vehicles. Their families sued the manufacturer under strict liability, alleging, "The design was defective and they didn't test it right. Also, they didn't give proper safety instructions and warnings." The vehicles went out of control during, as the families described, "normal use." Was the manufacturer liable under strict liability?

DECISION: **YOU'RE THE JUDGE!**

Sales of three-wheeled, all-terrain vehicles are now banned. Unsold three-wheelers were removed from stores. Consumers were given free training and warned of the risks of using them.

Similarly, the sale of lawn darts was also banned because of their unreasonably dangerous nature and for the numerous, serious injuries they inflicted. Lawn darts—similar in shape to board darts, only longer and much heavier—were made to be used in the yard.

How may a manufacturer avoid strict liability? A seller may avoid strict liability by giving proper instructions and warnings which, if followed, will make a product safe.

FACTS: Go Easy Co. manufactured powered bicycles that could go 10-15 m.p.h.

Frank was instructed how to ride the bike and warned, "Do not pedal while the motor is on. That will break the chain and cause a sudden forward lurch. When he did so anyway, he fell and broke his foot."

Wally was neither warned of this danger, nor received or read any written warnings on his bike (as were printed on Frank's). He pedaled while the motor was on and was injured. "Can we recover damages for our injuries?" they asked. **YOU'RE THE JUDGE!**

DECISION: Frank was given instructions and warned of the danger. He assumed the risk of his injury.

Wally did not know of the danger; he did not assume the risk. Contributory negligence will not apply as a defense in strict liability. Therefore, Wally may recover for his injury.

Were There Any Warnings?

An otherwise unreasonably dangerous product, such as a rifle, may be rendered safe by the use of adequate warnings.

Likewise, a reasonably safe product, such as a motorized bicycle, may be rendered dangerous without adequate warnings.

Does a manufacturer or seller having a duty to warn of a product's dangers, also have a duty to warn of obvious dangers? There is no duty to warn of obvious dangers or those entirely under the control of the buyer.

FACTS: Allen was injured when his snowmobile skidded off an icy road.

Vic shot himself in the foot. "I knew that there was a safety on the gun, but I didn't have it on," he acknowledged. Could either recover for their injuries from the manufacturer on the theory that they should have been better forewarned of the risks? **YOU'RE THE JUDGE!**

DECISION: No. Neither Allen nor Vic could recover for their injuries from such obvious dangers which were entirely within their control. They assumed the risk of, and contributed to, their injuries.

Express Warranty

Express warranty—the written guarantee given to purchasers of a product, clearly indicating that the manufacturer or seller will replace or repair a defective product free of charge for a certain period of time. It arises where the manufacturer or seller makes a direct, positive representation concerning any product sold.

FACTS: "That skateboard will easily hold your 200-pound son." Based on that statement by a store owner, Mrs. Lucas bought a skateboard for her son, Tony. The first time Tony got on it, two of the wheels collapsed and he broke his leg. Did the store owner make an express warranty? Was he liable for Tony's injury? **YOU'RE THE JUDGE!**

DECISION: The store owner was liable for Tony's injury. Tony need only prove a breach of the express warranty.

Warranty Of Merchantability

For a product under an **implied warranty of merchantability,** the manufacturer or seller warrants or promises that its products are fit for the ordinary purposes for which they are used.

FACTS: Judy was injured when, "I sat at that new picnic table at the park and it collapsed."

Al was replacing a light bulb by standing on his golf bag. He fell and sprained an ankle. Could either recover from the manufacturer for their injuries? **YOU'RE THE JUDGE!**

DECISION: Judy could recover for her injury. The table was not fit for its intended use.

Standing on the golf bag was not an ordinary purpose of the bag. Al could not recover.

Warranty Of Fitness For A Particular Purpose

An implied **warranty of fitness for a particular purpose** is a promise that exists where the manufacturer or seller has reason to know the purpose for which a product will be used. Here, a purchaser relies on the seller's skill and judgment.

FACTS: To help stabilize his racing car, Rick ordered custom-made wind skirts. When they failed, his car became airborne and crashed into a retaining wall. Rick broke his collarbone and bruised his ribs. Did Rick assume the risk of such injuries?

DECISION: **YOU'RE THE JUDGE!**

Do these warranties have to be expressly given to any purchaser of a product by the manufacturer or seller? Both implied warranties arise by law. Words or actions are not necessary to prove a breach. They may only be excluded by conspicuous language, if at all.

Was The Design Defective?

A product's design is defective if, when used as intended or foreseeable, it fails to perform as safely as expected. A design is also defective if it causes an injury and the manufacturer can't show that the benefits of the design outweigh the risk or danger from it.

FACTS: Judy bought a bow. It snapped, injuring her shoulder.

Guy was injured riding his new bike down a bumpy, dirt road. "The rear tire just fell off!" he said in disbelief.

When his bike fell over, Jean cut his leg on his new motorcycle's mudguard.

Each of them sued the manufacturer, alleging defective products. Could they recover? **YOU'RE THE JUDGE!**

DECISION: Judy and Guy may recover. Their injuries resulted from intended or reasonably foreseeable uses. Jean may not recover. The benefits of the mudguard, to prevent objects from being thrown up at the driver or a passenger, outweighed the risk of the injury that it caused.

Ace Co. would like to avoid lawsuits regarding the manufacture of football helmets. Should they consider how rough the sport is, or the misuse that the helmets might get? If so, what other considerations should this manufacturer take into account in designing and making helmets?

In designing any product, a manufacturer must consider the amount of contact involved, the types of injuries in the sport, any necessary warnings for the product's use, the product's durability (considering misuse and wear and tear), and whether the risk of injury will be increased due to the way the product is manufactured.

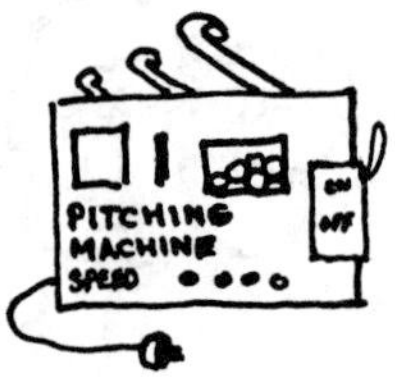

Baseball Pitching Machine

FACTS: While sweeping the gym floor, Sherwood, 16, was seriously injured by the sudden descent of the pitching arm of an automatic baseball pitching machine. "It hit me in the face. I've got these permanent scars," sobbed Sherwood.

Although the throwing arm could be unintentionally released while unplugged as a result of even a slight vibration, no operating instructions were provided. The only warning referred to the nonexistent instructions. Was the manufacturer negligent? **YOU'RE THE JUDGE!**

DECISION: Yes. The hidden danger could only be understood by someone with knowledge not ordinarily possessed by a 16 year-old. The manufacturer was guilty of negligence in the design, manufacture and sale of the machine, and for not giving adequate warning.

Without a safety guard or shield, the machine was "a hazard likely to occur at any moment," commented the court.

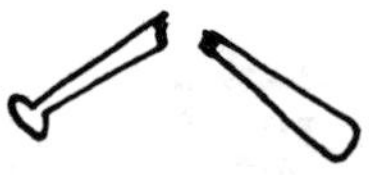

Baseball Bat

Will a manufacturer of baseball bats be liable where a broken bat made of defective wood breaks and injures a player?

FACTS: Shawn, the pitcher, was struck by a piece of a baseball bat which broke off when the batter hit a pitch. Shawn sued the bat's manufacturer, claiming, "The bat wasn't safe, and they didn't warn me that it could break." Did Shawn assume the risk of such an injury? **YOU'RE THE JUDGE!**

DECISION: Yes. The court noted, "It is common knowledge that bats frequently break, and immaterial that a properly made bat ordinarily will splinter with the grain while one made of defective wood may break across the grain. The risk of injury is not materially altered."

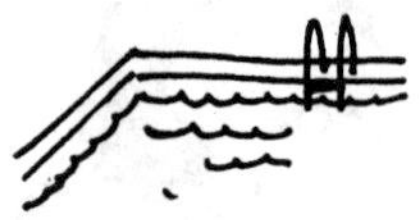

Swimming Pools

Product liability may arise out of a number of hazards from the use of swimming pools.

FACTS: Abe and Ben were injured when they dove into the swimming pools at their schools and struck their heads on the bottom.

The pool at Abe's school was marked 6'. Unknown to Abe, the water was only 5' deep. Expert testimony was given that, "Had the water been 6' deep, Abe would not have been injured."

Ben dove into his school's pool from the diving board, assuming that the water would be deep enough, although there were no depth markings.

When Judy began thrashing about in the deep end of a pool, a non-swimmer attempted to reach her with the safety hook, but it broke. She drowned.

Bob was injured when he slipped while running on the pool-side deck. Who was liable for these injuries?

DECISION: **YOU'RE THE JUDGE!**

Could the operator of the swimming pool be jointly liable with a manufacturer where they contributed to an injury, such as by not checking the depth of the water, or by not inspecting safety equipment?

Football Equipment

FACTS: A high school football player, Vincent, used a helmet and shoulder pads that he knew were "just a bit loose." When injured, he brought suit claiming that the equipment was defective. "Did I assume the risk of injury?" asked Vincent. **YOU'RE THE JUDGE!**

DECISION: Vincent had the opportunity to return any of the equipment if it was unfit, which was not shown. He voluntarily decided to use it and, therefore, assumed the risk of injury.

Similar results have been reached where injuries resulted when participants failed to wear prescribed protective equipment. Will liability result where defective equipment, or no required equipment, is provided?

FACTS: Fisher, a 17 year-old defensive back for his high school football team, was paralyzed after breaking his neck tackling an opponent. The tackle causing the injury was said to be a "spear" tackle. Such tackles were judged improper and are now banned.

Fisher sued the helmet manufacturer for negligent design, strict liability, and breach of warranty in that the helmet didn't protect him. Was the manufacturer liable for the injury? **YOU'RE THE JUDGE!**

DECISION: The helmet was defective in design, unreasonably dangerous, and did not perform as expected. Comparative negligence—where the negligence or fault of the injured player may reduce any recovery—reduced Fisher's recovery.

Another high school football player, Daniels, received permanent brain damage when his helmet caved in during a collision with a teammate. In deciding a suit against the manufacturer, the court commented that "the failure to warn that the helmet would not protect against head and brain injuries exposed the player to an unreasonable risk of harm."

Where a manufacturer fails to warn of such potentially serious injuries, may a court award punitive damages to punish the wrongdoer?

Punitive damages were awarded for gross negligence. The court described the conduct of the defendant as "knowingly indifferent to the player's rights, welfare and safety."

Hockey helmets have also been the subject of product liability litigation.

FACTS: Evan, 17, fractured his skull playing hockey. "I fell down to block the puck. It went through the gap in the helmet that I was given to wear." He sued the manufacturer, alleging a negligent design. Was the manufacturer negligent? **YOU'RE THE JUDGE!**

DECISION: The court found the manufacturer, "Guilty for the negligent manufacture of the helmet." The defense of assumption of the risk was denied as Evan was not aware of the danger involved. The gaps were not open and obvious.

In another case, an experienced hockey player, Manny, was injured when a puck struck him on the plastic chin strap of a helmet that he had purchased. He sued the helmet manufacturer.

The court found that, "The player, aware of the obvious danger, assumed the risk. There was no duty to warn, as that would not have discouraged him from playing a sport so fraught with risk of injury."

Gym Equipment

Injuries arising out of the use of gymnastic equipment have also lead to numerous product liability suits.

FACTS: Andrea was injured while using the uneven parallel bars. For no apparent reason, "They separated and I fell, landing on my back." she testified. Was the manufacturer liable under strict liability? **YOU'RE THE JUDGE!**

DECISION: The apparatus was inherently dangerous and defective when it left the manufacturer's plant, thus subjecting the manufacturer to strict liability (liability without regard to fault).

What duty do manufacturers of gym equipment owe to users? Manufacturers and sellers of gym equipment have a duty to use ordinary, reasonable care, to warn of any hidden dangers and risks, and to give any necessary instructions.

However, a manufacturer or seller does not insure a user's safety. There is no duty to warn of obvious dangers.

FACTS: Susan was injured attempting to vault over a horse. Judy was injured during her approach to the spring board. Both were given proper instructions and warned of the dangers of using the equipment. Did Susan and Judy contribute to their injuries? **YOU'RE THE JUDGE!**

DECISION: Yes. The defenses of assumption of the risk and contributory negligence prevented recovery. Susan and Judy were aware of and appreciated the risks, and, in addition, contributed to their injuries by using the equipment improperly.

Negligence has been found for injuries resulting from the use of defectively designed or manufactured trampolines (i.e. open space in the frame, weak seams, defective springs or supporting frame), or inadequate or non-existent warnings or instructions.

Other gym equipment also has been responsible for injuries.

FACTS: Lenny injured his back attempting to do a flip. "The gym mat wasn't supposed to slip." moaned Lenny.

Dominique injured her hip when a weight pulley collapsed and she fell to the floor. Did Lenny and Dominique assume the risk of such injuries? **YOU'RE THE JUDGE!**

DECISION: No. Both products were improperly designed or manufactured and unable to withstand the expected use. Strict liability applied. The manufacturers were liable for the injuries.

One court stated that, "Some manufacturers, fully aware of the dangers of a product and of past injuries, would rather risk liability than provide a warning which might reduce sales. Therefore, in addition to compensatory damages, they should be liable for punitive damages—to punish them in an effort to prevent further selling of such equipment without proper warnings and instruction."

FACTS: Wally Palmer, an 18 year-old university student, struck and injured his head against a gym wall while attempting a maneuver on a horizontal bar. He sued the manufacturer, alleging that for an inherently dangerous product, adequate warnings and instructions must be provided. The manufacturer felt that any dangers were open and obvious. "Weren't they liable?" he asked. **YOU'RE THE JUDGE!**

DECISION: The company had conducted tests which showed that the bar should be placed thirty inches from the wall, not eighteen inches as was the bar when Palmer was injured. Failing to warn of this hazard or to include instructions as to the proper use of the equipment made the company liable for punitive as well as compensatory damages.

How may a manufacturer avoid liability? A manufacturer may avoid liability where, after giving proper instructions, the equipment then was improperly installed or supervised.

The age and experience of participants, and the type of equipment in use may be factors in determining any liability.

FACTS: Hank, 12, was injured when, "One of the uneven parallel bars broke. I never used them before."

Jane, 18, was injured when she fell while doing a flip on a mat. She had performed the exercise successfully many times before. Would their different ages and experience help determine liability?

DECISION: **YOU'RE THE JUDGE!**

Golf, Equipment & Wheels

Product liability in golf may arise out of products used to maintain a course.

FACTS: Greg grabbed his clubs and headed for the golf course. Although in tip-top shape, on arriving home after playing, he felt sick.

His wife, in shock, cried, "A rash developed into blisters. His skin began peeling off. Then his internal organs failed and he died after two weeks."

An investigation revealed, "Greg's shoes, clubs and golf balls and the golf course were covered with a chemical sprayed on the course to remove brown spots." Testimony was that the chemical caused Greg's death. Was the golf course operator or the manufacturer of the chemical liable for Greg's death?

DECISION: **YOU'RE THE JUDGE!**

Product liability may also attach for injuries arising out of the use of golf equipment.

FACTS: Fred, 13, received permanent brain damage when a golf ball, attached to a training device, struck him.

"Golfing Gizmo" was designed to aid unskilled golfers improve their games. The labels on the carton and the instruction booklet read, COMPLETELY SAFE BALL WILL NOT HIT PLAYER.

Fred took his normal swing with and was struck by the ball, attached to a cord, as it rebounded.

An expert testified, "Fred caught the cord on his upward swing, thus drawing the cord and ball toward him on his follow-through." Was the manufacturer liable? **YOU'RE THE JUDGE!**

DECISION: The warranties that the product would perform in a safe manner and could be used safely was breached. Strict liability attached because of the defective and dangerous product. Also, the manufacturer was found guilty of fraudulent misrepresentation for the statement, COMPLETELY SAFE BALL WILL NOT HIT PLAYER.

Numerous cases have involved allegations of defective brakes or steering on golf carts.

FACTS: "The brakes just locked and the steering came loose on the new golf cart that we rented," explained John and Bob. "We got hurt when the cart overturned and we were thrown out." They sued the manufacturer for a breach of the warranty of fitness for a particular purpose.

Andy was injured when the golf cart that he rented hit a wall. He admitted, "I knew that the steering was getting loose, but I wanted to finish." Could John, Bob or Andy recover for their injuries? **YOU'RE THE JUDGE!**

DECISION: John and Bob had no knowledge of any defect. The manufacturer was liable for a breach of a warranty. The cart should have performed as required for its intended use.

Andy voluntarily assumed a known risk. Therefore, the manufacturer was not liable. If the golf course operator knew, or should have known, of the problem, he could share in the liability.

Strict liability has been found where a golf cart was inherently dangerous and defective as designed. The manufacturer could have used four wheels, for instance (instead of three), to increase the stability of the cart. Strict liability may also apply to snowmobiles, motorcycles, boats, and off-road vehicles.

Liability also attached to a manufacturer where defective tires were found responsible for a race-car driver's death.

Ski Equipment

FACTS: Ken Sanders purchased new skis. When the bindings failed to release during a fall, he broke his leg. He sued the manufacturer, alleging a breach of the warranty that the skis would perform as expected, and strict liability for not giving a warning.

One ad stated that, "The binding releases when it's supposed to."

"Was the manufacturer liable?" asked Sanders. **YOU'RE THE JUDGE!**

DECISION: No. The ad did not create an express warranty that the binding would release in every situation. The bindings could not be set to release during a slow fall and still keep the skier on his skis during normal skiing. The failure of the bindings to release was not the cause of the injury.

Other cases have denied liability where skis were used improperly, or where free lessons were refused and injury then followed.

Who might be liable where injuries result from ski lift accidents?

FACTS: Robinson and Jones, avid skiers, were "clowning around" when the ski lift started to move. They fell out and were injured. They sued the operator, alleging that the safety bar was not secured properly.

Several other skiers were injured when the ski lift they were riding "stopped suddenly and began to fall." There was no apparent defect.

Molly was injured when she fell off a ski lift after receiving improper instructions on how to secure the safety bar. Could any of these skiers recover for their injuries? If so, against whom? **YOU'RE THE JUDGE!**

DECISION: By clowning around, Robinson and Jones, experienced skiers, assumed the risk of their injuries.

With no apparent defect that the operator could have corrected, the manufacturer may be found liable for a negligently designed or manufactured ski lift.

The operator of the premises was liable for Molly's injuries.

Sunglasses, Pole Vaults &....

Who might be liable for injuries resulting from the use of sunglasses, a pole vault, a chin-up bar or pogo stick?

FACTS: Although he flipped down his "Baseball Sunglasses" which would give "instant eye protection," Palmer lost a fly ball in the sun. The ball struck and shattered the sunglasses, blinding Palmer in the right eye. Was the manufacturer liable? **YOU'RE THE JUDGE!**

DECISION: Yes. Since the sunglasses lacked the necessary safety features, they were not fit for baseball—the very purpose for which they had been sold. That was a breach of an implied warranty of fitness for a particular purpose.

Strict liability—liability without regard to fault—may be applied where a manufacturer is negligent in the design or manufacture of a product, or where there is a risk of injury from a hidden defect.

It applied where a pogo stick, a chin-up bar and a pole-vaulter's pole all broke, causing injuries. Users of these and similar products only assume the ordinary and apparent risks from such products, not the risk of injury from a hidden defect.

Were The Products Maintained?

There is ad uty to maintain equipment, either by checking it before use or by proper maintenance. Any failure of this duty may result in liability, either for the manufacturer; seller or lessor, or; for the user under assumption of the rusk or contributory negligince.

FACTS: Mark, a scuba diver, rented a tank from Jake's Scuba Shop. He said, "The tank's air supply line didn't work right. While I was diving, I couldn't get any air. When I began thrashing about trying to get Bill's attention, I accidentally knocked him unconscious." Bill was rescued, but suffered permanent brain damage.

Wally, also an experienced diver, rented a tank. In trying to reach the top after running out of air, he received a concussion from hitting the bottom of his boat.

Jan said, "I rented a spear gun and threw it in the boat. Later, it misfired and gashed me after bouncing off a rock." Was Jake's liable for any of these injuries? **YOU'RE THE JUDGE!**

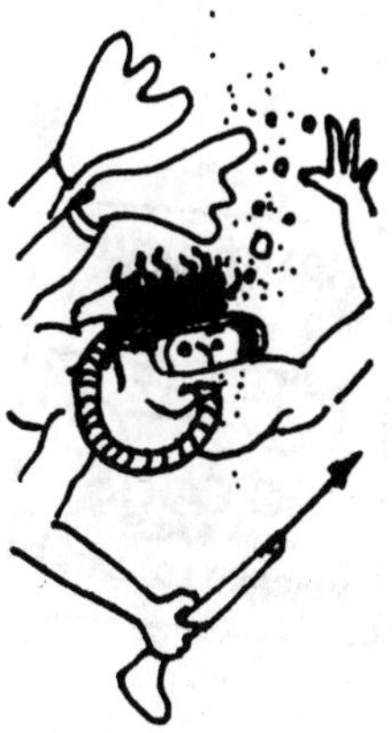

DECISION: Jake's was liable for Mark's injury. Jake had a duty to exercise reasonable care to make the scuba tank safe for use. This could have been done by a reasonable inspection.

Wally, by not checking his capacity gauge, contributed to, and assumed, the risk of injury from such an obvious oversight.

Jan also contributed to and assumed the risk of his injury by throwing the spear gun in the boat, thus damaging it.

Dive Tables

A diving instructional agency prepared and distributed a diver's manual for beginners. It had Dive Tables in it giving divers the ranges they should stay within while diving to prevent injury.

One diver, within the ranges of the tables, got the "bends" (bubbles in the bloodstream), causing paralysis. He sued the agency, alleging the tables did not adequately warn beginning divers of the number of injuries from the bends.

The agency defended that the manual warned divers to stay well within the tables' ranges, a hole in some diver's hearts makes them more susceptible to injury, and it was the diver's duty to ascertain if they had such a defect. Did the diver assume the risk of such an injury or was the instructional agency guilty of negligence?

ODDS & ENDS....

An ad in a local newspaper read:

FACTS: Relying on this ad, several young children bought the go-carts from Ace and set up a racecourse in a nearby field.

Ace had purchased the go-carts with instructions and warnings that they be "used only on flat surfaces." But Ace didn't pass these warnings on, only telling the boys that the carts should "probably be used in a parking lot." Ace put a metal shield on the bottom for protection from sharp objects, "souped" them up and then resold them.

Several accidents occurred while the children were racing on the rough terrain in the field. Tommy's cart suddenly shot forward when a branch stuck the accelerator open. He crashed through a fence.

Dennis' brakes failed and he crashed when the brake line was punctured by a rock.

All of the children sued Ace, charging, "He didn't give us proper instructions and warnings." Was Ace liable for the injuries? **YOU'RE THE JUDGE!**

DECISION: The children were young and inexperienced. Ace misrepresented the carts as being GUARANTEED SAFE and altered them against their intended use. And, although the children may have assumed the normal risks of using the go-carts, they did not assume the risk of injury from defective and improper alterations.

An express warranty, or warranties of merchantability or fitness for a particular purpose, may apply equally to other than sports products, such as appliances or a television.

9

PREMISES - CLEAR & SAFE

WHAT'S IT ABOUT?

Premises—Clear & Safe spells out and illustrates the duty of the owner or operator of a sports facility, such as a football stadium or bowling alley, to exercise reasonable care for the protection and safety of those using their facilities.

This duty may be somewhat greater where it concerns young children. Do you know what an attractive nuisance is?

PREMISE LIABILITY

The owner or operator of a sports facility or a place or facility of public amusement or entertainment is bound to exercise reasonable care for the safety and protection of patrons (that is, the care which an ordinarily reasonable and cautious person would exercise under the same or similar circumstances).

Although a participant may be prevented from recovering if he contributed to any injury, or assumed the risk of an open and obvious danger, a participant will not assume the risk of injury resulting from the negligence of the owner or operator of the premises used.

FACTS: A plaintiff explained how he was injured. "I was shagging fly balls when it began to rain. I ran toward the dugout, but stopped. The underground, automatic tarp, making no noise, came up and rolled over my leg, breaking my ankle. I never saw it."

"Was I liable because I failed to make sure no one was near the tarp before it was activated?" asked the ballpark operator.

DECISION: **YOU'RE THE JUDGE!**

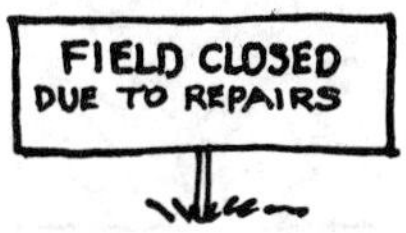

The owner or operator is not, however, the insurer of a participant's safety. Although he must be able to anticipate the normal actions of the sport or activity, he cannot be required to foresee every possible accident. Participants have a duty to use reasonable care for their own protection and safety.

FACTS: Even though ditches were being dug for new watering pipes, several high school athletes decided to use the local college's baseball field. Signs warned, FIELD CLOSED DUE TO REPAIRS. One of the players, Vinnie, was injured when he fell into a ditch while chasing a foul ball. Did he assume the risk of his injury?

DECISION: **YOU'RE THE JUDGE!**

The ordinary dangers of a particular sport may include the dangers common to a particular premises. However, such dangers must be obvious for a valid defense of assumption of the risk or contributory negligence.

FACTS: A baseball player ran into a clearly visible steel cable, constructed around the baseball field to restrain spectators from coming onto the field. He was injured and sued. He asked, "Did I assume the risk of such an injury?" **YOU'RE THE JUDGE!**

DECISION: Yes. The danger was obvious. Although the cable was not a risk normally inherent in a game of baseball, it became so where the player was aware of its existence and of the possibility of running into it.

A basketball player who had observed the first half of a basketball game, was judged to have assumed the risk of injury when he fell on the bleachers next to the court during the second half. He encountered a known and obvious danger.

The court indicated, "The duty to give attention to one's safety in a position of obvious danger is imposed because the ordinary man gives that attention. It is not careful conduct to pay no heed to the demands of safety."

An operator must provide facilities or premises properly designed and safely constructed for the use for which they are intended, and they must be maintained in a reasonably safe condition to avoid potential danger to users.

Will a participant assume the risk of a hidden danger or defect? A participant may assume the risk of injury from a danger or defect that is obvious, but not from a defect that is hidden.

FACTS: Albert, 19, was injured while playing basketball when he collided with a door jamb in a brick wall two feet from the basket. "I couldn't stop." explained Albert. He sued the gym operator for negligence for putting the basket too close to the wall.

Stevens, 17, was injured during a basketball practice for his high school team when his momentum carried him past the end line and into a glass window, which shattered.

In both cases, the players had played there before, and were aware of the hazards involved. Did they assume the risk of injury from such hazards? **YOU'RE THE JUDGE!**

DECISION: Albert had run into the wall numerous times before. He assumed the risk of his injury.

Stevens had also faced that risk before. However, he did not assume the risk that the panel would be of ordinary glass. He could have reasonably assumed that because of the closeness of the glass to the basket, it would be resistant to impact.

DEFENSE! DEFENSE!

The owner or operator of premises used for sports may rely on the defenses of assumption of the risk and contributory negligence.

Assumption of the risk requires that the participant have actual knowledge of the defect, a reasonable appreciation and awareness of all the dangers produced by the defect, and that the participant then voluntarily assumes such dangers.

FACTS: Ashcroft, an experienced jockey, suffered catastrophic injuries when, "My horse veered across the race track through an open exit gap." He sued the track, alleging that the accident resulted from the negligent placement of the exit gap which, in turn, resulted in the horse's behavior. Who was liable for the injury? **YOU'RE THE JUDGE!**

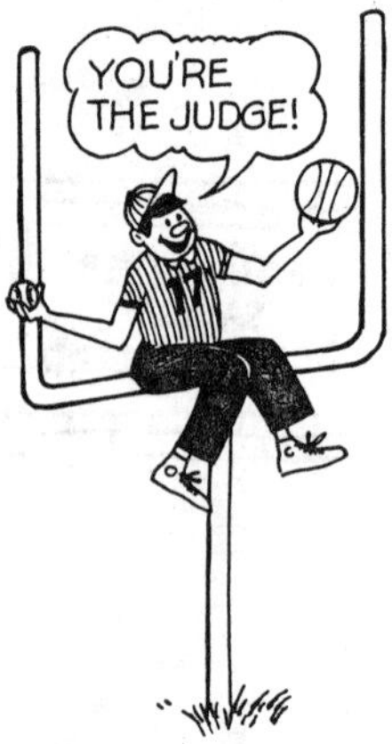

DECISION: Although Ashcroft was familiar with the horse, the track and the location of the exit gap, and was an experienced jockey, he did not assume the risk of such an injury from an open exit gate. He was not aware of that danger. The track was held liable.

Contributory negligence is a lack of proper care by an injured person for his own protection and safety which contributes to an injury.

Will contributory negligence apply if an injury would have occurred despite any reasonable action by an injured person?

FACTS: A number of participants were injured where the management of horse and auto racetracks allowed: horses to run in the opposite direction; restraining barriers not properly secured; exit gates, through which a horse could run during a race, left open; "dead" cars and other debris and equipment left on the track; and improper or no barriers for an auto race.

Would contributory negligence prevent recovery of damages for those injured in these situations? **YOU'RE THE JUDGE!**

DECISION: Where management improperly maintained or constructed the premises, negligence would be found. However, there would be contributory negligence by the participants where they failed to exercise reasonable care for their own protection and safety.

Participants may assume the risk of injury from ordinary dangers. But, will they assume that risk from an extraordinary danger?

A jockey was killed when he was thrown from his horse and struck his head on the concrete footing of a post supporting the track railing. The elevated footing was non-existent at any other race track. The court found that, although the jockey may have assumed the risk of being thrown from his mount, he did not assume the risk of injury from an extraordinary danger or negligent design.

The duty owed by an owner or operator of premises or facilities will apply to many different sports or activities.

BOWLING ALLEY

The proprietor of a bowling alley owes a duty to patrons to exercise ordinary and reasonable care to keep the premises in a safe condition. If he fails to discover or correct a problem which might place patrons in danger, there may be liability.

FACTS: One proprietor failed to inspect for, or clean up, drinks and gum on the floor and approaches of his bowling alley.

Herb, an unsuspecting bowler, groaned, "The approach was wet. I slipped and wrenched my back."

When another proprietor failed to fix an approach after it became worn and splintered, a bowler, Jerry, was injured when his foot stuck. Were the proprietors liable for these injuries?

DECISION: **YOU'RE THE JUDGE!**

However, a proprietor is not an insurer of a patron's safety. Where a danger was not obvious and the owner either didn't know it existed, or a reasonable inspection would not have revealed the danger, the owner will not be charged with a breach of his duty to provide a safe place.

FACTS: A bowler, Sykes, explained how he was injured. "My foot got caught in a space between the ball return and the floor." This type of construction was standard. Some alleys, aware of the danger, had closed it off. Prior to the accident, hundreds of thousands of games were bowled without incident. "Was I liable for that injury?" asked the operator. **YOU'RE THE JUDGE!**

DECISION: No. Neither the danger, nor the risk was obvious. Sykes assumed the risk of such an injury.

SKATING RINKS

Proprietors of ice and roller skating rinks have a duty to exercise reasonable care in maintaining their premises in a reasonably safe condition to guard patrons from unreasonable risks. Some specific steps to be taken include the elimination of overcrowding, keeping the skating surface clear of debris, and posting or repairing holes or soft spots in the rink as well as all approaches or aisles.

Do patrons have the right to assume that the premises they are using are reasonably safe?

FACTS: An iceskater was injured when, "I tripped when my skate struck a wooden ledge. I was reaching for the handrail."

An expert testified, "The handrail should have been moved to the very edge of the skating area."

A rollerskater was injured when he slipped and fell through a window. There were two windows adjacent to the rink. One was protected by an iron grating. The other had a bench placed under it in an attempt to protect the skaters. Were the operators of these premises negligent? **YOU'RE THE JUDGE!**

DECISION: Yes. The defects created obvious and unnecessary risks to the skaters who had a right to expect premises safe for their intended use (skating). The rink operators were liable for not using reasonable care in protecting the skaters.

An operator cannot be required to foresee every possible accident. Where a skater left the skating area and tripped and fell through a window in the spectator area, the proprietor was found not liable.

SWIMMING POOLS

The proprietor of a swimming facility must exercise ordinary or reasonable care to maintain the premises in a reasonably safe condition. This includes all swimming pools, deck areas, rescue and other equipment, fences and bathhouses.

FACTS: At one swimming pool, there was broken glass both in and next to the pool. Another pool was closed because of the condition of the water. A warning sign was posted, but there were no depth markers. At still another pool, there was one lifeguard on duty for more than fifty kids.

If an injury resulted from any of these situations, could the proprietor be found liable for improperly maintaining or supervising such premises?

DECISION: **YOU'RE THE JUDGE!**

A patron has a right to assume that the operator has provided a place that is reasonably safe for its intended use.

FACTS: Two children, ages 6 and 13, were trying to reach an errant ball knocked into a closed public pool.

The pool's walls and floor were slimy and slippery. The children waded into seven feet of dirty water at the deep end where they drowned after trying in vain to climb out.

"The entire pool was dry except for the deep end. There's a great drop-off, slanting down at an angle." said a policeman.

A neighborhood boy had warned them not to climb the chain link fence to the pool. A similar accident had happened two years earlier when two brothers, who had climbed the fence, drowned.

Did the children assume the risk of, or contribute to, their deaths? Was a greater duty of care owed to protect the children? Was the city liable?

DECISION: **YOU'RE THE JUDGE!**

AMUSEMENT RIDES

Will certain potentially dangerous activities require more care? Certain types of rides, such as amusement park rides and go-carts, because of their potential danger, may require a higher degree of care beyond reasonable and ordinary care.

FACTS: Minnie, confined to a wheelchair, was put aboard the merry-go-round at an amusement park. After about two revolutions, she and her wheelchair—with the brakes locked—were thrown from the ride. Minnie died from head injuries. Was the operator liable for her death?

DECISION: **YOU'RE THE JUDGE!**

The more dangerous the ride, the more care that is required to see that the ride is properly constructed, inspected, operated and maintained.

FACTS: Eight youths were trapped inside the Haunted Castle, a ride at the Great Adventure Amusement Park, when a fire broke out. They all died. Was the operator liable?

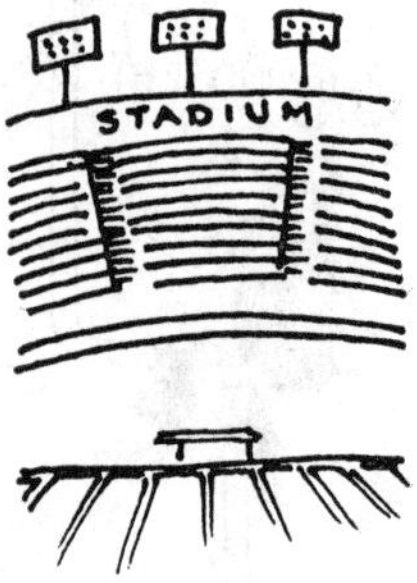
STADIUM

DECISION: **YOU'RE THE JUDGE!**

SEATS & BLEACHERS

An operator of premises used for sports and other activities is also under a duty to exercise reasonable care for the safety and protection of patrons with regard to seats, chairs or benches.

If they are known to be defective, or if defects should have been known by a timely and reasonable inspection, liability may attach.

YOU'RE THE JUDGE!

FACTS: A wooden soccer grandstand caught fire, killing many soccer fans. The club had been warned that the grandstand was a fire risk.

One witness testified, "Under the seats there were holes in the floorboards. You could see loads of litter which built up over the years."

When the fire broke out, probably under one of the wooden seats, the fans couldn't get out. The gates had been padlocked to keep out those who had not paid for admission. Was the operator negligent?

DECISION: **YOU'RE THE JUDGE!**

SKI LIFTS & SLOPES

The operator of premises used for skiing has a duty to exercise reasonable and ordinary care to maintain the premises, including slopes and equipment, such as lifts, in a reasonably safe condition.

FACTS: A lift operator failed to warn Ann Forman, 16, that the lift was closing down for the night. She was stranded when the chair stopped moving. Becoming hysterical at the prospect of being stranded overnight, "I jumped 25 feet to the ground and shattered my hip," she testified.

HELP

At another ski lift, an operator failed to lock the safety bar for Sally, 9, causing her injury from a fall. And Bob's injury was the result of a failure to inspect the lift, which needed repair.

Johnson was injured when he was unable to get onto a moving chairlift. There were no instructions. Were any of the operators liable for any of these injuries? **YOU'RE THE JUDGE!**

DECISION: "Operators owe the highest degree of care to invitees," commented one court.

The lift operators were held liable for failing to warn Forman that the lift was closing; for not locking Sally's safety bar; for not properly inspecting the lift Bob was using, and; for not giving Johnson proper instructions.

What if the skiers were aware of the dangers? Where skiers are aware of, and appreciate, the dangers involved and fail to act for their own safety and protection, they may not recover.

FACTS: When a ski lift operator failed to lock a safety bar, Ray, an experienced skier, fell and injured his neck.

Hank was injured when the ski lift he was riding on collapsed. It could not be foreseen that the bolt would fracture.

An inattentive skier, Paul, was injured when he was unable to get on a moving chairlift. Were the proprietors liable for any of these injuries? **YOU'RE THE JUDGE!**

DECISION: Ray assumed the risk of his injury. Although the manufacturer may be, the operator was not liable for Hank's injury. And there was no negligence by the operator where inattention caused Paul's injury.

MAINTENANCE OF SLOPES

FACTS: White, an experienced skier, said, "While coming down an intermediate trail, I hit a stump which was covered with snow, fell, and fractured my leg." White sued the ski resort for improperly maintaining the skiing premises. "Did I assume the risk of injury?" asked White. **YOU'RE THE JUDGE!**

DECISION: The court found that White assumed the risk of encountering such a hazard and being injured.

Another court sustained an award for a 25-year-old novice skier whose skis became entangled in a clump of brush encroaching three to four feet in from the edge of a novice trail. The court pointed out that, "The risk of encountering brush or other such hazards on the trail was not an inherent and assumed danger or risk of the sport."

However, a ski operator does not guarantee the safety of all its patrons. Skiers still assume the risk of injury from open and obvious dangers.

Will an operator be liable where a skier is confronted with an extraordinary risk or danger?

FACTS: An expert skier and racer, Philips, told how he was injured. "I was in a tuck position skiing down the lower half of an intermediate run, when I collided with a snow-cat which was traveling up the slope. I tore ligaments in my knee and cut my face."

Philips sued the operator, who defended, "He was out of control when he made a sweeping turn into the equipment."

Another skier, Thompson, was injured when he ran into a chairlift tower. The tower was obstructing a passage down a slope and was not padded. Were the operators liable for not exercising reasonable care for the skier's safety? **YOU'RE THE JUDGE!**

DECISION: Philips had skied that run many times before without seeing a snow-cat at that place. He could not foresee it being there and, therefore, did not assume the risk of such an injury. The operator was negligent in allowing the snow-cat on the ski slope while skiers were in the area.

The operator was liable for Thompson's injury. Skiing should have been prohibited in that area.

Negligence was also found where a novice skier was injured when struck from behind by a sled coming down a run next to the ski slope. The runs were separated for the first forty feet, after which there was no barrier to keep the sledders and skiers apart. The court stated, "Allowing skiing and sledding next to each other created added dangers which were not inherent in each sport individually."

BASKETBALL

FACTS: Dawson, a pro basketball player for the Magicians, slipped on a puddle of water while playing in a game. The puddle was the result of leaks in the roof. Dawson sued for career ending injuries, alleging negligence against the operator of the auditorium for not fixing the leak. Was the operator liable? **YOU'RE THE JUDGE!**

DECISION: The roof was known to be riddled with leaks. The owner, aware of the defects, owed a duty of reasonable care to the player, but failed to exercise that duty.

An operator may be found negligent for failing to correct a known problem, but not where the problem did not create an unreasonably dangerous condition.

FACTS: Walter, a pro basketball player, slipped and injured his knee when condensation formed on a newly waxed floor due to the combination of heat in the building and the ice (for hockey games) under the portable basketball floor.

Elliot and Rupert, pro baseball players, were injured when one crashed into an unpadded outfield wall and the other tripped on an uneven outfield surface.

Should professional players be required to assume greater risks than an average participant would assume? What if they were aware of the defects? Did they play there voluntarily? Should the owner be liable for not correcting the defects?

DECISION: **YOU'RE THE JUDGE!**

BALLFIELDS

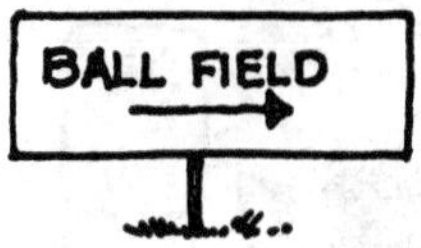

Players have a right to assume that a field will be safe for its intended or anticipated use. But what if the danger is obvious?

FACTS: A player, Sal Luckman, in a softball game, tripped over a hole and suffered a broken leg. "The hole was clearly visible," he admitted. "Didn't he assume the risk of the injury?" questioned the operator of the field. **YOU'RE THE JUDGE!**

DECISION: Yes. While the field was poorly designed, the condition was unmistakably evident and the danger obvious. Luckman had a duty to use reasonable care for his own protection and safety.

Neither could another baseball player recover damages when he was injured in a game after tripping on a cement curbing around the field. He had played there many times before.

In holding that momentary forgetfulness of the certain dangers was one of the risks that a player assumes, the court noted, "One who takes part in a sport accepts the inherent dangers in so far as they are obvious and necessary, just as a fencer accepts the risk of a thrust by his opponent."

BOWLING

A risk which might ordinarily be assumed, may not be assumed under certain circumstances, such as in the excitement of the sport.

FACTS: Murphy, a bowler, was assigned the last alley in a bowling house. Parallel to and lower than the alley was a walkway to the rear of the lanes. "After delivering my ball, I turned and walked back looking over my shoulder at the pins. I stepped off the edge of the alley and fell, hurting my leg and hip," swore Murphy. Did Murphy assume the risk of such an injury? **YOU'RE THE JUDGE!**

DECISION: No. What may have been perfectly obvious to a person walking normally is likely to be forgotten by a bowler in the excitement of a game. The design presented an obvious danger. "An owner must be able to anticipate the normal actions of a participant of a sport," remarked the court.

WHAT A RACKET!

Participants using tennis facilities may be held to have assumed the risk of, or contributed to, an injury where a danger was open and obvious. In the case of hidden dangers, they will not. Negligence against a proprietor of a tennis facility has been found for not keeping the court in a reasonably safe condition (clear of leaves, pine needles, and the like).

Should a professional be more aware of the dangers of a sport than the average player?

FACTS: Jane Heldman, a pro tennis player, severely injured her knee. She alleged that her injury was caused by a defect in the tennis floor. The tape used to hold the "Roll A Way" tennis floor down was not sticking, thus creating gaps or spaces in the court. Also, there were air pockets and a few problems with water drainage. Did Heldman assume the risk of injury? **YOU'RE THE JUDGE!**

DECISION: The court held that a pro should have a higher degree of knowledge and awareness of such dangers than would the average player. After appeal, the case was settled in favor Heldman.

Another player, Joe Smith, was guilty of contributory negligence even though he was not aware that a tennis court was constructed too close to a wall which he ran into.

The court commented, "It is needless to say that there are many cases holding that one is charged with the duty of seeing that which he ought to have seen, had he looked."

In a similar case involving a ping pong game, it was held that a player observed or should have observed that the table was too close to a window, through which he put his arm. He was guilty of contributory negligence. But what if the danger was not so obvious?

FACTS: Courts for handball, where players batted the ball with their hands, were now being used for racketball. Cheney was injured when one of his opponents' rackets rebounded off the wall and struck Cheney in the head. He sued, arguing, "I was not aware that the courts were too small for players with rackets." Was the operator liable?

DECISION: **YOU'RE THE JUDGE!**

GOLF COURSES

Proprietors or operators of golf courses have a duty to exercise reasonable care for the safety and protection of patrons. This includes the duty to make reasonable and timely inspections, and to correct any defects.

FACTS: Brian was hit by a following player's golf ball. Joe—believing the yardage on the par 4 to be correct—hit away. "I knew that I couldn't hit it that far," said Joe. The yardage given was much more than the actual distance. Was the operator liable? **YOU'RE THE JUDGE!**

DECISION: The operator, aware of the incorrect yardage, was grossly negligent in maintaining the premises. Punitive damages were awarded "to punish the wrongdoer."

Where a bridge collapsed, sending a golfcart and players into a canal, the operator was found liable for not maintaining the premises. The patrons had a right to expect reasonably safe premises.

Does the operator's duty to exercise reasonable care extend to those who are not patrons?

FACTS: When the water sprinklers on a golf course were turned on, a startled passerby on an adjacent public way was hit by the water, crashed his car, and broke his leg. Was the operator of the golf course liable?

DECISION: **YOU'RE THE JUDGE!**

Where a golfer slipped and fell on his way to the locker room, the operator was found negligent for not, at least, putting a strip of non-slip material on which the golfers could walk to enter the locker area.

However, an operator was found not liable for injuries received outside the locker room, such as where a golfer slipped on a walkway. The golfer had no right to expect such an area to be non-slip. Should a cart path be non-slip?

FACTS: Steve said, "I slipped on a cart path, shattering my right elbow. The path was worn and slippery. No one warned me, and I didn't see it." Was the proprietor negligent in failing to correct any defect, or did the golfer assume such a risk?

DECISION: **YOU'RE THE JUDGE!**

Whether or not an operator may be liable for injury from a defect in premises will depend upon the awareness of the patron, whether the operator knew or should have known of the condition, and either corrected or warned patrons of the danger, or knowingly left it unsafe.

Even if an operator was negligent, any injured patron must still

show that a hazard was the cause of the injury, not his own contributory negligence. Furthermore, if the patron knew of the condition, he may be held to have assumed the risk.

FACTS: Willy and Ernie were injured when they rode into protruding branches on a cart path and then hit a rock, crashing the cart. The dangers were open and obvious.

Richard was injured when his golf cart overturned in a sand trap. Did these golfers contribute to or assume the risk of injury? Was the operator liable?

DECISION: **YOU'RE THE JUDGE!**

GOLF COURSE DESIGN

A golf course owner or operator may be liable for failing to exercise reasonable care for the protection and safety of patrons, such as where adjacent holes or other areas of a golf course endanger players there.

Golfers assume the normal and inherent risks in the game, but do they assume extraordinary ones?

FACTS: Golfers were allowed to use woods on the driving range. Hank belted a drive out of the range, striking and injuring a golfer on the third hole.

Paul "duck hooked" one off the range, striking and injuring a golfer on the second hole. Did the golfers assume the risk of such injuries? Was the proprietor liable?

DECISION: **YOU'RE THE JUDGE!**

A golf course owner or operator also has a duty to exercise reasonable care in the use of powered carts. Liability may even attach if negligence is shown for giving the cart to someone who uses it improperly.

FACTS: Mildred suffered multiple leg fractures from a runaway golfcart. Her husband told what happened. "Another cart hit the one that she was riding in, causing it to hit and pin her against a restroom wall." Was the owner of the golf cart liable for Mildred's injuries? **YOU'RE THE JUDGE!**

DECISION: The court held that even if the owner exercised due care, he could still be liable. The court decided, "A golf cart, when negligently operated, has the same ability to cause serious injury as does any motor vehicle. The golf cart is a 'dangerous instrumentality' which imposes liability upon the owner when he entrusts it to someone who negligently operates it."

WAS IT AN ATTRACTIVE NUISANCE?

An **attractive nuisance** is a condition, device, machine or other agency, which is dangerous to young children (generally those under the age of 12) because of their inability to appreciate danger, and which may reasonably be expected to attract them to the premises.

A possessor of land owes a duty to exercise reasonable care to protect children from such dangers. He may be liable for any injury to a child trespassing where:

- the place or its condition is one which the landowner knows or should know that children are likely to trespass on—such as a swimming hole;
- the condition is one which the landowner knows or should know involves an unreasonable risk of death or serious injury to children—such as hidden obstacles or protruding objects;
- the children, because of their youth, either do not realize, or fail to discover the danger;
- the risk and danger to the children outweighs the usefulness of the condition, and;
- the landowner fails to exercise reasonable care to eliminate the danger or otherwise protect the safety of the children.

FACTS: Howie, 13, and other youths, were using the swimming hole on Mr. Jensen's land. Although it was dangerous, they had used the pond in past summers. Mr. Jensen knew that the kids were there. Howie was swimming when Hank fell out of a dead tree and landed on him. Howie drowned.

Bobbie, 12, was sledding down Mrs. Magruder's hill. "I hit an old car fender buried under the snow and broke my collarbone!" he cried. Mrs. Magruder knew that the kids sledded there.

Jane Sweeney, 9, skating on Grady's pond near her house, moaned, "I hit a tree stump and fell through the ice. I broke my arm."

Witkowski's farm was next to the park's picnic area. A container of fertilizer had been left near the fence. Kim, 5, reached through the open fence and drank some. She became violently ill.

Did the landowners know or should they have known of the youths' presence? Did these conditions create attractive nuisances?

DECISION: **YOU'RE THE JUDGE!**

What if the danger or hazard was obvious and the children were older? The age of a child and the obvious nature of the risk or hazard could prevent the use of the attractive nuisance doctrine.

FACTS: Kirk, 17, was hit by a golf ball while practicing soccer on a golf course. There was no fence or sign prohibiting Kirk from entering the course. Did Kirk assume the risk of and contribute to his injury?

DECISION: **YOU'RE THE JUDGE!**

ODDS & ENDS....

FACTS: Dick and Joe were at an annual golf outing. "We were having a great time drinking a few beers and trying to play," muttered Dick.

In attempting to cross a narrow bridge on the way to the 10th tee, they crashed their cart. Joe broke his ankle and Tom gashed his arm and leg.

They both sued the operator of the golf course for negligently maintaining the premises. They alleged, "The bridge was too narrow and unsafe, the boards old and decayed from years of use and harsh winters, and there was no railing."

The operator countered, "Dick and Joe were aware of the dangers. Furthermore, they contributed to their injuries by drinking and by 'swerving to and fro,' as one witness put it." Was the operator liable for the injuries? **YOU'RE THE JUDGE!**

DECISION: Yes. The golfers had the right to assume that the premises would be in a safe condition for their expected use. And, although they contributed to their injuries by their condition, the accident may have occurred anyway, even had they not been drinking. Had they noticed the condition of the bridge before attempting to cross, they would have assumed the risk of their injuries.

To prevent attractive nuisances, property owners should be keenly aware of their responsibility and duty for the protection of children.

10

MEDICAL TREATMENT

WHAT'S IT ABOUT?

Medical Treatment defines and outlines the duty owed by schools, doctors, medical personnel and others, such as coaches or park supervisors, to provide proper medical assistance to injured participants or others.

Do people who are injured have to give their consent to be treated for an injury?

Medical Providers Group A
4530 West Park Ave.
Worcester, MA 01201

Dear Athletes and Others:

We, the schools, team owners, doctors and others, who may be called upon to render medical assistance to you, recognize our duty to render such assistance in a proper and timely manner in order to ensure your protection and safety.

However, there will be injuries that are the result of the negligence of a small number of our members. We will be negligent where we have breached our duty to use the care and skill rightfully expected and necessary for your protection and safety, and that breach results in an injury and damages.

Not to minimize the seriousness of any injuries, but they are few in number. However, they are the ones that receive the attention of the courts.

Yours truly,

Medical Providers Group

WHAT DUTY IS OWED?

Medical treatment, or the lack of it, which results in an injury or the further aggravation of one, may result in liability.

FACTS: While watching a baseball game, Allen, 15, was struck above the left ear by a hard-hit foul ball. At first, he slumped forward in his seat, "out like a light." Then, he came, groggy and stuttering.

He staggered to the ballpark's first aid station where he was examined by a doctor. The doctor advised him that he had a bump on the head, but that he appeared to be all right and could resume his activities. The doctor did not take his blood pressure nor did he inquire as to Allen's reaction after being hit.

After the game, Allen began stuttering again, crying and shaking. After he was refused admittance at two hospitals, he was admitted at a third.

He was examined by a neurosurgeon and given medication for cerebral hemorrhaging. His condition deteriorated. A test revealed a mass in the brain. Nine hours later, Alan suffered a convulsion which made his condition terminal. When he died three days later, his parents sued the team, the park's doctor and the hospital for providing negligent emergency medical services.

An autopsy revealed that Allen had suffered a fracture when he was hit by the baseball. Bleeding from the time of the accident had resulted in the hemorrhage and his death.

Expert testimony was, "If Allen had been put at rest after arriving at the first aid station, instead of being allowed to move about freely, it was more likely than not that the bleeding would have stopped. He'd be alive today."

Other testimony was that the hospital had opportunities to perform surgery to prevent Allen's death. Was either the team or the park's doctor negligent? Was the hospital negligent?

DECISION: **YOU'RE THE JUDGE!**

Even if the hospital breached its duty to use that degree of care and skill expected, its failure did not relieve the doctor or team of liability for any negligence on their part. Were they both negligent?

LIABILITY OF SCHOOLS & OTHERS

What is the duty of those who conduct sports activities? Their duty is to provide reasonable medical assistance to injured participants or spectators as soon as possible under the circumstances. This includes providing safe facilities and equipment, and persons with the necessary skill and experience. However, they are not insurers of a participant's or others safety.

FACTS: Matt, participating in a bobsled run, failed to negotiate a curve. He received severe fractures of his left leg, a collapsed lung and some bruises.

Following the accident, Matt was transported down the slope on a stretcher and then to the nearest hospital eight miles away. The leg was placed in a cast. However, normal circulation did not return. When gangrene set in, the leg had to be amputated.

Matt sued, alleging negligence in the state's failure to provide sufficiently prompt medical assistance after the accident. He claimed, "I suffered undue exposure through an unreasonable delay in removing me from the snow and cold."

Was the state liable? **YOU'RE THE JUDGE!**

DECISION: No. The court held that the state had adequately discharged its duty after the accident. They promptly produced blankets, a stretcher and a doctor, and promptly transferred Matt to the hospital. Matt assumed the risk of the original injury, as well as the complications.

What if prompt assistance is not rendered? Even in such a case, there may be no liability where the delay does not cause or aggravate an injury.

For example, a football player, who had injured his ankle, was told to "wait on the sidelines until practice is over," before being given medical attention. There was no liability because the delay in receiving medical assistance did not aggravate the injury.

Where there is an injury, must those in control always first summon assistance?

Where a football player, Jim Duda, knocked his shoulder out of place during practice and the coach snapped it back, and sent him to the doctor, there was no liability for failing to obtain medical assistance. The injury did not appear serious and the court felt that there was no need to first summon assistance.

The duty of care, to provide or render assistance in a timely manner in order to insure a participant's protection and safety, will also require that any injured party be properly cared for until medical attention can be obtained.

FACTS: A football player, Scott, suffered a neck injury. Testimony indicated, "The player had been able to move his hands and feet before the coach ordered players to carry him from the field without a stretcher, but not after." Was the coach negligent for improperly rendered medical assistance? **YOU'RE THE JUDGE!**

DECISION: The court found that such conduct on the part of the coach was negligent, not only for allowing the player to be moved, but for failing to wait for a doctor.

Transportation to a hospital may be preferable to summoning a doctor to the scene, particularly where an injury, such as an ankle injury, would not be aggravated and time could be saved.

Liability may attach for negligent or unnecessary medical assistance that is rendered in a non-emergency situation.

FACTS: A high school football player's death resulted after a heat stroke, suffered during practice. Instead of cooling the player's body, an assistant coach placed him in a shower with room temperature water and then wrapped him in a blanket. This increased his accumulation of heat and caused his death. Was the school negligent? **YOU'RE THE JUDGE!**

DECISION: The court held, "The duty to secure reasonable medical assistance was breached. The school was negligent in not providing medical assistance, and in plying ill-chosen, improper first aid."

Similarly, where a teacher immersed an athlete's infected finger in a pan of boiling water, causing permanent disfigurement, liability for negligence was found for rendering unnecessary, forced medical care in a non-emergency situation. Trained medical assistance should have been summoned.

"A school should not assume the role of the physician," noted a court. Thus, liability was found where a physical education teacher overruled a doctor's opinion and note, and forced a student to participate in a broad jump class. The student was then injured.

Similarly, a coach was negligent where he determined—without a release from the doctor for a previous injury—that a boy was fit to play, and then re-injury resulted.

What if an injured athlete does not want medical assistance from non-medical personnel, but it is given anyway?

FACTS: A baseball player injured his leg during practice. "I do not want assistance from anyone except a doctor," he insisted.

An assistant then rendered medical assistance which aggravated the injury. Was this negligence? **YOU'RE THE JUDGE!**

DECISION: Yes. Where non-medical personnel is requested by an injured athlete not to give non-emergency medical assistance and gives it anyway, liability may then apply. The assistant was liable for the aggravation of the injury.

If a physical problem is not known of or could not be discovered by a reasonable person, then there may be no liability.

FACTS: Winthrop had a defect in his circulatory system. An examination did not reveal the problem and Winthrop did not divulge it. He was then struck in the head by a basketball and died, the re-

sult of participating in such condition. His family sued the school. Was the school liable for allowing Winthrop to play? **YOU'RE THE JUDGE!**

DECISION: The injury was not the responsibility of either the school or its personnel.

Liability may attach where a required examination of participants is either done improperly or not at all and such an examination would have revealed a problem which caused an injury.

Furthermore, it may be a school's duty to ensure that students not physically or mentally mature enough to participate for a particular sport or activity do not participate where injury might result.

If the sport or activity does not warrant an examination, then the failure to do so may not result in liability.

FACTS: A physical exam was neither required nor warranted for a try-out for the golf team. Had Jones been given one, it would have discovered a spinal problem. When he injured his spine while playing for the team, he sued the school for not examining him and discovering the problem. Was the school liable?

DECISION: **YOU'RE THE JUDGE!**

LIABILITY OF DOCTORS & OTHERS

What is the duty of a doctor who is rendering medical assistance?

A doctor is under a duty to use that degree of care and skill expected of a reasonably competent doctor in the same class of the medical profession to which he belongs, acting in the same or similar circumstances.

A doctor who holds himself out as an expert, will be held to a higher degree of care, as utilized by experts in that field.

Will it make a difference if a doctor provides medical assistance for a fee or for free?

FACTS: Dr. Adams was the school's football doctor. He was paid a fee for his services.

Dr. Bellows volunteered his services at a free medical clinic.

Dr. Charles, on his way home, stopped to help a jogger who had been hit by a car. Will the degree of care required by each doctor be different depending on the circumstances under which it was rendered? **YOU'RE THE JUDGE!**

DECISION: Legally, with few exceptions, it makes no difference whether the doctor undertakes the care for a fee, honorarium, or out of the kindness of his heart.

A doctor does not insure the success of all treatments, and will not be responsible for honest mistakes of judgment where the proper treatment is open to reasonable doubt. Liability will only occur where there has been negligence in following the standard and established procedures for treatment of an injury.

What must one injured show in order to recover for an injury alleged to be the fault of a doctor?

It must be shown that the doctor breached his duty to provide competent care, which resulted in an injury and damages.

FACTS: Johnson, a former football player and now coach, complained of back spasms. The doctor gave him an injection just below the left shoulder blade. It punctured one of his lungs.

"Yes, I did it," the doctor admitted. "I guess I misjudged the thickness of his chest wall. Usually, athletes have a lot thicker wall. I guess coaches aren't as thick as quarterbacks."

Was this competent care, an honest mistake of judgment for which the doctor was not liable?

DECISION: **YOU'RE THE JUDGE!**

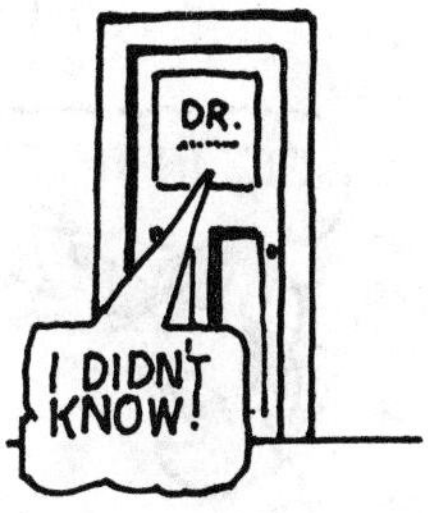

Failure To Recognize An Injury

Does a doctor have a duty to determine the nature of an injury before further injury results?

FACTS: A high school football player, Martin, while attempting a quarterback sneak, was tackled and slammed to the ground. He didn't move. Since he could still move his hands and feet, his spinal cord was not severed.

A doctor then allowed Martin to be carried from the field without a stretcher. It was then discovered that the spinal cord was severed. Was the doctor negligent? **YOU'RE THE JUDGE!**

DECISION: Yes. Severance could only have happened when Martin was carried from the field. The court found, "A doctor of reasonable skill and knowledge would have treated the athlete immediately to determine the nature of the injury and would have instructed that he be removed in a manner that would not cause further injury."

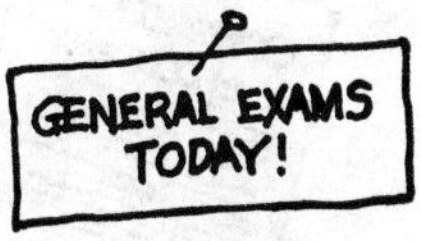

Physical Examinations

The type and extent of any physical examination required will depend in part on the reason for which it is given.

FACTS: Incoming school athletes were given a general exam. The next day a football player, Ed Wardell, was injured when his left

knee gave way. The exam had not revealed any problem with the knee.

A boxer, Juan Mendolina, died from a blow received during a prize fight. The doctor who had examined the fighter after two previous losses by technical knockouts failed to discover a preexisting brain injury.

Were the exams extensive enough? Was either doctor liable for the injury? **YOU'RE THE JUDGE!**

DECISION: A general examination given to all incoming school athletes would not be required to be as extensive as one required of boxers who had been knocked out and needed clearance before being allowed to fight again.

Where Wardell was injured the day after an examination which should have revealed the defect which caused the injury, then liability could attach to the doctor.

However, if the injury would have occurred even where the doctor treated Wardell, there can be no liability.

In a questionable decision, the doctor who examined Mendolina was found not liable for an honest error of judgment.

Another's Conduct

It might also be shown that another's conduct was a "substantial factor" in bringing about an injury.

FACTS: An athlete died from a severe concussion received in basketball practice the day after an examination should have revealed the concussion. The coach had allowed the boy to play after he complained of severe headaches. Who was liable? The doctor, the coach or both? **YOU'RE THE JUDGE!**

DECISION: The coach may be equally as liable as the doctor who failed to diagnose the concussion. The coach's conduct was a "substantial factor" in bringing about the death.

Do I Have Your Consent?

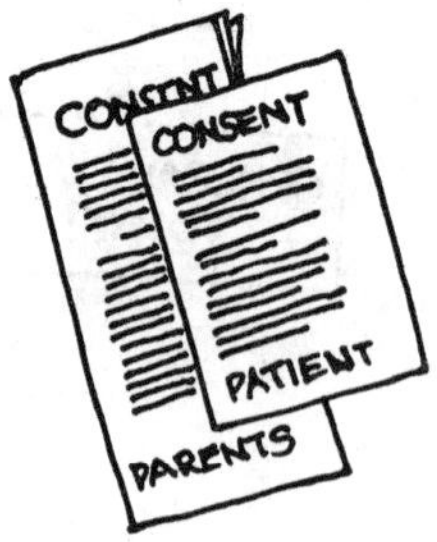

Usually, a doctor must obtain the consent of an adult patient before medical treatment can be given.

Must a doctor obtain the consent of a minor before giving medical treatment?

The general rule for minors is that since minors are deemed to be incapable of giving valid consent, consent for their treatment must be obtained from a minors' parents or guardians.

FACTS: John, 15, broke his ankle. He was sent to the hospital for medical treatment. Frances, 16, had a stroke while playing field hockey and needed immediate medical attention. Was parental consent needed in either situation? **YOU'RE THE JUDGE!**

DECISION: Parental consent was needed for John, but not for Frances. The general rule is subject to the following exceptions which allow a minor to give valid consent where: an emergency exists, a parent or guardian is inaccessible, or the minor is near majority and able to give a knowingly informed consent.

For consent to be valid, it must be the **informed consent** of the patient. A patient will be informed after a reasonable disclosure of any available alternative procedures and all dangers, advantages and disadvantages are made known to the patient.

Must consent be obtained in an emergency situation?

FACTS: While returning from a soccer game, Hans was injured and rendered unconscious in an auto accident. There was no time to reach his parents. Therefore, a doctor gave necessary emergency medical attention. Hans later sued the doctor for acting without his permission. Was the doctor negligent? **YOU'RE THE JUDGE!**

DECISION: No. If consent cannot be obtained, it may be implied from the circumstances in which treatment is given. This is especially true in emergency situations.

Disclosure of Medical Information

In order to make decisions concerning their bodies, athletes have a constitutional right to be informed of their medical condition.

Informed consent requires a doctor or others to inform an athlete of his condition or be liable for any subsequent injury resulting from an undisclosed risk.

What if the interests of a team conflict with an athlete's right to be informed of his physical condition?

FACTS: The Whalers football coach ordered the doctor, "Don't tell Killer what's wrong with him. I need him for Sunday's game. If you tell him, he might not play hurt."

Killer played and, due to his condition, aggravated the injury to his shoulder. He sued the team and the doctor. Were they liable for the additional injury? **YOU'RE THE JUDGE!**

DECISION: Both the doctor and the team were found liable. Although Killer may have decided to play while hurt, there still was a duty to inform him of his condition.

Similarly, another pro football player recovered damages against his team and the team's doctor for their "fraudulent" concealment of the severity of an injury to the player's knees. They prescribed a diet of pain killers and steroids so that the player could continue playing. The court commented, "The team and its doctor had a duty to inform the player of everything about his injury and they did not."

Where a doctor claims, "It won't get any worse," or "You're OK, no injury," or words to that effect, or nothing at all (where there is an injury), liability may attach.

FACTS: Edwards injured his knee during a pro football game. The team doctor recommended treatment. Edwards sat out the season, but returned the next pre-season. After being released, he underwent surgery to the knee. The surgeon found that he had sustained extensive damage to the knee, which was aggravated by his continuing to play football, and that surgery should have been performed at the time of the original injury. Was the team's doctor liable? **YOU'RE THE JUDGE!**

DECISION: The court awarded Edwards a judgment against the team's orthopedic surgeon for medical malpractice. Upon appeal, the case was settled.

Similar actions, alleging a conflict of interest, between a doctor's duty to a team and his duty to inform a player of his condition, have been brought.

FACTS: Jim Cranston, a baseball player, alleged that a team physician examined him before spring practice and discovered a symptomatic blood condition, but failed to treat it or report the condition to him. Soon after Cranston was released from the team the following year, he was hospitalized with a kidney disorder and died. If the disorder resulted from the blood condition, was the doctor liable?

DECISION: **YOU'RE THE JUDGE!**

Confidential Information

A doctor may be held liable for the disclosure of confidential information relating to a patient.

What if such an opinion is rendered in good faith or gratuitously? This is so even though it is rendered in good faith, and even if gratuitously.

Where the disclosure of confidential information about a patient is given with knowledge that another will rely upon it, the doctor may be responsible for damages incurred because of any innaccuracies of the opinion.

What if a doctor intentionally gives a false statement concerning a patient's condition, which leads to further suffering?

FACTS: After Davis had recovered from a blood clot, the team doctor was alleged to have announced, "Davis is suffering from a rare blood disease which will prevent him from playing pro football again."

This was printed in the newspapers. Davis read the article and became panic-stricken. He suffered from extreme emotional distress and torment. He sued the team and its doctor for the false statement. Was the doctor liable for causing Davis' further injuries? **YOU'RE THE JUDGE!**

DECISION: The court held that there was evidence to find that the doctor intentionally or recklessly inflicted mental stress by a false statement concerning the supposedly fatal disease.

Permission To Play

Liability may also attach where a doctor grants permission to an injured athlete to participate when his condition does not warrant it, or where there is a premature termination of treatment.

FACTS: Homer had suffered several concussions. He was warned by the team doctor, "Don't play tackle football." Nevertheless, his parents gave their signed permission. The doctor certified Homer's participation.

When Homer received another concussion, resulting in part from his previous condition, he sued the school. They defended, "The parents signed a letter of consent." Who was liable—the doctor or Homer and his parents?

Rusty suffered permanent brain damage as a result of a head injury received during a high school football game. His parents sued his doctor, alleging that he had been "improperly allowed to return to contact sports after an initial treatment for a related head injury." The doctor had recommended that he could return, but to "take it easy." Was the doctor liable? **YOU'RE THE JUDGE!**

DECISION: Both doctors were negligent for allowing Homer and Rusty to return to play. If the doctors thought that they had not sufficiently recovered, it should have been evident that returning to a contact sport would only place them in an unreasonably dangerous situation, with the possibility for further injury more likely.

Liability was also found where a high school football player was allowed to play a few days after his release from a hospital after suffering fainting spells. The negligence consisted of: the premature termination of treatment, a failure to advise the player that he was unfit to play, and allowing his return where his condition did not warrant it.

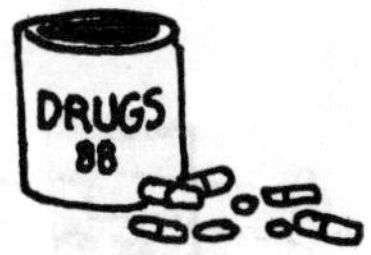

DRUGS

FACTS: Several athletes charged that owners, trainers and physicians negligently administered illegal and harmful drugs so that the athletes would perform while hurt and play more violently.

One coach testified, "The emphasis on maximum performance in sports leads to a demand that drugs be utilized, not only to maximize performance for the healthy, but also to delay the need for corrective surgery."

Another doctor testified, "While a painkiller may serve to inhibit pain, such a practice may cause or worsen an existing injury by inhibiting the natural warning system of the body, thereby increasing the risk of further injury."

Would such practices constitute negligence by those administering the drugs? Will your decision depend upon whether or not the players had informed consent?

DECISION: **YOU'RE THE JUDGE!**

Where there is an absence of a clear disclosure to an athlete of the dangers that drugs might pose, the athlete cannot validly consent to such prescription. This would be negligence by whomever administers the drugs.

What if a drug given to one participant causes injury to another?

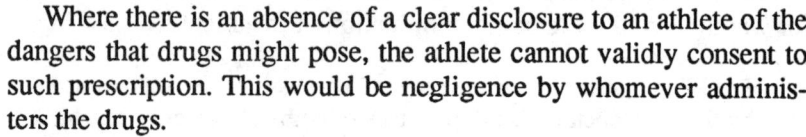

FACTS: A jockey, Mario, was killed when a horse (not the one ridden by Mario), broke down during a race, causing a pile-up. The jockey's estate sued the owner and trainer of the horse that broke down for improperly administering drugs to the horse. They alleged, "The horse was given a large dosage of an anesthetizing drug to numb pain so that he would continue running until he broke down."

Would such a practice, if it was the cause of the pile-up, be negligence?

DECISION: **YOU'RE THE JUDGE!**

"Blood doping" and the use of steroids to enhance the performance of athletes, with the alleged aid or approval of coaches, trainers and doctors may be negligence. Furthermore, steroids are included in a list of substances that are banned by both the NCAA, the Olympics and professional sports. Using any of these substances may lead to a suspension of the player from participation in school athletics, the Olympics or professional sports.

FACTS: A football team's trainer recommended that certain team members, in order to maximize their performance, use steroids. He obtained their consent. Later, when the athletes developed health problems, they sued the trainer and school for medical malpractice. They alleged that it was negligence to recommend such a practice to them. They further alleged, "Future health consequences were not explained—such as heart and liver problems."

The trainer defended by testifying as to the alleged "consent." Was the consent informed? Was the trainer negligent?

DECISION: **YOU'RE THE JUDGE!**

WARRANTY

FACTS: A doctor promised Seve that surgery on his injured knee would make it "as good as new." The surgery, although performed with all the care and skill expected of the doctor, with results as good as could be hoped for, left Seve with a bum knee. His career was over.

Seve sued the doctor for a breach of warranty —the doctor's promise, guarantee or assurance—to make his knee "as good as new." Seve relied upon this promise in consenting to the operation. Was the doctor liable for his failure to bring about the expected result?

DECISION: **YOU'RE THE JUDGE!**

There must be promissory language by the doctor. This language may be implied. And there must not only be a promise, but some reliance by the athlete upon that promise.

FACTS: Hugo needed surgery on his knee to have any chance of continuing to play pro football. He asked his doctor, "Will I be able to play after the surgery and rehabilitation?" The doctor didn't answer; he just smiled and nodded his head. When after the surgery, Hugo had to retire, he sued the doctor, alleging, "I relied on the doctor's warranty to correct my knee." Was the doctor liable? **YOU'RE THE JUDGE!**

DECISION: Yes. The doctor, by saying nothing, but implying by his actions that the surgery would allow Hugo to play, was liable. Hugo relied on that promise.

What if a doctor guarantees a certain result? What if he only predicts what the result may be?

Generally, a doctor does not warrant certain results. However, where a doctor does guarantee certain results, there may be liability for non-performance. However, liability will not attach for mere predictions of outcomes.

FACTS: Jack's doctor told him, "Surgery could correct your knee." And later added, "I think that everything will be okay, but if you would like, I can do the procedure again."

Another doctor told an athlete, "Don't worry about the stitches coming undone." Did the doctors promise certain results, or were these statements just opinions of the outcome? **YOU'RE THE JUDGE!**

DECISION: Courts are reluctant to hold that everytime a doctor tells the patient that a certain treatment will fix the patient up fine, or not to worry about it, that the doctor has warranted his curing the patient.

The courts found that such language implied uncertainty. They were mere opinions, not promises.

Doctors have to be allowed to calm or help patients without fear of warranting results. However, there is a limit as to what type of reassurance a doctor can give without warranting his work.

FACTS: "I guarantee that your leg will be fine after recovery from this surgery," and "I promise that there will be no complications." Did these statements, made to athletes by their doctors, warranty certain results? **YOU'RE THE JUDGE!**

DECISION: Yes. The statements go beyond normal assurances and may lead to liability where the results are not as warranted. A doctor must remember that what the patient may think of as success may be completely different from what the doctor thinks of as success.

Just as opinions and some assurances may not be promises, an offer of information to a patient is unlikely to be found as a guarantee of certain results.

FACTS: A star female athlete, desiring not to have children, had a tubal ligation (tubes tied). The doctor stated that this was permanent. When the athlete became pregnant, and thus unable to compete, she sued the doctor, alleging that his promise of permanency meant that she would never become pregnant. Did the doctor promise such a result? **YOU'RE THE JUDGE!**

DECISION: The doctor's statement was non-promissory. It was only intended to inform the patient that the operation was nonreversible.

There are no strict guidelines as to what constitutes a warranty or promise. The test appears to be: What did the patient think that the doctor was or was not promising?

Where doctors stated that: "Treatments would not leave a permanent scar," or "would make a patient's arm 100% perfect," or, "Treatments were perfectly safe," or, "Treatment would please the patient to her personal satisfaction," promises were found. Such statements contained less prediction and more warranty.

FACTS: A dentist assured a hockey player that his difficulty would be over. With his new dentures, he would be able to eat normally—including corn on the cob. When the hockey player could not eat normally, he sued the doctor, alleging that the doctor breached "his promise to end my difficulty." The doctor felt that he "was only reassuring the patient." Was the doctor liable for damages for a breach of promise? **YOU'RE THE JUDGE!**

DECISION: Yes. The hockey player was not a worried patient facing a serious health situation where a reassurance might be needed. It was an elective treatment where no reassurance was needed. The language was a breach of warranty.

CONSENT FORMS

Is a doctor shielded from liability by a written disclaimer in a consent form which the patient signs?

FACTS: Les, injured in a football game, needed surgery. He signed a consent form stating, "No guarantee or assurance has been given by anyone as to the results that may be obtained."

Kirby, injured playing soccer, signed a consent form providing, in part, "No result has been guaranteed."

Both doctors, when asked about the potential results, said reassuringly, "Don't worry, everything will be just fine."

If the results obtained by Les and Kirby were not what they expected, and they sued, would the consent forms that they had signed release the doctors of any liability? **YOU'RE THE JUDGE!**

DECISION: Even though there were signed consent forms, the courts may look to see whether there was an oral guarantee. Therefore, a doctor is not shielded from liability by a written disclaimer, unless it is also coupled with an oral disclaimer.

A doctor's best defense in preventing liability would be by the use of statements such as, "Assuming no complications," or, "Except for the unlikely event of a complication," instead of "I promise!" or "I guarantee!"

ODDS & ENDS....

Weight Control

Attempts at weight control occur most frequently where an athlete either desires to lose weight to qualify for a team, or where a weight loss is necessary to compete at a desired level.

FACTS: Several athletes, in an attempt to make the wrestling, boxing and 150-pound football teams (only for players weighing

150 pounds or less), went on crash diets. They all became too weak to compete competitively and, as a result, were injured.

Testimony showed that, in some instances the school either participated in, directed, or condoned the crash dieting. In others, the school did not know of the dieting. When could a school be held responsible for an athlete's injury which was the result of dieting? **YOU'RE THE JUDGE!**

DECISION: Where crash dieting is directed, condoned, or participated in, by a school or doctor—negligence may be found where injury results. And this may be so even where the coach or other school personnel did not direct it, but knew of the attempt and did nothing to stop it.

When possible, anyone being treated for an injury, or seeking or needing medical care, should receive a reasonable disclosure of their medical condition and any available alternative procedures, including all dangers, advantages and disadvantages. Only then can an individual give an informed consent for themself or another.

11

CONTRACTS - PROMISES! PROMISES!

WHAT'S IT ABOUT?

An agreement to do or not to do a particular thing—that is a contract. *Contracts—Promises! Promises!* gives samples and interprets a professional athlete's player contract, including no-cut and guaranteed contracts and bonuses. It also discusses a player's duty to perform.

Can a team breach a player's guaranteed contract? What is misrepresentation? What is fraud?

CONTRACTS

FACTS:

CONTRACT

I, ____________________, agree to play basketball for the Boston Blues. They agree to pay me $100,000 a year for 3 years.

DATE	YOU the PLAYER	Boston Blues

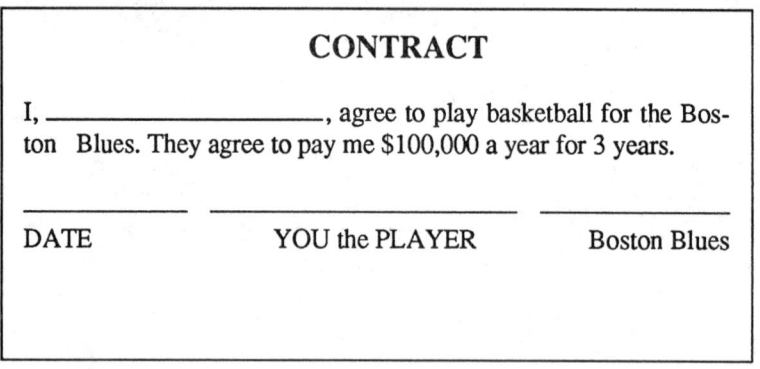

Do you think that this **contract** —an agreement to do or not to do a particular thing—between YOU and the Boston Blues fulfills the legal requirements for: a valid and enforceable contract of an offer, an acceptance of that offer, and consideration (your services as a player for money)?

DECISION: **YOU'RE THE JUDGE!**

Does a contract have to be in writing? An **express contract** is one that may be formed by either written or oral language. Thus, had you and the Blues orally agreed to a contract, that may have been a valid contract.

The Blues have made YOU an **offer**—a promise to enter into a contract that is clear and that is communicated to YOU. YOU may accept their offer, reject it or make a counter-offer. Or, the Blues could withdraw their offer at any time before YOU accept it.

If YOU decide to accept their offer, the **acceptance** must comply with the Blues terms. If YOU add or omit any terms, such as by insisting, "I accept, but I want a bonus," then a **counter-offer** is created, which the Blues may then accept, reject or counter-offer.

Both you and the Blues must give **consideration**—something of legal value. The considerations are your services as a player and the Blues' payment of money.

Lastly, in order to have formed a valid and enforceable contract, no defenses must exist. These defenses may apply to not just a contract between an athlete and a professional team, but also in other contracts, such as between an agent and an athlete.

FACTS: You and the Blues signed the contract. What if there was an absence of consideration—you didn't play or they didn't pay?

What if there was: **fraud**—intentional deception or dishonesty; **misrepresentation**—false statements by YOU or the Blues; **duress**—high pressure or threats; **unconscionable conduct**—unreasonable, dishonest or conniving? May any of these defenses be used to void the contract? **YOU'RE THE JUDGE!**

DECISION: If any of these defenses are present, then the contract may be voided by the offended party.

Will this contract between YOU and the Boston Blues resolve questions, such as:

- "What if I report in bad shape?"
- "Will I get a bonus if I play well?"
- "What if the team doesn't pay me?"
- "What happens if I don't try or if I'm injured?"
- "What if I am fined, suspended, waived, traded or fired?"

Although a simple contract may fulfill the basic requirements of an offer, acceptance and consideration, it may not solve all of the problems that may arise. That is why professional sports teams and their players sign a uniform or standard player contract similar to this:

UBA PLAYER CONTRACT

THIS **CONTRACT** is between YOU, herein called the Player, and the Boston Blues, herein called the Club, a member of the UNITED BASKETBALL ASSOCIATION.

In consideration of the promises made to each other, Player and Club agree as follows:

TERM This contract is for one year, August 1 to July 31. The Club is entitled to a one-year renewal option under the same terms and conditions as the original contract.

COMPENSATION For Player's services and other promises, the Club will pay the Player $1,000,000, earned BONUSES, and expenses for traveling, meals and lodging.

SERVICES The Club employs Player as a skilled basketball player. Player agrees to give his best efforts, and to behave and abide by fair play and good sportsmanship.

OTHER SPORTS & SERVICES Player has exceptional and unique skill, and will not, without permission, play for any other team or participate in any dangerous activity, including wrestling, boxing, racing, hockey, sky diving, football, bullriding or mountain climbing.

PHYSICAL CONDITION Player represents that he has no physical or mental defects and that he will maintain himself in first-class physical condition.

PICTURES, PUBLICITY & PUBLIC APPEARANCES Player grants Club permission to use his picture for publicity and promotion. Player will make public appearances, cooperate with media and will make ads only with the Club's permission.

INJURY If Player is injured, he will receive medical care and pay, as long as unable to play, but only for the remainder of the season. If Player is dismissed while unable to play, see Collective Bargaining Agreement (CBA) for grievance procedure.

PERFORMANCE, CONDUCT & DISMISSAL If Player's performance is unsatisfactory, or his conduct adversely reflects on the Club or the integrity of the League, then Club may fine, suspend or dismiss Player. CBA grievance procedure will govern.

RULES & DISPUTES Player will abide by all rules. Any disputes will be submitted to arbitration under the CBA, except that the commissioner shall have sole authority with regard to conduct involving the integrity of the game.

ASSIGNMENT Unless otherwise agreed, Club may assign this contract and Player's services to any other Club in the League.

APPROVAL The commissioner shall have the right to approve or disapprove this contract on reasonable grounds.

OTHER AGREEMENTS This contract and any attachments contain all that the parties have agreed to, and along with the Collective Bargaining Agreement, League Constitution and Rules, will govern the relationship between the Player and the Club.

SPECIAL PROVISIONS

A. Player's compensation is guaranteed. He may not be cut or traded during this contract.

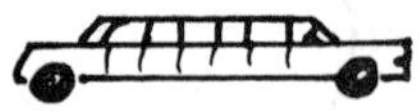

B. Player will receive a signing bonus of $50,000, and an interest-free loan of $250,000.

C. Player will receive bonuses for the following: games played, points scored, rebounds, victories, awards and home attendance.
Player will have free use of a chauffeured limo and a house for one year and of the arena for one night. A buy-out provision will be in effect for the option year of this contract. The Club will grant a scholarship to the Player for further study.

PLAYER—YOU	CLUB—Boston Blues by	Date

This contract—a product of the collective bargaining process between a league and its players—plays the predominant role in defining the rights and responsibilities of the professional team athlete.

FACTS: After signing this contract, you were injured during preseason. The team doctor said, "You will be out for the year." Will you receive your pay?

The Club argued, "You were injured playing checkers during the off-season." They decided to waive you. Can they waive you while you are injured?

DECISION: **YOU'RE THE JUDGE!**

General rules concerning contracts in professional team sports may also apply to contracts in other employment situations (such as individual sports, agent representation, endorsements and public appearances).

What are the rights and responsibilities of the parties to a contract?

A contract involving an athlete is sometimes called a **personal service contract**—agreement exchanging an act (personal performance) for a promise (to pay).

FACTS: Marilyn (a pro ping pong player), John (a pro basketball player), and Sid (a pro football coach), all signed personal service contracts.

Marilyn couldn't make a match. She asked, "Can my husband take my place?"

John had an endorsement appearance to attend, but wanted to play golf instead. He wanted a teammate to take his place.

Sid needed a vacation. He asked his assistant, "Will you take my place for a week?" May any of these pros assign their duties to others?

The Club would like to assign John's contract to another team. Can they? **YOU'RE THE JUDGE!**

DECISION: Personal service contracts call for the performance of services and the exercise of skill and judgment that may only be performed by the person with whom made. The athlete or coach may not assign (transfer to another) his or her duties to be performed.

However, unless the player has a no-trade provision in his contract, a team has the right to assign a player's contract to any other team in the league.

Other Agreements?

Will a court, in interpreting a contract between a professional player and his team, allow oral evidence as to what the parties agreed to?

In interpreting contracts where the parties have different views, the **Parol Evidence Rule** may come into play. It reads: "If the parties intended the contract—and any attached or referred to documents—to be their whole agreement, then the court will not allow any evidence of other agreements."

FACTS: In negotiating his contract, Pedro, a major league baseball player, was promised, "We'll give you a bonus!" However, when the season ended, he discovered that the bonus was not in his contract. In attempting to collect the bonus, may Pedro introduce evidence of the oral promise? **YOU'RE THE JUDGE!**

DECISION: No. Pedro should have made sure that the bonus was in the contract before he signed.

There are exceptions. Prior agreements, such as last year's contract between the parties, may sometimes be used—not to change the agreement—but to explain or define any unclear terms.

Approval

Approval of a contract by the commissioner or president of a league is generally required. This power is given to ensure that the interests of the player and the league are protected, such as to prevent improper bonuses.

FACTS: Max, a pro football player, signed a three year contract to play for the Rams. The contract required the commissioner's approval. When, after one year, Max declared, "I want to play elsewhere!" the team sought to enjoin him from doing so. The commissioner had given his approval only for the first of the three years on the contract. "Can I play somewhere else?" asked Max. **YOU'RE THE JUDGE!**

DECISION: Yes. Max could play elsewhere. There was no contract as commissioner approval was not obtained for the last two years of the contract.

Today, although commisssioner approval is still necessary, it is not required to complete a contract. The contract is binding when both the player and the club have signed it.

Term

FACTS: Marcel, a pro football player, wanted to play tennis during the off-season. His contract prohibited tennis. Did the contract cover the off-season? **YOU'RE THE JUDGE!**

DECISION: The term of the contract was for one year. This prevents Marcel from participating in prohibited conduct during the off-season.

When a contract does not prohibit a specific activity, a player may participate—such as a talented professional athlete participating in pro football and baseball in the same season.

Some professional sports leagues, such as major league baseball, limit the length of contracts between teams and their players.

Compensation

Contracts specify that players have a right to a definite salary. However, any action by the player's club to fine or discipline a player for his conduct may reduce that salary.

This may be so even where the player has a no-cut contract.

FACTS: Tom, a pro hockey player, got into a fight and was injured. The team stopped his pay, fined and suspended him. His contract did not cover this situation. Tom sued for his salary and asked, "Can I recover?" **YOU'RE THE JUDGE!**

DECISION: The general rule is that where a player's salary has been terminated for an injury which occurred while playing for the team, the player may recover for the remainder of that year.

Players will not be paid when they are on strike. Also, they may not be paid if an owner locks out his players when, through their representatives, they can't agree on a new Collective Bargaining Agreement. Some player contracts may allow for payment during a strike or lockout.

Bonuses

A player's right to receive any bonus will depend upon whether the bonus is awarded for signing or for performance, and whether the player has performed, if required.

May a player keep a signing bonus if he is cut from the team without performing?

Signing bonuses, offered as inducements to get players to sign, generally only require that players sign the contract and be "ready,

willing and able to perform." If cut, a player may retain the bonus. If not ready, willing and able to perform or, if required to perform and the player does not, then the player may have to return part or all of the bonus.

FACTS: Two pro football players, Brown and Sable, signed to play in a new football league starting the next year. The team had financial difficulties and, as the players never played, there was a dispute as to their bonuses. The team sought to recover the bonuses, claiming, "The players didn't even attend camp, let alone play in any games!" Could Brown and Sable keep the bonuses? **YOU'RE THE JUDGE!**

DECISION: Yes. The players were prohibited from signing with any other team (for play during the contract), and furthermore, the players' names were used for publicity purposes (selling tickets). This was of benefit to the team and was consideration by the players for the bonuses.

However, a player may forfeit a bonus if he fails to fulfill an obligation of his contract—such as when his contract calls for the player to report at a certain weight and he reports overweight.

Power To Terminate

Can a player terminate his contract if his team doesn't pay him? A player's ability to terminate a contract generally involves disputes concerning salary or medical care.

FACTS: Dan, the quarterback for the Marlins, injured his knee. The team decided not to pay his salary or medical expenses. His contract had a payment of salary clause. Could he terminate the contract for non-payment of his salary? **YOU'RE THE JUDGE!**

DECISION: The most widely used payment of salary clause reads: "If the team fails to pay the player or otherwise fails to perform a material obligation (provide for required and necessary medical care), then, under arbitration, if the decision is for the player, the team shall have the opportunity to make the payment before the player can terminate the contract."

Renegotiate

What if a player feels that, because he performed beyond that expected of him, he deserves to have his contract renegotiated? May he?

FACTS: Tony, a late-round draft choice, was offered a long term "take-it-or-leave-it" contract for a minimum salary. By the end of his first season, he was a star running back for the Indians. He walked out of training camp when the team wouldn't renegotiate his contract. The Indians first fined, and then threatened to release him. Could they do so? **YOU'RE THE JUDGE!**

DECISION: By not playing, Tony was in violation of his contract. Tony should have attempted to negotiate a clause into his contract calling for renegotiation if a certain level of performance was reached. Also, he could have negotiated an incentive or performance bonus to be based upon his play.

No-Cut, No-Trade & Guarantee?

Under a **no-cut contract,** will a player be paid even if he is in poor physical condition and cut from the team?

A no-cut provision ensures that a player's salary will not be affected by his performance, even if he is cut from the roster. And, absent a more specific agreement (denying salary for injury due to certain defects), a no-cut clause would entitle a player to his salary even if he were in poor physical condition or even if he were injured during the off-season.

FACTS: A clause in your contract read, "This is a no-cut contract. Player shall not be traded without his permission. Player's salary is guaranteed."

What if your performance was poor or you were subject to disciplinary action (suspension)? The team would like to terminate your contract, without pay, by cutting or trading you. Could they do so?

DECISION: **YOU'RE THE JUDGE!**

May players be fined? Although a team is entitled to a player's best efforts, poor performance, due solely to attitude, would be very difficult to prove. As to discipline which is necessary in maintaining control of players, it is doubtful that a team would restrict a coach's authority by giving a player a clause prohibiting discipline. Therefore, players may be fined.

FACTS: Harry signed a guaranteed contract with the Bulldogs. After violating curfew for the third time, the team suspended him without pay. Could he recover the salary provided for in his contract? Could he be fined? **YOU'RE THE JUDGE!**

DECISION: As with a no-cut contract, Harry must make a good faith effort to perform. He is subject to discipline, which may include a fine or suspension (with loss of pay).

May a player with a no-cut contract be traded? Absent a more specific agreement, a player with a **no-trade provision** may not be traded without his consent. If he is, then he may void the trade. Major league baseball players with ten years in the majors and five years for their present team may veto any trade involving them.

A **salary guarantee** may provide, "The player's salary will not be affected by his performance or by his physical condition, even if due to an off-season injury." A majority of professional athletes in team sports (except most NFL players) have contracts guaranteeing pay in the event of their being cut or injured. In the NHL, teams may buy out a player's contract.

FACTS: "Mad Mike" signed a contract with the Steamrollers pro football team. He was cut after the last exhibition game. Could he recover his salary? **YOU'RE THE JUDGE!**

DECISION: Mad Mike's contract was not guaranteed. When he did not make the team, the contract was voided; no further salary had to be paid.

And, if a player moves to another team or retires, it is doubtful that the parties intended that the player receive his salary.

A more standard form no-cut provision may provide that inadequate physical condition, whether due to improper conditioning or an off-season injury, may be grounds for terminating a contract. A player's salary would not be affected by performance, as long as the performance was a good faith effort.

What is arbitration? Disputes concerning injuries and salary may be settled by **arbitration**—a process whereby owners and players submit their dispute to an impartial third party or parties for resolution.

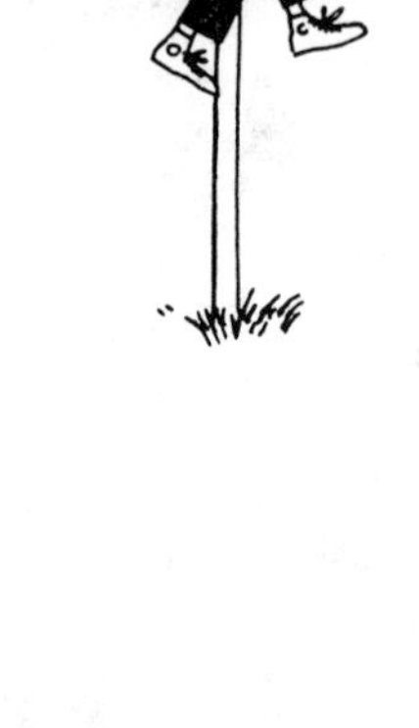

FACTS: Tom, a pro football player, had a no-cut contract which could only be terminated for off-season injuries which hampered his play. Tom reported to training camp unable to play, asserting, "The injury that I received at the end of last year still bothers me."

The team refused to pay his salary, arguing, "He injured himself in the off-season playing basketball."

How will this dispute be resolved? **YOU'RE THE JUDGE!**

DECISION: The matter will go to arbitration to determine whether Tom's off-season activity created a new injury or whether last year's injury was responsible for Tom's inability to play. Doctors will provide the necessary information for arbiters to make a decision.

Injury & Physical Condition

A professional athlete's ability to perform is the basis of his livelihood and of the contract with his team. Therefore, his physical condition and the risk of injury are primary concerns.

Upon signing a contract a player, in effect, warrants, "I have unique skill and ability. I am in, and will stay in, good physical condition. If I am injured and cannot perform due to a violation of any of these promises, or if I fail the pre-season physical exam, the team may have the right to terminate my contract."

If a player is injured while performing for the team, how long will the team pay him?

FACTS: Al, a pro football player, was injured in a game. John, a teammate, was hurt during the off-season working on his house. Hank, another teammate, was injured when he fell off a stage during a required public appearance. They all failed pre-season physical exams and were forced to retire.

What type of injuries will the team cover or pay for? For how long will the team pay for these injuries? **YOU'RE THE JUDGE!**

DECISION: Generally, a team will accept liability for injuries to players sustained in performance of their contract. That would include all games. Thus, Al could recover his salary for that season.

Activities unrelated to the contract, such as John's, are not covered, even if the injury had happened during the season.

However, a contract may provide that a player is covered in other situations where he is "carrying out an obligation of his contract" (making a required public appearance or speech). Hank could recover his salary.

For injuries covered, the team will generally pay medical expenses and salary for the remainder of that season only. A multi-year contract with a no-cut provision may guarantee payment for the remainder of the contract.

What if a player was injured trying to stay in shape during the off-season?

FACTS: An NBA player, Gene, was told by his team that he did not work out enough in the off-season. So Gene decided to join a summer basketball league. When he was injured while playing in the league, his team refused to pay his guaranteed salary, saying, "You played without our consent." Should the team have had to pay Gene?

DECISION: **YOU'RE THE JUDGE!**

Often, an injury may be the result of the combined effects of several blows, and then may not appear until some later time.

FACTS: Gabe, a pro football player, passed his team's pre-season physical exam, but then he was injured. The team terminated his contract, claiming, "The injury was the result of Gabe's debilitating back injury from a previous year, and for which we are not responsible." Gabe sued for his salary. Was the team liable? **YOU'RE THE JUDGE!**

DECISION: Gabe had reported to camp in good condition and the team physician certified this condition, noting that Gabe did not suffer from any symptoms of his previous injury. The team was liable.

A player who fails a pre-season exam may face termination or suspension without pay. A player will be examined after an injury to determine his ability to play and, if he is found unable to play due to the injury, the team physician will determine when he is fit to return to play.

FACTS: Kevin, a pro baseball player, was injured. After missing three months, he was declared fit to play by the team physician. His ability and skill in playing had been lessened by the injury and he was cut from the team. He sued for his salary, alleging, "I should have been paid throughout the period of my rehabilitation." Should he have? **YOU'RE THE JUDGE!**

DECISION: If Kevin, after rehabilitation, was still unable to perform at the level required of him, he could be terminated without pay. If, however, his ability to perform was still subject to improvement from an injury as a result of his playing for the team, then he would be entitled to his salary throughout his rehabilitation, but only for the remainder of the season, unless he had a guaranteed contract.

Any dispute regarding a player's physical fitness may be submitted to arbitration, where an independent medical review will determine the player's fitness.

Conduct & Rules

Who may discipline a player? The player's team? The commissioner? A player, in signing a contract—and subject to fine, suspension or dismissal—in effect agrees, "I will abide by rules intended to govern my conduct and to discourage activities, such as fighting, abusing officials or gambling." Any fine will be determined by the amount thought necessary to punish and to deter others from similar conduct. A commissioner or president may review a team's discipline and meet out any additional discipline thought to be necessary.

Is the player being disciplined entitled to due process? A player's contract or league rules may provide for arbitration, or **due process**—the right to notice and a fair and impartial hearing with representation.

Who will determine if any discipline is fair and reasonable? An independent arbitrator may ensure that any disciplinary rule is related to the league's interest in protecting the integrity of the sport, that the rule is fair and reasonable, and that it is exercised in good faith, not due to a vindictive motive or other personal reason.

FACTS: Jack, a pro basketball player, admitted, "I gambled on my team's games."

Without notice and a hearing, the team suspended him. Jack's contract provided for a hearing before any disciplinary action. Should Jack's suspension have been lifted and Jack given a hearing?

Paul, a pro baseball player, was fined and suspended for fighting during a game. He was given a hearing with the commissioner, who upheld the fine and suspension. Paul asked for "review by either the court or an independent arbitrator." Should Paul have been given a second hearing? **YOU'RE THE JUDGE!**

DECISION: Jack's suspension was upheld. The court applied the **"unclean hands" doctrine,** which holds that "one doing something wrong (having dirty hands) cannot ask for relief."

Jack had caused irreparable harm to the players, team, league, fans and youth. Therefore, because Jack had bet on the games in which he played, he was denied the due process procedures provided for in his contract. However, Jack should have been given an opportunity to mitigate the seriousness of the offense.

Paul, as provided by his contract, had the right to the grievance procedure, which entitled him to a hearing and review by an independent arbitrator.

You're Fired!

Tenure (permanent employment) rarely applies to a professional athlete. "Survival of the fittest" does.

It is in an owner's or promoter's interests to have only the very best players performing for them, but with no more security than is necessary. What are a team's or player's rights and duties regarding termination?

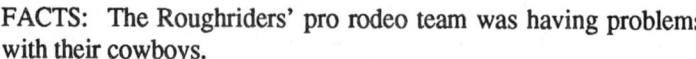

FACTS: The Roughriders' pro rodeo team was having problems with their cowboys.

Bronco Billy reported for the season "out of shape"; Randy could no longer stay on the bull; Bill continued to violate curfew; Larry intentionally missed the bus for the regional championship, and; Swen didn't show up for a public appearance. "Can we terminate any of the cowboys' contracts?" asked the Roughriders' owner. **YOU'RE THE JUDGE!**

DECISION: The team retained the right to terminate the cowboys' contracts for failing to: "maintain good physical condition, exhibit sufficient skill and ability and observe disciplinary rules, or for otherwise materially breaching their contracts."

Refusing to participate in scheduled competition may be material, but failure to show up for one public appearance probably would not be a material breach. Only Swen's contract wasn't terminated.

A player may be given the right to terminate a contract, especially where his team fails to pay his salary. And if a team discharges a player without good cause, then the player will be excused from performance, while still having a proper demand for his salary.

A team terminating a player's contract for good cause will be under no further obligation to employ or pay the player, except if the termination was for an injury occurring during play or in fulfilling other duties, or where the player had a no-cut contract guaranteeing his salary. Will a no-cut contract save a player from being terminated for disciplinary reasons?

FACTS: Due to continual disciplinary problems, Speedy, a star running back for the Tigers, was unable to perform to the satisfaction of the team. The Tigers considered terminating his contract, but the contract had a no-cut clause. "Can we terminate Speedy's contract? Should we?" asked the Tigers. **YOU'RE THE JUDGE!**

DECISION: Although the Tigers could terminate Speedy's contract, it is doubtful that they would let a player with marketable skill go. Generally, a team will attempt to sell the player's contract, trade him, or at least place him on waivers for a stated price to other interested teams.

Ability To Perform?

Who determines a player's ability to perform? Discretion to determine a player's skill or ability to play is given to a team through their head coach, manager or the team physician.

A player may be concerned that a coach's or doctor's loyalty to the team may influence any decision, thus negating "good faith" in determining the player's ability to perform. Therefore, where physical condition is at issue, a player's contract may provide for an independent exam and arbitration.

The **"good faith test"**—where "as long as the team acted in good faith and with honesty, its discretion will be upheld"—is generally used where a team has discretion as to whether or not it is "satisfied" with a player's ability.

FACTS: Pro football players, Tillman and Gambrell, after recovering from knee injuries, were pronounced fit to play by their team physicians. After failures to perform satisfactorily, they were dismissed. "Can we recover our salaries?" they asked. **YOU'RE THE JUDGE!**

DECISION: The court held, "The players were properly dismissed under a clause in their contracts permitting the clubs to dismiss them if they were not in proper physical condition." They had recovered as fully as possible, but not enough to satisfactorily play. The physicians had exercised good faith in examining the players.

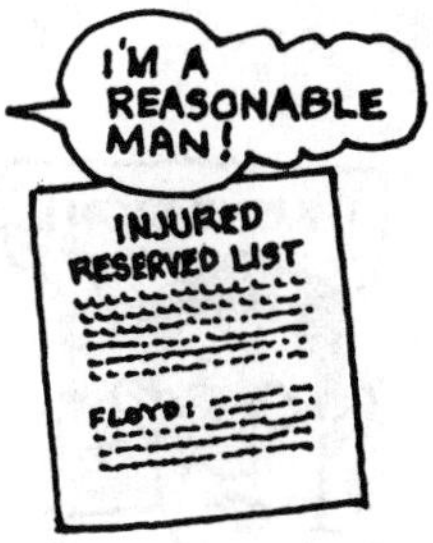

A second test used to determine if a team's decision concerning a player's ability to perform is reasonable is the **"reasonable man standard."** It states, "If a reasonable man would have been dissatisfied with a player's ability, then his club's discretion in dismissing the player will be honored"—unless the player's ability was hampered by an injury received while playing for the team.

FACTS: Floyd, a pro football player, was placed on the injured reserve list. He was later ordered back to duty and promptly cut from the team, allegedly due to his inability to perform sufficiently. He sued for his salary, contending, "I should be paid while I'm still recovering from that injury." Was he awarded his back pay? **YOU'RE THE JUDGE!**

DECISION: Yes. The evidence did not establish if the team doctor had stated that Floyd was physically able to perform. Floyd was advised by the trainer that he had been placed on the active or ready to play list on the advice from "higher up." Although a reasonable man may have been dissatisfied with Floyd's ability, it was due to an injury previously incurred while playing for his team.

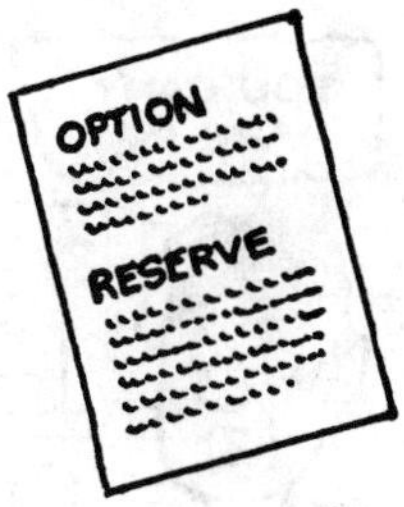

Option & Reserve

FACTS: Dave's contract to play for the Orioles contained an option clause allowing the team to renew his contract for one year without his consent.

YOU'RE
THE JUDGE!

Ed's contract with the Blue Sox had a reserve clause allowing the team to renew Ed's contract without his consent for as many years as he played. Could the teams use such clauses to prevent Dave and Ed from playing for other teams? **YOU'RE THE JUDGE!**

DECISION: Under the typical **option clause,** a club may renew an exclusive right to a player's services without his consent for one year after the expiration of the present contract. Although certain veterans may be exempt, the option clause is a part of every contract and may not be stricken through private negotiation.

Provisions that give a team rights to a player's services for an indefinite period are referred to as **reserve clauses.** Unless a player and his team contract for the player's services for an indefinite period of time (life contract), reserve clauses are no longer allowed.

If a player signs a new contract, then the option year will extend to the year after the contract expires.

What should a player do if he intends to "play out" his option so that he may negotiate with other teams?

I WON'T SIGN!

If a player intends to play out his option, he should leave the new contract unsigned, thereby forcing the club to exercise it's option if it intends to keep the player for another year.

In some sports (NBA), the option clause has been replaced with a right of first refusal clause giving a club the right to match any salary offered to one of their players by another team. This applies unless the player is a five-year veteran. There, a player automatically becomes a free agent with no right of first refusal clause in his contract. If a player is not a five-year veteran, any new contract must include a twenty-five percent pay raise for his team to retain the right of first refusal.

Was There A Breach Of Contract?

YOU CAN'T
MAKE ME!

FACTS: D.J. and Tommy Lee sued their team, the Blues, charging, "We weren't paid our salaries."

Due to a pre-season injury, D.J. wasn't able to play. Tommy Lee was ready, willing and able to perform for the team. Could they recover their salaries? **YOU'RE THE JUDGE!**

DECISION: Yes. Both contracts were breached. D.J. was unable to play due to an injury received while fulfilling duties under his contract. Tommy Lee was ready, willing and able to perform his duties.

Can a player be "forced" to perform? **Specific performance** requires a party to perform. But, as a general rule, this is inappropriate as it violates the Thirteenth Amendment to the Constitution which prohibits involuntary service. It is difficult to force compliance, and furthermore there is the undesirability of forcing two opposing parties to work together.

FACTS: Although the Whales were ready, willing and able to pay "Shark," he wanted to play water polo elsewhere. He asserted, "I won't play until they agree to trade me." Could the Whales force Shark to play for them? If not, could they prevent him from playing for another team in their league? **YOU'RE THE JUDGE!**

DECISION: The Whales could not force Shark to play for them.
A pro sports team enforces its contracts by an **injunction**—order of a court preventing a party (player) from doing or continuing an act (playing for another team), done in order to prevent injury (to the team). The injunction may be temporary until a trial can be had to determine the rights of the player and the team.

A court may issue a permanent injunction preventing a player from playing for another team. The team seeking an injunction must show that money damages are inadequate and that irreparable harm is likely if the injunction is not granted. The difficulty in replacing a player after rosters have been filled and the season has begun provides substantial proof of irreparable harm.

What if a contract is too one-sided or harsh? Enforcement may be denied where a contract is too one-sided or harsh, or where an injunction would seriously inhibit a player's opportunity to realize the fair value of his services.

FACTS: A pro basketball player, Randy Heyman, entered into a contract to play semi-pro ball for a minimum salary. After a successful season, he signed a contract with the ABA, a new pro league, with a substantial increase in salary. Could his former team get an injunction to prevent him from playing for the ABA? **YOU'RE THE JUDGE!**

DECISION: The former team might be entitled to damages for breach of contract, but not to an injunction. The old contract was too harsh and one-sided to permit enforcement. Any restraining order would seriously inhibit Heyman's opportunity to realize the fair value of his services in the "big" league.

Equity is justice administered by the court according to what is fair. "He who comes into equity must have clean hands." Thus, where a party seeking an injunction comes into court with unclean hands (has done something wrong), the court may then deny relief.

FACTS: Jack, a pro football player under contract to the Cougars, "jumped" to the Whalers, but then attempted to return to the Cou-

gars. Could the Whalers enjoin Jack from going back to the Cougars?

The Cougars asserted the defense of unclean hands. "The Whalers interfered with our original contract with Jack, and because of this, they should not be able to enforce any contract with him." **YOU'RE THE JUDGE!**

DECISION: The Whalers, who enticed Jack to abandon an existing commitment to the Cougars, could not complain when Jack decided not to honor the improperly secured contract with the Whalers. The Whalers came into equity with unclean hands.

May this defense be used where a party seeking an injunction has deceived a player into signing a contract?

FACTS: Jack, a pro basketball player under contract to the Hoopsters wanted to play for the Dribblers. The Hoopsters, who had signed Jack to a contract in violation of NCAA rules, sought to enjoin Jack from leaving. The Dribblers asserted, "The Hoopster's had unclean hands in signing Jack while he still had college eligibility left." Were the Hoopsters granted an injunction? **YOU'RE THE JUDGE!**

DECISION: No. The court refused to grant injunctive relief to the Hoopsters, ruling that their action was intended to deceive others. Jack could play for the Dribblers.

If another team or league signs or seeks to sign a player already under contract for services to begin after his present contract expires, this may be interference. Can it be enjoined?

FACTS: Ken, a star quarterback for the Bulls, signed to play for the Fumblers in a new football league. His services were to begin after his contract with the Bulls expired. The Fumblers announced the signing and had Ken begin promoting Fumblers' season tickets. Although Ken would not play for the Fumblers until his present contract expired, could the Bulls enjoin Ken from such publicity for the Fumblers? **YOU'RE THE JUDGE!**

DECISION: Ken's primary duty was to the Bulls until his contract expired. The promotional work interfered with the Bull's right to his services. An injunction was granted.

However, where there has not been any publicity which unreasonably interfered with a player's present duties, then no injunction would be issued for a contract which was to take effect after a player's present contract expires.

AGENTS

SECTION C **Worcester Times** SPORTS

SPORTS AGENTS

In the early days of sports, players did not need representation in negotiating contracts with their teams. The reserve clause bound the players to one team for as long as that team desired. Players were given a "take-it-or-leave-it" offer. The players were happy to do what they did best and get paid for it, with free travel, publicity and short work hours.

Then, sports exploded. Enormous revenues from attendance and T.V. helped professional leagues to expand. Along with new teams came new stadiums.

The demand for players became greater than the supply. Salaries rose. Teams fought for players' services. Along with the rise in salaries came other benefits, such as "no-trade" and "no-cut" clauses. Unions were formed and players sought "free agency." They challenged the clubs for more freedom to choose for whom they would play. They now had bargaining power.

And, thus was born the **sports agent**—one who, with consent, represents an athlete in negotiating a contract for the player's services. And, although most dealings between players and agents have been proper and to the benefit of the players, not all have.

HAVE I GOT A DEAL FOR YOU!
CONTRACT
AGENT

Rights & Duties Of Agent & Player

I WON'T PAY!

What are the rights and duties of players and the agents who represent them in negotiations with their teams?

FACTS: John and Billie Joe, pro basketball players, hired agents to represent them in negotiations with the Knickerbockers.

John's agent, Cal, negotiated a substantial pay raise and incentives. But John fumed, "I'm not the highest paid forward, so I'm not paying him."

Billie Joe's agreement with his agent, Al, called for Al to manage Billie Joe's money. When it was found out that Al had used the money for his own private investments, Billie Joe sued. Al had made a substantial profit. What were Cal's and Billie Joe's remedies? **YOU'RE THE JUDGE!**

DECISION: Cal may sue for the agreed upon fee. Unless the agreement called for the agent to obtain the highest paid contract, he had fulfilled his duties to John.

Billie Joe was discharged from the obligation to pay his agent. He could rescind the contract, recover the ill-gotten profits made by Al and recover any other damages that he suffered.

An agent is required to use reasonable care and skill, to act in good faith and with loyalty, and to disclose all relevant information to the player. The player is under a duty to pay the agent, as agreed, for his services.

FACTS: Sidney, an agent, agreed to represent Paul and Bob in contract negotiations with pro hockey clubs. Without the player's knowing, Sid agreed to give the Slashers "first crack" at his clients in return for a fee. Paul and Bob then signed with the Slashers.

Paul and Bob found out about Sid's deal with the Slashers and also that his fee was too high."Can we rescind our contract with Sid and recover wages lost due to Sid not dealing with any other teams?" asked Paul and Bob.

In addition, Sid encouraged Dave to break his contract with his agent and let Sid represent him. Could Dave's agent recover damages from Sid? **YOU'RE THE JUDGE!**

DECISION: Paul and Bob should have agreed that they, and not the team, would pay the fee, and then, only as the players received their salary. The team should not have paid Sid's fee as this would suggest a conflict of interest—was the agent working for the team or the players?

Paul and Bob could rescind their agreements with Sid and receive any lost pay. Giving a team "first crack" at the player's services was a breach of the duties of reasonable care, good faith and loyalty. Sid failed to disclose information that the players should have had in negotiating their contracts.

If Paul and Bob can prove that had it not been for Sid's actions, they could have received higher wages and benefits, then Sid will be liable.

Furthermore, if Dave, at Sid's encouragement, broke his present contract with his agent and signed with Sid, Sid may be liable for any damages the other agent may have suffered in lost fees. This was contractual interference.

May an agent recover money that he gave a player while the player still had college eligibility remaining? An arbitrator ruled that the player did not have to repay the agent. The arbitrator voided the contract between the player and the agent because the agent violated regulations regarding agents soliciting collegiate players.

NCAA Rules

NCAA rules and regulations forbid an athlete from agreeing to be represented by an agent until his collegiate eligibility has expired.

FACTS: Frank orally agreed to have an agent represent him. "You can represent me after the college season is over," he said.

Bob signed an "offer sheet," offering to allow an agent to represent him in negotiations for a pro contract. To prevent Bob from violating NCAA rules, the agent didn't sign the agreement until Bob had completed his amateur eligibility. Did either of these athletes violate the rule prohibiting representation before their eligibility has expired? **YOU'RE THE JUDGE!**

DECISION: Yes. Representation, whether written or oral, is prohibited. This prohibition includes entering into agreements (offer sheets) not effective until eligibility is up Both athletes violated the rule which is rationally related to the NCAA's objective of preserving amateurism in collegiate athletics.

All participants in Division I, NCAA basketball tournaments are now required to sign an affidavit stating that they have not signed with an agent (nor will they), during the tournament.

This action allows the NCAA to not just penalize the athlete's school, but to pursue the player and his agent for any damages which the school might suffer (loss of revenue from television coverage).

If, when signing an offer sheet, an athlete ceases to perform for his school, would the offer sheet would be enforceable by either the athlete or agent against the other?

FACTS: An offer sheet between a college star, Rudy, and an agent was not disclosed. Rudy continued to play. Upon completing his amateur eligibility, Rudy signed with another agent. The first agent sued Rudy for breach of contract. Could the first agent recover the fees that he would have earned as Rudy's agent? **YOU'RE THE JUDGE!**

DECISION: The defense of unclean hands was used in denying enforcement of the contract. The agent was wrong in signing Rudy before his eligibility was up, and, therefore, he should not benefit from his wrong.

NCAA rules also prohibit an athlete from: negotiating or signing a contract in a sport in which he intends to compete; asking to be placed on a draft list; accepting expenses or gifts from an agent; or receiving preferential treatment or benefits because of outstanding athletic ability.

FACTS: A college player, Frank, who had signed with an agent after his junior year, confessed, "I accepted cash and other favors. Can I still play for my college?" **YOU'RE THE JUDGE!**

DECISION: Frank was in violation of NCAA rules prohibiting him from signing with, or accepting anything of value from, an agent. He forfeited his remaining eligibility. Furthermore, the school could be required to forfeit games in which Frank had played.

However, recent rulings may alter these rules.

FACTS: Chris and Eddy, college football players, admitted, "We took money from agents." They both were declared ineligible to compete further for their college.

Chris petitioned the NFL for entry. NFL rules prohibit eligibility before an athlete's college class has graduated or before four years from when the athlete entered college.

Eddy wanted to have his college eligibility restored. Was either player successful? **YOU'RE THE JUDGE!**

DECISION: Previously, the NFL allowed the drafting of underclassmen who were either kicked out of school or off their team for infractions.

Here, the NFL agreed to draft Chris, made ineligible because of dealings with an agent.

Eddy was permitted to pay back the agent and—by becoming free of any contractual obligations—resumed his collegiate career.

To avoid prosecution, the players agreed to pay back part of their scholarships.

Does this mean that a college athlete can now violate the NFL draft eligibility rules and then, without any consequences, determine whether he wants to remain an amateur or turn pro?

An athlete may compete as a pro in any sport in which he does not participate as an amateur. But he is no longer eligible for any athletic scholarship. He may retain or talk to an agent for that sport only, provided he does not agree to be represented or does not accept anything of value. And an athlete may ask a pro league about his eligibility to be drafted.

FACTS: Tommy, a pro basketball player represented by an agent, John, signed a contract to play in a new league for a team partly owned by John. John had also represented Tommy in attempting to sign with his old team, the Dunkers.

Tommy protested, "John didn't represent me properly. He withheld information which would have affected my decision. I didn't know that he owned the new team." Tommy signed with the new league. Could Tommy rescind his contract with John and play for the Dunkers? **YOU'RE THE JUDGE!**

DECISION: Yes. "No man can faithfully serve two masters" whose interests are in conflict, noted one court. John had a duty to provide Tommy with the best representation. He also had a duty to provide his own team with the best players. These duties conflicted. John may be more interested in Tommy as a player than as a client. The failure to inform Tommy of every material fact that might have influenced his decision, was a breach of duty.

This duty may also be violated where an agent, who represents several players competing for positions on the same team, fails to inform the players of his competing representation.

Misrepresentation & Fraud

An agent may be guilty of **misrepresentation** if he intentionally makes a known and false misrepresentation of an important fact to the player which the player then relies on to his detriment.

FACTS: An agent represented his services to players as one of "total services." The agent said, "I will negotiate your contracts, take your paychecks and bonuses, pay your bills, make investments and put the remainder in trust for you."

The agent signed players and then lost their money through gambling and bad investments. Was this fraud and misrepresentation? **YOU'RE THE JUDGE!**

DECISION: The agent, who deceived players into signing such agreements and misrepresented facts, was convicted of grand larceny. The players received judgments for the lost money, but never collected.

There have also been numerous cases where agents were able to recover commissions earned after the players they represented refused to pay for proper services.

Tampering

An agent who makes improper payments to an athlete may be charged with **tampering**—improperly interfering with another's rights (such as the rights of a school or of those presenting a game).

FACTS: Murray played college football for the Winitoka Tigers. While Murray had college eligibility remaining, an agent, Jansen, gave him money in hopes of representing him in the pros.

When it was discovered that Murray had received the money, he lost his remaining eligibility and was disqualified from playing in his college's bowl game. Jansen was charged with tampering with a sports event by improperly influencing the bowl game. Did Jansen improperly influence the game? **YOU'RE THE JUDGE!**

DECISION: Yes. Jansen was sentenced to one year in jail. He appealed. To avoid prosecution, Murray agreed to pay back part of his scholarship.

ODDS & ENDS....

Bye-Bye!

Unless otherwise agreed, a player is bound by the contract that grants his team the right to assign the player's contract to any other team in the league. However, as it is an individual performance that is bargained for, an athlete may not assign his duties to another.

FACTS: Dink, a pro basketball player for the Hoopsters, objected to being traded to the Ice Breakers. "The trade will disrupt my family and business. And, as my style of play will not fit in with the Ice Breakers, my ability to improve and my pay will suffer." Could Dink prevent the trade? **YOU'RE THE JUDGE!**

DECISION: Unless Dink had a no-trade provision in his contract, his consent to assignment in his contract and promise to "perform for his new team" will generally preclude any objections, including having to move, disruption of family, social and business ties, new climate or city or new teammates or management.

In order to be able to improve, a team needs this right to trade a player. Therefore, a team has broad discretion as to when and whether or not to assign a player's contract.

Regulation

The NCAA has adopted a registration program intended to help athletes select honest and competent representation.

FACTS: Jack, an agent, signed Dana to a contract representing her in negotiations for the Women's Pro Basketball League. Dana signed a contract before her college eligibility had expired. When she graduated, the agent began negotiations, but Dana had decided on another agent. Was the contract enforceable? **YOU'RE THE JUDGE!**

DECISION: No. An agent must register with the school of any player he seeks to represent and state on the contract, "Amateur athletes may jeopardize their athletic eligibility by signing this contract." And, to prevent early, undisclosed signings, an agent must, within five days, file any contract with an athlete with the school, or else it is void and unenforceable.

The NFL now requires all agents, seeking to represent players, to be certified. The maximum fees that may be charged for representation are set by the NFL. Arbitration may be used to settle any dispute.

Other sports provide some protection by requiring signed agreements between a player and an agent be filed. The NBA prevents any team from contacting players until their collegiate eligibility has expired.

In several states, agents must register and are subject to an investigation. Upon proper notice and hearing, their license or registration may be denied, revoked or suspended. This law does not cover agents for athletes in individual sports, such as golf or tennis.

In other states, agents who contact college athletes must obtain a license or face criminal charges.

The same basic principles for the formation of a contract—offer, acceptance and consideration—involving professional athletes applies to everyday agreements, such as those used to buy a home or car.

12

WE'RE IN LABOR

WHAT'S IT ABOUT?

A **union**—called a player's association in professional sports—represents players in bargaining with team owners concerning the player's wages, discipline, safety and other conditions of work in hopes of reaching a Collective Bargaining Agreement. *We're In Labor* explains this process and discusses unfair labor practices, arbitration and strikes.

Can a team renew a player's contract indefinitely? Do you know how players finally became "free agents?"

LET'S ORGANIZE!

The right to form a **union**—a group of people, organized to bargain with their employer concerning wages, hours, grievances, and other terms and conditions of employment—is given by the National Labor Relations Act (NLRA) of 1935.

FACTS: You played pro volleyball for the Spikers in the newly formed American Volleyball League (AVL). You and the other players were concerned about wages, hours, bonuses, job security, rules, safety, equipment and discipline. Several of the players announced, "We'll form a union to help us negotiate an agreement with the owners!" Could you do so?

DECISION: **YOU'RE THE JUDGE!**

This NLRA grew out of the decades of labor strife between labor and management, beginning in the late 1800's and early 1900's when workers attempted to organize the steel mills in Pittsburgh, railroad yards in Chicago and auto manufacturing plants in the Midwest.

Prior to the NLRA, there was no such requirement that employers bargain. Such refusals to bargain led to strikes which, in turn, led to violence as workers set up picket lines in an attempt to keep out non-union workers. Management "blacklisted" the strike leaders, hired non-union labor and employed strike breakers. Often, the purpose of these actions was to create violence rather than prevent it.

Labor disputes also began in sports at this time. The first baseball player's union, The Brotherhood, was formed to deal with owners of baseball teams in the National League over such issues as the reserve clause and salaries. When an agreement couldn't be reached, the players formed their own league. But when the new league failed, the players were offered higher salaries by the National League.

The **National Labor Relations Act (NLRA)** gave employees, "The right to form a union, to bargain collectively, and to engage in other activities necessary for their aid and protection."

FACTS: A majority of the players in the American Volleyball League (AVL) formed a union and elected you president. Must the owners bargain with you over wages and other concerns? **YOU'RE THE JUDGE!**

DECISION: If a majority of the workers (players) in a bargaining unit wish to be represented by a union, then the employers (league and clubs) are required to bargain with the union.

Enforcement?

The NLRA established a **National Labor Relations Board** (Board) to hear charges of, and to prevent, unfair labor practices, as well as to monitor elections to determine if a majority of employees (players) desire union representation. Must the two sides bargain in good faith?

FACTS: One AVL owner admitted, "We cut that player because of his union involvement." The owners also refused to bargain in good faith (make an honest effort to resolve differences and reach an agreement) with the player's union. "What can we do?" you asked. **YOU'RE THE JUDGE!**

DECISION: You would file an unfair labor practice charge. The employers may be guilty of not bargaining with you and for cutting a player due to his union activity. Both of those practices are prohibited.

PLAYER'S ASSOCIATIONS

How does a union become the representative of a group of players?

In professional sports, a player's union is called an association. At a secret election, if a **player's association**—such as all of the players in the AVL—receives a majority vote, then bargaining with the league may begin. If an agreement (Collective Bargaining Agreement) can't be reached—settling disputes between the players and the owners—a strike is likely to follow.

Disputes in professional sports grew out of player demands for more freedom and higher salaries. Babe Ruth was supposedly asked in the midst of the great depression if he felt badly asking for a larger salary than that of the President. "No," replied Ruth, "I had a better year than he did."

Were baseball owners required to bargain with any union representing their players?

FACTS: In 1946, the modern era of sports labor history began. Newspapers reported, BASEBALL PLAYERS ORGANIZE THE AMERICAN BASEBALL GUILD!

When the owners refused to bargain, the Baseball Guild went to the Board. Should the owners, subject to a strike, fine and injunction, be forced to bargain with the Guild? **YOU'RE THE JUDGE!**

DECISION: For the NLRA to apply, labor practices had to involve **interstate commerce**—play or trade among more than one state. Although baseball was played among the states, the Supreme Court held, "Baseball was not interstate commerce!"

Therefore, the Act did not apply. Owners could not be forced to bargain.

However, baseball then changed some league practices, instituting a pension plan, minimum salary, player representation system and a spring training allowance (called "Murphy Money" after the man who organized the Guild).

Player reps took requests and suggestions to the owners, but the owners were not required to bargain. Although a long way from being a union, this system was the forerunner to present day players' associations.

Professional sports leagues have been around for many years, The National League of baseball goes back to 1876. The National Hockey League (NHL) began in 1917. The National Football League (NFL)—first the American Professional Football Association—began in 1920. And the National Basketball Association (NBA) dates to 1946. However, unions representing professional athletes only date back to the 1950's and 1960's.

"How can we get more money and other benefits out of the owners?" asked the players.

FACTS: The key is to become a free agent—able to negotiate with any team—and thus have teams bid up your salary.

Owners fought to prevent free agency. "Through the draft and reserve clause, where the player was reserved to play for only that team holding his contract, his bargaining power was limited. He couldn't sell his services to any other team." How could the players become free agents? **YOU'RE THE JUDGE!**

DECISION: There were two ways a player might accomplish this. One was an antitrust suit, alleging that the player was being prevented from selling his service to the highest bidder. Second was a collective bargaining approach, in which the players would bargain with the owners in hopes of reaching an agreement that would give them free agency status.

It was not until the 1960's that the first collective bargaining agreements in sports were signed. But, it was still unclear whether the Board would hear disputes in pro sports.

The players' union in baseball asked the Board, "Will you please take jurisdiction and hear our cases?"

FACTS: In two cases, one involving the hiring of a union band at an Athletics' baseball game and the other involving major league umpires who wanted an election for union representation, the Board was again asked to hear the cases. Would the Board order an election to allow the umpires to bargain collectively with the owners? **YOU'RE THE JUDGE!**

DECISION: Yes. The Board indicated, "We find that professional baseball (as other pro sports) is an industry affecting commerce, and is subject to our jurisdiction." The Board ordered an election among the umpires, and in so doing markedly altered the future of player-league relations.

Players in all professional sports were now entitled to all of the rights and protection of the National Labor Relations Act (NLRA)—the right to: organize, designate a representative (Player's Association), and bargain collectively with the owners and the league.

NEGOTIATING AN AGREEMENT

Collective bargaining is the process of negotiations between labor (the league) and a union (the players) concerning the mandatory subjects of wages, hours, and other terms and conditions of employment with the goal of arriving at an agreement or settling a dispute.

Any agreement between owners and a player's association covering wages, hours, and other terms and conditions of employment is called a **Collective Bargaining Agreement (CBA).**

Will any agreement reached bind all of the players, even those who are unhappy with it?

FACTS: The players of the AVL now had a player's association. In bargaining with the Owner's Council (representing the owners) a CBA was reached. Tony and several other players asked, "We're unhappy with the agreement. Is it binding on us? Can we negotiate for ourselves?" **YOU'RE THE JUDGE!**

DECISION: If the bargaining process produced an agreement, reached by good faith bargaining over mandatory subjects, in representations of the majority of the players, then the agreement will be binding upon all players, whether or not individual players are satisfied with all of the terms of the agreement.

UNFAIR LABOR PRACTICE?

The NLRA makes it an **unfair labor practice** for an employer (owner) to "interfere with employees (players) in the exercise of the players' rights to organize, to discourage membership or to refuse to bargain collectively." If an owner does so, will they be required to take whatever action is necessary to remedy the unfair labor practice?

FACTS: Several players testified, "The owners, in trying to break our union, cut players during a strike, disciplined others for taking part in union activities, interfered with our activities by trading and eliminating player reps, and advised players that any discussion of strike-related issues would result in a fine, suspension, or other disciplinary action." Were any of these acts unfair labor practices? **YOU'RE THE JUDGE!**

DECISION: All of these acts were unfair labor practices. The teams and their owners were enjoined from such actions, and were also required to take back the players with reinstatement of back pay.

Is it also an unfair labor practice for an employer or employees to refuse to bargain over mandatory subjects?

FACTS: NBA owners, in collective bargaining with the NBA Player's Association, offered, "Let's discuss the college draft, the option clause and compensation for free agents signed by another team."

The player's association refused to bargain, contending, "These subjects are non-mandatory. They all restrain players from bargaining freely for the rendering of their services." Did the player's union have to bargain? **YOU'RE THE JUDGE!**

DECISION: The college draft, option clause, and free agent compensation, all have a direct and substantial impact upon employment, duration, salary, and the ability to transfer between teams, and thus fall within "hours, and other terms and conditions of employment." Therefore, the player's association was under a duty to bargain over these subjects. Their refusal to do so was an unfair labor practice.

WAS THERE GOOD FAITH BARGAINING?

Good faith bargaining is the mutual obligation to meet at reasonable times, to make "relevant and necessary" information available and to confer in "good faith" over mandatory subjects.

FACTS: In bargaining, neither the AVL Player's Association, nor the owners would make concessions, nor could they reach an agreement. In addition, the owners refuse to negotiate over the colors and logos of the league's teams. Was this good faith bargaining? **YOU'RE THE JUDGE!**

DECISION: The players' union and the league only have to bargain in good faith; they are not required to either make concessions or to reach an agreement. Both parties must bargain over mandatory subjects, but are not required to bargain over permissive subjects, such as team colors or logos.

MANDATORY BARGAINING SUBJECTS

Mandatory bargaining subjects, which have to be bargained over by the player's association and owners, are those subjects covered by "wages, hours, and other matters affecting the terms and conditions of employment."

FACTS: The NBA established a maximum salary cap—the maximum amount any NBA team could pay its players.

When the N.J. Nets reached their salary cap, they were only permitted to offer their number one draft pick a one-year contract for a much smaller amount than other similar draft picks were receiving.

The player sued, alleging, "The draft and the salary cap are illegal restraints of trade—preventing me from earning my full, free market value." Did the draft and salary cap illegally restrain trade? **YOU'RE THE JUDGE!**

DECISION: No. The draft and salary cap were mandatory subjects—requiring them to be bargained over. They were bargained over in good faith between the league and the player's association. Therefore, they are protected by labor laws. They could not be challenged as being antitrust—restraints of trade.

Mandatory subjects may cover a very wide range of items, from artificial turf to certain league rules. An employer may institute unilateral changes concerning permissive subjects of bargaining. For example, if playing rules are permissive subjects of bargaining, sports leagues could change them without first bargaining with the player's union.

FACTS: Major league baseball team owners instituted random drug-testing clauses into players' contracts. The players contended, "This is a mandatory subject, requiring bargaining and an agreement before they may be inserted into our contracts." Did the owners have to negotiate over the testing clauses? **YOU'RE THE JUDGE!**

DECISION: An arbitrator ruled that teams violated the collective bargaining agreement by including the testing clauses without negotiation with the player's union. However, testing would still be allowed where there was probable cause to believe that a player was using drugs.

The problem is distinguishing between what is mandatory and what is not. A player's union may think that most matters bear some relationship to wages, hours, and other terms and conditions of employment. Owners objected to this view "We shouldn't have to bargain over every little thing," they contended.

FACTS: The first major sports cases concerning mandatory bargaining subjects involved an NFL rule which fined any player who left the bench while a fight was in progress on the field.

As to the use of artificial turf, the players felt it was responsible for a number of injuries. Were these mandatory subjects requiring bargaining in good faith before their implementation? **YOU'RE THE JUDGE!**

DECISION: Yes. The Board held, "The rule to fine players was unilaterally implemented by the owners. It was an unfair labor practice."

The Board further concluded, "Artificial turf was a condition of employment and, therefore, a mandatory bargaining subject, but that the council had met its obligation of good faith bargaining by discussing the matter with the union."

Several years later, the NFL implemented both "sudden death" (to eliminate ties), and a new punt rule. The NFL Player's Association felt, "Both rules subject the players to an undue risk of injury and are a change in work conditions which should have been discussed beforehand." Should they have?

It was decided, "The playing rules were mandatory subjects for bargaining, but that the owners' invitation for the association's views satisfied their duty to bargain in good faith."

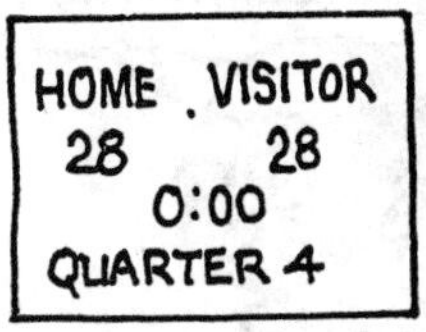

FACTS: Which of the following are mandatory subjects: wages, hours and other terms and conditions of employment? Which will require bargaining between owners and players?

- Disciplinary and safety rules.
- Scheduling—game rules and season length.
- Arbitration—salary, grievance & injury.
- Reserve system-draft, option, trades & free agency.
- Contract negotiations—salary, bonuses, guaranteed, no-cut, no-trade. **YOU'RE THE JUDGE!**

DECISION: Except for individual contract negotiations, all of these subjects require mandatory bargaining before they may be included in a collective bargaining agreement between owners and a player's association.

AN ATHENS NEWS
SECTION B

RESERVED!

"Through collective bargaining, the reserve system was drastically changed. For the first time, players were given rights concerning the draft, option clauses, free agency and salary.

The option clause and salary issues became subject to arbitration with results that were to 'free' the players from the restrictive reserve system of the past. Thus was born the **'free agent'**—a player playing out his option and becoming eligible to negotiate and sign with any team."

Collective bargaining led to agreements between owners and players providing for much less compensation for free agents.

In the NBA and NFL, a team with a restricted free agent player who has signed with another team in the league, may have a **right of first refusal**—where the losing team has the option of signing the free agent for the amount agreed upon between the player and the other team. However, in the NBA, this right will not apply to five year veterans. They automatically become free agents with no compensation to the player's former team.

If the player is not re-signed in the NBA, there is no compensation. In the NFL, the team losing a restricted free agent receives draft choices from the signing team. Unrestricted free agents, those not on a protected list, may bargain freely with any team. If signed, the losing team receives no compensation.

In baseball and soccer, there is no compensation for a lost free agent. In the NHL, if the two teams can't agree on compensation, then an arbitrator decides.

Although some sports require more compensation than others, all have helped players to increase their value by making their services more readily available to other competing teams.

PROTECTION FOR AGREEMENTS?

Antitrust laws might make **restraints of trade**—restrictions on a player's ability to trade his services with other teams—illegal. However, the labor law exemption to the antitrust laws provides, "Any agreement between owners and a player's association over mandatory subjects, if negotiated in good faith, is protected from antitrust laws."

FACTS: Players in the AVL contended, "Restrictions on our mobility to move between teams were illegal restraints of trade."

The owners replied, "The restrictions were mandatory subjects of bargaining, were bargained for, and therefore are protected by the labor exemption." The owner's negotiations were "take-it-or-leave-it." Was any agreement reached protected? **YOU'RE THE JUDGE!**

DECISION: The courts found that negotiations were unilateral and not bargained for in good faith. Therefore, the reserve system, including draft and compensation rules, was illegal. The labor exemption would not protect them until they were negotiated over in good faith bargaining.

To encourage resolve of disputes between owners and players over terms and conditions of work or the players' right to organize, "No injunction shall be granted, except as necessary, to prevent an irreparable injury."

ARBITRATION & GRIEVANCES

What is arbitration? **Arbitration** is a method of resolving disputes between owners and players in which parties submit their dispute to an impartial third party (arbitrator) for resolution— a decision. Will a court enforce any decision?

FACTS: The owners and players in the AVL negotiated an agreement (CBA) which had an arbitration clause to resolve disputes concerning salaries, injury and discipline. When Jose, a star forward for the Rockets, was suspended for abusing an official, he snapped, "I'll sue in court for reinstatement!" Could he? **YOU'RE THE JUDGE!**

DECISION: No. Where the parties agree to arbitration, the player and club lose the right to go to court, with narrow exceptions. Only if the arbitration clause does not extend to a particular claim can an injured party use the courts. However, the courts can be used to enforce any arbitration award.

A court will seldom vacate an arbitration award, unless the arbitrator "exceeded his authority, did not have jurisdiction to hear the matter, or where there was fraud or misconduct." If no jurisdiction is found, then a court will resolve any dispute.

IMPARTIAL ARBITRATION?

FACTS: The players in the AVL maintained, "We were forced to settle for a grievance system which calls for arbitration before the commissioner of all disputes dealing with discipline, salary, performance and trades. The commissioner was selected and paid for by the owners." Was this impartial arbitration? **YOU'RE THE JUDGE!**

DECISION: No. The commissioner had acted without authority and was not fair and impartial.

Collective bargaining agreements had diminished the commisssioner's or president's power to matters relating to player contracts, discipline and the integrity of the game. They were replaced by the impartial arbitrator. Baseball, in 1970, selected its first impartial arbitrator for handling disputes.

Player contracts now had salary, injury, performance, conduct, dismissal and dispute clauses calling for impartial grievance or arbitration procedures.

GIVE ME FREEDOM!

Disputes over the reserve system in baseball led to the beginning of "freedom" for all professional athletes in team sports.

Generally, teams released a player only when he was no longer of use to them or of value on the trading block. Such was not the case with Ken Harrelson, who got into a dispute with Mr. Finley, the owner of the A's, for whom he played. Harrelson was fired, thus becom-

ing a free agent. The bidding was fierce; he wound up signing with the Red Sox for a substantial salary increase.

A few years later, Catfish Hunter and Finley also had a disagreement.

FACTS: In 1974, Hunter negotiated a contract with the A's. Finley refused to make some of the payments. Hunter claimed, "Since Finley breached the contract, it was void." The dispute went to arbitration.

Finley argued, "The arbitrators should allow me to make the payments due, thereby forcing Hunter to continue to play for my team." Did Finley breach the contract, making Hunter a free agent, and consequently able to deal with any team? **YOU'RE THE JUDGE!**

DECISION: The independent arbitrator treated the contract as void and released Hunter from any services under the contract, thus making him a free agent.

Bidding for Hunter's services was also fierce. Finally, the Yankees won out, paying Catfish substantially more than what he had earned with the A's.

Players were now aware of the gains to be made as free agents. They began to bargain more vigorously. Several refused to sign new contracts, deciding instead to play out their option year. And, although most eventually signed, a few didn't.

NORTHEASTERN LAW REPORTER

The year was 1975. Andy Messersmith, a pitcher for the Dodgers, decided not to sign a contract, but instead to play out his option. The Dodgers exercised their option to renew the contract for 1975 and Messersmith played under those conditions. When the season ended, Messersmith declared, "I am now a free agent, free to negotiate with any team for my services!"

Dave McNally, a pitcher for Montreal, also refused to sign a contract for the 1975 season, thereby forcing Montreal to renew his contract under the option clause.

The player's association filed a grievance, asserting, "Both players should be declared free agents." And to prevent other clubs from blacklisting them, they argued, "The language in the Player's Contract, 'The Club shall have the right to renew this contract for the period of one year on the same terms,' gave the club the right to extend the contract for one year only, at which time the player's relationship with the club was terminated."

The Dodgers responded, "When we exercised our option to renew the contract, the renewal was of all the terms in the contract, including the term which gave us the right to renew again, thus we could renew perpetually. Furthermore, Messersmith was on our reserve list, thereby preventing other teams from negotiating with him."

Were Messersmith and McNally free agents, or could the teams renew their contracts again, and again, and again?

The Arbitrator ruled that Messersmith and McNally were indeed free agents, free to bargain with any club, and that they were no longer on any reserve list, as that list applied only to players under contract. "The clubs did not have the right to renew any contract beyond the renewal period of one year."

McNally had retired, but Messersmith, after spirited bidding for his services, signed with Atlanta for a substantial salary increase.

This decision ended the reserve system as it had existed. Many players began to play out their options and negotiate with other teams for increased salaries.

In order to promote competition, fan interest and team identity, the baseball owners and the player's association created a new reserve system. Thus, although the reserve system remained, protected by the labor exemption to the antitrust laws, it was less restrictive. It gave players much more freedom to bargain with other teams.

What if the baseball owners decided to "hold down" the free agency market by not signing them?

FACTS: Owners of major league baseball teams refused to offer contracts to free agents, thus forcing them to re-sign with their original teams for less money.

The owners were found guilty of collusion and conspiracy in holding down salaries by stifling the free agency market. But what damages would the players receive? Monetary damages? Free agency again? **YOU'RE THE JUDGE!**

DECISION: Those players who did not have the opportunity to become free agents were declared free. Any team signing them would not have to compensate the losing team. Any free agent not signed could remain with his present team. All affected players could file for money damages.

Arbitration was now used to resolve many disputes such as: free agency compensation, contract disputes, performance, salary, discipline, waivers, fines, and injury grievances.

FACTS: "Johnson, a pro basketball player, was acting defiant, uncooperative and peculiar," testified an official. He was given a disciplinary suspension for his conduct.

The player's association explained, "Medical testimony at an arbitration hearing will show that Johnson should have been placed on the disabled list because of an emotional illness." Should the team have been required to submit the dispute to arbitration? **YOU'RE THE JUDGE!**

DECISION: Yes. The matter was submitted to arbitration. It was concluded, "Johnson should have been placed on the disabled list, instead of given a disciplinary suspension for conduct resulting from emotional illness."

STRIKES & LOCKOUTS

A **strike** (the primary weapon of the players)—is the act of refusing to work—as a means of forcing owners or a league to give in to player demands.

The primary economic weapon of the owners is the **lockout**—locking the players out of work—as a means of forcing them to agree with the owners.

Unless otherwise agreed, a lockout clause in a professional athlete's contract would prevent the player from being paid in the event of a labor dispute.

Collective bargaining agreements typically include a "no strike-no lockout" provision in which the player's union agrees not to engage in any strike or other action interfering with the operation of the league, and the league or any of its clubs agree that they will not engage in any lockout of players. When may players strike or owners lockout the players?

FACTS: Players in the AVL were unhappy with their Collective Bargaining Agreement (CBA). The agreement contained a no strike-no lockout provision. "Can we strike? What will happen if we strike before the agreement expires?" they asked. **YOU'RE THE JUDGE!**

DECISION: Strikes and lockouts will generally occur after a collective bargaining agreement containing the no strike—no lockout provision has expired.

The NLRA guarantees players the right to engage in strikes. Generally, no restraining order or injunction prohibiting a strike or lockout will be issued unless the strike or lockout occurs while an agreement is in effect.

Without the ability to enjoin strikes or lockouts, the effectiveness of arbitration or collective bargaining agreements would be greatly reduced.

There have been numerous strikes and lockouts in professional sports, most of them leading to additional benefits and to more freedom for players from the reserve system.

ODDS & ENDS....

Arbitration

FACTS: Babe and Lou couldn't agree with their baseball teams on salaries. They asked for salary arbitration. How will an arbitrator decide the matter?

Speedy, a star running back for the Dolphins, had an injury grievance with his team. The team warned, "He's ready to play. If he doesn't, we'll cut him."

Speedy responded, "I haven't recovered from an injury that I got while playing, and therefore, I should still be paid." How will arbitration resolve this matter?

A number of players from all sports were found to be gambling and fighting. How would they be dealt with? **YOU'RE THE JUDGE!**

DECISION: Baseball salary arbitration uses a "high-low" system where qualified players and their teams submit their offers to the arbitrator. The arbitrator chooses one or the other, with no room for change.

For injury grievances in football, each party presents his own medical opinion to an arbitrator. If the opinions differ, an impartial physician renders an opinion. These three opinions are then given to the arbitrator for a decision.

Matters involving the integrity of the game or player discipline are under the sole authority of the commissioner or president, whose decision is final and binding. A player or team may appeal the decision only to the commissioner or president, who may then conduct a hearing, receiving evidence upon which he will base his final decision.

The rulings that made baseball players free agents have had a great effect not only on professional team players' and others' salaries, but also on the price that you pay to see professional team sports.

13

ANTITRUST - ANTIWHO?

WHAT'S IT ABOUT?

Antitrust—AntiWho? examines **antitrust** in sports—practices designed to illegally monopolize a sport by restraining or preventing players from competing or by stifling competition.

Do you know which major sport is exempt from antitrust laws, or how such laws affect other sports?

ANTITRUST

FACTS: The Spikers were part of the new National Volleyball League (NVL), which had franchises in most major markets. Attendance and TV ratings were booming and, with no competition or large salaries, ticket prices were kept up.

Along came the United Volleyball League (UVL), attempting to franchise teams into some of the remaining markets. One UVL owner grumbled, "We're having problems competing with the NVL. They've signed most of the quality players." Even so, NVL attendance and TV ratings began to fall.

The NVL owners suggested, "Let's expand into the markets where the UVL has teams."

The NVL "proposed" to its arenas and equipment dealers, "Only sell your products and rent space to the NVL. After the UVL is driven out of business, there will be no competition. We'll take care of you." They all agreed.

The UVL contended, "The NVL and its arenas and equipment dealers are attempting to monopolize pro volleyball by illegally conspiring to restrain trade (by not renting the arenas and selling equipment to the UVL at a fair price), and by expanding with the sole purpose of eliminating us from competition."

The players of the NVL wanted increased salaries, more freedom and other benefits. But, because of the draft and reserve clause, the players couldn't deal with anyone else. This kept salaries down. The NVL attempted to stop the players from forming a union by breaking up meetings and refusing to bargain with them.

In an attempt to end these problems, the NVL considered offering the UVL the chance to be taken over by, or to merge their most solvent teams into, the NVL, thus eliminating the need for high salaries. With no competition, the NVL could once again have a monopoly in pro volleyball.

Was this **antitrust**—practices designed to prevent full and free competition in an attempt to eliminate competition, illegally monopolize pro volleyball, restrain competitors from competing for players, arenas and fans, and restrain players from trading their services to other teams?

DECISION: **YOU'RE THE JUDGE!**

Professional sports leagues have used the draft and reserve clause to distribute superstars among teams and thus maintain interest, balance and competition. This attempt to monopolize players' services by restraining their mobility is opposite the players' interest in being free to sell their services to the highest bidder.

Furthermore, a league may also attempt to exclude or restrain weaker competitors from competition for fans and media support.

These competing interests between players, teams and competitors may involve activity that is contrary to fair competition.

What must be shown to prove that an activity is unlawful? In determining whether any activity is unlawful, it must be shown that the activity unreasonably restrained trade or commerce, and that it was not exempt from antitrust laws.

FAIR COMPETITION & MONOPOLY

The first known case dealing with antitrust was decided in 1414.

FACTS: Richard was sued for breaching an agreement to not "use his art of a cloth dyer's craft within the town for half a year." He had sold the business and agreed, "I will ply my trade elsewhere so as to not take customers away from the new owner." Did such an agreement restrain Richard from his trade? **YOU'RE THE JUDGE!**

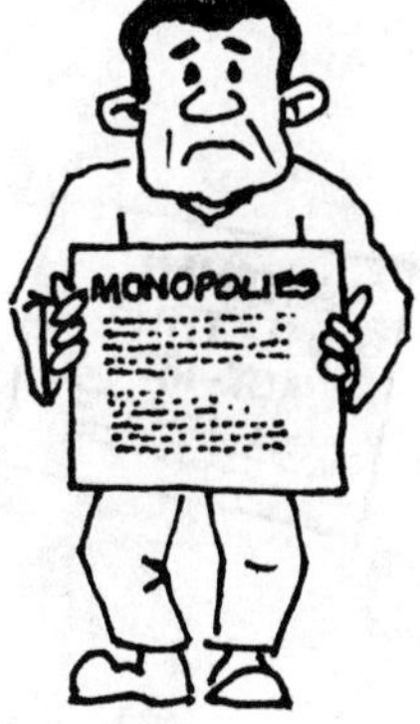

DECISION: The court reasoned that this was an attempt at a restraint which was void as being against common law supporting fair competition and protection of a free market.

Now the year was 1602. You were a judge in the courts of England and were called upon to hear the following case.

FACTS: Allen made and sold playing cards. But Queen Elizabeth had granted Darcy "the sole right to sell playing cards in England."

Darcy took Allen to court, alleging, "Allen is infringing on my exclusive right to sell playing cards." He asked that you "restrain Allen from his trade."

Allen responded, "Darcy's grant from the Queen amounted to a **monopoly**—exclusive control of goods (cards) or services (advice on using goods). Darcy's grant limits and restricts my right to purchase, sell, or exchange cards or advice." Will you dismiss Darcy's suit? **YOU'RE THE JUDGE!**

DECISION: Yes. You applied the common law and decided, "Darcy was attempting to monopolize the business of selling playing cards. This practice infringed on Allen's right, privilege, freedom and opportunity to engage in a trade. Darcy's grant, if it were allowed to stand with no competition, might lead to higher priced and poorer quality cards."

Furthermore, it would harm not only Allen and any future competitors, but would deprive the public of a choice of playing cards. Darcy's suit was dismissed. Allen could make and sell playing cards.

This developing law and the Statute of Monopolies (making most monopolies void or voidable) was merged into the common law of the new colonies in America.

Dissatisfaction with the common law's protection and, with concern over the abusive practices by corporate giants in the mid to late 1800's, led to not only the Sherman Antitrust Act, but to other antitrust laws as well.

SHERMAN ANTITRUST ACT

John Sherman, a U.S. Senator, felt that "businesses must conform to rules" to prevent unfair competition and, thus, promote free and fair competition and protect the public. This would give the little man a chance to compete with the giants.

So that the public might have better prices, service, quality, choice and innovative products, Senator Sherman proposed a bill to deal with illegal **trusts**—business firms combined for the purpose of controlling prices or eliminating competition—and, **combinations**—groups of businesses—that prevent full and free competition and tend to increase the costs to the consumer.

The bill, passed in 1890, was known as the **Sherman Antitrust Act.** It was an act opposing and aimed against trusts—antitrust—that would protect trade and interstate commerce against unlawful restraints and monopolies.

FACTS: Testimony proved, "The World Croquet League (WCL) illegally monopolized that sport throughout the U.S., and; the Western Horseshoe League (WHL) illegally monopolized that sport in California." Would the Sherman Antitrust Act prevent these monopolies? **YOU'RE THE JUDGE!**

DECISION: The Sherman Antitrust Act is a federal antitrust law, concerned with the regulation of activity in **interstate commerce**—trade of goods or services among different states. This act would prevent the WCL's monopoly.

If a monopoly exists solely within one state—**intrastate**—such as by the WHL, enforcement would have to be by state antitrust acts.

Section 1 of the Sherman Antitrust Act provides that every contract, combination of companies (teams), or conspiracy, which restrains interstate trade or commerce is illegal. This section requires that there be an agreement by more than one person or team.

FACTS: Did the NVL violate this section by conspiring to control prices (to eliminate competition) by restraining interstate trade and commerce between the UVL and the arenas and equipment dealers, and by expansion, designed to eliminate competition? **YOU'RE THE JUDGE!**

DECISION: These were violations of section 1 of the Sherman Act. There was an agreement between the owners and teams in the NVL.

Section 2 of the Sherman Antitrust Act provides that every person or team who monopolizes, or attempts, or conspires to monopolize interstate commerce shall be found guilty. Here, one person or team may act alone.

FACTS: Did the NVL conspire in an attempt to monopolize interstate trade or commerce in the professional volleyball market? **YOU'RE THE JUDGE!**

DECISION: The NVL, equipment dealers and arenas all violated Section 2 of the Sherman Act prohibiting conspiracies to monopolize.

Furthermore, the NVL's draft may have violated the Sherman Act as an attempt to monopolize pro volleyball by restraining players from trading their services to other teams.

A court may issue an injunction prohibiting such conduct.

CLAYTON ANTITRUST ACT

This act supplements the Sherman Antitrust Act and other existing laws against unlawful restraints and monopolies.

Section 2 of the **Clayton Antitrust Act** (1914) prohibits **price discrimination**—where a different price is charged to similarly situated buyers.

> FACTS: The equipment dealers and arena operators announced to the UVL, "You can buy our equipment or rent our arenas, but at higher prices than we charge the NVL." Was this discrimination? **YOU'RE THE JUDGE!**

> DECISION: The equipment dealers and arenas were guilty of price discrimination.

Section 3 of the Clayton Antitrust Act makes it unlawful to sell, or offer to buy, goods or services on the condition that the buyer will not buy from a competitor of the seller, or that the seller will not sell to any other, where the effect is to lessen competition and create a monopoly.

> FACTS: Were the NVL, equipment dealers and arenas in violation of this section where the NVL offered to the arenas and equipment dealers, "We'll rent or buy from you, if you will refuse to deal with NVL competitors." Would such practices be illegal? **YOU'RE THE JUDGE!**

> DECISION: As these practices will lessen competition and promote a monopoly, they are violations and illegal.

This is called a **boycott**— an agreement refusing or refraining to deal—sometimes called a group boycott or blacklisting.

Are player's unions permitted to solicit members or to strike? Must a league bargain with them?

Section 6 of the Clayton Antitrust Act permits unions (player's associations) and its members to carry out legitimate objectives, such as bargaining, soliciting and striking. Furthermore, the Act prohibits any injunction involving a dispute over terms or conditions of employment. This allows bargaining, soliciting and strikes, free from restraint.

Thus, the NVL can't prevent players from attempting to unionize, and the NVL would be required to bargain in good faith with any elected player's union.

> FACTS: Were the attempts by the NVL to prevent players from soliciting for union members, and their refusal to bargain, in violation of this section?

DECISION: **YOU'RE THE JUDGE!**

Section 7 of the Clayton Antitrust Act prohibits **acquisitions** (acquiring) or **mergers** (joining together) of teams where the effect may be to substantially lessen competition and create a monopoly.

FACTS: Will any acquisition by the NVL of any of the UVL teams, or any merger between the two leagues, be in violation of this section?

DECISION: **YOU'RE THE JUDGE!**

On a showing of irreparable harm, the Clayton Antitrust Act provides for an **injunction**—either a temporary or permanent restraining order prohibiting illegal activities.

FACTS: May the NVL, dealers and the arenas be enjoined from any of their practices? **YOU'RE THE JUDGE!**

DECISION: If it is likely that the UVL will prevail, the court will issue a temporary restraining order, enjoining the NVL from illegal activities which may cause irreparable harm. If the UVL should win at trial on any of the above violations, the court would then issue a permanent injunction.

FEDERAL TRADE COMMISSION ACT

The Federal Trade Commission Act declares that unfair or deceptive practices in interstate commerce are unlawful. It established the **Federal Trade Commission** to aid in the enforcement of the Sherman and Clayton Antitrust Acts in protecting consumers as well as competitors.

THIS IS A TEST!

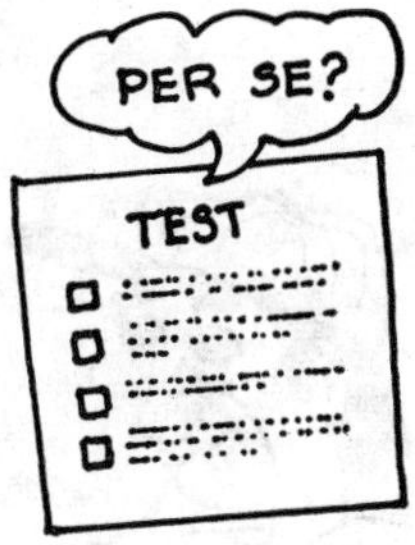

A court may use two tests in helping it determine if restraints on trade or commerce are unlawful.

The first is called the **per se** (by itself) **rule.** It holds that, "Certain agreements or practices, because of their deadly effect on competition and lack of any redeeming value, are unreasonable and illegal, without inquiry as to the harm they have caused or the reason for their use."

FACTS: The NVL, in order to restrain trade (keep the UVL from competing), agreed to fix prices with the dealers and arenas, allocate territory and boycott the UVL. They also offered to acquire or merge with the UVL. Should these practices be governed by the per se rule? **YOU'RE THE JUDGE!**

DECISION: Agreements having no objective other than to restrain trade and whose principal effect is to govern prices or foreclose markets are undue restraints of trade and per se illegal.

The second test is called the **rule of reason.** It holds that, "The legality of restraints on trade is determined by weighing all factors, such as the effect of any restraints on competition, the power of the parties and the economic conditions or the evil believed to exist."

FACTS: Did the NVL, dealers and arenas, by their agreements and practices designed to close out the UVL, violate the rule of reason?

DECISION: **YOU'RE THE JUDGE!**

ANTITRUST EXEMPTIONS

There are exemptions to the antitrust laws, the most notable being baseball. All other sports fall under the umbrella of antitrust protection.

The effect of an exemption is to make "certain conduct free from the obligations of antitrust laws." These exemptions are permitted in the interest of promoting competition.

Baseball

When an arbitrator's ruling held that baseball's reserve clause only bound a player for a one-year option, the perpetual right to renew a player's contract after it expired (which the club owners had for ninety years) was eliminated.

In collective bargaining, a compromise was reached between the clubs and the players. The clubs retained exclusive rights to its players for a number of years, after which the players would become free agents. This allowed players greater mobility in selling their services to other teams.

Even though its reserve clause has been modified, baseball still enjoys its long-standing immunity from the antitrust laws.

FACTS: In 1922, the National League (NL) sought to monopolize baseball by buying some clubs and inducing the others in a rival league, except one, to join them. The one club left alleged, "This is a conspiracy to monopolize baseball by eliminating competition. Isn't it a violation of the Sherman Act?" **YOU'RE THE JUDGE!**

DECISION: The court held that baseball was purely a state affair. Any transportation across state lines was not the essential thing, that being the business of giving exhibitions of baseball.

The court reasoned, "Because the travel was incidental, it was not interstate travel and the exhibitions were personal effort and not trade or commerce." Therefore, the Sherman Act didn't apply!

Would the courts, in more modern times, do away with baseball's exemption to antitrust laws?

The Supreme Court affirmed baseball's exemption when Curt Flood, a major league baseball player, brought an action charging that the reserve clause in his contract significantly impaired his ability to sell his services. The Court applied the doctrine of **stare decisis**—a policy whereby the court does not disturb previous case rulings. And so, baseball remained an exception to the general rule applying antitrust laws to sports.

Would You Like To Merge?

FACTS: The Clayton Act prohibits mergers whose effect may be to lessen competition and create a monopoly. The American Football League (AFL) and the National Football League (NFL) wanted to merge, as did the American Basketball Association (ABA) and the National Basketball Association (NBA). Would such mergers lessen competition and create a monopoly? Should they have been allowed to merge? **YOU'RE THE JUDGE!**

DECISION: Congress approved the mergers, deciding, "Antitrust laws shall not apply to an agreement by which two leagues combine into an expanded league, if this would increase rather than decrease the number of professional clubs so operating." The assumption was that the other leagues would otherwise have folded.

Collective Bargaining Agreements

The Clayton Act provides, "Antitrust laws shall not forbid or restrain unions from carrying out their activities."

If a player's union and league undertake to settle player-related issues, and if they reach an agreement which is the result of good faith bargaining—**collective bargaining agreement** (CBA),—will the labor exemption to antitrust laws prevent a court from reviewing the agreement?

FACTS: The players of the NVL organized a player's association and then began bargaining with the owners. After reaching agreement on a draft, the reserve system and other matters, the players—by majority vote—approved the agreement. The players, for these concessions to the league, received increased salaries, better retirement benefits, and less restrictive work conditions and rules.

Several players, unhappy with the agreement, sued, arguing, "The draft and reserve system are a violation of the antitrust laws prohibiting the restraint of players from selling their services." Was the Collective Bargaining Agreement (CBA) a violation of antitrust laws? **YOU'RE THE JUDGE!**

DECISION: Although some issues, such as player-related rules and movement of clubs are not protected by the labor exemption, the players will have to abide by the agreement.

The judge noted, "The labor exemption reflects a policy strongly favoring negotiation between clubs and players in order to resolve disputes." The union's interest in insuring employment for the players may require accepting restraints—such as a draft and option clause—on player mobility in return for the concessions of increased pay and other benefits.

Will any such agreement bind players who are not members of the association (such as unsigned draft picks)?

Even though an amateur athlete is not part of the bargaining unit, the courts have held that a player's association may bind these new entrants to a league.

But, where leagues did not conduct good faith bargaining, the courts rejected the league's right to protect its draft and reserve systems within the labor exemption. Proper bargaining then resulted in exempt agreements.

What kind of approval is needed by a union? The labor exemption will only be applied to those agreements which have been approved by the union. Approval must be more than passive consent; it must be the product of serious, good faith bargaining.

FACTS: Kapp, Smith, Mackey and other players alleged, "The draft system, Rozelle Rule (which gave the commissioner authority to determine compensation to a team for loss of a free agent), and the standard player contract restrained our ability to market our services among competing teams." The player's union's approval of these practices was not the product of good faith bargaining. Would the labor exemption apply to these practices? **YOU'RE THE JUDGE!**

DECISION: The court held, "These practices were not the product of good faith, serious bargaining and therefore, not immune from antitrust laws.

The annual player draft was a group boycott. The Rozelle rule was a nonmandatory, illegal subject. The labor law exemption only applies to mandatory subjects of collective bargaining, wages, hours and other terms and conditions of employment. "The league might avoid further antitrust problems by entering into meaningful collective bargaining with the player's union," commented the court.

Sports Broadcasting Act

The **Sports Broadcasting Act of 1961** exempted professional sports leagues from antitrust attack for controlling the broadcasting rights to sporting events. This allowed each major pro sports league to pool and sell the rights of its clubs, as a package, to networks. Congress granted a limited antitrust exemption, but only to leagues.

FACTS: Several boxing promoters acquired all broadcasting and movie revenues from fights involving champions and contenders, and in all of the principal arenas where championships could be successfully held. They required each title contender to agree, as a condition to fighting for the championship, that if he won, he would only take part in title fights promoted by them. As a result, they had promoted 19 of the last 21 championship fights.

The Government charged, "The defendant promoters were engaged in interstate commerce because of their negotiations and ticket sales across state lines. By their acts and by eliminating the leading competing promoter, they restrained and monopolized trade." Did they? **YOU'RE THE JUDGE!**

DECISION: The defendants restrained trade (prevented other promoters from competing) and monopolized the promotion of championship fights, both in violation of the Sherman Act.

Blackouts

The Sports Broadcasting Act's exemption also covered television blackouts of NFL regular season and play-off games to protect ticket sales.

But this limited exemption is denied for any agreement prohibiting the televising of other games.

FACTS: NFL bylaws provided that no team would have their game broadcast by television or radio, within 75 miles of another team's home game or, away game broadcast at home without permission from the home team. The commissioner had an unlimited power to prevent any team from broadcasting any of its games.

The U.S. Government alleged, "This practice illegally restrains trade by restraining teams from the choice of where to broadcast their games." Was this practice illegal? **YOU'RE THE JUDGE!**

DECISION: The league's bylaws restrained the sale of broadcasting (trade) in interstate commerce, and were illegal. A new contract restricting the individual teams from determining where their games would be broadcast was also prohibited.

Furthermore, the Sports Broadcasting Act's exemption prohibits the televising of any NFL football game on a Friday eve or on any Saturday between the second Friday in September and the second Saturday in December from any station located within 75 miles of any college or high school football game. The purpose of this statute is to protect attendance at such school's games.

And pro football games not sold out 72 hours before the start of the game may be blacked out.

Can an NFL team prevent the televising of their games within their "home territory?"

FACTS: Two TV stations, one within 40 miles of Miami, and one not, wanted to televise Dolphins home games. Both signals reached into the 40 mile area. The NFL prohibited such televising.

The stations wanted to know, "Is such a prohibition an illegal restraint of trade—restraining us from carrying the games?" **YOU'RE THE JUDGE!**

DECISION: Agreements prohibiting the televising of an NFL home game, without permission, from within or without a team's home territory—40 miles in any direction—on the day when the team is playing at home are exempt from the antitrust laws. Teams needed this protection in order to protect gate sales.

Is baseball broadcasting also exempt from antitrust laws? Broadcasting of baseball does not fall within that sports exemption to the antitrust laws.

FACTS: An owner of a baseball team breached a contract with one radio station and then conspired with another to eliminate competition for the game's radio audience. Did baseball's exemption to the antitrust laws protect this conspiracy to restrain competition from broadcasting the games? **YOU'RE THE JUDGE!**

DECISION: Broadcasting, although related, is separate and distinct from baseball. It is not protected. The conspiracy could be enjoined or prohibited.

OTHER PROFESSIONAL SPORTS

Professional sports affect interstate trade by the sale of broadcast rights to games, and by employing and dealing with organizations, people and player's associations located throughout the country.

In cases involving the attempt to exclude or eliminate competition—monopoly (the refusal to deal with others)—group boycotts, and the use of a draft, courts have held that, except for baseball, all other sports are subject to antitrust laws.

Some cases have ruled on underlying issues in addition to holding that antitrust laws apply to that sport and therefore, the sport is not exempt from antitrust laws.

Auto Racing

FACTS: In an Indianapolis 500 race, the STP car completely outran the competition. Following that race, the United States Auto Club (USAC), sanctioning organization for professional championship auto races, changed its rules and required modification of the car's engines.

STP challenged the rule change as, "An unlawful exercise of monopolistic power in restraint of trade, in that it discriminated against us and is unreasonable." Would the court enjoin USAC from enforcing this rule? **YOU'RE THE JUDGE!**

DECISION: No. The court decided, "The rule change was a proper exercise of USAC's power to promote equal competition in auto racing." Furthermore, USAC did not have monopoly power as membership in USAC was not required and the rule change applied equally to all participants.

Bowling

FACTS: Several bowling centers brought an antitrust action against Brunswick, one of the two largest equipment manufacturers and the largest operator of bowling centers in the U.S.

They contended, "The defendant Brunswick, by acquiring competing bowling centers that could not pay for equipment bought from Brunswick, might lessen competition and create a monopoly." Was this a monopoly? **YOU'RE THE JUDGE!**

DECISION: No. Had the acquired centers secured financing elsewhere and remained open, the plaintiffs would have suffered the same loss. "Mere size, without unlawful intent or conduct, is not a violation of antitrust laws," noted the court.

Boxing

Several boxing promoters were found in violation of the Sherman Act for monopolizing the promotion of championship fights, and for restraining others from promoting such fights.

Football

FACTS: A pro football player broke the reserve clause of his contract and signed with a team in a rival league. When suspended from playing in the NFL, he brought an action arguing, "The NFL conspired to monopolize pro football by blacklisting me from playing."

The NFL countered, "Pro football was not meant to be included within the reach of the antitrust laws." Was pro football subject to the antitrust laws? **YOU'RE THE JUDGE!**

DECISION: Yes. The court held that pro football operated in interstate commerce and was not exempt from such laws.

Golf

The Professional Golfers Association (PGA), which sponsors professional golf tournaments, adopted eligibility rules limiting entry by excluding golfers who did not meet certain requirements. This was thought necessary because there was neither enough time nor space on the golf courses to accommodate a large field.

Art, a pro golfer, complained, "My contract to play on the tour was terminated because of my lousy play." He brought an action alleging, "The PGA conspired to monopolize professional golf tournaments. Furthermore, they restrained me from my trade—playing golf."

The court held, "The PGA is entitled to adopt reasonable measures to keep tournaments to a manageable number. In so doing, they treated all golfers alike." There was no attempt to restrain golf pros or to monopolize tournament golf.

Several other cases have dealt with golf equipment.

FACTS: Polara developed a golf ball that was said to limit hooking and slicing by self-correcting in flight.

The U.S. Golf Association (USGA) refused to approve the ball for its competitions, stating, "A legitimate goal of the USGA is to preserve the character and integrity of the game."

Polara sued, claiming the USGA conspired to restrain and restrict the sale of their ball. Was this an illegal restraint of trade? **YOU'RE THE JUDGE!**

DECISION: The court found no illegal restraint of trade. It held that the USGA acted "solely in accordance with its responsibilities to the game of golf" in refusing to approve the golf ball. The USGA felt that the ball would change the competitive nature of the game.

Polara appealed and the case was settled. The USGA will continue to make specifications for equipment.

In other cases involving golf equipment, the USGA has challenged putters and "square-grooved" golf clubs, which allegedly allow a player more control of the ball.

FACTS: The USGA adopted a new method of measuring the grooves and was considering outlawing clubs with such grooves in

USGA tournaments. The manufacturers contended that the USGA conspired to restrain and restrict the sale of their clubs. Was this an illegal restraint of trade?

DECISION: **YOU'RE THE JUDGE!**

Hockey

Peters wanted to enter a hockey team in the NHL. When denied, he brought an action alleging that the defendants, owners of three of the six teams in the only pro hockey league, conspired to restrain commerce and to establish a monopoly of pro hockey teams. Did they?

The action was barred by the **statute of limitations**—requiring that actions not brought within a specified time are to be dismissed.

Soccer

FACTS: The NFL, in the interest of protecting its clubs, sought a ban requiring NFL owners who also owned North American Soccer League (NASL) teams to sell their interests in the NASL clubs.

The NASL alleged that this would deprive them of owners and thus restrain the business of pro soccer. Would the ban violate the antitrust laws? **YOU'RE THE JUDGE!**

DECISION: Yes. The rule of reason test required the court to consider all factors of the case, such as: effect on competition, power of parties, whether the ban was reasonable, and its purpose. The ban might lessen competition if the NASL couldn't find acceptable new owners. The NFL was the more powerful of the two leagues. The ban was held anticompetitive, thus NFL team owners did not have to sell their interests in NASL teams.

Tennis

A manufacturer brought suit against the United States Tennis Association (USTA) for banning its "double-strung (spaghetti) racket." The USTA claimed, "The racket will significantly alter the flight of a tennis ball by imparting exaggerated topspin, thus defeating competitive goals of the game."

The court found no restraint of trade. It was a legitimate goal of the USTA to preserve the character and integrity of the game of tennis.

Wrestling

FACTS: Harold was a pro wrestler and a promoter. He was informed, "You have to pay a 'booking fee' to the Wrestling Alli-

ance before you can promote any matches in which you wrestle."

Harold alleged that this action prevented him in his business of promoting wrestling matches. "It damaged my ability to earn an income," he fumed. Was this a conspiracy to monopolize pro wrestling? **YOU'RE THE JUDGE!**

DECISION: No. The court found that the group did not have the power to remove or exclude Harold. It only received a small booking fee. In fact, Harold's income increased the year after the action was brought.

ACQUISITIONS & NATURAL MONOPOLIES

Before the American Football League (AFL) and the American Basketball Association (ABA) were absorbed into the NFL and the NBA respectively, there was litigation. Both AFL and ABA teams alleged that the older leagues were restraining trade by preventing them from flourishing, and that mergers might lessen competition and create a monopoly.

The court, in the AFL versus the NFL case, looked to see how many desirable, potential franchise areas were open to the newer AFL. They found that the NFL had not dominated the market. There were many desirable areas still open. The AFL's case was further weakened by its ability to obtain a television contract and to sign star college players. Thus, the NFL succeeded.

Do you know what a natural monopoly is?

FACTS: You owned the only sporting goods store in Worcester, a small rural town. You trained your employees to "properly fit and instruct customers."

A new sporting goods store, Mr. Compete, moved into town. When unsuccessful, Mr. Compete sued, alleging, "You monopolized the sporting goods business in Worcester, prevented us from competing, and restrained trade by hiring all of the competent employees." Did you restrain trade by creating a monopoly? **YOU'RE THE JUDGE!**

DECISION: Your sporting goods store may be what is called a "natural monopoly." It is in a town where only one store can survive. As long as you have done nothing to abuse this power that you have, there will be no antitrust problems.

Such may also be the case where a new professional sports league challenges the power of an older, more established league. There may not be enough interest to support two leagues and the fans will naturally want to see the best perform.

FACTS: The United States Football League (USFL) filed an antitrust suit against the NFL, alleging that the NFL monopolized player and TV contracts and stadium leases, thus making successful entry into pro football impossible. They asked the court to break up this monopoly and permit the USFL to have access to stadiums. Did the NFL have a natural monopoly? **YOU'RE THE JUDGE!**

DECISION: The court found that the NFL had a "natural monopoly," which is permitted. Only one league could survive. The USFL, because of mismanagement, was responsible for its own downfall. The USFL was awarded $3 in damages!

The USFL then decided to suspend their football operations.

ODDS & ENDS....

Baseballs & Bubblegum

FACTS: Rawlings had a contract to manufacture all Major League Baseball (MLB) baseballs. MacGregor, who wanted to bid on the ball contract, alleged, "By only allowing one manufacturer of balls, MLB is restraining trade."

For quality control reasons, MLB insisted on only one supplier. Was this a restraint of trade in denying others an opportunity to furnish the baseballs?

DECISION: **YOU'RE THE JUDGE!**

Selling baseball trading cards packaged with bubblegum has also brought charges of a restraint of trade.

FACTS: Fleer, a bubble gum manufacturer, sued another manufacturer, Topps, and MLB, contending that "Licensing agreements between Topps and MLB excluded Fleer from selling baseball trading cards."

The agreement between Topps and MLB had no effect on the sale of trading cards with low-cost products other than bubblegum. Furthermore, Fleer could negotiate with minor league players, and could also attempt to persuade major league players from renewing their agreement with Topps. Was such an agreement a restraint of trade? **YOU'RE THE JUDGE!**

DECISION: The court found no unreasonable restraint of trade, nor any conspiracy to monopolize the trade of baseball cards.

Through negotiations, there are now several manufacturers selling packaged bubble gum and baseball cards.

The Sherman Antitrust Act—to promote free competition—was passed so that the public might have better prices, service, quality, choice and innovative products.

14

AM I ELIGIBLE?

WHAT'S IT ABOUT?

Am I Eligible? reveals attempts by professional athletes to become eligible to participate in individual sports, such as tennis and golf; or to participate, by way of a draft, in team sports, such as baseball. It also discusses "hardship," discipline and players' rights. Do you know what the hardship rule is?

BOYLSTON NEWS JUNE 7, 1972

Jan cried, "I failed to qualify at qualifying school for the PGA pro golf tour!"

"I had my playing rights taken away because of poor play." said Ben sadly.

"I've always dreamed of playing pro football," Michael sighed, "but I wasn't drafted or given a try-out."

Johnson explained, "I wanted to play pro ball at home for the Cowboys, but was drafted by the Saints."

All of these players felt that the rules governing their eligibility and participation either boycotted them from participating at all or restrained them from playing for the team of their choice. Should the players have been allowed to participate, or to play or negotiate with any team?

ELIGIBILITY & THE DRAFT

Athletes participating in individual sports are limited by rules governing both admittance and the retention of any right to participate.

In team sports, athletes are limited both in their entrance to league and in their freedom to negotiate with teams in that league. And, they are required to participate in a player draft. This is a system where, generally, teams select players in the inverse order of how the teams finished in the previous year's standings.

Do you know how a professional sports team drafts its players?

FACTS: The Bucs finished with the worst record in pro football and the Cavaliers with the worst record in pro basketball. Who will receive the first draft pick in each sport? **YOU'RE THE JUDGE!**

DECISION: In football, the team with the worst record chooses first, and so on, with the championship team selecting last. However, any team may trade its draft choice. The team receiving it, even if the championship team, will then draft in that team's place.

In basketball, a lottery is used in which the bottom teams draw for the first several picks. The remaining teams then draft in inverse order of their finish, with the champs drafting last. Again, draft picks may be traded.

This procedure is continued throughout. However, many "rounds" are necessary. A round is completed when each team, or a team receiving that team's draft choice, has selected a player.

The team drafting a player has exclusive negotiating rights to that athlete. No other team in that league may negotiate with the player without the drafting team's permission. If there is a competing league, an athlete may be chosen and negotiate with either league. What if a drafted player won't sign?

FACTS: Holloway was drafted by the Celtics, but declared, "I won't sign!" How long would the Celtics hold their rights to sign him? Did Holloway become a free agent by not signing? **YOU'RE THE JUDGE!**

DECISION: A team's rights to a drafted player are no longer perpetual. If a team does not sign a drafted player within one year, the player could then be drafted by any team in the next draft. If, again, the player is not signed, he would become a **free agent**- able to negotiate and sign with any team.

Thus, eligibility rules may restrict an athlete in different ways. An athlete in an individual sport is restricted in his ability to enter a sport, while an athlete in a team sport may be restricted in his choice of a team.

TEAM SPORTS

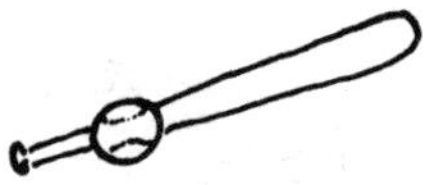

Each professional team sport has its own eligibility rules concerning an athlete's ability to participate.

Baseball

Major league baseball holds two drafts a year, one for high school and four-year college players, the other for junior college players.

FACTS: Abe went to high school, Ben to a four-year college and Charlie to a junior college. They all wanted to play pro baseball. "When will we be eligible to be drafted?" they all asked. **YOU'RE THE JUDGE!**

DECISION: High school seniors or students whose eligibility has expired are eligible for the draft.

Any draft choice who enters and remains in a four-year college without signing a contract cannot be drafted again until after his junior year or until he turns 21. A four-year college student may become eligible by quitting school or transferring to a junior college.

A junior college player is eligible for the draft at any time, except during the school's baseball season.

If any one of them is drafted, but not signed, they are again eligible for the next draft.

Basketball

When does an athlete become eligible for the NBA draft? Generally, a player becomes eligible for the NBA draft when his college eligibility expires. However, any player, including a high school senior, may give up his remaining amateur eligibility to be drafted.

This is called the **hardship rule.** An athlete simply declares "hardship" and becomes eligible for the draft.

FACTS: The NBA "Four Year Rule" provided, "No player is eligible to be drafted, or to play in the NBA until four years after his class has graduated from high school."

Haywood signed a contract with an NBA team. The commissioner rejected the contract as Haywood had only been out of high school for 3 years. Haywood sued, arguing that the rule restrained trade "by denying me the opportunity to earn a living." Was the rule illegal? **YOU'RE THE JUDGE!**

DECISION: Yes. The court held, "The rule preventing Haywood from being drafted or negotiating with any team was an unreasonable restraint of Haywood's right to earn a living by selling his services to play basketball." The rule was illegal.

For similar reasons, the court also found that the NBA draft violated antitrust laws. However, through collective bargaining, a modified draft was agreed to between the league and players.

If a player asks to be drafted, but isn't, is he still eligible to play in college?

A player asking to be placed on the league's draft list forfeits any remaining college eligibility, even if he withdraws his name from the draft or is not drafted.

Hockey

FACTS: An NHL rule prohibited a player with only one eye, Weldon, from playing professional hockey. Weldon sued, alleging a group boycott for restraining him from playing. Was the rule illegal? **YOU'RE THE JUDGE!**

DECISION: "No. It was a valid safety precaution," ruled the court.

Any amateur who turns 18 by September 15 is eligible for the NHL draft. If a drafted player enters college rather than sign a contract, he remains the property of the team that drafted him until six months after he graduates or leaves school. Unsigned players not entering college are subject to two more drafts, after which they become free agents, able to negotiate with any team.

The World Hockey Association (WHA) used to have a different age limit.

FACTS: Ken Linesman, 19, was prevented from playing in the WHA due to a rule prohibiting persons under the age of 20 from playing. He sued, arguing, "The rule denied me the opportunity to earn a living. It's a group boycott in that the NHL conspired to refuse to deal with athletes under the age of 20." Was the rule a boycott? **YOU'RE THE JUDGE!**

DECISION: Yes. This was a classic case of a **per se illegal group boycott**—the WHA and its teams refusing to deal with certain players. If an injunction was not granted, Linesman would have suffered irreparable harm in not being able to earn a livelihood.

Soccer

The Major Indoor Soccer League (MISL) holds its draft after the end of the college season. Any drafted, but unsigned player, is eligible for the next draft. A player then drafted, but unsigned until the next draft, becomes a free agent, able to negotiate with any team.

Football

The NFL's rules are the most restrictive. They hold that only players whose college eligibility is up or whose college class has graduated are eligible for their draft. Loss of eligibility (by dismissal, withdrawal or by signing with another league) generally does not qualify a player for the NFL draft, unless he otherwise meets their eligibility rules.

Several players have been admitted after petitioning the league for early eligibility. Would a challenge to the NFL's eligibility rules for preventing an athlete from earning a living be successful?

FACTS: Walt Glen, a star college player, said, "Players in other sports are allowed to play before their college eligibility is up. I want to play in the NFL after my junior year." He challenged the NFL's eligibility rule as being a group boycott for refusing to deal with him, alleging, "The rule is preventing me from earning a living." Was the eligibility rule a restraint of trade?

DECISION: **YOU'RE THE JUDGE!**

Any player eligible for the NFL draft, but not then chosen, immediately becomes a free agent able to negotiate with any team. However, this is generally because the player lacked sufficient skills. Therefore, the demand for his services may be minimal.

For a player who has been drafted, the original drafting team retains exclusive rights for two years, after which the player becomes a free agent, able to negotiate with any team. However, a player may be drafted and negotiate with a team in another league.

FACTS: Jim Cousins, who was drafted by the Bills, explained, "I signed with the Canadian Football League (CFL) for two years. After that contract expired, Houston, in the NFL, offered me a contract. Can I negotiate with them or any other team in the NFL?" asked Cousins. **YOU'RE THE JUDGE!**

DECISION: Cousins could negotiate with any team, subject to the original team's right to match any offer the player received. The Bills matched the offer and then traded Cousins.

The USFL, which suspended operations, had eligibility rules similar to those of the NFL, but their eligibility rule was challenged.

FACTS: Walker sought an exception to the USFL's eligibility rule prohibiting him from playing before his college eligibility was up.

He sued, arguing, "The USFL's rule prohibiting the signing of underclassmen is a group boycott—a refusal to deal—and illegally restrains the players' opportunity to earn a living." Was Walker allowed to play? **YOU'RE THE JUDGE!**

DECISION: Yes. The USFL's regulation barring the signing of underclassmen was declared an "illegal restraint of trade." The USFL allowed Walker to play after his junior year of college.

Will the draft deprive an athlete of being able to negotiate with any team to earn the best living possible?

FACTS: Smith was drafted by, and played for, the Redskins. After a career-ending neck injury, he filed an antitrust suit claiming, "If it had not been for the draft, I could have negotiated a contract containing injury protection provisions." Should Smith have recovered any damages for not being able to negotiate a better contract? **YOU'RE THE JUDGE!**

DECISION: Although the court found the draft to be an illegal group boycott and an unreasonable restraint of trade, it nevertheless ruled, "There was not enough evidence to show that had there been no draft, that Smith could have negotiated a better contract."

INDIVIDUAL SPORTS

Athletes in individual sports, such as bowling, golf and tennis, may also allege that eligibility rules improperly restrained or prevented them from the opportunity to earn a living by participating.

FACTS: The Women's Tennis Association (WTA) announced that, "Girls of any age are allowed to participate in professional tennis tournaments, but those under a certain age must take rest periods from the tour to pursue an education."

Christina, 16, didn't want to miss any tournaments, nor did she desire to continue with school. The state law where she lived allows the "discontinuance of school at age 16."

Christina challenged the WTA rule as being a boycott which denied her the right to earn a living. "Do I have to continue school?" she asked.

DECISION: **YOU'RE THE JUDGE!**

Operators of a bowling house and a billiards hall attempted to induce competitors to refuse to deal with other establishments. When the competitors competed at other establishments and then sought to enter the operators' tournaments, they were refused. The courts found these practices illegal boycotts.

Other players, deprived of their livelihood, have not been so successful in alleging that a rule excluding them from participation was an unreasonable refusal to deal with them.

FACTS: A U.S. Lawn Tennis Association (USLTA) rule threatened to bar any player from sanctioned tournaments if the player

signed to play in non-association sanctioned tournaments. Heldman felt that her threatened suspension would cause her a financial loss. Was the rule illegal? **YOU'RE THE JUDGE!**

DECISION: No. Uniformity in playing rules and competition of high caliber and ethical standards were proper concerns. Players were given **due process**—a fair and impartial hearing, with the right to be represented and the right to appeal.

In a similar case, U.S. Trotting Association (USTA) members were prohibited from racing horses in non-association sponsored meets. They alleged a group boycott—that they were being illegally prohibited from racing—but the court found the rule reasonable and necessary to ensure that races were free from illegal or improper conduct.

Can an athlete be suspended for having a "physical disability"?

FACTS: Juan had been a competent jockey for several years before it was discovered that he had only one eye. When suspended, he sued, alleging a group boycott for preventing his playing. Was the rule prohibiting him from competing a valid safety rule?

DECISION: **YOU'RE THE JUDGE!**

Pro golfers have also been denied eligibility for not meeting performance requirements. One court observed, "PGA rules are reasonable in attempting to keep the number of players at a manageable number so as to maintain a high level of competition, free from being bogged down by incompetent players."

Rules regarding racing cars have also been found to be reasonable.

FACTS: An STP car, which had outrun its competition in the Indy 500, was required to change engine specifications. The rule applied to all participants. Was the rule reasonable? **YOU'RE THE JUDGE!**

DECISION: The rule, adopted to achieve competitive races, was reasonable and not in restraint of trade.

HAVE YOU BEEN BEHAVING?

Disciplinary rules involving suspension from competition may be ruled an illegal boycott. Restraining an athlete from the right to play and earn a living is, in effect, refusing to deal with the athlete during the suspension.

FACTS: Lillian, a pro golfer, was suspended from the Ladies Professional Golf Association (LPGA) for allegedly cheating (moving her ball). Initially, a board comprised of fellow players heard Lillian during an investigation, then issued a fine and probation. Later, without a hearing, Lillian was suspended for one year. She sought an injunction preventing her suspension on the grounds that the LPGA's action illegally prevented her from earning a living. Did it? **YOU'RE THE JUDGE!**

DECISION: Yes. Suspending Lillian was a per se restraint of trade. There was no hearing or due process, and since members of the board were fellow competitors, they stood to gain financially from her suspension. The plaintiff was granted an injunction preventing the association from suspending her from play.

A league or association needs, however, to have self-regulation in order to insure that their competitions remain free of illegal and fraudulent activities which might erode fan support.

FACTS: A pro basketball player admitted placing bets on his team to win. He was suspended under a clause in his contract prohibiting gambling.

When he applied for reinstatement and was denied, he brought an action, charging, "The NBA conspired to restrain me from earning a living." Was the rule reasonable and necessary? **YOU'RE THE JUDGE!**

DECISION: The court found that the rule was reasonable and necessary for the survival of the league in avoiding even the slightest connection with gambling. There was no conspiracy in restraint of trade.

Must a player faced with suspension for an alleged violation be given a hearing?

A court must determine if the interest an authority seeks to protect is proper, if reasonable procedures were followed in determining whether a violation had occurred, and if the player was given due process—a fair and impartial hearing with representation.

FACTS: Bill Nance, a pro bowler, was suspended for knowingly bowling with another bowler who had changed his name in order to obtain a higher handicap, and for accepting ill-gotten prize money.

Nance sued for readmittance, charging, "The suspension is unfair. They're preventing me from earning a living." Were the restrictions an illegal restraint of trade? **YOU'RE THE JUDGE!**

DECISION: The court found no conspiracy, and furthermore, followed a general policy of the court not to review a suspension from voluntary associations unless there is bad faith, which was not found.

YOU'RE RESERVED!

An option clause generally gives a club in professional team sports the right to renew a player's contract for one additional year. And a club could renew a contract for as long as it chose to. Players had to sign the contracts containing this clause or not play.

FACTS: You were a pro baseball player and asked to sign a contract containing the following clause:

"The Player grants the Club a perpetual right to renew the Player's contract. If the Club renews the Player's contract, it will contain the same terms, except as to salary, which shall be determined by mutual agreement.

The Player agrees that the Club shall have the right to enjoin him by injunction from playing for any other team."

Was this an illegal restraint of trade, perpetually prohibiting you from dealing with any other team?

DECISION: **YOU'RE THE JUDGE!**

Reserve and option clauses have since been changed. Players now have more freedom to trade their services. But first, a bit of history leading up to the modern day "reserve system."

In the first reserve system in 1879, the National League baseball clubs adopted a secret agreement. Each owner could reserve or protect players who were placed on a reserved list, with other teams agreeing not to negotiate or attempt to hire another team's players unless given permission.

When this clause was inserted into players' contracts, the players objected.

They organized the first union, the National Brotherhood of Professional Players. The union demanded the end of the reserve clause. When the owners refused, the Player's League was formed.

FACTS: When two players, Ewing and Ward, sought to "jump" to the Player's League, their owners attempted to prevent them by pointing to the reserve clause in their contracts.

Ewing and Ward contended, "The agreement has nothing to do with the Player's League. Besides, the reserve clause is unfair." Would the court prevent Ewing and Ward from jumping leagues? **YOU'RE THE JUDGE!**

DECISION: The reserve clause could not prevent the players from playing for a team that was not part of that agreement. The teams in the Player's League had not agreed to reserve players.

The court also held that the right to reserve was perpetual and, therefore, "too unfair and vague to enforce."

The owners then changed the reserve clause to permit them to renew the players' contracts. Later leagues in other pro sports adopted similar restraints on players' mobility.

How would the courts interpret this "right to renew" option? Was it too harsh or one-sided in favor of the owners?

FACTS: Heyman played semi-pro basketball for the Capitols. When he signed to play in the newly formed ABA, the Capitols sought an injunction to restrain him. Heyman had signed a contract giving the Capitols the option to renew the contract for a one-year period. Did the court grant the injunction? **YOU'RE THE JUDGE!**

DECISION: No. The contract provided that if the Capitols exercised their option and renewed the contract, Heyman's salary could be fixed by the club. And, while binding Heyman for one year, the Capitols could terminate the contract at will. The court found this to be too harsh and one-sided.

When several players in the NBA attempted to sign contracts with teams in the American Basketball League, NBA teams sued, alleging, "Under the players' contracts, the clubs have a 'right to renew' option, binding the players to play for them for the next season, whether or not they signed new contracts."

Could this option be perpetually renewed? When the players sued, the court held that the right to renew was valid, but only for one year.

FACTS: Harris had played football for the Cowboys in the NFL. In violation of the option clause in his contract, he signed and began playing for the Dallas Texans of the AFL.

Peters, under contract to the Islanders, sought to jump to the newly formed World Hockey Association (WHA). Could Harris and Peters be enjoined from playing for the new leagues? **YOU'RE THE JUDGE!**

DECISION: The courts granted temporary injunctions, finding, "The clubs' exercise of their options granted them a right to renew the contracts for one year."

The players had voluntarily accepted employment. The "balance of hardship" was on the club's side as they would lose the money paid for the rights to the players' services if they never played for them.

Players are now prevented from jumping to new leagues, at least until their contracts have expired. Reserve, option clauses have also been enforced in cases between teams and players in the same league.

PLAYERS' RIGHTS ARE BORN!

When players began to successfully challenge draft and eligibility rules, their rights took a turn for the better.

Football

When NFL teams could not agree on compensation for a free agent, the "Rozelle Rule" was then used.

> FACTS: Kapp had come to the Patriots from the Vikings. When Kapp declared, "I refuse to sign a contract!" the commissioner ordered him to either sign or not play.
>
> If agreement as to compensation could not be reached between the teams, then the commissioner determined it. This practice was known as the "Rozelle Rule."
>
> Kapp didn't sign, but instead sued the NFL. He alleged that the Rozelle Rule was unreasonable and that the NFL was blacklisting players by refusing to deal with them. Did the rule unreasonably restrain a player's ability to seek work? **YOU'RE THE JUDGE!**

> DECISION: Yes. The Rozelle Rule was not the product of collective bargaining. It applied to players even if they had become free agents by playing out their contracts. And, as other teams could not deal with a player unless giving compensation, it restrained a player for an unlimited time. "This went far beyond any need for protection of a team's interests. Impartial arbitration to decide on compensation, if any, would be necessary."

The NFL owners were forced to bargain with the NFL Player's Association. The result was an agreement liberalizing the draft and changing the Rozelle Rule.

Now, if a player becomes a free agent and is given an "offer sheet" by another team, the team that may lose the player has a **"right of first refusal"** and may sign the player for the offered salary. If not done, the losing team is then compensated by future draft choice(s), depending upon the free agent's new salary. Very few "free agents" have been signed.

When the Collective Bargaining Agreement between the owners and players expired in 1987, without agreement on a new one, the players went out on strike.

They wanted "unrestricted free agency"—the ability to move to another team after their contract had expired without the new team having to compensate the player's old team for their loss. After several weeks, the striking players, without a new agreement, returned to work. Without an agreement, did the players become free agents?

The NFL instituted a new free agency plan. Each team would protect a certain number of its players. Those not on this restricted list became unrestricted free agents—able to sign with any team—with no compensation to their former team.

Basketball

FACTS: Several NBA players sought an injunction preventing the NBA from enforcing its draft and option clause.

They maintained, "The draft restrained us from bargaining freely for employment. The reserve or option clause could be renewed perpetually. If we played out our contracts and sought to play with other teams, we were blacklisted—no one would deal with us." Were these practices group boycotts by the NBA teams? **YOU'RE THE JUDGE!**

DECISION: The court found that these practices were, in effect, group boycotts by their refusal to deal with the players, except through these restrictive practices.

The NBA owners and the NBA Player's Association agreed to a Collective Bargaining Agreement (CBA). The draft remained, but if a team did not sign a drafted player before the next draft, the player would again be eligible to be drafted. If again, the athlete was not signed before the next draft, he became a free agent.

Would a team continue to have the right to renew a player's contract perpetually? No. At the end of a contract and one-year option, a player became a free agent. And, if an NBA player is a five-year veteran, he automatically becomes a free agent.

FACTS: Jake asserted, "I'm a free agent. I played out my contract and one-year option with the Bulls. I then received an offer from the Kings." Did the Bulls still have any rights to sign Jake? Did the Kings have to compensate the Bulls? **YOU'RE THE JUDGE!**

DECISION: If a team offered Jake a contract, the original team had a "right of first refusal." They could match any offer that Jake received. If the original team did not match that offer, the new team would no longer be required to compensate them.

The Bulls decided to match the Kings' offer, signed, and then traded Jake to the Kings.

Hockey

The NHL also replaced their perpetual reserve clause with a one-year option.

Collective bargaining produced a method whereby the team signing a free agent would make an "equalization payment" to the losing team. If the teams could not agree on a player(s), cash, or draft pick (s) (or any combination of these) for payment, then a neutral arbitrator would select, without change, one of the two teams' proposals.

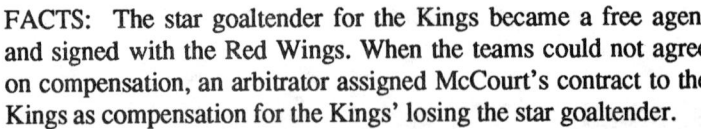

FACTS: The star goaltender for the Kings became a free agent and signed with the Red Wings. When the teams could not agree on compensation, an arbitrator assigned McCourt's contract to the Kings as compensation for the Kings' losing the star goaltender.

McCourt brought suit alleging, "This equalization payment restricted my ability to choose who I would play for." Would the court prohibit the compensation? **YOU'RE THE JUDGE!**

DECISION: No . The labor exemption holds that if the reserve clause was the product of bona fide, good faith bargaining, over a mandatory subject (employment), then it was exempt from the antitrust laws and could not be enjoined as a restraint of trade.

Baseball

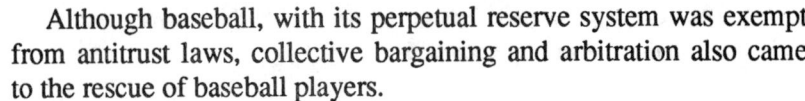

Although baseball, with its perpetual reserve system was exempt from antitrust laws, collective bargaining and arbitration also came to the rescue of baseball players.

Finley, owner of the A's, fired one of his players, Harrelson. Later, an arbitrator released another A's player, Hunter, from his contract. They both became free agents, signed with other teams, and received substantial pay raises.

While this did not change the reserve clause, other players now demanded higher salaries. Several refused to sign their contracts. Most players eventually signed, but one did not.

FACTS: Messersmith, a pitcher for the Dodgers did not sign his 1975 contract, but instead played out his option. He challenged the team's right to perpetually renew his contract and the reserved list, prohibiting other teams from dealing with him. Was Messersmith a free agent? **YOU'RE THE JUDGE!**

DECISION: Yes. An impartial arbitrator ruled that by playing out his option, Messersmith had become a free agent. The team could not renew his contract beyond the option year. Furthermore, other teams could deal with him as the reserve list applied only to players under contract.

A new Collective Bargaining Agreement (CBA) allowed players who play out their option after six years of service to become free agents. Players now may, in certain instances, veto a trade involving them.

RULES! RULES!

Playing rules may have several objectives: to heighten fan interest; to promote fairness of competition and for the integrity of the game, and; to insure the safety of the players.

FACTS: The American League (AL) decided to do away with the designated hitter rule, thus several players who couldn't play in the field would be cut.

Football changed its tackling rules, creating the need for quicker defensive players.

New tennis rackets and golf balls were prohibited from being used in tournaments.

Those affected—players and manufacturers—sued, protesting that, "The rules' changes illegally restrained our ability to earn a living." Would the changes be permitted? **YOU'RE THE JUDGE!**

DECISION: Someone will be affected no matter what rules' changes are made. Uniformity in regulating and improving the games is essential to hold fan interest. And, as long as a league is not attempting to suppress competition by eliminating certain players or products, then restraints designed to promote the game and protect competitors will be justified.

SQUAD SIZE

Can professional sports teams limit the number of players on each team?

Restrictions on squad size, while limiting the employment of some players, are necessary for competitive balance. Otherwise, one owner might be forced to hire more players to compete with another owner who had the resources to increase his roster, and thus his ability to win.

FACTS: The NFL cut its roster limit to forty-three players. Basketball cut its squad size to eleven. Golf cut the entrants for any tournament to one hundred-twenty-five. Those participants who now didn't qualify sued, complaining, "The reduced limits prevented us from trading our services. The rules were illegal group boycotts." What limit should apply? **YOU'RE THE JUDGE!**

DECISION: If a league or association sets a limit in the interest of maximizing profits and competitive balance, and not solely to restrict competition for players, then there will be no restraint of trade.

TRADE DEADLINES

Can teams be prohibited from acquiring players after a certain point in the season?

Although trade or acquisition deadlines may restrict the movement of players, they also prevent teams in play-off or pennant contention from "buying up" stars to assure winning. These restraints are

are only for a limited time, as they disappear when the season is over. They are necessary for competitive balance.

What if a deadline is not for competitive balance, but to lock out certain players?

FACTS: The NFL sought to prevent WFL players from entering the NFL after the WFL had folded. The regular trading deadline date was October 28. The NFL set a date of October 22 as the deadline for acquiring WFL players. Did this improperly interfere with those WFL players' trying to sign with NFL teams? **YOU'RE THE JUDGE!**

DECISION: Yes. The players were granted an injunction preventing the NFL from interfering with their attempt to secure employment in the NFL. Had the NFL set the same acquisition date for WFL players as its regular trading deadline, then the injunction may not have been granted.

ODDS & ENDS....

Ticket Tying

A **tying** arrangement "ties" the purchase of one product to the required purchase of another. Is this legal?

FACTS: You wanted to buy season tickets to see the Bills. The team only sold a package including tickets for pre and regular-season home games. You sued the Bills, objecting, "This is illegal! I only want regular-season tickets." Should you be able to buy a season ticket for only regular-season games? **YOU'RE THE JUDGE!**

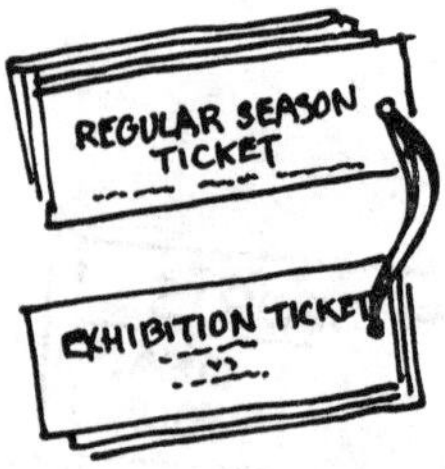

DECISION: The court held that teams may sell season ticket packages which include pre-season tickets.

The purchasers of season ticket packages received special privileges, such as preferred-location seats and parking. Individual game tickets were available, however, so fans were not compelled to buy something that they did not want.

Professional sports leagues and associations must balance their concern over eligibility rules, fairness of competition and player safety with an individual's right to earn a living.

15

MOVING ON

WHAT'S IT ABOUT?

Moving On tells how antitrust laws may affect attempts by professional sports' leagues to prevent their teams from moving from one city to another. Also discussed is **eminent domain**—a city's attempt to take private property (professional sports team) for public use.

May teams break their leases with stadiums in order to move? May leagues regulate who can own teams in their sport?

Section A

PAXTON NEWS

PRO TEAM GONE!

As one fan sighed, "It's like losing one of your kids to college ... it's hard to adjust to life without them. But at least your kid will come back for visits. When you've lost a team, they're gone for good." Fans everywhere have lost pro teams to other cities ... and to other fans.

Franchise free agency now allows teams to move... but it wasn't always that way.

CAN WE MOVE?

FACTS: The NHL's San Francisco Seals wanted to move to Vancouver. The St. Louis Blues wanted to move to Saskatchewan. There were no NHL teams in either place.

When the NHL denied permission for the teams to move, both teams sued, alleging, "The NHL is restraining trade by preventing us from moving." Should the teams have been allowed to move? **YOU'RE THE JUDGE!**

DECISION: The Sherman Antitrust Act provides that any agreement in restraint of trade is illegal. It prohibits competitors from restraining trade.

The courts held that the individual teams in the NHL were not competitors, but were acting together as one business enterprise. Therefore, there could be no agreement and, hence, no restraint. The teams could not move.

Furthermore, the teams could not successfully allege that the NHL was attempting to monopolize pro hockey. The teams were part of that monopoly and the law requires that one desiring to recover must be injured. The court pointed out, "The teams wished to continue to enjoy the protection of monopoly by the league, but wanted to enjoy it in different cities."

FACTS: What if the arena owners in Saskatchewan and Vancouver joined the teams in the antitrust suit as competitors to the arenas in St. Louis and San Francisco and as competitors to the NHL? Would there then be the necessary competition to show a restraint of trade?

DECISION: **YOU'RE THE JUDGE!**

Could other teams and arenas be more successful in showing that teams can be competitors and therefore, a league can restrain trade by preventing a team from moving to another city?

Rule 4.3 of the NFL Constitution required approval by three-fourths of the NFL clubs before another club could move within the home territory (within 75 miles) of any other NFL club.

The rule, similar to those used by other sports' leagues, was designed to keep owners from arbitrarily moving their teams to new locations, or to another team's home territory.

Such rules were subject to abuse by owners intent on denying an unpopular owner the necessary permission to move. Such was the case when Bill Veeck was denied permission by the AL to move his baseball team. Two days after Veeck sold the club, the new owner was given permission for the move.

In 1978, the L.A. Rams announced that they were leaving the Coliseum to play in nearby Anaheim. The Coliseum Commission then sought to have the Oakland Raiders move there. Were they successful?

FACTS: The commission and the Raiders sued the NFL, contending, "Rule 4.3 violates the antitrust law's prohibition against any agreement in restraint of trade."

The major issue was whether the NFL was a single business enterprise—which could not combine or agree with itself—or whether the NFL was comprised of 28 separate member clubs—who could combine, or agree, to restrain trade.

The NFL argued, "We are a single enterprise as evidenced by uniform playing rules, scheduling, the player draft, and sharing of television revenues and ticket receipts." Was the NFL a single business enterprise? **YOU'RE THE JUDGE!**

DECISION: No. The court found that the NFL was an association of 28 separate clubs. It further commented, "The clubs did not share all revenues, nor did they share their profits or losses. They were managed independently, each making its own decisions concerning ticket prices, player acquisitions and salaries, hiring of coaches and administrators and the terms of their stadium leases." The teams competed against each other for players, fans and the media.

The court, in mentioning a suit between the NFL and the NASL, noted, "The single entity defense fails where two teams compete in the same area for fans. League restraint of that competition often damages a stadium operator."

Now that the court held that the NFL could combine or agree to prevent a team from moving, the next question was, "Did they?"

FACTS: Did the NFL unlawfully combine or agree to restrain trade by denying the Raiders permission to play in the Coliseum and, thus, also restrain the Coliseum Commission from having another NFL team to replace the departed LA Rams? **YOU'RE THE JUDGE!**

DECISION: Yes. Rule 4.3, requiring clubs to approve any move, was arbitrary and unreasonable. It contained no considerations, such as the impact a team move would have on the new location or another NFL team, to guide owners in the approval process. It was subject to abuse, as owners could deny permission to move without using good faith.

The NFL and its members unreasonably restrained trade. They were permanently enjoined from interfering with the Raiders in their transfer to play in the L.A. Coliseum.

Other professional sports teams have moved or attempted to move. When the New York Nets desired to move to New Jersey, the New York Knicks objected. Because NBA rules required the consent of the team (Knicks) into whose territory a move is to be made, the Nets could not move. They sued. The suit was settled, and the Nets moved.

In a similar confrontation, the Colorado Rockies moved to New Jersey, with the Islanders, Rangers, and Flyers being paid indemnification fees for the profits that they would lose from having another team in their territory to draw away fans and TV revenues.

Would professional sports leagues now be prevented from restricting team movement?

The court in the Raiders case suggested that had there existed necessary, objective and reasonable restrictions on team movement, they would have been enforceable—whether in football or in any other league.

EMINENT DOMAIN?

In addition to leagues, cities have attempted to prevent teams from moving by using **eminent domain**—the power of a state or city to take private property for public use for fair compensation. It is commonly used to condemn land for public roads, bridges, railroads and airports. Land to build many sports stadiums was acquired by eminent domain.

FACTS: The city of Oakland objected to the Raiders' moving and brought an action in eminent domain.

The city asserted, "We should be allowed to acquire the Raiders as property necessary for providing recreation and sports for our residents."

The city of Oakland felt that, "If acquiring, erecting, and operating a sports stadium was a permissible municipal function, then owning a sports franchise to play in the stadium should also be permitted." Was the city allowed to take the Raiders? **YOU'RE THE JUDGE!**

DECISION: No. Oakland's condemnation was "not for a valid public purpose." The court decided, "A pro football team was not what the Constitution intended as private property that may be taken by eminent domain for public use."

If the city of Oakland were allowed to do so, then every city might do the same. And every city could condemn any business that considered moving.

FACTS: Springfield attempted to condemn a theater group and its hit play, "The Babe," and prevent its going on tour.

Another city, Harrison, wanted to condemn a sporting goods manufacturer (who employed many of the town's people) and prevent its moving. Another city, Westfield, wanted to prevent you from moving your ticket and program print shop to another town. Should the cities be allowed to take these businesses by eminent domain?

DECISION: **YOU'RE THE JUDGE!**

LEASES

Most professional sports teams are tied to their stadiums and arenas by a long-term **lease**—an agreement for exclusive possession of property for a specific period of time.

Teams attempting to leave a city before their leases expired have been enjoined, as in the case of the San Francisco Giants, when they attempted to move to Toronto. Others have settled the matter as did: New York City and the Jets, San Diego and the NL, and the Braves and the city of Buffalo. When the Seattle Pilots became the Milwaukee Brewers, the city complained and was awarded a new franchise, the Seattle Mariners.

If a team left before their lease expired, could they be forced to return?

FACTS: The New Orleans Jazz moved to Utah before their lease was up. The stadium manager fumed, "I want an injunction preventing the move and forcing the Jazz to return to New Orleans, at least until their lease expires." Did the Jazz have to return? **YOU'RE THE JUDGE!**

DECISION: The stadium manager was denied an injunction as, by the time a petition was filed, the team had moved. They settled on the issue of damages for lost rent and profit.

With this new found freedom of movement, teams could now obtain more favorable lease concessions and lower rent in return for long-term leases of a stadium or arena. Such concessions even include allowing a team to break its lease where attendance does not reach a specified level.

One team was trying to enter a lease, not break one.

FACTS: Holden sought to lease RFK Stadium in Washington to use for an AFL pro football team. He contended, "The stadium is the only one in the area suitable for pro football." The operators of the stadium had signed a lease prohibiting use of the stadium by any pro football team other than the Redskins. Was this an attempt to monopolize pro football in that area? **YOU'RE THE JUDGE!**

DECISION: The Redskins combined with the operator of the stadium to improperly restrain trade, and to monopolize pro football in the Washington area by excluding competition from using the stadium.

"WE DON'T WANT YOU"

Professional sports leagues have rules regulating who may own a franchise in their leagues. Such rules may prohibit ownership by those involved with gambling or by those having an interest in another team.

FACTS: Brown and Stone purchased the Celtics and then applied to the NBA for the transfer. When they were denied, they sued, alleging, "Our application was unreasonably denied."

One owner said, "You're with Harry. He's been a crawl in the throat of these owners. He's a renegade and a troublemaker, and they are worried that you'll side with him on any matters before the NBA."

The NBA contended, "We rejected the application because of business dealings between the three, practices which created potential conflicts of interest." Was this a restraint of trade for preventing the purchase? **YOU'RE THE JUDGE!**

DECISION: The judge ruled that the antitrust laws were for the protection of competition, and the plaintiffs, Brown and Stone, wanted to join with the other owners, not compete with them. Therefore, the antitrust laws did not apply. Brown and Stone had to sell their interest in the Celtics.

In a similar ruling, another court found that the Mid-South Grizzlies were not competitors of the NFL. There was no anticompetitive behavior in rejecting their application for admission into the NFL.

These cases assumed that the league was a single entity, which could not combine or agree with itself to restrain or monopolize trade.

Would the decisions have been different had these cases been decided after the Raiders' case held that teams do compete with each other and, therefore, could agree to prevent approval?

FACTS: Fisher reached an agreement to buy the NBA's Chicago Bulls. When agreement to lease Chicago Stadium (19,000 seats) for play could not be reached, Fisher arranged a lease to play in the Amphitheatre (10,500 seats).

"Because I couldn't use the Stadium, the NBA rejected my application." Fisher said. The team was then purchased by the group who owned the Stadium.

Fisher sued that group and the NBA for "restraining competition, conspiring to monopolize pro basketball, and for boycotting me to prevent approval of the sale." Should Fisher have been allowed to lease the Stadium? **YOU'RE THE JUDGE!**

DECISION: "The Stadium is an essential and scarce facility." Far superior to the Amphitheatre, it could not (practically) be duplicated. Its owners must share its use on fair terms.

The court ruled, "The evidence of conspiracy was overwhelming and showed that the group intended to dictate who the next owner of the Bulls would be."

The defendants, in failing to outbid Fisher for the team, conspired to monopolize (with other owners) and to obtain a negative vote from the NBA, and thus restrained Fisher from his fairly won victory.

Damages, including punitive, were awarded. The NBA was a defendant until a settlement was reached.

STATE LAWS

May states use their antitrust laws in dealing with professional sports teams?

The potential burden on **interstate commerce**—trade between several states—by professional sports teams outweighs any one state's interest in regulating professional sports. Therefore, federal antitrust laws will apply.

When Wisconsin attempted to use state antitrust laws to prevent the Milwaukee Braves from moving, the court found that baseball was not only exempt from federal antitrust laws, but from any antitrust laws.

Where amateur sports do not deal in interstate commerce, state antitrust laws may apply.

FACTS: Grant, a high school student, attended a summer baseball camp for three weeks. His high school association had a rule providing that, "Any student attending a summer camp specializing in one sport for more than two weeks during the summer shall lose his eligibility for the following year."

When Grant lost his eligibility, he sued, alleging that the rule restrained him from developing his skills for college. Was the rule unreasonable? **YOU'RE THE JUDGE!**

DECISION: The court held that the rule was reasonable and did not violate state antitrust laws. It was necessary to prevent one student gaining an unfair advantage over others who could not attend, and to prevent their being "burned out" from exploitation and undue pressure.

THE NCAA & ANTITRUST

The majority of NCAA rules and regulations are for the protection of amateurism and education in college athletics. This pursuit may prevent the use of antitrust laws in any challenge to such rules.

FACTS: An NCAA rule limited the number of assistant coaches a school could employ in its football and basketball programs. This forced the firing of a number of assistant coaches. Did the rule unreasonably restrain trade by preventing some coaches from working? **YOU'RE THE JUDGE!**

DECISION: No. The court decided, "The NCAA's goal of preserving and fostering competition by preventing wealthy and powerful schools from having an unfair advantage over others—by hiring extra coaches—was a reasonable one."

The NCAA also attempted to limit squad sizes in those same sports, but after several suits, they voted to abandon those restrictions.

Would the NCAA be subjected to the antitrust laws where its member schools established interstate commerce by: nationwide recruitment, team travel for games, and interstate TV broadcasting and sale of tickets?

FACTS: English played quarterback for Tulane. When the NCAA ruled him ineligible for not sitting out a year after his transfer from another college, English sued, alleging that the NCAA unfairly attempted to restrain him from playing. Did English have to sit out a year? **YOU'RE THE JUDGE!**

DECISION: English could not play. Antitrust laws did not apply to prevent the NCAA from enforcing its rules pertaining to recruitment, transfer and eligibility to preserve and foster competition in college sports.

The NCAA had limited its jurisdiction to men's athletics until 1981, when they voted to extend its activities into women's athletics.

FACTS: The Association for Intercollegiate Athletics for Women (AIAW), formed prior to 1981 to regulate women's athletics, sued the NCAA, alleging they expanded into women's athletics in order to monopolize and restrain trade in women's sports.

Many association members left and joined the NCAA. This loss of membership resulted in a substantial loss of revenue and prestige. Did the NCAA restrain the AIAW? Was this an illegal monopoly? **YOU'RE THE JUDGE!**

DECISION: The court found no antitrust violations. "The AIAW loss was the result of direct competition with the NCAA. The latter offered a superior product, management and promotional resources, and uniform rules for both men and women."

The NCAA also sought to govern the televising of college football games by granting an exclusive right to networks to carry games live.

In the interest of protecting attendance, NCAA rules limited both the number of games to be broadcast each season, and also the number of times any school could appear.

Could NCAA schools make their own deals for televising their games?

FACTS: Most of the major football programs formed the College Football Association (CFA) and made their own deals for broadcasting games in which they played.

The NCAA announced disciplinary action for any member that complied with the CFA television contract. The schools could have withdrawn from the NCAA, but they were dependent upon the NCAA for administration in other sports.

Instead, they sued, alleging, "The NCAA limitations are illegal and restrain us from making our own deals." Were the NCAA limitations illegal? **YOU'RE THE JUDGE!**

DECISION: Yes. The court found that the NCAA plan was an illegal restraint of trade for: limiting the number of times a team could appear, fixing prices paid to the teams, and prohibiting members from selling TV rights on their own. The NCAA plan neither protected live, in-person attendance, nor equalized competition among its members.

In commenting on protecting the "small guy's" right to compete, one judge commented, "Where, by unfair and illegal practices—intent on monopolizing and restraining trade—the right to enter and compete is restricted, antitrust laws will be available to see that the 'small guy' gets an equal shot with the 'big guy' at selling his services or products."

ODDS & ENDS....

FACTS: You were the President of All-American U. Your football team had just completed an undefeated season.

You wanted to play in the Flower Bowl. However, because you were neither a member of the Big Eleven, nor of the Pac 9, you were not eligible to be selected.

You sued the Flower Bowl Committee, the NCAA and the Pac 9 and Big Eleven football conferences, arguing, "They restrained trade, conspired to monopolize the Flower Bowl game and boycotted us, all in violation of the antitrust laws."

The Flower Bowl defended, "You are eligible for other bowl games." Would a court enjoin the Flower Bowl's practice of only considering the Pac 9 and Big Eleven conferences in selecting schools to play in the Flower Bowl?

DECISION: **YOU'RE THE JUDGE!**

Although eminent domain may not be used by a city to take a professional sports team, it is used to take land for stadiums, roadways and airports.

16

SPORTSMANLIKE CONDUCT

WHAT'S IT ABOUT?

Sportsmanlike Conduct deals with the regulation of professional sports and their rules governing play, conduct and discipline, in order to protect the game and its participants.

Does the commissioner or president of a professional sports league or association have complete authority over the conduct and discipline of teams and players?

SPORTSMANLIKE CONDUCT

FACTS: Jimmy, a pro tennis player, was upset at a linesman's call. He screamed at the umpire, "If you don't overrule that call, I'll quit!"

When the umpire did not overrule the call, Jimmy walked off the court, defaulting the match. He was later fined and suspended from tournament play.

Johnnie, also a pro tennis player, was fined and suspended for abuse of officials and equipment.

Hank was banished from pro football for gambling on his team's games.

John and Mike were suspended from pro basketball and baseball for taking drugs. They were given sufficient warnings and rehabilitation.

Dale, a pro race car driver, and Jose, a jockey, were fined and placed on probation for improperly causing accidents by cutting off others.

Brad, Jan (pro hockey coaches), and numerous professional athletes, were fined and suspended for fighting or encouraging fighting. Were the fines, suspensions and probation proper and necessary? **YOU'RE THE JUDGE!**

DECISION: Yes. In order to protect the game's interest, its integrity, safety of participants, and to help promote and ensure orderly and fair play, discipline is necessary to regulate conduct which might be detrimental to a game and its participants. All pro sports will make, define and enforce such rules and regulations.

PUBLIC REGULATION

Public regulation by athletic commissions may be established to prevent abuses and promote and protect the public's interest in the legitimate and sportsmanlike conduct of certain sports. Those sports subject to such public control include: horse, dog and automobile racing, jai-alai, boxing and wrestling.

Licensing of all persons or organizations involved in a sport enables a commission to maintain proper control over that sport and its activities.

Athletic commissions issue licenses, provide reasonable rules governing the sport and enforce such rules by appropriate discipline.

The court remarked of the following case that the facts revealed a scenario "that might have been authored by Alfred Hitchcock."

FACTS: In a case referred to as the "Belmont Ringer Case," Matt, a veterinarian, arranged for the purchase of two horses from South America. One, Lebon, was worth very little; the other, Cinzano, was very valuable. Shortly after the horses were quartered at Matt's farm, an "accident" befell Cinzano. He was quickly destroyed.

Some time after, Lebon, who bore a striking resemblance to the deceased horse, went off in the ninth race at Belmont at odds of 57-1. He won by four lengths. Among the "lucky bettors" was Matt, who won $77,000. No one doubted that the "Lebon" who won the race was really Cinzano. Was this fraudulent? **YOU'RE THE JUDGE!**

DECISION: Yes. The court convicted Matt, sentencing him to a fine and imprisonment.

A commission may revoke, or suspend, a license previously issued, or impose other sanctions, such as fines.

Before the rights of those involved in a regulated sport are affected, is due process required? What if the loss is minimal?

FACTS: Tony, a promoter, was fined and his license suspended for allegedly fixing boxing matches. The Boxing Commission did

this after hearing from boxers and promoters; the commission deemed it urgent to preserve the fans' interest and the game's integrity. They offered Tony a hearing after the suspension. "Should I have been given a hearing before the suspension?" asked Tony. **YOU'RE THE JUDGE!**

DECISION: The court concluded, "The seriousness of the fine and suspension—jeopardizing Tony's ability to earn a living—required notice and the opportunity to a fair and impartial hearing with representation before the suspension."

PRIVATE REGULATION

The NCAA and college conferences govern most amateur collegiate sports. Each professional sport not subject to public regulation has its own rules governing eligibility, play, conduct, discipline and other matters. The goals of each are the same: the safety of the players and preserving the integrity of the game.

How may players or coaches who join a fight be disciplined?

FACTS: Ray and Matty, opponents in a college basketball game, got into a fight and were ejected from the game. Several players and one of the coaches came off the bench to join the melee. Could the players and coach be disciplined? **YOU'RE THE JUDGE!**

DECISION: Unsportsmanlike conduct results in an automatic one game suspension for the players and for any bench personnel—other than a head coach—who come onto the floor. For a second incident involving fighting, a player will be suspended for the next game; and for the third incident the player will sit out for the remainder of that year.

Will a court review a league or association's disciplinary rules?

Generally, rules defining conduct and disciplinary measures, as long as they are necessary to carry out the legitimate needs of a sport, will not be reviewed by courts if minimum due process is given (notice and a fair and impartial hearing with representation).

Any person affected by enforcement action may waive those safeguards by knowing and voluntary action.

FACTS: When Mike, a pro golfer, used clubs in competition that did not meet PGA specifications, of which he was aware, he was immediately suspended from further play without a hearing. The purpose of the rule was "to protect the integrity and fairness of the game."

"Why didn't I get a hearing?" asked Mike. **YOU'RE THE JUDGE!**

DECISION: Unlike Tony, the promoter, who was not scheduled to immediately promote another fight, Mike was in competition that would continue into the next day. The suspension was proper. A later hearing could be given to determine the validity of any violation.

COMMISSIONER & PRESIDENT

In 1920, baseball owners chose self-regulation by electing their first commissioner, Judge "Mountain" Landis. He was given broad and complete authority to investigate anything detrimental to the best interest of the sport, and to punish as he saw fit.

One court noted, "As long as a commissioner or president acts within his authority, and in the best interest of the sport, his decisions will not be overruled."

Will a voluntary and good faith agreement to arbitrate a controversy before a commissioner or president, with no access to the courts, be binding?

FACTS: A soccer play-off game was tied and went into overtime. The Sockers' coach, confused as to who had been declared eligible for the shoot-out, questioned the referees. They declared, "Jacques is eligible."

When the Sockers won, the Strikers protested that Jacques was ineligible. The referees were wrong; Jacques was not eligible to play in the shoot-out. Should the commissioner have awarded the game to the Strikers? Would a court decide the controversy? **YOU'RE THE JUDGE!**

DECISION: The Sockers had used an ineligible player. The commissioner awarded the game to the Strikers. This was not a judgment call (one that could be overturned), but a violation of procedures. The commissioner's decision was final; a court would not act.

All pro sports now have a commissioner or president who oversees the conduct of teams and players. Their authority includes the approval of contracts, resolution of disputes, discipline of teams and players for rules' violations and any other action deemed necessary for the best interests of the sport.

May players wear uniforms "different" from those approved by the league ?

FACTS: The NFL Cardinals decided to try to change their luck by wearing all maroon socks, instead of the usual maroon and white.

Tino, a soccer goalkeeper for the Strikers, painted his pants several different colors. He said, "I got tired of wearing black all the time." Another goalie wore polka dots and patches with his sponsor's logos on them. Could the commissioner ban such attire as "eyesores"? **YOU'RE THE JUDGE!**

DECISION: The Cardinal's socks violated the league's standard uniform code and the commissioner could ban them.

Goalkeepers are required to wear uniforms different from their teammates. Such uniforms were permitted.

Where the head of a league fails to respect the limits of his authority, courts will be available for a review of the controversy. Any authority must have a legitimate purpose, such as to protect the integrity of the game or sport.

FACTS: The commissioner of baseball warned all clubs to refrain from tampering with free agents prior to a special draft. One owner let it be known publicly that he intended to sign one of the free agents. After a hearing, the commissioner suspended the owner from baseball for one season and directed that his team forfeit their first-round amateur draft choice for the following year. The owner alleged, "The commissioner overstepped his authority in depriving me of the draft choice." Were the suspension and forfeiture upheld by the court? **YOU'RE THE JUDGE!**

DECISION: The court held that the suspension was within the commissioner's authority to invoke the no-tampering rule; the power to deprive the team of their draft choice was not within the commissioner's power.

Other owners have also been fined for tampering with players. One coach was fined for tampering with a game by allowing the opposing team to score so that one of the coach's players would have a chance to break a scoring record.

WILL I BE DISCIPLINED?

FACTS: James, a pro tennis player, was coached by Manny, who gave signals to James throughout his matches. Could either the player or the coach be disciplined for such conduct? **YOU'RE THE JUDGE!**

DECISION: Both were subject to discipline for violation of the rule which prohibited coaching during a professional tennis match.

A league in team sports, and an association in individual sports, establishes disciplinary rules governing conduct. These rules provide for specific sanctions—fines, suspension and termination—for violations and conduct detrimental to the integrity of the game.

FACTS: Kirk was fined and suspended from baseball by the commissioner for substance abuse. "The suspension was too harsh and the fine too much," he grumbled. He appealed. Who handled the appeal? **YOU'RE THE JUDGE!**

DECISION: Kirk's appeal was handled by the same commissioner. Any further appeal could be to an independent arbitrator.

If there was no provision in his contract providing for appeal to an independent arbitrator, appeal would be to a court. However, unless the rule was illegal or illegally applied, the commissioner's decision would be upheld.

Discipline may be used to discourage gambling, as in the case of an NBA player suspended for gambling on games. The court refused to enjoin the suspension for lack of a hearing, finding that the player was "morally dishonest. The appearance of players betting was enough to destroy public confidence in the integrity of the game."

May discipline be used to discourage other activity as well?

FACTS: Ray, coach of the NBA Stingers, was irate over a referee's decision which cost him a game. He shrieked at the ref, "You blew the call! That cost me the game. Go read the rules book."

Pete, a baseball manager, irate over a call, bumped and pushed the umpire.

Rick, upset over a ref's call during a hockey game, yelled, "The ref is a no-good, vindictive - - who deliberately cheated us!" Could the commissioner fine or suspend the coaches for their conduct or comments? **YOU'RE THE JUDGE!**

DECISION: Yes. Coaches, owners and players have been fined and suspended for conduct not in the best interest of the game—where they have publicly criticized umpires and referees concerning a decision, or physically abused an official.

Players, managers and teams may also be fined or suspended for instigating brawls and riots.

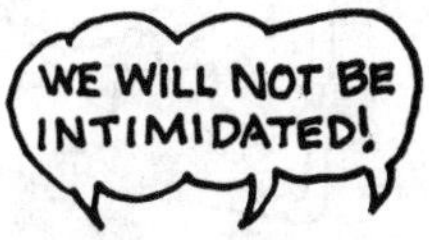

FACTS: In separate incidents involving fights by their teams, a baseball manager and a hockey coach both snarled, "We will not be intimidated!"

When brawls broke out, and spilled out into the stands, players, refs and fans were injured. Could the coaches be fined or suspended for instigating the fights?

DECISION: **YOU'RE THE JUDGE!**

Players are required to play within the rules. Conduct intended to injure an opposing player, or which reflects unfavorably on the game, is prohibited. As a result of flagrant, unsportsmanlike conduct players in all major sports have been fined and suspended.

How is the type and amount or length of punishment determined?

Punishment is determined by the severity of any injury, the seriousness of the act, any defenses (self-defense), and any previous similar conduct. The more severe the act or injury, the more severe will be the penalty. In hockey, abuse of players is still permitted—although there now are more severe fines and suspensions for flagrant acts of violence or bench-clearing brawls (one player was even given a one day jail sentence for hitting another player with his hockey stick).

FACTS: At a soccer game, players assaulted each other and insulted the referees. Then the fans pelted each other with rocks and fought, causing the stands to collapse, killing and injuring spectators. Were the players and teams subject to fines and suspensions for their misconduct? **YOU'RE THE JUDGE!**

DECISION: Yes. Clubs, players and coaches have been fined and suspended for their own misconduct, as well as that of fans, which resulted in injury. In assaulting other players and insulting the referee, they incited the fans to act in a violent manner.

Another soccer player was fined and suspended for not wearing shin guards, as required to prevent the possible contraction of AIDS from an open wound.

A suspension is legal if it is intended to accomplish a legitimate goal, such as subjecting all players to the same rules. It must be reasonable, no more extensive than necessary, and follow procedural safeguards (including adequate notice and a fair and impartial hearing with the opportunity for representation).

FACTS: Dena was suspended from the LPGA for allegedly cheating by improperly marking her golf ball on the putting green. A group of her fellow players, in a closed hearing, suspended her. Could Dena have the suspension enjoined because she was not given a fair and impartial hearing? **YOU'RE THE JUDGE!**

DECISION: Yes. The members who suspended her were her own competitors and had a financial interest in whether or not she played. Such action was unfair and, therefore, prohibited.

Players must use their best efforts to observe the rules and conduct themselves in a professional manner which will reflect favorably on their sport. Were the following acts "good conduct"?

FACTS: John, a pro tennis player, was upset with an umpire's calls. He slammed his racket, hit balls into the stands and called the umpire a "jerk," his opponent a "cheat" and several people—

including the president of the tennis association—"idiots."

Evan was wearing a product endorsement patch, not approved of by the USTA, on his tennis shorts.

Rashina, an Olympic skier, wore an oversized logo on her headband. Red, a pro football player, wore a headband with a company's name on it.

Bull, a pro golfer, decided (after nine holes of a tournament) to change into shorts. Bob, not liking the course, called it an "overgrown parking lot" and also criticized the commissioner, calling him a "thief."

Gary, a pro bowler, drinking while bowling, kicked and broke the ball return during a tournament. Afterwards, he played cards in the locker room. Could any of these competitors be fined, disqualified or otherwise disciplined for their conduct? **YOU'RE THE JUDGE!**

DECISION: Yes, for: unsportsmanlike conduct; abuse of equipment, officials, players and fans; improper clothing; improper product endorsement or logo; improper comments; and drinking and card playing. Each of these competitors was subject to fines, suspension, disqualification or termination for his or her conduct, (which were all prohibited by the rules governing play in their respective sports). Such conduct was not in the best interests of their sports.

A commissioner or president in a team sport may also be given the authority to approve or disapprove player contracts, or other transactions between teams.

This is to insure that teams negotiate proper terms, that competitive balance between teams is maintained, and to preserve equal treatment of players. For example, a league may have an interest in insuring that players only receive proper bonuses, or that every player is subject to the same disciplinary rules and punishments as other players.

May a commissioner void the sale of baseball players from one team to another?

FACTS: Finley, owner of the A's, decided to sell three of his star players to the Red Sox for cash only; no players were to be exchanged between the clubs.

After conducting a hearing, the commissioner disapproved the deal. Finley went to court, asserting the commissioner had overstepped his authority by voiding the sale. Should Finley have been able to sell his players to the Red Sox? **YOU'RE THE JUDGE!**

DECISION: The court ruled, "The commissioner's decision to void the sale of the players was proper. The transaction was inconsistent with the best interests and integrity of the game." If ap-

proved, the sale would have lessened competitive balance between the A's and other teams by weakening the A's ability to perform. The sale would have contributed to destroying public confidence in a home team.

In resolving any disciplinary disputes, independent arbitration may be used to determine the fairness and reasonableness of any disciplinary action.

Review by a court will be limited to cases where the commissioner or president clearly overstepped their power or failed to give due process.

As one court noted, "It is intended that the commissioner or president will continue to wield strong authority, this necessary to protect the best interests of, and the public confidence in, professional sports."

ODDS & ENDS....

Gambling does not always have to result in a fine, at least not to the winner.

FACTS: Fred traveled from California to Pennsylvania for a friendly round of golf with Lloyd. The trip was worth his while because Fred won $24,000 on several bets concerning their skills. When Lloyd didn't pay, Fred sued.

Lloyd said, "Gambling is illegal. I don't have to pay." Did Lloyd have to pay? **YOU'RE THE JUDGE!**

DECISION: Yes. The court quoted from the state gambling statutes which defined gambling as including, "A sporting event, over which the person taking a risk has no control." Here, the court reasoned, "There was a golf match, where each player, by his playing, had control over the outcome. The wagering on this golf match did not constitute gambling." Lloyd was, in effect, fined $24,000.

Another golfer was charged with "hooliganism" and fined, after his drive hit a bird that then smashed into the windshield of a jet taking off from an air force base next to the golf course. The jet, in mid take-off, bounced off the runway and destroyed five planes.

Any enforcement of disciplinary rules by the heads of professional sports leagues and associations must have a legitimate purpose, such as to protect the integrity of the game.

17

WAR & PEACE!

WHAT'S IT ABOUT?

War & Peace! details "wars" between competing professional sports leagues for players, cities, stadiums, owners and TV coverage.

Are professional sports leagues allowed to merge in order to end a war?

Philadelphia News
August 10, 1976

SPORTS LEAGUES AT WAR!

There have been "wars" between professional sports leagues since 1871 when the National League began its "battles" with competing baseball leagues—with only the American League surviving.

The National Basketball Association (NBA) was formed in 1949 after a war between two competing leagues. Later, after a battle with the American Basketball League (ABA), the NBA admitted four ABA teams, thus ending the ABA.

And, in the face of litigation with the World Hockey Association (WHA), the NHL voted to admit four WHA teams.

What about the teams that weren't admitted—were they illegally banished from participating?

BATTLES FOR PLAYERS, CITIES.... & SURVIVAL

FACTS: The ABA and WHL teams that were not merged into the NBA and NHL complained, "By locking us out, the older leagues restrained trade and monopolized the sports." How could the older leagues attempt to prevent antitrust litigation? **YOU'RE THE JUDGE!**

DECISION: Teams left out of the mergers were compensated monetarily in hopes of preventing antitrust litigation for restraining trade and monopolizing the sport by eliminating some teams.

The National Football League (NFL), formed in 1920, had a monopoly in pro football until the American Football Conference (AFC) appeared. The two battled until, in 1950, the NFL absorbed three AFC teams, and thus resumed its monopoly ... that is, until the American Football League (AFL) appeared. Then, the NFL-AFL "war" lasted until 1966, when the two leagues were allowed to merge.

The NFL then engaged in a short-lived war with the World Football League (WFL)—which folded—before warring with the United States Football League (USFL).

The USFL began in 1983. They competed with the NFL for star players, not under contract, and for college stars.

When it became evident that spring football would not support the USFL, they challenged the NFL in the courts.

FACTS: The USFL filed an antitrust suit against the NFL, alleging, "The NFL monopolized pro football by controlling stadiums and the major TV networks."

A network broadcasting contract was necessary to stay afloat financially. They argued, "The NFL practices were an attempt to boycott us from competing in pro football." Did the NFL unreasonably restrain trade and attempt to monopolize pro football? **YOU'RE THE JUDGE!**

DECISION: The court held that the NFL did not monopolize the networks. Furthermore, the NFL was a "natural monopoly"—only one league could survive. The USFL was awarded $3 in damages! They suspended operations in 1986.

Wars between competing leagues involved battles for players, interference with players' contracts and competition for cities, arenas, owners and TV contracts.

Players

How could these battles between warring sports leagues benefit players?

The battles provided players with an opportunity for increased salaries and benefits. Teams, in an attempt to lock up players, signed and paid them before their college eligibility was up—a violation of NCAA rules—and offered contracts and money (sometimes far different from that which appeared in the contract). Some players signed with more than one team or agent.

FACTS: Tom signed to play for the Tigers in the new World Football League (WFL). He then received a better offer and re-signed with his old team, the Blitzers, in the NFL.

The Tigers contended that the contract they had with Tom was valid and that the Blitzers interferred with that contract.

Tom insisted, "I was persuaded by the Tigers to sign for a bonus which they didn't pay."

The Blitzers reasoned, "We knew nothing of Tom's dealing with the Tigers. Tom still had to fulfill his option year with us." Which team would Tom play for? **YOU'RE THE JUDGE!**

DECISION: The Blitzers had an existing contract with Tom. And even if they didn't, there would be no interference—as the Tigers came into court with "unclean hands." They were aware that Tom was under contract and should not have been negotiating with him for the current year. Tom would play for the Blitzers, at least until his new contract and any option ran out.

Stadiums

Teams cannot exist without stadiums and arenas that will seat large crowds. And, as these stadiums and arenas are expensive to build, most cities have only one. Thus, team owners in new sports leagues often have to settle for a lesser facility when a desired facility is under contract with an existing team in a competing league.

Despite head-to-head competition with established leagues, new leagues are attracted to the biggest cities. These large cities may be able to support more than one franchise and will already have existing stadiums and arenas.

Although it may be possible to share a stadium or arena with another team by juggling schedules, the existing league will often attempt to "tie up" a playing site by employing an "exclusive use" arrangement with the facility. Such arrangements have been found illegal.

An **"essential" facility**—one that could not practicably be duplicated—will not have to be shared if it would be impractical—as where a baseball team plays more games and more regularly than a football team, or where time may be needed to properly prepare the facility for the next game and another's use will not leave enough time. What if a stadium is privately owned? Must it still be shared?

Even where a stadium is privately owned, a duty exists to lease an "essential" facility where no other suitable facility exists for a pro sports team.

Cities

Success for a pro sports team will depend upon the support of fans. Experience has shown that the larger the city, the greater the likelihood for sufficient attendance.

As any existing league generally already has franchises in most large cities, a new league will have to fight with the existing league in order to locate franchises in these cities.

FACTS: The AFL tried to show that the NFL was monopolizing pro football by locating and expanding into all of the major cities, thus preventing the AFL from competing for fans in the largest cities. "Was this an illegal monopoly?" asked the AFL. **YOU'RE THE JUDGE!**

DECISION: The court decided, "There were still cities available with enough fans to potentially support teams. And those cities where the NFL already had teams might support a second pro football team. The NFL did not have monopoly power and, furthermore, had not undertaken expansion into new cities with the intent to destroy the AFL as a competitor."

The AFL could not prevent the NFL from expanding into new cities or from expanding its television coverage in order to protect part of the market for themselves.

FACTS: Did the USFL, in its battle with the NFL, have a similar problem in trying to show that the NFL had monopolized pro football by locating teams in all of the major cities? **YOU'RE THE JUDGE!**

DECISION: The USFL had franchises in, or near, the major cities, but several of them failed economically, then folded or were moved.

Owners

Professional sports leagues have attempted to "protect" themselves. Such a case was when the NFL attempted to ban ownership of teams by its club owners of teams in any competing sports league.

The court found that the ban unreasonably restrained trade, thus making it difficult for other leagues to find potential owners, thereby subjecting them to potential failure for lack of financial support.

Media

Sports are played at different levels: from sandlot or pick-up games, to collegiate sports, and ultimately to the highest level of ability and success—professional sports. Different leagues may vie, but eventually the fans will support the best league.

FACTS: A new volleyball league challenged the established United Volleyball League (UVL). As the fans preferred to see the

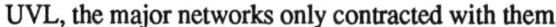

UVL, the major networks only contracted with them.

The new league claimed, "The networks locked us out. We won't be able to continue." Must the networks contract with the new league to cover their games? **YOU'RE THE JUDGE!**

DECISION: The media, to exist, will follow the fan's preference in deciding which games to broadcast. Leagues with lesser fan appeal will not be able to contract for television coverage as extensive as the desired league, or maybe not at all. As long as the networks did not conspire among themselves—or with the UVL—to lock out the new league, there will be no restraint of trade.

What will happen to the unwanted league? The ultimate outcome will likely be that one league will predominate while the other will disappear (or be merged or absorbed by the dominant league).

Merger

Merger or acquisition has settled several wars between competing leagues in pro sports.

Congress gave the NFL and AFL immunity from the antitrust laws prohibiting monopoly, thus clearing the way for them to end their war, declare a truce, and merge on the condition that the new league would have more teams than the two separate leagues. What if the players who were left out objected?

FACTS: After a long war, the ABA agreed to merge four ABA teams into the NBA.

Some ABA players objected, "The merger and the NBA's draft and reserve system monopolized pro basketball and prevented us from selling our services." They obtained an injunction preventing the two leagues from merging. Could the leagues still merge? **YOU'RE THE JUDGE!**

DECISION: After collective bargaining between the NBA and its player's association gave the players free agent status—with no unilateral right to renew by the losing team—the leagues were allowed to merge.

ODDS & ENDS....

FACTS: Before rumors of a new volleyball league, the UVL considered expanding. Could any new volleyball league successfully allege that any UVL expansion would prevent the new league from becoming established? Should the UVL have to forego expansion? **YOU'RE THE JUDGE!**

DECISION: Unless expansion was directly aimed at locking out a competing league, it is doubtful that such expansion could be enjoined.

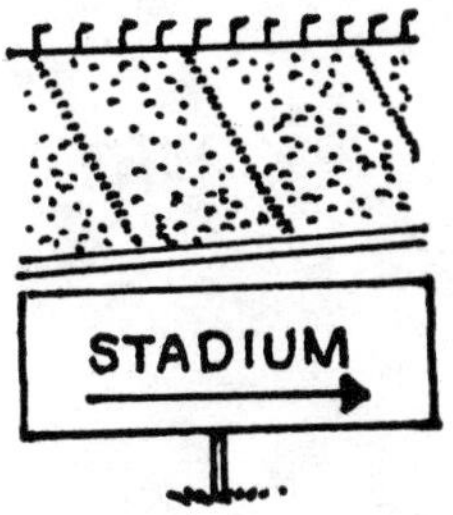

The effect of a league passing up expansion opportunities would be to deny fans in potential expansion cities the right to enjoy live pro sports, to deny qualified athletes and others the opportunity to earn a living, and to deny itself the opportunity to increase revenue. This could lessen the quality of the league.

18

OFFICIALS, REFEREES & UMPIRES

WHAT'S IT ABOUT?

All sports officials have a duty to provide fair and safe sporting events. *Officials, Referees & Umpires* considers who may be liable where an injury results to either a participant or an official during a sporting event.

Can an official's decision made during a sporting event be changed after the event is over?

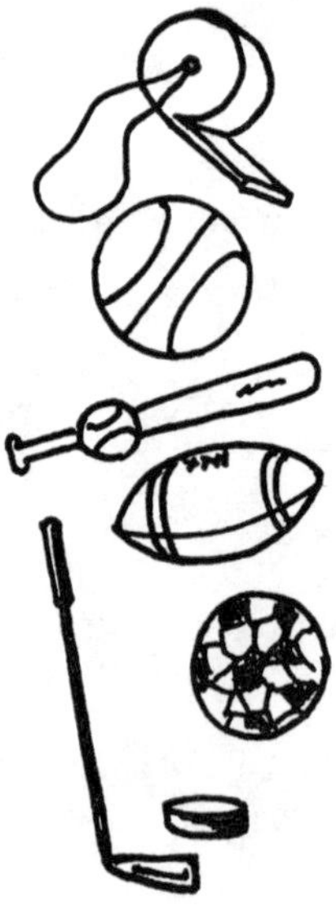

Officials, Referees & Umpires' Union
5647 Fair Place, Plantation, FL 33324

Dear players, coaches, managers, fans and others:

This is our **OFFICIALS' CHECKLIST.** In the interest of providing a contest that (regardless of the result) will be: enjoyed by all, fair and safe, and leave you saying, "The ref did a great job!"—we will do our best to abide by it. We promise to:

BE SMART & WORK HARD

We will know the rules of the sport and give our best effort to keep ourselves and the contest under control with proper calls.

NOT BE "TOUGH" GUYS

If a coach, manager or player is on our back, but not enough to warrant a penalty, we won't be threatening or irritating by standing nearby just to "show 'em."

GET INTO THE "FLOW"

We will concentrate on players' reactions and the tempo of the game to prevent a "smooth" game from turning into a "ragged or rough" one.

LISTEN

We won't yell, but will treat everyone politely, answering all sensible questions. We will be firm, but relaxed, and accept some criticism. But we won't be "told off."

FORGET THE FANS

We will ignore the fans unless they interrupt the contest or our job. They may not know the rules, may be emotional and partisan, or merely delight in antagonizing us.

BE COOL & CONFIDENT

We will establish a calm atmosphere for the game by remaining "cool" under pressure. We will exude confidence and command respect. But we will not be cocky.

Officials, Referees & Umpires' Union

WAS THE OFFICIAL LIABLE?

FACTS: Two basketball referees worked hard to control a game. But then, a scuffle broke out. An injury resulted when a player was elbowed in the face. Were the officials liable?

DECISION: **YOU'RE THE JUDGE!**

What must an injured participant prove in order to recover damages against an official? What is an official's duty?

In order to recover damages from an official for an injury, an injured participant must prove **negligence.** That is, the participant must show that the official owed a duty to exercise due and proper care for a player's safety, that the official breached that duty, and that an injury and damages would not have occurred "but for" the action or inaction of the official.

However, officials do not insure participant's safety. Participants have a duty for their own protection and safety.

An official's **defenses** may be that any injured player assumes the risk of injury as one ordinary or common to the contest or sport, or that the player contributed to his injury by taking part in the contest.

FACTS: Cater, a pro boxer, died several days after being knocked out in a fight. Many observers felt, "The referee should have stopped the fight. Cater was so dazed that he remained seated on his stool after the bell rang for his last round."

During an investigation, a neurologist testified that "fight officials displayed gross malpractice of their official duties" by allowing Cater to continue.

Cater's widow sued for "negligent supervision in failing to stop the fight." The referee and others defended by contending, "The boxer assumed the risk of injury by knowing, being aware of, and appreciating the risk." Was Cater aware in his condition? Was the referee liable?

DECISION: **YOU'RE THE JUDGE!**

After a high school wrestling match, the referee was sued for a failure of adequate supervision and control. The referee allegedly allowed a wrestler to continue with an illegal hold. As a result, the opponent was rendered a quadraplegic. The referee and other defendants settled out of court.

FACTS: While another wrestling referee's attention was distracted by a yelling fan, one of the wrestlers applied an illegal hold, resulting in a severe injury to his opponent, Guererro. "Was the referee liable?" asked Guererro. **YOU'RE THE JUDGE!**

DECISION: A referee may be liable, not because of a failure to act in a proper manner, but rather because of a failure to act at all. The referee should not have allowed the fan to distract him.

A referee's job is to ensure that a game is played within the rules. If he allows a game to get out of control, or to be played in violation of rules, a new peril arises—injury to a player due to a lack of control or to rules violations.

May participants assume the risk of, or contribute to, any injury by participating?

FACTS: The Colts were playing the Steelers. Jones was running full speed as a play reached the sideline. He claimed, "I struck the aluminum down marker which was still stuck in the ground. The collision ruined my knee and cut short my career. The referees should have known that the equipment was dangerous and moved it out of the way. They didn't properly supervise and control their duties to protect the players." Were the referees liable for Jones' injuries? **YOU'RE THE JUDGE!**

DECISION: Apparently the jury was not convinced by Jones' allegations. They returned a verdict in favor of the referees. Jones—in playing football—had contributed to and assumed the risk of such an injury.

The care officials owe to a participant depends upon how apparent any risk is and their ability to prevent it.

FACTS: During a hockey game, a referee observed extremely rough play, but failed to sufficiently supervise it. He also failed to enforce rules designed to protect players from injuries from high sticking and slashing. Injuries resulted.

During a football game, a quarterback was injured by an intentional punch after throwing the ball.

Were either of these risks of harm apparent? Could the referees have prevented the injuries? **YOU'RE THE JUDGE!**

DECISION: The first risk was apparent and the injury could have been prevented. The risk of injury to the quarterback was not apparent.

What was the referee's ability to prevent injury? In certain sports, such as boxing and wrestling, a referee has a greater capacity for control than in others. In team contact sports, such as football or hockey, control is more difficult.

In team sports, only a referee's continual failure to control player misconduct should be declared a breach of his duty to care for a player's safety.

FACTS: The Bruisers and the Bumpers, in their quest for the Hockey Championship Cup, met in a play-off game. The referees were kept busy breaking up minor scuffles. When another scuffle broke out at one point, the referees decided not to interfere.

One of them thought, "Maybe if we let these two players go at it and get it out of their systems, everyone will calm down and the game will go on smoothly."

One of the players fighting was severely injured. Were the referees liable for letting the fight go on? Did they have control?

DECISION: **YOU'RE THE JUDGE!**

Officials do not insure a sports participant's safety. Where certain hazards and unavoidable accidents occur, against which a referee may not guard by the greatest degree of caution, liability may not attach.

FACTS: Karby, 16, died from a head injury received during a basketball game. He was hurt when a ball, thrown by a fellow player, hit him in the head. Did Karby assume the risk of injury? **YOU'RE THE JUDGE!**

DECISION: Yes. There was no liability by the referee for what was an unavoidable accident.

Will a participant assume the risk of injury from an unknown danger? A participant never assumes the risk from unknown danger. The fact that a participant is aware of one danger (player irresponsibility) cannot serve to extend assumption of the risk to another danger—a negligent referee.

FACTS: Ed received a severe injury during a scrimmage football game when Peter, who had been playing recklessly for some time, improperly ran into him. There were referees at the scrimmage. "Did I assume the risk of injury?" asked Ed. **YOU'RE THE JUDGE!**

DECISION: No. A player will not assume the risk of a referee's careless supervision. The injury would not have resulted had the referee's supervision been adequate. The referee's negligent supervision resulted in a foreseeable type of injury from an out of control situation.

However, if a participant, such as a professional, has skill, knowledge and training—beyond that of the average participant—assumption of the risk will be easier to prove.

INJURY TO AN OFFICIAL

Stiffer penalties, including suspension, have been used in an attempt to prevent attacks on, and abuse of, officials.

FACTS: A fan leaving a baseball game explained what happened. "The home plate umpire was in the parking lot after the game. The losing team's coach was yelling at the umpire and then hit him in the face." Was this contact part of the game, or was it an intentional assault? **YOU'RE THE JUDGE!**

DECISION: The coach was convicted of assault on a sports official and fined under a law intended to protect officials of sports contests.

An official only consents to, and assumes the risk of injury from, acts that are "part of the game" (such as where he is unintentionally run into). But where an official is shoved or struck, in an action clearly apart from the game, recovery of damages for injury may be possible.

FACTS: Toone, an umpire, ruled that a Cap outfielder had trapped a flyball. The opposing manager charged onto the field vehemently protesting. "If there is another bad call, I'll incite the crowd!" he warned.

In the ninth inning, the manager and his players charged onto the field after a close play. The manager refused to control his players and refused to help after several fans challenged Toone.

One fan injured Toone, who then sued the fan, the team, and the manager, claiming, "They owed me a duty to conduct themselves so as not to incite the crowd against me, and also to provide me with safe passage after the game." Who was liable for Toone's injury? **YOU'RE THE JUDGE!**

DECISION: Although the court held against the fan, it found that the assault was not the result of the manager's unsportsmanlike conduct. "It would be an intolerable burden on the club to hold it responsible for the actions of any emotionally unstable persons who might attend the game. The injury may have occurred even without the manager's conduct," commented the court.

Officials will be charged with knowledge of the danger involved in officiating sports, such as where athletes will cut back and forth. One court stated, "Referees who voluntarily participate must accept the risks to which their roles expose them."

Such was the case where football and baseball officials were "run over," and hockey and baseball officials were injured by pucks and balls. They assumed the risks of injury, having knowledge, awareness and appreciation of the risk involved.

FACTS: Umpire Dillard was standing behind the plate in a Little League baseball game when a ball bounced past the catcher and went out of play. Dillard yelled, "Time out!"

While time was called, the pitcher threw another pitch which struck the plate and then Dillard, who was not wearing shin guards or a groin protector.

Dillard sued the league for failing to provide him with adequate equipment, and he sued the pitcher for failing to heed the time out. "Who was liable?" asked Dillard. **YOU'RE THE JUDGE!**

DECISION: The risk of being struck by a baseball while umpiring was reasonably foreseeable, as was errant play from players so young. It was not the practice of the league to supply umpires with equipment. He assumed the risk of such an injury.

These players were young and inexperienced. Where such a situation involves an older, more experienced player, will an official still be held to assume the risk of injury?

FACTS: A volunteer track official was struck in the head by the shot put at the state championships. He stammered, "I was facing the track, standing in my assigned spot while officiating a race. The events were staged together in a small area. I never saw the shotput." Did the official assume the risk of such an injury?

DECISION: **YOU'RE THE JUDGE!**

WORKMEN'S COMPENSATION

State **workmen's compensation** laws compensate employees for injuries incident to their employment, without regard to the neglect or fault of their employer. An employee need only show that his injury arose from, and in the course of, his employment.

FACTS: An umpire, Clark, injured by an irate player, applied for workmen's compensation benefits. He explained, "I wasn't an employee of the Umpire Association or a school, but was an independent contractor. I worked for myself and could accept or refuse any assignment. The association or school had no control in directing my work or how it was done." Could Clark receive benefits? **YOU'RE THE JUDGE!**

DECISION: No. Clark was not an employee of the association or school. He could sue the player, the player's coach or parents, or the school.

However, where an official, such as an official for professional sports, is employed by an association or league and cannot refuse to officiate a certain game without jeopardizing his job, workmen's compensation may be available.

BAD FAITH

The general rule that officials' decisions will not be disturbed will not apply where a decision involves corruption or bad faith.

FACTS: A horse won a close race. But before the winner was announced, one of three judges separately told each of the others that he and the third judge had agreed that another horse had won. Since each of the other judges believed that a majority of the judges was in favor of the second horse, they agreed. The second horse was declared the winner. Could the court overturn such a decision? **YOU'RE THE JUDGE!**

DECISION: The court concluded, "Such conduct was fraudulent. The decision cannot stand. The power to correct corrupt or fraudulent decisions is necessary to insure public confidence in the honest and competent officiating of athletic games and contests."

ODDS & ENDS....

"We Contest The Decision"

The desire to win may provide the motivation to challenge an official's decision thought to be wrong. Generally, such challenges will amount to little more than verbal protestations.

FACTS: Officials erred in not giving an automatic first down after the punter was "roughed" during a high school football game.

The losing team protested, "That error led to our defeat. The last seven minutes, which determined qualification for the state playoffs, should be played over." Would the game, in part, be replayed? **YOU'RE THE JUDGE!**

DECISION: No. The court ruled, "Football games are meant to be played on the gridiron and not in the courts. Players have no property right in the playing of the game by the rules. Decisions of officials do not present a controversy that can be heard by the courts."

Suits involving officials' errors in professional sports have also been denied.

The general rule is, "In the absence of bad faith or corruption, the decisions of sports officials will be final." That is so because of an official's experience, fairness and closeness to the action. However, there have been exceptions.

FACTS: In a high school basketball tournament, St. Michaels thought it beat Walther 67-66. St. Michaels scored at the first half buzzer, but Walther maintained that the buzzer went off several seconds after the clock had run out. The referees said the basket counted, but—after the game—reversed their decision, giving Walther the victory.

St. Michaels went to court seeking a ruling that the second half should be replayed. They asserted, "We certainly would have played differently had we known that the basket would not be counted." Should a court refuse to hear such a case, opening itself to appeal for every loss where an official's decision may be wrong? **YOU'RE THE JUDGE!**

DECISION: The second half was replayed, with St. Michaels again on the short end, 64-63.

Now matter how well officials perform their job in officiating sports events, they are sure to be booed.

19

DISHES, SATELLITES & PIRATES

WHAT'S IT ABOUT?

Dishes, Satellites & Pirates traces the history of television and cable in sports, explains who owns the TV and radio rights to sports broadcasts and discusses royalties and "piracy" of broadcast signals.

Do you know how the first "blackout" practice came about?

Section C - Sports **NY Observer** May 18, 1939

TELEVISION IS BORN!

In a baseball game yesterday, Princeton battled Columbia and won 2-1. Most of the 5,000 people who saw the game couldn't see the green grass, nor did they have to "dodge" foul balls. They didn't see the game in person, but watched it as the first sports event ever shown on TV!

TELEVISION SIGNALS

How would people receive a television signal? In the beginning, the only way a television signal could be received was by over-the-air transmission. The TV broadcasting station sent out a signal by antenna, which was received by another antenna—usually on the roof of a house—within range of the station. This is still the most common way by which most people receive television signals and programs.

But, with the advent of cable TV (CATV), television and sports became almost one. How did CATV begin?

CABLE TV

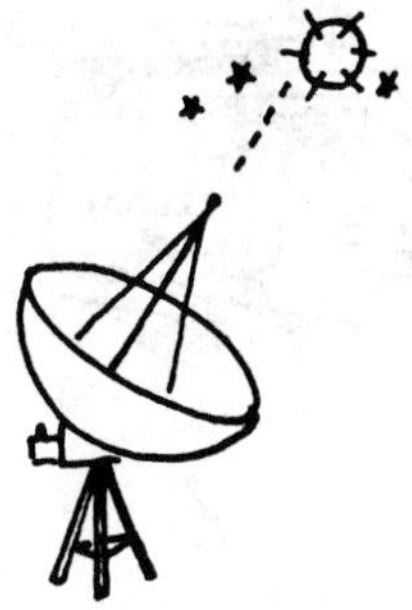

In the late 1940's, John Walson, an appliance salesman in Pennsylvania, realized that before he could sell new-fangled TV's to customers deep in mountain country—cut off from the broadcast signals in Philadelphia and Pittsburgh—he would have to guarantee reception. "How could I do that?" he asked.

Walson ran a wire to an antenna atop a nearby mountain, hooked his customers to it, and thus was born CATV!

That worked fine then, but how are CATV signals now brought into people's homes?

A cable station, such as ESPN or USA, after negotiating for broadcasting rights to a sporting event, sends the game's signal over Western Union land lines to the nearest city with the necessary transmitting microwave dish antenna (or directly from the game site if a dish is present).

From there, the signal is passed through the dish up to a satellite. At ESPN or USA, the signal is received back by another dish. The commercials, promos, and special effects are added, and then the complete show is beamed back up through the antenna of the dish to the satellite. Antennae at earth stations, set up by local cable companies that subscribe to the cable stations, then pull back down the completed signal and the picture is fed through cables to subscribers' living rooms.

These over-the-air and national cable broadcasts are supplemented by other forms of distributing signals for sports events. What are some of these other ways to distribute sports events?

"Superstations," like WTBS, WGN and WOR (which are local TV stations owning broadcast rights to local professional teams' games), beam signals by satellite to other cable operators. Thus, the Braves, Cubs and Mets can be seen coast to coast.

There also are: local cable companies; per-channel pay cable—such as HBO, subscription TV (where a decoder is needed to unscramble a signal), per-program home pay cable, and closed circuit for arenas and theatres—such as for a boxing match or other special event.

FACTS: People would now pay to watch sports at home, thus increasing the TV stations' revenue from commercials. TV began to dictate not only when games would be shown, but even when time-outs would be called during a game.

But what stations would be allowed to broadcast what games? And did the teams or the league own the rights to broadcast games?

DECISION: **YOU'RE THE JUDGE!**

TV & RADIO RIGHTS

> "This telecast is presented by authority of the National Football League. It is intended solely for the private use of our audience, and any rebroadcast or other use of this telecast without the express written consent of the National Football League is prohibited."

This announcement is virtually identical to those used in other professional sports. Major League Baseball (MLB), in an effort to prevent unauthorized broadcasts, began making such a statement in connection with radio broadcasts of their games even before TV was in widespread use.

The first incident involving the unauthorized broadcast of a sporting event happened at the 1934 World Series—between the Cardinals and Tigers.

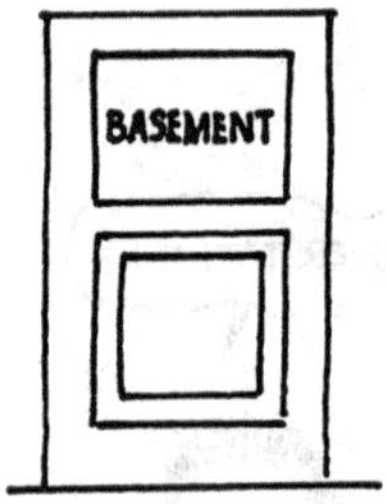

FACTS: Newton operated a radio station, WOCL, from the basement of his home. He would listen to the authorized radio broadcasts of games and, by using the information that he heard, give his audience a "play-by-play." His license renewal was challenged on the claim that he had improperly presented an unauthorized broadcast. "Can I still get my radio station license renewed?" asked Newton. **YOU'RE THE JUDGE!**

DECISION: Major League Baseball (MLB) had authorized the broadcast of World Series games by various radio stations, but not by Newton. Newton's conduct violated the Communications Act, which prohibits rebroadcasting, without consent, another station's programming. Newton's conduct was found to be a "dishonest, unfair utilization of another's labor and deceptive to the public." However, because the unauthorized broadcast had occurred only once, Newton's license was renewed.

Some early decisions denied the right of sports teams to control the broadcast of their games. Those decisions were few and not later followed.

FACTS: In 1938, radio station KQV stationed observers who watched baseball games over the fences at the Pirate's Forbes Field. These observers then relayed the information to KQV announcers, who then broadcast play-by-play descriptions of the games. The Pirates sued to enjoin KQV from the unauthorized broadcasts. KQV argued that the accounts of sports events constituted news and that any person had the right to disseminate the news. Was KQV enjoined from broadcasting the games? **YOU'RE THE JUDGE!**

DECISION: Yes. The court enjoined KQV from broadcasting the games without permission, commenting, "The Pirates—by going to great expense in creating the game, maintaining the baseball park and paying the players—had a **property right** in the news of the games. They could sell that right to others to broadcast the games, and could also restrict others from disseminating news of the game. KQV was guilty of unfair competition, unjust enrichment of another's property rights and of a fraud on the public."

Now teams could sell or license this right and prevent others from unauthorized live broadcasts of their games.

FACTS: Martin explained how he helped rebroadcast Giants baseball games. "I teletyped authorized reports of the games to radio stations across the country for immediate rebroadcast. The stations would pick up these broadcasts without paying the team and then insert their own play-by-play, complete with background sound effects of crowds, ball on bat and made up reasons for crowd noise." Was this legal? **YOU'RE THE JUDGE!**

DECISION: No. The court concluded, "Although some of these re-creations were more exciting than the game itself, they were unauthorized and illegal as a misappropriation of the Giants' property rights to control the broadcast of its baseball games. Martin was enjoined from sending the reports.

Teams could now control the broadcast of their games. But could they control any rebroadcast made after a game?

The right of teams to control the broadcast of their games extended not only to the live broadcast of the game but, also, for a reasonable time following the game or event, to any rebroadcast. Practices, other than reporting the game as part of a news broadcast, were prohibited. Incorporating film of games into movies or highlight films and supplying "up to the minute, ringside descriptions" of boxing matches were also prohibited.

To help protect this right to control an event's broadcast, sports teams began printing on the back of tickets:

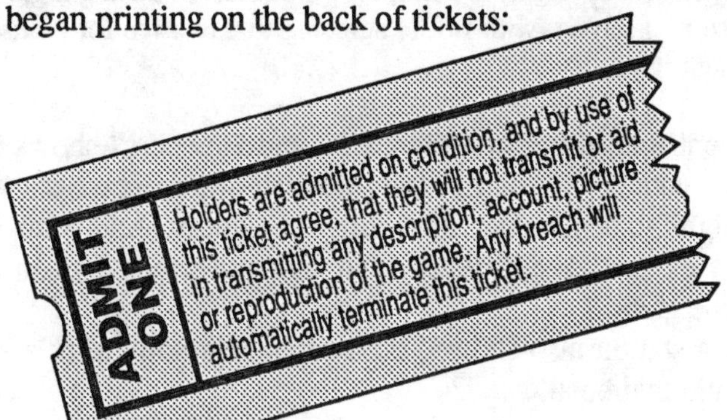

This sports property right concept was strengthened by a case concerning the celebrated "Flying" Zacchini's human cannon ball performance.

FACTS: On a nightly news show, a TV station broadcasted Zacchini's entire performance without his permission. The performer sued the station for "stealing my right to control who would see my performance." The station felt that it was only showing the news, a right given by the First Amendment. "Did the station misappropriate Zacchini's property right? **YOU'RE THE JUDGE!**

DECISION: Yes. Zacchini had the right to control the publicizing of his performance. The court found the station guilty of misappropriation and awarded damages to Zacchini.

What if the station had only broadcast part of the performance on its sports show?

The court explained, "Had the station only broadcast part of the performance, its right to do so would have been protected by the right to free speech and the right to disseminate the news."

Broadcasters, with the aid of satellite dishes (earth stations), have a wide variety of sports highlights to chose from in their daily sports shows. To what extent can a TV station rebroadcast highlights of a sporting event without the consent of the clubs or the clubs' licensees?

FACTS: Without consent, ESPN taped WSBK-TV telecasts of Red Sox and Bruins games. They excerpted highlights for their "Sportscenter" show, which was delivered via satellite to cable systems throughout the country—including those in the Boston area where WSBK had been selling their highlights to local TV stations. Was this practice an infringement on the team's right to control the broadcast of their own games? **YOU'RE THE JUDGE!**

DECISION: ESPN's action was an infringement of WSBK's property right (copyright) to control the broadcast of the highlights. The case was settled, with ESPN agreeing to pay a fee for its use of the highlights.

To prevent the selling of "Highlights and Bloopers" shows of its copyrighted games, Major League Baseball limits news shows to showing highlights no older than thirty-six hours. And total highlights can't exceed five minutes, with no more than two minutes from any one game.

What if a station also showed an awards ceremony after a sports event? Would that be allowed?

FACTS: Mason, president of WXXZ-TV, said, "Filming of the entire championship boxing match was sold for a delayed broadcast. But critical footage was excerpted without permission, showing highlights before the delayed broadcast. Also, the awards ceremony after the match was shown." Could either of these practices be enjoined? **YOU'RE THE JUDGE!**

DECISION: Yes. Both practices were enjoined. The right to a delayed broadcast may also extend to any highlights or awards ceremony taking place after the event.

WILL WE SEE THE GAME?

Increasingly, professional sports leagues and other professional sports have been selling their broadcast rights to pay cable TV.

The typical home viewer is being asked to pay for what was always free television.

Leagues and other sports asserted, "The broadcasts are our property to sell as we please." Should the sports and leagues have to provide free TV coverage of games and other sports events to the public, without whom the leagues and other sports could not survive?

EXCLUSIVE RIGHT TO PERFORM!

The **Copyright Act of 1976** gave professional sports leagues copyright protection—the exclusive right to "perform publicly" live sports events and control all broadcasts of their games.

FACTS: Superstation WZEZ simultaneously rebroadcasted a local station's coverage of the home baseball team without altering the programming or advertising. WZEZ had no control over the content or selection of the broadcast. They solely provided communication channels for the use of others. Was this a copyright infringement of the local station's right to control the broadcast? **YOU'RE THE JUDGE!**

DECISION: No. The Copyright Act allowed cable systems to convey such "secondary" broadcasts of copyrighted works. This is called "passive" broadcasting and is not copyright infringement. In return, each cable system must pay a fee which is distributed to the copyright owners.

Cable systems—the only media permitted to retransmit professional sports games without negotiating for the rights to do so—now negotiate for game broadcasting rights. Because of this "compulsory" license, a team's only right of control (other than scrambling signals) over cable's rebroadcast, comes from Federal Communications Commission (FCC) rules restricting some cable sports telecasts.

Baseball now scrambles some signals. Stations desiring to televise such games must obtain permission from the commissioner and pay a rights' fee. Those granted permission then buy a decoder.

RULES! RULES!

As cable systems had the right to carry an almost unlimited number of sporting events, teams and cable systems became concerned that the availability of too many games would hurt gate receipts and broadcast revenues. But how could the teams control the broadcasts of their games?

In addition to scrambling signals, two rules provide clubs with some control over the numbers and kinds of games that cable systems may carry.

FACTS: The Celtics, playing at home against the 76er's, were not televising the game in Boston. They requested that cable systems in the Boston area delete the telecast of the game by the 76er's. One cable station decided to carry the game locally. Could the Celtics enjoin the station from carrying the game? **YOU'RE THE JUDGE!**

DECISION: Yes. The "Sports" or "Same Game" Rule requires cable systems within 35 miles to delete the distant signal telecast of that club's home game—provided that the home game is not televised locally.

This rule protects a club's decision not to televise a particular home game, at the same time protecting the home gate and club's pay cable or subscription TV contracts.

FACTS: The Red Sox wanted to establish a network of local stations in New England to carry its games through its flagship station—the one carrying its home games. These local stations wanted to prevent local cable stations from duplicating their telecast of games. Could they prevent the cable stations from carrying Red Sox games? **YOU'RE THE JUDGE!**

DECISION: The second rule allows local stations to prevent local cable systems from duplicating a local station's broadcast.

The Atlanta Braves' flagship superstation, WTBS, sought to distribute play-off games nationwide by satellite. ABC, which held the exclusive nationwide broadcast rights, sued to prevent WTBS from carrying the games. WTBS was enjoined. Only local outlets of the participating teams were permitted to carry the games.

WHO GETS THE ROYALTIES?

As copyright owners of their games' telecasts, sports teams are entitled to all of the **royalties** or revenues from the telecasts. Although broadcasters have an interest in the commentary of the announcers, the public tunes into sports broadcasts mainly to see the event and the athletes.

FACTS: Many pro athletes asserted, "We are the show. Without our performance, there would be no game, no broadcast and no royalties. We should get a share of the royalties." Should the players share in the royalties? **YOU'RE THE JUDGE!**

DECISION: No. The "works made for hire" rule in the Copyright Act provides that a player's contribution to a copyrighted work (the games) becomes the property of the team. Furthermore, the players, in their contracts, agreed that all rights pertaining to pictures of the players are the property of the team.

Players, through bargaining with their team owners, could attempt to negotiate for broadcast revenues in addition to those already contributed to the players' retirement fund.

SCHOOLS & BROADCASTING RIGHTS

If schools competing in sports cannot resolve the distribution of any broadcast rights to their games, the home team will have exclusive rights in its home territory, and the visiting team in its home territory.

FACTS: The Holy Cross Crusaders played at home against the Boston College Eagles in the schools' annual fall football classic.

TV and radio stations approached both schools for the broadcast rights to the game—both locally, in Worcester, and back to the Boston area. Which school owned the rights to distribute the accounts and descriptions of the game locally? **YOU'RE THE JUDGE!**

DECISION: Holy Cross had the broadcast rights in the Worcester area; Boston College had the broadcast rights in the Boston area. If either sold its rights to a station which broadcasted to the other's area, the home school's rights would prevail.

Which school would own the rights to a national broadcast of the game? Neither school, alone, has the right to control the broadcasting rights in the other's area. Regional or national coverage supersedes local coverage and will only be carried upon agreement between both schools and the network or cable station seeking to purchase those rights.

SUPERSTATIONS

What is a "superstation"? A superstation is a local TV station whose signal is picked up by distant cable systems throughout the country and beyond. Stations such as WTBS (Atlanta), WGN (Chicago), and WOR (NJ) are superstations.

These stations show sports programming, which they and distant cable systems may carry without the consent of clubs or other copyright owners.

FACTS: The Mets brought suit against WOR for carrying Mets games, which were then picked up by distant cable systems without consent or compensation to the club. Would WOR be allowed to continue this practice? **YOU'RE THE JUDGE!**

DECISION: Yes. The court found this practice to be permitted under the "passive carrier" rule, and ruled, "Where WOR had no control over the content or selection of the broadcast, or the cable systems picking up its signal, and whose activity was solely to provide the channel for the use of others, then WOR could carry and make available the Mets' games without violating the law."

This made programing available to the public, which might otherwise not be available. Now, however, superstations and the teams whose games they carry have agreed to compensate other teams for lost attendance and TV revenues brought about by the intrusion of TV coverage into the other teams' home markets. In addition, baseball teams may now scramble their games. To obtain a decoder, stations must receive permission from the commissioner and pay a rights' fee.

PIRACY!

Teams, leagues and their licensed broadcasters use satellites to relay telecasts of games from the home site to the visiting club's home market or to network control points. Anyone having a satellite dish might intercept these telecasts.

However, the **Communications Act of 1934** prohibits the "interception and retransmission of broadcasts not intended for the use of the general public."

Later, in 1984, the U.S. Congress enacted the **Cable Communications Policy Act.** This act prohibits satellite transmissions except when they are made public or where the viewing is private. Home private viewing directly via satellite dish, without authorization from the cable programmer is permitted.

What is private viewing? Private viewing means viewing for private use in an individual home by means of equipment owned, or operated, by such individual.

Is public viewing by motel, bar, hotel and restaurant owners for the enjoyment of their customers permitted without the authorization of satellite programmers?

FACTS: The Miami Dolphins sued bars for intercepting and showing blacked-out telecasts of Dolphin home games, in violation of the NFL rule banning the broadcast of blacked-out games within 75 miles of the stadium where the home team is playing. The bars picked up the "clean feed" (without commercials) from a satellite to get around the ban.

The Dolphins argued, "This practice lessened game attendance and ticket sales. The game was our product and property. We don't like anyone stealing our property!"

The bars answered, "The games were news events that we could show. Nothing in the laws banned the use of satellite dishes." Could the bars continue to intercept the blacked-out games and broadcast them within the Dolphins home territory? **YOU'RE THE JUDGE!**

DECISION: No. The game telecast was the Dolphins' property and could be protected by copyright. The bars were enjoined from carrying any future games by such a practice. Now, some broadcasters scramble signals, reception for which requires permission, a rights' fee, and a fee for a decoder to unscramble the signals.

"POOLING" OF TV RIGHTS

The **Sports Broadcasting Act** allows certain professional sports leagues to pool all of the broadcast rights to their games.

By pooling rights, the NFL could prevent the networks from not televising games of "weaker" clubs. The act allows the networks to determine where the broadcasts will be seen.

Before this Act, pooling broadcast rights was illegal.By preventing networks from dealing only with successful clubs, it restrained trade.

Did the Sports Broadcasting Act offer any protection for high school and college football games?

FACTS: What if the NFL decided to begin Friday Night Football? Games would be carried nationwide every Friday during the season, with occasional Saturday games. Would this be allowed? **YOU'RE THE JUDGE!**

DECISION: No. The Sports Broadcasting Act protects high school and college football games by preventing any NFL telecasts on Friday evenings and Saturdays, from the second Friday in September to the second Saturday in December, from any station within 75 miles of the game site of a high school or college game.

The Sports Broadcasting Act only allows professional leagues, excepting soccer, to pool their broadcast rights. Colleges are not permitted such an arrangement.

FACTS: The NCAA restricted its member schools from negotiating on their own, prohibited them from televising games (except through the NCAA), and fixed prices of televised college football games. Was this an illegal monopoly of the televising of college football games? **YOU'RE THE JUDGE!**

DECISION: Yes. The court called the NCAA action a "commandeering" of schools' property rights in football games.

The court held, "The NCAA monopolized the market of televised college football games; it restrained trade by limiting schools' freedom to negotiate their own TV deals for coverage of their games."

The NCAA was still permitted to restrict Friday night games, impose TV sanctions against schools violating NCAA rules, and have its own TV plan, in which any school might participate.

BLACKOUTS!

In the 1930's, Judge "Mountain" Landis, the first baseball commissioner, prohibited radio broadcasts of major league games into minor league towns where the local team objected.

This rule was later expanded to prohibit radio or TV broadcasts into home territories of other teams, without permission, but "only when the other team was playing at home or telecasting an away game back to its home territory."

This, the first actual **blackout,** was repealed, but later followed by a similar NFL rule.

FACTS: The NFL rule prohibited a team from broadcasting its games into another team's home territory when the other team was either playing at home or broadcasting its away game back to its home territory. Could the NFL enforce such a rule? **YOU'RE THE JUDGE!**

DECISION: No. The Sports Broadcasting Act provided for a home territory blackout on a day when a team is playing at home, but not when the home team is playing away. For example, if the Dolphins were playing at home and chose to blackout a game not sold out, then a network could not televise the game in Miami's home territory, but could televise it elsewhere. They could televise other games into the Dolphins' home territory.

The act applies equally as well to blackouts in other major sports, and to play-off or championship games, as well as regular season games.

Another case helped to further define the 75 mile "home territory."

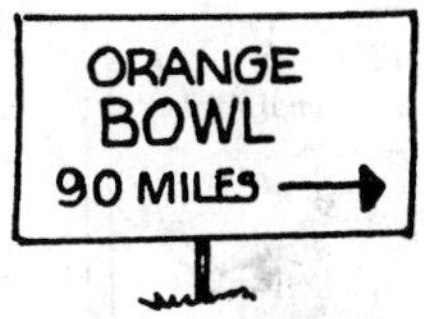

FACTS: A TV station, WTWV, sought to televise the Dolphins' home games which weren't sold out. The Sport's Broadcasting Act prohibited non-sold out games from being televised within the Dolphins' home territory, 75 miles in all directions from the game site, the Orange Bowl.

WTWV claimed, "The rule does not apply to us. Our transmitter is located 90 miles from the Orange Bowl, and, therefore, we should be allowed to broadcast the games."

"Can we blackout WTWV's signal?" asked the Dolphins. **YOU'RE THE JUDGE!**

DECISION: Yes. The 75 mile home territory protected the Dolphins from any television signal that reached into that protected area. It did not matter that the TV station was outside the 75 mile territory.

Blackout Lifting

In 1973, professional sports leagues were required to lift a local blackout of any pooled telecast of a game if all of the tickets available for purchase five days before the game were sold 72 hours or more in advance (unless the broadcast conflicted with a protected high school or college game). This law expired, but the NFL continues to follow it. And cable stations agreed to blackout hockey games in the participating team's home markets.

Owners have, on occasion, lifted a blackout although a game was not sold out within the required time.

ODDS & ENDS....

FACTS: Universal Studios sued Sony, alleging that Sony's videotape recorder (VCR) was being used to "copy Universal's copyrighted materials (movies)." Universal challenged the practice of home taping of TV programming."

Tom had a satellite dish in his backyard with which he picked up numerous sporting events. He paid for the dish, but paid no other fees. It, like the VCR, was for his private use, not for presenting a public performance of the game. Were these practices illegal? **YOU'RE THE JUDGE!**

DECISION: The court, noting that sports interests did not object to home recording, held that home taping for private, non-commercial use is permitted.

Although satellite dish reception for "private viewing" is legal, broadcasters are now scrambling their signals. In these cases, reception requires a fee for a decoder to unscramble the signals.

Many of us, with our VCRs, are virtual "pirates."

20

ENDORSEMENTS & TRADEMARKS

WHAT'S IT ABOUT?

Endorsements & Trademarks is an in-depth look at the marketing of sports products, trademarks, endorsements in advertising by "experts," and misrepresentations of products.

Can teams or players prevent the use of their nicknames or logos in selling products, such as T-shirts or hats?

U.S. Tomorrow

Section C
SPORTS

DO PROS USE THE SAME PRODUCTS AS YOU?

Can you match pro athletes with the products they endorse in advertisements on TV and in newspapers, magazines and elsewhere? Do pros have to use the products that they endorse in commercials?

ENDORSEMENTS

Endorsements are advertising messages (statements, demonstrations, or the use of a name, likeness or nickname) which consumers are likely to believe reflect the beliefs of the endorser.

Endorsements appear in advertising—a description of a product or service to induce the public to buy or use it.

Sports figures are used to endorse products because of the public's infatuation with them and with sports. Companies hope that fans will then buy their products for identity, image and to show allegiance for a team, player or sport.

As the public may place great faith and belief in sports stars, care must be taken to ensure that any product or service they promote is promoted properly, and that it performs as advertised.

Many of the products and services endorsed by athletes are not superior to a competitor's, but are endorsed and used by athletes because of the compensation paid.

Does an athlete have to talk about a product in order for there to be an endorsement?

FACTS: A manufacturer of tennis racquets employed a pro tennis player to praise the ability of their racket to produce overspin and keep the ball in play.

An ad for golf balls had a pro hitting a manufacturer's golf balls, but saying nothing. Were these endorsements? **YOU'RE THE JUDGE!**

DECISION: Yes. If consumers think the advertising message reflects the tennis player's or golfer's personal views and those of the sponsoring advertiser, then even if no verbal statements are made, it is an endorsement.

The importance of this is that, to protect the public, endorsements are governed by strict rules.

FACTS: Ken and Tony, NBA stars, were asked, "Will you endorse our beer, chewing tobacco and whiskey?" Were the athletes permitted to appear in such ads? **YOU'RE THE JUDGE!**

DECISION: No. Most sports prohibit active athletes from being involved in any endorsement of alcoholic beverages or tobacco products. Such endorsements would convey the wrong impression that use of such products is conducive to the development of athletic skill or physical prowess.

Also, to protect the public, the Federal Trade Commission (FTC) established restrictions on the use of celebrity endorsements.

The FTC has the power over "unfair or deceptive acts or practices." They investigate any celebrity representations in endorsements that are false, misleading or deceptive.

What if a company uses an athlete's likeness for an endorsement—is this permitted?

Using a sports figure's name or likeness for commercials, without consent, may create liability.

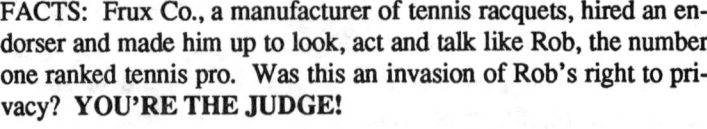

FACTS: Frux Co., a manufacturer of tennis racquets, hired an endorser and made him up to look, act and talk like Rob, the number one ranked tennis pro. Was this an invasion of Rob's right to privacy? **YOU'RE THE JUDGE!**

DECISION: Yes. Rob had a valuable "right to publicity," earned by years of experience, which may be protected, contracted away or "left alone." The ad was an invasion of Rob's privacy. It was enjoined and Rob was awarded damages.

An advertiser must also refrain from falsely stating or implying that a celebrity endorser uses a product when he does not.

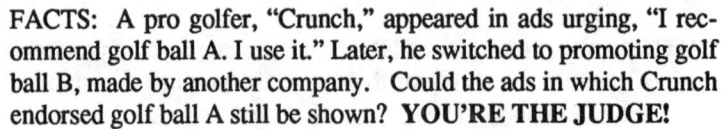

FACTS: A pro golfer, "Crunch," appeared in ads urging, "I recommend golf ball A. I use it." Later, he switched to promoting golf ball B, made by another company. Could the ads in which Crunch endorsed golf ball A still be shown? **YOU'RE THE JUDGE!**

DECISION: Ads in which Crunch endorsed golf ball A would be false. They can no longer be shown. The endorser, in any ad representing that he uses a product, must be a **bona fide user** —one who uses a product because he likes and approves of it at the time the endorsement is given.

A golfer could endorse two different golf balls, but it is unlikely that a company would allow the golfer to simultaneously endorse a competitor's product while endorsing the company's.

It should be determined at reasonable intervals whether the endorser still endorses the product. This is especially so where an athlete or sports celebrity endorses a product because of certain reasons and the product is later changed. If not determined, the endorsement may no longer be used.

FACTS: Slasher, a pro hockey player, presented his views in a "blind comparison test" of a soft drink. This was not designed to represent Slasher as a bona fide user. Must Slasher use the product? "Must we periodically check to see if Slasher still uses the drink?" asked the company. **YOU'RE THE JUDGE!**

DECISION: It is only when an endorser is held out as a bona fide user that tests for use requirements and checks on the endorser's views at "reasonable intervals" are required.

An endorsement used only once will not require further approval or use inquiry. However, a longer endorsement contract will require questioning at reasonable intervals.

What if the advertising message is by an announcer who is unfamiliar to the general public, except as a spokesman for a company's product? Are the rules then different?

FACTS: Dirk, unfamiliar to the public, endorsed a product, "Our whiffle balls can be thrown faster and they break more than any other." The ad ran for three years. Was this an endorsement? Must the company periodically check to see if Dirk still holds the same opinion of the whiffle ball? **YOU'RE THE JUDGE!**

DECISION: The ad was not represented as, or likely to be believed by consumers as, reflecting the opinion and beliefs of Dirk, but was represented as the opinion of the company. It was not an endorsement. Therefore, the company could continue to use the ad without checking Dirk's present opinion.

MISREPRESENTATION

Must an endorsement contain the exact words of an endorser? Endorsements may not contain deceptive representations. An ad that represents that the message is phrased in the exact words of the endorser must contain the precise language of the endorser.

FACTS: An advertiser for golf balls quoted an endorser, a pro golfer, as saying, "This ball won me the U.S. Open." What the golfer actually said was, "I used this ball when I won the U.S. Open." Was this a deceptive ad? **YOU'RE THE JUDGE!**

DECISION: Yes. The representation may deceive the public. It is not permitted.

An endorsement may be permitted even if not factually true in all respects. Allowing only partially true endorsements enables advertisers and endorsers to proclaim, for example, "This drink will make you a winner!"

This may be acceptable for some products, but not for those involving health, safety or children. There, the strictest standards apply, to ensure that there are no misrepresentations of any kind—no matter how slight.

Endorsers are generally free to comment on taste without requiring any substantiation, as by tests.

"I'M AN EXPERT!"

What is an expert? An **expert** is one who, because of education, training, knowledge or experience, has acquired special skills.

FACTS: The following, represented as experts in their fields, endorsed certain products: a race car driver for car performance products; a golfer for golf clubs and a tennis racquet; a tennis pro for golf balls; and, a basketball player for tennis shoes. Could these experts endorse those products? **YOU'RE THE JUDGE!**

DECISION: "Whenever an endorser is represented as an expert in an ad, then the expert must have such expertise." The golfer and tennis player cannot endorse each other's products.

If an organization endorses a product, then the endorsement must reflect the collective judgment of the group. And, an expert must judge the merits of any product endorsed.

FACTS: The Major Volleyball League (MVL) selected Juice-Aid as its "Official Drink." In ads promoting the drink, the MVL endorsed the product. "What must we do before we endorse the product?" asked the MVL. **YOU'RE THE JUDGE!**

DECISION: If a consumer is left with the impression that the product has nutritional value because of the connection between performance and diet, then the MVL must employ and rely on an expert in the field of nutrition before endorsing the product.

Furthermore, use of the words "selects" and "official" imply that the endorsement was based on a comparison against competing brands. Therefore, to avoid an assertion of a deceptive ad, side-by-side comparisons must have concluded that the product was at least equal to its competitor's. If a product is represented as being superior to other products, then scientific testing must substantiate that.

For an individual expert endorsement, an expert's opinion is required and "must be supported by an actual exercise of his expertise in evaluating the product, taking into consideration how an ordinary consumer would use the product."

FACTS: A novice skier endorsed skis, "These skis give you the feel and ease of movement needed in championship racing." Would this require an expert? Was this misleading? **YOU'RE THE JUDGE!**

DECISION: Yes. The ad required an expert who had used and examined the skis. The statements by the novice were false representations which may mislead the public.

"I'M A NON-EXPERT!"

A non-expert endorser and an advertiser must make "reasonable inquiry into the truthfulness of any endorsement." Reasonable inquiry means having information evaluated by competent, reliable and independent sources. This may lead to less confusion and deception.

However, as this will increase the time needed to respond to a competitor's endorsements, experts may be used where a quick reply to the competition is desired.

Is an expert opinion needed in advertising health or safety products?

Endorsing a product related to health or safety without proper reliance upon an expert evaluation may lead to a false and deceptive ad. Whereas, if an expert opinion is not needed, the endorser may rely upon personal experience.

FACTS: Bruno, a pro boxer, endorsed an acne medicine, saying, "This made my skin clear up." Sly, a pro wrestler, also endorsed the medicine, "The medicine's ingredients reacted with my skin to clear it up almost immediately."

Christine, a pro tennis player, endorsed a new car, "It runs great!" she said. "Hooker," a pro golfer, also endorsed the car, "It's the safest car there is."

Must any of these endorsers rely upon expert advice? **YOU'RE THE JUDGE!**

DECISION: Bruno's endorsement will not require expert advice, while Sly's endorsement of the acne medication will require the evaluation of an expert for Sly to rely upon.

Christine's endorsement of the car only required her personal evaluation, while expert advice must be relied upon by Hooker.

Sports celebrities or athletes who endorse a product relating to health or safety without relying upon expert opinion may subject themselves to personal liability.

Payment to an expert or well-known endorser need not be disclosed as long as the advertiser does not represent that the endorsement was given without compensation, or as long as there is no other financial interest in the sale of the product or service used in the endorsement.

FACTS: Mike Eagle, a pro golfer, was also the president of Par Busters, Inc., makers and promoters of Wind Breaker golf balls—guaranteed to fly lower and straighter in wind. Mike endorsed the golf balls in advertisements and received a share of the product's sales. Should Mike have been required to disclose his relationship with Par Busters in any ads that he appeared in? **YOU'RE THE JUDGE!**

DECISION: Yes. Any relationship which might "materially affect the credibility of the endorsement" must be disclosed. If the public were aware that the endorser had a financial interest, other than a payment not dependent upon the success of sales of the product, it might conclude that the endorser would "puff" his endorsement to increase his financial gain from the sale of the product.

What if the endorser, an athlete, also agrees to use the product? Such might be the case where a tennis or golf pro, as part of an endorsement contract, agrees to wear certain clothing or logos or to use the advertiser's equipment.

FACTS: Gary, a pro basketball player, in violation of an agreement to use certain tennis shoes, wore a competitor's. What could the advertiser do?
Larry complained, "The shoe didn't perform as it was supposed to. It fell apart!" What could Larry do? **YOU'RE THE JUDGE!**

DECISION: If Gary broke his endorsement contract, then there may be a separate action to either enforce the contract or sue for damages for the breach.

If the shoes fell apart, Larry could break the contract, but without any damages.

TRADEMARKS

Professional teams, associations and athletes, in order to satisfy the public's desire to identify with them, expend money and effort to develop goodwill and a favorable reputation. This goodwill and reputation is then marketed by attaching their logos and names to merchandise which the public will buy.

To protect these names, logos, and other identifying marks, they are registered as **trademarks**—any word, name, symbol, or other mark or any combination, used to identify one's goods and distinguish them from another's.

FACTS: Big Mike owned a sporting goods store in Falmouth. He admitted, "I created consumer demand by 'copying' and then attaching pro and college logos, names, and pictures of pro sports teams and players to many items. Then I sold them, without permission, for a lower price than 'official' items were sold for." Was Big Mike guilty of **trademark infringement? YOU'RE THE JUDGE!**

DECISION: Yes. Big Mike would be guilty of trademark infringement if a federal trademark had been registered and he had used a copy or duplication of the trademark—without consent—in interstate commerce, in connection with the sale (or offer for sale, distribution or advertisement of goods), and that such use was likely to cause confusion with the public.

This practice tarnishes the image of the trademark owner and confuses the consumer, who relies on quality goods bearing the official trademarks of their favorite athletes and teams.

FACTS: A manufacturer's umbrella, the "Capabrella," looked like an oversized baseball cap. Another manufacturer, Ace Co., made a similar-looking umbrella. The similarity between these trademarks and products created confusion. Could Ace Co. be enjoined from making such an umbrella? **YOU'RE THE JUDGE!**

DECISION: Yes. This was an infringement of the Capabrella trademark. Ace Co. could be enjoined from manufacturing a similar looking umbrella, one which would confuse the public as to whose it was.

Trademark infringement is just one type of unfair competition. If the mark has acquired a secondary meaning, then the test becomes whether the activities of the infringer have created a likelihood of confusion. What is a secondary meaning?

FACTS: Georgia University sued a manufacturer for selling products which had on them a picture of a "Battlin' Bulldog." It was strikingly similar to the picture of Ulga, the "Georgia Bulldog," the university's mascot. Would the picture of the school's mascot, which was recognized as such without the words, or vice versa, be confused with the picture and words of "Battlin' Bulldog?" **YOU'RE THE JUDGE!**

DECISION: Yes. The school's mascot and his name had each acquired a secondary meaning as being the mark of the school. The manufacturer's picture and name would confuse the public. The manufacturer was enjoined from using the name or the picture.

An often used defense to a trademark infringement charge is the contention, "The mark is functional and, therefore, can't be protected." Any feature of a product which is essential to the usefulness of the product is **functional**—necessary for the product's use.

FACTS: Ace Golf Co. designed two golf carts. One had a regular looking steering wheel. The other, designed like a bent golf club, was very distinctive. Were these steering wheels functional?

The Tucci Tennis Shoe Co. used velcro instead of shoelaces to secure its tennis shoes. Was this functional? **YOU'RE THE JUDGE!**

DECISION: The regular steering wheel was essential to the use of the cart; it was functional and could not be protected as a trademark. The other steering wheel was very distinctive; its design could be protected.

The use of velcro was functional and essential to the use of the shoes. It could not be protected by a trademark.

Any feature that is not related to identification or individuality is functional.

FACTS: The Bombers hockey team wore all white uniforms. Could they obtain a trademark on the uniform and then prevent anyone from selling such uniforms?

The Slashers used a unique combination of several colors for their uniforms.

The Trippers used another identifying mark with their colors—an emblem of a hockey player being tripped. Were these marks functional, or could they be protected by trademarks? **YOU'RE THE JUDGE!**

DECISION: The Bombers' uniform is not related to identification or individuality and, thus, may not be protected.

The Slashers' and Trippers' uniforms may be protected. They have certain color combinations and other identifying marks which are not functional.

If a product would be desired, regardless of the feature, then the feature is functional and cannot be protected by a trademark. For example, an article of clothing, such as a football jersey, or an emblem shaped as a football or baseball, with no logo or team colors, may not be protected. These are functional items.

INSIGNIAS, SYMBOLS & EMBLEMS

Trademark infringement may also involve a name, word, or phrase, either alone or in combination with goods or services.

FACTS: Dallas Emblem Co. duplicated and sold NHL team symbols on patches. The NHL sued for trademark infringement, claiming, "This was done without our consent. There would have been no market for a patch without the NHL's symbols. This use would confuse or deceive the public."

Dallas argued, "The insignia was an aesthetically pleasing feature of the patch, essential to its usefulness, and therefore could not be protected by a trademark." Should the NHL, or any other league, team, or other association be able to protect their insignias for their own use? **YOU'RE THE JUDGE!**

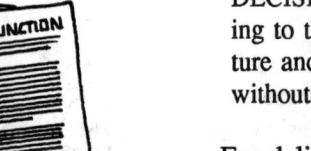

DECISION: Yes. "Dallas misappropriated a valuable right belonging to the NHL." They were enjoined from any further manufacture and sale of such emblems, without consent. The bare patch, without the NHL team symbols, would have no market.

For deliberate and fraudulent infringement, a court may, in addition to granting an injunction, award punitive damages. Such marks—as NFL, NBA, PGA and others—took substantial amounts of money and time to establish. To allow someone else to improperly use such marks is a serious misappropriation of a valuable and protected right to publicity in the mark. Can such a mark be functional, as well as a trademark?

Such marks acquired a strong secondary meaning of identification of the teams. A patch, without such an insignia, is of little, if any, value. Thus, the symbols have aesthetic value as well as indicating their source or origin. The marks are a functional component of the product as well as a trademark.

UNIFORMS

FACTS: A clothing manufacturer sold "replicas" of NFL jerseys—football shirts with large numerals, NFL team colors and either the name of an NFL city, team or player. The NFL contended, "Such jerseys, sold without our consent, confused the public since they desired and purchased the jersey believing that it was an 'official' NFL jersey—one made or authorized by the NFL."

Would the public be likely to buy the jerseys without the official NFL team colors, numerals, design, and city or player's name? Was this trademark infringement? **YOU'RE THE JUDGE!**

DECISION: The public purchased the jerseys because of the NFL colors, design, and name, and because they thought that they were purchasing "Official" NFL jerseys. The manufacturer confused and deceived the public. A functional feature, such as a fanciful nickname or design, can also serve as a trademark. The manufacturer was enjoined from the manufacturing and sale of the jerseys.

A cinema showed a movie in which uniforms strikingly similar to those worn by the Dallas Cowboy Cheerleaders, were worn.

The cinema argued that the uniform was purely functional as an article of clothing. The court held that the uniform had taken on a secondary meaning as that of the Cowboy Cheerleaders and, as such, could be protected from unconsented use. The improper use confused and deceived the public into believing that the Cowboy Cheerleaders were taking part in the movie.

In general, a uniform or color is not capable of becoming a trademark. But a certain combination of colors, as in team insignias, can become a trademark when recognized by the public as that of a certain team or group. Therefore, trademark rights are recognized for pro sports teams' uniforms.

Colleges may similarly protect their name and identifying marks.

FACTS: The University of Pittsburgh sued a manufacturer for selling clothing and other items with the school's colors and name on those products. Could the manufacturers be enjoined from selling such clothing or other items? **YOU'RE THE JUDGE!**

DECISION: The court enjoined the manufacturer. It found that the demand for a product with Pitt's name on it resulted from the efforts of PItt, not the manufacturer. The public wanted a Pitt T-shirt or other item, not the manufacturer's.

Infringement involving other products has also been found. Thus, manufacturers of tennis racquets were enjoined from using the name Seiko. Dad's Root Beer Co. was enjoined from using Cincinnati Reds trademarks on placemats. Another manufacturer was enjoined from using Titleist trademarks on golf balls and other equipment.

One court commented, "Fair competition requires that those developing goodwill and a recognizable name, symbol, or insignia be allowed to protect those marks. The public desires products authorized by their favorite teams, league, players or others, not those of an infringer. Infringement of a trademark tarnishes the owner's reputation and confuses and deceives the public."

WORDS, NAMES & PHRASES

FACTS: The state of Delaware devised a football lottery called "Scoreboard," which included different games based on picking winners of NFL games, some against the spread.

The NFL sued, charging, "The lottery misappropriated the name of the NFL (unfairly capitalizing on our success and popularity), infringed on our trademark in that name, was unfair competition, and harmed us by forced association with gambling." Was Delaware enjoined from running the lottery? **YOU'RE THE JUDGE!**

DECISION: Since gambling in the state of Nevada existed without harm to the NFL's reputation, there was no misappropriation. Confusion existed among the public as to whether the NFL was directly associated with the lottery, therefore the court ruled that the lottery tickets must explicitly declare that the NFL was in no way connected with the lottery.

The game, where fixed payoffs were paid dependent upon the number of games bet, was to be discontinued. This was similar to the "card," which is illegally wagered upon during college and pro football seasons.

Others have been more successful in preventing the use of their name, nickname or identifying phrase.

Wilson, holder of a trademark for "Advantage" tennis racquets, balls and golf equipment, could not enjoin Arthur Ashe from endorsing "Advantage Ashe" sunglasses. The products were not similar, and the public would not be confused or misled as to the origination of either product. Ashe had developed considerable goodwill in the term "Advantage Ashe," which was also the title of his autobiography.

FACTS: Drew "Bundini" Brown registered a trademark on the phrase, "Float like a butterfly, sting like a bee," a reference to the boxing abilities of Muhammad Ali.

When Kawasaki Motors began using the phrase in its ads,

Brown sued for an infringement of his trademark. Could Kawasaki be enjoined from use of the phrase?

DECISION: **YOU'RE THE JUDGE!**

In addition to teams, players and organizations may also claim trademark protection of their names or nicknames with which they have come to be identified with. Elroy "Crazylegs" Hirsch was thus able to prevent the use of that nickname, and the Olympic Committee could prevent the use of the word Olympics as an infringement on their trademark of the name.

ODDS & ENDS....

Who Dat doesn't own that which it thought it owned, a judge ruled. Own what?

FACTS: Who Dat Inc. claimed that it owned the football cheer: "Who dat say dey gonna beat dem Saints? Who dat?"

Who Dat sued a company that sold T-shirts imprinted with the cheer. Who Dat owned the rights to a recording, popular in New Orleans, in which some NFL's Saints sang the cheer between verses of "When The Saints Go Marching In." Could Who Dat enjoin the making of the T-shirts? **YOU'RE THE JUDGE!**

DECISION: The court ruled that the "Who Dat" cheer had been around for many years and was now in the public domain— anyone could use the phrase.

Sneakers & Patches

FACTS: Nell, an NBA coach, wore socks and sneakers which had the manufacturers' logos on them. Bert, a pro quarterback, had a logo patch on his jersey. Ernie, a pro tennis player, had a large logo patch on his shirt. Dunk, an NBA player, had logo patches on his uniform and wrist and head bands. Could any of these players be prohibited from such product endorsements? **YOU'RE THE JUDGE!**

DECISION: Although product endorsements may, in certain sports and in a specified manner, be permitted, rules prohibited Nell and Dunk from wearing such logos. Although the coach

couldn't, some players could endorse such products during a game. Rules also prohibited Bert from displaying any patch and Ernie from wearing a patch of that size.

Professional athletes, by their product endorsements, play a major role in the buying attitudes of the public.

21

PRIVACY

WHAT'S IT ABOUT?

Privacy tells how the **right of privacy**—the right to be left alone—came about and developed.

Can a fan's picture, without the fan's permission, be published or used in a magazine, newspaper or other media?

Worcester News June 22, 1905
Section A

Yellow Journalism!

The late 1800's was an era of vicious newspaper circulation battles and sensational, but often deceptive, press coverage in an attempt to win readership.

One such newspaper wrote of the private social affairs of a prominent attorney, thus prompting an article arguing for a **right of privacy** –"the right to be left alone, free from intrusion or invasion of one's private rights"–except as could be justified by freedom of the press and speech–guaranteed by the First amendment to the Constitution.

RIGHT OF PRIVACY

The first case testing this theory of a right of privacy involved a flour mill.

FACTS: The mill ordered, without consent, a woman's portrait lithographed on its boxes. The woman, Roberson, complained, "I didn't like being referred to as the 'Flour of the Family,' so I sued."

"Was the use of the picture without my permission an invasion of my right to privacy?" she asked the court. **YOU'RE THE JUDGE!**

DECISION: No. The court held that no right of privacy existed.

The following year, the first right of privacy law made it "wrong to use the name or likeness of any person for trade purposes (publishing or making public)" without that person's consent.

"Any person who unreasonably interferes with any others' interests in not having their affairs known, or their picture or likeness exhibited to the public, is liable to the others." The first case recognizing this new **right of privacy,** came in 1905.

FACTS: A newspaper ad for an insurance company contained a photograph of Pavesich. It quoted him as saying, "Buy James Company's life insurance."

Pavesich had not consented to either the picture or the quote and sued. Was this an invasion of Pavesich's right of privacy? **YOU'RE THE JUDGE!**

DECISION: Yes. The court found an invasion of Pavesich's right of privacy and awarded him damages.

A right of privacy must be balanced against freedom of the press and the public's right to know anything of "legitimate news value," especially if it concerns a **"public figure"**—any person who has achieved fame or notoriety, and who commands substantial public interest, such as an athlete.

However, where published matter deals with one's private life or is malicious and without consent, recovery for invasion of privacy may be had even if the story is true.

The right of privacy is divided into four separate branches:

Intrusion

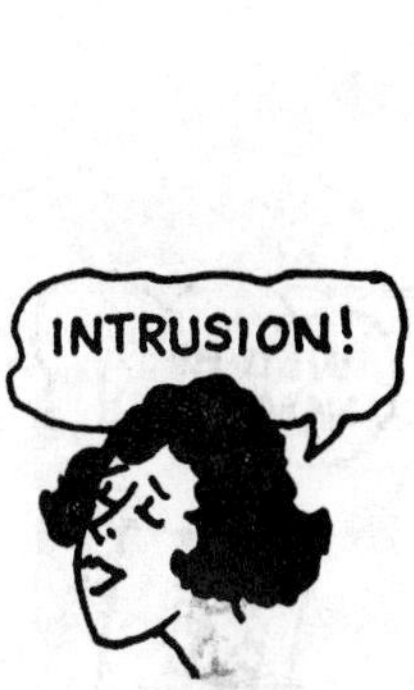

Was there an unreasonable **intrusion** upon one's privacy or individual life?

If so, this may be a violation of the right to privacy.

FACTS: Two newspaper reporters went to the home of Jack, "The Mad Healer," a famous wrestler who practiced healing. By lying, they gained admittance to Jack's home, where one of them complained of "tennis elbow."

While examining the elbow with an assortment of gadgets, Jack

was secretly photographed and the conversation was recorded by a hidden microphone.

When the photos and tape recording were published as part of a story on Jack's practice, and also used to charge Jack with quackery, Jack sued the newspaper for an "invasion of my privacy." The newspaper asked, "Were we guilty of an unreasonable intrusion into Jack's private life?" **YOU'RE THE JUDGE!**

DECISION: Yes. The court reasoned, "A privilege might exist for the publication of the pictures and story as news of a public figure, but it does not extend to the intrusion." The newspaper was liable to Jack for damages.

Often an intrusion is not physical, but consists of eavesdropping in private areas, such as a home or maybe a locker room. When an athlete is in a public area or a private area (locker room) opened to the public (reporters), only a reasonable photo or recording may be taken.

Would it be an intrusion if such a photo or recording was not published?

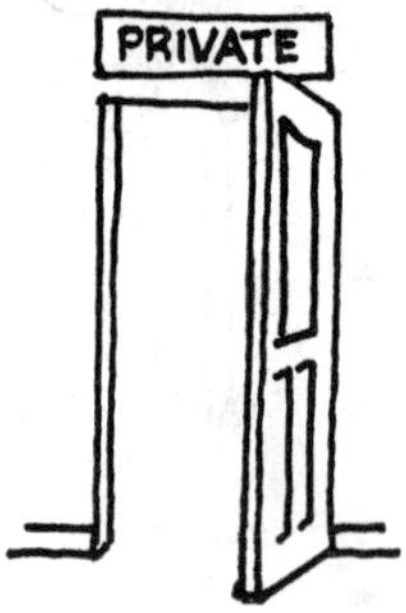

The invasion of privacy is the intrusion itself. Thus, taking pictures or recording statements of athletes at a private party or in a closed locker room, without permission, would be an intrusion into the private affairs of the athlete, and this would be so even if the pictures or story were not published.

May a newspaper publish a photo or recording gathered by an invasion of privacy by another?

FACTS: Hank admitted, "Without permission, and by using a telescopic lens, I took pictures of athletes and their guests at a private pool party. Also, I used a sensitive recorder hidden in the sauna to record players talking about officials and other matters. I then sold the material to a local newspaper. They printed it." Was the newspaper or Hank guilty of an invasion of privacy? **YOU'RE THE JUDGE!**

DECISION: The media simply published the work of another's intrusion. The courts usually will not hold the newspaper liable, although Hank may be.

What if the newspaper were aware of the intrusion? Even if the media was aware of the intrusion, the courts generally will not hold them liable. The reasoning is that the news gathering process would be severely hampered if the media were required to consider how independent sources obtained the news.

What if the media encouraged or aided an illegal invasion of privacy?

FACTS: A local newspaper drove Hank, not an employee, to an athlete's home where, with the camera that the newspaper had given him, Hank took pictures of the athlete through the window. Was the newspaper guilty of an unreasonable intrusion into the athlete's private life? **YOU'RE THE JUDGE!**

DECISION: The newspaper encouraged and aided Hank in acts of an unreasonable intrusion. They were liable to Hank for damages.

If the media is on private property, its license to report "newsworthy" items is limited to engaging in directly related activities, not to unrelated business.

FACTS: A reporter, Sandra, was invited to a team owner's office for a private celebration. While there, she took pictures. Could her newspaper print the pictures without an invasion of the privacy of those at the private party? **YOU'RE THE JUDGE!**

DECISION: Any printing of the pictures taken at the party would be an invasion of privacy. The pictures were of an unrelated, private nature. That is not permitted.

Public Disclosure

Was there an unreasonable **public disclosure** of embarrassing private facts?

If so, and even if true, this may violate the right to privacy.

It may be difficult to determine when publicity is unreasonable, when facts are private, or when private facts are offensive and objectionable. Truth is not a defense from liability since it is the publication of private facts that creates the liability.

FACTS: Tom, 16, a child prodigy in mathematics and golf, amid considerable public attention, gave up both and attempted to live down his fame and success. He succeeded in concealing his identity until a magazine published a story under the title: WHERE ARE THEY NOW. The article recounted Tom's unusual background, traced his attempts to hide his identity, described his menial employment and detailed certain conduct, such as his collecting old beer cans. Was Tom's privacy invaded? **YOU'RE THE JUDGE!**

DECISION: The court held, "The facts disclosed were not offensive or objectionable to reasonable persons."

However, there are limits to what a court will allow in balancing the public's interest in publicity against an individual's right to privacy.

FACTS: Vance was a bodysurfer at the "Tunnel" in California, the world's most dangerous site. Vance, the greatest daredevil, consented to an interview for an article on bodysurfing, but later withdrew his permission when he found out that the article would detail bizarre incidents about his lifestyle—such as diving down stairs to impress women, or eating insects.

The magazine, referring to Vance as abnormal, claimed, "The story was newsworthy."

Vance sued, arguing, "The article, which I didn't consent to, was an unreasonable public disclosure of embarrassing private facts. My right to privacy was invaded?" Was it? **YOU'RE THE JUDGE!**

DECISION: Yes. The court decided, "The magazine pried into the strictly private affairs of Vance's private life, reporting details that were not news. Truth was no defense."

However, the media may be protected in publishing almost anything true about individuals which has any "legitimate news value."

The limitation on what the media may publish may depend upon whether an area is private or open to the public.

FACTS: The Times newspaper published a picture of Bubby, star football player for the Hamilton Bears, while he was undressing in the locker room. The press had not been admitted, but the door was ajar. Bubby sued the Times for making an unreasonable and embarrassing public disclosure.

The newspaper claimed, "The picture was publicity that was public. The door was open." Could Bubby recover for an invasion of his right to privacy? **YOU'RE THE JUDGE!**

DECISION: Yes. Ordinarily, publicity of what is already public, and what anyone present would be free to see, is not an invasion of privacy. However, the press had not yet been admitted and there was nothing of legitimate news value. Caution and discretion should be used with "good taste."

False Light

Was there publicity or a publication of facts—by words or photos—which placed one in a **"false light"?**

If so, this may violate the right to privacy. False light exists where views not held, or actions not taken by a person, are attributed to that person.

FACTS: A magazine depicted a nude black man seated in the corner of a boxing ring. Ali, the former heavyweight boxing champ, sued the magazine, alleging that the depiction, without permission, was a picture of him which placed him in a false light. Was this a newsworthy item which the magazine could publish without permission? Did it place Ali in a false light? **YOU'RE THE JUDGE!**

DECISION: The court found that the depiction was a portrait or picture of Ali. Moreover, "There was no newsworthy dimension to this unauthorized use of such likeness. It placed the boxer in a 'false light' by attributing to him actions which he had not taken."

Would the intentional fictionalization of activities involving identifiable persons or places create liability?

FACTS: Notre Dame sought to enjoin the release of a book and movie involving the school's name and symbols, alleging that the movie and book placed the school in a "false light" by attributing to it views not held, and actions not taken, by the school.

The story was of a fictional female player who ran for the winning touchdown when Notre Dame players would not tackle her. Could the school prevent the release of the book and movie? **YOU'RE THE JUDGE!**

DECISION: No. The court decided, "The work was a form of expression of social and literary criticism, protected by the freedom of the press to disseminate 'newsworthy news' to the waiting public."

One may not fictionalize dialogues by attributing to another words not spoken.

FACTS: A book fictionalized the great baseball pitcher, Warren Spahn, and his relationships with others. The author invented dialogues involving, not only Spahn's life in baseball (in which Spahn was deemed a "public personality," and of which there was a legitimate public interest), but also fictionalized Spahn's personal and private life. Could Spahn recover damages for an invasion of privacy? **YOU'RE THE JUDGE!**

DECISION: Yes. Spahn's life could not be fictionalized. Nor could he be placed in a false light in the public's eyes by attributing to him innacurate, distorted, and fanciful words and acts. This is not protected by the freedoms of speech and the press. It was an invasion of Spahn's right to privacy.

A publication placing one in a false light, which is not an intentional or reckless falsification, but an innocent mistake or negligent act, may not be actionable. Such would be the case where a picture was accidentally published or views were attributed by mistake, and then retracted.

Appropriation

Was there an **appropriation**—unauthorized use of a name, picture or likeness of another for profit?

If so, this may violate the right to privacy—sometimes called the **right of publicity.**

The media are seldom sued for appropriation in reporting the news to the public. Invasion of privacy suits for misappropriation of one's name or likeness are usually connected with ads or promotions for products or services.

> FACTS: "Big Mike," a former football star, consented to allow his picture and name to be used in connection with honoring outstanding college football players and in promoting college football. When his name and likeness appeared without his consent in an ad for a soft drink, Big Mike sued. Was this an appropriation of Big Mike's right to publicity? **YOU'RE THE JUDGE!**

> DECISION: The court ruled, "The privacy of a public figure may not be lawfully invaded by the use of his name or picture for commercial purposes without his consent, unless it is of legitimate news value, which here it was not."

Similar decisions were reached where other manufacturers attempted to enhance the sale of games by using pro golfers' and baseball players' pictures and accomplishments without permission.

Although an athlete's right to privacy is more limited than that of the average person, athletes are entitled to relief where their names and pictures are used improperly. Athletes have invested years of practice and competition to build a recognizable and marketable personality—a valuable **right of publicity.**

> FACTS: Elroy "Crazylegs" Hirsch sued Johnson for marketing a shaving gel for women named "Crazylegs." Hirsch alleged, "The company appropriated a nickname that I made famous for my own use. I had a property right in the publicity value of my nickname, which was my identity." Did Hirsch have a property right in his nickname? **YOU'RE THE JUDGE!**

> DECISION: Yes. The court found that the publicity value in Hirsch's name gave him interest in controlling commercial uses of his name and the prevention of others from profiting from the use of his name without his consent. Any improper use would confuse the public as to whether Hirsch had approved the product.

What if an athlete's name or likeness is used, but is reasonably related to a matter of legitimate public interest? Then, unless the matter is an ad, it's use is not actionable.

Such was the case where a book included on the cover, without his permission, the likeness of former football great, Johnny Unitas. Unitas sued, but was unsuccessful. The court found that, "The subject matter of the book was of legitimate public interest and reasonably related to the use of Unitas' picture."

FACTS: Sports Illustrated used Namath's name and picture in ads designed to sell subscriptions. The ads read, "How to get Close to Joe Namath" and, "The man you love loves Joe Namath." Namath sued, alleging a wrongful use of his photograph without his consent, which deprived him of income from a right to publicity in his name and picture. Was this an invasion of privacy? **YOU'RE THE JUDGE!**

DECISION: No—as long as the picture was only used to illustrate the quality and content of the magazine in which it originally appeared many times, and where the use of Namath's picture was merely "incidental" to advertising of the magazine. He must also have been fairly depicted, and the language of the ads could not indicate an endorsement of the magazine.

Where athletes gave unrestricted permission to have their photos taken and distributed to the public, generally, actions for invasion of privacy were dismissed when their photos appeared on a calendar distributed by a beer wholesaler. An example of which had a player posed only in a bowling shirt and holding a bowling ball. A beer bottle was later engraved onto the photo for an ad campaign.

FACTS: Cepeda, a pro baseball star, gave Wilson Sporting Goods an exclusive right to use his photo to sell baseballs and gloves, and to license others to sell the same. When Wilson contracted with Swift to sell Cepeda baseballs for $1.00 off when customers sent in a label from a hot dog package, Cepeda sued Swift for invasion of privacy for using his name without his permission. Did Swift invade Cepeda's right to privacy? **YOU'RE THE JUDGE!**

DECISION: The court dismissed the suit, noting that Cepeda had given his permission to Wilson to license others to sell baseballs. Swift had not attempted to indicate that Cepeda either used or endorsed its products.

Where the use of an athlete's picture exceeds the consent granted, or an athlete's or performer's entire act, is published, recovery for an invasion of privacy may be awarded.

Such was the case where Ettore fought Joe Louis in 1936 and consented to motion pictures of the fight. In 1950, when NBC broadcast that fight as one of the "Greatest Fights of The Century," Ettore sued for an invasion of privacy.

The court held, "The consent given by Ettore could not be used for a later TV show not contemplated at the time of the fight." The court did note, "Ettore only got upset when the third round, his best, was cut from the show."

FACTS: Morrison performed his diving act at a circus. A TV station, against Morrison's wishes, filmed and showed the entire act on a news program. Morrison sued for an invasion of privacy—the publicity right to the value of his performance.

Could Morrison recover for the right of publicity value in his performance? **YOU'RE THE JUDGE!**

DECISION: Yes. Although the press may have a right to freely cover newsworthy events which the public has an interest in, it is not permitted to carry a performer's entire act, no matter how short.

Athletes in professional team sports sign a contract which grants to their teams the right to use players' pictures or likenesses for promotional and publicity purposes.

A professional athlete also has a right to publicity in his name and picture or likeness, which the athlete may sell.

After one baseball player sold the right to use his picture to Topp's baseball cards, a competing company attempted to use the player's picture. Topps successfully sued, preventing the competing company from using the player's picture.

SURVIVAL, JOKES & IMPERSONATIONS

Does the right to publicity survive an athlete's death?

FACTS: After Jesse, a well-known track star, passed away, a book on his life was published. His estate sued, alleging that the book was an invasion of Jesse's right to publicity which now belonged to the estate. Could any sale of the book be enjoined? **YOU'RE THE JUDGE!**

DECISION: No. The right of publicity does not survive an athlete's death. Cases involving the right of privacy can only be asserted by the person whose privacy is involved.

What if an alleged invasion of privacy occurred as an obvious joke?

Recovery was also denied where "Groucho" Marx, in one of his comedy routines, joked, "I once managed a prizefighter, Canvasback Cohen. I brought him out here, he got knocked out, and I made him walk back to Cleveland."

The comment was limited to public facts. Cohen, by entering the

The comment was limited to public facts. Cohen, by entering the ring, sought publicity, became known by his nickname and lost his right to privacy in that respect.

Is a voice impersonation an invasion of the right to publicity?

FACTS: A former pro athlete, Babe, waged a satirical campaign for political office. Without his permission, a company sold posters and a factual biography of Babe. In commercials promoting a product, another company used a voice impersonation of Babe. Was Babe's right of publicity invaded or misappropriated? **YOU'RE THE JUDGE!**

DECISION: Babe was a newsworthy public figure, and, therefore, did not possess a right of publicity. He could not enjoin the posters, a factual or truthful biography or commercials which did not use a name or likeness. Use of the voice in impersonation could be enjoined.

ODDS & ENDS....

The back of most tickets to sporting events grants permission for the use of a fan's image or likeness in any display of the game to which the ticket admits the fan. But, as a spectator is not a public figure, use of such a photo without consent will be limited to situations deemed "newsworthy" and in the interest of the public.

FACTS: A photo of a spectator at a football game, "hammimg it up" with his fly unzippered, was shown in a national sports magazine article on football fans entitled, "A Strange Kind of Love." The article implied that the spectator was a "crazy, drunken slob."

The spectator sued for, "An invasion of my right to privacy. The photo, an appropriation of my picture, subjected me to ridicule, placed me in a false light and embarrassed me." Was the photo newsworthy? **YOU'RE THE JUDGE!**

DECISION: Yes. The publication of the spectator's photo, taken with his encouragement and participation, even though taken without the spectator's express consent, was protected by the First Amendment freedom of the press to publish news of legitimate public interest. The spectator was in full view of the fans, drinking beer, waving a banner, and after being told who the photographer was, began to scream and holler. imploring the photographer to take more pictures. There was no invasion of privacy.

The different branches of invasion of privacy often overlap one another. For instance, the appropriation of an athlete's name or pic-

ture for an ad endorsing an alcoholic beverage may also place the athlete in a false light as a serious drinker. And, an act of intrusion into the private affairs of an athlete may be followed by the publication of private facts which may embarrass the athlete.

The right to privacy—the right to be left alone, free from intrusion of one's private rights—applies equally to all.

22

INSULTS & LIES

WHAT'S IT ABOUT?

Insults & Lies explains defamation and how it can injure others, whether done in writing or speaking by attacking another's reputation.

Do you know the difference between a public and a private figure?

Superior Court of New York

JJ Jock, plaintiff
v
NY Telegram, TV Sports Channel (TVSC),
Larry Libel and Sam Slander, defendants

COMPLAINT

Here comes the plaintiff, JJ Jock, who states as follows:

1. This is an action for **defamation** —a statement that injures the reputation and diminishes the esteem and respect in which the plaintiff is held by exposing him to public hatred or disgrace; or that excites adverse, derogatory or evil feelings or opinions against him.

2. JJ plays professional kickball for the NY Playgrounders. Larry Libel and Sam Slander are reporters for the NY Telegram and TVSC.

3. JJ alleges that the defendants made defamatory, unwarranted and untruthful attacks on his character by the following:

a. a defamatory statement made in writing—**libel.** A story in the Telegram reported by Larry Libel, "JJ couldn't kick a ball as well as minor leaguers. He's a second rate reserve who couldn't fight his way out of a paper bag. And he bet on his team to lose."

b. a defamatory statement made in speaking—**slander.** TVSC repeated a statement made by Sam Slander, "JJ couldn't beat my 10-year-old kid in kickball. He's on drugs. His performance wasn't even up to his usual standard—lousy."

4. These statements were communicated to other persons by publishing and broadcasting them in the Telegram and over TVSC.

5. JJ's good reputation is essential to his ability to make a living. These accusations will diminish that ability, thereby causing injury to his reputation, subjecting him to hatred and disgrace, and to unpleasant comments and opinions.

Wherefore, JJ, asks this court to award damages for injury to his reputation and character in an amount that the court deems necessary and proper.

FACTS: JJ Jock filed the above complaint for defamation against Larry Libel and Sam Slander, and the newspaper and TV station that they worked for.

Did the statements by Larry Libel and Sam Slander defame JJ?

DECISION: **YOU'RE THE JUDGE!**

IS AN ATHLETE A PUBLIC FIGURE?

A **public figure** is one who commands a substantial amount of public interest, has achieved widespread fame or notoriety, or has searched for public adulation and acclaim.

To recover for defamation, a public figure must prove that a defendant's statements were made with **malice**—knowledge that they were false, or made with reckless disregard for the truth.

FACTS: Cepeda, a star baseball player with the Giants, sued a magazine for an article which portrayed him as an ineffective and unpopular team player.

Chuy, a football player with the Eagles, claimed, "A false statement to a sportswriter, stating that I was suffering from a rare blood disease, injured my reputation." Were Cepeda and Chuy public figures? **YOU'RE THE JUDGE!**

DECISION: Regarding one's playing career, an athlete is a public figure and, therefore, must prove malice to recover for defamation. "An athlete's choice to engage in a profession which attracts wide public attention, and where the athlete invites such attention and seeks public acclaim, makes the athlete a public figure."

Chuy was denied recovery for defamation because of the court's misinterpretation of the law. Cepeda lost because he could not prove malice; that is, that the article was false or made with a reckless disregard for the truth.

Also, a coach portrayed in an article as one who "incited crowds to such a point of hysteria as to result in physical abuse of the referees," was unable to recover as he too, was unable to prove that the statements were published maliciously.

Another coach was more successful in his defamation suit.

FACTS: In an article, Butts, the athletic director at Georgia, was accused of conspiring to rig or fix a football game. The article was entitled: THE STORY OF A COLLEGE FOOTBALL FIX, and it accused Butts of giving "Bear" Bryant, the coach of Alabama, Georgia's plays.

The article revealed that an insurance salesman had accidentally overheard a telephone conversation between Butts and Bryant, in which (according to the article), "The Georgia players, their moves analyzed like those of rats in a maze, took a frightful physical beating."

Butts sued, charging, "The truth of the article was a serious departure from good investigative standards and the accuracy of its charges amounted to reckless and wanton conduct." Was Butts defamed? **YOU'RE THE JUDGE!**

DECISION: Yes. The magazine assigned the story to a writer who was not a football expert. He made no attempt to have such an expert check the story. Interested in cultivating an image "designed to provoke people, make them mad," the magazine ignored precautions to insure publication of the truth. The magazine's "highly unreasonable conduct" established that it had acted in reckless disregard in determining whether the article was false or not, thus proving malice. Punitive damages were awarded "to deter the wrong-doer from repeating the trespass."

Others may also be public figures where they are drawn into a public controversy, such as an agent in negotiations for a player, especially where contact with the media was sought out. Is a coach a public figure?

FACTS: "Sam is a despicable human being. He's a fat liar!" This statement was screamed at an owner's meeting by an opposing owner of another pro basketball team. The statement could not be supported. Was the coach a public figure? Was the statement defamatory? **YOU'RE THE JUDGE!**

DECISION: The coach was a public figure. The remarks were not privileged and were defamatory.

A member of a team may also be defamed. True magazine published a story entitled: THE PILL THAT KILLED SPORTS, which discussed the taking of drugs by athletes. Evidence showed that the substance given to the football players was "spirits of peppermint," a harmless substance used for the relief of dryness of the mouth. The article exposed the entire football team to public hatred and contempt.

What if a statement made about a public figure is deemed to be "fair comment"?

FACTS: A boxer's reputation as a "canvasback," unable to fight, was the subject of a comedy routine. Was the athlete defamed? **YOU'RE THE JUDGE!**

DECISION: No. Recovery was denied where malice could not be proved. The comments were limited to public facts and were "fair comment" about matters of legitimate public interest concerning a public figure.

Is name calling of those, considered public figures, defamation? Although it may be, it is not always.

FACTS: A sports agent, Harris, sued a former NFL football coach, Damon, for slander, alleging, "He called me a 'sleezebag' who 'slimed up from the bayou.'" Was this slander or constitutionally protected speech? **YOU'RE THE JUDGE!**

DECISION: The judge commented, "While it may not be a compliment to be called a sleezebag, the mere absence of complimentary effect does not make a statement defamatory." The judge added, "It is all too rare today to hear the clear, clean ring of a really original insult."

PRIVATE FIGURES

The public may have a legal right to information about public figures, but not as to private figures, or as to the private and personal life of a public figure.

This may be partly true because private figures rarely have access to the media as do public figures; they cannot fight back.

Athletes found to be private figures, as regarding their private and personal lives, need only show mere negligence or fault to prove defamation.

In a case involving a fictitious biography about the famed baseball pitcher, Warren Spahn, the court held that he was a public figure only in his professional career, thus upholding a verdict for "unauthorized exploitation" of his private and personal life.

How is it determined if one is a public or private figure? One's exposure to the public may determine whether he is a public or private figure.

FACTS: A high school wrestling coach sued a newspaper for libel. The newspaper had written that the coach lied in court when testifying about his part in a fight at a wrestling match. Was the coach a public figure? **YOU'RE THE JUDGE!**

DECISION: The court ruled that the coach was not a public figure. His exposure as a high school wrestling coach was not enough to make him a public figure.

DEFENSE! DEFENSE!

Although a statement may be defamatory, if the defamed party gave **consent** to the statement, or if the statement was truthful, recovery may be denied.

What if a truthful statement is used to hurt another? An exception exists where truthful information is used to hurt another.

FACTS: Bruiser, a pro football player, had a mental illness. A reporter, to whom Bruiser would not grant an interview, wrote, " Bruiser suffers from a mental illness, the possible side effects of which are physical outbursts. I'd stay away from Bruiser!" Was the statement, although true, defamatory? **YOU'RE THE JUDGE!**

DECISION: Truthful information, used for the sole purpose of hurting the defamed party, would be malicious and defamatory. Bruiser could recover damages.

To protect the public's interest, judicial and administrative proceedings are given absolute immunity from liability. Thus, where a report concerning gambling in professional sports was posted on a bulletin board, it was immune from liability for defamation.

And a statement made in a kidding manner, intended as a joke, such as, "Heck, Joe would never have to throw a game, but just pitch normal," may not be with malice. An athlete or other public figure must accept a harsher degree of criticism about their performance than would a private person.

For how long after an athlete's career will "fair comment" be allowed?

FACTS: Dempsey, a former boxing champ, sued a magazine for libel for the cover headline, "Dempsey's Gloves Were Loaded" and the inside story entitled, "He Didn't Know the Gloves Were Loaded." The story suggested that Dempsey won his championship by using "loaded gloves."

Allegedly, Dempsey's manager put plaster of paris mixed with water on Dempsey's bandaged hands. Did the privilege of fair comment about athletes protect the magazine from liability for defamation? **YOU'RE THE JUDGE!**

DECISION: No. Unless malice can be proven, fair comment, even about an athlete's pro activity after he had retired, will be allowed so long as it is newsworthy and of public interest. However, reaching back forty-five years was too great a period of time. Such statements were not fair comment.

Lies in a newspaper article which are stated as facts are libelous. How about lies in cartoons?

Lies which are stated as such by the use of cartoons, satire or parody are considered "kidding." Such statements are protected by the First Amendment's freedom of speech and are not libelous.

FACTS: A sports magazine had an ad parody purportedly quoting well-known Coach Pete discussing a fictitious beating of his mother by him, and a habit of "getting drunk" before games. Should the courts find a way to balance free speech rights with legal protection against offensive attacks or insults which "go too far"? **YOU'RE THE JUDGE!**

DECISION: The court ruled, "The ad was not libelous," and did not award damages for emotional distress. The ad was protected by the First Amendment's right to free speech.

Although not defenses, if an alleged defamatory statement is retracted, or if the anger of the speaker was—in part—due to provocation by the alleged defamed party, such factors could lessen any damages.

MALICIOUS PROSECUTION

Malicious prosecution is the misuse of the law or courts with the desire to inflict injury on another.

FACTS: Dave and Guy, owners of opposing NBA teams, were bitter rivals. Dave, in a suit against the league to move his team, named Guy personally as a defendant. Guy charged that by naming him personally as a defendant, Dave was guilty of malicious prosecution. "That was a malicious, spiteful and vindictive abuse of process. I suffered a heart attack because of it." The jury agreed that Dave's actions were indeed malicious. Could Guy recover damages for his heart attack? **YOU'RE THE JUDGE!**

DECISION: Guy had a right to freedom from the deliberate misuse of the law or the courts. He should not have been named a defendant in Dave's suit. Dave was found responsible for Guy's heart attack and had to pay damages, including punitive damages—to deter future wrongdoing.

ODDS & ENDS....

Statements made on TV or radio may be **slander** because they are spoken, or **libel** because, as with printed statements, they may be recorded.

Do any of the following allegations fall within the definition of **defamation**—a statement that injures the reputation and diminishes the esteem and respect in which the plaintiff is held by exposing him to public hatred or disgrace, or that excites adverse, derogatory or evil feelings or opinions against him?

FACTS: Michaels, a star professional soccer goaltender for the Sockers, sued several writers, sportscasters and others for defamation of his reputation and character for their statements and actions following the World Soccer Bowl. Michaels had allowed all eight goals in a 8-3 loss.

Michaels, in a complaint, alleged the following as being defamatory:

- Statements made at a post-game gathering and on TV that Michaels "choked" and appeared to be throwing the game;
- A picture in the paper showing Michaels lying on the ground with a following story entitled: MICHAELS LYING DOWN ON THE JOB!;
- A drawing of Michaels walking off the field, showing fans making indecent gestures and the choke sign while others pointed towards him;
- Cartoons showing Michaels giving the choke sign, accepting cash from a shady looking character and leaning on the side of the net as soccer balls whizzed by;
- The placing of a statue of his likeness in front of the stadium with his hands around his neck, in a choking position; and,
- The burning in effigy of a likeness similar to Michaels at a public meeting called by the team's booster club.

Which of these acts could be considered slander (spoken), libel (written), both, or neither? **YOU'RE THE JUDGE!**

DECISION: Pictures, cartoons, drawings, statues or other likenesses—where either reference (by use of writing), is made to a picture or there is no accompanying writing—may be considered libel as it is the publication or printing that creates potential liability for defamation.

The picture, drawing and statue are considered statements or writings; the words are inferred by what one might think when seeing them.

Only the statements at the post-game gathering and the cartoon showing him accepting money were found to be actionable libel for which Michaels could recover damages if the statements were proved false.

Cartoons, satires, parodies and jokes, such as you might find on the sports, comic or editorial pages, are considered "kidding." Such statements are protected by the First Amendment's freedom of speech.

23

YOUR TICKET PLEASE

WHAT'S IT ABOUT?

May spectators be denied admission to sports events? *Your Ticket Please* discusses this, ticket prices, seating and "scalping."

If you lose your ticket to a sports event, will you still be admitted?

Section C — WORLD NEWSPAPER — July 10, 1978

SPECTATOR VIOLENCE!!

Spectator violence is hardly new. As far back as 70 A.D., spectators at the games in Pompeii broke into wild sword fights, resulting in many deaths. Gladiator events were banned for a decade. Centuries later, thousands of people were killed when rival chariot-racing groups set off a series of riots that nearly destroyed Constantinople.

In more recent times at soccer games, referees' calls resulting in a home team's loss, and a late goal by a home team (after which the departing fans rushed back, while others tried to leave), resulted in hundreds of deaths. Other injuries and deaths were caused by fans pelting each other with rocks. Moats and fences had to be built to separate the fans from players, referees and the field.

And at hockey and baseball games promoting "Disco Night" and 10¢ beer, spectator violence also led to injuries.

These and many more incidents like them, most less severe, involving fans intent on interfering with the orderly and safe procession of a sports event, have brought about a need for increased security and stricter enforcement of admittance and expulsion procedures regarding spectators.

YOU CAN'T COME IN!

May spectators be denied admission to sports events? Operators of athletic facilities and other places of public amusement may, in the absence of law, admit or exclude persons at their pleasure, and also make such rules and regulations as they see fit to govern the admission of persons to their premises.

FACTS: When you go to most any sporting event, the back of the ticket will generally have a provision—in small type—to the effect that:

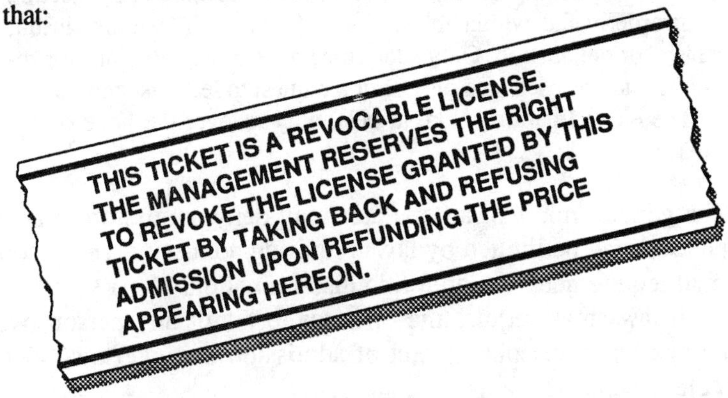

THIS TICKET IS A REVOCABLE LICENSE.
THE MANAGEMENT RESERVES THE RIGHT
TO REVOKE THE LICENSE GRANTED BY THIS
TICKET BY TAKING BACK AND REFUSING
ADMISSION UPON REFUNDING THE PRICE
APPEARING HEREON.

What would your rights be if you were excluded from a sporting event by such a provision? **YOU'RE THE JUDGE!**

DECISION: The ticket does not give the right to enter or remain in the facility. It is a mere license, revocable at the will of the operator, who may decline to permit the holder to enter, or remove him after he has taken his seat. And, unless the denial of admittance or expulsion is accompanied by insult or more force than is reasonably necessary, a spectator's only recourse would be to recover the price of admission on the ticket.

Thus, spectators have been refused admittance or ejected from sports events for any conduct which interferes with the event or other patrons' enjoyment of it, or is in violation of the law. Such exclusion promotes the protection of other spectators and the participants in the sporting event.

FACTS: "I was kicked out of the racetrack" Jake explained, "for trying to fix races and for illegal betting."

Paddy growled, "I was ejected from a hockey game for throwing bottles!"

Grady was kicked out of a baseball game for being "objectionable" to other fans, for paying players and for buying tickets from scalpers.

Stan was ejected from a basketball arena for swearing. Striker was banned from the bowling alley after admitting, "I beat up another bowler."

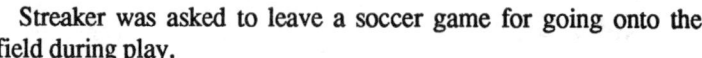

Streaker was asked to leave a soccer game for going onto the field during play.

Killer snarled, "I was kicked out of the football stadium and charged with rioting for encouraging the crowd to tear down the goalposts!" Were these expulsions proper? Could those expelled recover damages? **YOU'RE THE JUDGE!**

DECISION: Persons admitted to sporting events are required to conduct themselves in an orderly and proper manner. A proprietor may use reasonable steps to end any improper conduct or disturbance, as by requesting the offending person to stop, or by ejecting a disorderly fan within the limits of good order, without insult, abuse, or defamation. Only such force as may be necessary for removal may be used, and only after a request to leave is ignored

The ejected patron could, at best, only recover the price of admission.

The general rule that an operator may deny admission to anyone he pleases may be limited by laws requiring admission, or by constitutional requirements which forbid discrimination.

Such laws may require the operator to admit any person over a given age who presents a ticket of admission and whose conduct is not offensive.

TICKET PRICE

FACTS: A local theatre was charging $500 for a ticket to the closed circuit viewing of a heavyweight championship boxing match. Another theatre was charging $10, but only allowing 25 people to attend. Theatre held 200. Could you do anything about such an outrageous price, or the few number of people allowed in? **YOU'RE THE JUDGE!**

DECISION: Proprietors may charge what they choose for admission, limit the number admitted and, generally, regulate the terms and conditions of admission in any reasonable way. As one proprietor remarked, "If the terms of admission are unsatisfactory, no one is obliged to buy a ticket."

WHERE'S MY SEAT?

The right to a seat by a spectator depends upon the ticket that he holds. If the ticket is not for a reserved seat, he may take any unoccupied seat which has not been previously sold to another. But he cannot, after being notified by the proprietor to vacate it, continue to occupy a specially located seat for which an extra charge is made.

FACTS: Joey bought a reserved seat for a basketball game, but the proprietor failed to give him his seat. Joey's conduct was in no way offensive and the proprietor gave no reason for denying him the seat. Could Joey recover damages in excess of the ticket price?

DECISION: **YOU'RE THE JUDGE!**

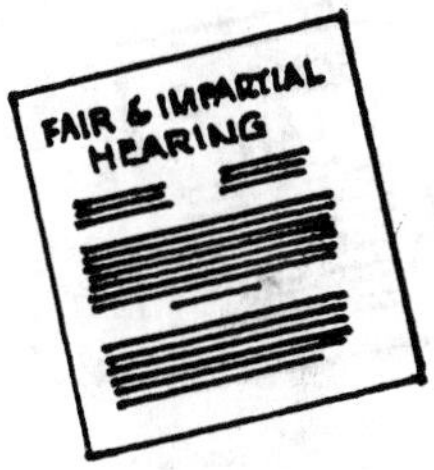

Generally, a spectator ejected from a sport's facility will be unable to recover damages in excess of the ticket price.

However, an action may be maintained against a proprietor or security for a breach of the duty to give proper treatment and protection to patrons not guilty of any misconduct, or for any improper ejectment.

Due process—a fair and impartial hearing with representation—may be required to determine whether there was a reasonable basis for excluding any person from a public facility. Such a hearing may not be required for exclusion from a private facility.

HANDS UP!

May fans entering a sporting event be searched?

FACTS: Fans attending a sporting event were subjected to warrantless, pat-down searches by police officers. Upon entering another stadium, other patrons were warned by a tape recording, "A search for drugs, alcohol, weapons and other contraband will be made of fans and their belongings."

Not everyone was searched, just those suspected of carrying prohibited materials. When these fans were confronted by the police, they gave their "consent" to be searched. Were these pat-down searches legal? **YOU'RE THE JUDGE!**

DECISION: No. The pat-down searches were unconstitutional, a violation of the Fourth Amendment's protection from unreasonable search and seizure. Searches could not be made on mere hunches. Probable cause to believe that an unlawful act was being committed was necessary. An injunction stopping the searches was granted.

WE WERE SCALPED!

Generally, **scalping** is selling an admission ticket for a price higher than the original price of the ticket.

A scalper acquires tickets and holds them until other buyers have exhausted the box office supply. Then the scalper offers to resell his tickets at a price higher than the original price. Those wishing to attend the event are compelled to either pay the scalper or not attend.

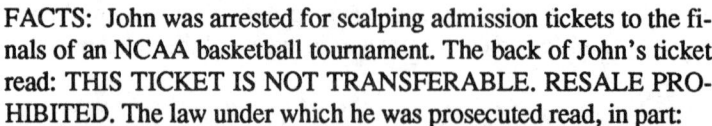

FACTS: John was arrested for scalping admission tickets to the finals of an NCAA basketball tournament. The back of John's ticket read: THIS TICKET IS NOT TRANSFERABLE. RESALE PROHIBITED. The law under which he was prosecuted read, in part:

> IT IS UNLAWFUL FOR ANY PERSON TO SCALP AN ADMISSION TICKET TO ANY AUDITORIUM, STADIUM, RINK, ATHLETIC FIELD OR ANY OTHER PLACE TO WHICH TICKETS ARE REQUIRED FOR ADMITTANCE.
>
> TO SCALP ADMISSION TICKETS MEANS TO SELL ANY TICKET AT A PRICE ABOVE THE PRICE PRINTED THEREON OR AT A PRICE HIGHER THAN THE STANDARD RETAIL PRICE FOR WHICH SUCH TICKET WAS ISSUED OR OFFERED FOR SALE.

John purchased tickets and then offered them for sale at inflated prices. He alleged that the law unreasonably interfered with his right to conduct a legitimate private business for profit. Was John guilty of scalping tickets? **YOU'RE THE JUDGE!**

DECISION: John was convicted of "scalping" tickets. The court commented, "There is a legitimate public interest in the regulation of such events and in enabling all of the members of the public desiring to attend such events to have an equal and fair opportunity to obtain admission tickets for the proper price. Such laws protect the general public from the abuses of ticket speculators, and the evils, fraud and theft that generally go with scalping."

Do states regulate the selling of tickets to sporting events? Yes. Several states have laws regulating the resale price of tickets to these events. These statutes either prohibit a resale price in excess of the original box office price, or establish a maximum profit for resales.

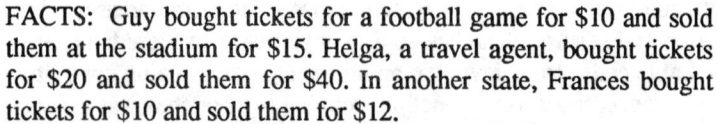

FACTS: Guy bought tickets for a football game for $10 and sold them at the stadium for $15. Helga, a travel agent, bought tickets for $20 and sold them for $40. In another state, Frances bought tickets for $10 and sold them for $12.

John and his family were attending a game. John said, "Our son couldn't make it, so we sold his $22 ticket for $25. Jimmy was offered $50 for his $25 play-off ticket. He accepted. Were any of these people guilty of scalping? **YOU'RE THE JUDGE!**

DECISION: Guy was guilty; his state prohibited the resale of tickets for any price in excess of the face value. Helga was not guilty. Travel agents are not covered by the law.

Frances was not guilty. Her state allowed resale not exceeding two dollars over the face value of the ticket. Neither was John guilty. He was not familiar with the law. His was an isolated incident, not one by a regular scalper. And, neither was Jimmy guilty. He didn't offer to sell the ticket.

Generally, any anti-scalping law is enforceable. Some may allow scalping anywhere in the state, or from outside the state, except at the game site on the day of the game. Other states may only make selling (not offering to sell) tickets at a profit, a violation.

TICKET TYING!

FACTS: Fans brought suits against NFL teams, claiming that, "Ticket selling practices illegally 'tied' the purchase of one product (the season ticket) to the purchase of another product (exhibition game tickets)." The teams only sold season tickets to purchasers who also bought tickets to all pre-season exhibition games. Was this a permitted practice? **YOU'RE THE JUDGE!**

DECISION: Yes. There were individual tickets available to each regular season game and, therefore, fans were not compelled to buy an exhibition game ticket to get a regular season game ticket.

Professional teams have a "legitimate monopoly" over the presentation of regular season and exhibition games. Such teams could not be found guilty of restraining free competition for exhibition games as no one else presented them.

LOST TICKETS!

What happens if you lose your ticket? Will you still be admitted?

FACTS: Sloan had a season ticket for the Rangers' hockey games. Upon purchase of the season ticket, Sloan signed a form which provided, in part:

SEASON TICKET FORM

UPON RECEIPT OF TICKETS PURCHASED, RISK OF LOSS OR THEFT OF TICKETS SHALL PASS TO THE SUBSCRIBER. MADISON SQUARE GARDEN SHALL NOT BE OBLIGATED TO ADMIT THE SUBSCRIBER TO GAMES UNLESS TICKETS ARE PRESENTED.

Sloan, having either misplaced or lost his ticket to a game, was denied entry. The Garden offered, "We'll sell him a ticket to the same seat and refund the admission price if the ticket is later found."

Sloan sued the Garden, protesting, "The demand of two payments for the same seat unfairly benefits the Garden. Should I have had to pay for the same seat twice?" **YOU'RE THE JUDGE!**

DECISION: Sloan failed to produce his ticket, as agreed. He must pay twice for the same seat (if he wants to attend), unless he is able to later produce the ticket.

The fact that the seat might be empty is no assurance that the ticket has not been used. "It is likely that if someone had the ticket, they would hide amongst the crowd of some 20,000 and not sit in the proper seat!" commented the judge.

CROWD CONTROL

What would happen if fans deliberately delayed a game by throwing debris onto the court?

FACTS: Central New England College was playing a basketball game against Eastern U. Eastern's fans, excited over their team's comeback from a large deficit, threw toilet paper and other debris onto the court. The game was delayed. Could the officials penalize Eastern for their fans' behavior? **YOU'RE THE JUDGE!**

DECISION: Under NCAA rules, Eastern was assessed a technical foul. Central was awarded two free throws and control of the ball. Central won the game, 80-79.

Similarly, another college team, Vanderbilt, lost a game when, with one second remaining in the game and a two point lead, its fans threw tennis balls onto the court. Vanderbilt was assessed a technical foul. The opposing team, Florida, made the two free throws and then won the game in overtime!

FOUL BALL!

If you were at a Major League Baseball game and caught a foul ball, would you have to return it to the field?

No, you wouldn't ... but it wasn't always that way.

At a game back in 1925, Reuben—a spectator— caught a foul ball. When he wouldn't return it, a court was called upon to settle the dispute.

The judge, in holding that spectators now could keep foul balls, reasoned that the "safety of the spectators and the disturbance to the game caused by the continued stoppage to retrieve the balls" called for such a ruling. "Besides, teams would not want to risk the loss of fans if the disputes continued."

A DAY IN COURT

Numerous fans have had their day in court concerning incidents involving sports contests.

One case in a Georgia traffic court involved a baseball fan ticketed for ignoring a DO NOT ENTER sign.

FACTS: Barry and several of his friends testified, "Whenever we went to Braves' games, about thirty-five a year, we didn't notice the sign." Did Barry have to pay the fine? **YOU'RE THE JUDGE!**

DECISION: The judge asked if the fans, by claiming to see so many games, were using this as an insanity defense. He dismissed the charges, figuring that Barry had suffered enough.

Two men cracked the formula for a promotional contest which called for finding matching numbers on cards. The men rounded up about 4,000 winning tickets, claimed more than $20 million in winnings and free trips to the Super Bowl. The sponsoring company cancelled the football-theme contest after learning of the winning tickets. Did the company have to pay?

A number of baseball fans, angry over a strike, filed suit when games for which they had purchased tickets were cancelled.

The fans listed damages as: "Interference with personal and vacation plans; mental anguish and tension, and; our safety is now jeopardized by individuals who might react violently when now unable to rid themselves of their tensions and problems by attending baseball games." The suit was dismissed.

Other fans have had better success in courts.

FACTS: Jimmy, unhappy that the Dolphins were "trying to make me use my ticket to see NFL replacement games during the strike," sued the team for a refund.

The team argued that Jimmy was only entitled to half of his money back because he enjoyed other amenities besides his club-seat (such as air conditioning, a lounge and preferred parking). Was Jimmy entitled to a full refund? **YOU'RE THE JUDGE!**

DECISION: The judge agreed that replacement games did not constitute real NFL games, which Jimmy had paid to see. He ruled that, "The club violated its contract with the ticketholders by fielding the replacement team." Jimmy got a full refund.

ODDS & ENDS....

Fan Clubs

FACTS: Dana, with help from Jimmy (a pro tennis player), ran a fan club for the latter. For a minimal fee, she wrote a newsletter and distributed photos and souvenirs.

An article in a tennis magazine quoted Jimmy's brother as saying, "Jimmy sued Dana because she was hindering him from starting his own club." After realizing that there was no suit, the magazine promised a retraction.

Fan club members demanded money back, calling the club a fraud. Another pro became hesitant about having Terry start his fan club.

Dana charged Jimmy and his family with violating their agreement, interfering with her club members and damaging her reputation. Could she recover damages?

DECISION: **YOU'RE THE JUDGE!**

Dwarf Tossing?

Dwarf tossing is a contest where—nowadays—the "tossed" wear helmets when hurled down a padded sidewalk. This sport originated in England where it is now banned.

The city of Chicago would not issue a permit to have such a contest at a local bar. The bar was offering prizes for the longest toss over the thirty foot record. And they would furnish a "house dwarf" for any contestants without a dwarf!

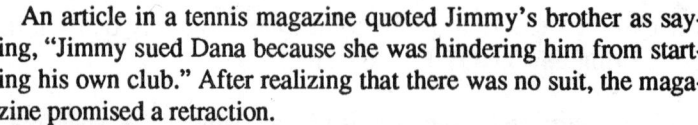

Tortillas! Peanuts!

FACTS: Fans at sporting events hurled tortillas, beach balls, fireworks, stink bombs and other objects into the crowd. Vendors hurled peanuts and other products. Could these activities be prohibited? **YOU'RE THE JUDGE!**

DECISION: After complaints from fans who said that they were hit by tortillas and peanuts, one city—for safety reasons—enacted an ordinance banning the throwing of any objects at sporting events. Vendors were exempted from the ban.

Other fans complained about beer drinking which they alleged caused fights and other "rowdyism." Some professional sports teams now offer seating in sections where alcoholic beverages are prohibited, or prohibit the sale of alcohol during the later part of the sports contests.

A crowd at a sports event may play an essential role in determining the outcome—from cheering for their favorite team or athlete to more directly affecting the outcome by disturbing play.

24

FANS & INJURIES

WHAT'S IT ABOUT?

You were a spectator at a sports event and were injured. Who was liable for the injury—a player, the player's team, the operator of the facility, or another spectator? Did you assume the risk of your injury or contribute to it? *Fans & Injuries* discusses injuries to spectators and who may be liable.

Should a spectator at a baseball game assume the risk of injury from a ball that may be traveling in excess of 100 m.p.h.?

Chicago Gazette
Section C - Sports

FANS INJURED - WHO'S LIABLE?

The danger that a sports activity will cause injury to spectators has existed from the time of the gladiators. As one court commented:

"A defect inherent in the nature of man is that perversity of spirit which attracts us to spectacles of danger in which the participants risk injury and death for our amusement. As far back as the events in the coliseums of ancient Rome, spectators were subject to risks for there must have been occasions when a lion escaped the arena to prowl amongst the patrons, or a gladiator lost control of his weapon to the detriment of a front row observer."

The dangers have changed, but so too have the rights of spectators. In the days of gladiators, an injured spectator had no rights. The spectator of today may seek recovery for an injury by proving that the injury was due to the negligence of another and not the result of a known and appreciated danger (thus not one that they assumed the risk of injury from).

An owner or operator of a sports facility, a player or participant or another spectator may be liable where they breach their duty to care for the protection and safety of spectators. What are the duties of an operator of a sports facility or a participant?

WHO'S LIABLE?

Except for injuries due to another's negligence, spectators will assume the risk of most injuries.

In the eyes of the court, the spectator "is a hearty and ruddy-complexioned Greek god, with a spirit that sets him apart from mere mortal men. He is deemed to foresee a ball, puck or other object that comes speeding in an unfamiliar orbit towards him. And, he is expected to be patient and forebearing—slightly ruffled, but unconcerned by the freshly imprinted baseball seams on his forehead."

FACTS: Fans at baseball and hockey games and at a golf tournament were struck by errantly thrown or hit balls or pucks. Other fans were injured when bats, sticks or clubs "slipped" from players' hands. Still others were injured when a racing car went out of control, and also, when players left the field in pursuit of another player or a ball. Will fans assume the risk of such injuries?

DECISION: **YOU'RE THE JUDGE!**

The owner or operator of a sports facility is bound to exercise ordinary or reasonable care for the protection and safety of spectators at a sporting event.

I ACTED REASONABLY!

FACTS: Frank, an usher at the town hall, explained what happened on roller derby night, "The place was packed with 3,000 screaming, rowdy fans. But the security was minimal. Some fans were hurt when, because of the lack of security to break up several scuffles, a big fight broke out!" Was this reasonable care? **YOU'RE THE JUDGE!**

DECISION: No. Such security was not that care which could reasonably be expected. Operators must employ a sufficient number of qualified personnel to maintain their premises in a reasonably safe condition.

However, as long as he acts reasonably, the owner or operator is not an insurer of a spectator's safety. Spectators will assume the ordinary risks of the sport or from attendance at a sports facility.

YOU ASSUMED THE RISK!

If the crowds at the roller derby games had been pretty quiet, and then suddenly, without warning, a fight broke out, and several fans sitting nearby, but not involved, were injured—and no amount of care would have prevented the injuries—would the spectators then be held to have assumed the risk of such injury? Yes. A proprietor will not be liable even though security may have been inadequate.

FACTS: Phillips was injured during a fight in the stadium parking lot following a baseball game. When he saw two drunks sitting on his car, he yelled at them. "One of them hit me," he complained. Phillips sued the Dodgers for not having proper security to protect him. There had been other fights and related mischief in the parking area during preceding games. Was the team liable for Phillips' injury? **YOU'RE THE JUDGE!**

DECISION: No. The court found Phillips primarily responsible for his own injury. The security was adequate. The court observed, "It's an easy matter to know whether a stairway is defective and what repairs will put it in order, but how can one know what measures will protect against the thug, the addict, the degenerate, the psychopath and the psychotic?"

NEGLIGENCE

What are the elements of negligence? To find an owner or operator of a sports facility or another guilty and liable for a **tort**—civil wrong committed against an individual—an injured spectator must prove **negligence**—that is, that the defendant owner, operator or another had a duty of care for the protection and safety of the spectator, that there was a breach of that duty which caused an injury, and that the injury and damages would not have occurred but for the acts or conduct of the defendant.

DEFENSE! DEFENSE!

The owner or operator of sports facilities, or another, may allege the defenses that: the spectator was guilty of **assumption of the risk**—the spectator assumed the risk of injury—having had actual knowledge and appreciation of the ordinary and inherent dangers of the sport, but chose to face them anyway; was guilty of **contributory negligence**—the spectator acted in a way that contributed to the injury (as by remaining when in danger) or took part in the activity which resulted in injury. Does a spectator have a duty to protect himself, such as by leaving when injury is imminent?

FACTS: Jan, a spectator at a football game, groaned, "I was injured when another spectator taking part in a fight fell on me." The crowd had been unruly for the whole game. Did Jan assume the risk of such an injury? **YOU'RE THE JUDGE!**

DECISION: Jan had the last clear chance to avoid the injury. He knew that the crowd was getting rowdy. He assumed the risk of, and contributed to, the injury by remaining. Security had kept the unruliness to mostly shouting until the injury.

Furthermore, if an injury was the result of an unavoidable accident, as where a spectator unintentionally bumped into another causing an injury, there would be no liability by the operator of the facility.

Can injured spectators recover even if they were party at fault for their injuries?

Comparative negligence compares the negligence of the spectator with that of the defendant, and allows the spectator to still recover, although his recovery may be reduced by his own negligence.

FACTS: Junior said, "I was injured at a football game, when I slipped in the aisle." Junior was found to be 60% at fault—he knew the liquid had been spilled—a common occurrence at such a game. The operator was found to be 40% at fault—he could have cleared the mess away. Could Junior recover for his injury? What if Junior were only 40% at fault? **YOU'RE THE JUDGE!**

DECISION: In some states, a spectator's recovery is denied where he is found to be more than 50% at fault. In others, irregardless of Junior's fault, he could recover 40% of the total recovery awarded by the court.

Still, in others, if Junior were 40% at fault, he would only recover 20% of the total award. In this case, the court compares the two, subtracting Junior's 40% fault from the operator's 60% fault.

SAFE FLOORS & AISLES?

The owner or operator of a sports facility represents that, except for unknown defects not discoverable by reasonable means, his facility is reasonably safe. Is he relieved of liability merely because he had no precise knowledge of a defective condition?

FACTS: Several spectators at a basketball game were injured when they slipped on a spilled liquid or on a worn and loose carpet in an entranceway. Spectators at a football game were injured by splinters in the bleachers and by loose nails. Did these spectators assume the risk of such injuries? Were the operators liable for the injuries? **YOU'RE THE JUDGE!**

DECISION: As to the spill and the carpet, the operator either knew or should have known of the defective condition. He was liable. Likewise, the operator of the football stadium should have attended to the loose nails.

However, the spectators assumed the risk of injury from splinters, common in wooden bleachers. The condition was not bad enough to require immediate attention.

However, where something not connected with the operation of a facility and not placed there by an operator, makes the premises unsafe, an operator is not under a continuing duty of inspection. He is not responsible unless he knew or should have known of the condition.

FACTS: Fran testified, "I was injured when I tripped on an umbrella in the aisle."

Hughey was injured when he tripped over cans in the aisle. Was the operator liable for such injuries? **YOU'RE THE JUDGE!**

DECISION: Fran assumed the risk of his injury. Hughey could recover for his. The operator should have corrected the condition. The condition was either known of, or should have been known of.

An operator must use reasonable care to ensure that aisles and floors are in a reasonably safe condition.

FACTS: A statute read, "No temporary seats or persons are allowed to remain in the aisles."

John was struck by a foul ball while walking up an aisle crowded by fans sitting in it. The accident had occurred in the split second when John saw the ball and turned up against the rail. "Can I recover for my injury?" he asked. **YOU'RE THE JUDGE!**

DECISION: No. John assumed the ordinary risks and hazards of the game. Even had there been no fans in the aisle, the accident could have occurred.

However, where a spectator was unable to move out of the way of a prohibited crowd in an aisle and was injured, an operator may be liable.

Has an operator exercised proper care for spectators' safety by merely posting warning signs?

FACTS: Warning signs at all entrances to an arena read, NO BOTTLES, CANS OR OTHER CONTAINERS ALLOWED. There was no security check at these entrances. A fan received a fractured skull when he was hit by a bottle. Was the operator of the arena liable for the injury? **YOU'RE THE JUDGE!**

DECISION: The operator should have provided at least a minimum check, which may have prevented such an injury. He was liable.

SAFE STAIRWAYS & RAILINGS?

Although there is no duty to warn of obvious dangers, an owner or operator of a sports facility has a duty to warn spectators of any known dangers, or those which could be discovered by inspection or supervision.

FACTS: Martin was injured when a broken railing at a hockey rink collapsed from the pressure of other spectators leaning on it. It was foreseeable that the spectators would act as such in an attempt to see the game. Another spectator broke his foot when he tripped over a step under repair. He could not see the AREA UNDER REPAIR sign, as the lighting was out in the walkway. Were the operators liable for these injuries? **YOU'RE THE JUDGE!**

DECISION: Yes. The operators violated their duty of care to the spectators by not taking the proper precautions necessary to alleviate the dangers.

SAFETY LAWS

If an injury to a spectator at a sports facility results from a defect, which violates a safety law designed to provide for the safety of premises used for sporting events, liability may be found against the owner or operator of the facility.

FACTS: A law made it UNLAWFUL TO PERMIT INTOXICATED, BOISTEROUS, OR DISORDERLY PERSONS TO ENTER OR REMAIN ON THE PREMISES. Another law required "handrails on all stairwells." Another required a "safe place" for spectators. If spectators were injured due to a violation of one of these laws, would the operator be liable?

DECISION: **YOU'RE THE JUDGE!**

ORDER!

The owner or operator of a sports facility has a duty to maintain order on his premises. If he does nothing to restrain or control improper conduct after he knows, or should have known of it, and injury results, he may be liable.

However, there will be no liability where the owner or operator could not have reasonably anticipated an assault.

FACTS: Roy, 17, attending a Harlem Globetrotters basketball game, was assaulted in a dimly-lit public restroom. It happened suddenly. There had not been any assaults during prior events on the premises. Was the operator liable? **YOU'RE THE JUDGE!**

DECISION: Roy was denied recovery where the defendant sports arena could not have reasonably anticipated the danger which caused the injury. The court noted, "Reasonable care requires intervention only when more than ordinary rudeness and jostling takes place."

An operator must provide adequate security or other protective measures to prevent harm to spectators.

Promoters of wrestling or boxing matches, or even operators of hockey arenas or football stadiums may anticipate more fan rowdiness than would be present at a basketball or baseball game. Therefore, proper security will be required to handle such conduct.

FACTS: Phillips cried, "I was struck by a broken bottle while at a baseball game!" It was not expected that the games would be rowdy.

Johnson, while trying to leave a wrestling match, was hit and injured by a soda-pop bottle that was thrown by a spectator. For several minutes, before Johnson was injured, a group of spectators were fighting and throwing bottles. Could either spectator recover for his injuries? **YOU'RE THE JUDGE!**

DECISION: Phillips could not recover. His injury was not foreseeable; there was neither prior notice nor ample time to prevent the occurrence. Johnson could recover; there was ample notice and time for the operator to prevent such conduct.

Another fan recovered damages when she was injured after falling on a broken bottle. Evidence showed that the bottle was "probably there before the crowd began leaving. Reasonable inspection would have discovered it or prevented fans from leaving with bottles."

But where proper supervision would not have detected the bottle, there would be no recovery. Could such a fan recover if bottles were prohibited from the sports facility?

Maintaining order may also require that an operator be aware of a fan's condition.

FACTS: A man rocking on an upper deck railing, while shouting obscenities at one of the teams, fell and plunged to his death before thousands of horrified fans. Another spectator was injured in the fall. It was reported that the decedent had been drinking heavily. Was there time to foresee the potential for injury and remove the fan? Was the operator liable for the death and the related injury?

DECISION: **YOU'RE THE JUDGE!**

STOP PUSHING!

The owner or operator of a sports facility has a duty to use reasonable care to keep the premises safe.

FACTS: The arena was overflowing—standing room only—for the state basketball play-offs. Mrs. Petry broke her elbow when she was pushed while trying to get through the crowd in the aisles to her seat. Were these reasonably safe premises?

DECISION: **YOU'RE THE JUDGE!**

Is an owner or operator of a sports facility liable for injuries produced by dangerous conditions which the operator knew or should have known of?

FACTS: Lee was injured when she was pushed off her chair and trampled on by other spectators who were attempting to recover a foul ball. An usher assigned to keep order wasn't there. Did Lee assume the risk of such an injury? **YOU'RE THE JUDGE!**

DECISION: The club was liable for the injury for not providing supervision and could have prevented it by warning spectators to keep their seats when foul balls came. The operator knew, or should have known, of the dangerous condition.

However, an owner or operator of a sports facility may not be liable for injuries resulting from a dangerous condition not known of (or reasonably foreseen).

FACTS: Shayne was injured when he was pushed from the balcony by a crowd surging for the exits after a boxing match. Adequate precautions for policing the crowd had been taken. "Was the operator liable for my injury?" asked Shayne. **YOU'RE THE JUDGE!**

DECISION: A panic would not be a foreseeable danger, unless the negligence of the owner or operator had created the condition. Recovery was denied.

The duty to care for a spectator's safety also requires warning of dangerous conditions.

IT'S CROWDED!

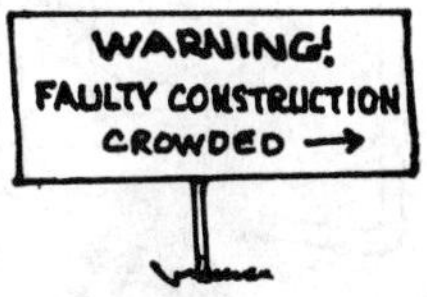

Will an owner or operator of a sports facility be liable for an injury to a spectator resulting from a crowded facility?

FACTS: Kallish explained, "I was injured when another spectator fell on me in an aisle." The club had oversold the game and additional spectators were seated in the aisles. Was the operator liable? **YOU'RE THE JUDGE!**

DECISION: The court found, "The injury was due to the unforeseeable, unexpected and unpreventable conduct of the spectators, not their numbers or presence in the aisles.

However, a duty to prevent crowding may arise where where such a condition has led to problems in the past.

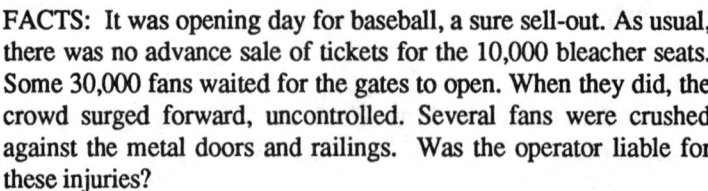

FACTS: It was opening day for baseball, a sure sell-out. As usual, there was no advance sale of tickets for the 10,000 bleacher seats. Some 30,000 fans waited for the gates to open. When they did, the crowd surged forward, uncontrolled. Several fans were crushed against the metal doors and railings. Was the operator liable for these injuries?

DECISION: **YOU'RE THE JUDGE!**

At a wrestling match a spectator, Camp, was injured when, "The crowd surged backward in anticipation of a wrestler being thrown from the ring." The promoter was found liable for "not bolting the seats to the floor, as required by law." Had they been bolted, the crowd could not have surged backwards.

WRONG PLACE!

Determining what is proper care for the protection and safety of spectators may, in part, depend on the nature of the sport. The more dangerous the sport, the more care that is required. Also, where a sport (not particularly dangerous), may create danger when played in a different place, more care may be required.

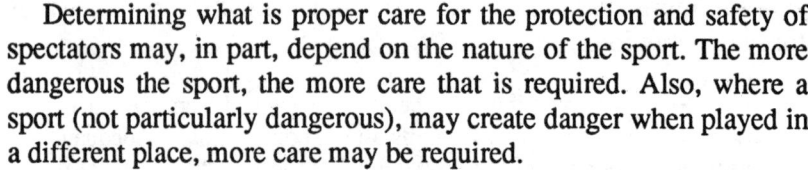

FACTS: The operator of a fair allowed baseball to be played away from the usual field, close to a picnic area. Two picnickers were injured; one by a thrown ball, the other by a player who was chasing a foul ball. They sued the operator for negligently allowing the game in an improper area. The operator claimed that the picnickers assumed the risk of injury. Who was liable? **YOU'RE THE JUDGE!**

DECISION: Although some picnickers may have been spectators, those who were not did not assume the risk of injury where they were not given notice or warning of the danger. They had the right to expect that the picnic area was safe. The operator, by allowing the game in an improper location, and otherwise failing to protect those using the picnic area, was liable for the injuries.

HAVE A SEAT!

The owner or operator of a sports facility has a duty to inspect the premises from time to time to see that they are safe. He may be charged with knowledge if a reasonable inspection would have disclosed a defect.

FACTS: Fredericks complained, "I broke my leg when I fell from the bleachers. I stumbled on a loose board."

The school in charge of the facility made inspections of the seats two or three times a year. They defended that Fredericks contributed to his injury by using a seat which he knew or should have known was defective. Fredericks charged that the school breached its duty to discover the defect. Was the school liable? **YOU'RE THE JUDGE!**

DECISION: The school was liable. A reasonable inspection for such a defect, which could not have happened over night, but only over a period of time, would have revealed it.

The duty is to furnish seats both safe for ordinary seating and that will withstand rough usage by spectators.

Sweikert was injured at a racetrack from a fall when a rotten board in a bleacher seat gave way. The court held that the track's owner had a duty to maintain the seats in reasonably safe condition—not only as seats but also as 2 steps—where evidence showed that seats were customarily used as steps.

What if spectators were injured when a railing they had been sitting on gave way?

FACTS: Juan and several other boys stood on the top seat of the bleachers. All of the other seats were taken. When they sat on the railing, it broke and they fell to the ground. Juan, injured, alleged that the school was liable for "not securing the railing." The school alleged that Juan was guilty of contributory negligence. Who was liable? **YOU'RE THE JUDGE!**

DECISION: The school district had met its duty to care for the safety of the spectators. Even if it had been aware, or should have been aware, of such use of the railing, it could not be held to know that it would give way. Could Juan recover from the manufacturer of the bleachers?

In some cases, a higher degree of care is required, such as at an amusement park.

FACTS: An inspection of seats on an amusement park ride, "The Snake," revealed them to be in reasonably good condition. But, because one of the seats was a bit loose, Jackson was thrown off the ride and injured. The park operator asked, "Was I liable?" **YOU'RE THE JUDGE!**

DECISION: As the risk of injury from an amusement park ride is much more probable, a higher degree of care is required. The operator was liable.

A spectator, although noticing a slight defect, may still use a seat and not be guilty of contributory negligence. A spectator has no duty to inspect his seat. He may assume that the operator has exercised reasonable care for his safety. However, using a seat in an abnormal manner may be contributory negligence, which will relieve an operator of any liability.

FACTS: A contestant, "Chubby," claimed, "I was in a national lap-sitting contest. I broke my hip when a chair collapsed and the twelve girls who were sitting on my lap fell on me." Did Chubby assume the risk of such an injury? **YOU'RE THE JUDGE!**

DECISION: Chubby was found guilty of both contributory negligence and assumption of the risk from such a use of the chair.

Also, recovery was denied where a spectator, without permission, chose to sit in an unassigned seat which he should have seen was in need of repair.

THE THING SPEAKS!

The doctrine of **res ipsa locquitor**—the thing speaks for itself—may be applied to find an operator liable for an injury to a spectator where the injury does not normally occur unless someone is negligent, the thing causing the injury was under the control of the owner or operator and the spectator was not at fault.

FACTS: At an indoor tennis match, a folding chair, under ordinary use, collapsed, injuring Gurney. Could he recover for his injury? **YOU'RE THE JUDGE!**

DECISION: Yes. The court ruled, "In the ordinary course of things, such seats or bleachers do not collapse if proper care in their construction and maintenance is used. Their collapse is reasonable evidence, in the absence of explanation by the operator, that the accident arose from a lack of care."

PUBLIC WAYS

The risk of injury to those neighboring a sports facility requires that reasonable precautions be taken for their safety. An owner or operator of a sports facility may be liable if it is shown that harm ought to have been foreseen, either because of past experience, inadequate barriers or a dangerous location.

FACTS: The operators of several baseball facilities had ample notice that baseballs were frequently knocked into adjacent public streets. At one facility, the fence wasn't high enough. At another, there was no fence or backstop. At still another, the distance to the sidewalk was too short. Several passersby were injured by batted balls. Were the operators liable for the injuries? **YOU'RE THE JUDGE!**

DECISION: Yes. "The playing of baseball itself, on land next to a public way, does not create a nuisance. It is the failureto tkereason-ble preautios here it s knwn or should be known that balls frequent-ly fly out of the stadium and into the public way," commented one court.

Suppose that one of the passersby regularly walked by the field and was well aware of the risk. Would he then have assumed the risk of injury?

Liability will not be found where it could not be anticipated that a ball would be knocked from a field into a public way, where it hap-pened infrequently or where the injured was aware of the risk.

May a player or his team be held liable for an injury to a passer-by?

FACTS: When the Double Play Tavern's left fielder dropped a high pop fly, the winning run scored. In anger, the fielder picked up the ball and threw it out of the park. The ball struck and injured Betty as she was walking across the street. Was the player or his team liable for the injury? **YOU'RE THE JUDGE!**

DECISION: The court, in a questionable decision, decided, "The player was acting within the scope of his employment for the Tav-ern and, therefore, the Tavern was liable for Betty's injuries." Was the fielder hired to throw baseballs onto a public way?

Those traveling by car or on foot next to golf courses have also been injured by errant golf balls.

FACTS: One golfer explained what happened. "I sliced a ball onto the street next to the course. The ball struck the windshield of a car, injuring the driver, Walton."

Walton sued for his injury. The golf course defended that Wilton assumed the risk of injury by using the road and by having notice of the possibility of such an occurrence by a posted warning sign. Was the golf course liable? **YOU'RE THE JUDGE!**

DECISION: Yes . The operator of the golf course knew or should have known, of the risk of injury to those using an adjacent public way. The particular hole was too close to the way and there had been similar accidents previously.

A golf course, without proper barriers to prevent balls from reach-ing a public way, may be a dangerous condition. Those using the way have a right to assume that they may do so free of risk of injury from an errant ball.

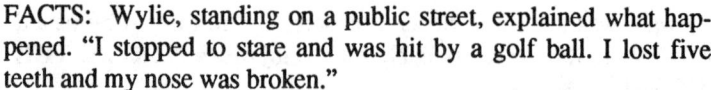

FACTS: Wylie, standing on a public street, explained what happened. "I stopped to stare and was hit by a golf ball. I lost five teeth and my nose was broken."

Wylie sued the club, which defended that he assumed the risk, as might a paying customer. Did he? **YOU'RE THE JUDGE!**

DECISION: Wylie did not assume the risk of such an injury. The judge noted, "It is the legitimate pleasure of a pedestrian to stop and stare. He had no cause to foresee that he was in danger." The club was liable for the injury.

Likewise, where a club permitted a dangerous, defective condition—by not having a fence to protect persons using a parking lot from golf balls—then liability may also be found.

But, there will be no liability when it is not likely that a ball will be knocked onto a public way, and sufficient barriers are in place.

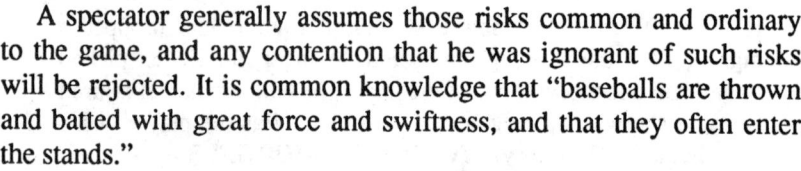

BASEBALL

A spectator generally assumes those risks common and ordinary to the game, and any contention that he was ignorant of such risks will be rejected. It is common knowledge that "baseballs are thrown and batted with great force and swiftness, and that they often enter the stands."

Will a spectator who voluntarily chooses an unprotected seat, with full knowledge of the risks and dangers of the game, be guilty of contributory negligence if injured?

FACTS: Crane said, "I chose an unprotected seat so that I could avoid any annoying obstructions. I was then hit by a foul ball."

Other fans were injured by batted balls while sitting in box seats, the upper deck, (down the foul line) and standing behind a fence along the third-base line. Could any of these fans recover for their injuries? **YOU'RE THE JUDGE!**

DECISION: No . The clubs were not negligent in failing to protect all of the seats. It was enough to screen the most dangerous seats. Fans assume the ordinary risks of the game. Furthermore, if injured while sitting or standing in unprotected areas, they will be guilty of contributory negligence.

If an injury occurs (during pregame practice or a game) while a spectator is in the aisle, moving to or from a seat, or where a passageway or seating area is crowded, will the fan still assume the risk for any injury resulting from batted or thrown balls?

FACTS: Baker was injured when struck by a foul ball while being lead by an usher through an aisle to his reserved seat in the unscreened section of the stadium. Should the usher have waited until play was halted? Could Baker recover for his injury? **YOU'RE THE JUDGE!**

DECISION: The court found that Baker had assumed the risk of such an injury. It is "well settled that a spectator at a baseball game assumes the risk of being struck by a foul or wildly thrown ball when sitting elsewhere than behind the screen in back of home plate."

Another court commented, "If a plaintiff knew, or should have known, of the risk of injury from a batted ball while in an unprotected seat, then he should have known of the same danger in the aisle by which he approached his seat."

Similarly, a spectator assumed the risk of injury when, although requesting a seat behind the screen, she agreed to the usher's suggestion that she sit in an unprotected place.

Entrance & Exitways

FACTS: Olson explained, "I was seated behind the screen at a baseball game but while leaving at an exit not in the screened section, was injured by a batted ball." Did Olson assume the risk of such an injury? **YOU'RE THE JUDGE!**

DECISION: There is a duty to provide a reasonably safe means of entering and exiting a screened area without having to walk through an unscreened area. The operator of the facility was liable for the injury.

Liability for an operator was also found where a spectator was struck by a ball while standing in a walkway. At the spot where Jones was injured, she could see neither home plate nor the ball coming towards her. She could not assume the risk of injury from a risk not ordinary to the game—faulty construction or inadequate supervision, for example. Was the stadium manufacturer also liable?

Screen

While a screen is not needed for all seats, there is a duty to provide screened seats for spectators desiring such protection. The duty is only to provide as many of these seats as may reasonably be expected to be needed. Only the most dangerous section of the ballpark (generally behind home plate) must be screened.

FACTS: Tony snarled, "I was hit in the head while seated behind home plate. The screen went straight up, but didn't extend overhead. A foul ball came down on my head!" Should Tony have been warned of the dangers of the game? Was the operator liable

for Tony's injury for not providing a screen extending overhead? **YOU'RE THE JUDGE!**

DECISION: "The timid may stay away!" commented the judge. The lower screen protected the fans from the most dangerous foul balls, subjecting them to no more risk than the rest of the fans.

Another court remarked, "It would be absurd, and no doubt resented by many spectators, if a ticket seller, or other employee, had warned each person entering the park that he or she would be imperiled by errant baseballs."

What if there was a hole in a protective screen?

FACTS: A spectator at a Mets' game, explained how she was injured. "I was struck by a foul ball while sitting behind the home plate screen. The ball went through a hole in the screen!" "Can I recover for my injury?" she asked. **YOU'RE THE JUDGE!**

DECISION: The court held, "A spectator, while seated behind a screen, has a right to receive protection from a foreseeable danger such as a foul ball. The team was negligent under the theory of res ipsa loquitor—the acts speaks for itself." It was not necessary for the plaintiff to show that the team knew, or should have known, of the defect.

Bullpen

Maynard, while seated near the third base dugout watching a game, was struck on the head by a ball thrown by a pitcher warming up in the bullpen. Could he recover damages against the player or his team?

The court found the team negligent for locating the bullpen in a dangerous place—along the left field line, close to the grandstand—and for allowing the pitcher to experiment with new pitches while in the bullpen. It noted, "A spectator does not assume the risk of every batted or thrown ball, only from those which are ordinary to the game."

What if a player intentionally throws a ball which injures a spectator?

FACTS: Grimes, a pitcher, was warming up in the bullpen during a game in Boston. Fans seated behind the wire mesh fence next to the bullpen heckled him continuously. Grimes then threw a pitch at an angle of 90 degrees from the mound to home plate. The pitch passed through the mesh fence and struck a fan who then sued Grimes and his team, the Orioles. Were the pitcher and the team liable for the injury? **YOU'RE THE JUDGE!**

DECISION: Yes. The court found that Grimes was within the scope of his employment when he threw the pitch, attempting to stop the interference with his doing his job. Both he and the Orioles were liable for the injury.

However, where a player left the field to assault a spectator in the stands who had "ragged" him and criticized his play, the assault was not committed within the scope of the players duties, but was a personal act. Although the team was not held liable, the player could be.

I Can't See!

FACTS: Janice, attending a baseball game at the Astrodome, was struck in the face by a foul ball. She claimed that, "The glare conditions inside the domed stadium kept me from following the flight of baseballs hit toward the stands."

Smith, sitting in the left field stands at another game, was injured when he also couldn't follow the flight of the ball. A number of the lights were out. Did Janice and Smithy assume the risk of such injuries? **YOU'RE THE JUDGE!**

DECISION: As to Janice, the court found no liability by the operator of the facility. She assumed such a risk. However, in the case of Smith, where there was insufficient lighting, the operator was found liable.

Extraordinary Risks?

A spectator's broken arm was caused by the rough play of boys hired to pick up seat cushions and backs after a baseball game. The owner had warned them against such rough play. Was the owner liable for the injury?

The operator was liable. This was a breach of the duty to exercise reasonable care for the safety of the spectators. It was foreseeable that rough play might endanger a spectator. Such conduct was not a risk common to the game.

FACTS: Margaret testified, "While sitting in my seat, I was struck in the head by a canvas banner." She argued that the team failed to exercise due care when they permitted the banner in the spectator area and failed to supervise and control the spectators.

Mary received severe and painful burns during a scheduled fireworks display when a firework landed near her box seat. She claimed that the Pirates were negligent for "permitting a dangerous and explosive display of fireworks too close to the spectators." Did the operators breach their duty to exercise reasonable care for the protection and safety of the spectators?

DECISION: **YOU'RE THE JUDGE!**

Ordinary Risk?

A spectator at a major league baseball game was struck in the face by a foul ball while sitting behind first base. In a suit for damages, the court held that the team failed to show that it provided a sufficient number of screened seats, but damages were not awarded.

FACTS: Loren, 11, was struck by a foul ball at a major league baseball game. She suffered a broken facial bone and an eye injury.

A 12 year-old boy was left brain damaged when he was struck by a foul ball. Could they recover damages for their injuries? **YOU'RE THE JUDGE!**

DECISION: A jury award in Loren's favor was overruled. "Spectators will assume the risk of injury from an ordinary or inherent risk of that sport," held the courts. It was held that a foul ball was an ordinary risk.

GOLF COURSE

The owner or operator of a golf course has a duty to exercise ordinary or reasonable care for the protection and safety of spectators. Although not insurers of the safety of the spectators, they may be liable for a spectator's injury where they create new hazards not common to the sport.

FACTS: Mary explained how she was injured. "While watching a golf tournament, I stepped in a hole in the cart path and broke my foot. The hole was hidden by overgrown grass." Did Mary assume the risk of such an injury? **YOU'RE THE JUDGE!**

DECISION: The operator of the golf course was found liable. The hole, there for a long time, should have been tended to.

In holding that another spectator could not recover for an injury, the judge commented, "It is common knowledge that golf balls do not always go where aimed. This is the very challenge of the game which spectators come to see. Errant shots will happen, and, on occasion, will land in an area where spectators are to be expected." This is a common and ordinary risk of the sport, and one which a spectator assumes the risk of.

FACTS: Greene, a spectator at a golf tournament, was struck by a ball where balls did not normally land. Another spectator was injured when a player overhit a green. Still another was hurt when he ran inside a roped off area and was struck by a ball. Could these spectators recover for their injuries? **YOU'RE THE JUDGE!**

DECISION: No. All of the spectators assumed the risk of injury.

Spectators have the right to assume that those in control exercised their duty to best protect the spectators, and that they are reasonably safe, except for an occasional errant shot.

FACTS: Duffy was struck by a golf ball at a pro golf tournament. She charged, "The sponsor of the tournament and the golf club were negligent in placing a concession stand in a dangerous position between two fairways."

The defendants claimed that the spectator assumed the risk of being hit by an occasional errant shot. A member of the club testified, "Balls had been hit daily in that area in the past." Did Duffy assume the risk of her injury? **YOU'RE THE JUDGE!**

DECISION: The spectator assumed the risk of injury from an occasional errant shot, but not while standing in an area where she expected to be safe. The judge suggested, "Sponsors have to redefine areas where spectators can go."

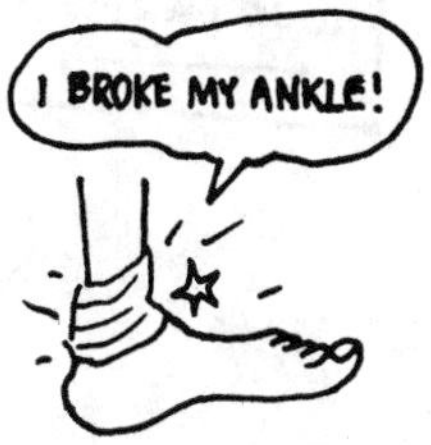

Another spectator assumed the risk of injury where she tripped over a rock concealed by tall grass and broke her ankle while walking down a rocky hill instead of on a well-defined pathway, as instructed. Similarly, another spectator assumed the risk of injury when, in broad daylight, she slipped and fell on a stone covered parking lot.

A major network was found negligent where a spectator tripped on a TV wire laid across a walkway and suffered permanent injuries. "Proper precautions must be taken to ensure the safety of the spectators," cautioned the court.

AUTOMOBILE RACING

FACTS: Carlton and Joanne, while videotaping their son in a demolition derby, were killed when a car spun out of control and into the barrier where they were filming. Allegedly, security had asked them and others to move from the area. Was the operator of the track liable for allowing spectators to remain in a known dangerous area?

DECISION: **YOU'RE THE JUDGE!**

The owner or operator of a racetrack has a duty to exercise reasonable care for the protection and safety of spectators, and to keep the racetrack and adjacent premises in a reasonably safe condition. This duty includes timely inspections to ensure their safety.

FACTS: Several spectators were injured when a race car went out of control. The car skidded when it ran into oil and debris, left on the track from a previous accident. Was the operator liable for the injuries?

DECISION: **YOU'RE THE JUDGE!**

An operator also has a duty to erect sufficient protective barriers between the track and spectators. In cases where the only barriers were a row of automobiles, a four foot fence or one that collapsed, or empty barrels, liability was found where spectators were injured as a result of such negligence in not providing sufficient barriers. This would be especially so where there had been previous injuries caused by such a lack of protection.

However, an operator of a racetrack is not an insurer of a spectator's safety. Spectators will assume the risk of injury by knowing and appreciating a danger.

FACTS: McPherson was injured while attending a stock car race when a car went out of control and crashed into the infield and pit area where he was standing. Did he assume the risk of such an injury? **YOU'RE THE JUDGE!**

DECISION: The court held, "One, knowing and comprehending danger and who voluntarily exposes himself to it, assumes the risk of such injury." Even though the protection in the infield area was less than that of the stands, he cannot recover.

What if there were no warnings? An owner or operator of a racetrack has been found liable for injuries where spectators were permitted to enter dangerous areas without being given proper warnings.

FACTS: Sisco, while walking from the pit area of a stock car racetrack, was struck by a pickup truck and killed. There were no speed limit signs, no lines denoting passenger lanes or pedestrian crosswalks and no other controls over traffic. The driver of the pickup had been drinking and unknowingly, drove through an unattended gate into the pit area. The estate of Sisco sued the track and the driver. Was the track liable for not controlling the area? Was the driver liable?

DECISION: **YOU'RE THE JUDGE!**

Negligence by an owner or operator of a racetrack has also been found where there was a failure to make a safety inspection of a race car (which later crashed and injured spectators), Also, where another race car was not equipped with a required safety shield to prevent the scattering of parts (which also caused an injury after a crash), negligence was found.

Liability for an operator of a racetrack may also exist where injuries are the result of a crash caused by the improper design of a track.

FACTS: A race car went out of control when it couldn't negotiate a turn. It crashed into the stands, injuring several spectators. The cars were traveling far in excess of the speed cars traveled when the track was built. Was the operator liable for running the race on a track not designed for such speeds?

DECISION: **YOU'RE THE JUDGE!**

A racecar driver may also be held liable for injuries to spectators where he or she acts in a negligent manner.

FACTS: One bystander told what happened, "In preparation for a race, O'Neil was doing a 'burnout'—revving the engine and spinning the tires—when the car went out of control and crashed into a concession stand, killing one and injuring other spectators."

The burnout was performed at the entrance to the track, instead of on the main race track, where it was usually performed. There were no guardrails or other barriers separating the entrance area from the stands. Was the operator of the track liable for a lack of barriers? Was the driver liable for negligence in performing in an improper area?

DECISION: **YOU'RE THE JUDGE!**

HORSE RACING

The owner or operator of a horse racing track has a duty to keep his premises in a reasonably safe condition for the protection and safety of spectators.

FACTS: Spectators at racetracks were injured by horses where there was: no entrance attendant; a lack of sufficient barriers or warning for a passageway across the track or other area leading onto or from a track; an attendant who invited a spectator to attempt a crossing; or an attendant who gave assurance that the track was clear. Did any of these situations create liability for the track operators? **YOU'RE THE JUDGE!**

DECISION: These were negligent acts for which the track operators were found liable for the spectators' injuries.

In holding that a spectator will not assume the risk of injury for not constantly watching for horses along a track or entry area, one judge remarked, "This is very different from merely crossing a public highway. There, the person crossing, unlike a spectator at a horse track who has a right to expect that reasonable efforts have been made for the spectators' protection and safety, has no assurance, but from his own careful observation, that the way is clear."

What if an injury to a spectator is the result of an unforseeable accident?

FACTS: Several spectators were injured at a racetrack when a horse bolted over a seven foot barrier fence and another fence six feet behind that.

The track president exclaimed, "I've never seen anything like it. I've talked to a lot of old-timers who have been around longer than I and they have never seen anything like it either!" Was the track operator liable for the injuries? **YOU'RE THE JUDGE!**

DECISION: Where the fence or rail was reasonably safe and suitable, there will be no liability for such an unforeseeable accident.

However, where it was a more common occurrence for horses to bolt over a particular fence, or through an opening, liability may be found for the failure to construct a fence or railing of sufficient height to protect spectators.

HOCKEY

The owner or operator of a hockey rink or team has a duty to exercise reasonable care for the protection and safety of spectators. This may not only include providing sufficient barriers where necessary, but may also include a duty in the selection or control of players.

Spectators will assume the risk of injury from the ordinary risks of the game or open and obvious dangers.

FACTS: While watching an ice hockey game, Kennedy (with knowledge and appreciation of the risks and danger inherent in the game), was injured by a flying puck. Could he recover for his injuries? **YOU'RE THE JUDGE!**

DECISION: Recovery was denied. Kennedy was sitting in the fourth row and the wooden dasher and plexiglass only protected spectators in the first three rows. He had attended many games before and was aware of the risks involved.

But where another spectator, Riley, was struck by a puck while seated in the first row of the balcony, he could recover. There were no signs warning of danger, and danger would not be apparent to one sitting so far from the ice.

Does it matter if a spectator had ever been to a hockey game before?

FACTS: The Pucksters were playing their first hockey game ever in Ft. Lauderdale. John, who had never attended a game, was injured when he was struck by a puck. Barbara was similarly injured, but she had been to many games before. Could they recover damages for their injuries. **YOU'RE THE JUDGE!**

DECISION: Although recovery has been denied where a spectator lived in an area where hockey was extensively played, recovery may be had where there was unfamiliarity with hockey and its dangers. It is expected that the puck will be batted along the surface, not in the air as in baseball.

Protective Barriers

Liability has been found where spectators were injured by pucks where screens or other protective barriers were not high enough, nor extended far enough. If protective devices were improperly maintained and boards collapsed, or where the safety glass broke after players crashed into it, liability may also be found.

One court, in finding for an injured spectator, held that the failure to provide adequate protection to spectators at a hockey game "constituted a dangerous condition that presented a foreseeable risk of injury."

Another spectator recovered for an injury received when struck by a puck while walking along the promenade. He did not know of the risk; the owner did. And where a spectator had a seat in a protected area, there was a duty to provide a safe and protected entrance and exit from that seat.

What if an injury was the result of an unforseeable accident?

FACTS: A spectator, Rich, was injured by a hockey stick which flew out of the hands of one of the players when the player collided with an opponent. Did Rich assume the risk of such an injury? **YOU'RE THE JUDGE!**

DECISION: Yes. The court held that such an occurrence was very rare since, in the course of the game, the stick was not intended to leave the hands of a player. And, as this was unforseeable, the duty to protect spectators was not violated.

Were The Players Controlled?

A team or league which encourages or condones improper behavior, or that is otherwise negligent in hiring or supervising players, may be liable for any resulting injury to spectators.

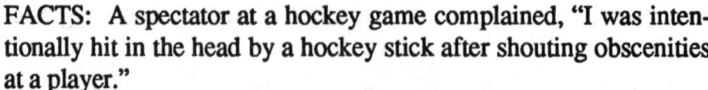

FACTS: A spectator at a hockey game complained, "I was intentionally hit in the head by a hockey stick after shouting obscenities at a player."

Another spectator, Walter, was injured when a player "thrust his hockey stick through a screen and struck me." The injuries were alleged to have occurred due to the encouragement by the team and hockey association of improper behavior. Could the spectators recover for their injuries? **YOU'RE THE JUDGE!**

DECISION: Both spectators recovered in settlements with the player and the hockey association. Spectators only assume the ordinary risks of the game.

Where a team or league does not condone or encourage improper behavior, then a player will not be acting within the scope of his duties where such acts are not done in furtherance of a his job. Thus, **respondeat superior**—holding a team liable for the acts of its employees—will not apply.

Where a player acts in self-defense of himself or another, will intentional contact with spectators be permitted?

FACTS: At the conclusion of a hockey game between the Bruins and the Rangers, an on the ice argument erupted into a brawl which grew to involve a few of the fans. Several spectators claimed, "We were hit with hockey sticks, assaulted, punched, kicked, choked and stepped on by the players who climbed into the stands."

The league and team were charged with negligence in condoning and encouraging violence, and for having inadequate security.

The players maintained that by climbing into the stands, "We were acting in self-defense and in defense of our teammates, who were being attacked by the fans." Were the players liable? Was the team or league liable for the acts of their players?

DECISION: **YOU'RE THE JUDGE!**

BOXING & WRESTLING

The duty of the owner or operator of a boxing or wrestling facility also includes maintaining the premises and equipment in a safe condition, warning of hidden hazards, and policing participants as well as spectators.

A spectator may assume the risk of injury or be guilty of contributory negligence where he knew, or should have known (from past experience), that wrestlers or boxers will leave the ring, but nevertheless sat in a front row seat and was injured. But, that is not always so.

FACTS: DeSilva, a spectator at a wrestling match told what happened, "I had a seat in the first row from the ring. One of the wrestlers picked up his opponent and threw him over the ropes. He landed on me, breaking my arm."

DeSilva had never observed a wrestler knocked out of the ring into the spectators. He sued the operator for not exercising proper care for his safety. Did DeSilva assume the risk of or contribute to his injury by sitting in a seat next to the ring when other safer seats were available? **YOU'RE THE JUDGE!**

DECISION: The risk of being struck by a wrestler or boxer leaving the ring was not an ordinary and inherent risk of the two sports. The operator was negligent for failing to warn DeSilva of such danger and for failing to place the front row seat a safer distance from the ring.

Similarly, where a wrestler struck a referee, who then fell from the ring and injured a spectator, the spectator could recover.

When a wrestler and a referee jumped from the ring and assaulted spectators in reaction to insults, although the wrestler or referee could be found liable, the promoters were not. The assaults were held to be outside the scope of the wrestler's or referee's employment. They were not employed to assault spectators.

FOOTBALL

FACTS: Mary, a spectator at a football game, was standing on the sideline when a player crashed into her and injured her. She sued the stadium operator and the player's team for negligence in not providing a barrier and not giving special warnings and protection. "Who was liable?" asked the team. **YOU'RE THE JUDGE!**

DECISION: As with any sport, a spectator assumes injury from the ordinary and inherent risks of the game, especially where the spectator chooses to sit or stand at an unsafe place despite the availability of a safer place. Mary assumed the risk of her injury.

Other spectators similarly injured have also been denied recovery. One court reasoned, "Football is a rough and rugged game requiring much brawn, physical effort and contact. The ball carrier is constantly forced out of bounds by the defense, and cannot avoid this. As a result, accidents may occur. The plaintiff was, or should have been, aware of such conditions. He knowingly placed himself in a position of danger and, therefore, assumed the risk of, and contributed to, his injury."

What if the injury was from an act by a player that was not part of the game?

FACTS: Rowan, a photographer, suffered neck injuries when he was struck in the head by a football that had been spiked into the ground by a Patriots player. He alleged that the act was not one ordinary to the game, therefore, the team and the player were negligent.

The team argued, "Rowan was familiar with the risks of covering sports events and, furthermore, he was warned." Was the team or the player liable for the injury? **YOU'RE THE JUDGE!**

DECISION: The jury found that Rowan assumed the risk of, and contributed to, his injury by placing himself near the action.

However, where a cheerleader was similarly injured at a Patriots game, she recovered damages after settling her suit. Was it more foreseeable that a cheerleader would be in such a place than the reporter and, thus, more care should have been taken to insure her safety?

May a team or one of its players be held liable where one fan injures another?

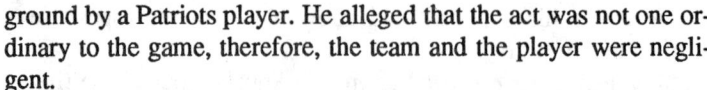

FACTS: Lenny, celebrating his game winning TD reception, threw the ball into the stands. In a wild fight for the ball, Irene was trampled and injured. She said, "I was just sitting there." Did she assume the risk of such an injury? **YOU'RE THE JUDGE!**

DECISION: Throwing a football into the stands is prohibited as a safety measure. The player was fined and the team liable for the injury.

Injuries to spectators have also been caused by "tools" of the sport.

FACTS: John was attending a pro football game. During a halftime demonstration, a radio controlled model airplane went out of control, striking and killing him. His family sued the team and stadium operator for negligently and carelessly selecting halftime entertainment that was "highly dangerous and hazardous," and for failing to adequately supervise the demonstration or warn the fans of the potential danger. Was the team or the operator liable?

DECISION: **YOU'RE THE JUDGE!**

BASKETBALL

Spectators at a basketball game generally assume the risk of injuries which might occur from an errant ball, or from being run into by an out-of-control player where the acts were unintentional. A spectator near a court, other safer places being available, may also be guilty of contributory negligence.

But what if a player intentionally runs into a spectator or throws the ball into a crowd?

FACTS: A basketball player for the Globetrotters, while clowning around in one of the team's acts, faked a pass and deliberately threw the ball into the stands, striking a spectator in the face and injuring her. Was the defendant liable? **YOU'RE THE JUDGE!**

DECISION: The court found that if the ball was negligently thrown towards the audience, and that as a result the plaintiff was injured, liability would attach. "The plaintiff had no choice between a protected and unprotected seat as she might have had at a baseball or hockey game. Also, there is no real danger of injury to spectators at a basketball game from balls entering the crowd in the usual course of a game."

SKIING

Spectators injured at ski areas have assumed the risk of, or contributed to, injuries from: falling on snow or ice, being struck by a loose ski, and from injury caused by a falling skier. Also, where the operator provided a roped off area and a spectator was injured while standing along the rope, operators were not found liable.

But liability may be found where there is a failure to provide a reasonably safe barrier to protect or adequately warn spectators of a danger, such as from snowmobiles.

BOWLING

FACTS: A bowler, Kirk, struck and injured a spectator by taking a practice swing in the open area between the alleys and the ball storage room. There were no warning signs prohibiting such practice. Was the operator liable? Was Kirk liable? **YOU'RE THE JUDGE!**

DECISION: Although the bowler may be liable, the owner could not be found negligent. The act was entirely unanticipated and unforseeable. Nor was there negligence for failing to post a sign prohibiting such practice.

SOCCER

Spectators at a soccer game, while standing on the sidelines, will assume the risk of injury as ordinary to the game (such as from an errantly kicked soccer ball).

However, where protective barriers provided are insufficient or non-existent, liability may attach.

FACTS: Wilson asserted, "There was a three-foot barrier surrounding the indoor soccer field. A ball struck and injured me. I was in the third row." "Should I have provided a higher barrier for the protection of spectators?" asked the operator. **YOU'RE THE JUDGE!**

DECISION: The barrier was of insufficient height to protect the safety of those spectators closest to the playing area,and the most likely spot for an injury to result from an errantly kicked soccer ball. The operator was liable.

TENNIS

Spectators unintentionally struck by a tennis ball, racket or player, are generally held to have assumed the risk of or contributed to any such injury. This is especially so where a fan is near the court, other safer places being available.

SWIMMING

As in the other sports, a spectator will assume the ordinary risks of the sport.

FACTS: "I slipped near the pool while going to my seat at a swim meet," said a spectator, Tom. At another meet, a contestant, late for the meet, ran into a spectator, Kena, who was standing next to the viewing stands. Both Tom and Kena were injured and sued the pool operator. Could either recover for their injuries? **YOU'RE THE JUDGE!**

DECISION: Tom assumed the risk of such an injury. It is common knowledge that water will leave the pool. Furthermore, he contributed to his injury by walking too close to the pool.

Kena was in an area of expected use for spectators. The operator was found liable for not protecting spectators with a proper set-off area for contestants to enter the pool area.

SKATING RINK

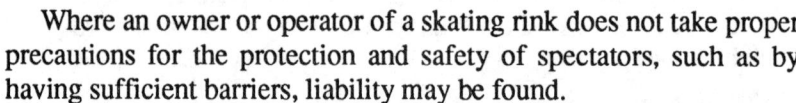

Where an owner or operator of a skating rink does not take proper precautions for the protection and safety of spectators, such as by having sufficient barriers, liability may be found.

FACTS: The owner of a skating rink allowed spectators to stand around the edge of the ice to view speed contests. One contestant, out of control, barreled into an unsuspecting spectator. Was the owner liable? **YOU'RE THE JUDGE!**

DECISION: Yes. Although a spectator might be held to be aware of such a possibility, the owner may be found liable for not prohibiting the spectators from what he knew or should have known was a dangerous area.

A spectator has a right to expect that the area that he is allowed into is a reasonably safe one. However, if a spectator stays in such an area after being on notice of a risk of injury, contributory negligence and assumption of the risk may prevent any recovery.

ODDS & ENDS....

Sky Diving

At a sky diving exhibition, one of the parachutists landed on a stack of loudspeakers placed on the perimeter of the landing area. The speakers toppled and landed on a spectator, Susan, injuring her. Susan was standing in an area designated for the spectators. Did Susan assume the risk of such an injury? Was the operator of the premises liable for the injury?

Supreme Court Justice Cardozo, in a case denying recovery for one injured at an amusement park, commented, "The rough and boisterous joke, the horseplay of the crowd evokes its own guffaws, but they are not the pleasures of tranquility. The plaintiff was not seeking a retreat for meditation. One who takes part in sports accepts the dangers that inhere in it so far as they are deemed obvious and necessary, just as the fencer accepts the risk of a thrust by his antagonist or a spectator at a ball game the chance of contact with the ball. The timorous may stay at home. "

But should spectators, especially those unable to realize or protect themselves from the dangers involved, continue to be held to assume the risk of injury from balls which might be traveling in excess of 100 m.p.h.?

Should proprietors of sports facilities be required to take better precautions for the protection and safety of spectators—such as by signs warning of the dangers, by advising fans that they have a right to a protected seat, or by extending or adding protected areas?

Should spectators, short of not attending, have a right to assume that they will be protected from hazards that they in no way could avoid, except by not attending?

25

YOU WAIVE THE RIGHT....

WHAT'S IT ABOUT?

You Waive The Right.... depicts attempts by those in charge of sports activities to have spectators waive any right to recover damages for an injury which is the fault of those in charge. Also discussed is product liability and improper warnings and instructions concerning the use of sports products which may injure a spectator.

Do you know when manufacturers may not waive any liability on their part?

WAS THERE A WAIVER?

A **waiver** is an intentional or voluntary surrender of a known right (the right to recover damages for an injury) with both knowledge of its existence and an intention to relinquish it. If valid, it will relieve another of an obligation to exercise care for one's protection.

FACTS: A ticket to most any sporting event has on the back of it a waiver of liability provision:

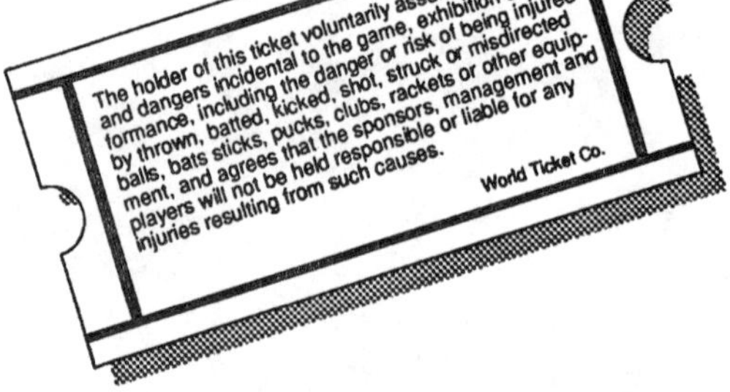

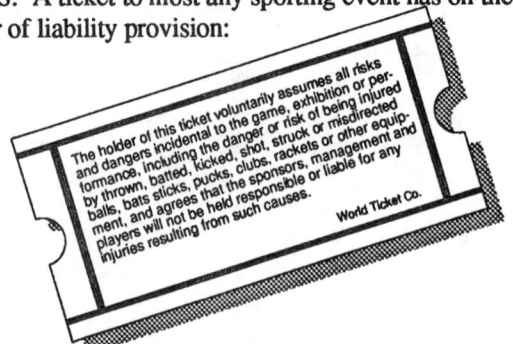

Do you think that by accepting this ticket that spectators would be prevented from recovering damages for any injury to them caused by the sponsors, managements or players' negligence?

DECISION: **YOU'RE THE JUDGE!**

For any waiver by a spectator to be valid in preventing liability by those in charge of sports activities, it must be voluntary.

FACTS: For the annual company outing, employees were required to purchase several tickets each. The tickets had waiver of liability provisions.

If an employee was injured while watching the events, would the purchase of such a ticket be considered a voluntary waiver of any right to recover damages? **YOU'RE THE JUDGE!**

DECISION: No. The waiver is not voluntary if it comes out of a relationship with unequal bargaining power, such as between an employer and employee. Such a waiver is invalid.

For a waiver to be enforced in preventing liability, it must be shown that the spectator had or should have had knowledge of the waiver.

FACTS: John, a spectator at a hockey match, said, "I didn't read the waiver of liability provision on the ticket." When John was hit by an errant puck and injured, he sued.

"John knew or should have known of the waiver on the ticket," insisted the promoter. Did John know of the waiver? **YOU'RE THE JUDGE!**

DECISION: John could be held to have had knowledge of the waiver. However, before liability could be waived, it would have to be determined whether or not he intended to waive his right to recover for any injury Even if the waiver were not valid, John may have assumed the risk of his injury.

It must also be shown that a spectator had the intention to waive any right to recover damages for an injury.

FACTS: Jason's ticket to the boxing matches had a waiver of liability provision. "I read and understood it," he admitted.

Kiwi's and Toni's tickets to a baseball game also had waiver of liability provisions. Kiwi read the waiver, although he didn't understand it. Toni didn't read it, but answered, "Sure!" when asked if he would abide by all of the provisions on the ticket. "I thought the usher was referring to sitting in the seat that the ticket was for," said Toni. Did Jason, Kiwi or Toni intend to waive any right they might have to recover if they were injured? **YOU'RE THE JUDGE!**

DECISION: No. Ignorance negates a waiver as does consent given by mistake or through a misunderstanding. Oversight or thoughtlessness does not create a waiver. Neither does reading and understanding the waiver, by itself, prevent a claim for injuries where there was no intent to waive any right to recover damages.

Where substantial rights, such as the right to recover damages for injuries caused by the negligence of another, are involved, will it be necessary to support any waiver with consideration for it to be valid?

FACTS: "Flash," a photographer, admitted, "I agreed to a waiver of liability provision on my admittance card in return for being able to sit up front to take pictures of the World Wrestling Championships." When a wrestler was thrown from the ring and fell on Flash, he sued. "Was the permission to be up front consideration for the waiver?" asked the promoter. **YOU'RE THE JUDGE!**

DECISION: The permission to get up close to the action, only granted to Flash, was consideration for the waiver, which consideration was necessary to support the waiver. Flash couldn't recover for his injury.

RACETRACKS & WRESTLING

Kotar, a paying spectator at a racetrack, signed a waiver in order to enter the "pit" area. The waiver released the track operator from liability for any injury. When Kotar was injured and sued the track, the court held, "In the absence of any concealment or false representation as to the contents of the waiver, the operator was not liable. The consideration for the waiver was admittance to the pit area."

What if a spectator were injured after being given a free pit pass?

FACTS: Lee, a spectator at an auto racetrack, was given a free pit pass. He was then injured due to the negligence of the operator. He had signed a waiver form. "Can I recover?" asked Lee. **YOU'RE THE JUDGE!**

DECISION: The operator was not released from liability, even though Lee had signed a waiver form. There was no consideration for the waiver. The pass was free to anyone who held it.

May more than ordinary negligence by those in control of a race also bring liability?

FACTS: Jack, attending an auto race, signed a waiver releasing the track from liability. When a car went out of control and struck an empty barrel (which was supposed to be filled with water to make it stable and thus protect those in the pit area), the barrel flew in the air, striking and killing Jack.

His wife sued, charging, "The sponsor was negligent in not filling the barrels. That caused Jack's death." Did the waiver release the track from liability? **YOU'RE THE JUDGE!**

DECISION: The waiver only released the track from ordinary negligence. The jury found that the sponsor, who testified that the sport was "perhaps the most dangerous in the world," was guilty of willful and wanton negligence for telling his subordinates, "Don't worry about filling all of the barrels with water."

In another case involving a waiver of liability provision, three spectators were injured when a car skidded into the pit area of a racetrack. The promoter sought to avoid liability for not having proper protective barriers on the basis of a release in the pit passes issued to the spectators. It provided that spectators "release every and any claim for injuries."

The court, in holding, "The release did not waive any claims for negligence," questioned whether public policy—the best interests of the public—would permit enforcement of a provision printed in such small type and designed to permit a wrongdoer to shift the risk of injury to the victims.

Do other spectators have the right to demand the exercise of ordinary and reasonable care for their protection and safety?

FACTS: Wright explained, "I was injured when the wrestlers carried the match from the ring to the aisles where I was sitting. I was knocked to the floor." His ticket had a waiver of liability provision on it. Did the waiver prevent Wright from recovering for his injury? **YOU'RE THE JUDGE!**

DECISION: No. The court, in ruling that Wright could recover damages for his injury, reasoned, "The waiver of liability on the ticket was no more than an attempt to whittle away at spectators' given rights to demand the exercise of ordinary and reasonable care for their protection and safety."

Wright had not, without any other conduct, voluntarily released, with knowledge and intent, his right to hold another liable for the other's negligence.

Because of this overriding policy against any attempt to have spectators waive their rights, personal injury claims by spectators are generally defended by alleging that an injured spectator voluntarily assumed the risk of injury, apart from the printing on the ticket.

An operator or promoter of a sporting event owes a duty to exercise ordinary and reasonable care for a spectator's safety and protection. However, he is not an insurer of a spectator's safety.

Where a spectator can be held to have had knowledge and appreciation of a risk, and then voluntarily encountered that risk and was injured, may recovery be denied?

FACTS: Billy Joe bought a ticket to the drag races. The ticket had a waiver of liability provision on it which Billy read and understood When asked by the operator if he would "waive the right to recover for ordinary negligence," he answered, "Yes."

Billy Joe was then injured when a car crashed, spewing parts into the air, one of which carried over the barrier and struck him. Could Billy Joe recover for his injury if the barrier was inadequate? **YOU'RE THE JUDGE!**

DECISION: Billy Joe read the language, understood it, and then voluntarily gave away the right to be compensated for injuries due to another's negligence. He could not recover.

PRODUCT LIABILITY

"Caveat emptor"— buyer beware—once put the burden on a buyer to be aware of any defects in a product which was bought. The buyer, in effect, waived any right to recover damages for an injury arising out of the use of that product.

Now, manufacturers and sellers must use reasonable care to make certain that their products do not harm users. If they do, then there may be **product liability**—liability of a manufacturer or seller of a product for an injury caused by their product.

What is the manufacturer's duty? A manufacturer has a duty to make products that are safe and fit for their intended or reasonably foreseeable uses. Any breach of that duty which causes injury and damages may be negligence.

FACTS: James, a spectator at a baseball game, explained, "I was cut by a piece of the bat which broke off when the batter swung." James alleged a breach of duty by the manufacturer of the bat to provide a safe product. "Was the manufacturer liable for my injury?" asked James. **YOU'RE THE JUDGE!**

DECISION: The judge commented, "It is common knowledge that bats frequently break, and immaterial that a properly made bat ordinarily will splinter with the grain while one made of defective wood may break across the grain. The risk of injury is not materially altered. James assumed the risk of such an injury."

Although the court didn't comment, should the manufacturer have been liable if the bat broke across the grain, inferring a defectively made bat?

Use, Instructions, Warnings, Upkeep & Old Age

A user of a product may waive any right to recover damages for any injury arising out of the use of a manufacturer's product in the following cases where: the product was used improperly, instructions or warnings were not followed, improper changes were made, proper maintenance was not given, or there was predictable deterioration.

FACTS: John injured a spectator at a golf tournament when, after an errant drive, he smashed his club against a tree. It snapped and hit the spectator.

Several other spectators and Bobby were injured when Bobby blew his engine and crashed his street car while drag racing. Could the spectators and Bobby recover for their injuries by alleging product liability—that the products were defective? **YOU'RE THE JUDGE!**

DECISION: A manufacturer will not be liable for injuries caused by uses other than those for which the product was intended. Bobby was guilty of contributory negligence. He could not recover. Both John and Bobby were liable to the injured spectators.

Is there a duty to warn of obvious dangers? Although a manufacturer or seller of a product has a duty to warn of hidden dangers, there is no duty to warn of obvious dangers, or of a danger entirely under the control of the buyer.

Judy failed to follow explicit instructions in setting up and using a home gymnastics weight set. She was injured when she used too much weight and it collapsed on her leg. She could not recover in a suit for damages.

John failed to follow a bold warning recommending that the pitching machine be run through a few cycles before inserting balls. It malfunctioned, hurling several balls in rapid succession, hitting John. The manufacturer was not liable for injuries caused by John's failure to follow the warning or instructions.

What if a user alters a product, or fails to adequately maintain it, and injury then results?

FACTS: Peter admitted, "I altered the engine in my new car." When the car went out of control, Peter broke his collarbone and leg. He sued, contending, "The vehicle should have been made to take the change without affecting performance."

"A snowmobile went out of control and crashed, breaking a spectator's arm," said Jan, the driver. The steering had been loose for some time. Could Peter or Jan successfully allege that the manufacturers were liable for product liability? **YOU'RE THE JUDGE!**

DECISION: A manufacturer will not be liable for injuries caused by subsequent changes in a product or by improper maintenance. Peter was guilty of contributory negligence. He could not recover. Jan was liable to the injured spectator.

What if a product was just simply old? Brent was injured when several spokes broke and his 10-year-old bicycle collapsed. When he sued, the court held that the manufacturer was "not liable for injuries caused by predictable deterioration of a product at the end of its useful life." Brent assumed the risk of such an injury.

TESTING 1...2...3

A manufacturer's duty to make products that are safe and fit for the ordinary uses of such products may include a duty to test the products.

FACTS: The Get Strong Co. made a product designed to test the strength of different muscles. Testing of the product was minimal. Jim, the supervisor, and Alex, who was being tested, were injured when a spring snapped.

When sued, the company defended, "They should have known that the product was unsafe by inspecting it." Was contributory negligence a valid defense? **YOU'RE THE JUDGE!**

DECISION: No. Contributory negligence is not a defense when such negligence consists merely of a failure to discover a defect in a product or to guard against the possibility of its existence. The company had a duty to test the product.

The buyer or user of a product has a right to expect that a product will perform as intended or may be reasonably expected.

STRICT LIABILITY

Strict liability is liability without regard to fault. Liability here is based upon the unreasonably dangerous nature of a product, not a manufacturer's conduct. If a defectively manufactured product causes an injury where there was a duty to make it safe, strict liability will attach.

Where strict liability applies, a manufacturer may not waive this liability for any negligence on his part.

FACTS: A chair lift at a ski resort malfunctioned, throwing and seriously injuring spectators being brought up the slope to view a race. The bull wheel which guided the lift's cable—and which had been inspected and certified safe—collapsed, causing the cable to snap like a rubber band.

Was the operator or manufacturer liable? Will res ipsa locquitor (the act speaks for itself), or strict liability, apply—either of which would allow recovery without regard to fault?

DECISION: **YOU'RE THE JUDGE!**

When a product (such as a car or motorcycle) is sold, a seller may avoid strict liability by giving proper instructions and warnings which, when followed, make the product safe.

ODDS & ENDS....

FACTS: Sports Inc., a manufacturer of sports products, was sued when several athletes were injured by the company's products. The company was found not liable.

During the trial, Sports Inc.'s attorney asked the owner, "In evaluating the effectiveness of a product's design, and in attempting to prevent injury and avoid liability, what are your considerations in making a product?" **YOU'RE THE JUDGE!**

DECISION: "Considerations may vary depending upon the product. The following questions should be asked and satisfactorily resolved prior to actual sales.

- What type of sport is the product for? Is physical contact involved?
- What type of injury is the product, or any warning, designed to prevent?
- How durable is the product?
- Will the risk of injury be increased if the product is defective?"

The more a product is designed to prevent injury, such as a football helmet, the greater is the care that is required in its manufacture, and the need for warnings and instructions as to its proper use.

Spectators do not assume the risk of all injuries received at sports events, as is insinuated by the use of a waiver on the back of most tickets

26

THAT'S A NUISANCE!

WHAT'S IT ABOUT?

You have a right to the quiet enjoyment of your property. Any interference with that right may be a nuisance. *That's A Nuisance!* explores nuisances—private and public.

Do property owners have a special duty to help prevent injuries to children?

Springfield News

People Bombed With Balls, Noise & Lights!!

You have a right to the unrestricted, "quiet enjoyment" and use of your property—free from any unreasonable risk of harm. This right protects you not only from trespass by uninvited persons, but also from certain acts that cause excessive annoyance, interference or injury.

These are called **nuisances**—the creation of a condition that will or may result in an interference with the rights of others to enjoy their property.

There are two kinds of nuisances —private and public.

PRIVATE & PUBLIC NUISANCES

A **private nuisance** is one that interferes with your interest only.

FACTS: An unusually high number of soccer balls were being kicked onto your property from an adjacent field. Several windows were broken. When the kids wouldn't stop, you asked, "What are my remedies? Was this a nuisance?" **YOU'RE THE JUDGE!**

DECISION: Your remedies are an **injunction**—court order preventing someone from beginning or continuing an offensive conduct—and damages for any harm caused by the nuisance. The court enjoined the playing of soccer at the field, at least until a fence could be built, and also awarded you damages for the broken windows.

Where a nuisance is a public one, laws may prohibit the activity causing the nuisance. A **public nuisance** is one that may affect or interfere with the general public, not just you.

FACTS: S&W Co. opened a driving range for its employees. One employee explained what happened: "Sea gulls, apparently mistaking the golf balls for shells (and in attempting to break them open), began swooping down, scooping up the balls and dropping them on unsuspecting neighbors and nearby streets." Was the range a public nuisance? **YOU'RE THE JUDGE!**

DECISION: Yes. After losing 500 balls thinking that the "golfers were hitting them all over the place!" the owner then realized, "People in their right minds wouldn't hit them there," and closed the range—at least until a solution could be found.

How will a court determine whether a condition is a nuisance?

The court will "balance the interests"- balancing the social value of the land use and the impracticality of preventing an invasion of another's rights against the harm and burden placed on an injured person. If the seriousness of the harm outweighs the usefulness of the condition, then an injured party may seek relief and damages for a nuisance.

A **mixed nuisance** is one that may interfere with both private and public interests, such as a drag racing strip.

STADIUMS & BALLFIELDS

Complaints charging that a ballfield or stadium is a nuisance generally involve situations where there is glare from lights, excessive noise or where balls leave the facility.

FACTS: Mrs. Kunerth filed for an injunction to halt play at the park next to her house. "The baseballs were sailing onto my property," she complained. "They caused damage to my house and injured someone in my yard!" Was she granted an injunction? **YOU'RE THE JUDGE!**

DECISION: Evidence showed that batted or thrown balls entered Mrs. Kunerth's yard fairly frequently, causing damage and injury.

An injunction was granted to halt the play of baseball at the park—at least until a higher fence was constructed to afford adequate protection.

May a passerby, injured by an errant ball, recover damages? Where batted or thrown balls often land on a road, and there have been insufficient precautions, a passerby may recover for injuries.

Generally, though, courts have concluded that baseball—even if close to a public roadway—does not constitute a nuisance which would make the operator of the field an insurer of the safety of persons lawfully using their property or the public roadway.

FACTS: "I was working in my garden next to the public ballpark. I was struck by a ball," John groaned. He brought suit, seeking an injunction preventing baseball from being played there, and for damages for his injuries. Evidence showed,"Only a few balls had landed in his yard since he moved there years ago." Was this a nuisance? **YOU'RE THE JUDGE!**

DECISION: No. Because the intrusion was an infrequent occurrence, a nuisance was not established. There could be no injunction or recovery of damages.

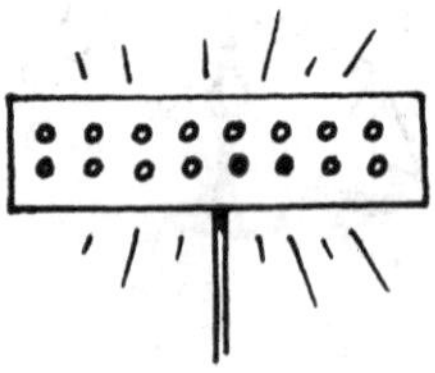

Neither will baseball be judged a nuisance where it was unforseeable that a ball would reach a roadway, (or did so) but infrequently.

Night Baseball

FACTS: Landowners next to a baseball park sought to enjoin, as a nuisance, the use of the park for night baseball. They alleged that the floodlights created "glare." All games were over by 10:30 and there was no undue noise or rowdyism. Was an injunction granted? **YOU'RE THE JUDGE!**

DECISION: The court observed that the field was used for the "sound development of boys." Night games were permitted as long as the glare could be reasonably eliminated by a screen. If not, an injunction would be granted.

Would a court view such a case differently where a professional team sought to build next to homeowners, or add lights to an existing field?

A court will balance the interests of homeowners—"Our property values will be diminished by lights and noise, and this will interfere with our comfort and enjoyment."—and the interests of the team—"We need a place suitable for playing, and which may benefit the community as a whole, bringing in fans and revenue."

FACTS: A Chicago ordinance prohibited professional sports contests at night in open stadiums, containing more than 15,000 seats that are located in a residential neighborhood.

In an attempt to install lights for night baseball, the Cubs challenged the law. Wrigley Field, the oldest in baseball, is located in a predominately residential neighborhood. Traffic to games flows through the neighborhood of people who supported day baseball, and felt, "The lights, traffic and noise would infringe on our right to peace and enjoyment, and would deteriorate the neighborhood." Was the ordinance reasonable? **YOU'RE THE JUDGE!**

DECISION: The court, in holding that the ordinance was reasonable and valid in preserving individual and community rights, joked, "Justice is a southpaw, and the Cubs just don't hit lefties."

But when the Cubs were offered the 1989 All-Star game, to be played at night, the Chicago City Council voted to allow a limited number of night games.

What if a landowner's property is "trampled" or littered on?

A ballfield may be a nuisance where neighboring property is continually trampled on by spectators or participants going to or coming from the ballfield. This could be corrected by erecting a fence or other suitable barrier. And where "rash was continually dumped on another landowner's property, the operator of the field had to clean it up or be subject to an injunction preventing the sale of products causing the problem.

FACTS: A ballfield was constructed with the backstop too close to homeplate and the bleachers too close to the field. Were these nuisances interfering with the rights of the players and fans to have a facility which wouldn't endanger their safety? Would they assume the risk of any resulting injury?

DECISION: **YOU'RE THE JUDGE!**

GOLF COURSES

Relief for injuries from errantly hit golf balls may be sought against a golf facility on the basis that it is a nuisance.

FACTS: Poorly hit golf balls landed in Lynn's yard once or twice a week. However, no one had been hit by a ball on the property for twelve years. Was this a nuisance? **YOU'RE THE JUDGE!**

DECISION: This did not constitute a nuisance to the landowners next to the golf course. It happened too infrequently. No injunction would be issued, nor could there be recovery for injuries. "The

risks and dangers of living next to a golf course are readily apparent, the occasional annoyance of an errant shot to be accepted," said the judge.

Neither would an injunction be issued to prevent the construction of a miniature golf course. The court held, "Neither lights nor noise from traffic or crowds constitute a nuisance when done at reasonable times and kept at reasonable levels."

Where it is shown that an injury was the result of a deficient layout of a golf course, could the injured recover damages?

FACTS: At two tees—where play continued from 6 a.m. until twilight—crowds collected while waiting to tee off. The residents next to the tees said they were "constantly annoyed, endangered and restricted in the use of our property by the golfers who demanded absolute silence and immobility of everything in sight when teeing off." They asked, "Are the tees a nuisance?" **YOU'RE THE JUDGE!**

DECISION: Yes. An injunction was granted. "This is an unreasonable interference with the use and enjoyment of land. The tees would have to be relocated. When the plaintiffs purchased their homes, a brochure given to them did not indicate the nearness of the tees, and neither was that pointed out to them," ruled the court.

Similarly, where many golf balls were hit onto other private property, a nuisance was found. The purchasers of the property did not agree to assume the risk of injury to themselves or their property. The builders would have to construct a suitable fence to keep the balls off of adjacent landowners' properties.

Does a passerby have a right to the free and unmolested use of a roadway?

FACTS: Bob was driving a taxi cab along a public street near the 13th tee of the St. Augustine Golf Course. An errant tee shot broke his windshield, causing the loss of an eye. Was the hole a nuisance? **YOU'RE THE JUDGE!**

DECISION: Yes. Balls from that tee had frequently landed on the highway and, on several occasions, struck other vehicles. The risk of balls being sliced onto the highway was a danger and a nuisance. It interfered with the right of the public to pass safely. Bob recovered for his injury.

Fairways that are too close to a roadway—including one that cuts across a golf course between two adjacent fairways—will be a nuisance if they interfere with the public's right to free and unmolested use of the roadway.

RACETRACKS

Where racing activities result in an unreasonable and foreseeable risk of injury to persons or property near a racetrack, may a nuisance be found?

FACTS:

BOLTON NEWS

Various residents, businesses and churchgoers, who lived and worked near racetracks, complained of the following: squealing brakes; yelling and screaming crowds (heard up to three miles from the track and requiring residents to close their windows); pollution from exhaust fumes and dust clouds; smells from burnt motor fuels and tires; glaring lights; horns and roaring engines, and; shouting over the public address system.

They contended that such behavior and activities were nuisances that turned their properties into a "defening whirlpool of sound." Did the court grant injunctions to prevent racetracks from such conduct?

Did the court grant injunctions to prevent racetracks from such conduct? **YOU'RE THE JUDGE!**

DECISION: Yes. The racetracks were mixed nuisances, interfering with both private and public interests They disturbed the peace, enjoyment, comfort, health, safety and welfare of passersby as well as residents, and depreciated the resident's property. The residents had a right to the full use and enjoyment of their property—free from any such annoyance or interference.

Where noise from a track is minimal and the distance to residences an acceptable length, a nuisance will not be found.

One court commented, "No one is entitled to absolute quiet, but only to the comfort prevailing in that neighborhood. Where one lived in a quiet neighborhood—as opposed to a noisy and busy one—a nuisance would be more likely to be found. And where one builds next to an existing track, he may assume the risk of the accompanying interferences."

Does racing on public streets constitute a nuisance?

FACTS: Some of the local kids raced their cars on the public streets. Nancy (who was racing) and John (a pedestrian), not involved in the racing, were injured when Speedy hit a pothole and went out of control. Both alleged, "The accident was due to improper control of the racing and maintenance of the streets." Was this a public nuisance? Did either Nancy or John assume the risk of or contribute to their injury? **YOU'RE THE JUDGE!**

DECISION: A nuisance was found for the interference with John's right to enjoy the public ways without undue risk. John did not assume the risk of, or contribute, to his injury; Nancy did.

SWIMMING POOLS

A swimming pool may be a nuisance where it deprives adjacent landowners of their right to the full use and enjoyment of their property. Such would be the case where there is excessive noise, glare from lights, traffic congestion, or the pool is frequently a source of annoyance and irritation to the adjoining landowners.

FACTS: Mike and Marion Wilson lived next to the town swimming pool. In the summer, the pool—open until 9 P.M.—was lighted, crowded and noisy. Would the court enjoin the use of the pool at night for being a nuisance? **YOU'RE THE JUDGE!**

DECISION: No. As with other potential nuisances, where the rights of the parties are balanced and the inconvenience and any annoyance is minimal, especially when compared with the purpose of the pool to promote public health, happiness, and welfare, there will be no nuisance.

WAS IT AN ATTRACTIVE NUISANCE?

Attractive nuisance applies to a situation where a child on another's property is injured by the condition, nature or use of the property. If an injury occurs, recovery is usually sought on the basis that the landowner has created a nuisance that attracts children—an attractive nuisance.

FACTS: Grega Co. had dug a large hole for a new watering system for some football and baseball fields. The hole was left without a barrier or warning. A neighborhood child, Tommy, 10, playing there (as was his custom), whined, "I fell in the hole and broke my leg!"

Grega Co. also had a pond on the premises which the kids used as a swimming hole. After the company dumped some chemicals in the pond, several of the kids swimming there became ill. Was the property an attractive nuisance? **YOU'RE THE JUDGE!**

DECISION: Both of the situations were attractive nuisances.

The attractive nuisance doctrine holds that one who maintains a condition which is dangerous to children (generally those under age 12) because of the children's inability to appreciate the danger, and which may reasonably be expected to attract them to the premises, is under a duty to exercise reasonable care for their protection and safety.

Attractive nuisance subjects a possessor of land to liability for injuries to children where: (1) the possessor knows or should know that children may trespass, and that a condition on the land may create an unreasonable risk of death or serious bodily harm to such children; (2) the children, because of their youth, do not discover the condition or realize the risk; (3) the burden of eliminating the danger is slight, and; (4) the possessor of the land fails to exercise reasonable care to protect the children.

FACTS: Larry, 7, was injured when he was hit by a golf ball. Susan, 10, was injured when she cut herself swimming at a pond next to a privately owned golf course. There were warning signs posted on a broken down fence. Children often played on the golf course and at the pond, and their presence was known by golfers and the owners.

Tim explained how his brother Jay, 8, was hurt. "He was cut by a broken bottle. It was in the broad jump pit next to the playing field." Were the golf course, pond and field attractive nuisances? Could the children recover damages for their injuries? **YOU'RE THE JUDGE!**

DECISION: All were attractive nuisances. The golf course owner had a special duty to care for the protection and safety of those who they could foresee using their property. The children played there often. The warning may have been beyond the children's comprehension. The owner was guilty of negligence and even golfers (in certain situations) may be held liable.

Jay's use of the broad jump pit was also foreseeable. There was a breach of the duty to maintain the premises by adequate inspection to prevent such an injury. All could recover.

What if the children were older? Could they still recover damages?

The age of a child and the obvious nature of any risk may prevent the use of the attractive nuisance doctrine. For example, where a 13-year-old child was injured while diving in a neighbor's pond, where it was obvious that the water was too shallow, he was held to have both contributed to, and assumed the risk of, such an injury. He could not recover damages from the neighbor.

ODDS & ENDS....

Would you want a bunch of tough guys fighting in your neighborhood?

FACTS: You lived next to Kendrick Field which was used for sports by the local high schools and neighborhood kids. On occasion, the city granted a permit for an outdoor concert at the field.

The town newspaper's headline read: TOUGH MAN CONTEST AT KENDRICK FIELD. Men would fight until one of them couldn't continue. The contest was to take place two nights a week over a two month period.

You would like to have the contest enjoined as a nuisance. You alleged, "It will attract an evil public gathering—those of idle, vicious and criminal habits—who will contaminate the youth and disturb the peaceful pursuits and happiness of citizens unwilling to attend such an event."

Will the court grant an injunction, stopping the contest as being a potential nuisance?

DECISION: **YOU'RE THE JUDGE!**

May an animal be considered to be a public nuisance?

FACTS: Harvey, who lived in an apartment next to a golf course, complained, "Those roosters just strut around the course making noise." Harvey claimed that the roosters were a nuisance. Were they? **YOU'RE THE JUDGE!**

DECISION: The state attorney threw the case out. The roosters only bothered Harvey, not the public—and the noise was too infrequent.

You have a right to the "quiet enjoyment" and use of your property, free from any unreasonable intrusions.

27

HERE'S MY PROPERTY

WHAT'S IT ABOUT?

When you leave your bicycle, tennis racket or other sports equipment at a shop to be fixed, or your car at a parking lot while attending a sports event, a **bailment**—a contract to deliver personal property for some purpose—is formed. *Here's My Property* discusses bailments and who may be liable for any damage to such properties.

If you find personal property, do you have a duty to protect it and try to find its owner?

BAILMENTS, BAILORS & BAILEES?

FACTS: Frank admitted, "I was trying to fix Wally's bicycle and baseball glove and ruined them."

Bernie fumed, "While at the health club, I left my clothes in a locker and my valuables in the safe. They were stolen. Both services were provided as a courtesy." Could Wally or Bernie recover damages?

Suppose that you borrowed your friend's golf clubs, or loaned him your boat, and they were returned damaged? Or, suppose that you left your golf cart in the repair shop, rented fishing equipment, parked your car at a garage while at a game, rented a room, or checked your baggage or clothing, and....

What would everyone's rights and responsibilities be if any of these properties were damaged?

DECISION: **YOU'RE THE JUDGE!**

All of these situations involve a **bailment**—a contract providing for the delivery of personal property by its owner to another for some specific use or purpose.

The owner of the property is called the **bailor;** the person who receives the property is called the **bailee.** Only possession is transferred. Title and ownership are retained by the owner.

FACTS: You brought your tennis racket to a repair shop and your son's baseball uniform to the cleaners. Both shops were busy. In a hurry, you left the racket and uniform on the counters. When you called later, both were missing.

You sued, charging, "The tennis shop and cleaners were negligent bailees, they breached their duty to take reasonable care of our property." Could you recover for the loss of the racket and uniform? **YOU'RE THE JUDGE!**

DECISION: No. A bailment does not arise until you deliver possession to the bailee, and he accepts. Leaving the property on the counters did not create a bailment.

Bailments fall into three classes: those for the benefit of the bailor; those for the benefit of the bailee, and; those for the benefit of both.

BENEFIT OF BAILOR

The promise to fix the bike and glove, and the leaving of clothing in the locker room and valuables in the safe were all for the sole benefit of the bailor—the owners of the property.

If a bailee gets no compensation for the services he renders to a bailor's property, then he is a gratuitous bailee—merely undertaking to do it as a courtesy to the bailor.

If the bailee gets no compensation, can he be held to his promise? Not unless he accepts possession of the bailor's property. Once he has accepted possession of the property, he is required to perform.

FACTS: You, as the bailee, undertook to fix the bike and glove. The health club, also as a bailee, accepted your clothes and valuables. Did either of you owe a duty to care for the property that was entrusted to you? **YOU'RE THE JUDGE!**

DECISION: A duty was now owed by the bailees—you and the health club—to use reasonable care to prevent reasonably foreseeable harm to the property.

What if the bailed property were lost or used improperly by the bailee? If bailed property is lost, stolen, damaged or destroyed, a bailee would be liable for the loss if he failed to use proper care. Likewise, if the harm was sustained during an improper use of the property by the bailee, he would also be liable. Otherwise, the bailor bears the loss.

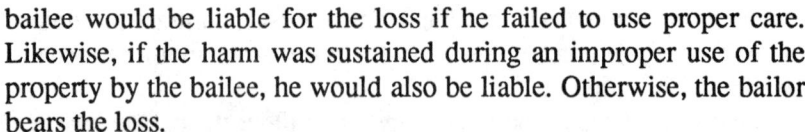

FACTS: "I left the glove and bike in my unlocked garage. They were stolen," you sadly reported. The health club burned to the ground. It was caused by an arsonist. Who was liable for the properties? **YOU'RE THE JUDGE!**

DECISION: You were liable for the glove and bike. You didn't use reasonable care. You should have either locked the garage or put the equipment in a safe place.

The club was not liable for the clothes and valuables. They took reasonable care of your property. The loss was caused by the willful act of a third person. Even if the fire were no one's fault, or a third person's negligence, the club would bear no responsibility. However, the club may be covered by insurance.

A bailee may not use property left with him unless it is necessary for its proper care, or unless the bailor grants permission. Such permission does not, however, relieve the bailee of liability for any failure of his duty to exercise reasonable care for the property. The bailee has a duty to return the identical property.

FACTS: After fixing the bike, you decided, without permission, to test it out. You rode it into a parked car. Were you liable for the damages to the bike? If the bike couldn't be repaired, could you replace it with another used bike?

DECISION: **YOU'RE THE JUDGE!**

A bailment for the benefit of the bailor may be terminated by either the bailor or the bailee. However, if a bailee agreed to keep the property for a certain time or to transport or deliver it, he must complete his requirement or be responsible for any resulting damages.

FACTS: After fixing John's glove, you delivered it as promised to the field, leaving it with a teammate. It was stolen before John arrived. "Was I liable?" you asked.

DECISION: **YOU'RE THE JUDGE!**

BENEFIT OF BAILEE

In a bailment for the sole benefit of the bailee, a bailor delivers property to be used and then returned by the bailee. If you promised to lend out your bike, your neighbor has no right to it—and there is no bailment—until you surrender possession and he accepts. Because the bailor gets no compensation, he can not be held to his promise.

Any departure from an agreed upon or expected use is at the peril of the bailee.

FACTS: After using your friend's golf clubs and tennis racket, you loaned them to Joe. He lost one of the golf clubs and used the tennis racket to play racketball, damaging it against a wall. "Who was liable for the damages?" asked Joe. **YOU'RE THE JUDGE!**

DECISION: A bailee is required to exercise great care in using and keeping property loaned to him. He is responsible for any loss caused by his negligence and will only be absolved of liability for loss, damage or theft, if he can show that it was not due to any negligence on his part. You should not have loaned the equipment to Joe without your friend's permission.

MUTUAL BENEFIT

What is a mutual benefit bailment? Renting a sports car or taking your snowmobile to a repair shop would be bailments for a mutual benefit. One party is given possession of another's property for a specific purpose, time and for a mutual advantage—you get the benefit of using the car or getting your snowmobile repaired, the rental company or repair shop gets money.

The bailee, required to use ordinary care, is responsible if he is negligent in his care of the property. What if a loss occurs which is beyond his control?

FACTS: Fires damaged both your snowmobile in the shop and your clothes in the cleaners, you lost the fishing equipment that you rented, your baggage was misplaced by a hotel, and your car was stolen from a secured parking garage. "Was I liable for these damages?" you asked. **YOU'RE THE JUDGE!**

DECISION: The loss of the snowmobile and clothes was not due to the negligence of the bailee. However, he may have been covered by insurance. The bailee was liable for the car and the baggage. You were liable for the fishing equipment.

If due to his negligence, a bailee injures another with bailed property—such as by running into another with a motorcycle—the bailee is liable as though he owned the property. A bailee is not liable for any injury caused by a thief who steals bailed property even though the theft was possible because the bailee was negligent. May a bailor be liable for an injury?

FACTS: Without giving proper warning, you, the bailor, entrusted a bailee with your golf cart, knowing that he was ignorant of the danger, and that he was reckless. The cart was not in good repair. Were you liable when the bailee injured another in an accident? **YOU'RE THE JUDGE!**

DECISION: You, the bailor, were liable. However, if the bailee were injured, he would assume the risk or be contributorily negligent if, in spite of knowledge of a defect, he made use of the property and was injured due to the defect (bad brakes).

If a bailee fails to complete the work on your property by the time promised, your damages are minimal unless you can show that it was understood that time was of the utmost importance.

A bailee is given a lien or the right to retain possession of bailed property until he has been paid for any storage or repairs.

A PAWN?

A **pawn** is a pledge or bailment of personal property by the bailor to the bailee to secure a loan from the bailee to the bailor.

FACTS: Randy exclaimed, "I needed money to pay the rent. So I took my golf clubs to the pawn shop where I got money for them. When I went back to pay the loan and get my clubs, they had been sold." Was the pawn shop liable for Randy's loss? **YOU'RE THE JUDGE!**

DECISION: The bailee or pawnbroker must exercise reasonable or ordinary care for the property, or be liable for any loss. However, if Randy did not pay the money back within a specified time, the pawnbroker could sell the clubs, upon any necessary notice to Randy.

Is a storekeeper responsible if a customer's property must be removed to try on merchandise, and then was misplaced or stolen?

FACTS: You went to a pawn shop looking for a fur coat to wear to a football game. Your coat, which you left on the counter while trying on the fur coat, was stolen. "Was the pawnbroker liable?" you asked. **YOU'RE THE JUDGE!**

DECISION: The pawnbroker was liable for the loss. He had a duty to exercise reasonable care for your coat, which necessarily had to be removed.

Are arenas or restaurants responsible for clothing left there by a patron?

Arenas, restaurants and the like are ordinarily not responsible for a patron's clothing, even if it was left at a place provided for such clothing, and even if someone employed there helps. However, liability may attach where there is a failure to take reasonable precautions to safeguard a patron's property, and this may be so despite any waiver of liability on a claim check.

BAILMENT FOR HIRE

A **bailment for hire** is an agreement by which a bailor rents out his property to the bailee for a specific purpose and warrants that the article is fit for the purpose intended.

FACTS: You rented a tractor from Andy's Store to work on your new golf course. There was an unknown defect in the tractor which caused it to go out of control. It damaged a new green and injured you. Who was liable for the damages and injury? **YOU'RE THE JUDGE!**

DECISION: The bailor, Andy's Store, was liable for any breach of his warranty or for any damages resulting from that breach. The manufacturer may also be liable.

A bailee is responsible for necessary repairs (tune-up), while a bailor is responsible for extraordinary or special repairs (transmission).

Another type of bailment for hire is where a bailor leaves personal property to be serviced by a bailee—repaired, altered or made into another product.

In the following example, who would be liable for any loss or destruction of the property?

FACTS: "I left cloth with the Brown Uniform Co. to be made into softball uniforms. A fire then destroyed the factory," said Marv. Who was liable for the loss? **YOU'RE THE JUDGE!**

DECISION: Ownership was still with the bailor, Marv. Only possession was with the bailee company. Therefore, unless the bailee was negligent, the loss was the bailor's. However, the bailee may be covered by insurance.

SPACE FOR RENT!

Where space is rented from a bailee to store personal property of a bailor, the bailee performs no service other than storing the bailor's property.

FACTS: Rich said, "I rented space in a self-service storage area to store my boat for the winter. I kept the keys and had the exclusive right to use the space." If Rich's property were damaged, who would be responsible? **YOU'RE THE JUDGE!**

DECISION: The renting of space in a locker or building does not constitute a bailment. Here, there is no delivery, merely rental with no liability to the owner of the space (other than that arising from gross negligence).

What if the owner of a storage area keeps a key to each storage area—does he then have some responsibility?

Where an owner of a space for rent has some control over that space—as by having a key to the storage area—then a bailment is formed. Then, there is a duty to exercise reasonable care to protect the property. Any breach may result in liability to the bailee, unless the loss is not due to his negligence, such as from a fire.

TRUNKS & BACK SEATS

In the absence of an express disclaimer, articles normally found in a vehicle are regarded as bailed. That is, a bailee—such as a parking garage—may have a duty to safeguard not only any vehicle parked there, but also to safeguard the vehicles contents, unless the garage clearly indicates a refusal to do so.

If an article is not normally found in an auto and its presence is unknown, then there is no bailment of the article, hence, no duty to safeguard.

FACTS: "I parked my car at the local garage," testified Wilma. "There were valuable drawings and sports equipment on the back seat and in the trunk. Everything was stolen." Who was liable for the loss? **YOU'RE THE JUDGE!**

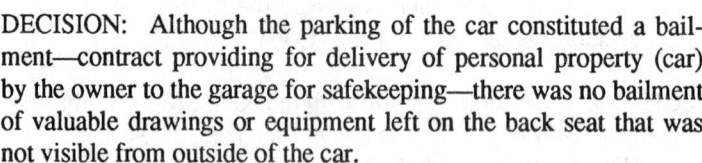

DECISION: Although the parking of the car constituted a bailment—contract providing for delivery of personal property (car) by the owner to the garage for safekeeping—there was no bailment of valuable drawings or equipment left on the back seat that was not visible from outside of the car.
When a car is bailed with the trunk locked, there is ordinarily a bailment of whatever is locked in the trunk. Wilma was liable for the valuables left on the back seat; the garage was liable for the car and the valuables left in the trunk.

Some courts have held that the operator of a parking lot has a duty of reasonable care for the protection of the auto regardless of whether or not there is a bailment.

PASSENGERS & BAGGAGE

A private carrier of passengers operates on the basis of a contract with the people whom he transports. Since he does not offer his services to the public, he has the right to choose with whom he will do business.

A common carrier of passengers serves the public. Does a common carrier have the right to to choose with whom he will do business?

FACTS: After a football game, the fans headed for the buses. Infuriated by his team's loss, one driver refused to allow any fans of the winning team on his bus. Could he do so? **YOU'RE THE JUDGE!**

DECISION: No. The driver may not discriminate. As a common carrier, he must carry all persons who request his services, only refusing those whose behavior is objectionable or who do not pay.

A person becomes a passenger when he enters the premises intending to use the carrier's services. And this is so even though he has yet to purchase a ticket.

A carrier has a duty to provide reasonable care for the protection and safety of his passengers. Is a carrier responsible for any delay in service?

FACTS: The Tigers' football fans wanted to reach the stadium for the kick-off. The carrier, knowing that there would be a delay, but wanting to sell his service, promised, "You'll be there on time." When the fans didn't arrive until the second quarter, they demanded a refund. "Weren't we entitled to one?" they asked. **YOU'RE THE JUDGE!**

DECISION: Although a carrier is not ordinarily responsible for any delay in service, this carrier was liable because of his knowledge of the probable delay and his promise.

A carrier is responsible for checked baggage, but not for baggage carried by a passenger. Passengers have a duty to declare excess value.

Any attempt to limit liability by a waiver of liability printed on a ticket or baggage claim check will not be binding where it was not brought to the passenger's attention and his proper consent obtained to waive any right to recover.

INNKEEPER

A hotel, motel, inn or other place of boarding is a public place—open to all. Accommodations are furnished to all who request them and who comply with reasonable rules, including payment.

FACTS: Mary requested accommodations at the Sportswomen's Club. While waiting in line to register, her luggage was stolen from the lobby. Was she a guest of the club? Was the club liable for the loss? **YOU'RE THE JUDGE!**

DECISION: A traveler requesting accommodations at a hotel becomes a guest immediately, even before registering or entering the building.

In the absence of a valid limitation, the management of a hotel generally insures the safety of goods of a guest and is liable for any loss due to its negligence, unless the loss was due to an act not under the control of the hotel—such as an act of God or negligence of the guest.

Innkeepers may limit liability by bringing any limitation to the attention of the guests—by posting such limitations and providing a safe. Liability for valuables left in a hotel safe may also be limited by the management.

FACTS: A sports equipment salesman, Eddy, lost his job after, "The company's receipts were stolen from the safe of the hotel where I was staying." Could he recover his lost wages because of the hotel's negligence? **YOU'RE THE JUDGE!**

DECISION: Even where the hotel may have been liable for the loss of the receipts, the hotel was not liable for lost wages.

A hotel or inn has a lien on any property brought in by a guest for all charges owed and may hold that property as security for such charges.

ODDS & ENDS....

"I Found It!"

FACTS: Andy found Joe's Super Bowl watch. What if he tired of keeping the watch and threw it in the trash? What obligation did Andy owe to Joe? **YOU'RE THE JUDGE!**

DECISION: Andy had no duty to keep the watch, but once he decided to, he only had the right to possess it. He had a duty to keep it safe. Treating it as trash, when it clearly had great value, was gross negligence.

Andy's duty was to search for the true owner, holding the watch until there was no reasonable expectation of the true owner showing up.

The more expensive the watch was, the longer Andy would have to hold it and search for the owner before he could throw it away or keep it.

FACTS: Andy admitted, "I wore the watch while swimming, had it cleaned, and then loaned it to a drunk." Would Andy be liable if the watch were damaged?

DECISION: **YOU'RE THE JUDGE!**

The care required of a finder is slight. This is because of the slight benefit to a finder. But, the degree of care owed may rise as the benefit goes from slight to something more—such as if the watch had diamonds in it and it appeared that the owner would not be found.

If Andy wore Joe's watch while swimming, he would be liable for any damages that resulted. Andy could undertake reasonable expenses to preserve the watch and charge them to Joe if he later claimed his watch.

If Andy loaned the watch to a drunk who then broke it, he would be liable for any loss in value or cost of repair.

FACTS: If Joe showed up to claim the watch, what procedure should Andy use to determine if Joe was the true owner? **YOU'RE THE JUDGE!**

DECISION: Andy would not have to give up the watch on demand. He could ask questions as to the identity of the watch in order to meet his duty to safeguard it for the true owner. Depending on the answers, Andy may be able to withhold the watch from Joe, at least until a court decided otherwise.

Understanding bailments is instrumental to protecting your personal property, and knowing your responsibilities towards the property of others.

IN CLOSING

Well folks, that's it! There is no more. I trust that you thoroughly enjoyed *You're The Judge!*

I have fallen in love with sports and the law and hope that you have too. My sincerest wish for you, and my reason for writing this book is that it will increase your knowledge, understanding and appreciation of the law—and how it concerns not only sports, but your everyday life.

This will help lead to a lifetime of enjoyment of sports. Furthermore, you will be able to apply this new knowledge to better protect the safety of yourself and others while appreciating how the law, rules and regulations are used to mete out justice. You will begin to better understand how this body of law, applied to sports, is the same law that touches so many non-sporting aspects of your life.

Give yourself time to understand the legal concepts in *You're The Judge!* Keep it in a handy spot; refer to it as needed or desired.

Remember that laws, rules and regulations may change as people's attitudes and the needs of society change. And a judge or jury may rule differently on similar facts. Remember also that any decision or information given in *You're The Judge!* is not intended to to be a substitute for proper legal or other advice. Use the book as an informational guide only; then seek out competent legal or other advice as necessary.

Your decisions, comments, thoughts and suggestions are welcomed.

WORDS & TERMS

Words & Terms contains definitions of the important legal and other words and terms used in *You're The Judge!* To assist the reader, these may be defined as they relate to sports or athletic activities. For a further discussion, see the page reference indicated in the definition. Words or terms that appear in SMALL CAPITALS are defined elsewhere in *Words & Terms.*

A

acceptance, 213 Receiving a thing that is offered, such as with the intention to make a contract.

acquisition, 259 Obtaining possession of professional sports teams by one league, whereby the acquired teams and its league cease to exist. Also, see MERGER.

act Written law formally passed by legislative power. See LAW; STATUTE.

action, 13 Judicial proceeding to enforce or protect a right, or to prevent a wrong. See SUIT.

adult Person who has attained the age of majority (generally 18-21), and is entitled to the management of his own affairs and to the enjoyment of common rights.

agent, 229 Person, with consent, authorized to act for another (principal), such as a professional sports agent who represents an athlete or player in negotiating a contract for the athlete's or player's services. See PRINCIPAL.

agreement Meeting of minds for a thing done or to be done; mutual obligation. See CONTRACT.

allegation Formal written statement by a party to a legal action, telling what is expected to be proven. See CASE.

amateur, 19 Athlete competing in athletic activity as a hobby, not as an occupation. Must compete for fun, not for pay. Also, see PROFESSIONAL.

answer, 13 Document answering a complaint and containing any denial and defenses. See COMPLAINT; DEFENSE.

antitrust Practices designed to prevent full and free competition, such as by: illegally monopolizing a sport, restraining and preventing players or athletes from competing, or stifling competition. See MONOPOLY; RESTRAINT OF TRADE.

antitrust acts, 255 Laws protecting commerce and trade from monopolies and illegal restraints of trade.

appeal Taking of a case to a higher court for a correction or reversal of a lower court's decision.

arbitration, 13, 220, 246 Process where parties, such as professional team owners and players, submit a dispute to an arbitrator for resolution.

arbitrator Private, impartial person(s) chosen by parties to a dispute to resolve the matter.

assault, 81 Unlawful, intentional threat or attempt, with force, to do physical harm to another. See BATTERY.

assumption of the risk, 88, 137 Defense to a charge of negligence where one injured is held to assume the risk of injury from a known and appreciated danger by voluntarily proceeding anyway. See NEGLIGENCE.

attractive nuisance, 193, 430 Rule holding that one maintaining on his premises a condition which is dangerous to young children (generally those under the age of 12) because of their inability to appreciate danger and may reasonably be expected to attract them to the premises, owes a duty to exercise reasonable care to protect them against such dangers. Also, see NUISANCE.

B

bailee, 435 Person receiving personal property of another under a bailment.

bailment, 435 Contract to deliver personal property by one person (bailor) to another (bailee) for a special purpose, such as delivering to be repaired, or renting, sports equipment.

bailor, 435 Person who owns and delivers personal property to bailee under a bailment.

battery, 81 Unlawful use of force by one person upon another without consent. See ASSAULT.

blackout, 263 Practice by professional sports leagues and others permitting them to prohibit the broadcast or televising of certain sports events which they control.

blue laws, 11 Laws regulating religious and personal conduct.

bona fide, 28 In or with good faith or honesty, as in good faith bargaining.

boycott, 258 Agreement refraining or refusing to deal as a means of coercion; sometimes called a group boycott.

breach Failure to perform a promise, warranty or duty.

breach of contract, 226 Failure to perform any or all terms of an agreement.

breach of warranty Failure to perform a promise or guaranty, such as by a manufacturer to make a product safe.

burden of proof, 16, 82 Duty to prove those facts necessary to win a judgment by a clear majority of the believable evidence.

C

case General term for an action or suit at law or in equity. See SUIT.

case law, 11 Law based on earlier court decisions. See PRECEDENT.

cause of action Facts which if proved in a suit would, in the absence of an effect defense, enable a plaintiff to obtain a judgement.

caveat emptor, 165, 418 "Let the buyer beware." Principle under which a buyer was held to have assumed all risks of injury from any defects in a product.

charitable immunity, 136 Immunity of charitable organizations and other non-profit organizations from being sued. See IMMUNITY.

civil action See ACTION; SUIT.

Civil Rights Act, 74 Act entitling all persons to full and equal enjoyment of any public place without discrimination or segregation on the grounds of race or color. See DISCRIMINATION.

claim, 13 Demand for something due or believed due, such as damages or a right.

Clayton Antitrust Act, 258 Act opposing unlawful restraints and monopolies so as to protect trade and commerce.

coercion To enforce or attempt to enforce by threat.

collective bargaining, 241 Process of negotiations between employers (professional sports team owners, league) and employees or others (player's association) concerning wages, hours and other terms and conditions of work.

collective bargaining agreement, 242, 261 Agreement reached between employers (owners) and employees (player's association) or others which regulates terms and conditions of work.

commission, 57 Group of officials authorized to perform certain acts or duties, such as an athletic commission authorized to promote and protect the interests of the public.

commissioner, 301 Person appointed by a sport and given authority to regulate and oversee the best interests of that sport, particularly concerning resolution of disputes and the conduct of teams and participants.

common law, 10 Law developed from custom, tradition and decisions by judges and juries, rather than from written laws.

comparative negligence, 90, 139 Defense where the negligence of the plaintiff is compared to that of the defendant. Any damages are based on this comparison. See NEGLIGENCE.

complaint, 13 Initial pleading in a suit, setting forth facts on which plaintiff bases claim for relief. See PLAINTIFF; SUIT.

consent, 81, 367 To give approval or permission. Also, see INFORMED CONSENT.

consideration, 213 Thing given or done, or refrained from, from one party and intended as the inducement to another to perform his part of a contract. See CONTRACT.

conspiracy Combination by two or more individuals or businesses (teams) for the purpose of illegally restraining trade or commerce.

Constitution, U. S. Fundamental laws and principles that determine the powers and duties of the government, which along with its amendments (Bill of Rights) guarantees certain rights to the people. Also, see DUE PROCESS; EQUAL PROTECTION.

contract, 212 Agreement to do or not to do a particular thing; offer, acceptance of that offer, and consideration, such as an agreement between a professional sports team and player.

contract, express Agreement, the terms of which are openly declared, either by written or oral language.

contract, no-cut, 219 Contract under which a player's salary, generally, will not be affected by his condition or performance, even if cut from the roster.

contract, no-trade, 220 Contract under which a player may not be traded without his consent.

contract, personal services, 215 Contract exchanging personal services (play) of an athlete for a promise to pay.

contributory negligence, 90, 138 Defense to a charge of negligence where one injured is held to have contributed to his injury by knowning of and appreciating a danger or risk, but then voluntarily proceeding anyway. See NEGLIGENCE.

copyright Author's or owner's exclusive legal right to reproduce, publish or sell literary, musical or artistic work.

counterclaims, 14 Claim alleged by a defendant that seeks to reduce plaintiff's claim or provide grounds for a judgement in favor of the defendant. See CLAIM.

court, 13 Governmental body whose function is to administer justice.

D

damages, 16, 89 Compensation for a loss or injury suffered.

decision Judgment of a court or jury of a legal dispute before them. See JUDGMENT.

defamation, 366 Statement that injures a person's reputation or character by false and malicious statements. See LIBEL; SLANDER.

defendant, 13 Person against whom plaintiff's complaint is brought. Also, see COMPLAINT.

defense Answer by a defendant; that which is offered to diminish or defeat plaintiff's complaint.

defense of others, 81 Defense in negligence where force used in defending others is that force the others could have used to defend themselves.

defraud To cheat, trick or swindle another out of property.

depositions, 14 Testimony of a witness recorded outside of court for use at trial. See TESTIMONY.

discovery, 14 Disclosure of facts, documents and the like to use in presenting a case to the court.

dismissal Order or judgement by a court terminating a suit without a complete trial. See TRIAL.

discrimination, 63 Failure to treat all people equally. Attempts to discriminate or differentiate in favor or against athletes or others in sports on the basis of prejudice because of race, sex, color or disability are illegal. See EQUAL PROTECTION.

draft, 273 System used in professional team sports whereby, generally, teams select players eligible for play in their sport in the inverse order of how the teams finished in the previous year's standings.

due process of law, 54, 65 Phrase used in 14th Amendment to the U.S. Constitution limiting a governments power to deprive a person of life, liberty or property without notice and an opportunity to be heard and to defend oneself—a fair and impartial hearing.

duress, 213 Unlawful coercion in forcing one to do something which he otherwise would not have done. See COERCION.

E

eminent domain, 291 Power of a state to take private property for public use.

endorsement, 340 Advertising message which consumers are likely to believe reflects the beliefs of the endorser, such as a professional athlete.

enjoin To command or prohibit, by court order, some act. See INJUNCTION.

equal protection of the laws 55, 65 Phrase used in the 14th amendment to the U.S. Constitution requiring every state to extend to all persons within its jurisdiction equal treatment and protection. It is intended to insure that all persons similarly situated shall be treated alike.

Equal Rights Amendment (ERA), 69 Amendment declaring that equality of rights and responsibility shall not be denied or taken away on account of sex. See DISCRIMINATION.

equity, 227 Justice administered by a court according to what is fair.

evidence Anything that gives or tends to give proof at trial of an issue, such as testimony of witnesses, documents and objects.

expert, 343 One who, because of education, training, knowledge or experience, has acquired special skills.

exploitation, 59 Unjust or improper use of another person for one's own profit or advantage.

express Clear, explicit or definite, such as an express warranty. See WARRANTY.

F

fair comment Statement by a writer in an honest belief of truth, even though it is not, relating to acts that are official, newsworthy and of public interest. See DEFAMATION.

financial aid See SCHOLARSHIP.

foreseeable Ability to see or know in advance,

such as that an injury may result from an existing danger.

fraud, 213 Intentional act of trickery, deceipt or misrepresentation intended to induce another to part with a right or something else of value. See MISREPRESENTATION.

free agent, 245 Professional sports team player who plays out his option, thus becoming free to negotiate and sign with any team concerning his services. Compensation (player, draft pick, money) to the team losing a free agent may be required.

functional, 347 Feature of a product necessary for the product's use, and which cannot be protected by a trademark. See TRADEMARK.

G

good faith Honest effort and intention.

good faith bargaining, 243 Mutual obligation between labor and a union (professional sports team owners and player's association) to meet at reasonable times, make relevant information available and confer with honest effort and intention over mandatory subjects. See MANDATORY SUBJECTS.

guardian, 34 Person who is legally assigned care of an individual not competent to act for himself, such as a minor.

H

hardship rule, 274 Rule allowing undergraduate athletes to give up their remaining amateur eligibility and enter the National Basketball Association (NBA) draft.

hung jury, 85 Jury so divided that it is unable to agree upon a verdict. See VERDICT.

I

imminent danger Term used regarding self-defense. Denotes immediate danger that must be instantly met and cannot wait upon the assistance of others or the protection of the law. See SELF-DEFENSE.

immunity Freedom or protection from legal action or duties which the law generally requires others to perform. See CHARITIBLE IMMUNITY; SOVEREIGN IMMUNITY.

implied Suggested or understood, but not directly or clearly stated, such as an implied warranty. See WARRANTY.

independent contractor Person working on his own without control of another, except as to the result of the work.

informed consent, 203 Consent given by a patient after a reasonable disclosure by medical personnel of any available alternative procedures and the dangers, advantages and disadvantages to the patient.

infringement Violation of a law or regulation; invasion of a right.

injunction, 259, 425 Order of a court directing a person or business to do, or refrain from doing, a particular thing, such as an illegal activity.

injury See PERSONAL INJURY.

intent State of mind with which one acts.

interrogatories, 14 Written questions used in judicial examination of a party or witness.

interstate commerce, 257 Commerce or trade among more than one state.

issue Single essential point to be decided at the conclusion of a trial. See TRIAL.

J

judgment Final decision or order of a court upon the rights and claims of parties to a suit. See SUIT.

jurisdiction, 13 Power of a court to hear and decide a claim. See CLAIM.

jury, 10 Group of people selected to hear evidence and decide a legal matter before them.

K

knowledge Truth or condition of knowing, being aware of, or understanding something.

L

laches, 14 Unreasonable delay in filing a complaint to the harm of a defendant.

last clear chance, 90 Defense holding that a person who has the last clear chance or opportunity to avoid injury to another is liable if he does not. See DEFENSE.

law, 8 Rule to be followed or obeyed, subject to legal penalty.

lawsuit See SUIT.

lease, 292 Agreement for the exclusive possession, use and enjoyment of land or property for a specific period of time, such as a sports facility.

legislation Power to make laws.

letter of intent, national, 34 Letter signed by student-athlete, parent or legal guardian making known the athlete's intent to attend a certain college.

liability, legal Obligation or responsibility for damages for an intentional or negligent act.

liable Obligated or responsible according to law or equity.

libel, 366 Form of defamation made in writing, pictures or other graphic representation that damages a person's reputation by holding him up to public ridicule, contempt, shame or disgrace. See DEFAMATION.

liberty, 52 Freedom from bodily restraint; freedom to be educated and of opportunity.

lockout, 250 Act by professional team sports owners of refusing to allow players to practice or play as a means of forcing them to agree over some matter.

M

majority See ADULT.

malice, 90 Intentional and wrongful conduct, without proper cause or excuse, with an intent to harm another. See DEFAMATION.

malicious prosecution, 371 Misuse of law or courts, without proper cause, with the desire to inflict injury on another.

mandatory subjects Collective bargaining subjects covered by wages, hours, and other terms and conditions of work. See COLLECTIVE BARGAINING.

merger, 259 Joining together of professional sports leagues into one, whereby the other then ceases to exist. Also, see ACQUISITION.

minor Person under the age of legal majority. See ADULT.

misrepresentation, 213, 223, 353 Statement by words or other conduct that misleads the person to whom made. See FRAUD.

mistake Unintentional act or omission done out of ignorance or misunderstanding.

mistrial, 85 Trial that has no legal effect, such as one cancelled due to error or misconduct.

monopoly, 256 Exclusive right, power or control to carry on a particular business or trade, such as manufacturing products or providing services (sports activities).

municipality City, town or other governmental branch.

N

National Collegiate Athletic Association (NCAA), 20 Voluntary organization of major colleges and universities, formed to regulate and supervise collegiate athletics in the U.S.

National Labor Relations Act (NLRA), 239 Act giving employees (professional athletes) the right to form a union or association (player's association), to bargain collectively, and to engage in other activities for their aid and protection. Also, see PLAYER'S ASSOCIATION.

negligence, 88, 166 Failure to exercise the standard of care which a reasonable person in the same or similar circumstances would exercise, and which breach causes an injury and damages. See BREACH.

nuisance, 424 Creation of a condition that annoys or disturbs one in possession of his property, rendering its ordinary use uncomfortable. Also, see ATTRACTIVE NUISANCE.

O

offer, 213 Promise to do a thing, such as to make a contract, which if accepted creates the contract.

opinion Decision reached by a judge or court detailing the reasons upon which a judgment is based. See JUDGMENT.

option clause, 226 System giving professional sports team owners the right to renew a player's services without consent for one year after the player's present contract expires. See CONTRACT; PERSONAL SERVICES.

P

parol evidence rule, 216 Rule prohibiting change, in the absence of fraud or mistake, in an agreement where the parties intended to merge all oral agreements into a written one.

pawn, 438 Bailment of personal property to secure a loan. See BAILMENT.

per se By itself or taken alone.

per se rule, 259, 275 Rule holding that certain agreements or practices, because of their deadly effect on competition, are per se illegal.

personal injury Hurt or damage to a person's body, as distinguished from injury to one's reputation or property. See DEFAMATION.

plaintiff, 13 Complaining party bringing a legal action. See ACTION; COMPLAINT

player's association Group of professional sports team players, organized to bargain with their employer (team owners) concerning wages, hours, grievances and other terms and conditions of work.

precedent, 11 Utilization of previous court decisions in judging a court action with similar facts.

premise liability, 179 Liability of the owner or operator of land and buildings, such as a sports facility, or place of public amusement or entertainment, to exercise reasonable care for the safety and protection of patrons. See LIABILITY; REASONABLE CARE.

preponderance of evidence, 16 Evidence by one party to a suit, which when fairly considered, produces the stronger impression and is more believable.

president, 301 Person appointed by a sport and given authority to regulate and oversee the best interests of that sport, particularly concerning resolution of disputes and the conduct of team or participants.

price discrimination, 258 Policy where a different price is charged to similarly situated buyers. Also, see CONSPIRACY.

principal Employer of an agent; the source of authority or right. See AGENT.

privacy, right of Right to let alone, free from unwarranted publicity or public scrutiny.

privilege Right, benefit or power enjoyed by a person or business, but not enjoyed by all.

procedure, 12 Method for enforcing legal rights and seeking damages for an injury

product liability, 165, 418 Liability of a manufacturer or seller of a product for an injury caused by their product. See LIABILITY.

professional Person working or competing in a profession for pay, not as a hobby, such as a professional athlete. Also, see AMATEUR.

proof Establishment of a fact by evidence. See EVIDENCE.

property Something exclusively owned or possessed, including rights.

property interest, 52 Claim or right in property, such as a right to participate in athletics.

property right Right to control some property, to do with as the owner desires, such as the right of a team or league to control the broadcast of their games.

proximate cause Negligent conduct without which an injury would not have happened. See NEGLIGENCE.

public figure, 355, 367 Person who has achieved fame or notoriety, and who commands substantial public interest, such as an athlete.

punitive damages, 84 Damages intended to serve as a deterent to, or to make an example of, the defendant or others for evil behavior. See DAMAGES.

pure accident, 90 Accident that is unforseeable or that could not be prevented by reasonable caution. See UNFORSEEABLE.

R

rational basis test, 55 Requires that any rule or classification, such as to regulate athletics or athletes, must be reasonable so that all persons similarly situated are treated alike.

reasonable care That care which an ordinary, reasonable and cautious person would exercise under the same or similar circumstances.

reasonable doubt Apprehension or suspicion which would make a reasonable man hesitate to act or accept the truth of a claim or accusation.

redshirting, 26 Intentional retention or keeping back of athletes, generally to extend athletic eligibility.

regulate To control or direct; to subject to rules or laws.

Rehabilitation Act, 73 Act holding that no otherwise qualified handicapped individual shall, solely by reason of a handicap, be excluded from participation in, be denied benefits of, or be subject to discrimination in athletics. See DISCRIMINATION.

remedy Legal means used to enforce a right, or; compensate for, or prevent, an injury, such as money damages or an injunction. See INJUNCTION.

reply See ANSWER.

res ipsa locquitor, 394 "The thing speaks for itself." Expression inferring negligence where the defendant had exclusive control of that which caused an injury and, further, that the injury would not ordinarily happen without negligence. See NEGLIGENCE.

rescind To annul, make void or cancel, such as a contract or agreement. See CONTRACT.

reserve clause, 226 System giving a professional sports team owner the right to reserve a player's services for an indefinite period. Unless agreed to, reserve clauses are no longer allowed.

respondeat superior, 146 "Let the master answer." Expression holding employers responsible for the negligent acts of their employees, such as a city or school's responsibility for the acts of its teachers and coaches.

restraint of trade Contract or conspiracy which tends, or is designed, to stifle or eliminate competition—illegal monopoly, such as restrictions on a professional team player's ability to trade his services with other teams. See CONSPIRACY.

right of first refusal, 282 Right of a professional sports team to sign a free agent they are about to lose for the amount agreed upon between the player and another team. See FREE AGENT.

right of privacy, 355 Right to be left alone, free from intrusion of one's private life.

right of publicity, 360 Right to a recognizable and marketable personality, such as a professional athlete.

risk Danger or hazard, such as which a person may knowingly accept, thus preventing recovery for any injury suffered as a result. See ASSUMPTION OF THE RISK.

rule Established legal standard or regulation directing or prohibiting certain conduct. See LAW.

rule of reason, 260 Rule holding that the legality of restraints on trade is determined by weighing certain factors. See RESTRAINT OF TRADE.

S

save-harmless statutes, 136 Laws permitting or requiring schools to protect, indemnify or grant immunity from prosecution to teachers and coaches from financial loss in cases alleging negligence against them. See IMMUNITY.

scalping, 377 Practice of generally selling a ticket to a sports event for a price higher than the original price of the ticket.

scholarship, 21 Authorized funds to a student by a college—grant-in-aid, loan or on-campus work—such as an athletic scholarship.

scope of employment Responsibility assigned to an individual by superiors or employer.

self-defense, 81 Conduct to protect or defend one's person or property against injury attempted by another. See PERSONAL INJURY.

settlement, 13 Agreement settling a matter without further need for a decision by a court.

sex discrimination, 64 Discrimination based solely on sex. See DISCRIMINATION.

Sherman Antitrust Act, 256 Act opposing unlawful restraints and monopolies so as to protect trade and commerce.

slander, 366 Oral statement of false and malicious words that injures another's reputation. See DEFAMATION.

sovereign immunity, 135 Freedom or protection from legal action for municipalities and schools. See IMMUNITY.

specific performance, 226 Performance of a contract according to the precise terms agreed upon. See CONTRACT.

stare decisis, 261 Practice whereby a court does not disturb previous case rulings.

state action, 49, 51 State involvement in providing public education, such as to public schools. These schools are bound by the requirements of the Constitution. See DUE PROCESS; EQUAL PROTECTION.

statute, 110 Act or law of a legislature declaring, commanding or prohibiting something. See ACT; LAW.

Statute of Limitations, 14, 134 Statute limiting the time in which a suit must be brought. See SUIT.

strict liability, 166, 420 Absolute liability, regardless of any fault or improper care by a product's user, will apply if a potentially dangerous, defectively manufactured product causes injury. There is an absolute duty to make it safe. See LIABILITY.

strict scrutiny test, 56 Requires that where a suspect class (race, sex, color) or fundamental interest (marriage, interstate travel) is involved, any rule, such as to regulate athletics or athletes, will be unconstitutional unless there is a compelling interest to be protected or promoted.

strike, 250 Act of refusing to work as a means of forcing an employer to give in to employees' demands, such as professional team players demanding of team owners less restrictive free agency or better work conditions. See FREE AGENCY.

suit Proceeding in a court where the plaintiff seeks compensation for injury or enforcement of a right.

T

tampering, 223 Improperly interfering with another's rights, such as a professional sports team's rights to one of its player's services.

testify, 15 To give testimony—evidence or statement—as a witness.

tort, 81 Private or civil wrong or injury. See PERSONAL INJURY; DEFAMATION.

trademark, 346 Distinctive word, name, mark or other symbol of authenticity through which products of one manufacturer may be distinguished or identified from those of others.

trademark infringement, 346 Act of using, without consent, a registered trademark which use is likely to cause confusion with the public.

trial, 14 Legal proceeding of issues before a court that has jurisdiction. See ACTION; SUIT.

U

unavoidable accident See PURE ACCIDENT.

unconstitutional In violation of the constitution and, therefore, unenforceable or illegal.

undue influence Improper or wrongful persuasion which induces one to do something which he would not do if acting freely.

unfair labor practice, 242 Practice where an employer or employees refuse to bargain, or bargain in good faith, such as where a professional sports team owner interferes with a player's associations' right to organize or encourage membership, or refuses to bargain. See COLLECTIVE BARGAINING.

unforseeable Not expected, seen or known of in advance.

union, 238 Group of people (association or player's association) organized to bargain with their employer (team owner or others) concerning discipline, wages, hours, grievances or other terms and conditions of work. See PLAYER'S ASSOCIATION.

V

valid Legally sufficient or binding.

venue, 13 Geographical place where a trial must be held; place where the plaintiff files a complaint.

verdict, 16 See JUDGMENT.

vicarious liability, 86 Liability for another's negligent acts.

voidable Capable of being voided—no legal force, unenforceable—such as a contract. See CONTRACT.

Voir dire, 14 Method by which a jury is selected.

volition, 115 Voluntary; acting or done of one's own free will or choice.

W

waiver, 123, 414 Voluntary surrender of a right with both knowledge of its existence and an intention to surrender it, such as a right to recover damages for a personal injury. See PERSONAL INJURY.

warranty, 168, 169, 207 Promise or guarantee, such as warranties given by a manufacturer or seller regarding the condition of their products.

witness, 15 Person who personally testifies to what he has seen, heard or observed.

workmen's compensation statutes, 110, 321 Statutes providing that employees (professional team athletes and others), with certain exceptions, may receive compensation for injuries related to their employment.

INDEX

Bold page references indicate where topics are defined and discussed. See *Words & Terms* for a complete list of definitions with page references of important legal and other words and terms used in *You're The Judge!*

Java 6 Illuminated

An Active Learning Approach

SECOND EDITION

Julie Anderson
Capitol College

Hervé Franceschi
Capitol College

JONES AND BARTLETT PUBLISHERS
Sudbury, Massachusetts
BOSTON TORONTO LONDON SINGAPORE

World Headquarters
Jones and Bartlett Publishers
40 Tall Pine Drive
Sudbury, MA 01776
978-443-5000
info@jbpub.com
www.jbpub.com

Jones and Bartlett Publishers Canada
6339 Ormindale Way
Mississauga, Ontario L5V 1J2
Canada

Jones and Bartlett Publishers International
Barb House, Barb Mews
London W6 7PA
United Kingdom

Jones and Bartlett's books and products are available through most bookstores and online booksellers. To contact Jones and Bartlett Publishers directly, call 800-832-0034, fax 978-443-8000, or visit our website www.jbpub.com.

Substantial discounts on bulk quantities of Jones and Bartlett's publications are available to corporations, professional associations, and other qualified organizations. For details and specific discount information, contact the special sales department at Jones and Bartlett via the above contact information or send an email to specialsales@jbpub.com.

Production Credits
Acquisitions Editor: Timothy Anderson
Production Director: Amy Rose
Senior Marketing Manager: Andrea DeFronzo
Editorial Assistant: Melissa Elmore
Manufacturing Buyer: Therese Connell
Cover Design: Kristin E. Ohlin
Composition: Northeast Compositors, Inc.
Printing and Binding: Replika Press
Cover Printing: Replika Press

Library of Congress Cataloging-in-Publication Data
Anderson, Julie.
Java 6 illuminated / Julie Anderson, Hervé Franceschi. — 2nd ed.
p. cm.
ISBN-13: 978-0-7637-4963-7
ISBN-10: 0-7637-4963-X
1. Java (Computer program language) I. Franceschi, Hervé. II. Title.
QA76.73.J3A532 2007
005.13'3—dc22

2007031406

6048

Printed in India
11 10 09 08 07 10 9 8 7 6 5 4 3 2 1

Dedications

To the memory of my parents, Glenn and Rosemary Austin, my first teachers. – *Julie Anderson*

A ma mère, trop tôt disparue, et à mon père. – *Hervé Franceschi*

Preface

The Purpose of This Book and Its Audience

Java 6 Illuminated, Second Edition covers all of the material required for the successful completion of an introductory course in Java. While the focus is on the material required for the Computer Science I (CS1) and Computer Science II (CS2) curricula, students enrolled in Information Systems, Information Technology, or self-directed study courses will find the book useful as well. It has been written to provide introductory computer science students with a comprehensive overview of the fundamentals of programming using Java as the teaching language. In addition, the book presents other topics of interest, including graphical user interfaces (GUI), data structures, file input and output, and applets.

Throughout the book, we have attempted to take an "active learning" approach to presenting the material. Instead of merely presenting the concepts to students in a one-sided, rote manner, we have asked them to take an active role in their understanding of the language through the use of numerous interactive examples, exercises, and projects.

Coverage and Approach

Our approach is to teach object-oriented programming in a progressive manner. We start in Chapter 1 by presenting an overview of object-oriented programming. In Chapter 3, we delve a little deeper into the concepts of classes and objects and introduce the student to many of the useful classes in the Java class library. Our emphasis at this point is on using classes; we teach the student how to read APIs in order to determine how to instantiate objects and call methods of the classes. In Chapter 7, we move on to designing user-defined classes, and in Chapter 10, we present inheritance, polymorphism, and interfaces. Throughout the book, we present concepts in an object-oriented context.

Our philosophy is to emphasize good software engineering practices by focusing on designing and writing correct, maintainable programs. As such, we discuss pseudocode, testing techniques, design trade-offs, and other software engineering tips.

We teach the student basic programming techniques, such as accumulation, counting, calculating an average, finding maximum and minimum values, using flag and toggle variables, and basic searching and sorting algorithms. In doing so, we emphasize the patterns inherent in programming. Concepts are taught first, followed by fully implemented examples with source code. We promote Java standards, conventions, and methodologies.

This book supports the important features of the latest version of Sun Microsystems' Java 6.0. The *Scanner* class is used to simplify user input from the keyboard and in reading from files. The *enum* functionality is presented as a user-defined data type in Chapter 7. Autoboxing and unboxing concepts are introduced in Chapter 3 with the Java wrapper classes. We demonstrate generic types and the enhanced *for* loop in the Chapter 9 coverage of *ArrayLists*, and we explain how to write a class using generic types in Chapter 14.

Learning Features

Recognizing today's students' growing interest in animation and visualization, we distribute techniques for producing graphical output and animation throughout the book, starting in Chapter 4 with applets. An example using either animation or graphical output is included in most chapters. Instructors who are not interested in incorporating graphics into their curriculum can simply skip these sections. In addition, some of our examples are small games, which we find motivational for students.

In each chapter, we include one or two Programming Activities, which are designed to provide visual feedback to the students so that they can assess the correctness of their code. In most Programming Activities, we provide a framework, usually with a graphical user interface, to which the student adds code to complete the application. The student should be able to finish the Programming Activity in about 15 to 20 minutes; thus, these activities can be used in the classroom to reinforce the topics just presented. Each Programming Activity also includes several discussion questions that test the student's understanding of the concepts the activity illustrates. The Programming Activities are also appropriate for a closed or open laboratory environment. In short, this book can be used in a traditional lecture environment, a computer-equipped classroom, or a lab environment.

In addition, we supplement each chapter with a browser-based module that animates sample code, illustrating visually the assignment of variable values, evaluation of conditions, and flow of control.

Java 6 Illuminated, Second Edition provides the instructor and students with an extensive variety of end-of-chapter material: multiple-choice questions, examples that ask the student to predict the output of prewritten code or to fill in missing code, debugging activities, short exercises, programming projects, technical writing assignments, and a higher-difficulty group project.

Chapter-by-Chapter Overview

The chapters are logically organized from simple to more difficult topics, while incorporating object orientation as needed, taking into account the specifics of the Java language. Here is a brief summary of the topics covered in each chapter:

Chapter 1: Introduction to Programming and the Java Language

We introduce the student to the concept of programming, first covering computer hardware and operating systems, and following with a brief evolution of programming languages, including an introduction to object-oriented programming. We explain programming basics and pseudocode as a program design technique. The student writes, compiles, and debugs their first program using an integrated development environment.

Chapter 2: Programming Building Blocks—Java Basics

In this chapter, we concentrate on working with variables and constants of primitive data types and composing arithmetic expressions. We illustrate the differences between integer and floating-point calculations and introduce operator precedence.

Chapter 3: Object-Oriented Programming, Part 1: Using Classes

Chapter 3 introduces classes from the user, or client, standpoint and discusses the benefits of encapsulation and code reuse. The student learns how to instantiate objects and call methods. We also demonstrate useful Java classes for console input and output, dialog boxes, formatting output, performing mathematical calculations, and generating random numbers.

Chapter 4: Introduction to Applets and Graphics

Chapter 4 presents several methods of the *Graphics* class that can be used to create graphical output by drawing shapes and text. The windowing graphics coordinate system is explained and using color is also explored. We demonstrate these graphics methods in applets because an applet window provides an easy-to-use palette for drawing. Instructors wishing to postpone or skip graphics coverage altogether can use as little or as much of this chapter as they desire.

Chapter 5: Flow of Control, Part 1: Selection

Various forms of the *if*, *if/else*, and *if/else if* statements are presented, along with the appropriate situations in which to use each form. We also demonstrate nested *if/else* statements and testing techniques. We begin our coverage of scope by introducing block scope. Later chapters build upon this foundation. As part of our object-oriented programming coverage, we teach the importance of comparing objects using the *equals* method. This chapter also covers the conditional operator and the *switch* statement.

Chapter 6: Flow of Control, Part 2: Looping

This is probably the most important chapter in the book. We have found that looping and repetition are the most difficult basic programming concepts for the average student to grasp. We try to ease the student's understanding of looping techniques by presenting patterns to follow in coding basic algorithms: accumulation, counting, calculating an average, and finding minimum and maximum values. We present a motivational and engaging example of repetition in the animation of a ball rolling across the screen. Looping is further explored as a tool for validation of input values. We continue our coverage of scope by illustrating the scope of variables declared within the *while* loop body and *for* loop header. We concentrate on using the *while* loop for event-controlled and sentinel-controlled repetition and the *for* loop for count-controlled looping. A large section focuses on constructing loop conditions, which is often a challenging task for the student. Sections are also provided on testing techniques for *while* loops and for *for* loops. In this chapter, we also introduce reading data from a text file using the *Scanner* class.

Chapter 7: Object-Oriented Programming, Part 2: User-Defined Classes

In this chapter, we teach the student to write classes, as well as client applications, that use the instantiated objects and call methods of the class. We present class design techniques and standard patterns for writing constructors, mutators and accessors, and the *toString*, *equals*, and other user-defined methods. We further explain scope in the context of class members and method parameters. We also explain how and when to use the keywords *this* and *static*. *Enum* is also covered as a user-defined class type. Finally, we teach the student how to use Javadoc and how to create a package.

Chapter 8: Single-Dimensional Arrays

This chapter begins with the declaration, instantiation, and initialization of single-dimensional arrays. From there, the student learns to perform the basic programming techniques (accumulation, counting, calculating an average, and finding maximum and minimum values) on array elements. We also cover arrays as instance variables of a class, and demonstrate maintaining encapsulation while accepting arrays as method parameters and returning arrays from methods. Basic searching and sorting algorithms are also presented, including sequential and binary searches and Selection and Insertion sorts.

Chapter 9: Multidimensional Arrays and the *ArrayList* Class

We focus in this chapter on two-dimensional array processing, including techniques for processing all the elements in the entire array, or the elements in a specific column or row. We also demonstrate the extra processing needed to handle arrays with rows of different lengths. A bar chart of the data in each row of the array is also demonstrated. In addition, we extrapolate the concepts from two-dimensional arrays to discuss multidimensional arrays.

We present the *ArrayList* class as an expandable array and demonstrate using classes with generic types, the enhanced *for* loop, as well as autoboxing and unboxing.

Chapter 10: Object-Oriented Programming, Part 3: Inheritance, Polymorphism, and Interfaces

Continuing our object-oriented programming coverage, we discuss the important concepts and benefits of inheritance and the design of class hierarchies, including abstract classes. We cover inherited members of a class, constructing objects of a subclass, adding specialization to a subclass, overriding inherited methods, and calling methods of the superclass. We discuss the trade-offs of declaring members as *protected* versus *private*. We demonstrate polymorphism with a graphical example, and introduce the student to interfaces, which are used extensively in Graphical User Interfaces. (See Chapter 12.)

Chapter 11: Exceptions and Input/Output Operations

Recognizing that building robust applications requires error handling, we present exception handling as a tool for validating user input and recovering from errors at run time. We demonstrate handling predefined exceptions and writing user-defined exceptions.

With this knowledge, the student is ready to perform file input and output operations. We demonstrate reading and writing *Strings* and primitive data types to text files, and reading and writing objects directly to files. The *StringTokenizer* class is also presented for parsing input from structured text files.

Chapter 12: Graphical User Interfaces

This chapter introduces the student to event-driven programming and writing event handlers for text fields, buttons, radio buttons, checkboxes, lists, combo boxes, and mouse activities. We also demonstrate panels and several layout managers for organizing GUI components, as well as how to nest components. In our examples, we illustrate how to separate the graphical user interface code from the underlying data and program logic.

Chapter 13: Recursion

Recursion is presented as a design technique, reducing the size of a problem until an easy-to-solve problem is reached. We demonstrate recursive methods with one base case and with multiple base cases, and with and without return values. Specific examples provided include computing the factorial of a number, finding the greatest common divisor, performing a binary search, determining if a phrase is a palindrome, calculating combinations, solving the Towers of Hanoi problem, and performing animation. The benefits and trade-offs of recursion versus iteration are also discussed.

Chapter 14: An Introduction to Data Structures

In this chapter, we cover data structures by exploring the concepts and implementations of various types of linked lists, stacks, and queues. We demonstrate many types and uses of linked lists: a singly linked list, a linked list as a stack, a linked list as a queue, a doubly linked list, a sorted linked list, and a recursively defined linked list. Arrays as stacks and circular arrays as queues are also covered in detail.

We begin with a list of primitive types (*int*) and progress to a list consisting of objects of a user-defined *Player* class. Then we cover defining a class using generic types to demonstrate how a list can be defined to hold generic objects.

Chapter 15: Running Time Analysis

We explain how to evaluate the performance of an algorithm in this chapter. We explain the Big-Oh notation and orders of magnitude. Students learn various methods for deriving performance estimates: counting statements in loops, iterative, handwaving, and proof by induction analyses for recursive methods. We demonstrate how the coding of an algorithm influences its running time. Worst-case, best-case, and average-case performance are explained and illustrated.

What's New in *Java 6 Illuminated*

In this edition, we have refined the existing material and incorporated new material as a result of feedback we received from instructors who have adopted the textbook. We have reorganized Chapter 3 to provide a more logical introduction to using classes. We focus first on classes (*String, DecimalFormat, Random, Scanner*) that use constructors to create objects. We then explain the concept of *static* methods and *static* class variables using the *Math* class as an example and introduce factory methods as a way of creating objects using the *NumberFormat* class. We also renamed our author-written *Date* class to *SimpleDate* to avoid confusion with the *Date* class in the Java class library.

In Chapter 4, we added the *Polygon* class in response to our students, who have requested the ability to draw more complex shapes than ovals and rectangles.

We have expanded our coverage of scope by introducing block scope in Chapters 5 and 6, leading into our discussion of class member and parameter scope in Chapter 7.

Because of the simplicity of the *Scanner* class, we now use *Scanner* methods to read from files in Chapter 11.

In Chapter 12, we have separated the GUI interface code from the program logic for many examples to better illustrate object-oriented design and the Model-View-Controller design.

In Chapter 14, we begin our illustration of lists by using a list of primitive types. Once the student is familiar with the concepts of nodes and references to the next element, we add elements of a specific author-written class, then move on to supporting generic objects with parameterized types.

Chapter 15, Running Time Analysis, is new to this edition. We added it for completeness because we found that many instructors were using this text for both CS1 and CS2.

Pedagogy

Concepts are always taught first, followed by complete, executable examples illustrating these concepts. Most examples demonstrate real-life applications so that the student can understand the need for the concept at hand. The example code is colored to better illustrate the syntax of the code and to reflect the use of colors in today's IDE tools, as shown in this example from Chapter 3:

```
/*  A demonstration of reading from the console using Scanner
    Anderson, Franceschi
*/

import java.util.Scanner;

public class DataInput
{
  public static void main( String [ ] args )
  {
     Scanner scan = new Scanner( System.in );

     System.out.print( "Enter your first name > " );
     String firstName = scan.next( );
```

```
        System.out.println( "Your name is " + firstName );

        System.out.print( "\nEnter your age as an integer > " );
        int age = scan.nextInt( );
        System.out.println( "Your age is " + age );

        System.out.print( "\nEnter your GPA > " );
        float gpa = scan.nextFloat( );
        System.out.println( "Your GPA is " + gpa );
    }
}
```

EXAMPLE 3.9 Reading from the Console using *Scanner*

Figures and tables are used to illustrate or summarize the concept at hand, such as these from Chapters 6 and 7:

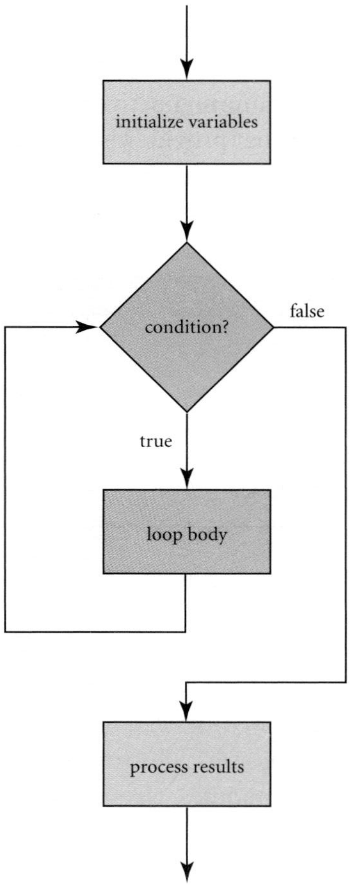

Figure 6.1
Flow of Control of a *while* Loop

TABLE 7.1 Access Modifiers

Access Modifier	Class or member can be referenced by . . .
public	methods of the same class, as well as methods of other classes
private	methods of the same class only
protected	methods in the same class, as well as methods of subclasses and methods in classes in the same package
no modifier (package access)	methods in the same package only

SOFTWARE ENGINEERING TIP

Define instance variables of a class as *private* so that only methods of the class will be able to set or change their values.

COMMON ERROR TRAP

Be sure that both operands of the logical AND and logical OR operators are *boolean* expressions. Expressions such as this: `x < y && z`, with *x*, *y*, and *z* being numeric types, are illegal. Instead, use the expression:

`x < y && x < z`

In each chapter, we emphasize good design concepts using "Software Engineering Tips," such as the one to the left from Chapter 7.

We also provide "Common Error Traps," such as the one to the left from Chapter 5, to alert students against common syntax and logic errors.

In each chapter, "active learning" programming activities reinforce concepts with enjoyable, hands-on projects that provide visual feedback to the students. These activities can be done in lab-type classrooms or can be assigned as projects. A header for a Programming Activity looks like this:

6.9 Programming Activity 1: Using *while* Loops

In this activity, you will work with a sentinel-controlled *while* loop, performing this activity:

> Write a *while* loop to process the contents of a grocery cart and calculate the total price of the items. It is important to understand that, in this example, we do not know how many items are in the cart.

Supplementing each chapter, we provide a browser-based module implemented as a Flash animation on the CD-ROM, which illustrates the execution of code that implements the concepts taught in the chapter. Each movie animates a brief code sample, one line at a time, and is controlled by the user via a "Next Step" button. These modules can be beneficial for students who learn best with visual aids, graphs, illustrations, and at their own pace outside the classroom. The modules are announced in each chapter using a special icon as in the sample at the top of the next page.

CODE IN ACTION

To see two step-by-step illustrations of do/while loops, look for the Chapter 6 Flash movie on the CD-ROM included with this book. Click on the link for Chapter 6 to start the movie.

Graphics Coverage

Graphics are distributed throughout the book and are used to engage the student and reinforce the chapter concepts. The Graphics coordinate system, methods for drawing shapes and text, and color concepts are presented with simple applets in Chapter 4. Animation using loops is demonstrated in Chapter 6, while drawing a bull's-eye target illustrates both looping and using a toggle variable. Classes for displayable objects are presented in Chapter 7; drawing a bar chart of array data is illustrated in Chapters 8 and 9; polymorphism is demonstrated using a Tortoise and Hare Race in Chapter 10; GUIs are covered in Chapter 12; and animation using recursion is demonstrated in Chapter 13. The two figures that follow illustrate graphical examples from Chapters 7 and 8.

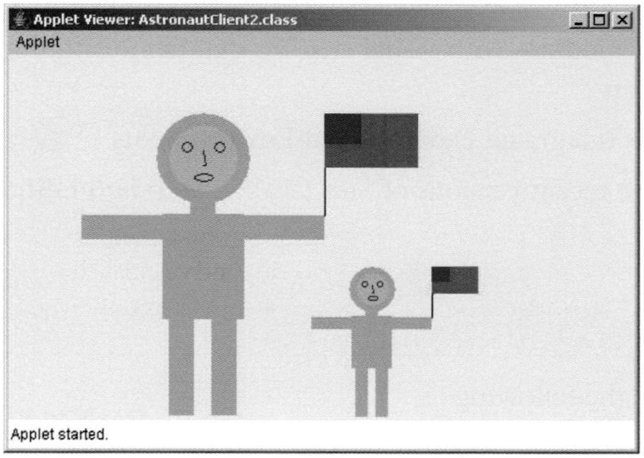

Figure 7.10
The *AstronautClient2* Window

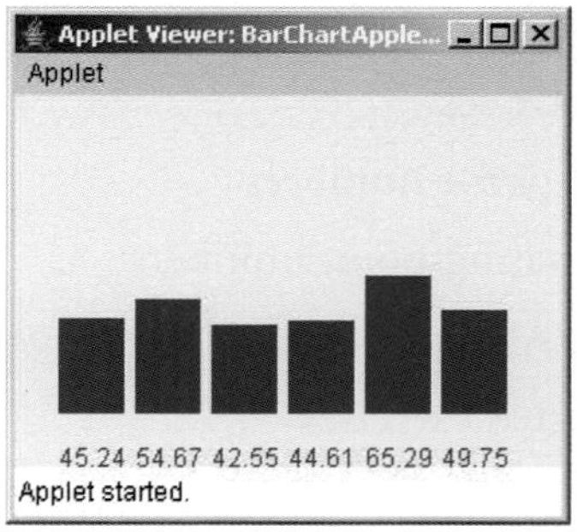

Figure 8.15
The *cellBills* Array as a Bar Chart

End-of-Chapter Exercises and Problems

A large collection of exercises and problems is proposed at the end of each chapter. Short exercises cover programming from a variety of angles: multiple choice concept questions, reading and understanding code segments, filling in some code, correcting errors, and interpreting compiler error messages to diagnose application bugs. Many programming projects are proposed with an emphasis on writing *classes*, not just a *program*. A more challenging group project is proposed in each chapter, allowing students to work as a group and develop communication skills, in accordance with recommendations from accreditation organizations. Small, essay-type questions are also proposed to enable students to acquire proficiency in technical writing and communication.

CD-ROM Accompanying This Book

Included in the CD-ROM accompanying this book are:

- Programming Activity framework code
- Full example code from each chapter
- Browser-based modules with visual step-by-step demonstrations of code execution
- Links to various Integrated Development Environments
- Link to the most recent versions of Sun Java™ 2 Standard Edition V. 6.0 JDK

Appendices

The appendices include the following:

- Java reserved words and keywords
- Operator precedence
- Unicode character set
- Representing negative numbers
- Representing floating-point numbers
- Java classes and APIs presented in this book
- Answers to selected exercises

Instructor Resources

These materials are available to instructors on the Jones and Bartlett website (http://www.jbpub.com/catalog/9780763749637/), and include

- Programming activity solution code (for instructors only)
- Answers to many end-of-chapter exercises
- PowerPoint slides for each chapter
- Test Items

Contacting the Authors

We have checked and rechecked the many technical details in this book. Despite our best efforts, however, we realize that some errors may have been missed. If you discover a technical error in the book, please contact us at jaanderson@capitol-college.edu or hfranceschi@capitol-college.edu. We will post any corrections on the book's website: http://www.jbpub.com/catalog/9780763749637/.

Acknowledgments

We would like to acknowledge the contributions of many partners, colleagues, and family members to this book.

First and foremost, we would like to thank our publisher, Jones and Bartlett, especially Tim Anderson, Acquisitions Editor; Amy Rose, Production Director; and Laura Pagluica, Editorial Assistant. We also want to thank Sarah Bayle, Production Assistant; Roya Millard, Production Assistant; Mike and Sigrid Wile of Northeast Compositors; Jenny Bagdigian, who copyedited the manuscript; and Kristin E. Ohlin, who designed the text and cover.

Second, we extend our thanks to the reviewers: Katrin Becker, University of Calgary; Yonshik Choi, Illinois Institute of Technology; Raj Gill, Anne Arundel Community College; Mark M. Meysenburg, Doane College; Roberta Evans Sabin and James Glenn, Loyola College of Maryland; Aaron Stevens, Boston University; Robert Burton, Brigham Young University; Barbara Guillott, Louisiana State University; James Brzowski, University of Massachusetts, Lowell; Paul Tymann, Rochester Institute of Technology; Daniel Joyce, Villanova University; Paolo Bucci, The Ohio State University; Gian Mario Basani, DePaul University; and Hans Peter Bischof, Rensselaer Polytechnic Institute. We have taken your thoughtful comments to heart and we think the book is better for them.

Julie Anderson would also like to acknowledge the pedagogical insight of Richard Rasala and Viera Proulx of Northeastern University. Thanks also to Jon Dornback, Damian Hart, and our colleagues Pat Smit and Earl Gottsman.

I am extremely grateful for the help extended by many family members: my father, Glenn Austin, son Brian Anderson, daughter-in-law Silvia Eckert, sister Kathleen Harmeyer, and mother-in-law Virginia Anderson. And of course, much gratitude goes to my loving husband, Tom, for his support and encouragement.

—Julie Anderson

I also recognize the support of my family. In particular, my brother, Paul, provided feedback on our sample chapter and the movies, and my wife, Kristin, gave her support and provided advice.

—Hervé Franceschi

Contents

CHAPTER 1

Introduction to Programming and the Java Language

CHAPTER CONTENTS

Introduction

Computer applications touch almost every aspect of our lives. They run automated teller machines, the grocery store's checkout register, the appointment calendar at your doctor's office, airport kiosks for flight check-in, a restaurant's meal-ordering system, and online auctions, just to name a few applications. On your personal computer, you may run a word processor, virus detection software, a spreadsheet, computer games, and an image processing system.

Someone, usually a team of programmers, wrote those applications. If you're reading this book, you're probably curious about what's involved in writing applications, and you would like to write a few yourself. Perhaps you have an idea for the world's next great application or computer game.

In this book, we'll cover the basics of writing applications. Specifically, we'll use the Java programming language. Keep in mind, however, that becoming a good programmer requires more than mastering the rules, or **syntax**, of a programming language. You also must master basic programming techniques. These are established methods for performing common programming operations, such as calculating a total, finding an average, or arranging a group of items in order.

You also must master good software engineering principles, so that you design code that is readable, easily maintained, and reusable. By readable, we mean that someone else should be able to read your program and figure out what it does and how it does it. Writing readable code is especially important for programmers who want to advance in their careers, because it allows someone else to take over the maintenance of your program while you move on to bigger and better responsibilities. Ease of maintenance is also an important aspect of programming, because the specifications for any program are continually changing. How many programs can you name that have had only one version? Not many. Well-designed code allows you and others to incorporate prewritten and pretested modules into your program, thus reducing the time to develop a program and yielding code that is more robust and has fewer bugs. One useful feature of the Java programming language is the large supply of prewritten code that you are free to use in your programs.

Programming is an exciting activity. It's very satisfying to decompose a complex task into computer instructions and watch your program come alive. It can be frustrating, however, when your program either doesn't run at all or produces the wrong output.

Writing correct programs is critical. Someone's life or life savings may depend on the correctness of your program. Reusing code helps in developing correct programs, but you must also master effective testing techniques to verify that the output of your program is correct.

In this book, we'll concentrate not only on the syntax of the Java language, but also on basic programming techniques, good software engineering principles, and effective testing techniques.

Before you can write programs, however, it's important to understand the platform on which your program will run. A platform refers to the computer hardware and the operating system. Your program will use the hardware for inputting data, for performing calculations, and for outputting results. The operating system will start your program running and will provide your program with essential resources, such as memory, and services, such as reading and writing files.

1.1 Basic Computer Concepts

1.1.1 Hardware

As shown in Figure 1.1, a computer typically includes the following components:

- a CPU, or central processing unit, which executes the instructions of a program
- a memory unit, which holds the instructions and data of a program while it is executing
- a hard disk, used to store programs and data so that they can be loaded into memory and accessed by the CPU
- a keyboard and mouse, used for input of data
- a monitor, used to display output from a program
- an Ethernet port and wireless networking transceiver for connecting to the Internet or a Local Area Network (LAN)
- other components (not shown) such as a graphics card and a DVD drive

Figure 1.1
A Typical Design of a Personal Computer

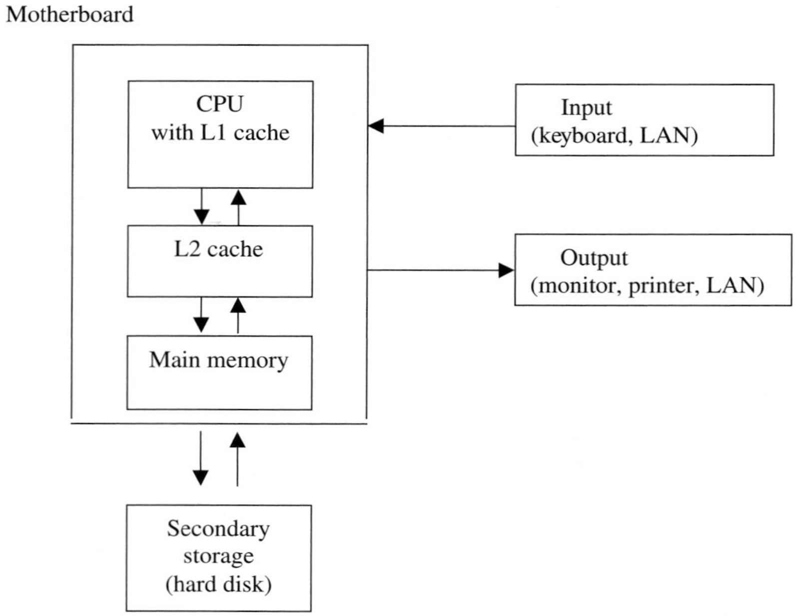

For example, if you were to go to a computer store in search of the latest personal computer, you might be shown a computer with this set of specifications:

- a 2.4-GHz Intel Core 2 Duo™ or AMD Turion™ 64 processor
- 1 MB of L2 cache memory
- 1 GB of RAM (Random Access Memory)
- a 200-GB hard disk

In these specifications, the Intel Core 2 Duo™ or AMD Turion™ 64 processor is the CPU. Other processors used as CPUs in desktop computers and servers include the Sun Microsystems SPARC, the Hewlett-Packard PA-RISC processor, and the IBM POWER processor.

CPUs consist of an Arithmetic Logic Unit (ALU) [also called an Integer Unit (IU)], which performs basic integer arithmetic and logical operations; a Floating Point Unit (FPU), which performs floating-point arithmetic; a set of hardware registers for holding data and memory addresses; and other supporting hardware, including a control unit to sequence the instructions. Each CPU comes with its own set of instructions, which are the operations that it can perform. The instructions typically perform arithmetic and logic operations, move data from one location to another, and change the flow of the program (that is, determine which instruction is to be executed next).

The first step in executing a program is loading it into memory. The CPU then fetches the program instructions from memory one at a time and executes them. A program consists of many instructions. An Instruction Pointer register (also called a Program Counter) keeps track of the current instruction being executed.

The speed of a CPU is related to its clock cycle, typically rated in MHz (Megahertz) or even GHz (Gigahertz); at the time of this edition, a high-end CPU speed would be rated at 3.4 GHz. It takes one clock cycle for a processor to fetch an instruction from memory, decode an instruction, or execute it. Current RISC processors feature pipelining, which allows the CPU to process several instructions at once, so that while one instruction is executing, the processor can decode the next instruction, and fetch the next instruction after that. This greatly improves performance of applications.

A CPU rated at 500 MHz is capable of executing 500 million instructions per second. That translates into executing one instruction every two 10^{-9} seconds (or two nanoseconds).

A CPU rated at 2 GHz is capable of executing 2 billion instructions per second. That translates into executing one instruction every 0.5 10^{-9} seconds (or half a nanosecond).

Memory or storage devices, such as L2 cache, memory, or hard disk, are typically rated in terms of their capacity, expressed in bytes. A byte is eight binary digits, or bits. A single bit's value is 0 or 1. Depending on the type of memory or storage device, the capacity will be stated in Kilobytes, Megabytes, or Gigabytes. The sizes of these units are shown in Table 1.1.

TABLE 1.1 Memory Units and Their Sizes

Memory Unit	Size
KB, or Kbytes, or Kilobytes	About 1,000 bytes (exactly 2^{10} or 1,024 bytes)
MB, or Mbytes, or Megabytes	About 1 million bytes (exactly 2^{20} or 1,048,576 bytes)
GB, or Gbytes, or Gigabytes	About 1 billion bytes (exactly 2^{30} or 1,073,741,824 bytes)

For the CPU to execute at its rated speed, however, instructions and data must be available to the CPU at that speed as well. Instructions and data come directly from the L1 cache, which is memory directly located on the CPU chip. Since L1 cache is located on the CPU chip, it runs at the same speed as the CPU. However, L1 cache typically is small, for example, 32 Kbytes, and eventually the CPU will need to process more instructions and data than can be held in the L1 cache at one time. At that point, the CPU typically brings data from what is called the L2 cache, which is located on separate memory chips connected to the CPU. A typical speed for the L2 cache would be 10 nanoseconds access time, and this will considerably slow down the rate at which the CPU can execute instructions. L2 cache size today is typically 256 Kbytes or 512 Kbytes, and again, the CPU will eventually need more space for instructions and data than the L2 cache can hold at one time. At that point, the CPU will bring data and instructions from main memory, also located outside, but connected to, the CPU chip. This will slow down the CPU even more, because main memory typically has an access time of about 50 nanoseconds. Main memory, though, is significantly larger in size than the L1 and L2 caches, typically anywhere between 128 and 512 Mbytes. When the CPU runs out of space again, it will have to get its data from the hard disk, which is typically between 20 and 80 Gbytes in size, but with an access time in the milliseconds range.

As you can see from these numbers, a considerable amount of speed is lost when the CPU goes from main memory to disk, which is why having sufficient memory is very important for the overall performance of applications.

Another factor that should be taken into consideration is cost per Kilobyte. Typically the cost per Kilobyte decreases significantly stepping down from L1 cache to hard disk, so high performance is often traded for low price.

Main memory (also called RAM) uses DRAM, or Dynamic Random Access Memory technology, which maintains data only when power is applied to the memory and needs to be refreshed regularly in order to retain data. L1 and L2 cache use SRAM, or Static Random Access Memory technology, which also needs power but does not need to be refreshed in order to retain data. Memory capacities are typically stated in powers of 2. For instance, 256 Kbytes of memory is 2^{18} bytes, or 262,144 bytes.

Memory chips contain cells, each cell containing a bit, which can store either a 0 or a 1. Cells can be accessed individually or as a group of typically

TABLE 1.2 A Comparison of Memory Types

Device	Location	Type	Speed	Capacity (MB)	Cost/KB
L1 cache	On-chip	SRAM	Very fast	Very small	Very high
L2 cache	Off-chip	SRAM	Fast	Small	High
Memory	Off-chip	DRAM	Moderate	Moderate	Moderate
Hard disk	Separate	Disk media	Slow	Large	Small

4, 8, or 16 cells. For instance, a 32-Kbit RAM chip organized as $8K \times 4$ is composed of exactly 2^{13}, or 8,192 units, each unit containing four cells. This RAM chip will have four data output pins (or lines) and 13 access pins (or lines), enabling access to all 8,192 cells because each access pin can have a value of 0 or 1. Table 1.2 compares the features of various memory types.

1.1.2 Operating Systems

An operating system (OS) is a software program that

- controls the peripheral devices (for instance, it manages the file system)
- supports multitasking, by scheduling multiple programs to execute during the same interval
- allocates memory to each program, so that there is no conflict among the memory of any programs running at the same time
- prevents the user from damaging the system. For instance, it prevents user programs from overwriting the OS or another program's memory

The operating system loads, or **boots**, when the computer system is turned on and is intended to run as long as the computer is running.

Examples of operating systems are MacOS for the Macintosh computers, Microsoft Windows, Unix, and Linux. Windows has evolved from a single-user, single-task DOS operating system to the multiuser, multitasking Windows Vista. Unix and Linux, on the other hand, were designed from the beginning to be multiuser, multitasking operating systems.

1.1.3 Application Software

Application software consists of the programs written to perform specific tasks. These programs are run by the operating system, or as is typically said, they are run "on top of" the operating system. Examples of applications are word processors, such as Microsoft Word or Corel WordPerfect; spreadsheets, such as Microsoft Excel; database management systems, such as Oracle or Microsoft SQL Server; Internet browsers, such as Mozilla Firefox and Microsoft Internet Explorer; and most of the programs you will write during your study of Computer Science.

1.1.4 Computer Networks and the Internet

Computer Networks

Computer networks connect two or more computers. A common network used by many corporations and universities is a LAN, or Local Area Network. A typical LAN connects several computers that are geographically close to one another, often in the same building, and allows them to share resources, such as a printer, a database, or a file system. In a LAN, most user computers are called **clients**, and one or more computers act as a **server**. The server controls access to resources on the network and can supply services to the clients, such as answering database requests, storing and serving files, or managing email.

The Internet

The Internet is a network of networks, connecting millions of computers around the world. The Internet evolved from ARPANET, a 1969 U.S. military research project whose goal was to design a method for computers to communicate. Most computers on the Internet are clients, typically requesting resources, such as web pages, through an Internet browser. These resources are provided by web servers, which store web pages and respond to these requests.

For example, when you, acting as a client, type *www.yahoo.com/index.html* into your web browser, you are requesting a resource. Here that resource is a web page (*index.html*), from the web server located at *www.yahoo.com*. That request will make its way to the server with the help of routers—special computers that find a path through the Internet networks from your computer to the correct destination.

Every machine on the Internet has a unique ID, called its IP address (IP stands for Internet Protocol). A computer can have a static IP address, which is dedicated to that machine, or a dynamic IP address, which is assigned to the computer when it connects to the Internet. An IP address is made up of four octets, whose values in decimal notation are between 0 and 255. For instance, 58.203.151.103 could represent such an IP address. In binary notation, this IP address is 111010.11001011.10010111.1100111. Later in this chapter, we will learn how to convert a decimal number, such as 103, to its binary equivalent, 1100111.

Most people are familiar with URL (Uniform Resource Locator) addresses that look like *www.yahoo.com*. URLs are actually Internet domain names. Domain name resolution servers, which implement the Domain Name System (DNS), convert domain names to IP addresses, so that Internet users don't need to know the IP addresses of websites they want to visit. The World Wide Web Consortium (W3C), an international group developing standards for Internet access, prefers the term Uniform Resource Identifier (URI) rather than URL, because URI covers future Internet addressing schemes.

Skill Practice
with these end-of-chapter questions

1.7.1 Multiple Choice Exercises

Questions 1, 2, 3, 4

1.7.3 General Questions

Questions 21, 22, 23

1.7.4 Technical Writing

Questions 31, 32, 33

1.2 Practice Activity: Displaying System Configuration

We have explored hardware and operating systems in general. Now, let's discover some information about the hardware and operating system on your computer. Depending on whether you're using a Windows operating system or a Linux operating system, choose the appropriate directions that follow to display the operating system's name, the CPU type, how much memory the computer has, and your home directory (for Unix/Linux users).

1.2.1 Displaying Windows Configuration Information

To display system configuration information on a Windows computer, run *msinfo32.exe* from the command line. From the *Start* menu, select *Run* and type *msinfo32* into the text box. You will get a display similar to the one in Figure 1.2, although the information displayed varies, depending on your hardware and the version of Windows you are running.

As you can see in Figure 1.2, this computer is running Windows Vista. The CPU is an AMD Turion™ 64 processor running at 2.4 GHz, and the computer has 2 GB of memory, 1 GB of which is not being used at the time of the display.

1.2.2 Displaying Unix/Linux Configuration Information

1. To retrieve the name of the operating system, at the $ prompt, type `echo $OSTYPE`.

```
$ echo $OSTYPE
linux-gnu
```

   This tells you that the machine is running the GNU version of the Linux operating system.

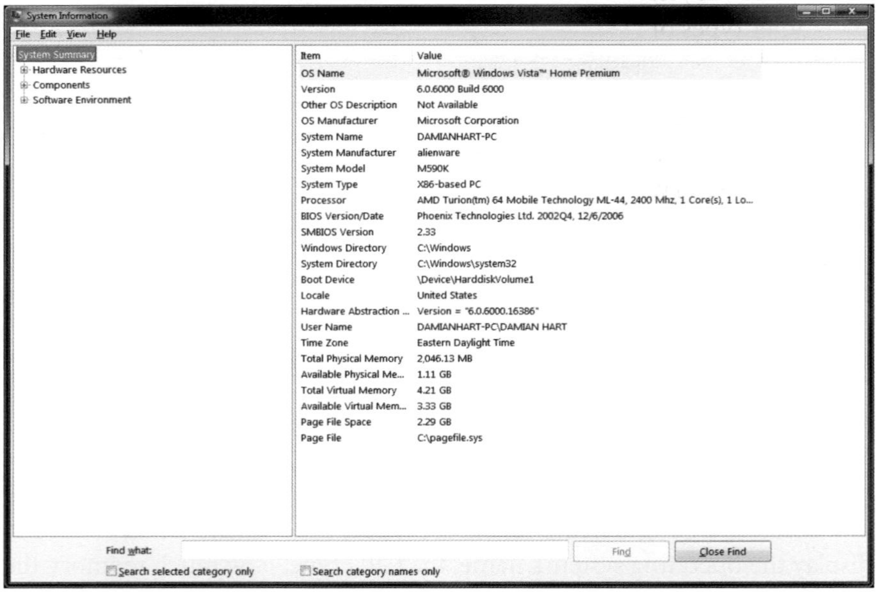

Figure 1.2
System Information

2. To retrieve the name of your home directory, at the prompt, type `echo $HOME`.

```
$ echo $HOME
/home/username
```

3. To retrieve information about your computer's main memory, at the prompt, type `cat /proc/meminfo`. This will display the contents of the file *meminfo* in the *proc* directory.

```
$ cat /proc/meminfo
      total:    used:     free:    shared:  buffers: cached:
Mem:  131158016 120090624 11067392 17285120 13152256 91246592
Swap: 271425536 3055616   268369920
MemTotal:      128084 kB
MemFree:        10808 kB
MemShared:      16880 kB
Buffers:        12844 kB
Cached:         89108 kB
SwapTotal:    265064 kB
SwapFree:     262080 kB
```

From this display, we see that the computer has 128 Mbytes of memory, 10 Mbytes of which is not being used at the time of the display. Other types of memory are also shown here, but discussion of these types of memory is beyond the scope of this course.

4. To retrieve information on your computer's CPU, type `cat /proc/cpuinfo`. This will display the contents of the file *cpuinfo* in the *proc* directory.

```
$ cat /proc/cpuinfo
processor       : 0
vendor_id       : GenuineIntel
cpu family      : 6
model           : 1
model name      : Pentium Pro
stepping        : 7
cpu MHz         : 199.459
cache size      : 256 KB
fdiv_bug        : no
```

```
hlt_bug          : no
sep_bug          : no
f00f_bug         : no
coma_bug         : no
fpu              : yes
fpu_exception    : yes
cpuid level      : 2
wp               : yes
flags            : fpu vme de pse tsc msr pae mce cx8 sep mtrr pge
                   mca cmov
bogomips         : 397.31
```

From this display, we see that the computer's CPU is an Intel Pentium Pro, running at 200 MHz. Again, discussion of the other information displayed is beyond the scope of this course.

DISCUSSION QUESTIONS ?

1. Compare the system information on several computers. Is it the same or different from computer to computer? Explain why the information is the same or different.
2. In the sample display for Windows Vista, the computer has 2 GB of memory, but only 1 GB of memory is available. Why do you think some memory is not available?
3. Compare your computer to the ones on the previous pages shown here. Which do you think would have better performance? Explain your answer.

1.3 Data Representation

1.3.1 Binary Numbers

As mentioned earlier, a CPU understands only binary numbers, whose digits consist of either 0 or 1. All data is stored in a computer's memory as binary digits. A bit holds one binary digit. A byte holds eight binary digits.

Binary numbers are expressed in the base 2 system, because there are only 2 values in that system, 0 and 1. By contrast, most people are used to the decimal, or base 10, system, which uses the values 0 through 9.

There are other number systems, such as the octal, or base 8, system, which uses the digits from 0 to 7, and the hexadecimal, or base 16, system, which uses the digits 0 to 9 and the letters A to F.

As we know it in the decimal system, the number 359 is composed of the following three digits:

3, representing the hundreds, or 10^2
5, representing the tens, or 10^1
9, representing the ones, or 10^0

Therefore, we can write 359 as

$$359 = 3*10^2 + 5*10^1 + 9*10^0$$

Thus, the decimal number 359 is written as a linear combination of powers of 10 with coefficients from the base 10 alphabet, that is the digits from 0 to 9. Similarly, the binary number 11011 is written as a linear combination of powers of 2 with coefficients from the base 2 alphabet, that is, the digits 0 and 1.

For example, the binary number 11011 can be written as

$$11011 = 1*2^4 + 1*2^3 + 0*2^2 + 1*2^1 + 1*2^0$$

Table 1.3 lists the binary equivalents for the decimal numbers 0 through 8, while Table 1.4 lists the decimal equivalents of the first 15 powers of 2.

TABLE 1.3 Binary Equivalents of Decimal Numbers 0 Through 8

Decimal	Binary
0	0000
1	0001
2	0010
3	0011
4	0100
5	0101
6	0110
7	0111
8	1000

TABLE 1.4 Powers of 2 and Their Decimal Equivalents

2^{14}	2^{13}	2^{12}	2^{11}	2^{10}	2^9	2^8	2^7	2^6	2^5	2^4	2^3	2^2	2^1	2^0
16,384	8,192	4,096	2,048	1,024	512	256	128	64	32	16	8	4	2	1

Note that in Table 1.3, as we count in increments of 1, the last digit alternates between 0 and 1. In fact, we can see that for even numbers, the last digit is always 0 and for odd numbers, the last digit is always 1.

Because computers store numbers as binary, and people recognize numbers as decimal values, conversion between the decimal and binary number systems often takes place inside a computer.

Let's try a few conversions. To convert a binary number to a decimal number, multiply each digit in the binary number by $2^{\text{position}-1}$, counting the rightmost position as position 1 and moving left through the binary number. Then add the products together.

Using this method, let's calculate the equivalent of the binary number 11010 in our decimal system.

$$
\begin{aligned}
11010 &= 1*2^4 + 1*2^3 + 0*2^2 + 1*2^1 + 0*2^0 \\
&= 16 + 8 + 0 + 2 + 0 \\
&= 26
\end{aligned}
$$

Now let's examine how to convert a decimal number to a binary number. Let's convert the decimal number 359 into its binary number equivalent. As we can see from the way we rewrote 11011, a binary number can be written as a sum of powers of 2 with coefficients 0 and 1.

The strategy to decompose a decimal number into a sum of powers of 2 is simple: first find the largest power of 2 that is smaller than or equal to the decimal number, subtract that number from the decimal number, then do the same with the remainder, and so on, until you reach 0.

The largest power of 2 that is smaller than 359 is 256 or 2^8 (the next larger power of 2 would be 512, which is larger than 359). Subtracting 256 from 359 gives us 103 ($359 - 256 = 103$), so we now have

$$359 = 2^8*1 + 103$$

Now we apply the same procedure to 103. The largest power of 2 that is smaller than 103 is 64 or 2^6. That means that there is no factor for 2^7, so that digit's value is 0. Subtracting 64 from 103 gives us 39.

Now we have

$$359 = 2^8*1 + 2^7*0 + 2^6*1 + 39$$

Repeating the procedure for 39, we find that the largest power of 2 smaller than 39 is 32 or 2^5. Subtracting 32 from 39 gives us 7.

So we now have

$$359 = 2^{8}*1 + 2^{7}*0 + 2^{6}*1 + 2^{5}*1 + 7$$

Repeating the procedure for 7, the largest power of 2 smaller than 7 is 2^2, or 4. That means that there are no factors for 2^4 or 2^3, so the value for each of those digits is 0. Subtracting 4 from 7 gives us 3, so we have

$$359 = 2^{8}*1 + 2^{7}*0 + 2^{6}*1 + 2^{5}*1 + 2^{4}*0 + 2^{3}*0 + 2^{2}*1 + 3$$

Repeating the procedure for 3, the largest power of 2 smaller than 3 is 2 or 2^1 and we have:

$$359 = 2^{8}*1 + 2^{7}*0 + 2^{6}*1 + 2^{5}*1 + 2^{4}*0 + 2^{3}*0 + 2^{2}*1 + 2^{1}*1 + 1$$

1 is a power of 2; it is 2^0, so we finally have

$$359 = 2^{8}*1 + 2^{7}*0 + 2^{6}*1 + 2^{5}*1 + 2^{4}*0 + 2^{3}*0 + 2^{2}*1 + 2^{1}*1 + 2^{0}*1$$

Removing the power of 2 multipliers, 359 can be represented in the binary system as

$$\begin{aligned} 359 &= 2^{8}*1 + 2^{7}*0 + 2^{6}*1 + 2^{5}*1 + 2^{4}*0 + 2^{3}*0 + 2^{2}*1 + 2^{1}*1 + 2^{0}*1 \\ &= 1 \quad 0 \quad 1 \quad 1 \quad 0 \quad 0 \quad 1 \quad 1 \quad 1 \end{aligned}$$

or

```
1 0110 0111
```

CODE IN ACTION

To see a step-by-step demonstration of converting between decimal and binary numbers, look for the Flash movie on the CD-ROM included with this book. Click on the link for Chapter 1 to start the movie.

In a computer program, we will use both positive and negative numbers. Appendix D explains how negative numbers, such as –34, are represented in the binary system. In a computer program, we also use floating-point numbers, such as 3.75. Appendix E explains how floating-point numbers are represented using the binary system.

1.3.2 Using Hexadecimal Numbers to Represent Binary Numbers

As you can see, binary numbers can become rather long. With only two possible values, 0 and 1, it takes 16 binary digits to represent the decimal value +32,768. For that reason, the hexadecimal, or base 16, system is often used as a shorthand representation of binary numbers. The hexadecimal system uses 16 digits: 0 to 9 and A to F. The letters A to F represent the values 10, 11, 12, 13, 14, and 15.

The maximum value that can be represented in four binary digits is $2^4 - 1$, or 15. The maximum value of a hexadecimal digit is also 15, which is represented by the letter F. So you can reduce the size of a binary number by using hexadecimal digits to represent each group of four binary digits.

Table 1.5 displays the hexadecimal digits along with their binary equivalents.

To represent the following binary number in hexadecimal, you simply substitute the appropriate hex digit for each set of four binary digits.

```
0001 1010 1111 1001 1011 0011 1011 1110
 1    A    F    9    B    3    B    E
```

TABLE 1.5 Hexadecimal Digits and Equivalent Binary Values

Hex Digit	Binary Value
0	0000
1	0001
2	0010
3	0011
4	0100
5	0101
6	0110
7	0111
8	1000
9	1001
A	1010
B	1011
C	1100
D	1101
E	1110
F	1111

Here's an interesting sequence of hexadecimal numbers. The first 32 bits of every Java applet are:

```
1100 1010 1111 1110 1011 1010 1011 1110
```

Translated into hexadecimal, that binary number becomes:

```
CAFE BABE
```

1.3.3 Representing Characters with the Unicode Character Set

Java represents characters using the Unicode Worldwide Character Standard, or simply Unicode. Each Unicode character is represented as 16 bits, or two bytes. This means that the Unicode character set can encode 65,536 characters.

The Unicode character set was developed by the Unicode Consortium, which consists of computer manufacturers, software vendors, the governments of several nations, and others. The consortium's goal was to support an international character set, including the printable characters on the standard QWERTY keyboard, as well as international characters such as é or λ.

Many programming languages store characters using the ASCII (American Standard Code for Information Interchange) character set, which uses 7 bits to encode each character, and thus, can represent only 128 characters. For compatibility with the ASCII character set, the first 128 characters in the Unicode character set are the same as the ASCII character set.

Table 1.6 shows a few examples of Unicode characters and their decimal equivalents.

For more information on the Unicode character set, see Appendix C or visit the Unicode Consortium's website at *http://www.Unicode.org.*

Skill Practice
with these end-of-chapter questions

1.7.1 Multiple Choice Exercises

Questions 5, 6, 7, 8

1.7.2 Converting Numbers

Questions 15, 16, 17, 18, 19, 20

1.7.3 General Questions

Questions 24, 25, 26

TABLE 1.6 Selected Unicode Characters and Their Decimal Equivalents

Unicode Character	Decimal Value
NUL, the null character (a nonprintable character)	0
*	42
1	49
2	50
A	65
B	66
a	97
b	98
}	125
delete (a nonprintable character)	127

1.4 Programming Languages

1.4.1 High- and Low-Level Languages

Programming languages can be categorized into three types:

- machine language
- assembly language
- high-level language

In the early days of computing, programmers often used machine language or assembly language. Machine language uses binary codes, or strings of 0s and 1s, to execute the instruction set of the CPU and to refer to memory addresses. This method of programming is extremely challenging and time consuming. Also, the code written in machine language is not portable to other computer architectures. Machine language's early popularity can be attributed largely to the fact that programmers had no other choices. However, programmers rarely use machine language today.

Assembly languages are one step above machine language, using symbolic names for memory addresses and mnemonics for processor instructions, for example: *BEQ* (branch if equal), *SW* (store), or *LW* (load). An Assembler program converts the code to machine language before it is executed. Like machine language, assembly languages are also CPU-dependent and are not portable among computers with different processors (for instance, between Intel and SPARC). Assembly language is easier to write than machine language, but still requires a significant effort, and thus is usually used only when the program requires features, such as direct hardware access, that are not supported by a high-level language.

High-level languages, such as Fortran, Pascal, Perl, C, C++, and Java, are closer to the English language than they are to machine language, making them a lot easier to use for software development and more portable among CPU architectures. For this reason, programmers have embraced high-level languages for more and more applications.

Characteristics of high-level languages, such as Java, are

- The languages are highly symbolic. Programmers write instructions using keywords and special characters and use symbolic names for data.
- The languages are somewhat portable (some more portable than others) among different CPUs.
- The languages can be specialized, for instance:
  - C, C++, and Java are used for general-purpose applications.
  - Perl is used for Internet applications.
  - Fortran is used for scientific applications.
  - COBOL is used for business applications and reports.
  - Lisp and Prolog are used for artificial intelligence applications.

High-level languages are compiled, interpreted, or a combination of both. A program written in a compiled language, such as C or C++, is converted by a compiler into machine code, then the machine code is executed.

By contrast, a program written using an interpreted language, such as Perl, is read and converted to machine code, line by line, at execution time. Typically, a program written in an interpreted language will run more slowly than its equivalent written in a compiled language.

Java uses a combination of a compiler and an interpreter. A Java program is first compiled into processor-independent byte codes, then the byte code file is interpreted at run time by software called the Java Virtual Machine (JVM).

1.4.2 An Introduction to Object-Oriented Programming

Initial high-level languages, such as Fortran or Pascal, were procedural. Typically, programmers wrote task-specific code in separate procedures, or functions, and invoked these procedures from other sections of the program in order to perform various tasks. The program's data was generally shared among the procedures.

In the mid-1970s, the first object-oriented programming language, Smalltalk, was introduced, enabling programmers to write code with a different approach. Whereas procedures or functions dealt mainly with basic data types such as integers, real numbers, or single characters, Smalltalk provided the programmer with a new tool: classes and objects of those classes.

A class enables the programmer to encapsulate data and the functions needed to manipulate that data into one package. A class essentially defines a template, or model, from which objects are created. Creating an object is called **instantiation**. Thus, objects are created—instantiated—according to the design of the class.

A class could represent something in real life, such as a person. The class could have various attributes such as, in the example of a "person" class, a first name, a last name, and an age. The class would also provide code, called **methods**, that allow the creator of the object to set and retrieve the values of the attributes.

One big advantage to object-oriented programming is that well-written classes can be reused by new programs, thereby reducing future development time.

Smalltalk was somewhat successful, but had a major deficiency: its syntax was unlike any syntax already known by most programmers. Most programmers who knew C, were attracted by the object-oriented features of Smalltalk, but were reluctant to use it because its syntax was so different from C's syntax. C++ added object-oriented features to C, but also added complexity.

Meanwhile, the Internet was growing by leaps and bounds and gaining popularity daily. Web developers used HTML to develop web pages and soon felt the need to incorporate programming features not only on the server side, but also directly on the client side. Fortunately, Java appeared on the scene.

1.4.3 The Java Language

On May 23, 1995, Sun Microsystems introduced Java, originally named Oak, as a free, object-oriented language targeted at embedded applications for consumer devices. A Java Virtual Machine was incorporated immediately into the Netscape Navigator Internet browser, and as the Internet grew, small Java programs, known as applets, began to appear on web pages in increasing numbers. Java syntax is basically identical (with some minor exceptions) to that of C++, and soon programmers all over the world started to realize the benefits of using Java. Those benefits include

- syntax identical to that of C++, except that Java eliminates some of C++'s more complex features
- object orientation
- Internet-related features, such as applets, which are run by the browser, and servlets, which are run by the web server
- an extensive library of classes that can be reused readily, including Swing classes for providing a Graphical User Interface and Java Database Connectivity (JDBC) for communicating with a database
- portability among every platform that supports a Java Virtual Machine
- built-in networking
- open source availability of the Java Development Kit

As we mentioned earlier, a Java program is first compiled into processor-independent byte codes, then the byte codes are interpreted at run time by the Java Virtual Machine (JVM). As its name implies, the JVM simulates a virtual processor with its own instruction set, registers, and instruction pointer. Thus, to run a Java program, you only need a JVM. Fortunately, JVMs are available on every major computing platform.

Because Java programs are interpreted at run time, they typically run more slowly than their C++ counterparts. However, many platforms provide Java compilers that convert source code directly to machine code. This results in greater execution speed, but with an accompanying loss of portability. Just-in-Time (JIT) compilers are also available. These JITs compile code at run time so that subsequent execution of the same code runs much faster.

Java programs can be written as applets, servlets, or applications.

Java applets are small programs designed to add interactivity to a web page. Applets are launched by an Internet browser; they cannot run standalone. As the user requests a web page that uses an applet, the applet is downloaded to the user's computer and run by the JVM in the browser. Due to browser incompatibilities, limitations imposed by security features, and slow download times, however, applets have fallen out of favor.

Java servlets are invoked by the web server and run on the server, without being downloaded to the client. Typically, servlets dynamically generate web content by reading and writing to a database using JDBC.

Java applications run standalone on a client computer. In this book, we will write a few applets, but mainly we will write Java applications.

Sun Microsystems provides a valuable website (*www.java.sun.com*), which has information on using the prewritten classes, a tutorial on Java, and many more resources for the Java programmer. We will refer you to that site often in this book.

1.5 An Introduction to Programming

1.5.1 Programming Basics

In many ways, programming is like solving a puzzle. You have a task to perform and you know the operations that a computer can perform (input, calculations, comparisons, rearranging of items, and output). As a programmer, your job is to decompose a task into individual, ordered steps of inputting, calculating, comparing, rearranging, and outputting.

For example, suppose your task is to find the sum of two numbers. First, your program needs to read (input) the numbers into the computer. Next, your program needs to add the two numbers together (calculate). Finally, your program needs to write (output) the sum.

Notice that this program consists of steps, called **instructions**, which are performed in order ("First," "Next," "Finally"). Performing operations in order, one after another, is called **sequential processing**.

The order in which instructions are executed by the computer is critical in programming. You can't calculate the sum of two numbers before you have read the two numbers, and you can't output a sum before you have calculated it. Programming, therefore, requires the programmer to specify the ordering of instructions, which is called the **flow of control** of the program. There are four different ways that the flow of control can progress through a program: sequential execution, method call, selection, and looping. We've just seen sequential execution, and we'll discuss the other types of flow of control in the next section.

Because getting the flow of control correct is essential to getting a program to produce correct output, programmers use a tool called **pseudocode** (pronounced *sue dough code*) to help them design the flow of control before writing the code.

1.5.2 Program Design with Pseudocode

Pseudocode, from *pseudo*, which means "appearing like," is a method for expressing a program's order of instructions in English language, rather than a programming language. In this way, the programmer can concentrate on designing a program without also being bogged down in the syntax of the particular programming language.

The pseudocode for calculating the sum of two numbers would look like Example 1.1.

```
read first number
read second number
set total to (first number + second number)
output total
```

EXAMPLE 1.1 Pseudocode for Summing Two Numbers

Fortunately, the rules for writing pseudocode are not rigid. Essentially, you can use any wording that works for you.

Let's look at another example. Suppose your program needs to calculate the square root of an integer. The instructions for calculating a square root are rather complex; fortunately, Java provides prewritten code that computes the square root of any integer. The prewritten code is called a **method**, and your program can execute that code by **calling the method**. As part of the method call, you tell the method which integer's square root you want to calculate. This is called **passing an argument to the method**. When the method finishes executing its instructions, control is passed back to your program just after the method call. Another way of looking at method calls is to consider what happens when you're reading a book and find a word you don't understand. You mark your place in the book and look up the word in a dictionary. When you're finished looking up the word, you go back to the book and continue reading.

Example 1.2 shows the pseudocode for calculating the square root of an integer.

```
read an integer
call the square root method, passing the integer and receiving the square root
output the square root of the integer
```

EXAMPLE 1.2 Using a Method Call to Calculate a Square Root

The order of operations is still input, calculate, and output, but we're calling a method to perform the calculation for us.

Now suppose your task is to determine whether a number is positive or negative. First, your program should input the number into the computer. Next, you need to determine whether the number is positive or negative. You know that numbers greater than or equal to 0 are positive and numbers less than 0 are negative, so your program should compare the number to 0. Finally, your program should write a message indicating whether the number is positive or negative.

Like Examples 1.1 and 1.2, the operations are input, calculate, and output, in that order. However, depending on whether the number is positive or negative, your program should write a different message. If the number is greater than or equal to 0, the program should write a message that the number is positive, but if the number is less than 0, the program should write a message that the number is negative. Code used to handle this situation is called **selection**; the program selects which code to execute based on the value of the data.

The pseudocode for this program could be written as that shown in Example 1.3.

```
read a number
if the number is greater than or equal to 0
   write "Number is positive."
else
   write "Number is negative."
```

EXAMPLE 1.3 Using Selection

Notice the indentation for the code that will be selected based on the comparison of the number with 0. Programmers use indentation to make it easier to see the flow of control of the program.

Now let's get a little more complicated. Suppose your program needs to find the sum of a group of numbers. This is called **accumulating**. To accomplish this, we can take the same approach as if we were adding a group of numbers using a calculator. We start with a total of 0 and add each number, one at a time, to the running total. When we have no more numbers to add, the running total is the total of all the numbers.

Translating this into pseudocode, we get the code shown in Example 1.4.

```
set total to 0
read a number
while there was a number to read, repeat next two instructions
  add number to total
  read the next number
write total
```

EXAMPLE 1.4 Accumulating a Total

The indented code will be repeated for each number read until there are no more numbers. This repeated execution of the same code is called **looping**, or **iteration**, and is used extensively in programming whenever the same processing needs to be performed on each item in a set.

Accumulating a total and determining whether a number is positive or negative are just two of many commonly performed operations. In programming, you will often perform tasks for which there are standard methods of processing, called **algorithms**. For example, the algorithm for accumulation is to set a total to 0, use looping to add each item to the total, then output the total. More generally, you can think of an algorithm as a strategy to solve a problem. Earlier in the chapter, we used an algorithm to convert a decimal number to its binary representation.

Other common programming tasks are counting items, calculating an average, sorting items into order, and finding the minimum and maximum values. In this book, you will learn the standard algorithms for performing these common operations. Once you learn these algorithms, your programming job will become easier. When you recognize that a program requires these tasks, you can simply plug in the appropriate algorithm with some minor modifications.

Programming, in large part, is simply reducing a complex task to a set of subtasks that can be implemented by combining standard algorithms that use sequential processing, method calls, selection, and looping.

SOFTWARE ENGINEERING TIP

Looking for patterns will help you determine the appropriate algorithms for your programs.

The most difficult part of programming, however, is recognizing which algorithms to apply to the problem at hand. This requires analytical skills and the ability to see patterns. Throughout this book, we will point out common patterns wherever possible.

1.5.3 Developing a Java Application

Writing a Java application consists of several steps: writing the code, compiling the code, and executing the application. Java source code is stored in a text file with the extension *.java*. Compiling the code creates one or more *.class* files, which contain processor-independent byte codes. The Java Virtual Machine (JVM) translates the byte codes into machine-level instructions for the processor on which the Java application is running. Thus, if a Java application is running on an Intel Pentium 4 processor, the JVM translates the byte codes into the Pentium 4's instruction set.

Sun provides a Java SE Development Toolkit (JDK) on its website (*www.java.sun.com*), which is downloadable free of charge. The JDK contains a compiler, JVM, and an applet viewer, which is a minimal browser. In addition, the JDK contains a broad range of prewritten Java classes that programmers can use in their Java applications.

If you are downloading and installing Java yourself, be sure to follow the directions on the Sun Microsystems website, including the directions for setting the path for *javac*, the Java compiler. You need to set the path correctly so that you can run the Java compiler from any directory on your computer.

To develop an application using the JDK, write the source code using any text editor, such as Notepad, Wordpad, or the vi editor. To compile the code, invoke the compiler from the command line:

```
javac ClassName.java
```

where *ClassName.java* is the name of the source file.

If your program, written in the file *ClassName.java*, compiles correctly, a new file, *ClassName.class*, will be created in your current directory.

To run the application, you invoke the JVM from the command line:

```
java ClassName
```

Typically, programmers use an Integrated Development Environment (IDE) to develop applications. An IDE consists of a program editor, a compiler, and a run-time environment, integrated via a Graphical User Interface. The advantage to using an IDE is that errors in the Java code that are found by the compiler or the Java Virtual Machine can be linked directly to the program editor at the line in the source file that caused the error. Additionally, the Graphical User Interface enables the programmer to switch among the editor, compiler, and execution of the program without launching separate applications.

Some of the many available IDEs include Eclipse from the Eclipse Foundation, Inc.; JGrasp, developed at Auburn University; NetBeans, downloadable from Sun Microsystems; and TextPad from Helios Software Solutions. Some IDEs are freely available, while others require a software license fee. We include several IDEs on the CD-ROM included with this book.

Skill Practice
with these end-of-chapter questions

1.7.1 Multiple Choice Exercises

Questions 9, 10, 11, 12, 13, 14

1.7.3 General Questions

Questions 27, 28, 29, 30

1.7.4 Technical Writing

Question 34

1.5.4 Programming Activity 1: Writing a First Java Application

Let's create our first Java program. This program prints the message, "Programming is not a spectator sport!" on the screen.

Start by launching your IDE and open a new editor window. This is where you will write the code for the program.

Before we type any code, however, let's name the document. We do this by saving the document as *FirstProgram.java.* Be sure to capitalize the F and the P and keep the other letters lowercase. Java is case-sensitive, so Java considers *firstprogram.java* or even *Firstprogram.java* to be a different name.

Keeping case sensitivity in mind, type in the program shown in Example 1.5.

```
1 // First program in Java
2 // Anderson, Franceschi
3
4 public class FirstProgram
5 {
6   public static void main( String [ ] args )
7   {
8      System.out.println( "Programming is not a spectator sport!" );
9
10     System.exit( 0 );
11  }
12 }
```

EXAMPLE 1.5 A First Program in Java

At this point, we ask that you just type the program as you see it here, except for the line numbers, which are not part of the program. Line numbers are displayed in this example to allow easy reference to a particular line in the code. We'll explain a little about the program now; additional details will become clear as the semester progresses.

The first two lines, which start with two forward slashes, are comments. They will not be compiled or executed; they are simply information for the programmer and are used to increase the readability of the program.

COMMON ERROR TRAP

Java is case-sensitive. The class name and the file name must match exactly, including capitalization.

Line 4 defines the class name as *FirstProgram.* Notice that the class name must be spelled exactly the same way—including capitalization—as the file name, *FirstProgram.java.*

The curly braces in lines 5 and 12 mark the beginning and ending of the *FirstProgram* class, and the curly braces in lines 7 and 11 mark the beginning and ending of *main.* Every Java application must define a class and a *main* method. Execution of a Java application always begins with the code inside *main*. So when this application begins, it will execute line 8, which writes the message "*Programming is not a spectator sport!*" to the system console. Next, it executes line 10, *System.exit(0)*, which exits the program. Including this line is optional; if you omit this line, the application will exit normally.

As you type the program, notice that your IDE automatically colors your text to help you distinguish comments, *String* literals ("*Programming is not a spectator sport!*"), Java class names (*String, System*), and keywords (*public, class, static*), which are reserved for specific uses in Java. Curly braces, brackets, and parentheses, which have syntactical meaning in Java, are usually displayed in color as well. Your IDE may use different colors than those shown in Example 1.5.

When you have completed typing the code in Example 1.5, compile it. If everything is typed correctly, the compiler will create a *FirstProgram.class* file, which contains the byte codes for the program.

If you received any compiler errors, check that you have entered the code exactly as it is written in Example 1.5. We give you tips on finding and fixing the errors in the next section.

If you got a clean compile with no errors, congratulations! You're ready to execute the application. This will invoke the Java Virtual Machine and pass it the *FirstProgram.class* file created by the compiler. If all is well, you will see the message, *Programming is not a spectator sport!*, displayed on the **Java console,** which is the text window that opens automatically. Figure 1.3 shows the correct output of the program.

```
Programming is not a spectator sport!
```

Figure 1.3
Output from Example 1.5

Debugging Techniques

If the compiler found syntax errors in the code, these are called **compiler errors**, not because the compiler caused them, but because the compiler found them. When the compiler detects errors in the code, it writes diagnostic information about the errors.

For example, try typing *println* with a capital P (as *Println*), and recompiling. The compiler displays the following message:

```
FirstProgram.java:8: cannot find symbol
symbol  : method Println  (java.lang.String)
location: class java.io.PrintStream
      System.out.Println( "Programming is not a spectator sport!" );
                ^

1 error
```

The first line identifies the file name that contains the Java source code, as well as the line number in the source code where the error occurred. In this case, the error occurred on line 8. The second line identifies the symbol *Println* as being the cause of the error. As further help, the location information in the third and fourth lines display line 8 from the source code, using a caret (^) to point to *Println*. All these messages point you to line 8, especially emphasizing the spelling of *Println*. With most IDEs, double-clicking on the first line in the error message transfers you to the source code window with your cursor positioned on line 8 so you can correct the error.

Many times, the compiler will find more than one error in the source code. When that happens, don't panic. Often, a single problem, such as a missing semicolon or curly brace, can cause multiple compiler errors.

For example, after correcting the preceding error, try deleting the left curly brace in line 7, then recompiling. The compiler reports four errors:

```
FirstProgram.java:7: ';' expected
        public static void main( String [ ] args )
                                                 ^

FirstProgram.java:10: <identifier> expected
        System.exit( 0 );
                   ^

FirstProgram.java:10: illegal start of type
        System.exit( 0 );
                     ^
```

```
FirstProgram.java:12: class, interface or enum expected
}
^
4 errors
```

As you can see, the compiler messages do not always report the problem exactly. When you receive a compiler message, looking at the surrounding lines will often help you find the error. Depending on your IDE, you might see messages other than those shown here because some IDEs attempt to interpret the error messages from the compiler to provide more relevant information on the errors.

It is sometimes easier to fix one error at a time and recompile after each fix, because the first fix might eliminate many of the reported errors.

Software Engineering Tip

Because one syntax error can cause multiple compiler errors, correct only the obvious errors and recompile after each correction.

When all the compiler errors are corrected, you're ready to execute the program.

It is possible to get a clean bill of health from the compiler, yet the program still won't run. To demonstrate this, try eliminating the brackets in line 6 after the word *String*. If you then compile the program, no errors are reported. But when you try to run the program, you get a **run-time error**.

Instead of *Programming is not a spectator sport!*, the following message is displayed on the Java console:

```
Exception in thread "main" java.lang.NoSuchMethodError: main
```

When you see this error, it typically means that the *main* method header (line 6) was not typed correctly.

Thus, we've seen that two types of errors can occur while you are developing a Java program: compiler errors, which are usually caused by language syntax errors or misspellings, and run-time errors, which are often caused by problems using the prewritten classes. Run-time errors can also be caused by exceptions that the JVM detects as it is running, such as an attempt to divide by zero.

Testing Techniques

Once your program compiles cleanly and executes without run-time errors, you may be tempted to conclude that your job is finished. Far from it—you must also verify the results, or output, of the program.

In the sample program, it's difficult to get incorrect results—other than misspelling the message or omitting the spaces between the words. But

TABLE 1.7 Types of Program Errors and Their Causes

Type of Error	Usual Causes
Compiler errors	Incorrect language syntax or misspellings
Run-time errors	Incorrect use of classes
Logic errors	Incorrect program design or incorrect implementation of the design

any nontrivial program should be tested thoroughly before declaring it production-ready.

To test a program, consider all the possible inputs and the corresponding correct outputs. It often isn't feasible to test every possible input, so programmers usually test **boundary conditions**, which are the values that sit on the boundaries of producing different output for a program.

For example, to test the code that determines whether an integer is negative or nonnegative, you would feed the program −1 and 0. These are the boundaries of negative and nonnegative integers. In other words, the boundary between negative and nonnegative integers is between −1 and 0.

When a program does not produce the correct output, we say the program contains **logic errors**. By testing your program thoroughly, you can discover and correct most logic errors. Table 1.7 shows types of program errors and their usual causes.

We'll talk more about testing techniques throughout the book.

DISCUSSION QUESTIONS ?

1. In the Debugging Techniques section, we saw that making one typo could generate several compiler errors. Why do you think that happens?
2. Explain why testing boundary conditions is an efficient way to verify a program's correctness.
3. Did any errors occur while you were developing the first application? If so, explain whether they were compiler or run-time errors and what you did to fix them.

1.6 Chapter Summary

- Basic components of a computer include the CPU, memory, a hard disk, keyboard, monitor, and mouse.
- Each type of CPU has its own set of instructions for performing arithmetic and logical operations, moving data, and changing the order of execution of instructions.
- An operating system controls peripheral devices, supports multitasking, allocates memory to programs, and prevents the user from damaging the system.
- Computer networks link two or more computers so that they can share resources, such as files or printers.
- The Internet connects millions of computers around the world. Web servers deliver web pages to clients running Internet browsers.
- Binary numbers are composed of 0s and 1s. A bit holds one binary digit. A byte holds eight binary digits.
- To convert a binary number to a decimal number, multiply each digit in the binary number by $2^{\text{position}-1}$, counting the rightmost position as position 1 and moving left through the number. Then add the products together.
- To convert a decimal number into a binary number, first find the largest power of 2 that is smaller than or equal to the decimal number, subtract that number from the decimal number, then do the same with the remainder, and so on, until you reach 0.
- Hexadecimal digits can be used to represent groups of four binary digits.
- The Unicode character set, which Java uses, can encode up to 65,536 characters using 16 bits per character.
- Machine language and assembly language are early forms of programming languages that require the programmer to write to the CPU's instruction set. Because this low-level programming is time consuming, difficult, and the programs are not portable to other

CHAPTER SUMMARY

CPU architectures, machine language and assembly language are rarely used.

- High-level languages are highly symbolic and somewhat portable. They can be compiled, interpreted, or as in the case of Java, converted to byte codes, which are interpreted at run time.
- A good program is readable, easily maintained, and reusable.
- Object-oriented programming uses classes to encapsulate data and the functions needed to manipulate that data. Objects are instantiated according to the class design. An advantage to object-oriented programming is reuse of the classes.
- Programs use a combination of sequential processing, method calls, selection, and iteration to control the order of execution of instructions. Performing operations in order, one after another, is called sequential processing. Temporarily executing other code, then returning, is called a method call. Selecting which code to execute based on the value of data is called selection. Repeating the same code on each item in a group of values is called iteration, or looping.
- Pseudocode allows a programmer to design a program without worrying about the syntax of the language.
- In programming, you will often perform tasks for which there are standard methods of processing, called algorithms. For example, accumulating is a common programming operation that finds the sum of a group of numbers.
- Programming, in large part, is reducing a complex task to a set of subtasks that can be implemented by combining standard algorithms that use sequential processing, selection, and looping.
- Java source code is stored in a text file with an extension of *.java.* Compiling the code produces one or more *.class* files.
- An Integrated Development Environment (IDE) consists of a program editor, a compiler, and a run-time environment, integrated via a Graphical User Interface.

- Compiler errors are detected by the compiler and are usually caused by incorrect Java syntax or misspellings. Run-time errors are detected by the Java Virtual Machine and are usually caused by exceptions or incorrect use of classes. Logic errors occur during program execution and are caused by incorrect program design.

1.7 Exercises, Problems, and Projects

1.7.1 Multiple Choice Exercises

1. Which one of these is not an operating system?
   - ❑ Linux
   - ❑ Java
   - ❑ Windows
   - ❑ Unix
2. Which one of these is not an application?
   - ❑ Word
   - ❑ Internet Explorer
   - ❑ Linux
   - ❑ Excel
3. How many bits are in three bytes?
   - ❑ 3
   - ❑ 8
   - ❑ 24
   - ❑ 0
4. In a network, the computers providing services to the other computers are called
   - ❑ clients
   - ❑ servers
   - ❑ laptops

5. A binary number ending with a 0
   - ❑ is even
   - ❑ is odd
   - ❑ cannot tell
6. A binary number ending with a 1
   - ❑ is even
   - ❑ is odd
   - ❑ cannot tell
7. A binary number ending with two 0s
   - ❑ is a multiple of 4
   - ❑ is not a multiple of 4
   - ❑ cannot tell
8. Using four bits, the largest positive binary number we can represent is 1111
   - ❑ true
   - ❑ false
9. Which one of these is not a programming language?
   - ❑ C++
   - ❑ Java
   - ❑ Windows
   - ❑ Fortran
10. Which one of these is not an object-oriented programming language?
    - ❑ C
    - ❑ Java
    - ❑ C++
    - ❑ Smalltalk
11. What is the file extension for a Java source code file?
    - ❑ .java
    - ❑ .exe
    - ❑ .class

12. What is the file extension of a compiled Java program?
    - ❑ .java
    - ❑ .exe
    - ❑ .class
13. In order to compile a program named *Hello.java*, what do you type at the command line?
    - ❑ java Hello
    - ❑ java Hello.java
    - ❑ javac Hello
    - ❑ javac Hello.java
14. You have successfully compiled *Hello.java* into *Hello.class*. What do you type at the command line in order to run the application?
    - ❑ java Hello.class
    - ❑ java Hello
    - ❑ javac Hello
    - ❑ javac Hello.class

1.7.2 Converting Numbers

15. Convert the decimal number 67 into binary.
16. Convert the decimal number 1,564 into binary.
17. Convert the binary number 0001 0101 into decimal.
18. Convert the binary number 1101 0101 0101 into decimal.
19. Convert the binary number 0001 0101 into hexadecimal.
20. Convert the hexadecimal number D8F into binary.

1.7.3 General Questions

21. A RAM chip is organized as $\times$ 8 memory, i.e., each unit contains 8 bits, or a byte. There are 7 address pins on the chip. How many bytes does that memory chip contain?
22. If a CPU is rated at 750 MHz, how many instructions per second can the CPU execute?

23. If a CPU can execute 100 million instructions per second, what is the rating of the CPU in MHz?

24. Suppose we are using binary encoding to represent colors. For example, a black-and-white color system has only two colors and therefore needs only 1 bit to encode the color system as follows:

Bit	Color
0	black
1	white

With 2 bits, we can encode four colors as follows:

Bit pattern	Color
00	black
01	red
10	blue
11	white

With 5 bits, how many colors can we encode?

With *n* bits (*n* being a positive integer), how many colors can we encode? (Express your answer as a function of *n*.)

25. In HTML, a color can be coded in the following hexadecimal notation: #*rrggbb* where

rr represents the amount of red in the color

gg represents the amount of green in the color

bb represents the amount of blue in the color

rr, *gg*, and *bb* vary between 00 and FF in hexadecimal notation, i.e., 0 and 255 in decimal equivalent notation. Give the decimal values of the red, green, and blue values in the color #33AB12.

26. RGB is a color system representing colors: R stands for red, G for green, and B for blue. A color can be coded as *rgb* where *r* is a number between 0 and 255 representing how much red there is in the color; *g* is a number between 0 and 255 representing how much green there is in the color, and *b* is a number between 0 and 255 representing how

much blue there is in the color. The color grey is created by using the same value for *r*, *g*, and *b*. How many shades of grey are there?

27. List three benefits of the Java programming language.
28. What is the name of the Java compiler?
29. Write the pseudocode for a program that finds the product of two numbers.
30. Write the pseudocode for a program that finds the sums of the numbers input that are greater than or equal to 10 and the numbers input that are less than 10.

1.7.4 Technical Writing

31. List the benefits of having a Local Area Network vs. standalone computer systems.
32. For one day, keep a diary of the computer applications that you use. Also note any features of the applications that you think should be improved or any features you'd like to see added.
33. You are looking at two computers with the following specifications, everything else being equal:

PC # 1	PC # 2
2.4-GHz CPU	2-GHz CPU
256 KB L2 cache	256 KB L2 cache
128 MB RAM	512 MB RAM
60-GB Hard drive	60-GB Hard drive
$999	$999

Which PC would you buy? Explain the reasoning behind your selection.

34. Go to the Sun Microsystems Java site (*http://java.sun.com*). Explain what resources are available there for someone who wants to learn Java.

1.7.5 Group Project (for a group of 1, 2, or 3 students)

35. In the octal system, numbers are represented using digits from 0 to 7; a 0 is placed in front of the octal number to indicate that the octal

system is being used. For instance, here are some examples of the equivalent of some octal numbers in the decimal system:

Octal	Decimal
000	0
001	1
007	7
010	8
011	9

In the hexadecimal system, numbers are represented using digits from 0 to 9 and letters A to F; 0x is placed in front of the hexadecimal number to indicate that the hexadecimal system is being used. For instance, here are some examples of the decimal equivalents of some hexadecimal numbers:

Hexadecimal	Decimal
0x0	0
0x1	1
0x9	9
0xA	10
0xB	11
0xF	15
0x10	16
0x11	17
0x1C	28

1. Convert 0xC3E (in hexadecimal notation) into an octal number.
2. Convert 0377 (in octal notation) into a hexadecimal number.
3. Discuss how, in general, you would convert a hexadecimal number into an octal number and an octal number into a hexadecimal number.

CHAPTER 2

Programming Building Blocks—Java Basics

CHAPTER CONTENTS

Introduction

If you boil it down to the basics, a program has two elements: instructions and data. The instructions tell the CPU what to do with the data.

The data may be different in each execution of the program, but the instructions stay the same. In a word processor, the words (data) are different from document to document, but the operation (instructions) of the word processor remains the same. When a line becomes full, for example, the word processor automatically wraps to the next line. It doesn't matter which words are on the line, only that the line is full. When you select a word and change the font to bold, it doesn't matter which word you select, it will become bold.

In Chapter 1, we discussed the types of operations that the computer can perform: input, calculation, comparisons of data and subsequent changes to the flow of control, data movement, and output. The Java language provides a syntax for expressing instructions using keywords, operators, and punctuation. In this chapter, we'll look at basic Java syntax for defining data and performing calculations, data movement, and output.

The Java language also provides a syntax for describing a program's data using keywords, symbolic names, and data types. The data used by a program can come from a variety of sources. The user can enter data from the keyboard, as happens when you type a new document into a word processor. The program can read the data from a file, as happens when you load an existing document into the word processor. Or the program can generate the data itself, as happens when a computer card game deals hands. Finally, some data is already known, for example, the number of hours in a day is 24, the number of days in December is 31, and the value of pi is 3.14159. This type of data is constant. In this chapter, we'll discuss how to define the data to be used in the program, how to perform calculations on that data, and how to output program results to the screen.

2.1 Java Application Structure

Every Java program consists of at least one class. It is impossible to write a Java program that doesn't use classes. As we said in Chapter 1, classes describe a logical entity that has data as well as methods (the instructions) to manipulate that data. An object is a physical instantiation of the class that contains specific data. We'll begin to cover classes in detail in the next chapter. For now, we'll just say that your source code should take the form of the shell code in Example 2.1.

```
1 /*  An application shell
2     Anderson, Franceschi
3 */
4 public class ShellApplication
5 {
6    public static void main( String [ ] args ) //required
7    {
8       // write your code here
9    }
10 }
```

EXAMPLE 2.1 A Shell for a Java Application

In Example 2.1, the numbers to the left of each line are not part of the program code; they are included here for your convenience. IDEs typically allow you to display line numbers.

From application to application, the name of the class, *ShellApplication*, will change, because you will want to name your class something meaningful that reflects its function. Each Java source code file must have the same name as the class name with a *.java* extension. In this case, the source file must be *ShellApplication.java.* Whatever name you select for a class must comply with the Java syntax for identifiers.

Java **identifiers** are symbolic names that you assign to classes, methods, and data. Identifiers must start with a **Java letter** and may contain any combination of letters and digits, but no spaces. A Java letter is any character in the range *a–z* or *A–Z*, the underscore (_), or the dollar sign ($), as well as many Unicode characters that are used as letters in other languages. Digits are any character between 0 and 9. The length of an identifier is essentially unlimited. Identifier names are case-sensitive, so *Number1* and *number1* are considered to be different identifiers.

In addition, none of Java's **reserved words** can be used as identifiers. These reserved words, which are listed in Appendix A, consist of keywords used in Java instructions, as well as three special data values: *true, false,* and *null.* Given that Java identifiers are case-sensitive, note that it is legal to use *True* or *TRUE* as identifiers, but *true* is not a legal variable name. Table 2.1 lists the rules for creating Java identifiers.

The shell code in Example 2.1 uses three identifiers: *ShellApplication, main,* and *args.* The remainder of Example 2.1 consists of comments, Java keywords, and required punctuation.

TABLE 2.1 Rules for Creating Identifiers

Java Identifiers
▪ Must start with a Java letter (*A–Z, a–z*, _, $, or many Unicode characters)
▪ Can contain an almost unlimited number of letters and/or digits (0–9)
▪ Cannot contain spaces
▪ Are case-sensitive
▪ Cannot be a Java reserved word

The basic building block of a Java program is the **statement**. A statement is terminated with a semicolon and can span several lines.

Any amount of **white space** is permitted between identifiers, Java keywords, operands, operators, and literals. White space characters are the space, tab, newline, and carriage return. Liberal use of white space makes your program more readable. It is good programming style to surround identifiers, operands, and operators with spaces and to skip lines between logical sections of the program.

SOFTWARE ENGINEERING TIP

Liberal use of white space makes your program more readable. It is good programming style to surround identifiers, operands, and operators with spaces and to skip lines between logical sections of the program.

A **block**, which consists of 0, 1, or more statements, starts with a left curly brace ({) and ends with a right curly brace (}). Blocks are required for class and method definitions and can be used anywhere else in the program that a statement is legal. Example 2.1 has two blocks: the class definition (lines 5 through 10) and the *main* method definition (lines 7 through 9). As you can see, nesting blocks within blocks is perfectly legal. The *main* block is nested completely within the class definition block.

Comments document the operation of the program and are notes to yourself and to other programmers who read your code. Comments are not compiled and can be coded in two ways. **Block comments** can span several lines; they begin with a forward slash-asterisk (/*) and end with an asterisk-forward slash (*/). Everything between the /* and */ is ignored by the compiler. Note that there are no spaces between the asterisk and forward slash. Lines 1–3 in Example 2.1 are block comments and illustrate the good software engineering practice of providing at the beginning of your source code a few comments that identify yourself as the author and briefly describe what the program does.

The second way to include comments in your code is to precede the comment with two forward slashes (//). There are no spaces between the forward slashes. The compiler ignores everything from the two forward slashes to the end of the line. In Example 2.1, the compiler ignores all of line 8, but only the part of line 6 after the two forward slashes.

SOFTWARE ENGINEERING TIP

Include a block comment at the beginning of each source file that identifies the author of the program and briefly describes the function of the program.

2.2 Data Types, Variables, and Constants

For the data in your program, you need to assign a symbolic name (an identifier) that you will use to refer to that data item. You must also specify to the compiler the data type. Java supports eight **primitive data types**: *byte*, *short*, *int*, *long*, *float*, *double*, *char*, and *boolean*. They are called primitive data types because they are not classes.

The data type you specify tells the compiler how much memory to allocate and the format in which to store the data. For example, if you specify that a data item is an *int*, then the compiler will allocate four bytes of memory for it and store its value as a 32-bit signed binary number. If, however, you specify that a data item is a double-precision floating-point number, then the compiler will allocate 8 bytes of memory and store its value as an IEEE 754 floating-point number.

Once you declare a data type for a data item, the compiler will monitor your use of that data item. If you attempt to perform operations that are not allowed for that type or are not compatible with that type, the compiler will generate an error. Because the Java compiler monitors the operations on each data item, Java is called a **strongly typed language**.

Take care in selecting identifiers for your programs. The identifiers should be meaningful and should reflect the data that will be stored in a variable, the concept encapsulated by a class, or the function of a method. For example, the identifier *age* clearly indicates that the variable will hold the age of a person. When you select meaningful variable names, the logic of your program is more easily understood, and you are less likely to introduce errors. Sometimes, it may be necessary to create a long identifier in order to clearly indicate its use, for example, *numberOfStudentsWhoPassedCS1*. Although the length of identifiers is essentially unlimited, avoid creating extremely long identifiers because they are more cumbersome to use. Also, the longer the identifier, the more likely you are to make typos when entering the identifier into your program. Finally, although it is legal to use identifiers, such as *TRUE*, which differ from Java keywords only in case, it isn't a good idea because they easily can be confused with Java keywords, making the program logic less clear.

SOFTWARE ENGINEERING TIP

When selecting identifiers, choose meaningful names that reflect the use of the identifier in the program; this will make your code self-documented. Use as many characters as necessary to make the identifier clear, but avoid extremely long identifiers. Also, for clarity in your program logic, avoid identifiers that resemble Java keywords.

2.2.1 Declaring Variables

Every variable must be given a name and a data type before it can be used. This is called **declaring a variable**. The data item is called a **variable** if its value can be changed during the program's execution, or if its value can be different from one execution of the program to another. A variable is like a box that can hold one item at a time. You can put an item in the box and later replace that item with a different item, but the box remains the same. Similarly, a variable can hold one data value at a time. You can change the data value it holds, but at any time, a variable has one value.

The syntax for declaring a variable is:

```
dataType identifier; // this declares one variable
```

or

```
dataType identifier1, identifier2, ...; // this declares multiple
                                        // variables of the same
                                        // data type
```

Note that a comma follows each identifier in the list except the last identifier, which is followed by a semicolon.

By convention, the identifiers for variable names start with a lowercase letter. If the variable name consists of more than one word, then each word after the first should begin with a capital letter. For example, these identifiers are conventional Java variable names: *number1*, *highScore*, *booksToRead*, *ageInYears*, and *xAxis*. Underscores conventionally are not used in variable names; they are reserved for the identifiers of constants, as we shall discuss later in the chapter. Similarly, do not use dollar signs to begin variable names. The dollar sign is reserved for the first letter of programmatically generated variable names; that is, variable names generated by software, not people. Although this may sound arbitrary now, the value of

SOFTWARE ENGINEERING TIP

Begin variable names with a lowercase letter. If the variable name consists of more than one word, begin each word after the first with a capital letter. Avoid underscores in variable names, and do not begin a variable name with a dollar sign.

following these conventions will become clearer as you gain more experience in Java and your programs become more complex.

2.2.2 Integer Data Types

An integer data type is one that evaluates to a positive or negative whole number. Java provides four integer data types, *int, short, long,* and *byte.*

The *int, short, long,* and *byte* types differ in the number of bytes of memory allocated to store each type, and therefore, the maximum and minimum values that can be stored in a variable of that type. All of Java's integer types are signed, meaning that they can be positive or negative; the high-order, or leftmost, bit is reserved for the sign.

Table 2.2 summarizes the integer data types, their sizes in memory, and their maximum and minimum values.

In most applications, the *int* type will be sufficient for your needs, since it can store positive and negative numbers up into the 2 million range. The *short* and *byte* data types typically are used only when memory space is critical, and the *long* data type is needed only for data values larger than 2 million.

Let's look at some examples of integer variable declarations. Note that the variable names clearly indicate the data that the variables will hold.

```
int testGrade;
int numPlayers, highScore, diceRoll;
short xCoordinate, yCoordinate;
long cityPopulation;
byte ageInYears;
```

TABLE 2.2 Integer Data Types

Integer Data Type	Size in Bytes	Minimum Value	Maximum Value
byte	1	−128	127
short	2	−32,768	32,767
int	4	−2,147,483,648	2,147,483,647
long	8	−9,223,372,036,854,775,808	9,223,372,036,854,775,807

2.2.3 Floating-Point Data Types

Floating-point data types store numbers with fractional parts. Java supports two floating-point data types: the single-precision *float* and the double-precision *double.*

REFERENCE POINT

Floating-point numbers are stored using the IEEE 754 standard, which is discussed in Appendix E.

The two types differ in the amount of memory allocated and the size of the number that can be represented. The single-precision type (*float*) is stored in 32 bits, while the double-precision type (*double*) is stored in 64 bits. *Floats* and *doubles* can be positive or negative.

Table 2.3 summarizes Java's floating-point data types, their sizes in memory, and their maximum and minimum positive nonzero values.

Because of its greater precision, the *double* data type is usually preferred over the *float* data type. However, for calculations not requiring such precision, *floats* are often used because they require less memory.

Although integers can be stored as *doubles* or *floats*, it isn't advisable to do so because floating-point numbers require more processing time for calculations.

Let's look at a few examples of floating-point variable declarations:

```
float salesTax;
double interestRate;
double paycheck, sumSalaries;
```

2.2.4 Character Data Type

REFERENCE POINT

The encoding of ASCII and Unicode characters is discussed in Appendix C.

The *char* data type stores one Unicode character. Because Unicode characters are encoded as unsigned numbers using 16 bits, a *char* variable is stored in two bytes of memory.

Table 2.4 shows the size of the *char* data type, as well as the minimum and maximum values. The maximum value is the character whose encoding is equal to the unsigned hexadecimal number *FFFF*. At this time, no Unicode character has been assigned the encoding of *FFFF*.

TABLE 2.3 Floating-point Data Types

Floating-point Data Type	Size in Bytes	Minimum Positive Nonzero Value	Maximum Value
float	4	1.4E-45	3.4028235E38
double	8	4.9E-324	1.7976931348623157E308

TABLE 2.4 The Character Data Type

Character Data Type	Size in Bytes	Minimum Value	Maximum Value
char	2	The character encoded as *0000*, the *null* character	The character encoded as *FFFF*, currently unused

Obviously, since the *char* data type can store only a single character, such as a *K*, a *char* variable is not useful for storing names, titles, or other text data. For text data, Java provides a *String* class, which we'll discuss later in this chapter.

Here are a few declarations of *char* variables:

```
char finalGrade;
char middleInitial;
char newline, tab, doubleQuotes;
```

2.2.5 Boolean Data Type

The *boolean* data type can store only two values, which are expressed using the Java reserved words *true* and *false*, as shown in Table 2.5.

Booleans are typically used for decision making and for controlling the order of execution of a program.

Here are a few declarations of *boolean* variables:

```
boolean isEmpty;
boolean passed, failed;
```

2.2.6 Initial Values and Literals

When you declare a variable, you can also assign an initial value to the data. To do that, use the **assignment operator** (=) with the following syntax:

```
dataType variableName = initialValue;
```

TABLE 2.5 The *boolean* Data Type

boolean Data Type	Possible Values
boolean	*true*
	false

COMMON ERROR TRAP

Although Unicode characters occupy two bytes in memory, they still represent a single character. Therefore, the literal must also represent only one character.

COMMON ERROR TRAP

Commas, dollar signs, and percent signs (%) cannot be used in integer or floating-point literals.

or

```
dataType variable1 = initialValue1, variable2 = initialValue2;
```

Notice that assignment is right to left. The initial value is assigned to the variable.

One way to specify the initial value is by using a **literal value**. In the following statement, the value *100* is an *int* literal value, which is assigned to the variable *testGrade*.

```
int testGrade = 100;
```

Table 2.6 summarizes the legal characters in literals for all primitive data types.

TABLE 2.6 Literal Formats for Java Data Types

Data Type	Literal Format
int, short, byte	Optional initial sign (+ or −) followed by digits 0–9 in any combination. A literal in this format is an *int* literal; however, an *int* literal may be assigned to a *byte* or *short* variable if the literal is a legal value for the assigned data type. An integer literal that begins with a 0 digit is considered to be an octal number (base 8) and the remaining digits must be 0–7. An integer literal that begins with 0x is considered to be a hexadecimal number (base 16) and the remaining digits must be 0–F.
long	Optional initial sign (+ or −) followed by digits 0–9 in any combination, terminated with an *L* or *l*. It's preferable to use the capital *L*, because the lowercase *l* can be confused with the number *1*. An integer literal that begins with a 0 digit is considered to be an octal number (base 8) and the remaining digits must be 0–7. An integer literal that begins with 0x is considered to be a hexadecimal number (base 16) and the remaining digits must be 0–F.
float	Optional initial sign (+ or −) followed by a floating-point number in fixed or scientific format, terminated by an *F* or *f*.
double	Optional initial sign (+ or −) followed by a floating-point number in fixed or scientific format.
char	▪ Any printable character enclosed in single quotes. ▪ A decimal value from 0–65,535. ▪ '\m', where \m is an escape sequence. For example, '\n' represents a newline, and '\t' represents a tab character.
boolean	*true* or *false*

Notice in Table 2.6 under the literal format for *char*, that *n* and *t* can be used to format output. We'll discuss these and other escape sequences in the next section of this chapter.

Example 2.2 shows a complete program illustrating variable declarations, specifying a literal for the initial value of each.

```
/* Variables Class
   Anderson, Franceschi
*/

public class Variables
{
 public static void main( String [ ] args )
 {
   // This example shows how to declare and initialize variables

   int testGrade = 100;
   long cityPopulation = 425612340L;
   byte ageInYears = 19;

   float  salesTax = .05F;
   double interestRate = 0.725;
   double avogadroNumber = +6.022E23;
   // avogadroNumber is represented in scientific notation;
   //     its value is 6.022 x 10 to the power 23

   char finalGrade = 'A';
   boolean isEmpty = true;

   System.out.println( "testGrade is " + testGrade );
   System.out.println( "cityPopulation is " + cityPopulation );
   System.out.println( "ageInYears is " + ageInYears );
   System.out.println( "salesTax is " + salesTax );
   System.out.println( "interestRate is " + interestRate );
   System.out.println( "avogadroNumber is " + avogadroNumber );
   System.out.println( "finalGrade is " + finalGrade );
   System.out.println( "isEmpty is " + isEmpty );
 }
}
```

EXAMPLE 2.2 Declaring and Initializing Variables

Line 9 shows a single-line comment. Line 17 declares a *double* variable named *avogadroNumber* and initializes it with its value in scientific notation. The Avogadro number represents the number of elementary particles in one mole of any substance.

Figure 2.1 shows the output of Example 2.2.

Another way to specify an initial value for a variable is to assign the variable the value of another variable, using this syntax:

```
dataType variable2 = variable1;
```

Two things need to be true for this assignment to work:

- *variable1* needs to be declared and assigned a value before this statement appears in the source code.
- *variable1* and *variable2* need to be compatible data types; in other words, the precision of *variable1* must be lower than or equal to that of *variable2*.

For example, in these statements:

```
boolean isPassingGrade = true;
boolean isPromoted = isPassingGrade;
```

isPassingGrade is given an initial value of *true*. Then *isPromoted* is assigned the value already given to *isPassingGrade*. Thus, *isPromoted* is also assigned the initial value *true*. If *isPassingGrade* were assigned the initial value *false*, then *isPromoted* would also be assigned the initial value *false*.

Figure 2.1
Output of Example 2.2

```
testGrade is 100
cityPopulation is 425612340
ageInYears is 19
salesTax is 0.05
interestRate is 0.725
avogadroNumber is 6.022E23
finalGrade is A
isEmpty is true
```

And in these statements:

```
float salesTax = .05f;
double taxRate = salesTax;
```

the initial value of .05 is assigned to *taxRate*. It's legal to assign a *float* value to a *double*, because all values that can be stored as *floats* are also valid *double* values. However, these statements are *not* valid:

```
double taxRate = .05;
float salesTax = taxRate; // invalid; float is lower precision
```

Even though *.05* is a valid *float* value, the compiler will generate a "`possible loss of precision`" error.

Similarly, you can assign a lower-precision integer value to a higher-precision integer variable.

Table 2.7 summarizes compatible data types; a variable or literal of any type in the right column can be assigned to a variable of the data type in the left column.

Variables need to be declared before they can be used in your program, but be careful to declare each variable only once; that is, specify the data type of the variable only the first time that variable is used in the program. If you attempt to declare a variable that has already been declared, as in the following statements:

```
double twoCents;
double twoCents = 2; // incorrect, second declaration of twoCents
```

TABLE 2.7 Valid Data Types for Assignment

Data Type	Compatible Data Types
byte	*byte*
short	*byte, short*
int	*byte, short, int, char*
long	*byte, short, int, char, long*
float	*byte, short, int, char, long, float*
double	*byte, short, int, char, long, float, double*
boolean	*boolean*
char	*char*

COMMON ERROR TRAP

Declare each variable only once, the first time the variable is used. After the variable has been declared, its data type cannot be changed.

you will receive a compiler error similar to the following:

```
twoCents is already defined
```

Similarly, once you have declared a variable, you cannot change its data type. Thus, these statements:

```
double cashInHand;
int cashInHand; // incorrect, data type cannot be changed
```

will generate a compiler error similar to the following:

```
cashInHand is already defined
```

CODE IN ACTION

On the CD-ROM included with this book, you will find a Flash movie showing a step-by-step illustration of how to convert between decimal and binary numbers. Click on the link for Chapter 2 to view the movie.

2.2.7 String Literals and Escape Sequences

In addition to literals for all the primitive data types, Java also supports *String* literals. *Strings* are objects in Java, and we will discuss them in greater depth in Chapter 3.

A ***String* literal** is a sequence of characters enclosed by double quotes. One set of quotes "opens" the *String* literal and the second set of quotes "closes" the literal. For example, these are all *String* literals:

```
"Hello"
"Hello world"
"The value of x is "
```

We used a *String* literal in our first program in Chapter 1 in this statement:

```
System.out.println( "Programming is not a spectator sport!" );
```

We also used *String* literals in output statements in Example 2.2 to label the data that we printed:

```
System.out.println( "testGrade is " + testGrade );
```

The + operator is the ***String* concatenation operator**. Among other uses, the concatenation operator allows us to print primitive data types along with *Strings*. We'll discuss the concatenation operator in more detail in Chapter 3.

String literals cannot extend over more than one line. If the compiler finds a newline character in the middle of your *String* literal, it will generate a compiler error. For example, the following statement is not valid:

```
System.out.println( "Never pass a water fountain
          without taking a drink." );
```

In fact, that statement will generate several compiler errors:

```
StringTest.java:9: unclosed string literal
     System.out.println( "Never pass a water fountain
                         ^

StringTest.java:10: unclosed string literal
          without taking a drink." );
                                 ^

StringTest.java:10: ')' expected
          without taking a drink." );
                                    ^
```

If you have a long *String* to print, break it into several strings and use the concatenation operator. This statement is a correction of the invalid statement above:

```
System.out.println( "Never pass a water fountain,"
                + " without taking a drink." );
```

Another common programming error is omitting the closing quotes. Be sure that all open quotes have matching closing quotes on the same line.

COMMON ERROR TRAP

All open quotes for a *String* literal should be matched with a set of closing quotes, and the closing quotes must appear before the line ends.

Now that we know that quotes open and close *String* literals, how can we define a literal that includes quotes? This statement

```
System.out.println( "She said, "Java is fun"" ); // illegal quotes
                                                 // within literal
```

generates this compiler error:

```
StringTest.java:24: ')' expected
     System.out.println( "She said, "Java is fun."" ); // illegal quotes
                                     ^
```

And since *String* literals can't extend over two lines, how can we create a *String* literal that includes a newline character? Java solves these problems by providing a set of escape sequences that can be used to include a special character within *String* and *char* literals. The escape sequences *\n, \t, \b, \r,* and *\f* are nonprintable characters. Table 2.8 lists the Java escape sequences.

In Example 2.3, we show how escape sequences can be used in *Strings.*

```
1  /*  Literals Class
2      Anderson, Franceschi
3  */
4
5  public class Literals
6  {
7    public static void main( String [ ] args )
8    {
9      System.out.println( "One potato\nTwo potatoes\n" );
10     System.out.println( "\tTabs can make the output easier to read"  );
11     System.out.println( "She said, \"Java is fun\"" );
12   }
13 }
```

EXAMPLE 2.3 Using Escape Sequences

Figure 2.2 shows the output of Example 2.3. Line 9 shows how *\n* causes the remainder of the literal to be printed on the next line. The tab character, *\t,*

TABLE 2.8 Java Escape Sequences

Character	Escape Sequence
newline	\n
tab	\t
double quotes	\"
single quote	\'
backslash	\\
backspace	\b
carriage return	\r
form feed	\f

```
One potato
Two potatoes

        Tabs can make the output easier to read
She said, "Java is fun"
```

Figure 2.2
Output of Example 2.3

used in line 10, will cause the literal that follows it to be indented one tab stop when output. Line 11 outputs a sentence with embedded double quotes; the embedded double quotes are printed with the escape sequence \".

2.2.8 Constants

Sometimes you know the value of a data item, and you know that its value will not (and should not) change during program execution, nor is it likely to change from one execution of the program to another. In this case, it is a good software engineering practice to define that data item as a **constant.**

Defining constants uses the same syntax as declaring variables, except that the data type is preceded by the keyword *final.*

```
final dataType CONSTANT_IDENTIFIER = assignedValue;
```

Assigning a value is optional when the constant is defined, but you must assign a value before the constant is used in the program. Also, once the constant has been assigned a value, its value cannot be changed (reassigned) later in the program. Any attempt by your program to change the value of a constant will generate the following compiler error:

```
cannot assign a value to final variable
```

Think of this as a service of the compiler in preventing your program from unintentionally corrupting its data.

By convention, *CONSTANT_IDENTIFIER* consists of all capital letters, and embedded words are separated by an underscore. This makes constants stand out in the code and easy to identify as constants. Also, constants are usually defined at the top of a program where their values can be seen easily.

Example 2.4 shows how to use constants in a program.

```
 1 /* Constants Class
 2    Anderson, Franceschi
 3 */
 4
 5 public class Constants
 6 {
 7   public static void main( String [ ] args )
 8   {
 9     final char ZORRO = 'Z';
10     final double PI = 3.14159;
11     final int DAYS_IN_LEAP_YEAR = 366, DAYS_IN_NON_LEAP_YEAR = 365;
12
13     System.out.println( "The value of constant ZORRO is " + ZORRO );
14     System.out.println( "The value of constant PI is " + PI );
15     System.out.println( "The number of days in a leap year is "
16                         + DAYS_IN_LEAP_YEAR );
17     System.out.println( "The number of days in a non-leap year is "
18                         + DAYS_IN_NON_LEAP_YEAR );
19
20     // PI = 3.14;
21     // The statement above would generate a compiler error
22     // You cannot change the value of a constant
23   }
24 }
```

EXAMPLE 2.4 Using Constants

SOFTWARE ENGINEERING TIP

Use all capital letters for a constant's identifier; separate words with an underscore (_). Declare constants at the top of the program so their value can be seen easily.

SOFTWARE ENGINEERING TIP

Declare as a constant any data that should not change during program execution. The compiler will then flag any attempts by your program to change the value of the constant, thus preventing any unintentional corruption of the data.

Lines 9, 10, and 11 define four constants. On line 11, note that both *DAYS_IN_LEAP_YEAR* and *DAYS_IN_NON_LEAP_YEAR* are constants. You don't need to repeat the keyword *final* to define two (or more) constants of the same data types. Lines 13 to 18 output the values of the four constants. If line 20 were not commented out, it would generate a compiler error because once a constant is assigned a value, its value cannot be changed. Figure 2.3 shows the output of Example 2.4.

Constants can make your code more readable: PI is more meaningful than 3.14159 when used inside an arithmetic expression. Another advantage of using constants is to keep programmers from making logic errors: Let's say

```
The value of constant ZORRO is Z
The value of constant PI is 3.14159
The number of days in a leap year is 366
The number of days in a non-leap year is 365
```

Figure 2.3
Output of Example 2.4

we set a constant to a particular value and it is used at various places throughout the code (for instance, a constant representing a tax rate); we then discover that the value of that constant needs to be changed. All we have to do is make the change in one place, most likely at the beginning of the code. If we had to change the value at many places throughout the code, that could very well result in logic errors or typos.

Skill Practice
with these end-of-chapter questions

2.7.1 Multiple Choice
Questions 1, 2

2.7.2 Reading and Understanding Code
Questions 4, 5, 6

2.7.3 Fill In the Code
Questions 23, 24, 25, 26

2.7.4 Identifying Errors in Code
Questions 33, 34, 38, 39

2.7.5 Debugging Area
Questions 40, 41

2.7.6 Write a Short Program
Question 46

2.7.8 Technical Writing
Question 52

2.3 Programming Activity 1: Exploring Data Types

For Programming Activity 1, let's explore the Java data types by finding and printing their maximum and minimum values.

Open the *ShellApplication.java* source code shown in Example 2.1. You will find this file on the CD-ROM accompanying this book.

Replace the class name, *ShellApplication*, with the name *DataTypeValues*. Since this is now the name of our class, save the source file as the name *DataTypeValues.java*. Also replace the comment in the first line with a description of what this application will do: "Java data types and their values," and add your name to the second line. Your source file should look like Example 2.5

```
/*  Java data types and their values
    your name here
*/
public class DataTypeValues
{
  public static void main( String [ ] args ) // required
  {
    // write your code here
  }
}
```

EXAMPLE 2.5 *DataTypeValues*, Version 1

The maximum and minimum values for the numeric data types are available for use in our program as the Java predefined constants shown in Table 2.9.

Let's start by declaring two variables of the *byte* data type. We'll assign one variable the minimum value and the other variable the maximum value. Include these declarations following the comment:

```
// write your code here

byte minByte = Byte.MIN_VALUE, maxByte = Byte.MAX_VALUE;
```

Following the declarations, type these lines to print the minimum and maximum byte values.

```
System.out.println( "The minimum byte value is " + minByte );
System.out.println( "The maximum byte value is " + maxByte );
```

In these statements, we're using *String* literals (the words enclosed in quotes) and the *String* concatenation operator (+) to join the *String* literals to the

COMMON ERROR TRAP

Forgetting to add a blank space to the end of a *String* literal before concatenating a value makes the output more difficult to read.

TABLE 2.9 Predefined Constants for Minimum and Maximum Values

Data Type	Minimum Value	Maximum Value
Integers		
byte	Byte.MIN_VALUE	Byte.MAX_VALUE
short	Short.MIN_VALUE	Short.MAX_VALUE
int	Integer.MIN_VALUE	Integer.MAX_VALUE
long	Long.MIN_VALUE	Long.MAX_VALUE
Floating Point		
float	Float.MIN_VALUE	Float.MAX_VALUE
double	Double.MIN_VALUE	Double.MAX_VALUE

value of the variables. Note that the last character in each *String* literal is a space. If you omit the space, the minimum and maximum values will begin immediately after the "is," which makes the output more difficult to read.

Compile the program and run it. Your output should look like Figure 2.4.

SOFTWARE ENGINEERING TIP

Developing and testing your programs in steps makes it easier to find and fix errors.

To print the *short* minimum and maximum values, declare two *short* variables:

```
short minShort = Short.MIN_VALUE, maxShort = Short.MAX_VALUE;
```

and include these two statements to print the values:

```
System.out.println( "The minimum short value is " + minShort );
System.out.println( "The maximum short value is " + maxShort );
```

At this point, your program should look like Example 2.6.

```
The minimum byte value is -128
The maximum byte value is 127
```

Figure 2.4
Minimum and Maximum *byte* Values

```java
/*  Java data types and their values
    your name here
*/
public class DataTypeValues
{
  public static void main( String [ ] args ) // required
  {
     // write your code here
     byte maxByte = Byte.MAX_VALUE, minByte = Byte.MIN_VALUE;
     System.out.println( "The minimum byte value is " + minByte );
     System.out.println( "The maximum byte value is " + maxByte );

     short maxShort = Short.MAX_VALUE, minShort = Short.MIN_VALUE;
     System.out.println( "The minimum short value is " + minShort );
     System.out.println( "The maximum short value is " + maxShort );
  }
}
```

EXAMPLE 2.6 *DataTypeValues*, Version 2

Compile and run the program and check your output. If your output is correct, define two variables for each remaining numeric data type and follow the pattern to print the minimum and maximum values for each numeric data type. You can even copy and paste these statements, changing the data type as appropriate. Compile and run the program after adding each data type to your program. When you are finished, your output should look like Figure 2.5.

Figure 2.5
Minimum and Maximum Data Type Values

```
The minimum byte value is -128
The maximum byte value is 127
The minimum short value is -32768
The maximum short value is 32767
The minimum int value is -2147483648
The maximum int value is 2147483647
The minimum long value is -9223372036854775808
The maximum long value is 9223372036854775807
The minimum float value is 1.4E-45
The maximum float value is 3.4028235E38
The minimum double value is 4.9E-324
The maximum double value is 1.7976931348623157E308
```

DISCUSSION QUESTIONS

1. What are the advantages of having different data types?
2. Why do you think it's important to be able to find the maximum and minimum values of each data type?

2.4 Expressions and Arithmetic Operators

2.4.1 The Assignment Operator and Expressions

In the previous section, we mentioned using the assignment operator to assign initial values to variables and constants. Now let's look at the assignment operator in more detail.

The syntax for the assignment operator is:

```
target = expression;
```

An expression consists of operators and operands that evaluate to a single value. The value of the expression is then assigned to *target*, which must be a variable or constant having a data type compatible with the value of the expression.

If *target* is a variable, the value of the expression replaces any previous value the variable was holding. For example, let's look at these instructions:

```
int numberOfPlayers = 10; // numberOfPlayers value is 10
numberOfPlayers = 8;      // numberOfPlayers value is now 8
```

The first instruction declares an *int* named *numberOfPlayers*. This allocates four bytes in memory to a variable named *numberOfPlayers* and stores the value 10 in that variable. Then, the second statement changes the value stored in the variable *numberOfPlayers* to 8. The previous value, 10, is discarded.

An expression can be a single variable name or a literal of any type, in which case, the value of the expression is simply the value of the variable or the literal. For example, in these statements,

```
int legalAge = 18;
int voterAge = legalAge;
```

the literal *18* is an expression. Its value is *18*, which is assigned to the variable *legalAge*. Then, in the second statement, *legalAge* is an expression, whose value is *18*. Thus the value *18* is assigned to *voterAge*. So after these statements have been executed, both *legalAge* and *voterAge* will have the value *18*.

One restriction, however, is that an assignment expression cannot include another variable unless that variable has been defined previously. The definition of the *height* variable that follows is **invalid,** because it refers to *weight*, which is not defined until the next line.

```
int height = weight * 2; // invalid, weight is not yet defined
int weight;
```

The compiler flags the definition of *height* as an error

```
cannot find symbol
```

because *weight* has not yet been defined.

An expression can be quite complex, consisting of multiple variables, constants, literals, and operators. Before we can look at examples of more complex expressions, however, we need to discuss the *arithmetic operators*.

2.4.2 Arithmetic Operators

Java's arithmetic operators are used for performing calculations on numeric data. The operators are shown in Table 2.10.

All these operators take two operands; thus, they are called **binary operators**.

Example 2.7 shows how these operators can be used in a program.

TABLE 2.10 Arithmetic Operators

Operator	Operation
+	addition
–	subtraction
*	multiplication
/	division
%	modulus (remainder after division)

```
1 /* SimpleOperators Class
2    Anderson, Franceschi
3 */
4
5 public class SimpleOperators
6 {
7    public static void main( String [ ] args )
8    {
9       int a = 6;
10      int b = 2;
11      int result;
12
13      result = a + b;
14      System.out.println( a + " + " + b + " is " + result );
15
16      result = a - b;
17      System.out.println( a + " - " + b + " is " + result );
18
19      result = a * b;
20      System.out.println( a + " * " + b + " is " + result );
21   }
22 }
```

EXAMPLE 2.7 Using Arithmetic Operators

SOFTWARE ENGINEERING TIP

For readable code, insert a space between operators and operands.

Lines 9 and 10 declare and initialize two *int* variables. Line 13 adds them and assigns the result to the variable *result*, which was declared at line 11; thus, the value of the expression $a + b$ is assigned to *result*, which is then output at line 14. Lines 16 and 17, as well as lines 19 and 20, do the same with the subtraction and multiplication operators (– and *). Figure 2.6 shows the output when Example 2.7 is executed.

As shown in Example 2.7, variables—such as *a*, *b*, and *result*—can be used multiple times within a program and can be assigned different values as the program executes. Furthermore, the same variable that appears on the left side of the assignment operator (=) can also appear in the expression on

```
6 + 2 is 8
6 - 2 is 4
6 * 2 is 12
```

Figure 2.6
Output of Example 2.7

the right side of the assignment operator. For example, we could use these statements to assign 32 to the variable *age,* then later add 1 to that value.

```
int age = 32;
...
age = age + 1;   // now, age is 33
```

2.4.3 Operator Precedence

The statements in Example 2.7 perform simple calculations, but what if you want to calculate how much money you have in coins? Let's say you have two quarters, three dimes, and two nickels. To calculate the value of these coins in pennies, you might use this expression:

```
int pennies = 2 * 25 + 3 * 10 + 2 * 5;
```

In which order should the computer do the calculation? If the value of the expression were calculated left to right, then the result would be

```
= 2 * 25 + 3 * 10 + 2 * 5
=   50   + 3 * 10 + 2 * 5
=       53   * 10 + 2 * 5
=           530   + 2 * 5
=                532 * 5
=                  2660
```

Clearly, 2,660 pennies is not the right answer. To calculate the correct number of pennies, the multiplications should be performed first, then the additions. This, in fact, is the order in which Java will calculate the preceding expression.

The Java compiler follows a set of rules called **operator precedence** to determine the order in which the operations should be performed.

Table 2.11 provides the order of precedence of the operators we've discussed so far. The operators in the first row—parentheses—are evaluated first, then the operators in the second row (*, /, %) are evaluated, and so on

TABLE 2.11 Operator Precedence

Operator Hierarchy	Order of Same-Statement Evaluation	Operation
( )	left to right	parentheses for explicit grouping
*, /, %	left to right	multiplication, division, modulus
+, –	left to right	addition, subtraction
=	right to left	assignment

with the operators in each row. When two or more operators on the same level appear in the same expression, the order of evaluation is left to right, except for the assignment operator, which is evaluated right to left.

As we introduce more operators, we'll add them to the Order of Precedence chart. The complete chart is provided in Appendix B.

Using Table 2.11 as a guide, let's recalculate the number of pennies:

```
int pennies = 2 * 25 + 3 * 10 + 2 * 5;
            =  50    +  30    +  10
            =  90
```

As you can see, *90* is the correct number of pennies in two quarters, three dimes, and two nickels.

We also could have used parentheses to clearly display the order of calculation. For example,

```
int pennies = (2 * 25) + (3 * 10) + (2 * 5);
            =  50      +  30      +  10
            =  90
```

The result is the same, 90 pennies.

It sometimes helps to use parentheses to clarify the order of calculations, but parentheses are essential when your desired order of evaluation is different from the rules of operator precedence. For example, to calculate the value of this formula:

$$\frac{x}{2y}$$

you could write this code:

```
double result = x / 2 * y;
```

This would generate incorrect results because, according to the rules of precedence, *x/2* would be calculated first, then the result of that division would be multiplied by *y*. In algebraic terms, the preceding statement is equivalent to

$$\frac{x}{2} * y$$

To code the original formula correctly, you need to use parentheses to force the multiplication to occur before the division:

```
double result = x / ( 2 * y );
```

2.4.4 Integer Division and Modulus

Division with two integer operands is performed in the Arithmetic Logic Unit (ALU), which can calculate only an integer result. Any fractional part is truncated; no rounding is performed. The remainder after division is available, however, as an integer, by taking the modulus (%) of the two integer operands. Thus, in Java, the integer division (/) operator will calculate the quotient of the division, whereas the modulus (%) operator will calculate the remainder of the division.

```
1 /* DivisionAndModulus Class
2    Anderson, Franceschi
3 */
4
5 public class DivisionAndModulus
6 {
7   public static void main( String [ ] args )
8   {
9     final int PENNIES_PER_QUARTER = 25;
10    int pennies = 113;
11
12    int quarters = pennies / PENNIES_PER_QUARTER;
13    System.out.println( "There are " + quarters + " quarters in "
14            + pennies + " pennies" );
15
16    int penniesLeftOver = pennies % PENNIES_PER_QUARTER;
17    System.out.println( "There are " + penniesLeftOver
18            + " pennies left over" );
19
20    final double MONTHS_PER_YEAR = 12;
21    double annualSalary = 50000.0;
22
23    double monthlySalary = annualSalary / MONTHS_PER_YEAR;
24    System.out.println( "The monthly salary is " + monthlySalary );
25  }
26 }
```

EXAMPLE 2.8 How Integer Division and Modulus Work

In Example 2.8, we have 113 pennies and we want to convert those pennies into quarters. We can find the number of quarters by dividing 113 by 25. The *int* variable *pennies* is assigned the value 113 at line 10. At line 12, the variable *quarters* is assigned the result of the integer division of *pennies* by the constant *PENNIES_PER_QUARTER*. Since the quotient of the division of 113 by 25 is 4, *quarters* will be assigned 4. At line 16, we use the modulus operator to assign to the variable *penniesLeftOver* the remainder of the division of *pennies* by *PENNIES_PER_QUARTER*. Since the remainder of the division of 113 by 25 is 13, 13 will be assigned to *penniesLeftOver*. Notice that integer division and modulus are independent calculations. You

```
There are 4 quarters in 113 pennies
There are 13 pennies left over
The monthly salary is 4166.666666666667
```

Figure 2.7
Output of Example 2.8

can perform a division without also calculating the modulus, and you can calculate the modulus without performing the division.

At line 23, we divide a *double* by a *double;* therefore, a floating-point division will be performed by the floating-point unit (FPU), and the result will be assigned to the variable *monthlySalary*. Figure 2.7 shows the output of the program.

The modulus is actually a useful operator. As you will see later in this book, it can be used to determine whether a number is even or odd, to control the number of data items that are written per line, to determine if one number is a factor of another, and for many other uses.

CODE IN ACTION

To see arithmetic operators used in a program, look for the Chapter 2 Flash movie on the CD-ROM accompanying this book. Click on the link for Chapter 2 to start the movie.

Skill Practice
with these end-of-chapter questions

2.7.2 Reading and Understanding Code
Questions 7, 8, 9, 10, 11, 12, 13

2.7.3 Fill In the Code
Questions 27, 29, 32

2.7.4 Identifying Errors in Code
Question 35

2.7.6 Write a Short Program
Question 44

2.4.5 Division by Zero

As you might expect, Java does not allow integer division by 0. If you include this statement in your program:

```
int result = 4 / 0;
```

the code will compile without errors, but at run time, when this statement is executed, the JVM will generate an exception and print an error message on the Java console:

```
Exception in thread "main" java.lang.ArithmeticException: / by zero
```

In most cases, this stops the program. In Chapter 11, we'll show you how to handle the exception so that you can write a message to the user and continue running the program.

In contrast, floating-point division by zero does not generate an exception. If the dividend is non-zero, the answer is *Infinity*. If both the dividend and divisor are zero, the answer is *NaN*, which stands for "Not a Number."

Example 2.9 illustrates the three cases of dividing by zero. As we can see on the output shown in Figure 2.8, line 16 of Example 2.9 never executes. The exception is generated at line 15 and the program halts execution.

```
1 /* DivisionByZero Class
2    Anderson, Franceschi
3 */
4
5 public class DivisionByZero
6 {
7   public static void main( String [ ] args )
8   {
9     double result1 = 4.3 / 0.0;
10    System.out.println( "The value of result1 is " + result1 );
11
12    double result2 = 0.0 / 0.0;
13    System.out.println( "The value of result2 is " + result2 );
14
15    int result3 = 4 / 0;
16    System.out.println( "The value of result3 is " + result3 );
17  }
18 }
```

EXAMPLE 2.9 Results of Division by Zero

```
The value of result1 is Infinity
The value of result2 is NaN
Exception in thread "main" java.lang.ArithmeticException: / by zero
        at DivisionByZero.main(DivisionByZero.java:15)
```

Figure 2.8
Output of Example 2.9

Although floating-point division by zero doesn't bring your program to a halt, it doesn't provide useful results either. It's a good practice to avoid dividing by zero in the first place. We'll give you tools to do that in Chapter 5.

2.4.6 Mixed-Type Arithmetic and Type Casting

So far, we've used a single data type in the expressions we've evaluated. But life isn't always like that. Calculations often involve data of different primitive types.

When calculations of mixed types are performed, lower-precision operands are converted, or **promoted**, to the type of the operand that has the higher precision.

The promotions are performed using the *first* of these rules that fits the situation:

1. If either operand is a *double*, the other operand is converted to a *double*.
2. If either operand is a *float*, the other operand is converted to a *float*.
3. If either operand is a *long*, the other operand is converted to a *long*.
4. If either operand is an *int*, the other operand is promoted to an *int*.
5. If neither operand is a *double*, *float*, *long*, or an *int*, both operands are promoted to *int*.

Table 2.12 summarizes these rules of promotion.

This arithmetic promotion of operands is called **implicit type casting** because the compiler performs the promotions automatically, without our specifying that the conversions should be made. Note that the data type of any promoted variable is not permanently changed; its type remains the same after the calculation has been performed.

TABLE 2.12 Rules of Operand Promotion

Data Type of One Operand	Data Type of Other Operand	Promotion of Other Operand	Data Type of Result
double	*char, byte, short, int, long, float*	*double*	*double*
float	*char, byte, short, int, long*	*float*	*float*
long	*char, byte, short, int*	*long*	*long*
int	*char, byte, short*	*int*	*int*
short	*char, byte*	Both operands are promoted to *int*	*int*
byte	*char*	Both operands are promoted to *int*	*int*

Table 2.12 shows many rules, but essentially, any arithmetic expression involving integers and floating-point numbers will evaluate to a floating-point number.

Lines 9 to 12 of Example 2.10 illustrate the rules of promotion. At line 11, the expression *PI * radius * radius* is a mixed-type expression. This expression will be evaluated left to right, evaluating the mixed-type expression *PI * radius* first. *PI* is a *double* and *radius* is an *int.* Therefore, *radius* is promoted to a *double* (4.0) and the result of *PI * radius* is a *double* (12.56636). Then, the next calculation (*12.56636 * radius*) also involves a mixed-type expression, so *radius* is again promoted to a *double* (4.0). The final result, 50.26544, is a *double* and is assigned to *area.* Figure 2.9 shows the output of the complete program.

Sometimes, it's useful to instruct the compiler specifically to convert the type of a variable. In this case, you use **explicit type casting**, which uses this syntax:

```
(dataType) ( expression )
```

The expression will be converted, or type cast, to the data type specified. The parentheses around *expression* are needed only when the expression consists of a calculation that you want to be performed before the type casting.

Type casting is useful in calculating an average. Example 2.10 shows how to calculate your average test grade. Your test scores are 94, 86, 88, and 97, making the combined total score 365. We expect the average to be 91.25.

```
 1 /*  MixedDataTypes Class
 2     Anderson, Franceschi
 3 */
 4
 5 public class MixedDataTypes
 6 {
 7    public static void main( String [ ] args )
 8    {
 9       final double PI = 3.14159;
10       int radius = 4;
11       double area = PI * radius * radius;
12       System.out.println( "The area is " + area );
13
14       int total = 365, count = 4;
15       double average = total / count;
16       System.out.println( "\nPerforming integer division, "
17                           + "then implicit typecasting" );
18       System.out.println( "The average test score is " + average );
19       // 91.0 INCORRECT ANSWER!
20
21       average = ( double ) ( total / count );
22       System.out.println( "\nPerforming integer division, "
23                          +  "then explicit typecasting" );
24       System.out.println( "The average test score is " + average );
25       // 91.0 INCORRECT ANSWER!
26
27       average = ( double ) total / count;
28       System.out.println( "\nTypecast one variable to double, "
29                          +  "then perform division" );
30       System.out.println( "The average test score is " + average );
31       // 91.25 CORRECT ANSWER
32    }
33 }
```

EXAMPLE 2.10 Mixed Data Type Arithmetic

Line 15 first attempts to calculate the average, but results in a wrong answer because both *total* and *count* are integers. So integer division is

Figure 2.9
Output of Example 2.10

```
The area is 50.26544

Performing integer division, then implicit typecasting
The average test score is 91.0

Performing integer division, then explicit typecasting
The average test score is 91.0

Typecast one variable to double, then perform division
The average test score is 91.25
```

performed, which truncates any remainder. Thus, the result of *total / count* is 91. Then 91 is assigned to *average*, which is a *double*, so 91 becomes 91.0.

Line 21 is a second attempt to calculate the average; again, this code does not work correctly because the parentheses force the division to be performed before the type casting. Thus, because *total* and *count* are both integers, integer division is performed again. The quotient, 91, is then cast to a *double*, 91.0, and that *double* value is assigned to *average.*

At line 27, we correct this problem by casting only one of the operands to a *double.* This forces the other operand to be promoted to a *double.* Then floating-point division is performed, which retains the remainder. It doesn't matter whether we cast *total* or *count* to a *double.* Casting either to a *double* forces the division to be a floating-point division.

Figure 2.9 shows the output of the complete program.

CODE IN ACTION

To see the calculation of an average, look for the Chapter 2 Flash movie on the CD-ROM accompanying this book. Click on the link for Chapter 2 to view the movie.

2.4.7 Shortcut Operators

A common operation in programming is adding 1 to a number (**incrementing**) or subtracting 1 from a number (**decrementing**). For example, if you were counting how many data items the user entered, every time you read another data item, you would add 1 to a count variable.

Because incrementing or decrementing a value is so common in programming, Java provides shortcut operators to do this: `++` and `--`. (Note that there are no spaces between the two plus and minus signs.) The statement

```
count++;
```

adds 1 to the value of *count*, and the statement

```
count--;
```

subtracts 1 from the value of *count*. Thus,

```
count++;
```

is equivalent to

```
count = count + 1;
```

and

```
count--;
```

is equivalent to

```
count = count - 1;
```

Both of these operators have **prefix** and **postfix** versions. The prefix versions precede the variable name (`++a` or `--a`) whereas the postfix versions follow the variable name (`a++` or `a--`). Both increment or decrement the variable. If they are used as a single, atomic statement (as in the preceding statements), there is no difference between the two versions. So

```
a++;
```

is functionally equivalent to

```
++a;
```

and

```
a--;
```

is functionally equivalent to

```
--a;
```

However, if they are used inside a more complex expression, then they differ as follows. The prefix versions increment or decrement the variable first, then the new value of the variable is used in evaluating the expression. The postfix versions increment or decrement the variable after the old value of the variable is used in the expression.

Example 2.11 illustrates this difference.

```
 1 /* ShortcutOperators Class
 2    Anderson, Franceschi
 3 */
 4
 5 public class ShortcutOperators
 6 {
 7   public static void main( String [ ] args )
 8   {
 9     int a = 6;
10     int b = 2;
11
12     System.out.println( "At the beginning, a is " + a );
13     System.out.println( "Increment a with prefix notation: " + ++a );
14     System.out.println( "In the end, a is " + a );
15
16     System.out.println( "\nAt the beginning, b is " + b );
17     System.out.println( "Increment b with postfix notation: " + b++ );
18     System.out.println( "In the end, b is " + b );
19   }
20 }
```

EXAMPLE 2.11 Prefix and Postfix Increment Operators

Lines 9 and 10 declare and initialize two *int* variables, *a* and *b*, to 6 and 2, respectively. In order to illustrate the effect of both the prefix and postfix increment operators, we output their original values at lines 12 and 16. At line 13, we use the prefix increment operator to increment *a* inside an output statement; *a* is incremented before the output statement is executed, resulting in the output statement using the value 7 for *a*. At line 17, we use the postfix increment operator to increment *b* inside an output statement; *b* is incremented after the output statement is executed, resulting in the output statement using the value 2 for *b*. Lines 14 and 18 simply output the values of *a* and *b* after the prefix and postfix operators were used at lines 13 and 17. Figure 2.10 shows the output of this example.

Another set of shortcut operators simplify common calculations that change a single value. For example, the statement

```
a = a + 2: // add 2 to a
```

can be simplified as

```
a += 2; // add 2 to a
```

```
At the beginning, a is 6
Increment a with prefix notation: 7
In the end, a is 7

At the beginning, b is 2
Increment b with postfix notation: 2
In the end, b is 3
```

Figure 2.10
Output of Example 2.11

The value added to the target variable can be a variable name or a larger expression.

COMMON ERROR TRAP

No spaces are allowed between the arithmetic operator (+) and the equal sign. Note also that the sequence is +=, not =+.

The shortcut addition operator (+=) is a single operator; there are no spaces between the + and the =. Also, be careful not to reverse the order of the operators. For example, in the following statement, the operators are reversed, so the compiler interprets the statement as "assign a positive 2 to a."

```
a =+ 2 ; // Incorrect! Assigns a positive 2 to a
```

Java provides shortcut operators for each of the basic arithmetic operations: addition, subtraction, multiplication, division, and modulus. These operators are especially useful in performing repetitive calculations and in converting values from one scale to another. For example, to convert feet to inches, we multiply the number of feet by 12. So we can use the *= shortcut operator:

```
int length = 3; // length in feet
length *= 12;   // length converted to inches
```

Converting from one scale to another is a common operation in programming. For example, earlier in the chapter we converted quarters, dimes, and nickels to pennies. You might also need to convert hours to seconds, feet to square feet, or Fahrenheit temperatures to Celsius.

Example 2.12 demonstrates each of the shortcut arithmetic operators. The output is shown in Figure 2.11.

```
/*  Shortcut Arithmetic Operators
    Anderson, Franceschi
*/

public class ShortcutArithmeticOperators
{
   public static void main( String [ ] args )
   {
      int a = 5;
      System.out.println( "a is " + a );

      a += 10;     //  a = a + 10;
      System.out.println( "\nAfter a += 10;  a is " + a );

      a -= 3;       //  a = a - 3;
      System.out.println( "\nAfter a -= 3; a is " + a );

      a *= 2;       //  a = a * 2;
      System.out.println( "\nAfter a *= 2; a is " + a );

      a /= 6;       //  a = a / 6;
      System.out.println( "\nAfter a /= 6; a is " + a );

      a %= 3;      //  a = a % 3;
      System.out.println( "\nAfter a %= 3; a is " + a );
   }
}
```

EXAMPLE 2.12 ***Shortcut Arithmetic Operators***

Figure 2.11
Output of Example 2.12

```
a is 5

After a += 10; a is 15

After a -= 3; a is 12

After a *= 2; a is 24

After a /= 6; a is 4

After a %= 3; a is 1
```

Table 2.13 summarizes the shortcut operators and Table 2.14 shows where the shortcut operators fit into the order of operator precedence.

SOFTWARE ENGINEERING TIP

Learn the shortcut operators because Java programmers use them, and you will be able to read and understand their code.

TABLE 2.13 Shortcut Operators

Shortcut Operator	Example	Equivalent Statement
++	a++; or ++a;	a = a + 1;
--	a--; or --a;	a = a – 1;
+=	a += 3;	a = a + 3;
-=	a -=10;	a = a – 10;
*=	a *= 4;	a = a • 4;
/=	a /= 7;	a = a / 7;
%=	a %= 10;	a = a % 10;

TABLE 2.14 Order of Operator Precedence

Operator Hierarchy	Order of Same-Statement Evaluation	Operation
( )	left to right	parentheses for explicit grouping
++, --	**right to left**	**shortcut postincrement**
++, --	**right to left**	**shortcut preincrement**
*, /, %	left to right	multiplication, division, modulus
+, -	left to right	addition or *String* concatenation, subtraction
=, +=, -=, *=, /=, %=	right to left	assignment operator and **shortcut assignment operators**

Skill Practice
with these end-of-chapter questions

2.7.1 Multiple Choice Exercises
Question 3

2.7.2 Reading and Understanding Code
Questions 14, 15, 16, 17, 18, 19, 20, 21, 22

2.7.3 Fill In the Code
Questions 28, 30, 31

2.7.4 Identifying Errors in Code
Questions 36, 37

2.7.5 Debugging Area
Questions 42, 43

2.7.6 Write a Short Program
Question 45

2.7.8 Technical Writing
Question 51

2.5 Programming Activity 2: Exercising the Arithmetic Operators

In this Programming Activity, you will write a program that calculates the sum, difference, product, quotient, and modulus of two integers.

Open the *ShellApplication.java* source code shown in Example 2.1. You will find this file on the CD-ROM accompanying this book.

Replace the class name, *ShellApplication*, with the name *ArithmeticOperations*. Since this is now the name of our class, save the source file as the name *ArithmeticOperations.java*. Also replace the comment in line 1 with a description of what this application will do: "Exercising the Arithmetic Operators," and add your name. Your source file should look like Example 2.13.

```
/* Exercising the Arithmetic Operators
   your name here
*/

public class ArithmeticOperations
{
  public static void main( String [ ] args ) // required
  {
     // write your code here
  }
}
```

EXAMPLE 2.13 ***ArithmeticOperations*, Version 1**

After the comment

```
// write your code here
```

declare two integer variables, *number1* and *number2*, and assign them the initial values 10 and 3, respectively.

```
int number1 = 10, number2 = 3;
```

Let's start by printing the values of the variables:

```
System.out.println( "number1 is " + number1 );
System.out.println( "number2 is " + number2 );
```

Then define variables to hold the sum, difference, product, quotient, and modulus of these two numbers. Because these variables will hold the results of integer calculations, they should also be declared as *ints*. The variables don't need initial values, however, because we will assign values as we perform the calculations.

```
int sum, difference, product, quotient, modulus;
```

Now calculate the value of each variable and print the result. For example, here's the code for computing and printing the sum.

```
sum = number1 + number2;
System.out.println( "The sum is " + sum );
```

Remember to insert a space before the second quotation marks. Compile, run, and test your results. Then do the same for the remainder of the arithmetic operators. When you are finished, your output should look like Figure 2.12.

Figure 2.12
Output from *ArithmeticOperations*

```
number1 is 10
number2 is 3
The sum is 13
The difference is 7
The product is 30
The quotient is 3
The modulus is 1
```

DISCUSSION QUESTIONS ?

1. Explain how the division operator and the modulus operator perform complementary functions for integer division.
2. What happens if you omit the space at the end of the *String* literal in the *System.out.println* statements?

SUMMARY

2.6 Chapter Summary

- Java programs consist of at least one class.
- Identifiers are symbolic names for classes, methods, and data. Identifiers should start with a letter and may contain any combination of letters and digits, but no spaces. The length of an identifier is essentially unlimited. Identifier names are case sensitive.
- Java's reserved words cannot be used as identifiers.
- The basic building block of a Java program is the statement. A statement is terminated with a semicolon and can span several lines.
- Any amount of white space is permitted between identifiers, Java keywords, operands, operators, and literals. White space characters are the space, tab, newline, and carriage return.

- A block, which consists of 0, 1, or more statements, starts with a left curly brace and ends with a right curly brace. Blocks can be used anywhere in the program that a statement is legal.
- Comments are ignored by the compiler. Block comments are delineated by /* and */. Line comments start with // and continue to the end of the line.
- Java supports eight primitive data types: *double*, *float*, *long*, *int*, *short*, *byte*, *char*, and *boolean*.
- Variables must be declared before they are used. Declaring a variable is specifying the data item's identifier and data type. The syntax for declaring a variable is: `dataType identifier1, identifier2, ...;`
- Begin variable names with a lowercase letter. If the variable name consists of more than one word, begin each word after the first with a capital letter. Do not put spaces between words.
- An integer data type is one that evaluates to a positive or negative whole number. Java recognizes four integer data types: *int*, *short*, *long*, and *byte*.
- Floating-point data types store numbers with fractional parts. Java supports two floating-point data types: the single-precision type *float*, and the double-precision type *double*.
- The *char* data type stores one Unicode character. Because Unicode characters are encoded as unsigned numbers using 16 bits, a *char* variable is stored in two bytes of memory.
- The *boolean* data type can store only two values, which are expressed using the Java reserved words *true* and *false*.
- The assignment operator (=) is used to give a value to a variable.
- To assign an initial value to a variable, use this syntax when declaring the variable:

```
dataType variable1 = initialValue1;
```

- Literals can be used to assign initial values or to reassign the value of a variable.
- Constants are data items whose value, once assigned, cannot be changed. Data items that you know should not change throughout

CHAPTER SUMMARY

the execution of a program should be declared as a constant, using this syntax:

```
final dataType CONSTANT_IDENTIFIER = initialValue;
```

- Constant identifiers, by convention, are composed of all capital letters with underscores separating words.
- An expression consists of operators and operands that evaluate to a single value.
- The value of an expression can be assigned to a variable or constant, which must be a data type compatible with the value of the expression and cannot be a constant that has been assigned a value already.
- Java provides binary operators for addition, subtraction, multiplication, division, and modulus.
- Calculation of the value of expressions follows the rules of operator precedence.
- Integer division truncates any fractional part of the quotient.
- When an arithmetic operator is invoked with operands that are of different primitive types, the compiler temporarily converts, or promotes, one or both of the operands.
- An expression or a variable can be temporarily cast to a different data type using this syntax:

```
(dataType) ( expression )
```

- Shortcut operators ++ and –– simplify incrementing or decrementing a value by 1. The prefix versions precede the variable name and increment or decrement the variable, then use its new value in evaluation of the expression. The postfix versions follow the variable name and increment or decrement the variable after using the old value in the expression.
- Java provides shortcut operators for each of the basic arithmetic operations: addition, subtraction, multiplication, division, and modulus.

2.7 Exercises, Problems, and Projects

2.7.1 Multiple Choice Exercises

1. What is the valid way to declare an integer variable named *a*? (Check all that apply.)

   - ❑ `int a;`
   - ❑ `a int;`
   - ❑ `integer a;`

2. Which of the following identifiers are valid?

   - ❑ `a`
   - ❑ `sales`
   - ❑ `sales&profit`
   - ❑ `int`
   - ❑ `inter`
   - ❑ `doubleSales`
   - ❑ `TAX_RATE`
   - ❑ `1stLetterChar`
   - ❑ `char`

3. Given three declared and initialized *int* variables *a*, *b*, and *c*, which of the following statements are valid?

   - ❑ `a = b;`
   - ❑ `a = 67;`
   - ❑ `b = 8.7;`
   - ❑ `a + b = 8;`
   - ❑ `a * b = 12;`
   - ❑ `c = a - b;`
   - ❑ `c = a / 2.3;`
   - ❑ `boolean t = a;`

- ❑ `a /= 4;`
- ❑ `a += c;`

2.7.2 Reading and Understanding Code

4. What is the output of this code sequence?

```
double a = 12.5;
System.out.println( a );
```

5. What is the output of this code sequence?

```
int a = 6;
System.out.println( a );
```

6. What is the output of this code sequence?

```
float a = 13f;
System.out.println( a );
```

7. What is the output of this code sequence?

```
double a = 13 / 5;
System.out.println( a );
```

8. What is the output of this code sequence?

```
int a = 13 / 5;
System.out.println( a );
```

9. What is the output of this code sequence?

```
int a = 13 % 5;
System.out.println( a );
```

10. What is the output of this code sequence?

```
int a = 12 / 6 * 2;
System.out.println( a );
```

11. What is the output of this code sequence?

```
int a = 12 / ( 6 * 2 );
System.out.println( a );
```

12. What is the output of this code sequence?

```
int a = 4 + 6 / 2;
System.out.println( a );
```

13. What is the output of this code sequence?

```
int a = ( 4 + 6 ) / 2;
System.out.println( a );
```

14. What is the output of this code sequence?

```
double a = 12.0 / 5;
System.out.println( a );
```

15. What is the output of this code sequence?

```
int a = (int) 12.0 / 5;
System.out.println( a );
```

16. What is the output of this code sequence?

```
double a = (double) ( 12 ) / 5;
System.out.println( a );
```

17. What is the output of this code sequence?

```
double a = (double) ( 12 / 5 );
System.out.println( a );
```

18. What is the output of this code sequence?

```
int a = 5;
a++;
System.out.println( a );
```

19. What is the output of this code sequence?

```
int a = 5;
System.out.println( a-- );
```

20. What is the output of this code sequence?

```
int a = 5;
System.out.println( --a );
```

21. What is the output of this code sequence?

```
int a = 5;
a += 2;
System.out.println( a );
```

22. What is the output of this code sequence?

```
int a = 5;
a /= 6;
System.out.println( a );
```

2.7.3 Fill In the Code

23. Write the code to declare a *float* variable named *a* and assign *a* the value 34.2.

```
// your code goes here
```

24. Write the code to assign the value 10 to an *int* variable named *a.*

```
int a;
// your code goes here
```

25. Write the code to declare a *boolean* variable named *a* and assign *a* the value *false.*

```
// your code goes here
```

26. Write the code to declare a *char* variable named *a* and assign *a* the character B.

```
// your code goes here
```

27. Write the code to calculate the total of three *int* variables *a, b,* and *c* and print the result.

```
int a = 3;
int b = 5;
int c = 8;

// your code goes here
```

28. Write the code to calculate the average of two *int* variables *a* and *b* and print the result. The average should be printed as a floating-point number.

```
int a = 3;
int b = 5;

// your code goes here
```

29. Write the code to calculate and print the remainder of the division of two *int* variables with the values 10 and 3 (the value printed will be 1).

```
int a = 10;
int b = 3;

// your code goes here
```

30. This code increases the value of a variable *a* by 1, using the shortcut increment operator.

```
int a = 7;

// your code goes here
```

31. This code multiplies the value of a variable *a* by 3, using a shortcut operator.

```
int a = 7;

// your code goes here
```

32. Assume that we have already declared and initialized two *int* variables, *a* and *b*. Convert the following sentences to legal Java expressions and statements.

    - ❑ `b equals a plus 3 minus 7`
    - ❑ `b equals a times 4`
    - ❑ `a equals b times b`
    - ❑ `a equals b times 3 times 5`
    - ❑ `b equals the quotient of the division of a by 2`
    - ❑ `b equals the remainder of the division of a by 3`

2.7.4 Identifying Errors in Code

33. Where is the error in this code sequence?

```
int a = 3.3;
```

34. Where is the error in this code sequence?

```
double a = 45.2;
float b = a;
```

35. Where is the error in this code sequence?

```
int a = 7.5 % 3;
```

36. What would happen when this code sequence is compiled and executed?

```
int a = 5 / 0;
```

37. Where is the error in this code sequence?

```
int a = 5;
a - = 4;
```

38. Is there an error in this code sequence? Explain.

```
char c = 67;
```

39. Is there an error in this code sequence? Explain.

```
boolean a = 1;
```

2.7.5 Debugging Area—Using Messages from the Java Compiler and Java JVM

40. You coded the following on line 8 of class *Test.java*:

```
int a = 26.4;
```

When you compile, you get the following message:

```
Test.java:8: possible loss of precision
found : double
required: int
  int a = 26.4;
        ^
1 error
```

Explain what the problem is and how to fix it.

41. You coded the following on line 8 of class *Test.java*:

```
int a = 3
```

When you compile, you get the following message:

```
Test.java:8: ';' expected
        int a = 3
                ^
```

Explain what the problem is and how to fix it.

42. You coded the following in class *Test.java*:

```
int a = 32;
int b = 10;
double c = a / b;
System.out.println( "The value of c is " + c );
```

The code compiles properly and runs, but the result is not what you expected. The output is

```
The value of c is 3.0
```

You expected the value of *c* to be 3.2. Explain what the problem is and how to fix it.

43. You coded the following in class *Test.java*:

```
int a = 5;
a =+ 3;
System.out.println( "The value of a is " + a );
```

The code compiles properly and runs, but the result is not what you expected. The output is

```
The value of a is 3
```

You expected the value of *a* to be 8. Explain what the problem is and how to fix it.

2.7.6 Write a Short Program

44. Write a program that calculates and outputs the square of each integer from 1 to 9.

45. Write a program that calculates and outputs the average of integers 1, 7, 9, and 34.

46. Write a program that outputs the following:

```
****
```

2.7.7 Programming Projects

47. Write a program that prints the letter X composed of asterisks (*). Your output should look like this:

```
*   *
 * *
  *
 * *
*   *
```

48. Write a program that converts 10, 50, and 100 kilograms to pounds (1 lb = .454 kg).

49. Write a program that converts 2, 5, and 10 inches to millimeters (1 inch = 25.4 mm).

50. Write a program to compute and output the perimeter and the area of a circle having a radius of 3.2 inches.

2.7.8 Technical Writing

51. Some programmers like to write code that is as compact as possible, for instance, using the increment (or decrement) operator in the middle of another statement. Typically, these programmers document their programs with very few comments. Discuss whether this is a good idea, keeping in mind that a program "lives" through a certain period of time.

52. Compare the following data types for integer numbers: *int*, *short*, and *long*. Discuss their representation in binary, how much space they take in memory, and the purpose of having these data types available to programmers.

CHAPTER 3

Object-Oriented Programming, Part 1: Using Classes

CHAPTER CONTENTS

Introduction

Writing computer programs that use classes and objects is called **object-oriented programming**, or **OOP**. Every Java program consists of at least one class.

In this chapter, we'll introduce object-oriented programming as a way to use classes that have already been written. Classes provide services to the program. These services might include writing a message to the program's user, popping up a dialog box, performing some mathematical calculations, formatting numbers, drawing shapes in a window, or many other basic tasks that add a more professional look to even simple programs. The program that uses a class is called the **client** of the class.

One benefit of using a prewritten class is that we don't need to write the code ourselves; it has already been written and tested for us. This means that we can write our programs more quickly. In other words, we shorten the development time of the program. Using prewritten and pretested classes provides other benefits as well, including more reliable programs with fewer errors.

In Chapter 7, we'll show you how to write your own classes. For now, we'll explore how using prewritten classes can add functionality to our programs.

3.1 Class Basics and Benefits

In Java, classes are composed of data and operations—or functions—that operate on the data. Objects of a class are created using the class as a template, or guide. Think of the class as a generic description, and an object as a specific item of that class. Or you can think of a class as a cookie cutter, the objects of that class are the cookies made with the cookie cutter. For example, a *Student* class might have the following data: name, year, and grade point average. All students have these three data items. We can create an object of the *Student* class by specifying an identifier for the object (for example, *student1*) along with a name, year, and grade point average for a particular student (for example, *Maria Gonzales*, *Sophomore*, *3.5*). The identifier of the object is called the **object reference**. Creating an object of a class is called **instantiating an object**, and the object is called an **instance of the class**. Many objects can be instantiated from one class. There can be many instances of the *Student* class, that is, many *Student* objects can be instantiated from the *Student* class. For example, we could create a second object of the *Student* class, *student2,* with its data as *Mike Smith, Junior, 3.0.*

The data associated with an object of a class are called **instance variables**, or **fields**, and can be variables and constants of any primitive data type (*byte, short, int, long, float, double, char,* and *boolean*), or they can be objects of other classes.

The operations for a class, called **methods**, set the values of the data, retrieve the current values of the data, and perform other class-related functions on the data. For example, the *Student* class would provide methods to set the values of the name, year, and grade point average; retrieve the current values of the name, year, and grade point average; and perhaps promote a student to the next year. Invoking a method on an object is called **calling the method**. With a few exceptions, only class methods can directly access or change the instance variables of an object. Other objects must call the methods to set or retrieve the values of the instance variables. Together, the fields and methods of a class are called its **members**.

In essence, a class is a new data type, which is created by combining items of Java primitive data types and objects of other classes. Just as the primitive data types can be manipulated using arithmetic operators (+, –, *, /, and %), objects can be manipulated by calling class methods.

We like to think of classes as similar to M&M™ candies: a protective outer coating around a soft center. Because the methods to operate on the data are included in the class, they provide a protective coating around the data inside. In a well-designed class, only the class methods can change the data. Methods of other classes cannot directly access the data. We say that the data is *private* to the class. In other words, the class **encapsulates** the data and the methods provide the only interface for setting or changing the data values. The benefit from this encapsulation is that the class methods ensure that only valid values are assigned to an object. For example, a method to set a Student's grade point average would accept values only between 0.0 and 4.0.

Let's look at another example of a class. The *SimpleDate* class, written by the authors, has the instance variables *month, day,* and *year.* An object of this class, *independenceDay,* could be instantiated with data values of *7, 4,* and *1776.* Another object of that class, *examDay,* might be instantiated with the values *12*, *4*, and *2006*. Methods of the *SimpleDate* class ensure that only valid values are set for the month, day, and year. For example, the class methods would not allow us to set a date with a value of January 32. Other class methods increment the date to the next day and provide the date in *mm/dd/yyyy* format.

SOFTWARE ENGINEERING TIP

By convention, class names in Java start with a capital letter. Method names, instance variables, and object names start with a lowercase letter. In all of these names, embedded words begin with a capital letter.

Notice that the class names we used, *Student* and *SimpleDate*, begin with a capital letter, and the object names, *student1*, *independenceDay*, and *examDay*, start with a lowercase letter. By convention, class names start with a capital letter. Object names, instance variables, and method names conventionally start with a lowercase letter. Internal words start with a capital letter in class names, object names, variables, and methods.

There are many benefits to using classes in a program. Some of the most important benefits include reusability (not only in the current program but also in other programs), encapsulation, and reliability.

A well-written class can be reused in many programs. For example, a *SimpleDate* class could be used in a calendar program, an appointment-scheduling program, an online shopping program, and many more applications that rely on dates. Reusing code is much faster than writing and testing new code. As an added bonus, reusing a tested and debugged class in another program makes the program more reliable.

Encapsulation of a class's data and methods helps to isolate operations on the data. This makes it easier to track the source of a bug. For example, when a bug is discovered in an object of the *Student* class, then you know to look for the problem in the methods of the *Student* class, because no other code in your program can directly change the data in a *Student* object.

You do not need to know the implementation details of a class in order to use it in your program. Does the *SimpleDate* class store the date in memory as three integers, *month*, *day*, and *year*? Or is the date stored as the number of milliseconds since 1980? The beauty of object orientation is that we don't need to know the implementation of the class; all we need to know is the class **application programming interface** (**API**), that is, how to instantiate objects and how to call the class methods.

The benefits of using classes are clear. We will leave the details of creating our own classes until Chapter 7. In the meantime, let's explore how to use classes that are already written.

3.2 Creating Objects Using Constructors

A class describes a generic template for creating, or instantiating, objects. In fact, an object must be instantiated before it can be used. To understand how to instantiate an object of a class and how to call methods of the class, you must know the API of a class, which the creators of the class make public. Table 3.1 shows the API of the *SimpleDate* class, written by the authors of this textbook.

Instantiating an object consists of defining an object reference—which will hold the address of the object in memory—and calling a special method of the class called a **constructor**, which has the same name as the class. The job of the constructor is to assign initial values to the data of the class.

Example 3.1 illustrates how to instantiate objects of the *SimpleDate* class.

```
/*  A Demonstration of Using Constructors
    Anderson, Franceschi
*/

public class Constructors
{
  public static void main( String [ ] args )
  {
    SimpleDate independenceDay;
    independenceDay = new SimpleDate( 7, 4, 1776 );

    SimpleDate graduationDate = new SimpleDate( 5, 15, 2012 );

    SimpleDate defaultDate = new SimpleDate( );
  }
}
```

EXAMPLE 3.1 Demonstrating Constructors

Declaring an object reference is very much like declaring a variable of a primitive type; you specify the data type and an identifier. For example, to declare an integer variable named *number1*, you provide the data type (*int*) and the identifier (*number1*), as follows:

```
int number1;
```

TABLE 3.1 The *SimpleDate* Class API

SimpleDate Class Constructor Summary	
SimpleDate( )	
creates a *SimpleDate* object with initial default values of 1, 1, 2000.	
SimpleDate(int mm, int dd, int yy)	
creates a *SimpleDate* object with the initial values of *mm*, *dd*, and *yy*.	

SimpleDate Class Method Summary	
Return value	**Method name and argument list**
int	getMonth( ) returns the value of *month*.
int	getDay( ) returns the value of *day*.
int	getYear( ) returns the value of *year*.
void	setMonth(int mm) sets the *month* to *mm*; if *mm* is invalid, sets *month* to 1.
void	setDay(int dd) sets the *day* to *dd*; if *dd* is invalid, sets *day* to 1.
void	setYear(int yy) sets the *year* to *yy*.
void	nextDay( ) increments the date to the next day.
String	toString( ) returns the value of the date in the form: *month/day/year*.
boolean	equals(Object obj) compares this *SimpleDate* object to another *SimpleDate* object.

One notable difference in declaring an object reference is that its data type is a class, not a primitive data type. Here is the syntax for declaring an object reference:

```
ClassName objectReference1, objectReference2, ...;
```

In Example 3.1, lines 9, 12, and 14 declare object references for a *SimpleDate* object. *SimpleDate*, the class name, is the data type, and *independenceDay*, *graduationDate*, and *defaultDate* are the object references.

Object references can refer to **any** object of its class. For example, *SimpleDate* object references can point to any *SimpleDate* object, but a *SimpleDate* object reference cannot point to objects of other classes, such as a *Student* object.

Once an object reference has been declared, you instantiate the object using the following syntax:

```
objectReference = new ClassName( argument_list );
```

This calls a constructor of the class to initialize the data. The **argument list** consists of a comma-separated list of initial data values to assign to the object. Classes often provide multiple constructors with different argument lists. Depending on which constructor you call, you can accept default values for the data or specify initial values for the data. When you instantiate an object, your argument list—that is, the number of arguments and their data types—must match one of the constructors' argument lists.

As shown in Table 3.1, the *SimpleDate* class has two constructors. The first constructor, *SimpleDate( )*, is called the **default constructor**, because its **argument list is empty**. This constructor assigns default values to all data in the object. Thus, in line 14 of Example 3.1, which uses the default constructor, the data for the *defaultDate* object is set to the default values for the *SimpleDate* class, which are *1*, *1*, and *2000*.

We see from Table 3.1 that the second constructor for the *SimpleDate* class, *SimpleDate(int mm, int dd, int yy)*, takes three arguments, all of which should evaluate to integer values. The first argument is the value for the month, the second argument is the value for the day, and the third argument is the value for the year.

Lines 10 and 12 of Example 3.1 instantiate *SimpleDate* objects using the second constructor. In line 10, the argument list tells the constructor to give the value *7* to the month, *4* to the day, and *1776* to the year. In line 12, the argument list tells the constructor to give the value *5* to the month, *15* to the day, and *2012* to the year. Note that no data types are given in the argument list, only the initial values for the data. The data types of the arguments are specified in the API so that the client of the class knows what data types the constructor is expecting for its arguments.

Lines 12 and 14 also illustrate that you can combine the declaration of the object reference and instantiation of the object in a single statement.

When an object is instantiated, the JVM allocates memory to the new object and assigns that memory location to its object reference. Figure 3.1 shows the three objects instantiated in Example 3.1.

Figure 3.1
Three *SimpleDate* Objects after Instantiation

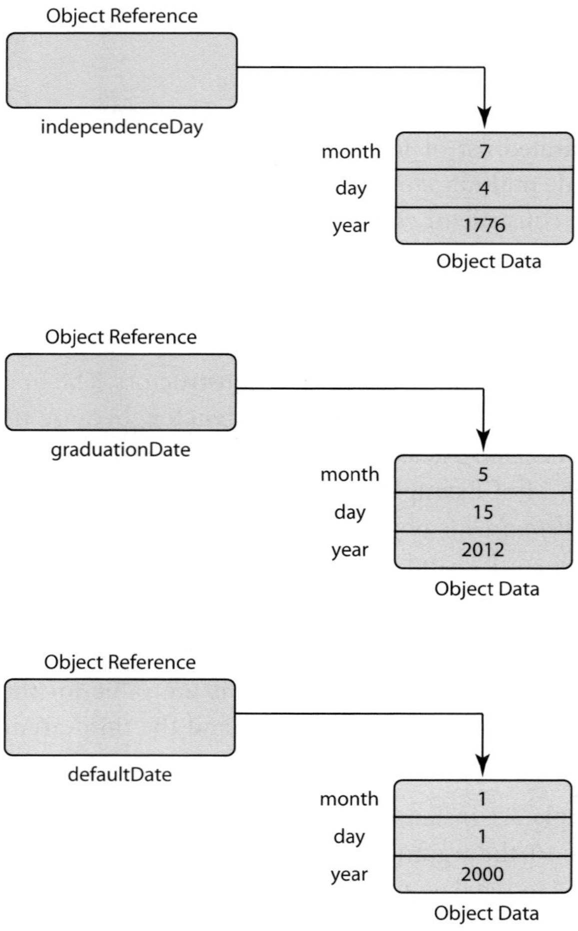

It's important to understand that an object reference and the object data are different: The object reference represents the memory location, and the object data are the data stored at that memory location. Notice in Figure 3.1 that the object references, *independenceDay*, *graduationDate*, and *defaultDate*, point to the locations of the object data.

COMMON ERROR TRAP

Do not forget to instantiate all objects that your program needs. Objects must be instantiated before they can be used.

3.3 Calling Methods

Once an object is instantiated, we can use the object by calling its methods. As we mentioned earlier, the authors of classes publish their API so that their clients know what methods are available and how to call those methods.

Figure 3.2 illustrates how calling a class method alters the flow of control in your program. When this program starts running, the JVM executes instruction 1, then instruction 2, then it encounters a method call. At that

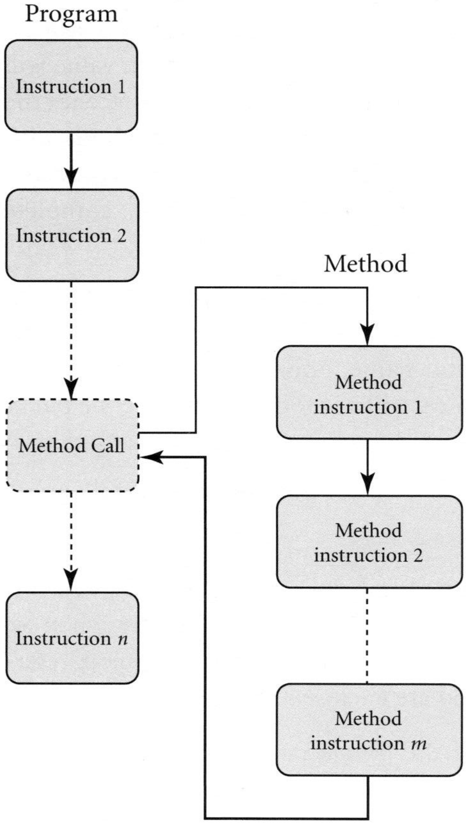

Figure 3.2
Flow of Control of a Method Call

point, the JVM **transfers control to the method** and starts executing instructions in the method. When the method finishes executing, the JVM transfers control back to the program immediately after the point the method was called and continues executing instructions in the program.

A class API consists of the class method names, their return values, and their argument lists. The argument list for a method indicates the order and number of arguments to send to the method, along with the data type of each argument. Each item in the argument list consists of a data type and a name. The arguments can be literals, constants, variables, or any expression that evaluates to the data type specified in the API of the method. For example, the API in Table 3.1 shows that the *setMonth* method takes one argument, which must evaluate to an integer value.

A method may or may not return a value, as indicated by a data type, class type, or the keyword **void** in front of the method name. If the method returns a value, then the data type or class type of its **return value** will precede the method's name. For instance, in Table 3.1, the *getDay* method returns an integer value. The call to a **value-returning method** will be used in an expression. When the method finishes executing, its return value will replace the method call in the expression. If the keyword *void* precedes the method name, the method does not return a value. Because methods with a *void* return type have no value, they cannot be used in an expression; instead, a method call to a method with a *void* return type is a complete statement. In Table 3.1, the *setYear* method is a *void* method.

Another keyword you will see preceding the method call in an API is *public*. This keyword means that any client of the class can call this method. If the keyword *private* precedes the method name, only other methods of that class can call that method. Although we will not formally include the *public* keyword in the API, all the methods we discuss in this chapter are *public*.

To call a method for an object of a class, we use **dot notation**, as follows:

```
objectReference.methodName( arg1, arg2, arg3, . . . )
```

The object reference is followed immediately by a **dot** (a period), which is followed immediately by the method name. (Later in the chapter, when we call *static* methods, we will substitute the class name for the object reference.) The arguments for the method are enclosed in parentheses.

Let's look again at the methods of the *SimpleDate* class. The first three methods in the *SimpleDate* class API take an empty argument list and return an *int*; thus, those methods have a return value of type *int*. You can call these methods in any expression in your program where you could use an *int*. The value of the first method, *getMonth( )*, is the value of the month in the object. Similarly, the value of *getDay( )* is the value of the day in the object, and the value of *getYear( )* is the value of the year. These "get" methods are formally called **accessor methods**; they enable clients to access the value of the instance variables of an object.

The next three methods in the *SimpleDate* class API take one argument of type *int* and do not return a value, which is indicated by the keyword *void*. These methods are called in standalone statements. The first method, *setMonth(int mm)*, changes the value of the month in the object to the value of the method's argument, *mm*. Similarly, *setDay(int dd)* changes the value of the day in the object, and *setYear(int yy)* changes the value of the year in the object to the value of the method's argument. These "set" methods are formally called **mutator methods**; they enable a client to change the value of the instance variables of an object.

Example 3.2 illustrates how to use some of the methods of the *SimpleDate* class. Line 10 calls the *getMonth* method for the *independenceDay* object. When line 10 is executed, control transfers to the *getMonth* method. When the *getMonth* method finishes executing, the value it returns (7) replaces the method call in the statement. The statement then effectively becomes:

```
int independenceMonth = 7;
```

In lines 15–16, we print the value of the day in the *graduationDate* object. Again, control transfers to the *getDay* method, then its return value (15) replaces the method call. So the statement effectively becomes:

```
System.out.println( "The current day for graduation is "
                    + 15 );
```

Line 18 calls the *setDay* method, which is used to change the value of the day for an object. The *setDay* method takes one *int* argument and has a *void* return value. Line 18 is a complete statement, because the method call to a method with a *void* return value is a complete statement. The method changes the value of the day in the *graduationDate* object, which we illustrate in lines 19–20 by printing the new value as shown in Figure 3.3. Then, on line 22, we instantiate another object, *currentDay*, with a day, month, and year of 9, 30, 2008, which we demonstrate by printing the values returned by calls to the *getDay*, *getMonth*, and *getYear* methods. On line 28, we call the *nextDay* method, which has a *void* return value, and increments the date to the next day, and then we print the new values of the *currentDay* object.

COMMON ERROR TRAP

When calling a method that takes no arguments, remember to include the empty parentheses after the method's name. The parentheses are required even if there are no arguments.

COMMON ERROR TRAP

When calling a method, include only values or expressions in your argument list. Including data types in your argument list will cause a compiler error.

```java
/*  A demonstration of calling methods
    Anderson, Franceschi
*/

public class Methods
{
  public static void main( String [ ] args )
  {
     SimpleDate independenceDay = new SimpleDate( 7, 4, 1776 );
     int independenceMonth = independenceDay.getMonth( );
     System.out.println( "Independence day is in month "
                         + independenceMonth );

     SimpleDate graduationDate = new SimpleDate( 5, 15, 2008 );
     System.out.println( "The current day for graduation is "
                         + graduationDate.getDay( ) );

     graduationDate.setDay( 12 );
     System.out.println( "The revised day for graduation is "
                         + graduationDate.getDay( ) );

     SimpleDate currentDay = new SimpleDate( 9, 30, 2008 );
     System.out.println( "The current day is "
                         + currentDay.getMonth( ) + '/'
                         + currentDay.getDay( ) + '/'
                         + currentDay.getYear( ) );

     currentDay.nextDay( );
     System.out.println( "The next day is "
                         + currentDay.getMonth( ) + '/'
                         + currentDay.getDay( ) + '/'
                         + currentDay.getYear( ) );
  }
}
```

EXAMPLE 3.2 Calling Methods

Figure 3.3
Output of Example 3.2

```
Independence day is in month 7
The current day for graduation is 15
The revised day for graduation is 12
The current day is 9/30/2008
The next day is 10/1/2008
```

For now, we'll postpone discussion of the last two methods in the class API, *toString* and *equals*, except to say that their functions, respectively, are to convert the object data to a printable format and to compare the object data to another object's data. All classes provide these methods.

Skill Practice
with these end-of-chapter questions

3.19.1 Multiple Choice Exercises

Questions 2, 3, 4, 5, 9, 10

3.19.8 Technical Writing

Questions 69, 70

3.4 Using Object References

As we have mentioned, an object reference points to the data of an object. The object reference and the object data are distinct entities. Any object can have more than one object reference pointing to it, or an object can have no object references pointing to it.

In Example 3.3, two *SimpleDate* object references, *hireDate* and *promotionDate*, are declared and their objects are instantiated at lines 9 and 14. Lines 10–12 and 15–18 output the respective data member values of *hireDate* and *promotionDate*. Then, line 20 uses the assignment operator to copy the object reference *hireDate* to the object reference *promotionDate*. After line 20, both object references have the same value and therefore point to the location of the same object, as shown in Figure 3.4. The second object, with values (9, 28, 2007), no longer has an object reference pointing to it and is now marked for **garbage collection**. The **garbage collector**, which is part of the Java Virtual Machine, releases the memory allocated to objects that

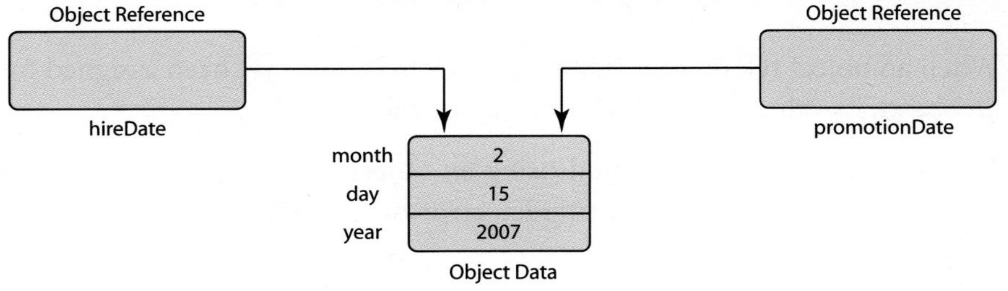

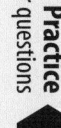

Figure 3.4
Two Object References Pointing to the Same Object

no longer have an object reference pointing to them. Lines 23–25 and 26–29 output the respective data member values of *hireDate* and *promotionDate* again. These are now identical, as shown in Figure 3.5.

```
 1 /*  A demonstration of object reference assignment
 2     Anderson, Franceschi
 3 */
 4
 5 public class ObjectReferenceAssignment
 6 {
 7   public static void main( String [ ] args )
 8   {
 9      SimpleDate hireDate = new SimpleDate( 2, 15, 2007 );
10      System.out.println( "hireDate is " + hireDate.getMonth( )
11                          + "/" + hireDate.getDay( )
12                          + "/" + hireDate.getYear( ) );
13
14      SimpleDate promotionDate = new SimpleDate( 9, 28, 2007 );
15      System.out.println( "promotionDate is "
16                          + promotionDate.getMonth( )
17                          + "/" + promotionDate.getDay( )
18                          + "/" + promotionDate.getYear( ) );
19
20      promotionDate = hireDate;
21      System.out.println( "\nAfter assigning hireDate "
22                          + "to promotionDate:" );
23      System.out.println( "hireDate is " + hireDate.getMonth( )
24                          + "/" + hireDate.getDay( )
25                          + "/" + hireDate.getYear( ) );
26      System.out.println( "promotionDate is "
27                          + promotionDate.getMonth( )
28                          + "/" + promotionDate.getDay( )
29                          + "/" + promotionDate.getYear( ) );
30   }
31 }
```

EXAMPLE 3.3 Demonstrating Object Reference Assignments

When an object reference is first declared, but has not yet been assigned to an object, its value is a special literal value, **null**.

If you attempt to call a method using an object reference whose value is *null*, Java generates either a compiler error or a run-time error called an

```
hireDate is 2/15/2007
promotionDate is 9/28/2007

After assigning hireDate to promotionDate:
hireDate is 2/15/2007
promotionDate is 2/15/2007
```

Figure 3.5
Output of Example 3.3

exception. The exception is a *NullPointerException* and results in a series of messages printed on the Java console indicating where in the program the *null* object reference was used. Line 10 of Example 3.4 will generate a compiler error, as shown in Figure 3.6, because *aDate* has not been instantiated.

```
 1 /*  A demonstration of trying to use a null object reference
 2     Anderson, Franceschi
 3 */
 4
 5 public class NullReference
 6 {
 7   public static void main( String [ ] args )
 8   {
 9      SimpleDate aDate;
10      aDate.setMonth( 5 );
11   }
12 }
```

EXAMPLE 3.4 Attempting to Use a *null* Object Reference

```
NullReference.java:10: variable aDate might not have been initialized
     aDate.setMonth( 5 );
     ^

1 error
```

Figure 3.6
Compiler error from Example 3.4

COMMON ERROR TRAP

Using a *null* object reference to call a method will generate either a compiler error or a *NullPointerException* at run time. Be sure to instantiate an object before attempting to use the object reference.

Java does not provide support for explicitly deleting an object. One way to indicate to the garbage collector that your program is finished with an object is to set its object reference to *null*. Obviously, once an object reference has the value *null*, it can no longer be used to call methods.

```
1 /*  A demonstration of trying to use a null object reference
2     Anderson, Franceschi
3 */
4
5 public class NullReference2
6 {
7   public static void main( String [ ] args )
8   {
9      SimpleDate independenceDay = new SimpleDate( 7, 4, 1776 );
10     System.out.println( "The month of independenceDay is "
11                           + independenceDay.getMonth( ) );
12
13     independenceDay = null;  // set object reference to null
14     // attempt to use object reference
15     System.out.println( "The month of independenceDay is "
16                           + independenceDay.getMonth( ) );
17   }
18 }
```

EXAMPLE 3.5 Another Attempt to Use a *null* Object Reference

Example 3.5 shows a *NullPointerException* being generated at run time. Line 9 instantiates the *independenceDay* object, and lines 10–11 print the month. Line 13 assigns *null* to the object reference and lines 15–16 attempt to print the month again. As Figure 3.7 shows, a *NullPointerException* is generated. Notice that the console message indicates the name of the application class (*NullReference2*), the method *main*, and the line number *15*, where the exception occurred. The JVM often prints additional lines in the message, depending on where in your program the error occurred.

Figure 3.7
Output of Example 3.5

```
The month of independenceDay is 7
Exception in thread "main" java.lang.NullPointerException
   at NullReference2.main(NullReference2.java:15)
```

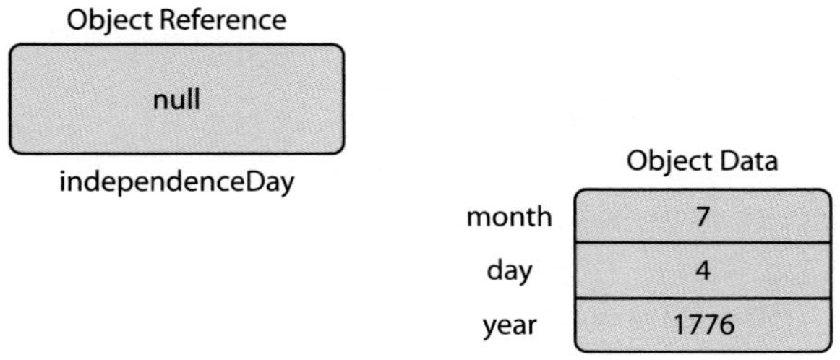

Figure 3.8
The *independenceDay* Object Reference Set to *null*

Figure 3.8 shows the *independenceDay* object reference and object data after setting the object reference to *null.*

3.5 Programming Activity 1: Calling Methods

Let's put this all together with a sample program that uses a *SimpleDate* object. In this Programming Activity, we'll use a program that displays the values of the object data as you instantiate the object and call the methods of the class.

In the Chapter 3 Programming Activity 1 folder on the CD-ROM accompanying this book, you will find three source files: *SimpleDate.java, SimpleDateClient.java,* and *Pause.java.* Copy all the *.java* and *.class* files to a directory on your computer. Note that all files should be in the same directory.

Open the *SimpleDateClient.java* source file. You'll notice that the class already contains some source code. Your job is to fill in the blanks. Search for five asterisks in a row (*****). This will position you to the places in the source code where you will add your code. This section of code is shown in Figure 3.9.

Notice that line 15 is a declaration of a *SimpleDate* object reference, *dateObj.* You will use this object reference for instantiating an object and for calling the methods of the *SimpleDate* class.

In the source file, you should see nine commented lines that instruct you to instantiate the object or call a method. You will also notice that there are eight lines that look like this:

```
// animate( "message" );
```

Figure 3.9

Partial Listing of *SimpleDateClient.java*

```
private int animationPause = 2; // 2 seconds between animations

SimpleDate dateObj; // declare Date object reference

public void workWithDates( )
{
  animate( "dateObj reference declared" );

  /***** Add your code here *****/
  /**** 1. Instantiate dateObj using an empty argument list  */


  //animate( "Instantiated dateObj - empty argument list" );

  /***** 2. Set the month to the month you were born */


  //animate( "Set month to birth month" );


  /***** 3. Set the day to the day of the month you were born */


  //animate( "Set day to birth day" );


  /***** 4. Set the year to the year you were born */


  //animate( "Set year to birth year" );


  /***** 5. Call the nextDay method */


  //animate( "Set the date to the next day" );


  /***** 6. Set the day to 32, an illegal value */


  //animate( "Set day to 32" );


  /***** 7. Set the month to 13, an illegal value */


  //animate( "Set month to 13" );


  /***** 8. Assign the value null to dateObj */


  //animate( "Set object reference to null" );


  /***** 9. Attempt to set the month to 1 */

}
```

These lines are calls to an *animate* method in this class that displays the object reference and the object data after you have executed your code. The *message* is a *String* literal that describes what action your code just took. The *animate* method will display the message, as well as the object data. Note that when you call a method in the same class, you don't use an object reference and dot notation.

To complete the Programming Activity, write the requested code on the line between the numbered instruction and the *animate* method call. Then **uncomment** (remove the two slashes from) the *animate* method call.

For example, after you've written the code for the first instruction, lines 22 through 25 should look like this. The line you write is shown in bold.

```
/* 1. Instantiate a dateObj using empty argument list */

dateObj = new SimpleDate( );
animate( "Instantiated dateObj - empty argument list" );
```

Compile and run the code and you will see a window that looks like the one in Figure 3.10.

As you can see, the *dateObj* reference points to the *SimpleDate* object, and the *month*, *day*, and *year* instance variables have been assigned default values.

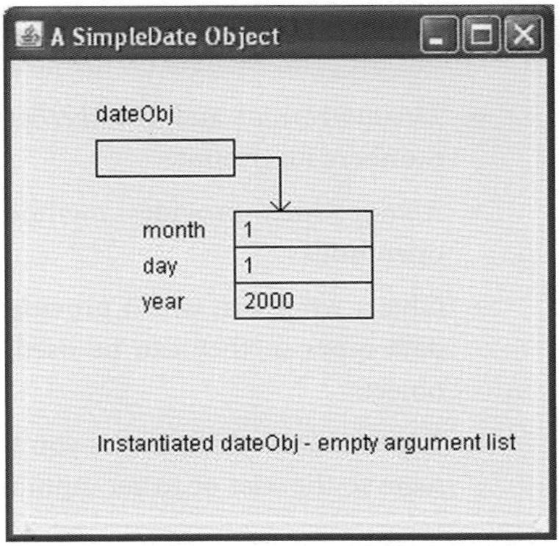

Figure 3.10
Programming Activity 1 Output

Write the code for the remaining instructions, compiling and running the program after completing each task. The program will display the changes you make to the object data.

The pause between animations is set by default to two seconds. To change the pause time, change the value assigned to *animationPause* on line 13 to the number of seconds you would like to pause between animations.

DISCUSSION QUESTIONS ?

1. After instructions 6 and 7 have executed, why do the day and month values get set to 1?
2. At the end of the execution of the program, a *NullPointerException* is generated. Which statement in the program causes this error? Explain why.

3.6 The Java Class Library

Java provides more than 2,000 predefined classes that you can use to add functionality to your program. In this chapter, we'll discuss a few commonly used Java classes:

- *String*, which provides a data type for character strings, along with methods for searching and manipulating strings
- *Random*, which generates random numbers
- *Scanner*, which provides methods for reading input from the Java console
- *System* and *PrintStream*, which provide data members and methods for printing data on the Java console
- *DecimalFormat* and *NumberFormat*, which allow you to format numbers for output
- *Math*, which provides methods for performing mathematical operations
- Object wrappers, which provide an object equivalent to primitive data types so they can be used in your program as if they were objects
- *JOptionPane*, which allows you to use dialog boxes to display messages to the user or to get input from the user

The Java classes are arranged in **packages**, grouped according to functionality.

TABLE 3.2 Commonly Used Java Packages

Package	Categories of Classes
java.lang	Basic functionality common to many programs, such as the *String* class, *Math* class, and object wrappers for the primitive data types
java.awt	Graphics classes for drawing and using colors, and old-style user interface components
javax.swing	New-style user interface components that have a consistent look and feel across platforms
java.text	Classes for formatting numeric output
java.util	the *Scanner* class, the *Random* class, and other miscellaneous classes
java.io	Classes for reading from and writing to files

Table 3.2 describes some of the Java packages that we will cover in this book. You can find more details on these classes on Sun Microsystems' Java website *http://java.sun.com.*

Many of the commonly used classes, such as *String* and *Math*, reside in the *java.lang* package. Any class in the *java.lang* package is automatically available to your program.

To use a class that is not in the *java.lang* package, you need to tell the compiler in which package the class resides; in other words, you need to tell the compiler where to find the class definition. To do this, you include an **import** statement in your program. The *import* statement is inserted at the top of the program after your introductory comments, but before the *class* statement that begins the program. (Yes, we've defined classes already in the programs we wrote in the previous two chapters.)

For example, if you want to use the *DecimalFormat* class to format a floating-point number for output, you would import the *DecimalFormat* class from the *java.text* package as follows:

```
import java.text.DecimalFormat;
```

If you're using more than one class from a package, you can import the whole package by using an asterisk in place of the class name, as follows:

```
import java.text.*;
```

3.7 The *String* Class

As we've discussed, Java provides the *char* primitive data type, which stores one character. Almost every program, however, needs a data type that stores more than one character. Programs need to process names, addresses, or labels of many kinds. For example, many programs involve a login procedure where the user has to enter a user ID and a password. The program reads the user ID and password, compares them to values stored in a database, and allows the user to continue only if the user ID and password match the database values.

To handle this type of data, Java provides a *String* class. Because the *String* class is part of the *java.lang* package, it is automatically available to any Java program and you do not need to use the *import* statement. The *String* class provides several constructors, as well as a number of methods to manipulate, search, compare, and concatenate *String* objects.

Let's look at two of the *String* class constructors shown in Table 3.3. Example 3.6 shows how to use these two constructors in a program.

```
/* Demonstrating the String methods
   Anderson, Franceschi
*/
public class StringDemo
{
  public static void main ( String [ ] args )
  {
    String s1 = new String( "OOP in Java " );
    System.out.println( "s1 is: " + s1 );
    String s2 = "is not that difficult. ";
    System.out.println( "s2 is: " + s2 );

    String s3 = s1 + s2; // new String is s1, followed by s2
    System.out.println( "s1 + s2 returns: " + s3 );

    System.out.println( "s1 is still: " + s1 ); // s1 is unchanged
```

TABLE 3.3 *String* Class Constructors

String Class Constructor Summary
`String( String str )` allocates a *String* object with the value of *str*, which can be a *String* object or a *String* literal.
`String( )` allocates an empty *String* object.

```
    System.out.println( "s2 is still: " + s2 ); // s2 is unchanged

    String greeting1 = "Hi"; // instantiate greeting1
    System.out.println( "\nThe length of " + greeting1 + " is "
                        + greeting1.length( ) );

    String greeting2 = new String( "Hello" ); // instantiate greeting2
    int len = greeting2.length( );  // len will be assigned 5
    System.out.println( "The length of " + greeting2 + " is " + len );

    String empty = new String( );
    System.out.println( "The length of the empty String is "
                        + empty.length( ) );

    String greeting2Upper = greeting2.toUpperCase( );
    System.out.println( );
    System.out.println( greeting2 + " converted to upper case is "
                        + greeting2Upper );

    String invertedName = "Lincoln, Abraham";

    int comma = invertedName.indexOf( ',' ); // find the comma
    System.out.println( "\nThe index of " + ',' + " in "
                        + invertedName + " is " + comma );

    // extract all characters up to comma
    String lastName = invertedName.substring( 0, comma );
    System.out.println( "Dear Mr. " + lastName );
  }
}
```

EXAMPLE 3.6 Demonstrating *String* Methods

When this program runs, it will produce the output shown in Figure 3.11.

```
s1 is: OOP in Java
s2 is: is not that difficult.
s1 + s2 returns: OOP in Java is not that difficult.
s1 is still: OOP in Java
s2 is still: is not that difficult.

The length of Hi is 2
The length of Hello is 5
The length of the empty String is 0

Hello converted to upper case is HELLO

The index of , in Lincoln, Abraham is 7
Dear Mr. Lincoln
```

Figure 3.11
Output from Example 3.6

The first constructor

```
String( String str )
```

allocates a *String* object and sets its value to the sequence of characters in the argument *str*, which can be a *String* object or a *String* literal. Line 8 instantiates the *String s1* and sets its value to "OOP in Java". Similarly, line 23 instantiates a *String* named *greeting2*, and assigns it the value "Hello".

The second constructor

```
String( )
```

creates an empty *String*, in other words, a *String* containing no characters. You can add characters to the *String* later. This constructor will come in handy in programs where we build up our output, piece by piece. Line 27 uses the second constructor to instantiate an empty *String* named *empty*.

Additionally, because *Strings* are used so frequently in programs, Java provides special support for instantiating *String* objects without explicitly using the *new* operator. We can simply assign a *String* literal to a *String* object reference. Lines 10 and 19 assign *String* literals to the *s2* and *greeting1* *String* references.

Java also provides special support for appending a *String* to the end of another *String* through the **concatenation operator** (+) and the **shortcut version of the concatenation operator** (+=). This concept is illustrated in Example 3.6. Lines 8–11 declare, instantiate, and print two *String* objects, *s1* and *s2*. Line 13 concatenates *s1* and *s2* and the resulting *String* is assigned to the *s3 String* reference, which is printed at line 14. Finally, we output *s1* and *s2* again at lines 16 and 17 to illustrate that their values have not changed.

Note that the *String* concatenation operator is the same character as the addition arithmetic operator. In some cases, we need to make clear to the compiler which operator we want to use. For example, this statement uses both the *String* concatenation operator and the addition arithmetic operator:

```
System.out.println( "The sum of 1 and 2 is " + ( 1 + 2 ) );
```

Notice that we put *1 + 2* inside parentheses to let the compiler know that we want to add two *ints* using the addition arithmetic operator (+). The addition will be performed first because of the higher operator precedence of parentheses. Then it will become clear to the compiler that the other +

TABLE 3.4 *String* Methods

String Class Method Summary	
Return value	**Method name and argument list**
`int`	`length( )`
	returns the length of the *String*
`String`	`toUpperCase( )`
	converts all letters in the *String* to uppercase
`String`	`toLowerCase( )`
	converts all letters in the *String* to lowercase
`char`	`charAt( int index )`
	returns the character at the position specified by *index*
`int`	`indexOf( String searchString )`
	returns the index of the beginning of the first occurrence of *searchString* or –1 if *searchString* is not found
`int`	`indexOf( char searchChar )`
	returns the index of the first occurrence of *searchChar* in the *String* or –1 if *searchChar* is not found
`String`	`substring( int startIndex, int endIndex )`
	returns a substring of the *String* object beginning at the character at index *startIndex* and ending at the character at index *endIndex – 1*

operator is intended to be a *String* concatenation operator because its operands are a *String* and an *int*.

Some useful methods of the *String* class are summarized in Table 3.4.

The length Method

The *length* method returns the number of characters in a *String*. Sometimes, the number of characters in a user ID is limited, for example, to eight, and this method is useful to ensure that the length of the ID does not exceed the limit.

The *length* method is called using a *String* object reference and the dot operator, as illustrated in lines 21, 24, and 29 of Example 3.6. At lines 21 and 29, the *length* method is called inside an output statement and the respective return values from the *length* method are output. At line 24, we call the *length* method for the *greeting2* object and assign the return value to the *int* variable *len*. Then at line 25, we output the value of the variable *len*. As shown in Figure 3.11, the length of "*Hi*" is 2, the length of "*Hello*" is 5, and the length of the empty *String* is 0.

The toUpperCase and toLowerCase Methods

The *toUpperCase* method converts all the letters in a *String* to uppercase, while the *toLowerCase* method converts all the letters in a *String* to lowercase. Digits and special characters are unchanged.

At line 31 of Example 3.6, the *toUpperCase* method is called using the object reference *greeting2*, and the return value is assigned to a *String* named *greeting2Upper*, which is then printed at lines 33 and 34.

The indexOf Methods

The *indexOf* methods are useful for searching a *String* to see if specific *Strings* or characters are in the *String*. The methods return the location of the first occurrence of a single *char* or the first character of a *String*.

The location, or **index**, of any character in a *String* is counted from the first position in the *String*, which has the index value of 0. Thus in this *String*,

```
String greeting = "Ciao";
```

the *C* is at index 0; the *i* is at index 1; the *a* is at index 2; and the *o* is at index 3. Because indexes begin at 0, the maximum index in a *String* is 1 less than the number of characters in the *String*. So the maximum index for *greeting* is `greeting.length( )–1`, which is 3.

In Example 3.6, line 38 retrieves the index of the first comma in the *String* *invertedName* and assigns it to the *int* variable *comma*; the value of *comma*, here 7, is then output at lines 39 and 40.

The charAt and substring Methods

The *charAt* and *substring* methods are useful for extracting either a single *char* or a group of characters from a *String*.

The *charAt* method returns the character at a particular index in a *String*. One of the uses of this method is for extracting just the first character of a *String*, which might be advantageous when prompting the user for an answer to a question. For example, we might ask users if they want to play again. They can answer "y," "yes," or "you bet!"

Our only concern is whether the first character is a *y*, so we could use this method to put the first character of their answer into a *char* variable. Assuming the user's answer was previously assigned to a *String* variable named *answerString*, we would use the following statement to extract the first character of *answerString*:

```
char answerChar = answerString.charAt( 0 );
```

In Chapter 5, we'll see how to test whether *answerChar* is a *y*.

The *substring* method returns a group of characters, or **substring**, from a *String*. The original *String* is unchanged. As arguments to the *substring* method, you specify the index at which to start extracting the characters and the index of the first character not to extract. Thus, the *endIndex* argument is one position past the last character to extract. We know this sounds a little awkward, but setting up the arguments this way actually makes the method easier to use, as we will demonstrate.

In Example 3.6, we want to extract the last name in the *String invertedName*. Line 38 finds the index of the comma and assigns it to the *int* variable *comma*, then line 43 extracts the substring from the first character (index 0) to the index of the comma (which conveniently won't extract the comma), and assigns it to the *String* variable *lastName*. When the variable *lastName* is output at line 44, its value is *Lincoln*, as shown in Figure 3.11.

When you are calculating indexes and the number of characters to extract, be careful not to specify an index that is not in the *String*, because that will generate a run-time error, *StringIndexOutOfBoundsException*.

COMMON ERROR TRAP

Specifying a negative start index or a start index past the last character of the *String* will generate a *StringIndexOutOfBoundsException*. Specifying a negative end index or an end index greater than the length of the *String* will also generate a *StringIndexOutOfBoundsException*.

REFERENCE POINT

You can read more about the *String* class on Sun Microsystems' Java website *http://java.sun.com*.

3.8 Formatting Output with the *DecimalFormat* Class

In a computer program, numbers represent a real-life entity, for instance, a price or a winning percentage. Floating-point numbers, however, are calculated to many decimal places and, as a result of some computations, can end up with more significant digits than our programs need. For example, the price of an item after a discount could look like 3.466666666666666,

TABLE 3.5 A *DecimalFormat* Constructor and the *format* Method

DecimalFormat Class Constructor	
`DecimalFormat( String pattern )`	
instantiates a *DecimalFormat* object with the output *pattern* specified in the argument.	
The *format* Method	
Return value	**Method name and argument list**
`String`	`format( double number )`
	returns a *String* representation of *number* formatted according to the *DecimalFormat* object used to call the method.

when all we really want to display is $3.47; that is, with a leading dollar sign and two significant digits after the decimal point. The *DecimalFormat* class allows you to specify the number of digits to display after the decimal point and to add dollar signs, commas, and percentage signs (%) to your output.

The *DecimalFormat* class is part of the *java.text* package, so to use the *DecimalFormat* class, you should include the following *import* statement in your program:

```
import java.text.DecimalFormat;
```

We can instantiate a *DecimalFormat* object using a simple constructor that takes a *String* object as an argument. This *String* object represents how we want our formatted number to look when it's printed. The API for that constructor is shown in Table 3.5.

The pattern that we use to instantiate the *DecimalFormat* object consists of special characters and symbols and creates a "picture" of how we want the number to look when printed. Some of the more commonly used symbols and their meanings are listed in Table 3.6.

```
/* Demonstrating the DecimalFormat class
     Anderson, Franceschi
*/

// import the DecimalFormat class from the java.text package;
import java.text.DecimalFormat;

```

TABLE 3.6 Special Characters for *DecimalFormat* Patterns

Common Pattern Symbols for a *DecimalFormat* Object	
Symbol	**Meaning**
0	Required digit. Do not suppress 0's in this position.
#	Optional digit. Do not print a leading or terminating digit that is 0.
.	Decimal point.
,	Comma separator.
$	Dollar sign.
%	Multiply by 100 and display a percentage sign.

```
public class DemoDecimalFormat
{
  public static void main( String [ ] args )
  {
     // first, instantiate a DecimalFormat object specifying a
     // pattern for currency
     DecimalFormat pricePattern = new DecimalFormat( "$#0.00" );

     double price1 = 78.66666666;
     double price2 = 34.5;
     double price3 = .3333333;
     int price4 = 3;
     double price5 = 100.23;

     // then print the values using the pattern
     System.out.println( "The first price is: "
                 + pricePattern.format( price1 ) );
     System.out.println( "\nThe second price is: "
                 + pricePattern.format( price2 ) );
     System.out.println( "\nThe third price is: "
                 + pricePattern.format( price3 ) );
     System.out.println( "\nThe fourth price is: "
                 + pricePattern.format( price4 ) );
     System.out.println( "\nThe fifth price is: "
                 + pricePattern.format( price5 ) );

     // instantiate another new DecimalFormat object
```

```
35      // for printing percentages
36      DecimalFormat percentPattern = new DecimalFormat( "#0.0%" );
37
38      double average = .980;
39      System.out.println( "\nThe average is: "
40                  + percentPattern.format( average ) );
41      // notice that the average is multiplied by 100
42      // to print a percentage.
43
44
45      // now instantiate another new DecimalFormat object
46      // for printing time as two digits
47      DecimalFormat timePattern = new DecimalFormat( "00" );
48
49      int hours = 5, minutes = 12, seconds = 0;
50      System.out.println( "\nThe time is "
51                  + timePattern.format( hours ) + ":"
52                  + timePattern.format( minutes ) + ":"
53                  + timePattern.format( seconds ) );
54
55      // now instantiate another DecimalFormat object
56      // for printing numbers in the millions.
57      DecimalFormat bigNumber = new DecimalFormat( "#,###" );
58
59      int millions = 1234567;
60      System.out.println( "\nmillions is "
61                  + bigNumber.format( millions ) );
62    }
63  }
```

EXAMPLE 3.7 Demonstrating the *DecimalFormat* Class

Once we have instantiated a *DecimalFormat* object, we format a number by passing it as an argument to the *format* method, shown in Table 3.5. Example 3.7 demonstrates the use of the *DecimalFormat* patterns and calling the *format* method. The output for this program is shown in Figure 3.12.

In Example 3.7, line 14 instantiates the *DecimalFormat* object, *pricePattern*, which will be used to print prices. In the pattern

```
"$#0.00"
```

the first character of this pattern is the dollar sign ($), which we want to precede the price. The # character specifies that leading zeroes should not be printed. The 0 specifies that there should be at least one digit to the left of the decimal point. If there is no value to the left of the decimal point,

```
The first price is: $78.67

The second price is: $34.50

The third price is: $0.33

The fourth price is: $3.00

The fifth price is: $100.23

The average is: 98.0%

The time is 05:12:00

millions is 1,234,567
```

Figure 3.12
Output from Example 3.7

then print a zero. The two 0's that follow the decimal point specify that two digits should be printed to the right of the decimal point; that is, if more than two digits are to the right of the decimal point, round to two digits; if the last digit is a 0, print the zero, and if there is no fractional part to the number, print two zeroes. Using this pattern, we see that in lines 23–24, *price1* is rounded to two decimal places. In lines 25–26, *price2* is printed with a zero in the second decimal place.

In lines 29–30, we print *price4*, which is an integer. The *format* method API calls for a *double* as the argument; however, because all numeric data types can be promoted to a *double*, any numeric data type can be sent as an argument. The result is that two zeroes are added to the right of the decimal point.

Finally, we use the *pricePattern* pattern to print *price5* in lines 31–32, which needs no rounding or padding of extra digits.

Next, line 36 instantiates a *DecimalFormat* object, *percentPattern*, for printing percentages to one decimal point (`"#0.0%"`). Lines 38–40 define the variable *average*, then print it using the *format* method. Notice that the *format* method automatically multiplies the value of *average* by 100.

REFERENCE POINT

You can read more about the *DecimalFormat* class on Sun Microsystems' Java website *http://java.sun.com*.

Line 47 defines another pattern, `"00"`, which is useful for printing the time with colons between the hour, minutes, and seconds. When the time is printed on lines 50–53, the hours, minutes, and seconds are padded with a leading zero, if necessary.

Line 57 defines our last pattern, `"#,###"`, which can be used to insert commas into integer values in the thousands and above. Lines 60–61 print the variable *millions* with commas separating the millions and thousands digits. Notice that the pattern is extrapolated for a number that has more digits than the pattern.

3.9 Generating Random Numbers with the *Random* Class

Random numbers come in handy for many operations in a program, such as rolling dice, dealing cards, timing the appearance of a nemesis in a game, or other simulations of seemingly random events.

There's one problem in using random numbers in programs, however: Computers are **deterministic**. In essence, this means that given a specific input to a specific set of instructions, a computer will always produce the same output. The challenge, then, is generating random numbers while using a deterministic system. Many talented computer scientists have worked on this problem, and some innovative and complex solutions have been proposed.

The *Random* class, which is in the *java.util* package, uses a mathematical formula to generate a sequence of numbers, feeding the formula a **seed** value, which determines where in that sequence the set of random numbers will begin. As such, the *Random* class generates numbers that appear to be, but are not truly, random. These numbers are called **pseudorandom** numbers, and they work just fine for our purposes.

Table 3.7 shows a constructor for the *Random* class and a method for retrieving a random integer. The default constructor creates a random number generator using a seed value. Once the random number generator is created, we can ask for a random number by calling the *nextInt* method. Other methods, *nextDouble*, *nextBoolean*, *nextByte*, and *nextLong*, which are not shown in Table 3.7, return a random *double*, *boolean*, *byte*, or *long* value, respectively.

To demonstrate how to use the random number generator, let's take rolling a die as an example. To simulate the roll of a six-sided die, we need to

TABLE 3.7 A *Random* Class Constructor and the *nextInt* Method

***Random* Class Constructor**	
`Random( )`	
Creates a random number generator.	
The *nextInt* Method	
Return value	**Method name and argument list**
`int`	`nextInt( int number )`
	returns a random integer ranging from 0 up to, but not including, *number* in uniform distribution

simulate random occurrences of the numbers 1 through 6. If we call the *nextInt* method with an argument of 6, it will return an integer between 0 and 5. To get randomly distributed numbers from 1 to 6, we can simply add 1 to the value returned by the *nextInt* method. Thus, if we have instantiated a *Random* object named *random,* we can generate random numbers from 1 to 6, by calling the *nextInt* method in this way:

```
int die = random.nextInt( 6 ) + 1;
```

In general, then, if we want to generate random numbers from n to m, we should call the *nextInt* method with the number of random values we need $(m - n + 1)$, and then add the first value of our sequence (n) to the returned value. Thus, this statement generates a random number between 10 and 100 inclusive:

```
int randomNumber =  random.nextInt( 100 - 10 + 1 ) + 10;
```

Line 18 of Example 3.8 will generate a random number between 20 and 200 inclusive.

```
1 /*  A demonstration of the Random class
2     Anderson, Franceschi
3 */
4 import java.util.Random;
5
6 public class RandomNumbers
7 {
8   public static void main( String [ ] args )
```

```
   {
     Random random = new Random( );

     // simulate the roll of a die
     int die = random.nextInt( 6 ) + 1;
     System.out.println( "\nThe die roll is " + die );

     // generate a random number between 20 and 200
     int start = 20, end = 200;
     int number = random.nextInt( end - start + 1 ) + start;
     System.out.println( "\nThe random number between " + start
                          + " and " +  end  + " is " + number );
   }
}
```

EXAMPLE 3.8 A Demonstration of the *Random* Class

```
The die roll is 2

The random number between 20 and 200 is 117
```

Figure 3.13
Output from Example 3.8

REFERENCE POINT

You can read more about the *Random* class on Sun Microsystems' Java website *http://java.sun.com*.

When the *RandomNumbers* program executes, it will produce output similar to the window shown in Figure 3.13. The output will vary from one execution of the program to the next because different random numbers will be generated.

3.10 Input from the Console Using the *Scanner* Class

As our programs become more complex, we will need to allow the users of our programs to input data. User input can be read into your program in several ways:

- from the Java console
- from a dialog box
- from a file
- through a Graphical User Interface (GUI)

The Java class library provides classes for all types of data input. In this chapter, we will concentrate on two ways to input data: from the Java console and from a dialog box. In Chapter 6 and Chapter 11, we explore how to input data from a file, and in Chapter 12, we learn how to input data through a GUI.

The *Scanner* class provides methods for reading *byte*, *short*, *int*, *long*, *float*, *double*, and *String* data types from the Java console. These methods are shown in Table 3.8.

TABLE 3.8 Selected Methods of the *Scanner* Class

A *Scanner* Class Constructor	
`Scanner( InputStream dataSource )`	
creates a *Scanner* object that will read from the *InputStream dataSource*. To read from the keyboard, we will use the predefined *InputStream System.in*.	
Selected Methods of the *Scanner* Class	
Return value	**Method name and argument list**
`byte`	`nextByte( )` returns the next input as a *byte*
`short`	`nextShort( )` returns the next input as a *short*
`int`	`nextInt( )` returns the next input as an *int*
`long`	`nextLong( )` returns the next input as a *long*
`float`	`nextFloat( )` returns the next input as a *float*
`double`	`nextDouble( )` returns the next input as a *double*
`boolean`	`nextBoolean( )` returns the next input as a *boolean*
`String`	`next( )` returns the next token in the input line as a *String*
`String`	`nextLine( )` returns the input line as a *String*

The *Scanner* class is defined in the *java.util* package, so your programs will need to include the following *import* statement:

```
import java.util.Scanner;
```

In order to use the *Scanner* class, you must first instantiate a *Scanner* object and associate it with a data source. We will use the *System.in* input stream, which by default is tied to the keyboard. Thus, our data source for input will be *System.in*. The following statement will instantiate a *Scanner* object named *scan* and associate *System.in* as the data source.

```
Scanner scan = new Scanner( System.in );
```

Once the *Scanner* object has been instantiated, you can use it to call any of the *next. . .* methods to input data from the Java console. The specific *next. . .* method you call depends on the type of input you want from the user. Each of the *next. . .* methods returns a value from the input stream. You will need to assign the return value from the *next. . .* methods to a variable to complete the data input. Obviously, the data type of the variable must match the data type of the value returned by the *next. . .* method.

The *next. . .* methods just perform input. They do not tell the user what data to enter. Before calling any of the *next* methods, therefore, you need to prompt the user for the input you want. You can print a prompt using *System.out.print*, which is similar to using *System.out.println*, except that the cursor remains after the printed text, rather than advancing to the next line.

When writing a prompt for user input, keep several things in mind. First, be specific. If you want the user to enter his or her full name, then your prompt should say just that:

```
Please enter your first and last names.
```

If the input should fall within a range of values, then tell the user which values will be valid:

```
Please enter an integer between 0 and 10.
```

Also keep in mind that users are typically not programmers. It's important to phrase a prompt using language the user understands. Many times, programmers write a prompt from their point of view, as in this bad prompt:

```
Please enter a String:
```

Users don't know, and don't care, about *Strings* or any other data types, for that matter. Users want to know only what they need to enter to get the program to do its job.

When your prompts are clear and specific, the user makes fewer errors and therefore feels more comfortable using your program.

Line 13 of Example 3.9 prompts the user to enter his or her first name. Line 14 captures the user input and assigns the word entered by the user to the *String* variable *firstName*, which is printed in line 15. Similarly, line 17 prompts for the user's age; line 18 captures the integer entered by the user and assigns it to the *int* variable *age*, and line 19 outputs the value of *age*. Reading other primitive data types follows the same pattern. Line 21 prompts for the user's grade point average (a *float* value). Line 22 captures the number entered by the user and assigns it to the *float* variable *gpa*, and line 23 outputs the value of *gpa*.

SOFTWARE ENGINEERING TIP

Provide the user with clear prompts for input. Prompts should be phrased using words the user understands and should describe the data requested and any restrictions on valid input values.

```
1 /*  A demonstration of reading from the console using Scanner
2     Anderson, Franceschi
3 */
4
5 import java.util.Scanner;
6
7 public class DataInput
8 {
9   public static void main( String [ ] args )
10  {
11     Scanner scan = new Scanner( System.in );
12
13     System.out.print( "Enter your first name > " );
14     String firstName = scan.next( );
15     System.out.println( "Your name is " + firstName );
16
17     System.out.print( "\nEnter your age as an integer > " );
18     int age = scan.nextInt( );
19     System.out.println( "Your age is " + age );
20
21     System.out.print( "\nEnter your GPA > " );
22     float gpa = scan.nextFloat( );
23     System.out.println( "Your GPA is " + gpa );
24  }
25 }
```

EXAMPLE 3.9 Reading from the Console using *Scanner*

Figure 3.14
Data Input with Example 3.9

```
Enter your first name > Syed
Your name is Syed

Enter your age as an integer > 21
Your age is 21

Enter your GPA > 3.875
Your GPA is 3.875
```

When this program executes, the prompt is printed on the console and the cursor remains at the end of the prompt. Figure 3.14 shows the output when these statements are executed and the user enters *Syed*, presses *Enter*, enters 21, presses *Enter*, and enters 3.875, and presses *Enter* again.

The methods *nextByte*, *nextShort*, *nextLong*, *nextDouble*, and *nextBoolean* can be used with the same pattern as *next*, *nextInt*, and *nextFloat*.

SOFTWARE ENGINEERING TIP

End your prompts with some indication that input is expected, and include a trailing space for better readability.

Note that we end our prompt with a space, an angle bracket, and another space. The angle bracket indicates that we are waiting for input, and the spaces separate the prompt from the input. Without the trailing space, the user's input would immediately follow the prompt, which is more difficult to read, as you can see in Figure 3.15.

As you review Table 3.8, you may notice that the *Scanner* class does not provide a method for reading a single character. To do this, we can use the *next* method, which returns a *String*, then extract the first character from the *String* using the *charAt(0)* method call, as shown in Example 3.10. Line 14 inputs a *String* from the user and assigns it to the *String* variable *initialS*, then line 15 assigns the first character of *initialS* to the *char* variable *initial*; *initial* is then output at line 16 as shown in Figure 3.16.

Figure 3.15
Prompt and Input Running Together

```
Enter your age as an integer >21
```

```
/*  A demonstration of how to get character input using Scanner
    Anderson, Franceschi
*/

import java.util.Scanner;

public class CharacterInput
{
  public static void main( String [ ] args )
  {
     Scanner scan = new Scanner( System.in );

     System.out.print( "Enter your middle initial > " );
     String initialS = scan.next( );
     char initial = initialS.charAt( 0 );
     System.out.println( "Your middle initial is " + initial );
  }
}
```

EXAMPLE 3.10 Using *Scanner* for Character Input

```
Enter your middle initial > A
Your middle initial is A
```

Figure 3.16
Output of Example 3.10

A *Scanner* object divides its input into sequences of characters called **tokens**, using **delimiters**. The default delimiters are the standard **white-space** characters, which among others include the space, tab, and newline characters. The complete set of Java whitespace characters is shown in Table 3.9.

By default, when a *Scanner* object tokenizes the input, it skips leading whitespace, then builds a token composed of all subsequent characters until it encounters another delimiter. Thus, if you have this code,

```
System.out.print( "Enter your age as an integer > " );
int age = scan.nextInt( );
```

and the user types, for example, three spaces and a tab, *21*, and a newline:

```
<space><space><space><tab>21<newline>
```

TABLE 3.9 Java Whitespace Characters

Character	Unicode equivalents
space	\u00A0, \u2007, \u202F
tab	\u0009, \u000B
line feed	\u000A
form feed	\u000C
carriage return	\u000D
file, group, unit, and record separators	\u001C, \u001D, \u001E, \u001F

then the *Scanner* object skips the three spaces and the tab, starts building a token with the character *2*, then adds the character *1* to the token, and stops building the token when it encounters the *newline*. Thus, *21* is the resulting token, which the *nextInt* method returns into the *age* variable.

An input line can contain more than one token. For example, if we prompt the user for his or her name and age, and the user enters the following line, then presses *Enter:*

```
<tab>Jon<space>Olsen,<space>21<space>
```

then, the leading whitespace is skipped and the *Scanner* object creates three tokens:

- *Jon*
- *Olsen,*
- *21*

Note that commas are not whitespace, so the comma is actually part of the second token. To input these three tokens, your program would use two calls to the *next* method to retrieve the two *String* tokens and a call to *nextInt* to retrieve the age.

To capture a complete line of input from the user, we use the method *nextLine*. Example 3.11 shows how *nextLine* can be used in a program. Figure 3.17 shows a sample run of the program with the user entering data.

```java
/*  A demonstration of using Scanner's nextLine method
    Anderson, Franceschi
*/

import java.util.Scanner;

public class InputALine
{
  public static void main( String [ ] args )
  {
    Scanner scan = new Scanner( System.in );

    System.out.print( "Enter a sentence > " );
    String sentence  = scan.nextLine( );
    System.out.println( "You said: \"" + sentence + "\"" );
  }
}
```

EXAMPLE 3.11 Using the *nextLine* Method

```
Enter a sentence > Scanner is useful.
You said: "Scanner is useful."
```

Figure 3.17
Output of Example 3.11

REFERENCE POINT

You can read more about the *Scanner* class on Sun Microsystems' Java web-site: *http://java.sun.com*.

If the user's input (that is, the next token) does not match the data type of the *next. . .* method call, then an *InputMismatchException* is generated and the program stops. Figure 3.18 demonstrates Example 3.9 when the program calls the *nextInt* method and the user enters a letter, rather than an

```
Enter your first name > Sarah
Your name is Sarah

Enter your age as an integer > a
Exception in thread "main" java.util.InputMismatchException
   at java.util.Scanner.throwFor(Unknown Source)
   at java.util.Scanner.next(Unknown Source)
   at java.util.Scanner.nextInt(Unknown Source)
   at java.util.Scanner.nextInt(Unknown Source)
   at DataInput.main(DataInput.java:18)
```

Figure 3.18
An Exception When Input Is Not the Expected Data Type

integer. In Chapter 6, we show you how to avoid this exception, and in Chapter 11, we show you how to intercept the exception and recover from it.

If the user doesn't type anything when prompted, or if the user types some characters but doesn't press *Enter*, the program will simply wait until the user does press *Enter*.

Skill Practice
with these end-of-chapter questions

3.19.1 Multiple Choice Exercises
Questions 1, 11

3.19.2 Reading and Understanding Code
Questions 14, 15, 16

3.19.3 Fill In the Code
Questions 24, 25, 26, 27

3.19.4 Identifying Errors in Code
Questions 36, 37, 38, 39, 43

3.19.5 Debugging Area
Questions 45, 49

3.19.6 Write a Short Program
Questions 50, 51, 52

3.11 Calling *Static* Methods and Using *Static* Class Variables

Classes can also define **static methods,** which can be called without instantiating an object. These are also called **class methods**. The API of these methods has the keyword *static* before the return type:

```
static dataType methodName( arg1, arg2, . . . )
```

One reason a class may define *static* methods is to provide some quick, one-time functionality without requiring the client to instantiate an object. For example, dialog boxes typically pop up only once in a program. Creating an object for a dialog box, when it is used only once, is a waste of memory and processor time. We'll see later in this chapter how it's possible to create dialog boxes and to perform mathematical calculations without creating an object.

Class, or *static*, methods are invoked using the class name, rather than an object reference, as in the following syntax:

```
ClassName.staticMethodName( argumentList );
```

For example, in this statement:

```
absValue = Math.abs( someNumber );
```

the class name is *Math*, and the *static* method is *abs*, which returns the absolute value of the argument (*someNumber*). We use the class name rather than an object reference, because *static* methods can be called without instantiating an object. Later in this chapter, we will explore some *static* methods of the *Math* class in greater detail.

Because *static* methods can be called without an object being instantiated, *static* methods cannot access the instance variables of the class (because instance variables are object data and exist only after an object has been instantiated). *Static* methods can access **static data**, however, and classes often declare *static* data to be used with *static* methods. *Static* data belong to the class, rather than to a particular object, or instance, of the class.

A common use of *static* class variables is to define constants for commonly used values or for parameters for the *static* class methods. For example, as we'll discuss in Chapter 4, the *Color* class provides *static* constants that can be assigned to a *Color* object reference.

Like *static* methods, *static* constants are also accessed using the class name and dot operator, as in this syntax:

```
ClassName.staticConstant
```

Thus, the *static* constant representing the color blue can be accessed this way:

```
Color.BLUE
```

At first, this may appear to go against our earlier discussion of encapsulation and the restrictions on clients directly accessing object data. Remember we said that the client needed to use accessor ("gets") and mutator ("sets") methods to access object data. The reasoning behind encapsulation is to protect the object data from corruption by the client. However, in this case, the *static* data is constant, so the client is unable to change it. For the client, directly accessing the class constant is easier and faster than calling a method.

3.12 Using *System.in* and *System.out*

In order to print program output to the screen, we have been using statements like

```
System.out.println( "The value of b is " + b );
```

and

```
System.out.print( "Enter your first name > " );
```

And to instantiate a *Scanner* object, we used this statement:

```
Scanner scan = new Scanner( System.in );
```

It is now time to look at these statements in depth and understand them completely.

System is an existing Java class in the *java.lang* package. One of its fields is a *static* constant, *out*, which represents the Java console by default. Another of its fields is a *static* constant, *in*, which represents the keyboard by default. Because *in* and *out* are *static*, we refer to them using the class name, *System*, and the dot notation:

```
System.out
System.in
```

Table 3.10 shows these static constants as well as the *static exit* method, which can be used to terminate a program. Calling *System.exit( )* at the end of a program is optional. After the last instruction is executed, the program will end in any case. However, the *exit* method of the *System* class can be useful if you want to stop execution at a place other than the end of the program.

System.out is an object of the *PrintStream* class, which is also an existing Java class; it can be found in the *java.io* package. The *out* object refers to the **standard output device**, which by default is the Java console.

The methods *print* and *println* belong to the *PrintStream* class and take arguments of any primitive type, a *String*, or an object reference. The only

TABLE 3.10 ***Static* Constants of the *System* Class and the *exit* Method**

Constant	Value
`in`	*static* constant that represents the standard input stream, by default the keyboard
`out`	*static* constant that represents the standard output stream, by default the Java console
A Useful *System* Method	
Return value	**Method name and argument list**
`void`	`exit( int exitStatus )` *static* method that terminates the Java Virtual Machine. A value of 0 for *exitStatus* indicates a normal termination. Any other values indicate abnormal termination and are used to signal that the program ended because an error occurred.

difference between *print* and *println* is that *println* will also print a *newline* character after it writes the output. Table 3.11 shows some methods of the *PrintStream* class, which can be used with *System.out.*

TABLE 3.11 ***PrintStream* Methods for Use with *System.out***

Useful *PrintStream* Methods	
Return value	**Method name and argument list**
`void`	`print( argument )` prints *argument* to the standard output device. The *argument* can be any primitive data type, a *String* object, or another object reference.
`void`	`println( argument )` prints *argument* to the standard output device, then prints a *newline* character. The *argument* can be any primitive data type, a *String*, or another object reference.
`void`	`println( )` prints a *newline* character. This method is useful for skipping a line in the program's output.

Example 3.12 demonstrates various ways to use the *print* and *println* methods:

```
1 /*  Testing the print and println methods
2     Anderson, Franceschi
3 */
4
5 public class PrintDemo
6 {
7   public static void main( String [ ] args )
8   {
9     System.out.println( "Combine the arguments using concatenation" );
10    System.out.println( "A double: " + 23.7 + ", and an int: " + 78 );
11
12    System.out.print( "\nJava is case sensitive: " );
13    System.out.println( 'a' + " is different from " + 'A' );
14
15    System.out.println( "\nCreate a variable and print its value" );
16    String s = new String( "The grade is" );
17    double grade = 3.81;
18    System.out.println( s + " " + grade  );
19
20    System.out.println( );  // skip a line
21    SimpleDate d = new SimpleDate( 4, 5, 2009 );
22    System.out.println( "Explicitly calling toString, d is "
23                        + d.toString( ) );
24    System.out.println( "Implicitly calling toString, d is " + d );
25
26    System.exit( 0 );  // optional
27  }
28 }
```

EXAMPLE 3.12 Demonstrating the *print* and *println* Methods

Lines 10 and 13 show how *print* or *println* can be used with various data types such as *double*, *int*, and *char*. Variables and expressions can also be used instead of literals, as shown in line 18, where the *String s* and the *double* variable *grade* are output.

We can also print objects. All classes have a *toString* method, which converts the object data to a *String* for printing. The *toString* method is called automatically whenever an object is used as a *String*. Notice that our *SimpleDate* class, introduced earlier in the chapter, had a *toString* method that returned the object data as a *String* in the format *mm/dd/yyyy*.

```
Combine the arguments using concatenation
A double: 23.7, and an int: 78

Java is case sensitive: a is different from A

Create a variable and print its value
The grade is 3.81

Explicitly calling toString, d is 4/5/2009
Implicitly calling toString, d is 4/5/2009
```

Figure 3.19
The Output from Example 3.12

The *toString* method's API is

```
String toString( )
```

REFERENCE POINT

You can read more about the *System* and *PrintStream* classes on Sun Microsystems' Java website *http://java.sun.com*.

After the *SimpleDate* object reference *d* is instantiated at line 21, it is printed at lines 22–23 and again at line 24. At lines 22–23, the method *toString* is called explicitly; at line 24, it is called automatically. The output of Example 3.12 is shown in Figure 3.19. Finally, we terminate the program by calling the *exit* method of the *System* class.

3.13 The *Math* Class

The *Math* class is also part of the *java.lang* package. As such, it is automatically available to any Java program; you do not need to use the *import* statement. The *Math* class provides two *static* constants (*E* and *PI*), as well as a number of *static* methods that save the programmer from writing some complex mathematical code.

The two constants, *E* and *PI*, are both *doubles* and represent, respectively, ***e*** (the base of the natural logarithm, i.e., log e = 1) and ***pi***, the ratio of the circumference of a circle to its diameter. Approximate values of *e* and *pi*, as we know them, are 2.78 and 3.14, respectively. These constants are shown in Table 3.12.

Because *E* and *PI* are *static* data members of the *Math* class, they are referenced using the name of the *Math* class and the dot notation as follows:

```
Math.E
Math.PI
```

TABLE 3.12 *Static* Constants of the *Math* Class

Constant	Value
`E`	*e*, the base of the natural logarithm
`PI`	*pi*, the ratio of the circumference of a circle to its diameter

Useful methods of the *Math* class are shown in Table 3.13. All the methods of the *Math* class are *static*; so they are called using the class name, *Math*, and the dot notation as follows:

```
Math.abs( -5 )
```

TABLE 3.13 Useful Methods of the *Math* Class

Math Class Method Summary	
Return value	**Method name and argument list**
`dataTypeOfArg`	`abs( arg )`
	static method that returns the absolute value of the argument *arg*, which can be a *double*, *float*, *int*, or *long*.
`double`	`log( double a )`
	static method that returns the natural logarithm (in base e) of its argument, *a*. For example, log(1) returns 0 and log(*Math.E*) returns 1.
`dataTypeOfArgs`	`min( argA, argB )`
	static method that returns the smaller of the two arguments. The arguments can be *doubles*, *floats*, *ints*, or *longs*.
`dataTypeOfArgs`	`max( argA, argB )`
	static method that returns the larger of the two arguments. The arguments can be *doubles*, *floats*, *ints*, or *longs*.
`double`	`pow( double base, double exp )`
	static method that returns the value of *base* raised to the *exp* power.
`long`	`round( double a )`
	static method that returns the closest integer to its argument, *a*.
`double`	`sqrt( double a )`
	static method that returns the positive square root of *a*.

Example 3.13 demonstrates how the *Math* constants and the *abs* method can be used in a Java program. In lines 9 and 10, we print the values of *e* and *pi* using the *static* constants of the *Math* class. Then in lines 12 and 15, we call the *abs* method, which returns the absolute value of its argument. We then print the results in lines 13 and 16. The output of Example 3.13 is shown in Figure 3.20.

```
1 /*  A demonstration of the Math class methods and constants
2     Anderson, Franceschi
3 */
4
5 public class MathConstants
6 {
7   public static void main( String [ ] args )
8   {
9     System.out.println( "The value of e is " + Math.E );
10    System.out.println( "The value of pi is " + Math.PI );
11
12    double d1 = Math.abs( 6.7 ); // d1 will be assigned 6.7
13    System.out.println( "\nThe absolute value of 6.7 is " + d1 );
14
15    double d2 = Math.abs( -6.7 ); // d2 will be assigned 6.7
16    System.out.println( "\nThe absolute value of -6.7 is " + d2 );
17  }
18 }
```

EXAMPLE 3.13 *Math* Class Constants and the *abs* Method

```
The value of e is 2.718281828459045
The value of pi is 3.141592653589793

The absolute value of 6.7 is 6.7

The absolute value of -6.7 is 6.7
```

Figure 3.20
Output from Example 3.13

The operation and usefulness of most *Math* class methods are obvious. But several methods—*pow, round*, and *min/max*—require a little explanation.

The pow Method

Example 3.14 demonstrates how some of these *Math* methods can be used in a Java program.

```
 1 /*  A demonstration of some Math class methods
 2     Anderson, Franceschi
 3 */
 4
 5 public class MathMethods
 6 {
 7   public static void main( String [ ] args )
 8   {
 9     double d2 = Math.log( 5 );
10     System.out.println( "\nThe log of 5 is " + d2 );
11
12     double d4 = Math.sqrt( 9 );
13     System.out.println( "\nThe square root of 9 is " + d4 );
14
15     double fourCubed = Math.pow( 4, 3 );
16     System.out.println( "\n4 to the power 3 is " + fourCubed );
17
18     double bigNumber = Math.pow( 43.5, 3.4 );
19     System.out.println( "\n43.5 to the power 3.4 is " + bigNumber );
20   }
21 }
```

EXAMPLE 3.14 A Demonstration of Some *Math* Class Methods

The *Math* class provides the *pow* method for raising a number to a power. The *pow* method takes two arguments, the first is the base and the second is the exponent.

Although the argument list for the *pow* method specifies that the base and the exponent are both *doubles,* you can, in fact, send arguments of any numeric type to the *pow* method because all numeric types can be promoted to a *double.* No matter what type the arguments are, however, the return value is always a *double.* Thus, when line 15 calls the *pow* method with two integer arguments, the value of *fourCubed* will be *64.0.* If you prefer that the return value be 64, you can cast the return value to an *int.*

Line 18 shows how to use the *pow* method with arguments of type *double.* The output of Example 3.14 is shown in Figure 3.21.

```
The log of 5 is 1.6094379124341003

The square root of 9 is 3.0

4 to the power 3 is 64.0

43.5 to the power 3.4 is 372274.65827529586
```

Figure 3.21
Output from Example 3.14

The round Method

The *round* method converts a *double* to its nearest integer using these rules:

- any factional part .0 to .4 is rounded down
- any fractional part .5 and above is rounded up

Lines 9–13 in Example 3.15 use the *round* method with various numbers. Figure 3.22 shows the output.

```
 1 /*  A demonstration of the Math round method
 2     Anderson, Franceschi
 3 */
 4
 5 public class MathRounding
 6 {
 7   public static void main( String [ ] args )
 8   {
 9     System.out.println( "23.4 rounded is " + Math.round( 23.4 ) );
10     System.out.println( "23.49 rounded is " + Math.round( 23.49 ) );
11     System.out.println( "23.5 rounded is " + Math.round( 23.5 ) );
12     System.out.println( "23.51 rounded is " + Math.round( 23.51 ) );
13     System.out.println( "23.6 rounded is " + Math.round( 23.6 ) );
14   }
15 }
```

EXAMPLE 3.15 A Demonstration of the *Math round* method

```
23.4 rounded is 23
23.49 rounded is 23
23.5 rounded is 24
23.51 rounded is 24
23.6 rounded is 24
```

Figure 3.22
Output from Example 3.15

The min and max Methods

The *min* and *max* methods return the smaller or larger of their two arguments, respectively. Example 3.16 demonstrates how the *min* and *max* methods can be used in a Java program. Figure 3.23 shows the output. Thus the statement on line 9 of Example 3.16

```
int smaller = Math.min( 8, 2 );
```

will assign 2 to the *int* variable *smaller*. At line 12, a similar statement using the *max* method will assign 8 to the *int* variable *larger*.

```
1 /*  A demonstration of min and max Math class methods
2     Anderson, Franceschi
3 */
4
5 public class MathMinMaxMethods
6 {
7   public static void main( String [ ] args )
8   {
9     int smaller = Math.min( 8, 2 );
10    System.out.println( "The smaller of 8 and 2 is " + smaller );
11
12    int larger = Math.max( 8, 2 );
13    System.out.println( "The larger of 8 and 2 is " + larger );
14
15    int a = 8, b = 5, c = 12;
16    int tempSmaller = Math.min( a, b );   // find smaller of a & b
17    int smallest = Math.min( tempSmaller, c ); // compare result to c
18    System.out.println( "The smallest of " + a + ", " + b + ", and "
19                        + c + " is " + smallest );
20  }
21 }
```

EXAMPLE 3.16 A Demonstration of the *min* and *max* Methods

Figure 3.23
Output from Example 3.16

```
The smaller of 8 and 2 is 2
The larger of 8 and 2 is 8
The smallest of 8, 5, and 12 is 5
```

The *min* method can also be used to compute the smallest of three variables. After declaring and initializing the three variables (*a*, *b*, and *c*) at line 15, we assign to a temporary variable named *tempSmaller* the smaller of the first two variables, *a* and *b*, at line 16. Then, at line 17, we compute the smaller of *tempSmaller* and the third variable, *c*, and assign that value to the *int* variable *smallest*, which is output at lines 18 and 19.

The pattern for finding the largest of three numbers is similar, and we leave that as an exercise at the end of the chapter.

REFERENCE POINT

You can read more about the *Math* class on Sun Microsystems' Java website *http://java.sun.com*.

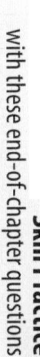

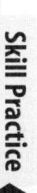

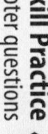

Skill Practice
with these end-of-chapter questions

3.19.1 Multiple Choice Exercises

Questions 6, 7, 8, 13

3.19.2 Reading and Understanding Code

Questions 17, 18, 19, 20, 21, 22, 23

3.19.3 Fill In the Code

Questions 28, 29, 30, 31, 32, 34

3.19.4 Identifying Errors in Code

Questions 40, 41, 42

3.19.5 Debugging Area

Questions 46, 47, 48

3.19.6 Write a Short Program

Questions 53, 54

CODE IN ACTION

To see a step-by step illustration of how to instantiate an object and call both instance and *static* methods, look for the Chapter 3 Flash movie on the CD accompanying this book. Click on the link for Chapter 3 to view the movie.

3.14 Formatting Output with the *NumberFormat* Class

Like the *DecimalFormat* class, the *NumberFormat* class can also be used to format numbers for output. The *NumberFormat* class, however, provides specialized *static* methods for creating objects specifically for formatting currency and percentages.

The *NumberFormat* class is part of the *java.text* package, so you need to include the following *import* statement at the top of your program.

```
import java.text.NumberFormat;
```

The static methods of the *NumberFormat* class to format currency and percentages are shown in Table 3.14.

As you can see from the first two method headers, their return type is a *NumberFormat* object. These *static* methods, called **factory methods**, are used instead of constructors to create objects. Thus, instead of using the *new* keyword and a constructor, we will call one of these methods to create our *formatting* object.

The *getCurrencyInstance* method returns a formatting object that reflects the local currency. In the United States, that format is a leading dollar sign and two digits to the right of the decimal place. The *getPercentInstance* method returns a formatting object that prints a fraction as a percentage by multiplying the fraction by 100, rounding to the nearest whole percent, and adding a percent sign (%).

TABLE 3.14 Useful Methods of the *NumberFormat* Class

NumberFormat Method Summary	
Return value	**Method name and argument list**
NumberFormat	getCurrencyInstance( ) *static* method that creates a format object for money.
NumberFormat	getPercentInstance( ) *static* method that creates a format object for percentages.
String	format(double number) returns a *String* representation of *number* formatted according to the object used to call the method.

We then use the *format* method from the *NumberFormat* class to display a value either as money or a percentage. The *format* method takes one argument, which is the variable or value that we want to print; it returns the formatted version of the value as a *String* object, which we can then print.

Example 3.17 is a complete program illustrating how to use these three methods.

```
/*  Demonstration of currency and percentage formatting
    using the NumberFormat class.
    Anderson, Franceschi
*/

// we need to import the NumberFormat class from java.text
import java.text.NumberFormat;

public class DemoNumberFormat
{
  public static void main( String [ ] args )
  {
     double winningPercentage = .675;
     double price = 78.9;

     // get a NumberFormat object for printing a percentage
     NumberFormat percentFormat = NumberFormat.getPercentInstance( );

     // call format method using the NumberFormat object
     System.out.print( "The winning percentage is " );
     System.out.println( percentFormat.format( winningPercentage ) );

     // get a NumberFormat object for printing currency
     NumberFormat priceFormat = NumberFormat.getCurrencyInstance( );

     // call format method using the NumberFormat object
     System.out.println( "\nThe price is: "
                           + priceFormat.format( price ) );
  }
}
```

EXAMPLE 3.17 Demonstrating the *NumberFormat* Class

The output of this program is shown in Figure 3.24.

Figure 3.24
Output from Example 3.17

```
The winning percentage is 68%

The price is: $78.90
```

3.15 The *Integer*, *Double*, and Other Wrapper Classes

In Chapter 2, we discussed primitive data types and how they can be used in a program. In this chapter, we've discussed classes and class methods and how useful and convenient classes are in representing and encapsulating data into objects.

Most programs use a combination of primitive data types and objects. Some class methods, however, will accept only objects as arguments, so we need some way to convert a primitive data type into an object. Conversely, there are times when we need to convert an object into a primitive data type. For example, let's say we have a Graphical User Interface where we ask users to type their age into a text box or a dialog box. We expect the age to be an *int* value; however, text boxes and dialog boxes return their values as *Strings*. To perform any calculations on an age in our program, we will need to convert the value of that *String* object into an *int*.

For these situations, Java provides **wrapper classes**. A wrapper class "wraps" the value of a primitive type, such as *double* or *int*, into an object. These wrapper classes define an instance variable of that primitive data type, and also provide useful constants and methods for converting between the objects and the primitive data types. Table 3.15 lists the wrapper classes for each primitive data type.

All these classes are part of the *java.lang* package. So, the *import* statement is not needed in order to use them in a program.

To convert a primitive *int* variable to an *Integer* wrapper object, we can instantiate the *Integer* object using the *Integer* constructor.

```
int intPrimitive = 42;
Integer integerObject = new Integer( intPrimitive );
```

However, because this is a common operation, Java provides special support for converting between a primitive numeric type and its wrapper class. Instead of using the *Integer* constructor, we can simply assign the *int* vari-

TABLE 3.15 Wrapper Classes for Primitive Data Types

Primitive Data Type	Wrapper Class
double	Double
float	Float
long	Long
int	Integer
short	Short
byte	Byte
char	Character
boolean	Boolean

able to an *Integer* object reference. Java will automatically provide the conversion for us. This conversion is called **autoboxing**. In Example 3.18, the conversion is illustrated in lines 9 and 10. The *int* variable, *intPrimitive*, and the *Integer* object, *integerObject*, are output at lines 12 and 13 and have the same value (42). The output is shown in Figure 3.25.

Similarly, when an *Integer* object is used as an *int*, Java also provides this conversion, which is called **unboxing**. Thus, when we use an *Integer* object in an arithmetic expression, the *int* value is automatically used. Line 15 of Example 3.18 uses the *Integer* object *integerObject* in an arithmetic expression, adding the *Integer* object to the *int* variable *intPrimitive*. As shown in Figure 3.25, the result is the same as if both operands were *int* variables.

Similar operations are possible using other numeric primitives and their associated wrapper classes.

In addition to automatic conversions between primitive types and wrapper objects, the *Integer* and *Double* classes provide methods, shown in Table 3.16, that allow us to convert between primitive types and objects of the *String* class.

The *parseInt*, *parseDouble*, and *valueOf* methods are *static* and are called using the *Integer* or *Double* class name and the dot notation. The *parse* methods convert a *String* to a primitive type, and the *valueOf* methods convert a *String* to a wrapper object. For example, line 18 of Example 3.18 converts the *String* "*76*" to the *int* value 76. Line 19 converts the *String* "*76*" to an *Integer* object.

```java
/*  A demonstration of the Wrapper classes and methods
    Anderson, Franceschi
*/

public class DemoWrapper
{
  public static void main( String [ ] args )
  {
    int intPrimitive = 42;
    Integer integerObject = intPrimitive;

    System.out.println( "The int is " + intPrimitive );
    System.out.println( "The Integer object is " + integerObject );

    int sum = intPrimitive + integerObject;
    System.out.println( "The sum is " + sum );

    int i1 = Integer.parseInt( "76" );    // convert "76" to an int
    Integer i2 = Integer.valueOf( "76" ); // convert "76" to Integer
    System.out.println( "\nThe value of i1 is " + i1 );
    System.out.println( "The value of i2 is " + i2 );

    double d1 = Double.parseDouble( "58.32" );
    Double d2 = Double.valueOf( "58.32" );
    System.out.println( "\nThe value of d1 is " + d1 );
    System.out.println( "The value of d2 is " + d2 );
  }
}
```

EXAMPLE 3.18 A Demonstration of the Wrapper Classes

Figure 3.25
Output from Example 3.18

```
The int is 42
The Integer object is 42
The sum is 84

The value of i1 is 76
The value of i2 is 76

The value of d1 is 58.32
The value of d2 is 58.32
```

TABLE 3.16 Methods of the *Integer* and *Double* Wrapper Classes

Useful Methods of the *Integer* Wrapper Class	
Return value	**Method name and argument list**
`int`	`parseInt( String s )`
	static method that converts the *String s* to an *int* and returns that value
`Integer`	`valueOf( String s )`
	static method that converts the *String s* to an *Integer* object and returns that object

Useful Methods of the *Double* Wrapper Class	
Return value	**Method name and argument list**
`double`	`parseDouble( String s )`
	static method that converts the *String s* to a *double* and returns that value
`Double`	`valueOf( String s )`
	static method that converts the *String s* to a *Double* object and returns that object

Similarly, line 23 converts the *String* "*58.32*" to a *double*, and line 24 converts the same *String* to a *Double* object.

The usefulness of these wrappers will become clear in the next section of this chapter, where we discuss dialog boxes.

REFERENCE POINT

You can read more about the wrapper classes on Sun Microsystems' Java website *http://java.sun.com*.

3.16 Input and Output Using *JOptionPane* Dialog Boxes

Java provides the *JOptionPane* class for creating dialog boxes—those familiar pop-up windows that prompt the user to enter a value or notify the user of an error. The *JOptionPane* class is in the *javax.swing* package, so you will need to provide an *import* statement in any program that uses a dialog box.

TABLE 3.17 Input and Output Methods of the *JOptionPane* Class

Useful Methods of the *JOptionPane* Class	
Return value	**Method name and argument list**
`String`	`showInputDialog( Component parent, Object prompt )`
	static method that pops up an input dialog box, where *prompt* asks the user for input. Returns the characters typed by the user as a *String.*
`void`	`showMessageDialog( Component parent, Object message )`
	static method that pops up an output dialog box with *message* displayed

Most classes in the *javax.swing* package are designed for GUIs, but *JOptionPane* dialog boxes can be used in both GUI and non-GUI programs.

Table 3.17 lists some useful *JOptionPane static* methods.

The *showInputDialog* method is used for input, that is, for prompting the user for a value and inputting that value into the program. The *showMessageDialog* method is used for output, that is, for printing a message to the user. Although Java provides several constructors for dialog boxes, it is customary to create dialog boxes that will be used only once using the *static* methods and the *JOptionPane* class name.

Let's look first at the method *showInputDialog*, which gets input from the user. It takes two arguments: a parent component object and a prompt to display. At this point, our applications won't have a parent component object, so we'll always use *null* for that argument.

The second argument, the prompt, is usually a *String*, and lets the user know what kind of input our program needs. Next, notice that the return value of the *showInputDialog* method is a *String*.

Example 3.19 shows how the *showInputDialog* method is used to retrieve user input through a dialog box.

```
/* Using dialog boxes for input and output of Strings
   Anderson, Franceschi
*/

import javax.swing.JOptionPane;

public class DialogBoxDemo1
```

```
 8 {
 9   public static void main( String [ ] args )
10   {
11     String name = JOptionPane.showInputDialog( null,
12                   "Please enter your first and last names" );
13     JOptionPane.showMessageDialog( null, "Hello, " + name );
14   }
15 }
```

EXAMPLE 3.19 Using Dialog Boxes with *Strings*

When lines 11 and 12 are executed, the dialog box in Figure 3.26 appears. The user types his or her name into the white box, then presses either the *Enter* key or clicks the *OK* button. At that time, the *showInputDialog* method returns a *String* representing the characters typed by the user, and that *String* is assigned to the variable *name*.

To output a message to the user, use the *showMessageDialog* method. The *showMessageDialog* method is similar to the *showInputDialog* method in that it takes a parent component object (*null* for now) and a *String* to display. Thus, in Example 3.19, line 13 uses the variable *name* to echo back to the user a greeting.

Notice that because the *showMessageDialog* is a method with a *void* return value, you call it as a standalone statement, rather than using the method call in an expression.

If the user typed "Syed Ali" when prompted for his name, the output dialog box shown in Figure 3.27 would appear.

To input an integer or any data type other than a *String*, however, you need to convert the returned *String* to the desired data type. Fortunately, as we saw in the previous section, you can do this using a wrapper class and its associated *parse* method, as Example 3.20 demonstrates.

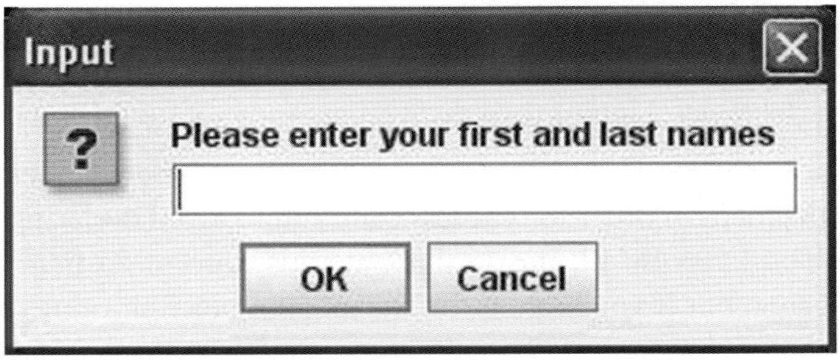

Figure 3.26
Dialog Box Prompting for First and Last Names

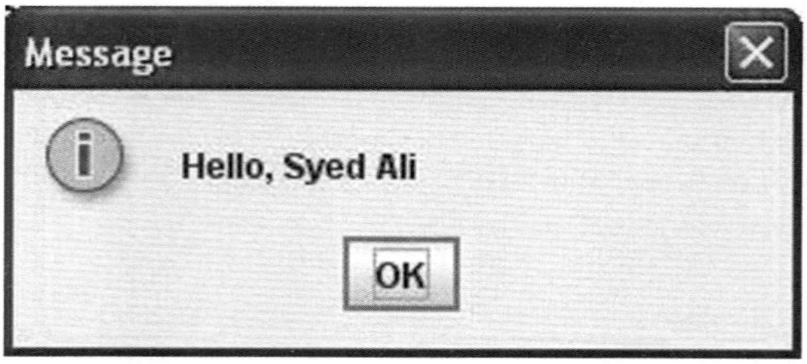

Figure 3.27
Output Dialog Box from Example 3.19

```
1 /* Demonstrating dialog boxes for input and output of numbers
2    Anderson, Franceschi
3 */
4
5 import javax.swing.JOptionPane;
6
7 public class DialogBoxDemo2
8 {
9   public static void main( String [ ] args )
10   {
11      String input = JOptionPane.showInputDialog( null,
12            "Please enter your age in years" );
13      int age = Integer.parseInt( input );
14      JOptionPane.showMessageDialog( null, "Your age is  " + age );
15
16      double average = Double.parseDouble(
17            JOptionPane.showInputDialog( null,
18            "Enter your grade point average between 0.0 and 4.0" ) );
19      JOptionPane.showMessageDialog( null, "Your average is "
20            + average );
21   }
22 }
```

EXAMPLE 3.20 Converting Input *Strings* to Numbers

Lines 11 and 12 pop up an input dialog box and assign the characters entered by the user to the *String input.* Line 13 uses the *parseInt* method of the *Integer* class to convert *input* to an integer, which is assigned to the *int* variable *age.* Line 14 then displays the value of *age* in an output dialog box.

Java programmers often combine multiple related operations into one statement in order to type less code and to avoid declaring additional variables. Lines 16, 17, and 18 illustrate this concept. At first it may look confusing, but if you look at the statement a piece at a time, it becomes clear what is happening. The *showInputDialog* method is called, returning a

String representing whatever the user typed into the dialog box. This *String* then becomes the argument passed to *parseDouble*, which converts the *String* to a *double*. Lines 19–20 display the value of *average* in another dialog box.

In this prompt, we included a range of valid values to help the user type valid input. However, including a range of values in your prompt does not prevent the user from entering other values. The *parseDouble* method will accept any *String* that can be converted to a numeric value. After your program receives the input, you will need to verify that the number entered is indeed within the requested range of values. In Chapter 6, we will show you techniques for verifying whether the user has entered valid values.

REFERENCE POINT

You can read more about the *JOptionPane* class on Sun Microsystems' Java website *http://java.sun.com*.

With either *Double.parseDouble* or *Integer.parseInt*, the value the user types must be convertible to the appropriate data type. If not, an exception is generated. For example, if the user enters *A* for the grade point average, the method generates a *NumberFormatException*. We'll discuss how you can intercept and handle exceptions in Chapter 11.

The various input and output dialog boxes from a sample run of Example 3.20 are shown in Figure 3.28.

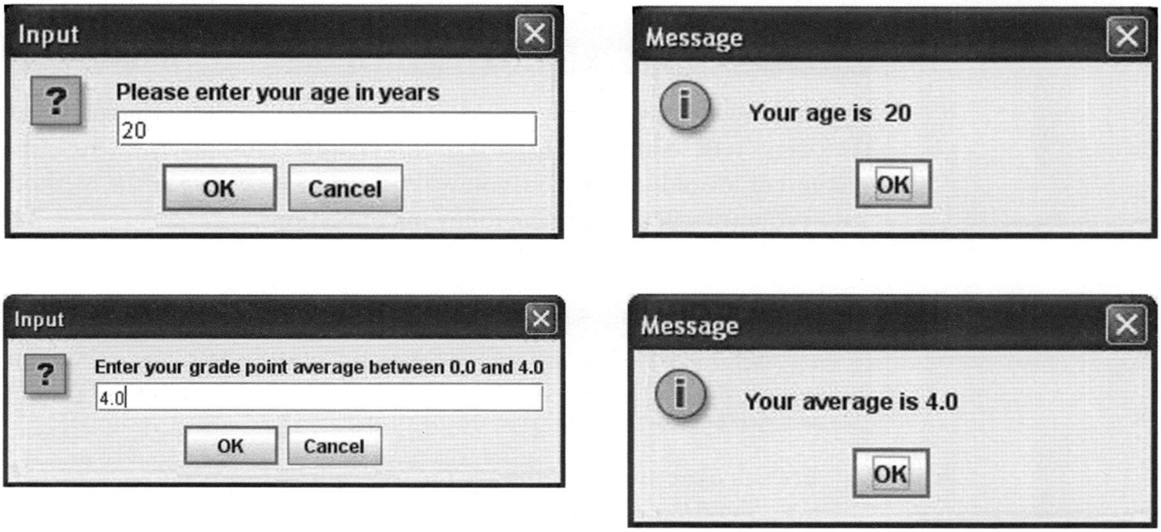

Figure 3.28
Dialog Boxes from Example 3.20

Skill Practice
with these end-of-chapter questions

3.19.1 Multiple Choice Exercises

Question 12

3.19.3 Fill In the Code

Question 33

3.19.3 Identifying Errors in Code

Question 35

3.19.5 Debugging Area

Question 44

3.19.6 Write a Short Program

Questions 55, 56

3.19.8 Technical Writing

Questions 71, 72

3.17 Programming Activity 2: Using Predefined Classes

In this Programming Activity, you will write a short program using some of the classes and methods discussed in this chapter. Plus, given the API of a method of an additional class, you will determine how to call the method. Your program will perform the following operations:

1. a. Prompt the user for his or her first name
   b. Print a message saying hello to the user
   c. Tell the user how many characters are in his or her name
2. a. Ask the user for the year of his or her birth
   b. Calculate and print the age the user will be this year
   c. Declare a constant for average life expectancy; set its value to 77.9
   d. Print a message that tells the user the percentage of his or her expected life lived so far

3. a. Generate a random number between 1 and 20
   b. Pop up a dialog box telling the user that the program is thinking of a number between 1 and 20 and ask for a guess
   c. Pop up a dialog box telling the user the number

To complete this Programming Activity, copy the contents of the Chapter 3 Programming Activity 2 folder on the CD-ROM accompanying this book. Open the *PracticeMethods.java* file and look for four sets of five asterisks (*****), where you will find instructions to write *import* statements and items 1, 2, and 3 for completing the Programming Activity.

Example 3.21 shows the *PracticeMethods.java* file, and Figures 3.29 and 3.30 show the output from a sample run after you have completed the

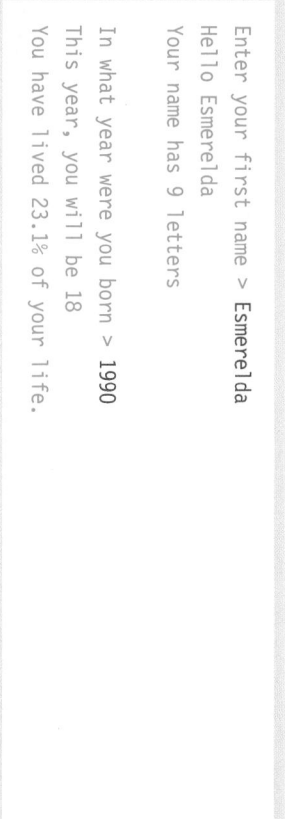

```
Enter your first name > Esmerelda
Hello Esmerelda
Your name has 9 letters

In what year were you born > 1990
This year, you will be 18
You have lived 23.1% of your life.
```

Figure 3.29
Console Output from a Sample Run of Programming Activity 2

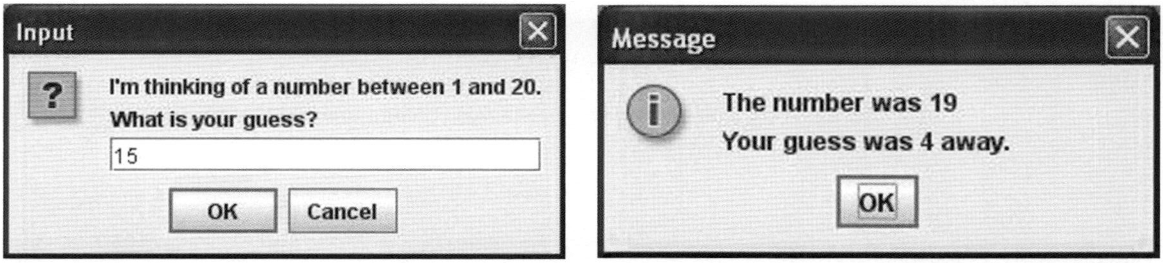

Figure 3.30
Dialog Boxes from a Sample Run of Programming Activity 2

Programming Activity. Because item 3 generates a random number, your output may be different.

```
/* Chapter 3 Programming Activity 2
   Calling class methods
   Anderson, Franceschi
*/

// ***** add your import statements here

public class PracticeMethods
{
  public static void main( String [ ] args )
  {
    //*****
    // 1.  a. Create a Scanner object to read from the console
    //     b. Prompt the user for his or her first name
    //     c. Print a message that says hello to the user
    //     d. Print a message that says how many letters
    //               are in the user's name
    // Your code goes here

    //*****
    // 2.  a. Skip a line, then prompt the user for the year
    //            of birth
    //     b. Calculate and print the age the user will be this year
    //     c. Declare a constant for average life expectancy,
    //            set its value to 77.9
    //     d. Print a message that tells the user the percentage
    //            of his or her expected life lived
    //       Use the DecimalFormat class to format the percentage

    //*****
    // 3.  a. Generate a random integer between 1 and 20
    //     b. Pop up an input dialog box and ask the user for a guess.
    //     c. Pop up an output dialog box telling the user the number
    //          and how far from the number the guess was (hint: use Math.abs)

  }
}
```

EXAMPLE 3.21 ***PracticeMethods.java***

? DISCUSSION QUESTIONS

1. Which methods of the *Scanner* class did you choose for reading the user's name and birth year? Explain your decisions.
2. How would you change your code to generate a random number between 10 and 20?

3.18 Chapter Summary

CHAPTER SUMMARY

- Object-oriented programming entails writing programs that use classes and objects. Using prewritten classes shortens development time and creates more reliable programs. Programs that use prewritten classes are called clients of the class.
- Benefits of object-oriented programming include encapsulation, reusability, and reliability.
- Classes consist of data, plus instructions that operate on that data. Objects of a class are created using the class as a template. Creating an object is called instantiating an object, and the object is an instance of the class. The *new* keyword is used to instantiate an object.
- The object reference is the variable name for an object and points to the data of the object.
- The data of a class are called instance variables or fields, and the instructions of the class are called methods. Methods of a class get or set the values of the data or provide other services of the class.
- The name of a method, along with its argument list and return value, is called the Application Programming Interface (API) of that method. Methods that are declared to be *public* can be called by any client of the class.
- By convention, class names in Java start with a capital letter. Method names, instance variables, and object names start with a lowercase letter. In all these names, embedded words begin with a capital letter.
- When your program makes a method call, control transfers to the instructions in the method until the method finishes executing. Then control is transferred back to your program.

CHAPTER SUMMARY

- Instance methods are called using the object reference and the dot notation.
- A constructor is called when an object is instantiated. A constructor has the same name as the class and its job is to initialize the object's data. Classes can have multiple constructors. Constructors have no return values.
- A method's data type is called the method's return type. If the data type is anything other than the keyword *void*, the method returns a value to the program. When a value-returning method finishes executing, its return value replaces the method call in the expression.
- Accessor methods, also called *gets*, allow clients to retrieve the current value of object data. Mutator methods, also called *sets*, allow clients to change the value of object data.
- When an object reference is first declared, its value is *null*. Attempting to use a *null* object reference to call a method generates an error.
- The garbage collector runs occasionally and deletes objects that have no object references pointing to them.
- Java packages are groups of classes arranged according to functionality. Classes in the *java.lang* packages are automatically available to Java programs. Other classes need to be imported.
- The *String* class can be used to create objects consisting of a sequence of characters. *String* constructors accept *String* literals, *String* objects, or no argument, which creates an empty *String*. The *length* method returns the number of characters in the *String* object. The *toUpperCase* and *toLowerCase* methods return a *String* in upper or lower case. The *charAt* method extracts a character from a *String*, while the *substring* method extracts a *String* from a *String*. The *indexOf* method searches a *String* for a character or substring.
- The *DecimalFormat* class, in the *java.text* package, formats numeric output. For example, you can specify the number of digits to display after the decimal point or add dollar signs and percentage signs (%).

- The *Random* class, in the *java.util* package, generates random numbers.
- The *Scanner* class, in the *java.util* package, provides methods for reading input from the Java console. Methods are provided for reading primitive data types and *Strings*.
- When prompting the user for input, phrase the prompt in language the user understands. Describe the data requested and any restrictions on valid input values
- *Static* methods, also called class methods, can be called without instantiating an object. *Static* methods can access only the *static* data of a class.
- *Static* methods are called using the class name and the dot notation.
- *System.out.println* prints primitive data types or a *String* to the Java console and adds a *newline* character. *System.out.println* with no argument skips a line. *System.out.print* prints the same data types to the Java console, but does not add a *newline*. Classes provide a *toString* method to convert objects to a *String* in order to be printed.
- The *Math* class provides *static* constants *PI* and *E* and *static* methods to perform common mathematical calculations, such as finding the maximum or minimum of two numbers, rounding values, and raising a number to a power.
- The *NumberFormat* class, in the *java.text* package, provides *static* methods for formatting numeric output as currency or a percentage.
- Wrapper classes provide an object interface for a primitive data type. The *Integer* and *Double* wrapper classes provide *static* methods for converting between *ints* and *doubles* and *Strings*.
- The *JOptionPane* class, in the *javax.swing* package, provides the *static* methods *showMessageDialog* for popping up an output dialog box and *showInputDialog* for popping up an input dialog box.

3.19 Exercises, Problems, and Projects

3.19.1 Multiple Choice Exercises

1. If you want to use an existing class from the Java class library in your program, what keyword should you use?
   - ❑ `use`
   - ❑ `import`
   - ❑ `export`
   - ❑ `include`
2. A constructor has the same name as the class name.
   - ❑ true
   - ❑ false
3. A given class can have more than one constructor.
   - ❑ true
   - ❑ false
4. What is the keyword used to instantiate an object in Java?
   - ❑ `make`
   - ❑ `construct`
   - ❑ `new`
   - ❑ `static`
5. In a given class named *Quiz*, there can be only one method with the name *Quiz*.
   - ❑ true
   - ❑ false
6. A *static* method is
   - ❑ a class method
   - ❑ an instance method
7. In the *Quiz* class, the *foo* method has the following API:

   ```
   public static double foo( float f )
   ```

   What can you say about *foo*?

- ❑ It is an instance method.
- ❑ It is a class field.
- ❑ It is a class method.
- ❑ It is an instance variable.

8. In the *Quiz* class, the *foo* method has the following API:

   `public static void foo( )`

   How would you call that method?

   - ❑ `Quiz.foo( );`
   - ❑ `Quiz.foo( 8 );`
   - ❑ `Quiz( foo( ) );`

9. In the *Quiz* class, the *foo* method has the following API:

   `public double foo( int i, String s, char c )`

   How many arguments does *foo* take ?

   - ❑ 0
   - ❑ 1
   - ❑ 2
   - ❑ 3

10. In the *Quiz* class, the *foo* method has the following API:

    `public double foo( int i, String s, char c )`

    What is the return type of method *foo*?

    - ❑ `double`
    - ❑ `int`
    - ❑ `char`
    - ❑ `String`

11. *String* is a primitive data type in Java.

    - ❑ true
    - ❑ false

12. Which one of the following is not an existing wrapper class?
    - ❑ `Integer`
    - ❑ `Char`
    - ❑ `Float`
    - ❑ `Double`

13. What is the proper way of accessing the constant *E* of the *Math* class?
    - ❑ `Math.E( );`
    - ❑ `Math.E;`
    - ❑ `E;`
    - ❑ `Math( E );`

3.19.2 Reading and Understanding Code

14. What is the output of this code sequence?

```
String s = new String( "HI" );
System.out.println( s );
```

15. What is the output of this code sequence?

```
String s = "A" + "BC" + "DEF" + "GHIJ";
System.out.println( s );
```

16. What is the output of this code sequence?

```
String s = "Hello";
s = s.toLowerCase( );
System.out.println( s );
```

17. What is the output of this code sequence?

```
int a = Math.min( 5, 8 );
System.out.println( a );
```

18. What is the output of this code sequence?

```
System.out.println( Math.sqrt( 4.0 ) );
```

19. What is the output of this code sequence? (You will need to actually compile this code and run it in order to have the correct output.)

```
System.out.println( Math.PI );
```

20. What is the output of this code sequence?

```
double f = 5.7;
long i = Math.round( f );
System.out.println( i );
```

21. What is the output of this code sequence?

```
System.out.print( Math.round( 3.5 ) );
```

22. What is the output of this code sequence?

```
int i = Math.abs( -8 );
System.out.println( i );
```

23. What is the output of this code sequence?

```
double d = Math.pow( 2, 3 );
System.out.println( d );
```

3.19.3 Fill In the Code

24. This code concatenates the three *Strings* "Intro", "to", and "Programming" and outputs the resulting *String*. (Your output should be "Intro to Programming.")

```
String s1 = "Intro ";
String s2 = "to";
String s3 = " Programming";
// your code goes here
```

25. This code prints the number of characters in the *String* "Hello World."

```
String s = "Hello World";
// your code goes here
```

26. This code prompts the user for a *String*, then prints the *String* and the number of characters in it.

```
// your code goes here
```

27. This code uses only a single line *System.out.println* . . . statement in order to print

    "Welcome to Java Illuminated"

    on one line using (and only using) the following variables:

```
String s1 = "Welcome ";
String s2 = "to ";
String s3 = "Java ";
String s4 = "Illuminated";
// your code goes here
```

28. This code uses exactly four *System.out.print* statements in order to print

    "Welcome to Java Illuminated"

on the same output line.

```
// your code goes here
```

29. This code assigns the maximum of the values 3 and 5 to the *int* variable *i* and outputs the result.

```
int i;
// your code goes here
```

30. This code calculates the square root of 5 and outputs the result.

```
double d = 5.0;
// your code goes here
```

31. This code asks the user for two integer values, then calculates the minimum of the two values and prints it.

```
// your code goes here
```

32. This code asks the user for three integer values, then calculates the maximum of the three values and prints it.

```
// your code goes here
```

33. This code pops up a dialog box that prompts the user for an integer, converts the *String* to an *int*, adds 1 to the number, and pops up a dialog box that outputs the new value.

```
// your code goes here
```

34. This code asks the user for a *double*, then prints the square of this number.

```
// your code goes here
```

3.19.4 Identifying Errors in Code

35. Where is the error in this statement?

```
import text.NumberFormat;
```

36. Where is the error in this statement?

```
import java.util.DecimalFormat;
```

37. Where is the error in this code sequence?

```
String s = "Hello World";
system.out.println( s );
```

38. Where is the error in this code sequence?

```
String s = String( "Hello" );
System.out.println( s );
```

39. Where is the error in this code sequence?

```
String s1 = "Hello";
String s2 = "ello";
String s = s1 - s2;
```

40. Where is the error in this code sequence?

```
short s = Math.round( 3.2 );
System.out.println( s );
```

41. Where is the error in this code sequence?

```
int a = Math.pow( 3, 4 );
System.out.println( a );
```

42. Where is the error in this code sequence?

```
double pi = Math( PI );
System.out.println( pi );
```

43. Where is the error in this code sequence?

```
String s = 'H';

System.out.println( "s is " + s );
```

3.19.5 Debugging Area—Using Messages from the Java Compiler and Java JVM

44. You coded the following program in file *Test.java:*

```
public class Test
{
  public static void main( String [ ] args )
  {
    int a = 6;
    NumberFormat nf = NumberFormat.getCurrencyInstance( );
  }
}
```

When you compile, you get the following message:

```
Test.java: 6: cannot find symbol
  symbol : class NumberFormat
  location: class Test
  NumberFormat nf = NumberFormat.getCurrencyInstance( );
  ^
Test.java: 6: cannot find symbol
  symbol : variable NumberFormat
```

```
  location: class Test
  NumberFormat nf = NumberFormat.getCurrencyInstance( );
                                                    ^
2 errors
```

Explain what the problem is and how to fix it.

45. You coded the following on lines 10–12 of class *Test.java:*

```
String s;                          // line 10
int l = s.length( );               // line 11
System.out.println( "length is " + l );      // line 12
```

When you compile, you get the following message:

```
Test.java:11: variable s might not have been initialized.
  int l = s.length( );   // line 11
          ^
1 error
```

Explain what the problem is and how to fix it.

46. You coded the following on lines 10 and 11 of class *Test.java:*

```
double d = math.sqrt( 6 );            // line 10
System.out.println( "d = " + d );     // line 11
```

When you compile, you get the following message:

```
Test.java: 10: cannot find symbol
  symbol : variable math
  location: class Test
double d = math.sqrt( 6 ); // line 10
               ^
  1 error
```

Explain what the problem is and how to fix it.

47. You coded the following on lines 10 and 11 of class *Test.java:*

```
double d = Math.PI( );              // line 10
System.out.println( "d = " + d );   // line 11
```

When you compile, you get the following message:

```
Test.java:10: cannot find symbol
symbol : method PI ( )
location: class java.lang.Math
  double d = Math.PI( );   // line 10
                 ^
1 error
```

Explain what the problem is and how to fix it.

48. You coded the following on lines 10 and 11 of class *Test.java:*

```
double d = Math.e;                  // line 10
System.out.println( "d = " + d );   // line 11
```

When you compile, you get the following message:

```
Test.java:10: cannot find symbol
  symbol : variable e
  location: class java.lang.Math
       double d = Math.e;                 // line 10
                      ^
  1 error
```

Explain what the problem is and how to fix it.

49. You imported the *DecimalFormat* class and coded the following in the class *Test.java:*

```
double grade = .895;
DecimalFormat percent =
  new DecimalFormat( "#.0%" );

System.out.println( "Your grade is "
  + grade );
```

The code compiles properly and runs, but the result is not what you expected. You expect this output:

```
Your grade is 89.5%
```

But instead, the output is

```
Your grade is 0.895
```

Explain what the problem is and how to fix it.

3.19.6 Write a Short Program

50. Write a program that reads two words representing passwords from the Java console and outputs the number of characters in the smaller of the two. For example, if the two words are *open* and *sesame*, then the output should be *4*, the length of the shorter word, *open.*

51. Write a program that reads a name that represents a domain name from the Java console. Your program should then concatenate that name with *www.* and *.com* in order to form an Internet domain name and output the result. For instance, if the name entered by the user is *yahoo*, then the output will be *www.yahoo.com.*

52. Write a program that reads a word from the Java console. Your program should then output the same word, output the word in uppercase letters only, output that word in lowercase letters only, and then, at the end, output the original word.

53. Write a program that generates two random numbers between 0 and 100 and prints the smaller of the two numbers.

54. Write a program that takes a *double* as an input from the Java console, then computes and outputs the cube of that number.

55. Write a program that reads a filename from a dialog box. You should expect that the filename has one . (dot) character in it, separating the filename from the file extension. Retrieve the file extension and output it. For instance, if the user inputs *index.html*, you should output *html*; if the user inputs *MyClass.java*, you should output *java*.

56. Write a program that reads a full name (first name and last name) from a dialog box; you should expect the first name and the last name to be separated by a space. Retrieve the first name and output it.

3.19.7 Programming Projects

57. Write a program that reads three integer values from the Java console representing, respectively, a number of quarters, dimes, and nickels. Convert the total coin amount to dollars and output the result with a dollar notation.

58. Write a program that reads from the Java console the radius of a circle. Calculate and output the area and the perimeter of that circle. You can use the following formulas:

    $\text{area} = \pi * r^2$

    $\text{perimeter} = 2 * \pi * r$

59. Write a program that generates five random integers between 60 and 100 and calculates the smallest of the five numbers.

60. Write a program that generates three random integers between 0 and 50, calculates the average, and prints the result.

61. Write a program that reads two integers from the Java console: one representing the number of shots taken by a basketball player, the other representing the number of shots made by the same player.

Calculate the shooting percentage and output it with the percent notation.

62. Write a program that takes three *double* numbers from the Java console representing, respectively, the three coefficients a, b, and c of a quadratic equation. Solve the equation using the following formulas:

    $x1 = (-b + \text{square root } (b^2 - 4\,ac)) \,/\, (2a);$

    $x2 = (-b - \text{square root } (b^2 - 4\,ac)) \,/\, (2a);$

    Run your program on the following sample values:

    $a = 1.0, b = 3.0, c = 2.0$

    $a = 0.5, b = 0.5, c = 0.125$

    $a = 1.0, b = 3.0, c = 10.0$

    Discuss the results for each program run, in particular what happens in the last case.

63. Write a program that takes two numbers from the Java console representing, respectively, an investment and an interest rate (you will expect the user to enter a number such as .065 for the interest rate, representing a 6.5% interest rate). Your program should calculate and output (in $ notation) the future value of the investment in 5, 10, and 20 years using the following formula:

    $\text{future value} = \text{investment} * (1 + \text{interest rate})^{\text{year}}$

    We will assume that the interest rate is an annual rate and is compounded annually.

64. Write a program that reads from the Java console the (x,y) coordinates for two points in the plane. You can assume that all numbers are integers. Using the *Point* class from Java (you may need to look it up on the Web), instantiate two *Point* objects with your input data, then output the data for both *Point* objects.

65. Write a program that reads a *char* from the Java console. Look up the *Character* class on the Web, in particular the method *getNumericValue*. Using the *getNumericValue* method, find the corresponding Unicode encoding number and output the character along with its corresponding Unicode value. Find all the Unicode values for characters a to z and A to Z.

66. Write a program that reads a telephone number from a dialog box; you should assume that the number is in this format: nnn-nnn-nnnn. You should output this same telephone number but with spaces instead of dashes, that is: nnn nnn nnnn.

67. Write a program that reads a sentence from a dialog box. The sentence has been encrypted as follows: only the first five even-numbered characters should be counted; all other characters should be discarded. Decrypt the sentence and output the result. For example, if the user inputs "Hiejlzl3ow", your output should be *Hello.*

68. Write a program that reads a commercial website URL from a dialog box; you should expect that the URL starts with *www* and ends with *.com*. Retrieve the name of the site and output it. For instance, if the user inputs *www.yahoo.com*, you should output *yahoo*.

3.19.8 Technical Writing

69. At this point, we have written and debugged many examples of code. When you compile a Java program with the Java compiler, you get a list of all the errors in your code. Do you like the Java compiler? Do the error messages it displays when your code does not compile help you determine what's wrong?

70. Computers, computer languages, and application programs existed before object-oriented programming. However, OOP has become an industry standard. Discuss the advantages of using OOP compared to using only basic data types in a program.

71. Explain and discuss a situation where you would use the method *parseInt* of the class *Integer*.

72. In addition to the basic data types (*int*, *float*, *char*, *boolean*, . . .), Java provides many prewritten classes, such as *Math*, *NumberFormat*, and *DecimalFormat*. Why is this an advantage? How does this impact the way a programmer approaches a programming problem in general?

3.19.9 Group Project (for a group of 1, 2, or 3 students)

73. Write a program that calculates a monthly mortgage payment; we will assume that the interest rate is compounded monthly.

You will need to do the following:

- ❑ Prompt the user for a *double* representing the annual interest rate.
- ❑ Prompt the user for the number of years the mortgage will be held (typical input here is 10, 15, or 30).
- ❑ Prompt the user for a number representing the mortgage amount borrowed from the bank.
- ❑ Calculate the monthly payment using the following formulas:
  - Monthly payment = $(mIR * M) / (1 - (1 / (1 + mIR)^{(12*nOY)}))$, where:
    - mIR = monthly interest rate = annual interest rate / 12
    - nOY = number of years
    - M = mortgage amount
- ❑ Output a summary of the mortgage problem, as follows:
  - the annual interest rate in percent notation
  - the mortgage amount in dollars
  - the monthly payment in dollars, with only two significant digits after the decimal point
  - the total payment over the years, with only two significant digits after the decimal point
  - the overpayment, i.e., the difference between the total payment over the years and the mortgage amount, with only two significant digits after the decimal point
  - the overpayment as a percentage (in percent notation) of the mortgage amount

CHAPTER 4

Introduction to Applets and Graphics

CHAPTER CONTENTS

Introduction

To this point, we've written Java applications, which run as standalone programs. Now we'll write a few Java applets, which are run by an Internet browser or an applet viewer.

As we discussed in Chapter 1, applets were originally designed to add interactivity to a web page. For example, a computer chess game on the Web can be run as an applet.

Another advantage to applets is the ease with which you can add graphics to a program. Up to this point, the input and output of our applications have been text—words and numbers. There was one exception, however: Programming Activity 1 in Chapter 3. That application opened a window and drew figures along with the text. How did we do that? We used graphics.

Graphical output is an integral part of many programs today. One compelling reason for using graphics in a program is the ability to present data in a format that is easy to comprehend. For example, our application could output average monthly temperatures as text, like this:

```
Jan   31
Feb   24
Mar   45
Apr   56
May   69
Jun   76
Jul   88
Aug   87
Sep   75
Oct   65
Nov   43
Dec   23
```

Or we could produce the bar chart shown in Figure 4.1.

The bar chart presents the same information as the text output, but it adds a visual component that makes it easier to compare the monthly temperatures—for example, to find the highest or lowest temperature or to spot temperature trends throughout the year. The colors also add information,

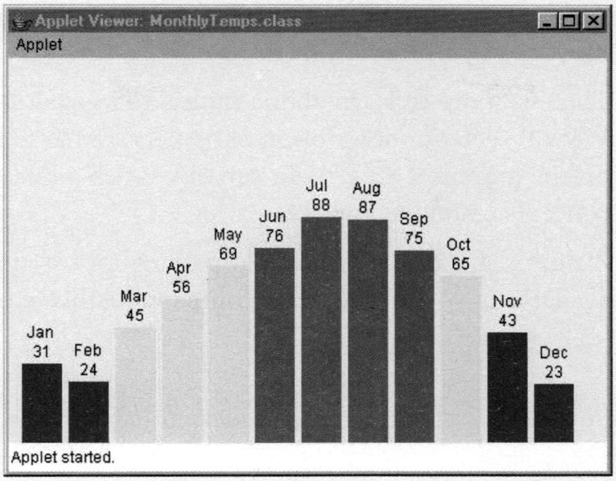

Figure 4.1
Bar Chart of Monthly Temperatures

with the low temperatures shown in blue, the moderate temperatures shown in yellow, and the high temperatures shown in red.

In this chapter, we begin by adding graphical output to applets. Later, when we cover GUIs in Chapter 12, we'll show you how to add graphical output to a Java application.

4.1 Applet Structure

The *JApplet* class, an existing Java class of the *javax.swing* package, provides the basic functionality of an applet. An applet class that we write is an extension of the *JApplet* class. In Java, the *extends* keyword specifies that one class is an extension of another and *inherits* the properties of the other class. Inheritance is one of the ways to reuse classes. We will cover inheritance in detail in Chapter 10.

An applet automatically opens a window where your program can draw shapes and text. The *main* method is not used in applets. Instead, we will use the *paint* method for our drawing code. The *paint* method is called automatically when the browser or applet viewer launches the applet, as well as any time the applet window needs to redraw itself. An applet might need to redraw itself if the user resizes the applet window or after another window, which was covering all or part of the applet window, is closed or is moved away from the applet window.

There is more to learn about applets than what is covered in this chapter. We will keep our description of applets simple so that you can concentrate on the graphical aspects. In subsequent chapters, we will cover additional concepts related to applets.

Example 4.1 shows a minimal pattern for an applet. This applet shell is available to you on the CD accompanying this book.

```
 1 /* An applet shell
 2    Anderson, Franceschi
 3 */
 4
 5 import javax.swing.JApplet;
 6 import java.awt.Graphics;
 7
 8 public class ShellApplet extends JApplet
 9 {
10   public void paint( Graphics g )
11   {
12     super.paint( g );
13     // include graphics code here
14   }
15 }
```

EXAMPLE 4.1 The *ShellApplet* Class

Lines 5 and 6 import the two classes that are used in this example: *JApplet*, used at line 8, and *Graphics*, used at line 10. The *Graphics* class is part of the *awt* (Abstract Window Toolkit) package.

Line 8 looks similar to the class header in our Java applications, but it includes two additional words: *extends JApplet*. In this case, we are inheriting from the *JApplet* class. Among other things, our *ShellApplet* class inherits the methods of the *JApplet* class. This means that we don't need to start from scratch to create an applet, so we can write applets that much faster. The *JApplet* class is called the **superclass**, and the *ShellApplet* is called the **subclass**.

The *paint* method, at lines 10–14, is where you put code to display words and graphics that should appear in the applet window. The first statement in the *paint* method is *super.paint(g)*. This statement calls the *paint* method of our superclass, the *JApplet* class, so that it can perform its initialization of the applet window.

The *paint* method's only parameter is a *Graphics* object. This object is automatically generated by the browser or applet viewer, which sends it to the *paint* method. The *Graphics* object represents the graphics context, which, among other things, includes the applet window. The *Graphics* class contains the methods we will need to make text and shapes appear in the applet window.

Skill Practice
with these end-of-chapter questions

4.7.1 Multiple Choice Exercises
Questions 1, 2, 3, 4

4.7.4 Identifying Errors in Code
Questions 26, 27

4.7.5 Debugging Area
Question 28

4.7.8 Technical Writing
Question 38

4.2 Executing an Applet

Like applications, applets need to be compiled before they are run. Once compiled, however, applets are unlike applications in that they do not run standalone. Applets are designed to be run by an Internet browser or an applet viewer. We tell the browser to launch an applet by opening a web page that includes an *APPLET* tag as part of the HTML code. We tell the applet viewer to run the applet by specifying a minimum web page that contains an *APPLET* tag.

If you are not familiar with HTML coding, the language consists of pairs of **tags** that specify formatting for the web page. The opening tag begins the

TABLE 4.1 HTML Tags

HTML Tags	Meaning
<HTML></HTML>	Marks the beginning and end of the web page.
<HEAD></HEAD>	Marks the beginning and end of the header portion of the web page. The header contains general descriptive information about the page.
<TITLE></TITLE>	Marks the beginning and end of the text that will be displayed on the title bar of the browser or applet viewer window.
<BODY></BODY>	Marks the beginning and end of the body of the web page. The body contains the content of the web page.
<APPLET></APPLET>	Identifies the applet to launch in the browser or applet viewer window. The <APPLET> tag supports attributes for specifying the applet name, location of the class file, and size of the applet window. Each attribute consists of the attribute's name followed by an equals sign (=) and the value assigned to that attribute. CODE = the class name of the applet CODEBASE = the directory in which to search for the class file WIDTH = the width of the applet's window in pixels HEIGHT = the height of the applet's window in pixels

specific formatting; the closing tag, which is identical to the opening tag except for a leading forward slash (/), ends that formatting. The basic HTML tags used with applets are described in Table 4.1.

Example 4.2 shows a minimal HTML file that you can modify to launch an applet.

```
<HTML>
<HEAD>
   <TITLE>TitleName</TITLE>
</HEAD>
<BODY>
   <APPLET CODE="ClassName.class" CODEBASE="." WIDTH=w
             HEIGHT=h></APPLET>
</BODY>
</HTML>
```

EXAMPLE 4.2 Minimal HTML Page for Launching an Applet

The *CODE* attribute of the *APPLET* tag is the name of the applet class. The *CODEBASE* attribute is the directory in which the JVM should look for the class file. In Example 4.2, the dot (.) for the *CODEBASE* value means that the class file is in the same directory as the HTML page. The *WIDTH* and *HEIGHT* attributes specify in pixels (or picture elements) the width and height of the applet window.

For example, if we had a class called *FirstApplet*, we could use a simple text editor to create the HTML file shown in Example 4.3. In this case, the applet window will be 400 pixels wide and 300 pixels high.

```
<HTML>
<HEAD>
   <TITLE>My First Applet</TITLE>
</HEAD>
<BODY>
   <APPLET CODE="FirstApplet.class" CODEBASE="." WIDTH=400
            HEIGHT=300></APPLET>
</BODY>
</HTML>
```

EXAMPLE 4.3 HTML Page for Launching an Applet Named *FirstApplet*

An applet viewer is provided as part of Sun Microsystems' Java SE Development Kit (JDK). The applet viewer is a minimal browser that enables us to view the applet without needing to open a web browser.

If the name of the web page is *FirstApplet.html*, we can run the applet viewer from the command line as follows:

```
appletviewer FirstApplet.html
```

If you are using an Integrated Development Environment (IDE) such as TextPad, JGrasp, or Eclipse, you can run the applet viewer directly without opening a command line window. In addition, IDEs typically create a minimum web page that contains an *APPLET* tag so that you don't need to create an HTML file for each applet you write.

4.3 Drawing Shapes with *Graphics* Methods

Java's *Graphics* class, in the *java.awt* package, provides methods to draw figures such as rectangles, circles, and lines; to set the colors for drawing; and to write text in a window.

Each drawing method requires you to specify the location in the window to start drawing. Locations are expressed using an (x,y) coordinate system. Each coordinate corresponds to a pixel. The x coordinate specifies the horizontal position, beginning at 0 and increasing as you move across the window to the right. The y coordinate specifies the vertical position, starting at 0 and increasing as you move down the window. Thus for a window that is 400 pixels wide and 300 pixels high, the coordinate (0, 0) corresponds to the upper-left corner; (399, 0) is the upper-right corner; (0, 299) is the lower-left corner, and (399, 299) is the lower-right corner. Figure 4.2 shows a window with a few sample pixels and their (x,y) coordinates.

Table 4.2 shows some useful methods of the *Graphics* class for drawing shapes and displaying text in a window.

As you can see, all these methods have a *void* return type, so they do not return a value. Method calls to these methods should be standalone statements; that is, the method call should be terminated by a semicolon.

The pattern for the method names is simple. The *draw* methods render the outline of the figure, while the *fill* methods render solid figures. The *clearRect* method draws a rectangle in the background color, which effectively erases anything drawn within that rectangle.

Figure 4.3 shows the relationship among the method arguments and the figures drawn.

Figure 4.2
The Graphics Coordinate System

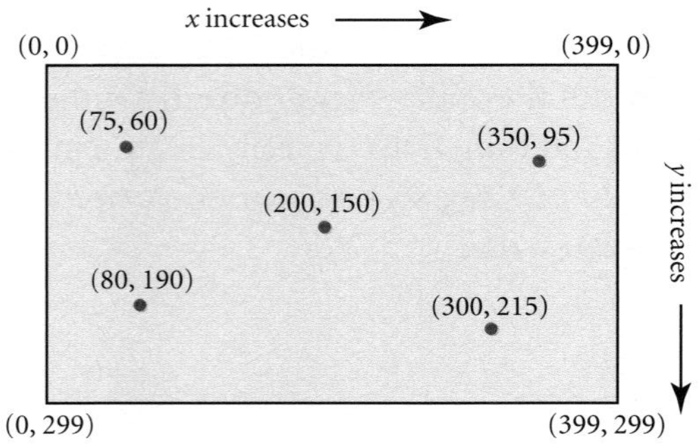

TABLE 4.2 Methods of the *Graphics* Class

Useful Methods of the *Graphics* Class	
Return value	**Method name and argument list**
`void`	`drawLine( int xStart, int yStart, int xEnd, int yEnd )` draws a line starting at (*xStart*, *yStart*) and ending at (*xEnd*, *yEnd*).
`void`	`drawRect( int x, int y, int width, int height )` draws the outline of a rectangle with its top-left corner at (*x*, *y*), with the specified *width* and *height* in pixels.
`void`	`fillRect( int x, int y, int width, int height )` draws a solid rectangle with its top-left corner at (*x*, *y*), with the specified *width* and *height* in pixels.
`void`	`clearRect( int x, int y, int width, int height )` draws a solid rectangle in the current background color with its top-left corner at (*x*, *y*), with the specified *width* and *height* in pixels.
`void`	`drawOval( int x, int y, int width, int height )` draws the outline of an oval inside an invisible, bounding rectangle with the specified *width* and *height* in pixels. The top-left corner of the rectangle is (*x*, *y*).
`void`	`fillOval( int x, int y, int width, int height )` draws a solid oval inside an invisible, bounding rectangle with the specified *width* and *height* in pixels. The top-left corner of the rectangle is (*x*, *y*).
`void`	`drawString( String s, int x, int y )` displays the *String s*. If you were to draw an invisible, bounding rectangle around the first letter of the *String*, (*x*, *y*) would be the lower-left corner of that rectangle.
`void`	`drawPolygon( Polygon p )` draws the outline of *Polygon p*.
`void`	`fillPolygon( Polygon p )` draws the *Polygon p* and fills its area with the current color

Figure 4.3
The Arguments for Drawing Lines, Rectangles, Ovals, and Text

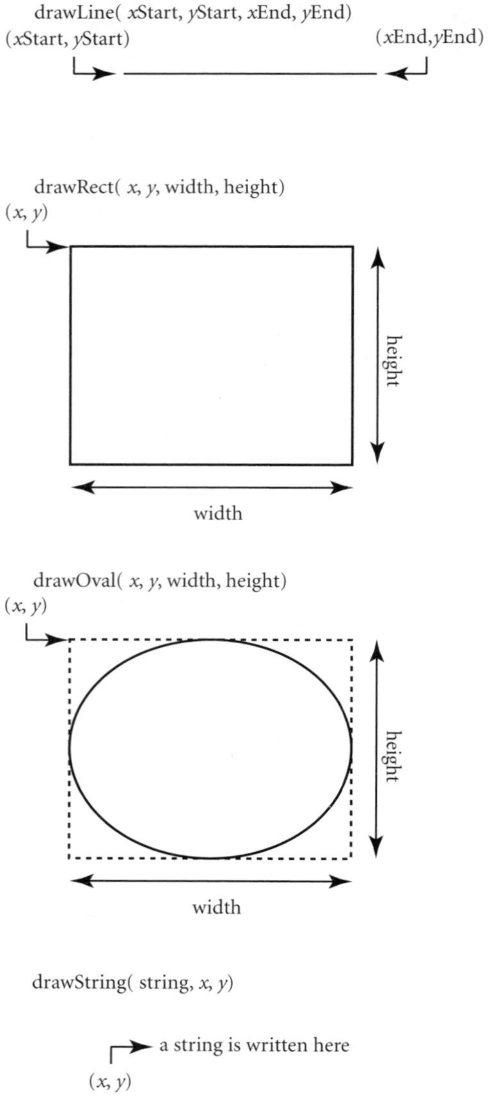

Example 4.4 shows how to use the *drawString* method. The coordinate you specify is the lower-left corner of the first character in the *String*. If you want to display more than one line of text in the default font, add 15 to the *y* value for each new line. For example, the statements at lines 13 and 14 print the message "Programming is not a spectator sport!" on two lines.

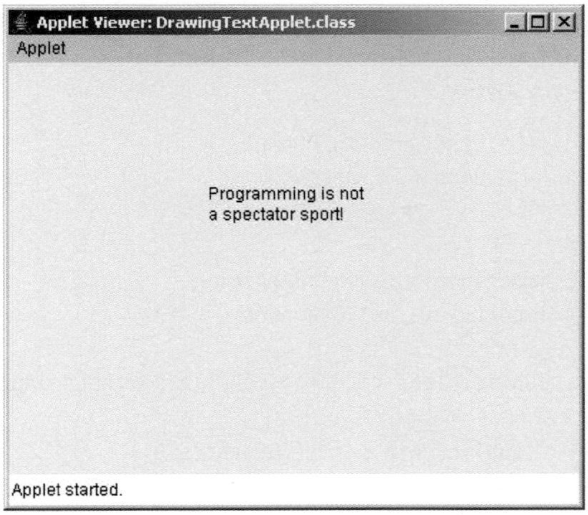

Figure 4.4
An Applet Displaying Two Lines of Text

Figure 4.4 shows the output of the applet.

```
/* Drawing Text
   Anderson, Franceschi
*/

import javax.swing.JApplet;
import java.awt.Graphics;

public class DrawingTextApplet extends JApplet
{
  public void paint( Graphics g )
  {
    super.paint( g );
    g.drawString( "Programming is not", 140, 100 );
    g.drawString( "a spectator sport!", 140, 115 );
  }
}
```

EXAMPLE 4.4 An Applet That Displays Text

To draw a line, you call the *drawLine* method with the coordinates of the beginning of the line and the end of the line. Lines can be vertical, horizontal, or at any angle. In vertical lines, the *startX* and *endX* values are the same, while in horizontal lines, the *startY* and *endY* values are the same. Statements at lines 14–16 in Example 4.5 draw a few lines.

```
 1 /* A Line Drawing Applet
 2    Anderson, Franceschi
 3 */
 4
 5 import javax.swing.JApplet;
 6 import java.awt.Graphics;
 7
 8 public class LineDrawingApplet extends JApplet
 9 {
10   public void paint( Graphics g )
11   {
12     super.paint( g );
13
14     g.drawLine( 100, 150, 100, 250 );  // a vertical line
15     g.drawLine( 150, 75, 275, 75 );    // a horizontal line
16     g.drawLine( 0, 0, 399, 299 );      // a diagonal line from
17                                        // the upper-left corner
18                                        // to the lower-right corner
19   }
20 }
```

EXAMPLE 4.5 An Applet That Draws Lines

Figure 4.5 shows these lines drawn in an applet window.

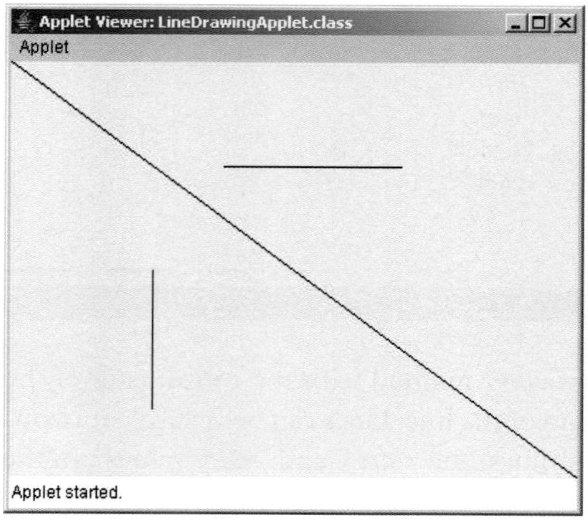

Figure 4.5
Vertical, Horizontal, and Diagonal Lines

Example 4.6 shows how to use the methods for drawing shapes in an applet. To draw a rectangle, call the *drawRect* or *fillRect* methods with the (*x*,*y*) coordinate of the upper-left corner, as well as the width in pixels and the height in pixels. Obviously, to draw a square, you specify equal values for the width and height. Line 14 draws a rectangle 40 pixels wide and 100 pixels high; line 15 draws a solid square with sides that are 80 pixels in length.

Drawing an oval or a circle is a little more complex. As you can see in Figure 4.3, you need to imagine a rectangle bounding all sides of the oval or circle. Then the (*x*,*y*) coordinate you specify in the *drawOval* or *fillOval* method is the location of the upper-left corner of the bounding rectangle. The width and height are the width and height of the bounding rectangle. Line 17 in Example 4.6 draws a filled oval whose upper-left corner is at coordinate (100, 50) and is 40 pixels wide and 100 pixels high; this filled oval is drawn exactly inside the rectangle drawn at line 14. Line 18 draws an oval 100 pixels wide and 40 pixels high, the same dimensions as the oval drawn at line 17, but rotated 90 degrees.

You draw a circle by calling the *drawOval* or *fillOval* methods, specifying equal values for the width and height. If it seems more natural to you to identify circles by giving a center point and a radius, you can convert the center point and radius into the arguments for Java's *drawOval* or *fillOval* methods as done in lines 21–25.

```
 1 /* A Shape Drawing Applet
 2    Anderson, Franceschi
 3 */
 4
 5 import javax.swing.JApplet;
 6 import java.awt.Graphics;
 7
 8 public class ShapeDrawingApplet extends JApplet
 9 {
10   public void paint( Graphics g )
11   {
12     super.paint( g );
13
14     g.drawRect( 100, 50, 40, 100 );    // rectangle
15     g.fillRect( 200, 70, 80, 80 );     // solid square
16
17     g.fillOval( 100, 50, 40, 100 );    // oval inside the rectangle
18     g.drawOval( 100, 200, 100, 40 );   // same-size oval
19                                        // rotated 90 degrees
```

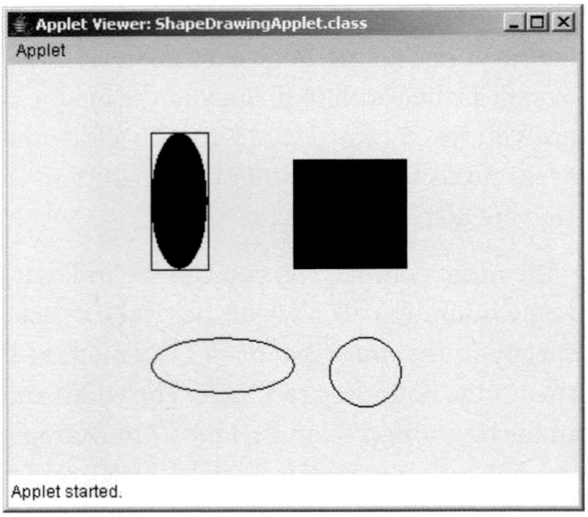

Figure 4.6
Geometric Shapes and Fills

```
    int centerX = 250, centerY = 225;
    int radius = 25;
    g.drawOval( centerX - radius, centerY - radius,
                radius * 2, radius * 2 );  // circle using radius
                                           // and center
  }
}
```

EXAMPLE 4.6 An Applet That Draws Shapes

Figure 4.6 shows the ovals and rectangles drawn in Example 4.6.

CODE IN ACTION

To see a demonstration of the *Graphics* drawing methods, look for the Chapter 4 Flash movie on the CD-ROM accompanying this book. Click on the link for Chapter 4 to view the movie.

The *Polygon* class, which is in the *java.awt* package, allows us to draw custom shapes. The *Polygon* class represents a polygon as an ordered set of (*x*,*y*) coordinates; each (*x*,*y*) coordinate defines a vertex in the polygon. A line, called an edge, connects each (*x*,*y*) coordinate to the next one in the

TABLE 4.3 A Constructor and Method of the *Polygon* Class

Polygon Constructor	
`Polygon( )`	
creates an empty *Polygon*	
A Useful Method of the *Polygon* Class	
Return value	**Method name and argument list**
`void`	`addPoint( int x, int y )`
	appends the coordinate to the polygon

set. Finally, there is a line connecting the last (*x*,*y*) coordinate to the first one. Table 4.3 describes a constructor for the *Polygon* class, as well as a method for adding (*x*,*y*) coordinates to the polygon. To draw the polygon, we call the *drawPolygon* or *fillPolygon* methods of the *Graphics* class, shown in Table 4.2.

Example 4.7 demonstrates creating and drawing polygons. On line 7 we import the *Polygon* class from the *java.awt* package. On lines 15–18, we instantiate an empty *Polygon* named *triangle* and add three coordinates to it. Then we draw the triangle as an outlined polygon on line 19. On lines 21–27 we instantiate another *Polygon*, *hexagon*, and add six points to it. We draw this polygon as a solid figure on line 28. The output of this applet is shown in Figure 4.7.

```
 1 /* An applet that draws polygons
 2    Anderson, Franceschi
 3 */
 4
 5 import javax.swing.JApplet;
 6 import java.awt.Graphics;
 7 import java.awt.Polygon;
 8
 9 public class DrawingPolygons extends JApplet
10 {
11   public void paint( Graphics g )
12   {
```

```
      super.paint( g );

      Polygon triangle = new Polygon( );
      triangle.addPoint( 75, 50 );
      triangle.addPoint( 25, 150 );
      triangle.addPoint( 125, 150 );
      g.drawPolygon ( triangle );

      Polygon hexagon = new Polygon( );
      hexagon.addPoint( 150, 100 );
      hexagon.addPoint( 200, 13 );
      hexagon.addPoint( 300, 13 );
      hexagon.addPoint( 350, 100 );
      hexagon.addPoint( 300, 187 );
      hexagon.addPoint( 200, 187 );
      g.fillPolygon ( hexagon );
   }
}
```

EXAMPLE 4.7 Drawing Polygons

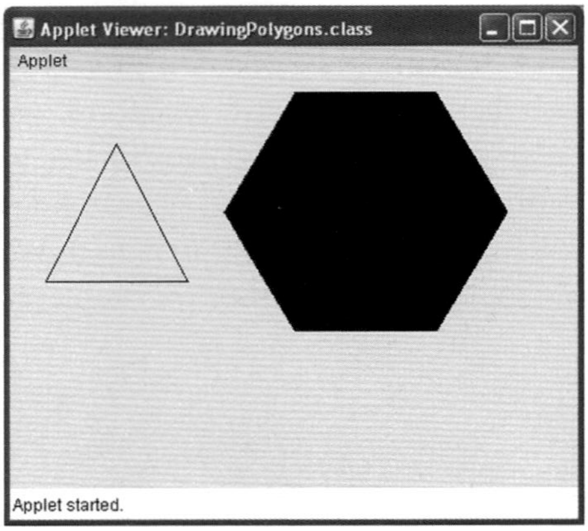

Figure 4.7
Output of Example 4.7

COMMON ERROR TRAP

Do not call the *paint* method. It is called automatically when the applet starts and every time the window contents need to be updated.

What happens if the (*x*,*y*) coordinate you specify for a figure isn't inside the window? If a figure's coordinates are outside the bounds of the window, no error will be generated, but the figure won't be visible. If the user resizes the window so that the coordinates are now within the newly sized window, then the figure will become visible.

Now we can write an applet that draws a picture. We've decided to draw an astronaut. Example 4.8 shows the code to do that. Notice that we never call the *paint* method; it is called automatically by the applet viewer or web browser.

```
/* An applet with graphics
   that draws an astronaut
   Anderson, Franceschi
*/

import javax.swing.JApplet;
import java.awt.Graphics;

public class Astronaut extends JApplet
{

  public void paint( Graphics g )
  {
     super.paint( g );

     int sX = 95, sY = 20; // starting x and y coordinate

     // helmet
     g.drawOval( sX + 60, sY, 75, 75 );
     g.drawOval( sX + 70, sY + 10, 55, 55 );

     // face
     g.drawOval( sX + 83,  sY + 27, 8, 8 );
     g.drawOval( sX + 103, sY + 27, 8, 8 );
     g.drawLine( sX + 97, sY + 35, sX + 99, sY + 43 );
     g.drawLine( sX + 97, sY + 43, sX + 99, sY + 43 );
     g.drawOval( sX + 90, sY + 48, 15, 6 );

     // neck
     g.drawRect( sX + 88, sY + 70, 20, 10 );

     // torso
     g.drawRect( sX + 65, sY + 80, 65, 85 );

     // arms
     g.drawRect( sX, sY + 80, 65, 20 );
     g.drawRect( sX + 130, sY + 80, 65, 20 );

     // legs
     g.drawRect( sX + 75, sY + 165, 20, 80 );
     g.drawRect( sX + 105, sY + 165, 20, 80 );
```

```
42
43      // flag
44      g.drawLine( sX + 195, sY + 80, sX + 195 , sY );
45      g.drawRect( sX + 195, sY, 75, 45 );
46      g.drawRect( sX + 195, sY, 30, 25 );
47
48      // caption
49      g.drawString( "One small step for man. . .",
50                          sX + 25, sY + 270 );
51   }
52 }
```

EXAMPLE 4.8 An Applet that Draws an Astronaut

When the applet in Example 4.8 runs, our astronaut will look like the one in Figure 4.8.

To draw our astronaut, we used rectangles for the body, arms, legs, and flag; lines for the nose and the flag's stick; circles for the helmet and eyes; and an oval for the mouth. Then we used the *drawString* method to print "One small step for man..."

SOFTWARE ENGINEERING TIP

When drawing a figure using graphics, specify coordinates as offsets from a starting (*x*, *y*) coordinate.

In line 16, we declare and initialize two variables, *sX* and *sY*. These are the starting *x* and *y* values for the astronaut. The *x* and *y* arguments we send to the *drawRect*, *drawLine*, *drawOval*, and *drawString* methods are specified relative to this starting (*sX*, *sY*) coordinate. By specifying these values, such as *sX* + 60, we are using **offsets**. By using offsets from the starting (*sX*, *sY*) coordinate, we can easily change the position of the astronaut on the screen

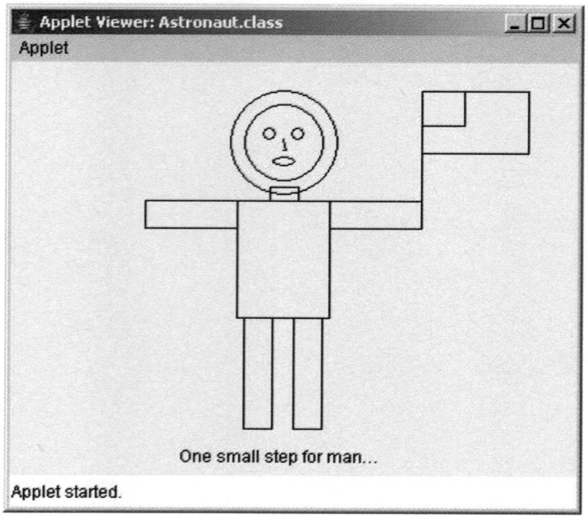

Figure 4.8
An Astronaut Made from Rectangles, Ovals, Lines, and Text

by simply changing the values of *sX* and *sY*. We don't need to change any of the arguments sent to the *Graphics* methods. To demonstrate this, try changing the values of *sX* and *sY* and re-running the applet.

Skill Practice
with these end-of-chapter questions

4.7.1 Multiple Choice Exercises

Questions 6, 7, 8, 9

4.7.2 Reading and Understanding Code

Questions 12,13,14,15

4.7.3 Fill In the Code

Questions 17, 18, 19, 20

4.7.4 Identifying Errors in Code

Questions 21, 22

4.7.6 Write a Short Program

Questions 31, 32, 33

4.7.8 Technical Writing

Question 39

4.4 Using Color

All the figures we have drawn were black. That's because when our applet starts, the default drawing color is black. We can add color to the drawing by setting the **current color**, also called the **foreground color**, which is part of the graphics context represented by the *Graphics* object sent to the *paint* method. The *draw* and *fill* methods draw the figures in the current color. The current color remains in effect until it is set to another color. For example, if you set the current color to blue—then call the *drawRect*, *fillOval*, and *drawLine* methods—the rectangle, oval, and line will all be drawn in blue. Then if you set the color to yellow and call the *drawRect* method, that rectangle will be drawn in yellow.

To set the current color, use the *setColor* method of the *Graphics* class as shown in Table 4.4. This method takes a *Color* object as an argument.

TABLE 4.4 The *setColor* Method of the *Graphics* Class

Another Useful Method of the *Graphics* Class	
Return value	**Method name and argument list**
`void`	`setColor( Color c )`
	sets the current foreground color to the *Color* specified by *c*.

The *Color* class, which is in the *java.awt* package, defines colors using an RGB (Red, Green, Blue) system. Any RGB color is considered to be composed of red, green, and blue components. Each component's value can range from 0 to 255; the higher the value, the higher the concentration of that component in the color. For example, a color with red = 255, green = 0, and blue = 0 is red, and a color with red = 0, green = 0, and blue = 255 is blue.

Gray consists of equal amounts of each component. The higher the value of the components, the lighter the color of gray. This makes sense because white is (255, 255, 255), so the closer a color gets to white, the lighter that color will be. Similarly, the closer the gray value gets to 0, the darker the color, because (0, 0, 0) is black.

The *Color* class provides a set of *static Color* constants representing 13 common colors. Table 4.5 lists the *Color* constants for these common colors and their corresponding red, green, and blue components.

Each color constant is a predefined *Color* object, so you can simply assign the constant to your *Color* object reference.You do not need to instantiate a new *Color* object. *Color* constants can be used wherever a *Color* object is expected. For example, this statement assigns the *Color* constant *Color.RED* to the object reference *red*:

```
Color red = Color.RED;
```

And this statement sets the current color to orange:

```
g.setColor( Color.ORANGE );
```

TABLE 4.5 *Color* Constants and Their Red, Green, and Blue Components

Color Constant	Red	Green	Blue
Color.BLACK	0	0	0
Color.BLUE	0	0	255
Color.CYAN	0	255	255
Color.DARK_GRAY	64	64	64
Color.GRAY	128	128	128
Color.GREEN	0	255	0
Color.LIGHT_GRAY	192	192	192
Color.MAGENTA	255	0	255
Color.ORANGE	255	200	0
Color.PINK	255	175	175
Color.RED	255	0	0
Color.WHITE	255	255	255
Color.YELLOW	255	255	0

In addition to using the *Color* constants, you can instantiate your own custom colors using any of the 16 million possible combinations of the component values. The *Color* class has a number of constructors, but for our purposes, we'll need only the constructor shown in Table 4.6.

TABLE 4.6 A *Color* Class Constructor

Color Constructor
`Color( int rr, int gg, int bb )`
Allocates a *Color* object with an *rr* red component, *gg* green component, and *bb* blue component.

Now let's add color to our astronaut drawing. Example 4.9 shows our modified applet.

```
/* An applet with graphics
   that draws an astronaut in color
   Anderson, Franceschi
*/

import javax.swing.JApplet;
import javax.swing.JOptionPane;
import java.awt.Graphics;
import java.awt.Color;

public class AstronautWithColor extends JApplet
{

  public void paint( Graphics g )
  {
    super.paint( g );

    // instantiate a custom color
    Color spacesuit = new Color( 195, 175, 150 );

    int sX = 100;  // the starting x position
    int sY = 25;   // the starting y position

    // helmet
    g.setColor( spacesuit );
    g.fillOval( sX + 60, sY, 75, 75 );
    g.setColor( Color.LIGHT_GRAY );
    g.fillOval( sX + 70, sY + 10, 55, 55 );

    // face
    g.setColor( Color.DARK_GRAY );
    g.drawOval( sX + 83,  sY + 27, 8, 8 );
    g.drawOval( sX + 103, sY + 27, 8, 8 );
    g.drawLine( sX + 97, sY + 35, sX + 99, sY + 43 );
    g.drawLine( sX + 97, sY + 43, sX + 99, sY + 43 );
    g.drawOval( sX + 90, sY + 48, 15, 6 );

    // neck
    g.setColor( spacesuit );
    g.fillRect( sX + 88, sY + 70, 20, 10 );

    // torso
```

```
        g.fillRect( sX + 65, sY + 80, 65, 85 );

        // arms
        g.fillRect( sX, sY + 80, 65, 20 );
        g.fillRect( sX + 130, sY + 80, 65, 20 );

        // legs
        g.fillRect( sX + 75, sY + 165, 20, 80 );
        g.fillRect( sX + 105, sY + 165, 20, 80 );

        // flag
        g.setColor( Color.BLACK );
        g.drawLine( sX + 195, sY + 80, sX + 195 , sY );
        g.setColor( Color.RED );
        g.fillRect( sX + 195, sY, 75, 45 );
        g.setColor( Color.BLUE );
        g.fillRect( sX + 195, sY, 30, 25 );

        // caption
        g.setColor( Color.BLACK );
        g.drawString( "One small step for man...",
                              sX + 25, sY + 270 );
    }
}
```

EXAMPLE 4.9 An Applet That Draws an Astronaut in Color

Figure 4.9 shows our astronaut in color.

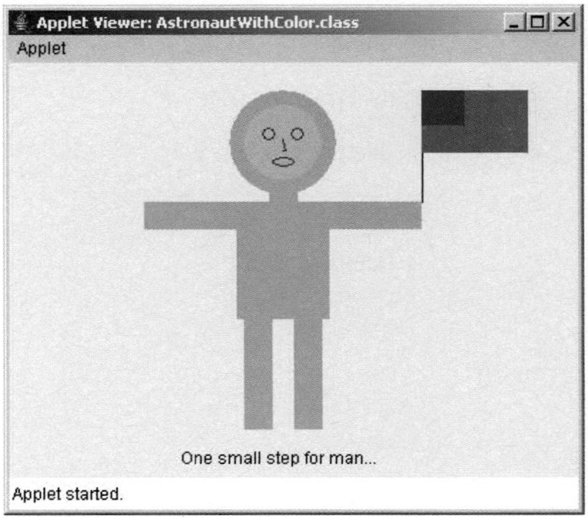

Figure 4.9
Our Astronaut in Color

On line 9, we include an *import* statement for the *Color* class in the *java.awt* package.

For the space suit, we instantiate a custom *Color* object named *spacesuit* on line 19 using the constructor shown in Table 4.6. To draw the astronaut in color, we change the *draw* methods to *fill* methods, and when we draw any figure that is part of the space suit, we make sure the current color is our custom color, *spacesuit.*

It's important to realize that the rendering of the figures occurs in the order in which the *draw* or *fill* methods are executed. Any new figure that occupies the same space as a previously drawn figure will overwrite the previous figure. In this drawing, we intentionally draw the red rectangle of the flag before drawing the blue rectangle. If we drew the rectangles in the opposite order, the blue rectangle would not be visible because the red rectangle, drawn second, would cover the blue rectangle.

Skill Practice
with these end-of-chapter questions

4.7.1 Multiple Choice Exercises

Questions 5,10

4.7.2 Reading and Understanding Code

Question 11

4.7.3 Fill In the Code

Question 16

4.7.4 Identifying Errors in Code

Questions 23, 24, 25

4.7.5 Debugging Area

Questions 29, 30

4.5 Programming Activity 1: Writing an Applet with Graphics

In this Programming Activity, you will write an applet that uses graphics. You will draw a picture of your own design. The objective of this programming activity is to gain experience with the window coordinate system, the *draw* and *fill* graphics methods, and using colors.

1. Start with the *ShellApplet* class, change the name of the class to represent the figure you will draw, and add an *import* statement for the *Color* class.
2. Create a drawing of your own design. It's helpful to sketch the drawing on graph paper first, then translate the drawing into the coordinates of the applet window. Your drawing should include at least two each of rectangles, ovals, circles, and lines, plus a polygon. Your drawing should also use at least three colors, one of which is a custom color.
3. Label your drawing using the *drawString* method.

Be creative with your drawing!

? DISCUSSION QUESTIONS

1. If you define the starting (*x*, *y*) coordinate of the drawing as (400, 400) you might not be able to see the drawing. Explain why and what the user can do to make the drawing visible.
2. What is the advantage to drawing a figure using a starting (*x*, *y*) coordinate?

4.6 Chapter Summary

- Applets are Java programs that are run from an applet viewer or an Internet browser. Applets are invoked via the HTML *APPLET* tag.
- When an applet begins executing, the *paint* method is called. The *paint* method is used to display text and graphics on the applet window.
- The *Graphics* class in the *java.awt* package provides methods to draw figures, such as rectangles, circles, polygons, and lines; to set the colors for drawing; and to write text in a window.

- An (*x*,*y*) coordinate system is used to specify locations in the window. Each coordinate corresponds to a pixel (or picture element). The *x* value specifies the horizontal position, beginning at 0 and increasing as you move right across the window. The *y* value specifies the vertical position, starting at 0 and increasing as you move down the window.
- All drawing on a graphics window is done in the current color, which is changed using the *setColor* method.
- Objects of the *Color* class, in the *java.awt* package, can be used to set the current color. The *Color* class provides *static* constants for common colors.
- Custom *Color* objects can be instantiated by using a constructor and specifying the red, green, and blue components of the color.

4.7 Exercises, Problems, and Projects

4.7.1 Multiple Choice Exercises

1. What package does the *Graphics* class belong to?
   - ❑ *Graphics*
   - ❑ *java.awt*
   - ❑ *swing*
   - ❑ *Applet*
2. How does a programmer typically get access to a *Graphics* object when coding an applet?
   - ❑ One must be created with the *Graphics* constructor.
   - ❑ It is an instance variable of the class *JApplet*.
   - ❑ It is a parameter of the *paint* method.
3. An applet is a standalone application.
   - ❑ true
   - ❑ false
4. In an applet, the *paint* method is called automatically even if the programmer does not code the method call.
   - ❑ true
   - ❑ false

5. Look at the following code:

```
Color c = Color.BLUE;
```

What is *BLUE*?

- ❑ a *static* field of the class *Color*
- ❑ an instance variable of the class *Color*
- ❑ a *static* method of the class *Color*
- ❑ an instance method of the class *Color*

6. What can be stated about the line drawn by the following code?

```
g.drawLine( 100, 200, 300, 200 );
```

- ❑ The line is vertical.
- ❑ The line is horizontal.
- ❑ The line is a diagonal.
- ❑ none of the above.

7. What do the arguments 10, 20 represent in the following statement?

```
g.drawRect( 10, 20, 100, 200 );
```

- ❑ the (*x*,*y*) coordinate of the upper-left corner of the rectangle we are drawing
- ❑ the width and height of the rectangle we are drawing
- ❑ the (*x*,*y*) coordinate of the center of the rectangle we are drawing
- ❑ the (*x*,*y*) coordinate of the lower-right corner of the rectangle we are drawing

8. What do the arguments 100, 200 represent in the following statement?

```
g.drawRect( 10, 20, 100, 200 );
```

- ❑ the (*x*,*y*) coordinate of the upper-left corner of the rectangle we are drawing
- ❑ the width and height of the rectangle we are drawing
- ❑ the height and width of the rectangle we are drawing
- ❑ the (*x*,*y*) coordinate of the lower-right corner of the rectangle we are drawing

9. How many arguments does the *fillOval* method take?

   ❑ 0

   ❑ 2

   ❑ 4

   ❑ 5

10. In RGB format, a gray color can be coded as *A A A* where the first *A* represents the amount of red in the color, the second *A* the amount of green, and the third *A* the amount of blue. *A* can vary from 0 to 255, including both 0 and 255; how many possible gray colors can we have?

    ❑ 1

    ❑ 2

    ❑ 255

    ❑ 256

    ❑ 257

4.7.2 Reading and Understanding Code

11. In what color will the rectangle be drawn?

```
g.setColor( Color.BLUE );
g.drawRect( 10, 20, 100, 200 );
```

12. What is the length of the line being drawn?

```
g.drawLine( 50, 20, 50, 350 );
```

13. What is the width of the rectangle being drawn?

```
g.fillRect( 10, 20, 250, 350 );
```

14. What is the (*x*,*y*) coordinate of the upper-right corner of the rectangle being drawn?

```
g.fillRect( 10, 20, 250, 350 );
```

15. What is the (*x*,*y*) coordinate of the lower-right corner of the rectangle being drawn?

```
g.drawRect( 10, 20, 250, 350 );
```

4.7.3 Fill In the Code

16. This code sets the current color to red.

```
// assume you have a Graphics object named g
// your code goes here
```

17. This code draws the *String* "Fill in the Code" with the lower-left corner of the first character (the *F*) being at the coordinate (100, 250).

```
// assume you have a Graphics object called g
// your code goes here
```

18. This code draws a filled rectangle with a width of 100 pixels and a height of 300 pixels, starting at the coordinate (50, 30).

```
// assume you have a Graphics object called g
// your code goes here
```

19. This code draws a filled rectangle starting at (50, 30) for its upper-left corner with a lower-right corner at (100, 300).

```
// assume you have a Graphics object called g
// your code goes here
```

20. This code draws a circle of radius 100 with its center located at (200, 200).

```
// assume you have a Graphics object called g
// your code goes here
```

4.7.4 Identifying Errors in Code

21. Where is the error in this code sequence?

```
Graphics g = new Graphics( );
```

22. Where is the error in this code sequence?

```
// we are inside method paint
g.drawString( 'Find the bug', 100, 200 );
```

23. Where is the error in this code sequence?

```
// we are inside method paint
g.setColor( GREEN );
```

24. Where is the error in this code sequence?

```
// we are inside method paint
g.setColor( Color.COBALT );
```

25. Where is the error in this code sequence?

```
// we are inside method paint
g.color = Color.RED;
```

26. Where is the error in this statement?

```
import Graphics;
```

27. Where is the error in this statement?

```
import java.awt.JApplet;
```

4.7.5 Debugging Area—Using Messages from the Java Compiler and Java JVM

28. You coded the following program in the file *MyApplet.java*:

```
import javax.swing.JApplet;
import java.awt.Graphics;

public class MyApplet extends JApplet
{
    public static void paint( Graphics g )    // line 6
    {
        // some code here
    }
}
```

When you compile, you get the following message:

```
MyApplet.java:6: paint(java.awt.Graphics) in MyApplet cannot
override paint(java.awt.Graphics) in java.awt.Container;
overriding method is static
public static void paint( Graphics g )    // line 6
                   ^

1 error
```

Explain what the problem is and how to fix it.

29. You imported the *Color* class and coded the following on line 10 of the class *MyApplet.java*:

```
Color c = new Color( 1.4, 234, 23 );    // line 10
```

When you compile, you get the following message:

```
MyApplet.java:10: cannot find symbol
symbol  : constructor Color (double,int,int)
location : class java.awt.Color

Color c = new Color( 1.4, 234, 23 );    // line 10
                    ^

1 error
```

Explain what the problem is and how to fix it.

30. You coded the following on line 10 of the class *MyApplet.java*:

```
Color c = Color.Blue; // line 10
```

When you compile, you get the following message:

```
MyApplet.java:10: cannot find symbol
symbol  : variable Blue
location: class java.awt.Color
      Color c = Color.Blue;    // line 10
                     ^

1 error
```

Explain what the problem is and how to fix it.

4.7.6 Write a Short Program

31. Write an applet that displays the five Olympic rings.
32. Write an applet that displays a tic-tac-toe board. Include a few X's and O's.
33. Write an applet that displays a rhombus (i.e., a parallelogram with equal sides). Your rhombus should not be a square.

4.7.7 Programming Projects

34. Write an applet that displays two eyes. An eye can be drawn using an oval, a filled circle, and lines. On the applet, write a word or two about these eyes.
35. Write an applet that displays the following coins: a quarter, a dime, and a nickel. These three coins should be drawn as basic circles (of different diameters) with the currency value inside (for instance, $.25).
36. Write an applet that displays a basic house, made up of lines (and possibly rectangles). Your house should have multiple colors. On the applet, give a title to the house (for instance, "Java House").
37. Write an applet that displays a black and red bull's eye target, typically made up of several concentric circles.

4.7.8 Technical Writing

38. On the World Wide Web, an applet is a program that executes on the "client side" (a local machine such as your own PC) as opposed to the "server side" (such as a server at *www.yahoo.com*). Do you see any potential problem executing the same program, such as an applet, on possibly millions of different computers worldwide?

39. If the *drawRect* method did not exist, but you still had the *drawLine* method available, explain how you would be able to draw a rectangle.

4.7.9 Group Project (for a group of 1, 2, or 3 students)

40. Write an applet and one HTML file calling the applet.

    The applet should include the following:

    - a drawing of a chessboard piece (it can be in a single color).
    - a description of a particular piece of a chessboard (for instance, a rook) and its main legal moves.

    In order to make the description visually appealing, you should use several colors and several fonts. You will need to look up the following on Sun's Java website:

    - the *Font* class
    - how the *Font* class constructors work
    - the method *setFont* of the *Graphics* class

CHAPTER 5

Flow of Control, Part 1: Selection

CHAPTER CONTENTS

Introduction

In Chapter 1, we said that the order of a program's instructions is critical to producing correct results. The order in which the instructions are executed is called the **flow of control** of the program. There are essentially four types of flow of control: sequential execution, method calls, selection, and looping. Most programs use a combination of all types of flow of control.

So far, our programs have used sequential execution and method calls exclusively. In our Java applications, the JVM executed the first instruction in the *main* method, then executed the next instruction in *main*, and continued executing instructions in order until there were no more instructions to execute. Whenever one of the instructions included a method call, the instructions in the method were executed until the method returned and we resumed execution of instructions in order.

Sometimes, however, you don't want to execute every instruction. Some instructions should be executed only for certain input values, but not for others. For example, we may want to count only the odd numbers or perform only the operation that the user selects from a menu. For these applications, we need a way to determine at run time the input values we have and, therefore, which instructions we should execute.

In this chapter, we'll discuss **selection**, which gives us a way to test for certain conditions and to select the instructions to execute based on the results of the test. To perform selection, Java provides a number of alternatives: *if*, *if/else*, *if/else if*, the conditional operator (?:), and *switch*.

5.1 Forming Conditions

Often in a program, we need to compare variables or objects. For instance, we could be interested in knowing if a person's age is over 18, or if a student's average test score is above 90. If the age is over 18, that person would be allowed to shop online. If a student has an average of 90 or better, that student will be placed on the honor roll, or if a student's grade is below 60, he or she will be sent a warning.

Java provides equality, relational, and logical operators to evaluate and test whether an expression is true or false. It also provides selection statements to transfer control to a different part of the program depending on the result of that test.

5.1.1 Equality Operators

A common operation is to compare two variables or values of the same data type to determine if their values are equal. For example, we need to compare the user's input to a 'y' to determine whether he or she wants to play again. Or if we want to print a list of students who will continue next year, we need to eliminate the students who are graduating seniors.

To compare values of primitive data types, Java provides the equality operators shown in Table 5.1. Both are binary operators, meaning that they take two operands. The operands may be expressions that evaluate to a primitive numeric or *boolean* type or an object reference. The result of an expression composed of a relational operator and its two operands is a *boolean* value, that is, *true* or *false*.

For instance, if an *int* variable *age* holds the value 32, then

> the expression `( age == 32 )` will evaluate to *true*, and
> the expression `( age != 32 )` will evaluate to *false*.

The following expression can be used to eliminate seniors by testing whether the value of the *int* variable *yearInCollege* is not equal to 4:

```
yearInCollege != 4
```

The following expression can be used in a game program to determine whether the user wants to play again:

```
playAgain  == 'y'
```

TABLE 5.1 Equality Operators

Equality Operator	Type	Meaning
==	binary	is equal to
!=	binary	is not equal to

Assuming the user's input is stored in the *char* variable *playAgain*, then if the user typed 'y', the expression evaluates to *true*; with any other input value, the expression evaluates to *false*.

A common error is to use the assignment operator instead of the equality operator. For example:

```
playAgain = 'y'
```

COMMON ERROR TRAP

Do not confuse the equality operator == (double equal signs) with the assignment operator = (one equal sign).

assigns the value *y* to the variable *playAgain*. Confusing the assignment and equality operators is easy to do; so easy, in fact, that we can almost guarantee that you will make this mistake at least once.

Although the equality operators can be used to compare object references, these operators cannot be used to compare objects. We discuss the comparison of objects later in the chapter.

5.1.2 Relational Operators

To compare values of primitive numeric types, Java provides the relational operators shown in Table 5.2. These operators are binary, meaning that they take two operands, each of which is an expression that evaluates to a primitive numeric type. The relational operators cannot be used with *boolean* expressions or with object references.

Again, if an *int* variable *age* holds the value 32, then

the expression `( age < 32 )` will evaluate to *false*,
the expression `( age <= 32 )` will evaluate to *true*,
the expression `( age > 32 )` will evaluate to *false*, and
the expression `( age >= 32 )` will evaluate to *true*.

TABLE 5.2 Relational Operators

Relational Operator	Type	Meaning
`<`	binary	is less than
`<=`	binary	is less than or equal to
`>`	binary	is greater than
`>=`	binary	is greater than or equal to

This expression tests whether an *int* variable *testScore* is at least 90:

```
testScore >= 90
```

This code tests whether that test score is less than 60:

```
testScore < 60
```

5.1.3 Logical Operators

A common operation in a program is to test whether a combination of conditions is true or false. For these operations, Java provides the logical operators !, &&, and ||, which correspond to the Boolean logic operators NOT, AND, and OR. These operators, which are shown in Table 5.3, take *boolean* expressions as operands. A *boolean* expression can be any legal combination of *boolean* variables; a condition using relational operators that evaluates to *true* or *false;* or a call to a method that returns a *boolean* value.

The NOT operator (!) takes one *boolean* expression as an operand and inverts the value of that operand. If the operand is *true*, the result will be *false*; and if the operand is *false*, the result will be *true*.

The AND operator (&&) takes two *boolean* expressions as operands; if both operands are *true*, then the result will be *true*; otherwise, it will be *false*.

The OR operator (||) also takes two *boolean* expressions as operands. If both operands are *false*, then the result will be *false*; otherwise, it will be *true*. The OR operator consists of two vertical bars with no intervening space. On the PC keyboard, the vertical bar is the shifted character above the *Enter* key.

The truth table for these logical operators is shown in Table 5.4.

The order of precedence of the relational and logical operators is shown in Table 5.5, along with the arithmetic operators. Note that the Unary NOT

REFERENCE POINT

The complete Operator Precedence Chart is provided in Appendix B.

TABLE 5.3 Logical Operators

<table>
<tr><th>Logical Operator</th><th>Type</th><th>Meaning</th></tr>
<tr><td>!</td><td>unary</td><td>NOT</td></tr>
<tr><td>&&</td><td>binary</td><td>AND</td></tr>
<tr><td>||</td><td>binary</td><td>OR</td></tr>
</table>

TABLE 5.4 Truth Table for Logical Operators

<table>
<tr><th colspan="2">Operands</th><th colspan="3">Operations</th></tr>
<tr><td>a</td><td>b</td><td>!a</td><td>a && b</td><td>a || b</td></tr>
<tr><td>true</td><td>true</td><td>false</td><td>true</td><td>true</td></tr>
<tr><td>true</td><td>false</td><td>false</td><td>false</td><td>true</td></tr>
<tr><td>false</td><td>true</td><td>true</td><td>false</td><td>true</td></tr>
<tr><td>false</td><td>false</td><td>true</td><td>false</td><td>false</td></tr>
</table>

TABLE 5.5 Operator Precedence

<table>
<tr><th>Operator Hierarchy</th><th>Order of Same-Statement Evaluation</th><th>Operation</th></tr>
<tr><td>( )</td><td>left to right</td><td>parentheses for explicit grouping</td></tr>
<tr><td>++, --</td><td>right to left</td><td>shortcut postincrement</td></tr>
<tr><td>++, --, !</td><td>right to left</td><td>shortcut preincrement, logical unary NOT</td></tr>
<tr><td>*, /, %</td><td>left to right</td><td>multiplication, division, modulus</td></tr>
<tr><td>+, -</td><td>left to right</td><td>addition or String concatenation, subtraction</td></tr>
<tr><td><, <=, >, >=</td><td>left to right</td><td>relational operators: less than, less than or equal to, greater than, greater than or equal to</td></tr>
<tr><td>==, !=</td><td>left to right</td><td>equality operators: equal to and not equal to</td></tr>
<tr><td>&&</td><td>left to right</td><td>logical AND</td></tr>
<tr><td>||</td><td>left to right</td><td>logical OR</td></tr>
<tr><td>=, +=, -=, *=, /=, %=</td><td>right to left</td><td>Assignment operator and shortcut assignment operators</td></tr>
</table>

operator (!) has the highest precedence of the relational and logical operators, followed by the relational operators, then the equality operators, then AND (&&), then OR (||).

Example 5.1 shows these operators at work.

```
/* Using Logical Operators
   Anderson, Franceschi
*/

public class LogicalOperators
{
 public static void main( String [ ] args )
 {
  int age = 75;
  boolean test;

  test = ( age > 18 && age < 65 );
  System.out.println( age + " > 18 && " + age + " < 65 is " + test );

  // short circuitry with AND
  test = ( age < 65 && age > 18 );
  System.out.println( age + " < 65 && " + age + " > 18 is " + test );

  // short circuitry with OR
  test = ( age > 65 || age < 18 );
  System.out.println( age + " > 65 || " + age + " < 18 is " + test );

  // AND has higher precedence than OR
  test = ( age > 65 || age < 18  && false );
  System.out.println( age + " > 65 || " + age
                        + " < 18 && false is " + test );

  // use of parentheses to force order of execution
  test = ( ( age > 65 || age < 18 )  && false );
  System.out.println( "( " + age + " > 65 || " + age
                        + " < 18 ) && false is " + test );
 }
}
```

EXAMPLE 5.1 How Logical Operators Work

Line 12 evaluates whether the variable *age* is greater than 18 and less than 65 and assigns the result to the *boolean* variable *test*. Since line 9 set the value of *age* to 75, the first operand (*age* > *18*) evaluates to *true*. The second operand (*age* < *65*) evaluates to *false*; finally,

```
true && false
```

evaluates to *false*, and *false* is assigned to *test*, which is printed at line 13. Line 16 evaluates the same expression as in line 12, but in reverse order. Now the first operand (*age* < *65*) evaluates to *false*, and therefore, since the operator is the logical AND, the overall expression evaluates to *false*, independently of the value of the second operand. Because (*false* && something) always evaluates to *false*, the second operand (*age* > *18*) will never be evaluated by the Java compiler. This is called **short-circuit evaluation**.

Line 20 shows an example of short-circuit evaluation for the logical OR operator. The first operand (*age* > *65*) evaluates to *true*, resulting in the overall expression evaluating to *true*, independently of the value of the second operand. Because (*true* || something) always evaluates to *true*, the second operand will never be evaluated by the Java compiler.

As shown in Table 5.5, the logical AND operator has higher precedence than the logical OR operator. Thus, the expression in line 24 is not evaluated from left to right; rather, the second part of the expression (*age* < *18* && *false*) is evaluated first, which evaluates to *false*. Then (*age* > *65* || *false*) evaluates to *true*, which is assigned to *test*, and then output at lines 25–26. If we want to evaluate the expression from left to right, we have to use parentheses to force this, as in line 29. Then, (*age* > *65* || *age* < *18*) is evaluated first and evaluates to *true*; (*true* && *false*) is evaluated next and evaluates to *false*.

Figure 5.1 shows the output of Example 5.1.

Figure 5.1
Output from Example 5.1

```
75 > 18 && 75 < 65 is false
75 < 65 && 75 > 18 is false
75 > 65 || 75 < 18 is true
75 > 65 || 75 < 18  && false is true
( 75 > 65 || 75 < 18 ) && false is false
```

Suppose we have three *ints: x, y,* and *z,* and we want to test if *x* is less than both *y* and *z.* A common error is to express the condition this way:

```
x < y && z // incorrect comparison of x to y and z
```

Because *z* is not a *boolean* variable, this statement will generate a compiler error. Both operands of the logical AND and logical OR operators must evaluate to a *boolean* expression. The correct expression is the following: `x < y && x < z`.

COMMON ERROR TRAP

Be sure that both operands of the logical AND and logical OR operators are *boolean* expressions. Expressions such as this: `x < y && z`, with *x, y,* and *z* being numeric types, are illegal. Instead, use the expression: `x < y && x < z`

There are often several ways to express the same condition using the Java logical operators. For instance, suppose we have two *boolean* variables called *flag1* and *flag2* and we want to test if at least one of them is *false.*

In plain English, we would translate it as *flag1 is false OR flag2 is false.*

Table 5.6 provides several equivalent expressions for the preceding test.

Although all the expressions in Table 5.6 are equivalent, the first expression, which is the simplest translation of the condition to test, is the easiest to understand and would be the best selection for readability.

DeMorgan's Laws

Thanks to the work of the British mathematician Augustus DeMorgan, we have a set of rules to help develop expressions that are equivalent. DeMorgan, who is known for his work in Boolean algebra and set theory, developed what are known as DeMorgan's Laws. They are the following:

```
1.  NOT( A AND B ) = ( NOT A ) OR ( NOT B )
2.  NOT( A OR B ) = ( NOT A ) AND ( NOT B )
```

TABLE 5.6 Examples of Equivalent Expressions

Equivalent Expressions	English Meaning
`( flag1 == false ) || ( flag2 == false )`	*flag1* is false OR *flag2* is false
`!flag1 || !flag2`	*!flag1* is true OR *!flag2* is true
`! ( flag1 && flag 2 )`	not both *flag1* and *flag2* are true

In Java, therefore, using the first law, we see that

`!( a && b )` is equivalent to `!a || !b`

Using the second law, we see that

`!( a || b )` is equivalent to `!a && !b`

These laws can be verified simply by the extended truth table shown in Table 5.7.

Thus, to use DeMorgan's Laws, you need to change the AND operator to OR and change the OR operator to AND, and apply the NOT operator (!) to each operand of a logical operator. When the operands are expressions using relational or equality operators, the negated expressions are shown in Table 5.8.

TABLE 5.7 Truth Table for DeMorgan's Laws

<table>
<tr><th>a</th><th>b</th><th>!a</th><th>!b</th><th>a && b</th><th>a || b</th><th>!(a && b)</th><th>!a || !b</th><th>!(a || b)</th><th>!a && !b</th></tr>
<tr><td>true</td><td>true</td><td>false</td><td>false</td><td>true</td><td>true</td><td>false</td><td>false</td><td>false</td><td>false</td></tr>
<tr><td>true</td><td>false</td><td>false</td><td>true</td><td>false</td><td>true</td><td>true</td><td>true</td><td>false</td><td>false</td></tr>
<tr><td>false</td><td>true</td><td>true</td><td>false</td><td>false</td><td>true</td><td>true</td><td>true</td><td>false</td><td>false</td></tr>
<tr><td>false</td><td>false</td><td>true</td><td>true</td><td>false</td><td>false</td><td>true</td><td>true</td><td>true</td><td>true</td></tr>
</table>

TABLE 5.8 The Logical NOT Operator Applied to Relational and Equality Operators

Expression	! (Expression)
a == b	a != b
a != b	a == b
a < b	a >= b
a >= b	a < b
a > b	a <= b
a <= b	a > b

TABLE 5.9 More Examples of Equivalent Expressions

<table>
<tr><th>Equivalent Expressions</th><th>English Meaning</th></tr>
<tr><td><code>(age <= 18 || age >= 65)</code></td><td>age is less than or equal to 18 or age is greater than or equal to 65</td></tr>
<tr><td><code>!(age > 18 && age < 65)</code></td><td>age is not between 18 and 65</td></tr>
<tr><td><code>!(age > 18) || !(age < 65)</code></td><td>age is not greater than 18 or age is not less than 65</td></tr>
</table>

For instance, suppose we have an *int* variable named *age*, representing the age of a person, and we want to assess whether *age* is less than or equal to 18 or greater than or equal to 65.

Table 5.9 provides several equivalent expressions for the preceding test.

Again, although all the expressions in Table 5.9 are equivalent, the first expression, which is the simplest translation of the condition to test, is the easiest to read.

SOFTWARE ENGINEERING TIP

Compose Boolean expressions so that they are easy to read and understand.

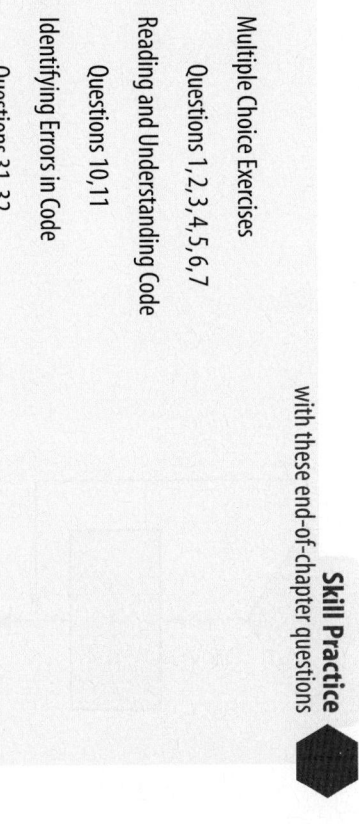

Skill Practice
with these end-of-chapter questions

5.14.1 Multiple Choice Exercises

Questions 1, 2, 3, 4, 5, 6, 7

5.14.2 Reading and Understanding Code

Questions 10, 11

5.14.4 Identifying Errors in Code

Questions 31, 32

5.2 Simple Selection with *if*

The simple selection pattern is appropriate when your program needs to perform an operation for one set of data, but not for all other data. For this situation, we use a simple *if* statement, which has this pattern:

```
if ( condition )
{
  true block
}
next statement
```

The true block can contain one or more statements and is executed only if the condition evaluates to *true*. After the true block executes, the instruction following the *if* statement is executed. If the condition is *false,* the true block is skipped and execution picks up at the next instruction after the *if* statement. If the true block contains only one statement, the curly braces are optional. Figure 5.2 illustrates the flow of control of a simple *if* statement.

In Example 5.2, we first prompt the user to enter a grade at lines 12–13. Then we prompt the user for any extra credit points at lines 15–16. At line 18, we test whether the extra credit points are greater than 0. If so, we add the extra credit points to the test grade at line 19. Then, no matter what the extra credit was, lines 21–22 are executed, which print the final grade. Figures 5.3 and 5.4 show two runs of the program, one with extra credit greater than 0, and one with no extra credit.

Figure 5.2
Flow of Control of a Simple *if* Statement

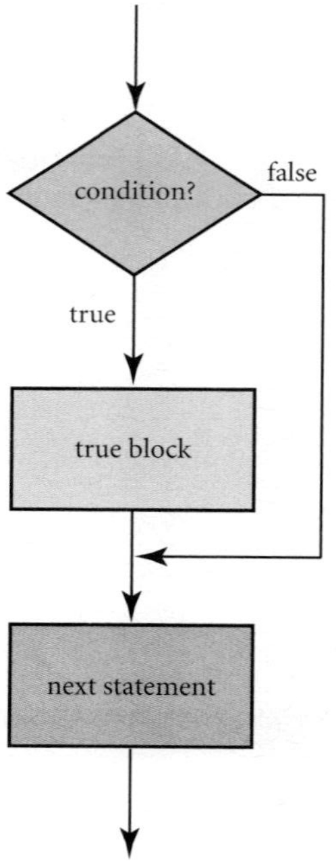

Figure 5.3
Output of Example 5.2 with 10 Extra Credit Points

```
Enter your test grade > 85
Enter your extra credit > 10
Your final test grade is 95
```

```
Enter your test grade > 85
Enter your extra credit > 0
Your final test grade is 85
```

Figure 5.4
Output of Example 5.2 with No Extra Credit

```
1 /* Using if to calculate a final test grade
2    Anderson, Franceschi
3 */
4 import java.util.Scanner;
5
6 public class TestGrade
7 {
8   public static void main( String [ ] args )
9   {
10    Scanner scan = new Scanner( System.in );
11
12    System.out.print( "Enter your test grade > " );
13    int grade = scan.nextInt( );
14
15    System.out.print( "Enter your extra credit > " );
16    int extraCredit = scan.nextInt( );
17
18    if ( extraCredit > 0 )
19        grade += extraCredit;
20
21    System.out.println( "Your final test grade is "
22                  + grade ) ;
23  }
24 }
```

EXAMPLE 5.2 Working with *if* Statements

Notice the indentation of the true block (line 19). Indenting clarifies the structure of the program. It's easy to see that we add the extra credit to the test grade only if the condition is true. Notice also that we skipped a line after the end of the *if* statement; this further separates the true block from the instruction that follows the *if* statement, making it easier to see the flow of control.

SOFTWARE ENGINEERING TIP

Indent the true block in an *if* statement for clarity.

Many software engineers believe it's a good practice to include the curly braces even if only one statement is included in the true block, because it increases clarity and ease of maintenance. The curly braces increase clarity because they highlight the section of code to be executed when the condition is *true*. Program maintenance is easier because if the program requirements change and you need to add a second statement to the true block, the curly braces are already in place.

Note that there is no semicolon after the condition. If you place a semicolon after the condition, as in this **incorrect** statement,

```
if ( grade >= 60 );  // incorrect to place semicolon here
     System.out.println( "You passed" );
```

COMMON ERROR TRAP

Adding a semicolon after the condition of an *if* statement indicates that the true block is empty and can cause a logic error at run time.

the compiler will not generate an error. Instead, it will consider the semicolon to indicate that the *if* statement is empty, because a semicolon by itself indicates a statement that does nothing. In this case, the compiler concludes that there is no instruction to execute when the condition is *true*. As a result, when the program runs, the statement

```
System.out.println( "You passed" );
```

is treated as though it follows the *if* statement, and therefore, the message "You passed" will be printed regardless of the value of *grade*.

5.3 Selection Using *if/else*

The second form of an *if* statement is appropriate when the data falls into two mutually exclusive categories and different instructions should be executed for each category. For these situations, we use an *if/else* statement, which has the following pattern:

```
if ( condition )
{
   true block
}
else
{
   false block
}
next statement
```

If the condition evaluates to *true*, the true block is executed and the false block is skipped. If the condition evaluates to *false*, the true block is skipped and the false block is executed. In either situation, the statement following the *if* statement is executed next. Figure 5.5 illustrates the flow of control of an *if/else* statement.

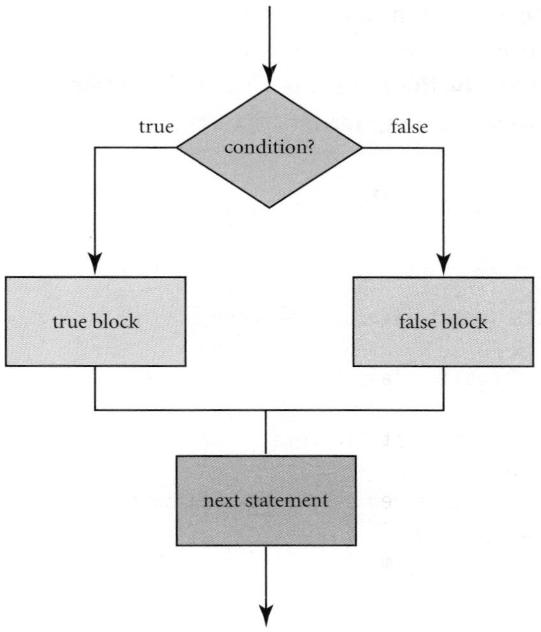

Figure 5.5
Flow of Control of an *if/else* Statement

If the true or false block contains only one statement, the curly braces are optional for that block.

Again, notice the indentation of the true and false blocks and that the *else* and curly braces line up under the *if*. This coding style makes it easy to see which statements belong to the true block and which belong to the false block. If the indentation is incorrect, a reader of your program may misunderstand which statements will be executed. In any event, the compiler ignores the indentation; the indentation is designed only to make it easier for humans to understand the logic of the code.

In Example 5.3, we test a grade to determine whether it is a passing grade (>=60) or a failing grade (any other value). This is a case where the data is mutually exclusive: either the grade is a passing grade or it is not. We want to print a different message depending on the grade status. After prompting the user for a numeric grade, we declare a *String* to hold the appropriate message (line 16), which will be determined in our *if/else* statement. If the *if* condition, `(grade >= 60)`, is true, then we assign "You passed" to *message*. If the condition is false, we assign "You failed" to *message*. On line 22, after the *if/else* statement completes, we print whatever *String* we have assigned to *message*. Figures 5.6 and 5.7 show two runs of the program, first with a grade greater than or equal to 60, and then with a grade less than 60.

```
1 /* Using if/else
2    Anderson, Franceschi
3 */
4
5 import java.util.Scanner;
6
7 public class PassingGrade
8 {
9  public static void main( String [ ] args )
10  {
11     Scanner scan = new Scanner( System.in );
12
13     System.out.print( "Enter a grade > " );
14     int grade = scan.nextInt( );
15
16     String message;
17     if ( grade >= 60 )
18      message = "You passed";
19     else
20      message = "You failed ";
21
22     System.out.println( message ) ;
23  }
24 }
```

EXAMPLE 5.3 Working with *if/else* Statements

Figure 5.6
Output from Example 5.3 with *grade* >= 60

```
Enter a grade > 60
You passed
```

Figure 5.7
Output from Example 5.3 with *grade* < 60

```
Enter a grade > 59
You failed
```

Note that we could have used two sequential *if* statements, as in:

```
if ( grade >= 60 )
   message = "You passed";

if ( grade < 60 )
   message = "You failed ";
```

However, if the first condition, `(grade >= 60)`, is false, the second condition, `(grade < 60)`, must be true. So an *if/else* simplifies our processing and avoids unnecessarily testing two conditions when only one of the conditions can be true.

Block Scope

The scope of a variable is the region within a program where the variable can be **referenced**, or used. When we declare a variable, its scope extends from the point at which it is declared until the end of the block in which we declared it. A method, such as *main*, is a block. Thus, in Example 5.3, the scope of the object reference *scan* extends from line 11 through the end of *main*. Thus, we can legally reference *scan* on line 14. Similarly, the scope of *grade* extends from its declaration (line 14) through the end of *main*, and we can legally reference it on line 17 in the *if* condition. Finally, the scope of the *String message* extends from line 16 through the end of *main*, and thus we can legally reference *message* on lines 18, 20, and 22.

The true blocks and false blocks for *if* statements are also blocks. Thus, if instead of declaring the *String message* on line 16, we declare it inside the true block of the *if* statement as in the following,

```
if ( grade >= 60 )
{
   String message = "You passed";
}
else
   message = "You failed ";

System.out.println( message );
```

then the scope of *message* extends from its declaration only until the end of the true block. In this case, the compiler will generate "cannot find symbol" error messages for the references to *message* inside the false block and for the *System.out.println* statement after the *if* statement because *message* is out of scope outside of the true block.

CODE IN ACTION

On the CD-ROM included with this book, you will find a Flash movie illustrating step-by-step how to use an *if/else* statement. Click on the link for Chapter 5 to view the movie.

Skill Practice
with these end-of-chapter questions

5.14.2 Reading and Understanding Code

Questions 12,13

5.14.3 Fill In the Code

Questions 20, 21, 22, 23, 24, 25, 26, 27, 28, 29, 30

5.14.4 Identifying Errors in Code

Questions 33, 34, 35

5.14.5 Debugging Area

Question 40

5.14.6 Write a Short Program

Questions 42, 43, 46, 48

5.14.8 Technical Writing

Question 54

5.4 Selection Using *if/else if*

The last form of an *if* statement is appropriate when the data falls into more than two mutually exclusive categories and the appropriate instructions to execute are different for each category. For this situation, Java provides the *if/else if* statement.

The *if/else if* statement follows this pattern:

```
if ( condition 1 )
{
     true block for condition 1
}
else if ( condition 2 )
```

```
{
      true block for condition 2
}
. . .
else if ( condition n )
{
      true block for condition n
}
else
{
      false block for all conditions being false
}
next statement
```

The flow of control for this form of the *if* statement is shown in Figure 5.8.

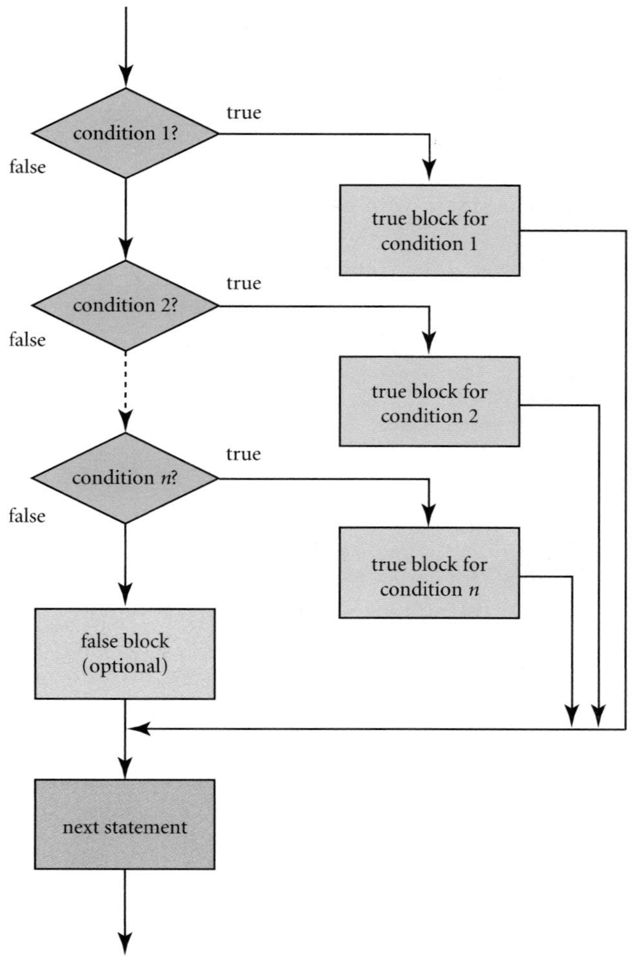

Figure 5.8
Flow of Control of an *if/else if* Statement

There can be any number of conditions in an *if/else if* statement. As you can see, once a condition evaluates to *true* for any value, control moves to the true block for that condition, then skips the remainder of the conditions, continuing execution at any statement that follows the *if/else if* statement. The final false block (along with the final *else*) is optional and is executed only when none of the conditions evaluates to *true.*

We can use the *if/else if* statement to determine a student's letter grade based on his or her numeric grade. Example 5.4 demonstrates a Java application that prompts a student for a test grade and translates that grade into a letter grade.

```
/* A program to translate a numeric grade into a letter grade
   Anderson, Franceschi
*/

import java.util.Scanner;

public class LetterGrade
{
  public static void main( String [ ] args )
  {
    Scanner scan = new Scanner( System.in );

    char letterGrade;

    System.out.print( "Enter your test grade: " );
    int grade = scan.nextInt( );

    if ( grade >= 90 )
         letterGrade = 'A';

    else if ( grade >= 80 )
         letterGrade = 'B';

    else if ( grade >= 70 )
         letterGrade = 'C';

    else if ( grade >= 60 )
         letterGrade = 'D';

```

```
30     else  // grade fits none of the conditions
31         letterGrade = 'F';
32
33     System.out.println( "Your test grade of " + grade
34                         + " is a letter grade of " + letterGrade );
35   }
36 }
```

EXAMPLE 5.4 A Demonstration of *if/else if*

```
Enter your test grade: 83
Your test grade of 83 is a letter grade of B
```

Figure 5.9
Output from Example 5.4

Figure 5.9 shows the output from the program when a student enters a grade of 83.

Notice that each condition is a simple relational expression. Even though we assign a *B* letter grade when the numeric grade is between 80 and 89, the condition for a *B* letter grade (line 21) is simply:

```
if ( grade >= 80 )
```

We don't need to write the condition as

```
if ( grade >= 80 && grade < 90 )
```

because by the time the condition is tested at line 21, all numeric grades greater than or equal to 90 have been eliminated by the test condition at line 18. Any grade greater than or equal to 90 causes the condition at line 18, `( grade >= 90 )`, to evaluate to *true*. For those grades, the flow of control is to assign an *A* to *letterGrade* at line 19, then skip the remainder of the conditions, continuing execution at the statement following the *if/else if* statement, which is line 33 in this example. Thus, if the condition at line 21 is evaluated, we know that the *grade* must be less than 90.

CODE IN ACTION

On the CD-ROM included with this book, you will find a Flash movie illustrating step-by-step how to use an *if/else if* statement. Click on the link for Chapter 5 to view the movie.

Skill Practice
with these end-of-chapter questions

5.14.1 Multiple Choice Exercises

Question 8

5.14.2 Reading and Understanding Code

Question 15

5.14.4 Identifying Errors in Code

Questions 36, 37, 38

5.5 Sequential and Nested *if/else* Statements

When you need the results of one *if* statement's processing before you can evaluate the next condition, you can write multiple *if* statements either sequentially or nested within other *if* statements.

5.5.1 Sequential *if/else* Statements

Finding the Minimum or Maximum Values

To illustrate sequential *if* statements, let's look at the problem of finding the smallest of three numbers.

In Chapter 3, we found the smallest of three numbers using the *min* method of the *Math* class. We first found the smaller of two numbers, then found the smaller of that result and the third number. We can use that same logic to find the smallest of three numbers with multiple, sequential *if* statements. First we find the smaller of the first two numbers, then we find the smaller of that result and the third number. The pseudocode for this application is:

```
read number1
read number2
read number3

if number1 is less than number2
   smallest is number1
else
   smallest is number2
```

```
if number3 is less than smallest
  smallest is number3
```

Translating the pseudocode into Java, we get the application in Example 5.5, which prompts the user for three integers and outputs the smallest of the three numbers. In this application, we use two *if* statements. The first *if* statement (lines 23–26) uses an *if/else* statement to find the smaller of the first two integers and stores that value into the variable *smallest.* Then, the second *if* statement (lines 28–29) compares the third integer to the value stored in *smallest.* In the second *if* statement, we don't use an *else* clause, because we need to change the value in *smallest* only if the condition is *true,* that is, if the third number is less than *smallest.* Otherwise, the smallest value is already stored in *smallest.*

```
1  /* Find the smallest of three integers
2     Anderson, Franceschi
3  */
4
5  import java.util.Scanner;
6
7  public class FindSmallest
8  {
9    public static void main( String [ ] args )
10   {
11       int smallest;
12       int num1, num2, num3;
13
14       Scanner scan = new Scanner( System.in );
15
16       System.out.print( "Enter the first integer: " );
17       num1 = scan.nextInt( );
18       System.out.print( "Enter the second integer: " );
19       num2 = scan.nextInt( );
20       System.out.print( "Enter the third integer: " );
21       num3 = scan.nextInt( );
22
23       if ( num1 < num2 )
24          smallest = num1;
25       else
26          smallest = num2;
27
```

```
      if ( num3 < smallest )
         smallest = num3;

      System.out.println( "The smallest is " + smallest );
   }
}
```

EXAMPLE 5.5 An Application with Sequential *if* Statements

When the program in Example 5.5 is run using *6*, *7*, and *5* for the three integers, the output is as shown in Figure 5.10.

One more point. The code only checks that one number is less than another. What happens if two or more of the numbers are equal? The code still works! We only need to find the smallest value; we don't care which of the variables holds that smallest value.

5.5.2 Nested *if/else* Statements

If statements can be written as part of the true or false block of another *if* statement. These are called nested *if* statements. Typically, you nest *if* statements when more information is required beyond the results of the first *if* statement.

One difficulty that arises with nested *if* statements is specifying which *else* clause pairs with which *if* statement, especially if some *if* statements have *else* clauses and others do not. The compiler matches any *else* clause with the most previous *if* statement that doesn't already have an *else* clause. If this matching is not what you want, you can use curly braces to specify the desired *if/else* pairing.

In this code, we have one *if* statement nested within another *if* statement.

```
if ( x == 2 )
      if ( y == x )
        System.out.println( "x and y equal 2" );
      else
        System.out.println( "x equals 2, but y does not" );
```

Figure 5.10
Output from Example 5.5

```
Enter the first integer: 6
Enter the second integer: 7
Enter the third integer: 5
The smallest is 5
```

Without curly braces, the entire second *if* statement comprises the true block of the first condition (`x == 2`), and the *else* is paired with the second condition (`y == x`), because this is the most previous *if* condition that doesn't have an *else*.

However, we can force the *else* clause to be paired with the first condition by using curly braces, as follows:

```
if ( x == 2 )
{
   if ( y == x )
      System.out.println( "x and y equal 2" );
}
else
   System.out.println( "x does not equal 2" );
```

With the curly braces added, the *if* condition (`y == x`), along with its true block, becomes the complete true block for the condition (`x == 2`), and the *else* clause now belongs to the first *if* condition (`x == 2`).

Why can't we just alter the indentation to indicate our meaning? Remember that indentation increases the readability of the code for humans. The compiler ignores indentation and instead follows Java's syntactic rules.

Dangling Else

A common error is writing *else* clauses that don't match any *if* conditions. This is called a **dangling else**. For example, the following code, which includes three *else* clauses and only two *if* conditions, will generate this compiler error:

```
    'else' without 'if'
```

```
if ( x == 2 )

  if ( y == x )
      System.out.println( "x and y equal 2" );

  else // matches y==x
      System.out.println( "y does not equal 2" );

else // matches x==2
  System.out.println( "x does not equal 2" );

else // no matching if!
  System.out.println( "x and y are not equal" );
```

COMMON ERROR TRAP

Be sure that all *else* clauses match an *if* condition. Writing *else* clauses that don't match *if* conditions will generate an `'else' without 'if'` compiler error.

For a more complex and real-world example of nested *if* statements, let's generate a random number between 1 and 10. We did something similar to this in Programming Activity 2 in Chapter 2, but we just displayed the number. Using some nested *if* statements, however, we can make this program a little more interesting. After we generate the random number, we'll prompt the user for a guess. First we'll verify that the guess is between 1 and 10. If it isn't, we'll print a message. Otherwise, we'll check whether the user has guessed the number. If so, we'll print a congratulatory message. If the user has not guessed the number, we'll display the number, then determine whether the guess was close. We'll define "close" as within three numbers. We'll print a message informing the user whether the guess was close, then we'll wish the user better luck next time. The pseudocode for this program looks like this:

```
generate a secret random number between 1 and 10
prompt the user for a guess

if guess is not between 1 and 10
    print message
else
  if guess equals the secret number
    print congratulations
  else
    print the secret number
    if  guess is not within 3 numbers
      print "You missed it by a mile!"
    else
      print "You were close."

    print "Better luck next time."
```

This pseudocode uses three nested *if* statements; the first determines if the guess is within the requested range of numbers. If it isn't, we print a message. Otherwise, the second *if* statement tests whether the user has guessed the secret number. If so, we print a congratulatory message. If not, we print the secret number, and our last nested *if* statement determines whether the guess was not within 3 numbers of the secret number. If not, we print "You missed it by a mile!"; otherwise, we print "You were close." In either case, we print "Better luck next time."

Example 5.6 is the result of translating this pseudocode into a Java application.

```
/* Guess a number between 1 and 10
   Anderson, Franceschi
*/

import java.util.Random;
import java.util.Scanner;

public class GuessANumber
{
  public static void main( String [ ] args )
  {
    Random random = new Random( );
    int secretNumber = random.nextInt( 10 ) + 1;

    Scanner scan = new Scanner( System.in );

    System.out.print( "I'm thinking of a number"
               + " between 1 and 10. What is your guess? " );
    int guess = scan.nextInt( );

    if ( guess < 1 || guess > 10 )
    {
       System.out.println( "Well, if you're not going to try,"
                                     + " I'm not playing." );
    }
    else
    {
       if ( guess == secretNumber )
           System.out.println( "Hoorah. You win!" );
       else
       {
           System.out.println( "The number was " + secretNumber );

           if ( Math.abs( guess - secretNumber ) > 3 )
               System.out.println( "You missed it by a mile!" );
           else
               System.out.println( "You were close." );

           System.out.println( "Better luck next time." );
       }
    }
  }
}
```

EXAMPLE 5.6 Nested *if* Statements

```
I'm thinking of a number between 1 and 10. What is your guess? 2
The number was 10
You missed it by a mile!
Better luck next time.
```

Figure 5.11
Output from the *GuessANumber* Program in Example 5.6

On line 34, we used the *abs* method of the *Math* class to determine whether the guess was within three integers of the secret number. By taking the absolute value of the difference between the guess and the secret number, we don't need to worry about which number is higher than the other; we will always receive a positive difference from the *abs* method.

Figure 5.11 shows the output of a sample run of this program.

5.6 Testing Techniques for *if/else* Statements

When an application uses *if/else* statements, the application's flow of control depends on the user's input or other data values. For one input value, the application may execute the true block, while for another input value, the application may execute the false block. Obviously, running an application only once is no guarantee that the program is correct, because if the true block was executed, then the false block was not executed, and therefore, was not tested. Similarly, if the false block was executed, then the true block was not executed, and therefore was not tested.

To test an application for correctness, we could attempt to test all execution paths. To do this, we devise a **test plan** that includes running the application with different data values designed to execute all the statements in the application.

For example, an application that determines whether an integer is positive or negative might have this code:

```
System.out.print( "Enter an integer > " );
int x = scan.nextInt( );
if  ( x > 0 )
   System.out.println( x + " is positive" );
else
   System.out.println( x + " is negative" );
```

We could test this code by running the application twice, the first time entering the value 1, and the second time entering the value −1. We see that the results for those two values are correct: 1 is positive and −1 is negative. We have executed all the statements successfully, but can we say for certain that the program is correct? What if we entered the value 0, which is considered neither a positive nor a negative integer? As written, our program determines that 0 is negative, which is incorrect.

We see, then, that testing the true and false blocks is not sufficient; we need to test the condition of the *if/else* statement as well. There are three possibilities: x is less than 0, x is equal to 0, or x is greater than 0. To test the condition, we should run the application with input values that meet these three criteria. So we should run the application one more time with the input value of 0. This will show us that the program is incorrect, because our code identifies 0 as a negative number.

To correct the program, we should add another condition (`x < 0`) so we can separate 0 from the negative numbers. The code would then become:

```
System.out.print( "Enter an integer > " );
int x = scan.nextInt( );
if  ( x > 0 )
   System.out.println( x + " is positive" );
else if ( x < 0 )
   System.out.println( x + " is negative" );
else
   System.out.println( "The integer is 0" );
```

Now if we retest the program with input values −1, 1, and 0, we get correct results for each of these values.

Another testing method is to treat the program like a black box, that is, as if the program's inner workings are unknown and unknowable to us. We devise our test plan based solely on the specifications of the program and develop input values that test the program logically. Thus, if our specifications are that we should determine whether an integer is positive or negative, we deduce that we should run the program with inputs that are a negative number, a positive number, and the special case, 0.

Both testing methods work together to ensure that a program is correct.

SOFTWARE ENGINEERING TIP

When testing your program, develop input values that test all execution paths and confirm that the logic implements the program specifications.

5.7 Programming Activity 1: Working with *if/else*

In this activity, you will write an *if/else* selection statement to decide how a golfer's score compares to par.

Copy to a directory on your computer all the files in the Chapter 5 Programming Activity 1 folder on the CD-ROM accompanying this book.

Open the *PathClient.java* source file. You will add your code to the *workWithIfElse* method. Part of the method has been coded for you. Search for ***** in the source file.

You should be positioned at the code shown in Example 5.7.

```
public void workWithIfElse( int score )
{
      String result = "???";
      // ***** Student code starts here
      // If score is greater than 72, assign "over par" to result
      // If score is equal to 72, assign "par" to result
      // If score is less than 72, assign "below par" to result




      //
      // Student code ends here
      //

      firstTime = false;
      animate( score, result );
}
```

EXAMPLE 5.7 The Student Code Portion of Programming Activity 1

Where indicated in the code, you should write an *if/else* statement to perform the following function:

- In the method header of the method *workWithIfElse*, you see "`( int score )`". The *int* variable *score* represents a golf score. This variable will be an input from the user; the dialog box that prompts the user for the score has already been coded for you and stores the user's input in the variable *score*, which is available to your code as a parameter of the *workWithIfElse* method. Do not declare the variable *score* inside the method; just use it.

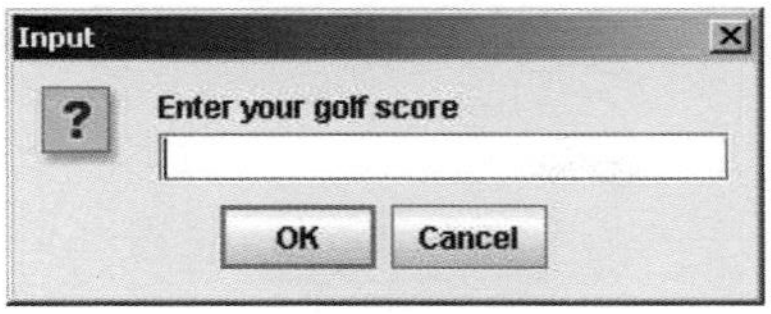

Figure 5.12
The Beginning of the Application

- We want to know if the golf score is "over par," "par," or "below par." Par is 72.
- Inside the *if/else* statement, you need to assign a value to the *String* variable named *result*, as follows:

  If *score* is higher than 72, then assign "over par" to *result*; if score is exactly 72, assign "par" to *result*; and if score is lower than 72, assign "below par" to *result*.
- You do not need to write the code to call the method *animate*; that part of the code has already been written for you.

Animation: The application window will display the correct path of the *if/else* statement (in green), which may or may not be the same as your path, depending on how you coded the *if/else* statement. The animation will also assess your result, that is, the value of the variable *result*, and give you feedback on the correctness of your result.

To test your code, compile and run the application and enter an integer in the dialog box. Try the following input values for *score*: 45, 71, 72, 73, and 89. Be sure your code produces the correct result for all input values.

When the program begins, you will see an empty graphics window and the dialog box of Figure 5.12, prompting you for an integer value.

Figure 5.13 demonstrates the correct code path when the input value is 82 and assesses that the student's code is correct.

Figure 5.14 again demonstrates the correct code path when the input value is 82, but in this case, the student's code is incorrect.

? DISCUSSION QUESTIONS

1. How many conditions did you use in the complete *if/else* statement?
2. Your code should be correct if the application gets correct results for the input values 71, 72, and 73. Explain why.

Figure 5.13
A Correct *if/else* Statement

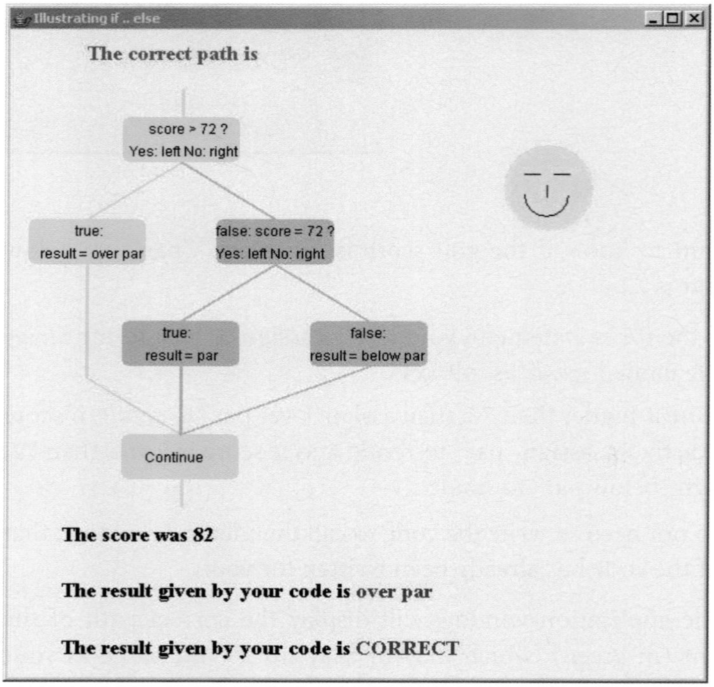

Figure 5.14
An Incorrect *if/else* Statement

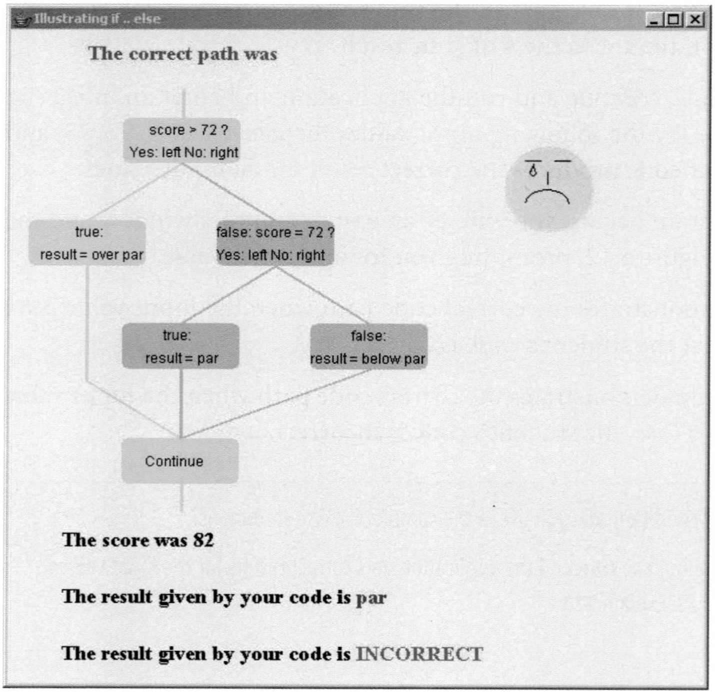

5.8 Comparing Floating-Point Numbers

As we explain in Appendix E, *floats* and *doubles* are stored using IEEE 754 standard format, which can introduce minor rounding errors when arithmetic is performed. That said, it is not advisable to simply rely on the equality operators to compare floating-point numbers.

REFERENCE POINT

Binary representation of floating-point numbers is discussed in Appendix E.

Let's take a look at Example 5.8, which computes 11 * .1 two ways. First, at line 11, we assign .0 to a *double* variable, *d1*, and at lines 12–22 we add .1 to *d1* eleven times. Then, at line 24, we declare a second *double* variable, *d2*, and assign it the result of multiplying .1 times 11. You would expect, then, that *d1* and *d2* would have the same value. Not so, as the output of the program shows in Figure 5.15.

You can also see the effects of rounding when comparing a *float* to a *double*. For example, at lines 35 and 36 of Example 5.8, we assign the same floating-point number (PI) to a double variable *piD* and to a float variable *piF*, then compare the two values at line 40. As you can see from the output in Figure 5.15, they do not compare as equal. The reason is that double-precision floating-point numbers are able to store a larger number of significant digits than single-precision floating-point numbers.

```
 1 /* Using equality operators on floating-point numbers
 2    Anderson, Franceschi
 3 */
 4
 5 public class EqualityFloatingPoint
 6 {
 7  public static void main( String [ ] args )
 8  {
 9   // Part 1: Compute 11 * .1 two ways
10
11   double d1 = .0; // add .1 to 0 eleven times
12   d1 += .1;  // 1
13   d1 += .1;  // 2
14   d1 += .1;  // 3
15   d1 += .1;  // 4
16   d1 += .1;  // 5
17   d1 += .1;  // 6
18   d1 += .1;  // 7
19   d1 += .1;  // 8
20   d1 += .1;  // 9
21   d1 += .1;  // 10
```

```
      d1 += .1;  // 11

      double d2 = .1 * 11; // compute 11 * .1

      System.out.println( "d1 = " + d1 );
      System.out.println( "d2 = " + d2 );
      if ( d1 == d2 )
         System.out.println( "d1 and d2 are equal" );
      else
         System.out.println( "d1 and d2 are not equal" );

      // Part 2: Compare float and double with same value

      float  piF = 3.141592653589793f;
      double piD = 3.141592653589793;

      System.out.println( "\npiF = " + piF );
      System.out.println( "pid = " + piD );
      if ( piF == piD )
          System.out.println( "piF and piD are equal" );
      else
          System.out.println( "piF and piD are not equal" );
   }
}
```

EXAMPLE 5.8 Using the Equality Operator to Compare Floating-Point Numbers

Figure 5.15
Output from Example 5.8

```
d1 = 1.0999999999999999
d2 = 1.1
d1 and d2 are not equal

piF = 3.1415927
pid = 3.141592653589793
piF and piD are not equal
```

Instead of using the equality operator to compare floating-point numbers, it's better to compare the absolute value of the difference to a small value, called a **threshold**. The value of the threshold should be the difference we can tolerate and still consider the numbers equal. Let's redo Example 5.8. Instead of using the equality operator, we'll use the *Math.abs* method to compute a difference between the two numbers and compare the difference to a threshold value. We'll set the threshold at .0001, meaning that if the numbers differ by less than .0001, we'll consider them equal. The results of this approach are shown in Example 5.9 and the output is given in Figure 5.16.

```
/* Using a threshold to compare floating-point numbers
   Anderson, Franceschi
*/

public class ComparingFloatingPoint
{
 public static void main( String [ ] args )
 {
   final double THRESHOLD = .0001;

   // Part 1: Compute 11 * .1 two ways
   double d1 = .0; // add .1 to 0 eleven times
   d1 += .1;  // 1
   d1 += .1;  // 2
   d1 += .1;  // 3
   d1 += .1;  // 4
   d1 += .1;  // 5
   d1 += .1;  // 6
   d1 += .1;  // 7
   d1 += .1;  // 8
   d1 += .1;  // 9
   d1 += .1;  // 10
   d1 += .1;  // 11

   double d2 = .1 * 11; // compute 11 * .1

   System.out.println( "d1 = " + d1 );
   System.out.println( "d2 = " + d2 );
   if ( Math.abs( d1 - d2 ) < THRESHOLD )
       System.out.println( "d1 and d2 are considered equal" );
   else
       System.out.println( "d1 and d2 are not equal" );

   // Part 2: Compare float and double with same value
   float  piF = 3.141592653589793f;
   double piD = 3.141592653589793;
```

```

    System.out.println( "\npiF = " + piF );
    System.out.println( "piD = " + piD );
    if ( Math.abs( piF - piD ) < THRESHOLD )
       System.out.println( "piF and piD are considered equal" );
    else
       System.out.println( "piF and piD are not equal" );
  }
}
```

Example 5.9 Comparing Floating-Point Numbers Using a Threshold

When you need exact precision in calculations with decimal numbers, you can use the *BigDecimal* class in the Java Class Library. The *BigDecimal* class, which is in the *java.math* package, provides methods that perform addition, subtraction, multiplication, and division of *BigDecimal* objects so that the results are exact, without the rounding errors caused by floating-point operations. Table 5.10 shows a constructor of the *BigDecimal* class and several useful methods for performing calculations and comparing *BigDecimal* objects.

REFERENCE POINT

You can read more about the *BigDecimal* class on Sun Microsystems' Java website *http://java.sun.com.*

In Example 5.10, we perform the same calculations as in Example 5.9, but we use *BigDecimal* objects instead of *doubles.* On lines 11 and 12, we instantiate two *BigDecimal* objects, *d1* and *pointOne*, to represent 0.0 and .1, respectively. Then on lines 16–26, we call the *add* method to add .1 to *d1* 11 times. We instantiate two more *BigDecimal* objects on lines 29 and 30, then call the *multiply* method to multiply .1 * 11. On line 35, we compare the resulting *BigDecimal* objects by calling the *compareTo* method, and find

Figure 5.16
Output of Example 5.9

```
d1 = 1.0999999999999999
d2 = 1.1
d1 and d2 are considered equal

piF = 3.1415927
piD = 3.141592653589793
piF and piD are considered equal
```

TABLE 5.10 The *BigDecimal* Class API

BigDecimal Class Constructor Summary
`BigDecimal( String ddd )` creates a *BigDecimal* object equivalent to the decimal number expressed as a *String*.

BigDecimal Class Method Summary	
Return value	**Method name and argument list**
`BigDecimal`	`add( BigDecimal num )` returns a *BigDecimal* object equal to the current *BigDecimal* object plus *num*
`BigDecimal`	`subtract( BigDecimal num )` returns a *BigDecimal* object equal to the current *BigDecimal* object minus *num*
`BigDecimal`	`multiply( BigDecimal num )` returns a *BigDecimal* object equal to the current *BigDecimal* object times *num*
`BigDecimal`	`divide( BigDecimal num )` returns a *BigDecimal* object equal to the current *BigDecimal* object divided by *num*
`int`	`compareTo( BigDecimal num )` returns 0 if the current *BigDecimal* object is equal to *num*; -1 if the current *BigDecimal* object is less than *num*; and 1 if the current *BigDecimal* object is greater than *num*

that the two results are in fact equal. The output of Example 5.10 is shown in Figure 5.17.

```
/* Using BigDecimal to compute precise decimal numbers
   Anderson, Franceschi
*/

import java.math.BigDecimal;

```

```java
public class UsingBigDecimal
{
 public static void main( String [ ] args )
 {
   BigDecimal  d1 = new BigDecimal( "0.0"  );
   BigDecimal  pointOne = new BigDecimal( "0.1"  );

   // Compute 11 * .1 two ways
   // add .1 to 0 eleven times
   d1 = d1.add( pointOne ); // 1
   d1 = d1.add( pointOne ); // 2
   d1 = d1.add( pointOne ); // 3
   d1 = d1.add( pointOne ); // 4
   d1 = d1.add( pointOne ); // 5
   d1 = d1.add( pointOne ); // 6
   d1 = d1.add( pointOne ); // 7
   d1 = d1.add( pointOne ); // 8
   d1 = d1.add( pointOne ); // 9
   d1 = d1.add( pointOne ); // 10
   d1 = d1.add( pointOne ); // 11

   // multiply .1 * 11
   BigDecimal  d2 = new BigDecimal( "0.1"  );
   BigDecimal  eleven = new BigDecimal( "11"  );
   d2 = d2.multiply( eleven );

   System.out.println( "d1 = " + d1 );
   System.out.println( "d2 = " + d2 );
   if ( d1.compareTo( d2 ) == 0 )
       System.out.println( "d1 and d2 are equal" );
   else
       System.out.println( "d1 and d2 are not equal" );
 }
}
```

EXAMPLE 5.10 Comparing Floating-Point Numbers Using *BigDecimal*

Figure 5.17
Output of Example 5.10

```
d1 = 1.1
d2 = 1.1
d1 and d2 are equal
```

5.9 Comparing Objects

5.9.1 The *equals* Method

Often, you'll want to compare whether two objects are equal; typically, we will say that two objects are equal if they have the same data. If you use the equality operator (==) to compare object references, however, you are comparing the value of the object references. In other words, you are comparing whether the object references point to the same object, that is, the same memory location. To compare object data, you need to use the *equals* method, which all classes inherit from the *Object* class. We will cover inheritance in greater detail in Chapter 10. Many classes provide a custom version of the *equals* method. The API of the *equals* method, which is an instance method, is the following:

```
public boolean equals( Object ob )
```

Typically, the *equals* method returns *true* if the data in the parameter object matches the data in the object for which the method was called.

The program in Example 5.11 creates the *SimpleDate* object references and objects shown in Figure 5.18. The program compares the object references using the equality operator and then compares the object data using the *equals* method. The output from this program is shown in Figure 5.19.

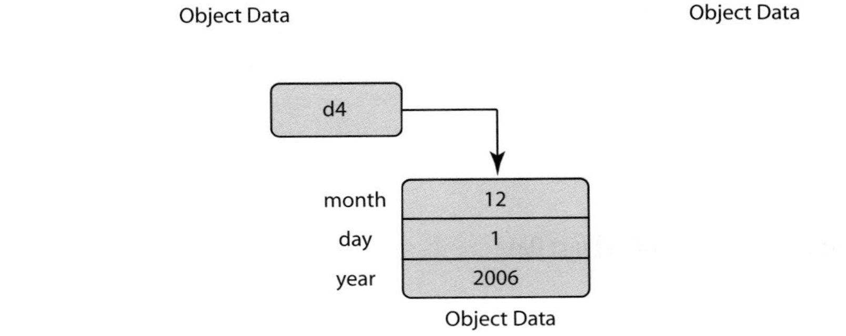

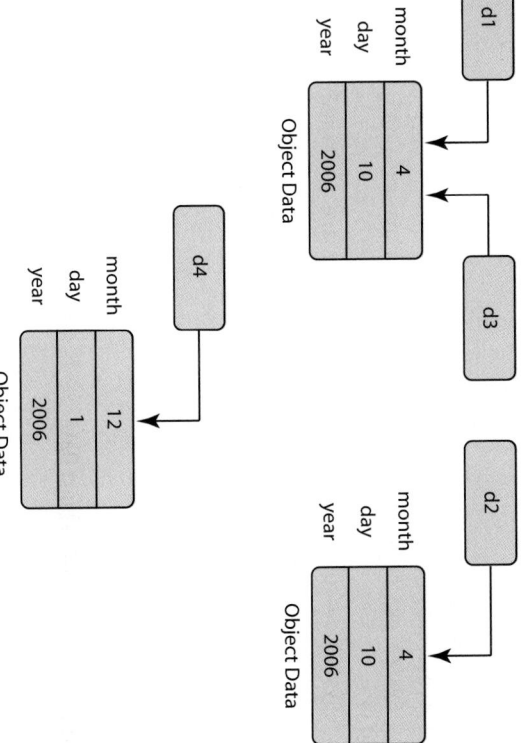

Figure 5.18
***SimpleDate* Objects and References**

```
/*  Comparing object references and data
    Anderson, Franceschi
*/

public class ComparingObjects
{
  public static void main( String [ ] args )
  {
    // instantiate two SimpleDate objects with identical data
    SimpleDate d1 = new SimpleDate( 4, 10, 2006 );
    SimpleDate d2 = new SimpleDate( 4, 10, 2006 );

    // assign object reference d1 to d3
    SimpleDate d3 = d1;  // d3 now points to d1

    // instantiate another object with different data
    SimpleDate d4 = new SimpleDate( 12, 1, 2006 );

    // compare references using the equality operator
    if ( d1 == d2 )
       System.out.println( "d1 and d2 are equal\n" );
    else
       System.out.println( "d1 and d2 are not equal\n" );

    if ( d1 == d3 )
       System.out.println( "d1 and d3 are equal\n" );
    else
       System.out.println( "d1 and d3 are not equal\n" );

    // compare object data using the equals method
    if ( d1.equals( d2 ) )
       System.out.println( "d1 data and d2 data are equal\n" );
    else
       System.out.println( "d1 data and d2 data are not equal\n" );

    if ( d1.equals( d4 ) )
       System.out.println( "d1 data and d4 data are equal" );
    else
       System.out.println( "d1 data and d4 data are not equal" );
  }
}
```

EXAMPLE 5.11 Comparing Object Data

```
d1 and d2 are not equal

d1 and d3 are equal

d1 data and d2 data are equal

d1 data and d4 data are not equal
```

Figure 5.19
Output from Example 5.11

Lines 10 and 11 instantiate two *SimpleDate* objects with the same data. Line 14 sets the *d3* object reference to point to the *d1* object. Line 17 instantiates the *d4* object with different data.

In line 20, when we compare *d1* and *d2* using the equality operator, the result is *false*, because the object references *d1* and *d2* point to two different objects. However, when we compare *d1* and *d3* (line 25), the result is *true*, because *d1* and *d3* point to the same object. Thus, object references are equal only when they point to the same object.

COMMON ERROR TRAP

Do not use the equality operators to compare object data; instead, use the *equals* method.

We get different results using the *equals* method. When line 31 compares *d1* and *d2* using the *equals* method, the result is *true*, because *d1* and *d2* have identical data. As you would expect, *d1* and *d4* are not equal (line 36) because the objects have different data.

5.9.2 *String* Comparison Methods

Because *Strings* are objects, you can also compare *Strings* using the *equals* method. In addition, the *String* class provides two other methods, *equalsIgnoreCase* and *compareTo*, for comparing the values of *Strings*. These methods, along with the *equals* method are summarized in Table 5.11.

The *equalsIgnoreCase* method is similar to the *equals* method, except that it is insensitive to case. Thus, the *equalsIgnoreCase* method returns *true* if the two *String* objects have the same sequence of characters, regardless of capitalization. For example, the *equalsIgnoreCase* method considers *ABC*, *AbC*, and *abc* to be equal.

The *compareTo* method returns an integer value, rather than a *boolean* value. The *compareTo* method's return value represents whether the *String* object is less than, equal to, or greater than the *String* argument passed to

TABLE 5.11 Comparison Methods of the *String* Class

String Methods for Comparing *String* Values	
Return value	**Method name and argument list**
`boolean`	`equals( String str )`
	compares the value of two *Strings*. Returns *true* if the *Strings* are equal; *false* otherwise.
`boolean`	`equalsIgnoreCase( String str )`
	compares the value of two *Strings*, treating upper and lower case characters as equal. Returns *true* if the *Strings* are equal; *false* otherwise.
`int`	`compareTo( String str )`
	compares the value of the two *Strings* in lexicographic order. If the *String* object is less than the *String* argument, *str*, a negative integer is returned. If the *String* object is greater than the *String* argument, a positive number is returned; if the two *Strings* are equal, 0 is returned.

REFERENCE POINT

The first 128 Unicode values are given in Appendix C.

the *compareTo* method. The *compareTo* method uses lexicographic order—the Unicode collating sequence—to compare the *Strings*. Using the Unicode collating sequence means that a character with a lower Unicode numeric value is considered less than a character with a higher Unicode numeric value. Thus, an *a* is lower than a *b;* an *A* is lower than a *B;* and *0* is lower than *1*.

The *compareTo* method scans the two *Strings* from left to right. If it finds different characters in the same position in the two *Strings*, it immediately returns an integer value representing the difference between the Unicode values of those characters. For example, the distance between *a* and *c* is −2; the distance between *K* and *F* is 5.

If the *Strings* differ in length, but the characters they have in common are identical, then the *compareTo* method returns the difference in the length of the *Strings*.

In most cases, however, the exact return value is not important; it is sufficient to know whether the *String* object is less than, greater than, or equal to the *String* argument. In other words, all that we usually need to know is whether the return value is positive, negative, or 0.

Example 5.12 demonstrates how these methods can be used in a Java application to compare *Strings*. The output of the program is shown in Figure 5.20.

```
/* Demonstration of the String comparison methods
   Anderson, Franceschi
*/

public class ComparingStrings
{
  public static void main( String [ ] args )
  {
    String title1 = "Green Pastures";
    String title2 = "Green Pastures II";
    String title3 = "green pastures";

    System.out.print( "Using equals: " );
    if ( title1.equals( title3 ) )
      System.out.println( title1 + " equals " + title3 );
    else
      System.out.println( title1 + " is not equal to " + title3 );

    System.out.print( "Using equalsIgnoreCase: " );
    if ( title1.equalsIgnoreCase( title3 ) )
      System.out.println( title1 + " equals " + title3 );
    else
      System.out.println( title1 + " is not equal to " + title3 );

    System.out.print( "Using compareTo: " );
    if ( title1.compareTo( title3 ) > 0 )
      System.out.println( title1 + " is greater than " + title3 );
    else if ( title1.compareTo ( title3 ) < 0 )
      System.out.println( title1 + " is less than " + title3 );
    else
      System.out.println( title1 + " is equal to " + title3 );

    System.out.print( "Using compareTo: " );
    if ( title1.compareTo( title2 ) > 0 )
      System.out.println( title1 + " is greater than " + title2 );
    else if ( title1.compareTo( title2 ) < 0 )
      System.out.println( title1 + " is less than " + title2 );
    else
      System.out.println( title1 + " is equal to " + title2 );
  }
}
```

EXAMPLE 5.12 Comparing *Strings*

Figure 5.20
Output from Example 5.12

```
Using equals: Green Pastures is not equal to green pastures
Using equalsIgnoreCase: Green Pastures equals green pastures
Using compareTo: Green Pastures is less than green pastures
Using compareTo: Green Pastures is less than Green Pastures II
```

In Example 5.12, we define three similar *Strings*: *title1 (Green Pastures)*, *title2 (Green Pastures II)*, and *title3 (green pastures)*. When we compare *title1*, *Green Pastures*, to *title3*, *green pastures*, using the *equals* method (line 14), the result is *false*, because the *Strings* do not match in case. When we perform the same comparison using the *equalsIgnoreCase* method (line 20), however, the result is *true*, because except for capitalization, these two *Strings* are identical in character sequence and length.

Using the *compareTo* method (line 34), *Green Pastures* evaluates to less than *Green Pastures II*. Although all the characters of the first *String* are found in the second *String* in the same order, the first *String* has fewer characters than the second *String*. The reason that *Green Pastures* evaluates to less than *green pastures* (line 26) is not so obvious—until you look at the Unicode character chart. The capital letters have lower numeric values than the lowercase letters, so a capital *G* is less than a lowercase *g*.

5.10 The Conditional Operator (?:)

The conditional operator (?:), while not a statement in itself, can be used in expressions. It evaluates a condition and contributes one of two values to the expression based on the value of the condition. The conditional operator is especially useful for handling invalid input and for outputting similar messages. The syntax of the conditional operator is shown here:

```
( condition ?  expression1 : expression2 )
```

The value of an expression containing a conditional operator is determined by evaluating the condition, which is any expression that evaluates to *true* or *false*. If the condition evaluates to *true*, *expression1* becomes the value of the expression; if the condition evaluates to *false*, *expression2* becomes the value of the expression.

When assigning the result of that expression to a variable, the statement:

```
variable = ( condition ? expression1 : expression2 );
```

is equivalent to

```
if ( condition )
      variable = expression1;
else
      variable = expression2;
```

Some programmers like to use the conditional operator because it enables them to write compact code; other programmers feel that an *if/else* sequence is more readable.

Suppose that we want to write a simple game where we ask the user to pick between two doors. Behind one door is a prize and behind the other door is nothing. Example 5.13 shows some code to do this. We first use the conditional operator on line 17 to validate the user input. If the user enters anything other than a 2, we assign the value 1 to the variable *door*. The statement at line 17 is equivalent to this code:

```
int door;
if ( inputNum == 2 )
   door = inputNum;
else
   door = 1;
```

So, instead of using five lines to declare the variable *door* and perform the *if* statement, the conditional operator performs the same function in only one line.

We then print a message about whether the chosen door was correct (Figure 5.21). If the user has selected door number 1, we print:

```
You have chosen the wrong door
```

Otherwise, we print:

```
You have chosen the correct door
```

as shown in Figure 5.22. As you can see, depending on the value of *door*, the messages we want to print differ only in one word (*correct* or *wrong*). So on lines 19–20, we use the conditional operator in the argument of the *println* method to determine which word to insert into the message.

```
1 /* Using the conditional operator
2    Anderson, Franceschi
3 */
4
```

```java
import java.util.Scanner;

public class DoorPrize
{
 public static void main( String [ ] args )
 {
  Scanner scan = new Scanner( System.in );

  System.out.print( "Enter 1 or 2 to pick a door: " );
  int inputNum = scan.nextInt( );
  System.out.println( "You entered " + inputNum + "\n" );

  int door = ( inputNum == 2 ? inputNum : 1 );

  System.out.println( "You have chosen the "
            + ( door == 1 ? "wrong" : "correct" ) + " door" );
 }
}
```

EXAMPLE 5.13 Using the Conditional Operator

Table 5.12, Operator Precedence, shows that the conditional operator is low in precedence, being just above the assignment operators.

Figure 5.21
A Run of Example 5.13

```
Enter 1 or 2 to pick a door: 8
You entered 8

You have chosen the wrong door
```

Figure 5.22
Another Run of Example 5.13

```
Enter 1 or 2 to pick a door: 2
You entered 2

You have chosen the correct door
```

TABLE 5.12 Operator Precedence

Operator Hierarchy	Order of Same-Statement Evaluation	Operation
( )	left to right	parentheses for explicit grouping
++, --	right to left	shortcut postincrement
++, --, !	right to left	shortcut preincrement, logical unary NOT
*, /, %	left to right	multiplication, division, modulus
+, -	left to right	addition or *String* concatenation, subtraction
<, <=, >, >=	left to right	relational operators: less than, less than or equal to, greater than, greater than or equal to
==, !=	left to right	equality operators: equal to and not equal to
&&	left to right	logical AND
||	left to right	logical OR
?:	**left to right**	**conditional operator**
=, +=, -=, *=, /=, %=	right to left	assignment operator and shortcut assignment operators

5.11 The *switch* Statement

The *switch* statement can be used instead of an *if/else if* statement for selection when the condition consists of comparing the value of an expression to constant integers (*byte, short,* or *int*) or characters (*char*). The syntax of the *switch* statement is the following:

```
switch ( expression )
{
   case constant1:
         statement1;
         . . .
         break; // optional
   case constant2:
```

```
            statement1;
            . . .
            break; // optional
      . . .
      default:  // optional
            statement1;
            . . .
}
```

The expression is first evaluated, then its value is compared to the *case* constants in order. When a match is found, the statements under that *case* constant are executed in sequence. The execution of statements continues until either a *break* statement is encountered or the end of the *switch* block is reached. If other *case* statements are encountered before a *break* statement, then their statements are also executed. This allows you to execute the same code for multiple values of the expression.

As you can see in the preceding syntax, the *break* statements are optional. Their job is to terminate execution of the *switch* statement. The *default* label and its statements, which are also optional, are executed when the value of the expression does not match any of the *case* constants. The statements under a *case* constant are also optional, so multiple *case* constants can be written in sequence if identical operations will be performed for those values. We'll use this feature in our examples of the *switch* statement.

Let's look at how a *switch* statement can be used to implement a simple calculator. We can prompt the user for two numbers on which they want to perform a calculation, and a single letter for the operation they want to perform: *a* for addition, *s* for subtraction, *m* for multiplication, or *d* for division. We can use a *switch* statement with the selected operation as the expression and *case* constants for each possible operation. For example, here's the beginning of the *switch* statement:

```
switch ( operation )
{
      case 'a':
            // perform the addition
            break;
      case 's':
            // perform the subtraction
            break;
      . . .
}
```

But what if the user enters an *A* instead of an *a*? For usability, we want to allow the user to enter the operation as either a lowercase letter or an uppercase letter. We can handle this by providing two *case* constants for each operation—the lowercase letter and the uppercase letter. Then the beginning of the *switch* statement looks like this:

```
switch ( operation )
{
      case 'a':
      case 'A':
          // perform the addition
          break;
      case 's':
      case 'S':
          // perform the subtraction
          break;
      . . .
}
```

If the user enters an uppercase *A*, we perform the addition, then the *break* ends execution of the *switch* block. If the user enters a lowercase *a*, we also perform the addition. Again, the *break* ends execution of the *switch* block.

What if the user doesn't enter any of the valid letters for the operation to perform? This is where the *default* case comes in handy. We can use the *default* case to write an error message to the user.

Example 5.14 shows the code for our simple calculator.

```
/*  A simple calculator
    Anderson, Franceschi
*/

import java.text.DecimalFormat;
import java.util.Scanner;

public class Calculator
{
  public static void main( String [ ] args )
  {
    double fp1, fp2;
    String operationS;
    char operation;

    Scanner scan = new Scanner( System.in );
```

```

    // set up the output format of the result
    DecimalFormat twoDecimals = new DecimalFormat( "#,###,###.##" );

    // print a welcome message
    System.out.println( "Welcome to the Calculator" );

    // read the two operands
    System.out.print( "Enter the first operand: " );
    fp1 = scan.nextDouble( );
    System.out.print( "Enter the second operand: " );
    fp2 = scan.nextDouble( );

    // print a menu, then prompt for the operation
    System.out.println( "\nOperations are: "
                      + "\n\t A for addition"
                      + "\n\t S for subtraction"
                      + "\n\t M for multiplication"
                      + "\n\t D for division" );
    System.out.print( "Enter your selection: " );
    operationS = scan.next( );
    operation = operationS.charAt( 0 );

    // perform the operation and print the result
    switch ( operation )
    {
     case 'A':
     case 'a':
         System.out.println( "The sum is "
                 + twoDecimals.format( fp1 + fp2 ) );
         break;
     case 'S':
     case 's':
         System.out.println( "The difference is "
                 + twoDecimals.format( fp1 - fp2 ) );
         break;
     case 'M':
     case 'm':
         System.out.println( "The product is "
                 + twoDecimals.format( fp1 * fp2 ) );
         break;
     case 'D':
     case 'd':
         if ( fp2 == 0 )
           System.out.println( "Dividing by 0 is not allowed" );
         else
```

```
63             System.out.println( "The quotient is "
64                     + twoDecimals.format( fp1 / fp2 ) );
65             break;
66         default:
67             System.out.println( operation + " is not valid." );
68     }
69   }
70 }
```

EXAMPLE 5.14 A Simple Calculator

Figure 5.23 shows the output from Example 5.14 when the user selects multiplication, and Figure 5.24 shows the output when the user enters an unsupported operation.

We declared the two numbers on which to perform the operation as *doubles* (line 12) and prompt the user using the *nextDouble* method of the *Scanner* class (lines 25–28). Because a *double* variable can hold any numeric value equal to or lower in precision than a *double*, using *doubles* for our calculator allows the user to enter two *ints*, or two *doubles*, or any combination of integers and floating-point numbers. Conversely, if we used *int* variables and the *nextInt* method of the *Scanner* class, the user would be restricted to entering integers only.

When the calculator begins, we set up a *DecimalFormat* pattern for outputting the result to a maximum of two decimal places (line 19).

We also use the newline (*n*) and tab (*t*) escape characters to format the menu message (lines 30–35). To read the user's selection (lines 36–38), we

```
Welcome to the Calculator
Enter the first operand: 23.4
Enter the second operand: 3

Operations are:
    A for addition
    S for subtraction
    M for multiplication
    D for division
Enter your selection: m
The product is 70.2
```

Figure 5.23
The Calculator Performing Multiplication

Figure 5.24
The Calculator with an Invalid Entry for the Operation

```
Welcome to the Calculator
Enter the first operand: 52
Enter the second operand: 34.5

Operations are:
   A for addition
   S for subtraction
   M for multiplication
   D for division
Enter your selection: f
f is not valid.
```

use the *next* method of the *Scanner* class, which returns a *String*. We then extract just the first character of the *String* (via the *charAt* method of the *String* class) to produce a *char* to use as our *switch* variable.

One more note on the calculator. We need to check whether the divisor is 0 before performing division (line 60). Although we discussed earlier in the chapter that we should compare floating-point numbers by comparing the difference between the two numbers with a threshold value, in this case, we care only if the second operand is exactly 0, so we can safely compare its value to 0.0. If the second operand is 0.0, we print an error message; otherwise, we perform the division.

Let's look at an example that performs a *switch* on an integer. We'll create an applet that simulates rolling a die and drawing the die corresponding to the roll. Example 5.15 shows the code to do this.

```
/*  An applet that rolls and draws a die
    Anderson, Franceschi
*/

import javax.swing.JApplet;
import java.awt.Graphics;
import java.awt.Color;
import java.util.Random;

public class RollDie extends JApplet
{
  public void paint( Graphics g )
```

```
{
    super.paint( g );

    Random random = new Random( );
    int roll = random.nextInt( 6 ) + 1;

    int startX = 150, startY = 100;

    g.setColor( Color.PINK ); // die will be pink
    g.fillRect( startX, startY, 60, 60 ); // draw the die

    g.setColor( Color.BLACK ); // dots will be black
    switch ( roll )
    {
       case  1:   // draw the center dot
         g.fillRect( startX + 25, startY + 25, 10, 10 );
         break;

       case  3:   // draw center dot, continue through 2
         g.fillRect( startX + 25, startY + 25, 10, 10 );
       case  2:   // draw diagonal corner dots
         g.fillRect( startX + 5, startY + 5, 10, 10 );
         g.fillRect( startX + 45, startY + 45, 10, 10 );
         break;

       case  5:   // draw center dot, continue through 4
         g.fillRect( startX + 25, startY + 25, 10, 10 );
       case  4:   // draw four corner dots
         g.fillRect( startX + 5, startY + 5, 10, 10 );
         g.fillRect( startX + 45, startY + 45, 10, 10 );
         g.fillRect( startX + 5, startY + 45, 10, 10 );
         g.fillRect( startX + 45, startY + 5, 10, 10 );
         break;

       case  6:   // draw all six dots
         g.fillRect( startX + 5, startY + 5, 10, 10 );
         g.fillRect( startX + 45, startY + 45, 10, 10 );
         g.fillRect( startX + 5, startY + 45, 10, 10 );
         g.fillRect( startX + 45, startY + 5, 10, 10 );
         g.fillRect( startX + 5, startY + 25, 10, 10 );
         g.fillRect( startX + 45, startY + 25, 10, 10 );
    }
  }
}
```

EXAMPLE 5.15 Using *switch* to Draw a Die

In Example 5.15, we first generate a random number between 1 and 6 to simulate the roll of a die (lines 16–17). We set *startX* and *startY* values that we will use as the upper left corner of the die (line 19), and then draw the die itself as a 60-by-60 pink square (lines 21–22). We set the color to black for drawing the dots (line 24) and we will use a *switch* statement on *roll* (lines 25–54) to determine which dots we should draw.

If we look at a die, we see that many of the rolls cause one or more of the same dots to be drawn. For example, a 3 consists of the center dot and the two diagonal dots, whereas the 2 consists of just the two diagonal dots. One advantage to the *switch* statement is that once a match is found between the *switch* variable and a *case* constant, all following statements are executed until a *break* is encountered. Using this feature, we can set up *case* 3 to draw just the center dot without using a *break* statement, then follow immediately with *case* 2, which draws the two diagonal dots and *breaks* (lines 31–36). When a roll of 3 is generated, the *switch* statement will match the *case* for 3, draw the center dot, and then fall through to the *case* 2 statements, which draws the two diagonal dots and *breaks.* When a roll of 2 is generated, we draw only the two diagonal dots and *break.* We do similar processing for rolls of 5 and 4 (lines 38–45). For *case* 5, we draw the center dot, then fall through to *case* 4, which draws the four corner dots and *breaks*. Many other combinations are possible. Note that we don't need a *default* case because the random generator will only generate values from 1 to 6, and we have provided *case* statements to handle each of those values. The output from one roll of the die is shown in Figure 5.25.

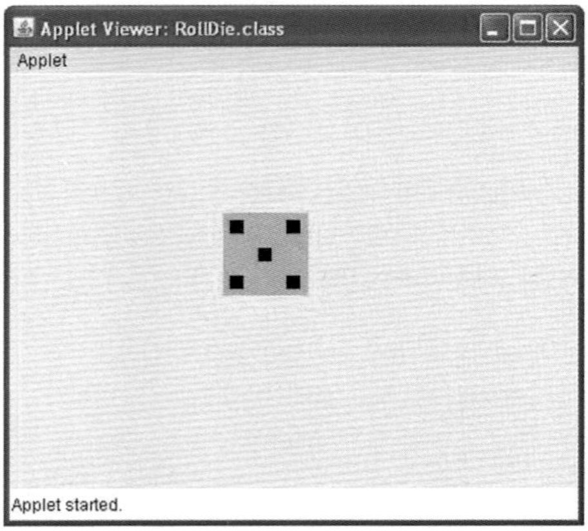

Figure 5.25
Output of Example 5.15

CODE IN ACTION

To see a step-by-step illustration of using a *switch* statement, look for the Chapter 5 Flash movie on the CD-ROM included with this book. Click on the link for Chapter 5 to start the movie.

Skill Practice
with these end-of-chapter questions

5.14.1 Multiple Choice Exercises
Question 9

5.14.2 Reading and Understanding Code
Questions 14,16,17,18,19

5.14.5 Debugging Area
Questions 39,41

5.14.6 Write a Short Program
Questions 44,45,47

5.14.8 Technical Writing
Question 53

5.12 Programming Activity 2: Using the *switch* Statement

In this activity, you will write a *switch* statement that selects a path depending on an input value. The framework will animate your code so that you can watch the path that the code takes in the *switch* block.

Copy to a directory on your computer all the files in the Chapter 5 Programming Activity 2 directory on the CD-ROM accompanying this book.

Search for five stars (*****) in the *MultiPathClient.java* source code to find where to add your code. The five stars are inside the method *workWithSwitch* (the method header has already been coded for you).

You should be positioned at the code shown in Example 5.16.

```
// ***** 1 student writes this method
public void workWithSwitch( int value )
{
```

```
  //
  // Student code starts here
  //




  //
  // Student code ends here
  //

  mp.setControl( false );
  mp.resetPath( );
  mp.setCount( 0 );
  mp.setCurrent( -1 );

}
// end of workWithSwitch
```

EXAMPLE 5.16 The Student Code Portion of Programming Activity 2

Where indicated in the code, write a *switch* statement, as follows:

- In the method header of the method *workWithSwitch*, you see `( int value )`. The *int* variable *value* represents the input from the user; the dialog box that prompts the user and reads the score has already been coded for you. This variable, *value*, is the input value for the *switch* statement; it is available to your code as a parameter of the *workWithSwitch* method. Do not declare the variable *value* inside the method; just use it.
- Write *case* statements for the following integer constants: *0*, *1*, *2*, *3*, *4*, as well as a *default* statement.
- Within each *case* statement, you should do two things:
  - Print a message to the screen indicating which value was input. The message for the *default* case should indicate that the input value is not one of the valid values.
  - Call the *animate* method. The API for the *animate* method is

    `void animate( int caseConstant, int value )`

    The first argument is the *case* constant, the second argument is the input variable, *value*. For instance, for the statement `case 2:`, your *animate* method call is

    `animate( 2, value );`

For the default case, the method call should be

```
animate( -1, value );
```

To test your code, compile and run the *MultiPathClient* application. When the program begins, you will see an empty graphics window and the dialog box of Figure 5.26, prompting you for an integer value.

To execute your *switch* statement, enter an integer in the dialog box. Depending on how you coded the *case* statements, the *break* statements, and the input value, the window will display (in green) the path of execution of your code. For example, Figure 5.27 demonstrates the code path when the input value is 3. If the path is not what you expected, you will need to correct your code.

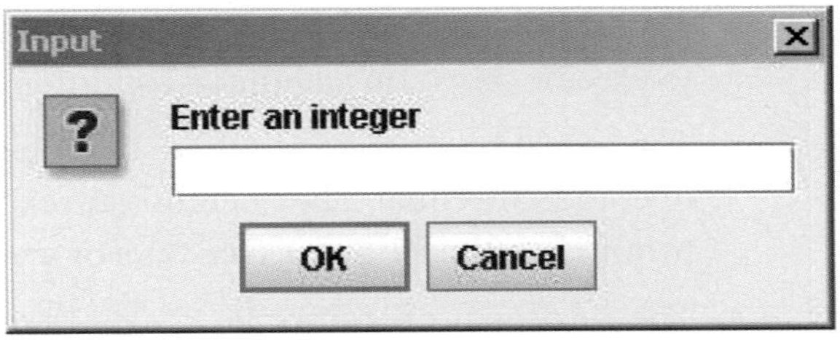

Figure 5.26
The Input Box of the *MultiPathClient* Application

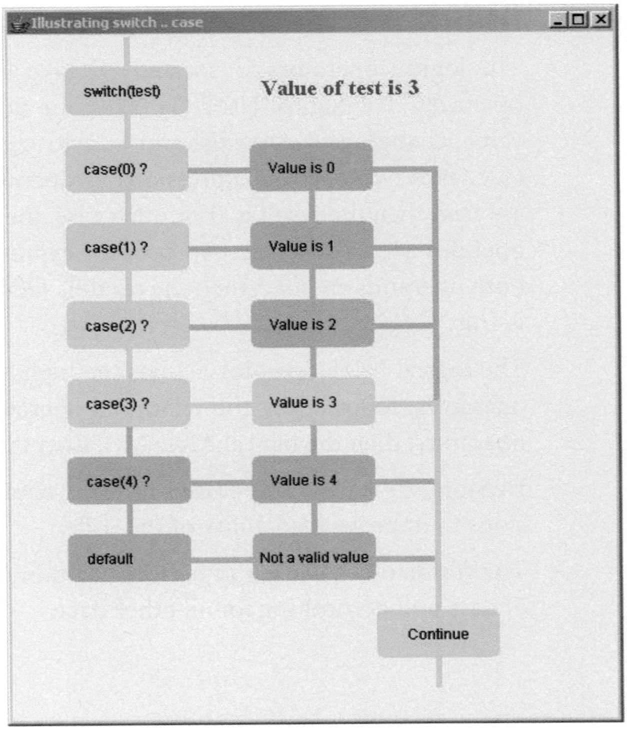

Figure 5.27
A Sample Run of the *MultiPathClient* Application

After each execution of the *switch* statement, the dialog box will reappear, prompting you for another integer. To test your code, enter each integer from 0 to 4 into the dialog box, plus some other integer value. To exit the application, click the *Cancel* button on the dialog box.

DISCUSSION QUESTIONS ?

1. Explain the purpose of the *default* case in a *switch* statement.
2. Explain what happens when you omit a *break* statement in a *case* statement.

CHAPTER SUMMARY

5.13 Chapter Summary

- Java provides equality, relational, and logical operators to evaluate a condition, and selection statements to choose which instructions to execute based on whether a condition evaluates to *true* or *false*.
- The equality operators (==, !=) are used to test whether two operands are equal. The operands are expressions that evaluate to a primitive numeric or *boolean* type or an object reference.
- The relational operators (<, <=, >, >=) compare the values of two operands that are expressions that evaluate to a primitive numeric type.
- The logical operators (!, &&, and ||) take *boolean* expressions as operands. The logical NOT (!) takes one operand, and inverts its value, changing *true* to *false* and *false* to *true*. The AND operator (&&) takes two *boolean* expressions as operands; if both operands are *true*, then the result is *true*; otherwise, the result is *false*. The OR operator (||) also takes two *boolean* expressions as operands. If both operands are *false*, then the result is *false*; otherwise, the result is *true*.
- The logical NOT operator (!) has the highest precedence of these operators, followed by the relational operators, then the equality operators, then the logical AND (&&), then the logical OR(||).
- DeMorgan's Laws can be used to form equivalent logical expressions to improve readability of the code.
- The *if* statement is used to perform certain operations for one set of data and do nothing for all other data.

- Curly braces are required when the true or false block of an *if* statement consists of more than one statement.
- The *if/else* statement is used to perform certain operations for one set of data and other operations for all other data.
- The *if/else if* statement is appropriate when the data falls into more than two mutually exclusive categories and the appropriate instructions to execute are different for each category.
- *if/else* statements can be coded sequentially and can be nested inside other *if/else* statements.
- When *if* statements are nested, the compiler matches any *else* clause with the most previous *if* condition that doesn't already have an *else* clause.
- Because rounding errors can be introduced in floating-point calculations, do not use the equality operators to compare two floating-point numbers. Instead, compare the absolute value of the difference between the numbers to some threshold value.
- When you need exact precision in calculations with decimal numbers, you can use the *BigDecimal* class in the Java Class Library.
- Using the equality operator on object references compares the values of the references, not the object data. Two object references will be equal only if they point to the same object.
- Use the *equals* method to determine whether the data in two objects is equal.
- In addition to the *equals* method, two *Strings* can also be compared using the *equalsIgnoreCase* method and the *compareTo* method of the *String* class.
- The conditional operator (?:) is used in expressions where one of two values should be used depending on the evaluation of a condition. The conditional operator is useful for validating input and for outputting similar messages.
- The *switch* statement evaluates an integer or character expression, then compares the expression's value to *case* constants. When a match is found, it executes the statements until either a *break* statement or the end of the *switch* block is encountered.

5.14 Exercises, Problems, and Projects

5.14.1 Multiple Choice Exercises

1. Given the following code declaring and initializing two *int* variables *a* and *b* with respective values 3 and 5, indicate whether the value of each expression is *true* or *false*.

```
int a = 3;
int b = 5;
```

Expression	true	false
❑ `a < b`	___	___
❑ `a != b`	___	___
❑ `a == 4`	___	___
❑ `( b - a ) <= 1`	___	___
❑ `Math.abs( a - b ) >= 2`	___	___
❑ `( b % 2 == 1 )`	___	___
❑ `b <= 5`	___	___

2. Given the following code declaring and initializing three *boolean* variables *a*, *b*, and *c*, with respective values *true*, *true*, and *false*, indicate whether the value of each expression is *true* or *false*.

```
boolean a = true;
boolean b = true;
boolean c = false;
```

Expression	true	false
❑ `!a`	___	___
❑ `a && b`	___	___
❑ `a && c`	___	___
❑ `a || c`	___	___
❑ `!( a || b )`	___	___
❑ `!a || b`	___	___
❑ `!( !( a && c ) )`	___	___
❑ `a && !( b || c )`	___	___

3. Given two *boolean* variables *a* and *b*, are the following expressions equivalent?

   - ❑ `!( !a )`
   - ❑ `a`

4. Given two *boolean* variables *a* and *b*, are the following expressions equivalent?

   - ❑ `!( a && b )`
   - ❑ `!a || !b`

5. Given two *boolean* variables *a* and *b*, are the following expressions equivalent?

   - ❑ `!( !a && !b )`
   - ❑ `a && b`

6. Given two *boolean* variables *a* and *b*, are the following expressions equivalent?

   - ❑ `!( !a && !b )`
   - ❑ `a || b`

7. Given the following code declaring and initializing two *int* variables *a* and *b* with respective values 3 and 5, indicate whether the operand (`b < 10`) will be evaluated.

```
int a = 3;
int b = 5;
```

Expression	yes	no
❑ `a < b || b < 10`	____	____
❑ `a != b && b < 10`	____	____
❑ `a == 4 || b < 10`	____	____
❑ `a > b && b < 10`	____	____

8. Mark all the valid Java selection keywords.

   - ❑ `if`
   - ❑ `else if`
   - ❑ `else`
   - ❑ `elsif`

9. How do we compare the value of two *String* objects in Java? (Mark all that apply.)
   - ❏ using the = operator
   - ❏ using the == operator
   - ❏ using the *equals* method

5.14.2 Reading and Understanding Code

10. What is the output of this code sequence?

```
boolean a = true;
System.out.println( a );
```

11. What is the output of this code sequence?

```
boolean a = ( true && false );
System.out.println( a );
```

12. What is the output of this code sequence?

```
if ( ( true || false ) && ( false || true ) )
   System.out.println( "Inside true block" );
System.out.println( "End of sequence" );
```

13. What is the output of this code sequence?

```
if ( 27 % 3 == 0 )
   System.out.println( "27 is divisible by 3" );
else
   System.out.println( "27 is not divisible by 3" );
System.out.println( "End of sequence" );
```

14. What is the output of this code sequence?

```
String s = "Hello";
if ( s.equals( "hello" ) )
   System.out.println( "String is hello" );
else
   System.out.println( "String is not hello" );
System.out.println( "End of sequence" );
```

15. What is the output of this code sequence?

```
int grade = 77;
if ( grade >= 90 )
   System.out.println( "A" );
else if ( grade >= 80 )
   System.out.println( "B" );
```

```
else if ( grade >= 70 )
   System.out.println( "C" );
else
   System.out.println( "D or lower" );
System.out.println( "Done" );
```

16. What is the output of this code sequence?

```
int a = 65;
boolean b = false;

if ( a >= 70 )
{
   System.out.println( "Hello 1" );
   if ( b == true )
      System.out.println( "Hello 2" );
}
else
{
   System.out.println( "Hello 3" );
   if ( b == false )
      System.out.println( "Hello 4" );
}
System.out.println( "Done" );
```

17. What is the output of this code sequence?

```
int season = 3;
switch ( season )
{
   case  1:
         System.out.println( "Season is Winter" );
         break;
   case  2:
         System.out.println( "Season is Spring" );
         break;
   case  3:
         System.out.println( "Season is Summer" );
         break;
   case  4:
         System.out.println( "Season is Fall" );
         break;
   default:
         System.out.println( "Invalid Season" );
}
```

18. What is the output of this code sequence?

```
char c = 'e';
switch ( c )
{
   case 'H':
        System.out.println( "letter 1" );
        break;
   case 'e':
        System.out.println( "letter 2" );
        break;
   case 'l':
        System.out.println( "letters 3 and 4" );
        break;
   case 'o':
        System.out.println( "letter 5" );
        break;
   default:
        System.out.println( "letter is not in Hello" );
}
```

19. What is the output of this code sequence?

```
int n = 3;
switch ( n )
{
   case 1:
     System.out.println( "Number 1" );
   case 2:
     System.out.println( "Number 2" );
   case 3:
     System.out.println( "Number 3" );
   case 4:
     System.out.println( "Number 4" );
   default:
     System.out.println( "Other number" );
}
```

5.14.3 Fill In the Code

For Exercises 20 through 30, assume that a *boolean* variable named *a* has been declared and assigned the value *true* or *false*. You should also assume that two *int* variables named *b* and *c* have been declared and assigned some integer values.

20. If *a* is *true*, increment *b* by 1.

```
// your code goes here
```

21. If *a* is *true*, increment *b* by 2; if *a* is *false*, decrement *b* by 1.

```
// your code goes here
```

22. If *a* is *true*, change *a* to *false*; if *a* is *false*, change *a* to *true*.

```
// your code goes here
```

23. If *b* is equal to *c*, then assign *true* to *a*.

```
// your code goes here
```

24. If *b* is less than *c*, increment *b* by 1; otherwise, leave *b* unchanged.

```
// your code goes here
```

25. If *b* is a multiple of *c*, set *a* to *true*; otherwise, set *a* to *false*.

```
// your code goes here
```

26. If *c* is not equal to 0, assign to *b* the value of *b* divided by *c*.

```
// your code goes here
```

27. If the product *b* times *c* is greater than or equal to 100, then invert *a* (if *a* is *true*, *a* becomes *false*; if *a* is *false*, *a* becomes *true*) otherwise, assign *true* to *a*.

```
// your code goes here
```

28. If *a* is *true* and *b* is greater than 10, increment *c* by 1.

```
// your code goes here
```

29. If both *b* and *c* are less than 10, then assign *true* to *a*; otherwise, assign *false* to *a*.

```
// your code goes here
```

30. If *b* or *c* is greater than 5, then assign *true* to *a*; otherwise, assign *false* to *a*.

```
// your code goes here
```

5.14.4 Identifying Errors in Code

For Exercises 31 through 38, assume that two *boolean* variables named *b1* and *b2* have been declared and assigned the value *true* or *false* earlier in the program. You should also assume that two *int* variables named *a1* and *a2* have been declared and assigned some integer values earlier in the program.

31. Where is the error in this code sequence?

```
b1 = a1 && a2;
```

32. Where is the error in this expression?

```
( b2 == b1 ) AND ( a1 <= a2 )
```

33. Where is the logical error in this code sequence?

```
if ( a1 == 4 );
    System.out.println( "a1 equals 4" );
```

34. Where is the error in this code sequence?

```
boolean b1 = true;
if b1
    System.out.println( "b1 is true" );
```

35. Where is the error in this code sequence?

```
if { b2 == true }
    System.out.println( "b2 is true" );
```

36. Where is the error in this code sequence?

```
if ( b1 == true )
    System.out.println( "b1 is true" );
else
    System.out.println( "b1 is false" );
else if ( a1 < 100 )
    System.out.println( "a1 is <= 100" );
```

37. Is there an error in this code sequence? Explain.

```
if ( b2 == b1 )
      System.out.println( "b2 and b1 have the same value" );
else if ( a1 == a2 )
      System.out.println( "a1 and a2 have the same value" );
else
      System.out.println( "All variables are different" );
```

38. Is there an error in this code sequence? Explain.

```
if ( b2 )
      System.out.println( "b2 is true" );
else if ( a1 <= 10 || a2 > 50 )
{
      System.out.print( "a1 <= 10 or " );
      System.out.println( "a2 > 50" );
}
else
      System.out.println( "none of the above" );
```

5.14.5 Debugging Area—Using Messages from the Java Compiler and Java JVM

39. You coded the following in class *Test.java:*

```
boolean b = true;
if ( b )
      System.out.println( "Inside true block" );
      System.out.println( "b was true" );
else         // line 12
      System.out.println( "Inside false block" );
```

At compile time, you get the following error:

```
Test.java:12: 'else' without 'if'

   else       // line 12
   ^
      1 error
```

Explain what the problem is and how to fix it.

40. You coded the following in the class *Test.java:*

```
int a = 32;
if ( a = 31 )     // line 9
      System.out.println( "The value of a is 31" );
else
      System.out.println( "The value of a is not 31" );
```

At compile time, you get the following error:

```
Test.java:9: incompatible types
found   : int
required: boolean
  if ( a = 31 )    // line 9
         ^
1 error
```

Explain what the problem is and how to fix it.

41. You coded the following in the class *Test.java:*

```
boolean b = true;
if ( b )
{
      System.out.println( "Inside true block" );
      System.out.println( "b was true" );
else         // line 13
      System.out.println( "Inside false block" );
}
System.out.println( "Done" );
```

At compile time, you get the following error:

```
Test.java:13: 'else' without 'if'.
else        // line 13
^
1 error
```

Explain what the problem is and how to fix it.

5.14.6 Write a Short Program

42. Write a program that takes two *ints* as input from the keyboard, representing the number of hits and the number of at-bats for a batter. Then calculate the batter's hitting percentage and check if the hitting percentage is above .300. If it is, output that the player is eligible for the All Stars Game; otherwise, output that the player is not eligible.

43. Write a program that reads a *char* as an input from the keyboard and outputs whether it comes before or after the letter *b* in Unicode order.

44. Write a program that calculates the area of the following figures:

    ❑ a square of side 0.666666667

    ❑ a rectangle of sides $\frac{1}{9}$ and 4

    Test the two calculated areas for equality; discuss your result.

45. Write a program that reads a sentence using a dialog box. Depending on the last character of the sentence, output another dialog box identifying the sentence as declarative (ends with a period), interrogative (ends with a question mark), exclamatory (ends with an exclamation point), or other.

46. An email address contains the @ character. Write a program that takes a word from the keyboard and outputs whether it is an email address based on the presence of the @ character. Do not worry about what else is in the word.

47. Write a program that takes two words as input from the keyboard, representing a password and the same password again. (Often, websites ask users to type their password twice when they register to make sure there was no typo the first time around.) Your program should do the following:

    ❑ if both passwords match, then output "You are now registered as a new user"

    ❑ otherwise, output "Sorry, there is a typo in your password"

48. Write a program that takes a word as input from the keyboard, representing a user ID. (Often, websites place constraints on user IDs.) Your program should do the following:
    - ❑ if the user ID contains between 6 and 10 characters inclusive, then output "Welcome barbara" (assuming *barbara* is the user ID entered)
    - ❑ otherwise, output "Sorry, user ID invalid"

5.14.7 Programming Projects

49. Write a program that reads a web address (for instance, *www.yahoo.com*) from the keyboard and outputs whether this web address is for a government, a university, a business, an organization, or another entity.
    - ❑ If the web address contains *gov*, it is a government web address.
    - ❑ If the web address contains *edu*, it is a university web address.
    - ❑ If the web address contains *com*, it is a business web address.
    - ❑ If the web address contains *org*, it is an organization web address.
    - ❑ Otherwise, it is a web address for another entity.
50. Write a program that reads a temperature as a whole number from the keyboard and outputs a "probable" season (winter, spring, summer, or fall) depending on the temperature.
    - ❑ If the temperature is greater than or equal to 90, it is probably summer.
    - ❑ If the temperature is greater than or equal to 70 and less than 90, it is probably spring.
    - ❑ If the temperature is greater than or equal to 50 and less than 70, it is probably fall.
    - ❑ If the temperature is less than 50, it is probably winter.
    - ❑ If the temperature is greater than 110 or less than −5, then you should output that the temperature entered is outside the valid range.
51. Write a program that takes a *String* as input from the keyboard, representing a year. Your program should do the following:
    - ❑ If the year entered has two characters, convert it to an *int*, add 2000 to it, and output it.

- ❑ If the year entered has four characters, just convert it to an *int* and output it.
- ❑ If the year entered has neither two nor four characters, output that the year is not valid.

52. Write a program that takes two words as input from the keyboard, representing a user ID and a password. Your program should do the following:
    - ❑ If the user ID and the password match "admin" and "open," respectively, then output "Welcome."
    - ❑ If the user ID matches "admin" and the password does not match "open," output "Wrong password."
    - ❑ If the password matches "open" and the user ID does not match "admin", output "Wrong user ID."
    - ❑ Otherwise, output "Sorry, wrong ID and password."

5.14.8 Technical Writing

53. When comparing two *doubles* or *floats* for equality, programmers calculate the difference between the two numbers and check if that difference is sufficiently small. Explain why and give a real-life example.

54. Look at the following code segment:

```
int b = 44;
if ( b = 23 )
     System.out.println( "Inside true block" );
```

In Java, this code will generate the following compiler error:

```
Test.java:9: Incompatible types
found   : int
required: boolean
if ( b = 23 )
       ^
1 error
```

In the C++ programming language, the equivalent code will compile and run and will give you the following output:

```
Inside true block
```

Discuss whether Java handles this situation better than C++ and why.

5.14.9 Group Project (for a group of 1, 2, or 3 students)

55. We want to build a simple "English language" calculator that does the following:

    - takes three inputs from the keyboard, two of them single digits (0 to 9)
    - takes a *char* from the keyboard, representing one of five operations from the keyboard: + (addition), – (subtraction), * (multiplication), / (division), and ^ (exponentiation)
    - outputs the description of the operation in plain English, as well as the numeric result

    For instance, if the two numbers are 5 and 3, and the operation is *, then the output should be

    ```
    five multiplied by three is 15
    ```

    Note that the result is given as a number, not a word.

    If the two numbers are 2 and 9, and the operation is –, then the output should be

    ```
    two minus nine is -7
    ```

    Hint: to perform the exponentiation, use the *pow* method of the *Math* class.

    If the two numbers are 5 and 2, and the operation is ^, then the output should be

    ```
    five to the power two is 25
    ```

    Hint: to perform the exponentiation, use the *pow* method of the *Math* class.

    If the two numbers are 5 and 0, and the operation is /, then the output should be

    ```
    Division by zero is not allowed
    ```

    Here the operation will not be performed.

    If the two numbers are 25 and 3, and the operation is +, then the output should be

    ```
    Invalid number
    ```

As for the operators, they should be translated into English as follows:

+	plus
–	minus
*	multiplied by
/	divided by
^	to the power

You should use the *switch* ... *case* selection statement to translate the input values into words.

You need to consider these special situations:

- ❑ for division, there is a special constraint: you cannot divide by 0, and you should therefore test whether the second number is 0. If it is 0, then you should output a message saying that you are not allowed to divide by 0.
- ❑ the "operator" is not one of the preceding five operators; in that case, output a message saying that the operator is not a valid one.
- ❑ one or two of the numbers is not a valid digit; again, you should output a message to that effect.

Hint: You can deal with these special situations in the *default* statement of the *switch* block and possibly use some *boolean* variables to keep track of this information, as you may need it later in your program.

CHAPTER 6

Flow of Control, Part 2: Looping

CHAPTER CONTENTS

Introduction

Have you ever watched the cashier at the grocery store? Let's call the cashier Jane. Jane's job is to determine the total cost of a grocery purchase. To begin, Jane starts with a total cost of $0.00. She then reaches for the first item and scans it to record its price, which is added to the total. Then she reaches for the second item, scans that item to record its price, which is added to the total, and so on. Jane continues scanning each item, one at a time, until there are no more items to scan. Usually, the end of an order is signaled by a divider bar laying across the conveyor belt. When Jane sees the divider bar, she knows she is finished. At that point, she tells us the total cost of the order, collects the money, and gives us a receipt.

So we see that Jane's job consists of performing some preliminary work, processing each item one at a time, and reporting the result at the end.

In computing, we often perform tasks that follow this same pattern:

1: initialize values

2: process items one at a time

3: report results

The flow of control that programmers use to complete jobs with this pattern is called **looping**, or **repetition**.

6.1 Event-Controlled Loops Using *while*

If we attempt to write pseudocode for the grocery store cashier, we may start with something like this:

```
set total to $0.00
reach for first item
if item is not the divider bar
    add price to total
reach for next item
if item is not the divider bar
    add price to total
reach for next item
if item is not the divider bar
    add price to total
... (finally)
reach for next item
item is the divider bar,
    tell the customer the total price
```

We can see a pattern here. We start with an order total of $0.00. Then we repeat a set of operations for each item. We reach for the item and check whether it's the divider bar. If the item is not the divider bar, we add the item's price to the order total. We reach for the next item and check whether it's the divider bar, and so on. When we reach for the item and find that it is the divider bar, we know there are no more items to process, so the total we have at that time is the total for the whole order. In other words, we don't know the number of items that will be placed on the conveyor belt. We just process the order, item by item, until we see the divider bar, which we do not process.

In Java, the *while* loop is designed for repeating a set of instructions for each input value when we don't know at the beginning how many input values there will be. We simply process each input value, one at a time, until a signal—an event—tells us that there is no more input. This is called **event-controlled looping**. In the cashier's case, the signal for the end of input was the divider bar. In other tasks, the signal for the end of the input may be a special value that the user enters, called a **sentinel value**, or it may be that we've reached the end of an input file.

6.2 General Form for *while* Loops

The *while* loop has this syntax:

```
// initialize variables
while ( condition )
{
    // process data; loop body
}
// process the results
```

The condition is a *boolean* expression, that is, any expression that evaluates to *true* or *false*. When the *while* loop statement is encountered, the condition is evaluated; if the value is *true*, the statements in the **loop body** are executed. The condition is then reevaluated and, if *true*, the loop body is executed again. This repetition continues until the loop condition evaluates to *false*, at which time, the loop body is skipped and execution continues at the instruction following the loop body.

The curly braces are needed only if the loop body has more than one statement; that is, if more than one statement should be executed if the condition evaluates to *true*.

The scope of any variable defined within the *while* loop body extends from its declaration to the end of the *while* loop. Thus, any variable that is declared within a *while* loop body cannot be referenced after the *while* loop ends.

The flow of control of a *while* loop is shown in Figure 6.1.

Each execution of the loop body is called an **iteration** of the loop. Thus, if the loop body executes five times before the condition evaluates to *false*, we say there were five iterations of the *while* loop.

What happens if the loop condition is *false* the first time it is evaluated? Because the loop condition is evaluated before executing the *while* loop body, and the loop body is executed only if the condition is *true*, it is possible that the *while* loop body is never executed. In that case, there would be **zero iterations** of the loop.

Figure 6.1
Flow of Control of a *while* Loop

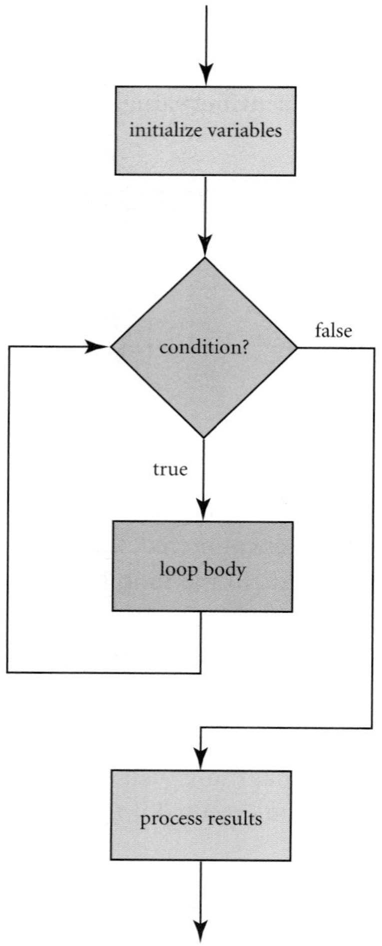

Using a *while* loop construct, the pseudocode for the cashier would look like this:

```
set total to $0.00
reach for first item
while item is not the divider bar
{
   add price to total
   reach for next item
}
// if we get here, the item is the divider bar
output the total price
```

It is also possible to construct a *while* loop whose condition *never* evaluates to *false*. That results in an **endless loop**, also known as an **infinite loop**. Because the condition always evaluates to *true*, the loop body is executed repeatedly, without end. This might happen if items other than the divider bar were placed continuously on the conveyor belt. One symptom of an endless loop is that the program doesn't terminate; it appears to "hang." However, if the program writes some output in the loop body, you will see that output spewing out on the Java console. Normally, the only recourse is for the user to abort the program.

The way to ensure that the condition will eventually evaluate to *false* is to include code, called a **loop update statement**, within the loop body that appropriately changes the variable that is being tested by the loop condition. If, for example, the loop condition tests for reading the sentinel value, the loop update statement should read the next input value.

COMMON ERROR TRAP

Avoid putting a semicolon after the condition of a *while* loop. Doing so creates an empty loop body and could result in an endless loop.

One common logic error that causes an endless loop is putting a semicolon after the condition, as in the following:

```
while ( condition );  // semicolon causes endless loop if condition is true
```

A semicolon immediately following the condition indicates an empty loop body. Although some advanced programming techniques call for the use of an empty loop body, we will not be using those techniques in this book.

6.3 Event-Controlled Looping

The *while* loop is used when we don't know how many times the loop will execute; that is, when the loop begins, we don't know how many iterations of the loop will be required. We rely on a signal, or **event**, to tell us that we have processed all the data. For example, when the cashier begins checking out an order, she doesn't (necessarily) know how many items are in the grocery cart; she only knows to stop when she sees the divider bar on the conveyor belt. We call this an event-controlled loop because we continue processing data until an event occurs, which signals the end of the data.

When we're prompting the user to enter data from the console, and we don't know at the beginning of the loop how much data the user has to be processed, we can define a special value, called the sentinel value. The sentinel value can vary from task to task and is typically a value that is outside the normal range of data for that task.

Sometimes the data our program needs is in a text file. For example, a file could store a company's monthly sales for the last five years. We may want to calculate average monthly sales or perform other statistical computations on that data. In this case, we need to read our data from the file, instead of asking the user to enter the data from the keyboard. Typically, we use a file when a large amount of data is involved because it would be impractical for a user to enter the data manually.

Reading from a file is also an event-controlled loop because we don't know at the beginning of the program how much data is in the file. Thus, we need some way to determine when we have finished processing all the data in the file. Java, and other languages, provides some indicator that we have reached the end of the file. Thus, for input from a file, sensing the end-of-file indication is the event that signals that there is no more data to read.

6.3.1 Reading Data from the User

Let's look at the general form for using a *while* loop to process data entered from the user.

```
initialize variables
read the first data item // priming read
while data item is not the sentinel value
{
   process the data

   read the next data item // update read
}
report the results
```

After performing any initialization, we attempt to read the first item. We call this the **priming read** because, like priming a pump, we use that value to feed the condition of the *while* loop for the first iteration. If the first item is not the sentinel value, we process it. Processing may consist of calculating a total, counting the number of data items, comparing the data to previously read values, or any number of operations. Then we read the next data item. This is called the **update read** because we update the data item in preparation for feeding its value into the condition of the *while* loop for the next iteration. This processing, followed by an update read, continues until we do read the sentinel value, at which time, we do not execute the *while* loop body. Instead, we skip to the first instruction following the *while* loop. Note that the sentinel value is not meant to be processed. Like the divider bar for the cashier, it is simply a signal to stop processing.

We illustrate this pattern in Example 6.1, which prompts the user for integers and echoes to the console whatever the user enters. We chose the sentinel value to be –1, that is, when the user enters a –1, we stop processing.

```
/*  Working with a sentinel value
    Anderson, Franceschi
*/
import java.util.Scanner;

public class EchoUserInput
{
   public static void main( String [ ] args )
   {
      final int SENTINEL = -1;
      int number;

      Scanner scan = new Scanner( System.in );

      // priming read
      System.out.print( "Enter an integer, or -1 to stop > " );
      number = scan.nextInt( );

      while ( number != SENTINEL )
      {
         // processing
         System.out.println( number );

         // update read
         System.out.print( "Enter an integer, or -1 to stop > " );
```

```
26          number = scan.nextInt( );
27      }
28
29      System.out.println( "Sentinel value detected. Goodbye" );
30    }
31 }
```

EXAMPLE 6.1 Echoing Input from the User

Figure 6.2 shows the output from this program when the user enters 23, 47, 100, and –1.

On line 10, we declare the sentinel value, –1, as a constant because the value of the sentinel will not change during the execution of the program, and it lets us clearly state via the *while* loop condition (line 19) that we want to execute the loop body only if the input is not the sentinel value.

Then on lines 16–17, we perform the priming read. The *while* loop condition on line 19 checks for the sentinel value. If the user enters the sentinel value first, we skip the *while* loop altogether and execute line 29, which prints a message that the sentinel value was entered, and we exit the program. If the user enters a number other than the sentinel value, we execute the body of the *while* loop (lines 21–26). In the *while* loop, we simply echo the user's input to the console, then perform the update read. Control then skips to the *while* loop condition, where the value the user entered in the update read is compared to the sentinel value. If this entry is the sentinel value, the loop is skipped; otherwise, the body of the loop is executed: The value is echoed, then a new value is read. This same processing continues until the user does enter the sentinel value.

Figure 6.2

Output from Example 6.1, Using a Sentinel Value

```
Enter an integer, or -1 to stop > 23
23
Enter an integer, or -1 to stop > 47
47
Enter an integer, or -1 to stop > 100
100
Enter an integer, or -1 to stop > -1
Sentinel value detected. Goodbye
```

A common error in constructing *while* loops is forgetting the update read. Without the update read, the *while* loop continually processes the same data item, leading to an endless loop.

COMMON ERROR TRAP

Omitting the update read may result in an endless loop.

Another common error is omitting the priming read and, instead, reading data inside the *while* loop before the processing, as in the following pseudocode:

```
initialize variables
while data item is not the sentinel value
{
   read the next data
   process the data
}
report the results
```

This structure has several problems. The first time we evaluate the *while* loop condition, we haven't read any data, so the result of that evaluation is unpredictable. Second, when we do read the sentinel value, we will process it, leading to incorrect results.

COMMON ERROR TRAP

Omitting the priming read leads to incorrect results.

6.3.2 Reading Data from a Text File

The *Scanner* class enables us to read data easily from a text file. Java also provides a whole set of classes in the *java.io* package to enable programmers to perform user input and output from a file. We will cover many of these classes in Chapter 11.

REFERENCE POINT

The *java.io* package, which contains classes to perform input and output from various data streams, including files, is discussed in Chapter 11.

For the *Scanner* class, the general form for reading data from a text file is a little different from reading the data from the user. First, instead of reading a value and checking whether it is the sentinel value, we check whether there is more data in the file, then read a value. Second, we don't need to print a prompt because the user doesn't enter the data; we just read the next value from the file. For the *Scanner* class, the pseudocode for reading from a text file is shown here:

```
initialize variables
while we have not reached end of file
```

```
{
  read the next data item
  process the data
}
report the results
```

Scanner class methods, including a constructor for reading from a text file, are shown in Table 6.1. Another class we will use is the *File* class, which associates a file name with a file. The constructor for the *File* class is shown in Table 6.2.

The constructor shown in Table 6.1 can be used to associate a *Scanner* object with a file. The *Scanner* object will tokenize the contents of the file and return the tokens as we call the *next* methods. The *hasNext* method in the *Scanner* class returns *true* if the input has another token, and *false* otherwise. Thus, when the *hasNext* method returns *false*, we know we have reached the end of the file.

```
23
47
100
```

Figure 6.3
Contents of *input.txt*

Example 6.2 reads integers from a file named *input.txt* and echoes the integers to the console. The contents of *input.txt* are shown in Figure 6.3 and the output from the program is shown in Figure 6.4.

On line 14 of Example 6.2, we use the constructor of the *File* class to convert the filename, *input.txt*, to a platform-independent filename. Because we are specifying the simple filename, the JVM will look for the file in the same directory as our source file. If the file is located in another directory, we need to specify the path as well as the filename. For example, if the file were located on a flash drive in a Windows system, we would pass the *String* "*e:\\input.txt*" to the constructor. Notice that we need to use an escape sequence of two backslashes in order to specify the pathname, *e:\input.txt*.

The *File* class belongs to the *java.io* package, so we include an *import* statement for that class in line 5.

REFERENCE POINT

The *String* escape sequences are discussed in Chapter 2.

In line 15, we construct a *Scanner* object associated with the *inputFile* object. If the file is not found, the constructor generates a *FileNotFoundException*. It is also possible that an *IOException* may be generated if we encounter problems reading the file. Java requires us to acknowledge that these exceptions may be generated. One way to do that is to include the phrase `"throws IOException"` in the header for *main* (line 10). In Chapter 11, we will discuss other ways to handle exceptions. We also import the *IOException* class on line 6.

TABLE 6.1 Selected Methods of the *Scanner* Class

Selected Methods of the *Scanner* Class	
Constructor	
`Scanner( File file )`	
creates a *Scanner* object and associates it with a file	
Return value	**Method name and argument list**
`boolean`	`hasNext( )` returns *true* if there is another token in the input stream; *false,* otherwise
`byte`	`nextByte( )` returns the next input as a *byte*
`short`	`nextShort( )` returns the next input as a *short*
`int`	`nextInt( )` returns the next input as an *int*
`long`	`nextLong( )` returns the next input as a *long*
`float`	`nextFloat( )` returns the next input as a *float*
`double`	`nextDouble( )` returns the next input as a *double*
`boolean`	`nextBoolean( )` returns the next input as a *boolean*
`String`	`next( )` returns the next token in the input line as a *String*

TABLE 6.2 *File* Class Constructor

A Constructor for the *File* Class
`File( String pathname )`
constructs a *File* object with the *pathname* file name so that the file name is platform-independent

REFERENCE POINT

Exceptions are discussed extensively in Chapter 11. You can read more about the *Scanner* class on Sun Microsystems' Java website: *http://java.sun.com*.

On line 17, the first time our *while* loop condition is evaluated, we check whether there is any data in the file. If the file is empty, the *hasNext* method will return *false*, and we will skip execution of the loop body, continuing at line 25, where we print a message and exit the program.

The body of the *while* loop (lines 19–22) calls the *nextInt* method to read the next integer in the file and echoes that integer to the console. We then reevaluate the *while* loop condition (line 17) to determine if more data is in the file. When no more integers remain to be read, the *hasNext* method returns *false*, and we skip to line 25, where we print a message and exit the program.

Notice that we do not use a priming read because the *hasNext* method essentially peeks ahead into the file to see if there is more data. If the *hasNext* method returns *true*, we know that there is another integer to read, so we perform the read in the first line of the *while* loop body (line 20).

```
1 /* Reading a Text File
2    Anderson, Franceschi
3 */
4 import java.util.Scanner;
5 import java.io.File;
6 import java.io.IOException;
7
8 public class EchoFileData
9 {
10    public static void main( String [ ] args ) throws IOException
11    {
12       int number;
13
14       File inputFile = new File( "input.txt" );
15       Scanner scan = new Scanner( inputFile );
16
17       while ( scan.hasNext( ) )
18       {
19          // read next integer
20          number = scan.nextInt( );
21          // process the value read
22          System.out.println( number );
23       }
24
25       System.out.println( "End of file detected. Goodbye" );
26    }
27 }
```

EXAMPLE 6.2 Echoing Input from a File

```
23
47
100
End of file detected. Goodbye
```

Figure 6.4
Output from Example 6.2, Reading from a File

6.4 Looping Techniques

You will find that the *while* loop is an important tool for performing many common programming operations on a set of input values. For example, the *while* loop can be used to calculate the sum of values, count the number of values, find the average value, find the minimum and maximum values, animate an image, and other operations.

6.4.1 Accumulation

Let's look at a common programming operation for which a *while* loop is useful: calculating the sum of a set of values. To do this, we will build a simple calculator that performs one function: addition. We will prompt the user for numbers one at a time. We'll make the sentinel value a 0; that is, when the user wants to stop, the user will enter a 0. At that point, we will print the total.

The calculator can be developed using an event-controlled *while* loop and a standard computing technique: **accumulation**. In the accumulation operation, we initialize a *total* variable to 0. Each time we input a new value, we add that value to the *total*. When we reach the end of the input, the current value of *total* is the total for all the input.

Here is the pseudocode for the addition calculator:

```
set total to 0
read a number   // priming read
while the number is not the sentinel value
```

```
{
   add the number to total
   read the next number   // update read
}
output the total
```

Notice that this operation is almost identical to the grocery cashier's job in that we perform a priming read before the *while* loop. Inside the *while* loop, we process each number one at a time—adding each number to the total, then we read the next value, until we see the sentinel value, which is the signal to stop.

Example 6.3 provides the code for the addition calculator and Figure 6.5 shows the output for a sample execution of the calculator.

```
/*  Addition Calculator
    Anderson, Franceschi
*/

import java.util.Scanner;

public class Calculator
{
   public static void main( String [ ] args )
   {
      final int SENTINEL = 0;
      int number;
      int total = 0;

      Scanner scan = new Scanner( System.in );

      System.out.println( "Welcome to the addition calculator.\n" );

      System.out.print( "Enter the first number"
                        + " or 0 for the total > " );
      number = scan.nextInt( );

      while ( number != SENTINEL )
      {
         total += number;

         System.out.print( "Enter the next number"
                           + " or 0 for the total > " );
         number = scan.nextInt( );
      }
```

```
31
32         System.out.println( "The total is " + total );
33     }
34 }
```

EXAMPLE 6.3 An Addition Calculator

```
Welcome to the addition calculator.

Enter the first number or 0 for the total > 34
Enter the next number or 0 for the total > -10
Enter the next number or 0 for the total > 2
Enter the next number or 0 for the total > 5
Enter the next number or 0 for the total > 8
Enter the next number or 0 for the total > 0
The total is 39
```

Figure 6.5
Output from a Sample Run of the Addition Calculator

Line 13 declares and initializes the *total* to *0*. This is an important step because the loop body will add each input value to the total. If the total is not set to 0 before the first input, we will get incorrect results. Furthermore, if *total* is declared but not initialized, our program will not compile.

COMMON ERROR TRAP

Forgetting to initialize the total to 0 will produce incorrect results.

Lines 19–21 read the first input value (the priming read). The *while* loop begins at line 23, and its condition checks for the sentinel value. The first time the *while* loop is encountered, this condition will check the value of the input from the priming read.

The loop body processes the input (line 25), which consists of adding the input value to the *total*. The final step in the loop body (lines 27–29) is to read the next input (the update read).

When the end of the loop body is reached, control is transferred back to line 23, where the loop condition is again tested with the input value read on line 29. If the condition is *true*, that is, if the input just read is not the sentinel value, then the loop body is reexecuted and the condition is retested, continuing until the input *is* the sentinel value, which causes the condition to evaluate to *false*. At that time, the loop body is skipped and line 32 is executed, which reports the results by printing the *total*.

SOFTWARE ENGINEERING TIP

Indent the body of a *while* loop to clearly illustrate the logic of the program.

Notice that the body of the *while* loop is indented and that the opening and closing curly braces are aligned in the same column as the *w* in the *while*. This style lets you easily see which statements belong to the *while* loop body.

COMMON ERROR TRAP

Choosing the wrong sentinel value may result in logic errors.

It is important to choose the sentinel value carefully. Obviously, the sentinel value cannot be a value that the user might want to be processed. In the addition calculator, we want to allow the user to enter positive or negative integers. We chose 0 as the sentinel value for two reasons. First, adding 0 to a total has no effect, so it is unlikely that the user will want to enter that value to be processed. Second, to the user, it is logical to enter a 0 to signal that there are no more integers to be added.

CODE IN ACTION

To see a step-by-step illustration of a *while* loop with a sentinel value, look for the Flash movie in the Chapter 6 folder on the CD-ROM included with this book. Click on the link for Chapter 6 to start the movie.

6.4.2 Counting Items

Counting is used when we need to know how many items are input or how many input values fit some criterion, for example, how many items are positive numbers or how many items are odd numbers. Counting is similar to accumulation in that we start with a count of 0 and increment (add 1 to) the count every time we read a value that meets the criterion. When there are no more values to read, the count variable contains the number of items that meet our criterion.

For example, let's count the number of students who passed a test. The pseudocode for this operation is as follows:

```
set countPassed to 0
read a test score
while the test score is not the sentinel value
{
  if the test score >= 60
  {
    add 1 to countPassed
  }
  read the next test score
}
output countPassed
```

The application in Example 6.4 counts the number of students that passed a test. We also calculate the percentage of the class that passed the test. To do this, we maintain a second count: the number of scores entered. This value will be incremented each time we read a score, whereas the *countPassed* value will be incremented only if the score is greater than or equal to 60. The sentinel value is –1. A sample run of this program is shown in Figure 6.6.

```
/* Counting passing test scores
   Anderson, Franceschi
*/

import java.util.Scanner;
import java.text.DecimalFormat;

public class CountTestScores
{
   public static void main( String [ ] args )
   {
     int countPassed = 0;
     int countScores = 0;
     int score;
     final int SENTINEL = -1;

     Scanner scan = new Scanner( System.in );

     System.out.println( "This program counts "
                 + "the number of passing test scores." );
     System.out.println( "Enter a -1 to stop." );

     System.out.print( "Enter the first score > " );
     score = scan.nextInt( );

     while ( score != SENTINEL )
     {
         if ( score >= 60 )
         {
               countPassed++;
         }

         countScores++;

         System.out.print( "Enter the next score > " );
         score = scan.nextInt( );
     }

```

```
39      System.out.println( "You entered " + countScores + " scores" );
40      System.out.println( "The number of passing test scores is "
41                          + countPassed );
42      if ( countScores != 0 )
43      {
44         DecimalFormat percent = new DecimalFormat( "#0.0%" );
45         System.out.println(
46           percent.format( (double) ( countPassed ) / countScores )
47           + " of the class passed the test." );
48      }
49    }
50 }
```

EXAMPLE 6.4 Counting Passing Test Scores

```
This program counts the number of passing test scores.
Enter a -1 to stop.
Enter the first score > 98
Enter the next score > 75
Enter the next score > 60
Enter the next score > 59
Enter the next score > 45
Enter the next score > 88
Enter the next score > 94
Enter the next score > 96
Enter the next score > 56
Enter the next score > 77
Enter the next score > 82
Enter the next score > 89
Enter the next score > 100
Enter the next score > 78
Enter the next score > 95
Enter the next score > -1
You entered 15 scores
The number of passing test scores is 12
80.0% of the class passed the test.
```

Figure 6.6
Counting Passing Test Scores

COMMON ERROR TRAP

Forgetting to initialize the count variables will produce a compiler error.

Lines 12 and 13 declare the variables *countPassed* and *countScores* and initialize both to 0. Initializing these values to 0 is critical; otherwise, we will get the wrong results or a compiler error. We initialize these values to 0 because at that point, we have not yet processed any test scores.

Our *while* loop framework follows the familiar pattern. We perform the priming read for the first input (lines 23–24); our *while* loop condition checks for the sentinel value (line 26); and the last statements of the *while* loop (lines 35–36) read the next value.

In the processing portion of the *while* loop, line 28 checks if the score just read is a passing score, and if so, line 30 adds 1 to *countPassed*. For each score entered, regardless of whether the student passed, we increment *countScores* (line 33).

When the sentinel value is entered, the *while* loop condition evaluates to *false* and control skips to line 39, where we output the number of scores entered and the number of passing scores. So that we avoid dividing by 0, note that line 42 checks whether no scores were entered. Note also that in line 46 we type cast *countPassed* to a *double* to force floating-point division, rather than integer division, so that the fractional part of the quotient will be maintained.

6.4.3 Calculating an Average

Calculating an average is a combination of accumulation and counting. We use accumulation to calculate the total and we use counting to count the number of items to average.

Here's the pseudocode for calculating an average:

```
set total to 0
set count to 0
read a number
while the number is not the sentinel value
{
   add the number to total
   add 1 to the count

   read the next number
}
set the average to total / count
output the average
```

Thus, to calculate an average test score for the class, we need to calculate the total of all the test scores, then divide by the number of students who took the test.

```
average = total / count;
```

It's important to remember that if we declare *total* and *count* as integers, then the *average* will be calculated using integer division, which truncates the remainder. To get a floating-point average, we need to type cast one of the variables (either *total* or *count*) to a *double* or a *float* to force the division to be performed as floating-point.

```
double average = (double) ( total ) / count;
```

The application in Example 6.5 calculates an average test score for a class of students. The output is shown in Figure 6.7.

```
/* Calculate the average test score
   Anderson, Franceschi
*/

import java.util.Scanner;
import java.text.DecimalFormat;

public class AverageTestScore
{
  public static void main( String [ ] args )
  {
    int count = 0;
    int total = 0;
    final int SENTINEL = -1;
    int score;

    Scanner scan = new Scanner( System.in );

    System.out.println( "To calculate a class average," );
    System.out.println( "enter each test score." );
    System.out.println( "When you are finished, enter a -1" );

    System.out.print( "Enter the first test score > " );
    score = scan.nextInt( );

    while ( score != SENTINEL )
    {
       total += score;    // add score to total
       count++;           // add 1 to count of test scores

       System.out.print( "Enter the next test score > " );
       score = scan.nextInt( );
    }

    if ( count != 0 )
    {
       DecimalFormat oneDecimalPlace = new DecimalFormat( "##.0" );
       System.out.println( "\nThe class average is "
         + oneDecimalPlace.format( (double) ( total ) / count ) );
    }
```

```
41      else
42          System.out.println( "\nNo grades were entered" );
44    }
45 }
```

EXAMPLE 6.5 Calculating an Average Test Score

```
To calculate a class average,
enter each test score.
When you are finished, enter a -1
Enter the first test score > 88
Enter the next test score > 78
Enter the next test score > 96
Enter the next test score > 75
Enter the next test score > 99
Enter the next test score > 56
Enter the next test score > 78
Enter the next test score > 84
Enter the next test score > 93
Enter the next test score > 79
Enter the next test score > 90
Enter the next test score > 85
Enter the next test score > 79
Enter the next test score > 92
Enter the next test score > 99
Enter the next test score > 94
Enter the next test score > -1

The class average is 85.3
```

Figure 6.7
Calculating the Average Test Score

In Example 6.5, lines 12 and 13 declare both *count* and *total* variables as *ints* and initialize each to 0. Again, our *while* loop structure follows the same pattern. Lines 23–24 read the first input value; the *while* loop condition (line 26) checks for the sentinel value; and the last statements in the *while* loop (lines 31–32) read the next score. For the processing portion of the *while* loop, we add the score to the total and increment the count of scores (lines 28–29). When the sentinel value is entered, we stop executing the *while* loop and skip to line 35.

COMMON ERROR TRAP

Forgetting to check whether the denominator is 0 before performing division is a logic error.

In line 35, we avoid dividing by 0 by checking whether *count* is 0 (that is, if no scores were entered) before performing the division. If *count* is 0, we

REFERENCE POINT

The difference between floating-point division and integer division is explained in Chapter 2.

simply print a message saying that no grades were entered. If *count* is not 0, we calculate and print the average. We first instantiate a *DecimalFormat* object (line 37) so that we can output the average to one decimal place. Remember that we need to type cast the *total* to a *double* (lines 38–39) to force floating-point division, rather than integer division.

6.4.4 Finding Maximum or Minimum Values

In Chapter 5, we illustrated a method for finding the maximum or minimum of three numbers. But that method won't work when we don't know how many numbers will be input. To find the maximum or minimum of an unknown number of input values, we need another approach.

In previous examples, we calculated a total for a group of numbers by keeping a running total. We started with a total of 0, then added each new input value to the running total. Similarly, we counted the number of input items by keeping a running count. We started with a count of 0 and incremented the count each time we read a new value. We can apply that same logic to calculating a maximum or minimum. For example, to find the maximum of a group of values, we can keep a "running," or current, maximum. We start by assuming that the first value we read is the maximum. In fact, it is the largest value we have seen so far. Then as we read each new value, we compare it to our current maximum. If the new value is greater, we make the new value our current maximum. When we come to the end of the input values, the current maximum is the maximum for all the input values.

Finding the minimum value, of course, uses the same approach, except that we replace the current minimum only if the new value is less than the current minimum.

Here's the pseudocode for finding a maximum value in a file:

```
read a first number and make it the maximum
while there is another number to read
{
   read the next number
   if number > maximum
```

```
  {
    set maximum to number
  }
}
output the maximum
```

Example 6.6 shows the code to find a maximum test grade in a file. As shown in Figure 6.8, the grades are stored as integers, one per line, in the file *grades.txt*. When this program runs, its output is shown in Figure 6.9.

```
/* Find the maximum test grade
   Anderson, Franceschi
*/

import java.util.Scanner;
import java.io.*;

public class FindMaximumGrade
{
   public static void main( String [ ] args ) throws IOException
   {
     int maxGrade;
     int grade;

     Scanner scan = new Scanner( new File( "grades.txt" ) );

     System.out.println( "This program finds the maximum grade "
                         + "for a class" );

     if ( ! scan.hasNext( ) )
     {
          System.out.println( "No test grades are in the file" );
     }
     else
     {
         maxGrade = scan.nextInt( );  // make first grade the max

         while ( scan.hasNext( ) )
         {
            grade = scan.nextInt( );  // read next grade
```

```
88
78
96
75
99
56
78
84
93
79
90
85
79
90
85
79
92
99
94
```

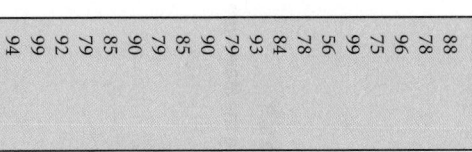

Figure 6.8
The Contents of *grades.txt*

```
31
32             if ( grade > maxGrade )
33                maxGrade = grade;     // save as current max
34          }
35
36          System.out.println( "The maximum grade is " + maxGrade );
37       }
38    }
39 }
```

EXAMPLE 6.6 Finding the Maximum Value

```
This program finds the maximum grade for a class
The maximum grade is 99
```

Figure 6.9
Finding the Maximum Value

In line 20, we call the *hasNext* method to test whether the file is empty. If so, we print a message (line 22) and the program ends. If, however, the file is not empty, we read the first value and automatically make it our maximum by storing the grade in *maxGrade* (line 26). In line 28, our *while* loop condition tests whether we have reached end of file. If not, we execute the body of the *while* loop (lines 30–33). We read the next grade and check whether that grade is greater than the current maximum. If so, we assign that grade to *maxGrade*; otherwise, we leave *maxGrade* unchanged. Then control is transferred to line 28 to retest the *while* loop condition.

When we do reach end of file, the *while* loop condition becomes *false*, and control is transferred to line 36, and we output *maxGrade* as the maximum value.

COMMON ERROR TRAP

Initializing a maximum or a minimum to an arbitrary value, such as 0 or 100, is a logic error and could result in incorrect results.

A common error is to initialize the maximum or minimum to an arbitrary value, such as 0 or 100. This will not work for all conditions, however. For example, let's say we are finding the maximum number and we initialize the maximum to 0. If the user enters all negative numbers, then when the end of data is encountered, the maximum will still be 0, which is clearly an error. The same principle is true when finding a minimum value. If we initialize the minimum to 0, and the user enters all positive numbers greater than 0, then at the end of our loop, our minimum value will still be 0, which is also incorrect.

Skill Practice
with these end-of-chapter questions

6.14.1 Multiple Choice Exercises
Question 1

6.14.2 Reading and Understanding Code
Questions 5, 6, 7, 8, 20

6.14.3 Fill In the Code
Questions 21, 22, 23, 24, 25, 26

6.14.4 Identifying Errors in Code
Questions 30, 31

6.14.5 Debugging Area
Question 37

6.14.6 Write a Short Program
Questions 44, 45

6.14.8 Technical Writing
Questions 70, 71

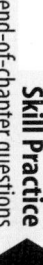

6.4.5 Animation

Animation is another operation that can be performed using *while* loops. For example, to move an object across a graphics window, we change the x or y values and draw the object in a new position in each iteration of the loop. We stop moving the object when we reach the edges of the window. Therefore, the sentinel value for the loop is that the x- or y-coordinate has reached the edge of the window.

If we want to roll a ball from left to right along an imaginary line, we can represent the ball by a filled circle. We start with an x value of 0 and some y value; our *while* loop draws the object at the current x, y position, then increments the x value.

Thus, to test for the sentinel value—that is, whether the ball has reached the right edge of the window—we add the diameter of the ball to the current x position of the ball and compare that result to the x-coordinate of the right edge of the window.

For this animation, we'll use a *Circle* class written by the authors. Table 6.3 shows the constructors and methods of the *Circle* class.

Example 6.7 shows a *while* loop that simulates rolling a ball from the left edge of the window to the right edge.

```
/* RollABall, Version 1
   Anderson, Franceschi
*/

import java.awt.Graphics;
import java.awt.Color;
import javax.swing.JApplet;

public class RollABall1 extends JApplet
{
  public void paint( Graphics g )
  {
     super.paint( g );

     final int X = 0;          // the x value of the ball
     final int Y = 50;         // the y value of the ball
     final int DIAMETER = 15;  // the diameter of the ball
     final Color COLOR = Color.BLUE; // the color of the ball
     final int SPACER = 5;     // space between balls

     // instantiate the ball as a Circle object
     Circle ball = new Circle( X, Y, DIAMETER, COLOR );

     // get ball diameter
     int ballDiameter = ball.getDiameter( );
     int sentinel = getWidth( ); // edge of the window is sentinel

```

TABLE 6.3 The *Circle* Class API

The *Circle* Class API	
Constructors	
`Circle( )`	
constructs a *Circle* object with default values; *x* and *y* are set to 0, diameter to 10, and color to black	
`Circle( int startX, int startY, int sDiameter, Color circleColor )`	
constructs a *Circle* object; sets *x* and *y* to *startX* and *startY*, respectively; diameter to *sDiameter*; and color to *circleColor*	
Return value	**Method name and argument list**
`int`	`getX( )` returns the ball's current *x* value
`int`	`getY( )` returns the ball's current *y* value
`int`	`getDiameter( )` returns the current diameter of the circle
`Color`	`getColor( )` returns the current color of the circle
`void`	`setX( int newX )` sets the *x* value to *newX*
`void`	`setY( int newY )` sets the *y* value to *newY*
`void`	`setDiameter( int newDiameter )` sets the diameter to *newDiameter*
`void`	`setColor( Color newColor )` sets the circle color to *newColor*
`void`	`draw( Graphics g )` draws a filled circle with *x* and *y* being the upper-left corner of a bounding rectangle, with the diameter and color set in the object

```
28       while ( ball.getX( ) + ballDiameter < sentinel )
29       {
30          ball.draw( g );    // draw the ball
31
32          // set x to next drawing location
33          ball.setX( ball.getX( ) + ballDiameter + SPACER );
34       }
35    }
36 }
```

EXAMPLE 6.7 Roll a Ball, Version 1

In the *paint* method, we instantiate the ball (line 22). It will start with an *x* value of 0 (the left edge of the screen), *y* value of 50, diameter of 15, and a blue color. We use a *while* loop (lines 28–34) to repeatedly draw a ball and increment the *x* value. The sentinel value occurs when the *x* value of the next ball (x + *ballDiameter*) reaches the right edge of the applet window. We determine the value of the right edge of the window by calling the *getWidth* method of the *JApplet* class (line 26), which returns the width of the applet window.

We chose to increment the *x* value by the width of the ball (the diameter) plus 5 pixels so that each ball is 5 pixels apart (line 33). Let's take a closer look at that statement:

```
ball.setX( ball.getX( ) + ballDiameter + SPACER );
```

We call the *setX* method of the *Circle* class to set the *x* value of the next ball. In order to set the *x* value to a new value, we need to get the current *x* value of the *ball* object and the current diameter. We do that by calling the *getX* method and adding the *ballDiameter* value we got earlier from the *getDiameter* method (line 25). Thus, by adding the diameter of the ball to the current *x* value, we calculate the *x* value of the right side of the ball. Adding the constant *SPACER* to that result puts a space of 5 pixels between the last ball drawn and the next.

Figure 6.10 shows the output when the applet is run.

This is fine for a first effort, but it isn't the effect we want. The result is just a series of balls drawn from left to right. There's another problem with *RollABall1*, which you can appreciate only if you run the applet: all

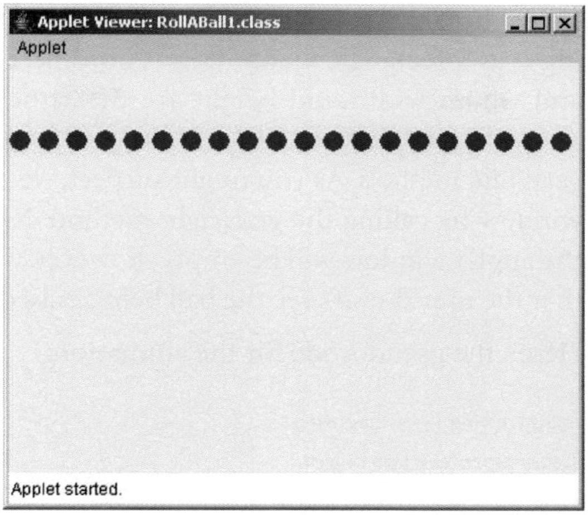

Figure 6.10
Roll a Ball, Version 1

the balls appear at once. There's no visual effect of the ball moving from left to right.

To get a rolling movement, we need to slow down the execution of the applet. To do that, we can use the *Pause* class provided by the authors and available in the directory on the CD containing this code. The *wait* method of the *Pause* class has the following API:

```
static void wait( double seconds )
```

Because the *wait* method is *static*, we invoke it using the *Pause* class name. For example, the following statement will pause the applet for approximately 3/100th of a second:

```
Pause.wait( .03 );
```

Also, we want to see only one ball at any time, and that should be the ball at the current (*x*, *y*) coordinate. To get this effect, we need to "erase" the previous ball before we draw the next ball in the new location. To erase the ball, we have two options: we can redraw the ball in the background color or we can clear the whole window by calling the *clearRect* method, which draws a rectangle in the background color. The default background color for the *JApplet* class is not one of the *Color* constants (*Color.BLUE*, etc.), so it's a difficult color to match. That being the case, we opt for the *clearRect* method, which has the following API:

```
void clearRect( int x, int y, int width, int height )
```

Using the *clearRect* method, we can erase the whole applet window by treating it as a rectangle whose (x, y) coordinate is the upper-left corner (0, 0) and whose width and height are the same as the applet window. We've already seen that we can get the width of the window by calling the *getWidth* method. As you might suspect, we can get the height of the applet window by calling the *getHeight* method. Note that after we call *clearRect*, the applet window will be empty; however, we draw the next ball so quickly that the user doesn't see the ball being erased.

Here's the pseudocode for the animation:

```
set starting (x, y) coordinate
instantiate the ball object
while the x value is not the edge of the window
{
  draw the ball
  pause
  erase the ball
  set (x, y) coordinate to next drawing position
}
```

Example 6.8 shows the revised version of the rolling ball.

```
/* RollABall, version 2
   Anderson, Franceschi
*/

import java.awt.Graphics;
import java.awt.Color;
import javax.swing.JApplet;
import javax.swing.JOptionPane;

public class RollABall2 extends JApplet
{
  public void paint( Graphics g )
  {
     super.paint( g );

     final int X = 0;           // the x value of the ball
     final int Y = 50;          // the y value of the ball
```

```
18       final int DIAMETER = 15;  // the diameter of the ball
19       final Color COLOR = Color.BLUE; // the color of the ball
20       final int SPACER = 5;     // space between balls
21
22       // instantiate the ball as a Circle object
23       Circle ball = new Circle( X, Y, DIAMETER, COLOR );
24
25       // get ball diameter and width & height of the applet window
26       int ballDiameter = ball.getDiameter( );
27       int windowWidth = getWidth( );
28       int windowHeight = getHeight( );
29
30       // rolling horizontally
31       // check whether ball is at right edge of window
32       while ( ball.getX( ) + ballDiameter < windowWidth )
33       {
34            ball.draw( g );  // draw the ball
35
36            Pause.wait( 0.03 ); // wait 3/100th of a second
37
38            // clear the window
39            g.clearRect( 0, 0, windowWidth, windowHeight );
40
41            // position to next location for drawing ball
42            ball.setX( ball.getX( ) + SPACER ); // increment x by 5
43       }
44
45       ball.draw( g );  // draw the ball in the current position
46    }
47 }
```

EXAMPLE 6.8 Roll a Ball, Version 2

In the *paint* method, we now draw a ball (line 34), pause for approximately 3/100ths of a second (line 36), then use the *clearRect* method to erase the window (line 39) before positioning *x* to the next location for drawing the ball (line 42). Now, only one ball is visible at any time, and the ball appears to roll across the screen, as shown in Figure 6.11. After the *while* loop completes, we draw the ball one more time (line 45) because when the *while* loop ends, the last ball drawn will have been erased.

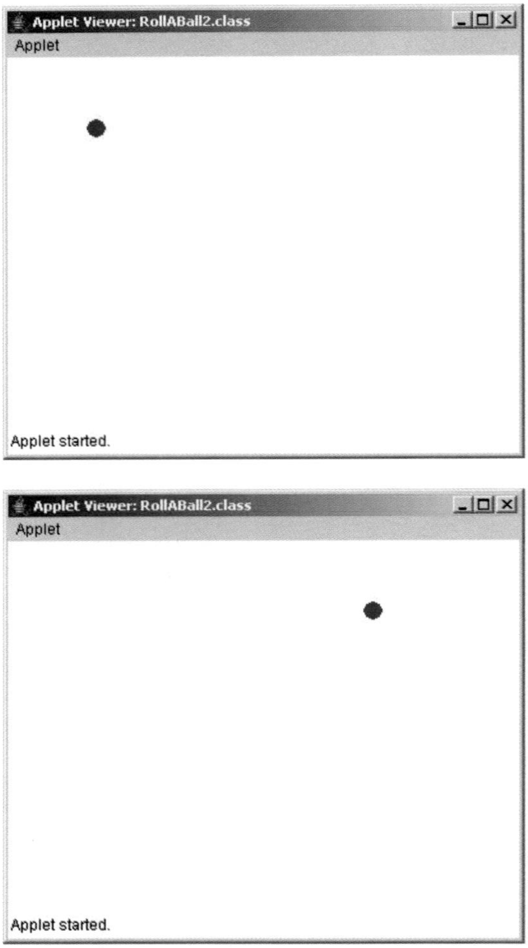

Figure 6.11
Roll a Ball, Version 2

6.5 Type-Safe Input Using *Scanner*

One problem with reading input using *Scanner* is that if the next token does not match the data type we expect, an *InputMismatchException* is generated, which stops execution of the program. This could be caused by a simple typo on the user's part; for example, the user may type a letter or other nonnumeric character when our program prompts for an integer. To illustrate this problem, Example 6.9 shows a small program that prompts the user for an integer and calls the *nextInt* method of the *Scanner* class to read the integer, and Figure 6.12 shows the *InputMismatchException* generated when the user enters an *a* instead of an integer. Notice that the program ends when the exception is generated; we never execute line 15, which echoes the age to the console.

```
1 /* Reading an integer from the user
2    Anderson, Franceschi
3 */
4 import java.util.Scanner;
5
6 public class ReadInteger
7 {
8    public static void main( String [ ] args )
9    {
10         Scanner scan = new Scanner( System.in );
11
12         System.out.print( "Enter your age as an integer > " );
13         int age = scan.nextInt( );
14
15         System.out.println( "Your age is " + age );
16    }
17 }
```

EXAMPLE 6.9 Reading an Integer

```
Enter your age as an integer > a
Exception in thread "main" java.util.InputMismatchException
        at java.util.Scanner.throwFor(Unknown Source)
        at java.util.Scanner.next(Unknown Source)
        at java.util.Scanner.nextInt(Unknown Source)
        at java.util.Scanner.nextInt(Unknown Source)
        at ReadInteger.main(ReadInteger.java:13)
```

Figure 6.12
Input Failure

We can make our program more robust by checking, before we read, that the next token matches our expected input. The *Scanner* class provides *hasNext* methods for doing this, which are shown in Table 6.4. The *hasNext* methods return *true* if the next token can be read as the data type specified. For example, if we expect an integer, we can test whether the user has typed characters that can be interpreted as an integer by calling the *hasNextInt* method. If that method returns *true*, it is safe to read the value using the *nextInt* method. If the next token is not what we need, that is, if the *hasNextInt* method returns *false*, then reading that value as an *int* will

TABLE 6.4 ***Scanner*** **Methods for Testing Tokens**

Selected Input Stream Testing Methods of the *Scanner* Class	
Return value	**Method name and argument list**
`boolean`	`hasNext( )` returns *true* if there is another token in the input stream; *false*, otherwise
`boolean`	`hasNextByte( )` returns *true* if the token in the input stream can be read as a *byte*; *false*, otherwise
`boolean`	`hasNextShort( )` returns *true* if the token in the input stream can be read as a *short*; *false*, otherwise
`boolean`	`hasNextInt( )` returns *true* if the token in the input stream can be read as an *int*; *false*, otherwise
`boolean`	`hasNextLong( )` returns *true* if the token in the input stream can be read as a *long*; *false*, otherwise
`boolean`	`hasNextFloat( )` returns *true* if the token in the input stream can be read as a *float*; *false*, otherwise
`boolean`	`hasNextDouble( )` returns *true* if the token in the input stream can be read as a *double*; *false*, otherwise
`boolean`	`hasNextBoolean( )` returns *true* if the token in the input stream can be read as a *boolean*; *false*, otherwise
`String`	`nextLine( )` returns the remainder of the input line as a *String*

generate the *InputMismatchException.* In that case, we need to notify the user that the value typed is not valid and reprompt for new input. But first we need to clear the invalid input. We can flush the invalid input by calling the *nextLine* method of the *Scanner* class, which returns any remaining tokens on the input line as a *String.* Then we just ignore that *String.* Example 6.10 shows a revised version of Example 6.9 that is type-safe, meaning we guarantee we have an integer to read before reading it.

On line 14 of Example 6.10, we prompt for the integer. Then on line 15, the *while* loop condition checks whether the user has, indeed, typed an integer value. If not, we ignore whatever the user did type by calling the *nextLine* method (line 17). On line 18, we reprompt the user. The *while* loop continues executing until the user does enter an integer and the *hasNextInt* method returns *true.* At that point, we execute line 20, which reads the integer into the *age* variable. Figure 6.13 shows the output of this program when the user enters data other than integers, then finally enters an integer.

```
 1  /* Type-Safe Input Using Scanner
 2     Anderson, Franceschi
 3  */
 4
 5  import java.util.Scanner;
 6
 7  public class TypeSafeReadInteger
 8  {
 9     public static void main( String [ ] args )
10     {
11        Scanner scan = new Scanner( System.in );
12        String garbage;
13
14        System.out.print( "Enter your age as an integer > " );
15        while ( ! scan.hasNextInt( ) )
16        {
17              garbage = scan.nextLine( );
18              System.out.print( "\nPlease enter an integer > " );
19        }
20        int age = scan.nextInt( );
21        System.out.println( "Your age is " + age );
22     }
23  }
```

EXAMPLE 6.10 Type-Safe Input

Figure 6.13
Reprompting Until the User Enters an Integer

```
Enter your age as an integer > asd

Please enter an integer > 12wg

Please enter an integer > 12.4

Please enter an integer > 23
Your age is 23
```

6.6 Constructing Loop Conditions

Constructing the correct loop condition may seem a little counterintuitive. The loop executes as long as the loop condition evaluates to *true*. Thus, if we want our loop to terminate when we read the sentinel value, then the loop condition should check that the input value is *not* the sentinel value. In other words, the loop continuation condition is the inverse of the loop termination condition. For a simple sentinel-controlled loop, the condition normally follows this pattern:

```
while ( inputValue != sentinel )
```

In fact, you can see that the loop conditions in many of the examples in this chapter use this form of *while* loop condition. Examples 6.7 and 6.8 use a similar pattern. We want to roll the ball as long as the ball is completely within the window. The loop termination condition is that the starting *x* value plus the diameter of the ball is greater than or equal to the *x* value of the right side of the window. The loop continuation condition, therefore, is that the *x* value of the ball plus the diameter is less than the *x* value of the right side of the window.

```
while ( ball.getX( ) + ballDiameter < windowWidth )
```

For some applications, there may be multiple sentinel values. For example, suppose we provide a menu for a user with each menu option being a single character. The user can repeatedly select options from the menu, with the sentinel value being *S* for stop. To allow case-insensitive input, we want to recognize the sentinel value as either *S* or *s*. To do this, we need a compound loop condition, that is, a loop condition that uses a logical AND (`&&`) or logical OR (`||`) operator.

Our first inclination might be to form the condition this way, which is **incorrect**:

```
while ( option != 'S' || option != 's' )  // INCORRECT
```

With this condition, the loop will execute forever. Regardless of what the user enters, the loop condition will be *true*. If the user types *S*, the first expression (`option != 'S'`) is *false*, but the second expression (`option != 's'`) is *true*. Thus, the loop condition evaluates to *true* and the *while* loop body is executed. Similarly, if the user types *s*, the first expression (`option != 'S'`) is *true*, so the loop condition evaluates to *true* and the *while* loop body is executed.

An easy method for constructing a correct *while* loop condition consists of three steps:

1. Define the loop termination condition; that is, define the condition that will make the loop stop executing.
2. Create the loop continuation condition—the condition that will keep the loop executing—by applying the logical NOT operator (!) to the loop termination condition.
3. Simplify the loop continuation condition by applying DeMorgan's Laws, where possible.

REFERENCE POINT

DeMorgan's Laws are explained in Chapter 5.

Let's use these three steps to construct the correct loop condition for the menu program.

1. Define the loop termination condition:

   The loop will stop executing when the user enters an *S* or the user enters an *s*. Translating that into Java, we get

   ```
   ( option == 'S' || option == 's' )
   ```

2. Create the loop continuation condition by applying the ! operator:

   ```
   ! ( option == 'S' || option == 's' )
   ```

3. Simplify by applying DeMorgan's Laws:

   To apply DeMorgan's Laws, we change the == equality operators to !=

and change the logical OR operator (`||`) to the logical AND operator (`&&`), producing an equivalent, but simpler expression:

```
( option != 'S' && option != 's' )
```

We now have our loop condition.

To illustrate, let's write an application that calculates the cost of cell phone service. We'll provide a list of options, and the user will select options one at a time until the user enters *S* or *s* to stop. This is an accumulation operation because we are accumulating the total cost of the cell phone service. Example 6.11 shows the code for this application and Figure 6.14 shows the output of a sample run.

```
/* Calculate price for cell phone service
   Anderson, Franceschi
*/

import java.util.Scanner;
import java.text.DecimalFormat;

public class CellService
{
   public static void main( String [ ] args )
   {
      String menu = "\nAvailable Options";
      menu += "\n\tA  1,000 anytime minutes: $25.49";
      menu += "\n\tU  Unlimited weekend minutes: $6.99";
      menu += "\n\tN  Nationwide long distance: $12.99";
      menu += "\n\tT  Text messaging: $5.99";

      String optionS;
      char option;
      double cost = 10.99; // base cost

      DecimalFormat money = new DecimalFormat( "$###.00" );
      Scanner scan = new Scanner( System.in );

      System.out.println( "Select the options "
                       + "for your cell phone service: " );
      System.out.println( "Base cost: " + money.format( cost ) );

      System.out.println( menu ); // print the menu
      System.out.print( "Enter an option, "
                      + "or \"S\" to stop > " );
      option = scan.next( ).charAt( 0 );

```

```
      while ( option != 'S' && option != 's' )
      {
         switch ( option )
         {
            case 'a':
            case 'A':
               System.out.println( "1,000 anytime minutes: "
                                   + "$25.49" );
               cost += 25.49;
               break;
            case 'u':
            case 'U':
               System.out.println( "Unlimited weekend minutes: "
                                   + "$6.99" );
               cost += 6.99;
               break;
            case 'n':
            case 'N':
               System.out.println( "Nationwide long distance: "
                                   + "$12.99" );
               cost += 12.99;
               break;
            case 't':
            case 'T':
               System.out.println( "Text messaging: "
                                   + "$5.99" );
               cost += 5.99;
               break;
            default:
               System.out.println( "Unrecognized option" );
         }

         System.out.println( "Current cost: "
                             + money.format( cost ) );

         System.out.println( menu ); // print the menu
         System.out.print( "Enter an option, "
                           + "or \"S\" to stop > " );
         option = scan.next( ).charAt( 0 );
      }

      System.out.println( "\nTotal cost of cell service is "
                          + money.format( cost ) );
   }
}
```

EXAMPLE 6.11 A Compound Loop Condition

Figure 6.14
Calculating Cell Phone Service

```
Select the options for your cell phone service:
Base cost: $10.99

Available Options
       A  1,000 anytime minutes; $25.49
       U  Unlimited weekend minutes: $6.99
       N  Nationwide long distance; $12.99
       T  Text messaging: $5.99
Enter an option, or "S" to stop > a
1,000 anytime minutes: $25.49
Current cost: $36.48

Available Options
       A  1,000 anytime minutes: $25.49
       U  Unlimited weekend minutes: $6.99
       N  Nationwide long distance: $12.99
       T  Text messaging: $5.99
Enter an option, or "S" to stop > U
Unlimited weekend minutes: $6.99
Current cost: $43.47

Available Options
       A  1,000 anytime minutes: $25.49
       U  Unlimited weekend minutes: $6.99
       N  Nationwide long distance: $12.99
       T  Text messaging: $5.99
Enter an option, or "S" to stop > s

Total cost of cell service is $43.47
```

In Example 6.11, we use the compound condition in the *while* loop (line 34). Then within the *while* loop, we use a *switch* statement (lines 36–64) to determine which menu option the user has chosen. We handle case-insensitive input of menu options by including *case* constants for both the lowercase and uppercase versions of each letter option.

COMMON ERROR TRAP

Do not check for the sentinel value inside a *while* loop. Let the *while* loop condition detect the sentinel value.

Note that we don't provide *case* statements for the sentinel values. Instead, we use the *while* loop condition to detect when the user enters the sentinel values.

Animation is another operation that may require a *while* loop with a compound condition. For example, suppose that instead of rolling our ball horizontally, we roll it diagonally down and to the right. To roll the ball diagonally down and to the right, we need to change both the *x* and the *y* values in the *while* loop body. Thus, within the while loop, we increment both *x* and *y*. We continue as long as the ball has not rolled beyond the right edge of the window and the ball has also not rolled beyond the bottom of the window.

Let's develop the condition by applying our three steps:

1. The loop termination condition is that the ball has rolled beyond either the right edge of the window or the bottom edge of the window.

```
// the ball is out of bounds
( ball.getX( ) + ballDiameter > windowWidth
    || ball.getY( ) + ballDiameter > windowHeight )
```

2. The loop continuation condition is created by applying the logical NOT operator (!) to the loop termination condition:

```
// the ball is not out of bounds
!  ( ball.getX( ) + ballDiameter > windowWidth
       || ball.getY( ) + ballDiameter > windowHeight )
```

3. Simplifying the condition by applying DeMorgan's Law, we get:

```
// the ball is in bounds
( ball.getX( ) + ballDiameter <= windowWidth
    && ball.getY( ) + ballDiameter <= windowHeight )
```

Example 6.12 shows the *RollABall3* class, which uses four *while* loops to roll the ball diagonally down to the right (*x* is incremented, *y* is incremented), then diagonally down to the left (*x* is decremented, *y* is incremented); then diagonally up to the left (*x* is decremented, *y* is decremented), and finally diagonally up to the right (*x* is incremented, *y* is decremented). We set the starting *y* value to 10 and the starting *x* value two-thirds of the way across the window. When the program runs, the ball appears to bounce off the walls of the window, as shown in Figure 6.15.

```
/* RollABall, Version 3
   Rolls the ball diagonally
   Anderson, Franceschi
*/

import java.awt.Graphics;
import java.awt.Color;
import javax.swing.JApplet;

public class RollABall3 extends JApplet
```

```
{
   public void paint( Graphics g )
   {
      super.paint( g );

      final int Y = 10;          // the y value of the ball
      final int DIAMETER = 15;  // the diameter of the ball
      final Color COLOR = Color.BLUE; // the color of the ball
      final int SPACER = 2;      // space between balls

      // get width & height of the applet window
      int windowWidth = getWidth( );
      int windowHeight = getHeight( );

      // start x 2/3 across the window
      int x =  windowWidth * 2 / 3;

      // instantiate the ball as a Circle object
      Circle ball = new Circle( x, Y, DIAMETER, COLOR );

      // get ball diameter
      int ballDiameter = ball.getDiameter( );

      // rolling diagonally down to the right
      while ( ball.getX( ) + ballDiameter <= windowWidth
                && ball.getY( ) + ballDiameter <= windowHeight )
      {

         ball.draw( g );  // draw the ball

         Pause.wait( 0.03 ); // pause for 3/100 of a second
         // erase the ball
         g.clearRect( 0, 0, windowWidth, windowHeight );

         ball.setX( ball.getX( ) + SPACER ); // move right
         ball.setY( ball.getY( ) + SPACER ); // and down
      }

      // rolling diagonally down to the left
      while ( ball.getY( )  + ballDiameter < windowHeight
               && ball.getX( ) > 0 )
      {
         ball.draw( g );  // draw the ball

```

```
            Pause.wait( 0.03 ); // pause for 3/100 of a second
            // erase the ball
            g.clearRect( 0, 0, windowWidth, windowHeight );

            ball.setX( ball.getX( ) - SPACER ); // move left
            ball.setY( ball.getY( ) + SPACER ); // and down
         }

         // rolling diagonally up to the left
         while ( ball.getY( ) > 0 && ball.getX( ) > 0 )
         {
            ball.draw( g );  // draw the ball

            Pause.wait( 0.03 ); // pause for 3/100 of a second
            // erase the ball
            g.clearRect( 0, 0, windowWidth, windowHeight );

            ball.setX( ball.getX( ) - SPACER ); // move left
            ball.setY( ball.getY( ) - SPACER ); // and up
         }

         // rolling diagonally up to the right
         while ( ball.getY( )  > 0
                 && ball.getX( ) + ballDiameter < windowWidth )
         {
            ball.draw( g );  // draw the ball

            Pause.wait( 0.03 ); // pause for 3/100 of a second
            // erase the ball
            g.clearRect( 0, 0, windowWidth, windowHeight );

            ball.setX( ball.getX( ) + SPACER ); // move right
            ball.setY( ball.getY( ) - SPACER ); // and up
         }

         ball.draw( g );  // draw the ball
      }
   }
```

EXAMPLE 6.12 The *RollABall3* Class

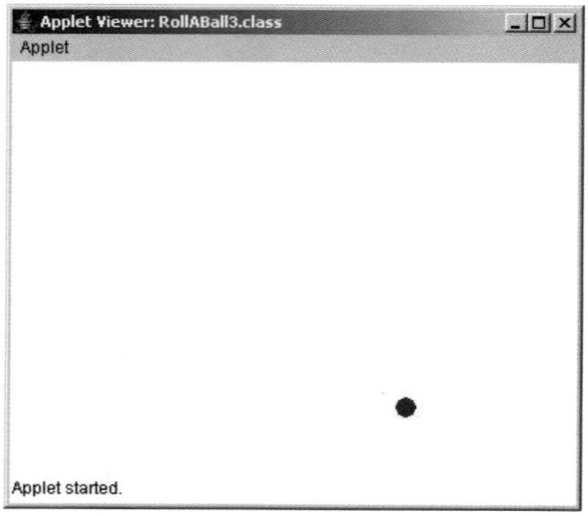

Figure 6.15
Output from *RollABall3*

Skill Practice
with these end-of-chapter questions

6.14.1 Multiple Choice Exercises

Questions 9, 10

6.14.3 Fill In the Code

Question 28

6.14.4 Identifying Errors in Code

Question 34

6.14.5 Debugging Area

Question 36

6.14.6 Write a Short Program

Question 53

6.7 Testing Techniques for *while* Loops

It's a good feeling when your code compiles without errors. Getting a clean compile, however, is only part of the job for the programmer. The other part of the job is verifying that the code is correct; that is, that the program produces accurate results.

It usually isn't feasible to test a program with all possible input values, but we can get a reasonable level of confidence in the accuracy of the program by concentrating our testing in three areas:

1. Does the program produce correct results with a set of known input?

2. Does the program produce correct results if the sentinel value is the first and only input?
3. Does the program deal appropriately with invalid input?

Let's take a look at these three areas in more detail:

1. Does the program produce correct results with known input?

To test the program with known input, we select valid input values and determine what the results should be by performing the program's operation either by hand or by using a calculator. For example, to test whether a total or average is computed correctly, enter some values and compare the program's output to a total or average you calculate by entering those same values into a calculator.

It's especially important to select input values that represent boundary conditions; that is, values that are the lowest or highest expected values. For example, to test a program that determines whether a person is old enough to vote in a presidential election (that is, the person is 18 or older), we should select test values of 17, 18, and 19. These values are the boundary conditions for `age >= 18`; the test values are one integer less, the same value, and one integer greater than the legal voting age. We then run the program with the three input values and verify that the program correctly identifies 17 as an illegal voting age and 18 and 19 as legal voting ages.

2. Does the program produce correct results if the sentinel value is the first and only input?

In our *while* loops, when we find the sentinel value, the flow of control skips the *while* loop body and picks up at the statement following the *while* loop. When the sentinel value is the first input value, our *while* loop body does not execute at all. We simply skip to the statement following the *while* loop. In cases like this, the highly respected computer scientist Donald Knuth recommends that we "do exactly nothing, gracefully."

In many programs that calculate a total or an average for the input values, when no value is input, your program should either report the total or average as 0 or output a message that no values were entered. Thus, it's important to write your program so that it tolerates no input except the sentinel value and, therefore, we need to test our programs by entering the sentinel value first.

Let's revisit the earlier examples in this chapter to see how they handle the case when only the sentinel value is entered.

SOFTWARE ENGINEERING TIP

Expect that the user might enter the sentinel value first. Your program needs to handle this special case.

In the addition calculator (Example 6.3), we set the total to 0 before the *while* loop and simply report the value of total after the *while* loop. So we get the correct result (0) with only the sentinel value.

In Example 6.4 where we count the percentage of passing test scores, we handle the sole sentinel value by performing some additional checking after the *while* loop. If only the sentinel value is entered, the count will be 0. We check for this case and if we find a count of 0, we skip reporting the percentage so that we avoid dividing by 0. We use similar code in Example 6.5, where we calculate the average test score. If we detect a count of 0, we also skip the calculation of the average to avoid dividing by 0 and simply report the class average as 0.

3. Does the program deal appropriately with invalid input?

If the program expects a range of values or certain discrete values, then it should notify the user when the input doesn't fit the expected values.

In Example 6.11, we implemented a menu for calculating the cost of cell phone service. The user could enter *s*, *a*, *u*, *n*, or *t* (or the corresponding capital letters) representing their desired service options. If the user enters a letter other than those expected values, we use the *default* clause of the *switch* statement to issue an error message, "*Unrecognized option.*"

In the next section, we explain how to validate that user input is within a range of values using a *do/while* loop.

6.8 Event-Controlled Loops Using *do/while*

Another form of loop that is especially useful for validating user input is the *do/while* loop. In the *do/while* loop, the loop condition is tested at the end of the loop (instead of at the beginning, as in the *while* loop). Thus the body of the *do/while* loop is executed at least once.

The syntax of the *do/while* loop is the following:

```
// initialize variables
do
{
   // body of loop
} while ( condition );
// process the results
```

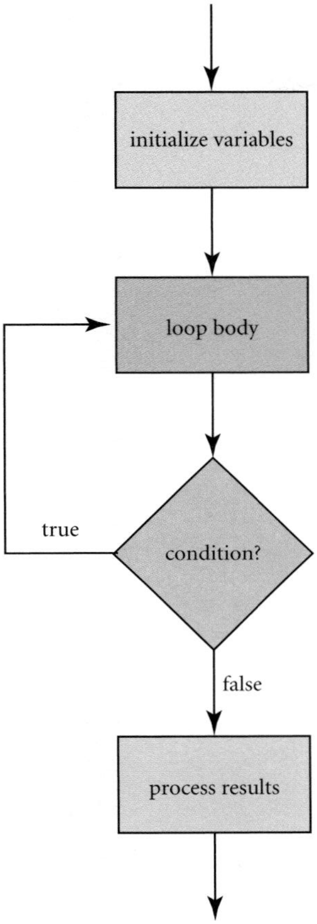

Figure 6.16
The Flow of Control of a *do/while* Statement

Figure 6.16 shows the flow of control of a *do/while* loop.

To use the *do/while* loop to validate user input, we insert the prompt for the input inside the body of the loop, then use the loop condition to test the value of the input. Like the *while* loop, the body of the loop will be reexecuted if the condition is *true*. Thus, we need to form the condition so that it's *true* when the user enters invalid values.

Example 6.13 implements a *do/while* loop (lines 14–18) that prompts the user for an integer between 1 and 10. Figure 6.17 shows the output of the program. If the user enters a number outside the valid range, we reprompt the user until the input is between 1 and 10. Thus the condition for the *do/while* loop (line 18) is

```
while ( number < 1 || number > 10 )
```

Figure 6.17
Validating Input

```
Enter a number between 1 and 10 > 20
Enter a number between 1 and 10 > -1
Enter a number between 1 and 10 > 0
Enter a number between 1 and 10 > 11
Enter a number between 1 and 10 > 5
Thank you!
```

```
 1 /* Validate input is between 1 and 10
 2    Anderson, Franceschi
 3 */
 4
 5 import java.util.Scanner;
 6
 7 public class ValidateInput
 8 {
 9   public static void main( String [ ] args )
10   {
11     int number;   // input value
12     Scanner scan = new Scanner( System.in );
13
14     do
15     {
16        System.out.print( "Enter a number between 1 and 10 > "  );
17        number = scan.nextInt( );
18     } while ( number < 1 || number > 10 );
19
20     System.out.println( "Thank you!" );
21   }
22 }
```

EXAMPLE 6.13 Validating User Input

For validating input, you may be tempted to use an *if* statement rather than a *do/while* loop. For example, to perform the same validation as Example 6.13, you may try this **incorrect** code:

```
System.out.print( "Enter a number between 1 and 10 > " );
number = scan.nextInt( );
```

```
if ( number < 1 || number > 10 ) // INCORRECT!
{
    System.out.print( "Enter a number between 1 and 10 > " );
    number = scan.nextInt( );
}
```

The problem with this approach is that the *if* statement will reprompt the user only once. If the user enters an invalid value a second time, the program will not catch it. A *do/while* loop, however, will continue to reprompt the user as many times as needed until the user enters a valid value.

COMMON ERROR TRAP

Do not use an *if* statement to validate input because it will catch invalid values entered the first time only. Use a *do/while* loop to reprompt the user until the user enters a valid value.

CODE IN ACTION

To see two step-by-step illustrations of *do/while* loops, look for the Flash movie in the Chapter 6 folder on the CD-ROM included with this book. Click on the link for Chapter 6 to start the movie.

6.9 Programming Activity 1: Using *while* Loops

In this activity, you will work with a sentinel-controlled *while* loop, performing this activity:

> Write a *while* loop to process the contents of a grocery cart and calculate the total price of the items. It is important to understand that, in this example, we do not know how many items are in the cart.

The framework will animate your code and display the current subtotal so that you can check the correctness of your code. The window will display the various *Item* objects moving down a conveyor belt toward a grocery bag. It will also display the unit price of the item and your current subtotal, as well as the correct subtotal.

For example, Figure 6.18 demonstrates the animation: We are currently scanning the first item, a milk carton, with a unit price of $2.00; thus, the correct subtotal is $2.00.

As the animation will show, *Item* objects could be milk, cereal, orange juice, or the divider bar. The number of *Item* objects in the cart is determined randomly; as you watch the animation, sometimes you will find that there are two items in the cart, sometimes six, sometimes three, and so forth. Scanning the divider bar signals the end of the items in the cart.

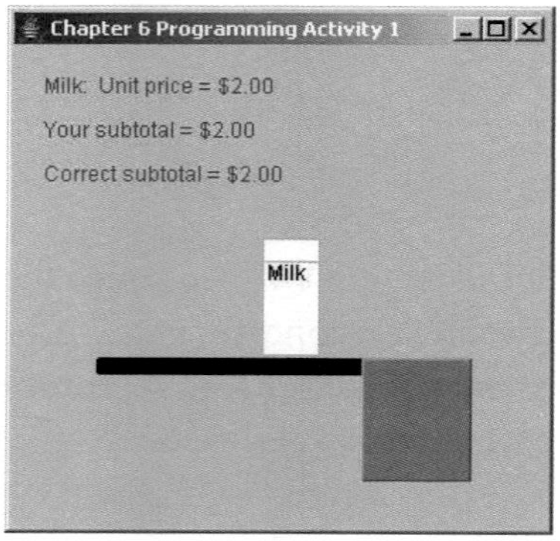

Figure 6.18
Animation of the *Cashier* Application

Task Instructions

Copy the files in the Chapter 6 Programming Activity 1 directory on the CD-ROM accompanying this book to a directory on your computer. Searching for five stars (*****) in the *Cashier.java* source code will show you where to add your code. You will add your code inside the *checkout* method of the *Cashier* class (the method header for the *checkout* method has already been coded for you). Example 6.14 shows a fragment of the *Cashier* class, where you will add your code:

```
public void checkout( )
{
 /* ***** Student writes the body of this method ***** */
 //
 //  Using a while loop, calculate the total price
 //  of the groceries.
 //
 // The getNext method (in this Cashier class) returns the
 // next item on the conveyor belt, which is an Item object
 // (we do not know which item and we do not know how many items
 // are in the cart - this is randomly generated).
 // getNext does not take any arguments. Its API is:
 //       Item getNext( )
 //
 // Right after you update the current subtotal,
 // you should call the animate method.
 // The animate method takes one parameter: a double,
 // which is your current subtotal.
 // For example, if the name of your variable representing
 // the current subtotal is total, your call to the animate
 // method should be:
 //    animate( total );
```

```
  //
  // The instance method getPrice of the Item class
  // returns the price of the Item object.
  // The method getPrice does not take any arguments.
  // Its API is:
  //        double getPrice( )
  //
  // The cart is empty when the getNext method returns
  // the divider Item.
  // You detect the divider Item because its price
  // is -0.99. So an Item with a price of -0.99
  // is the sentinel value for the loop.
  //
  // After you scan the divider, display the total
  // for the cart in a dialog box.

  // End of student code
}
```

EXAMPLE 6.14 The *checkout* Method in *Cashier.java*

- You can access items in the cart by calling the *getNext* method of the *Cashier* class, which has the following API:

  ```
  Item getNext( )
  ```

  The *getNext* method returns an *Item* object, which represents an *Item* in the cart. As you can see, the *getNext* method does not take any arguments. Since we call the method *getNext* from inside the *Cashier* class, we call the method without an object reference. For example, a call to *getNext* could look like the following:

  ```
  Item newItem;

  newItem = getNext( );
  ```

  The *getNext* method is already written and contains code to generate the animation; it is written in such a way that the first *Item* object on the conveyor belt may or may not be the divider. (If the first *Item* is the divider, the cart is empty.)

- After you get a new *Item*, you can "scan" the item to get its price by calling the *getPrice* method of the *Item* class. The *getPrice* method has this API:

  ```
  double getPrice( )
  ```

Thus, you would get an item, then get its price using code like the following:

```
Item newItem;
double price;

newItem = getNext( );
price = newItem.getPrice( );
```

- After adding the price of an item to your subtotal, call the *animate* method of the *Cashier* class. This method will display both your subtotal and the correct subtotal so that you can verify that your code is correct.

  The animate method has the following API:

  ```
  void animate( double subtotal )
  ```

  Thus, if your variable representing the current total is *total*, you would call the animate method using the following code:

  ```
  animate( total );
  ```

- We want to exit the loop when the next *Item* is the divider. You will know that the *Item* is the divider because its price will be –0.99 (negative 0.99); thus, scanning an *Item* whose price is –0.99 should be your condition to exit the *while* loop.
- After you scan the divider, display the total for the cart in a dialog box. Verify that your total matches the correct subtotal displayed.
- To test your code, compile and run the application from the *Cashier* class.

Troubleshooting

If your method implementation does not animate or animates incorrectly, check these items:

- Verify that you have correctly coded the priming read.
- Verify that you have correctly coded the condition for exiting the loop.
- Verify that you have correctly coded the body of the loop.

DISCUSSION QUESTIONS ?

1. What is the sentinel value of your *while* loop?
2. Explain the purpose of the priming read.

6.10 Count-Controlled Loops Using *for*

Before the loop begins, if you know the number of times the loop body should execute, you can use a *count-controlled loop*. The *for* loop is designed for count-controlled loops, that is, when the number of iterations is determined before the loop begins.

6.10.1 Basic Structure of *for* Loops

The *for* loop has this syntax:

```
for ( initialization; loop condition; loop update )
{
      // loop body
}
```

Notice that the initialization, loop condition, and loop update in the *for* loop header are separated by semicolons (not commas). Notice also that there is no semicolon after the closing parenthesis in the *for* loop header. A semicolon here would indicate an empty *for* loop body. Although some advanced programs might correctly write a *for* loop with an empty loop body, the programs we write in this book will have at least one statement in the *for* loop body.

COMMON ERROR TRAP

Use semicolons, rather than commas, to separate the statements in a *for* loop header.

The scope of any variable declared within the *for* loop header or body extends from the point of declaration to the end of the *for* loop body.

COMMON ERROR TRAP

Adding a semicolon after the closing parenthesis in the *for* loop header indicates an empty loop body and will likely cause a logic error.

The flow of control of the *for* loop is shown in Figure 6.19. When the *for* loop is encountered, the initialization statement is executed. Then the loop condition is evaluated. If the condition is true, the loop body is executed, then the loop update statement is executed, and the loop condition is reevaluated. Again, if the condition is true, the loop body is executed, followed by the loop update, then the reevaluation of the condition, and so on, until the condition is false.

The *for* loop is equivalent to the following *while* loop:

```
// initialization
while ( loop condition )
{
   // loop body
   // loop update
}
```

As you can see, *while* loops can be used for either event-driven or count-controlled loops. A *for* loop is especially useful for count-controlled loops,

Figure 6.19
Flow of Control of the *for* Loop

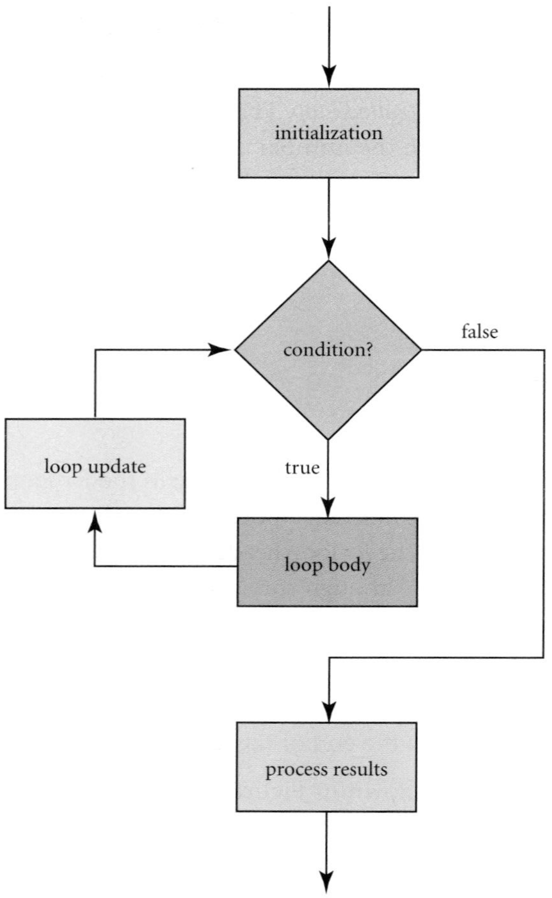

however. Because all the loop control is contained in the *for* loop header, you can easily see what condition will stop the loop and how the condition will be updated after each iteration.

6.10.2 Constructing *for* Loops

Typically, we use a **loop control variable** in a *for* loop; that control variable is usually used for counting. We set its initial value in the initialization statement, increment or decrement its value in the loop update statement, and check its value in the loop condition.

For example, if we want to find the sum of five integers, we know the loop body should execute five times—once for each integer. We set our loop control variable to 1 in the initialization statement, increment the loop control variable by 1 in the loop update statement, and check if its value is less than or equal to 5 in the loop condition. When the loop update statement increments the control variable's value to 6, we will have executed the loop body five times. The pseudocode for this program is the following:

```
set total to 0
for i = 1 to 5 by 1
{
  read integer
  add integer to total
}
print the total
```

With a *for* loop, we do not need to perform a priming read because the condition for exiting the loop is controlled by a counter, not by an input value.

Example 6.15 shows the *for* loop for calculating the sum of five integers.

```
/* Find the total of 5 numbers
   Anderson, Franceschi
*/

import java.util.Scanner;

public class Sum5Numbers
{
  public static void main( String [ ] args )
  {
    int total = 0;  // stores the sum of the 5 numbers
    int number;     // stores the current input

    Scanner scan = new Scanner( System.in );

    for ( int i = 1; i <= 5; i++ )
    {
      System.out.print( "Enter an integer > " );
      number = scan.nextInt( );

      total += number;  // add input to total
    }

    // process results by printing the total
```

```
25     System.out.println( "The total is " + total );
26   }
27 }
```

EXAMPLE 6.15 Finding the Sum of Five Numbers

In this example, which is a standard accumulation operation, the *for* loop initialization statement declares *i*, which will be our loop control variable. We start *i* at 1, and after each execution of the loop body, we increment *i* by 1 in the loop update statement. The loop condition checks if the value of *i* is less than or equal to 5; when *i* reaches 6, we have executed the loop body five times. Figure 6.20 shows the execution of this *for* loop.

Note that because we declare our loop counter variable *i* in the *for* loop header, that we cannot reference *i* after the *for* loop ends. Thus, this code would generate a compiler error, because *i* is out of scope on line 24:

```
16     for ( int i = 1; i <= 5; i++ )
17     {
18       System.out.print( "Enter an integer > " );
19       number = scan.nextInt( );
20
21       total += number;  // add input to total
22     }
23
24     System.out.println( "The total for " + ( i - 1 )
25                         + " number is " + total );
```

Defining a new variable using the same name as a variable already in scope is invalid and generates a compiler error. However, a variable name can be reused when a previously defined variable with the same name is no longer in scope. In the code above, the scope of the variable *i* defined in line 16 is

Figure 6.20
Finding the Sum of Five Integers

```
Enter an integer > 12
Enter an integer > 10
Enter an integer > 5
Enter an integer > 7
Enter an integer > 3
The total is 37
```

limited to the *for* loop on lines 16–22. We cannot define another variable named *i* in that *for* loop; however, as shown here, we could reuse the name *i* in a subsequent *for* loop (lines 24–29), because the first *i* is no longer in scope. In fact, programmers often reuse the variable name *i* for the counter variable in their *for* loops.

```
16     for ( int i = 1; i <= 5; i++ )
17     {
18       System.out.print( "Enter an integer > " );
19       number = scan.nextInt( );
20
21       total += number;  // add input to total
22     }
23
24     for ( int i = 1; i <= 10; i++ )
25     {
26       System.out.print( "Enter integer " + i + " > " );
27       number = scan.nextInt( );
28     }
```

If you do want to refer to the loop variable after the loop ends, you can define the variable before the *for* loop, as shown in the following code.

```
int i;
for ( i = 1; i <= 5; i++ )
{
  System.out.print( "Enter an integer > " );
  number = scan.nextInt( );

  total += number;  // add input to total
}

System.out.println( "The total for " + ( i - 1 )  // i is 6
                    + " numbers is " + total );
```

We can also increment the loop control variable by values other than 1. Example 6.16 shows a *for* loop that increments the control variable by 2 to print the even numbers from 0 to 20.

The pseudocode for this program is the following:

```
set output to an empty String
for i = 0 to 20 by 2
{
  append i and a space to the output String
}
print the output String
```

We start with an empty *String* variable, *toPrint*, and with each iteration of the loop we append the next even number and a space. When the loop completes, we output *toPrint*, which prints all numbers on one line, as shown in Figure 6.21.

```
/* Print the even numbers from zero to twenty
   Anderson, Franceschi
*/

public class PrintEven
{
  public static void main( String [ ] args )
  {
    String toPrint = "";  // initialize output String

    for ( int i = 0; i <= 20; i += 2 )
    {
       toPrint += i + " "; // append current number and a space
    }

    System.out.println( toPrint ); // print results
  }
}
```

EXAMPLE 6.16 Printing Even Numbers

Figure 6.21
Printing Even Numbers from 0 to 20

```
0 2 4 6 8 10 12 14 16 18 20
```

In this example, we initialize the loop control variable to 0, then increment *i* by 2 in the loop update statement (`i += 2`) to skip the odd numbers. Notice that we used the value of the loop control variable *i* inside the loop. The loop control variable can perform double duty such as this because the loop control variable is available to our code in the loop body.

The loop control variable also can be used in our prompt to the user. For example, in Example 6.15, we could have prompted the user for each integer using this statement:

```
System.out.print( "Enter integer " + i  + " > " );
```

```
Enter integer 1 > 23
Enter integer 2 > 12
Enter integer 3 > 10
Enter integer 4 > 11
Enter integer 5 > 15
The total is 71
```

Figure 6.22
Adding the Loop Control Variable to the Prompt

Then the user's prompt would look like that shown in Figure 6.22.

CODE IN ACTION

To see a step-by-step illustration of a *for* loop, look for the Flash movie in the Chapter 6 folder on the CD-ROM included with this book. Click on the link for Chapter 6 to start the movie.

We can also decrement the loop control variable. Example 6.17 shows an application that reads a sentence entered by the user and prints the sentence backward.

The pseudocode for this program is the following:

```
set backwards to an empty String
read a sentence

for i = ( length of sentence – 1 ) to 0 by –1
{
  get character at position i in sentence
  append character to backwards
}
print backwards
```

To print a sentence backward, we treat the sentence, a *String*, like a stream of characters; each iteration of the loop extracts and processes one character from the *String*, using the *charAt* method of the *String* class. Line 10 declares two *Strings*: *original*, to hold the sentence the user enters, and *backwards* (initialized as an empty *String*) to hold the reverse of the user's sentence. Lines

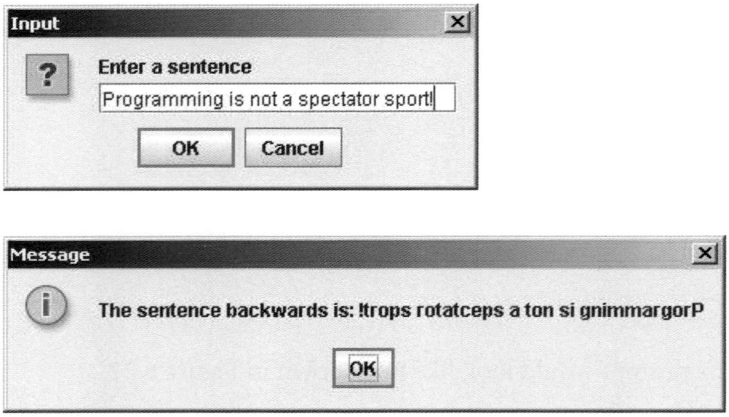

Figure 6.23
Printing a Sentence Backward

12–13 prompt the user for a sentence. Lines 15 through 18 make up the *for* loop, whose purpose is to copy the original sentence backward into the *String backwards.* We do this by starting the copying at the last character in the original *String* and moving backward in the *String* one character at a time until we have copied the first character in *original.* Thus, we initialize our loop variable to the position of the last character in *original* (`original.length( ) – 1`) and extract one character at a time, appending it to *backwards.* The loop update statement (`i--`) moves the loop variable backward by one position, and our loop condition (`i >= 0`) checks whether we have reached the beginning of the *String original.* Figure 6.23 shows the execution of the program with the user entering the sentence, "*Programming is not a spectator sport!*"

```
1 /* Print a sentence backward
2    Anderson, Franceschi
3 */
4 import javax.swing.JOptionPane;
5
6 public class Backwards
7 {
8   public static void main( String [ ] args )
9   {
10    String original, backwards = "";
11
12    original = JOptionPane.showInputDialog( null,
13                              "Enter a sentence" );
14
15    for ( int i = original.length( ) - 1; i >= 0; i-- )
16    {
17       backwards += original.charAt( i );
```

```
    }

    JOptionPane.showMessageDialog( null,
                "The sentence backwards is: " + backwards );
  }
}
```

EXAMPLE 6.17 Printing a Sentence Backward

We can display some interesting graphics using *for* loops. The applet in Example 6.18 draws the bull's-eye target shown in Figure 6.24. To make the bull's-eye target, we draw 10 concentric circles (circles that have the same center point), beginning with the largest circle and successively drawing a smaller circle on top of the circles already drawn. Thus, the bull's-eye target circles have the same center point, but different diameters. The pseudocode for this program is

```
for diameter = 200 to 20 by –20
{
   instantiate a circle
   draw the circle
   if color is black
      set color to red
   else
      set color to black
}
```

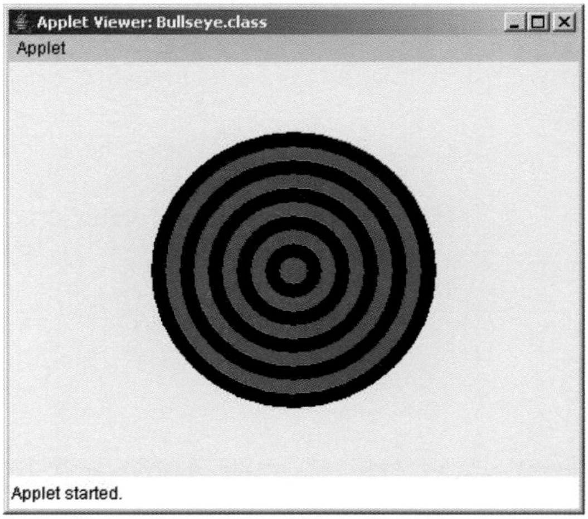

Figure 6.24
Drawing a Bull's-Eye Target

REFERENCE POINT

The API for the *Circle* class is given in Section 6.4.5

We can again use the *Circle* class introduced in Section 6.4.5, when we rolled a ball.

Translating the pseudocode into Java, we get the code shown in Example 6.18.

```
/* Bull's-eye target
   Anderson, Franceschi
*/

import javax.swing.JApplet;
import java.awt.Color;
import java.awt.Graphics;

public class Bullseye extends JApplet
{
   // center of bullseye
   private int centerX = 200, centerY = 150;
   // color of first circle
   private Color toggleColor = Color.BLACK;
   // each circle will be a Circle object
   private Circle circle;

   public void paint( Graphics g )
   {
     super.paint( g );

     for ( int diameter = 200; diameter >= 20; diameter -= 20 )
     {
       // instantiate circle with current diameter and color
       circle = new Circle( centerX - diameter / 2,
                            centerY - diameter / 2,
                            diameter, toggleColor );

       circle.draw( g ); // draw the circle

       if ( toggleColor.equals( Color.BLACK ) )
         toggleColor = Color.RED;   // if black, change to red
       else
         toggleColor = Color.BLACK; // if red, change to black
     }
   }
}
```

EXAMPLE 6.18 Drawing a Bull's-Eye Target

Our *for* loop initialization statement in line 22 sets up the diameter of the largest circle as 200 pixels and the loop update statement decreases the diameter of each circle by 20 pixels. The smallest circle we want to draw should have a diameter of 20 pixels, so we set the loop condition to check that the diameter is greater than or equal to 20. We need to start with the largest circle rather than the smallest circle so that new circles we draw don't hide the previously drawn circles.

Drawing the bull's-eye target circles illustrates two common programming techniques: conversion between units and a toggle variable.

We need to convert between units because the *Circle* class constructor takes as its arguments the upper-left (*x*, *y*) coordinate and the width and height of the circle's bounding rectangle (this is consistent with the *fillOval* method of the *Graphics* class). However, all our circles have the same center point, but not the same upper-left *x* and *y* coordinates. Given the diameter and the center point of the circle, however, we can calculate the (*x*, *y*) coordinate of the upper-left corner. Figure 6.25 shows how we make the conversion.

The difference between the center point and the upper-left corner of the bounding rectangle is the radius of the circle, which is half of the diameter

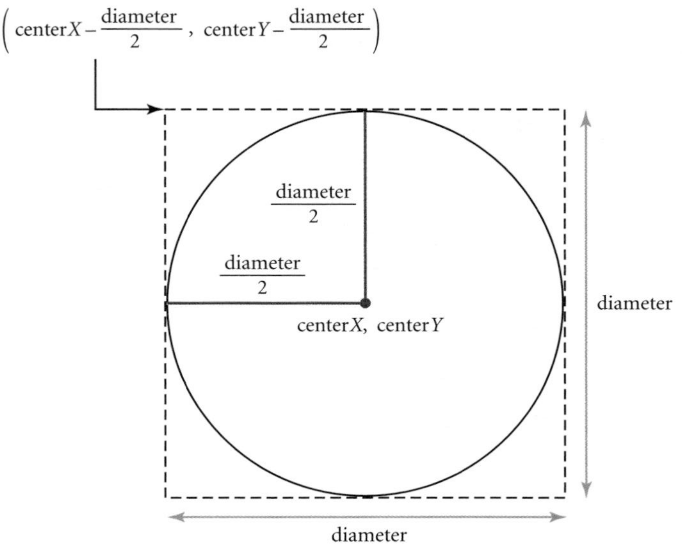

Figure 6.25
Converting Circle Coordinates

(`diameter / 2`). So, the upper-left *x* value is the *x* value of the center point minus half the diameter (`centerX – diameter / 2`). Similarly, the upper-left *y* value is the *y* value of the center point minus half the diameter (`centerY – diameter / 2`).

Thus, we instantiate each circle using the following statement:

```
circle = new Circle( centerX - diameter / 2,
                     centerY - diameter / 2,
                     diameter, toggleColor );
```

SOFTWARE ENGINEERING TIP

Use a toggle variable when you need to alternate between two values.

To alternate between red and black circles, we use a **toggle variable**, which is a variable whose value alternates between two values. We use a *Color* object for our toggle variable, *toggleColor*, and initialize it to *Color.BLACK*. After drawing each circle, we switch the color (lines 31–34). If the current color is black, we set it to red; otherwise, the color must be red, so we set the color to black.

Skill Practice
with these end-of-chapter questions

6.14.1 Multiple Choice Exercises

Questions 2, 3, 4

6.14.2 Reading and Understanding Code

Questions 11, 12, 13, 14, 15, 16, 17, 18, 19

6.14.3 Fill In the Code

Questions 27, 29

6.14.5 Identifying Errors in Code

Questions 32, 33, 35

6.14.5 Debugging Area

Questions 38, 39, 40, 41, 42

6.14.6 Write a Short Program

Questions 43, 46, 47, 48, 49, 50, 51, 52

6.10.3 Testing Techniques for *for* Loops

One of the most important tests for *for* loops is that the starting and ending values of the loop variable are set correctly. For example, to execute a *for* loop five times, we could set the initial value of the loop variable to 0 and use the condition (`i < 5`), or we could set the initial value of the loop variable to 1 and use the condition (`i <= 5`). Either of these *for* loop headers will cause the loop to execute five times.

```
for ( int i = 0; i < 5; i++ ) // executes 5 times
```

or

```
for ( int i = 1; i <= 5; i++ ) // executes 5 times
```

However, the following *for* loop header is incorrect; the loop will execute only four times.

```
for ( int i = 1; i < 5; i++ ) // INCORRECT! executes only 4 times
```

Thus to test the *for* loop in Example 6.15 that prompts for five integers, we need to verify that the program outputs exactly five prompts. To test that we are prompting the user five times, we can enter the integers 1, 2, 3, 4, and 5 at the prompts. Another option, shown in Figure 6.26, is to append a number to the prompt, which does double duty. Besides keeping the user informed of the number of integers entered so far, it also helps to verify that we have the correct number of prompts.

Like *while* loops, the body of a *for* loop may not be executed at all. If the loop condition is *false* the first time it is tested, the body of the *for* loop is skipped. Thus, when testing, we want to simulate input that would cause the loop condition to be *false* when the *for* loop statement is first encountered. For example, in the *Backwards* class in Example 6.17, we need to test

```
Enter integer 1 > 23
Enter integer 2 > 12
Enter integer 3 > 10
Enter integer 4 > 11
Enter integer 5 > 15
The total is 71
```

Figure 6.26
Counting Five Prompts

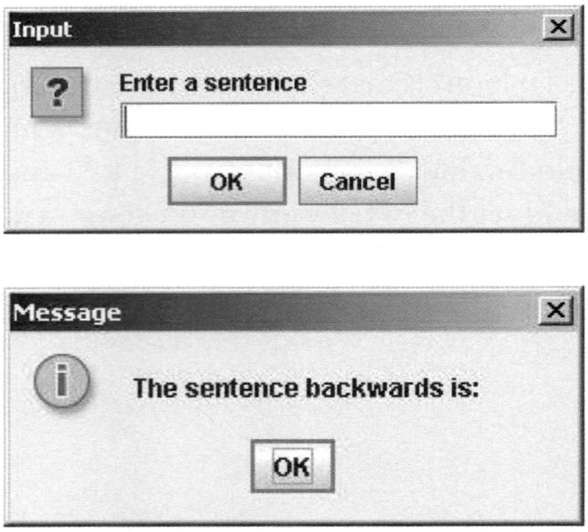

Figure 6.27
The Backwards Class with an Empty Sentence

the *for* loop with an empty sentence. In other words, when the prompt appears to enter a sentence, we simply press the *OK* button. If you try this, you will find that the application still works, as Figure 6.27 shows.

The program works correctly with an empty sentence because the *for* loop initialization statement is

```
int i = original.length( ) – 1;
```

Because the length of an empty *String* is 0, this statement sets *i* to –1. The loop condition (`i >= 0`) is *false*, so the loop body is never executed. The flow of control skips to the statement following the loop,

```
JOptionPane.showMessageDialog( null,
          "The sentence backwards is: " + backwards );
```

which prints an empty *String*. Although it would be more user-friendly to check whether the sentence is empty and print a message to that effect, the program does indeed do exactly nothing, gracefully.

6.11 Nested Loops

Loops can be nested inside other loops; that is, the body of one loop can contain another loop. For example, a *while* loop can be nested inside another *while* loop or a *for* loop can be nested inside another *for* loop. In fact, the nested loops do not need to be the same loop type; that is, a *for* loop can be nested inside a *while* loop and a *while* loop can be nested inside a *for* loop.

Nested loops may be useful if you are performing multiple operations, each of which has its own count or sentinel value. For example, we may be interested in processing data in a statistics table containing rows and columns. In order to process all the data, we could loop from the first row to the last row; inside that loop, we would process each row by looping from the first column to the last column of that row. A statistics table can be stored in what is called a two-dimensional array, a subject we discuss in Chapter 9.

REFERENCE POINT

Nested *for* loops are useful for processing data stored in two-dimensional arrays, which are discussed in Chapter 9. Simple *for* loops are useful to process data stored in standard arrays; standard arrays are discussed in Chapter 8.

Going back to Jane, our grocery cashier, her workday can be modeled using nested loops. In Programming Activity 1, we wrote the code for our cashier to calculate the total cost of the contents of one customer's grocery cart. But cashiers check out multiple customers, one after another. While the line of people in front of the cashier is not empty, she will help the next customer. For each customer, she will set the total order to $0.00 and start scanning items and add the prices to the total. While the current customer still has items in the cart, Jane will scan the next item. When Jane finishes processing a customer's cart, she will check to see if there is a customer waiting in line. If there is one, she will set the total to $0.00 and start scanning the next customer's items.

Thus, the cashier's job can be described using a *while* loop nested inside another *while* loop. The pseudocode for these nested loops is shown here:

```
look for a customer
while there is a customer in line
{
  set total to $0.00
  reach for first item
  while item is not the divider bar
  {
      add price to total
      reach for next item
  }
  // if we get here, the item is the divider bar
  output the total price

  look for another customer
}
```

The important point to understand with nested loops is that the inner (or nested) loop executes completely (executes all its iterations) for each single iteration of the outer loop.

Let's look at a simple example that uses nested *for* loops. Suppose we want to print five rows of numbers as shown here:

```
1
1 2
1 2 3
1 2 3 4
1 2 3 4 5
```

We can see a pattern here. In the first line, we print one number; in the second line, we print two numbers, and so on. In other words, the quantity of numbers we print and the line number are the same. The pseudocode for this pattern is the following:

```
for line = 1 to 5 by 1
{
  for number = 1 to line by 1
  {
   print number and a space
  }
  print a new line
}
```

Translating this pseudocode into nested *for* loops, we get the code shown in Example 6.19.

```
/*  Printing numbers using nested for loops
    Anderson, Franceschi
*/

public class NestedForLoops
{
  public static void main( String [ ] args )
  {
     // outer for loop prints 5 lines
     for ( int line = 1; line <= 5; line++ )
     {
       // inner for loop prints one line
       for ( int number = 1; number <= line; number++ )
```

```
14          {
15            // print the number and a space
16            System.out.print( number + " " );
17          }
18
19          System.out.println( );     // print a newline
20        }
21    }
22 }
```

EXAMPLE 6.19 Nested *for* Loops

Notice that the inner *for* loop (lines 12–17) uses the value of *line*, which is set by the outer *for* loop (lines 9–20). Thus, for the first iteration of the outer loop, *line* equals 1, so the inner loop executes once, printing the number 1 and a space. Then we print a newline character because line 19 is part of the outer *for* loop. The outer loop then sets the value of *line* to 2, and the inner loop starts again at 1 and executes two times (until *number* equals the line number in the outer loop). Then we again print a newline. This operation continues until the *line* exceeds 5, when the outer loop terminates. The output from Example 6.19 is shown in Figure 6.28.

Note that we needed to use different names for our *for* loop control variables. The loop control variable *line* is in scope from lines 10 to 20, which includes the inner *for* loop.

Let's look at another example of a nested loop. We'll let the user enter positive integers, with a 0 being the sentinel value. For each number, we'll find all its factors; that is, we will find all the integers that are evenly divisible into the number, except 1 and the number itself.

If a number is evenly divisible by another, the remainder after division will be 0. The modulus operator (%) will be useful here, because it calculates the remainder after integer division. Thus, to find all the factors of a number,

```
1
1 2
1 2 3
1 2 3 4
1 2 3 4 5
```

Figure 6.28
Output from Example 6.19

we can test all integers from 1 up to the number to see if the remainder after division is 0. But let's think about whether that's a good approach. The number 1 will be a factor for every number, because every number is evenly divisible by 1. So we can test integers beginning at 2. Then, because 2 is the smallest factor, there's no need to test integers higher than *number / 2*. Thus, our range of integers to test will be from 2 to *number / 2*.

For this example, we'll use a *for* loop nested inside a *while* loop. The pseudocode for this example is

```
read first number  // priming read
while number is not 0
{
  print "The factors for number are "
  for factor = 2 to ( number / 2 ) by 1
  {
   if number % factor is 0
     print factor and a space
  }
  print a new line

  read next number  // update read
}
```

But what happens if we don't find any factors for a number? In that case, the number is a prime number. We can detect this condition by using a *boolean* variable called a **flag**. We set the flag to *false* before starting the *for* loop that checks for factors. Inside the *for* loop, we set the flag to *true* when we find a factor. In other words, we signal (or flag) the fact that we found a factor. Then after the *for* loop terminates, we check the value of the flag. If it is still *false*, we did not find any factors and the number is prime. Our pseudocode for this program now becomes

```
read first number  // priming read
while number is not 0
{
  print "The factors for number are "
  set flag to false
```

```
    for factor = 2  to ( number / 2 ) by 1
    {
      if number % factor is 0
      {
        print factor and a space
        set flag to true
      }
    }

    if  flag is false
      print "number is prime"

    print a new line

    read next number   // update read
}
```

Since we want to read positive numbers only, the lines "read first number" and "read next number" in the preceding pseudocode will actually be more complex than a simple statement. Indeed, we will prompt the user to enter a positive number until the user does so. In order to do that, we will use a *do/while* loop to validate the input from the user. Therefore, inside the *while* loop, we nest not only a *for* loop, but also a *do/while* loop. In the interest of keeping the pseudocode simple, we did not show that *do/while* loop. However, it is included in the code in Example 6.20 at lines 17–23 and 45–51.

Translating this pseudocode into Java, we get the code shown in Example 6.20; the output of a sample run of the program is shown in Figure 6.29.

```
1 /* Factors of integers
2    with checks for primes
3    Anderson, Franceschi
4 */
5 import java.util.Scanner;
6
7 public class Factors
8 {
9   public static void main( String [ ] args )
10  {
```

```
    int number;           // positive integer entered by user
    final int SENTINEL = 0;
    boolean factorsFound; // flag signals whether factors are found

    Scanner scan = new Scanner( System.in );

    // priming read
    do
    {
      System.out.print( "Enter a positive integer "
                         + "or 0 to exit > " );
      number = scan.nextInt( );
    } while ( number < 0 );

    while ( number != SENTINEL )
    {
      System.out.print( "Factors of " + number + ":  " );
      factorsFound = false;  // reset flag to no factors

      for ( int factor = 2; factor <= number / 2; factor++ )
      {
        if ( number % factor == 0 )
        {
           System.out.print( factor + " " );
           factorsFound = true;
        }
      } // end of for loop

      if ( ! factorsFound )
          System.out.print( "none, " + number + " is prime" );

      System.out.println( );  // print a newline
      System.out.println( );  // print a second newline

      // read next number
      do
      {
         System.out.print( "Enter a positive integer "
                            +  "or 0 to exit > " );
         number = scan.nextInt( );
      } while ( number < 0 );
    } // end of while loop
  }
}
```

EXAMPLE 6.20 Finding Factors

```
Enter a positive integer or 0 to exit > 100
Factors of 100:  2 4 5 10 20 25 50

Enter a positive integer or 0 to exit > 25
Factors of 25:  5

Enter a positive integer or 0 to exit > 21
Factors of 21:  3 7

Enter a positive integer or 0 to exit > 13
Factors of 13:  none, 13 is prime

Enter a positive integer or 0 to exit > 0
```

Figure 6.29
Output of Finding Factors

6.12 Programming Activity 2: Using *for* Loops

In this activity, you will write a *for* loop:

> For this Programming Activity, we will again calculate the total cost of the items in a grocery cart. This time, however, we will write the program for the Express Lane. In this lane, the customer is allowed up to 10 items. The user will be asked for the number of items in the grocery cart. Your job is to write a *for* loop to calculate the total cost of the items in the cart.

Like Programming Activity 1, the framework will animate your *for* loop, displaying the items in the cart moving down a conveyor belt toward a cashier station (a grocery bag). It will also display the unit price of the item, the correct subtotal, and your current subtotal. By comparing the correct subtotal to your subtotal, you will be able to check whether your code is calculating the correct value.

Figure 6.30 demonstrates the animation. The cart contains five items. The third item, a carton of orange juice, is being scanned at a unit price of $3.00, bringing the correct subtotal for the cart to $8.50.

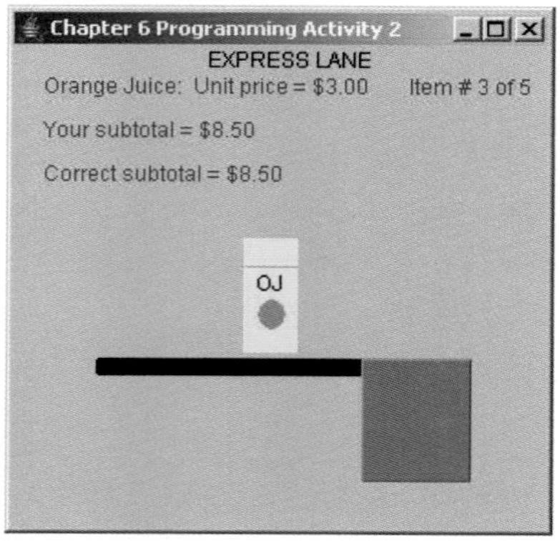

Figure 6.30
Sample Animation

Instructions

Copy the files in the Chapter 6 Programming Activity 2 directory on the CD-ROM accompanying this book to a directory on your computer. Searching for five stars (*****) in the *Cashier.java* code will show you where to add your code. You will add your code inside the *checkout* method of the *Cashier* class (the method header for the *checkout* method has already been coded for you). Example 6.21 shows a fragment of the *Cashier* class, where you will add your code:

```
public void checkout( int numberOfItems )
{
   /* ***** Student writes the body of this method ***** */
   //
   //  The parameter of this method, numberOfItems,
   //  represents the number of items in the cart. The
   //  user will be prompted for this number.
   //
   //  Using a for loop, calculate the total price
   //  of the groceries for the cart.
   //
   //  The getNext method (in this Cashier class) returns the next
   //  item in the cart, which is an Item object (we do not
   //  know which item will be returned; this is randomly generated).
   //  getNext does not take any arguments. Its API is
   //      Item getNext( )
   //
```

```
//  As the last statement of the body of your for loop,
//  you should call the animate method.
//  The animate method takes one parameter:  a double,
//  which is your current subtotal.
//  For example, if the name of your variable representing
//  the current subtotal is total, your call to the animate
//  method should be:
//      animate( total );
//
//  The getPrice method of the Item class
//  returns the price of the Item object as a double.
//  The getPrice method does not take any arguments. Its API is
//     double getPrice( )
//
//  After you have processed all the items, display the total
//  for the cart in a dialog box.



 //
 //  End of student code
 //
}
```

EXAMPLE 6.21 The *checkout* Method in the *Cashier* Class

To write the body of your *for* loop, you can use the following methods:

- You can access items in the cart using the *getNext* method of the *Cashier* class, which has the following API:

  ```
  Item getNext( )
  ```

  The *getNext* method returns an *Item* object, which represents an *Item* in the cart. As you can see, the *getNext* method does not take any arguments. Since we call the method *getNext* from inside the *Cashier* class, we can simply call the method without an object reference. For example, a call to *getNext* could look like the following:

  ```
  Item newItem;

  newItem = getNext( );
  ```

- After you get a new *Item*, you can "scan" the item to get its price by calling the *getPrice* method of the *Item* class. The *getPrice* method has this API:

  ```
  double getPrice( )
  ```

  Thus, you would get the next item, then get its price using code like the following:

  ```
  Item newItem;
  double price;

  newItem = getNext( );
  price = newItem.getPrice( );
  ```

When you have finished writing the code for the *checkout* method, compile and run the application from the *Cashier* class. When the application finishes executing, verify that your code is correct by:

- checking that your subtotal matches the correct subtotal displayed
- checking that you have processed all the items in the cart by verifying that the current item number matches the total number of items. For example, if the cart has five items, check that the message in the upper-right corner of the screen displays: `Item # 5 of 5`.

Troubleshooting

If your method implementation does not animate or animates incorrectly, check these items:

- Verify that you have correctly coded the header of your *for* loop.
- Verify that you have correctly coded the body of the loop.

DISCUSSION QUESTIONS ?

1. Explain why a *for* loop is appropriate for this activity.
2. Explain how you set up your *for* loop, that is, what initialization statement did you use, what was your condition, and what was the loop update statement?

6.13 Summary

- Looping repeats a set of operations for each input item while a condition is *true.*
- The *while* loop is especially useful for event-controlled looping. The *while* loop executes a set of operations in the loop body as long as the loop condition is *true.* Each execution of the loop body is an iteration of the loop.
- If the loop condition evaluates to *false* the first time it is evaluated, the body of the *while* loop is never executed.
- If the loop condition never evaluates to *false*, the result is an infinite loop.
- In event-controlled looping, processing of items continues until the end of input is signaled either by a sentinel value or by reaching the end of the file.
- A sentinel value is a special input value that signals the end of the items to be processed. With a sentinel value, we perform a priming read before the *while* loop. The body of the loop processes the input, then performs an update read of the next data item.
- When reading data from an input file, we can test whether we have reached the end of the file by calling a *hasNext* method of the *Scanner* class.
- In the accumulation programming technique, we initialize a total variable to 0 before starting the loop. In the loop body, we add each input value to the total. When the loop completes, the current total is the total for all processed input values.
- In the counting programming technique, we initialize a count variable to 0 before starting the loop. In the loop body, we increment the count variable for each input value that meets our criteria. When the loop completes, the count variable contains the number of items that met our criteria.
- To find an average, we combine accumulation and counting. We add input values to the total and increment the count. When the

CHAPTER SUMMARY

loop completes, we calculate the average by dividing the total by the count. Before computing the average, however, we should verify that the divisor (that is, the count) is not 0.

- To find the maximum or minimum values in a set of input, we assign the first input to a running maximum or minimum. In the loop body, we compare each input value to our running maximum or minimum. If the input value is less than the running minimum, we assign the input value to the running minimum. Similarly, if the input value is greater than the running maximum, we assign the input value to the running maximum. When the loop completes, the running value is the maximum or minimum value of all the input values.
- To animate an image, the loop body draws the image, pauses for a short interval, erases the image, and changes the starting *x* or *y* values to the next location for drawing the image.
- To avoid generating exceptions when the user types characters other than the data type expected, use the *hasNext* methods of the *Scanner* class.
- To construct a loop condition, construct the inverse of the loop termination condition.
- When testing a program that contains a loop, test that the program produces correct results by inputting values and comparing the results with manual calculations. Also test that the results are correct if the *while* loop body never executes. Finally, test the results with input that is invalid.
- The *do/while* loop checks the loop condition after executing the loop body. Thus, the body of a *do/while* loop always executes at least once. This type of loop is useful for validating input.
- The *for* loop is useful for count-controlled loops, that is, loops for which the number of iterations is known when the loop begins.
- When the *for* loop is encountered, the initialization statement is executed. Then the loop condition is evaluated. If the condition is *true,* the loop body is executed. The loop update statement is then executed and the loop condition is reevaluated. Again, if the condition is *true,* the loop body is executed, followed by the loop update,

then the reevaluation of the condition, and so on, until the condition evaluates to *false*.

- Typically, we use a loop counting variable in a *for* loop. We set its initial value in the initialization statement, increment or decrement its value in the loop update statement, and check its value in the loop condition.
- The loop update statement can increment or decrement the loop variable by any value.
- In a *for* loop, it is important to test that the starting and ending values of the loop variable are correct. Also test with input for which the *for* loop body does not execute at all.

6.14 Exercises, Problems, and Projects

6.14.1 Multiple Choice Exercises

1. How do you discover that you have an infinite loop in your code?
   - ❑ The code does not compile.
   - ❑ The code compiles and runs but gives the wrong result.
   - ❑ The code runs forever.
   - ❑ The code compiles, but there is a runtime error.
2. If you want to execute a loop body at least once, what type of loop would you use?
   - ❑ *for* loop
   - ❑ *while* loop
   - ❑ *do/while* loop
   - ❑ none of the above
3. What best describes a *for* loop?
   - ❑ It is a count-controlled loop.
   - ❑ It is an event-controlled loop.
   - ❑ It is a sentinel-controlled loop.
4. You can simulate a *for* loop with a *while* loop.
   - ❑ true
   - ❑ false

6.14.2 Reading and Understanding Code

5. What is the output of this code sequence? (The user successively enters 3, 5, and –1)

```
System.out.print( "Enter an int > " );
int i = scan.nextInt( );
while ( i != -1 )
{
   System.out.println( "Hello" );

   System.out.print( "Enter an int > " );
   i = scan.nextInt( );
}
```

6. What is the output of this code sequence? (The user successively enters 3, 5, and –1.)

```
int i = 0;
while ( i != -1 )
{
    System.out.println( "Hello" );
    System.out.print( "Enter an int > " );
    i = scan.nextInt( );
}
```

7. What is the output of this code sequence? (The user successively enters 3, 5, and –1.)

```
System.out.print( "Enter an int > " );
int i = scan.nextInt( );
while ( i != -1 )
{
   System.out.print( "Enter an int > " );
   i = scan.nextInt( );

   System.out.println( "Hello" );
}
```

8. What are the values of *i* and *sum* after this code sequence is executed?

```
int sum  = 0;
int i = 17;
while ( i % 10 != 0 )
{
  sum += i;
  i++;
}
```

9. What are the values of *i* and *product* after this code sequence is executed?

```
int i = 6;
int product = 1;
do
{
    product *= i;
    i++;
} while ( i < 9 );
```

10. What are the values of *i* and *product* after this code sequence is executed?

```
int i = 6;
int product = 1;
do
{
    product *= i;
    i++;
} while ( product < 9 );
```

11. What is the output of this code sequence?

```
for ( int i = 0; i < 3; i++ )
   System.out.println( "Hello" );
System.out.println( "Done" );
```

12. What is the output of this code sequence?

```
for ( int i = 0; i <= 2; i++ )
   System.out.println( "Hello" );
System.out.println( "Done" );
```

13. What is the value of *i* after this code sequence is executed?

```
int i = 0;
for ( i = 0; i <= 2; i++ )
   System.out.println( "Hello" );
```

14. What is the value of *i* after this code sequence is executed?

```
int i = 0;
for ( i = 0; i < 2034; i++ )
   System.out.println( "Hello" );
```

15. What are the values of *i* and *sum* after this code sequence is executed?

```
int i = 0;
int sum  = 0;
for ( i = 0; i < 5; i++ )
{
   sum += i;
}
```

16. What are the values of *i* and *sum* after this code sequence is executed?

```
int i = 0;
int sum  = 0;
for ( i = 0; i < 40; i++ )
{
   if ( i % 10 == 0 )
       sum += i;
}
```

17. What is the value of *sum* after this code sequence is executed?

```
int sum  = 0;
for ( int i = 1; i < 10; i++ )
{
    i++;
    sum += i;
}
```

18. What is the value of *sum* after this code sequence is executed?

```
int sum  = 0;
for ( int i = 10; i > 5; i-- )
{
    sum += i;
}
```

19. What is printed when this code sequence is executed?

```
for ( int i = 0; i < 5; i++ )
{
   System.out.println( Math.max( i, 3 ) );
}
```

20. What are the values of *i* and *sum* after this code sequence is executed?

```
int i = 0;
int sum  = 0;
while ( i != 7 )
{
   sum += i;
   i++;
}
```

6.14.3 Fill In the Code

21. This *while* loop generates random integers between 3 and 7 until a 5 is generated and prints them all out, excluding 5.

```
Random random = new Random( );
int i =  random.nextInt( 5 ) + 3;
```

22. This *while* loop takes an integer input from the user, then prompts for additional integers and prints all integers that are greater than or equal to the original input until the user enters 20, which is not printed.

```
System.out.print( "Enter a starting integer > " );

int start = scan.nextInt( );

// your code goes here
```

23. This *while* loop takes integer values as input from the user and finds the sum of those integers until the user types in the value –1 (which is not added).

```
System.out.print( "Enter an integer value, "
                  + "enter -1 to stop > " );
int value = scan.nextInt( );
// your code goes here
```

24. This loop calculates the sum of the first four positive multiples of 7 using a *while* loop (the sum will be equal to 7 + 14 + 21 + 28 = 70)

```
int sum = 0;
int countMultiplesOf7 = 0;
int count = 1;
// your code goes here
```

25. This loop takes words as input from the user and concatenates them until the user types in the word "end" (which is not concatenated). The code then outputs the concatenated *String.*

```
String sentence = "";
String word;
// your code goes here

while ( ! word.equals( "end" ) )
{
    // and your code goes here

}
System.out.println( "The sentence is " + sentence );
```

26. This loop reads integers from a file (already associated with the *Scanner* object reference *scan*) and computes the sum. We don't know how many integers are in the file.

```
int sum = 0;
// your code goes here
```

27. Here is a *while* loop; write the equivalent *for* loop.

```
int i = 0;
while ( i < 5 )
{
   System.out.println( "Hi there" );
   i++;
}

// your code goes here
```

28. This loop reads integers from the user until the user enters either 0 or 100. Then it prints the sum of the numbers entered (excluding the 0 or 100).

```
// your code goes here
```

29. This loop calculates the sum of the integers from 1 to 5 using a *for* loop.

```
int sum = 0;
// your code goes here
```

6.14.4 Identifying Errors in Code

30. Where is the problem with this code sequence (although this code sequence does compile)?

```
int i = 0;
while ( i < 3 )
   System.out.println( "Hello" );
```

31. Where is the error in this code sequence that is supposed to read and echo integers until the user enters –1?

```
int num;
while ( num != -1 )
{
   System.out.print( "Enter an integer > " );
   num = scan.nextInt( );
   System.out.println( num );
}
```

32. The following code sequence intends to print *Hello* three times; however, it does not. Where is the problem in this code sequence?

```
for ( int i = 0; i < 3; i++ );
   System.out.println( "Hello" );
```

33. Where is the error in this code sequence, which is intended to print *Hello* 10 times?

```
for ( int i = 10; i > 0; i++ )
   System.out.println( "Hello" );
```

34. Where is the problem with this code sequence? The code is intended to generate random numbers between 1 and 10 until the number is either a 7 or a 5.

```
Random random = new Random( );
int number  =  1 + random.nextInt( 10 );
while ( number != 5 || number != 7 )
{
    number  =  1 + random.nextInt( 10 );
}
System.out.println( "The number is " + number );
```

35. Where is the error with this code sequence?

```
int sum = 0;
for ( int i = 1; i < 6; i++ )
     sum += i;

System.out.println( "The value of i is " + i );
```

6.14.5 Debugging Area—Using Messages from the Java Compiler and Java JVM

36. You coded the following in the class *Test.java*:

```
int i = 0;
int sum = 0;
do
{
     sum += i;
     i++;
} while ( i < 3 )    // line 10
```

At compile time, you get the following error:

```
Test.java:10: ';' expected
while( i < 3 )   // line 10
              ^

1 error
```

Explain what the problem is and how to fix it.

37. You coded the following in the class *Test.java*:

```
int i = 0;
while ( i < 3 )
{
   System.out.println( "Hello" );
   i--;
}
```

The code compiles but never terminates.

Explain what the problem is and how to fix it.

38. You coded the following in the class *Test.java*:

```
for ( int i = 0; i++; i < 3 )     // line 5
   System.out.println( "Hello" );
```

At compile time, you get the following error:

```
Test.java:5: not a statement
for ( int i = 0; i++; i < 3 )     // line 5
                        ^

1 error
```

Explain what the problem is and how to fix it.

39. You coded the following in the class *Test.java*:

```
for ( int i = 1; i < 3; i++ )        // line 5
   System.out.println( "Hello" );
```

The code compiles and runs, but only prints *Hello* twice, whereas we expected to print *Hello* three times.

Explain what the problem is and how to fix it.

40. You coded the following in the class *Test.java*:

```
int product = 1;
for ( int i = 1, i < 5, i++ )          // line 8
   product *= i;
System.out.println( "Product is " + product ); // line 10
```

At compile time, you get the following errors:

```
Test.java:8: ';' expected
  for ( int i = 1, i < 5, i++ )         // line 8
                    ^
Test.java:8: illegal start of type
  for ( int i = 1, i < 5, i++ )         // line 8
                        ^
2 errors
```

Explain what the problem is and how to fix it.

41. You coded the following in the class *Test.java*:

```
for ( int i = 0; i < 3; i++ )
   System.out.println( "Hello" );
System.out.println( "i = " + i );   // line 8
```

At compile time, you get the following error:

```
Test.java:8: cannot find symbol
symbol  : variable i
location: class Test
       System.out.println( "i = " + i ); // line 8
                                    ^
1 error
```

Explain what the problem is and how to fix it.

42. You coded the following in the class *Test.java*:

```
int i = 0;
for ( int i = 0; i < 3; i++ ) // line 6
   System.out.println( "Hello" );
```

At compile time, you get the following error:

```
Test.java:6: i is already defined in main( java.lang.String[] )
for( int i = 0; i < 3; i++ )       // line 6
         ^
1 error
```

Explain what the problem is and how to fix it.

6.14.6 Write a Short Program

43. Write a program that prompts the user for a value greater than 10 as an input (you should loop until the user enters a valid value) and finds the square root of that number and the square root of the result, and continues to find the square root of the result until we reach a

number that is smaller than 1.01. The program should output how many times the square root operation was performed.

44. Write a program that expects a word containing the @ character as an input. If the word does not contain an @ character, then your program should keep prompting the user for a word. When the user types in a word containing an @ character, the program should simply print the word and terminate.

45. Write a program that reads *double* values from a file named *input.txt* and outputs the average.

46. Write a program that uses a *for* loop to output the sum of all the integers between 10 and 20, inclusive, that is, 10 + 11 + 12 . . . + 19 + 20.

47. Write a program that uses a *for* loop to output the product of all the integers between 3 and 7, inclusive, that is, 3 * 4 * 5 * 6 * 7.

48. Write a program that uses a *for* loop to count how many multiples of 7 are between 33 and 97, inclusive.

49. Write a program that reads a value (say *n*) from the user and outputs *Hello World* *n* times. Verify that the user has entered an integer. If the input is 3, the output will be *Hello World* printed three times.

50. Write a program that takes a word as an input from the keyboard and outputs each character in the word, separated by a space.

51. Write a program that takes a value as an input from the keyboard and outputs the factorial of that number; the factorial of an integer *n* is $n * (n-1) * (n-2) * \ldots * 3 * 2 * 1$. For instance, the factorial of 4 is $4 * 3 * 2 * 1$, or 24.

52. Using a loop, write a program that takes 10 integer values from the keyboard and outputs the minimum value of all the values entered.

53. Write an applet that displays a rectangle moving horizontally from the right side of the window to the left side of the window.

6.14.7 Programming Projects

54. Write a program that inputs a word representing a binary number (0s and 1s). First, your program should verify that it is indeed a binary

number, that is, the number contains only 0s and 1s. If that is not the case, your program should print a message that the number is not a valid binary number. Then, your program should count how many 1s are in that word and output the count.

55. Perform the same operations as Question 54, with the following modification: If the word does not represent a valid binary number, the program should keep prompting the user for a new word until a word representing a valid binary number is input by the user.

56. Write a program that inputs a word representing a binary number (0s and 1s). First, your program should check that it is indeed a binary number, that is, the number contains only 0s and 1s. If that is not the case, your program should output that the number is not a valid binary number. If that word contains exactly two 1s, your program should output that that word is "accepted," otherwise that it is "rejected."

57. Perform the same operations as Question 56, with the following modification: If the word does not represent a valid binary number, the program should keep prompting the user for a new word until a word representing a valid binary number is input by the user.

58. Write a program that inputs a word representing a binary number (0s and 1s). First, your program should check that it is indeed a binary number, that is, that it contains only 0s and 1s. If that is not the case, your program should output that the number is not a valid binary number. If that word contains at least three consecutive 1s, your program should output that that word is "accepted," otherwise that it is "rejected."

59. Perform the same operations as Question 58 with the following modification: If the word does not represent a valid binary number, the program should keep prompting the user for a new word until a word representing a valid binary number is input by the user.

60. Write a program that takes website names as keyboard input until the user types the word *stop* and counts how many of the website names are commercial website names (i.e., end with *.com*), then outputs that count.

61. Using a loop, write a program that takes 10 values representing exam grades (between 0 and 100) from the keyboard and outputs the minimum value, maximum value, and average value of all the values entered. Your program should not accept values less than 0 or greater than 100.

62. Write a program that takes an email address as an input from the keyboard and, using a loop, steps through every character looking for an @ sign. If the email address has exactly one @ character, then print a message that the email address is valid; otherwise, print a message that it is invalid.

63. Write a program that takes a user ID as an input from the keyboard and steps through every character, counting how many digits are in the user ID; if there are exactly two digits, output that the user ID is valid, otherwise that it is invalid.

64. Write a program that takes an integer value as an input and converts that value to its binary representation; for instance, if the user inputs 17, then the output will be 10001.

65. Write a program that takes a word representing a binary number (0s and 1s) as an input and converts it to its decimal representation; for instance, if the user inputs 101, then the output will be 5; you can assume that the *String* is guaranteed to contain only 0s and 1s.

66. Write a program that simulates an XOR operation. The input should be a word representing a binary number (0s and 1s). Your program should XOR all the digits from left to right and output the results as "True" or "False." In an XOR operation, *a* XOR *b* is *true* if *a* or *b* is *true* but not both; otherwise, it is *false.* In this program, we will consider the character "1" to represent true and a "0" to represent false. For instance, if the input is 1011, then the output will be 1 (1 XOR 0 is 1, then 1 XOR 1 is 0, then 0 XOR 1 is 1, which causes the output to be "True"). You can assume that the input word is guaranteed to contain only 0s and 1s.

67. Write a program that takes a sentence as an input (using a dialog box) and checks whether that sentence is a palindrome. A palindrome is a word, phrase, or sentence that is symmetrical; that is, it is spelled the

same forward and backward. Examples are "otto," "mom," and "Able was I ere I saw Elba." Your program should be case-insensitive; that is, "Otto" should also be counted as a palindrome.

68. Write a program that takes an HTML-like sequence as an input (using a dialog box) and checks whether that sequence has the same number of opening brackets (<) and closing brackets (>).

69. Write an applet that shows a small circle getting bigger and bigger. Your applet should allow the user to input the starting radius and the ending radius (and also verify that the starting radius is smaller than the ending radius).

6.14.8 Technical Writing

70. In programming, a programmer can make syntax errors that lead to a compiler error; these errors can then be corrected. Other errors can lead to a runtime error; these errors can also be corrected. Logic errors, however, can lead to an incorrect result or no result at all. Discuss examples of logic errors that can be made when coding loops and the consequences of these logic errors.

71. Discuss how you would detect whether you have an infinite loop in your code.

6.14.9 Group Project (for a group of 1, 2, or 3 students)

72. Often on a web page, the user is asked to supply personal information, such as a telephone number. Your program should take an input from the keyboard representing a telephone number. We will consider that the input is a valid telephone number if it contains exactly 10 digits and any number of dash (-) and whitespace characters. Keep prompting the user for a telephone number until the user gives you a valid one. Once you have a valid telephone number, you should assume that the digits (only the digits, not the hyphen[s] nor the whitespace) in the telephone number may have been encrypted by shifting each number by a constant value. For instance, if the shift is 2, a 0 becomes a 2, a 1 becomes a 3, a 2 becomes a 4, . . . , an 8 becomes a 0, and a 9 becomes a 1. However, we know that the user is from New York where the decrypted area code (after the shift is

applied), represented by the first three digits of the input, is 212. Your program needs to decrypt the telephone number and output the decrypted telephone number with the format 212-xxx-xxxx, as well as the shift value of the encryption. If there was an error in the input and the area code cannot be decrypted to 212, you should output that information.

CHAPTER 7

Object-Oriented Programming, Part 2: User-Defined Classes

CHAPTER CONTENTS

Introduction

When you see the title of this chapter, you might say, "Finally, we get to write our own classes." Actually, we've been writing classes all along. All Java source code belongs to a class. The classes we've been writing are application and applet classes. Now it's time to write some service classes—classes that encapsulate data and methods for use by applications, applets, or even other service classes. These are called **user-defined classes** because we, rather than the Java authors, create them.

First, let's take a moment to examine why we want to create user-defined classes.

We have written a lot of programs using Java's primitive data types (*boolean, char, int, double,* etc.), but the real world requires manipulation of more complex data than just individual *booleans* or *ints.* For example, if you are the programmer for an online bookstore, you will need to manipulate data associated with books. Books typically have an ISBN, a title, an author, a price, an in-stock quantity, and perhaps other pieces of data. We can create a *Book* class so that each object will hold the data for one book. For example, the ISBN, the title, and the author can be represented by *Strings,* the price by a *double,* and the in-stock quantity by an *int.* If we create this *Book* class, our program will be able to store and manipulate all the data of a book as a whole. This is one of the concepts of object-oriented programming.

By incorporating into the class the methods that work with the book data, we also are able to hide the details involved with handling that data. An application can simply call the methods as needed. Thus, creating your own classes can simplify your program.

Finally, a well-written class can be reused in other programs. Thus, user-defined classes speed up development.

7.1 Defining a Class

Classes encapsulate the data and functionality for a person, place, or thing, or more generally, an object. For example, a class might be defined to represent a student, a college, or a course.

To define a class, we use the following syntax:

```
accessModifier class ClassName
{
    // class definition goes here
}
```

This syntax should look familiar as the first line in our applications and applets. You may also notice that our class names have been nouns and have started with a capital letter: *Astronaut*, *Calculator*, *CellService*, and so forth. These names follow the conventions encouraged by the Java developers.

SOFTWARE ENGINEERING TIP

Use a noun for the class name and start the class name with a capital letter.

Inside the curly braces we define the data of the class, called its **fields**, and the methods. An important function performed by the class methods is maintaining the values of the class data for the **client programs**, which are the users of the class, in that the clients create objects and call the methods of the class. Our applications and applets have been clients of many Java classes, such as *String*, *DecimalFormat*, and *Math*. The fields and methods of a class are called the **members** of the class.

For each class and for each member of a class, we need to provide an **access modifier** that specifies where the class or member can be used (see Table 7.1). The possible access modifiers are *public*, *private*, and *protected*, or no modifier at all, which results in package access. The *public* access modifier allows the class or member to be used, or **referenced**, by methods of the same or other classes. The *private* access modifier specifies that the class or member can be referenced only by methods of the same class. Package access specifies that the

TABLE 7.1 Access Modifiers

Access Modifier	Class or member can be referenced by . . .
public	methods of the same class, as well as methods of other classes
private	methods of the same class only
protected	methods in the same class, as well as methods of subclasses and methods in classes in the same package
no modifier (package access)	methods in the same package only

class or member can be accessed by methods in classes that are in the same package. Later in the chapter, we will learn how to create our own package. We'll defer discussing the *protected* access modifier until Chapter 10, where we cover inheritance.

Typically, the *accessModifier* for a class will be *public*, and we know that a *public* class must be stored in a file named *ClassName.java* where *ClassName* is the name of the class. Not all classes will be *public*, however; we will introduce *private* classes in Chapter 12, where we cover GUIs.

Let's start to define a class that represents an automobile, which we can use to calculate miles per gallon. We'll name the class *Auto*, and we'll use the *public* access modifier so that any application can use this class. The class header will look like the following:

```
public class Auto
{
}
```

When we write a class, we will make known the *public* method names and their APIs so that a client program will know how to instantiate objects and call the methods of the class. We will not publish the implementation (or code) of the class, however. In other words, we will publish the APIs of the methods, but not the method bodies. This is called **data hiding**. A client program can use the class without knowing how the class is implemented, and we, as class authors, can change the implementation of the methods as long as we don't change the interface, or APIs.

7.2 Defining Instance Variables

The instance variables of a class hold the data for each object of that class. Thus, we also say that the instance variables represent the properties of the object. Each object, or instance of a class, gets its own copy of the instance variables, each of which can be given a value appropriate to that object. The values of the instance variables, therefore, can represent the state of the object.

SOFTWARE ENGINEERING TIP

Define instance variables of a class as *private* so that only methods of the class will be able to set or change their values.

Instance variables are defined using the following syntax:

```
accessModifier dataType identifierList;
```

The *private* modifier is typically used for the nonconstant instance variables of the class. This permits only methods of the same class to set or change the values of the instance variables. In this way, we achieve encapsulation; the class provides a protective shell around the data.

The data type of an instance variable can be any of Java's primitive types or a class type.

The *identifierList* consists of one or more names for instance variables of the same data type and can optionally assign initial values to the instance variables. If more than one instance variable name is given, a comma is used as a separator. By convention, identifier names for instance variables are nouns and begin with a lowercase letter; internal words begin with a capital letter. Each instance variable and class variable must be given a name that is unique to the class. It is legal to use the same names for instance variables in different classes, but within a class, the same name cannot be used for more than one instance variable or class variable. Thus, we say that the fields of a class have **class scope**.

Optionally, you can declare an instance variable to be a constant (*final*).

SOFTWARE ENGINEERING TIP

Use nouns for identifier names for instance variables. Begin the identifier with a lowercase letter and capitalize internal words.

The following statements are examples of instance variable definitions:

```
private String name = "";    // an empty String
private final int PERFECT_SCORE = 100, PASSING_SCORE = 60;
private int startX, startY, width, height;
```

What criteria should you use to select the instance variables of the class? The answer is to select the data that all objects will have in common. For example, for a *Student* class, you might select the student name, grade point average, and projected graduation date. For a *Calculator* class, you might select two operands, an operator, and a result.

Thus, for our *Auto* class, we will define instance variables to hold the model of the automobile, the number of miles the auto has been driven, and the gallons of gas used. Thus, our *Auto* class definition now becomes the following:

SOFTWARE ENGINEERING TIP

Define instance variables for the data that all objects will have in common.

```
public class Auto
{
   private String model;
   private int milesDriven;
   private double gallonsOfGas;
}
```

7.3 Writing Class Methods

We declared the instance variables of the *Auto* class as *private* so that only the methods of the *Auto* class will be able to access or change the values of the instance variables directly. Clients of the *Auto* class will need to use the methods of the class to access or change any of the instance variables. So we'll need to write some methods.

Methods have this syntax:

```
accessModifier returnType methodName( parameter list ) // method header
{
      // method body
}
```

where *parameter list* is a comma-separated list of data types and variable names.

The method header syntax should be familiar because we've seen the API for many class methods. One difference is just a matter of semantics. The method caller sends **arguments**, or **actual parameters**, to the method; the method refers to these arguments as its **formal parameters**.

SOFTWARE ENGINEERING TIP

Use verbs for method names. Begin the method name with a lowercase letter and begin internal words with a capital letter.

Because methods provide a function for the class, typically method names are verbs. Like instance variables, the method name should begin with a lowercase letter with internal words beginning with a capital letter.

The access modifier for methods that provide services to the client will be *public.* Methods that provide services only to other methods of the class are typically declared to be *private.*

SOFTWARE ENGINEERING TIP

Declare methods that provide services to clients as *public.* Methods that will be called only by other methods of the class should be declared *private.*

The return type of a method is the data type of the value that the method returns to the caller. The return type can be any of Java's primitive data types, any class type, or *void.* Methods with a return type of *void* do not return a value to the caller.

The body of each method, which consists of the code that performs the method's function, is written between the beginning and ending curly braces. Unlike *if* statements and loops, however, these curly braces are not optional; the curly braces are required, regardless of the number of statements in the method body.

COMMON ERROR TRAP

Forgetting to enclose the body of a method in curly braces generates one or more compiler errors.

Several compiler errors can result from forgetting one or both of the curly braces. You might receive either of these messages:

```
illegal start of expression
```

or

```
';' expected
```

In the method body, a method can declare variables, call other methods, and use any of the program structures we've discussed: *if/else* statements, *while* loops, *for* loops, *switch* statements, and *do/while* loops.

All objects of a class share one copy of the class methods.

We have actually written methods already. For example, we've written the method *main*. Its definition looks like this:

```
public static void main( String [ ] args )
{
      // application code
}
```

We know that the *static* keyword means that the Java Virtual Machine can call *main* to start the application running without first instantiating an object. The return type is *void* because *main* does not return a value. The parameter list expects one argument, a *String* array. We discuss arrays in the next chapter.

We have not previously written a value-returning method. A value-returning method sends back its results to the caller using a *return* statement in the method body. The syntax for the *return* statement is

```
return expression;
```

As you would expect, the data type of the expression must match the return type of the method. Recall that a value-returning method is called from an expression, and when the method completes its operation, its return value replaces the method call in the expression.

If the data type of the method is *void*, as in *main*, we have a choice of using the *return* statement without an expression, as in this statement:

```
return;
```

or omitting the *return* statement altogether. Given that control automatically returns to the caller when the end of the method is reached, most programmers omit the *return* statement in *void* methods.

7.4 Writing Constructors

A constructor is a special method that is called when an object is instantiated using the *new* keyword. A class can have several constructors. The job of the class constructors is to initialize the fields of the new object.

The syntax for a constructor follows:

```
accessModifier ClassName( parameter list )
{
    // constructor body
}
```

Notice that a constructor has the same name as the class and has no return type—not even *void*.

SOFTWARE ENGINEERING TIP

Define constructors to be *public* so that clients can instantiate objects of the class.

It's important to use the *public* access modifier for the constructors so that applications can instantiate objects of the class.

The constructor can either assign default values to the instance variables or the constructor can accept initial values from the client through parameters when the object is instantiated.

Providing a constructor for a class is optional. If you don't write a constructor, the compiler provides a **default constructor**, which is a constructor that takes no arguments. This default constructor assigns default initial values to all instance variables; this is called **autoinitialization**. Numeric variables are given the value of 0, characters are given the value *space*, *boolean* variables are given the value *false*, and object references are given the value *null*. Table 7.2 shows the values the default constructor assigns to instance variables.

If we do provide a constructor, any instance variables our constructor does not initialize will still be given the predefined default value.

TABLE 7.2 Default Initial Values of Instance Variables

Data Type	Initial Value
byte	0
short	0
int	0
long	0
float	0.0
double	0.0
char	*space*
boolean	*false*
object reference	*null*

Example 7.1 shows Version 1 of our *Auto* class with two constructors.

```
/* Auto class, Version 1
   Anderson, Franceschi
*/

public class Auto
{
    // instance variables
    private String model;          //  model of auto
    private int milesDriven;       //  number of miles driven
    private double gallonsOfGas;   //  number of gallons of gas

    // Default constructor:
    //  initializes model to "unknown";
    //  milesDriven is autoinitialized to 0
    //        and gallonsOfGas to 0.0
    public Auto( )
    {
       model = "unknown";
    }

    // Overloaded constructor:
    // allows client to set beginning values for
    //   model, milesDriven, and gallonsOfGas.
    public Auto( String startModel,
                 int startMilesDriven,
                 double startGallonsOfGas )
    {
       model = startModel;

       // validate startMilesDriven parameter
       if ( startMilesDriven >= 0 )
           milesDriven = startMilesDriven;
       else
       {
           System.err.println( "Miles driven is negative." );
           System.err.println( "Value set to 0." );
       }

       // validate startGallonsOfGas parameter
       if ( startGallonsOfGas >= 0.0 )
           gallonsOfGas = startGallonsOfGas;
       else
```

```
43         {
44              System.err.println( "Gallons of gas is negative" );
45              System.err.println( "Value set to 0.0." );
46         }
47     }
48 }
```

EXAMPLE 7.1 The *Auto* Class, Version 1

Our default constructor (lines 12–19) does not set values for the *milesDriven* and *gallonsOfGas* instance variables. Because *ints* and *doubles* are autoinitialized to 0 and 0.0, respectively, we just accept those default values.

However, it is necessary for our constructor to set the *model* instance variable to a valid *String* value. Because *Strings* are object references, they are autoinitialized to *null*. Any attempt to call a method using the *model* instance variable with a *null* value would generate a *NullPointerException*.

As mentioned earlier, you can provide multiple constructors for a class. We provide a second constructor (lines 21–47) that lets the client set initial values for all the instance variables. Because the class is the caretaker of its fields, it is the class's responsibility to ensure that the data for each object is valid. Thus, when the constructor sets initial values for the instance variables, it should first check whether its parameters are, indeed, valid values. What constitutes a valid value for any instance variable depends in part on the data type of the variable and in part on the class and is a design decision. For our *Auto* class, we have decided that *milesDriven* and *gallonsOfGas* cannot be negative. If the constructor finds that the *startMilesDriven* or *startGallonsOfGas* parameters are negative, it prints an error message to *System.err*—which by default is the Java console—and sets the instance variables to default values. Some methods in the Java class library generate an exception when a parameter value is invalid; others substitute a default value for the invalid parameter. Again, how your classes handle invalid argument values is a design decision.

REFERENCE POINT

Exceptions are covered in Chapter 11.

When we provide multiple constructors, we are **overloading** a method. To overload a method, we provide a method with the same name but with a different number of parameters, or with the same number of parameters but with at least one parameter having a different data type. The name of the method, along with the number, data types, and order of its parameters, is called the method's **signature**. Thus, to overload a method, the new method must have a different signature. Notice that the return type is not part of the signature.

When a client calls a method that is overloaded, Java determines which version of the method to execute by looking at the number, data types, and order of the arguments in the method call. Example 7.2 shows a client program that instantiates three *Auto* objects.

```
 1 /* Auto Client, Version 1
 2    Anderson, Franceschi
 3 */
 4
 5 public class AutoClient
 6 {
 7   public static void main( String [ ] args )
 8   {
 9      System.out.println( "Instantiate sedan" );
10      Auto sedan = new Auto( );
11
12      System.out.println( "\nInstantiate suv" );
13      Auto suv = new Auto( "Trailblazer", 7000, 437.5 );
14
15      System.out.println( "\nInstantiate mini" );
16      // attempt to set invalid value for gallons of gas
17      Auto mini = new Auto( "Mini Cooper", 200, -1.0 );
18   }
19 }
```

EXAMPLE 7.2 The *Auto* Client, Version 1

Line 10 causes the default constructor to be called because no arguments are passed to the constructor. Line 13 causes the overloaded constructor to be called because it passes three arguments to the constructor. If the client attempted to instantiate a new object with a number of parameters other than 0 or 3, the compiler would generate an error because there is no constructor that matches those arguments. In general, the arguments sent to an overloaded method must match the formal parameters of some version of that method.

SOFTWARE ENGINEERING TIP

Provide, at the minimum, a default constructor and a constructor that accepts initial values for all instance variables.

The number of constructors you provide is a design decision and depends on the class. Providing multiple constructors gives the client a choice of ways to create an object. It is good practice to provide, at minimum, a default constructor. The reason for this will become clear as we explore

Figure 7.1
Output from *Auto* Client, Version 1

```
Instantiate sedan

Instantiate suv

Instantiate mini
Gallons of gas is negative
Value set to 0.0.
```

classes in more depth. It is also good practice to provide another constructor that accepts values for all the instance variables.

On line 17, we instantiate an *Auto* object with an invalid argument for gallons of gas. As Figure 7.1 shows, the constructor prints an error message. The object is still created, but the value of its *gallonsOfGas* instance variable is 0.0.

Beware of this common error: declaring a *void* return type for a constructor. Remember that constructors have no return type at all. For example, the following invalid constructor definition declares a return type of *void:*

```
// Error! void return value specified
public void Auto( String model,
                  int startMilesDriven,
                  double startGallonsOfGas )
{
     // body of constructor
}
```

This is a difficult error to find. The class file will compile without an error because the compiler doesn't recognize this method as a constructor. Instead, the client program will get a compiler error when it attempts to instantiate an *Auto* object. For example, this statement in a client program

```
Auto gm = new Auto( "Prius", 350, 15.5 );
```

would generate this compiler error:

```
C:\AutoClient.java:15: cannot find symbol
symbol  : constructor Auto (java.lang.String,int,double)
location: class Auto
            Auto gm = new Auto("Prius", 350, 15.5 );
                      ^
1 error
```

COMMON ERROR TRAP

Specifying a return value for a constructor will cause a compiler error in the client program when the client attempts to instantiate an object of that class.

Notice that both constructors access the instance variables directly. Remember that instance variables have class scope, which means that they can be accessed anywhere in the class. Thus, any method of the class can access any of the instance variables directly. In our *Auto* class, any method can access the instance variables *model*, *milesDriven*, and *gallonsOfGas*.

Methods have class scope as well. Any method can call any of the methods in the class, regardless of whether the methods have been declared *private*, *public*, or *protected*.

In addition to accessing the instance variables, a method can also access its own parameters. When a method begins executing, its parameters have been declared and have been given the values of the arguments sent by the caller of the method.

The parameters have **local scope** in that a method can access its parameters directly. We call this local scope because the parameters are local to a method; that is, a method can access its own parameters, but attempting to access another method's parameters generates a compiler error.

Table 7.3 summarizes the rules of scope.

Attempting to use an identifier that is not in scope will generate the following compiler error:

```
cannot find symbol
```

TABLE 7.3 Rules of Scope

A method in a class can access

- the instance variables of its class
- any parameters sent to the method
- any variable the method declares within its body from the point of declaration until the end of the method or until the end of the block in which the variable was declared, whichever comes first
- any methods in the class

You may wonder why the compiler calls an identifier a **symbol**. The Java compiler generates a **symbol table** as it reads your code. Each identifier you declare is put into the symbol table, along with the identifier's data type and where in the program it was defined. This symbol table allows the compiler to track the identifiers that are in scope at any given time. Thus, if an identifier is not in scope, the compiler will not be able to find that symbol in its table for that section of code.

When the client in Example 7.2 runs, it instantiates three objects, but there is nothing more our application can do with them. To allow our client to manipulate the *Auto* objects further, we need to provide more methods.

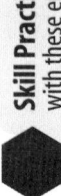

Skill Practice
with these end-of-chapter questions

7.18.1 Multiple Choice Exercises

Questions 1, 2, 3, 4, 5, 6, 7

7.18.3 Fill In the Code

Questions 28, 30, 31

7.18.5 Debugging Area

Questions 47, 48, 49

7.18.8 Technical Writing

Question 73

7.5 Writing Accessor Methods

Because clients cannot directly access *private* instance variables of a class, classes usually provide *public* accessor methods for the instance variables. These methods have a simple, almost trivial, standard form:

```
public returnType getInstanceVariable( )
{
   return instanceVariable;
}
```

The standard name of the method is *get*, followed by the instance variable's name with an initial capital letter. The method takes no arguments and simply returns the current value of the instance variable. Thus, the return type is the same data type as the instance variable.

You can see this simple pattern in the accessor methods for Version 2 of our *Auto* class, shown in Example 7.3 (lines 49–68).

```
 1 /* Auto class, Version 2
 2    Anderson, Franceschi
 3 */
 4
 5 public class Auto
 6 {
 7     // instance variables
 8     private String model;           //  model of auto
 9     private int milesDriven;        //  number of miles driven
10     private double gallonsOfGas;    //  number of gallons of gas
11
12     // Default constructor:
13     //  initializes model to "unknown";
14     //  milesDriven is autoinitialized to 0
15     //        and gallonsOfGas to 0.0
16     public Auto( )
17     {
18        model = "unknown";
19     }
20
21     // Overloaded constructor:
22     // allows client to set beginning values for
23     //   model, milesDriven, and gallonsOfGas.
24     public Auto( String startModel,
25                  int startMilesDriven,
26                  double startGallonsOfGas )
27     {
28        model = startModel;
29
30        // validate startMilesDriven parameter
31        if ( startMilesDriven >= 0 )
32           milesDriven = startMilesDriven;
33        else
34        {
35           System.err.println( "Miles driven is negative." );
36           System.err.println( "Value set to 0." );
37        }
```

```

      // validate startGallonsOfGas parameter
      if ( startGallonsOfGas >= 0.0 )
         gallonsOfGas = startGallonsOfGas;
      else
      {
         System.err.println( "Gallons of gas is negative" );
         System.err.println( "Value set to 0.0." );
      }
   }

   // Accessor method:
   // returns current value of model
   public String getModel( )
   {
      return model;
   }

   // Accessor method:
   // returns current value of milesDriven
   public int getMilesDriven( )
   {
      return milesDriven;
   }

   // Accessor method:
   //  returns current value of gallonsOfGas
   public double getGallonsOfGas( )
   {
      return gallonsOfGas;
   }
}
```

EXAMPLE 7.3 *Auto* Class, Version 2

In the client code in Example 7.4, we've added a few statements to call the accessor methods for the two *Auto* objects we've instantiated. Then we print the values, as shown in Figure 7.2.

```
/* Auto Client, Version 2
   Anderson, Franceschi
*/

public class AutoClient
```

```
{
    public static void main( String [ ] args )
    {
        Auto sedan = new Auto( );
        String sedanModel = sedan.getModel( );
        int sedanMiles = sedan.getMilesDriven( );
        double sedanGallons = sedan.getGallonsOfGas( );
        System.out.println( "sedan: model is " + sedanModel
                  + "\n miles driven is " + sedanMiles
                  + "\n gallons of gas is " + sedanGallons );

        Auto suv = new Auto( "Trailblazer", 7000, 437.5 );
        String suvModel = suv.getModel( );
        int suvMiles = suv.getMilesDriven( );
        double suvGallons = suv.getGallonsOfGas( );
        System.out.println( "suv: model is " + suvModel
                  + "\n miles driven is " + suvMiles
                  + "\n gallons of gas is " + suvGallons );
    }
}
```

EXAMPLE 7.4 ***Auto* Client, Version 2**

```
sedan: model is unknown
 miles driven is 0
 gallons of gas is 0.0
suv: model is Trailblazer
 miles driven is 7000
 gallons of gas is 437.5
```

Figure 7.2
Output from *Auto* Client, Version 2

SOFTWARE ENGINEERING TIP

Provide *public* accessor methods for any instance variable for which the client should be able to retrieve the value. Each accessor method returns the current value of the corresponding instance variable.

Because the *sedan* object was instantiated by calling the default constructor, its model is *unknown* and the miles driven and gallons of gas are set to default values. On the other hand, the *suv* object data reflects the values sent to the overloaded constructor when the *suv* object was instantiated.

Thus, Version 2 of our *Auto* class lets our clients instantiate objects and get the values of the instance variables. But we still need to give the client a way to change the instance variables. In order to do this, we provide mutator methods.

7.6 Writing Mutator Methods

As we have discussed, we declare the instance variables as *private* to encapsulate the data of the class: We allow only the class methods to directly set the values of the instance variables. Thus, it is customary to provide a *public* **mutator** method for any instance variable that the client will be able to change.

The general form of a mutator method is the following:

```
public void setInstanceVariable( dataType newValue )
{
    // validate newValue, then assign to the instance variable
}
```

SOFTWARE ENGINEERING TIP

Provide a mutator method for any instance variable that you want to allow the client to change. If the argument sent to the method is not a valid value for the instance variable, one option is for the mutator method to print a message to *System.err* and leave the value of the instance variable unchanged.

We declare mutator methods as *public* so that client programs can use the methods to change the values of the instance variables. We do not return a value, so we declare the return type as *void*. By convention, the name of each mutator method starts with the lowercase word, *set*, followed by the instance variable name with an initial capital letter. For obvious reasons, the data type of the method's parameter should match the data type of the instance variable being set.

Whenever possible, the body of your mutator method should validate the parameter value passed by the client. If the parameter value is valid, the mutator assigns that value to the instance variable; otherwise, one option is for the mutator to print a message on the system error device (*System.err*), which, by default, is the Java console.

Example 7.5 shows Version 3 of our *Auto* class.

```
/* Auto class, Version 3
   Anderson, Franceschi
*/

public class Auto
{
   // instance variables
   private String model;          //  model of auto
   private int milesDriven;       //  number of miles driven
   private double gallonsOfGas;   //  number of gallons of gas

   // Default constructor:
   //  initializes model to "unknown";
```

```
    //  milesDriven is autoinitialized to 0
    //        and gallonsOfGas to 0.0
    public Auto( )
    {
      model = "unknown";
    }

    // Overloaded constructor:
    // allows client to set beginning values for
    //   model, milesDriven, and gallonsOfGas.
    public Auto( String startModel,
                 int startMilesDriven,
                 double startGallonsOfGas )
    {
      model = startModel;
      setMilesDriven( startMilesDriven );
      setGallonsOfGas( startGallonsOfGas );
    }

    // Accessor method:
    // returns current value of model
    public String getModel( )
    {
      return model;
    }

    // Accessor method:
    // returns current value of milesDriven
    public int getMilesDriven( )
    {
      return milesDriven;
    }

    // Accessor method:
    //  returns current value of gallonsOfGas
    public double getGallonsOfGas( )
    {
      return gallonsOfGas;
    }

    // Mutator method:
    // allows client to set model
    public void setModel( String newModel )
    {
```

```
58       model = newModel;
59     }
60
61     // Mutator method:
62     // allows client to set value of milesDriven;
63     // prints an error message if new value is less than 0
64     public void setMilesDriven( int newMilesDriven )
65     {
66       if ( newMilesDriven >= 0 )
67         milesDriven = newMilesDriven;
68       else
69       {
70         System.err.println( "Miles driven cannot be negative." );
71         System.err.println( "Value not changed." );
72       }
73     }
74
75     // Mutator method:
76     // allows client to set value of gallonsOfGas;
77     // prints an error message if new value is less than 0.0
78     public void setGallonsOfGas( double newGallonsOfGas )
79     {
80       if ( newGallonsOfGas >= 0.0 )
81         gallonsOfGas = newGallonsOfGas;
82       else
83       {
84         System.err.println( "Gallons of gas cannot be negative." );
85         System.err.println( "Value not changed." );
86       }
87     }
88 }
```

EXAMPLE 7.5 *Auto* Class, Version 3

SOFTWARE ENGINEERING TIP

Write the validation code for instance variables in mutator methods and have the constructor call the mutator methods to set initial values.

The mutator methods for the *milesDriven* (lines 61–73) and *gallonsOfGas* (lines 75–87) instance variables validate that the parameter value is greater than 0. If not, the methods print a message to *System.err* and do not change the value of the instance variable. In previous versions of our *Auto* class, the constructor performed the same validation. Now that the mutator methods perform this validation, the constructor can call the mutator methods. In this way, we eliminate duplicate code; the validation of each parameter's value is performed in one place. If later we decide to impose other restrictions on any instance variable's value, we will need to change the code in only one place. In this way, a client cannot set invalid values for *milesDriven* or *gallonsOfGas*, either when the object is instantiated or by calling a mutator method.

```
1 /* Auto Client, Version 3
2    Anderson, Franceschi
3 */
4
5 public class AutoClient
6 {
7   public static void main( String [ ] args )
8   {
9      Auto suv = new Auto( "Trailblazer", 7000, 437.5 );
10
11     // print initial values of instance variables
12     System.out.println( "suv: model is " + suv.getModel( )
13            + "\n miles driven is " + suv.getMilesDriven( )
14            + "\n gallons of gas is " + suv.getGallonsOfGas( ) );
15
16     // call mutator method for each instance variable
17     suv.setModel( "Sportage" );
18     suv.setMilesDriven( 200 );
19     suv.setGallonsOfGas( 10.5 );
20
21     // print new values of instance variables
22     System.out.println( "\nsuv: model is " + suv.getModel( )
23            + "\n miles driven is " + suv.getMilesDriven( )
24            + "\n gallons of gas is " + suv.getGallonsOfGas( ) );
25
26     // attempt to set invalid value for milesDriven
27     suv.setMilesDriven( -1 );
28     // print current values of instance variables
29     System.out.println( "\nsuv: model is " + suv.getModel( )
30            + "\n miles driven is " + suv.getMilesDriven( )
31            + "\n gallons of gas is " + suv.getGallonsOfGas( ) );
32   }
33 }
```

EXAMPLE 7.6 *Auto* Client, Version 3

In Example 7.6, our client instantiates one *Auto* object, *suv* (line 9), and prints the values of its instance variables (lines 11–14). Then we call each mutator method, setting new values for each instance variable (lines 16–19). We again print the values of the instance variables (lines 21–24) to show that the values have been changed. Then, in line 27, we attempt to set an invalid value for *milesDriven*. As Figure 7.3 shows, the mutator method prints an error message and does not change the value, which we verify by again printing the values of the instance variables (lines 28–31).

When a method begins executing, the parameters have been defined and have been assigned the values sent by the client. When the client calls the *setModel* method at line 17, the *newModel* parameter has the value *Sportage* when the method starts executing.

A common error in writing mutator methods is using the instance variable name for the parameter name. When a method parameter has the same name as an instance variable, the parameter "hides" the instance variable. In other words, the parameter has **name precedence**, so any reference to that name refers to the parameter, not to the instance variable.

For example, the intention in this incorrectly coded method is to set a new value for the *model* instance variable:

```
// Incorrect!  parameter hides instance variable
public void setModel( String model )
{
    model = model;
}
```

Because the parameter, *model*, has the same identifier as the *model* instance variable, the result of this method is to assign the value of the parameter to the parameter! This is called a ***No-op***, which stands for "No operation," because the statement has no effect. To avoid this logic error, choose a different name

Figure 7.3
Output from *Auto* Client, Version 3

```
suv: model is Trailblazer
 miles driven is 7000
 gallons of gas is 437.5

suv: model is Sportage
 miles driven is 200
 gallons of gas is 10.5
Miles driven cannot be negative.
Value not changed.

suv: model is Sportage
 miles driven is 200
 gallons of gas is 10.5
```

for the parameter. To avoid name conflicts, we name each parameter using the pattern *newInstanceVariable*.

A similar common error is to declare a local variable with the same name as the instance variable, as shown in the following incorrectly coded method:

```
// Incorrect! declared local variable hides instance variable
public void setModel( String newModel )
{
      String model; // declared variable hides instance variable
      model = newModel;
}
```

Any variable that a method declares is a local variable because its scope is local to the method. Thus, the declared variable, *model*, is a local variable to the *setModel* method.

COMMON ERROR TRAP

Be aware that a method parameter or local variable that has the same name as an instance variable hides the instance variable.

With the preceding code, the *model* local variable hides the instance variable with the same name, so the method assigns the parameter value to the local variable, not to the instance variable. The result is that the value of the *model* instance variable is unchanged.

The instance variable, *model*, is defined already in the class. Thus, the method should simply assign the parameter value to the instance variable without attempting to declare the instance variable (again) in the method.

Finally, another common error is declaring the parameter, as shown below:

COMMON ERROR TRAP

Do not declare the parameters of a method inside the method body. When the method begins executing, the parameters exist and have been assigned the values set by the client in the method call.

```
// Incorrect! Declaring the parameter; parameters are declared already
public void setModel( String newModel )
{
      String newModel; // local variable has same name as parameter
      model = newModel;
}
```

This code generates this compiler error:

```
newModel is already defined in setModel(java.lang.String)
```

7.7 Writing Data Manipulation Methods

Now we finally get down to the business of the class. Usually you will define a class not only to encapsulate the data, but also to provide some service. Thus, you would provide one or more methods that perform the functionality of the class. These methods might calculate a value based on the instance variables or manipulate the instance variables in some way. The

API of these methods depends on the function being performed. If a method merely manipulates the instance variables, it requires no parameters because instance variables are accessible from any method and, therefore, are in scope.

For example, in our *Auto* class, part of the functionality of our class is to calculate miles per gallon, so we provide a *calculateMilesPerGallon* method in our *Auto* class, Version 4, shown in Example 7.7.

```
/* Auto class, Version 4
   Anderson, Franceschi
*/

public class Auto
{
    // instance variables
    private String model;           //  model of auto
    private int milesDriven;        //  number of miles driven
    private double gallonsOfGas;    //  number of gallons of gas

    // Default constructor:
    //  initializes model to "unknown";
    //  milesDriven is autoinitialized to 0
    //        and gallonsOfGas to 0.0
    public Auto( )
    {
       model = "unknown";
    }

    // Overloaded constructor:
    // allows client to set beginning values for
    //   model, milesDriven, and gallonsOfGas.
    public Auto( String startModel,
                 int startMilesDriven,
                 double startGallonsOfGas )
    {
       model = startModel;
       setMilesDriven( startMilesDriven );
       setGallonsOfGas( startGallonsOfGas );
    }

    // Accessor method:
    // returns current value of model
    public String getModel( )
```

```
    {
       return model;
    }

    // Accessor method:
    // returns current value of milesDriven
    public int getMilesDriven( )
    {
       return milesDriven;
    }

    // Accessor method:
    // returns current value of gallonsOfGas
    public double getGallonsOfGas( )
    {
       return gallonsOfGas;
    }

    // Mutator method:
    // allows client to set model
    public void setModel( String newModel )
    {
       model = newModel;
    }

    // Mutator method:
    // allows client to set value of milesDriven;
    // prints an error message if new value is less than 0
    public void setMilesDriven( int newMilesDriven )
    {
       if ( newMilesDriven >= 0 )
          milesDriven = newMilesDriven;
       else
       {
         System.err.println( "Miles driven cannot be negative." );
         System.err.println( "Value not changed." );
       }
    }

    // Mutator method:
    // allows client to set value of gallonsOfGas;
    // prints an error message if new value is less than 0.0
    public void setGallonsOfGas( double newGallonsOfGas )
    {
       if ( newGallonsOfGas >= 0.0 )
```

```
81           gallonsOfGas = newGallonsOfGas;
82         else
83         {
84           System.err.println( "Gallons of gas cannot be negative." );
85           System.err.println( "Value not changed." );
86         }
87       }
88
89       // Calculates miles per gallon.
90       //  if no gallons of gas have been used, returns 0.0;
91       //  otherwise, returns miles per gallon
92       //        as milesDriven / gallonsOfGas
93       public double calculateMilesPerGallon( )
94       {
95         if ( gallonsOfGas != 0.0 )
96           return milesDriven / gallonsOfGas;
97         else
98           return 0.0;
99       }
100  }
```

EXAMPLE 7.7 *Auto* Class, Version 4

Our class now provides the method to calculate mileage for an *Auto* object. The *calculateMilesPerGallon* method (lines 89–99) needs no parameters since it accesses only instance variables of the class, which are in scope. As you can see from the code, we guard against dividing by 0 by checking the value of *gallonsOfGas* before using it as the divisor. If *gallonsOfGas* is not equal to zero, we divide *milesDriven* by *gallonsOfGas* and return the result as a *double*. Otherwise, we return 0.0.

Example 7.8 shows a client program that instantiates an *Auto* object, calls the *calculateMilesPerGallon* method, and prints the return value, as shown in Figure 7.4.

Figure 7.4
Output from *Auto* Client, Version 4

```
Mileage for suv is 16.0
```

```
/* Auto Client, Version 4
   Anderson, Franceschi
*/

public class AutoClient
{
   public static void main( String [ ] args )
   {
     Auto suv = new Auto( "Trailblazer", 7000, 437.5 );

     double mileage = suv.calculateMilesPerGallon( );
     System.out.println( "Mileage for suv is "
                         + mileage );
   }
}
```

EXAMPLE 7.8 *Auto* Client, Version 4

Skill Practice
with these end-of-chapter questions

7.18.1 Multiple Choice Exercises

Questions 8, 9, 10, 11, 12, 13

7.18.2 Reading and Understanding Code

Questions 17, 18,19,20,24,26

7.18.3 Fill In the Code

Questions 32, 33, 36, 37

7.18.4 Identifying Errors in Code

Questions 38, 39, 43,45

7.18.5 Debugging Area

Question 52

7.8 Programming Activity 1: Writing a Class Definition, Part 1

In this programming activity, you will write the methods for an *Airport* class. Then you will run a prewritten client program that instantiates several *Airport* objects, calls the methods that you have written, and displays the values of the objects' data.

The *Airport* class has two instance variables: the airport code and the number of gates.

In the Chapter 7 Programming Activity 1 folder on the CD-ROM accompanying this book, you will find three source files: *Airport.java*, *AirportClient.java*, and *Pause.java*, as well as the *.class* files for *AirportClient* and *Pause*. Copy these files to a directory on your computer. Note that all files should be in the same directory.

Load the *Airport.java* source file; you'll notice that the class already contains some source code. The method names and APIs are described in comments. Your job is to define the instance variables and write the methods. It is important that you define the method headers exactly as described, including method name, return value, and parameters, because our *AirportClient* class will call each method to test it. Search for five asterisks in a row (*****). This will position you at the seven places in the class definition where you will add your code. The *Airport.java* code is shown here in Example 7.9.

```
/* Airport class
   Anderson, Franceschi
*/

public class Airport
{
  // 1. ***** Define the instance variables  *****
  //  airportCode is a String
  //  gates is an integer



   // 2. ***** Write this method *****
   // Default constructor:
   // method name: Airport
```

```
// return value:  none
// parameters: none
// function: sets the airportCode to an empty String



// 3. ***** Write this method *****
// Overloaded constructor:
// method name: Airport
// return value: none
// parameters:  a String startAirportCode and an int startGates
// function:
//      calls the setAirportCode method,
//      passing startAirportCode parameter;
//      calls the setGates method, passing startGates parameter




// 4. ***** Write this method *****
// Accessor method for the airportCode instance variable
// method name: getAirportCode
// return value: String
// parameters: none
// function: returns airportCode



// 5. ***** Write this method *****
// Accessor method for the gates instance variable
// method name: getGates
// return value: int
// parameters: none
// function: returns gates



// 6. ***** Write this method *****
// Mutator method for the airportCode instance variable
// method name: setAirportCode
// return value: void
// parameters: String newAirportCode
```

```
   // function: assigns airportCode the value of the
   //       newAirportCode parameter



   // 7. ***** Write this method *****
   // Mutator method for the gates instance variable
   // method name: setGates
   // return value:  void
   // parameters: int newGates
   // function: validates the newGates parameter.
   //   if newGates is greater than or equal to 0,
   //       sets gates to newGates;
   //       otherwise, prints an error message to System.err
   //       and does not change value of gates




 } // end of Airport class definition
```

EXAMPLE 7.9 ***Airport.java***

When you finish writing the methods for the *Airport* class, compile the source file. When *Airport.java* compiles without errors, load the *Airport-Client.java* file. This source file contains *main*, so you will execute the application from this file. When the application begins, you should see the window shown in Figure 7.5.

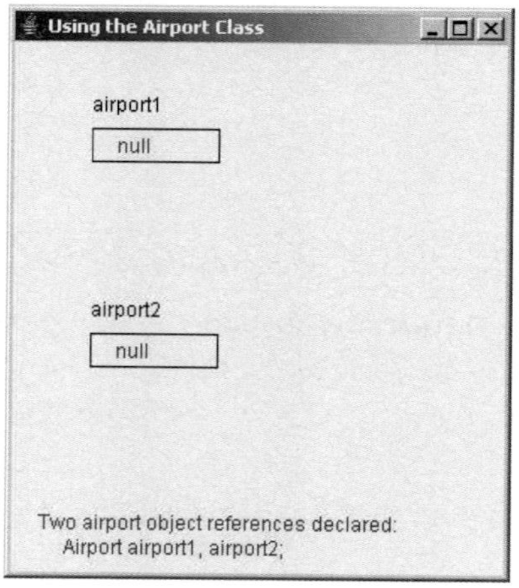

Figure 7.5
Programming Activity 1 Opening Window

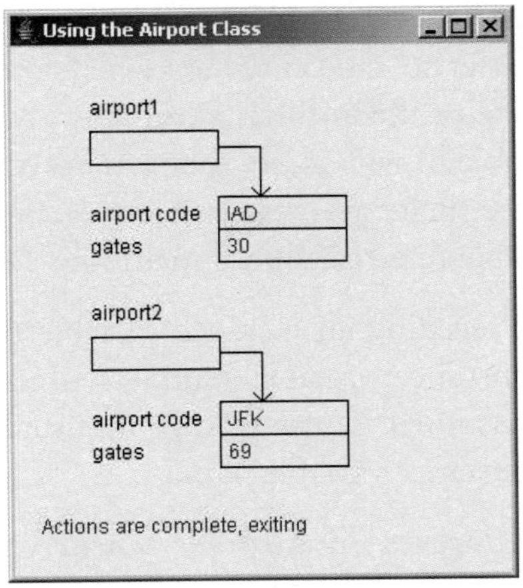

Figure 7.6
***AirportClient* When Complete**

As you can see, the *AirportClient* has declared two *Airport* object references, *airport1* and *airport2*. The references are *null* because no *Airport* objects have been instantiated.

The client application, *AirportClient*, will instantiate the *Airport* objects and call the methods you have written for the *Airport* class. As the application does its work, it displays a status message at the bottom of the window that indicates which method it has called. It also displays the current values of both *Airport* objects. You can check your work by comparing the values in the objects with the status message. Figure 7.6 shows the *AirportClient* application when it has finished instantiating *Airport* objects and calling *Airport* methods.

? DISCUSSION QUESTIONS

1. Why is *main* in a different source file from the *Airport* class definition?
2. Explain the importance of using standard naming conventions for accessor and mutator methods.

7.9 The Object Reference *this*

When an object is instantiated, a copy of each of the instance variables is created. However, all objects of a class share one copy of the methods. How, then, does a method know for which object the method was called? In other words, how does a method know which instance variables it should get, set, or use to calculate a value? The answer is the special object reference named *this*.

When a method begins executing, the JVM sets the object reference, *this*, to refer to the object for which the method has been called. That object is called the **implicit parameter**. When a method references an instance variable, it will access the instance variable that belongs to the object that the implicit parameter references. In other words, by default, any instance variable referred to by a method is considered to be *this.instanceVariable.*

Preceding an instance variable name with *this* is optional; when just the instance variable name is used (without any object reference), *this* is assumed. Consequently, we usually omit the *this* reference and use just the instance variable name.

However, in methods where you need to avoid ambiguity in variable names, you can precede an instance variable name with *this.* That approach comes in handy as a way to avoid one of the common errors we discussed earlier in the chapter: A parameter to a mutator method with the same name as the instance variable being changed hides the instance variable. We can eliminate this problem by using the *this* reference with the instance variable, which effectively "uncovers" the instance variable name.

For instance, some programmers would code the *setModel* mutator as follows:

```
public void setModel( String model )
{
   this.model = model;
}
```

Here we give the parameter, *model*, the same name as the instance variable it represents. Then in the assignment statement, we use the *this* reference to distinguish the instance variable from the parameter. Now it is clear that the parameter value, *model*, should be assigned to the instance variable, *this.model.*

7.10 The *toString* and *equals* Methods

In addition to constructors, mutator methods, and accessor methods, a well-designed class usually implements the *toString* and *equals* methods.

The *toString* method is called automatically when an object reference is used as a *String*. For example, the *toString* method for an object is called when the object reference is used with, or as, a parameter to *System.out.println*. The function of the *toString* method is to return a printable representation of the object data.

The *equals* method is designed to compare two objects for equality; that is, it typically returns *true* if the corresponding instance variables in both objects are equal in value. The *equals* method takes an *Object* reference parameter that is expected to be an *Auto* reference and returns *true* if the values of its fields are equal to the values of the fields of this *Auto* object, *false* otherwise.

All classes inherit a version of the *toString* and the *equals* methods from the *Object* class, but these versions do not provide the functionality we describe earlier. Thus, it is good practice to provide new versions of these methods. To do that, we use the same header as the methods in the *Object* class, but provide a new method body. This is called **overriding a method**. We discuss overriding methods in more detail in Chapter 10, where we cover inheritance.

The APIs of the t*oString* and *equals* methods are the following:

```
public String toString( )
public boolean equals( Object o )
```

Example 7.10 shows Version 5 of the *Auto* class with implementations of the *toString* method (lines 98–106) and the *equals* method (lines 108–125).

```
 1 /* Auto class, Version 5
 2    Anderson, Franceschi
 3 */
 4
 5 import java.text.DecimalFormat;
 6
 7 public class Auto
 8 {
 9     // instance variables
10     private String model;          //  model of auto
11     private int milesDriven;       //  number of miles driven
12     private double gallonsOfGas;   //  number of gallons of gas
13
14     // Constructors:
15     //  initializes model to "unknown";
16     //  milesDriven is autoinitialized to 0
17     //        and gallonsOfGas to 0.0
18     public Auto( )
19     {
20        model = "unknown";
21     }
22
23     // allows client to set beginning values for
```

```
   //   model, milesDriven, and gallonsOfGas.
   public Auto( String startModel,
                int startMilesDriven,
                double startGallonsOfGas )
   {
     model = startModel;
     setMilesDriven( startMilesDriven );
     setGallonsOfGas( startGallonsOfGas );
   }

   // Accessor methods:
   // returns current value of model
   public String getModel( )
   {
     return model;
   }

   // returns current value of milesDriven
   public int getMilesDriven( )
   {
     return milesDriven;
   }

   // returns current value of gallonsOfGas
   public double getGallonsOfGas( )
   {
     return gallonsOfGas;
   }

   // Mutator methods:
   // allows client to set model
   public void setModel( String newModel )
   {
     model = newModel;
   }

   // allows client to set value of milesDriven
   // prints an error message if new value is less than 0
   public void setMilesDriven( int newMilesDriven )
   {
     if ( newMilesDriven >= 0 )
       milesDriven = newMilesDriven;
     else
     {
       System.err.println( "Miles driven cannot be negative." );
       System.err.println( "Value not changed." );
     }
```

```
    }

    // allows client to set value of gallonsOfGas;
    // prints an error message if new value is less than 0.0
    public void setGallonsOfGas( double newGallonsOfGas )
    {
      if ( newGallonsOfGas >= 0.0 )
        gallonsOfGas = newGallonsOfGas;
      else
      {
        System.err.println( "Gallons of gas cannot be negative." );
        System.err.println( "Value not changed." );
      }
    }

    // Calculates miles per gallon.
    //  If no gallons of gas have been used, returns 0.0;
    //  otherwise, returns miles per gallon
    //        as milesDriven / gallonsOfGas
    public double calculateMilesPerGallon( )
    {
       if ( gallonsOfGas != 0.0 )
         return milesDriven / gallonsOfGas;
       else
         return 0.0;
    }

    // toString: returns a String of instance variable values
    public String toString( )
    {
       DecimalFormat gallonsFormat = new DecimalFormat( "#0.0" );
       return "Model: " + model
              + "; miles driven: " + milesDriven
              + "; gallons of gas: "
              + gallonsFormat.format( gallonsOfGas );
    }

    // equals: returns true if fields of parameter object
    //         are equal to fields in this object
    public boolean equals( Object o )
    {
        if ( ! ( o instanceof Auto ) )
              return false;
        else
        {
              Auto objAuto = ( Auto ) o;
              if ( model.equals( objAuto.model )
```

```
118                     && milesDriven == objAuto.milesDriven
119                     && Math.abs( gallonsOfGas - objAuto.gallonsOfGas )
120                                          < 0.0001 )
121                       return true;
122                 else
123                       return false;
124         }
125     }
126 }
```

EXAMPLE 7.10 *Auto* Class, Version 5

In the *toString* method (lines 98–106), we begin by instantiating a *DecimalFormat* object for formatting the gallons of gas as a floating-point number with one decimal place. Note that *gallonsFormat* is a local variable for the *toString* method; that is, only the *toString* method can use the *gallonsFormat* object. To use the *DecimalFormat* class, we import the class on line 5. We then build the *String* to return by concatenating labels for each instance variable with the values of the instance variables. The *toString* method can be used in a client class containing the *main* method, for instance, to print *Auto* objects using a single statement instead of calling all the class accessor methods.

To implement our *equals* method (lines 108–125), we first need to check that the parameter's type is *Auto*. The *instanceof* binary operator, whose left operand is an object reference and right operand is a class, returns *true* if the object reference can be cast to an instance of the class (for example, if it is an object reference of that class), *false* otherwise. (See Table 7.4.) We use the *instanceof* operator at line 112 to determine if the parameter *o* can be cast to an *Auto* object reference (most likely, when sent by a client, *o* will be an *Auto* reference). If it cannot, we return *false*, otherwise, we can proceed

TABLE 7.4 The *instanceof* Operator

Operator	Syntax	Operation
instanceof	*objectReference* instanceof *ClassName*	evaluates to *true* if *objectReference* is of *ClassName* type; *false* otherwise.

with comparing *o*'s fields and this *Auto* object's fields. Before performing the comparison, we must cast the *Object* reference *o* to an *Auto* (line 116). Otherwise, there would be a compiler error when trying to access the instance variable *model* with the *Object o*, because *model* is an instance variable of class *Auto* and not of class *Object*.

REFERENCE POINT

Type casting is discussed in Chapter 2.

We compare each instance variable in the parameter object, *objAuto*, with the same instance variable in this object. We return *true* if the corresponding instance variables in each object have the same values; otherwise, we return *false*.

Notice that line 117 calls the *equals* method of the *String* class to compare the values of *model* in the objects because *model* is a *String* object reference. Notice also that because instance variables are in scope for methods, our *equals* method is able to directly access the instance variables of both this object and the *Auto* object, *objAuto*.

Example 7.11 puts version 5 of the *Auto* class to work. We instantiate two objects that differ only in the model. On line 10, we explicitly call *toString* to print the fields of the *sporty* object. On line 14, we implicitly call the *toString* method; *toString* is called automatically because the *compact* object is the argument sent to the *println* method, which converts the object to a *String*. On lines 16–19, we compare the two objects using the *equals* method and print the results. The output is shown in Figure 7.7.

```
1  /* Auto Client, version 5
2     Anderson, Franceschi
3  */
4
5  public class AutoClient
6  {
7    public static void main( String [ ] args )
8    {
9       Auto sporty = new Auto( "Spyder", 0, 0.0 );
10      System.out.println( sporty.toString( ) );
11
12      Auto compact = new Auto( "Accent", 0, 0.0 );
13      System.out.println( );
14      System.out.println( compact );
15
```

```
      if ( compact.equals( sporty ) )
        System.out.println( "\nsporty and compact are equal" );
      else
        System.out.println( "\nsporty and compact are not equal" );
   }
}
```

EXAMPLE 7.11 *Auto* Client, Version 5

```
Model: Spyder; miles driven: 0; gallons of gas: 0.0

Model: Accent; miles driven: 0; gallons of gas: 0.0

sporty and compact are not equal
```

Figure 7.7
Output from Example 7.11

CODE IN ACTION

On the CD-ROM included with this book, you will find a Flash movie illustrating step-by-step how to define a class. Click on the link for Chapter 7 to view the movie.

7.11 *Static* Class Members

As we have mentioned, a separate set of instance variables is created for each object that is instantiated. In addition to instance variables, classes can define **class variables**, which are created only once, when the JVM initializes the class. Thus, class variables exist before any objects are instantiated, and each class has only one copy of its class variables.

You can designate a class variable by using the keyword *static* in its definition. Also, *static* variables that are constants are usually declared to be *public* because they typically are provided to allow the client to set preferences for the operations of a class. For example, we can directly use the *INFORMATION_MESSAGE static* constant in the *JOptionPane* class to specify the type of icon to display in a dialog box.

Another purpose for *static* variables is to make it easier to use the class. For example, the *PI* and *E static* constants in the *Math* class are provided so that our applications do not need to define those commonly used values. Also, as we saw in the programming activity in Chapter 2, the maximum and minimum values for data types are made available as the *MAX_VALUE* and *MIN_VALUE public static* constants of the *Integer*, *Double*, and *Character* wrapper classes.

If, however, you define a *static* variable for your class that is not a constant, it is best to define it as *private* and provide accessor and mutator methods, as appropriate, for client access to the *static* variable.

We finish our *Auto* class, with Version 6 shown in Example 7.12, by defining a *private static* variable to count the number of objects that have been instantiated during the application. We call this class variable *countAutos* and initialize it to 0 (line 14). Because a constructor is called whenever an object is instantiated, we can update the count by incrementing the value of *countAutos* in the class constructors (lines 24 and 37).

When you define a *static* variable for your class, its accessor and mutator methods must be defined as ***static* methods**, also called **class methods**. To do this, insert the keyword *static* in the method headers after the access modifier. We provide a *static* accessor method for the client to get the count of *Auto* objects (lines 59–63). We do not provide a mutator method, however, because clients of the class should not be able to update the value of *countAutos* except via the constructors, which update the count automatically.

Methods that are defined to be *static* are subject to the following important restrictions, which are summarized in Table 7.5:

- *static* methods can reference only *static* variables.
- *static* methods can call only *static* methods.
- *static* methods cannot use the object reference *this*.

TABLE 7.5 Access Restrictions for *static* and Non-*static* Methods

	static method	Non-*static* Method
Access instance variables?	no	yes
Access *static* class variables?	yes	yes
Call *static* class methods?	yes	yes
Call non-*static* instance methods?	no	yes
Use the reference *this*?	no	yes

Again, it makes sense that *static* methods cannot access instance variables because *static* methods are associated with the class, not with any object. Further, a *static* method can be called before any objects are instantiated, so there will be no instance variables to access. Attempting to access an instance variable *xxx* from a *static* method will generate this compiler error:

```
non-static variable xxx cannot be referenced from a static context
```

Notice that the *getCountAutos* method (lines 59–63) is declared to be *static* and references only the *static countAutos* variable.

A non-*static*, or **instance**, method, on the other hand, can reference both class variables and instance variables, as well as class methods and instance methods.

At this point, we can explain a little more about the *main* method. Its header is:

```
public static void main( String [ ] args )
```

Because *main* is defined as *static*, the JVM can execute *main* without first creating an object.

```
1 /* Auto class, Version 6
2    Anderson, Franceschi
3 */
4
5 import java.text.DecimalFormat;
6
7 public class Auto
8 {
9     // instance variables
10    private String model;         //  model of auto
11    private int milesDriven;      //  number of miles driven
12    private double gallonsOfGas;  //  number of gallons of gas
13
14    private static int countAutos = 0;  // static class variable
15
16    // Constructors:
17    //  initializes model to "unknown";
18    //  milesDriven is autoinitialized to 0
19    //        and gallonsOfGas to 0.0;
20    // increments countAutos
21    public Auto( )
22    {
23      model = "unknown";
24      countAutos++;     // increment static count of Auto objects
25    }
26
```

```
   // allows client to set beginning values for
   // model, milesDriven, and gallonsOfGas;
   // increments countAutos
   public Auto( String startModel,
                int startMilesDriven,
                double startGallonsOfGas )
   {
     model = startModel;
     setMilesDriven( startMilesDriven );
     setGallonsOfGas( startGallonsOfGas );
     countAutos++;    // increment static count of Auto objects
   }

   // Accessor methods
   // returns current value of model
   public String getModel( )
   {
     return model;
   }

   // returns current value of milesDriven
   public int getMilesDriven( )
   {
     return milesDriven;
   }

   // returns current value of gallonsOfGas
   public double getGallonsOfGas( )
   {
     return gallonsOfGas;
   }

   // returns countAutos
   public static int getCountAutos( )
   {
     return countAutos;
   }

   // Mutator methods:
   // allows client to set model
   public void setModel( String newModel )
   {
      model = newModel;
   }

```

```
   // allows client to set value of milesDriven;
   // prints an error message if new value is less than 0
   public void setMilesDriven( int newMilesDriven )
   {
      if ( newMilesDriven >= 0 )
         milesDriven = newMilesDriven;
      else
      {
         System.err.println( "Miles driven cannot be negative." );
         System.err.println( "Value not changed." );
      }
   }

   // allows client to set value of gallonsOfGas;
   // prints an error message if new value is less than 0.0
   public void setGallonsOfGas( double newGallonsOfGas )
   {
     if ( newGallonsOfGas >= 0.0 )
        gallonsOfGas = newGallonsOfGas;
     else
     {
        System.err.println( "Gallons of gas cannot be negative." );
        System.err.println( "Value not changed." );
     }
   }

   // Calculates miles per gallon.
   // If no gallons of gas have been used, returns 0.0;
   // otherwise, returns miles per gallon
   //   as milesDriven / gallonsOfGas
   public double calculateMilesPerGallon( )
   {
     if ( gallonsOfGas != 0.0 )
          return milesDriven / gallonsOfGas;
     else
          return 0.0;
   }

   // toString: returns a String with values of instance variable
   public String toString( )
   {
      DecimalFormat gallonsFormat = new DecimalFormat( "#0.0" );
      return "Model: " + model
            + "; miles driven: " + milesDriven
            + "; gallons of gas: "
```

```
            + gallonsFormat.format( gallonsOfGas );
  }

  // equals: returns true if fields of parameter object
  //          are equal to fields in this object
   public boolean equals( Object o )
   {
       if ( ! ( o instanceof Auto ) )
             return false;
       else
       {
             Auto objAuto = ( Auto ) o;
             if ( model.equals( objAuto.model )
                  && milesDriven == objAuto.milesDriven
                  && Math.abs( gallonsOfGas - objAuto.gallonsOfGas )
                                                 < 0.0001 )
                       return true;
             else
                       return false;
       }
   }
 }
```

EXAMPLE 7.12 ***Auto*** **Class, Version 6**

Example 7.13 shows Version 6 of our *AutoClient* class. In line 11, we call the *getCountAutos* method before instantiating any objects, then in line 17, we call the *getCountAutos* method again after instantiating one object. As Figure 7.8 shows, the *getCountAutos* method first returns 0, then 1. Notice that in both calls to the *static* method, we use the dot operator with the class name rather than an object reference.

```
 1  /* Auto Client, Version 6
 2     Anderson, Franceschi
 3  */
 4
 5  public class AutoClient
 6  {
 7    public static void main( String [ ] args )
 8    {
 9       System.out.println( "Before instantiating an Auto object:"
10                           + "\nthe count of Auto objects is "
11                           + Auto.getCountAutos( ) );
12
```

```
      Auto sporty = new Auto( "Spyder", 0, 0.0 );

      System.out.println( "\nAfter instantiating an Auto object:"
                          + "\nthe count of Auto objects is "
                          + Auto.getCountAutos( ) );
   }
}
```

EXAMPLE 7.13 *Auto* Client, Version 6

Figure 7.8
Output from Example 7.13

```
Before instantiating an Auto object:
the count of Auto objects is 0

After instantiating an Auto object:
the count of Auto objects is 1
```

Well, there it is. We've finished defining our *Auto* class. Although it's a large class, we were able to build the *Auto* class incrementally using stepwise refinement.

7.12 Graphical Objects

Let's revisit the astronaut from Chapter 4. We drew the astronaut in the *paint* method. The code for the astronaut and the applet was intertwined, or tightly coupled. We couldn't run the applet without drawing the astronaut, and we couldn't draw the astronaut without running the applet.

Now that we know how to design our own classes, we can separate the astronaut from the applet. We can define the astronaut as its own *Astronaut* class and make the applet the client of the *Astronaut* class. This will allow us to encapsulate the astronaut's data and the code for drawing the astronaut within the *Astronaut* class. It also promotes reuse of the *Astronaut* class by other programmers, who might want to create *Astronaut* objects for different applications.

The *Astronaut* class is shown in Example 7.14. We started by identifying the instance variables of the *Astronaut* class. Obviously, we need the starting (*x*, *y*) coordinate to draw the astronaut, so we define two *int* instance variables to hold those values (lines 11–12).

In addition, we added one more instance variable, *scale* (line 13), to allow the client to draw astronauts of different sizes. For example, a scaling factor of 1.0 will draw the astronaut at full size, 0.5 will draw the astronaut at half size, and 2.0 will draw a double-sized astronaut.

Our default constructor (lines 15–23) sets the starting *x* and *y* values to 0 and the scaling factor to 1.0 so that by default the astronaut is drawn in the upper-left corner of the window at full size. The overloaded constructor (lines 25–33) accepts values for these instance variables.

We provide one mutator method to change both *x* and *y* values (lines 36–40), as well as another mutator to change the scaling factor (lines 42–48).

We moved the code that draws the astronaut from the applet's *paint* method into its own method, which we named *draw* (lines 50–131). Because the astronaut is drawn using methods of the *Graphics* class, the applet client will need to pass its *Graphics* object as an argument to the *draw* method. Also, because the space suit color is used only in the *draw* method, we made it a local variable (line 59). If we wanted to let the client choose the space suit color, we could define another instance variable for it and add a corresponding parameter to the overloaded constructor.

Inside the *draw* method, we made a few changes to make the astronaut easier to scale. First, we converted the starting *x* and *y* coordinates to the center of the astronaut's head. In this way, the calculations for scaling the astronaut are simplified because we can capitalize on the astronaut's symmetry. Next we drew each part of the astronaut by multiplying any length measurement by the scaling factor. Finally, because the scaling factor is a *double* and the *Graphics* methods expect integer arguments, we type cast our calculated measurement to an *int* when needed.

We did not provide accessor methods or write a *toString* or an *equals* method for the *Astronaut* class. For a graphical object, these methods are less useful, given that the major purpose of graphical objects is to be drawn.

```
1 /* An Astronaut Class
2    Anderson, Franceschi
3 */
4
5 import java.awt.Graphics;
6 import java.awt.Color;
7
8 public class Astronaut
9 {
```

```
    // the starting x and y coordinates for the astronaut
    private int sX;
    private int sY;
    private double scale; // scaling factor, 1.0 is full size

    // Default constructor:
    // sets starting x and y coordinates to 0
    // sets scaling factor to 1.0
    public Astronaut( )
    {
      sX = 0;  // draw in upper-left corner
      sY = 0;
      scale = 1.0;  // draw full size
    }

    // Overloaded constructor:
    // sets starting x and y coordinates
    //  and scaling factor to values set by client
    public Astronaut( int startX, int startY, double startScale )
    {
      sX = startX;
      sY = startY;
      setScale ( startScale );
    }

    // Mutator methods:
    public void setCoordinates( int newX, int newY )
    {
      sX = newX;
      sY = newY;
    }

    public void setScale( double newScale )
    {
      if ( newScale > 0 )
          scale = newScale;
      else
          scale = 1.0;
    }

    // draw method:
    // draws astronaut using starting (x,y) coordinate
    //  and scaling factor
    public void draw( Graphics g )
    {
```

```
    // convert between starting x, y coordinates and center of head
    int oX = sX + (int) (65 * 2 * scale);
    int oY = sY + (int) (75 * scale);

    Color spacesuit = new Color( 195, 175, 150 );
    // helmet
    g.setColor( spacesuit );
    g.fillOval( oX - (int) (75 * scale / 2),
                oY - (int) (75 * scale / 2),
                (int) (75 * scale), (int) (75 * scale) );
    g.setColor( Color.LIGHT_GRAY );
    g.fillOval( oX - (int) (55 * scale / 2),
                oY - (int) (55 * scale / 2),
                (int) (55 * scale), (int) (55 * scale) );

    // face
    g.setColor( Color.DARK_GRAY );
    g.drawOval( oX - (int) ( (55 * scale / 4 )
                  + (8 * scale / 2) ),
                  oY - (int) (55 * scale / 4), (int) (8 * scale),
                  (int) (8 * scale) );
    g.drawOval( oX + (int) ( (55 * scale / 4)
                   -  (8 * scale / 2) ),
                  oY - (int) (55 * scale / 4), (int) (8 * scale),
                  (int) (8 * scale) );
    g.drawLine( oX,  oY - (int) (6 * scale),
                  oX + (int) (2  *  scale),
                  oY + (int) (6 * scale) );
    g.drawLine( oX, oY + (int) (6 * scale),
                  oX + (int) (2  *  scale),
                  oY + (int) (6 * scale) );
    g.drawOval( oX - (int) (15 * scale / 2),
                  oY + (int) (55 * scale / 4),
                  (int) (15 * scale), (int) (6 * scale) );

    // neck
    g.setColor( spacesuit );
    g.fillRect( oX - (int) (20 * scale / 2),
                oY + (int) (-1 + 75 * scale / 2),
                (int) (20 * scale), (int) (1 + 10 * scale) );

    // torso
    g.fillRect( oX - (int) (65 * scale / 2),
                oY +(int) (-1 + 75 * scale / 2 + 10 * scale),
                (int) (65 * scale), (int) (1 + 85 * scale) );
```

```
    // arms
    g.fillRect( oX - (int) (65 * 3 * scale / 2),
                 oY + (int) (75 * scale / 2 + 10 * scale),
                (int) (1 + 65 * scale), (int) (20 * scale) );
    g.fillRect( oX + (int) (-1 + 65 * scale / 2),
                 oY + (int) (75 * scale / 2 + 10 * scale),
                (int) (1 + 65 * scale), (int) (20 * scale) );

    // legs
    g.fillRect( oX - (int) (55 * scale / 2),
                 oY + (int) (-1 + 75 * scale / 2 + 95 * scale),
                (int) (20 * scale), (int) (80 * scale) );
    g.fillRect( oX + (int) (55 * scale / 2 - 20 * scale),
                oY + (int) (- 1 + 75 * scale / 2 + 95 * scale ),
                (int) (20 * scale), (int) (80 * scale) );

    // flag
    g.setColor( Color.BLACK );
    g.drawLine( oX + (int) (65 * scale / 2 + 65 * scale),
                    oY + (int) (75 * scale / 2 + 10 * scale),
                    oX + (int) (65 * scale / 2 + 65 * scale),
                    oY );
    g.setColor( Color.RED );
    g.fillRect( oX + (int) (65 * scale / 2 + 65 * scale),
                 oY - (int) (75 * scale / 2),
                 (int) (75 * scale), (int) (45 * scale) );
    g.setColor( Color.BLUE );
    g.fillRect( oX + (int) (65 * scale / 2 + 65 * scale ),
                 oY - (int) (75 * scale / 2),
                 (int) (30 * scale), (int) (25 * scale) );
  }
}
```

EXAMPLE 7.14 The *Astronaut* Class

Now, we can create the applet class, which will be the client of the *Astronaut* class. Our simplified *AstronautClient* applet is shown in Example 7.15. The applet has one instance variable, which is an *Astronaut* object reference, *astro*. We instantiate the *Astronaut* object in the *init* method (lines 13–17). The *init* method, which is part of the *JApplet* class and therefore is inherited by the *Astronaut* class, is a place to put initialization code, such as assigning initial values to instance variables. Similar to a constructor, the *init* method is called automatically when an applet begins running. We did not use the *init* method in applet examples in previous chapters; in fact, if your applet does not have any instance variables and so doesn't need to perform any initialization, then the *init* method is optional.

We call the *Astronaut*'s *draw* method in the applet's *paint* method (line 23), passing to *draw* the *Graphics* object reference *g* that was passed to *paint*. The applet window is shown in Figure 7.9.

```
1  /* Astronaut client
2     Anderson, Franceschi
3  */
4
5  import javax.swing.JApplet;
6  import java.awt.Graphics;
7
8  public class AstronautClient extends JApplet
9  {
10    // instance variable is an Astronaut
11    private Astronaut astro;
12
13    public void init( )
14    {
15       // instantiate the Astronaut object
16       astro = new Astronaut( 50, 12, 1 );
17    }
18
19    public void paint( Graphics g )
20    {
21       super.paint( g );
22
23       astro.draw( g ); // draw the astronaut
24    }
25 }
```

EXAMPLE 7.15 The *AstronautClient* Applet

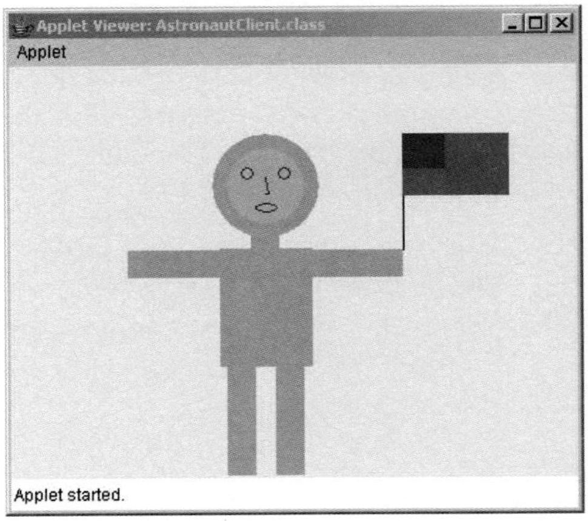

Figure 7.9
The *AstronautClient* Window

An advantage to separating the *Astronaut* class from the *AppletClient* class is that it is now easy to draw two or more astronauts. Example 7.16 shows the code for the *AstronautClient2* class, which draws two astronauts, one full size and one half size. To add a second astronaut, all we needed to do was declare a second *Astronaut* object reference (line 11), instantiate it in *init* (line 17), and call the *draw* method for the second astronaut in the applet's *paint* method (line 26).

There is one other small change we needed to make. With two astronauts, we need a larger window, so we call the *setSize* method (line 18), passing it the new width and height of the applet window. The *setSize* method is inherited from the *JApplet* class. As such, it is a method of our *Astronaut-Client2* class, so we call *setSize* without an object reference. Figure 7.10 shows the output from the applet.

```
1  /* Astronaut client with two astronauts
2     Anderson, Franceschi
3  */
4
5  import javax.swing.JApplet;
6  import java.awt.Graphics;
7
8  public class AstronautClient2 extends JApplet
9  {
10    // instance variables
11    private Astronaut astro1, astro2;
12
13    public void init( )
14    {
15       // instantiate the Astronaut objects
16       astro1 = new Astronaut( 25, 10, 1.0 );  // full size
17       astro2 = new Astronaut( 225, 155, 0.5 ); // half size
18       setSize( 500, 300 ); // set the window size
19    }
20
21    public void paint( Graphics g )
22    {
23        super.paint( g );
```

```
        astro1.draw( g ); // draw first Astronaut
        astro2.draw( g ); // draw second Astronaut
    }
}
```

EXAMPLE 7.16 The *AstronautClient2* Class with Two Astronauts

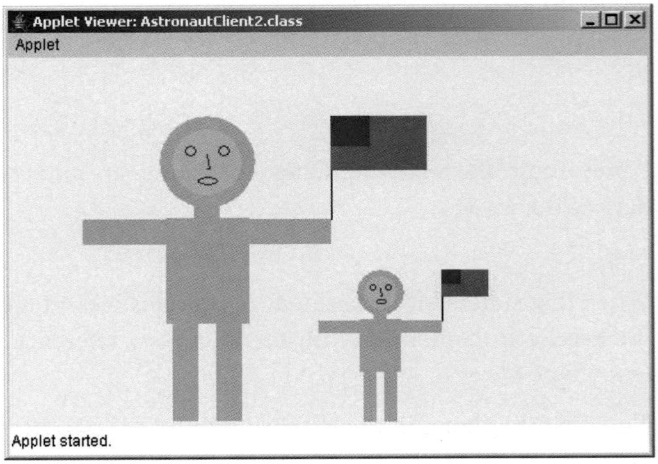

Figure 7.10
The *AstronautClient2* Window

7.13 Enumeration Types

Enumeration types are designed to increase the readability of programs. The enumeration type, *enum*, is a special kind of class declaration. It allows us to define a set of named constant objects that can be used instead of numbers in a program.

Enum types are useful for managing ordered sets where each member of the set has a name. Examples are the days of the week, months of the year, and playing cards. To represent these sets in a program, we often use numbers, such as 1 through 7 for the days of the week or 1 through 12 for the months of the year. The problem is that to input or output these values, we need to convert between our internal numeric representation (for example, 1–7) and the words that users recognize (Sunday, Monday, Tueday, etc.). The *enum* type allows us to instantiate a constant object for each value in a set. The set of objects will be ordered so that we can refer to the objects by name, without the need for using numbers.

The *enum* functionality is built into *java.lang*, so we can define *enum* types without using an *import* statement.

The syntax for creating a set of *enum* objects is

```
enum EnumName { obj1, obj2, . . . };

where obj1, obj2, etc. are names for the constant objects.
```

For example, the following statement defines an *enum* type to represent the days of the week:

```
enum Days { Sun, Mon, Tue, Wed, Thur, Fri, Sat };
```

When that statement is executed, an object is instantiated for each name in the list. Each name in the list, therefore, is a reference to an object of the *enum* type *Days*.

COMMON ERROR TRAP

Do not use *String* literals in the initialization list for *enum* types.

Note that the values in the initialization list are object references (*Sun*), not *String* literals ("*Sun*").

Each object has an instance variable that holds a numeric value, which is determined by its position in the list of *enum* objects. By default, the first object has the value 0, the second object has the value 1, and so on. Because the objects are an ordered set, for example, the object *Thur* is higher in value than *Wed*. We can use the *enum* objects, however, without relying on the specific value of each object.

The *enum* objects are instantiated as constant objects, meaning that their values cannot be changed.

To refer to any of the constant objects in an *enum* type, we use the following dot syntax:

```
enumType.enumObject
```

Thus, to refer to the *Wed* object in our *Days enum* type, we use this syntax:

```
Days.Wed
```

Once we have defined an *enum* type, we can declare an object reference of that type. For example, the following statement defines a *Days* object reference *d*:

```
Days d;
```

Like any other object reference, the value of *d* will be *null* initially. To assign a value to the reference *d*—for example, *Thur*—we use the following statement:

```
d = Days.Thur;
```

Table 7.6 lists some useful methods that can be called with *enum* objects, and Example 7.17 demonstrates the use of these methods.

TABLE 7.6 Useful Methods for *enum* Objects

Useful Methods for *enum* Objects	
Return type	**Method name and argument list**
`int`	`compareTo ( Enum eObj )`
	compares two *enum* objects and returns a negative number if *this* object is less than the argument, a positive number if *this* object is greater than the argument, and 0 if the two objects are the same
`boolean`	`equals( Object eObj )`
	returns *true* if this object is equal to the argument *eObj*; returns *false* otherwise
`int`	`ordinal( )`
	returns the numeric value of the *enum* object. By default, the value of the first object in the list is 0, the value of the second object is 1, and so on
`String`	`toString( )`
	returns the name of the *enum* constant
`enum`	`valueOf( String enumName )`
	static method that returns the *enum* object whose name is the same as the *String* argument *enumName*

```
1 /* Demonstration of enum
2    Anderson, Franceschi
3 */
4
5 public class EnumDemo
6 {
7   public enum Days { Sun, Mon, Tue, Wed, Thur, Fri, Sat };
8
9   public static void main( String [ ] args )
10  {
11     Days d1, d2;  // declare two Days object references
12
13     d1 = Days.Wed;
14     d2 = Days.Fri;
15
16     System.out.println( "Comparing objects using equals" );
17     if ( d1.equals( d2 ) )
18       System.out.println( d1 + " equals " + d2 );
19     else
20       System.out.println( d1 + " does not equal " + d2 );
21
22     System.out.println( "\nComparing objects using compareTo" );
23     if ( d1.compareTo( d2 ) > 0 )
24       System.out.println( d1 + " is greater than " + d2 );
25     else if ( d1.compareTo( d2 ) < 0 )
26       System.out.println( d1 + " is less than " + d2 );
27     else
28       System.out.println( d1 + " is equal to " + d2 );
29
30     System.out.println( "\nGetting the  ordinal value" );
31     System.out.println( "The value of " + d1 + " is "
32                         + d1.ordinal( ) );
33
34     System.out.println( "\nConverting a String to an object" );
35     Days day = Days.valueOf( "Mon" );
36     System.out.println( "The value of day is " + day );
37   }
38 }
```

EXAMPLE 7.17 A Demonstration of *enum* Methods

Line 7 defines the *enum* type *Days*; this instantiates the seven constant objects representing the days of the week. On line 11, we declare two object references of the *Days enum* type. Then on lines 13 and 14, we assign *d1* a reference to the *Wed* object, and we assign *d2* a reference to the *Fri* object.

```
Comparing objects using equals
Wed does not equal Fri

Comparing objects using compareTo
Wed is less than Fri

Getting the ordinal value
The value of Wed is 3

Converting a String to an object
The value of day is Mon
```

Figure 7.11
Output from Example 7.17

Line 17 compares *d1* and *d2* using the *equals* method. Because *Wed* and *Fri* are different objects, the *equals* method returns *false.* Lines 18 and 20 implicitly call the *toString* method, which prints the name of the objects.

Lines 23 and 25 call the *compareTo* method, which returns a negative number, indicating that *Wed* is lower in value than *Fri.*

We then retrieve the value of the *d1* object by calling the *ordinal* method (lines 31–32), which returns 3 because *Wed* is the fourth object in the *enum* list.

Finally, line 35 converts from a *String* to an *enum* object using the *valueOf* method. Notice that the *valueOf* method is *static,* so we call it using our *enum* type, *Days.*

If the *String* passed to the *valueOf* method is not a name in our set of defined *enum* objects, the *valueOf* method generates an *IllegalArgumentException.* In Chapter 11, we show you how to intercept an exception and reprompt the user for a valid name.

REFERENCE POINT

Exceptions are covered in Chapter 11.

The output from Example 7.17 is shown in Figure 7.11.

We can use *enum* objects in *switch* statements to make the *case* constants more meaningful, which in turn makes the code more readable. Example 7.18 uses our *Days enum* class to display the daily specials offered in the cafeteria.

```
/** Specials of the Day
    Anderson, Franceschi
*/

import java.util.Scanner;

public class DailySpecials
```

```
{
  public enum Days { Sun, Mon, Tue, Wed, Thur, Fri, Sat };

  public static void main( String [ ] args )
  {
    Scanner scan = new Scanner( System.in );

    System.out.print( "Enter a day\n"
                      + "(Sun, Mon, Tue, Wed, Thur, Fri, Sat) > " );
    String inputDay = scan.next( );
    Days day = Days.valueOf( inputDay );

    switch ( day )
    {
       case Mon:
            System.out.println( "The special for "
                                + day + " is barbeque chicken." );
            break;

       case Tue:
            System.out.println( "The special for "
                                + day + " is tacos" );
            break;

       case Wed:
            System.out.println( "The special for "
                                + day + " is chef's salad" );
            break;

       case Thur:
            System.out.println( "The special for "
                                + day + " is a cheeseburger" );
            break;

        case Fri:
            System.out.println( "The special for "
                                + day + " is fish fillet" );
            break;

        default: // if day is Sat or Sun
            System.out.println( "Sorry, we're closed on "
                                + day );
    }
  }
}
```

EXAMPLE 7.18 ***DailySpecials*** **Class**

```
Enter a day
(Sun, Mon, Tue, Wed, Thur, Fri, Sat) > Fri
The special for Fri is fish fillet
```

Figure 7.12
Output from *DailySpecials*

Figure 7.12 shows the output from Example 7.18 when the user enters *Fri.*

In the *DailySpecials* program, we prompt the user for a day (lines 15–17), then read the *String* entered by the user and convert it to an *enum* object by calling the *valueOf* method at line 18.

Once we have a valid *enum* value, we can use it as a *switch* variable (line 20).

Notice that we use each *enum* object name in a *case* label without qualifying it with the *Days* type. Including the *enum* type in a *switch* statement generates the following compiler error:

```
an enum switch case label must be the unqualified name of an
enumeration constant
```

Skill Practice
with these end-of-chapter questions

7.18.1 Multiple Choice Exercises
Questions 14,15,16

7.18.2 Reading and Understanding Code
Questions 21,22,23,25,27

7.18.3 Fill In the Code
Questions 29,34,35

7.18.4 Identifying Errors in Code
Questions 40,41,42,44,46

7.18.5 Debugging Area
Questions 50,51,53,54

7.18.6 Write a Short Program
Questions 55,56,57,58,59,60,61,62

7.18.8 Technical Writing
Question 72

7.14 Programming Activity 2: Writing a Class Definition, Part 2

In this programming activity, you will complete the definition of the *Airport* class. Then you will run a prewritten client program that instantiates several *Airport* objects, calls the methods that you have written, and displays the values of the objects' data.

Copy into a directory on your computer all the files from the Chapter 7 Programming Activity 2 folder on the CD-ROM accompanying this book. Note that all files should be in the same directory.

Load the *Airport.java* source file; you'll notice that the class already contains the class definition from Programming Activity 1. Your job is to complete the class definition by adding a *static* class variable (and its supporting code) and writing the *toString* and *equals* methods. It is important to define the *static* class variable and the methods exactly as described in the comments because the *AirportClient* class will call each method to test its implementation. Searching for five asterisks in a row (*****) will position you at the six places in the class definition where you will add your code. The *Airport.java* code is shown here in Example 7.19:

```
/* Airport class
   Anderson, Franceschi
*/

public class Airport
{

  // instance variables
  private String airportCode;
  private int gates;

  // 1. ***** Add a static class variable *****
  //  countAirports is an int
  //  assign an initial value of 0


  // 2. ***** Modify this method *****
  // Default constructor:
  // method name: Airport
  // return value:  none
  // parameters: none
  // function: sets the airportCode to a blank String
  //     ***** add 1 to countAirports class variable
```

```
public Airport( )
{
   airportCode = "";

}

// 3. ***** Modify this method *****
// Overloaded constructor:
// method name: Airport
// return value: none
// parameters:  a String airport code and an int startGates
// function: assigns airportCode the value of the
//      startAirportCode parameter;
//      calls the setGates method,
//      passing the startGates parameter
//    ***** add 1 to countAirports class variable
public Airport( String startAirportCode, int startGates )
{
   airportCode = startAirportCode;
   setGates( startGates );

}

// Accessor method for the airportCode instance variable
// method name: getAirportCode
// return value: String
// parameters: none
// function: returns airportCode
public String getAirportCode( )
{
   return airportCode;
}

// Accessor method for the gates instance variable
// method name: getGates
// return value: int
// parameters: none
// function: returns gates
public int getGates( )
{
   return gates;
}

// 4. ***** Write this method *****
// Accessor method for the countAirports class variable
```

```
// method name: getCountAirports
// return value: int
// parameters: none
// function: returns countAirports




// Mutator method for the airportCode instance variable
// method name: setAirportCode
// return value: void
// parameters: String newAirportCode
// function: assigns airportCode the value of the
//                    newAirportCode parameter
public void setAirportCode( String newAirportCode )
{
   airportCode = newAirportCode;
}

// Mutator method for the gates instance variable
// method name: setGates
// return value:  void
// parameters: int newGates
// function: validates the newGates parameter.
//   if newGates is greater than 0, sets gates to newGates;
//   otherwise, prints an error message to System.err
//   and does not change value of gates
public void setGates( int newGates )
{
   if ( newGates  >=  0 )
     gates = newGates;
   else
   {
     System.err.println( "Gates must be at least 0" );
     System.err.println( "Value of gates unchanged." );
   }
}

// 5. ***** Write this method *****
// method name:  toString
// return value: String
// parameters: none
// function:  returns a String that contains the airportCode
```

```
//    and gates

// 6. ***** Write this method *****
// method name: equals
// return value: boolean
// parameter:  Airport object
// function:  returns true if airportCode
//     and gates in this object
//    are equal to those in the parameter object;
//    returns false otherwise

} // end of Airport class definition
```

EXAMPLE 7.19 The *Airport.java* File

When you finish modifying the *Airport* class, compile the source file. When *Airport.java* compiles without any errors, load and compile the *AirportClient.java* file. This source file contains *main*, so you will execute the application from this file. When the application begins, you should see the window shown in Figure 7.13.

As you can see, the *AirportClient* has declared two *Airport* object references, *airport1* and *airport2*. The references are *null* because no *Airport* objects have been instantiated. Note also that the value of the *countAirports* class variable is displayed.

The *AirportClient* application will call methods of the *Airport* class to instantiate the two *Airport* objects, call the *toString* and *equals* methods, and get the value of the *static* class variable, *countAirports*. As the application does its work, it displays a status message at the bottom of the window indicating which method has been called and it also displays the current

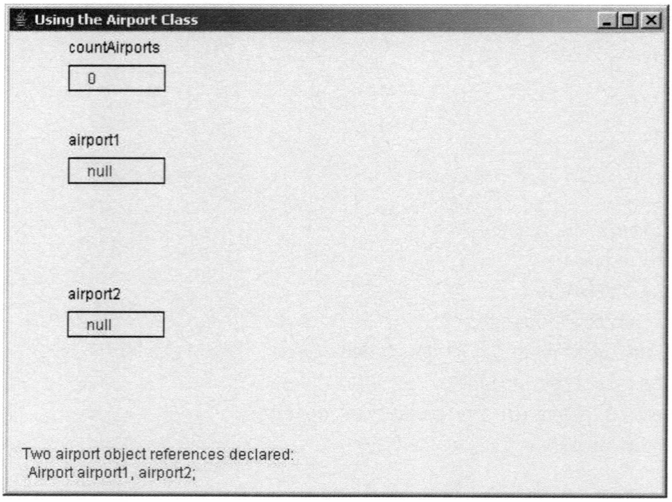

Figure 7.13
***AirportClient* Opening Window**

state of the *Airport* objects. You can check your work by comparing the state of the objects with the status message.

DISCUSSION QUESTIONS

1. Explain why the *countAirports* class variable has a value of 0 before any *Airport* objects have been instantiated.
2. How does a client call the *getCountAirports* method?
3. Explain why the client calls the *equals* method rather than directly comparing the object references *airport1* and *airport2* using the following *if* statement:

```
if ( airport1 == airport2 )
```

7.15 Creating Packages

As we have mentioned, one of the advantages of a well-written class is that it can be reused. Ideally, as you write programs, you will look for functionality that is common to many programs. It is a good practice to encapsulate this functionality into a class so that you can reuse that code in future programs. Java provides the concept of a package for easily reusing classes.

SOFTWARE ENGINEERING TIP

Put classes that provide reusable functionality into a package.

A **package** is a collection of related classes that can be imported into programs. We have imported classes from multiple Java packages: *java.awt*, *java.util*, *java.text*, and others. We can also create our own packages, which allows us to reuse a class without needing to physically store that class in the same directory as our other source files. Instead, we create the package and *import* the class from that package into our source file.

Let's look at an example of a class that can provide reusable functionality to our programs. In Chapter 6, we demonstrated how to detect and recover from an error when the user enters data that is a different type from what we expect. For example, if we prompt the user for an integer and the user enters a letter instead, the default behavior of the *Scanner* class is to generate an *InputMismatchException*. Our solution in Chapter 6 was to check whether the user's input matched our expected data type before attempting to read the value. For example, we inserted the following code to read an *int*:

```
System.out.print( "Enter . . . as an integer > " );
while ( ! scan.hasNextInt( ) )
{
   String garbage = scan.nextLine( );
   System.out.print( "\nPlease enter an integer > " );
}
int x = scan.nextInt( );
```

Although looping until the user enters a valid value solves the input mismatch problem, that's a lot of code to include in our program every time we need to read data that is a primitive data type.

Instead, we can create a class that provides the functionality we need, but which hides the complexity of the validation code. When we need input from the user, we'll call the methods of that class instead of coding the *while* loop. Example 7.20 shows the code for a *ConsoleIn* class that provides methods for type-safe reading of integers. That class can easily be expanded to include methods for type-safe reading of other primitive types.

```
/** Type-Safe Input Using Scanner
*   Anderson, Franceschi
*/
package com.jbpub.af;

import java.util.Scanner;

public class ConsoleIn
{
    private Scanner scan;

    public ConsoleIn( )
    {
```

```
14       scan = new Scanner( System.in );
15    }
16
17    public int readInt( String prompt )
18    {
19       System.out.print( prompt + " > " );
20       while ( ! scan.hasNextInt( ) )
21       {
22          String garbage = scan.nextLine( );
23          System.out.println( "Input is not an integer" );
24          System.out.print( prompt + " > " );
25       }
26       return scan.nextInt( );
27    }
28 }
```

EXAMPLE 7.20 *ConsoleIn* Class

We provide a constructor for the class (lines 12–15) that instantiates an object of the *Scanner* class and associates it with the console (*System.in*).

Although we only provide a method to read *ints*, we could easily provide *read* methods for each primitive data type; the general API would be the following:

```
public dataType readDataType( String prompt )
```

Let's look at the *readInt* method (lines 17–27). Its API is

```
public int readInt( String prompt )
```

Line 19 displays the prompt and appends a space, the > character, and another space. Lines 20 through 25 consist of a *while* loop that tests whether the input the user entered is an integer. The *hasNextInt* method of the *Scanner* class returns *true* if the input is an integer. So if the *hasNextInt* method returns *false*, we flush the bad input by calling the *nextLine* method of the *Scanner* class to ignore the returned data. We then print an error message and reprompt the user. This process repeats until the user types an integer, at which time, the *hasNextInt* method returns *true*. We then skip to line 26, which reads and returns the integer the user entered. The methods for reading the other primitive data types follow the same pattern.

Now that we have the *ConsoleIn* class, we can put the class into a package to make it available for use in other programs.

To create a package, you insert a *package* statement into the source file as the first line after the header comments. The *package* statement has the following syntax:

```
package packageName;
```

In the *ConsoleIn* class, we define our package as *com.jbpub.af* (line 4). Because many programmers create packages, we need to avoid a situation, called **name collision**, where multiple programmers choose the same name for their packages. The convention, therefore, is to name your package using your domain name. Specifically, the package name should use the reverse of the domain name (without the *www*). Thus, because our domain name is *www.jbpub.com*, we begin all our package names with *com.jbpub*. For this package, we append a dot and *af*. Each part of the package name represents a directory. So our package will be stored in the directory structure *com\jbpub\af* or *com/jbpub/af*, depending on the operating system. In an *import* statement, the dots in the package name separate the directory names in a platform-independent way.

The next step in creating a package is to create the directory where you want to place the package. Later on, as you create more classes you can put these classes in that same package or create a new package in the same or a different directory.

For our package, we created the *com* directory, then created a subdirectory, *jbpub*, and an *af* subdirectory in the *jbpub* directory.

The next step is to copy the source file into the package directory and compile it. We copied the *ConsoleIn.java* source file into the *af* directory and compiled it.

So that the compiler can find the package you just created, the final step is to modify your *CLASSPATH* environment variable, which tells the Java compiler where to look for packages. This step is system-dependent. We've included instructions for Windows 2000 and Linux systems. For other operating systems, consult your system documentation or Sun Microsystems' Java website.

For a Windows 2000 machine, we suggest the following steps:

> Let's assume that you have decided to put the packages you create into the *My Documents* folder. For the package *com.jbpub.af*, you would create the directories in such a way that *af* will be a subdirectory of *jbpub*, itself a subdirectory of *com*, itself a subdirectory of *My Documents*.

Open the *Control Panel* and select the *System* icon. (On Windows XP, in the *Control Panel*, you will need to select the *Performance and Maintenance* icon before you can select the *System* icon.) From the *Advanced* tab, select the *Environment Variables* button. You will see two windows. In the top window, labeled *User variables*, look for *classpath* under the *variable* column.

If you see *classpath*, click the *edit* button. Append a semicolon and the pathname to the *My Documents* folder to the value that *classpath* currently has.

If *classpath* does not appear under the *variable* column, click the *new* button. Type *classpath* into the *Variable name* text box and type the pathname to the *My Documents* folder into the *Variable value* text box. You will probably need to add the current directory, designated by a dot (.), to the value.

When you finish, the *classpath* variable value might look like this:

```
.;c:\documents and settings\yourusername\my documents\
```

The initial dot (.) indicates that the compiler should look first in the current directory for classes.

On a typical Linux machine, we suggest using the following steps:

Let's assume that you have decided to put the packages that you create in the following directory, where *studentName* would be your user ID:

```
/home/studentName/myOwnClasses
```

At the Unix prompt, type the following command. (We use the # sign below to represent the Unix prompt.)

```
# export CLASSPATH=$CLASSPATH:/home/studentName/myOwnClasses
```

This statement appends */home/studentName/myOwnClasses* to the *CLASSPATH* environment variable. To check that this command was successful, at the Unix prompt type:

```
# echo $CLASSPATH
```

Your result should look something like this:

```
/usr/local/java/jre/lib:.:/home/studentName/myOwnClasses
```

You can see three directory paths separated by a colon (:):

- `/usr/local/java/jre/lib` is the directory (depending on your machine and your versions of Unix and Java, it could very well be another one) where the Java Class Library is located.
- `.` (dot) is the current directory.

- `/home/studentName/myOwnClasses` is the directory where you are planning to place the packages that you create.

Once the package is created, you can import the class to use its functionality. Example 7.21 shows client code that uses the *ConsoleIn* class to read an integer.

```
1 /*  ConsoleIn Client
2     Anderson, Franceschi
3 */
4 import com.jbpub.af.ConsoleIn; // import ConsoleIn from package
5
6 public class ConsoleInClient
7 {
8    public static void main( String [ ] args )
9    {
10      ConsoleIn console = new ConsoleIn( );
11
12      int age = console.readInt( "Enter your age" );
13      System.out.println( "Your age is " + age );
14   }
15 }
```

EXAMPLE 7.21 ***ConsoleInClient* Class**

In Example 7.21, we import the *ConsoleIn* class on line 4. Line 10 instantiates a *ConsoleIn* object, then line 12 uses that object reference to call the *readInt* method. Figure 7.14 shows the output of the *ConsoleInClient* class when the user enters invalid input, then valid input.

```
Enter your age > abc
Input is not an integer
Enter your age > 23.4
Input is not an integer
Enter your age > 23
Your age is 23
```

Figure 7.14
Output from the *ConsoleInClient* Class

7.16 Generating Web-Style Documentation with Javadoc

In most corporations and organizations, programmers share code and frequently use classes developed by another programmer. If the class is well designed and well documented, it will be easy for others to use that class. After all, that is essentially what we have been doing by using existing Java classes. It has been easy to understand what functions these existing classes perform, what they encapsulate, how the constructors work, what the methods do, and how to use the classes. The reason that these classes are easy to understand and use is not only that they are well designed and written, but also that the available documentation, particularly on Sun Microsystems' Java website, is clear, easy to understand, complete, and represents these classes well.

We, too, will learn how to produce HTML-based documentation similar to the documentation available on Sun Microsystems' Java website.

Indeed, there is a tool, called **Javadoc**, provided in the Java Development Kit (JDK), to do just that. Javadoc is an executable program (actually *javadoc.exe*) located in the *bin* directory. It is invoked much the same way as the *javac* compiler, except that instead of creating *.class* files, it creates *.html* files that document the class.

For instance, to generate documentation for our *Auto* class, we would type the following at the command line:

```
javadoc Auto.java
```

If we want to generate documentation for all the source files in the directory, we would type:

```
javadoc *.java
```

Table 7.7 shows the files generated for the *Auto* class.

If you double-click on *index.html*, you will open a web page with the same look as the ones on Sun's Java website.

REFERENCE POINT

The full documentation for using Javadoc can be found at *http://java.sun.com*.

We will review a few basic Javadoc features here. Full documentation on Javadoc is available on Sun's website.

To write comments that will be included in the Javadoc documentation, we use a special form of block comment ahead of any class, field, constructor, or method. The syntax for including Javadoc comments follows.

TABLE 7.7 HTML Files Generated by Javadoc

File name	Short description
Auto.html	*Auto* class documentation (without frames)
allclasses-frame.html	List of the classes with links (with frames)
allclasses-noframe.html	List of the classes with links (without frames)
constant-values.html	Constants of the class with links
deprecated-list.html	List of deprecated methods
help-doc.html	How these files are organized
index-all.html	Links to class, constructors, methods
index.html	*Auto* class documentation (with frames)
overview-tree.html	Class hierarchy
package-frame.html	Frame for this package
package-tree.html	Class hierarchy
resources	Directory containing one or more GIFs
stylesheet.css	Style sheet
package-list	List of packages

```
/**
Javadoc comment here
*/
```

As we already know, the syntax for a Java block comment is

```
/*
Java block comment here
*/
```

So a Javadoc comment is just a special Java block comment. The *javac* compiler will simply ignore it, but the Javadoc executable will look for it and generate the appropriate documentation. Javadoc discards all whitespace characters and the * at the beginning of each line until a non–whitespace

TABLE 7.8 Selected Javadoc Tags

Tag	Most common syntax	Explanation
`@param`	`@param variableName description`	Adds a parameter to the parameter section
`@return`	`@return text`	Adds a description for the return type

character and non * character is encountered. The industry convention is to start every line of a Javadoc comment with a *. Therefore, we recommend the following syntax:

```
/**
*  A Javadoc comment here
*  A second Javadoc comment here
*  . . . .
*/
```

SOFTWARE ENGINEERING TIP

When coding a documentation block, use an * at the beginning of each line to indicate that this is a documentation comment.

Class documentation comprises two parts:

- A description section
- A tag section

Javadoc recognizes two types of tags: block tags and inline tags. We will discuss block tags only.

Block tags start with the character @. Table 7.8 lists two block tags, *@param* and *@return*, along with an explanation of each.

In the description section and inside the tag section, the text should be written in HTML; therefore, HTML tags such as
 (break) or <B> (bold) can be used. The tag <BR> inserts a new line; the tag <B> will change the text style to bold until the end tag </B> is encountered.

Example 7.22 shows a simplified version of our *Auto* class incorporating some documentation comments:

```
/*  Simplified Auto Class with Javadoc comments
    Anderson, Franceschi
*/

public class SimplifiedAuto
{
 private String model;
```

```
private int milesDriven;
private double gallonsOfGas;



/**
* Default constructor:<BR>
* initializes model to "unknown"<BR>
* milesDriven are autoinitialized to 0, and gallonsOfGas to 0.0
*/
public SimplifiedAuto( )
{
   model = "unknown";
}

/**
* Overloaded constructor:<BR>
* Allows client to set beginning values for model,
*   milesDriven, and gallonsOfGas<BR>
* This constructor takes three parameters<BR>
* Calls mutator methods to validate new values
* @param startModel the model of the car
* @param startMilesDriven the number of miles driven
* @param startGallonsOfGas the number of gallons of gas used
*/
public SimplifiedAuto( String startModel, int startMilesDriven,
                       double startGallonsOfGas )
{
    model = startModel;
    setMilesDriven( startMilesDriven );
    setGallonsOfGas( startGallonsOfGas );
}

/**
* Mutator method:<BR>
* Allows client to set value of milesDriven<BR>
* Prints an error message if new value is less than 0<BR>
* <B>setMilesDriven</B> does not change the value
* of <B>milesDriven</B> if newMilesDriven has negative value
* @param newMilesDriven the new number of miles driven
*/
public void setMilesDriven( int newMilesDriven )
{
   if ( newMilesDriven > 0 )
      milesDriven = newMilesDriven;
   else
```

```
   {
       System.err.println( "Miles driven cannot be negative." );
       System.err.println( "Value not changed." );
   }
}

/**
* Mutator method:<BR>
* Allows client to set value of gallonsOfGas<BR>
* If new value is less than 0, prints an error message<BR>
*    and does not change the value of <B>gallonsOfGas</B>
* @param newGallonsOfGas the new number of gallons of gas used
*/
public void setGallonsOfGas( double newGallonsOfGas )
{
   if ( newGallonsOfGas >= 0 )
        gallonsOfGas = newGallonsOfGas;
   else
   {
       System.err.println( "Gallons of gas cannot be negative." );
       System.err.println( "Value not changed." );
   }
}

/**
* equals method:<BR>
* Compares two SimplifiedAuto objects for the same field values
* @param a1 another SimplifiedAuto object
* @return a boolean, true if this object
* has the same field values as the parameter a1
*/
public boolean equals( Object a1 )
{
    if ( ! ( a1 instanceof SimplifiedAuto ) )
     return false;
    else
    {
       SimplifiedAuto objAuto = ( SimplifiedAuto ) a1;
       return ( model.equals( objAuto.model )
              && milesDriven == objAuto.milesDriven
              && Math.abs( gallonsOfGas - objAuto.gallonsOfGas )
                                  < 0.0001 );
    }
}
}
```

EXAMPLE 7.22 The *SimplifiedAuto* Class

SOFTWARE ENGINEERING TIP

When you write a class, add a few documentation comments, and generate the web-style documentation. Show the web pages to friends or colleagues and ask them if they fully understand what the class encapsulates and what it is about. Ask them a few questions about the constructor and the methods. This is a good way to check if your class is well designed and ready for reuse.

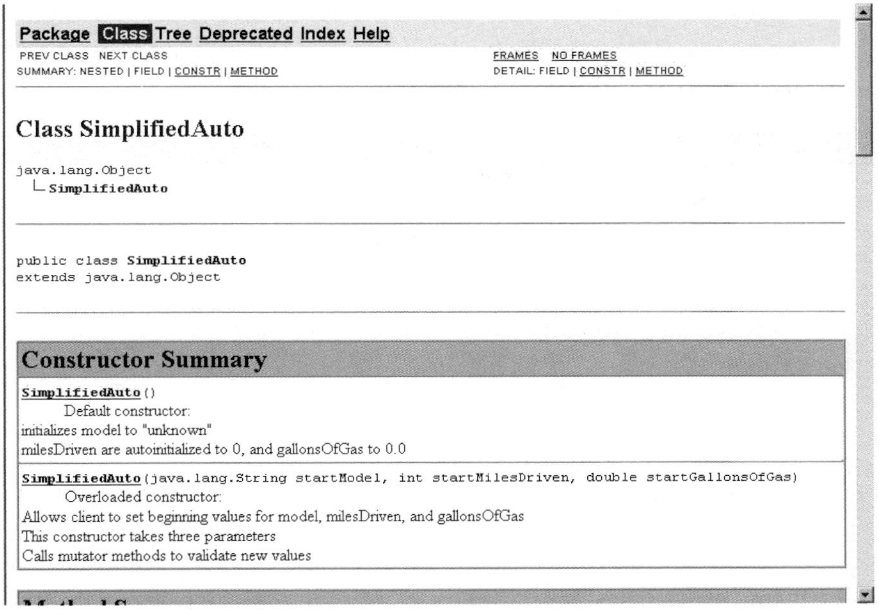

Package **Class** **Tree** **Deprecated** **Index** **Help**

PREV CLASS NEXT CLASS | FRAMES NO FRAMES

SUMMARY: NESTED | FIELD | CONSTR | METHOD | DETAIL: FIELD | CONSTR | METHOD

Class SimplifiedAuto

```
java.lang.Object
  └ SimplifiedAuto
```

```
public class SimplifiedAuto
extends java.lang.Object
```

Constructor Summary

SimplifiedAuto()
Default constructor:
initializes model to "unknown"
milesDriven are autoinitialized to 0, and gallonsOfGas to 0.0

SimplifiedAuto(java.lang.String startModel, int startMilesDriven, double startGallonsOfGas)
Overloaded constructor:
Allows client to set beginning values for model, milesDriven, and gallonsOfGas
This constructor takes three parameters
Calls mutator methods to validate new values

Figure 7.15
***SimplifiedAuto* Class Web-Style Documentation**

startMilesDriven - the number of miles driven
startGallonsOfGas - the number of gallons of gas used

Method Detail

setMilesDriven

```
public void setMilesDriven(int newMilesDriven)
```

Mutator method:
Allows client to set value of milesDriven
Prints an error message if new value is less than 0
setMilesDriven does not change the value of **milesDriven** if newMilesDriven has negative value

Parameters:
newMilesDriven - the new number of miles driven

setGallonsOfGas

```
public void setGallonsOfGas(double newGallonsOfGas)
```

Mutator method:
Allows client to set value of gallonsOfGas
If new value is less than 0, prints an error message
and does not change the value of **gallonsOfGas**

Parameters:
newGallonsOfGas - the new number of gallons of gas used

Figure 7.16
Web-Style Documentation for the *Mutator* Methods

Figure 7.15 shows part of the generated *index.html* file, and Figure 7.16 shows the generated documentation for the *setMilesDriven* and *setGallonsOfGas* methods.

7.17 Chapter Summary

CHAPTER SUMMARY

- The members of a Java class include its instance variables, class variables, and methods.
- One copy of each instance variable is created for every object instantiated from the class. One copy of each class variable and method is shared by all objects of the class.
- By convention, class names are nouns and begin with a capital letter; all internal words begin with a capital letter, and other letters are lowercase. Method names are verbs and begin with a lowercase letter; internal words begin with a capital letter, and all other letters are lowercase. Nonconstant instance variables are nouns and follow the same capitalization rules as methods. Constant fields have all capital letters with internal words separated by an underscore.
- The *public* access modifier allows the class or member to be accessed by other classes. The *private* access modifier specifies that the class or member can be accessed only by other members of the same class. Package access allows other classes in the same package to access the class or class members.
- Classes, constructors, *final* class variables, and class methods typically are declared as *public*, and instance variables typically are declared as *private.*
- Instance variables reflect the properties that all objects will have in common. Instance variables are defined by specifying an access modifier, data type, and identifier, and optionally, an initial value. Instance variables can be declared to be *final.*
- A method is defined by providing a method header, which specifies the access modifier, a return type, method name, and parameter list. The method body is enclosed in curly braces. Value-returning methods return the result of the method using one or more *return* state-

ments. A method with a *void* return type does not return a value.

- The scope of an identifier is the range of code in which that identifier can be accessed. Instance variables and methods have class scope in that they can be accessed anywhere in the class.
- A method can reference the instance variables of its class, the parameters sent to the method, and local variables declared by the method and can call other methods of its class.
- A method can be overloaded by defining another method with the same name but a different signature, that is, with a different number of parameters or with parameters of different data types.
- Constructors are responsible for initializing the instance variables of the class.
- If you don't provide a constructor, the compiler provides a default constructor, which is a constructor that takes no arguments. This default constructor assigns default initial values to all the instance variables. Numeric variables are given the value of 0, characters are given the value *space*, *boolean* variables are given the value of *false*, and object references are given the value of *null*. Local variables declared in methods are not given initial values automatically.
- Accessor methods are named *getIV*, where *IV* is an instance variable name; the return data type is the same as the instance variable and the body of the method simply returns the value of the instance variable.
- Mutator methods are named *setIV*, where *IV* is an instance variable name; the return data type is *void*, and the method takes one argument, which is the same data type as the instance variable and contains the new value for the instance variable. The body of the method should validate the new value and, if the new value is valid, assign the new value to the instance variable.
- When a method begins executing, the JVM sets the object reference *this* to refer to the object for which the method has been called.
- The *toString* method is called automatically when an object refer-

ence is used as a *String* and its job is to provide a printable representation of the object data.

- The *equals* method compares two objects for equality, that is, it should return *true* only if the corresponding instance variables in both objects are equal in value, and *false* otherwise.
- *Static* class variables are created when the class is initialized. Thus, class variables exist before any objects are instantiated, and each class has only one copy of the class variables. *Static* variables that are constants are usually declared to be *public* because they typically are provided to allow the client to set preferences for the operations of a class.
- *Static* class methods can reference only *static* variables, can call only *static* methods, and cannot use the object reference *this*.
- A non-*static*, or instance, method can reference both class and instance variables, as well as class and instance methods, and the reference *this*.
- A graphical object usually has instance variables for the starting (*x*, *y*) coordinate. It also provides a *draw* method that takes a *Graphics* object as a parameter and includes the code to draw the graphical object.
- Enumeration types can be defined to give meaning to ordered sets that are represented in a program by numbers. For each name in an *enum* type initialization list, a constant object is created with an instance variable having a sequential numeric value. References can be defined of the *enum* type. Objects of the *enum* type can be compared, printed, and requested to return their numeric value.
- Javadoc, which is part of the Java JDK, generates documentation for classes. To use Javadoc, you enclose a description of each class, method, and field in a block comment beginning with /** and ending with */. In addition, you can describe each parameter using the *@param* tag and return value using the *@return* tag.

7.18 Exercises, Problems, and Projects

7.18.1 Multiple Choice Exercises

1. What can you say about the name of a class?

- ❑ It must start with an uppercase letter.
- ❑ The convention is to start with an uppercase letter.

2. What can you say about the name of constructors?
   - ❑ They must be the same name as the class name.
   - ❑ They can be any name, just like other methods.
3. What is a constructor's return type?
   - ❑ *void*
   - ❑ *Object*
   - ❑ The class name
   - ❑ A constructor does not have a return type.
4. It is legal to have more than one constructor in a given class.
   - ❑ true
   - ❑ false
5. In a class, if a field is *private,*
   - ❑ it can be accessed directly from any class.
   - ❑ it can be accessed directly only from inside its class.
6. In a typical class, what is the general recommendation for access modifiers?
   - ❑ Instance variables are *private* and methods are *private.*
   - ❑ Instance variables are *private* and methods are *public.*
   - ❑ Instance variables are *public* and methods are *private.*
   - ❑ Instance variables are *public* and methods are *public.*
7. In a class, fields
   - ❑ can only be basic data types
   - ❑ can only be basic data types or existing Java types (from existing classes)
   - ❑ can be basic data types, existing Java types, or user-defined types (from user-defined classes)

8. Accessors and mutators are
   - ❑ instance variables of a class
   - ❑ used to access and modify field variables of a class from outside the class
   - ❑ constructor methods
9. Accessor methods typically take
   - ❑ no parameter
   - ❑ one parameter, of the same type as the corresponding field
10. Mutator methods typically take
    - ❑ no parameter
    - ❑ one parameter, of the same type as the corresponding field
11. Accessor methods typically
    - ❑ are *void* methods
    - ❑ return the same type as the corresponding field
12. Mutator methods typically
    - ❑ are *void* methods
    - ❑ return the same type as the corresponding field
13. When coding a method that performs calculations on fields of that class, then
    - ❑ these fields must be passed as parameters to the method.
    - ❑ these fields do not need to be passed as parameters to the methods because the class methods have direct access to them.
14. What is the keyword used for declaring a constant?
    - ❑ *static*
    - ❑ *final*
    - ❑ *constant*
15. What is the keyword used for declaring a class variable or method?
    - ❑ *static*
    - ❑ *final*

- ❑ *class*

16. What can you say about *enum*?
    - ❑ It is part of the package *java.lang*.
    - ❑ It can be used for self-documentation, improving the readability of your code.
    - ❑ An *enum* object is a constant object.
    - ❑ All of the above.

7.18.2 Reading and Understanding Code

For Questions 17 and 18, consider that inside the class *Sky*, we have already coded the following:

```
public class Sky
{
   private Color color;
   public Sky( Color c )
   {
      color = c;
   }
}
```

17. Consider the following method header:

```
public Color getColor( )
```

Is this method a constructor, mutator, or accessor?

18. Consider the following method header:

```
public void setColor( Color c )
```

Is this method a constructor, mutator, or accessor?

For Questions 19 to 24, consider that the class *Airplane* has two methods with the following method headers; we also have a default constructor already coded.

```
public static double foo1( String s )
public String foo2( char c )
```

19. What is the return type of method *foo1*?
20. What is the return type of method *foo2*?
21. Is method *foo1* a class or instance method? Explain.

22. Is method *foo2* a class or instance method? Explain.
23. Write a line or two of code to call method *foo1* from a client class.
24. Write a line or two of code to call method *foo2* from a client class. Assume we have instantiated an object named *a1*.
25. Inside method *main*, we see code like

    ```
    Airplane.foo3( 34.6 );
    ```

    From this, reconstruct the header of method *foo3* (which belongs to the class *Airplane*); make appropriate assumptions if necessary.
26. Inside method *main*, we see code like

    ```
    Airplane a = new Airplane( );
    int n = a.foo4( "Hello" );
    ```

    From this, reconstruct the header of method *foo4* (which belongs to class *Airplane*).
27. If you have defined the following *enum* constants:

    ```
    enum Seasons { Winter, Spring, Summer, Fall };
    ```

    What is the output of the following code sequence?

    ```
    System.out.println( Seasons.Spring.ordinal( ) );
    ```

7.18.3 Fill In the Code

28. Declare two instance variables *grade*, which is an integer, and *letterGrade*, which is a *char*.

    ```
    // declare grade here

    // declare letterGrade here
    ```
29. Declare a class field for a federal tax rate, a constant, with value .07.

    ```
    // declare federal tax rate constant; value is 0.07
    ```

    For Questions 30 to 37, we will assume that class *TelevisionChannel* has three fields: *name*, a *String*; *number*, an integer; and *cable*, a *boolean*, which represents whether the channel is a cable channel.
30. Code a default constructor for that class: initialize the fields to an empty string, 0, and *false*, respectively.

    ```
    // your default constructor code goes here
    ```

31. Code a constructor for that class that takes three parameters.

```
// your constructor code goes here
```

32. Code the three accessors for that class.

```
// your code goes here
```

33. Code the three mutators for that class.

```
// your code goes here
```

34. Code the *toString* method.

```
// your code goes here
```

35. Code the *equals* method.

```
// your code goes here
```

36. Code a method returning the number of digits in the channel number. For instance, if the channel number is 21, the method returns 2; if the channel number is 412, the method returns 3.

```
// your code goes here
```

37. Code a method returning the word *cable* if the current object represents a cable channel and returning the word *network* if the current object does not represent a cable channel.

```
// your code goes here
```

7.18.4 Identifying Errors in Code

For Questions 38 to 45, consider that inside the class *Gift*, we have already coded the following:

```
public class Gift
{
   private String description;
   private double price;
   private String occasion;
   private boolean taxable;

   public static final double TAX_RATE = 0.05;

   public Gift( String d, double p, String o, boolean t )
   {
```

```
      description = d;
      price = p;
      occasion = o;
      taxable = t;
   }

   public void setPrice( double p )
   {
      price = p;
   }

   public void setTaxable( boolean t )
   {
      taxable = t;
   }
}
```

38. We are coding the following inside the class *Gift*; where is the error?

```
public void getPrice( )
{
   return price;
}
```

39. We are coding the following inside the class *Gift*; where is the error?

```
public void setOccasion( String occasion )
{
   occasion = occasion;
}
```

40. We are coding the following inside the class *Gift*; where is the error?

```
public String toString( )
{
  System.out.println( "description = " + description );
  System.out.println( "price = " + price );
  System.out.println( "occasion = " + occasion );
  System.out.println( "taxable = " + taxable );
}
```

41. We are coding the following inside the class *Gift*; where is the error?

```
public boolean equals( Object g )
{
  return ( this == g );
}
```

42. We are coding the following inside the class *Gift*; where is the error?

```
public void setTaxRate( double newTaxRate )
{
   TAX_RATE = newTaxRate;
}
```

43. We are coding the following inside the class *Gift*; where is the error?

```
public double calcTax( TAX_RATE )
{
  return ( TAX_RATE * price );
}
```

44. We are coding the following in the *main* method inside the class *Gift-Client*; where is the error?

```
Gift g = new Gift( "radio", 59.99, "Birthday", false );
Gift.setPrice( 99.99 );
```

45. We are coding the following in the *main* method inside the class *Gift-Client*; where is the error?

```
Gift g = new Gift( "radio", 59.99, "Birthday", false );
g.setTaxable( ) = true;
```

46. Where are the errors in the following statement?

```
enum Months = { "January", "February", "March" };
```

7.18.5 Debugging Area—Using Messages from the Java Compiler and Java JVM

For Questions 47 and 48, consider the following class *Grade*:

```
public class Grade
{
  private char letterGrade;

  public Grade( char lg )
  {
    letterGrade = lg;
  }
  public char getLetterGrade( )
  {
    return  letterGrade;
  }
  public void setLetterGrade( char lg )
  {
    letterGrade = lg;
```

```
   }
}
```

47. In the *main* method of the class *GradeClient*, you have coded

```
Grade g = new Grade( 'B' );
g.letterGrade = 'A';          // line 10
```

When you compile, you get the following message:

```
GradeClient.java:10: letterGrade has private access in Grade
g.letterGrade = 'A';
 ^
1 error
```

Explain what the problem is and how to fix it.

48. In the *main* method of the class *GradeClient*, you have coded

```
Grade g = new Grade( "A" );  // line 10
```

When you compile, you get the following message:

```
GradeClient.java:10: cannot find symbol
symbol  : constructor Grade (java.lang.String)
location: class Grade
Grade g = new Grade( "A" );
          ^
1 error
```

Explain what the problem is and how to fix it.

49. You coded the following definition for the class *Grade*:

```
public class Grade
{
   private char letterGrade;

   public char Grade( char startLetter )
   {
      letterGrade = startLetter;
   } // line 10
}
```

When you compile, you get the following message:

```
Grade.java:10: missing return statement
 }
 ^
1 error
```

Explain what the problem is and how to fix it.

50. You coded the following definition for the class *Grade*:

```
public class Grade
{
  private char letterGrade;
  public Grade( char lg )
  {
    letterGrade = lg;
  }
  public String toString( )      // line 10
  {                              // line 11
     return letterGrade;         // line 12
  }                              // line 13
}
```

When you compile, you get the following message:

```
Grade.java:12: incompatible types
found   : char
required: java.lang.String
 return letterGrade;
        ^
1 error
```

Explain what the problem is and how to fix it.

51. You coded the following definition for the class *Grade*:

```
public class Grade
{
  private char letterGrade;
  public Grade( char lg )
  {
    letterGrade = lg;
  }
  public String toString( )    // line 10
  {                            // line 11
    return ( lg );             // line 12
  }                            // line 13
}
```

When you compile, you get the following message:

```
Grade.java:12: cannot find symbol
symbol  : variable lg
location: class Grade
 return lg;
        ^
Grade.java:10: illegal start of type
```

```
    return ( lg );          // line 12
                ^
2 errors
```

Explain what the problem is and how to fix it.

52. You coded the following definition for the class *Grade*:

```
public class Grade
{
  private char letterGrade;
  public Grade( char letterGrade )
  {
    letterGrade = letterGrade;
  }
  public char getLetterGrade( )
  {
    return letterGrade;
  }
}
```

In the *main* method of the class *GradeClient*, you have coded:

```
Grade g1 = new Grade( 'A' );
System.out.println( g1.getLetterGrade( ) );
```

The code compiles properly and runs, but the result is not what you expected.

The client's output is a space, not an *A*.

Explain what the problem is and how to fix it.

53. You have defined the following *enum* constants:

```
enum Seasons { Winter, Spring, Summer, Fall };
```

In the *main* method of the class *Test*, you have coded

```
Seasons s = Seasons.Spring;
if ( s.equals( Winter ) )    // line 10
      System.out.println( "It is cold" );
else
      System.out.println( "The weather is fine" );
```

When you compile, you get the following message:

```
Test.java:10: cannot find symbol
symbol  : variable Winter
location: class Test
  if ( s.equals( Winter ) )  // line 10
```

```
                    ^
1 error
```

Explain what the problem is and how to fix it.

54. You have defined the following *enum* constants:

```
enum Seasons { Winter, Spring, Summer, Fall };
```

In the *main* method of the class *Test*, you have coded

```
Seasons.Fall = Autumn;  // line 10
```

When you compile, you get the following message:

```
Test.java:10: cannot assign a value to final variable Fall
  Seasons.Fall = Autumn;  // line 10
         ^
Test.java:10: cannot find symbol
symbol  : variable Autumn
location: class Test
  Seasons.Fall = Autumn;  // line 10
                 ^
2 errors
```

Explain what the problem is and how to fix it.

7.18.6 Write a Short Program

55. Write a class encapsulating the concept of a team (for example, "Orioles"), assuming a team has only one attribute: the team name. Include a constructor, the accessor and mutator, and methods *toString* and *equals*. Write a client class to test all the methods in your class.

56. Write a class encapsulating the concept of a television set, assuming a television set has the following attributes: a brand and a price. Include a constructor, the accessors and mutators, and methods *toString* and *equals*. Write a client class to test all the methods in your class.

57. Write a class encapsulating the concept of a course grade, assuming a course grade has the following attributes: a course name and a letter grade. Include a constructor, the accessors and mutators, and methods *toString* and *equals*. Write a client class to test all the methods in your class.

58. Write a class encapsulating the concept of a course, assuming a course has the following attributes: a code (for instance, CS1), a description,

and a number of credits (for instance, 3). Include a constructor, the accessors and mutators, and methods *toString* and *equals.* Write a client class to test all the methods in your class.

59. Write a class encapsulating the concept of a student, assuming a student has the following attributes: a name, a social security number, and a GPA (for instance, 3.5). Include a constructor, the accessors and mutators, and methods *toString* and *equals.* Write a client class to test all the methods in your class.

60. Write a class encapsulating the concept of website statistics, assuming website statistics have the following attributes: number of visitors and type of site (commercial, government, etc.). Include a constructor, the accessors and mutators, and methods *toString* and *equals.* Write a client class to test all the methods in your class.

61. Write a class encapsulating the concept of a corporate name (for example, "IBM"), assuming a corporate name has only one attribute: the corporate name itself. Include a constructor, the accessors and mutators, and methods *toString* and *equals.* Also include a method returning a potential domain name by adding *www.* at the beginning and *.com* at the end of the corporate name (for instance, if the corporate name is IBM, that method should return *www.ibm.com*). Write a client class to test all the methods in your class.

62. Write a class encapsulating the concept of a file, assuming a file has only a single attribute: the name of the file. Include a constructor, the accessors and mutators, and methods *toString* and *equals.* Also, code a method returning the extension of the file, that is, the letters after the last dot in the file (for instance, if the filename is *Test.java*, then the method should return *java*); if there is no dot in the filename, then the method should return "*unknown extension.*" Write a client class to test all the methods in your class.

7.18.7 Programming Projects

63. Write a class encapsulating the concept of the weather forecast, assuming that it has the following attributes: the temperature and the sky conditions, which could be sunny, snowy, cloudy, or rainy. Include a constructor, the accessors and mutators, and methods *toString* and *equals.* Temperature, in Fahrenheit, should be between −50 and +150; the default value is 70, if needed. The default sky condition is

sunny. Include a method that converts Fahrenheit to Celsius. Celsius temperature = (Fahrenheit temperature − 32) * 5 / 9. Also include a method that checks whether the weather attributes are consistent (there are two cases where they are not consistent: when the temperature is below 32 and it is not snowy, and when the temperature is above 100 and it is not sunny). Write a client class to test all the methods in your class.

64. Write a class encapsulating the concept of a domain name, assuming a domain name has a single attribute: the domain name itself (for instance, *www.yahoo.com*). Include a constructor, the accessors and mutators, and methods *toString* and *equals*. Also include the following methods: one returning whether or not the domain name starts with *www*; another returning the extension of the domain name (i.e., the letters after the last dot, for instance *com*, *gov*, or *edu*; if there is no dot in the domain name, then you should return "*unknown*"); and another returning the name itself (which will be the characters between *www* and the extension; for instance, *yahoo* if the domain is *www.yahoo.com*—if there are fewer than two dots in the domain name, then your method should return "*unknown*"). Write a client class to test all the methods in your class.

65. Write a class encapsulating the concept of an HTML page, assuming an HTML statement has only a single attribute: the HTML code for the page. Include a constructor, the accessors and mutators, and methods *toString* and *equals*. Include the following methods: one checking that there is a > character following each < character, one counting how many images are on the page (i.e., the number of IMG tags), and one counting how many links are on the page (i.e., the number of times we have "A HREF"). Write a client class to test all the methods in your class.

66. Write a class encapsulating the concept of coins, assuming that coins have the following attributes: a number of quarters, a number of dimes, a number of nickels, and a number of pennies. Include a constructor, the accessors and mutators, and methods *toString* and *equals*. Also code the following methods: one returning the total amount of money in dollar notation with two significant digits after the decimal point, and others returning the money in quarters (for instance, 0.75 if there are three quarters), in dimes, in nickels, and in pennies. Write a client class to test all the methods in your class.

EXERCISES, PROBLEMS, AND PROJECTS

67. Write a class encapsulating the concept of a user-defined *double*, assuming a user-defined *double* has only a single attribute: a *double*. Include a constructor, the accessor and mutator, and methods *toString* and *equals*. Add a method, taking one parameter specifying how many significant digits we want to have, and returning a *double* representing the original *double* truncated so that it includes the specified number of significant digits after the decimal point (for instance, if the original *double* is 6.9872 and the argument of the method is 2, this method will return 6.98). Write a client class to test all the methods in your class.

68. Write a class encapsulating the concept of a circle, assuming a circle has the following attributes: a *Point* representing the center of the circle, and the radius of the circle, an integer. Include a constructor, the accessors and mutators, and methods *toString* and *equals*. Also include methods returning the perimeter ($2 * \pi *$ radius) and area ($\pi * \text{radius}^2$) of the circle. Write a client class to test all the methods in your class.

69. Write a class encapsulating the concept of a rational number, assuming a rational number has the following attributes: an integer representing the numerator of the rational number, and another integer representing the denominator of the rational number. Include a constructor, the accessors and mutators, and methods *toString* and *equals*. You should not allow the denominator to be equal to 0; you should give it the default value 1 in case the corresponding argument of the constructor or a method is 0. Also include methods performing multiplication of a rational number by another and addition of a rational number to another, returning the resulting rational number in both cases. Write a client class to test all the methods in your class.

70. Write a class encapsulating the concept of an investment, assuming the investment has the following attributes: the amount of the investment, and the interest rate at which the investment will be compounded. Include a constructor, the accessors and mutators, and methods *toString* and *equals*. Also include a method returning the future value of the investment depending on how many years we hold it before selling it, which can be calculated using the formula:

$$\text{future value} = \text{investment}\ (1 + \text{interest rate})^{\text{numberOfYears}}$$

We will assume that the interest rate is compounded annually. Write a client class to test all the methods in your class.

71. Write a class encapsulating the concept of a telephone number, assuming a telephone number has only a single attribute: a *String* representing the telephone number. Include a constructor, the accessor and mutator, and methods *toString* and *equals*. Also include methods returning the area code (the first three digits/characters of the phone number; if there are fewer than three characters in the phone number or if the first three characters are not digits, then this method should return "*unknown area code*"). Write a client class to test all the methods in your class.

7.18.8 Technical Writing

72. An advantage of object-oriented programming is code reuse, not just by the programmer who wrote the class, but by other programmers. Describe the importance of proper documentation and how you would document a class so that other programmers can use it easily.

73. Java has a number of naming conventions for classes, methods, and field variables. Is this important? Why is it good to respect these conventions?

7.18.9 Group Project (for a group of 1, 2, or 3 students)

74. Write a program that solves a quadratic equation in all cases, including when both roots are complex numbers. For this, you need to set up the following classes:

    Complex, which encapsulates a complex number

    ComplexPair, which encapsulates a pair of complex numbers

    Quadratic, which encapsulates a quadratic equation

    SolveEquation, which contains the *main* method

    Along with the usual constructors, accessors, and mutators, you will need to code additional methods:

    In the *Complex* class, a method that determines whether a complex object is real

    In the *ComplexPair* class, a method that determines whether both complex numbers are identical

In the *Quadratic* class, a method to solve the quadratic equation and return a *ComplexPair* object

Additionally, you need to include code in the *main* method to solve several examples of quadratic equations input from the keyboard. Your output should make comments as to what type of roots we get (double real root, distinct real roots, distinct complex roots). You should check that your code works in all four basic cases:

- ❑ The quadratic equation is actually a linear equation.
- ❑ Both roots are complex.
- ❑ There is a double real root.
- ❑ There are two distinct real roots.

CHAPTER 8

Single-Dimensional Arrays

CHAPTER CONTENTS

Introduction

Up to this point, we have been working with individual, or scalar, variables; that is, each variable has held one value at a time. To process a group of variables of the same type—for example, counting the number of odd integers entered by the user—we used a *while* loop or a *for* loop.

Thus, to find the average high temperature for the last year, we would use a *for* loop:

```
double dailyTemp;
double total = 0.0;
for ( int i = 1; i <= 365; i++ )
{
   System.out.print( "Enter a temperature" );
   dailyTemp = scan.nextDouble( );
   total += dailyTemp;
}
double average = total / 365;
```

We defined one variable, *dailyTemp*, to hold the data. We read each temperature into our *dailyTemp* variable, added the temperature to our total, then read the next value into the *dailyTemp* variable, added that temperature to the total, and so on, until we finished reading and processing all the temperatures. Each time we read a new temperature, it overwrote the previous temperature, so that at the end of the loop, we had access to the last temperature only.

But suppose we want to perform multiple operations on those temperatures. Perhaps we want to find the highest or lowest temperature or find the median. Or suppose we don't know what operations we will perform, or in what order, until the user chooses them from a menu. In those cases, one scalar variable, *dailyTemp*, won't work; we want to store all the temperatures in memory at the same time. An array allows us to do just that without declaring several variables individually.

An **array** is a sequence of variables of the same data type. The data type could be any Java primitive data type, such as *int*, *float*, *double*, *byte*, *boolean*, *char*, *short*, or *long*, or it could be a class. Each variable in the array, called an **element**, is accessed using the array name and a subscript, called an **index**, which refers to the element's position in the array.

Arrays are useful for many applications: for example, calculating statistics on a group of data values or processing data stored in tables, such as matrices or game boards.

8.1 Declaring and Instantiating Arrays

In Java, arrays are implemented as objects, so creating an array takes two steps:

1. Declaring the object reference for the array.
2. Instantiating the array.

In arrays of primitive types, each element in the array contains a value of that type. For example, in an array of *doubles*, each element contains a *double* value. In arrays of objects, each element is an object reference, which stores the location of an object.

SOFTWARE ENGINEERING TIP

An array's data type can be any primitive type or any predefined or user-defined class. The important thing to remember is that each element of an array with a class data type is a reference to the object; it is not the object itself.

8.1.1 Declaring Arrays

To declare an array, you specify the name of the array and the data type, as you would for any other variable. Adding an empty set of brackets ([ ]) indicates that the variable is an array.

Here is the syntax for declaring an array:

```
datatype [ ] arrayName;
```

For example, the following statement creates a reference to an array that will hold daily high temperatures:

```
double [ ] dailyTemps; // each element is a double
```

The brackets can be placed before or after the array name. So the following syntax is also valid:

```
datatype arrayName [ ];
```

Thus, we could have declared the preceding array using the following statement:

```
double dailyTemps [ ];
```

Although you will see Java code written using either syntax, we prefer the first format with the brackets right after the data type, because it's easier to read as "a *double* array."

To declare an array to hold the titles of all tracks on a CD, you might declare it this way:

```
String [ ] cdTracks; // each element is a String object reference
```

Similarly, this statement declares an array to hold the answers to a true/false test:

```
boolean [ ] answers; // each element is a boolean value
```

Using our *Auto* class from Chapter 7, this statement declares an array to hold *Auto* objects:

```
Auto [ ] cars; // each element is an Auto object reference
```

You can declare multiple arrays of the same data type in one statement by inserting a comma after each array name, using this syntax:

```
datatype [ ] arrayName1, arrayName2;
```

For example, the following statement will declare three integer arrays to hold quiz scores for current courses:

```
int [ ] cs101, bio201, hist102;  // all elements are int values
```

COMMON ERROR TRAP

Putting the size of the array inside the brackets in the array declaration will generate a compiler error.

Note that an array declaration does not specify how many elements the arrays will have. The declaration simply specifies an object reference for the array and the data type of the elements. Thus, **declaring an array does not allocate memory for the array**.

8.1.2 Instantiating Arrays

As we mentioned earlier, Java arrays are objects, so to allocate memory for an array, you need to instantiate the array using the *new* keyword. Here is the syntax for instantiating an array:

```
arrayName = new datatype [size];

      where size is an expression that evaluates to an integer and
      specifies the number of elements in the array.
```

The following statements will instantiate the arrays declared earlier:

```
dailyTemps = new double [365]; // dailyTemps has 365 elements

cdTracks = new String [15];    // cdTracks has 15 elements

int numberOfQuestions = 30;
answers = new boolean [numberOfQuestions]; // answers has 30 elements

cars = new Auto [3];           // cars has 3 elements

cs101 = new int [5];           // cs101 has 5 elements
bio201 = new int [4];          // bio201 has 4 elements

hist102 = new int [6];         // hist102 has 6 elements
```

TABLE 8.1 Default Initial Values of Array Elements

Element Data Type	Initial Value
double	0.0
float	0.0
int, long, short, byte	0
char	space
boolean	*false*
object reference	*null*

When an array is instantiated, the elements are given initial values automatically.

Numeric elements are set to 0, *boolean* elements are set to *false*, *char* elements are set to a space, and object references are set to *null*, as shown in Table 8.1.

Thus, all the elements in the *dailyTemps* array are given an initial value of 0.0; the elements in the *cs101*, *bio201*, and *hist102* arrays are given an initial value of 0; the elements of the *answers* array are given an initial value of *false*; and the elements of the *cdTracks* and *cars* arrays are given an initial value of *null*.

8.1.3 Combining the Declaration and Instantiation of Arrays

Arrays also can be instantiated when they are declared. To combine the declaration and instantiation of an array, use this syntax:

```
datatype [ ] arrayName = new datatype [size];

    where size is an expression that evaluates to an integer and
    specifies the number of elements in the array.
```

Thus, this statement:

```
double [ ] dailyTemps = new double [365];
```

is equivalent to:

```
double [ ] dailyTemps;
dailyTemps = new double [365];
```

Similarly, this statement:

```
String [ ] cdTracks = new String [15];
```

is equivalent to:

```
String [ ] cdTracks;
cdTracks = new String [15];
```

8.1.4 Assigning Initial Values to Arrays

Java allows you to instantiate an array by assigning initial values when the array is declared. To do this, you specify the initial values using a comma-separated list within curly braces:

```
datatype [ ] arrayName = { value0, value1, value2, ... };

    where valueN is an expression that evaluates to the data type
    of the array and is the value to assign to the element at index N.
```

Note that we do not use the *new* keyword and we do not specify a size for the array. The number of elements in the array is determined by the number of values in the initialization list.

For example, this statement declares and instantiates an array of odd numbers:

```
int nine = 9;
int [ ] oddNumbers = { 1, 3, 5, 7, nine, nine + 2, 13, 15, 17, 19 };
```

Because 10 values are given in the initialization list, this array has 10 elements. Notice that the values can be an expression, for example, *nine* and *nine + 2*.

Similarly, we can declare and instantiate an array of objects by providing objects in the list, as shown next. The *cars* array of *Auto* objects has three elements.

```
Auto sportsCar = new Auto( "Ferrari", 0, 0.0 );
Auto [ ] cars = { new Auto( "BMW", 100, 15.0 ), sportsCar, new Auto( ) };
```

COMMON ERROR TRAP

An initialization list can be given only when the array is declared. Attempting to assign values to an array using an initialization list after the array is instantiated will generate a compiler error.

COMMON ERROR TRAP

The *new* keyword is not used when an array is instantiated using an initialization list. No size is given; the number of values in the list specifies the size of the array.

8.2 Accessing Array Elements

Elements of an array are accessed using this syntax:

```
arrayName[exp]

  where exp is an expression that evaluates to an integer.
```

Exp is the element's position, or **index**, within the array. The index of the first element in the array is always 0; the index of the last element is always 1 less than the number of elements.

TABLE 8.2 Accessing Array Elements

Element	Syntax
Element 0	`arrayName[0]`
Element *i*	`arrayName[i]`
Last element	`arrayName[arrayName.length - 1]`

Arrays have a read-only, integer instance variable, **length**, which holds the number of elements in the array. To access the number of elements in an array named *arrayName*, use this syntax:

```
arrayName.length
```

Thus, to access the last element of an array, use this syntax:

```
arrayName[arrayName.length - 1]
```

Note that regardless of the data type of the elements in an array, the *length* of an array is always an integer, because *length* represents the number of elements in the array.

Table 8.2 summarizes the syntax for accessing elements of an array.

COMMON ERROR TRAP

Note that for an array, *length*—with no parentheses—is an instance variable, whereas for *Strings*, *length()*—with parentheses—is a method. Note also that the instance variable is named *length*, rather than *size*.

For example, suppose we want to analyze our monthly cell phone bills for the past six months. We want to calculate the average bill, the total payments for the six months, and the lowest and highest bills. We can use an array of *doubles* with six elements, as shown in Example 8.1.

```
/* Array of Cell Phone Bills
   Anderson, Franceschi
*/

public class CellBills
{
  public static void main( String [ ] args )
  {
     // declare and instantiate the array
     double [ ] cellBills = new double [6];

     // assign values to array elements
     cellBills[0] = 45.24;
     cellBills[1] = 54.67;
     cellBills[2] = 42.55;
```

```
16        cellBills[3] = 44.61;
17        cellBills[4] = 65.29;
18        cellBills[5] = 49.75;
19
20        System.out.println( "The first monthly cell bill is "
21                              + cellBills[0] );
22        System.out.println( "The last monthly cell bill is "
23                              + cellBills[cellBills.length - 1] );
24    }
25 }
```

EXAMPLE 8.1 The *cellBills* Array

In lines 9–10, we declare and instantiate the *cellBills* array. Because the elements of *cellBills* are *doubles*, instantiating the array also initializes each element to 0.0 and sets the value of *cellBills.length* to 6. Thus, Figure 8.1 represents the *cellBills* array after line 10 is executed.

Lines 12–18 store values into each element of the array. The element at index *i* of the array is *cellBills[i]*. Remember that the first element of an array is always at index 0. Thus, the last element is *cellBills[5]*, or equivalently, *cellBills[cellBills.length – 1]*. Figure 8.2 shows how the *cellBills* array looks after lines 13–18 are executed.

Lines 20–21 print the value of the first element, and lines 22–23 print the value of the last element. The output of Example 8.1 is shown in Figure 8.3.

Array indexes *must* be between 0 and *arrayName.length – 1*. Attempting to access an element of an array using an index less than 0 or greater than *arrayName.length – 1* will compile without errors, but will generate an *ArrayIndexOutOfBoundsException* at run time. By default, this exception halts execution of the program.

Figure 8.1
The *cellBills* Array After Instantiation

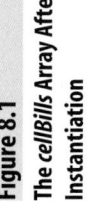

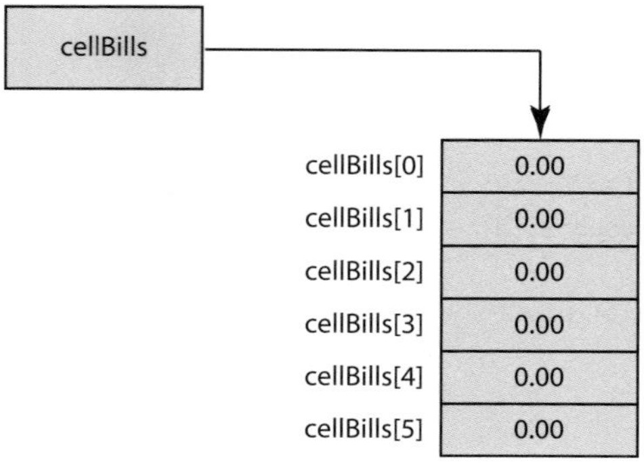

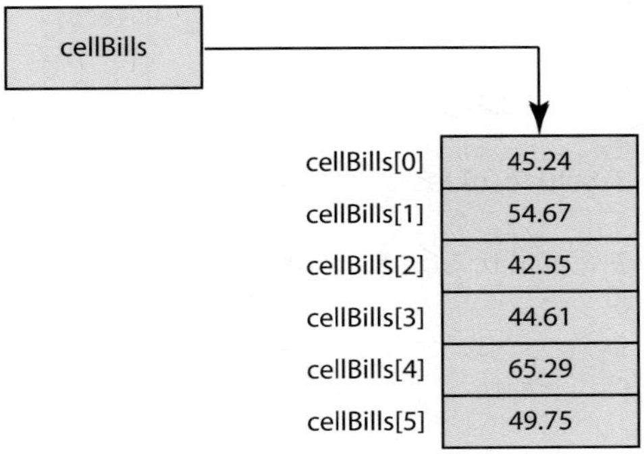

Figure 8.2
The *cellBills* Array After Assigning Values

```
The first monthly cell bill is 45.24
The last monthly cell bill is 49.75
```

Figure 8.3
Output of Example 8.1

For example, all the following expressions are invalid:

```
// invalid indexes for the cellBills array!!

cellBills[-1]                 // the lowest valid index is 0

cellBills[cellBills.length]   // the highest valid index is
                              // cellBills.length - 1

cellBills[150]                // the highest valid index is 5
```

Instantiating an array with a class data type involves two steps:

1. Instantiate the array.
2. Instantiate the objects.

Remember that the elements of an array with a class data type are object references. When the array is instantiated, all elements are set to *null*. Thus, the second step needs to be instantiating each object and assigning its reference to an array element.

Example 8.2 illustrates how to work with an array of objects. In this example, we reuse the *Auto* class from Chapter 7.

COMMON ERROR TRAP

Attempting to access an element of an array using an index less than 0 or an index greater than *arrayName.length - 1* will generate an *ArrayIndex-OutOfBoundsException* at run time.

```
 1 /* Working with an Array of Objects
 2    Anderson, Franceschi
 3 */
 4
 5 public class AutoArray
 6 {
 7   public static void main( String [ ] args )
 8   {
 9     // 1. instantiate cars array
10     Auto [ ] cars = new Auto [3];
11
12     // 2. instantiate Auto objects
13     Auto sportsCar = new Auto( "Ferrari", 100, 15.0 );
14     cars[0] = sportsCar;    // assign sportsCar to element 1
15     cars[1] = new Auto( );  // default Auto object
16     // cars[2] has not been instantiated and is null
17
18     // call Auto methods
19     System.out.println( "cars[0] is a " + cars[0].getModel( ) );
20
21     Auto myCar = cars[1];
22     System.out.println( "myCar has used " + myCar.getGallonsOfGas( )
23                         + " gallons of gas" );
24
25     // attempt to call method when Auto object is not instantiated
26     System.out.println( "cars[2] is a " + cars[2].getModel( ) );
27   }
28 }
```

EXAMPLE 8.2 Working with an Array of Objects

COMMON ERROR TRAP

With an array of objects, be sure that an array element points to an instantiated object before attempting to use that element to call a method of the class. Otherwise, a *NullPointer-Exception* will be generated.

At lines 9–10, we declare and instantiate *cars*, an array of three *Auto* objects. At this point, each element has the value of *null*. Thus, our second step is to instantiate objects of the *Auto* class and assign their references to the array elements.

At lines 13–14, we instantiate the *Auto* object *sportsCar* and assign the *sportsCar* reference to element 0. At line 15, we instantiate a default *Auto* object and assign its reference to element 1. We do not instantiate an object for element 2, which remains *null*.

We then call methods of the *Auto* class. Because the array elements are object references, to call a method for an object in an array, we use the array name and index, along with the dot notation. This is illustrated in line 19, where we print the model of element 0 by calling the *getModel* method. In

```
cars[0] is a Ferrari
myCar has used 0.0 gallons of gas
Exception in thread "main" java.lang.NullPointerException
        at AutoArray.main(AutoArray.java:26)
```

Figure 8.4
Output of Example 8.2

lines 21–23, we assign element 1 to the *Auto* reference *myCar*, then call the *getGallonsOfGas* method using the *myCar* reference.

Finally, line 26 attempts to retrieve the model of element 2; however, because *cars[2]* is *null*, a *NullPointerException* is generated. Figure 8.4 shows the output of this program.

Skill Practice
with these end-of-chapter questions

8.10.1 Multiple Choice Exercises
Questions 1,2,3,4,5,7,8

8.10.2 Reading and Understanding Code
Questions 13,14,15

8.10.4 Identifying Errors in Code
Questions 36,37,38,40,42,44

8.10.5 Debugging Area
Question 45

8.10.8 Technical Writing
Questions 73,75

8.3 Aggregate Array Operations

Once the array is declared and instantiated, it would be convenient if we could just use the array name to perform operations on the whole array, such as printing the array, copying the array to another array, inputting values to the array, and so on. Unfortunately, Java does not support these aggregate operations on arrays.

For example, attempting to print the array using the array name will *not* print all the elements of the array. Instead, this statement:

```
System.out.println( cellBills ); // incorrect attempt to print array!
```

calls the *toString* method of the *Array* class, which simply prints the name of the object's class and the hash code of the array name, for example, `[D@310d42`.

8.3.1 Printing Array Elements

To print all elements of an array, we need to use a loop that prints each element individually. A *for* loop is custom-made for processing all elements of an array in order. In fact, the following *for* loop header is a standard way to process all elements in an array:

```
for ( int i = 0; i < arrayName.length; i++ )
```

Note that the initialization statement:

```
int i = 0;
```

sets *i* to the index of the first element of the array.

The loop update statement:

```
i++;
```

increments *i* to the next index so that we process each element in order.

The loop condition:

```
i < arrayName.length
```

continues execution of the loop as long as the index is less than the *length* of the array.

COMMON ERROR TRAP

In a *for* loop, using the condition:

```
i <= arrayName.length
```

will generate an *ArrayIndexOutOfBoundsException* because the index of the last element of an array is *arrayName.length – 1*.

Note that we use the *less than* operator (<) in the condition. Using the *less than or equal to* operator (<=) would cause us to attempt to reference an element with an index of *arrayName.length*, which is beyond the end of the array.

Inside the *for* loop, we refer to the current element being processed as

```
arrayName[i]
```

Example 8.3, whose output is shown in Figure 8.5, demonstrates how to print each element in an array.

```
/* Printing Array Elements
   Anderson, Franceschi
*/
```

```
 4
 5 public class PrintingArrayElements
 6 {
 7   public static void main( String [ ] args )
 8   {
 9     double [ ] cellBills = new double [6];
10     cellBills[0] = 45.24;
11     cellBills[1] = 54.67;
12     cellBills[2] = 42.55;
13     cellBills[3] = 44.61;
14     cellBills[4] = 65.29;
15     cellBills[5] = 49.75;
16
17     System.out.println( "Element\tValue" );
18     for ( int i = 0; i < cellBills.length; i++ )
19     {
20       System.out.println( i + "\t" + cellBills[i] );
21     }
22   }
23 }
```

EXAMPLE 8.3 Printing All Elements of an Array

In lines 9–15, we instantiate the *cellBills* array and assign values to its six elements. In line 18, we use the standard *for* loop header. Inside the *for* loop (line 20), we print each element's index and value.

8.3.2 Reading Data into an Array

Similarly, we can use the standard *for* loop to input data into an array. In Example 8.4, we use a *for* loop to prompt the user for each monthly cell phone bill and to assign the input value to the appropriate array elements.

```
Element Value
0       45.24
1       54.67
2       42.55
3       44.61
4       65.29
5       49.75
```

Figure 8.5
Output of Example 8.3

```
1 /* Reading data into an array
2    Anderson, Franceschi
3 */
4
5 import java.util.Scanner;
6
7 public class ReadingDataIntoAnArray
8 {
9   public static void main( String [ ] args )
10  {
11    Scanner scan = new Scanner( System.in );
12
13    double [ ] cellBills = new double[6];
14    for ( int i = 0; i < cellBills.length; i++ )
15    {
16      System.out.print( "Enter bill amount for month "
17                        + ( i + 1 ) + "\t" );
18      cellBills[i] = scan.nextDouble( ); // read current bill
19    }
20  }
21 }
```

EXAMPLE 8.4 Reading Data from the Console into an Array

At lines 14–19, our *for* loop prompts the user for a value for each element in the *cellBills* array. Note that our prompt uses the expression ($i + 1$) for the month number. Although array indexes start at 0, people start counting at 1. If we used the array index in the prompt, we would ask the user for the bills for months 0 to 5. By adding 1 to the array index, we are able to prompt the user for months 1 through 6, which are the month numbers that the user expects.

SOFTWARE ENGINEERING TIP

Prompt for data in terms the user understands.

The output of Example 8.4 is shown in Figure 8.6.

Figure 8.6
Reading Data into an Array

```
Enter bill amount for month 1    63.33
Enter bill amount for month 2    54.27
Enter bill amount for month 3    71.19
Enter bill amount for month 4    59.03
Enter bill amount for month 5    62.65
Enter bill amount for month 6    65.08
```

8.3.3 Summing the Elements of an Array

To sum the elements of the array, we again use the standard *for* loop, as shown in Example 8.5.

```
 1 /* Summing Array Elements
 2    Anderson, Franceschi
 3 */
 4
 5 import java.text.NumberFormat;
 6
 7 public class SummingArrayElements
 8 {
 9  public static void main( String [ ] args )
10  {
11    double [ ] cellBills = new double [6];
12    cellBills[0] = 45.24;
13    cellBills[1] = 54.67;
14    cellBills[2] = 42.55;
15    cellBills[3] = 44.61;
16    cellBills[4] = 65.29;
17    cellBills[5] = 49.75;
18
19    double totalBills = 0.0;  // initialize total
20    for ( int i = 0; i < cellBills.length; i++ )
21    {
22      totalBills += cellBills[i];
23    }
24
25    NumberFormat priceFormat = NumberFormat.getCurrencyInstance( );
26    System.out.println( "Total for the bills: "
27                        + priceFormat.format( totalBills ) );
28  }
29 }
```

EXAMPLE 8.5 Summing the Elements of an Array

We fill the *cellBills* array with values at lines 12–17. We declare the *double* variable *totalBills* and initialize it to 0.0 at line 19. The *for* loop, at lines 20–23, adds each element of the array to *totalBills*. We use the *NumberFormat* class to format the value of *totalBills* as currency for output (lines 25–27). The output of Example 8.5 is shown in Figure 8.7.

Figure 8.7
Calculating the Total of All Elements

```
Total for the bills: $302.11
```

8.3.4 Finding Maximum or Minimum Values

Suppose we want to find the month that has the lowest bill. That would require finding a minimum value in the array and noting its index. Similarly, to find a month with the highest bill, we would need to find a maximum value in the array and note its index.

To find a maximum or minimum value in an array, we use a variation of the standard *for* loop. Example 8.6 finds the highest array value and its array index for our *cellBills* array of monthly cell bills.

```
/* Finding the maximum array value
   Anderson, Franceschi
*/

import java.text.NumberFormat;

public class MaxArrayValue
{
 public static void main( String [ ] args )
 {
   double [ ] cellBills = new double [6];
   cellBills[0] = 45.24;
   cellBills[1] = 54.67;
   cellBills[2] = 42.55;
   cellBills[3] = 44.61;
   cellBills[4] = 65.29;
   cellBills[5] = 49.75;

   int maxIndex = 0;   // initialize to index of first element
   for ( int i = 1; i < cellBills.length; i++ )
   {
    if ( cellBills[i] > cellBills[maxIndex] )
      maxIndex = i;  // save index of maximum value
   }

   NumberFormat priceFormat = NumberFormat.getCurrencyInstance( );
   System.out.println ( "The highest bill, "
```

```
28                         + priceFormat.format( cellBills[maxIndex] )
29                         + ", was found at index " + maxIndex );
30   }
31 }
```

EXAMPLE 8.6 Finding a Maximum Value in an Array

We start by assuming that the first element is a maximum value. So we initialize an integer variable, *maxIndex*, to 0, at line 19. Then, at lines 20–24, starting at element 1, we step through the array, comparing the value of each element with the element at *maxIndex*. Whenever we find a value higher than the current maximum, we assign its index to *maxIndex* (line 23). When the *for* loop completes, *maxIndex* holds the index of the array element with a highest value. We then print both that index and the corresponding array value at lines 26–29. The output is shown in Figure 8.8.

What happens if the array has only one value? Will we still get the correct result? The answer is yes, because the single element will be at index 0. We start by assigning 0 to *maxIndex*. Then the *for* loop body will not execute because the condition will evaluate to *false*. So *maxIndex* will not be changed and remains set to 0.

What happens if more than one element holds the highest value? We find the index of the first element only, because our condition requires that the element value must be greater than the current maximum to change *maxIndex*.

8.3.5 Copying Arrays

Suppose we create a second array to hold a copy of our cell phone bills, as shown in the following statement:

```
double [ ] billsBackup = new double [6];
```

At this point, all elements of the *billsBackup* array are initialized automatically to 0.0. Figure 8.9 shows the current state of the *cellBills* and *billsBackup* arrays.

```
The highest bill, $65.29, was found at index 4
```

Figure 8.8
Output of Example 8.6

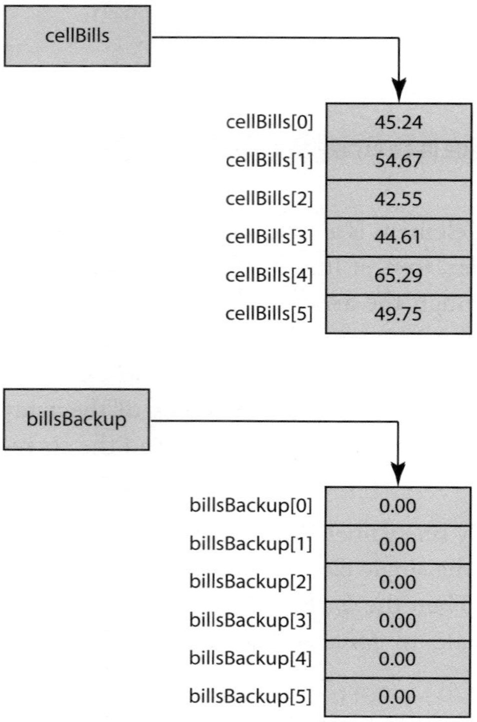

Figure 8.9
The *cellBills* and *billsBackup* Arrays

Then, if we want to copy the elements of the *cellBills* array to the corresponding elements of the *billsBackup* array, we might be tempted to use the assignment operator:

```
billsBackup = cellBills; // incorrect attempt to copy array elements!
```

This won't work. Because arrays are objects, the assignment operator copies the *cellBills* object reference to the *billsBackup* object reference. Both *cellBills* and *billsBackup* now point to the same object. The array data was not copied. In fact, we just lost the original *billsBackup* array. With no object reference pointing to it, the array is a candidate for garbage collection, as shown in Figure 8.10.

If we were to assign a new value to an element in the *billsBackup* array, we would change the element in the *cellBills* array also, because they are now the same array.

This statement:

```
billsBackup[4] = 38.00;
```

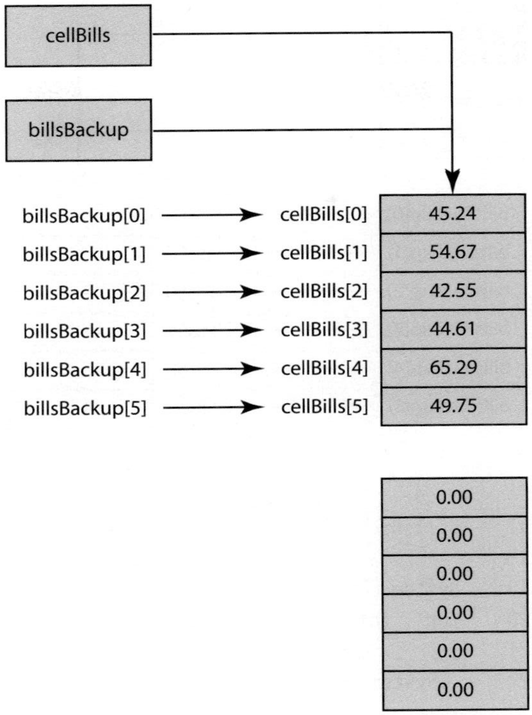

Figure 8.10
Assigning *cellBills* to *billsBackup*

has the effect shown in Figure 8.11.

Example 8.7 shows how to copy the elements in one array to another array.

```
/* Copying Array Elements to Another Array
   Anderson, Franceschi
*/

public class CopyingArrayElements
{
 public static void main( String [ ] args )
 {
   double [ ] cellBills = { 45.24, 54.67, 42.55, 44.61, 65.29, 49.75 };

   double billsBackup [ ] = new double [cellBills.length];
   for ( int i = 0; i < cellBills.length; i++ )
   {
     billsBackup[i] = cellBills[i]; // copy each element
   }

```

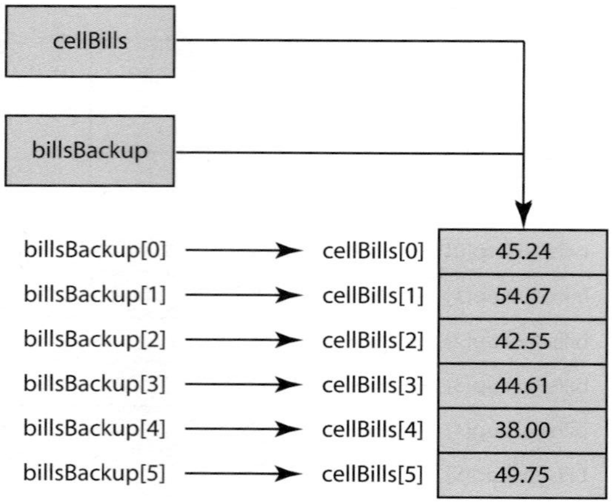

Figure 8.11
Altering *billsBackup* Alters *cellBills* Array

```
    billsBackup[4] = 38.00;  // change value in billsBackup

    System.out.println( "cellBills\nElement\tValue " );
    for ( int i = 0; i < cellBills.length; i++ )
    {
      System.out.println ( i + "\t" + cellBills[i] );
    }

    System.out.println( "\nbillsBackup\nElement\tValue " );
    for ( int i = 0; i < billsBackup.length; i++ )
    {
      System.out.println ( i + "\t" + billsBackup[i] );
    }
  }
}
```

EXAMPLE 8.7 Copying Array Elements into Another Array

At line 9, we instantiate the array *cellBills* using an initialization list. At line 11, we declare and instantiate the array *billsBackup* to have the same size as the original array *cellBills*. At lines 12–15, we use a standard *for* loop to copy one element at a time from the *cellBills* array to the *billsBackup* array.

Now the *billsBackup* array and the *cellBills* array are separate arrays with their own copies of the element values, as shown in Figure 8.12. Changing an element in one array will have no effect on the value of the corresponding element in the other array.

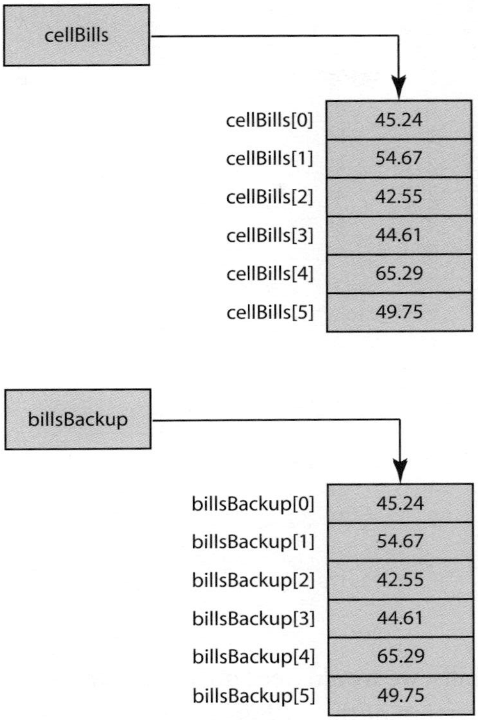

Figure 8.12
Arrays After Copying Each Element

We illustrate this by assigning a new value to an element in the array *bills-Backup* (line 17). Finally, we use two *for* loops to print the contents of both arrays. As Figure 8.13 shows, the value is changed only in the array *billsBackup*.

Be aware, however, that when you copy an array whose elements are objects, even using the *for* loop structure, you are copying object references. The result is that the corresponding elements of each array will point to the same object. If an object in one array is changed, that change will be reflected in the other array as well.

8.3.6 Changing the Size of an Array

Arrays are assigned a length when they are instantiated, and the *length* of an array becomes a constant value. But what if we want to change the number of elements in an array after it has been instantiated?

For example, our *cellBills* array contains six elements, holding six months' worth of cell phone bills. If we decide to collect a year's worth of cell phone

Figure 8.13
Output of Example 8.7

```
cellBills
Element Value
0       45.24
1       54.67
2       42.55
3       44.61
4       65.29
5       49.75

billsBackup
Element Value
0       45.24
1       54.67
2       42.55
3       44.61
4       38.0
5       49.75
```

bills, we would need an array with 12 elements. We could instantiate a new version of the *cellBills* array with 12 elements, using this statement:

```
cellBills = new double [12];
```

That statement instantiates a new array of *doubles* all initialized to 0.0. But what happened to the original array of six elements? Since the *cellBills* reference now refers to the new, 12-element array, the 6-element array has no object reference pointing to it, so there is no way we can access the array's values. That is not the result we intended!

To expand the size of an array while maintaining the values of the original array, we can use the following technique:

1. Instantiate an array with the new size, giving the new array a temporary reference.
2. Copy the elements from the original array to the new array.
3. Point the original array reference to the new array.
4. Assign a *null* value to the temporary array reference.

Thus, instead of immediately pointing *cellBills* to the new array, we should instantiate a 12-element array using a temporary array name, copy the six elements from the *cellBills* array into the 12-element array, assign the *cellBills* reference to the new array, and assign *null* to the temporary array reference. The following code will do that:

```
double [ ] temp = new double [12];  //instantiate new array

// copy all elements from cellBills to temp
for ( int i = 0; i < cellBills.length; i++ )
{
      temp[i] = cellBills[i]; // copy each element
}

cellBills = temp; // assign temp to cellBills
temp = null;      // temp no longer points to cellBills
```

The last statement sets *temp* to *null* so that we don't have two references to the *cellBills* array.

This is a tedious operation. And what if after having increased the size of an array, we find later in our program that we need to increase the size again? Clearly, arrays are not meant to be expanded via this artificial process. In Chapter 9, we introduce the *ArrayList* class, which allows for automatic expansion.

REFERENCE POINT

The *ArrayList* class is discussed in Chapter 9; it offers array functionality with automatic expansion as needed.

8.3.7 Comparing Arrays for Equality

To compare whether two arrays are equal, first determine if they are equal in length, and then use a *for* loop to compare the corresponding elements in each array, that is, compare element 0 in the first array to element 0 in the second array; compare element 1 in the first array to element 1 in the second array; and so on. If all elements in the first array are equal to the corresponding elements in the second array, then the arrays are equal. Example 8.8 compares two arrays of *doubles*, a primitive data type.

```
/* Comparing Arrays of basic data types
   Anderson, Franceschi
*/

public class ComparingArrays
{
```

```
7   public static void main( String [ ] args )
8   {
9    double [ ] cellBills1 = { 45.24, 54.67, 42.55, 44.61, 65.29, 49.75 };
10   double [ ] cellBills2 = { 45.24, 54.67, 41.99, 44.61, 65.29, 49.75 };
11
12   boolean isEqual = true;
13   if ( cellBills1.length != cellBills2.length )
14   {
15     isEqual = false; // arrays are not the same size
16   }
17   else
18   {
19     for ( int i = 0; i < cellBills1.length && isEqual; i++ )
20     {
21       if ( Math.abs( cellBills1[i] - cellBills2[i] ) > 0.001 )
22       {
23          isEqual = false; // elements are not equal
24       }
25     }
26   }
27
28   if ( isEqual )
29     System.out.println( "cellBills1 and cellBills2 are equal" );
30   else
31     System.out.println( "cellBills1 and cellBills2 are not equal" );
32  }
33 }
```

EXAMPLE 8.8 Comparing Arrays of Primitive Data Types

Before we begin the *for* loop, we declare at line 12 a *boolean* variable, *isEqual*, and set it to *true*. In this way, we assume the arrays are equal. Then, our first step is to compare whether the two arrays have the same length (line 13). If they are not the same size, the arrays cannot be equal, so we set *isEqual* to *false* and execution skips to line 28. If the two arrays are the same size, we use a *for* loop at lines 19–25 to test whether the corresponding elements in each array are equal. Note that we have added a second test to the *for* loop condition (*isEqual*). If any corresponding elements are not equal, we set *isEqual* to *false* at line 23. This will cause the condition of the *for* loop to evaluate to *false*, and we exit the *for* loop. Thus, when the *for* loop finishes executing, if any corresponding elements did not match, *isEqual* will be

```
cellBills1 and cellBills2 are not equal
```

Figure 8.14
Output of Example 8.8

false. If both arrays are the same size and all corresponding elements are equal, we never change the value of *isEqual,* so it remains *true.* The output from this example is shown in Figure 8.14.

Naturally, if the elements of the arrays are *ints, booleans,* or *chars,* we would use the equality operator (!=) at line 21 as in:

```
if ( intArray1[i] != intArray2[i] )
```

assuming the two arrays we are comparing have names *intArray1* and *intArray2.*

If the elements of the arrays are objects, your *for* loop should call the *equals* method of the objects' class. Thus, to compare two arrays of *Auto* objects, named *cars1* and *cars2,* we would use the following code instead of the condition at line 21:

```
if ( ! cars1[i].equals( cars2[i] ) )
```

A pitfall to avoid is attempting to test whether two arrays are equal using the equality operator (==). This code:

```
if ( cellBills == billsBackup )
```

will not compare the data of the two arrays. It will compare whether the *cellBills* and *billsBackup* object references are equal; that is, whether they point to the same array.

Similarly, the *equals* method inherited from *Object* also returns the wrong results.

This code:

```
if ( cellBills.equals( billsBackup ) )
```

will return *true* only if both object references point to the same array.

COMMON ERROR TRAP

Because arrays are objects, attempting to compare two arrays using the equality operator (==) will compare whether the two array references point to the same array in memory, not whether the data in the two arrays are equal. Calling the *equals* method inherited from the *Object* class yields similar results.

8.3.8 Displaying Array Data as a Bar Chart

One way to display array data is graphically, by drawing a bar chart. For example, the bar chart in Figure 8.15 displays the data in the *cellBills* array.

Each bar is simply a rectangle. Example 8.9 shows the code to generate Figure 8.15.

```
/* BarChart Applet
   Anderson, Franceschi
*/

import javax.swing.JApplet;
import java.awt.Graphics;
import java.awt.Color;

public class BarChartApplet extends JApplet
{
 final int LEFT_MARGIN = 20;        // starting x coordinate
 final int BASE_Y_BAR  = 150;       // bottom of the bars
 final int BASE_Y_VALUE = 175;      // bottom of the values
 final int BAR_WIDTH = 30;          // width of each bar
 final int SPACE_BETWEEN_BARS = 5;  // pixels between bars
 double [ ] cellBills = { 45.24, 54.67, 42.55, 44.61, 65.29, 49.75 };

 public void paint( Graphics g )
 {
  super.paint( g );

```

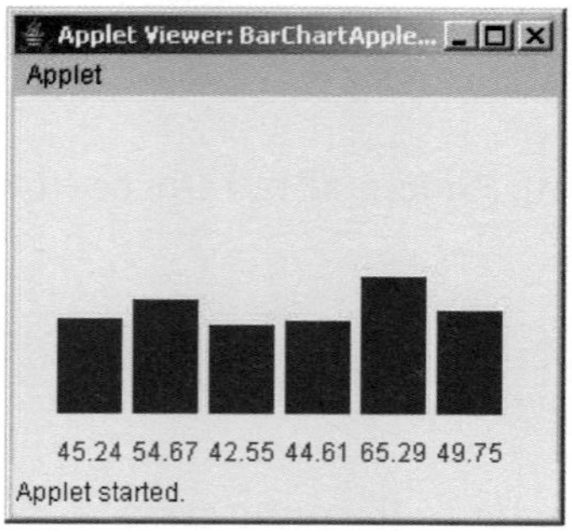

Figure 8.15
The *cellBills* Array as a Bar Chart

```
22   g.setColor( Color.BLUE );          // bars will be blue
23   int xStart = LEFT_MARGIN;          // x value for first bar
24
25   for ( int i = 0; i < cellBills.length; i++ )
26   {
27     g.fillRect( xStart, BASE_Y_BAR - ( int )( cellBills[i] ),
28                 BAR_WIDTH, ( int )( cellBills[i] ) );
29
30     g.drawString( Double.toString( cellBills[i] ),
31                   xStart, BASE_Y_VALUE );
32
33     // move to starting x value for next bar
34     xStart += BAR_WIDTH + SPACE_BETWEEN_BARS;
35   }
36  }
37 }
```

EXAMPLE 8.9 Displaying Array Values as a Bar Chart

To create the bar chart, we use our standard *for* loop at lines 25–35 in the *paint* method and call the *fillRect* method of the *Graphics* class to draw a rectangle for each element (lines 27–28). We use the *drawString* method at lines 30–31 to print the value of each element.

REFERENCE POINT

The *fillRect* and *drawString* methods of the *Graphics* class are discussed in Chapter 4.

As you recall, the *fillRect* method takes four arguments: the upper-left *x* value, the upper-left *y* value, the rectangle's width, and the rectangle's height.

We can determine the argument values for the *fillRect* method for each element using the following approach, as illustrated in Figure 8.16:

- Width: The width of the bar is a constant value. For our bar chart, we chose a width of 30 pixels; the constant *BAR_WIDTH* stores that value (line 14).
- Height: The height for each bar is the value of the array element being charted. Because the *fillRect* method expects an integer value for the height, however, we will need to type cast each *cellBills* element to an *int*. Thus, in the *fillRect* method call (lines 27–28), we represent the height of a bar as:

```
( int )( cellBills[i] )
```

- Upper-left *y* value: Similarly, the upper-left *y* value will be the height of the bar subtracted from the base *y* value for all the bars; the base *y* value for all the bars is the constant *BASE_Y_BAR* defined in line 12. We subtract the value of the element from the base of the bar because *y* values increase from the top of the window to the bottom. Thus, in our *fillRect* method call, we represent the upper-left *y* value of a bar as:

```
BASE_Y_BAR - ( int )( cellBills[i] )
```

- Upper-left *x* value: We'll start the first bar at the left side of the window, plus a left margin value, represented by the constant *LEFT_MARGIN* (line 11). After we draw each bar, our *for* loop needs to move the starting *x* value to the position of the next bar. To do this, at line 34, we increment the starting *x* value by the width of the bar, *BAR_WIDTH* (defined on line 14), plus the space between bars, *SPACE_BETWEEN_BARS* (defined on line 15).

The arguments to the *drawString* method of the *Graphics* class are the *String* to display and the base *x* and *y* values. At lines 30–31, we convert the *cellBills* element to a *String* using the *toString* method of the *Double* wrapper class. The base *x* value is the same as the starting *x* value for the

Figure 8.16
Arguments for Drawing Each Bar

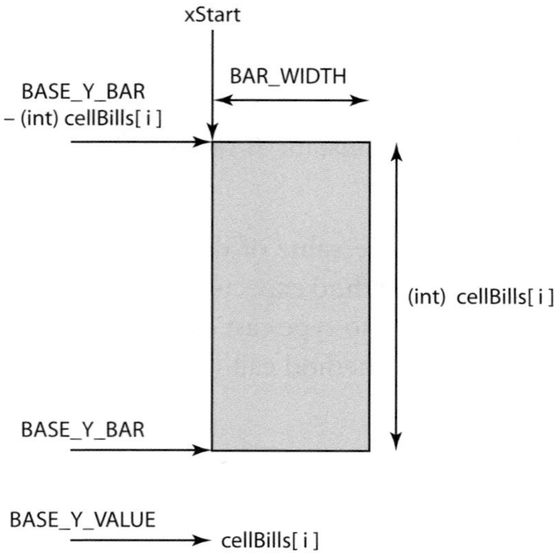

element's bar, and the base *y* coordinate, *BASE_Y_VALUE*, is the base position for printing the array values (defined on line 13).

CODE IN ACTION

On the CD-ROM included with this book, you will find a Flash movie with step-by-step illustrations of working with arrays. Click on the link for Chapter 8 to start the movie.

Skill Practice
with these end-of-chapter questions

8.10.1 Multiple Choice Exercises
Questions 6, 9, 10

8.10.2 Reading and Understanding Code
Questions 16, 17, 18, 19, 20, 21

8.10.3 Fill In the Code
Questions 27, 28, 29, 30, 31

8.10.4 Identifying Errors in Code
Questions 39, 41, 43

8.10.5 Debugging Area
Questions 46, 47, 48

8.10.8 Technical Writing
Question 76

8.4 Programming Activity 1: Working with Arrays

In this activity, you will work with a 15-element integer array. Specifically, you will write the code to perform the following operations:

1. fill the array with random numbers between 50 and 80
2. print the array
3. set every array element to a specified value

4. count the number of elements with a specified value
5. find the minimum value in the array

The framework for this Programming Activity will animate your algorithm so that you can check the accuracy of your code. For example, Figure 8.17 shows the application counting the elements having the value 73.

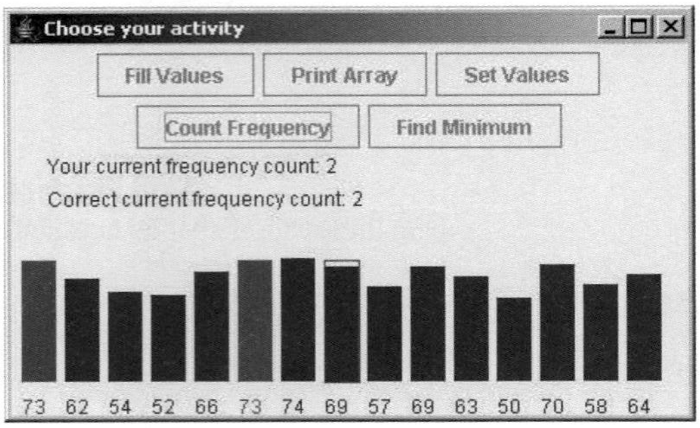

Figure 8.17
Animation of the Programming Activity

At this point, the application has found the value 73 in elements 0 and 5 and is comparing the value 73 with the value 69 in element 7.

Instructions

In the Chapter 8 Programming Activity 1 directory on the CD-ROM accompanying this book, you will find the source files needed to complete this activity. Copy all the files to a directory on your computer. Note that all files should be in the same directory.

Open the *ArrayPractice1.java* source file. Searching for five stars (*****) in the source code will position you at the sample method and the four other locations where you will add your code. We have provided the sample code for task number 1, which you can use as a model for completing the other tasks. In every task, you will fill in the code for a method that will manipulate an existing array of 15 integers. You should not instantiate the array; we have done that for you. Example 8.10 shows the section of the *ArrayPractice1* source code where you will add your code.

Note that for the *countFrequency* and *findMinimum* methods, we provide a dummy *return* statement (*return 0;*) We do this so that the source code will compile. In this way, you can write and test each method separately, using stepwise refinement. When you are ready to write the *countFrequency* and *findMinimum* methods, just replace the dummy *return* statements with the appropriate *return* statement for that method.

```
// ***** 1. The first method has been coded as an example
/** Fills the array with random numbers between 50 and 80.
*    The instance variable arr is the integer array
*    to be filled with values
*/
public void fillValues( )
{
    Random rand = new Random( );
    for ( int i = 0; i < arr.length; i++ )
    {
       arr[i] =  rand.nextInt( 31 ) + 50;
       animate( -1 );  // needed to create visual feedback
    }
}
// end of fillValues method

// ***** 2. student writes this method
/** Prints the array to the console with elements separated
*     by a space
*    The instance variable arr is the integer array to be printed
*/
public void printArray(  )
{
 // Note:  to animate the algorithm, put this method call as the
 // last statement in your for loop:
 //                 animate( i );
 //     where i is the index of the current array element
 // Write your code here:


} // end of printArray method

// ***** 3. student writes this method
/** Sets all the elements in the array to parameter value
*    The instance variable arr is the integer array to be processed
*    @param  value    the value to which to set the array elements
*/
public void setValues( int value )
{
 // Note:  to animate the algorithm, put this method call as the
 // last statement in your for loop
 //           animate( i );
 //      where i is the index of the current array element
```

```
 // Write your code here:


} // end of setValues method

// ***** 4. student writes this method
/** Counts number of elements equal to parameter value
*    The instance variable arr is the integer array to be processed
*      @param  value    the value to count
*      @return   the number of elements equal to value
*/
public int countFrequency( int value )
{
 // Note:  to animate the algorithm, put this method call as the
 // last statement in your for loop
 //          animate( i, count );
 //         where i is the index of the current array element
 //                 count is the variable holding the frequency
 // Write your code here:


     return 0; // replace this line with your return statement

} // end of countFrequency method

// ***** 5. student writes this method
/** Finds and returns the minimum value in arr
*    The instance variable arr is the integer array to be processed
*     @return the minimum value found in arr
*/
public int findMinimum(  )
{
 // Note:  to animate the algorithm, put this method call as the
 // last statement in your for loop
 //        animate( i, minimum );
 //            where i is the index of the current array element
 //               minimum is the variable holding the minimum
 // Write your code here:


     return 0; // replace this line with your return statement

} // end of findMinimum method

// End of student code
```

EXAMPLE 8.10 Location of Student Code in *ArrayPractice1*

Our framework will animate your algorithm so that you can watch your code work. For this to happen, be sure that your *for* loop calls the *animate* method. The arguments that you send to *animate* will differ depending on the task you are coding. Detailed instructions for each task are included in the code.

To test your code, compile and run the *ArrayPractice1* source code. Figure 8.18 shows the graphics window when the program begins. Because the values of the array are randomly generated, the values will be different each time the program runs. To test any method, click the appropriate button.

Troubleshooting

If your method implementation does not animate, follow these tips:

- Verify that the last statement in your *for* loop is a call to the *animate* method and that you passed the appropriate arguments to the *animate* method.
- Verify that your *for* loop has curly braces. For example, the *animate* method call is outside the body of this *for* loop:

```
for ( int i = 0; i< arr.length; i++ )
      System.out.println ( arr [i] );
      animate( i );  // this statement is outside the for loop
```

Remember that without curly braces, the *for* loop body consists of only the first statement following the *for* loop header. Enclosing both statements within curly braces will make the *animate* method call part of the *for* loop body.

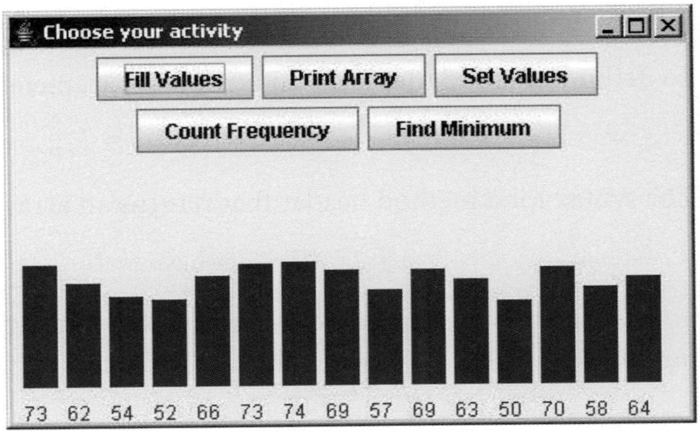

Figure 8.18
The Graphics Window When the Application Begins

```
for ( int i = 0; i < arr.length; i++ )
{
      System.out.println ( arr [i] );
      animate( i );
}
```

- Verify that you did not instantiate a new array. Perform all operations on the array passed to the method as a parameter.

DISCUSSION QUESTIONS ?

1. Could you use the following *for* loop header in every method? Explain why or why not.

   ```
   for ( int i = 0; i < arr.length; i++ )
   ```

2. How would you modify the *findMinimum* method to return the index of the minimum value?

8.5 Using Arrays in Classes

8.5.1 Using Arrays in User-Defined Classes

An array can be used inside a user-defined class just like any other variable. In particular,

- an array can be an instance variable.
- an array can be a parameter to a method.
- a method can return an array.
- an array can be a local variable inside a method.

COMMON ERROR TRAP

If you think of the brackets as being part of the data type of the array, then it's easy to remember that the brackets are included in the method header—where the data types of parameters are given—but that brackets are not included in method calls, where the data itself is given.

To define a method that takes an array as a parameter, use this syntax:

```
accessModifier returnType methodName( dataType [ ] arrayName )
```

The syntax for a method header that returns an array is

```
accessModifier dataType [ ] methodName( parameterList )
```

To pass an array as an argument to a method, just use the array name without brackets as the argument value:

```
methodName( arrayName )
```

In Example 8.11, we define a class named *CellPhone* that illustrates the use of arrays in a class.

```
/** CellPhone class
*   Anderson, Franceschi
*/

import java.text.DecimalFormat;

public class CellPhone
{
  public final int MONTHS = 6;  // default number of months
  private String phoneNumber;
  private double [ ] cellBills;

  /** Default constructor
  *   creates cellBills with MONTHS elements
  */
  public CellPhone( )
  {
     phoneNumber = "";
     cellBills = new double [MONTHS];
  }

  /** Constructor
  *  @param  number  cell phone number
  *  @param  bills   array of monthly bills
  */
  public CellPhone( String number, double [ ] bills )
  {
    phoneNumber = number;

    // instantiate array with same length as parameter
    cellBills = new double [bills.length];

    // copy parameter array to cellBills array
    for ( int i = 0; i < cellBills.length; i++ )
    {
      cellBills[i] = bills[i];
    }
  }

  /** Returns the phone number
  *   @return the phone number
  */
  public String getPhoneNumber( )
  {
```

```java
      return phoneNumber;
   }

   /** Returns an array of cell phone bills
   *   @return  copy of cellBills array
   */
   public double [ ] getCellBills( )
   {
      double [ ] temp = new double [cellBills.length];
      for ( int i = 0; i < cellBills.length; i ++ )
      {
        temp[i] = cellBills[i];
      }
      return temp;
   }

   /**  Calculates total of all cell phone bills
   *    @return  total of all elements in cellBills array
   */
   public double calcTotalBills( )
   {
      double total = 0.0;  // initialize total to 0.0

      for ( int i = 0; i < cellBills.length; i++ )
      {
        total += cellBills[i];  // add current element to total
      }
      return total;
   }

   /** Finds a maximum bill
   *  @return largest value in cellBills array
   */
   public double findMaximumBill( )
   {
      double max = cellBills[0]; // assume first element is max

      for ( int i = 1; i < cellBills.length; i++ )
      {
         if ( cellBills[i] > max )
            max = cellBills[i];  // save new maximum
      }
      return max;
   }

   /** Returns printable version of CellPhone object
   *   @return phone number plus each month's bill
```

```
92     */
93     public String toString( )
94     {
95       String returnValue = phoneNumber + "\n";
96       DecimalFormat money = new DecimalFormat( "$##0.00" );
97       for ( int i = 0; i < cellBills.length; i++ )
98       {
99          returnValue += money.format( cellBills[i] ) + "\t";
100      }
101      returnValue += "\n";
102
103      return returnValue;
104    }
105
106    /**  Compares two CellPhone objects for equality
107    *   @param c CellPhone object
108    *   @return  true if objects are equal; false, otherwise
109    */
110    public boolean equals( Object c )
111    {
112      if ( !( c instanceof CellPhone ) )
113          return false;
114      else
115      {
116          CellPhone objCP = ( CellPhone ) c;
117          if ( !( phoneNumber.equals( objCP.phoneNumber ) ) )
118            return false;
119
120          if ( cellBills.length != objCP.cellBills.length )
121            return false; // arrays are not the same length
122
123          for ( int i = 0; i < cellBills.length; i++ )
124          {
125             if ( cellBills[i] != objCP.cellBills[i] )
126               return false;
127          }
128          return true;
129      }
130    }
131 }
```

EXAMPLE 8.11 The *CellPhone* Class

Our *CellPhone* class defines three instance variables in lines 9–11: the phone number (a *String* named *phoneNumber*), monthly bills (an array of *doubles* named *cellBills*), and a constant named *MONTHS*, whose value, 6, represents the number of monthly cell bills, and therefore the length of the *cellBills* array if a *CellPhone* object is instantiated using the default constructor. Note that since *MONTHS* is a constant, we made it *public*.

When your class has instance variables that are arrays, you will need to take a little extra care to ensure that encapsulation is not violated.

Let's start with initialization of the array. The overloaded constructor of the *CellPhone* class, whose method header is at line 26, includes an array parameter. With parameters of primitive types, the constructor can simply assign the value of the parameter to the instance variable. As we have seen, however, the name of an array is an object reference, which contains the location of the array in memory. If the constructor merely assigns the array parameter, *bills*, to our array instance variable, *cellBills*, as in the following code:

```
cellBills = bills;  // incorrect! Client still has reference!
```

then *bills* and *cellBills* would point to the same array. That means that the client still has a reference to the array, and the client can change the array values without going through the mutator methods of the class. For example, if the client executes this statement:

```
bills[2] = 75.00;
```

then *cellBills[2]* also gets the value 75.00, because they are the same array. This is clearly a violation of encapsulation, which means that a client should be able to change the *private* fields of a class only by calling the mutator methods of the class.

SOFTWARE ENGINEERING TIP

Sharing array references with the client violates encapsulation. To return an array from a method, copy the elements of the instance variable array to a temporary array and return a reference to the temporary array. Similarly, to accept an array as a parameter to a method, instantiate a new array and copy the elements of the parameter array to the new array.

To avoid this problem, our constructor instantiates a new *cellBills* array that is the same size as the array passed as a parameter, and then copies the elements of the parameter array into the new *cellBills* array (lines 30–37).

There are similar considerations in implementing the accessor method of an array instance variable. With instance variables of primitive types, the accessor methods simply return the value of the instance variable. Our accessor for *cellBills* (lines 48–59) has an array as a return value. If we return the *cellBills* reference, however, we run into the same problem with encapsulation; that is, if our accessor for the *cellBills* instance variable uses this statement:

```
return cellBills; // incorrect! Client has reference to instance variable
```

we give the client a reference to the *cellBills* array, and the client can directly change the values of the array without calling the mutator methods of the class. Just as the constructor instantiated a new array and copied the parameter array's value to the new array, the accessor method should instantiate a new array, copy the *cellBills* array to it, and return a reference to the new array. Thus, at line 53, we declare and instantiate a local array variable named *temp*. At lines 54–57, we copy the contents of *cellBills* into *temp*, and return *temp* at line 58.

We also provide a method *calcTotalBills* (lines 61–73) that calculates the total of the monthly bills using the accumulation technique discussed earlier in the chapter and a *findMaximumBill* method (lines 75–88), which finds a maximum value in the *cellBills* array, also using techniques discussed earlier in the chapter.

Our *toString* method (lines 90–104) builds up a *String* named *returnValue* by first including *phoneNumber*, then formatting each bill using a *DecimalFormat* pattern for money and concatenating that value, plus a tab, to *returnValue*.

The *equals* method (lines 106–130) compares the phone number and each element of the *cellBills* array in the object with the phone number and corresponding element in the *cellBills* array in the parameter object.

We can test our *CellPhone* class with the client class shown in Example 8.12. The output is shown in Figure 8.19 on page 503.

```
/** Client to exercise the CellPhone class
* Anderson, Franceschi
*/

import java.text.DecimalFormat;

public class CellPhoneClient
{
  public static void main( String [ ] args )
  {
    double [ ] bills = new double[3]; // array of cell phone bills
    bills[0] = 24.60; // assign values
    bills[1] = 48.75;
    bills[2] = 62.50;

    // instantiate CellPhone object using default constructor
    CellPhone c1 = new CellPhone( );

    // instantiate two identical CellPhone objects
    CellPhone c2 = new CellPhone( "555-555-5555", bills );
    CellPhone c3 = new CellPhone( "555-555-5555", bills );

    // print data from c1 and c2
    System.out.println( "c1 = " + c1.toString( ) );
    System.out.println( "c2 = " + c2.toString( ) );

    // find and print maximum bill
```

```
28         DecimalFormat money = new DecimalFormat( "$##0.00" );
29         System.out.println( "\nThe highest bill is "
30                     + money.format( c2.findMaximumBill( ) ) );
31
32         // find and print total of all bills
33         System.out.println( "\nThe total of all bills is "
34                     + money.format( c2.calcTotalBills( ) ) );
35
36         System.out.println( ); // print blank line
37         // call equals method
38         if ( c2.equals( c3 ) )
39            System.out.println( "c2 and c3 are equal" );
40         else
41            System.out.println( "c2 and c3 are not equal" );
42
43         // test encapsulation
44         // set new value in original array
45         bills[2] = 100.00;
46         // print c2 to show value in object not changed
47         System.out.println( "\nafter client changes original array\n"
48                          + "c2 = "  + c2.toString( ) );
49
50         // test encapsulation further
51         // get array of cell bills and store in new array
52         double [ ] billsCopy = c2.getCellBills( );
53
54         billsCopy[1] = 50.00;  // change value of one element
55         // print c2 to show value in object not changed
56         System.out.println( "\nafter client changes returned array\n"
57                           + "c2 = "  + c2.toString( ) );
58     }
59 }
```

EXAMPLE 8.12 The *CellPhoneClient* Class

In the *CellPhoneClient*, we instantiate three *CellPhone* objects. We instantiate *c1* using the default constructor (line 17), giving it an empty phone number and six months of bills initialized to 0.00, as shown in line 24, when we use the *toString* method to print *c1*'s data. We set up a *bills* array with three values (lines 11–14) and pass *bills* to the overloaded constructor (lines 20–21) to instantiate *c2* and *c3* with identical data. We then use *toString* to print *c2*'s data (line 25).

We then call the *findMaximumBill* method and print its return value (lines 27–30). Next, we call the *calcTotalBills* method and print its return value (lines 32–34).

```
c1 =
$0.00   $0.00   $0.00   $0.00   $0.00   $0.00

c2 = 555-555-5555
$24.60  $48.75  $62.50Ï


The highest bill is $62.50

The total of all bills is $135.85

c2 and c3 are equal

after client changes original array
c2 = 555-555-5555
$24.60  $48.75  $62.50


after client changes returned array
c2 = 555-555-5555
$24.60  $48.75  $62.50
```

Figure 8.19
Output from the *CellPhoneClient* Class

A call to the *equals* method to compare *c2* and *c3* (lines 37–41) returns a value of *true*, because the two objects have the same data.

Finally, we test encapsulation two ways. First, we change a value in the *bills* array, then print *c2* again to verify that its data has not changed (lines 43–48). Second, we call the accessor method for the *cellBills* array and change a value in the array returned from the method call. We again print *c2* to verify that its data is unchanged (lines 50–57). Testing the *CellPhone* class with such an example is helpful in checking that we have correctly implemented the class.

8.5.2 Retrieving Command Line Arguments

The syntax of an array parameter for a method might look familiar to you. We've seen it repeatedly in Java applications in the header for the *main* method:

```
public static void main( String [ ] args )
```

As you can see, *main* receives a *String* array as a parameter. That array of *Strings* holds the arguments, if any, that the user sends to the program from the command line. An argument might be the name of a file for the program to read or some configuration parameters that specify preferences in how the application should perform its function.

The sample program in Example 8.13 demonstrates how to retrieve the parameters sent to a Java application. Because *args* is a *String* array, we can use the *length* field to get the number of parameters (lines 8–9), and we use our standard *for* loop format (lines 10–13) to retrieve and print each parameter, as shown in Figure 8.20.

```
1  /** Print Command Line arguments
2  *   Anderson, Franceschi
3  */
4  public class CommandLineArguments
5  {
6   public static void main( String [ ] args )
7   {
8     System.out.println( "The number of parameters is "
9                          + args.length );
10    for ( int i = 0; i < args.length; i ++ )
11    {
12        System.out.println( "args[" + i + "]: "  + args[i] );
13    }
14   }
15 }
```

EXAMPLE 8.13 Retrieving Command Line Arguments

Figure 8.20 shows the output produced when we invoke the program as

```
java CommandLineArguments input.txt output.txt
```

Skill Practice
with these end-of-chapter questions

8.10.1 Multiple Choice Exercises

Question 11

8.10.2 Reading and Understanding Code

Questions 22, 23, 24, 25, 26

8.10.3 Fill In the Code

Questions 32, 33, 34, 35

8.10.6 Write a Short Program

Questions 49, 50, 51, 52, 53, 54, 55, 56, 58, 59, 60, 61

```
The number of parameters is 2
args[0]: input.txt
args[1]: output.txt
```

Figure 8.20
Output from Example 8.13

8.6 Searching and Sorting Arrays

Arrays are great instruments for storing a large number of related values. As seen earlier in this chapter, we can use arrays to store daily temperatures, CD titles, telephone bills, quiz grades, and other sets of related values. Once the data is stored in an array, we will want to manipulate that data. A very common operation is searching an array for a specific value.

8.6.1 Sequential Search of an Unsorted Array

Let's assume you are the manager of a DVD rental store. Each member customer gets a card with a unique member ID. You have decided to pick five member IDs at random and give those members a free gift the next time they visit the store. So you set up a *DVDWinners* class with two array instance variables:

- An array of *ints* that holds the member IDs of the winners.
- An array of *Strings* that holds the corresponding prizes.

Note that both arrays have five elements and that there is a one-to-one correspondence between the two arrays. Winner #1 will receive prize #1, winner #2 will receive prize #2, and so on. This programming technique is called **parallel arrays**.

You fill the *winners* array with member IDs chosen randomly from entry cards members have filled out. You fill the *prizes* array with *Strings* representing prize descriptions. When a member rents a DVD, you can look through the *winners* array for the member's ID. If the member's ID is in the *winners* array, you use its array index in the *prizes* array to retrieve the prize that the member won. If the member ID is not found in the array, you know the member is not a winner.

The *DVDWinners* class is shown in Example 8.14.

```
/** Winners of Free DVD Rentals
*   Anderson, Franceschi
*/
```

```java

import java.util.Random;

public class DVDWinners
{
  // array to hold winning member numbers chosen at random
  private int [ ] winners;
  // parallel array that holds prizes
  private String [ ] prizes = { "3 free rentals!",
                                "2 free rentals!",
                                "1 free rental!",
                                "free popcorn!",
                                "a free box of candy!" };
  /** Default constructor instantiates winners array
  *    and randomly generates winning member IDs
  */
  public DVDWinners( )
  {
    winners  = new int [prizes.length];
    fillWinners( ); // generate winner member IDs
  }

  /** Utility method generates winner member IDs
  *     and stores them in the winners array
  */
  private void fillWinners( )
  {
    Random rand = new Random( );
    for ( int i = 0; i < winners.length; i++ )
    {
      winners[i] = rand.nextInt( 5000 ) + 1;
    }
  }

  /** Calls indexOfWinner with the member number
  *   then translates return value into the prize won
  *   @param memberNumber value to find
  *   @return prize
  */
  public String getPrize( int memberNumber )
  {
     int prizeIndex = indexOfWinner( memberNumber );
```

```
46       if ( prizeIndex == -1 )
47           return "Sorry, member is not a winner.";
48       else
49           return "You win " + prizes[prizeIndex];
50     }
51
52     /** Performs sequential search of winners array
53     *   @param key member ID to find in winners array
54     *   @return index of key if found, -1 if not found
55     */
56     private int indexOfWinner( int key )
57     {
58       for ( int i = 0; i < winners.length; i++ )
59       {
60          if ( winners[i] == key )
61              return i;
62       }
63       return -1;
64     }
65
66     /** Returns printable version of DVDWinners object
67     *   @return winning numbers separated by a tab
68     */
69     public String toString( )
70     {
71       String returnValue = "";
72       for ( int i = 0; i < winners.length; i++ )
73       {
74         returnValue += winners[i] + "\t";
75       }
76       return returnValue;
77     }
78 }
```

EXAMPLE 8.14 The *DVDWinners* Class

The constructor randomly generates values to fill the array by calling the utility method, *fillWinners* (lines 26–36). In the interest of keeping things simple, we have coded the *fillWinners* method in such a way that it does not necessarily generate different numbers; however, the likelihood of two winning numbers being equal is very small. We declare the *fillWinners* method as *private* because it is designed to be called only by the methods of this class.

Our *indexOfWinner* method (lines 52–64) performs a **Sequential Search**, which compares the member ID to each element in the array one by one. The *indexOfWinner* method accepts a parameter, *key*, which is the member ID to search for in the array. If *key* is found, *indexOfWinner* returns the index of that array element. If *key* is not found, that is, if none of the elements in the array matches the value of *key*, *indexOfWinner* returns –1. Since –1 is not a valid array index, it's a good value to use to indicate that the search was unsuccessful.

Notice that if the current array element matches the *key*, the *indexOfWinner* method returns immediately to the caller (line 61); that is, the method stops executing. The return value is the index of the element that matched the *key*. If, however, the method finishes executing all iterations of the *for* loop, then the method has looked at every element in the array without finding a match. In that case, the method returns -1 (line 63), indicating that the *key* was not found.

Our *getPrize* method (lines 38–50) calls *indexOfWinner* to check if its *memberNumber* parameter is a winning number; if it is, it uses the array index returned by *indexOfWinner* in order to return the corresponding element of the array *prizes* (line 49).

Example 8.15 shows a client application that uses our *DVDWinners* class.

```
/** Client for the DVDWinners class
    Anderson, Franceschi
*/
import java.util.Scanner;

public class DVDWinnersClient
{
  public static void main( String [ ] args )
  {
    // instantiate the winningIDs array
    DVDWinners winningIDs = new DVDWinners( );

    // prompt for the member ID
```

```
14     Scanner scan = new Scanner( System.in );
15     System.out.print( "Enter the member's ID "
16                           + "or 0 to stop > " );
17     int searchID = scan.nextInt( );
18
19     while ( searchID != 0 )
20     {
21       // determine whether member is a winner
22       System.out.println( winningIDs.getPrize( searchID ) );
23
24       System.out.print( "\nEnter the next member's ID "
25                             + "or 0 to stop > " );
26       searchID = scan.nextInt( );
27     }
28
29     System.out.println( "\nThe winners were "
30                             + winningIDs.toString( ) );
31   }
32 }
```

EXAMPLE 8.15 Client Application for the *DVDWinners* Class

We instantiate a *DVDWinners* object reference named *winningIDs* (lines 10–11). We then prompt for a member ID (lines 15–17) and call the *getPrize* method (line 22) in order to output any prize that may have been won by the current member. Figure 8.21 shows a possible output of running the *DVDWinnersClient* application.

SOFTWARE ENGINEERING TIP

When you write a class that uses corresponding lists of items with different data types, consider using parallel arrays.

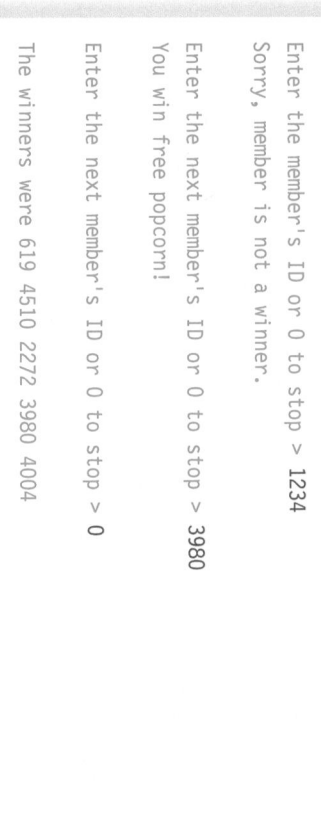

```
Enter the member's ID or 0 to stop > 1234
Sorry, member is not a winner.

Enter the next member's ID or 0 to stop > 3980
You win free popcorn!

Enter the next member's ID or 0 to stop > 0

The winners were 619 4510 2272 3980 4004
```

Figure 8.21
Output of Example 8.15

8.6.2 Selection Sort

The member IDs in the preceding *winners* array were in random order, so when a member was not a winner, our *findWinners* method needed to look at every element in the array before discovering that the ID we were looking for was not in the array. This is not efficient, since most members are not winners. The larger the array, the more inefficient a sequential search becomes. We could simplify the search by arranging the elements in numeric order, which is called **sorting the array**. Once the array is sorted, we can use various algorithms to speed up a search. Later in this chapter, we discuss how to search a sorted array.

In this chapter, we present two basic sorting algorithms, **Selection Sort** and **Insertion Sort**.

Selection Sort derives its name from the algorithm used to sort the array. We select a largest element in the array and place it at the end of the array. Then we select a next-largest element and put it in the next-to-last position in the array. To do this, we consider the unsorted portion of the array as a **subarray**. We repeatedly select a largest value in the current subarray and move it to the end of the subarray, then consider a new subarray by eliminating the elements that are in their sorted locations, until the subarray has only one element. At that time, the array is sorted.

In more formal terms, we can state the Selection Sort algorithm, presented here in pseudocode, in this way:

To sort an array with n elements in ascending order:

1. Consider m elements as a subarray with $m = n$ elements.
2. Find the index of a largest value in this subarray.
3. Swap the values of the element with the largest value and the element in the last position in the subarray.
4. Consider a new subarray of $m = m - 1$ elements by eliminating the last element in the previous subarray.
5. Repeat steps 2 through 4 until $m = 1$.

For example, let's walk through a Selection Sort on the following array. At the beginning, the entire array is the subarray (shown here with shading).

We begin by considering the entire array as an unsorted subarray. We find that the largest element is 26 at index 1.

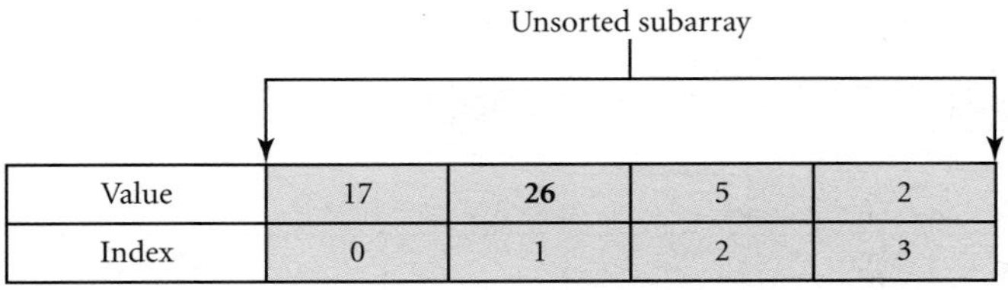

Next we move element 1 to the last element by swapping the values of the elements at indexes 1 and 3.

The value 26 is now in the right place, and we consider elements 0 through 2 as the unsorted subarray.

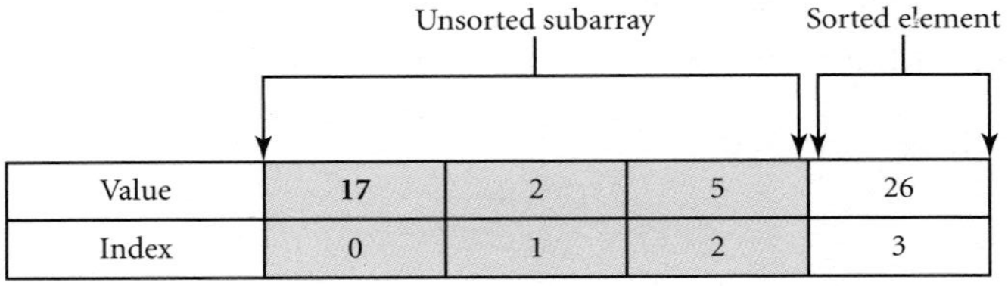

The largest element in the new subarray is 17 at index 0. So we move element 0 to the last index of the subarray (index 2) by swapping the elements at indexes 0 and 2.

The value 17 is now in the right place, and we consider elements 0 and 1 as the new unsorted subarray.

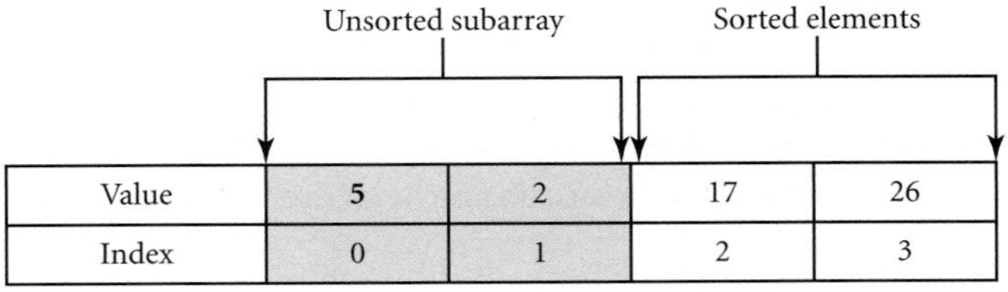

The largest element in the new subarray is 5 at index 0. We move element 0 to the last index of the subarray (index 1) by swapping the elements at indexes 0 and 1.

The value 5 is now in the right place, and we consider element 0 as the new subarray. But because there is only one element in the subarray, the subarray is sorted. Thus the whole array is sorted, and our job is done.

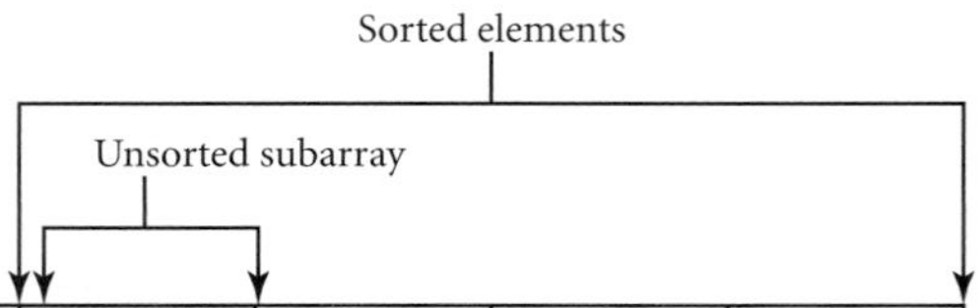

Value	2	5	17	26
Index	0	1	2	3

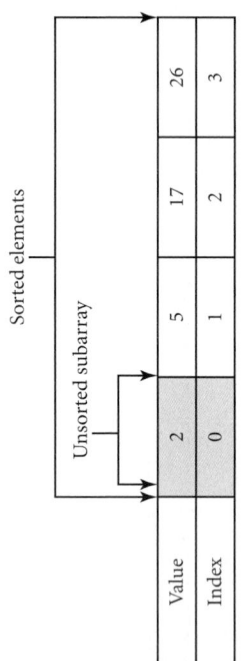

A critical operation in a Selection Sort is swapping two array elements. Before going further, let's examine the algorithm for swapping two array elements.

To swap two values, we need to define a temporary variable that is of the same data type as the values being swapped. This variable will temporarily hold the value of one of the elements, so that we don't lose the value during the swap.

The algorithm, presented here in pseudocode, involves three steps:

To swap elements a and b:

1. Assign the value of element *a* to the temporary variable
2. Assign the value of element *b* to element *a*
3. Assign the value in the temporary variable to element *b*

For instance, if an array named *array* has *int* elements, and we want to swap the element at index 3 with the element at index 6, we will use the following code:

```
int temp = array[3];     // line 1
array[3] = array[6];     // line 2
array[6] = temp;         // line 3
```

The order of these operations is critical; changing the order might result in loss of data and erroneous data stored in the array.

The following illustrates line by line what happens during the swap:

Before line 1 is executed, our array looks like this:

Value	23	45	7	33	78	90	82	80	90	66
Index	0	1	2	3	4	5	6	7	8	9

Line 1 assigns the value of element 3 to *temp*. After line 1 is executed, the value of *temp* is 33. The array is unchanged.

Value	23	45	7	33	78	90	82	80	90	66		33
Index	0	1	2	3	4	5	6	7	8	9		temp

Line 2 assigns the value of element 6 (82) to element 3. After line 2 is executed, both element 6 and element 3 have the same value. But that's OK, because we saved the value of element 3 in *temp*.

Value	23	45	7	82	78	90	82	80	90	66		33
Index	0	1	2	3	4	5	6	7	8	9		temp

Line 3 assigns the value we saved in *temp* to element 6. After line 3 is executed, the values of elements 3 and 6 have been successfully swapped.

COMMON ERROR TRAP

When swapping elements, be sure to save a value before replacing it with another value to avoid losing data.

Value	23	45	7	82	78	90	33	80	90	66		33
Index	0	1	2	3	4	5	6	7	8	9		temp

Example 8.16 shows the *Sorter* class, which provides a *static selectionSort* method for an integer array.

```
/* Sort Utility Class
*  Anderson, Franceschi
*/

public class Sorter
{
  /**  Uses Selection Sort to sort
  *      an integer array in ascending order
  *    @param array the array to sort
  */
  public static void selectionSort( int [ ] array )
  {
    int temp; // temporary location for swap
    int max;  // index of maximum value in subarray

    for ( int i = 0; i < array.length; i++ )
    {
```

```
18         // find index of largest value in subarray
19         max = indexOfLargestElement( array, array.length - i );
20
21         // swap array[max] and array[array.length - i - 1]
22         temp = array[max];
23         array[max] = array[array.length - i - 1];
24         array[array.length - i - 1] = temp;
25       }
26     }
27
28     /**  Finds index of largest element
29     *    @param    size  the size of the subarray
30     *    @param    array the array to search
31     *    @return   the index of the largest element in the subarray
32     */
33     private static int indexOfLargestElement( int [ ] array, int size )
34     {
35       int index = 0;
36       for( int i = 1; i < size; i++ )
37       {
38          if ( array[i] > array[index] )
39             index = i;
40       }
41       return index;
42     }
43 }
```

EXAMPLE 8.16 The *Sorter* Class

Part of the Selection Sort algorithm is finding the index of the largest element in a subarray, so we implement the Selection Sort with two methods. At lines 7–26, is the *selectionSort* method, which implements the Selection Sort algorithm. To perform its work, the *selectionSort* method calls the utility method, *indexOfLargestElement* (lines 28–42), which returns the index of the largest element in a subarray. This method uses the algorithm discussed earlier in the chapter for finding a maximum value in an array. We declare this method *private* because its only function is to provide a service to the *selectionSort* method. The *indexOfLargestElement* method must also be declared as *static* because the *selectionSort* method is *static*, and thus can call only *static* methods.

In Example 8.17, the client code instantiates an integer array and prints the array before and after the Selection Sort is performed. Because *selectionSort* is a *static* method, we call it using the *Sorter* class name. The output of a sample run is shown in Figure 8.22.

```
/** Client for Selection Sort
*   Anderson, Franceschi
*/
import java.util.Random;

public class SelectionSortClient
{
  public static void main( String [ ] args )
  {
    // instantiate an array and fill with random values
    int [ ] numbers = new int [6];
    Random rand = new Random( );
    for ( int i = 0; i < numbers.length; i++ )
    {
      numbers[i] = rand.nextInt( 5000 ) + 1;
    }

    System.out.println( "Before Selection Sort, the array is" );
    for ( int i = 0; i < numbers.length; i++ )
       System.out.print( numbers[i] + "\t" );
    System.out.println( );

    Sorter.selectionSort( numbers ); // sort the array

    System.out.println( "\nAfter Selection Sort, the array is"  );
    for ( int i = 0; i < numbers.length; i++ )
       System.out.print( numbers[i] + "\t" );
    System.out.println( );
  }
}
```

EXAMPLE 8.17 Using Selection Sort

```
Before Selection Sort, the array is
3394    279     1181    2471    3660     221

After Selection Sort, the array is
221     279     1181    2471    3394     3660
```

Figure 8.22
Using Selection Sort

8.6.3 Insertion Sort

Like Selection Sort, Insertion Sort also derives its name from the algorithm used to sort the array. The basic approach to an Insertion Sort is to sort elements much like a card player arranges the cards in sorted order in his or her hand. The player inserts cards one at a time in such a way that the cards on the left side of his or her hand are sorted at all times; the cards on the right side of his or her hand have not yet been inserted into the sorted part of the hand. As Figure 8.23a shows, the three yellow cards on the left (3, 5, and 9) are already arranged in sorted order, and the white cards on the right (4, 2, and 8) have yet to be inserted into their correct location. Note that the "sorted" yellow cards on the left side are not necessarily in their final position yet. We will now insert the 4. We first compare it to the 9; since 4 is smaller than 9, we shift the 9 to the right (Figure 8.23b). We then compare the 4 to the 5; since 4 is smaller than 5, we shift the 5 to the right

Figure 8.23a
The next card to insert is a 4

Figure 8.23b
9 is shifted to the right

Figure 8.23c
5 is shifted to the right

Figure 8.23d
4 is inserted

(Figure 8.23c). We then compare the 4 to the 3; since 4 is larger than 3, the 3 stays in place and we insert the 4 in the empty slot (Figure 8.23d). We are now ready to insert the next card, the 2.

To sort an array of n elements in ascending order, Insertion Sort implements a double loop:

- The outer loop executes $n - 1$ times and iterates through the array elements from indexes 1 through $n - 1$. If the variable i represents the counter of the outer loop, the array can be thought of as made of three parts:
  - a sorted subarray (although the elements may not be in their final position yet) from index 0 to $i - 1$,
  - the array element (at index i) that we are currently inserting,

    - a subarray (from index $i + 1$ to $n - 1$) of elements that have not yet been inserted.
- At each iteration of the outer loop, we insert the current array element at its proper place within the sorted subarray. The inner loop compares the current array element to the elements of the sorted array from right to left and shifts these elements to the right until it finds the proper insert location.
- After all elements have been inserted, the array is sorted.

The pseudocode for the Insertion Sort is

```
for i = 1 to last array index by 1
   j = i
   temp = element at index i
   while ( j != 0 and value of current element is less than value of element at index j – 1 )
      shift element at index j – 1 to the right
      decrement j by 1
   assign current element value (stored in temp) to element at index j
```

For example, let's walk through an Insertion Sort on the following array. At the beginning, the unsorted array is

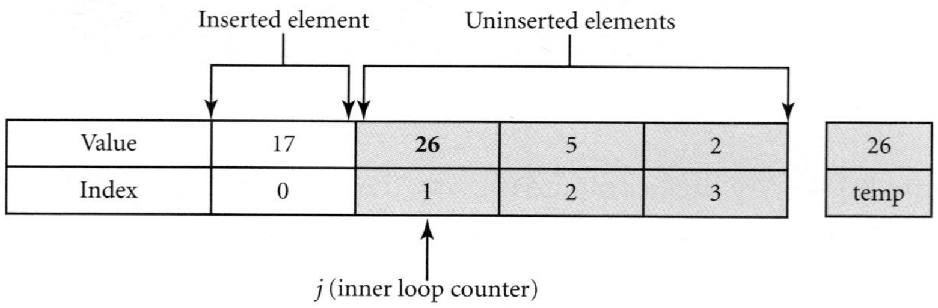

The first element of the array, 17, is automatically in the correct position when we consider the subarray as consisting of that element only. The value of the outer loop counter (i) is 1, and we will now insert the second array element, 26, into the left subarray. First, we save the value of the element to be inserted by storing it in *temp*. We need to save the value because it is possible that we will shift other values, in which case we would overwrite that element. The value of the inner loop counter (j) is set to the value of the outer loop counter (i), i.e., 1. We compare elements 26 (index $j = 1$) and 17 (index $j - 1 = 0$). Since 26 is larger than 17, we exit the inner loop (and therefore we do not shift 17 to the right). We then assign the value of the current element, 26, stored in *temp*, to the element at index $j = 1$; in this case, there is no change to the array. The value 26 has been inserted.

The outer loop counter (i) is incremented, and its value is 2. We will now insert the third array element, 5, into the left subarray (at this point comprised of the two inserted elements, 17 and 26).

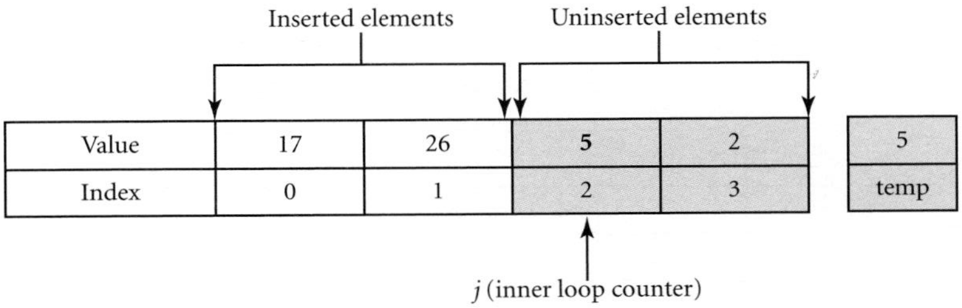

The value of the inner loop counter (j) is set to the value of the outer loop counter (i), i.e. 2. We compare the current element, 5, stored in *temp*, and 26 (index $j - 1 = 1$). Since 5 is smaller than 26, we shift 26 to the right and decrement j by 1; j now has the value 1.

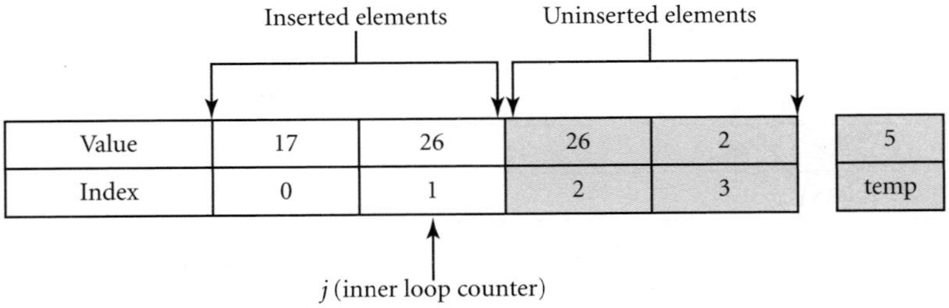

We then compare the current element, 5, stored in *temp*, and 17 (index $j - 1 = 0$). Since 5 is smaller than 17, we shift 17 to the right and decrement j by 1; j now has the value 0.

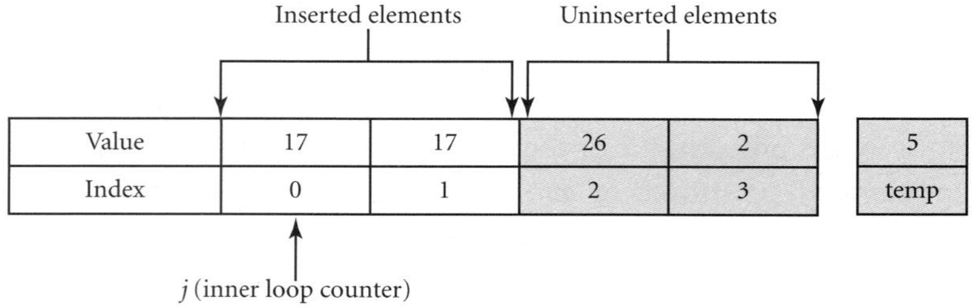

Since j is 0, we exit the inner loop and assign the value of the current element, 5, stored in *temp*, to the array element at index $j = 0$. The value 5 has now been inserted.

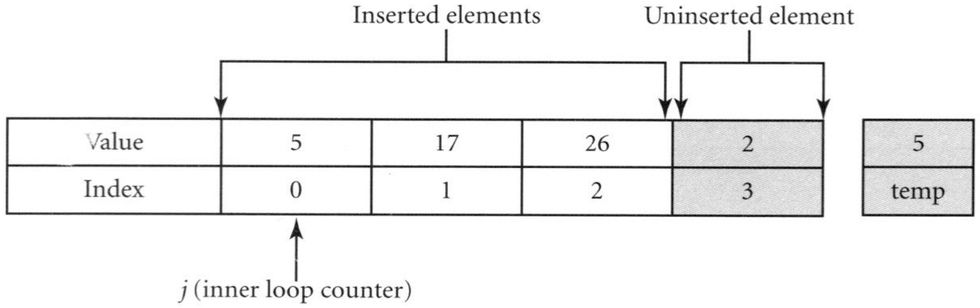

The outer loop counter (i) is incremented, and its value is 3. We will now insert the fourth array element, 2, into the left subarray (at this point comprised of the three inserted elements, 5, 17, and 26).

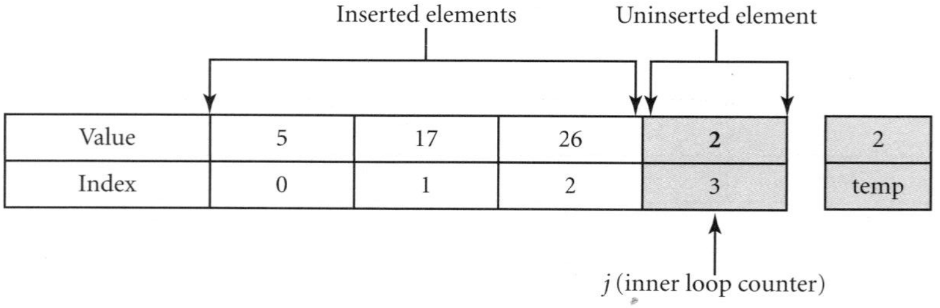

The value of the inner loop counter (j) is set to the value of the outer loop counter (i), i.e. 3. We compare the current element, 2, stored in *temp*, and 26 (index $j - 1 = 2$). Since 2 is smaller than 26, we shift 26 to the right and decrement j by 1; j now has the value 2.

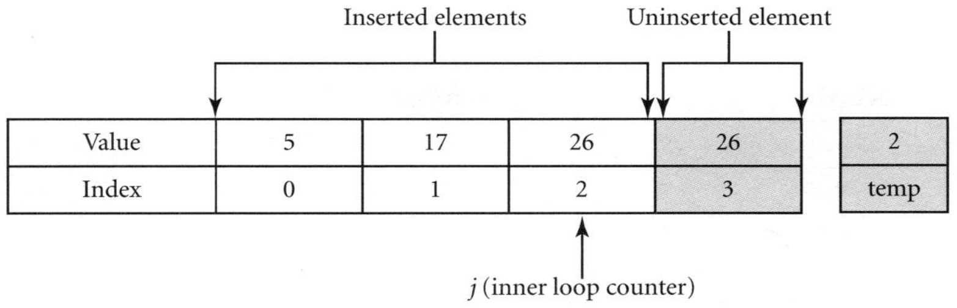

We then compare the current element, 2, stored in *temp*, and 17 (index $j - 1 = 1$). Since 2 is smaller than 17, we shift 17 to the right and decrement *j* by 1; *j* now has the value 1.

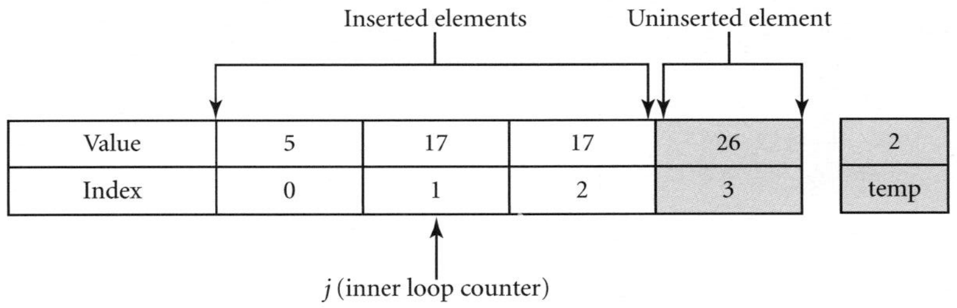

We then compare the current element, 2, stored in *temp*, and 5 (index $j - 1 = 0$). Since 2 is smaller than 5, we shift 5 to the right and decrement *j* by 1; *j* now has the value 0.

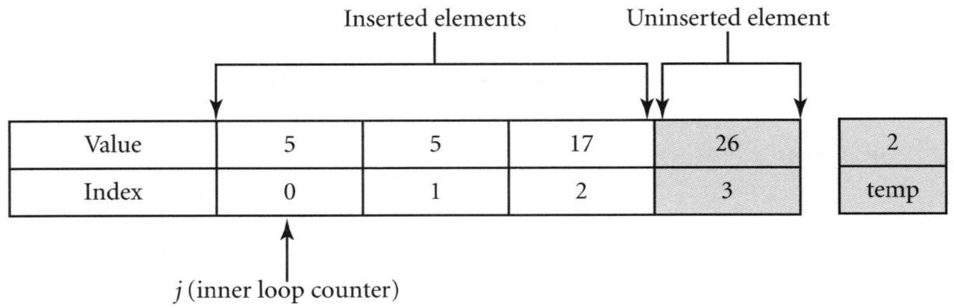

Since *j* is 0, we exit the inner loop and assign the value of the current element, 2, stored in *temp*, to the array element at index *j*. The value 2 has now been inserted.

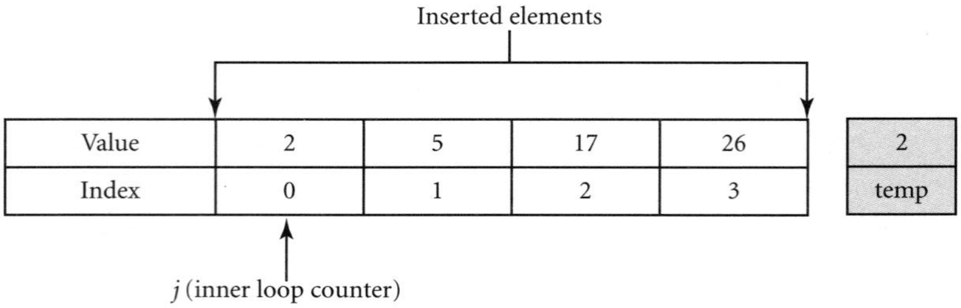

COMMON ERROR TRAP

When looping through an array, be careful not to access an element outside the bounds of the array. Your code will compile, but will generate an *ArrayIndexOutOfBoundsException* at run time.

The outer loop counter (i) is incremented, and its value is 4, which causes the outer loop to terminate. All the elements have been inserted; the array is now sorted.

Example 8.18 shows our *Sorter* class with the Insertion Sort algorithm implemented in lines 43–63.

```
 1 /* Sort Utility Class
 2    Anderson, Franceschi
 3 */
 4
 5 public class Sorter
 6 {
 7   /**  Performs a Selection Sort on
 8    *      an integer array
 9    *     @param the array to sort
10   */
11  public static void selectionSort( int [ ] array )
12  {
13     int temp; // temporary location for swap
14     int max;  // index of maximum value in subarray
15
16     for ( int i = 0; i < array.length; i++ )
17     {
18       // find index of largest value in subarray
19       max = indexOfLargestElement( array, array.length - i );
20
21       // swap array[max] and array[array.length - i - 1]
22       temp = array[max];
23       array[max] = array[array.length - i - 1];
24       array[array.length - i - 1] = temp;
25     }
26   }
27
```

```
/**  Finds index of largest element
*    @param     size  the size of the subarray
*    @return    the index of the largest element in the subarray
*/
private static int indexOfLargestElement( int [ ] array, int size )
{
   int index = 0;
   for( int i = 1; i < size; i++ )
   {
      if ( array[i] > array[index] )
         index = i;
   }
   return index;
}

/**  Performs an Insertion Sort on an integer array
*    @param array   array to sort
*/
public static void insertionSort( int [ ] array )
{
  int j, temp;

  for ( int i = 0; i < array.length; i++ )
  {
     j = i;
     temp = array[i];

     while ( j != 0 && array[j - 1] > temp )
     {
        array[j] = array[j - 1];
        j--;
     }

     array[j] = temp;
  }
}
}
```

EXAMPLE 8.18 Sorter Class with Insertion Sort

Example 8.19 shows a client program that instantiates an integer array, fills it with random values, and then prints the array before and after performing the Insertion Sort. Figure 8.24 shows a sample run, using the Insertion Sort algorithm to sort an array of integers.

```java
/** Client for Insertion Sort
*   Anderson, Franceschi
*/
import java.util.Random;

public class InsertionSortClient
{
  public static void main( String [ ] args )
  {
    // instantiate an array and fill with random values
    int [ ] numbers = new int [6];
    Random rand = new Random( );
    for ( int i = 0; i < numbers.length; i++ )
    {
      numbers[i] = rand.nextInt( 5000 ) + 1;
    }

    System.out.println( "Before Insertion Sort, the array is" );
    for ( int i = 0; i < numbers.length; i++ )
       System.out.print( numbers[i] + "\t" );
    System.out.println( );

    Sorter.insertionSort( numbers ); // sort the array

    System.out.println( "\nAfter Insertion Sort, the array is"  );
    for ( int i = 0; i < numbers.length; i++ )
        System.out.print( numbers[i] + "\t" );
    System.out.println( );
  }
}
```

EXAMPLE 8.19 Using Insertion Sort

Figure 8.24
Using Insertion Sort

```
Before Insertion Sort, the array is
2856    2384    3979    3088    1176    284

After Insertion Sort, the array is
284     1176    2384    2856    3088    3979
```

8.6.4 Sorting Arrays of Objects

We saw earlier in the chapter that data items to be sorted can be primitive data types, such as integers or *doubles*. But they can also be objects. With an array of objects, it is important to understand that we need to sort the objects themselves, not the array elements, which are merely the object references, or memory locations of the objects.

Arrays of objects are sorted using a sort key, which is one or more of the instance variables of the objects. For instance, if we have email objects, they can be sorted by date received, by author, by subject, and so on. It is important to note that when we sort objects, the integrity of the objects must be respected; for instance, when we sort a collection of email objects by sender, we sort a collection of email objects, not a collection of senders.

Thus, to perform the Insertion Sort on the *cars* array of *Auto* objects, we need to decide which field (or fields) of the *Auto* object determines the order of the objects. If we say that the *model* is the sort field, then the comparison statement would compare the models in two objects, that is, two *Strings*. As you recall from Chapter 5, the *compareTo* method of the *String* class compares the values of two *Strings*. It returns a positive number if the *String* for which the method is invoked is greater than the *String* passed as an argument.

REFERENCE POINT

The *compareTo* method of the *String* class is discussed in detail in Chapter 5.

To sort the *cars* array using an Insertion Sort, we would need to make several revisions to the *InsertionSort* method. First, the data type of the array must be declared as an *Auto* in the parameter list. Second, *temp* needs to be defined as an *Auto* reference, and finally, we need to substitute the *compareTo* method in the condition that compares array elements.

The revised Insertion Sort code becomes:

```
/* * Insertion sorts an array of Autos
*      @param arr an array of Autos
*/
public static void insertionSort( Auto [ ] arr )
{
  Auto temp;
  int j;

  for ( int i = 1; i < arr.length; i++ )
```

```
  {
     j = i;
     temp = arr[i];

     while ( j != 0 && ( temp.getModel( ) ).compareTo(
             arr[j - 1].getModel( ) )  < 0 )
     {
         arr[j] = arr[j - 1];
         j--;
     } // end while loop

     arr[j] = temp;

  } // end for loop
}  // end InsertionSort method
```

8.6.5 Sequential Search of a Sorted Array

Earlier in the chapter, the *DVDWinners* class sequentially searched an array. The algorithm assumed the elements were not in order. If we sort the array, a Sequential Search can be implemented more efficiently for the case when the search key is not present in the array. Instead of searching the entire array before discovering that the search key is not in the array, we can stop as soon as we pass the location where that element would be if it were in the array. In other words, if the array is sorted in ascending order, we can recognize an unsuccessful search when we find an element in the array that is greater than the search key. Because the array is sorted in ascending order, all the elements after that array element are larger than that element, and therefore are also larger than the search key.

To implement this algorithm, we can add another test to the *for* loop condition, so that we exit the loop as soon as we find an element that is greater than the search key. The improved algorithm shown next could be used to replace the *indexOfWinner* method shown in Example 8.14 for Sequential Search of a sorted *winners* array:

```
public int indexOfWinner( int key )
{
   for ( int i = 0; winners[i] <= key && i < winners.length; i++ )
   {
      if ( winners[i] == key )
```

```
            return i;
    }

    return -1; // end of array reached without finding key
               // or an element larger than the key was found
}
```

In fact, if the array is sorted, it can be searched even more efficiently using an algorithm called Binary Search, which we explain in the next section.

8.6.6 Binary Search of a Sorted Array

If you've played the "Guess a Number" game, you probably have used the concept of a **Binary Search**. In this game, someone asks you to guess a secret number between 1 and 100. For each number you guess, they tell you whether the secret number is larger or smaller than your guess. A good strategy is to guess the number in the middle, which in this example is 50. Whether the secret number is larger or smaller than 50, you will have eliminated half of the possible values. If the secret number is greater than 50, then you know your next guess should be 75 (halfway between 50 and 100). If the secret number is less than 50, your next guess should be 25 (halfway between 1 and 50). If you continue eliminating half the possible numbers with each guess, you will quickly guess the secret number. This approach works because we are "searching" a sorted set of numbers (1 to 100).

Similarly, a Binary Search of a sorted array works by eliminating half the remaining elements with each comparison. First, we look at the middle element of the array. If the value of that element is the search key, we return its index. If, however, the value of the middle element is greater than the search key, then the search key cannot be found in elements with array indexes higher than that element. Therefore, we will search the left half of the array only. Similarly, if the value of the middle element is lower than the search key, then the search key cannot be found in elements with array indexes lower than the middle element. Therefore, we will search in the right half of the array only. As we keep searching, the subarray we search keeps shrinking in size. In fact, the size of the subarray we search is cut in half at every iteration.

If the search key is not in the array, the subarray we search will eventually become empty. At that point, we know that we will not find our search key, and we return –1.

Example 8.20 shows our Binary Search algorithm.

```
/** Binary Search
*   Anderson, Franceschi
*/

import java.util.Scanner;

public class BinarySearcher
{
  public static void main( String [ ] args )
  {
    // define an array sorted in ascending order
    int [ ] numbers = { 3, 6, 7, 8, 12, 15, 22, 36, 45,
                        48, 51, 53, 64, 69, 72, 89, 95 };

    Scanner scan  = new Scanner( System.in );
    System.out.print( "Enter a value to search for > " );
    int key = scan.nextInt( );

    int index = binarySearch( numbers, key );
    if ( index != -1 )
         System.out.println( key + " found at index " + index );
    else
         System.out.println( key + " not found" );
  }

  public static int binarySearch( int [ ] arr, int key )
  {
    int start = 0;
    int end = arr.length - 1;
    int middle;

    while ( end >= start )
    {
      middle = ( start + end ) / 2; // element in middle of array

      if ( arr[middle] == key )
      {
         return middle;       // key found at middle
      }
      else if ( arr[middle] > key )
      {
         end = middle - 1;   // search left side of array
```

```
43         }
44         else
45         {
46            start = middle + 1; // search right side of array
47         }
48      }
49      return -1;
50    }
51 }
```

EXAMPLE 8.20 Binary Search of a Sorted Array

We start by declaring and initializing an integer array with 17 sorted elements (lines 12–13). We then prompt the user for a search key and call the *binarySearch* method (lines 16–19).

The *binarySearch* method is coded at lines 26–50. The local variables *start* and *end* store the first and last index of the subarray to search. Because we begin by searching the entire array, we initialize these to the indexes of the first and last element of the array that was passed as a parameter. The local variable *middle*, declared at line 30, will store the index of the middle element in the subarray to search.

The search is performed in a *while* loop (lines 32–48), whose condition determines whether the subarray is empty. If the subarray is not empty, we calculate the value for *middle* by adding the indexes of the first and last elements and dividing by 2 (line 34). Next we test whether the value at the *middle* index is equal to the key. If so, we have found the key and we return its index, which is *middle* (lines 36–39). If not, we test whether the value in the middle of the subarray is greater than the key. If so, we reduce the subarray to the elements with indexes less than *middle* (lines 40–43) and greater than or equal to *start*. If the value in the middle of the subarray is less than the key, we reduce the subarray to the elements with indexes greater than *middle* (lines 44–47) and smaller than or equal to *end*.

When the *while* loop continues, we reevaluate the condition to determine whether the subarray is empty, and if not, continue making our comparisons and either returning the index of the search key or reducing the size of the subarray. If the search key is not in the array, the subarray eventually becomes empty, and we exit the *while* loop and return –1 (line 49). Figure 8.25 shows the output when the search key is found.

Figure 8.25
Output from Example 8.20

```
Enter a value to search for > 64
64 found at index 12
```

Let's run through the Binary Search algorithm on the key 7 to illustrate how the algorithm works when the key is found in the array. Here is the array *numbers*:

Value	3	6	7	8	12	15	22	36	45	48	51	53	64	69	72	89	95
Index	0	1	2	3	4	5	6	7	8	9	10	11	12	13	14	15	16

When the *binarySearch* method is called, it sets *start* to 0 and *end* to *arr.length – 1*, which is 16. Thus, the value of *middle* is 8.

The element at index 8 (45) is greater than 7, so we set *end* to 7 (*middle – 1*), and we will now search the left subarray, highlighted next. The value of *middle* is now 3 ((0 + 7) / 2).

Value	3	6	7	8	12	15	22	36	45	48	51	53	64	69	72	89	95
Index	0	1	2	3	4	5	6	7	8	9	10	11	12	13	14	15	16

The element at index 3 (8) is greater than 7, so we set *end* to 2 (*middle – 1*) and keep searching in the left subarray, highlighted next. The value of *middle* is now 1 ((0 + 2) / 2).

Value	3	6	7	8	12	15	22	36	45	48	51	53	64	69	72	89	95
Index	0	1	2	3	4	5	6	7	8	9	10	11	12	13	14	15	16

The element at index 1 (6) is smaller than 7, so we set *start* to 2 (*middle + 1*) and search in the right subarray, highlighted next. The value of *middle* is now 2 ((2 + 2) / 2).

Value	3	6	7	8	12	15	22	36	45	48	51	53	64	69	72	89	95
Index	0	1	2	3	4	5	6	7	8	9	10	11	12	13	14	15	16

The element at index 2 (7) is equal to 7. We have found the value and return its index, 2.

Let's now run the preceding example on the key 34 to illustrate how the algorithm works when the key is not found in the array.

Here is the array *numbers* again:

Value	3	6	7	8	12	15	22	36	45	48	51	53	64	69	72	89	95
Index	0	1	2	3	4	5	6	7	8	9	10	11	12	13	14	15	16

Again, when the *binarySearch* method is called, it sets *start* to 0 and *end* to *arr.length – 1*, which is 16. Thus, *middle* is assigned the value 8 for the first comparison.

The element at index 8 (45) is greater than 34, so we set *end* to 7 (*middle – 1*), and keep searching in the left subarray. The value of *middle* becomes 3 for the next comparison.

Value	3	6	7	8	12	15	22	36	45	48	51	53	64	69	72	89	95
Index	0	1	2	3	4	5	6	7	8	9	10	11	12	13	14	15	16

The element at index 3 (8) is smaller than 34, so we search in the right subarray highlighted below. The value of *middle* is now 5.

Value	3	6	7	8	12	15	22	36	45	48	51	53	64	69	72	89	95
Index	0	1	2	3	4	5	6	7	8	9	10	11	12	13	14	15	16

The element at index 5 (15) is smaller than 34, so we search in the right subarray. The value of *middle* is now 6.

Value	3	6	7	8	12	15	22	36	45	48	51	53	64	69	72	89	95
Index	0	1	2	3	4	5	6	7	8	9	10	11	12	13	14	15	16

The element at index 6 (22) is smaller than 34, so we search in the right subarray. The value of *middle* is now 7.

Value	3	6	7	8	12	15	22	36	45	48	51	53	64	69	72	89	95
Index	0	1	2	3	4	5	6	7	8	9	10	11	12	13	14	15	16

At this point, *start*, *end*, and *middle* all have the value 7. The element at index 7 (36) is larger than 34, so we assign *end* the value *middle – 1*, which is 6. This makes *end* less than *start* and consequently makes the *while* loop condition evaluate to *false*. We have not found 34, so we return −1.

8.7 Programming Activity 2: Searching and Sorting Arrays

In this activity, you will work again with a 15-element integer array, performing these activities:

1. Write a method to perform a Sequential Search of an array.
2. Write a method to implement the Bubble Sort algorithm to sort an array.

The basic approach to a Bubble Sort is to make multiple passes through the array. In each pass, we compare adjacent elements. If any two adjacent elements are out of order, we put them in order by swapping their values.

To sort an array of *n* elements in ascending order, Bubble Sort implements a double loop:

- The outer loop executes $n - 1$ times.
- For each iteration of the outer loop, the inner loop steps through all the unsorted elements of the array and does the following:
  - Compares the current element with the next element in the array.
  - If the next element is smaller, it swaps the two elements.

Outer loop counter	Indexes of element(s) at the sorted position
0	$n - 1$
1	$n - 2, n - 1$
2	$n - 3, n - 2, n - 1$
...	...
$n - 3$	$2, 3, 4, \ldots, n - 3, n - 2, n - 1$
$n - 2$	$1, 2, 3, 4, \ldots, n - 3, n - 2, n - 1$

At this point, $n - 1$ elements have been moved to their correct positions. That leaves only the element at index 0, which is therefore automatically at the correct position within the array. The array is now sorted.

As the outer loop counter goes from 0 to $n - 2$, it iterates $n - 1$ times.

The pseudocode for the Bubble Sort is

```
for i = 0 to last array index – 1 by 1
   for j = 0 to ( last array index – i –1 ) by 1
      if (2 consecutive elements are in the wrong order)
         swap them
```

For example, let's walk through a Bubble Sort on the following array. At the beginning, the unsorted array is

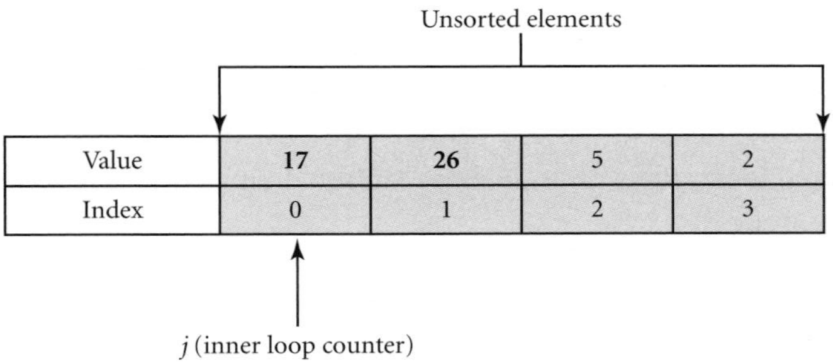

The value of the outer loop counter (i) is 0, and the value of the inner loop counter (j) is also 0. We compare elements 17 (index $j = 0$) and 26 (index $j + 1 = 1$). Since 17 is smaller than 26, we do not swap them.

The inner loop counter (j) is incremented, and its value is now 1.

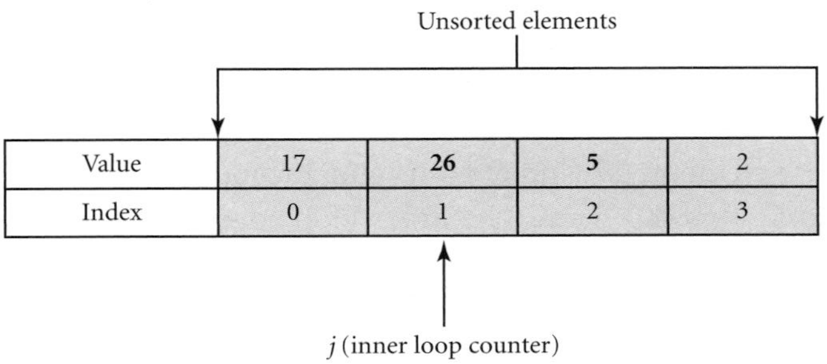

We compare elements 26 (index $j = 1$) and 5 (index $j + 1 = 2$). Since 26 is larger than 5, we swap them. The inner loop counter (j) is incremented, and its value is now 2.

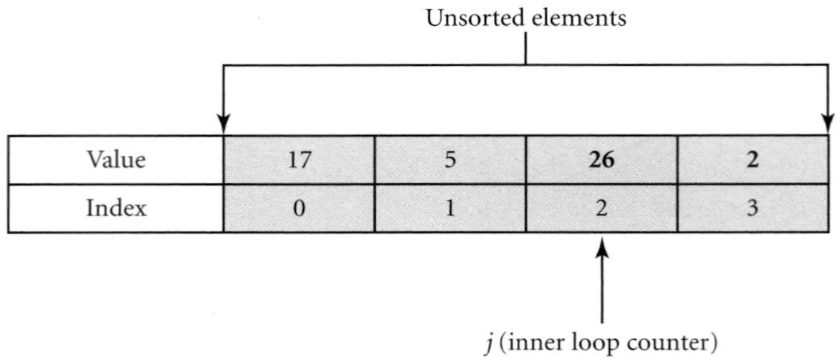

We compare elements 26 (index $j = 2$) and 2 (index $j + 1 = 3$). Since 26 is larger than 2, we swap them.

The inner loop counter (j) is incremented, and its value is now 3; therefore, we exit the inner loop. (We have reached the end of the unsorted subarray, which at this point is the whole array.) At the end of one execution of the inner loop, the value 26 has "bubbled up" to its correct position within the array.

We now go back to the outer loop, and the outer loop counter (i) is incremented; its value is now 1. We reenter the inner loop and the value of the inner loop counter (j) is reinitialized to 0.

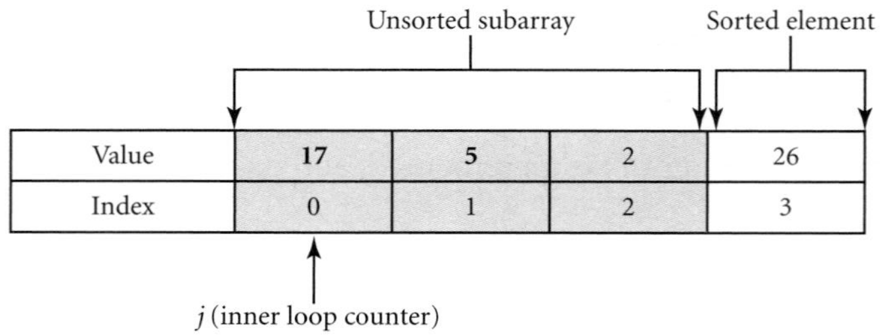

We compare elements 17 (index $j = 0$) and 5 (index $j + 1 = 1$). Since 17 is larger than 5, we swap them. The inner loop counter (j) is incremented, and its value is now 1.

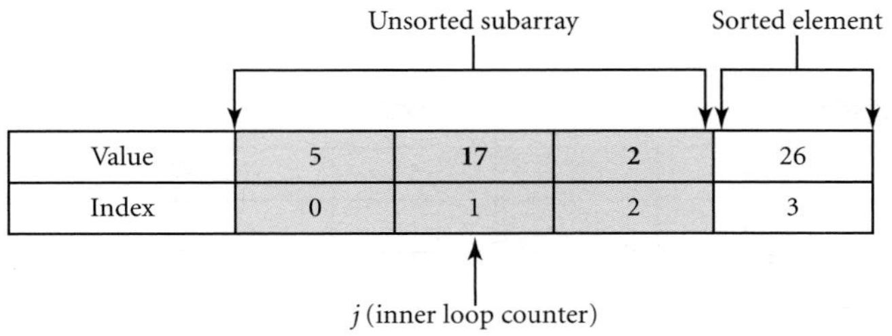

We compare elements 17 (index $j = 1$) and 2 (index $j + 1 = 2$). Since 17 is larger than 2, we swap them.

The inner loop counter (j) is incremented, and its value is now 2; therefore, we exit the inner loop. (We have reached the end of the unsorted subarray.) At this point, the element 17 has "bubbled up" to its correct position within the array.

We go back to the outer loop, and the outer loop counter (i) is incremented; its value is now 2, and this will be the last iteration of the outer loop. We reenter the inner loop and the value of the inner loop counter (j) is reinitialized to 0.

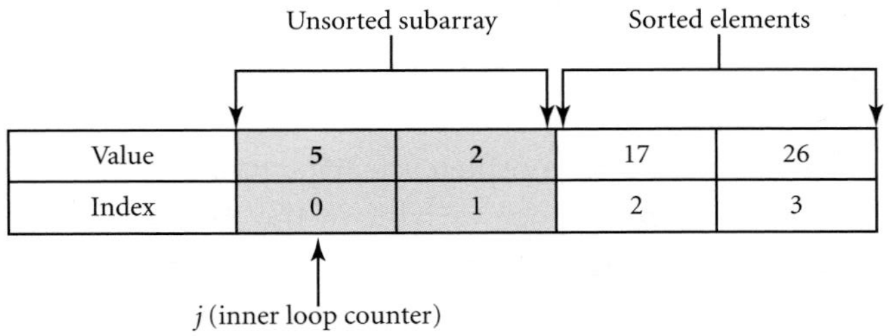

We compare elements 5 (index $j = 0$) and 2 (index $j + 1 = 1$). Since 2 is smaller than 5, we swap them.

The inner loop counter (j) is incremented, and its value is now 1; therefore, we exit the inner loop. (We have reached the end of the unsorted subarray.) At this point, the element 5 has "bubbled up" to its correct position within the array.

We go back to the outer loop, and the outer loop counter (i) is incremented; its value is now 3, and therefore, we exit the outer loop. For the four elements in the array; we executed the outer loop three times.

The array is now sorted.

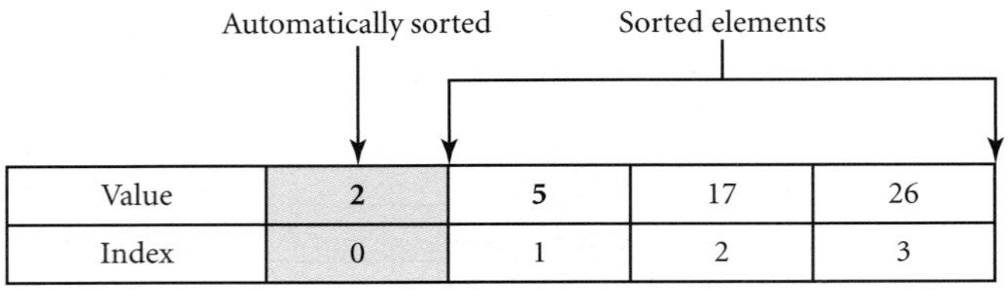

The framework for this Programming Activity will animate your algorithm so that you can watch your algorithm work and check the accuracy of your code. For example, Figure 8.26 demonstrates the Bubble Sort at work. At this point, the program has completed three passes through the array and is comparing the values of elements 5 and 6.

Instructions

In the Chapter 8 Programming Activity 2 directory on the CD-ROM accompanying this book, you will find the source files needed to complete this activity. Copy all the files to a directory on your computer. Note that all files should be in the same directory.

Open the *ArrayPractice2.java* source file. Searching for five stars (*****) in the source code will position you at the two locations where you will add your code. Your first task is to complete the *sequentialSearch* method, which searches the *arr* array, an instance variable of the *ArrayPractice2* class. The array *arr* has already been instantiated for you and filled with random values. The second task is to complete the *bubbleSort* method. Example 8.21 shows the section of the *ArrayPractice2* source code where you will add your code. Note that in each method, you are asked to call the *animate* method so that your method code can be animated as it works. Note also

Figure 8.26
The Bubble Sort at Work

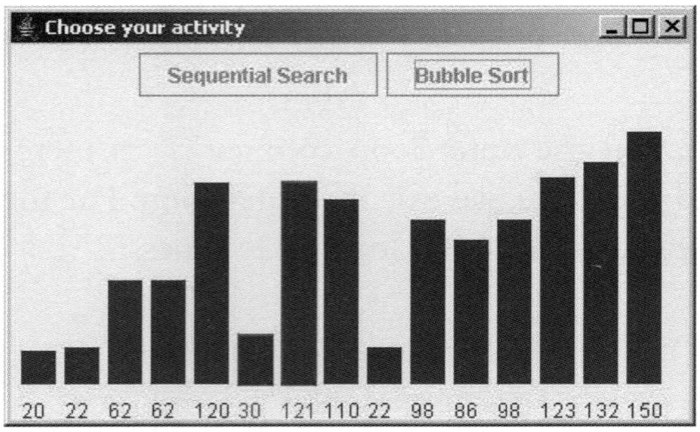

that for the *sequentialSearch* method, we provide a dummy *return* statement (*return 0;*). We do this so that the source code will compile. In this way, you can write and test each method separately, using stepwise refinement. When you are ready to write the *sequentialSearch* method, just replace the dummy *return* statement with the appropriate *return* statement for that method.

```
// 1 ***** student writes this method
/** Searches for key in integer array named arr
//    arr is an instance variable of the class and has been
//    instantiated and filled with random values.
// @param key value to search for
// @return  if key is found, the  index of the first element
//    in array whose value is key; if key is not found,
//     the method returns -1
*/
public int sequentialSearch( int key )
{
 // Note:  To animate the algorithm, put this method call as the
 // first statement in your for loop
 //  animate( i, 0 );
 //        where i is the index of the current array element


   return 0; // replace this statement with your return statement

} // end of sequentialSearch

// 2. *****  student writes this method
/**  Sorts arr in ascending order using the bubble sort algorithm
*/
public void bubbleSort( )
{
 // Note:  To animate the algorithm, put this method call as the
 // last statement in your innermost for loop
 //  animate( i, j );
 //          where i is the value of the outer loop counter
 //           and j is the value of the inner loop counter,
 //           or the index of the current array element


} // end of bubbleSort
```

EXAMPLE 8.21 Student Section of *ArrayPractice2*

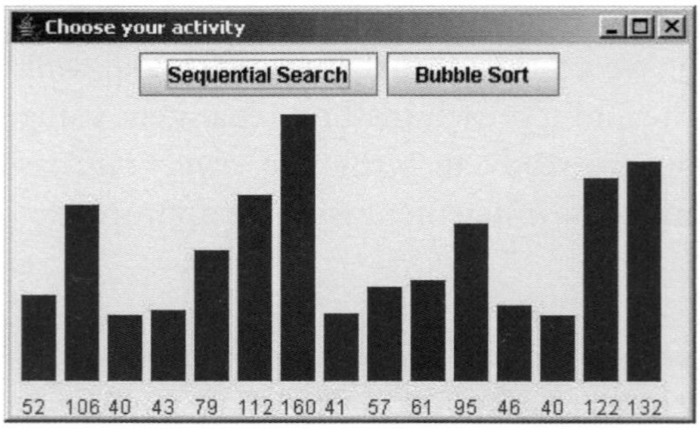

Figure 8.27
Opening Window of *ArrayPractice2*

When you have finished writing your code, compile and run the application. Figure 8.27 shows the graphics window when the application begins. To test any method, click on the appropriate button.

Troubleshooting

If your method implementation does not animate, consider these tips:

- Verify that your *for* loop calls the *animate* method as instructed in the method comments.
- Verify that you did not instantiate a new array. Perform all operations on the instance variable array named *arr*.

DISCUSSION QUESTIONS ?

1. The sequential search finds only the first occurrence of the parameter *key*. How would you modify the *sequentialSearch* method to count the occurrences of *key*?
2. It is possible that the array might be completely sorted before all the passes have been completed. How would you modify your code so that you exit the *bubbleSort* method as soon as possible?

8.8 Using Arrays as Counters

In some circumstances, it is useful to use an array of integers as an ordered group of accumulators, or counters. For example, suppose you are analyzing a survey that has four possible answers, 0 through 3. You want to count how many people selected each answer. You could set up four counters and use an *if/else* statement to increment the appropriate counter. The pseudocode would be:

```
read first survey
while ( not end of surveys )
{
  if answer is 0
    increment counter0
  else if answer is 1
    increment counter1
  else if answer is 2
    increment counter2
  else if answer is 3
    increment counter3

  read next survey
}
```

That would work if you have only a few possible answers, but what if you had 100 or more answers? You would end up writing a very long *if/else* statement.

Instead, you could set up an array of counters and let the counter for answer 0 be *array[0]*, the counter for answer 1 be *array[1]*, and so on. This approach—using an array of counters—is simpler to code and saves processing time.

As another example, suppose we want to throw a die 500 times and count the number of times each outcome occurs; that is, we want to count the number of ones, twos, threes, fours, fives, and sixes that are rolled. To do this, we set up a simple *Die* class shown in Example 8.22, with a method for rolling a value. Then we set up the client class, *DieCount*, shown in Example 8.23, that has an array with six integer elements; each element will hold the number of times a particular roll occurs.

```
/** Die class
*   Anderson, Franceschi
*/
import java.util.Random;

public class Die
{
    public final int SIDES = 6;
    private Random rand;

    /** default constructor
    *   instantiates the Random object
    */
    public Die( )
    {
```

```
      rand = new Random( );
   }

   /** rolls the die
   *  @return  the value of the roll
   */
   public int roll( )
   {
      return rand.nextInt( SIDES ) + 1;
   }
}
```

EXAMPLE 8.22 The *Die* Class

```
/** DieCount Class
*   Anderson, Franceschi
*/

public class DieCount
{
  public static void main( String [ ] args )
  {
     final int FACES = 6, NUMBER_OF_ROLLS = 500;

     // instantiate the counter array
     // which sets initial values to 0
     int [ ] rollCount = new int [FACES];

     // instantiate the Die
     Die d1 = new Die( );

     // roll the die 500 times
     for ( int i = 1; i <= NUMBER_OF_ROLLS; i++ )
     {
        int myRoll = d1.roll( );
        rollCount[myRoll - 1]++;  // increment the counter for roll
     }

     // print count for each roll
     System.out.println( "Roll\tCount" );
     for ( int i = 0; i < rollCount.length; i++ )
     {
        System.out.println( ( i + 1 ) + "\t" + rollCount[i] );
     }
  }
}
```

EXAMPLE 8.23 The *DieCount* Class

In the *Die* class constructor, we instantiate the *Random* object *rand*, which will be used by the *roll* method (lines 19–25), which in turn generates a random number between 1 and 6 to simulate the roll of a die.

In the *DieCount* class, we instantiate our array of six counters, *rollCount*, on line 13, which autoinitializes each element to 0—exactly what we want for counters.

To count the number of times each roll occurs, we use a *for* loop that iterates 500 times, with each iteration calling the *roll* method of the *Die* class. We then need to count each roll. That's where our array of counters, *rollCount*, comes in.

Since the *rollCount* array has six elements, the index of the first element is 0, and the index of the last element is 5. We will use *rollCount[0]* to hold the number of times we rolled a 1, *rollCount[1]* to hold the number of times we rolled a 2, and continue that way until we use *rollCount[5]* to hold the number of times we rolled a 6. Thus, to get the index of the appropriate counter, we need to decrement the roll by 1. So our statement to increment the count for a roll (line 22) becomes

```
rollCount[myRoll - 1]++;
```

After rolling the die 500 times and counting each roll, we print the total times each roll occurred (lines 25–30). Note that we increment the loop variable to convert between our counter index and the roll number. The output from a sample run of this program is shown in Figure 8.28. Because the program generates the rolls randomly, your output may be slightly different.

```
Roll    Count
1       81
2       82
3       89
4       78
5       87
6       83
```

Figure 8.28
Output from *DieCount*

Our algorithm is not ideal, however. We need to subtract 1 from the index in order to increment the counter, and we need to add 1 to the index to print the outcome.

A better approach would be to create the array with seven elements. Then we can use elements 1 through 6 as the counters for the rolls 1 through 6. The index and the roll number will be the same. What happens to element 0? Nothing. We just ignore it.

The revised *DieCount2* class is shown in Example 8.24.

```
/** DieCount2 Class
*   Anderson, Franceschi
*/

public class DieCount2
{
  public static void main( String [ ] args )
  {
     final int FACES = 7, NUMBER_OF_ROLLS = 500;

     // instantiate the counter array
     // which sets initial values to 0
     int [ ] rollCount = new int [FACES];

     // instantiate the Die
     Die d1 = new Die( );

     // roll the die 500 times
     for ( int i = 1; i <= NUMBER_OF_ROLLS; i++ )
     {
       int myRoll = d1.roll( );
       rollCount[myRoll]++;  // increment the counter for roll
     }

     // print count for each roll
     System.out.println( "Roll\tCount" );
     for ( int i = 1; i < rollCount.length; i++ )
     {
       System.out.println(  i  + "\t" + rollCount[i] );
     }
  }
}
```

EXAMPLE 8.24 The *DieCount2* Class

Notice the changes to the code in this example. First, we set *FACES* to 7 (line 9), so we will instantiate an array with seven elements. Then we can use the roll of the die as the index into the counter array to increment the appropriate count (line 22). One last change is that when we loop through the *rollCount* array to print the counters, we initialize our loop counter to 1 (line 27), since we are not using element 0 as a counter and we simply use *i* as the roll number.

It's true that we're allocating an extra integer (four bytes of memory) that is never used, but we're eliminating 500 subtract operations and 6 addition operations! The program is more efficient, easier to write, and easier to read.

Skill Practice
with these end-of-chapter questions

8.10.1 Multiple Choice Exercises

Question 12

8.10.4 Identifying Errors in Code

Question 44

8.10.6 Write a Short Program

Question 57

8.10.8 Technical Writing

Question 74

8.9 Chapter Summary

SUMMARY

- An array is a sequence of variables of the same data type. The data type can be any Java primitive data type, such as *int, float, double, byte, boolean,* or *char*, or it can be a class.
- Each element in the array is accessed using the array name and an index, which refers to the element's position in the array.
- Arrays are implemented as objects. Creating an array consists of declaring an object reference for the array and instantiating the array. The size of the array is given when the array is instantiated.
- In arrays of primitive types, each element of the array contains a value of that type. In arrays of objects, each element is an object reference.

CHAPTER SUMMARY

- When an array is instantiated, the elements are given initial values automatically, depending on the data type. Numeric types are set to 0; *boolean* types are set to *false*; *char* types are set to a space, and object references are set to *null*.
- Instantiating an array of object references involves two steps: instantiating the array and instantiating the objects.
- Arrays can be instantiated when they are declared by assigning initial values in a comma-separated list within curly braces. The number of values in the initialization list determines the number of elements in the array.
- Array elements are accessed using the array name and an index. The first element's index is 0 and the last element's index is the size of the array − 1.
- Arrays have an integer instance variable, *length*, which holds the number of elements in the array.
- Attempting to access an element of an array using an index less than 0 or greater than *arrayName.length – 1* will generate an *ArrayIndexOutOfBoundsException* at run time.
- Aggregate array operations, such as printing and copying arrays, are not supported for arrays. Using a *for* loop, you can process each array element individually.
- To change the size of an array, instantiate an array of the desired size with a temporary name, copy the appropriate elements from the original array to the new array, and assign the new array reference to the original array. Assign *null* to the temporary array name.
- Arrays can be passed as arguments to methods and can also be the return type of methods.
- When an array is an instance variable of a class, the constructor should instantiate a new array and copy the elements of the parameter array into the new array.
- A Sequential Search determines whether a particular value, the search key, is in an array by comparing the search key to each element in the array.
- A Selection Sort arranges elements in the array in order by value by reducing the array into successively smaller subarrays and placing

the largest element in each subarray into the last position of the subarray.

- An Insertion Sort arranges elements of an array much like a card player arranges cards in sorted order in his or her hand. The elements are inserted one at a time in ascending order into the left side of the array.
- To sort an array of objects, you can use the class method provided to compare objects' values.
- A sorted array can be searched more efficiently using a Binary Search, which successively reduces the number of elements to search by half.
- Arrays of integers can be used as an ordered group of counters.

8.10 Exercises, Problems, and Projects

8.10.1 Multiple Choice Exercises

1. What are the valid ways to declare an integer array named *a*? (Check all that apply.)

   ❑ `int [ ] a;`

   ❑ `int a[ ];`

   ❑ `array int a;`

   ❑ `int array a;`

2. What is the index of the first element of an array?

   ❑ –1

   ❑ 0

   ❑ 1

3. An array *a* has 30 elements; what is the index of its last element?

   ❑ 29

   ❑ 30

   ❑ 31

4. What is the default value of the elements in an array of *ints* after declaration and instantiation of the array?
   - ❑ 0
   - ❑ *null*
   - ❑ undefined
5. How do you access the element of array *a* located at index 6?
   - ❑ `a{6}`
   - ❑ `a( 6 )`
   - ❑ `a[6]`
6. Which of the following assertions is true?
   - ❑ An array cannot be sized dynamically.
   - ❑ An array can be sized dynamically, but cannot be resized without instantiating it again.
   - ❑ An array can be sized dynamically and can also be resized without instantiating it again.
7. How do you retrieve the number of elements in an array *a*?
   - ❑ `a.length( )`
   - ❑ `a.length`
   - ❑ `a.size( )`
   - ❑ `a.size`
8. All the elements of an array must be of the same type.
   - ❑ true
   - ❑ false
9. Array aggregate assignment is possible in Java.
   - ❑ true
   - ❑ false
10. Aggregate comparison of arrays is possible in Java.
    - ❑ true
    - ❑ false

11. An array can be returned by a method.

    ❑ true

    ❑ false

12. A Sequential Search on a sorted array is typically faster than a Sequential Search on an unsorted array.

    ❑ true

    ❑ false

8.10.2 Reading and Understanding Code

13. What is the output of this code sequence?

```
double [ ] a = { 12.5, 48.3, 65.0 };
System.out.println( a[1] );
```

14. What is the output of this code sequence?

```
int [ ] a = new int [6];
System.out.println( a[4] );
```

15. What is the output of this code sequence?

```
double [ ] a = { 12.5, 48.3, 65.0 };
System.out.println( a.length );
```

16. What is the output of this code sequence?

```
int [ ] a = { 12, 48, 65 };

for ( int i = 0; i < a.length; i++ )
   System.out.println( a[i] );
```

17. What is the output of this code sequence?

```
int [ ] a = { 12, 48, 65 };

for ( int i = 0; i < a.length; i++ )
   System.out.println( "a[" + i + "] = " + a[i] );
```

18. What is the output of this code sequence?

```
int s = 0;
int [ ] a = { 12, 48, 65 };

for ( int i = 0; i < a.length; i++ )
   s += a[i];

System.out.println( "s = " + s );
```

19. What is the output of this code sequence?

```
int [ ] a = new int[10];

for ( int i = 0; i < a.length; i++ )
  a[i] = i + 10;

System.out.println( a[4] );
```

20. What is the output of this code sequence?

```
double [ ] a = { 12.3, 99.6, 48.2, 65.8 };
double temp = a[0];

for ( int i = 1; i < a.length; i++ )
{
   if ( a[i] > temp )
      temp = a[i];
}
System.out.println( temp );
```

21. What is the output of this code sequence?

```
int [ ] a = { 12, 48, 65, 23 };
int temp = a[1];
a[1] = a[3];
a[3] = temp;

for ( int i = 0; i < a.length; i++ )
   System.out.print( a[i] + " " );
```

22. What does this method do?

```
public int foo( int [ ] a )
{
   int temp = 0;

   for ( int i = 0; i < a.length; i++ )
   {
         if ( a[i] == 5 )
               temp++;
   }
   return temp;
}
```

23. What does this method do?

```
public int foo( int [ ] a )
{
     for ( int i = 0; i < a.length; i++ )
     {
          if ( a[i] == 10 )
               return i;
     }
     return -1;
}
```

24. What does this method do?

```
public boolean foo( int [ ] a )
{
     for ( int i = 0; i < a.length; i++ )
     {
          if ( a[i] < 0 )
               return false;
     }
     return true;
}
```

25. What does this method do?

```
public String [ ] foo( String [ ] a )
{
     String [ ] temp = new String[a.length];
     for ( int i = 0; i < a.length; i++ )
     {
          temp[i] = a[i].toLowerCase( );
     }
     return temp;
}
```

26. What does this method do?

```
public boolean [ ] foo( String [ ] a )
{
     boolean [ ] temp = new boolean[a.length];

     for ( int i = 0; i < a.length; i++ )
     {
          if ( a[i].contains( "@" ) )
               temp[i] = true;
```

```
            else
                  temp[i] = false;
      }
      return temp;
}
```

8.10.3 Fill In the Code

27. This code assigns the value 10 to all the elements of an array *a*.

```
int [ ] a = new int[25];
for ( int i = 0; i < a.length; i++ )
{
      // your code goes here

}
```

28. This code prints all the elements of array *a* that have a value greater than 20.

```
double [ ] a = { 45.2, 13.1, 12.8, 87.4, 99.0, 100.1, 43.8, 2.4 };

for ( int i = 0; i < a.length; i++ )
{
      // your code goes here

}
```

29. This code prints the average of the elements of array *a*.

```
int [ ] a = { 45, 13, 12, 87, 99, 100, 43, 2 };
double average = 0.0;

for ( int i = 0; i < a.length; i++ )
{
      // your code goes here

}

// ... and your code continues here
```

30. This code calculates and prints the dot product of two arrays ($\Sigma\, a[i] * b[i]$).

```
int [ ] a = { 3, 7, 9 };
int [ ] b = { 2, 9, 4 };
```

```
int dotProduct = 0;

for ( int i = 0; i < a.length; i++ )
{
      // your code goes here

}
```

31. This code prints the following three lines:

```
a[0] = 3
a[1] = 6
a[2] = 10
```

```
int [ ] a = { 3, 6, 10 };

for ( int i = 0; i < a.length; i++ )
{
      // your code goes here

}
```

32. This method returns *true* if an element in an array of *Strings* passed as a parameter contains the substring *IBM*; otherwise, it returns *false*.

```
public boolean foo( String [ ] a )
{
   // your code goes here
}
```

33. This method returns the number of elements in an array passed as a parameter that are multiples of 7.

```
public int foo( int [ ] a )
{
   // your code goes here
}
```

34. This method returns *true* if the first two elements of the array passed as a parameter have the same value; otherwise, it returns *false*.

```
public boolean foo( String [ ] a )
{
      // your code goes here
}
```

35. This method takes an array of *ints* as a parameter and returns an array of *booleans*. For each element in the parameter array whose value is 0, the corresponding element of the array returned will be assigned *false*; otherwise, the element will be assigned *true*.

```
public boolean [ ] foo( int [ ] a )
{
 // your code goes here
}
```

8.10.4 Identifying Errors in Code

36. Where is the error in this code sequence?

```
double [ ] a = { 3.3, 26.0, 48.4 };
a[4] = 2.5;
```

37. Where is the error in this code sequence?

```
double [ ] a = { 3.3, 26.0, 48.4 };
System.out.println( a[-1] );
```

38. Where is the error in this code sequence?

```
double [ ] a = { 3.3, 26.0, 48.4 };
System.out.println( a{1} );
```

39. Where is the error in this code sequence?

```
double [ ] a = { 3.3, 26.0, 48.4 };
for ( int i = 0; i <= a.length; i++ )
      System.out.println( a[i] );
```

40. Where is the error in this code sequence?

```
double a[3] = { 3.3, 26.0, 48.4 };
```

41. Where is the error (although this code will compile and run) in this code sequence?

```
int a[ ] = { 3, 26, 48, 5 };
int b[ ] = { 3, 26, 48, 5 };

if ( a != b )
      System.out.println( "Array elements are NOT identical" );
```

42. Where is the error in this code sequence?

```
int [ ] a = { 3, 26, 48, 5 };
a.length = 10;
```

43. Where is the logic error in this code sequence?

```
int [ ] a = { 3, 26, 48, 5 };
System.out.println( "The array elements are " + a );
```

44. Where is the error in this code sequence?

```
Integer i1 = new Integer( 10 );
Integer i2 = new Integer( 15 );
Double d1 = new Double( 3.4 );
String s = new String( "Hello" );
Integer [ ] a = { i1, i2, d1, s };
```

8.10.5 Debugging Area—Using Messages from the Java Compiler and Java JVM

45. You coded the following on line 26 of the class *Test.java:*

```
int a[6] = { 2, 7, 8, 9, 11, 16 };   // line 26
```

When you compile, you get the following messages:

```
Test.java:26: ']' expected
      int a[6] = { 2, 7, 8, 9, 11, 16 };   // line 26
            ^
Test.java:26: not a statement
int a[6] = { 2, 7, 8, 9, 11, 16 };   // line 26
       ^
Test.java:26: ';' expected
int a[6] = { 2, 7, 8, 9, 11, 16 };   // line 26
        ^

3 errors
```

Explain what the problem is and how to fix it.

46. You coded the following on lines 26, 27, and 28 of the class *Test.java*:

```
int [ ] a = { 2, 7, 8, 9, 11, 16 };    // line 26 of class Test.java
for ( int i = 0; i <= a.length; i++ ) // line 27 of class Test.java
      System.out.println( a[i] );     // line 28 of class Test.java
```

The code compiles properly, but when you run, you get the following message:

```
Exception in thread "main" java.lang.ArrayIndexOutOfBoundsException
at Test.main ( Test.java:28 )
```

Explain what the problem is and how to fix it.

47. You coded the following in the class *Test.java*:

```
int [ ] a = { 1, 2, 3 };
int [ ] b = { 1, 2, 3 };
if ( a == b )
     System.out.println( "Arrays are equal" );
else
     System.out.println( "Arrays are NOT equal" );
```

    The code compiles properly and runs, but the result is not what you expected; the output is

```
Arrays are NOT equal
```

    Explain what the problem is and how to fix it.

48. You coded the following in the class *Test.java*:

```
int [ ] a = { 1, 2, 3 };
System.out.println( a );
```

    The code compiles properly and runs, but the result is not what you expected; the output is similar to the following:

```
[I@f0326267
```

    Explain what the problem is and how to fix it.

8.10.6 Write a Short Program

49. Write a value-returning method that returns the number of elements in an integer array.
50. Write a value-returning method that returns the product of all the elements in an integer array.
51. Write a *void* method that sets to 0 all the elements of an integer array.
52. Write a *void* method that multiplies by 2 all the elements of an array of *floats*.
53. Write a method that returns the percentage of elements greater than or equal to 90 in an array of *ints*.
54. Write a method that returns the difference between the largest and smallest elements in an array of *doubles*.
55. Write a method that returns the sum of all the elements of an array of *ints* that have an odd index.

56. Write a method that returns the percentage of the number of elements that have the value *true* in an array of *booleans.*

57. Write a method that returns *true* if an array of *Strings* contains the *String* "*Hello*"; *false* otherwise.

58. Write a method that prints all the elements of an array of *chars* in reverse order.

59. Write a method that returns an array composed of all the elements in an array of *chars* in reverse order.

60. Write an array-returning method that takes a *String* as a parameter and returns the corresponding array of *chars.*

61. Code an array-returning method that takes an array of *ints* as a parameter and returns an array of *booleans,* assigning *true* for any element of the parameter array greater than or equal to 100; and *false* otherwise.

8.10.7 Programming Projects

62. Write a class encapsulating the concept of statistics for a baseball team, which has the following attributes: a number of players, a list of number of hits for each player, a list of number of at-bats for each player.

    Write the following methods:

    - ❑ A constuctor with two equal-length arrays as parameters, the number of hits per player, and the number of at-bats per player.
    - ❑ Accessors, mutators, *toString,* and *equals* methods.
    - ❑ Generate and return an array of batting averages based on the attributes given.
    - ❑ Calculate and return the total number of hits for the team.
    - ❑ Calculate and return the number of players with a batting average greater than .300.
    - ❑ A method returning an array holding the number of hits, sorted in ascending order.

    Write a client class to test all the methods in your class.

63. Write a class encapsulating the concept of student grades on a test, assuming student grades are composed of a list of integers between 0 and 100.

    Write the following methods:

    - ❑ A constructor with just one parameter, the number of students; all grades can be randomly generated
    - ❑ Accessor, mutator, *toString*, and *equals* methods
    - ❑ A method returning an array of the grades sorted in ascending order
    - ❑ A method returning the highest grade
    - ❑ A method returning the average grade
    - ❑ A method returning the median grade (*Hint:* The median grade will be located in the middle of the sorted array of grades.)
    - ❑ A method returning the mode (the grade that occurs most often). (*Hint:* Create an array of counters; count how many times each grade occurs; then pick the maximum in the array of counters; the array index is the mode.)

    Write a client class to test all the methods in your class.

64. Write a class encapsulating the concept of daily temperatures for a week.

    Write the following methods:

    - ❑ A constructor accepting an array of seven temperatures as a parameter
    - ❑ Accessor, mutator, *toString*, and *equals* methods
    - ❑ A method returning how many temperatures were below freezing
    - ❑ A method returning an array of temperatures above 100 degrees
    - ❑ A method returning the largest change in temperature between any two consecutive days
    - ❑ A method returning an array of daily temperatures, sorted in descending order.

    Write a client class to test all the methods in your class.

65. Write a class encapsulating the concept of a tic-tac-toe game as follows:

    Two players will be playing, player 1 and player 2.

    The board is represented by an array of 9 integer elements: elements at indexes 0, 1, and 2 represent the first row; elements at indexes 3, 4, and 5 represent the second row; elements at indexes 6, 7, and 8 represent the third row.

    The value 0 in the array indicates that this space is available; the value 1 indicates the space is occupied by player 1; and the value 2 indicates that this space is occupied by player 2.

    In the *main* method of your client class, your program will simulate a tic-tac-toe game from the command line (or a *JOptionPane* dialog box), doing the following:

    - ❑ Create a *TicTacToe* object and instantiate it.
    - ❑ In a loop, prompt for plays, as *ints*, from the user. At each iteration of the loop, you will need to call methods of the *TicTacToe* class to update the *TicTacToe* object. You need to keep track of who is playing (player 1 or 2), enforce the rules, check if either player has won the game. It is clear that if anyone has won the game, it is the last player who played.
    - ❑ If a player wins, you will need to exit the loop and present the result of the game. If the game ends in a tie, you should output that result.

    In your *TicTacToe* class, you will need to code the following methods:

    - ❑ A default constructor instantiating the array representing the board.
    - ❑ A method that allows a player to make a move; it takes two arguments: the player number and the position played on the board.
    - ❑ A method checking if a play is legal.
    - ❑ A method checking if a player has won the game; you can break up that method into several methods if you like (for instance, check if a player has won the game by claiming an entire horizontal row).

- ❑ A method that checks whether the game is a tie (if no player has won and all squares have been played, the game is tied).
- ❑ A method that displays the results of the game ("Player 1 won," "Player 2 won," or "Tie game").

Write a client class, where the *main* method is located, to test all the methods in your class and enable the user to play.

66. When a new user logs in for the first time on a website, the user has to submit personal information, such as user_id, password, name, email address, telephone number, and so forth. Typically, there are two fields for passwords, requiring the user to enter the password twice, to ensure that the user did not make a typo in the first password field.

    Write a class encapsulating the concept of processing a form with the following elements:

    User_id

    Password

    Reenter password

    Email address

    Name

    Street address

    City

    State

    Zip

    Telephone

    In your class, write the following methods:

    - ❑ A constructor with one parameter, a sequence of 10 words in an array of *Strings*, your only instance variable.
    - ❑ Accessor, mutator, *toString*, and *equals* methods.
    - ❑ A method checking that no *Strings* in the array are empty. (All fields are mandatory.) If at least one is empty, it returns *false*, otherwise, it returns *true*.

- ❑ A method returning the number of characters in the user_id.
- ❑ A method checking if the two *Strings* representing the passwords (representing the password typed in twice) are identical; if they are, it returns *true*; if not, it returns *false*.
- ❑ A method checking if the *String* representing the email address actually "looks like" an email address; to simplify, we can assume that an email address contains one and only one @ character and contains one or more periods after the @ character. If it does "look like" an email address, then the method returns *true*; otherwise, it returns *false*.
- ❑ A method checking if the *String* representing the state has exactly two characters. If it does, it returns *true;* otherwise, it returns *false*.

Write a client class to test all the methods in your class.

67. We want to write a program that performs some syntax checking on HTML code; for simplicity reasons, we will assume that the HTML code is syntactically correct if the number of < characters in any word is the same as the number of > characters in that word. We will also assume that the syntax is correct if the first word is *<HTML>* and the last word is *</HTML>*.

    Write a class encapsulating that concept, including the following methods:

    - ❑ A constructor with one parameter, an array of the words in the HTML sentence, your only instance variable. Your constructor should then get user input from the console for that same number of words and store them in an array of *Strings*, your only data member.
    - ❑ Accessor, mutator, *toString*, and *equals* methods.
    - ❑ A method returning how many words are in the array.
    - ❑ A method returning *true* if the first word is *<HTML>* and the last word is *</HTML>*; *false* otherwise.
    - ❑ A method checking if each array element contains the same number of < characters as > characters; if that is the case, the

method returns *true*; otherwise, it returns *false*. For this, we suggest the following method to help you:

- Write an *int*-returning method that takes a *String* and a *char* as parameters and returns how many times that *char* appears in the *String*; you can convert the *String* to an array of *chars* and loop through it, or use another strategy of your choice.

❑ A method counting and returning the number of IMG tags overall.

Write a client class to test all the methods in your class.

68. Write a class encapsulating the concept of converting integer grades to letter grades (A, B, C, D, or F), assuming grades are composed of a list of integers between 0 and 100.

Write the following methods:

❑ A constructor with just one parameter, the number of students; all grades can be randomly generated.

❑ Accessor, mutator, *toString*, and *equals* methods.

❑ A method returning an array of *chars* corresponding to the integer grades (90 or above should be converted to A, 80 or above to B, 70 or above to C, 60 or above to D, and 59 or less to F).

❑ A method returning the number of A's.

❑ A method returning an array of *ints* counting how many A's, B's, C's, D's, and F's were received.

Write a client class to test all the methods in your class.

69. Write a class encapsulating the concept of printing a letter as a 7×5 grid of either spaces or asterisks (*). That letter is made up of a list of thirty-five 1's and 0's, which will be stored in an array representing the letter, the only instance variable of the class.

For instance, the following is what the input file would look like for the letter I. A 1 will print as a *, and a 0 as a space.

After every 5 elements have been printed, you will need to print a new line.

If the input is

```
0 1 1 1 0 0 0 1 0 0 0 0 1 0 0 0 0 1 0 0 0 0 1 0 0 0 0 1 0 0 0 1 1 1 0
```

when printed, that letter would look like this:

```
***
 *
 *
 *
 *
 *
***
```

Write the following methods:

- ❑ A constructor with 1 parameter, an array of thirty-five 0's or 1's, your only instance variable. Be sure to enforce the constraint of having only 1's and 0's.
- ❑ Accessor, mutator, *toString*, and *equals* methods.
- ❑ A method printing out the letter as in the output example above.
- ❑ A method returning the number of 1's.
- ❑ A method returning the percentage of 0's.

Write a client class to test all the methods in your class.

70. Write a class encapsulating the concept of a team of baseball players, assuming a baseball player has the following attributes: a name, a position, and a batting percentage. In addition to that class, you will need to design and code a *Player* class to encapsulate the concept of a baseball player.

    In your class encapsulating the team, you should write the following methods:

    - ❑ A constructor taking an array of *Player* objects as its only parameter and assigning that array to the array data member of the class, its only instance variable. In your client class, when you test all your methods, you can hard-code nine baseball *Player* objects.

- ❑ Accessor, mutator, *toString*, and *equals* methods.
- ❑ A method checking that all positions are different, returning *true* if they are, *false* if they are not.
- ❑ A method returning the batting percentage of the team.
- ❑ A method checking that we have a pitcher (that is, the name of the position) on the team; if we do not have any, it returns *false*; otherwise, it returns *true*.
- ❑ A method returning the array of *Player* objects sorted in ascending order using the batting percentage as the sorting key.
- ❑ A method checking if a certain person (a parameter of the method) is on the team, based on the name of that person. If the person is on the team, the method returns *true*; otherwise, it returns *false*.
- ❑ A method returning an array of *Player* objects, sorted in ascending order based on batting percentages.

Write a client class to test all the methods in your class.

71. Write a class encapsulating a similar concept to the one used in the die counting problem of Section 8.8. Here, we want to roll two dice; the total of the numbers rolled will be between 2 and 12. We want to keep track of how many times each possible roll was rolled.

Write the following methods:

- ❑ A constructor with no parameter; it randomly generates two numbers between 1 and 6, representing the dice.
- ❑ Accessor, mutator, *toString*, and *equals* methods.
- ❑ A method returning the total of the two dice.
- ❑ A method checking if the two dice have identical values; if they do, it returns *true*; otherwise, it returns *false*.

The number of times we roll the dice should be an input from the user at the command line (not inside the program). Your program should output the total for each possible roll (from 2 to 12), as well as the number of times the two dice had identical values.

Write a client class to test all the methods in your class.

72. Write an applet that creates two *Die* objects and rolls the two dice 5,000 times. Display the results showing the frequency of each possible total in a bar chart. Pick a scale that is appropriate for the maximum height of your bar chart.

8.10.8 Technical Writing

73. What do you think are advantages and disadvantages of arrays?
74. Write the pseudocode to perform a Selection Sort on an array of *Auto* objects based on the instance variable *model*.
75. When you try to use an array index that is out of bounds, your code will compile, but you will generate a run-time exception. Discuss whether this is an advantage or a disadvantage, and why.
76. When instantiating an array, you can assign the number of elements in the array dynamically, using a variable (as opposed to using a constant). Discuss a situation where that would be useful.

8.10.9 Group Project (for a group of 1, 2, or 3 students)

77. Security is an important feature of information systems. Often, text is encrypted before being sent, and then decrypted upon receipt. We want to build a class (or several classes) encapsulating the concept of encryption. You will need to test that class with a client program where the *main* method is located.

    For this project, encrypting consists of translating each character into another character. For instance, if we consider the English alphabet, including characters *a* through *z*, each character is randomly encrypted into another, which could be the same character. (If you like, you can design your program so that no character is encrypted into itself.) To represent this concept, we can have an array of characters for the original alphabet, and another array of characters for the encrypted alphabet. For example, we could have

Original alphabet	Encrypted alphabet
a	u
b	p
c	h
d	a
e	s
f	x
g	z
h	b
i	j
. . .	. . .

To encrypt a word, each letter in the word is replaced by the corresponding letter in the encryted alphabet. For example, the word *caged* would be encrypted into *huzsa.* To decrypt a word, the letters in the encrypted word are replaced by the corresponding letter in the original alphabet. For example, the encrypted word *xssa* would be decrypted as *feed.*

If we have 26 different characters in the original alphabet, then we will have 26 different characters in the encrypted alphabet. Furthermore, the encrypted alphabet should be randomly generated.

In your *main* method, you should prompt the user for a sentence. Your program should encrypt the sentence, output the encrypted sentence, then decrypt it, and output the decrypted sentence, which should be identical to the original sentence that was input by the user.

For extra credit, use an array to keep track of the number of occurrences of each character. Convert these occurrences to percentages, and then use these percentages to attempt to decrypt a large, encrypted message.

CHAPTER 9

Multidimensional Arrays and the *ArrayList* Class

CHAPTER CONTENTS

Introduction

In Chapter 8, we learned that arrays could be useful when we have a lot of data to store in memory. If we write a program to perform statistics on last year's temperatures, it is convenient to set up an array of *doubles* of size 365 to store the daily temperature data.

But what if in addition to analyzing daily temperatures, we want to analyze temperatures by the week, or by a particular day of the week? For instance, if we sail on weekends, we could want to know how many times the temperature was above 65 degrees on Saturdays and Sundays. If we are considering investing in air conditioning at home, we might be interested in knowing how many weeks had temperatures above 90 degrees. If we are avid skiers, we could be interested in the number of weeks with temperatures lower than 32 degrees.

In this situation, we would want to organize our data along two dimensions: weeks and days of the week. If we were to visualize the data as a table, we could imagine a table made up of 52 rows, each row representing a week. Each row would have seven columns, representing the days of the week. This table is shown in Figure 9.1. Or we could imagine a table of seven rows, each row representing a day of the week, and 52 columns, each column representing a week of the year. In either case, we can represent the rows and columns of our temperature table using a two-dimensional array. More generally, **multidimensional** arrays allow us to represent data organized along n dimensions with a single array.

Figure 9.1
Temperature Data for the Previous 52 Weeks

	Sunday	Monday	Tuesday	Wednesday	Thursday	Friday	Saturday
Week 1	35	28.6	29.3	38	43.1	45.6	49
Week 2	51.9	37.9	34.1	37.1	39	40.5	43.2
...							
...							
...							
...							
...							
Week 51	56.2	51.9	45.3	48.7	42.9	35.5	38.2
Week 52	33.2	27.1	24.9	29.8	37.7	39.9	38.8

9.1 Declaring and Instantiating Multidimensional Arrays

Just like single-dimensional arrays, multidimensional arrays are implemented as objects, so creating a multidimensional array takes the same two steps as creating a single-dimensional array:

1. declaring the object reference for the array
2. instantiating the array

In arrays with elements of primitive types, each element of the array contains a value of that type. For example, in an array of *doubles*, each element contains a *double* value. In arrays with a class data type, each element is an object reference, which points to the location of an object of that class.

9.1.1 Declaring Multidimensional Arrays

To declare a multidimensional array, we use the same syntax as for a single-dimensional array, except that we include an empty set of brackets for each dimension.

Here is the syntax for declaring a two-dimensional array:

```
datatype [ ][ ] arrayName;
```

Here is the syntax for declaring a three-dimensional array:

```
datatype [ ][ ][ ] arrayName;
```

In order to keep things simple, we will concentrate on two-dimensional arrays at this point. We will discuss three- and four-dimensional arrays later in the chapter.

The following statement declares an array to hold the daily high temperatures for the last 52 weeks:

```
double [ ][ ] dailyTemps;
```

The brackets can be placed before or after the array name. So the following syntax for declaring a two-dimensional array is also valid:

```
datatype arrayName [ ][ ];
```

We prefer to put the brackets right after the data type, because it's easier to read.

To store quiz grades for students, we could declare a two-dimensional array, where each row will store the quiz grades for a particular student and each column will store the grades for a particular quiz:

```
char [ ][ ] quizzes;   // each element is a char
```

The syntax is the same whether we declare arrays with basic data types or class types.

Imagine that we are interested in keeping track of a fleet of cars within a multinational corporation. The corporation operates in various countries, and in each of these countries, some employees have a company car. For this situation, we can declare a two-dimensional array where the first dimension will represent the country and the second dimension will represent the employee. Using our *Auto* class from Chapter 7, the following statement declares this two-dimensional array to hold *Auto* objects:

```
Auto [ ][ ] cars;
```

You can also declare multiple multidimensional arrays of the same data type in one statement by inserting a comma after each array name, using this syntax:

```
datatype [ ][ ] arrayName1, arrayName2;
```

For example, the following statement will declare two integer arrays to hold the number of stolen bases for two baseball players for each game in their career:

```
int [ ][ ] brian, jon;
```

The first dimension represents the games (per season), and the second dimension represents the season.

Notice that when we declare a multidimensional array, we do not specify how many elements the array will have. Declaring a multidimensional array does not allocate memory for the array; this is done in step 2, when we instantiate the array.

COMMON ERROR TRAP

Specifying the size of any of the dimensions of a multidimensional array in the declaration will generate a compiler error.

For example, this code from the file *Test.java:*

```
double [7][52] dailyTemps;
```

will generate the following compiler errors:

```
Test.java:5: ']' expected
  double [7][52] dailyTemps;
          ^
Test.java:5: not a statement
  double [7][52] dailyTemps;
         ^
Test.java:5: not a statement
  double [7][52] dailyTemps;
                  ^
3 errors
```

9.1.2 Instantiating Multidimensional Arrays

Just like instantiating single-dimensional arrays, you instantiate a multidimensional array using the *new* keyword. Here is the syntax for instantiating a two-dimensional array:

```
arrayName = new datatype [exp1][exp2];

   where exp1 and exp2 are expressions that evaluate to integers and
   specify, respectively, the number of rows and the number of columns in
   the array.
```

This statement allocates memory for the array. The number of elements in a two-dimensional array is equal to the sum of the number of elements in each row. When all the rows have the same number of columns, the number of elements in the array is equal to the number of rows multiplied by the number of columns.

For example, if we instantiate the following *dailyTemps* array with 52 rows and 7 columns, the array will have 52 * 7, or 364 elements:

```
dailyTemps = new double [52][7]; // dailyTemps has 52 rows
                                 // and 7 columns,
                                 // for a total of 364 elements
```

These statements will instantiate the other arrays declared above:

```
int numberOfStudents = 25;
int numberOfQuizzes = 10;
quizzes = new char [numberOfStudents][numberOfQuizzes];
// quizzes has 25 rows and 10 columns
// for a total of 250 elements

cars = new Auto [5][50];
// cars has 5 rows and 50 columns
// cars will store 250 Auto objects

brian = new int [80][20];
// brian has 80 rows and 20 columns
// there are 80 games per season
// brian played baseball for 20 seasons

jon = new int [80][10];
// jon has 80 rows and 10 columns
// jon played baseball for 10 seasons
```

REFERENCE POINT

The initial values automatically given to array elements depend on the data type of the array and are discussed in Chapter 8.

When a multidimensional array is instantiated, the elements are given initial values automatically. Elements of arrays with numeric types are initialized to 0, elements of *char* type are initialized to a space, elements of *boolean* type are initialized to *false*, and elements of class types are initialized to *null*.

9.1.3 Combining the Declaration and Instantiation of Multidimensional Arrays

Multidimensional arrays, like single-dimensional arrays, can also be instantiated when they are declared. To combine the declaration and instantiation of a two-dimensional array, use this syntax:

```
datatype [ ][ ] arrayName = new datatype [exp1][exp2];

   where exp1 and exp2 are expressions that evaluate to integers and
   specify, respectively, the number of rows and columns in the array.
```

Thus, this statement:

```
double [ ][ ] dailyTemps = new double [52][7];
```

is equivalent to:

```
double [ ][ ] dailyTemps;
dailyTemps = new double [52][7];
```

Similarly, this statement:

```
char [ ][ ] quizzes = new char [25][10];
```

is equivalent to:

```
char [ ][ ] quizzes;
quizzes = new char [25][10];
```

Furthermore, this statement:

```
Auto [ ][ ] cars = new Auto [5][50];
```

is equivalent to:

```
Auto [ ][ ] cars;
cars = new Auto [5][50];
```

9.1.4 Assigning Initial Values to Multidimensional Arrays

We can instantiate a two-dimensional array by assigning initial values when the array is declared. To do this, we specify the initial values using comma-separated lists of initial values, enclosed in an outer set of curly braces:

```
datatype [ ][ ] arrayName =
     { { value00, value01, ... }, { value10, value11, }, ... };
```

where *valueMN* is an expression that evaluates to the data type of the array and is the value to assign to the element at row M and column N.

The list contains a number of sublists, separated by commas. The number of these sublists determines the number of rows in the array. For each row, the number of values in the corresponding sublist determines the number of columns in the row. Thus, Java allows a two-dimensional array to have a different number of columns in each row. For example, in our *Auto* array, each country (row) could have a different number of employees (columns) with company cars.

Indeed, a two-dimensional array is an array of arrays. The first dimension of a two-dimensional array consists of an array of array references, with each reference pointing to a single-dimensional array. Thus, a two-dimensional array is composed of an array of rows, where each row is a single-dimensional array. Therefore, each row can have a different number of elements, or columns.

For example, this statement declares and instantiates a two-dimensional array of integers:

```
int [ ][ ] numbersList1 = { { 0, 5, 10 },
                            { 0, 3, 6, 9 } };
```

Because two sublists are given, this two-dimensional array has two rows. The first sublist specifies three values, and therefore, the first row will have three columns; the second sublist specifies four values, and therefore, the second row will have four columns.

Figure 9.2 shows the *numbersList1* array after the preceding statement is executed.

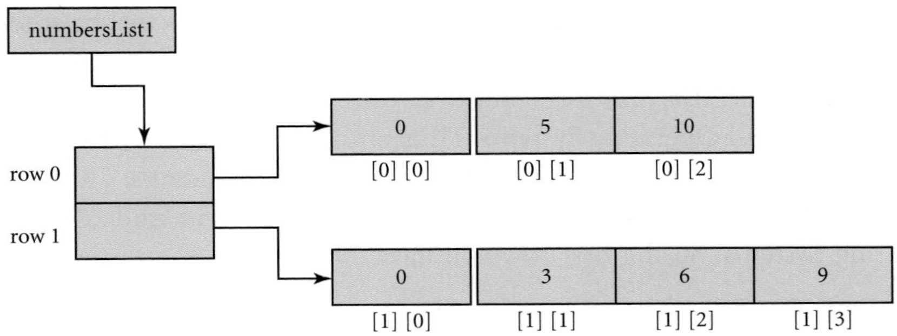

Figure 9.2
The *numbersList1* Array After Instantiation

An initialization list can be given only when the array is declared. If a two-dimensional array has already been instantiated, attempting to assign values to an array using an initialization list will generate a compiler error. For example, this code from the file *Test.java:*

```
int [ ][ ] grades = new int [2][3];
grades = { { 89, 73, 98 },
           { 88, 65, 92 } };
```

will generate the following compiler error:

```
Test.java:6: illegal start of expression
  grades = { { 89, 73, 98 },
           ^

1 error
```

We can declare and instantiate an array of objects by providing object references in the list:

```
Auto sportsCar = new Auto( "Ferrari", 0, 0.0 );
Auto sedan1 = new Auto( "BMW", 0, 0.0 );
Auto sedan2 = new Auto( "BMW", 100, 15.0 );
Auto sedan3 = new Auto( "Toyota", 0, 0.0 );
Auto rv1 = new Auto( "Jeep", 0, 0.0 );

Auto [ ][ ] cars = { { sportsCar, sedan1 },
                     { rv1, new Auto( ) },
                     { sedan2, sedan3 } };
```

COMMON ERROR TRAP

An initialization list can be given only when the two-dimensional array is declared. Attempting to assign values to an array using an initialization list after the array is instantiated will generate a compiler error.

This array of *Auto* objects has three rows with two columns in each row. The elements of the array *cars* are object references to *Auto* objects.

In most situations, the number of columns will be the same for each row. However, there are situations where it is useful to have a different number of columns for each row. For instance, Dr. Smith, a college professor, keeps track of grades using a two-dimensional array. The rows represent the courses she teaches and the columns represent the grades for the students in those sections. Grades are A, B, C, D, or F, so she declares the array with *char* elements. Dr. Smith teaches four courses: CS1, CS2, Database Management, and Operating Systems. Thus, she has four rows in the array. But in each course, Dr. Smith has a different number of students: There are 23 students in CS1, 16 in CS2, 12 in Database Management, and 28 in Operating Systems. So the first row will have 23 columns, the second row 16 columns, the third row 12 columns, and the fourth and last row will have 28 columns.

Using an initialization list, it is easy to instantiate a two-dimensional array with a different number of columns for every row. But sometimes the data is retrieved dynamically—read from a file, for example—and it is not possible to use an initialization list.

To instantiate a two-dimensional array with a different number of columns for each row, you can do the following:

- first, instantiate the two-dimensional array.
- second, instantiate each row, as a single-dimensional array.

For the preceding example, we can use the following code:

```
char [ ][ ] grades;           // declare the array
grades = new char [4][ ];     // instantiate the array
                              // grades has 4 null array elements

grades[0] = new char [23];    // instantiate row 0; 23 char elements
grades[1] = new char [16];    // instantiate row 1; 16 char elements
grades[2] = new char [12];    // instantiate row 2; 12 char elements
grades[3] = new char [28];    // instantiate row 3; 28 char elements
```

The second statement:

```
grades = new char [4][ ];
```

instantiates the two-dimensional array *grades* as an array having four rows, none of which has been instantiated yet. Because a two-dimensional array is an array of arrays, each element of the first dimension of the *grades* array is an array reference. Thus, before being instantiated, each element of the first dimension of the *grades* array has the value *null*.

As explained earlier, in a two-dimensional array, each row is a single-dimensional array. The last four statements instantiate each row, *grades[0]*, *grades[1]*, *grades[2]*, and *grades[3]*, each row having a different number of elements, or columns. The elements in these arrays are *chars*, initialized to a space.

Later in this chapter, we will define a general pattern for processing two-dimensional array elements so that it applies to all situations: an identical number of columns for each row, or a different number of columns for each row.

9.2 Accessing Multidimensional Array Elements

Elements of a two-dimensional array are accessed using this syntax:

```
arrayName[exp1][exp2]
   where exp1 and exp2 are expressions that evaluate to integers.
```

Exp1 is the element's row position, or **row index**, within the two-dimensional array. *Exp2* is the element's column position, or **column index**, within the two-dimensional array. The row index of the first row is always 0; the row index of the last row is always 1 less than the number of rows. The column index of the first column is always 0. The column index of the last column is always 1 less than the number of columns in that row.

Because a two-dimensional array is an array of arrays, the length of a two-dimensional array is its number of arrays, or rows. We access the number of rows in a two-dimensional array using the following syntax:

```
arrayName.length
```

Similarly, the length of each row is the number of columns (or elements) in that row's array. To access the number of columns in row *i* of a two-dimensional array named *arrayName*, use this syntax:

```
arrayName[i].length
```

Table 9.1 summarizes the syntax for accessing elements of a two-dimensional array.

TABLE 9.1 Accessing Two-Dimensional Array Elements

Array Element	Syntax
Row 0, column *j*	`arrayName[0][j]`
Row *i*, column *j*	`arrayName[i][j]`
Last row, column *j*	`arrayName[arrayName.length - 1][j]`
Last row, last column	`arrayName[arrayName.length - 1]` `[arrayName[arrayName.length - 1].length - 1]`
Number of rows in the array	`arrayName.length`
Number of columns in row *i*	`arrayName[i].length`

Suppose we want to analyze the monthly cell phone bills for the past three months for a family of four persons. The parents, Joe and Jane, each have a cell phone, and so do the children, Mike and Sarah. We want to calculate the average monthly bill for each person, the total payments for the three months, and determine which family member had the lowest and highest bills. We could use a two-dimensional array of *doubles* with three rows and four columns. The rows will represent the months and the columns will represent the family members. For example, we could have the following mapping for the row and column indexes:

row 0 : July
row 1 : August
row 2 : September

column 0 : Joe
column 1 : Jane
column 2 : Mike
column 3 : Sarah

We could visualize our two-dimensional array as the table shown in Table 9.2.

We'll name the array *familyCellBills*. Each element in the array will be referenced as *familyCellBills[i][j]*, where *i* is the index of the row (the month), and *j* is the index of the column (the person). Remember that the first element in a row or column is at index 0, so the first element in the first row is at index [0][0].

In lines 13–15 of Example 9.1, we declare and instantiate the *familyCellBills* array. Because the elements of *familyCellBills* are *doubles*, instantiating the array also initializes each element to 0.0. Lines 18–31 store values into each

TABLE 9.2 Visualizing a Two-Dimensional Array

	Joe	Jane	Mike	Sarah
July	45.24	54.67	32.55	25.61
August	65.29	49.75	32.08	26.11
September	75.24	54.53	34.55	28.16

element of the array. Figure 9.3 shows how the *familyCellBills* array looks after lines 18–31 are executed.

```
1 /* Two-Dimensional Array of Cell Phone Bills
2     Anderson, Franceschi
3 */
4
5 public class FamilyCellBills
6 {
7  public static void main( String [ ] args )
8  {
9   // declare constants for the number of rows and columns
10   final int NUMBER_OF_MONTHS = 3;
11   final int NUMBER_OF_PERSONS = 4;
12
13   // declare and instantiate the array
14   double [ ][ ] familyCellBills =
15      new double [NUMBER_OF_MONTHS][NUMBER_OF_PERSONS];
16
17   // assign values to array elements
18   familyCellBills[0][0] = 45.24;  // row 0
19   familyCellBills[0][1] = 54.67;
20   familyCellBills[0][2] = 32.55;
21   familyCellBills[0][3] = 25.61;
22
23   familyCellBills[1][0] = 65.29;  // row 1
24   familyCellBills[1][1] = 49.75;
25   familyCellBills[1][2] = 32.08;
26   familyCellBills[1][3] = 26.11;
27
28   familyCellBills[2][0] = 75.24;  // row 2
29   familyCellBills[2][1] = 54.53;
30   familyCellBills[2][2] = 34.55;
31   familyCellBills[2][3] = 28.16;
32
33   System.out.println( "The first monthly cell bill for the first "
34      + "family member is\n"
35      + familyCellBills[0][0] );
36   System.out.println( "The last monthly cell bill for the last "
37      + "family member is\n"
38      + familyCellBills[NUMBER_OF_MONTHS - 1][NUMBER_OF_PERSONS - 1] );
39
40   int numRows = familyCellBills.length;
41   System.out.println( "\nThe number of rows is " + numRows );
42
```

```
43   for ( int i = 0; i < numRows; i++ )
44   {
45    System.out.print( "The number of columns in row " + i + " is " );
46    System.out.println( familyCellBills[i].length );
47   }
48  }
49 }
```

EXAMPLE 9.1 The *familyCellBills* Array

Note that the last element is *familyCellBills[2][3]*, with a row index that is 1 less than *familyCellBills.length*, and a column index that is 1 less than *familyCellBills[2].length*, which is the number of columns in the last row. More generally, for a two-dimensional array named *arr*, the last element is:

```
arr[arr.length - 1][arr[arr.length - 1].length - 1]
```

Lines 33–38 output the first and last element of the array *familyCellBills*.

Line 40 assigns the number of rows in the *familyCellBills* array to the *int* variable *numRows*. The variable *numRows* now has the value 3 and is output at line 41.

At lines 43–47, a *for* loop outputs the number of columns in each row of *familyCellBills*. Figure 9.4 shows the output of this example.

Row indexes of a two-dimensional array *must* be between 0 and *arrayName.length – 1*. Attempting to access an element of an array using a row index less than 0 or greater than *arrayName.length – 1* will compile without errors, but will generate an *ArrayIndexOutOfBoundsException* at run time. By default, this exception halts execution of the program.

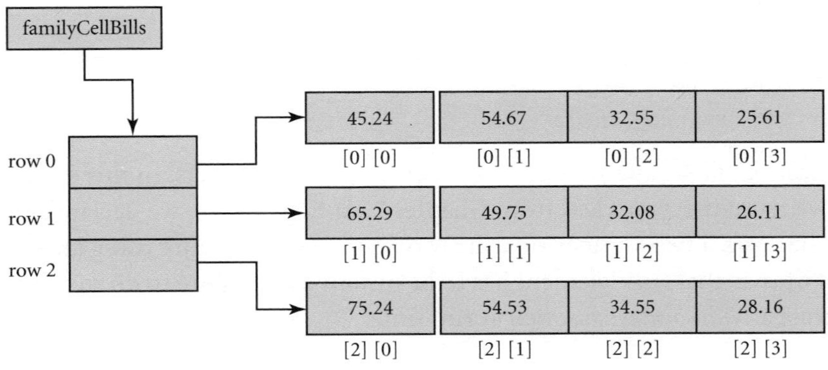

Figure 9.3
The *familyCellBills* Array After Assigning Values

Figure 9.4
Output of Example 9.1

```
The first monthly cell bill for the first family member is
45.24
The last monthly cell bill for the last family member is
28.16

The number of rows is 3
The number of columns in row 0 is 4
The number of columns in row 1 is 4
The number of columns in row 2 is 4
```

For example, all the following expressions are invalid:

```
// invalid row indexes for the familyCellBills array!!

familyCellBills[-1][2]
// the lowest valid row index is 0

familyCellBills[cellBills.length][2]
// the highest valid row index is familyCellBills.length - 1
```

Similarly, column indexes of a two-dimensional array *must* be between 0 and *arrayName[i].length – 1*, where *i* is the row index. Attempting to access an element of row *i* in a two-dimensional array using a column index less than 0 or greater than *arrayName[i].length – 1* will compile without errors, but will generate an *ArrayIndexOutOfBoundsException* at run time.

COMMON ERROR TRAP

Attempting to access an element of a two-dimensional array using a row index less than 0 or greater than *arrayName.length – 1* will generate an *ArrayIndexOutOfBoundsException* at run time. Similarly, attempting to access an element of row *i* of a two-dimensional array using a column index less than 0 or greater than *arrayName[i].length – 1* also will generate an *ArrayIndexOutOfBoundsException*.

For example, all the following expressions are invalid:

```
// invalid column indexes for the familyCellBills array!!

familyCellBills[1][-1]
// the lowest valid column index is 0

familyCellBills[1][familyCellBills[1].length]
// the highest valid column index of row i is
// familyCellBills[i].length - 1
```

Example 9.2 illustrates how to work with an array of objects. In this example, we reuse the *Auto* class from Chapter 7. At lines 17–20, we declare and initialize *cars*, a two-dimensional array of *Auto* objects. Before using an element of *cars*, that *Auto* element has to be instantiated; failure to do so could generate a *NullPointerException* at run time.

```
cars[1][0]'s description is:
Model: Ferrari; miles driven: 0; gallons of gas: 0.0
```

Figure 9.5
Output of Example 9.2

There are three rows in *cars*: the first row has three columns, and the second and third rows have two columns each. Line 22 retrieves the array element at row 1 and column 0—here *sportsCar*—and assigns it to the *Auto* object reference *retrievedCar*, which is then printed at lines 25–26, where *toString* is called implicitly. Figure 9.5 shows the output of this example.

```
1 /* Working with a Two-Dimensional Array of Objects
2    Anderson, Franceschi
3 */
4
5 public class TwoDimAutoArray
6 {
7  public static void main( String [ ] args )
8  {
9   // instantiate several Auto object references
10  Auto sedan1 = new Auto( "BMW", 0, 0.0 );
11  Auto sedan2 = new Auto( "BMW", 100, 15.0 );
12  Auto sedan3 = new Auto( "Toyota", 0, 0.0 );
13  Auto sportsCar = new Auto( "Ferrari", 0, 0.0 );
14  Auto rv1 = new Auto( "Jeep", 0, 0.0 );
15  Auto rv2 = new Auto( "Ford", 200, 30.0 );
16
17  // declare and initialize two-dimensional array of Autos
18  Auto [ ][ ] cars = { { sedan1, sedan2, sedan3 },
19                       { sportsCar, new Auto( ) },
20                       { rv1, rv2 } };
21
22  Auto retrievedCar = cars[1][0];
23  // retrievedCar gets the sportsCar object reference
24
25  System.out.println( "cars[1][0]'s description is:\n"
26                      + retrievedCar );
27  }
28 }
```

EXAMPLE 9.2 Two-Dimensional Array of *Auto* Objects

Skill Practice
with these end-of-chapter questions

9.10.1 Multiple Choice Exercises

Questions 1,2,3,4,5,6,7,8

9.10.2 Reading and Understanding Code

Questions 14,15,16,17,18

9.10.3 Fill In the Code

Questions 33,34

9.10.4 Identifying Errors in Code

Questions 50,51,52,53

9.10.5 Debugging Area

Question 59

9.10.6 Write a Short Program

Question 65

9.10.8 Technical Writing

Question 94

9.3 Aggregate Two-Dimensional Array Operations

As with single-dimensional arrays, Java does not support aggregate operations on multidimensional arrays. For example, you cannot print the contents of an array using only the array name. Instead, you need to process each element individually.

9.3.1 Processing All the Elements of a Two-Dimensional Array

To process all the elements of a two-dimensional array, we use nested *for* loops that access and process each element individually. Often, the most logical way to process all elements is in row order, and within each row, in column order. We could also process elements one column at a time if that is more logical for the problem at hand.

In our nested *for* loops, the outer *for* loop will process the rows and the inner *for* loop will process the columns within each row. We will use *i* for the row index and *j* for the column index.

For the outer *for* loop, we can use the same header as we use to process single-dimensional arrays:

```
for ( int i = 0; i < arrayName.length; i++ )
```

Note that the initialization statement of the outer loop:

```
int i = 0;
```

sets *i* to the index of the first row of the two-dimensional array. Then the outer loop update statement increments *i*, so that we process each row in order.

The outer loop condition:

```
i < arrayName.length
```

continues execution of the outer loop as long as the row index is less than the *length* of the two-dimensional array, which represents the number of rows. Note that we use the *less than* operator (<) instead of the *less than or equal to* operator (<=). Using the less than or equal to operator would cause us to illegally attempt to reference an element with a row index of *arrayName.length*.

The *for* loop header for the inner loop, which processes the columns of the current row, is as follows:

```
for ( int j = 0; j < arrayName[i].length; j++ )
```

The initialization statement of the inner loop:

```
int j = 0;
```

sets *j* to the index of the first column of the current row. Then the inner loop update statement increments *j* to the next column index, so that we process each column of the current row in order.

The inner loop condition:

```
j < arrayName[i].length
```

continues execution of the inner loop as long as the column index is less than the *length* of the current row (row *i*). Given that each row can have a different number of columns, this will ensure that we do not attempt to access an element beyond the last column index of the current row.

Note, again, that we use the *less than* operator (<), not the *less than or equal to* operator (<=), which would cause us to illegally attempt to reference an element with a column index of *arrayName[i].length.*

COMMON ERROR TRAP

In the outer *for* loop, using the following condition:

`i <= arrayName.length`

will generate an *ArrayIndexOutOfBoundsException* because the last row of a two-dimensional array is *arrayName.length – 1*. Similarly, in the inner *for* loop, using the condition:

`j <= arrayName[i].length`

will generate an *ArrayIndexOutOfBoundsException* because the last column of row *i* in a two-dimensional array is `arrayName[i].length – 1`.

Inside the inner *for* loop, we refer to the current element being processed as:

```
arrayName[i][j]
```

Thus, the general pattern for processing the elements of a two-dimensional array called *arrayName* in row-first, column-second order using nested *for* loops is:

```
for ( int i = 0; i < arrayName.length; i++ )
{
   for ( int j = 0; j < arrayName[i].length; j++ )
   {
      // process element arrayName[i][j]
   }
}
```

Example 9.3 illustrates how to print all the elements of the two-dimensional array *familyCellBills* in row order. The array is declared and initialized at lines 10–12. At lines 16–23, the nested *for* loops, using the standard pattern described earlier, print all the elements of the array. Figure 9.6 shows the output of the program.

```
1 /* Processing a Two-Dimensional Array of Cell Phone Bills
2     Anderson, Franceschi
3 */
4
5 public class OutputFamilyCellBills
6 {
7  public static void main( String [ ] args )
8  {
9   // declare and initialize the array
10  double [ ][ ] familyCellBills = { {45.24, 54.67, 32.55, 25.61},
11                                     {65.29, 49.75, 32.08, 26.11},
12                                     {75.24, 54.53, 34.55, 28.16} };
13
14  System.out.println( "\tData for family cell bills" );
15
16  for ( int i = 0; i < familyCellBills.length; i++ )
17  {
18    System.out.print( "\nrow " + i + ":\t" );
19    for ( int j = 0; j < familyCellBills[i].length; j++ )
20    {
```

```
      System.out.print( familyCellBills[i][j] + "\t" );
    }
  }
  System.out.println( );
 }
}
```

EXAMPLE 9.3 Two-Dimensional Array Processing

```
   Data for family cell bills

row 0:    45.24     54.67     32.55     25.61
row 1:    65.29     49.75     32.08     26.11
row 2:    75.24     54.53     34.55     28.16
```

Figure 9.6
Output of Example 9.3

9.3.2 Processing a Given Row of a Two-Dimensional Array

What if we want to process just one row of a two-dimensional array? For instance, we could be interested in calculating the sum of the cell bills for the whole family for a particular month, or identifying who had the highest cell bill in a particular month.

The general pattern for processing the elements of row *i* of a two-dimensional array called *arrayName* uses a single *for* loop:

```
for ( int j = 0; j < arrayName[i].length; j++ )
{
     // process element arrayName[i][j]
}
```

Example 9.4 shows how to sum all the elements of a particular row of the two-dimensional array *familyCellBills.*

```
/* Processing One Row of a Two-Dimensional Array
   Anderson, Franceschi
*/

import java.util.Scanner;
import java.text.NumberFormat;

public class SumARowFamilyCellBills
{
```

```
10 public static void main( String [ ] args )
11 {
12  // declare and initialize the array
13  double [ ][ ] familyCellBills = { {45.24, 54.67, 32.55, 25.61},
14                                    {65.29, 49.75, 32.08, 26.11},
15                                    {75.24, 54.53, 34.55, 28.16} };
16
17  String [ ] months = { "July", "August", "September" };
18  for ( int i = 0; i < months.length; i++ )
19     System.out.println( "Month " + i + " : " + months[i] );
20
21  Scanner scan = new Scanner( System.in );
22  int currentMonth;
23  do
24  {
25    System.out.print( "Enter a month number between 0 and 2 > " );
26    currentMonth = scan.nextInt( );
27  } while ( currentMonth < 0 || currentMonth > 2 );
28
29  double monthlyFamilyBills = 0.0;
30  for ( int j = 0; j < familyCellBills[currentMonth].length; j++ )
31  {
32    // add current family member bill to total
33    monthlyFamilyBills += familyCellBills[currentMonth][j];
34  }
35
36  NumberFormat priceFormat = NumberFormat.getCurrencyInstance( );
37  System.out.println( "\nThe total family cell bills during "
38                      + months[currentMonth] + " is "
39                      + priceFormat.format( monthlyFamilyBills ) );
40 }
41 }
```

EXAMPLE 9.4 Processing One Row in a Two-Dimensional Array

Since the rows correspond to the months, we declare and initialize at line 17 a single-dimensional *String* array named *months* in order to make our prompt more user-friendly. At lines 18–19, we print a menu for the user, providing month names and the corresponding indexes. At lines 23–27, we use a *do/while* loop to prompt the user for a month index until the user enters a valid value between 0 and 2.

To calculate the total of the family cell bills for the month index that the user inputs, we first initialize the variable *monthlyFamilyBills* to 0.0 at line 29. We then use a single *for* loop at lines 30–34, following the pattern

```
Month 0 : July
Month 1 : August
Month 2 : September
Enter a month number between 0 and 2 > 1

The total family cell bills during August is $173.23
```

Figure 9.7
Output of Example 9.4

described earlier, to sum all the family member bills for the month chosen by the user. We then format and output the total at lines 36–39. Figure 9.7 shows the output of the program when the user chooses 1 for the month.

9.3.3 Processing a Given Column of a Two-Dimensional Array

If we want to determine the highest cell bill for Mike or calculate the average cell bill for Sarah, we will need to process just one column of the two-dimensional array.

The general pattern for processing the elements of column *j* of a two-dimensional array called *arrayName* uses a single *for* loop:

```
for ( int i = 0; i < arrayName.length; i++ )
{
   if ( j < arrayName[i].length )
      // process element arrayName[i][j]
}
```

Because rows may have a different number of columns, a given row *i* may not have a column *j*. Thus, we need to check that the current column number is less than *arrayName[i].length* before we attempt to access *arrayName[i][j]*.

SOFTWARE ENGINEERING TIP

Before processing an element in a column, check whether the current row contains an element in that column. Doing so will avoid an *ArrayIndexOutOfBoundsException*.

Because our two-dimensional array *familyCellBills* has the same number of columns (4) in every row, no extra precaution is necessary here. It is a good software engineering practice, however, to verify that the column index is valid before attempting to process the array element.

Example 9.5 shows how to find the maximum value of all the elements of a particular column.

```
/* Processing One Column of a Two-Dimensional Array
   Anderson, Franceschi
*/

import java.util.Scanner;
```

```
6 import java.text.NumberFormat;
7
8 public class MaxMemberBill
9 {
10  public static void main( String [ ] args )
11  {
12   // declare and initialize the array
13   double [ ][ ] familyCellBills = { {45.24, 54.67, 32.55, 25.61},
14                                     {65.29, 49.75, 32.08, 26.11},
15                                     {75.24, 54.53, 34.55, 28.16} };
16
17   String [ ] familyMembers = { "Joe", "Jane", "Mike", "Sarah" };
18   for ( int i = 0; i < familyMembers.length; i++ )
19         System.out.println( "Family member " + i + " : "
20                             + familyMembers[i] );
21
22   Scanner scan = new Scanner( System.in );
23   int currentMember;
24   do
25   {
26    System.out.print( "Enter a family member between 0 and 3 > " );
27    currentMember = scan.nextInt( );
28   } while ( currentMember < 0 || currentMember > 3 );
29
30   double memberMaxBill = familyCellBills[0][currentMember];
31   for ( int i = 1; i < familyCellBills.length; i++ )
32   {
33    if ( currentMember < familyCellBills[i].length )
34    {
35      // update memberMaxBill if necessary
36      if ( familyCellBills[i][currentMember] > memberMaxBill )
37        memberMaxBill = familyCellBills[i][currentMember];
38    }
39   }
40
41   NumberFormat priceFormat = NumberFormat.getCurrencyInstance( );
42   System.out.println ( "\nThe max cell bill for "
43                        + familyMembers[currentMember] + " is "
44                        + priceFormat.format( memberMaxBill ) );
45  }
46 }
```

EXAMPLE 9.5 Processing a Column in a Two-Dimensional Array

At line 17, we declare and initialize a single-dimensional *String* array named *familyMembers* to make our prompt more user-friendly. At lines

24–28, we again use a *do/while* loop to prompt the user for a valid family member index.

To calculate the maximum value of the family member cell bills, we first initialize the variable *memberMaxBill* to the first element in the column (*familyCellBills[0][currentMember]*) at line 30. We then use a standard *for* loop at lines 31–39, following the pattern described earlier to update the value of *memberMaxBill* as necessary. There is one minor difference; we do not need to start the row at index 0 because we initialized *memberMaxBill* to the value of the element in row 0 of the column *currentMember*. Note that we assume that there is an element at column 0 of each row, that is, each row has been instantiated. The value of the variable *memberMaxBill* is then formatted and printed at lines 41–44. Figure 9.8 shows the output of the program.

9.3.4 Processing a Two-Dimensional Array One Row at a Time

Earlier, we calculated the sum of the elements of a given row of a two-dimensional array. But what if we are interested in calculating that sum for each row? In this case, we need to initialize our total variable before we process each row and print the results after we process each row.

The general pattern for processing each row of a two-dimensional array called *arrayName* using nested *for* loops is

```
for ( int i = 0; i < arrayName.length; i++ )
{
   // initialize processing variables for row i
   for ( int j = 0; j < arrayName[i].length; j++ )
   {
      // process element arrayName[i][j]
   }
   // finish the processing of row i
}
```

```
Family member 0 : Joe
Family member 1 : Jane
Family member 2 : Mike
Family member 3 : Sarah
Enter a family member between 0 and 3 > 2

The max cell bill for Mike is $34.55
```

Figure 9.8
Output of Example 9.5

There are two important additions to the general pattern for processing all elements of the array:

- Before processing each row, that is, before the inner loop, we need to initialize the processing variables for the current row. If we are summing elements, we initialize the total variable to 0. If we are calculating a minimum or maximum value, we initialize the current minimum or maximum to the value of the first element of the current row.
- When we reach the end of each row, that is, after each completion of the inner loop, we finish processing the current row. For instance, we may want to print the sum or maximum value for that row.

Example 9.6 shows how to sum the elements of each row of the two-dimensional array *familyCellBills.*

```
/* Processing Each Row of a Two-Dimensional Array
   Anderson, Franceschi
*/

import java.util.Scanner;
import java.text.NumberFormat;

public class SumEachRowFamilyCellBills
{
 public static void main( String [ ] args )
 {
  // declare and initialize the array
  double [ ][ ] familyCellBills = { {45.24, 54.67, 32.55, 25.61},
                                    {65.29, 49.75, 32.08, 26.11},
                                    {75.24, 54.53, 34.55, 28.16} };

  String [ ] months = { "July", "August", "September" };

  NumberFormat priceFormat = NumberFormat.getCurrencyInstance( );
  double currentMonthTotal;
  for ( int i = 0; i < familyCellBills.length; i++ )
  {
   currentMonthTotal = 0.0;  // initialize total for row
   for ( int j = 0; j < familyCellBills[i].length; j++ )
   {
    // add current family member bill to current monthly total
    currentMonthTotal += familyCellBills[i][j];
```

```
28     }
29     // print total for row
30     System.out.println( "The total for " + months[i] + " is "
31                      + priceFormat.format( currentMonthTotal ) );
32   }
33  }
34 }
```

EXAMPLE 9.6 Processing Each Row in a Two-Dimensional Array

Again, the rows correspond to the months, and we declare and initialize at line 17 a *String* array named *months* in order to make the output user-friendly.

To calculate the total of the family cell bills for each month, we use nested *for* loops at lines 21–32, following the pattern described earlier.

Inside the outer *for* loop, we initialize the *currentMonthTotal* at line 23 before processing each row. Without this statement, the variable *currentMonthTotal* would continue to accumulate, as if we were summing all the elements of the array instead of calculating a separate sum for each row.

After the inner loop finishes, we complete the processing of row *i* by printing the value of *currentMonthTotal* at lines 29–31. Figure 9.9 shows the output of the program.

COMMON ERROR TRAP

Failing to initialize the row processing variables before each row is a logic error and will generate incorrect results.

9.3.5 Processing a Two-Dimensional Array One Column at a Time

Processing each column of a two-dimensional array requires a little extra checking. If the number of columns in each row differs, we must be careful not to attempt to access an element with an out-of-bounds column index. Generally, we will need to determine the number of columns in the largest row in the array before coding the outer loop header.

For example, suppose you are keeping track of your test grades in three classes: Intro to Java, Database Management, and English Composition. You have two test grades in Intro to Java, four in Database Management,

```
The total for July is $158.07
The total for August is $173.23
The total for September is $192.48
```

Figure 9.9
Output of Example 9.6

and three in English Composition. We can use a two-dimensional array to store these test grades as follows:

```
int [ ][ ] grades = { { 89, 75 },
                      { 84, 76, 92, 96 },
                      { 80, 88, 95 } };
```

There are three rows in the array *grades.* The maximum number of columns in any row is four; therefore, in order to process all the columns, our outer loop should loop from column index 0 to column index 3. Our inner loop should check that the current column number exists in the row before attempting to process the element.

Let's assume, at this point, that we stored the maximum number of columns in an *int* variable called *maxNumberOfColumns.* The general pattern for processing elements of a two-dimensional array, *arrayName,* one column at a time is:

```
// maxNumberOfColumns holds the number of columns
// in the largest row of familyCellBills
for ( int j = 0; j < maxNumberOfColumns; j++ )
{
   for ( int i = 0; i < arrayName.length; i++ )
   {
      if ( j < arrayName[i].length )
      {
          // process element arrayName[i][j]
      }
   }
}
```

The outer loop condition:

```
j < maxNumberOfColumns
```

continues execution of the outer loop as long as the column index is less than the maximum number of columns of the two-dimensional array, which has been computed and assigned to the variable *maxNumberOfColumns.*

The inner loop condition:

```
i < arrayName.length
```

continues execution of the inner loop as long as the row index is less than the number of rows.

Again, because each row may have a different number of columns, a given row *i* may not have a column *j*. Thus, using the following *if* condition, we check that an element in column *j* exists—*j* is less than *arrayName[i].length*—before we attempt to access *arrayName[i][j]*:

```
if ( j < arrayName[i].length )
```

Example 9.7 shows how this pattern can be implemented in a program.

```
/* Processing Each Column in a Two-Dimensional Array
   Anderson, Franceschi
*/

public class GradesProcessing
{
 public static void main( String [ ] args )
 {
  int [ ][ ] grades = { { 89, 75 },
                        { 84, 76, 92, 96 },
                        { 80, 88, 95 } };

  // compute the maximum number of columns
  int maxNumberOfColumns = grades[0].length;
  for ( int i = 1; i < grades.length; i++ )
  {
   if ( grades[i].length > maxNumberOfColumns )
       maxNumberOfColumns = grades[i].length;
  }
  System.out.println( "The maximum number of columns in grades is "
                      + maxNumberOfColumns );

  for ( int j = 0; j < maxNumberOfColumns; j++ )
  {
   System.out.print( "\nColumn " + j + ": " );
   for ( int i = 0; i < grades.length; i++ )
   {
    if ( j < grades[i].length )
         System.out.print( grades[i][j] );
    System.out.print( "\t" );
   }
  }
  System.out.println( );
 }
}
```

EXAMPLE 9.7 Processing a Two-Dimensional Array in Column Order

Figure 9.10
The Output of Example 9.7

```
The maximum number of columns in grades is 4

Column 0: 89    84      80
Column 1: 75    76      88
Column 2:       92      95
Column 3:       96
```

The array *grades* is declared and initialized at lines 9–11. Lines 13–19 compute the maximum number of columns in a row and store the value in the *int* variable *maxNumberOfColumns.* First, we initialize *maxNumberOfColumns* to the number of columns of row 0 at line 14. At lines 15 to 19, we loop through each remaining row in *grades* and update *maxNumberOfColumns* if we find that the current row has more columns than *maxNumberOfColumns.*

At lines 23–32, we use nested loops to print all the elements of *grades* in column order, following the general pattern described earlier. The output of the program is shown in Figure 9.10.

9.3.6 Displaying Two-Dimensional Array Data as a Bar Chart

Another way to display two-dimensional array data is graphically, by drawing a bar chart. For example, the bar chart in Figure 9.11 displays the data in the *familyCellBills* array.

REFERENCE POINT

Chapter 8 provides instructions on drawing a bar chart from the data in a single-dimensional array.

Each bar is a rectangle. So to create a bar chart, we use our standard nested *for* loops, and call the *fillRect* method of the *Graphics* class to draw a rectangle for each element. We use the *drawString* method to print the value of each element. To change colors for each row, we set up an array of *Color* objects, and loop through the array to set the current color for each row iteration. Furthermore, each time we process a row, we must reset the (x, y) coordinate of the first bar of the current row.

Example 9.8 shows the applet code that displays the bar chart shown in Figure 9.11.

```
/* Displaying a Two-Dimensional Array as a Bar Chart
   Anderson, Franceschi
*/

```

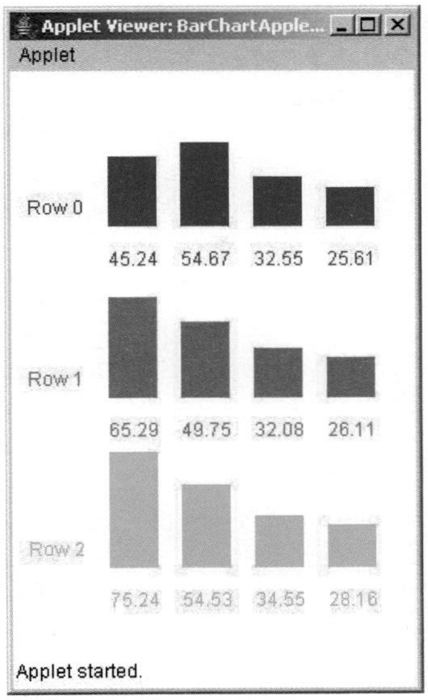

Figure 9.11
The *familyCellBills* Array as a Bar Chart

```
import javax.swing.JApplet;
import java.awt.Graphics;
import java.awt.Color;

public class BarChartApplet extends JApplet
{
 final int LEFT_MARGIN = 60;         // starting x value
 final int BASE_Y_BAR  = 100;        // bottom of the bars
 final int BASE_Y_VALUE = 125;       // bottom of the values
 final int BAR_WIDTH = 30;           // width of each bar
 final int SPACE_BETWEEN_BARS = 15; // pixels between bars
 final int ROW_HEIGHT = 110;         // pixels between rows
 double [ ][ ] familyCellBills = { { 45.24, 54.67, 32.55, 25.61 },
                                   { 65.29, 49.75, 32.08, 26.11 },
                                   { 75.24, 54.53, 34.55, 28.16 } };
 Color [ ] colors = { Color.BLUE, Color.RED, Color.GREEN };

 public void init( )
 {
   setSize( 250, 375 );
 }

 public void paint( Graphics g )
```

```
28  {
29   int xStart = LEFT_MARGIN;     // x value for 1st column (bars)
30   int yStart = BASE_Y_VALUE;    // y value for 1st row (data)
31   int yStartBar = BASE_Y_BAR;   // y value for 1st row (bars)
32
33   for ( int i = 0; i < familyCellBills.length; i++ )
34   {
35    g.setColor( colors[i] );    // set color for current row
36    g.drawString( "Row " + i, xStart - LEFT_MARGIN + 10,
37                  (int) ( yStart - .3 * ROW_HEIGHT ) );
38
39    for ( int j = 0; j < familyCellBills[i].length; j++ )
40    {
41      g.fillRect( xStart, yStartBar - (int) ( familyCellBills[i][j] ),
42                  BAR_WIDTH, (int) ( familyCellBills[i][j] ) );
43
44      g.drawString( Double.toString( familyCellBills[i][j] ),
45                    xStart, yStart );
46
47      // move to starting x value for next bar
48      xStart += BAR_WIDTH + SPACE_BETWEEN_BARS;
49    }
50
51    // new row:  increase yStart and yStartBar
52    yStart += ROW_HEIGHT;        // increment yStart for next row
53    yStartBar += ROW_HEIGHT;     // increment yStartBar for next row
54    xStart = LEFT_MARGIN;        // reset xStart for next row
55   }
56  }
57 }
```

EXAMPLE 9.8 Applet Displaying a Two-Dimensional Array as a Bar Chart

The *Color* single-dimensional array *colors* that we use to determine the color of each row of bars is declared and initialized at line 20. It has the same number of rows as *familyCellBills*. The first row of bars will be displayed in blue, the second row in red, and the third row in green.

In the *paint* method, at the beginning of the outer loop and before the inner loop, we set the color for the current row (line 35) by using the row number as an index into the *colors* array. At lines 36–37, we display the row number.

In the body of the inner loop (lines 39–49), we draw the rectangle for the element value at row *i* and column *j* of *familyCellBills*, then display a *String* representing the same value. We then increment *xStart* to the location of the next bar to draw.

After the inner loop and before restarting the outer loop, we update the values of *yStart*, *yStartBar*, and *xStart* (lines 51–54) so that they are properly set for processing the next row. Earlier, we said that initializing variable values for the next row is usually done at the beginning of the outer loop body before entering the inner loop, but it also can be done after the inner loop and before re-entering the outer loop, as shown here.

CODE IN ACTION

To see a step-by-step illustration showing how to use two-dimensional arrays, look for the Flash movie on the CD-ROM included with this book. Click on the link for Chapter 9 to start the movie.

Skill Practice
with these end-of-chapter questions

9.10.2 Reading and Understanding Code

Questions 19, 20, 21, 22, 23, 24, 25, 26, 27, 28

9.10.3 Fill In the Code

Questions 35, 36, 37, 38, 39, 40, 41, 42, 43, 44, 45

9.10.4 Identifying Errors in Code

Question 54

9.10.5 Debugging Area

Questions 60, 61, 62

9.10.6 Write a Short Program

Questions 66, 67, 68, 69, 70, 71, 72, 73, 74, 75, 76, 77, 78, 79

9.4 Two-Dimensional Arrays Passed to and Returned from Methods

Writing methods that take two-dimensional arrays as parameters and/or return two-dimensional arrays is similar to working with single-dimensional arrays.

The syntax for a method that accepts a two-dimensional array as a parameter is the following:

```
returnType methodName( arrayType [ ][ ] arrayParameterName )
```

The syntax for a method that returns a two-dimensional array is the following:

```
returnArrayType [ ][ ]  methodName( parameterList )
```

The caller of the method passes the argument list and assigns the return value to a reference to a two-dimensional array of the appropriate data type.

Combining both possibilities, the syntax for a method that accepts a two-dimensional array as a parameter and whose return value is a two-dimensional array is the following:

```
returnArrayType [ ][ ]  methodName( arrayType [ ][ ] arrayParameterName )
```

The caller of the method simply passes the name of the array without any brackets and assigns the return value to a reference to a two-dimensional array of the appropriate data type.

For example, suppose we want to tally votes in an election. We have four candidates running in six districts. We want to know how many votes each candidate received and how many votes were cast in each district. Thus, we can set up a two-dimensional array with each row representing a district and each column representing a candidate, with the values in each element representing the votes a candidate received in that district. We need to compute the sum of each row to find the number of votes per district and the sum of each column to find the number of votes per candidate.

To do this, we create a class, *Tally*, that has a two-dimensional array instance variable, *voteData*, storing the votes. The *Tally* class also has a method, *arrayTally*, that will compute the sums for each column and row of *voteData*. The sums will be returned from the method as a two-dimensional array with two rows. The first row will hold the totals for each column of *voteData*, and the second row will hold the totals for each row of *voteData*.

Example 9.9 shows the *Tally* class.

```
/** Two-Dimensional Arrays as Method Parameters
*   and Return Values: the Tally class
*   Anderson, Franceschi
*/

public class Tally
{
  int [ ][ ] voteData;

  /** overloaded constructor
  *   @param   newVoteData   an array of vote counts
  */
  public Tally( int [ ][ ] newVoteData )
  {
    voteData = new int [newVoteData.length][ ];
    for ( int i = 0; i < newVoteData.length; i++ )
         voteData[i] = new int [newVoteData[i].length];

    for ( int i = 0; i < newVoteData.length; i++ )
    {
      for ( int j = 0; j < newVoteData[i].length; j++ )
      {
        voteData[i][j] = newVoteData[i][j];
      }
    }
  }

  /** arrayTally method
  *   @return   a two-dimensional array of votes
  */
  public int [ ][ ] arrayTally( )
  {
    // create array of tallies, all elements are 0
    int [ ][ ] returnTally = new int [2][ ];
    returnTally[0] = new int [voteData[0].length];
    returnTally[1] = new int [voteData.length];

    for ( int i = 0; i < voteData.length; i++ )
    {
      for ( int j = 0; j < voteData[i].length; j++ )
      {
```

```
42          returnTally[0][j] += voteData[i][j];  // add to column sum
43          returnTally[1][i] += voteData[i][j];  // add to row sum
44        }
45      }
46      return returnTally;
47    }
48 }
```

EXAMPLE 9.9 The *Tally* Class

The overloaded constructor, coded at lines 10–26, receives the two-dimensional array argument *newVoteData*. After instantiating *voteData* at line 15, we copy *newVoteData* into *voteData* one element at a time at lines 19–25.

We coded the *arrayTally* method at lines 28–47. Our first job is to instantiate the *returnArray*, which is the array the method will return to the caller. We know that the array will have two rows, one holding the sums of the columns and one holding the sums of the rows. Because each row in the *returnArray* will have a different number of columns, we instantiate the array with two rows, but do not give a value for the number of columns (line 34). We then instantiate each row with the appropriate number of columns (lines 35–36). Row 0, the sums of the columns, will have the same number of columns as the *voteData* array. In the interest of keeping this example simple, we have assumed that *voteData* has the same number of columns in every row, that is, each candidate was on the ballot in each district. Thus, that number is therefore equal to the number of columns in the first row, *voteData[0].length* (line 35). Row 1, the sum of the rows, will have the same number of columns as the number of rows in the *voteData* array.

In lines 38–45, we loop through the parameter array, computing the sums. We add each element's value to the sum for its column (line 42) and the sum for its row (line 43). When we finish, we return the *returnTally* array to the caller (line 46).

Example 9.10 shows a client program that instantiates a *Tally* object reference and calls the *arrayTally* method.

```
/** Tally votes: the VoteTally class
*   Anderson, Franceschi
*/

public class VoteTally
{
```

```
7    public static void main( String [ ] args )
8    {
9      // votes are for 4 candidates in 6 districts.
10     int [ ][ ] votes = { { 150, 253, 125, 345 },
11                          { 250, 750, 234, 721 },
12                          { 243, 600, 212, 101 },
13                          { 234, 243, 143, 276 },
14                          { 555, 343, 297, 990 },
15                          { 111, 426, 834, 101 } };
16     // candidate names
17     String [ ] candidates = { "Smith", "Jones",
18                               "Berry", "Chase" };
19
20     // instantiate a Tally object reference
21     Tally tally = new Tally( votes );
22
23     // call arrayTally method to count the votes
24     int [ ][ ] voteCounts = tally.arrayTally( );
25
26     // print totals for candidates
27     System.out.println( "Total votes per candidate" );
28     for ( int i = 0; i < candidates.length; i++ )
29       System.out.print( candidates[i] + "\t" );
30     System.out.println( );
31     for ( int j = 0; j < voteCounts[0].length; j++ )
32       System.out.print( voteCounts[0][j] + "\t" );
33     System.out.println( );
34
35     // print totals for districts
36     System.out.println("\nTotal votes per district" );
37     for ( int i = 0; i < voteCounts[1].length; i++ )
38        System.out.print( ( i + 1 ) + "\t" );
39     System.out.println( );
40     for ( int i = 0; i < voteCounts[1].length; i++ )
41        System.out.print( voteCounts[1][i] + "\t" );
42     System.out.println( );
43   }
44 }
```

EXAMPLE 9.10 The *VoteTally* Class

We start by defining our two-dimensional array, *votes*, which holds the votes for each candidate for each district (lines 9–15). Most likely, we would read these values from a file, but for simplicity, we hard-coded the values in

Figure 9.12
Output from Example 9.10

```
Total votes per candidate
Smith    Jones    Berry    Chase
1543     2615     1845     2534

Total votes per district
1      2      3      4      5      6
873    1955   1156   896    2185   1472
```

the initialization list. We also define a single-dimensional array of *Strings*, *candidates*, which holds the candidates' names (lines 16–18). Each name in the *candidates* array corresponds to the column in the *votes* array that holds that candidate's votes.

On lines 20–21, we instantiate the *Tally* object *tally*, passing the two-dimensional array *votes* to the *Tally* overloaded constructor. Notice that for the argument, we use only the array name, *votes*, without brackets.

On line 24, we call the *arrayTally* method, assigning the return value to a two-dimensional array reference named *voteCounts*.

Lines 26–33 print the totals per candidate by printing the elements in row 0 of the returned array, and lines 35–42 print the totals per district by printing the elements in row 1 of the returned array. The output is shown in Figure 9.12.

9.5 Programming Activity 1: Working with Two-Dimensional Arrays

In this activity, you will work with a 4-row, 20-column, two-dimensional array of integers. Specifically, you will write methods to perform the following operations:

1. Fill the array with random numbers between 50 and 80.
2. Print the array.
3. Set every array element of a given row to a specified value. The value is a parameter of a method.
4. Find the minimum value in a given column of the array. The column is a parameter of a method.

5. Count the number of elements of the array having a specified value. The value is a parameter of a method.

The framework for this Programming Activity will animate your algorithm so that you can check the accuracy of your code. For example, Figure 9.13 shows the application counting the elements having the value 56:

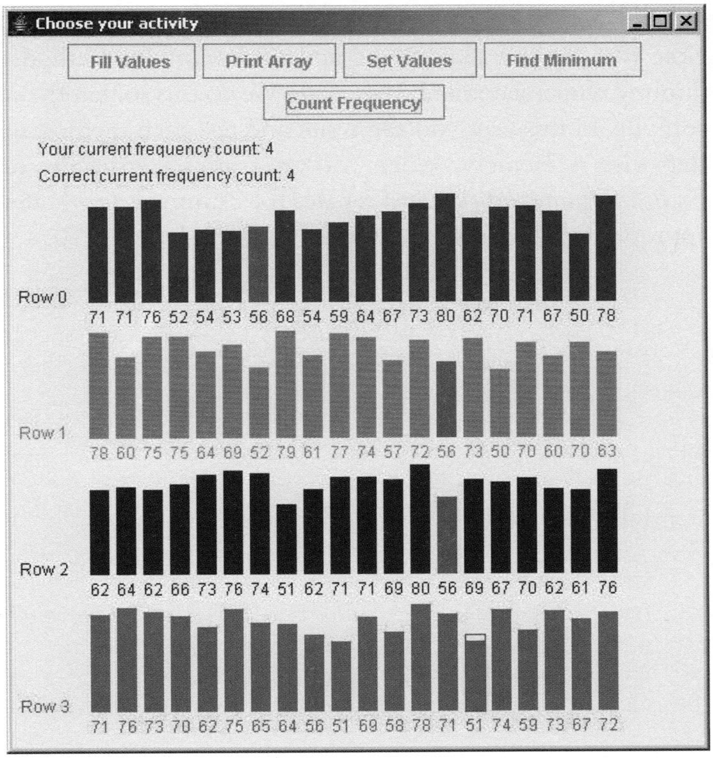

Figure 9.13
Animation of the Programming Activity

At this point, the application has found the value 56 in four array elements: one in each row.

Instructions

In the Chapter 9 Programming Activity 1 directory on the CD-ROM accompanying this book, you will find the source files needed to complete this activity. Copy all the files to a directory on your computer. Note that all files should be in the same directory.

Open the *TwoDimArrayPractice1.java* source file. Searching for five stars (*****) in the source code will position you at the sample method and the four other locations where you will add your code. We have provided the sample code for task number 1, which you can use as a model for completing the other tasks. In every task, you will fill in the code for a method that will manipulate an existing array of 4 rows and 20 columns. You should not instantiate the array; we have done that for you. Example 9.11 shows the section of the *TwoDimArrayPractice1* source code where you will add your code.

Note that for the *countFound* and *findMinimum* methods, we provide a dummy *return* statement: (*return 0;*) We do this so that the source code will compile. In this way, you can write and test each method separately, using step-wise refinement. When you are ready to write the *countFound* and *findMinimum* methods, just replace the dummy *return* statements with the appropriate *return* statement for that method.

```
// ***** 1.  This method has been coded as an example
/** Fills the array with random numbers between 50 and 80
*  The instance variable named intArray is the integer array to be
*  filled with values
*/
public void fillValues( )
{
 for ( int row = 0; row < intArray.length; row++ )
 {
     System.out.print( row + "\t" );
     for ( int column = 0; j < intArray[row].length; column++ )
     {
      intArray[row][column] = ( int ) ( Math.random( ) * 31 ) + 50;
      animate( row, column );  // needed for visual feedback
     }
     System.out.println( );
 }
} // end of fillValues method

// ***** 2.  Student writes this method
/** Prints array to the console, elements are separated by a space
*  The instance variable named intArray is the integer array to be
*  printed
*/
public void printArray( )
```

```
{
 // Note:  To animate the algorithm, put this method call as the
 // last element in your inner for loop
 //            animate( row, column );
 //      where row is the index of the array's current row
 //  and column is the index of the array's current column
 // Write your code here:

} // end of printArray method

// ***** 3.  Student writes this method
/** Sets all the elements in the specified row to the specified value
* The instance variable named intArray is the integer array
*  @param value      the value to assign to the element of the row
*  @param row        the row in which to set the elements to value
*/
public void setValues( int value, int row )
{
 // Note:  To animate the algorithm, put this method call as the
 // last element in your for loop
 //            animate( row, column );
 //      where row is the index of the array's current row
 //      where column is the index of the array's current column
 // Write your code here:

} // end of setValues method

// ***** 4.  Student writes this method
/** Finds minimum value in the specified column
*  The instance variable named intArray is the integer array
*  @param column     the column to search
*  @return           the minimum value found in the column
*/
public int findMinimum( int column )
{
 // Note:  To animate the algorithm, put this method call as the
 // last element in your for loop
 //            animate( row, column, minimum );
 //  where row is the index of the array's current row
 //        column is the index of the array's current column
 //        minimum is the variable storing the current minimum
 // Write your code here:
```

```
 return 0; // replace this line with your return statement

} // end of findMinimumn method

// ***** 5.  Student writes this method
/** Finds the number of times value is found in the array
*  The instance variable named intArray is the integer array
*  @param value      the value to count
*  @return           the number of times value was found
*/
public int countFound( int value )
{
 // Note:  To animate the algorithm, put this method call as the
 // last element in your inner for loop
 //          animate( row, column, num );
 // where row is the index of the array's current row
 //       column is the index of the array's current column
 //       num is the local variable storing the current frequency
 //        count
 // Write your code here:


 return 0;  // replace this line with your return statement

}
// end of countFound method
```

EXAMPLE 9.11 Location of Student Code in *TwoDimArrayPractice1*

The framework will animate your algorithm so that you can watch your code work. For this to happen, be sure that your single or nested *for* loops call the method *animate*. The arguments that you send to *animate* are not always the same and the location of the call to *animate* will differ depending on the task you are coding. Detailed instructions for each task are included in the code.

To test your code, compile and run the *TwoDimArrayPractice1* source code. Figure 9.14 shows the graphics window when the program begins. Because the values of the array are randomly generated, the values will be different each time the program runs. To test any method, click on the appropriate button.

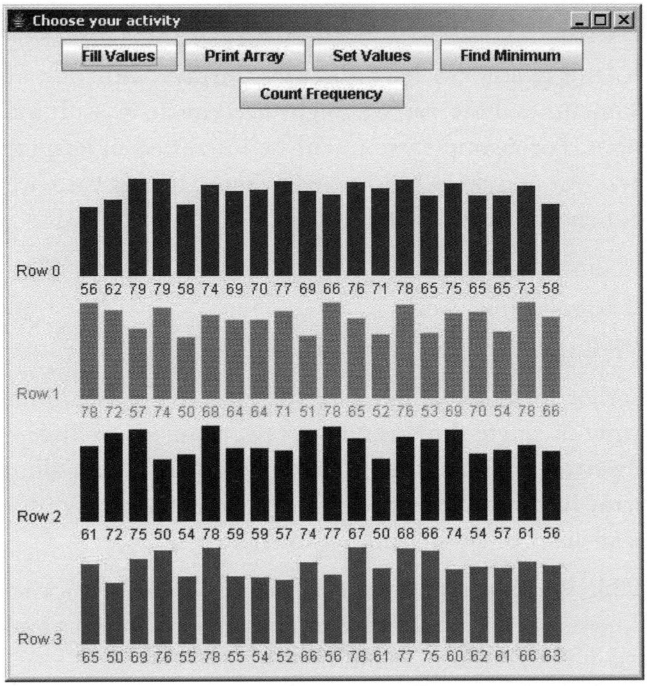

Figure 9.14
The Graphics Window When the Application Begins

Troubleshooting

If your method implementation does not animate, check these tips:

- Verify that the last statement in your single *for* loop or inner *for* loop is a call to the *animate* method and that you passed the appropriate arguments. For example:

```
animate( row, column );
```

- Verify that your exit conditions for your *for* loops are correct. Sometimes the exit condition depends on the length of the array (i.e., the number of rows in the array), and sometimes it depends on the number of columns in the current row of the array.

? DISCUSSION QUESTIONS

1. With a two-dimensional array, for which operations would you use nested *for* loops and for which operations would you use a single *for* loop?
2. When performing an operation on a given row, which index is fixed and which index is used as the looping variable? When performing an operation on a given column, which index is fixed and which index is used as the looping variable?

9.6 Other Multidimensional Arrays

To this point, we have discussed arrays with one and two dimensions. Sometimes, however, we might need an array with more than two dimensions. For example, we might be interested in keeping track of sales on a per-year, per-week, and per-day basis. In this case, we would use a three-dimensional array as follows:

1st dimension: year

2nd dimension: week

3rd dimension: day of the week

Earlier in this chapter, we explained that a two-dimensional array is an array of single-dimensional arrays. Similarly, a three-dimensional array is an array of two-dimensional arrays. And a four-dimensional array is an array of three-dimensional arrays. More generally, an *n*-dimensional array is an array of $(n - 1)$-dimensional arrays.

Table 9.3 shows how an *n*-dimensional array is structured dimension by dimension; $i_1, i_2, \ldots, i_n$ are used as generic indexes for the first dimension, second dimension, ..., and n^{th} dimensions.

If we keep track of sales over a period of 10 years, then we would have a 10-by-52-by-7 array. The principles discussed for a two-dimensional array still

TABLE 9.3 Structure of an *n*-Dimensional Array

Dimension	Array Element
first	$arrayName[i_1]$ is an (n − 1)-dimensional array
second	$arrayName[i_1][i_2]$ is an (n − 2)-dimensional array
k^{th}	$arrayName[i_1][i_2][i_3][..][i_k]$ is an (n − k) multi-dimensional array
$(n - 2)^{th}$	$arrayName[i_1][i_2][i_3][..][i_{n-2}]$ is a two-dimensional array
$(n - 1)^{th}$	$arrayName[i_1][i_2][i_3][..][i_{n-1}]$ is a single-dimensional array
n^{th}	$arrayName[i_1][i_2][i_3][..][i_{n-1}][i_n]$ is an array element

apply; we just have three dimensions instead of two. The following code sequence illustrates how to declare, instantiate, and access elements of this three-dimensional array:

```
double [ ][ ][ ] sales;              // declare a three-dimensional array

sales = new double [10][52][7];      // instantiate the array

sales[0][0][0] = 638.50;             // access the first element

sales[4][22][3] = 928.20;            // access another element

sales[9][51][6] = 1234.90;           // access the last element
```

To process elements of a single-dimensional array, we use a simple *for* loop; for a two-dimensional array, we use a double *for* loop. For a three-dimensional array, we use a triple *for* loop.

The general pattern for processing elements in a three-dimensional array is

```
for ( int i = 0; i < arrayName.length; i++ )
{
   for ( int j = 0; j < arrayName[i].length; j++ )
   {
      for ( int k = 0; k < arrayName[i][j].length; k++ )
      {
         // access and process the element arrayName[i][j][k]
      }
   }
}
```

The following code sequence will print the elements of the three-dimensional array *sales*:

```
for ( int i = 0; i < sales.length; i++ )
{
   for ( int j = 0; j < sales[i].length; j++ )
   {
      for ( int k = 0; k < sales[i][j].length; k++ )
      {
         // access the element at sales[i][j][k]
         System.out.println( sales[i][j][k] + "\t" );
      }
      // skip a line when second dimension index changes
      System.out.println( );
```

```
   }
   // skip a line when first dimension index changes
   System.out.println( );
}
```

If we are interested in keeping track of sales on a state-by-state basis, we can use a four-dimensional array as follows:

1st dimension: state

2nd dimension: year

3rd dimension: week

4th dimension: day of the week

The following code sequence illustrates how to declare, instantiate, and access the elements of such a four-dimensional array:

```
double [ ][ ][ ][ ] stateSales;              // declare a four-dimensional
                                             // array

stateSales = new double [50][10][52][7];     // instantiate the array

stateSales[0][0][0][0] = 58.50;              // access the first element

sales[34][4][22][3] = 98.30;                 // access another element

sales[49][9][51][6] = 137.70;                // access the last element
```

To process elements of a four-dimensional array, we use a quadruple *for* loop. That quadruple *for* loop pattern parallels the ones for the two-dimensional and three-dimensional arrays. For a four-dimensional array called *arrayName*, it is:

```
for ( int i = 0; i < arrayName.length; i++ )
{
    for ( int j = 0; j < arrayName[i].length; j++ )
    {
       for ( int k = 0; k < arrayName[i][j].length; k++ )
       {
          for ( int l = 0; l < arrayName[i][j][k].length; l++ )
          {
             // process element arrayName[i][j][k][l]
          }
       }
    }
}
```

9.7 The *ArrayList* Class

As we have seen, single-dimensional and multidimensional arrays are useful in many situations. However, they have limitations.

Let's say you are designing a search engine for a large website, for example, an online bookstore. The user will type a word in a text field box, your code will access a database, retrieve all the books with titles that contain this word, and return them to the user.

We could store the book information in an array of books. One problem, however, is that we don't know how many books we will have. There could be 3, 32, 500, or 5,000 books, or maybe even more. Without knowing the number of books, we do not know what size to make the array. The safest bet would be to create the array with the maximum possible number of elements, that is, the maximum number of books that we anticipate. If we actually have fewer books than we anticipated, however, we will waste space.

If we end up with more books than we anticipated, we would need to increase the size of an array. As we demonstrated in Chapter 8, changing the size of an array is a tedious process. We will have to instantiate a new array and copy the elements of the original array to the new array.

The *ArrayList* class, in the *java.util* package, solves these problems. An *ArrayList* object automatically expands its capacity as needed. The *ArrayList* class uses **generics**. Generics are **parameterized types**, meaning that the data type will be defined at the time a client class declares and instantiates an object of the class. Generics allow programmers to design and code classes that use objects without specifying the class—or data type—of the object.

REFERENCE POINT

Wrapper classes are explained in Chapter 3, along with the concepts of autoboxing and unboxing.

Thus, for example, we could have an *ArrayList* of *Book* objects, an *ArrayList* of *Auto* objects, or an *ArrayList* of *Strings*. The specified type must be a class, not a primitive type. If we want to store primitive data types in an *ArrayList*, then we need to use one of the wrapper classes such as *Integer*, *Double*, or *Character*.

The *ArrayList* class, and more generally a class using generics, can be used for many purposes. This is another facet of object-oriented programming that allows programmers to reuse code. In Chapter 14, we will discuss how to design a user-defined class using generics. In this chapter, we will focus on how to use the *ArrayList* class.

Because the *ArrayList* class is in the *java.util* package, programs using an *ArrayList* object will need to provide the following *import* statement:

```
import java.util.ArrayList;
```

9.7.1 Declaring and Instantiating *ArrayList* Objects

Here is the syntax for declaring an *ArrayList* of objects:

```
ArrayList<ClassName> arrayListName;
```

Inside the brackets, we declare the class type of the objects that will be stored in the *ArrayList*. A space is optional between the *ArrayList* class name and the opening bracket.

For example, these two statements declare an *ArrayList* of *Strings* and an *ArrayList* of *Auto* objects:

```
ArrayList<String> listOfStrings;
ArrayList<Auto> listOfCars;
```

If you try to declare an *ArrayList* object reference using a primitive data type instead of a class type, as in

```
ArrayList<int> listOfInts;
```

you will get this compiler error:

```
Test.java:7: unexpected type
found   : int
required: reference
  ArrayList<int> listOfInts;
           ^
1 error
```

Two constructors of the *ArrayList* class are shown in Table 9.4.

TABLE 9.4 *ArrayList* Constructors

ArrayList Constructor Summary
Constructor name and argument list
`ArrayList<ClassName>( )`
constructs an *ArrayList* object of *ClassName* type with an initial capacity of 10
`ArrayList<ClassName>( int initialCapacity )`
constructs an *ArrayList* object of *ClassName* type with the specified initial capacity

If you know how many elements you will store in the *ArrayList* object, you can use the overloaded constructor to specify the initial capacity; otherwise, simply use the default constructor. As you add elements to the *ArrayList* object, its capacity will increase automatically, as needed.

Here is the syntax for instantiating an *ArrayList* using the default constructor:

```
arrayListName = new ArrayList<ClassName>( );
```

where *ClassName* is the class type of the objects that will be stored in the *ArrayList* and *arrayListName* has been declared previously as an *ArrayList* reference for that class.

These statements will instantiate the *ArrayList* objects declared earlier, with an initial capacity of 10:

```
listOfStrings = new ArrayList<String>( );
listOfCars = new ArrayList<Auto>( );
```

If you try to instantiate an *ArrayList* object without specifying the object type, as in

```
listOfCars = new ArrayList( );
```

you will get the following warning from the compiler:

```
. . .

Test.java:11: warning: [unchecked] unchecked conversion
found   : java.util.ArrayList
required: java.util.ArrayList<Auto>
     listOfCars = new ArrayList();
                  ^
1 warning
```

In *ArrayLists*, there is a distinction between capacity and size. The **capacity** of an *ArrayList* is the number of elements allocated to the list. The **size** is the number of those elements that are filled with objects. Thus, when you instantiate an *ArrayList* using the default constructor, its capacity is 10, but its size is 0. In other words, the *ArrayList* has room for 10 objects, but no objects are currently stored in the list.

These statements will declare, then instantiate, an *ArrayList* of *Astronaut* objects with an initial capacity of 5, using the overloaded constructor:

```
ArrayList<Astronaut> listOfAstronauts1;
listOfAstronauts1 = new ArrayList<Astronaut>( 5 );
```

In this case, the capacity of *listOfAstronauts1* is 5 and its size is 0.

We can also combine the declaration and instantiation of an *ArrayList* object into one statement. Here is the syntax using the default constructor:

```
ArrayList<ClassName> arrayListName = new ArrayList<ClassName>( );
```

These statements will declare and instantiate two *ArrayList* objects, *Integers* and *Astronauts*, respectively:

```
ArrayList<Integer> listOfInts = new ArrayList<Integer>( );
ArrayList<Astronaut> listOfAstronauts2 = new ArrayList<Astronaut>( );
```

9.7.2 Methods of the *ArrayList* Class

Like arrays, the *ArrayList* class uses indexes to refer to elements. Among others, it provides methods that provide the following functions:

- add an item at the end of the list
- replace an item at a given index
- remove an item at a given index
- remove all the items in the list
- search the list for a specific item
- retrieve an item at a given index
- retrieve the index of a given item
- check to see if the list is empty
- return the number of items in the list, that is, its size
- optimize the capacity of the list by setting its capacity to the number of items in the list

Some of the most useful methods are shown in Table 9.5. Note that some of the method headers include *E* as their return type or parameter data type (as opposed to a class name or simply the *Object* class). *E* represents the data type of the *ArrayList*. Thus, for an *ArrayList* of *Integer* objects, *E* is an *Integer*; and the *get* method, for example, returns an *Integer* object. Similarly, for an *ArrayList* of *Auto* objects, *E* is an *Auto* object. In this case, the *get* method returns an *Auto* object.

TABLE 9.5 *ArrayList* Methods

Useful Methods of the *ArrayList* Class	
Return value	**Method name and argument list**
`boolean`	`add( E element )` appends the specified *element* to the end of the list
`void`	`clear( )` removes all the elements from this list
`int`	`size( )` returns the number of elements in this list
`E`	`remove( int index )` removes and returns the element at the specified *index* position in the list
`E`	`get( int index )` returns the element at the specified *index* position in the list; the element is not removed from the list
`E`	`set( int index, E element )` replaces the element at the specified *index* position in this list with the specified *element*
`void`	`trimToSize( )` sets the capacity to the list's current size

9.7.3 Looping Through an *ArrayList* Using an Enhanced *for* Loop

The general pattern for processing elements of an *ArrayList* of *ClassName* objects called *arrayListName* using a *for* loop is

```
ClassName currentObject;
for ( int i = 0; i < arrayListName.size( ); i++ )
{
      currentObject = arrayListName.get( i );
      // process currentObject
}
```

For instance, to process elements of an *ArrayList* of *Auto* object references called *listOfAutos* using a standard *for* loop, the general pattern is:

```
Auto currentAuto;
for ( int i = 0; i < listOfAutos.size( ); i++ )
{
      currentAuto = listOfAutos.get( i );
      // process currentAuto
}
```

Java provides a simplified way to process the elements of an *ArrayList*, called the **enhanced *for* loop**. The general pattern for processing elements of an *ArrayList* of *ClassName* objects called *arrayListName* using the enhanced *for* loop is:

```
for ( ClassName currentObject : arrayListName )
{
      // process currentObject
}
```

A variable of the class type of the objects stored in the *ArrayList* is declared in the enhanced *for* loop header, followed by a colon and name of the *ArrayList*. The enhanced *for* loop enables looping through the *ArrayList* objects automatically. Your code does not call the *get* method; inside the body of the loop, *currentObject* is directly available for processing.

For example, to process elements of an *ArrayList* of *Autos* called *cars* using the enhanced *for* loop, the general pattern is:

```
for ( Auto currentAuto : cars )
{
    // process currentAuto
}
```

Example 9.12 shows how to create and use an *ArrayList* of *Integers*. Line 11 declares and instantiates the *ArrayList* object reference *list* using the default constructor. Three elements are added to *list* using the *add* method at lines 12–14. As the argument to the *add* method, we use *Integer* object references at lines 12 and 13, and an *int* at line 14. As we explained in Chapter 3, the autoboxing feature of Java eliminates the need to convert an *int* to an *Inte-*

ger object. This is done automatically when an *int* variable is used where an *Integer* object is expected.

After an *ArrayList* object has been declared and instantiated as being of a certain class type, you cannot add an object of a different class type. For example, the statement

```
list.add ( new Double ( 6.7 ) );
```

would produce the following compiler error:

```
ArrayListOfIntegers.java:15: cannot find symbol
symbol  : method add(java.lang.Double)
location: class java.util.ArrayList<java.lang.Integer>
  list.add( new Double( 6.7 ) );
      ^
1 error
```

At lines 17–18, we print the elements of *list* using a traditional *for* loop, using the *get* method to retrieve the element at the current index. At lines 22–23, we use the enhanced *for* loop to print the elements. At lines 27–28, we also use the enhanced *for* loop to print the elements; but this time, we use an *int* as the looping variable, using the unboxing feature of Java, which converts *Integer* objects to *int* values, as needed. At line 31, we use the *set* method to change the value of the element at index 1 to 100, also using autoboxing. At line 37, we use the *remove* method to delete the element at index 0 and assign it to the variable *removed*, using unboxing again.

The output of this example is shown in Figure 9.15.

```
1 /* A Simple ArrayList of Integers
2    Anderson, Franceschi
3 */
4
5 import java.util.ArrayList;
6
7 public class ArrayListOfIntegers
8 {
```

```
public static void main( String [ ] args )
{
 ArrayList<Integer> list = new ArrayList<Integer>( );
 list.add( new Integer( 34 ) );
 list.add( new Integer( 89 ) );
 list.add( 65 ); // autoboxing

 System.out.println( "Using the traditional for loop:" );
 for ( int i = 0; i < list.size( ); i++ )
    System.out.print( list.get( i ) + "\t" );
 System.out.println( );

 System.out.println( "\nUsing the enhanced for loop:" );
 for ( Integer currentInteger : list )
    System.out.print( currentInteger + "\t" );
 System.out.println( );

 System.out.println( "\nUsing unboxing and enhanced for loop:" );
 for ( int currentInt : list ) // unboxing
    System.out.print( currentInt + "\t" );
 System.out.println( );

 list.set( 1, 100 );
 System.out.println( "\nAfter calling set( 1, 100 ):" );
 for ( int currentInt : list ) // unboxing
    System.out.print( currentInt + "\t" );
 System.out.println( );

 int removed = list.remove( 0 );
 System.out.println( "\nAt index 0, " + removed + " was removed" );
 System.out.println( "\nAfter removing the element at index 0:" );
 for ( int currentInt : list ) // unboxing
    System.out.print( currentInt + "\t" );
 System.out.println( );
}
}
```

EXAMPLE 9.12 Using *ArrayList* Methods

```
Using the traditional for loop:
34    89    65

Using the enhanced for loop:
34    89    65

Using unboxing and enhanced for loop:
34    89    65

After calling set( 1, 100 ):
34    100   65

At index 0, 34 was removed

After removing the element at index 0:
100   65
```

Figure 9.15
Output of Example 9.12

9.7.4 Using the *ArrayList* Class in a Program

Now let's see how we can use the *ArrayList* class in a Java program. Going back to our example of a bookstore and a search engine, we want to design and code a simple program that enables users to search for books.

We will have three classes in this program:

- a *Book* class, encapsulating the concept of a book
- a *BookStore* class, encapsulating the concept of a bookstore
- a *BookSearchEngine* class, including the *main* method, which provides the user interface.

In the interest of keeping things simple, our *Book* class will contain only three instance variables: the book title, which is a *String*; the book's author, which is also a *String*; and the book price, which is a *double*.

Example 9.13 shows a simplified *Book* class with constructors, accessor methods, and a *toString* method.

```
/* Book class
   Anderson, Franceschi
*/

public class Book
{
 private String title;
 private String author;
 private double price;

 /** default constructor
 */
 public Book( )
 {
  title = "";
  author = "";
  price  = 0.0;
 }

 /** overloaded constructor
 *  @param newTitle   the value to assign to title
 *  @param newAuthor  the value to assign to author
 *  @param newPrice   the value to assign to price
 */
 public Book( String newTitle, String newAuthor, double newPrice )
 {
  title = newTitle;
  author = newAuthor;
  price  = newPrice;
 }

 /** getTitle method
 *   @return the title
 */
 public String getTitle( )
 {
  return title;
 }

 /** getAuthor method
 *   @return the author
 */
 public String getAuthor( )
 {
```

```
  return author;
 }

 /** getPrice method
 *   @return the price
 */
 public double getPrice( )
 {
  return price;
 }

 /** toString
 * @return title, author, and price
 */
 public String toString( )
 {
  return ( "title: " + title + "\t"
           + "author: " + author + "\t"
           + "price: " + price );
 }
}
```

EXAMPLE 9.13 The *Book* Class

Our *BookStore* class, shown in Example 9.14, will simply have one instance variable: an *ArrayList* of *Book* objects, representing the collection of books in the bookstore, which we name *library*.

In most cases, when an *ArrayList* is filled with data, that data will come from a database or a file. In the interest of focusing on the *ArrayList* class and its methods, we have hard-coded the objects for the *ArrayList library* in the *BookStore* class, rather than reading them from a database or a file.

In the default constructor (lines 11 to 24), we instantiate the *library* instance variable, then add six *Book* objects to *library* using the *add* method from the *ArrayList* class. At line 23, we call the *trimToSize* method to set the capacity of *library* to its current size, which is 6, in order to minimize the memory resources used.

The *toString* method is coded from lines 26 to 37. It generates and returns a *String* representing all the books in *library*, one book per line. In order to do that, we use an enhanced *for* loop from lines 32 to 35. The header of that loop, at line 32, follows the general pattern of the enhanced *for* loop header by declaring a *Book* variable named *tempBook*, followed by a colon, followed by *library*, the *ArrayList* object to loop through.

The *searchForTitle* method, coded from lines 39 to 53, performs the task of searching for a keyword within the title of each *Book* object stored in *library*. The keyword, a *String*, is the parameter of the method and is named *searchString*. This method returns an *ArrayList* of *Book* objects. We create another *ArrayList* of *Books*, which we name *searchResult* at line 45 and loop through *library* using an enhanced *for* loop from lines 46 to 50. Inside the body of the loop, we use the *indexOf* method of the *String* class to test if the current *Book* object contains the keyword *searchString* in its *title* instance variable. If it does, we add that *Book* object to *searchResult*. Finally, we call the method *trimToSize* to set the capacity of *searchResult* to the current number of elements, then return the *ArrayList* to the caller.

```
 1 /*  BookStore class
 2     Anderson, Franceschi
 3 */
 4
 5 import java.util.ArrayList;
 6
 7 public class BookStore
 8 {
 9  private ArrayList<Book> library;
10
11  /** default constructor
12  *   instantiates ArrayList of Books
13  */
14  public BookStore( )
15  {
16   library = new ArrayList<Book>( );
17   library.add( new Book( "Intro to Java", "James", 56.99 ) );
18   library.add( new Book( "Advanced Java", "Green", 65.99 ) );
19   library.add( new Book( "Java Servlets", "Brown", 75.99 ) );
20   library.add( new Book( "Intro to HTML", "James", 29.49 ) );
21   library.add( new Book( "Intro to Flash", "James", 34.99 ) );
22   library.add( new Book( "Advanced HTML", "Green", 56.99 ) );
23   library.trimToSize( );
24  }
25
26  /** toString
27  *  @return  each book in library, one per line
28  */
29  public String toString( )
30  {
31   String result = "";
```

```
  for( Book tempBook : library )
  {
    result += tempBook.toString( ) + "\n";
  }
  return result;
}

/** Generates list of books containing searchString
*  @param searchString    the keyword to search for
*  @return         the ArrayList of books containing the keyword
*/
public ArrayList<Book> searchForTitle( String searchString )
{
  ArrayList<Book> searchResult = new ArrayList<Book>( );
  for ( Book currentBook : library )
  {
   if ( ( currentBook.getTitle( ) ).indexOf( searchString ) != -1 )
        searchResult.add( currentBook );
  }
  searchResult.trimToSize( );
  return searchResult;
 }
}
```

EXAMPLE 9.14 The *BookStore* Class

Our *BookSearchEngine* class, shown in Example 9.15, contains the *main* method: it creates a *BookStore* object, asks the user for a keyword, and searches for partial matches in our *BookStore* object.

A *BookStore* object, *bs*, is declared and instantiated at line 12. At lines 14–15, the user is then prompted for a keyword that will be used to search for books whose title contains that keyword. Lines 16 and 17 simply output the collection of *Books* in the *BookStore* object *bs*; later, when the search results are output, we can compare that output to the original list of *Books* to check our results. At line 19, we call the *searchForTitle* method with *keyword* as its argument; the *ArrayList* of *Book* objects returned is assigned to the variable *results*. At lines 23–24, we loop through *results* and output its contents, again using the enhanced *for* loop. Figure 9.16 shows a run of the program with the user searching for books containing the word "Java."

```
1 /* BookSearchEngine class
2    Anderson, Franceschi
3 */
4
5 import java.util.ArrayList;
```

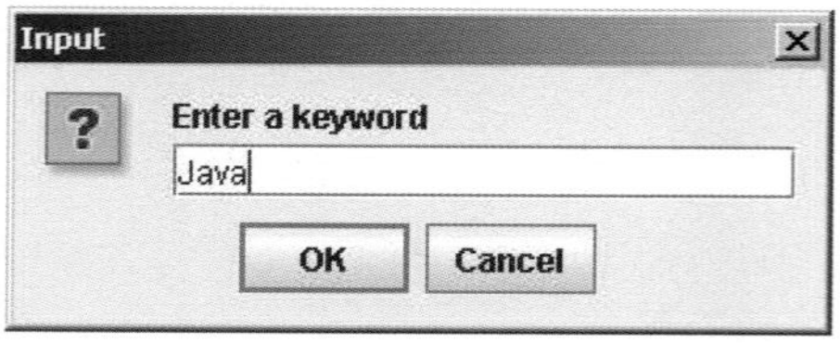

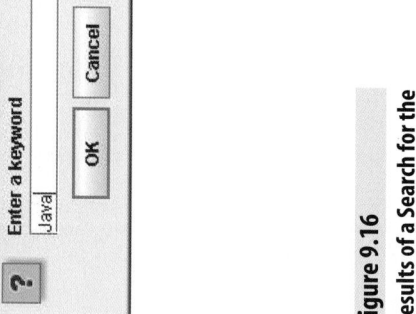

```
Our book collection is:
title: Intro to Java      author: James    price: 56.99
title: Advanced Java      author: Green    price: 65.99
title: Java Servlets      author: Brown    price: 75.99
title: Intro to HTML      author: James    price: 29.49
title: Intro to Flash     author: James    price: 34.99
title: Advanced HTML      author: Green    price: 56.99

The search results for Java are:
title: Intro to Java      author: James    price: 56.99
title: Advanced Java      author: Green    price: 65.99
title: Java Servlets      author: Brown    price: 75.99
```

Figure 9.16
Results of a Search for the Keyword "Java"

```java
import javax.swing.JOptionPane;

public class BookSearchEngine
{
 public static void main( String [ ] args )
 {
  BookStore bs = new BookStore( );

  String keyword = JOptionPane.showInputDialog( null,
                     "Enter a keyword" );
  System.out.println( "Our book collection is:" );
  System.out.println( bs.toString( ) );

  ArrayList<Book> results = bs.searchForTitle( keyword );

  System.out.println( "The search results for " + keyword
                      + " are:" );
  for( Book tempBook : results )
        System.out.println( tempBook.toString( ) );
 }
}
```

EXAMPLE 9.15 A Search Engine for Books

CODE IN ACTION

To see a step-by-step illustration showing how to use the *ArrayList* class, look for the Flash movie on the CD-ROM included with this book. Click on the link for Chapter 9 to start the movie.

9.8 Programming Activity 2: Working with the *ArrayList* Class

In this activity, you will work with an *ArrayList* object. Specifically, you will write the code to perform the following operations:

1. Fill the *ArrayList* object with *Auto* elements.
2. Print the *Auto* elements contained in the *ArrayList* object.
3. Set the *model* instance variable of every *Auto* element in the *ArrayList* object to a specified model.
4. Find the maximum number of miles of all *Auto* elements contained in the *ArrayList* object.
5. Count the number of *Auto* elements in the *ArrayList* objects with a specified model.

The framework for this Programming Activity will animate your algorithm so that you can check the accuracy of your code. For example, Figure 9.17 shows the application counting the number of *Auto* elements in the *ArrayList* object having a model value equal to "Ferrari." The application accesses each element in the *ArrayList* in order, checking the *model* for the desired value, "Ferrari." At this point, the current element being accessed is a *BMW* and the application has found two *Auto* elements with the *model* value, "Ferrari."

Instructions

In the Chapter 9 Programming Activity 2 directory on the CD-ROM accompanying this book, you will find the source files needed to complete this activity. Copy all the files to a directory on your computer. Note that all files should be in the same directory.

Figure 9.17
Animation of the Programming Activity

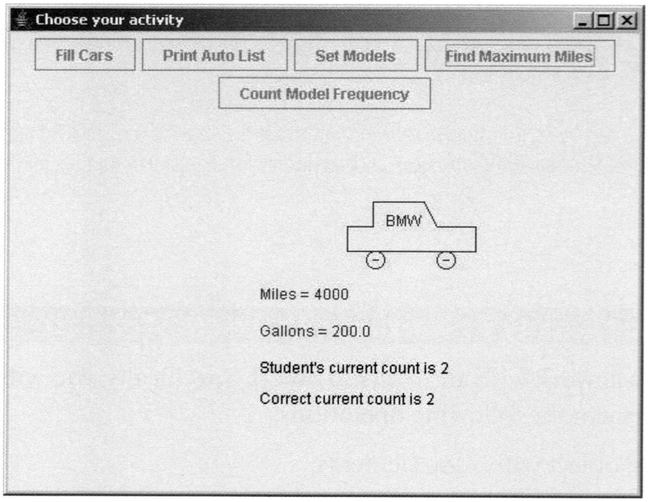

Open the *ArrayListPractice.java* source file. Searching for five stars (*****) in the source code will position you to the sample method and the four other locations where you will add your code. We have provided the sample code for task number 1. In every task, you will fill in the code for a method that will manipulate an existing *ArrayList* of *Auto* elements. You should not instantiate the *ArrayList* object; we have done that for you. Example 9.16 shows the section of the *ArrayListPractice* source code where you will add your code.

Note that for the *countFound* and *findMaximumMilesDriven* methods, we provide a dummy *return* statement (*return 0;*). We do this so that the source code will compile. In this way, you can write and test each method separately, using step-wise refinement. When you are ready to write the *countFound* and *findMaximumMilesDriven* methods, just replace the dummy *return* statements with the appropriate *return* statement for that method.

```
// ***** 1.  This method has been coded as an example
/** Fills the carList with hard-coded Auto objects
*    The instance variable carList is the ArrayList
*        to be filled with Auto objects
*/
public void fillWithCars( )
{
  // clear carList before adding cars
  carList.clear( );
  // Reset the number of Autos to 0
```

```
    // This is needed so that the animation feedback works correctly
    Auto.clearNumberAutos( );

    Auto car1 = new Auto( "BMW", 0, 0.0 );
    Auto car2 = new Auto( "Ferrari", 100, 500.0 );
    Auto car3 = new Auto( "Jeep", 1000, 90.0 );
    Auto car4 = new Auto( "Ferrari", 10, 3.0 );
    Auto car5 = new Auto( "BMW", 4000, 200.0 );
    Auto car6 = new Auto( "Ferrari", 1000, 50.0 );

    carList.add( car1 );
    carList.add( car2 );
    carList.add( car3 );
    carList.add( car4 );
    carList.add( car5 );
    carList.add( car6 );
    animate( );
  }
  // end of fillWithCars method

  // ***** 2.  Student writes this method
  /**  Prints carList to console, elements are separated by a space
  *    The instance variable carList is the ArrayList to be printed
  */
  public void printAutoList( )
  {
   // Note:  To animate the algorithm, put this method call as the
   // last statement in your for loop
   //             animate( car );
   //  where car is the variable name for the current Auto object
   //  as you loop through the ArrayList object
   // Write your code here:

  }
  // end of printAutoList method

  // ***** 3.  Student writes this method
  /** Sets the model of all the elements in carList to parameter value
  * The instance variable carList is the ArrayList to be modified
  *  @param model the model to assign to all Auto objects in carList
  */
  public void setModelValues( String model )
  {
   // Note:  To animate the algorithm, put this method call as the
   // last statement in your for loop
   //            animate( car );
   //  where car is the variable name for the current Auto object
   //  as you loop through the ArrayList object
```

```
  // Write your code here:

 }
 // end of setModelValues method

 // ***** 4.  Student writes this method
 /** Finds maximum number of miles driven
 *   Instance variable carList is the ArrayList to search
 *  @return     the maximum miles driven by all the Auto objects
 */
 public int findMaximumMilesDriven( )
 {
  // Note:  To animate the algorithm, put this method call as the
  // last statement in your for loop
  //            animate( car, maximum );
  //  where car is the variable name for the current Auto object
  //  and maximum is the int variable storing the current maximum
  //  number of miles for all Auto elements you have already tested
  //  as you loop through the ArrayList object
  // Write your code here:

   return 0; // replace this statement with your return statement

 }
 // end of findMaximumMilesDriven method

 // ***** 5.  Student writes this method
 /** Finds number of times parameter model is found in the carList
 *   Instance variable carList is the ArrayList in which we search
 *  @param model      the model to count
 *  @return           the number of times model was found
 */
 public int countFound( String model )
 {
  // Note:  To animate the algorithm, put this method call as the
  // last statement in your for loop
  //            animate( car, num );
  //  where car is the variable name for the current Auto object
  //  and num is the int variable storing the current number of
  //  Auto elements whose model is equal to the method's parameter
  //  as you loop through the ArrayList object
  // Write your code here:

   return 0; // replace this statement with your return statement

 }
 // end of countFound method
```

EXAMPLE 9.16 Location of Student Code in *ArrayListPractice*

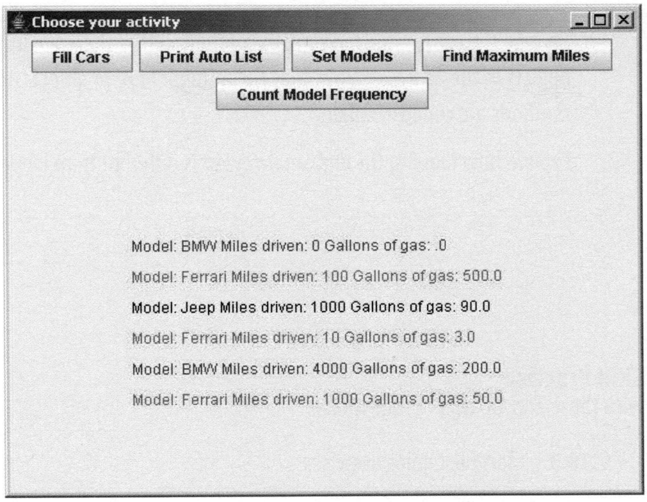

Figure 9.18
The Graphics Window When the Application Begins

The framework will animate your code so that you can watch it work. For this to happen, be sure that your *for* loops call the *animate* method. The arguments that you send to *animate* are not always the same, but the location of the call to *animate* is always the same, that is, the last statement of your *for* loop. Detailed instructions for each task are included in the code.

To test your code, compile and run the *ArrayPractice* source code. Figure 9.18 shows the graphics window when the program begins. Because the *Auto* elements of the *ArrayList* object are hard coded, the values will be the same each time the program runs. To test any method, click on the appropriate button.

Troubleshooting

If your method implementation does not animate, check these tips:

- Verify that the last statement in your single *for* loop or inner *for* loop is a call to the *animate* method and that you passed the loop variable(s) as the argument(s), as in the following:

```
animate( car );              // or
animate( car, maximum );     // or
animate( car, num );
```

- Verify that the headers of your *for* loops are correct. It should always be the same.
- Verify that you update the variables *maximum* and *num* correctly.

DISCUSSION QUESTIONS ?

1. Change the code in the *fillWithCars* method so that there are more or fewer *Auto* objects in the *ArrayList*. How does the number of *Auto* objects impact how the other methods are coded? Explain.
2. Explain how looping through an *ArrayList* is different from looping through an array.

Skill Practice
with these end-of-chapter questions

9.10.1 Multiple Choice Exercises

Questions 9,10,11,12,13

9.10.2 Reading and Understanding Code

Questions 29,30,31,32

9.10.3 Fill In the Code

Questions 46,47,48,49

9.10.4 Identifying Errors in Code

Questions 55,56,57,58

9.10.5 Debugging Area

Questions 63,64

9.10.6 Write a Short Program

Questions 80,81,82

9.10.8 Technical Writing

Question 95

9.9 Chapter Summary

- Arrays can be single-dimensional, two-dimensional, three-dimensional, or more generally *n*-dimensional.
- In a two-dimensional array, each row is an array.
- Each element in a two-dimensional array is accessed using the array name, a row index, and a column index that refer to the element's position in the array.
- Concepts such as declaration, instantiation, initial values, indexing, and aggregate operations from single-dimensional arrays also apply to two-dimensional arrays.
- Two-dimensional arrays can be instantiated by assigning initial values in a comma-separated list of comma-separated lists at the declaration.
- Each row in a two-dimensional array can have a different number of columns.
- A two-dimensional array has an instance variable, *length*, which holds the number of rows in the array.
- Each row of a two-dimensional array has an instance variable, *length*, which holds the number of elements in that row.
- The *ArrayList* class implements generics and is part of the *java.util* package.
- An *ArrayList* can be thought of as an expandable single-dimensional array of objects.
- To define an *ArrayList* to hold elements of primitive data types, use the wrapper classes.
- An *ArrayList* object expands automatically as needed as objects are added.
- We access an element of an *ArrayList* via its index.
- We can process each element in an *ArrayList* using the enhanced *for* loop.

9.10 Exercises, Problems, and Projects

9.10.1 Multiple Choice Exercises

1. What is/are the valid way(s) to declare a two-dimensional integer array named *a*? (Check all that apply.)
   - ❑ `int [ ][ ] a;`
   - ❑ `int a [ ][ ];`
   - ❑ `array [ ] int a;`
   - ❑ `int array [ ] a;`
2. A two-dimensional array is an array of arrays.
   - ❑ true
   - ❑ false
3. In a two-dimensional array, every row must have the same number of columns.
   - ❑ true
   - ❑ false
4. What is the default value of the elements of a two-dimensional array of *booleans* after declaration and instantiation of the array?
   - ❑ *true*
   - ❑ *false*
   - ❑ undefined
5. How do you access the element of array *a* located at row 2 and column 4?
   - ❑ `a{2}{4}`
   - ❑ `a( 2,4 )`
   - ❑ `a[2][4]`
   - ❑ `a[4][2]`
6. How do you retrieve the number of rows in a two-dimensional array *a*?
   - ❑ `a.rows`
   - ❑ `a.length`
   - ❑ `a.rows( )`
   - ❑ `a.size`

7. How do you retrieve the number of columns in row 2 in a two-dimensional array *a*?

   ❑ `a.length`

   ❑ `a[2].length`

   ❑ `a.size`

   ❑ `a[2].size`

8. All the elements of a two-dimensional array must be of the same type.

   ❑ true

   ❑ false

9. An *ArrayList* can be returned by a method.

   ❑ true

   ❑ false

10. It is possible to declare and instantiate an *ArrayList* of a user-defined class type.

   ❑ true

   ❑ false

11. As we add objects to an *ArrayList*, how can we be sure it has enough capacity?

   ❑ Use the *setCapacity* method.

   ❑ Use the *trimToSize* method.

   ❑ We don't need to do anything; capacity expands automatically as needed.

12. Where does the *add* method of the *ArrayList* class add an object?

   ❑ at the beginning of the list.

   ❑ at the end of the list.

13. To what package does the class *ArrayList* belong?

   ❑ *java.io*

   ❑ *java.util*

- ❑ *java.array*
- ❑ *java.list*

9.10.2 Reading and Understanding Code

For Questions 14 to 24, consider the following two-dimensional array declaration and initialization:

```
String [ ][ ] cities = { { "New York", "LA", "San Francisco", "Chicago" },
                         { "Munich", "Stuttgart", "Berlin", "Bonn" },
                         { "Paris", "Ajaccio", "Lyon" },
                         { "Montreal", "Ottawa", "Vancouver" } };
```

14. How many rows are in the array *cities*?
15. What is the value of the expression *cities[2][1]*?
16. What is the index of the last row in the array *cities*?
17. What are the row and column indexes of *Chicago* in the array *cities*?
18. What is the output of this code sequence?

```
System.out.println( cities[3][2] );
```

19. What is the output of this code sequence?

```
for ( int j = 0; j < cities[1].length; j++ )
   System.out.println( cities[1][j] );
```

20. What is the output of this code sequence?

```
for ( int i = 0; i < cities.length; i++ )
   System.out.println( cities[i][1] );
```

21. What is the output of this code sequence?

```
for ( int i = 0; i < cities.length; i++ )
{
   for ( int j = 0; j < cities[i].length; j++ )
         System.out.print( cities[i][j] + "\t" );
   System.out.println( );
}
```

22. What is the output of this code sequence?

```
for ( int i = 0; i < cities.length; i++ )
{
   for ( int j = 0; j < cities[i].length; j++ )
   {
         if ( cities[i][j].length( ) == 6 )
```

```
            System.out.println( cities[i][j] );
    }
}
```

23. What is the output of this code sequence?

```
int count  = 0;
for ( int i = 0; i < cities.length; i++ )
{
   for ( int j = 0; j < cities[i].length; j++ )
   {
         if ( cities[i][j].length( ) == 7 )
              count++;
   }
}
System.out.println( "count is " + count );
```

24. What is the output of this code sequence?

```
for ( int i = 0; i < cities.length; i++ )
{
   for ( int j = 0; j < cities[i].length; j++ )
   {
         if ( cities[i][j].charAt( 0 ) == 'S' )
              System.out.println( cities[i][j] );
   }
}
```

25. What does this method do?

```
public static int foo( double [ ][ ] a )
{
   int b = 0;
   for ( int i = 0; i < a.length; i++ )
   {
      for ( int j = 0; j < a[i].length; j++ )
           b++;
   }
   return b;
}
```

26. What does this method do?

```
public static boolean foo( char [ ][ ] a )
{
      int b = a[0].length;
      for ( int i = 1; i < a.length; i++ )
      {
         if ( a[i].length != b )
```

```
            return false;
    }
    return true;
}
```

27. What does this method do?

```
public static int foo( String [ ][ ] a )
{
      int b = 0;
      for ( int i = 0; i < a.length; i++ )
      {
            b++;
      }
      return b;
}
```

28. What does this method do?

```
public static int [ ] foo( float [ ][ ] a )
{
      int [ ] temp = new int [a.length];
      for ( int i = 0; i < a.length; i++ )
            temp[i] = a[i].length;
      return temp;
}
```

29. What does this method do?

```
public static int foo( ArrayList<Integer> a )
{
      int b = 0;
      for ( Integer i : a )
      {
         b++;
      }
      return b;
}
```

30. After the following code sequence is executed, what are the contents and index of each element of *a*?

```
ArrayList<Integer> a = new ArrayList<Integer>( );
a.add( 7 );
a.add( 4 );
a.add( 21 );
```

31. After the following code sequence is executed, what are the contents and index of each element of *a*?

```
ArrayList<Integer> a = new ArrayList<Integer>( );
a.add( 7 );
a.add( 4 );
a.add( 21 );
a.set( 1, 45 );
```

32. After the following code sequence is executed, what are the contents and index of each element of *a*?

```
ArrayList<Integer> a = new ArrayList<Integer>( );
a.add( 7 );
a.add( 4 );
a.add( 21 );
a.add( 1, 45 );
```

9.10.3 Fill In the Code

For Questions 33 to 37, consider the following statement:

```
String [ ][ ] geo = { { "MD", "NY", "NJ", "MA", "ME", "CA", "MI", "OR" },
                      { "Detroit", "Newark", "Boston", "Seattle" } };
```

33. This code prints the element at row index 1 and column index 2 of the two-dimensional array *geo*.

```
// your code goes here
```

34. This code prints the element of the array *geo* whose value is "CA."

```
// your code goes here
```

35. This code prints all the states (i.e., the first row) that start with an *M* in the array *geo*.

```
for ( int j = 0; j < geo[0].length; j++ )
{
      // your code goes here

}
```

36. This code prints all the cities (i.e., the second row) in the array *geo*.

```
for ( int j = 0; j < geo[1].length; j++ )
{
      // your code goes here

}
```

37. This code prints all the elements of the array *geo*.

```
for ( int i = 0; i < geo.length; i++ )
{
     // your code goes here

}
```

For Questions 38 to 41, consider the following statement:

```
int [ ][ ] a = { { 9, 6, 8, 10, 5 },
                 { 7, 6, 8, 9, 6 },
                 { 4, 8, 10, 6, 6 } };
```

38. This code calculates and prints the sum of all the elements in the array *a*.

```
int sum = 0;
for ( int i = 0; i < a.length; i++ )
{
     // your code goes here

}
System.out.println( "sum is " + sum );
```

39. This code counts and prints the number of times the value 8 appears in the array *a*.

```
int count = 0;
for ( int i = 0; i < a.length; i++ )
{
     // your code goes here

}
System.out.println( "# of 8s in a: " + count );
```

40. This code counts and prints the number of times the value 6 appears in the second row (i.e., the row whose index is 1) of array *a*.

```
int count = 0;

// your code for the for loop header goes here
{
     if ( a[1][j] == 6 )
           count++;
}
System.out.println( "# of 6s in the 2nd row: " + count );
```

41. This code calculates the sum of the elements in the second column (i.e, the column with index 1) of array *a*.

```
int sum  = 0;
for ( int i = 0; i < a.length; i++ )
{
      // your code goes here

}
System.out.println( "sum is " + sum );
```

42. This method returns *true* if an element in an array of *Strings* is equal to "Java"; otherwise, it returns *false*.

```
public static boolean foo( String [ ][ ] a )
{
      // your code goes here
}
```

43. This method returns the product of all the elements in an array.

```
public static int foo( int [ ][ ] a )
{
   // your code goes here
}
```

44. This method returns *true* if there is at least one row in the array that has exactly five columns; otherwise, it returns *false*.

```
public static boolean foo( char [ ][ ] a )
{
   // your code goes here
}
```

45. This method takes an array of *ints* as a parameter and returns a single-dimensional array of *booleans*. The length of the array returned should be equal to the number of rows in the two-dimensional array parameter. The element at index *i* of the returned array will be *true* if there is a 0 in the corresponding row of the parameter array; otherwise, it will be *false*. Assume that every row in *a* has the same number of columns.

```
public static boolean [ ] foo( int [ ][ ] a )
{
   // your code goes here
   // every row has the same number of columns

}
```

For Questions 46 to 49, consider the following statements:

```
ArrayList<String> languages = new ArrayList<String>( );
languages.add( "SQL" );
languages.add( "Java" );
languages.add( "HTML" );
languages.add( "PHP" );
languages.add( "Perl" );
```

46. This code prints the number of elements in *languages.*

```
// your code goes here
```

47. This code retrieves the *String* "HTML" from *languages* (without deleting it) and assigns it to the *String* variable *webLanguage.*

```
// your code goes here
```

48. This code replaces "HTML" *with* "C++" in *languages.*

```
// your code goes here
```

49. This code prints all the elements of *languages* that start with the letter *P.*

```
for ( String s : languages )
{
  // your code goes here

}
```

9.10.4 Identifying Errors in Code

50. Where is the error in this code sequence?

```
double [ ][ ] a = { 3.3, 26.0, 48.4 };
```

51. Where is the error in this code sequence?

```
int [ ][ ] a = { { 3, 26, 4 }, { 14, 87 } };
System.out.println( a[1][2] );
```

52. Where is the error in this code sequence?

```
double [ ][ ] a = new double [ ][10];
```

53. Where is the error in this code sequence?

```
int [ ][ ] a = { { 1, 2 },
                 { 10.1, 10.2 } };
```

54. Where is the error in this code sequence? (This code compiles and runs, but outputs garbage.)

```
int [ ][ ] a = { { 3, 26, 48 }, { 5, 2, 9 } };
System.out.println( "The array elements are " + a );
```

55. Where is the error in this code sequence?

```
ArrayList<double> al;
```

56. Where is the error in this code sequence?

```
ArrayList<Float> a1 = new ArrayList( )<Float>;
```

57. Where is the error in this code sequence? (The compiler may ask you to recompile.)

```
ArrayList<Double> a;
a = new ArrayList<Float>( );
```

58. Where is the error in this code sequence?

```
// a is an ArrayList of Strings
// a has already been declared and instantiated
a.size( ) = 10;
```

9.10.5 Debugging Area—Using Messages from the Java Compiler and Java JVM

59. You coded the following on line 14 of the *Test.java* class:

```
int a[2][ ] = { { 2, 7 }, { 9, 2 } };      // line 14
```

When you compile, you get the following message:

```
Test.java:14: ']' expected
  int a[2][ ] = { { 2, 7 }, { 9, 2 } };
       ^
Test.java:14: not a statement
  int a[2][] = {{ 2, 7 }, { 9, 2 } };
                ^
Test.java:14: ';' expected
  int a[2][] = {{ 2, 7 }, { 9, 2 } };
                 ^
Test.java:14: illegal start of expression
  int a[2][] = {{ 2, 7 }, { 9, 2 } };
                       ^
Test.java:14: not a statement
  int a[2][] = {{ 2, 7 }, { 9, 2 } };
                           ^
Test.java:14: ';' expected
  int a[2][] = {{ 2, 7 }, { 9, 2 } };
                            ^
6 errors
```

Explain what the problem is and how to fix it.

60. You coded the following in the *Test.java* class:

```
int [ ][ ] a = { { 1, 2, 3, 4 },
                 { 10, 20, 30 } };

for ( int i = 0; i < a.length; i++ )
{
      for ( int j = 0; j < a[0].length; j++ )
      {
            System.out.println( a[i][j] );    // line 14
      }
}
```

The code compiles properly but when you run, you get the following output:

```
 1
 2
 3
 4
10
20
30
Exception in thread "main" java.lang.ArrayIndexOutOfBoundsException: 3
        at Test.main(Test.java: 14)
```

Explain what the problem is and how to fix it.

61. You coded the following in the *Test.java* class in order to output the smallest element in the array *a.*

```
int [ ][ ] a = { { 9, 8, 7, 6 },
                 { 10, 20, 30, 40 } };

int min = a[0][0];
for ( int i = 1; i < a.length; i++ )
{
      for ( int j = 0; j < a[i].length; j++ )
      {
            if ( a[i][j] < min )
                  min = a[i][j];
      }
}
System.out.println( "The minimum is " + min );
```

The code compiles properly, but when you run, you get the following output:

```
The minimum is 9
```

You expected the value of *min* to be 6. Explain what the problem is and how to fix it.

62. You coded the following in file *Test.java*:

```
int [ ][ ] a = { { 9, 8, 7, 6 },
                 { 10, 20, 30, 40 } };

for ( int j = 0; j <= a[1].length; j++ )
{
  if ( a[1][j] == 20 )        // line 14
  {
      System.out.println( "Found 20 at column index " + j
                          + " of second row" );
  }
}
```

The code compiles properly, but when you run, you get the following output:

```
Found 20 at column index 1 of second row
Exception in thread "main" java.lang.ArrayIndexOutOfBoundsException: 4
        at Test.main(Test.java:14)
```

Explain what the problem is and how to fix it.

63. You coded the following in the *Test.java* class:

```
public static void main( String [ ] args )
{
  // cars is an ArrayList of Auto objects
  // cars has already been declared and instantiated
  for ( Auto a ; cars )      // line 12
  {
      System.out.println( a.toString( ) );
  }   // line 15
}     // line 16
```

When you compile, you get the following message :

```
Test.java:12: ';' expected
  for ( Auto a ; cars ) // line 12
                      ^
1 error
```

Explain what the problems are and how to fix them.

EXERCISES, PROBLEMS, AND PROJECTS

64. You coded the following in the *Test.java* class:

```
ArrayList<String> a = new ArrayList<String>( );
a.add( "Cloudy" );
a.add( "Snowy" );
a.add( "Cloudy" );
System.out.println( "Weather is " + a.get( 3 ) ); // line 14
```

The code compiles properly, but when you run, you get the following output:

```
   Exception in thread "main" java.lang.IndexOutOfBoundsException:
Index: 3, Size: 3
            at java.util.ArrayList.RangeCheck(ArrayList.java:547)
            at java.util.ArrayList.get(ArrayList.java:322)
            at Test.main(Test.java:14)
```

Explain what the problem is and how to fix it.

65. You coded the following in the file *Test.java:*

```
ArrayList<Integer> a = new ArrayList ( );
```

When you compile, you get the following warning message:

```
TestCompilerErrors.java:10: warning: [unchecked] unchecked conversion
found   : java.util.ArrayList
required: java.util.ArrayList<java.lang.Integer>
   ArrayList<Integer> a = new ArrayList ( );
                          ^
1 warning
```

Explain what the problem is and how to fix it.

66. You coded the following in the file *Test.java:*

```
ArrayList<Double> a = new ArrayList<Double>( );
a.add( new Double ( 2.3 ) );
a.add( 8.4 );
a.add( new Integer( 5 ) ); // line 11
```

When you compile, you get the following message:

```
Test.java:11: cannot find symbol
symbol  : method add(java.lang.Integer)
location: class java.util.ArrayList<java.lang.Double>
  a.add( new Integer( 5 ) );
   ^
1 error
```

Explain what the problem is and how to fix it.

67. You coded the following in the file *Test.java:*

```
ArrayList<Character> a = new ArrayList<Character>( );
a.add( 'X' );
a.add( 'A' );
a.add( 'V' );
a.add( 'A' );
a.set( 1, 'J' );
for( Character c : a )
  System.out.print( c + " " );
```

The code compiles properly, but when you run, you get the following output:

```
X J V A
```

when you expected:

```
J A V A
```

Explain what the problem is and how to fix it.

9.10.6 Write a Short Program

68. Write a value-returning method that returns the number of rows in a two-dimensional array of *doubles.* Include code to test your method.
69. Write a value-returning method that returns the number of elements in a two-dimensional array of *floats.* Include code to test your method.
70. Write a value-returning method that returns the number of columns that have two elements in a two-dimensional array of *booleans.* Include code to test your method.
71. Write a value-returning method that returns the number of columns with *n* elements in a two-dimensional array of *chars,* where *n* is a parameter of the method. Include code to test your method.
72. Write a value-returning method that returns the sum of all the elements in a two-dimensional array of *floats.* Include code to test your method.
73. Write a method with a *void* return value that sets to 0 all the elements of the even-numbered rows and sets to 1 all the elements of odd-numbered rows of a two-dimensional array of *ints.* Include code to test your method.

74. Write a value-returning method that returns the sum of the elements in the last column of each row in a two-dimensional array of *ints*. Include code to test your method.
75. Write a method with a *void* return value that inverts all the elements of a two-dimensional array of *booleans* (*true* becomes *false* and *false* becomes *true*). Include code to test your method.
76. Write a method that returns the number of elements having the value *true* in a two-dimensional array of *booleans*. Include code to test your method.
77. Write a method that returns the percentage of elements having the value *false* in a two-dimensional array of *booleans*. Include code to test your method.
78. Write a method that returns the average of all elements in a two-dimensional array of *ints*. Include code to test your method.
79. Write a method that returns the *String* "regular" if all the rows of a two-dimensional array of *floats* have the same number of columns; otherwise, it returns "irregular." Include code to test your method.
80. Write a method that returns the concatenation of all elements in a two-dimensional array of *Strings*. Include code to test your method.
81. Write an array-returning method that takes a two-dimensional array of *chars* as a parameter and returns a single-dimensional array of *Strings* as follows: The array returned should have a number of elements equal to the number of rows in the parameter array; every element of the array returned should be the concatenation of all the column elements of the corresponding row in the parameter array. Include code to test your method.
82. Write an array-returning method that takes a two-dimensional array of *ints* as a parameter and returns a two-dimensional array of *chars*, assigning a letter grade corresponding to the integer grade (A if 90 or above, . . ., F if less than 60). Include code to test your method.
83. Write a method that returns the sum of all the elements of an *ArrayList* of *Integer* objects. Include code to test your method.
84. Write a method that returns the *String* "odd" or "even" if the number of elements of an *ArrayList* of *Strings* is odd or even. Include code to test your method.

85. Write a method that takes an *ArrayList* of *Integer* objects and returns an *ArrayList* of *Character* objects of the same size. The returned elements of the *ArrayList* are assigned a letter grade corresponding to the integer grade of the same index element of the *ArrayList* parameter (A if 90 or above, . . ., F if less than 60). Include code to test your method.

9.10.7 Programming Projects

86. Write a class (and a client class to test it) that encapsulates statistics for summer job salaries for a group of people over several years. Your only instance variable should be a two-dimensional array of values representing salaries. Dimension 1 represents the people and dimension 2 represents the year of the summer job. Your constructor can simply take two integers representing the number of people and the number of years, then randomly generate the salaries and fill the array. You should include the following methods:

    - ❑ a method returning the index of the person having made the most money over the years
    - ❑ a method returning the year when the highest salary was earned
    - ❑ a method returning the total amount of money made by all the people over the years.

87. Write a class (and a client class to test it) that encapsulates the evolution of the passwords of three students over four months. Your only instance variable should be a two-dimensional array of values representing the passwords. Dimension 1 represents the student and dimension 2 represents the month. (Since we are concerned about security, we are assuming that people change their password once a month; we only care about the value of the password at the end of a given month.) Your constructor can simply take a single-dimensional array of words representing the 12 passwords; they can be assigned to the two-dimensional array elements one at a time, starting with the first row. You should include the following methods:

    - ❑ a method returning the index of the person who changed his or her password the most times
    - ❑ a method returning the longest password
    - ❑ a method changing all the passwords to "unlock"

- ❑ a method returning *true* if at least one person had a given word—the method's parameter—as his/her password in at least one month; *false* otherwise.

88. Write a class (and a client class to test it) that encapsulates the evolution of the sales tax rates in the 50 U.S. states over the last 10 years. Your only instance variable should be a two-dimensional array of values representing the sales tax rates. Dimension 1 represents the state and dimension 2 represents the year. Your constructor can simply be a default constructor, randomly generating the sales tax rates, which should be between 0 and 0.06. You should include the following methods:

    - ❑ a method returning the index of the state that has the biggest average tax rate over the years
    - ❑ a method returning an array of indexes of the states that have had at least one year with a tax rate less than 0.001
    - ❑ a method returning the highest sales tax rate over the years for a given state (which will be a parameter).

89. Write a class (and a client class to test it) that encapsulates the evolution of the quality ratings of various hotels over the years. Hotel ratings are represented by a number of stars, which can vary from one star (lowest quality) to five stars (highest quality). Your only instance variable should be a two-dimensional array of values representing the quality ratings. Dimension 1 represents the hotel and dimension 2 represents the year. Your constructor can take two parameters representing the number of hotels and the number of years. The ratings can simply be generated randomly. You should include the following methods:

    - ❑ a method returning an array of indexes of the hotels that have earned five stars at least once over the years
    - ❑ a method returning the average rating of all the hotels over the years
    - ❑ a method printing the indexes of the hotels that have earned five stars every year
    - ❑ a method returning *true* if at least one hotel earned five stars for at least one year; *false* otherwise.

90. Write a class (and a client class to test it) that encapsulates the value of the 26 letters of the English alphabet in the game of Scrabble in 10 countries. You should have three instance variables:

    - a two-dimensional array of integers representing the point values of the letters in the various countries
    - a single-dimensional array representing the alphabet from a to z
    - another single-dimensional array representing 10 countries.

    For the two-dimensional array, dimension 1 represents the letter and dimension 2 represents the country. Your constructor can simply be a default constructor, randomly generating the values between 1 and 10. You should include the following methods:

    - a method returning an array of letters with their highest point value in any country
    - a method printing the names of the countries that have at least one letter with a point value of 10
    - a method taking a *String* as a parameter and printing the score of the word represented by that *String* in every country.

91. Write a class (and a client class to test it) that encapsulates the numbers of the various chessboard pieces in a chess game. You should have two instance variables:

    - a two-dimensional array of integers; each array element represents how many of a particular chess piece of a particular color are on the board. In order to set it up, consider the following:
        - The first dimension represents the color of the pieces. On a chessboard, there are white and black pieces.
        - The second dimension represents the pieces themselves. On a chessboard, we have on each side: one king, one queen, two bishops, two knights, two rooks, and eight pawns.
    - a single-dimensional array describing the pieces (king, queen, etc.).

Your constructor can simply be a default constructor, declaring and instantiating the two arrays to match the preceding information. You should include the following methods:

- ❑ a method with a *void* return value, called *playerATakesPlayerB*, updating the array based on a piece being taken by the opponent. It takes two parameters:
  - a *boolean* parameter representing whether "white takes black" or "black takes white"
  - an *int* parameter representing which piece gets taken
- ❑ a method returning how many of a particular piece are on the board (this method takes a parameter representing the piece)
- ❑ a method taking a *boolean* as a parameter, representing a color and returning the value of the board for that particular color. You can consider that a king is worth 0 points, a queen is worth 6 points, a rook is worth 4 points, a knight and a bishop are each worth 3 points, and a pawn is worth 1 point.

92. Write a class (and a client class to test it) that encapsulates a deck of cards. A deck of cards is made up of 52 cards. You should have three instance variables:

- ❑ a two-dimensional array of values representing the cards
- ❑ a single-dimensional array describing the suit: spades, hearts, diamonds, and clubs
- ❑ an instance variable representing the trump suit.

For the two-dimensional array, dimension 1 represents the suit and dimension 2 represents the type of card (ace, two, three, . . ., jack, queen, king). Your constructor should take one parameter, which will represent the suit of the trump. Based on that, the cards should be given the following values:

- ❑ Non-trump from 2 to 10: 1 point
- ❑ Non-trump jack = 2
- ❑ Non-trump queen = 3
- ❑ Non-trump king = 4

- ❑ Non-trump ace = 5
- ❑ Any trump card = Non-trump value + 1

You should include the following methods:

- ❑ a method returning the trump suit, by name
- ❑ a method printing the whole deck of cards, suit by suit, with the value for each card
- ❑ a method taking a *String* as a parameter representing a suit, and returning the total value of the cards of that suit.

93. Write a class (and a client class to test it) that encapsulates a tic-tac-toe board. A tic-tac-toe board looks like a table of three rows and three columns partially or completely filled with the characters X and O. At any point, a cell of that table could be empty or could contain an X or an O. You should have one instance variable, a two-dimensional array of values representing the tic-tac-toe board.

    Your default constructor should instantiate the array so that it represents an empty board.

    You should include the following methods:

    - ❑ a method, returning a *boolean*, simulating a play with three parameters as follows: If the first parameter is *true*, then X is playing; otherwise, O is playing. The other two parameters represent what cell on the board is being played. If the play is legal, that is, the cell is a legal cell on the board and is empty, then the method should update the array and return *true*; otherwise, the array should not be updated and the method should return *false*
    - ❑ a method returning how many valid plays have been made so far
    - ❑ a method checking if a player has won based on the contents of the board; this method takes no parameter. It returns X if the "X player" has won, O if the "O player" has won, T if the game was a tie. A player wins if he or she has placed an X (or an O) in all cells in a row, all cells in a column, or all cells in one of the two diagonals.

94. Modify the *BookStore* and *BookSearchEngine* classes from the chapter.

    You should include the following additional methods and test them:

    - ❑ a method returning the book with the lowest price in the library
    - ❑ a method searching the library for *Books* of a given author and returning an *ArrayList* of such *Books*
    - ❑ a method returning an *ArrayList* of *Books* whose price is less than a given number.

95. Write a *Garage* class (and a client class to test it) with one instance variable: an *ArrayList* of *Autos* (you can use the *Auto* class from Chapter 7).

    You should include the following methods:

    - ❑ a method returning the average number of miles of all cars in the garage
    - ❑ a method returning "full" if the garage has 100 cars or more, "below minimum" if the garage has fewer than 25 cars, and "normal load" if the garage has between 25 and 100 cars in it
    - ❑ a method returning the total number of gallons of gas used by all cars in the garage.

96. Write a *ComputerPart* class and a *ComputerKit* class (and a client class to test them).

    The *ComputerPart* class has two instance variables: a *String* representing an item (for instance, "cpu" or "disk drive"), and a *double* representing the price of that item. The *ComputerKit* class has just one instance variable: an *ArrayList* of *ComputerPart* objects (they make up a computer) representing the list of parts for the computer kit.

    You should include the following methods:

    - ❑ a method returning "expensive" if the total of the prices of the *ComputerPart* objects is greater than 1,000, "cheap" if it is less than 250, "normal" if it is between 250 and 1,000
    - ❑ a method returning *true* if a certain item is included in the list of parts; *false* otherwise
    - ❑ a method returning how many times a particular item (for instance, "cpu," or "memory") is found in the list of parts.

9.10.8 Technical Writing

97. A two-dimensional array can have a different number of columns in every row. Do you see that as an advantage or a disadvantage? Discuss.

98. Discuss the pros and cons of using an array vs. using an *ArrayList*.

9.10.9 Group Project (for a group of 1, 2, or 3 students)

99. Design and code a program including the following classes, as well as a client class to test all the methods coded:

    A *Passenger* class, encapsulating a passenger. A passenger has two attributes: a name, and a class of service, which will be 1 or 2.

    A *Train* class, encapsulating a train of passengers: a train of passengers has one attribute, a list of passengers, which must be represented with an *ArrayList*. Your constructor will build the list of passengers by reading data from a file called *passengers.txt*. You can assume that *passengers.txt* has the following format:

    ```
    <name1>  <class1>
    <name2>  <class2>
    ...
    ```

    For instance, the file could contain:

    ```
    James    1
    Ben      2
    Suri     1
    Sarah    1
    Jane     2
    ...
    ```

    You should include the following methods in your *Train* class:

    - ❑ a method returning the percentage of passengers traveling in first class
    - ❑ a method taking two parameters representing the price of traveling in first and second class and returning the total revenue for the train
    - ❑ a method checking if a certain person is on the train; if he/she is, the method returns *true*; otherwise, it returns *false*.

CHAPTER 10

Object-Oriented Programming, Part 3: Inheritance, Polymorphism, and Interfaces

CHAPTER CONTENTS

Introduction

One of the most common ways to reuse a class is through inheritance. Inheritance helps us to organize related classes into **hierarchies**, or ordered levels of functionality. To set up a hierarchy, we begin by defining a class that contains methods and fields (instance variables and class variables) that are common to all classes in the hierarchy. Then we define new classes at the next lower level of the hierarchy, which inherit the behavior and fields of the original class. In the new classes, we define additional fields and more specific methods. The original class is called the **superclass**, and the new classes that inherit from the superclass are called **subclasses**. Some OOP developers call a superclass the **base class** and call a subclass the **derived class**.

As in life, a superclass (parent) can have multiple subclasses (children), and each subclass can be a superclass (parent) of other subclasses (children) and so on. Thus, a class can be both a subclass (child) and a superclass (parent). In contrast to life, however, Java subclasses inherit directly from only one superclass.

A subclass can add fields and methods, some of which may **override**, or hide, a field or method inherited from a superclass.

Let's look at an example. To represent a hierarchy of vehicle types, we define a *Vehicle* class as a superclass. We then define an *Automobile* class that inherits from *Vehicle.* We also define a *Truck* class, which also inherits from *Vehicle.* We further refine our classes by defining a *Pickup* class and a *TractorTrailer* class, both of which inherit from the *Truck* class. Figure 10.1 depicts our hierarchy using a UML (Unified Modeling Language) diagram. Arrows pointing from a subclass to a superclass indicate that the subclass refers to the superclass for some of its methods and fields. The boxes below the class name are available for specifying instance variables and methods for each class. For simplicity, we will leave those boxes blank. Later in the chapter, we will illustrate UML diagrams complete with fields and methods.

The Java class library contains many class hierarchies. At the root of all Java class hierarchies is the *Object* class, the superclass for all classes. Thus, all classes inherit from the *Object* class.

The most important advantage to inheritance is that in a hierarchy of classes, we write the common code only once. After the common code has

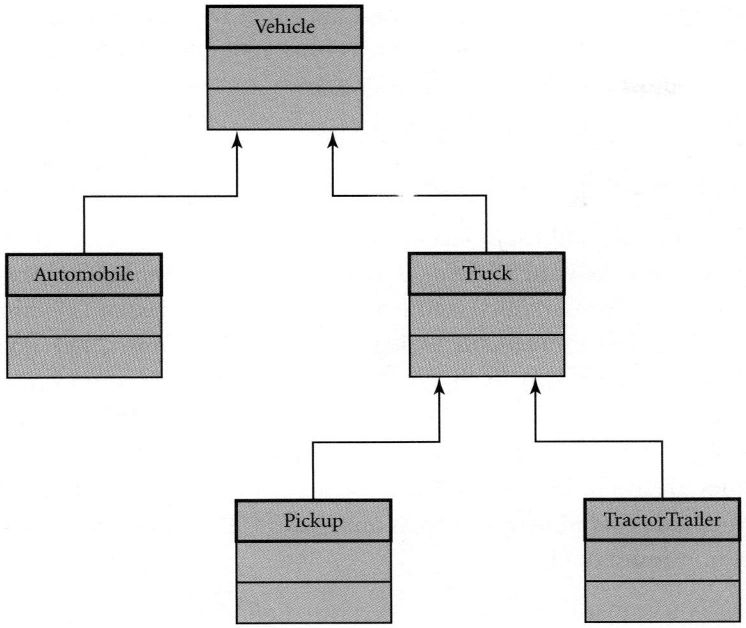

Figure 10.1
***Vehicle* Class Hierarchy**

been tested, we can reuse it with confidence by inheriting it into the subclasses. And when that common code needs revision, we need to revise the code in only one place.

10.1 Inheritance

The syntax for defining a subclass class that inherits from another class is to add an *extends* clause in the class header:

```
accessModifier class SubclassName extends SuperclassName
{
    // class definition
}
```

The *extends* keyword specifies that the subclass inherits members of the superclass. That means that the subclass begins with a set of predefined methods and fields inherited from its hierarchy of superclasses.

Let's look at an example of inheritance that we've already used. We've used the *extends* keyword whenever we wrote an applet. For example, we defined our rolling ball applet in Chapter 6 as:

```
public class RollABall extends JApplet
```

This means that the *RollABall* class inherits from the *JApplet* class.

Because our *RollABall* class extends *JApplet*, it inherits more than 275 methods and more than 15 fields. That's because the *JApplet* class is a subclass of *Applet*, which is a subclass of *Panel*, which is a subclass of *Container*, which is a subclass of *Component*, which is a subclass of *Object*. The *RollABall* class hierarchy is shown in Figure 10.2. All along the hierarchy, the subclasses inherit methods and fields, all of which become available to our applets. True, not every applet has a use for all the inherited methods and fields, but they are available if needed, and the benefit is that we don't need to write the methods or define the fields in our applets. Thus, we can build applets with a minimum of effort.

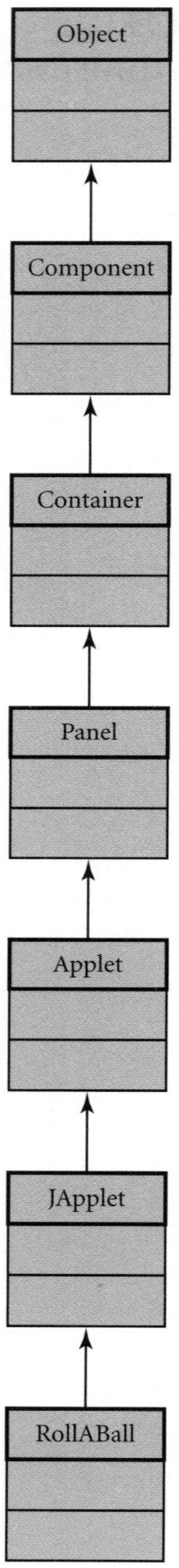

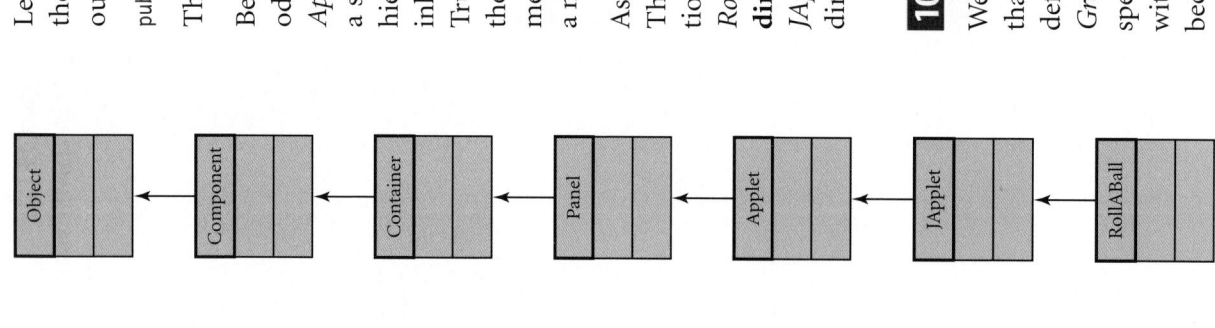

Figure 10.2
The *RollABall* Class Hierarchy

As you can see from Figure 10.2, our *RollABall* class has six superclasses. The class that a subclass refers to in the *extends* clause of the class definition is called its **direct superclass**. Thus, *JApplet* is the direct superclass of *RollABall*. Similarly, the class that *extends* the superclass is called the **direct subclass** of the superclass, so *RollABall* is a direct subclass of the *JApplet* class. A class can have multiple direct subclasses, but only one direct superclass.

10.2 Inheritance Design

We say that an "is a" relationship exists between a subclass and a superclass; that is, a subclass object "is a" superclass object. For example, we could define a student class hierarchy with a *Student* superclass and derive a *GraduateStudent* subclass. A graduate student "is a" student, but actually a special type of student. We could also define an employee class hierarchy with an *Employee* superclass and derive *Faculty* and *Staff* subclasses, because faculty and staff are both special types of employees.

To design classes for inheritance, our superclass should define fields and methods that will be common to all classes in the hierarchy. Each subclass will provide specialization by adding methods and fields. Where appropri-

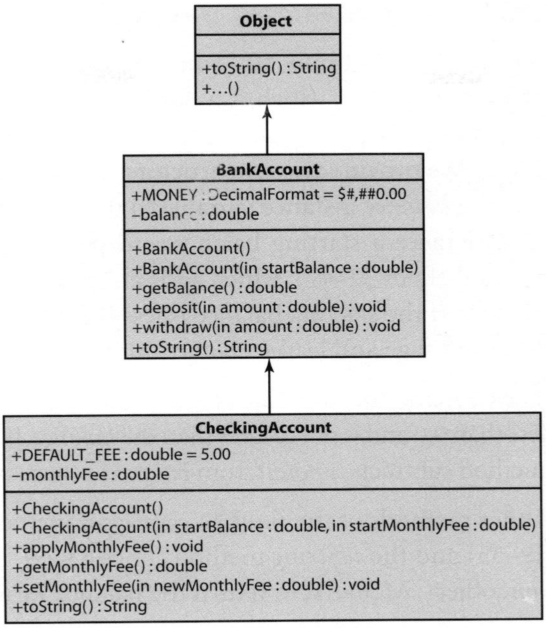

Figure 10.3
The *BankAccount* Class Hierarchy

ate, subclasses can also provide new versions of inherited methods, which is called **overriding methods**.

SOFTWARE ENGINEERING TIP

The superclasses in a class hierarchy should contain fields and methods common to all subclasses. The subclasses should add specialized fields and methods.

Let's build a bank account class hierarchy. We start by defining a generic *BankAccount* superclass. The *BankAccount* class will contain the fields and methods that are common to all bank accounts. Then we will define a *CheckingAccount* class that inherits from the *BankAccount* class. The *CheckingAccount* class will add instance variables and methods that specifically support checking accounts. Our class hierarchy is shown in the UML diagram in Figure 10.3. In this diagram, we display the instance variables in the box immediately below the class name and the methods in the next lower box. A "+" preceding a class member indicates that the member is *public*, while a "–" indicates that the member is *private.* Each method's signature is given with each parameter and its type within parentheses and the return type following a colon. The *Object* class has more methods than we indicate on the UML diagram. However, the *toString* method is the only method of *Object* that we will deal with in this hierarchy, so we have omitted the other methods of *Object* on the diagram and indicate that other methods exist (+...()).

10.2.1 Inherited Members of a Class

As shown in Example 10.1, our *BankAccount* class has two instance variables, the *balance*, which is a *double* (line 11), and a constant *DecimalFormat* object that we will use for formatting the *balance* as money (lines 9–10). We provide two constructors. The default constructor (lines 13–19) sets the *balance* instance variable to 0.0. The overloaded constructor (lines 21–27) takes a starting balance and passes that parameter to the *deposit* method (lines 37–47), which adds any non-negative starting balance to the *balance*. If the starting balance is less than 0.0, the *deposit* method prints an error message and leaves *balance* unchanged.

The *withdraw* method (lines 49–61) validates that the *amount* parameter is not less than 0.0 and is not greater than the *balance*. If *amount* is valid, the *withdraw* method subtracts *amount* from *balance*; otherwise, it prints an error message.

Other methods of the *BankAccount* class include the *balance* accessor (lines 29–35) and the *toString* method (lines 63–69), which uses the *DecimalFormat* object, *MONEY*, to return the balance formatted as money.

```
1 /**    BankAccount class, Version 1
2 *      Anderson, Franceschi
3 *      Represents a generic bank account
4 */
5 import java.text.DecimalFormat;
6
7 public class BankAccount
8 {
9   public final DecimalFormat MONEY
10                        = new DecimalFormat( "$#,##0.00" );
11  private double balance;
12
13  /** Default constructor
14  *   sets balance to 0.0
15  */
16  public BankAccount( )
17  {
18    balance = 0.0;
19  }
20
21  /** Overloaded constructor
```

```
* @param startBalance  beginning balance
*/
public BankAccount( double startBalance )
{
  deposit( startBalance );
}

/** Accessor for balance
*   @return  current account balance
*/
public double getBalance( )
{
  return balance;
}

/** Deposit amount to account
*   @param amount  amount to deposit;
*                  amount must be >= 0.0
*/
public void deposit( double amount )
{
  if ( amount >= 0.0 )
    balance += amount;
  else
    System.err.println( "Deposit amount must be positive." );
}

/** withdraw amount from account
*    @param amount   amount to withdraw;
*                    amount must be >= 0.0
*                    amount must be <= balance
*/
public void withdraw( double amount )
{
  if (  amount >= 0.0 && amount <= balance )
    balance -= amount;
  else
    System.err.println( "Withdrawal amount must be positive "
                        + "and cannot be greater than balance" );
}
```

```
  /** toString
  *  @return  the balance formatted as money
  */
  public String toString( )
  {
    return ( "balance is " + MONEY.format( balance ) );
  }
}
```

EXAMPLE 10.1 *BankAccount* Class, Version 1

Now we can derive our *CheckingAccount* subclass. Example 10.2 shows Version 1 of our *CheckingAccount* class. For this initial version, we simply define the *CheckingAccount* class as extending *BankAccount* (line 5). The body of our class is empty for now, so we can demonstrate the fields and methods that a subclass inherits from its superclass.

```
1 /* CheckingAccount class, Version 1
2    Anderson, Franceschi
3 */
4
5 public class CheckingAccount extends BankAccount
6 { }
```

EXAMPLE 10.2 *CheckingAccount* Class, Version 1

When a class *extends* a superclass, all the *public* fields and methods of the superclass (excluding constructors) are inherited. That means that the *CheckingAccount* class inherits the *MONEY* instance variable and the *getBalance, deposit, withdraw,* and *toString* methods from the *BankAccount* class. An inherited field is directly accessible from the subclass, and an inherited method can be called by the other methods of the subclass. In addition, *public* inherited methods can be called by a client application using a subclass object reference.

Any fields and methods that are declared *private* are not inherited, and therefore are not directly accessible by the subclass. Nevertheless, the *private* fields and methods are still part of the subclass object. Remember that a *CheckingAccount* object "is a" *BankAccount* object, so a *CheckingAccount* object has a *balance* instance variable. However, the *balance* is declared to be *private* in the *BankAccount* class, so the *CheckingAccount* methods cannot directly access the *balance*. The *CheckingAccount* methods must call the accessor and mutator methods of the *BankAccount* class to access or change the value of *balance*.

Calling methods to retrieve and change values of an instance variable may seem a little tedious, but it enforces encapsulation. Allowing the *CheckingAccount* class to set the value of *balance* directly would complicate maintenance of the program. The *CheckingAccount* class would need to be responsible for maintaining a valid value for *balance*, which means that the *CheckingAccount* class would need to know all the validation rules for *balance* that the *BankAccount* class enforces. If these rules change, then the *CheckingAccount* class would also need to change. As long as the *BankAccount* class ensures the validity of *balance*, there is no reason for the *CheckingAccount* class to duplicate that code.

Java provides the ***protected*** access modifier so that fields and methods can be inherited by subclasses (like *public* fields and methods), while still being hidden from client classes (like *private* fields and methods). In addition, any class in the same package as the superclass can directly access a *protected* field, even if that class is not a subclass. Because more than one class can directly access a *protected* field, *protected* access compromises encapsulation and complicates maintenance of a program. For that reason, we prefer to use *private*, rather than *protected*, for our instance variables. We will discuss the difference between *private* and *protected* in greater detail later in the chapter.

Table 10.1 summarizes the fields and methods that are inherited by a subclass. We will add to this table as we explain more about inheritance.

Example 10.3 shows a client for the *CheckingAccount* class. In line 9, we instantiate an object of the *CheckingAccount* class. After instantiation, the *c1* object has two fields: *balance* and *MONEY*, and it has four methods: *getBalance*, *deposit*, *withdraw*, and *toString*.

We illustrate this by using the *c1* object reference to call the *deposit* method in line 12 and the *withdraw* method in line 15, and to call the *toString* method implicitly in lines 13 and 16. Figure 10.4 shows the output from this program.

TABLE 10.1 Inheritance Rules

Superclass Members	Inherited by Subclass?	Directly Accessible by Subclass?	Directly Accessible by Client of Subclass?
public fields	yes	yes, by using field name	yes
public methods	yes	yes, by calling method from other subclass methods	yes
protected fields	yes	yes, by using field name	no, must use accessors and mutators
protected methods	yes	yes, by calling method from subclass methods	no
private fields	no	no, must use accessors and mutators	no, must use accessors and mutators
private methods	no	no	no

```
/* CheckingAccount Client, Version 1
   Anderson, Franceschi
*/

public class CheckingAccountClient
{
  public static void main( String [ ] args )
  {
    CheckingAccount c1 = new CheckingAccount( );
    System.out.println( "New checking account: " + c1 );

    c1.deposit( 350.75 );
    System.out.println( "\nAfter depositing $350.75: " + c1 );

    c1.withdraw( 200.25 );
    System.out.println( "\nAfter withdrawing $200.25: " + c1 );
  }
}
```

EXAMPLE 10.3 ***CheckingAccount* Client, Version 1**

Figure 10.4
Output from *Checking-AccountClient*, Version 1

```
New checking account: balance is $0.00

After depositing $350.75: balance is $350.75

After withdrawing $200.25: balance is $150.50
```

10.2.2 Subclass Constructors

Although constructors are *public*, they are not inherited by subclasses. However, to initialize the *private* instance variables of the superclass, a subclass constructor can call a superclass constructor either implicitly or explicitly.

When a class extends another class, the default constructor of the subclass automatically calls the default constructor of the superclass. This is called **implicit** invocation. Athough we did not code any constructors in our *CheckingAccount* class in Example 10.2, we were able to instantiate a *CheckingAccount* object (with a 0.0 *balance*) because the Java compiler provided a default constructor for the *CheckingAccount* class, which implicitly called the default constructor of the *BankAccount* class.

To **explicitly** call the constructor of the direct superclass, the subclass constructor uses the following syntax:

```
super( argument list );
```

Thus, if we want to instantiate a *CheckingAccount* object with a starting balance other than 0.0, we need to provide an overloaded constructor for the *CheckingAccount* class. That constructor will take the starting balance as a parameter and pass that starting balance to the overloaded constructor in the *BankAccount* class.

This call to the direct superclass constructor, if used, must be the first statement in the subclass constructor. Otherwise, the following compiler error is generated:

```
call to super must be first statement in constructor
```

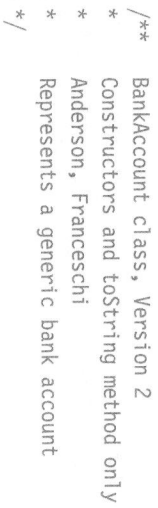

COMMON ERROR TRAP

In a constructor, the call to the direct superclass constructor, if used, must be the first statement.

Example 10.4 shows Version 2 of the *BankAccount* class, which for simplicity, and to help us focus on constructors, has only a default and overloaded constructor and the *toString* method. To illustrate the order in which the constructors execute, we print a message in each constructor (lines 21 and 33), indicating that it has been called.

```
1 /**   BankAccount class, Version 2
2 *     Constructors and toString method only
3 *     Anderson, Franceschi
4 *     Represents a generic bank account
5 */
6
```

```java
import java.text.DecimalFormat;

public class BankAccount
{
  public final DecimalFormat MONEY
                    = new DecimalFormat( "$#,##0.00" );
  private double balance;

  /** Default constructor
  *   sets balance to 0.0
  */
  public BankAccount( )
  {
    balance = 0.0;
    System.out.println( "In BankAccount default constructor" );
  }

  /** Overloaded constructor
  *   @param startBalance  beginning balance
  */
  public BankAccount( double startBalance )
  {
    if ( balance >= 0.0 )
        balance = startBalance;
    else
        balance = 0.0;
    System.out.println( "In BankAccount overloaded constructor" );
  }

  /** toString
  *  @return  the balance formatted as money
  */
  public String toString( )
  {
    return ( "balance is " + MONEY.format( balance ) );
  }
}
```

EXAMPLE 10.4 *BankAccount*, Version 2

Example 10.5 shows Version 2 of the *CheckingAccount* class, which has both a default constructor and an overloaded constructor. Again, we have inserted messages (lines 13–14 and 24–25) to indicate when a constructor is called.

```
 1 /* CheckingAccount class, Version 2
 2    Anderson, Franceschi
 3 */
 4
 5 public class CheckingAccount extends BankAccount
 6 {
 7    /** default constructor
 8    *   explicitly calls the BankAccount default constructor
 9    */
10    public CheckingAccount( )
11    {
12        super( ); // optional, call BankAccount constructor
13        System.out.println( "In CheckingAccount "
14                          + "default constructor" );
15    }
16
17    /** overloaded constructor
18    *   calls BankAccount overloaded constructor
19    *   @param  startBalance  starting balance
20    */
21    public CheckingAccount( double startBalance )
22    {
23        super( startBalance ); // call BankAccount constructor
24        System.out.println( "In CheckingAccount "
25                          + "overloaded constructor" );
26    }
27 }
```

EXAMPLE 10.5 *CheckingAccount* Class, Version 2

In the *CheckingAccount* default constructor, we explicitly call the default constructor of the *BankAccount* class (line 12). This statement is optional; without it, the *BankAccount* default constructor is still called implicitly.

In the *CheckingAccount* overloaded constructor, we pass the *startBalance* parameter to the *BankAccount* constructor (line 23) to initialize the

COMMON ERROR TRAP

An attempt by a subclass to directly access a *private* field or call a *private* method defined in a superclass will generate a compiler error. To set initial values for *private* variables, call the appropriate constructor of the direct superclass.

balance instance variable. Because *balance* has *private* access in the *BankAccount* class, our *CheckingAccount* class cannot access *balance* directly. If we attempted to initialize the *balance* directly using the following statement:

```
balance = startBalance;
```

the compiler would generate the following error:

```
balance has private access in BankAccount
```

SOFTWARE ENGINEERING TIP

Overloaded constructors in a subclass should explicitly call the direct superclass constructor to initialize the fields in its superclasses.

Example 10.6 shows Version 2 of our *CheckingAccount* client. On line 10, we instantiate a *CheckingAccount* object using the default constructor and print the balance by implicitly calling the *toString* method on line 11. Then on line 14, we instantiate a second *CheckingAccount* object with a starting balance of $100.00. Again we verify the result by printing the balance (line 15).

```
1 /* CheckingAccount Client, Version 2
2    Anderson, Franceschi
3 */
4
5 public class CheckingAccountClient
6 {
7   public static void main( String [ ] args )
8   {
9     // use default constructor
10    CheckingAccount c1 = new CheckingAccount( );
11    System.out.println( "New checking account: " + c1 + "\n" );
12
13    // use overloaded constructor
14    CheckingAccount c2 = new CheckingAccount( 100.00 );
15    System.out.println( "New checking account: " + c2 );
16  }
17 }
```

EXAMPLE 10.6 *CheckingAccountClient*, Version 2

Figure 10.5 shows the output from this program. As you can see, when we construct the *c1* object, the *BankAccount* default constructor runs. When it finishes, we print a message indicating that the *CheckingAccount* default

```
In BankAccount default constructor
In CheckingAccount default constructor
New checking account: balance is $0.00

In BankAccount overloaded constructor
In CheckingAccount overloaded constructor
New checking account: balance is $100.00
```

Figure 10.5
Output from Example 10.6

TABLE 10.2 Inheritance Rules for Constructors

Superclass Members	Inherited by Subclass?	Directly Accessible by Subclass?	Directly Accessible by Client of Subclass Using a Subclass Reference?
constructors	no	yes, using `super( arg list )` in a subclass constructor	no

constructor is running. Similarly, when we construct the *c2* object, the *BankAccount* overloaded constructor runs, then we print a message from the *CheckingAccount* overloaded constructor.

Table 10.2 summarizes the inheritance rules for constructors.

10.2.3 Adding Specialization to the Subclass

At this point, our *CheckingAccount* class provides no more functionality than the *BankAccount* class. But our purpose for defining a *CheckingAccount* class was to provide support for a specialized type of bank account. To add specialization to our *CheckingAccount* subclass, we define new fields and methods. For example, we can define a *monthlyFee* instance variable, as well as an accessor and mutator method for the monthly fee and a method to charge the monthly fee to the account.

Example 10.7 shows Version 3 of the *CheckingAccount* class with the specialization added. This version *extends* the complete *BankAccount* class shown in Example 10.1. We added the *monthlyFee* instance variable on line 8, as well as a constant default value for the monthly fee (line 7). Our default constructor (lines 10–18) still calls the default constructor of the *BankAccount* class to initialize the *balance*, but it also initializes the *monthlyFee* to the default value.

Similarly, the overloaded constructor (lines 20–30) passes the *startBalance* parameter to the overloaded constructor of the *BankAccount* class and adds a *startMonthlyFee* parameter to accept an initial value for the *monthlyFee*, which it passes to the *setMonthlyFee* mutator method (lines 48–57).

The *applyMonthlyFee* method (lines 32–38), which charges the monthly fee to the checking account, calls the *withdraw* method inherited from the *BankAccount* class to access the *balance* instance variable, which is declared *private* in the *BankAccount* class.

```
1 /* CheckingAccount class, Version 3
2    Anderson, Franceschi
3 */
4
5 public class CheckingAccount extends BankAccount
6 {
7    public final double DEFAULT_FEE = 5.00;
8    private double monthlyFee;
9
10   /** default constructor
11   *   explicitly calls the BankAccount default constructor
12   *   set monthlyFee to default value
13   */
14   public CheckingAccount( )
15   {
16       super( ); // optional
17       monthlyFee = DEFAULT_FEE;
18   }
19
20   /** overloaded constructor
21   *  calls BankAccount overloaded constructor
22   *  @param  startBalance  starting balance
```

```
   *  @param  startMonthlyFee starting monthly fee
   */
   public CheckingAccount( double startBalance,
                           double startMonthlyFee )
   {
     super( startBalance ); // call BankAccount constructor
     setMonthlyFee( startMonthlyFee );
   }

   /** applyMonthlyFee method
   * charges the monthly fee to the account
   */
   public void applyMonthlyFee( )
   {
    withdraw( monthlyFee );
   }

   /** accessor method for monthlyFee
   *  @return  monthlyFee
   */
   public double getMonthlyFee( )
   {
     return monthlyFee;
   }

   /** mutator method for monthlyFee
   *  @param newMonthlyFee new value for monthlyFee
   */
   public void setMonthlyFee( double newMonthlyFee )
   {
     if ( monthlyFee >= 0.0 )
        monthlyFee = newMonthlyFee;
     else
        System.err.println( "Monthly fee cannot be negative" );
   }
}
```

EXAMPLE 10.7 *CheckingAccount*, Version 3

Example 10.8 shows Version 3 of our client program, which instantiates a *CheckingAccount* object and charges the monthly fee. The output is shown in Figure 10.6.

Figure 10.6
Output from *CheckingAccountClient*, Version 3

```
New checking account:
balance is $100.00; monthly fee is 7.5

After charging monthly fee:
balance is $92.50; monthly fee is 7.5
```

```
/* CheckingAccount Client, Version 3
   Anderson, Franceschi
*/

public class CheckingAccountClient
{
   public static void main( String [ ] args )
   {
     CheckingAccount c3 = new CheckingAccount( 100.00, 7.50 );
     System.out.println( "New checking account:\n"
                         + c3.toString( )
                         + "; monthly fee is "
                         + c3.getMonthlyFee( ) );

     c3.applyMonthlyFee( );  // charge the fee to the account
     System.out.println( "\nAfter charging monthly fee:\n"
                         + c3.toString( )
                         + "; monthly fee is "
                         + c3.getMonthlyFee( ) );
   }
}
```

EXAMPLE 10.8 *CheckingAccountClient*, Version 3

10.2.4 Overriding Inherited Methods

When the methods our subclass inherits do not fulfill the functions we need, we can **override** the inherited methods by providing new versions of those methods. We have seen this feature in our applets. Whenever we wrote an *init* or *paint* method, we were overriding the corresponding method inherited from the *JApplet* class.

To override an inherited method, we provide a new method with the same header as the inherited method; that is, the new method must have the same name, the same number and type of parameters, and the same return type. Overriding a method makes the inherited version of the method invisible to the client of the subclass. We say that the overridden method is hidden from the client. When the client calls the method using a subclass object reference, the subclass version of the method is invoked.

Methods in a subclass can still access the inherited version of the method by preceding the method call with the *super* keyword, as in the following syntax:

```
super.methodName( argument list )
```

In our *CheckingAccount* class, we inherited the *toString* method from the *BankAccount* class. But this method returns only the *balance.* In Example 10.8, we needed to call the *CheckingAccount* method *getMonthlyFee* to print the value of *monthlyFee.* Furthermore, as Figure 10.6 shows, the *balance* value is formatted and the *monthlyFee* value is not. Instead, the *toString* method in the *CheckingAccount* class should return formatted versions of both the *balance* and the *monthlyFee.* We can accomplish this by overriding the inherited *toString* method.

Example 10.9 shows Version 4 of the *CheckingAccount* class with the new *toString* method (lines 59–67). To format the *balance,* we call the *toString* method of the *BankAccount* class (line 65), then add the formatted value of *monthlyFee* to the *String* being returned. Notice that we didn't need to instantiate a new *DecimalFormat* object in order to format the *monthlyFee* instance variable. Because the *MONEY* object is declared to be *public* in the *BankAccount* class, we inherited the *MONEY* object, so we can simply call the *format* method using the *MONEY* object reference. An advantage to making the *MONEY* object *public* is that both the balance and the monthly fee will be printed using the same formatting rules. Another advantage is that if we want to change the formatting for printing the data, we need to make only one change: We redefine the value of the *MONEY* constant in the *BankAccount* class.

```
1  /* CheckingAccount class, Version 4
2     Anderson, Franceschi
3  */
4
5  public class CheckingAccount extends BankAccount
6  {
```

```
public final double DEFAULT_FEE = 5.00;
private double monthlyFee;

/** default constructor
*   explicitly calls the BankAccount default constructor
*   set monthlyFee to default value
*/
public CheckingAccount( )
{
   super( ); // call BankAccount constructor
   monthlyFee = DEFAULT_FEE;
}

/** overloaded constructor
*  calls BankAccount overloaded constructor
*  @param  startBalance  starting balance
*  @param  startMonthlyFee starting monthly fee
*/
public CheckingAccount( double startBalance,
                        double startMonthlyFee )
{
   super( startBalance ); // call BankAccount constructor
   setMonthlyFee( startMonthlyFee );
}

/** applyMonthlyFee method
* charges the monthly fee to the account
*/
public void applyMonthlyFee( )
{
   withdraw( monthlyFee );
}

 /** accessor method for monthlyFee
 *  @return  monthlyFee
 */
 public double getMonthlyFee( )
 {
   return monthlyFee;
 }

/** mutator method for monthlyFee
*  @param newMonthlyFee new value for monthlyFee
*/
public void setMonthlyFee( double newMonthlyFee )
```

```
    {
      if ( monthlyFee >= 0.0 )
        monthlyFee = newMonthlyFee;
      else
        System.err.println( "Monthly fee cannot be negative" );
    }

    /* toString method
    *  @return String containing formatted balance and monthlyFee
    *     invokes superclass toString to format balance
    */
    public String toString( )
    {
      return super.toString( )
             + "; monthly fee is " + MONEY.format( monthlyFee );
    }
}
```

EXAMPLE 10.9 *CheckingAccount* Class, Version 4

Example 10.10 shows Version 4 of the *CheckingAccountClient* class. In this class, we again instantiate a *CheckingAccount* object with an initial balance of $100.00 and a monthly fee of $7.50 (line 9), then implicitly invoke the *toString* method to print the data of the object (line 10). This time, we invoke the *toString* method of the *CheckingAccount* class, which returns both the *balance* and *monthlyFee* values, formatted as money, as shown in Figure 10.7.

```
 1 /* CheckingAccount Client, Version 4
 2    Anderson, Franceschi
 3 */
 4
 5 public class CheckingAccountClient
 6 {
 7    public static void main( String [ ] args )
 8    {
 9      CheckingAccount c4 = new CheckingAccount( 100.00, 7.50 );
10      System.out.println( "New checking account:\n" + c4 );
11    }
12 }
```

EXAMPLE 10.10 *CheckingAccountClient*, Version 4

Figure 10.7
Output from *Checking-AccountClient*, Version 4

```
New checking account:
balance is $100.00; monthly fee is $7.50
```

COMMON ERROR TRAP

Do not confuse overriding a method with overloading a method. A subclass overriding a method provides a new version of that method, which hides the superclass version. A client calling the method using a subclass object reference will invoke the subclass version. A class overloading a method provides a new version of that method, which varies in the number and/or type of parameters. All *public* versions of overloaded methods are available to be called by the client of the class.

SOFTWARE ENGINEERING TIP

Methods that override inherited methods should explicitly call the direct superclass method whenever appropriate, in order to process inherited fields.

Table 10.3 summarizes the inheritance rules for inherited methods that have been overridden.

When you override a method, be sure that the method signature is identical to the inherited method. However, you can override an inherited method with a method that specifies a subclass object reference where the original method used a superclass reference. This is possible because a subclass object is a superclass object, so a subclass object reference can be substituted for any superclass object reference. If two methods of a class have the same name but different signatures (that is, if the number, order, or type of parameters is different), then the method is *overloaded*, not *overridden*.

For example, if in an applet we were to write the *init* method with the following header:

```
public void init( int a )
```

then our *init* method has a different signature from the *init* method we inherited from the *JApplet* class, which does not take any parameters. In this case, we are overloading the *init* method, not overriding it. In other words, we are providing an additional version of the *init* method. The inherited version is still visible and available to be called. When the applet starts executing, the browser or applet viewer would call the *init* method of the *JApplet* class, not our *init* method.

TABLE 10.3 Inheritance Rules for Overridden Methods

Superclass Members	Inherited by Subclass?	Directly Accessible by Subclass?	Directly Accessible by Client of Subclass Using a Subclass Reference?
public or *protected* inherited methods that have been overridden in the subclass	no	yes, using `super.methodName( arg list )`	no

TABLE 10.4 Overriding vs. Overloading Methods

	Method Names	Argument Lists	Return Types	Directly Accessible by Subclass Client Using a Subclass Object Reference?
Overriding a *public* Method	identical	identical	identical	only the subclass version can be called
Overloading a *public* Method	identical	different in number or type of parameters	identical	all versions of the overloaded method can be called

Skill Practice
with these end-of-chapter questions

10.10.1 Multiple Choice Exercises
Questions 1, 2, 4, 8, 9

10.10.3 Fill In the Code
Questions 21,22,23,34

10.10.5 Debugging Area
Questions 32, 34, 35

10.10.6 Write a Short Program
Questions 36,37,38,39,40,41,42,43,44,45,46

10.10.8 Technical Writing
Question 56

Table 10.4 illustrates the differences between overriding *public* methods and overloading *public* methods.

10.3 The *protected* Access Modifier

We have seen that the subclass does not inherit constructors or *private* members of the superclass. However, the superclass constructors are still available to be called from the subclass and the *private* fields of the superclass are implemented as fields of the subclass.

Although *private* fields preserve encapsulation, there is additional processing overhead involved with calling methods. Whenever a method is called, the JVM saves the return address and makes copies of the arguments. Then when a value-returning method completes, the JVM makes a copy of the return value available to the caller. The *protected* access modifier was designed to avoid this processing overhead and to facilitate coding by allowing the subclass to access any *protected* field without calling its accessor or mutator method.

Be aware, however, that *protected* fields and methods also can be accessed directly by other classes in the same package, even if the classes are not within the same inheritance hierarchy.

To classes outside the package, a *protected* member of a class has the same restrictions as a *private* member. In other words, a class outside the package in which the *protected* member is declared may not call any *protected* methods and must access any *protected* fields through *public* accessor or mutator methods.

The *protected* access modifier has tradeoffs. As we mentioned, any fields declared as *protected* can be accessed directly by subclasses. Doing so, however, compromises encapsulation because multiple classes can set the value of an instance variable defined in another class.

Thus, maintaining classes that define or use *protected* members becomes more difficult. For example, we need to verify that any class that has access to the *protected* instance variable either does not set the variable's value, or if the class does change the value, that the new value is valid. Because of this added maintenance complexity, we recommend that *protected* access be used only when high performance is essential.

SOFTWARE ENGINEERING TIP

Unless high performance is a critical requirement, avoid using the *protected* access modifier because doing so compromises encapsulation and complicates the maintenance of a program. Where possible, call superclass methods to change the values of *protected* instance variables.

We also recommend that subclass methods avoid directly setting the value of a *protected* instance variable. Instead, wherever possible, call superclass methods when values of *protected* variables need to be changed.

To illustrate how *protected* access can be used in class hierarchies, let's look closely at our *CheckingAccount* class. We have been calling the *withdraw* method inherited from the *BankAccount* class to apply the monthly fee. However, the *withdraw* method leaves the *balance* unchanged if the withdrawal amount is greater than the balance. Thus, if the account does not have sufficient funds, the monthly fee is not charged. We would like the *CheckingAccount* class to be able to charge the monthly fee to the account and let the balance become negative. When this happens, we will print a warning message that the account is overdrawn.

To accomplish this, we declare the *balance* instance variable to be *protected* instead of *private*. This allows us to directly access *balance* inside the *applyMonthlyFee* method of the *CheckingAccount* class, because *balance* is now inherited by *CheckingAccount*.

Example 10.11 shows the *BankAccount* class, Version 3. The only change, compared to version 1 (Example 10.1), is that the *balance* instance variable is declared as *protected*, rather than *private* (line 11).

```
1 /**    BankAccount class, Version 3
2 *      Anderson, Franceschi
3 *      Represents a generic bank account
4 */
5 import java.text.DecimalFormat;
6
7 public class BankAccount
8 {
9   public final DecimalFormat MONEY
10                  = new DecimalFormat( "$#,##0.00" );
11  protected double balance;
12
13  /** Default constructor
14  *   sets balance to 0.0
15  */
16  public BankAccount( )
17  {
18    balance = 0.0;
19  }
20
21  /** Overloaded constructor
22  *   @param startBalance  beginning balance
23  */
24  public BankAccount( double startBalance )
25  {
26    deposit( startBalance );
27  }
28
29  /** Accessor for balance
30  *   @return  current account balance
31  */
```

```
  public double getBalance( )
  {
    return balance;
  }

  /** Deposit amount to account
  *   @param amount  amount to deposit;
  *                  amount must be >= 0.0
  */
  public void deposit( double amount )
  {
    if ( amount >= 0.0 )
      balance += amount;
    else
      System.err.println( "Deposit amount must be positive." );
  }

  /** withdraw amount from account
  *    @param amount   amount to withdraw;
  *                    amount must be >= 0.0
  *                    amount must be <= balance
  */
  public void withdraw( double amount )
  {
    if (  amount >= 0.0 && amount <= balance )
      balance -= amount;
    else
      System.err.println( "Withdrawal amount must be positive "
                          + "and cannot be greater than balance" );
  }

  /** toString
  *  @return  the balance formatted as money
  */
  public String toString( )
  {
    return ( "balance is " + MONEY.format( balance ) );
  }
}
```

EXAMPLE 10.11 ***BankAccount* Class, Version 3**

Example 10.12 shows Version 5 of the *CheckingAccount* class, which inherits from the *BankAccount* class in Example 10.11 that declares the *balance* as *protected.* The *CheckingAccount* class now inherits *balance*, and our *CheckingAccount* methods can access the *balance* variable directly. Nevertheless, in the default and overloaded constructors, we still call the superclass constructor to set the value of *balance* (lines 16 and 28). Otherwise, to avoid setting *balance* to an invalid initial value, we would need to know the validation rules for *balance* in *BankAccount* and unnecessarily duplicate that code.

Also, in the *toString* method (lines 61–69), we call the *toString* method of the *BankAccount* class. Again, we do this to be consistent with the superclass functionality and to avoid duplicating code in the *BankAccount* class.

In the *applyMonthlyFee* method (lines 32–40), however, we access *balance* directly. For this checking account, our bank will charge the monthly fee even if it results in a negative balance for the account, so we subtract *monthlyFee* from *balance*, which allows the balance to be negative, and if so, we print a warning. Notice that we change the value of *balance* directly instead of calling the *getBalance* and *withdraw* methods.

```
1 /* CheckingAccount class, Version 5
2    Anderson, Franceschi
3 */
4
5 public class CheckingAccount extends BankAccount
6 {
7    public final double DEFAULT_FEE = 5.00;
8    private double monthlyFee;
9
10   /** default constructor
11   *   explicitly calls the BankAccount default constructor
12   *   set monthlyFee to default value
13   */
14   public CheckingAccount( )
15   {
16     super( );       // call BankAccount constructor
17     monthlyFee = DEFAULT_FEE;
18   }
19
20   /** overloaded constructor
21   *  calls BankAccount overloaded constructor
```

```
 *  @param  startBalance    starting balance
 *  @param  startMonthlyFee starting monthly fee
 */
public CheckingAccount( double startBalance,
                        double startMonthlyFee )
{
  super( startBalance );   // call BankAccount constructor
  setMonthlyFee( startMonthlyFee );
}

/** applyMonthlyFee method
* charges the monthly fee to the account
*/
public void applyMonthlyFee( )
{
  balance -= monthlyFee;
  if ( balance < 0.0 )
    System.err.println( "Warning: account is overdrawn" );
}

/** accessor method for monthlyFee
*  @return  monthlyFee
*/
public double getMonthlyFee( )
{
  return monthlyFee;
}

/** mutator method for monthlyFee
*  @param newMonthlyFee new value for monthlyFee
*/
public void setMonthlyFee( double newMonthlyFee )
{
  if ( monthlyFee >= 0.0 )
     monthlyFee = newMonthlyFee;
  else
     System.err.println( "Monthly fee cannot be negative" );
}

/* toString method
*  @return String containing formatted balance and monthlyFee
*    invokes superclass toString to format balance
*/
```

```
    public String toString( )
    {
      return super.toString( )
             + "; monthly fee is " + MONEY.format( monthlyFee );
    }
}
```

EXAMPLE 10.12 *CheckingAccount* Class, Version 5

Example 10.13 shows Version 5 of the *CheckingAccountClient* class. In this class, we again instantiate a *CheckingAccount* object with an initial balance of $100.00 and a monthly fee of $7.50 (line 9). We then call *withdraw* (line 12), so that the resulting balance is less than the monthly fee. Next we call the *applyMonthlyFee* method (line 16). When we print the state of the object in line 17, the *balance* is negative. The output of Example 10.13 is shown in Figure 10.8.

```
1 /* CheckingAccount Client, Version 5
2     Anderson, Franceschi
3 */
4
5 public class CheckingAccountClient
6 {
7    public static void main( String [ ] args )
8    {
9      CheckingAccount c5 = new CheckingAccount( 100.00, 7.50 );
10     System.out.println( "New checking account:\n" + c5 );
11
12     c5.withdraw( 95 );
13     System.out.println( "\nAfter withdrawing $95:\n" + c5 );
14
15     System.out.println( "\nApplying the monthly fee:" );
16     c5.applyMonthlyFee( );
17     System.out.println( "\nAfter charging monthly fee:\n" + c5 );
18   }
19 }
```

EXAMPLE 10.13 *CheckingAccountClient* Class, Version 5

Table 10.5 compiles all the inheritance rules we have discussed.

Figure 10.8
Output from *Checking-AccountClient*, Version 5

```
New checking account:
balance is $100.00; monthly fee is $7.50

After withdrawing $95:
balance is $5.00; monthly fee is $7.50

Applying the monthly fee:
Warning: account is overdrawn

After charging monthly fee:
balance is -$2.50; monthly fee is $7.50
```

TABLE 10.5 Inheritance Rules

Superclass Members	Inherited by Subclass?	Directly Accessible by Subclass?	Directly Accessible by Client of Subclass?
public fields	yes	yes, by using field name	yes
public methods	yes	yes, by calling method from other subclass methods	yes, by calling method using a subclass object reference
protected fields	yes	yes, by using field name	no, must use accessors and mutators
protected methods	yes	yes, by calling method from subclass methods	no
private fields	no	no, must use accessors and mutators	no, must use accessors and mutators
private methods	no	no	no
constructors	no	yes, using `super( arg list )` in a subclass constructor	no
public or *protected* inherited methods that have been overridden in the subclass	no	yes, using `super.methodName( arg list )`	no

Skill Practice
with these end-of-chapter questions

10.10.2 Reading and Understanding Code

Questions 12,13,14,15,16,17,18,19,20

CODE IN ACTION

On the CD-ROM included with this book, you will find a Flash movie with a step-by-step illustration of the use of inheritance in a program. Click on the link for Chapter 10 to start the movie.

10.4 Programming Activity 1: Using Inheritance

For this Programming Activity, you will create the *SavingsAccount* class, which inherits directly from the *BankAccount* class. The *SavingsAccount* class is similar to the *CheckingAccount* class in that both classes inherit from *BankAccount*. Figure 10.9 shows the resulting hierarchy.

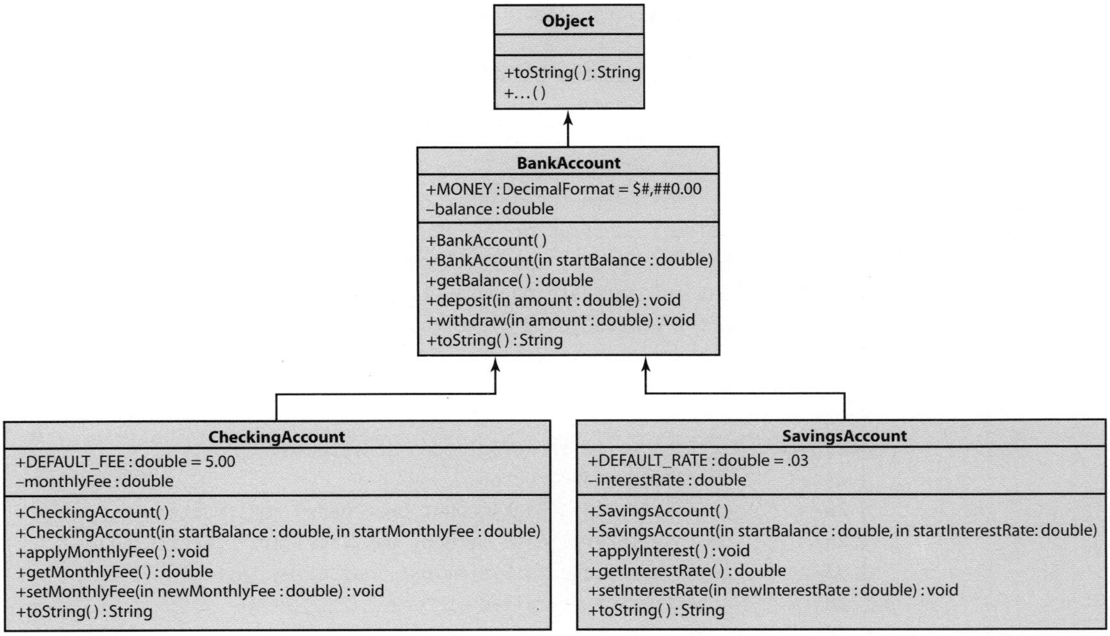

Figure 10.9
Bank Account Hierarchy

The *SavingsAccount* class inherits from the version of the *BankAccount* class in which the *balance* is declared to be *private*. The *SavingsAccount* subclass adds an annual *interestRate* instance variable, as well as supporting methods to access, change, and apply the interest rate to the account balance.

Instructions

Copy the source files in the Programming Activity 1 directory for this chapter to a directory on your computer. Load the *SavingsAccount.java* source file and search for five asterisks in a row (*****). This will position you to the six locations in the file where you will add code to complete the *SavingsAccount* class. The *SavingsAccount.java* file is shown in Example 10.14.

```
/* SavingsAccount class
   Anderson, Franceschi
*/

import java.text.NumberFormat;

// 1. ***** indicate that SavingsAccount inherits
//          from BankAccount
public class SavingsAccount
{
   public final double DEFAULT_RATE = .03;
   // 2. ****** define the private interestRate instance variable
   // interestRate, a double, represents an annual rate

   // 3. ***** write the default constructor
   /** default constructor
   *   explicitly call the BankAccount default constructor
   *   set interestRate to default value DEFAULT_RATE
   *   print a message to System.out indicating that
   *    constructor is called
   */

   // 4. ***** write the overloaded constructor
   /** overloaded constructor
   *   explicitly call BankAccount overloaded constructor
   *   call setInterestRate method, passing startInterestRate
   *   print a message to System.out indicating that
   *    constructor is called
   *  @param  startBalance      starting balance
   *  @param  startInterestRate starting interest rate
```

```
  */


  // 5. ****** write this method:
  /** applyInterest method, no parameters, void return value
  *  call the deposit method, passing a month's worth of interest
  *  remember that interestRate instance variable is annual rate
  */


  /** accessor method for interestRate
  *  @return  interestRate
  */
  public double getInterestRate( )
  {
    return interestRate;
  }

  /** mutator method for interestRate
  *  @param  newInterestRate new value for interestRate
  *          newInterestRate must be >= 0.0
  *            if not, print an error message
  */
  public void setInterestRate( double newInterestRate )
  {
    if ( interestRate >= 0.0 )
       interestRate = newInterestRate;
    else
       System.err.println( "Interest rate cannot be negative" );
  }

  // 6. *****  write this method
  /* toString method
  *  @return String containing formatted balance and interestRate
  *    invokes superclass toString to format balance
  *    formats interestRate as percent using a NumberFormat object
  *    To create a NumberFormat object for formatting percentages
  *    use the getPercentInstance method in the NumberFormat class,
  *    which has this API:
  *       static NumberFormat getPercentInstance( )
  */

}
```

EXAMPLE 10.14 ***SavingsAccount.java***

Figure 10.10
The Teller Window

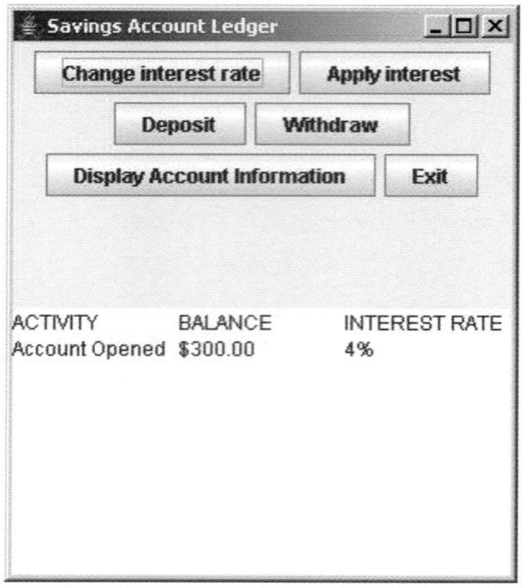

When you have completed the six tasks, load, compile, and run the Teller application (*Teller.java*), which you will use to test your *SavingsAccount* class. When the Teller application begins, you will be prompted with a dialog box for a starting balance. If you press "Enter" or the "OK" button without entering a balance, the Teller application will use the default constructor to instantiate a *SavingsAccount* object. If you enter a starting balance, the Teller application will prompt you for an interest rate and will instantiate a *SavingsAccount* object using the overloaded constructor. Once the *SavingsAccount* object has been instantiated, the Teller application will open the window shown in Figure 10.10, which provides buttons you can use to call the *SavingsAccount* methods to test your code.

Below the buttons is a ledger that displays the current state of the savings account. As you click on the various buttons, the ledger will display the operation performed and the values of the balance and the interest rate when that operation is complete.

The operations performed by each button are already coded for you and are the following:

- *Change Interest Rate*—prompts for a new interest rate and calls your *setInterestRate* method
- *Apply Interest*—calls your *applyInterest* method
- *Deposit*—prompts for the deposit amount and calls the *deposit* method inherited from *BankAccount*
- *Withdraw*—prompts for the withdrawal amount and calls the *withdraw* method inherited from *BankAccount*

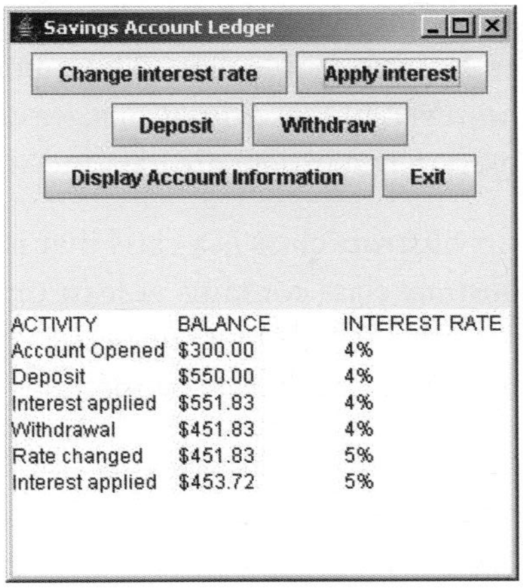

Figure 10.11
Sample Teller Window After Performing Several Operations

- *Display Account Information*—calls your *toString* method and displays the result in a dialog box
- *Exit*—exits the program.

Figure 10.11 shows the Teller window after several operations have been performed.

? DISCUSSION QUESTIONS

1. Explain why the Teller application can call the *withdraw* and *deposit* methods using a *SavingsAccount* object reference, even though we did not define these methods.
2. Explain why your *applyInterest* method in the *SavingsAccount* class needs to call the *deposit* method of the *BankAccount* class.

10.5 *Abstract* Classes and Methods

In our Bank Account hierarchy, we could instantiate *BankAccount* objects, *CheckingAccount* objects, and *SavingsAccount* objects. In some situations, however, we will design a class hierarchy where one or more classes at the top of the hierarchy specify patterns for methods that subclasses in the hierarchy must implement. The superclasses do not implement these methods, however. In these situations, we do not intend that these superclasses will be used to instantiate objects, and we define the superclasses as ***abstract***.

An ***abstract* class** is a class that is not completely implemented. Usually, an *abstract* class contains at least one ***abstract* method**, that is, a method that specifies an API that subclasses should implement, but does not provide an implementation for the method.

Because an *abstract* class is not complete, it cannot be used to instantiate objects. An *abstract* class can be extended, however, so that its subclasses can complete the implementation of the *abstract* methods and can be instantiated.

A class is declared to be *abstract* by including the *abstract* keyword in the class header, as shown in the following syntax:

```
accessModifier abstract class ClassName
```

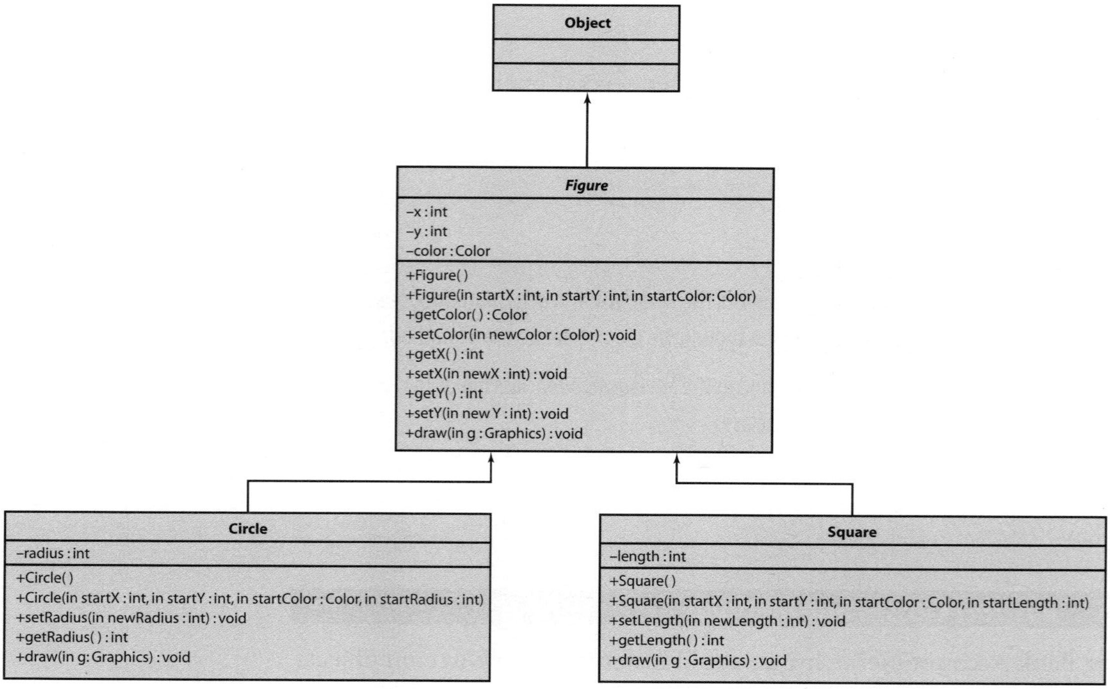

Figure 10.12
The *Figure* Hierarchy

An *abstract* method is defined by including the *abstract* keyword in the method header and by using a semicolon to indicate that there is no code for the method, as shown in the following syntax:

```
accessModifier abstract returnType methodName( argument list );
```

Note that we do not include opening and closing curly braces for the method body—just a semicolon to indicate that the *abstract* method does not have a body.

For example, to draw figures, we can set up the hierarchy shown in Figure 10.12. The root superclass under *Object* is the *abstract Figure* class, and we derive two subclasses: *Circle* and *Square*. In the UML diagram, the name of the *Figure* class is set in italics to indicate that it is an *abstract* class.

All figures will have an (*x*, *y*) coordinate and a color, so the *Figure* class defines three fields: two *ints*, *x* and *y*, and a *Color* object named *color*.

We want all classes in the hierarchy to provide a *draw* method to render the figure; however, the *Figure* class has nothing but a point to draw, so its *draw* method has nothing to do. Thus, we will not provide an implementation of the *draw* method in the *Figure* class; instead, we will define the *draw* method as an *abstract* method.

Let's look at the code for the *Figure* hierarchy in detail. Example 10.15 shows the *abstract Figure* class. We define the class as *abstract* in the class header (line 7). The constructors (lines 13–22 and lines 24–37) instantiate the *x* and *y* values and the *Color* object that all figures will have in common. The *Figure* class also provides accessor and mutator methods for its instance variables. The *abstract draw* method (lines 88–91) provides the API for the *draw* method, but no implementation—just a semicolon. The *Circle* and *Square* subclasses of the *Figure* class will provide appropriate implementations of the *draw* method.

```
1 /** abstract Figure superclass for drawing shapes
2 *   Anderson, Franceschi
3 */
4 import java.awt.Graphics;
5 import java.awt.Color;
6
7 public abstract class Figure
8 {
9   private int x;
10  private int y;
11  private Color color;
```

```java

/** default constructor
*   sets x and y to 0
*   sets color to black
*/
public Figure( )
{
  x = 0;
  y = 0;
  color = Color.BLACK;
}

/** overloaded constructor
*   sets x to startX
*   sets y to startY
*   sets the color to startColor
*   @param  startX      starting x pixel for figure
*   @param  startY      starting y pixel for figure
*   @param  startColor  figure color
*/
public Figure( int startX, int startY, Color startColor )
{
  x = startX;
  y = startY;
  color = startColor;
}

/** accessor method for color
*   @return current figure color
*/
public Color getColor( )
{
  Color tempColor = color;
  return tempColor;
}

/** mutator method for color
*   @param newColor  new color for figure
*/
public void setColor( Color newColor )
{
  color = newColor;
}

/** accessor method for x
```

```
    *   @return current x value
    */
    public int getX( )
    {
      return x;
    }

    /** mutator method for x
    *   @param newX  new value for x
    */
    public void setX( int newX )
    {
      x = newX;
    }

    /** accessor method for y
    *   @return current y value
    */
    public int getY( )
    {
      return y;
    }

    /** mutator method for y
    *   @param newY new y value
    */
    public void setY( int newY )
    {
      y = newY;
    }

    /** abstract draw method
    *   @param Graphics context for drawing figure
    */
    public abstract void draw( Graphics g );
}
```

EXAMPLE 10.15 The *abstract Figure* Class

COMMON ERROR TRAP

Do not include opening and closing curly braces in the definition of an *abstract* method. Including them would mean that the method is implemented, but does nothing. Instead, indicate an unimplemented method by using a semicolon.

COMMON ERROR TRAP

Attempting to instantiate an object of an *abstract* class will generate the following compiler error:

```
className is
abstract; cannot
be instantiated
```

where *className* is the name of the *abstract* class.

When a subclass inherits from an *abstract* class, it can provide implementations for any, all, or none of the *abstract* methods. If the subclass does not completely implement all the *abstract* methods of the superclass, then the subclass must also be declared *abstract*. If, however, the subclass implements all the *abstract* methods in the superclass, and the subclass is not declared *abstract*, then the class is not *abstract* and we can instantiate objects of that subclass.

Example 10.16 shows the *Circle* class, which inherits from the *Figure* class and adds a *radius* instance variable. In the overloaded constructor, we pass the *startX*, *startY*, and *startColor* parameters to the constructor of the *Figure* class (line 34). On lines 54–63, the *Circle* class implements the *draw* method. We get the (*x*, *y*) coordinate and the color for the circle by calling the accessor methods of the *Figure* class because the *x*, *y*, and *color* instance variables are declared *private*.

```
 1 /* Circle class
 2 *  inherits from abstract Figure class
 3 *  Anderson, Franceschi
 4 */
 5
 6 import java.awt.Graphics;
 7 import java.awt.Color;
 8
 9 public class Circle extends Figure
10 {
11    private int radius;
12
13    /** default constructor
14    *   calls default constructor of Figure class
15    *   sets radius to 0
16    */
17    public Circle( )
18    {
19      super( );
20      radius = 0;
21    }
22
23    /** overloaded constructor
24    *   sends startX, startY, startColor to Figure constructor
25    *   sends startRadius to setRadius method
26    *   @param startX      starting x pixel
27    *   @param startY      starting y pixel
28    *   @param startColor  color for circle
29    *   @param startRadius radius of circle
30    */
31    public Circle( int startX, int startY, Color startColor,
32                   int startRadius )
```

```
33    {
34       super( startX, startY, startColor );
35       setRadius( startRadius );
36    }
37
38    /** mutator method for radius
39    *   @param newRadius  new value for radius
40    */
41    public void setRadius( int newRadius )
42    {
43       radius = newRadius;
44    }
45
46    /** accessor method for radius
47    *   @return radius
48    */
49    public int getRadius( )
50    {
51       return radius;
52    }
53
54    /** draw method
55    *  sets color and draws a circle
56    *  @param g  Graphics context for drawing the circle
57    */
58    public void draw( Graphics g )
59    {
60        g.setColor( getColor( ) );
61        g.fillOval ( getX( ), getY( ),
62                     radius * 2, radius * 2 );
63    }
64 }
```

EXAMPLE 10.16 The *Circle* Class

Similarly, Example 10.17 shows the *Square* class, which also inherits from the *Figure* class. The *Square* class adds a *length* instance variable and uses code similar to the *Circle* class to call the constructors of the *Figure* class (lines 19 and 34) and to implement its own version of the *draw* method (lines 54–63).

```
1 /* Square class
2 *  inherits from abstract Figure class
3 *  Anderson, Franceschi
4 */
```

```java

import java.awt.Graphics;
import java.awt.Color;

public class Square extends Figure
{
   private int length;

   /** default constructor
   *   calls default constructor of Figure class
   *   sets length to 0
   */
   public Square( )
   {
     super( );
     length = 0;
   }

   /** overloaded constructor
   *   sends startX, startY, startColor to Figure constructor
   *   sets startLength to setLength method
   *   @param startX      starting x pixel
   *   @param startY      starting y pixel
   *   @param startColor  color for square
   *   @param startLength length of square
   */
   public Square( int startX, int startY, Color startColor,
                  int startLength )
   {
      super( startX, startY, startColor );
      setLength( startLength );
   }

   /** mutator method for length
   *   @param newLength  new value for length
   */
   public void setLength( int newLength )
   {
      length = newLength;
   }

   /** accessor method for length
   *   @return length
   */
   public int getLength( )
```

```
   {
      return length;
   }

   /** draw method
   *  sets color and draws a square
   *  @param g  Graphics context for drawing square
   */
   public void draw( Graphics g )
   {
      g.setColor( getColor( ) );
      g.fillRect( getX( ), getY( ),
                  length, length );
   }
}
```

EXAMPLE 10.17 The *Square* Class

REFERENCE POINT

For more information on *ArrayLists*, see Chapter 9.

Because we want to instantiate *Circle* and *Square* objects, we do not declare these classes *abstract* and they are forced to implement the *draw* method. Example 10.18 shows a client applet, *TrafficLight*, which paints a traffic light, shown in Figure 10.13. On lines 10 and 11, we declare two *ArrayLists*, one to hold *Circle* objects and one to hold *Square* objects. In the *init* method (lines 13–24), we instantiate both *ArrayLists* and add three *Square* objects to *squaresList* and three *Circle* objects to *circlesList*. Then in the *paint* method, we create the traffic light by calling the *draw* methods for all

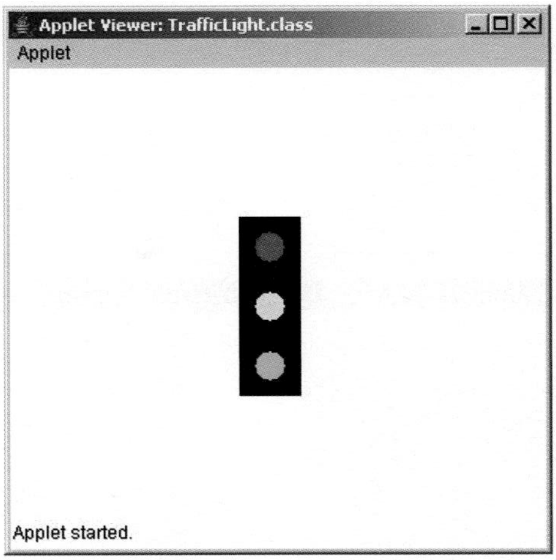

Figure 10.13
The *TrafficLight* Applet

the *Squares* in the *squaresList* (lines 28–29), then calling the *draw* method for all the *Circles* in the *circlesList* (lines 31–32).

```
 1 /* Figure Hierarchy Client
 2    Anderson, Franceschi
 3 */
 4 import javax.swing.JApplet;
 5 import java.awt.*;
 6 import java.util.ArrayList;
 7
 8 public class TrafficLight extends JApplet
 9 {
10   private ArrayList<Circle> circlesList;
11   private ArrayList<Square> squaresList;
12
13   public void init( )
14   {
15     squaresList = new ArrayList<Square>( );
16     squaresList.add( new Square( 150, 100, Color.BLACK, 40 ) );
17     squaresList.add( new Square( 150, 140, Color.BLACK, 40 ) );
18     squaresList.add( new Square( 150, 180, Color.BLACK, 40 ) );
19
20     circlesList = new ArrayList<Circle>( );
21     circlesList.add( new Circle( 160, 110, Color.RED, 10 ) );
22     circlesList.add( new Circle( 160, 150, Color.YELLOW, 10 ) );
23     circlesList.add( new Circle( 160, 190, Color.GREEN, 10 ) );
24   }
25
26   public void paint( Graphics g )
27   {
28     for ( Square s : squaresList )
29       s.draw( g );
30
31     for ( Circle c : circlesList )
32       c.draw( g );
33   }
34 }
```

EXAMPLE 10.18 The *TrafficLight* Applet

TABLE 10.6 Restrictions for Defining *abstract* Classes and Methods

abstract classes	• Classes must be declared *abstract* if the class contains any *abstract* methods. • *abstract* classes can be extended. • *abstract* classes cannot be used to instantiate objects.
abstract methods	• *abstract* methods can be declared only within an *abstract* class. • An *abstract* method must consist of a method header followed by a semicolon. • *abstract* methods cannot be called. • *abstract* methods cannot be declared as *private* or *static*. • A constructor cannot be declared *abstract*.

Java imposes a few restrictions on declaring and using *abstract* classes and methods. These rules are summarized in Table 10.6.

10.6 Polymorphism

An important concept in inheritance is that an object of a class is also an object of any of its superclasses. That concept is the basis for an important OOP feature, called **polymorphism**, which simplifies the processing of various objects in the same class hierarchy. The word *polymorphism,* which is derived from the word fragment *poly* and the word *morpho* in the Greek language, literally means "multiple forms."

Polymorphism allows us to use the same method call for any object in the hierarchy. We make the method call using an object reference of the superclass. At run time, the JVM determines to which class in the hierarchy the object actually belongs and calls the version of the method implemented for that class.

To use polymorphism in your application, the following conditions must be true:

- the classes are in the same hierarchy
- the subclasses override the same method

- a subclass object reference is assigned to a superclass object reference (that is, a subclass object is referenced by a superclass reference)
- the superclass object reference is used to call the method

For example, we can take advantage of polymorphism in our traffic light applet by calling the *draw* method for either a *Circle* or *Square* object using a *Figure* object reference. Although we cannot instantiate an object from an *abstract* class, Java allows us to define object references of an *abstract* class.

Example 10.19 shows the rewritten traffic light applet. Instead of using separate *ArrayLists* for *Circle* and *Square* objects, we can declare and instantiate only one *ArrayList* of *Figure* references (lines 10 and 14). As each *Circle* and *Square* object is instantiated, we add its object reference to the *ArrayList* of *Figure* references (lines 15–22).

This greatly simplifies the *paint* method (lines 25–29), which steps through *figuresList*, calling the *draw* method for each element. For the method call, it doesn't matter whether the object reference in *figuresList* is a *Circle* or *Square* reference. We just call the *draw* method using that reference. At run time, the JVM determines whether the object is a *Circle* or a *Square* and calls the appropriate *draw* method for the object type. Notice that we have interwoven the adding of *Circles* and *Squares* to *figuresList*, rather than adding all *Squares*, then adding all *Circles*. Because the *ArrayList* is composed of *Figure* references, any element can be either a *Circle* or a *Square*—because a *Circle* and a *Square* are both *Figures*. The output of this applet is identical to that of Example 10.18, as shown in Figure 10.13.

```
 1 /* Figure hierarchy Client
 2    Anderson, Franceschi
 3 */
 4 import javax.swing.JApplet;
 5 import java.awt.*;
 6 import java.util.ArrayList;
 7
 8 public class TrafficLightPolymorphism extends JApplet
 9 {
10   private ArrayList<Figure> figuresList;
11
12   public void init( )
13   {
14     figuresList = new ArrayList<Figure>( );
15     figuresList.add( new Square( 150, 100, Color.BLACK, 40 ) );
```

```
    figuresList.add( new Circle( 160, 110, Color.RED, 10 ) );

    figuresList.add( new Square( 150, 140, Color.BLACK, 40 ) );
    figuresList.add( new Circle( 160, 150, Color.YELLOW, 10 ) );

    figuresList.add( new Square( 150, 180, Color.BLACK, 40 ) );
    figuresList.add( new Circle( 160, 190, Color.GREEN, 10 ) );
  }

  public void paint( Graphics g )
  {
    for ( Figure f : figuresList )
        f.draw( g );
  }
}
```

EXAMPLE 10.19 Traffic Light Using Polymorphism

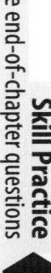

Skill Practice
with these end-of-chapter questions

10.10.1 Multiple Choice Exercises
Questions 7,10,11

10.10.4 Identifying Errors in Code
Question 31

10.10.5 Debugging Area
Questions 33,34,35

10.7 Programming Activity 2: Using Polymorphism

In this Programming Activity, you will complete the implementation of the Tortoise and the Hare race. The Tortoise runs a slow and steady race, while the Hare runs in spurts with rests in between. Figure 10.14 shows a sample run of the race. In this figure, we show only one tortoise and one hare; however, using polymorphism we can easily run the race with any number and combination of tortoises and hares.

The class hierarchy for this Programming Activity is shown in Figure 10.15.

Figure 10.14
A Sample Run of the Tortoise and the Hare Race

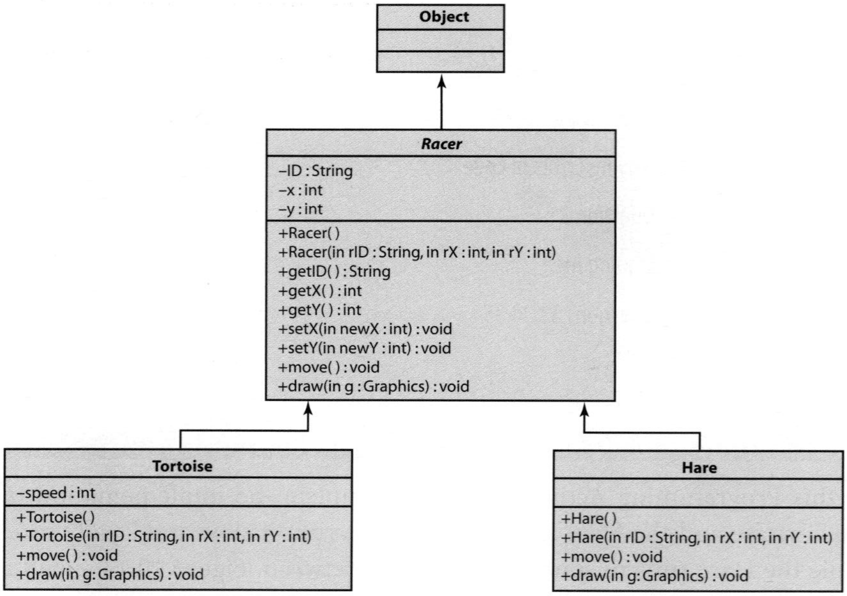

Figure 10.15
***Racer* Hierarchy**

The code for the *Racer* class, which is the superclass of the *Tortoise* and *Hare* classes, is shown in Example 10.20. The *Racer* class has three instance variables (lines 10–12): a *String ID*, which identifies the type of racer; and *x* and *y* positions, both of which are *ints*. The class has the usual constructors, as well as accessor and mutator methods for the *x* and *y* positions and ID. These instance variables and methods are common to all racers, so we put them in the *Racer* class. Individual racers, however, will differ in the way they move and in the way they are drawn. Thus, in line 8, we declare the *Racer* class to be *abstract*, and in lines 74–81, we define two *abstract* methods, *move* and *draw*. Classes that inherit from the *Racer* class will need to provide implementations of these two methods (or be declared *abstract* as well).

```
 1 /**  Racer class
 2 *    Abstract class intended for racer hierarchy
 3 *    Anderson, Franceschi
 4 */
 5
 6 import java.awt.Graphics;
 7
 8 public abstract class Racer
 9 {
10   private String ID;  // racer ID
11   private int x;      // x position
12   private int y;      // y position
13
14   /** default constructor
15   *    Sets ID to blank
16   */
17   public Racer( )
18   {
19     ID = "";
20   }
21
22   /** Constructor
23   *    @param rID   racer ID
24   *    @param rX    x position
25   *    @param rY    y position
```

```
*/
public Racer( String rID, int rX, int rY )
{
  ID = rID;
  x = rX;
  y = rY;
}

/** accessor for ID
*   @return  ID
*/
public String getID( )
{
  return ID;
}

/** accessor for x
*   @return  current x value
*/
public int getX( )
{
  return x;
}

/** accessor for y
*   @return  current y value
*/
public int getY( )
{
  return y;
}

/** mutator for x
*   @param  newX   new value for x
*/
public void setX( int newX )
{
  x = newX;
}

/** mutator for y
*   @param  newY   new value for y
*/
```

```
  public void setY( int newY )
  {
    y = newY;
  }

  /** abstract method for Racer's move
  */
  public abstract void move( );

  /** abstract method for drawing Racer
  *    @param   g    Graphics context
  */
  public abstract void draw( Graphics g );
}
```

EXAMPLE 10.20 The *abstract Racer* Class

The *Tortoise* and *Hare* classes inherit from the *Racer* class. Thus, their only job is to pass constructor arguments to the *Racer* class and implement the *draw* and *move* methods. For this Programming Activity, we have provided the *Tortoise* and *Hare* classes with the *draw* and *move* methods already written.

Your job is to add *Tortoise* and *Hare* objects to an *ArrayList* of *Racer* objects, as specified by the user. Then you will add code to run the race by stepping through the *ArrayList*, calling *move* and *draw* for each *Racer* object.

Instructions

Copy the source files in the Programming Activity 2 directory for this chapter to a directory on your computer.

1. Write the code to determine which racers will run the race. Load the *RacePoly.java* source file and search for five asterisks in a row (*****). This will position you inside the *prepareToRace* method.

   The dialog box to prompt the user for the racer type is already coded for you in the *getRacer* method. When your *switch* statement executes, the *getRacer* method has already been called and the *char* variable *input* contains the user's input. You do not need to call the *getRacer* method.

```
/** prepareToRace method
*   uses a dialog box to prompt user for racer types
*     and to start the race
*   racer types are 't' or 'T' for Tortoise,
*                   'h' or 'H' for Hare
*   's' or 'S' will start the race
*/
private void prepareToRace( )
{
   int yPos = FIRST_RACER;         // y position of first racer
   final int START_LINE = 40;      // x position of start of race
   final int RACER_SPACE = 50;     // spacing between racers
   char input;

   input = getRacer( ); // get input from user

   while ( input != 's' && input != 'S' )
   {
      /** 1. ***** Student writes this switch statement
      *  input local char variable contains the racer type
      *      entered by the user
      *  If input is 'T' or 't',
      *     add a Tortoise object to the ArrayList named racerList
      *            which is an instance variable of this class
      *  The API of the Tortoise constructor is:
      *          Tortoise( String ID, int startX, int startY )
      *   a sample call to the constructor is
      *          new Tortoise( "Tortoise", START_LINE, yPos )
      *          where START_LINE is a constant local variable
      *            representing the starting x position for the race
      *          and yPos is a local variable representing
      *             the next racer's y position
      *
      *  If input is 'H' or 'h',
      *      add a Hare object to the ArrayList named racerList
      *  The API of the Hare constructor is:
      *          Hare( String ID, int startX, int startY )
      *      a sample call to the constructor is
      *          new Hare( "Hare", START_LINE, yPos )
      *          where START_LINE is a constant local variable
      *            representing the starting x position for the race
      *          and yPos is a local variable representing
      *             the next racer's y position
      *
      *  After adding a racer to the ArrayList racerList,
```

```
     *          increment yPos by the value of
     *          the constant local variable RACER_SPACE
     *
     *  if input is anything other than 'T', 't',
     *          'H' or 'h', pop up an error dialog box
     *          a sample method call for the output dialog box is:
     *            JOptionPane.showMessageDialog( this, "Message" );
     */
     // write your switch statement here

      /** end of student code, part 1 */

      repaint( );
      input = getRacer( );  // get input from user

    } // end while

  } // end prepareToRace
```

2. Next, write the code to run the race. In the *RacePoly.java* source file, search again for five asterisks in a row (*****). This will position you inside the *paint* method, where you will perform tasks 2 and 3. For task 2, you will write code to loop through the *ArrayList* of *Racers* and call the *move* and *draw* methods for each racer as they run the race. When you finish that task, search again for five asterisks in a row (*****), which will position you at the location of task 3. This task is similar to task 2, in that you need to loop through the *ArrayList* of *Racers*. However, in this task you will only call the *draw* method for each *Racer*. This code will be executed before the race begins as racers are added to the start line.

   The portion of the *paint* method where you will add your code is shown here.

```
/** paint method
*    @param g   Graphics context
*    draws the finish line;
*    moves and draws racers
*/
public void paint( Graphics g )
{
  super.paint( g );
```

```
   // draw the finish line
   finishX = getWidth( ) - 20;
   g.setColor( Color.blue );
   g.drawLine( finishX, 0, finishX, getHeight( ) );

   if ( raceIsOn )
   {
      /* 2. ***** student writes this code
      *  loop through instance variable ArrayList racerList,
      *    which contains Racer object references,
      *    calling move, then draw for each racer
      *  The API for move is:
      *      void move( )
      *  The API for draw is:
      *      void draw( Graphics g )
      *        where g is the Graphics context
      *        passed to the paint method
      */

       /** end of student code, part 2 */
    }
    else  // display racers before race begins
    {
       /* 3. ***** student writes this code
       *  loop through instance variable ArrayList racerList,
       *    which contains Racer object references,
       *    calling draw for each element. (Do not call move!)
       *  The API for draw is:
       *      void draw( Graphics g )
       *        where g is the Graphics context
       *        passed to this paint method
       */
       // student code goes here

      /** end of student code, part 3 */
   }
}
```

When you have finished writing the code, compile the source code and run the *RacePoly* application. Try several runs of the race with a different number of racers and with a different combination of *Tortoises* and *Hares*. Figure 10.16 shows the race with four *Tortoises* and three *Hares*.

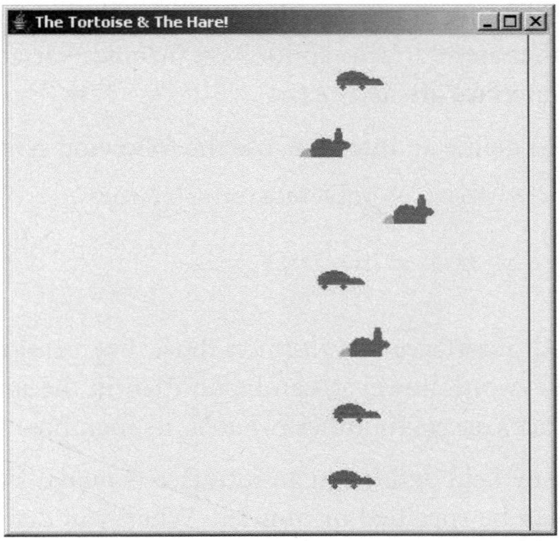

Figure 10.16
Another Run of the Race

DISCUSSION QUESTIONS

1. Explain how polymorphism simplifies this application.
2. If you wanted to add another racer, for example, an aardvark, explain what code you would need to write and what existing code, if any, you would need to change.

10.8 Interfaces

In Java, a class can inherit directly from only one class, that is, a class can *extend* only one class. To allow a class to inherit behavior from multiple sources, Java provides the **interface**.

An interface typically specifies behavior that a class will *implement*. Interface members can be any of the following:

- classes
- constants
- *abstract* methods
- other interfaces

Typically, interfaces define only constants and *abstract* methods. Notice that an interface cannot have instance variables and that all methods in an interface are *abstract*.

To define an interface, use the following syntax:

```
accessModifier interface InterfaceName
{
    // body of interface
}
```

All interfaces are *abstract*; thus, they cannot be instantiated. The *abstract* keyword, however, can be omitted in the interface definition. If the interface's access modifier is *public*, its members are implicitly *public* as well.

Any field defined in an interface is *public*, *static*, and *final*. These keywords can be specified or omitted. When you define a field in the interface, you must also assign a value to the field at that time.

All methods within an interface must be *abstract*, so the method definition must consist of only a method header and a semicolon. Like the interface header, the *abstract* keyword can be omitted from the method definition.

To inherit from an interface, a class declares that it *implements* the interface in the class definition, using the following syntax:

```
accessModifier class ClassName extends SuperclassName
                               implements Interface1, Interface2, ...
```

The *extends* clause is optional if the class inherits only from the *Object* class. A class can *implement* 0, 1, or more interfaces. If a class *implements* more than one interface, the interfaces are specified in a comma-separated list of interface names. When a class *implements* an interface, the class must provide an implementation for each method contained in the interface.

In the Programming Activity of the last section, we ran the Tortoise and the Hare Race. Each racer inherited from the *abstract Racer* class, which specified two *abstract* methods: *draw* and *move*. Thus, both the *Tortoise* and *Hare* classes implemented those two methods.

Below are brief, summarized versions of the *Racer* and *Tortoise* classes from Programming Activity 2:

```
// Racer defines move and draw as abstract methods
public abstract class Racer
{
```

```
  public abstract void move( );
  public abstract void draw( Graphics g );

  // other fields and methods
}

// Tortoise inherits from Racer and implements move and draw
public class Tortoise extends Racer
{
  public void move( )
  {
     // implementation here
  }

  public void draw( Graphics g )
  {
     // implementation here
  }

  // other fields and methods
}
```

That class hierarchy worked well for running the race, but suppose we just wanted to draw a tortoise or a hare, or another animal, without racing them. In other words, we don't want to implement the *move* method, just the *draw* method.

In this case, we can define an *abstract* class, *Animal*, which contains only one *abstract* method: *draw*. To provide the optional capability of running a race, we define an interface, named *Moveable*, which includes the *abstract* method *move*. Then, if we just want to draw an animal, we define a class that *extends* the *Animal* class. If we want to make our animal a racer, we implement the *Moveable* interface.

Following are brief, summarized versions of the *Animal* class; the *Moveable* interface; a racing animal class, which we call *TortoiseRacer*; and a *TortoiseNonRacer* class that can be used in another application where animal objects are drawn, but do not race.

```
// Animal defines only one abstract method: draw
public abstract class Animal
{
  public abstract void draw( Graphics g );
```

```
  // other fields and methods
}

// Moveable defines move as an abstract method
public interface Moveable
{
  // some constants defined here
  public void move( );

}

// TortoiseRacer inherits from Animal and Moveable
//  and implements both move and draw
public class TortoiseRacer extends Animal implements Moveable
{
  public void draw( Graphics g )
  {
     // implementation here
  }

  public void move( )
  {
     // implementation here
  }

  // other fields and methods here
}

// non-racing Tortoise inherits only from Animal
//  and implements draw method only
public class TortoiseNonRacer extends Animal
{
  public void draw( Graphics g )
  {
     // implementation here
  }

  // other fields and methods here
}
```

Example 10.21 shows the actual *Animal* class, which is similar to the *Racer* class shown in Example 10.20, except that its only *abstract* method is *draw* (lines 73–76).

```
/**  Animal class
*    Anderson, Franceschi
*/

import java.awt.Graphics;

public abstract class Animal
{
  private int x;       // x position
  private int y;       // y position
  private String ID;   // animal ID

  /** default constructor
  *    Sets ID to empty String
  */
  public Animal( )
  {
    ID = "";
  }

  /** Constructor
  *    @param rID   Animal ID
  *    @param rX    x position
  *    @param rY    y position
  */
  public Animal( String rID, int rX, int rY )
  {
    ID = rID;
    x = rX;
    y = rY;
  }

  /** accessor for ID
  *   @return  ID
  */
  public String getID( )
  {
    return ID;
  }

  /** accessor for x
  *   @return  x coordinate
  */
  public int getX( )
  {
```

```
    return x;
  }

  /** accessor for y
  *   @return  y coordinate
  */
  public int getY( )
  {
    return y;
  }

  /** mutator for x
  *   @param  newX  new value for x position
  */
  public void setX( int newX )
  {
    x = newX;
  }

  /** mutator for y
  *   @param  newY  new value for y position
  */
  public void setY( int newY )
  {
    y = newY;
  }

  /** abstract method for drawing Animal
  *   @param   g    Graphics context
  */
  public abstract void draw( Graphics g );
}
```

EXAMPLE 10.21 The *Animal* Class

Example 10.22 shows the actual *Moveable* interface, which specifies the API for the *move* method (line 10). Although all methods in an interface are *abstract*, we do not need to specify the *abstract* keyword. Also, all members of a *public* interface are *public*, so we do not need to specify an access modifier either.

In lines 7–8, we define two constants, which will be used by the racer in the *move* method to determine how fast the racer will move. A hare would increment its *x* value by the *FAST* value (5), and the tortoise would increment its *x* value by the *SLOW* value (1).

```
/** Moveable interface
*   Anderson, Franceschi
*/

public interface Moveable
{
  int FAST = 5; // static constant
  int SLOW = 1; // static constant

  void move( ); // abstract method
}
```

EXAMPLE 10.22 The *Moveable* Interface

Example 10.23 shows the actual *TortoiseRacer* class, which is functionally equivalent to the *Tortoise* class in the Programming Activity. It inherits from the *Animal* class and *implements* the *Moveable* interface (line 10). It provides bodies for both the *draw* method (lines 29–53), inherited from *Animal*, and the *move* method (lines 55–63), inherited through the *Moveable* interface. Because implementing the *Moveable* interface is optional, we can also define classes that inherit from *Animal*, but do not need to provide a *move* method. In this way, we have designed for more optimal reuse of our classes.

```
1 /**  TortoiseRacer class
2 *    inherits from abstract Animal class
3 *    implements Moveable interface
4 *    Anderson, Franceschi
5 */
6
7 import java.awt.Graphics;
8 import java.awt.Color;
9
10 public class TortoiseRacer extends Animal implements Moveable
11 {
12   /** Default Constructor: calls Animal default constructor
13   */
14   public TortoiseRacer( )
15   {
```

```
    super( );
  }

  /** Constructor
  *    @param rID  racer Id, passed to Animal constructor
  *    @param rX   x position, passed to Animal constructor
  *    @param rY   y position, passed to Animal constructor
  */
  public TortoiseRacer( String rID, int rX, int rY )
  {
    super( rID, rX, rY );
  }

  /** draw: draws the Tortoise at current (x, y) coordinate
  *       implements abstract method in Animal class
  *       @param g   Graphics context
  */
  public void draw( Graphics g )
  {
    int startX = getX( );
    int startY = getY( );

    g.setColor( new Color( 34, 139, 34 ) ); // dark green

    //body
    g.fillOval( startX, startY, 25, 15 );

    //head
    g.fillOval( startX + 20, startY + 5,  15, 10 );

    //flatten bottom
    g.clearRect( startX, startY + 11, 35, 4 );

    //feet
    g.setColor( new Color( 34, 139, 34 ) );  // brown
    g.fillOval( startX + 3, startY + 10,  5, 5 );
    g.fillOval( startX + 17, startY + 10, 5, 5 );
  }

  /** implements move method in Moveable interface
  *   move:  calculates the new x value for the racer
  *   Tortoise move characteristics: "slow & steady wins the race"
  *      increment x by SLOW (inherited from Moveable interface)
  */
```

```
    public void move( )
    {
        setX( getX( ) + SLOW );
    }
}
```

EXAMPLE 10.23 The *TortoiseRacer* Class

Example 10.24 shows a client applet that exercises the *TortoiseRacer* class. In this race, the tortoise, the only racer, always wins, as shown in Figure 10.17.

REFERENCE POINT

Interfaces are used extensively in GUI applications, as you will see in Chapter 12.

```
/** TortoiseRacer Client
*   Anderson, Franceschi
*/

import javax.swing.*;
import java.awt.*;

public class TortoiseRacerClient extends JApplet
{
  private TortoiseRacer t;

  public void init( )
  {
    t = new TortoiseRacer( "Tortoise", 50, 50 );
  }

  public void paint( Graphics g )
  {
    for ( int i = 0; i < getWidth( ); i++ )
    {
      t.move( );
      t.draw( g );

      Pause.wait( .03 );
      g.clearRect( 0, 0, getWidth( ), getHeight( ) );
    }
  }
}
```

EXAMPLE 10.24 A Client Applet for the *TortoiseRacer* Class

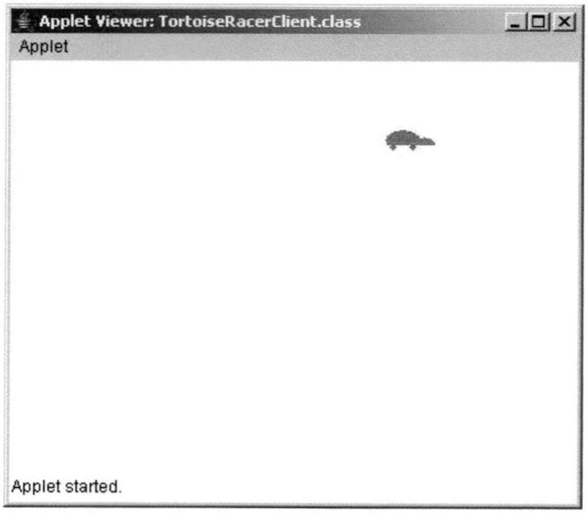

Figure 10.17
Output from Example 10.24

Skill Practice
with these end-of-chapter questions

10.10.1 Multiple Choice Exercises

Questions 3,5,6

10.10.3 Fill In the Code

Question 25

10.10.4 Identifying Errors in Code

Questions 26,27,28,29,30

10.10.8 Technical Writing

Question 57

CODE IN ACTION

On the CD-ROM included with this book, you will find a Flash movie with a step-by-step illustration of the use of *abstract* classes, polymorphism, and interfaces in a program. Click on the link for Chapter 10 to start the movie.

10.9 Chapter Summary

- Inheritance lets us organize related classes into ordered levels of functionality, called hierarchies. The advantage is that we write the common code only once and reuse it in multiple classes.
- A subclass inherits methods and fields of its superclass. A subclass can have only one direct superclass, but many subclasses can inherit from a common superclass.
- Inheritance implements the "is a" relationship between classes. Any object of a subclass is also an object of the superclass.
- All classes inherit from the *Object* class.
- To specify that a subclass inherits from a superclass, the subclass uses the *extends* keyword in the class definition, as in the following syntax:

  ```
  accessModifier class ClassName extends SuperclassName
  ```

- A subclass does not inherit constructors or *private* members of the superclass. However, the superclass constructors are still available to be called from the subclass, and the *private* fields of the superclass are implemented as fields of the subclass.
- To access private fields of the superclass, the subclass needs to use the accessor and mutator methods provided by the superclass.
- To call the constructor of the superclass, the subclass constructor uses the following syntax:

  ```
  super( argument list );
  ```

  If used, this statement must be the first statement in the subclass constructor.
- A subclass can override an inherited method by providing a new version of the method. The new method's API must be identical to the inherited method. To call the inherited version of the method, the subclass uses the *super* object reference using the following syntax:

  ```
  super.methodName( argument list )
  ```

- Any field declared using the *protected* access modifier is inherited by the subclass. As such, the subclass can directly access the field without calling its accessor or mutator method.

CHAPTER SUMMARY

- An *abstract* class can be used to specify APIs for methods that subclasses should implement. An *abstract* class cannot be used to instantiate objects. A class is declared to be *abstract* by including the *abstract* keyword in the class header.
- An *abstract* class typically has one or more *abstract* methods. An *abstract* method specifies the API of the method, but does not provide an implementation. The API of an *abstract* method is followed by a semicolon.
- When a subclass inherits from an *abstract* class, it can provide implementations for any, all, or none of the *abstract* methods. If the subclass does not implement all the *abstract* methods of the superclass, then the subclass must also be declared as *abstract*. If, however, the subclass implements all the *abstract* methods in the superclass and is not declared *abstract*, then the class is not *abstract* and we can instantiate objects of that subclass.
- Polymorphism simplifies the processing of various objects in a hierarchy by allowing us to use the same method call for any object in the hierarchy. We assign an object reference of a subclass to a superclass reference, then make the method call using the superclass object reference. At run time, the JVM determines to which class in the hierarchy the object actually belongs and calls the appropriate form of the method for that class.
- Interfaces allow a class to inherit behavior from multiple sources. Interface members can be classes, constants, *abstract* methods, or other interfaces.
- To define an interface, use the following syntax:

```
accessModifier interface InterfaceName
{
  // body of interface
}
```

- To use an interface, a class header should include the *implements* keyword and the name of the interface, as in the following syntax:

```
accessModifier class ClassName implements InterfaceName
```

- To specify that a subclass inherits from a superclass and uses an interface, a class header should include the *implements* keyword and the name of the interface, as in the syntax that follows.

```
accessModifier class ClassName extends SuperclassName
                                implements InterfaceName
```

10.10 Exercises, Problems, and Projects

10.10.1 Multiple Choice Exercises

1. The *extends* keyword applies to
   - ❑ a class inheriting from another class
   - ❑ a variable
   - ❑ a method
   - ❑ an expression
2. A Java class can inherit from two or more classes.
   - ❑ true
   - ❑ false
3. In Java, multiple inheritance is implemented using the concept of
   - ❑ an interface
   - ❑ an *abstract* class
   - ❑ a *private* class
4. Which of the following is inherited by a subclass?
   - ❑ all instance variables and methods
   - ❑ *public* instance variables and methods only
   - ❑ *protected* instance variables and methods only
   - ❑ *protected* and *public* instance variables and methods
5. What Java keyword is used in a class header when a class is defined as inheriting from an interface?
   - ❑ *inherits*
   - ❑ *includes*

- ❑ *extends*
- ❑ *implements*

6. A Java class can implement one or more interfaces.
   - ❑ true
   - ❑ false
7. How do you instantiate an object from an *abstract* class?
   - ❑ With any constructor.
   - ❑ With the default constructor only.
   - ❑ You cannot instantiate an object from an *abstract* class.
8. When a class overrides a method, what Java keyword is used to call the method inherited from the superclass?
   - ❑ *inherited*
   - ❑ *super*
   - ❑ *class*
   - ❑ *methodName*
9. Where should the following statement be located in the body of a subclass constructor?

   ```
   super( );
   ```
   - ❑ It should be the last statement.
   - ❑ It should be the first statement.
   - ❑ It can be anywhere.
10. If a class contains an *abstract* method, then
    - ❑ the class must be declared *abstract.*
    - ❑ the class is not *abstract.*
    - ❑ the class may or may not be *abstract.*
    - ❑ All of the above.
11. What can you tell about the following method?

    ```
    public void myMethod( )
    {
    }
    ```

- ❑ This method is *abstract.*
- ❑ This method is not *abstract.*

10.10.2 Reading and Understanding Code

For Questions 12 to 20, consider the following three classes:

```
public class A
{
 private int number;
 protected String name;
 public double price;

 public A( )
 {
   System.out.println( "A( ) called" );
 }

 private void foo1( )
 {
  System.out.println( "A version of foo1( ) called" );
 }

 protected int foo2( )
 {
  System.out.println( "A version of foo2( ) called" );
  return number;
 }

 public String foo3( )
 {
  System.out.println( "A version of foo3( ) called" );
  return "Hi";
 }
}

public class B extends A
{
  private char service;

  public B( )
  {
   super( );
   System.out.println( "B( ) called" );
  }
```

```
   public void foo1( )
   {
    System.out.println( "B version of foo1( ) called" );
   }

   protected int foo2( )
   {
    int n = super.foo2( );
    System.out.println( "B version of foo2( ) called" );
    return ( n + 5 );
   }

   public String foo3( )
   {
    String temp = super.foo3( );
    System.out.println( "B version of foo3( )" );
    return ( temp + " foo3" );
   }
 }

 public class C extends B
 {
   public C( )
   {
    super( );
    System.out.println( "C( ) called" );
   }

   public void foo1( )
   {
    System.out.println( "C version of foo1( ) called" );
   }
 }
```

12. Draw the UML diagram for the class hierarchy.
13. What fields and methods are inherited by which class?
14. What fields and methods are not inherited?
15. What is the output of the following code sequence?

```
B b1 = new B( );
```

16. What is the output of the following code sequence?

```
B b2 = new B( );
b2.foo1( );
```

17. What is the output of the following code sequence?

```
B b3 = new B( );
int n = b3.foo2( );
```

18. What is the output of the following code sequence?

```
// b4 is a B object reference
System.out.println( b4.foo3( ) );
```

19. What is the output of the following code sequence?

```
C c1 = new C( );
```

20. What is the output of the following code sequence?

```
// c2 is a C object reference
c2.foo1( );
```

10.10.3 Fill In the Code

For Questions 21 to 25, consider the following class *F* and the interface *I*:

```
public class F
{
 private String first;
 protected String name;

 public F( )
 { }

 public F( String f, String n )
 {
  first = f;
  name = n;
 }
 public String getFirst( )
 {
  return first;
 }
 public String getName( )
 {
  return name;
 }
 public String toString( )
 {
   return ( "first: " + first + "\tname: " + name );
 }
 public boolean equals( Object f )
 {
  if ( ! ( f instanceof F ) )
```

```
        return false;
    else
    {
        F objF = ( F ) f;
        return( first.equals( objF.first ) && name.equals( objF.name ) );
    }
}
```

```
public interface I
{
 public static final String TYPE = "human";
 public abstract int age( );
}
```

21. The *G* class inherits from the *F* class. Code the class header of the *G* class.

```
// your code goes here
```

22. Inside the *G* class, which inherits from the *F* class, declare a *private* instance variable for the middle initial and code a constructor with three parameters, calling the constructor of the *F* class and assigning the third parameter, a *char*, to the new instance variable.

```
// your code goes here
```

23. Inside the *G* class, which inherits from the *F* class, code the *toString* method, which returns a printable representation of a *G* object reference.

```
// your code goes here
```

24. Inside the *G* class, which inherits from the *F* class, code the *equals* method, which compares two *G* objects and returns *true* if they have identical instance variables; *false* otherwise.

```
// your code goes here
```

25. The *K* class inherits from the *F* class and the *I* interface; code the class header of the *K* class.

```
// your code goes here
```

10.10.4 Identifying Errors in Code

For Questions 26 to 31, consider the following two classes, *C* and *D*, and interface *I*:

```
public abstract class C
{
 private void fool( )
 {
  System.out.println( "Hello fool" );
```

```
 }
 public abstract void foo2( );
 public abstract int foo3( );
}

public class D extends C
{
 public void foo2( )
 {
  System.out.println( "Hello foo2( )" );
 }
 public int foo3( )
 {
  return 10;
 }
 private void foo4( )
 {
  System.out.println( "Hello D foo4( )" );
 }
}

public interface I
{
 public static final double PI = 3.14;
}
```

26. Where is the error in this code sequence?

```
C c1 = new C( );
```

27. Where is the error in this code sequence?

```
D d1 = new D( );
d1.foo1( );
```

28. Is there an error in this code sequence? Why or why not?

```
C c2;
c2 = new D( );
```

29. Where is the error in this new class?

```
public class E extends D
{
 public void foo4( )
 {
  super.foo4( );
  System.out.println( "Hello E foo4()" );
 }
}
```

30. Where is the error in this class?

```
public class J extends I
{
}
```

31. Where is the error in this class?

```
public class K
{
 public void foo( );
}
```

10.10.5 Debugging Area—Using Messages from the Java Compiler and Java JVM

32. You coded the following class

```
public class N extends String, Integer
{
}
```

When you compile, you get the following message:

```
N.java:1: '{' expected
public class N extends String, Integer
                             ^
1 error
```

Explain what the problem is and how to fix it.

For Exercises 33 to 35, consider the following class:

```
public abstract class M
{
 private int n;
 protected double p;
 public abstract void foo1( );
}
```

33. You coded the following class:

```
public class P extends M
{
}
```

When you compile, you get the following message:

```
P.java:1: P is not abstract and does not override abstract method
foo1() in M
public class P extends M
       ^
1 error
```

34. You coded the following class:

```
public class P extends M
{
 public void foo1( )
 {
  System.out.println( "n is: " + n );
 }
}
```

When you compile, you get the following message:

```
P.java:5: n has private access in M
  System.out.println( "n is: " + n );
                                 ^
1 error
```

35. You coded the following classes:

```
public class P extends M
{
 public P( double newP )
 {
  p = newP;
 }
 public void foo1( )
 {
 }
}

public class Q extends P
{
 private int z;
 public Q( double newP, int newZ )
 {
  z = newZ;
  super( newP );  // line 7
 }
}
```

When you compile, you get the following message:

```
Q.java:5: cannot find symbol
symbol  : constructor P()
location: class P
 {
 ^
Q.java:7: call to super must be first statement in constructor
```

```
  super( newP );
       ^
2 errors
```

10.10.6 Write a Short Program

36. Write an applet overriding the *init* and *paint* methods of the *JApplet* class with a simple output line to the screen, which will show in what order each method is called.

For Exercises 37 to 41, consider the following class:

```
public class Game
{
 private String description;

 public Game( String newDescription )
 {
  setDescription( newDescription );
 }

 public String getDescription( )
 {
  return description;
 }

 public void setDescription( String newDescription )
 {
  description = newDescription;
 }

 public String toString( )
 {
  return ( "description: " + description );
 }
}
```

37. Write a class encapsulating a PC-based game, which inherits from *Game*. A PC-based game has the following additional attributes: the minimum megabytes of RAM needed to play the game, the number of megabytes needed on the hard drive to install the game, and the minimum GHz performance of the CPU. Code the constructor and the *toString* method of the new class. You also need to include a client class to test your code.

38. Write a class encapsulating a board game, which inherits from *Game*. A board game has the following additional attributes: the number of players and whether the game can end in a tie. Code the constructor and the *toString* method of the new class. You also need to include a client class to test your code.

39. Write a class encapsulating a sports game, which inherits from *Game*. A sports game has the following additional attributes: whether the game is a team or individual game, and whether the game can end in a tie. Code the constructor and the *toString* method of the new class. You also need to include a client class to test your code.

40. Write a class encapsulating a trivia game, which inherits from *Game*. A trivia game has the following additional attributes: the ultimate money prize, and the number of questions that must be answered to win the ultimate money. Code the constructor and the *toString* method of the new class. You also need to include a client class to test your code.

41. Write a class encapsulating a board game, which inherits from *Game*. A board game has the following additional attributes: the minimum number of players, the maximum number of players, and whether there is a time limit to finish the game. Code the constructor and the *toString* method of the new class. You also need to include a client class to test your code.

For Exercises 42 to 46, consider the following class:

```
public class Store
{
 public final double SALES_TAX_RATE = 0.06;
 private String name;

 public Store( String newName )
 {
  setName( newName );
 }

 public String getName( )
 {
  return name;
 }
```

```
  public void setName( String newName )
  {
   name = newName;
  }

  public String toString( )
  {
   return ( "name: " + name );
  }
}
```

42. Write a class encapsulating a web store, which inherits from *Store.* A web store has the following additional attributes: an Internet address and the programming language in which the website was written. Code the constructor and the *toString* method of the new class. You also need to include a client class to test your code.

43. Write a class encapsulating a music store, which inherits from *Store.* A music store has the following additional attributes: the number of titles it offers and its address. Code the constructor and the *toString* method of the new class. You also need to include a client class to test your code.

44. Write a class encapsulating a bike store, which inherits from *Store.* A bike store has the following additional attributes: the number of bicycle brands that it carries and whether it sponsors a bike club. Code the constructor and the *toString* method of the new class. You also need to include a client class to test your code.

45. Write a class encapsulating a grocery store, which inherits from *Store.* A grocery store has the following additional attributes: annual revenues and whether it is an independent store or part of a chain. Code the constructor and the *toString* method of the new class; also code a method returning the annual taxes paid by the store. You also need to include a client class to test your code.

46. Write a class encapsulating a restaurant, which inherits from *Store.* A restaurant has the following additional attributes: how many people are served every year and the average price per person. Code the constructor and the *toString* method of the new class; also code a method returning the average taxes per year. You also need to include a client class to test your code.

10.10.7 Programming Projects

47. Write a superclass encapsulating a rectangle. A rectangle has two attributes representing the width and the height of the rectangle. It has methods returning the perimeter and the area of the rectangle. This class has a subclass, encapsulating a parallelepiped, or box. A parallelepiped has a rectangle as its base, and another attribute, its length; it has two methods that calculate and return its area and volume. You also need to include a client class to test these two classes.

48. Write a superclass encapsulating a circle; this class has one attribute representing the radius of the circle. It has methods returning the perimeter and the area of the circle. This class has a subclass, encapsulating a cylinder. A cylinder has a circle as its base, and another attribute, its length; it has two methods, calculating and returning its area and volume. You also need to include a client class to test these two classes.

49. Write an *abstract* superclass encapsulating a shape: A shape has two *abstract* methods: one returning the perimeter of the shape, another returning the area of the shape. It also has a constant field named PI. This class has two non-*abstract* subclasses: one encapsulating a circle, and the other encapsulating a rectangle. A circle has one additional attribute, its radius. A rectangle has two additional attributes, its width and height. You also need to include a client class to test these two classes.

50. Write an *abstract* superclass encapsulating a vehicle: A vehicle has two attributes: its owner's name and its number of wheels. This class has two non-*abstract* subclasses: one encapsulating a bicycle, and the other encapsulating a motorized vehicle. A motorized vehicle has the following additional attributes: its engine volume displacement, in liters; and a method computing and returning a measure of horsepower—the number of liters times the number of wheels. You also need to include a client class to test these two classes.

51. Write an *abstract* superclass encapsulating some food; it has two attributes: its description and the number of calories per serving. It also has an *abstract* method taking a number of servings as a parameter and returning the number of calories. This class has two non-*abstract* subclasses: one encapsulating a liquid food (such as a drink,

for instance), and the other encapsulating a fruit. A liquid food has an additional attribute: its viscosity. A fruit has an additional attribute: its season. You also need to include a client class to test these two classes.

52. Write an *abstract* superclass encapsulating a college applicant: A college applicant has two attributes: the applicant's name and the college the applicant is applying to. This class has two non-*abstract* subclasses: one encapsulating an applicant for undergraduate school, and the other encapsulating an applicant for graduate school. An applicant for undergraduate school has two additional attributes: an SAT score, and a GPA. An applicant for graduate school has one additional attribute: the college of origin. It also has a method which returns "from inside" if the college of origin is the same as the college applied to; otherwise, it returns "from outside." You also need to include a class to test these two classes.

53. Write an *abstract* superclass encapsulating a vacation: A vacation has two attributes: a budget and a destination. It has an *abstract* method returning by how much the vacation is over or under budget. This class has two non-*abstract* subclasses: one encapsulating an all-inclusive vacation, and the other encapsulating a vacation bought piece-meal. An all-inclusive vacation has three additional attributes: a brand (for instance ClubMed®); a rating, expressed as a number of stars; and a price. A piecemeal vacation has two additional attributes: a set of items (hotel, meal, airfare, . . .), and a set of corresponding costs. You also need to include a class to test these two classes.

54. Write an *abstract* superclass encapsulating a part, with two attributes: the part number, and a budget cost for it. This class has two non-*abstract* subclasses: one encapsulating a self-manufactured part, and the other encapsulating an outsourced part. A self-manufactured part has a cost and a drawing number; it has also a method returning whether it is over budget or under budget. An outsourced part has a set of suppliers, each with a price for the part. It also has a method to retrieve the lowest-cost supplier for a part and the corresponding cost. You also need to include a class to test these two classes.

55. Write an *abstract* superclass encapsulating a number; this class has one *abstract void* method: *square*. This class has two non-*abstract* subclasses: one encapsulating a rational number, and the other encapsulating a complex number. A rational number is represented by two integers, the numerator and the denominator of the rational number.

A complex number is represented by two real numbers, the real part and the complex part of the complex number. You also need to include a class to test these two classes.

10.10.8 Technical Writing

56. In a large organization, programmers develop a library of classes as they work on various projects. Discuss, in such an environment, how inheritance can be helpful in reusing code and therefore saving time.
57. Other programming languages allow multiple inheritance, that is, a class can inherit from several classes. In Java, a class can extend only one class, but can implement several interfaces. Discuss potential problems that can arise in other programming languages that allow inheritance from multiple classes.

10.10.9 Group Project (for a group of 1, 2, or 3 students)

58. Design and code a program, including the following classes, as well as a client applet class to test all the methods coded:

    An *abstract Shape* class, encapsulating a shape: a shape has one *abstract* method, *draw*, which takes one parameter, a *Graphics* object. *Shape* has three subclasses:

    - ❑ The *Line* class, encapsulating a line: A line can be represented by a starting (x, y) coordinate and an ending (x, y) coordinate. The *draw* method will draw a line between them.
    - ❑ The *Rectangle* class, encapsulating a rectangle: A rectangle can be represented by its (x, y) top-left corner of the rectangle, its width, and its height. The *draw* method will draw the corresponding rectangle.
    - ❑ The *Oval* class, encapsulating an oval: An oval can be represented by the (x, y) top-left corner coordinate of its bounding rectangle, its width, and its height. The *draw* method will draw the corresponding oval.

    Your applet class should prompt the user for the type of shape that the user wants to draw, prompt the user for the appropriate data, and then draw the figure in the applet window.

CHAPTER 11

Exceptions and Input/Output Operations

CHAPTER CONTENTS

Introduction

Up to now, whenever our programs needed data, we have supplied that data using one of several different methods:

- Assigning values to variables in our program. This is known as **hard coding** the values of variables.
- Prompting the user for values using the *Scanner* class.
- Reading data from a text file using the *Scanner* class.
- Prompting the user for values using a *JOptionPane* dialog box.
- Generating random numbers using the *Random* class.

Typically, whenever we prompted the user to supply values, we asked for one value at a time. If a program needs a large number of values, however, prompting the user for each value will take a long time and will be impractical. Furthermore, as the number of values increases, the potential for input errors increases as well.

Programs often use existing data accumulated by an organization, such as a university, a government, or a corporation. Typically, the volume of data is significant, and again, data entry through the keyboard is impractical.

Furthermore, these large amounts of data typically reside in two types of storage:

- disk files
- databases

Working with databases is beyond the scope of this book. In most of this chapter, we concentrate on reading from and writing to files.

But there is a prerequisite to all this: understanding the concept of exceptions, their associated classes, and exception handling.

11.1 Simple Exception Handling

By now you should have discovered that sometimes your program doesn't work, even though you didn't get any compiler errors. At run time, logic errors can surface. For example, we might attempt to divide an integer by 0 or try to access the 11th element in a 10-element array. Java is a robust language and does not allow these "illegal" operations to occur unnoticed.

These illegal operations generate **exceptions**. Some exceptions are generated by the Java Virtual Machine, while others are generated by constructors or other methods. For example, a method might generate an exception when it detects an attempted illegal operation or an illegal parameter.

By default, when an exception is generated in an application that does not have a graphical user interface, the program will terminate. In many cases, however, we can attempt to recover from the exception and continue running the program. This is called **handling the exception**. For the programmer to handle an exception, Java provides two tools:

- exception classes
- the *try*, *catch*, and *finally* blocks

The *Exception* class is the superclass of all exception classes, which encapsulate specific exceptions, such as integer division by 0, attempting to access an out-of-bounds array index, an illegal number format, using a *null* object reference to call a method, trying to open a file that does not exist, and others.

Figure 11.1 is an inheritance hierarchy showing only a few of the Java exception classes. The *Exception* class and *RuntimeException* and its subclasses are in the *java.lang* package. The *IOException* class and its subclass, *FileNotFoundException*, are in the *java.io* package.

11.1.1 Using *try* and *catch* Blocks

Throughout this book, we have used dialog boxes to prompt the user for input values. Example 11.1 shows a program that prompts the user for an integer. The *showInputDialog* method of the *JOptionPane* class returns the user's input as a *String* (lines 12–13), which we then convert to an *int* using the *parseInt* method of the *Integer* wrapper class (line 17).

```
1 /*  An exception generated by the parseInt method
2 *   Anderson, Franceschi
3 */
4
5 import javax.swing.JOptionPane;
6
7 public class DialogBoxInput
8 {
```

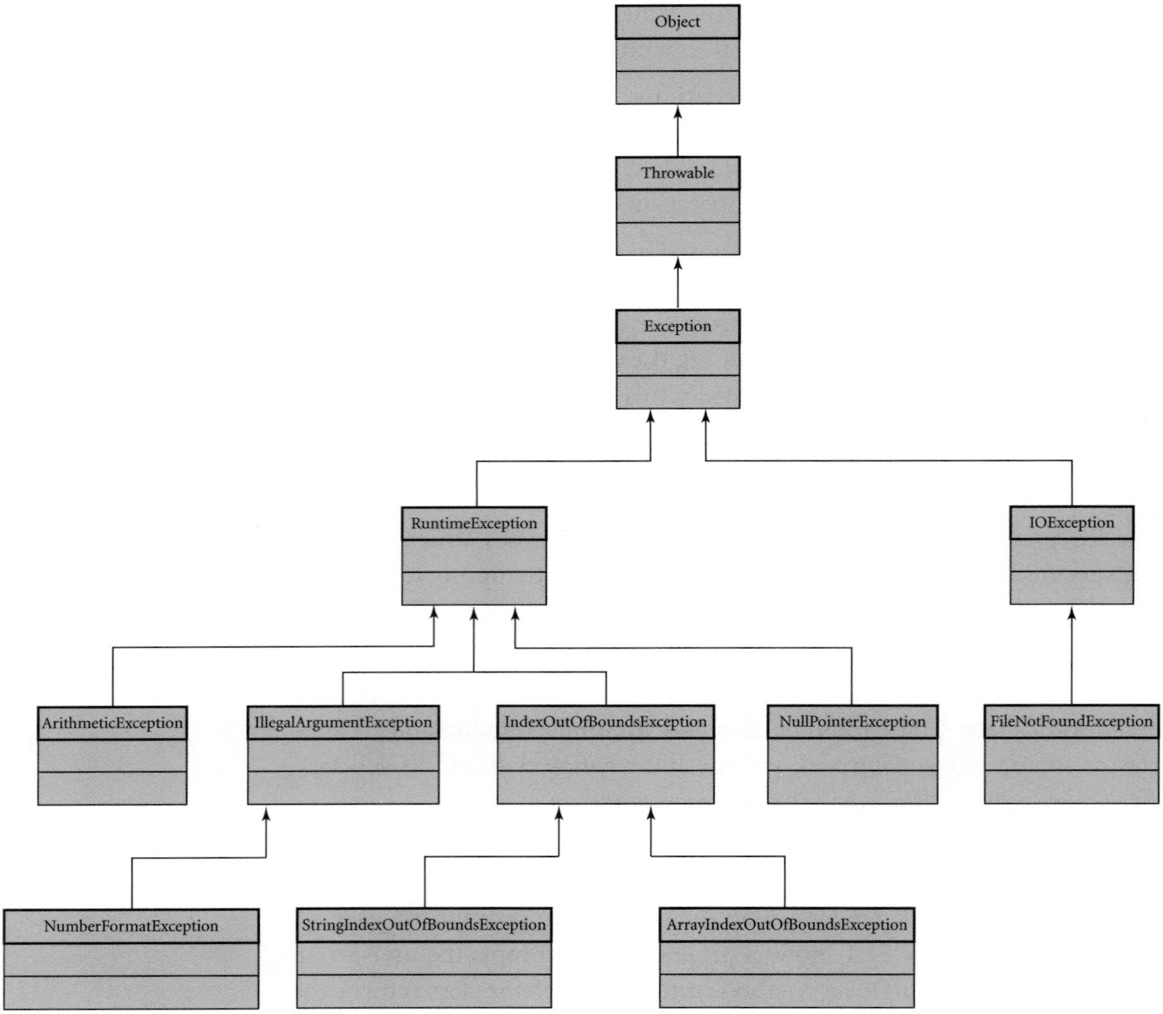

Figure 11.1

Inheritance Hierarchy for Various Exception Classes

```
 9   public static void main( String [ ] args )
10   {
11     // prompt for input; return value is a String
12     String s = JOptionPane.showInputDialog( null,
13                             "Enter an integer" );
14     System.out.println( "You entered " + s );
15
16     // attempt to convert the String to an int
17     int n = Integer.parseInt( s );
18     System.out.println( "Conversion was successful. "
19                         + "The integer is " + n );
20   }
21 }
```

EXAMPLE 11.1 Generating an Exception

Figure 11.2 shows a successful run of the program with the user input being 45.

Everything goes well as long as the user's input can be converted to an *int.* But what happens when the user types characters other than digits? Figure 11.3 shows the output from the same program when the user enters "a."

At run time, the call to the *parseInt* method (line 17) generates a *NumberFormatException*, which terminates the program. Lines 18–19 of the program are never executed. We can determine the line that generated the exception by reading the last line of the console output, which identifies the

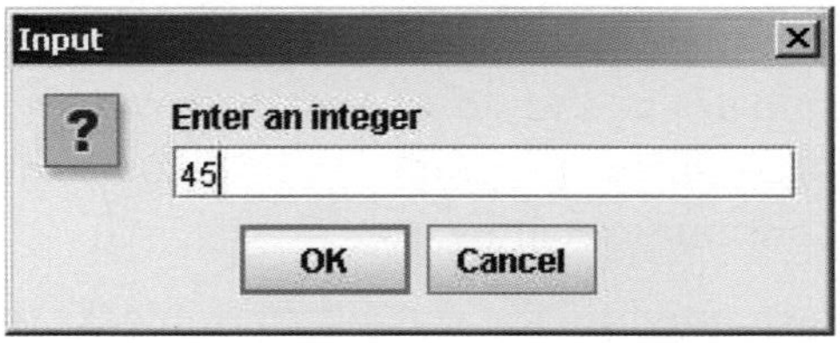

Figure 11.2
Successful Conversion of a *String* to an *int*

```
You entered 45
Conversion was successful. The integer is 45.
```

Figure 11.3
Output Showing *a* *NumberFormatException* at Run Time

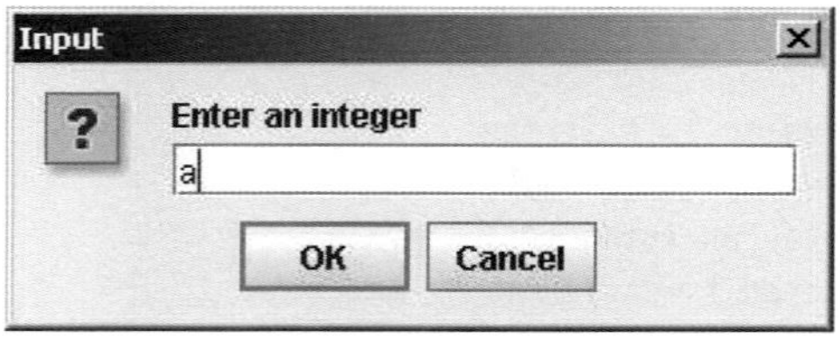


```
You entered a
Exception in thread "main" java.lang.NumberFormatException: For input string: "a"
       at java.lang.NumberFormatException.forInputString(NumberFormatException.java:48)
       at java.lang.Integer.parseInt(Integer.java:447)
       at java.lang.Integer.parseInt(Integer.java: 497)
       at DialogBoxInput.main(DialogBoxInput.java:17)
```

source of the exception: line 17 in the *main* method of the *DialogBoxInput* class.

Let's take a look at what happened here. The *parseInt* method has the following header:

```
public static int parseInt( String str ) throws NumberFormatException
```

The *throws NumberFormatException* clause indicates that the *parseInt* method may detect a situation for which it will generate a *NumberFormatException*. In fact, if the *String* argument cannot be converted to an *int*, the *parseInt* method will generate, or **throw**, a *NumberFormatException*.

Naturally, we would like to avoid the situation when invalid user input terminates execution of our program. Typos and invalid input values can occur in any program. We need to be able to recover from these errors and continue executing.

Java provides the *try* and *catch* blocks to allow us to handle exceptions so that our code can continue to run. We put the code that might generate an exception inside the *try* block, and we put the code to recover from the exception inside a *catch* block. If an exception is thrown by the code inside the *try* block, then execution will jump to the *catch* block, where we write code to handle that exception. If nothing illegal happens in the *try* block, the code in the *catch* block will be skipped.

The minimum syntax for a *try* and *catch* block is as follows:

```
try
{
  // code that might generate an exception
}
catch ( ExceptionClass exceptionObjRef )
{
  // code to recover from the exception
}
```

The curly braces are required for both the *try* body and the *catch* body even if the bodies have only one statement, or even no statements.

Note that the *ExceptionClass* parameter of the *catch* clause specifies one and only one *ExceptionClass*. Listing zero or two or more *ExceptionClasses* in the *catch* clause will generate a compiler error.

COMMON ERROR TRAP

Omitting curly braces around the *try* and *catch* blocks will generate a compiler error. A *catch* clause listing several *Exception* classes as parameters will also generate a compiler error.

Java distinguishes between two types of exceptions:

- unchecked, those that are subclasses of *Error* or *RuntimeException*
- checked, any other exception class

An **unchecked exception**, such as an *ArithmeticException* caused by attempting integer division by 0, a *NumberFormatException*, or a *NullPointerException*, does not have to be handled with a *try* and *catch* block. In other words, if you omit the *try* and *catch* blocks, your code will compile without an error. If one of these unchecked exceptions is generated at run time, however, the JVM will catch it and print output similar to that shown in Figure 11.3.

Code that could generate a **checked exception**, such as an *IOException*, must be coded within a *try* block. This is required; otherwise, the program will not compile. Thus, when we perform I/O on a file, our code must deal with a potential *IOException* by using *try* and *catch* blocks. We illustrate this later in the chapter.

In the *catch* block, we can use the *Exception* parameter as an object reference to get more information about what caused the exception. Table 11.1 shows three methods inherited by the *Exception* classes.

Example 11.2 shows Version 2 of the *DialogBoxInput* application, using a *try* and *catch* block to detect the exception if it occurs.

TABLE 11.1 Useful Methods of Exception Classes

Useful Methods of Exception Classes	
Return value	**Method name and argument list**
String	getMessage( )
	returns a message indicating the cause of the exception
String	toString( )
	returns a *String* containing the exception class name and a message indicating the cause of the exception
void	printStackTrace( )
	prints the line number of the code that caused the exception, along with the sequence of method calls leading up to the exception

We prompt the user and echo the input on lines 14–17. Then we define a *try* block (lines 19–24) and insert the *parseInt* method call that performs the conversion. The *catch* block (lines 25–35) contains the code we want to execute if the *parseInt* method *throws* an exception.

```
 1 /*  DialogBoxInput, Version 2
 2 *   Catching the exception generated by the parseInt method
 3 *   Anderson, Franceschi
 4 */
 5
 6 import javax.swing.JOptionPane;
 7
 8 public class DialogBoxInput
 9 {
10   public static void main( String [ ] args )
11   {
12     int n = 0;  // declare and initialize variable
13
14     // prompt for input
15     String s = JOptionPane.showInputDialog( null,
16                                  "Enter an integer" );
17     System.out.println( "You entered " + s );
18
19     try
```

```
20     {
21        // attempt to convert the String to an int
22        n = Integer.parseInt( s );
23        System.out.println( "Conversion was successful." );
24     }
25     catch ( NumberFormatException nfe )
26     {
27        System.out.println( "Sorry. incompatible data." );
28        System.out.println( "\nOutput from getMessage: \n"
29                            + nfe.getMessage( ) );
30
31        System.out.println( "\nOutput from toString: \n"
32                            + nfe.toString( ) );
33        System.out.println( "\nOutput from printStackTrace: " );
34        nfe.printStackTrace( );
35     }
36
37     System.out.println( "\nn is " + n );
38   }
39 }
```

EXAMPLE 11.2 ***DialogBoxInput* with *try* and *catch* Blocks**

Figure 11.4 shows the output when the user inputs a valid value. In this case, the *try* block completes without an exception being generated, and the *catch* block is not executed. Execution of the program skips to line 37, where we print the value of the converted integer.

In contrast, Figure 11.5 shows the output when the user inputs an invalid value. In this case, the *parseInt* method throws a *NumberFormatException*. As

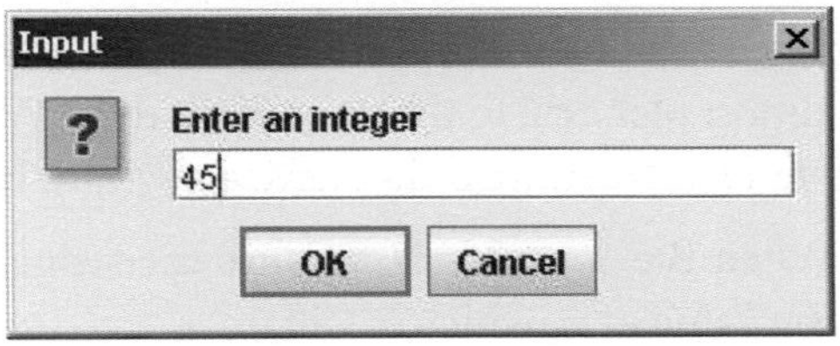

Figure 11.4
Output with No Exception Generated

```
You entered 45
Conversion was successful.

n is 45.
```

Figure 11.5
Output When an Exception Is Generated

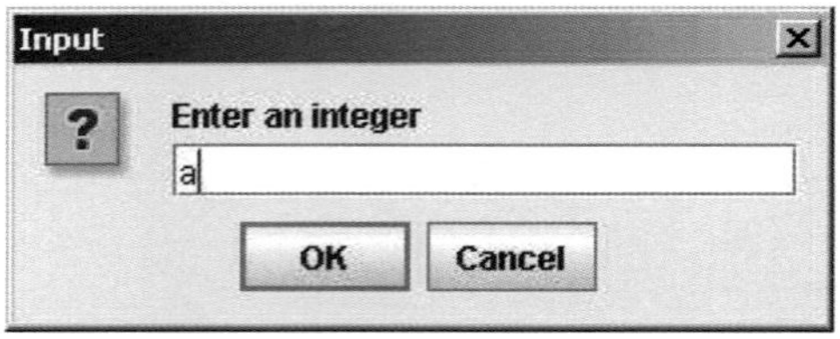


```
You entered a
Sorry. incompatible data.

Output from getMessage:
For input string: "a"

Output from toString:
java.lang.NumberFormatException: For input string: "a"

Output from printStackTrace:
java.lang.NumberFormatException: For input string: "a"
        at java.lang.NumberFormatException.forInputString(NumberFormatException.java:48)
        at java.lang.Integer.parseInt(Integer.java:447)
        at java.lang.Integer.parseInt(Integer.java: 497)
        at DialogBoxInput.main(DialogBoxInput.java:22)

n is 0
```

you can see, the *try* block stops executing at line 22, and we do not print the "Conversion was successful" message. Instead, the *catch* block is executed, and we print the values from the *getMessage*, *toString*, and *printStackTrace* methods of the *NumberFormatException* class. As you can see, the only difference between the return values from the *getMessage* and *toString* methods is that the *toString* method returns the exception class name, as well as the message. You may recognize the output of the *printStackTrace* method. It is almost identical to the message that the JVM printed to the console in Example 11.1, when we didn't have a *try/catch* block.

When the *catch* block finishes executing, we execute line 37, which prints the value of *n*, which is still 0.

COMMON ERROR TRAP

Failing to initialize a variable that is assigned a value in a *try* block, then accessed after the *try* block, will generate a compiler error.

Notice that we declare and initialize the variable *n* in line 12 before we enter the *try* block. If we do not initialize *n* and then try to access *n* after the *try/catch* blocks, we will receive the following compiler error:

```
variable n might not have been initialized
```

The error indicates that the only place where *n* is assigned a value is in the *try* block. If an exception occurs, the *try* block will be interrupted and we might not ever assign a value to *n*. Initializing *n*'s value before entering the *try* block solves this problem.

Although Example 11.2 detects the exception, it merely prints a message that the exception occurred; it does nothing to recover from—or handle—the exception. Example 11.3 shows Version 3 of the *DialogBoxInput* class, which handles the exception by putting the *try* and *catch* blocks inside a *do/while* loop so that we continue to prompt the user for a value until the input is valid.

```
/*  DialogBoxInput, Version 3
*   Handling an exception
*   Anderson, Franceschi
*/

import javax.swing.JOptionPane;

public class DialogBoxInput
{
  public static void main( String [ ] args )
  {
    // declare and initialize variables that will be
    // assigned values in the try block
    int n = 0;
    boolean goodInput = false; // flag variable

    // priming read
    String s = JOptionPane.showInputDialog( null,
                               "Enter an integer" );
    do
    {
      try
      {
        // attempt to convert the String to an int
        n = Integer.parseInt( s );
        goodInput = true;
      }
      catch ( NumberFormatException nfe )
      {
        s = JOptionPane.showInputDialog( null,
                               s + " is not an integer. "
                               + "Enter an integer" );
      }
    } while ( !goodInput );
```

```
35
36     JOptionPane.showMessageDialog( null, "The integer is " + n );
37   }
38 }
```

EXAMPLE 11.3 Recovering from the Exception

SOFTWARE ENGINEERING TIP

Write code to catch and handle exceptions generated by invalid user input. Although the methods of the *Exception* class are good debugging tools, they are not necessarily appropriate to use in the final version of a program. Always try to write code that is user-friendly.

On line 15, we declare a *boolean* variable, *goodInput*, which we will use as a flag variable to indicate whether the value entered by the user could be converted to an *int*. We initialize *goodInput* to *false*; its value will remain *false* until the *parseInt* method completes without an exception, at which time we will assign the value *true* (line 26). We use the value of *goodInput* in the *while* condition of the *do/while* loop (line 34) so that we continue to reprompt the user as long as the input is invalid. Remember that if an exception occurs in the *parseInt* method, line 26 will not be executed, so *goodInput* will be set to *true* only if no exception occurs. Now our application correctly detects and recovers from invalid user input and continues processing.

In Figure 11.6, the user first enters an invalid value. We reprompt the user, and the user enters a valid value. Notice that the user doesn't see that the

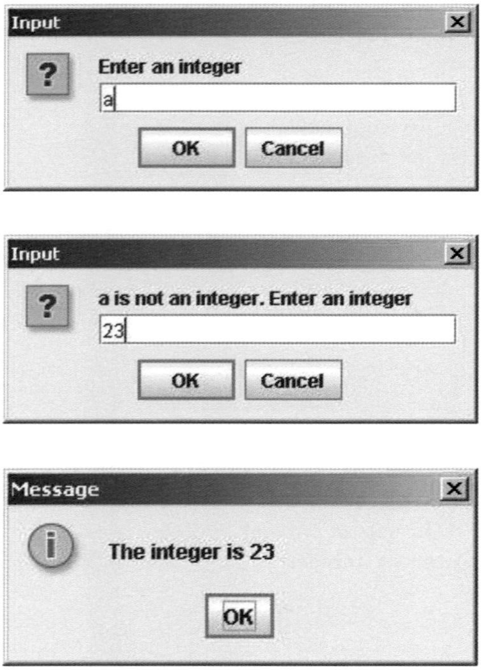

Figure 11.6
Handling the Exception

exception occurred, and also notice that our prompt clearly explains the problem to the user.

11.1.2 Catching Multiple Exceptions

If the code in the *try* block might generate multiple types of exceptions, we can provide multiple *catch* blocks, one for each possible exception. When an exception is generated, the JVM searches the *catch* blocks in order. The first *catch* block with a parameter that matches the exception thrown will execute; any remaining *catch* blocks will be skipped.

Remember that subclass objects are also objects of their superclasses, so an exception will match any *catch* block with a parameter that names any of its superclasses. For example, a *NumberFormatException* will match a *catch* block with a *RuntimeException* parameter, and all exceptions will match a *catch* block with an *Exception* parameter. Therefore, when coding several *catch* blocks, put the *catch* blocks for the specialized exceptions first, followed by more general exceptions.

SOFTWARE ENGINEERING TIP

Arrange *catch* blocks to handle the more specialized exceptions first, followed by more general exceptions.

Furthermore, after a *try* block and its associated *catch* blocks, you may optionally add a *finally* block, which will always be executed, whether an exception occurred or not. In the *finally* block, you can include some clean-up code. We will demonstrate a *finally* block when we read from a file later in this chapter.

Here is the syntax for using a *try* block, several *catch* blocks, and a *finally* block:

```
try
{
   // code that might generate an exception
}
catch ( Exception1Class e1 )
{
   // code to handle an Exception1Class exception
}
. . .
catch ( ExceptionNClass eN )
{
   // code to handle an ExceptionNClass exception
}
finally
{
   // code to execute regardless of whether an exception occurs
}
```

Again, the curly braces around the various blocks are required, whether these blocks contain zero, one, or more statements.

Example 11.4 shows a *Divider* class that catches two possible exceptions. First, we prompt the user for an integer (lines 20–22), then attempt to convert the input *String* to an *int* (lines 27–28). As we have seen, an invalid input value will generate a *NumberFormatException.* If we are successful in converting the input to an *int,* we use the *int* as the divisor in a division operation (lines 30–31). For simplicity, we use a predefined value (100) as the dividend. If the divisor is 0, line 31 will generate an *ArithmeticException.*

Thus, we put all this code into our *try* block (lines 25–34) and provide two *catch* blocks, one to handle the *NumberFormatException* (lines 35–40) and one to handle the *ArithmeticException* (lines 41–46).

```
 1 /* Divider
 2 *  Handling multiple exceptions
 3 *  Anderson, Franceschi
 4 */
 5
 6 import javax.swing.JOptionPane;
 7
 8 public class Divider
 9 {
10   public static void main( String [ ] args )
11   {
12     // declare and initialize variables
13     int divisor = 0;
14     int quotient = 0;
15     int dividend = 100;
16
17     // initialize flag variable
18     boolean goodInput = false;
19
20     // prompt for input
21     String s = JOptionPane.showInputDialog( null,
22                                "Enter an integer divisor" );
23     do
24     {
25       try
26       {
```

```
27          // attempt to convert the String to an int
28          divisor = Integer.parseInt( s );
29
30          // attempt the division
31          quotient = dividend / divisor;
32
33          goodInput = true;
34        }
35        catch ( NumberFormatException nfe )
36        {
37          s = JOptionPane.showInputDialog( null,
38                               s + " is not an integer. "
39                               + "Enter an integer divisor" );
40        }
41        catch ( ArithmeticException ae )
42        {
43          s = JOptionPane.showInputDialog( null,
44                             "Divisor cannot be 0. "
45                             + "Enter an integer divisor" );
46        }
47      } while ( !goodInput );
48
49      JOptionPane.showMessageDialog( null,
50                                  "The result is " + quotient );
51    }
52 }
```

EXAMPLE 11.4 The *Divider* Class

Figure 11.7 shows an execution of the program. At the first prompt, the user enters 45h, which causes the *parseInt* method to throw a *NumberFormatException*. The JVM starts scanning the *catch* blocks for a matching *Exception* parameter. The first *catch* block (lines 35–40) matches the exception thrown, so the code in that *catch* block is executed and we reprompt the user for a valid integer. We then skip the *catch* block for the *ArithmeticException* and line 47 is executed, which tests the value of *goodInput*._This will still be *false* at this point, so we repeat the *do/while* loop.

This time, the user enters 0, so the *parseInt* method successfully converts 0 to an *int*. Then line 31 is executed, where we attempt to divide by 0. This

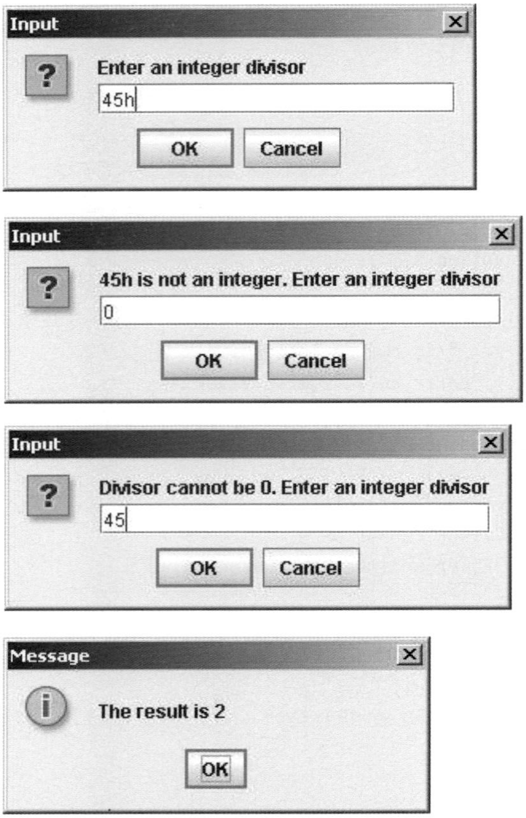

Figure 11.7
Output from Example 11.4

causes an *ArithmeticException*. Again, the JVM starts scanning *catch* blocks for a matching exception parameter. The JVM skips the first *catch* block, but finds a match in the second block (lines 41–46), so we execute that *catch* block. This time we inform the user that the divisor cannot be 0 and reprompt for a new value. Finally, the user enters a valid, nonzero value; we are now able to both convert the input to an *int* and perform the division without generating any exceptions. In this case, both *catch* blocks are skipped, and we display the result in a dialog box (lines 49–50).

SOFTWARE ENGINEERING TIP

Whenever possible, use a simple *if/else* statement to detect an unchecked exception, rather than *try* and *catch* blocks. This will improve the performance of your code.

Having provided several examples of exceptions, we must also consider this: Not every problem needs to be addressed by generating an exception. As a matter of fact, generating and handling exceptions considerably slows down execution of your code due to the processing overhead. Often, for example when using Java's I/O classes, we will have no choice but to use *try* and *catch* blocks. In Example 11.4, however, we could have used a simple *if/else* statement to test the value of the divisor before attempting the division. This would solve the problem simply and efficiently without generating an exception.

How do we know if a constructor or a method *throws* an exception and what type of exception it *throws*? As always, our best source of information is the Sun Microsystems website. After you have identified a constructor or a method that you would like to use, simply view its API in order to determine whether it *throws* any exceptions, and if so, which ones.

REFERENCE POINT

Consult the Sun Microsystems' Java website *www.java.sun.com* to see if a constructor or a method *throws* an exception and, if so, what type of exception.

11.1.3 User-Defined Exceptions

There will be times when we want to design our own exception class because the predefined Java exception classes do not fit our needs.

Suppose we are interested in designing a class encapsulating email addresses. We will call that class *EmailAddress*. To keep things simple, we will say that a legal email address is a *String* containing the @ character. In order to prevent instantiation of objects with illegal email addresses, we will design our *EmailAddress* constructor so that it throws an exception if its argument, a *String*, does not contain the @ character.

In order to do that, we first design an exception class that encapsulates an illegal email exception. We call our class *IllegalEmailException* and we will *throw* the exception when the argument to the *EmailAddress* constructor does not contain the @ character. Since Java already has an *IllegalArgumentException* class, we will define our *IllegalEmailException* class as a subclass of the *IllegalArgumentException* class.

More generally, when a user-defined exception class is defined as a subclass of an existing Java exception class, such as *Exception*, *NumberFormatException*, or *IllegalArgumentException*, our class inherits the functionality of the existing exception class, which simplifies coding the new class. We *extend* the *IllegalArgumentException* class so that we can associate a specific error message with the exception. We need to code only the constructor, and the constructor's job is to pass our message to the constructor of the superclass.

Thus, the general pattern of a user-defined exception class is:

```
public class ExceptionName extends ExistingExceptionClassName
{
  public ExceptionName( String message )
  {
    super( message );
  }
}
```

Example 11.5 shows our *IllegalEmailException* class.

```
 1 /* The IllegalEmailException class
 2    Anderson, Franceschi
 3 */
 4
 5 public class IllegalEmailException extends IllegalArgumentException
 6 {
 7   public IllegalEmailException( String message )
 8   {
 9     super( message );
10   }
11 }
```

EXAMPLE 11.5 The *IllegalEmailException* Class

The constructor for the class is coded at lines 7 to 10; it takes a *String* parameter and simply passes it to the superclass constructor.

The pattern for a method that throws a user-defined exception is:

```
accessModifier dataType methodName( parameter list )
                        throws ExceptionName
{
  if ( parameter list is legal )
      // process the parameter list
  else
      throw new ExceptionName( "Some message here" );
}
```

The message we pass to the *ExceptionName* constructor will identify the type of error we detected. When a client program catches the exception, the client can call the *getMessage* method of the exception class in order to retrieve that message.

Example 11.6 shows our *EmailAddress* class.

```
/* The EmailAddress class
   Anderson, Franceschi
*/

public class EmailAddress
{
  public static final char AT_SIGN = '@';
  private String email;

```

```
10   public EmailAddress( String newEmail )
11                      throws IllegalEmailException
12   {
13     if ( newEmail.indexOf( AT_SIGN ) != - 1 )
14          email = newEmail;
15     else
16          throw new IllegalEmailException
17                ( "Email address does not contain " + AT_SIGN );
18   }
19
20   public String getHost( )
21   {
22     int index = email.indexOf( AT_SIGN );
23     return email.substring( index + 1, email.length( ) );
24   }
25 }
```

EXAMPLE 11.6 The *EmailAddress* Class

We coded the constructor at lines 10–18. We test if the constructor's argument, *newEmail*, contains the character *AT_SIGN* (a constant equal to @) at line 13. If it does, we proceed normally and initialize the instance variable *email* at line 14. If it does not, we throw an *IllegalEmailException* with the appropriate message at lines 16–17. In addition to the constructor, we coded the *getHost* method at lines 20–24. The *getHost* method returns the substring comprising the characters of *email* after *AT_SIGN*. Thus, for an email address of *myEmailAddress@yahoo.com*, the *getHost* method will return *yahoo.com*.

Now that we have built our own exception class and a class including a method that *throws* that exception, we are ready to use them in a client program. This is identical to using a predefined Java exception. Example 11.7 shows our *EmailChecker* class.

```
/* The EmailChecker class
   Anderson, Franceschi
*/

import java.util.Scanner;

public class EmailChecker
{
  public static void main( String [ ] args )
  {
```

```
11     Scanner scan = new Scanner( System.in );
12     System.out.print( "Enter your email address > " );
13     String myEmail = scan.next( );
14     try
15     {
16       EmailAddress address = new EmailAddress( myEmail );
17       System.out.println( "Your host is " + address.getHost( ) );
18     }
19     catch ( IllegalEmailException iee )
20     {
21       System.out.println( iee.getMessage( ) );
22     }
23   }
24 }
```

EXAMPLE 11.7 The *EmailChecker* Class

We ask the user to input an email address, *myEmail*, at lines 12–13. We then try to instantiate the *EmailAddress* object *address* at line 16, passing *myEmail* to the constructor. If *myEmail* does not contain the @ character, our *EmailAddress* constructor *throws* an *IllegalEmailException*, which this program *catches* at line 19. In this *catch* block, we print the message the *EmailAddress* constructor sent to the *IllegalEmailException* constructor. If *myEmail* contains the @ character, we continue executing inside the *try* block. Figure 11.8 shows two runs of this example,

Figure 11.8
Two Sample Runs of Example 11.7

```
Enter your email address > mary.jb.com
Email address does not contain @
```

```
Enter your email address > john@jb.com
Your host is jb.com
```

the first generates the exception, the second completes without generating an exception.

CODE IN ACTION

On the CD-ROM included with this book, you will find a Flash movie with a step-by-step illustration of *try* and *catch* blocks. Click on the link for Chapter 11 to start the movie.

Skill Practice
with these end-of-chapter questions

11.10.1 Multiple Choice Exercises

Questions 1, 2, 3, 4

11.10.8 Technical Writing

Question 62

11.2 The *java.io* Package

In addition to the *Scanner* class in the *java.util* package, Java provides a number of classes in the *java.io* package for reading from files and for writing to files. We will use only a few of those classes here. Table 11.2 describes a group of classes designed for data input.

TABLE 11.2 Selected Classes for Input

Input Classes	
Class	**Description**
`InputStream`	*Abstract* superclass representing an input stream of raw bytes
`FileInputStream`	Input stream to read raw bytes of data from files
`ObjectInputStream`	Class to read/recover objects from a file written using *ObjectOutputStream*

Figure 11.9 shows an inheritance hierarchy for the Java classes described in Table 11.2.

Figure 11.9
The Inheritance Hierarchy for Input Classes

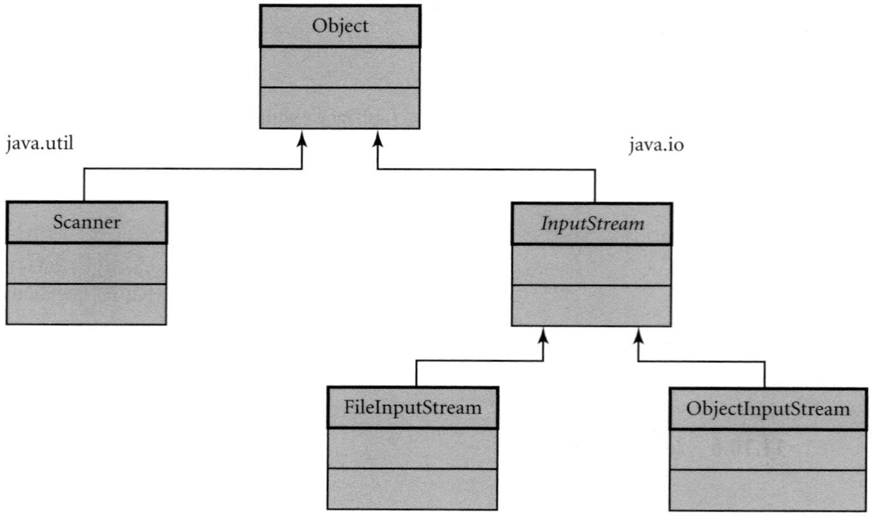

REFERENCE POINT

The *Scanner* class is discussed in Chapter 3 and Chapter 6.

Table 11.3 describes a group of classes designed for data output, and Figure 11.10 shows an inheritance hierarchy for output Java classes in Table 11.3.

TABLE 11.3 Selected Output Classes

Output Classes	
Class	**Description**
`Writer`	*Abstract* superclass for output classes
`OutputStreamWriter`	Class to write output data streams
`OutputStream`	*Abstract* superclass representing an output stream of raw bytes
`FileWriter`	Class for writing to character files
`BufferedWriter`	Class providing more efficient writing to character files
`PrintWriter`	Convenient class to print basic data types, *Strings*, and objects
`PrintStream`	Class providing ability to print various data types conveniently
`FileOutputStream`	Output stream to write raw bytes of data to files
`ObjectOutputStream`	Class to write objects to a file

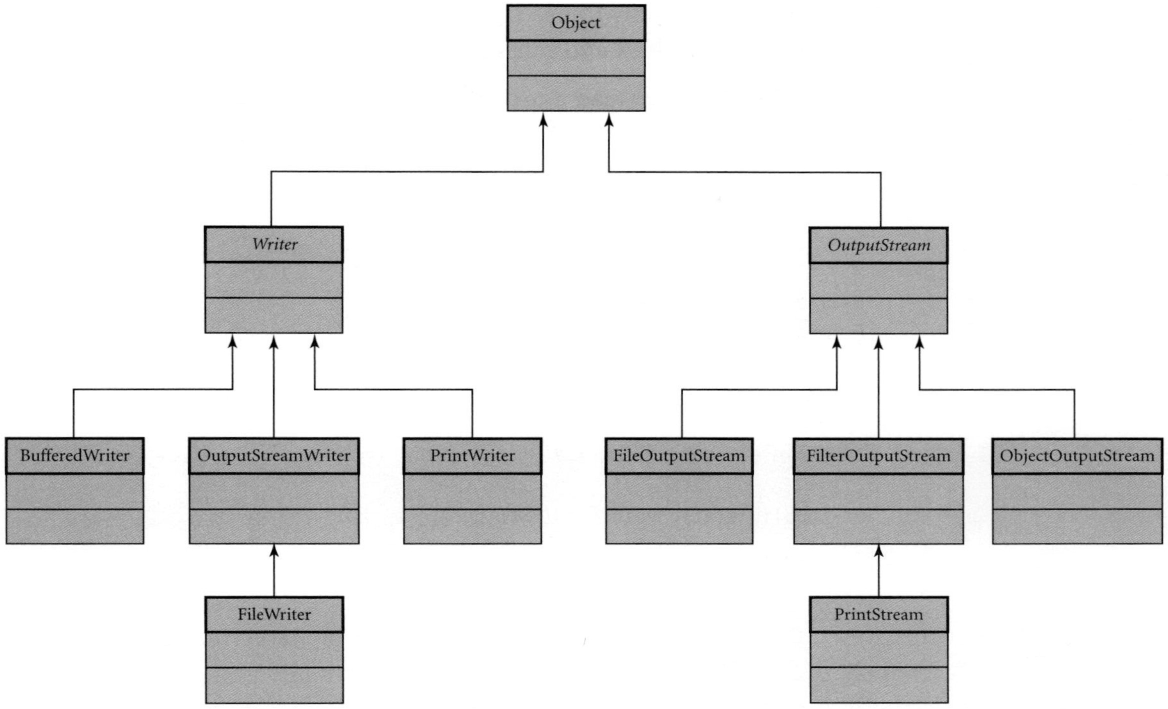

Figure 11.10

The Inheritance Hierarchy for Output Classes

11.3 Reading and Writing Text Files

Java supports two file types, text and binary. In text files, data is stored as characters; in binary files, data is stored as raw bytes. Different classes are used for writing and reading each file type. The type of a file is determined when the file is written to and depends on which classes were used to write to the file. Thus, to read from an existing file, you must know the file's type in order to select the appropriate classes.

In this section, we concentrate on text files.

11.3.1 Reading Text Files

In Chapter 6, we used the *Scanner* class to read from a text file. To avoid dealing with exceptions, we added the *throws IOException* clause to the header of *main*. If the file we wanted to read was not found, however, a *FileNotFoundException* was generated and the program terminated. Now that we have seen how to use *try* and *catch* blocks, we can put the *Scanner* code inside a *try* block and catch any exceptions that may occur.

In Example 11.8, we read a text file named *datafile.txt,* one line at a time, and echo each line to the console.

```
/* Demonstrating how to read from a text file
   Anderson, Franceschi
*/

import java.util.Scanner;
import java.io.File;
import java.io.FileNotFoundException;
import java.io.IOException;

public class ReadTextFile
{
  public static void main( String [ ] args )
  {
    try
    {
       Scanner file = new Scanner( new File ( "dataFile.txt" ) );

       while ( file.hasNext( ) ) // test for the end of the file
       {
          String stringRead = file.nextLine( );  // read a line
          System.out.println( stringRead );  // print the line read
       }

       // release resources associated with dataFile.txt
       file.close( );
    }

    catch ( FileNotFoundException fnfe )
    {
      System.out.println( "Unable to find dataFile.txt, exiting" );
    }

    catch ( IOException ioe )
    {
      ioe.printStackTrace( );
    }
  }
}
```

EXAMPLE 11.8 Demonstrating How to Read a Text File

Lines 5–8 import the four classes used by this program: *Scanner, File, FileNotFoundException,* and *IOException.* Line 16 instantiates a *Scanner* object from a *File* object, passing the name of the file to be read, *dataFile.txt,* as the argument to the *File* constructor.

The *File* object is used only as the argument of the *Scanner* constructor; it is not used anywhere else in the program. In this case, instead of creating a *File* object reference, many programmers prefer to use an anonymous *File* object as the argument of the *Scanner* constructor. In other words, instead of writing the following two statements:

```
File f = new File( "dataFile.txt" );
Scanner file = new Scanner( f );
```

we use the following single statement:

```
Scanner file = new Scanner( new File ( "dataFile.txt" ) );
```

It is a matter of preference as to which code you use.

SOFTWARE ENGINEERING TIP

Close files when you have finished processing their data. Do not close the standard input, output, or error devices.

When we associate a file with an input stream or output stream, we are **opening the file**. When we are finished with a file, we call the *close* method (shown in Table 11.4) to release the resources associated with the file. Calling the *close* method is optional. When the program finishes executing, all of its resources are released, including the resources of any unclosed files. Nevertheless, it is good practice, in general, to call the *close* method, especially if you will be opening a number of files (or opening the same file multiple times). In contrast, the standard input stream (*System.in*), the standard output stream (*System.out*), and the standard error stream (*System.err*) are open when the program begins. They are intended to stay open and should not be closed.

The *Scanner* constructor throws a *FileNotFoundException* if the file does not exist. We catch this exception at line 28. Since the program cannot continue without the file, we print a message to the user that we were not able to find the file and that the program is exiting (line 30). Thus, instead of

TABLE 11.4 The *close* Method of the *Scanner* Class

Return value	Method name and argument list
void	close( ) releases resources associated with an open input stream

facing a *FileNotFoundException* with a stack trace, the user now sees a friendly message explaining the problem.

If no exception is thrown, we begin to read the file. The *while* loop condition, at line 18, uses the *Scanner hasNext* method to test whether we have reached the end of the file. If not, *hasNext* returns *true*, and we execute the *while* loop body, which reads one line in the file by calling the *nextLine* method of the *Scanner* class, and echoes the *String* we read to the console.

We continue looping through the file until we receive a *false* return value from the *hasNext* method. We then exit the loop and call the *close* method on line 25 to release the file's resources.

Any attempt to access the file after it has been closed will generate an *IllegalStateException*. Also, if the *nextLine* method does not find data in the file, it throws a *NoSuchElementException*. We do not expect either of these exceptions to be thrown, and we would not be able to recover from those errors if they should occur, so we use *IOException* as the parameter of the *catch* block on lines 33–36, which will catch any I/O exception. Because we will not know the cause of the exception generated, we call the *printStackTrace* method, which outputs useful debugging information.

Note how we have ordered the two *catch* blocks. Remember that when an exception occurs, the *catch* blocks are scanned, in order, for a match between the *catch* block parameter and the type of exception that occurred. Because the *FileNotFoundException* is a subclass of *IOException*, a *FileNotFoundException* will also match a *catch* block for an *IOException*. Therefore, we need to put the *catch* block for the *FileNotFoundException* before the *catch* block for the *IOException*. This way, if the file *dataFile.txt* does not exist, the exception will match the first *catch* block, which handles the *FileNotFoundException*, and we will be able to print a meaningful message for the user.

Let's assume the file *dataFile.txt* contains the Gelett Burgess poem shown in Figure 11.11. When the program in Example 11.8 runs, it will produce the

Figure 11.11
Contents of *dataFile.txt*

```
I never saw a purple cow,
I never hope to see one;
But I can tell you, anyhow,
I'd rather see than be one!
```

```
I never saw a purple cow,
I never hope to see one;
But I can tell you, anyhow,
I'd rather see than be one!
```

Figure 11.12
Output of Example 11.8 When File is Found

```
Unable to find dataFile.txt, exiting
```

Figure 11.13
Output of Example 11.8 When File is Not Found

output shown in Figure 11.12 if the file is found, and the output in Figure 11.13 if the file is not found.

11.3.2 Writing to Text Files

In the previous section, we learned how to read data from a text file. But how did the data get into the file in the first place? It could be that someone put the data into the file using an editor, such as Notepad in Windows, or vi, pico, or emacs in Unix. Typing data into a file is convenient when the amount of data is small. But very often files contain a significant amount of data, typically written to the file by a computer program. For instance, a web server writes to log files to keep track of the visitors accessing the website, how they got to the website, the time they arrived, etc. If the web server comes under attack from a hacker, these log files can be consulted to determine where the hacker came from, who the hacker was, and other information.

In this section, we will learn how to write to a text file. But before going into the details, we must distinguish among several situations:

- Creating/writing to a new file, that is, the file does not exist.
- Writing to an existing file and replacing the contents of the file with new data.
- Writing to an existing file, but keeping the contents of the file and adding data at the end of the file. This is called **appending** to the file.

TABLE 11.5 Writing or Appending to an Existing or New File

Operation	If the file exists . . .	If the file does not exist . . .
write	the current contents of the file are deleted, and writing starts at the beginning of the file	the file is created and writing starts at the beginning of the file
append	data is added to the end of the file, keeping the existing contents	the file is created and writing starts at the beginning of the file

Java provides us with the necessary tools to perform all the preceding actions. Table 11.5 summarizes what will happen, depending on the action we perform.

To write to a file, we instantiate a *FileWriter* object, add buffering with a *BufferedWriter* object, write to the file, and *close* the *BufferedWriter* object to release the resources associated with it.

FileWriter, a subclass of the class *OutputStreamWriter*, itself a subclass of the class *Writer*, is designed to write characters to text files. *FileWriter* has several constructors, one of which takes as its two arguments a *String* file name and a *boolean* mode, representing whether we are writing (*false*) or appending (*true*) to the file.

However, a *FileWriter* writes just one byte at a time, and therefore is inefficient for writing entire lines of text. The class *BufferedWriter*, also a subclass of the *Writer* class, uses **buffering** for efficient writing. Both constructors of the *BufferedWriter* class take a *Writer* object as an argument. Because *FileWriter* is a subclass of *Writer*, a *FileWriter* object is a *Writer* object.

You may wonder what the word "buffering" means and how buffering applies to writing data. Writing data to the disk is much slower than writing data into main memory. When a class uses buffering, instead of writing one character at a time to the file, it accumulates the data in a temporary location in memory, called a **buffer**. Then when the buffer is full or is flushed, the accumulated data is written to the file in one operation. We use the method *write*, which takes one argument, a *String*. (There are other *write* methods, taking other arguments, but we will concentrate on just this one.) The classes, constructors, and methods discussed above are shown in Table 11.6.

Example 11.9 shows how these *FileWriter* and *BufferedWriter* classes can be used to write to a text file named *output.txt*.

TABLE 11.6 Useful Classes, Constructors, and Methods for Writing to a Text File

Class	Constructor	Exceptions Thrown
`FileWriter`	`FileWriter( String fileName, boolean mode )` constructs a *FileWriter* object from a *String* representing the name of a file; if *mode* is *false*, we will write to the file; if *mode* is *true*, we will append to the file	`IOException`
`BufferedWriter`	`BufferedWriter( Writer w )` constructs a *BufferedWriter* object from a *Writer* object	None
	Method APIs	
`BufferedWriter`	`void write( String s )` writes a *String* to the current *OutputStream* object. This method is inherited from the *Writer class*	`IOException`
`BufferedWriter`	`void newLine( )` writes a line separator	`IOException`
`BufferedWriter`	`void close( )` releases the resources associated with the *BufferedWriter* object	`IOException`

```
/* Demonstrating how to write to a text file
   Anderson, Franceschi
*/

import java.io.FileWriter;
import java.io.BufferedWriter;
import java.io.IOException;

public class WriteTextFile
{
  public static void main( String [ ] args )
  {
    try
    {
      FileWriter fw = new FileWriter( "output.txt", false );
      // false means we will be writing to output.txt,
      // rather than appending to it
```

```
18
19        BufferedWriter bw = new BufferedWriter( fw );
20
21        // write four lines
22        bw.write( "I never saw a purple cow," );
23        bw.newLine( );
24        bw.write( "I never hope to see one;" );
25        bw.newLine( );
26        bw.write( "But I can tell you, anyhow," );
27        bw.newLine( );
28        bw.write( "I'd rather see than be one!" );
29        bw.newLine( );
30
31        // release resources associated with output.txt
32        bw.close( );
33        System.out.println( "File written successfully" );
34      }
35
36      catch ( IOException ioe )
37      {
38        ioe.printStackTrace( );
39      }
40    }
41 }
```

EXAMPLE 11.9 Demonstrating How to Write to a Text File

Lines 5, 6, and 7 import the *FileWriter*, *BufferedWriter*, and *IOException* classes.

Line 15 instantiates a *FileWriter* object using two arguments: *output.txt*, the name of the file we will write to, and *false*, which means that we will be writing to the file, not appending to it. If the file *output.txt* exists, its contents will be deleted and overwritten, whereas if the file does not exist, it will be created. The *FileWriter* constructor throws an *IOException*; such an exception will be thrown, for instance, if we specify a filename that is a directory.

Line 19 instantiates a *BufferedWriter* object, which we will use to write text to the file. At line 22, using the *BufferedWriter* object *bw*, we call the *write* method, passing the *String* to be written to the file. Note that we call the *newLine* method after writing the *String* to the file. We do this because the *write* method does not insert a line separator into the file. Also, we call the *newLine*

```
I never saw a purple cow,
I never hope to see one;
But I can tell you, anyhow,
I'd rather see than be one!
```

Figure 11.14
Contents of *output.txt*

```
File written successfully
```

Figure 11.15
Console Output from Example 11.9

method, rather than appending a "*\n*" to our *String*, because the line separator can be different on different platforms. This makes our code more portable. At lines 24–29, we write three more lines of text and three more line separators.

At line 32, we call the *close* method to release the *BufferedWriter* resources. Any further attempt to write to the file using the *bw* object reference will result in an *IOException* being thrown (and caught at line 36). The *catch* block at lines 36–39 uses an *IOException* as its parameter, which also matches the type of exception thrown by the *FileWriter* constructor and the *write* method. Again, because we don't know where the *IOException* may have occurred, we include code to print a stack trace in the *catch* block to help diagnose the problem.

After this program is executed, the file *output.txt* will contain the text shown in Figure 11.14.

Because we wrote the text to the *output.txt* file, the only output to the console is generated by line 33, as shown in Figure 11.15.

11.3.3 Appending to Text Files

Appending text to a file is similar to writing text; the only difference is that the second argument of the *FileWriter* constructor is *true*, instead of *false*.

Example 11.10 shows how these *FileWriter* and *BufferedWriter* classes can be used in a Java program to append text to our file named *output.txt*.

```
/* Demonstrating how to append to a text file
   Anderson, Franceschi
*/
```

```
 4
 5 import java.io.FileWriter;
 6 import java.io.BufferedWriter;
 7 import java.io.IOException;
 8
 9 public class AppendTextFile
10 {
11   public static void main( String [ ] args )
12   {
13     try
14     {
15        FileWriter fw = new FileWriter( "output.txt", true );
16        // true means we will be appending to output.txt,
17        // rather than writing to it
18
19        BufferedWriter bw = new BufferedWriter( fw );
20
21        // write four more lines
22        bw.write( "Ah, yes! I wrote the \"Purple Cow\" --" );
23        bw.newLine( );
24        bw.write( "I'm sorry, now, I wrote it!" );
25        bw.newLine( );
26        bw.write( "But I can tell you anyhow," );
27        bw.newLine( );
28        bw.write( "I'll kill you if you quote it!" );
29        bw.newLine( );
30
31        // release resources associated with output.txt
32        bw.close( );
33        System.out.println( "File appended successfully" );
34     }
35
36     catch ( IOException ioe )
37     {
38       ioe.printStackTrace( );
39     }
40   }
41 }
```

EXAMPLE 11.10 Demonstrating How to Append to a Text File

Example 11.10 is similar to Example 11.9. The major difference is that when we instantiate the *FileWriter* object (line 15), the second argument is *true*, which means that we will append to the file *output.txt*, instead of

```
I never saw a purple cow.
I never hope to see one;
But I can tell you, anyhow,
I'd rather see than be one!
Ah, yes! I wrote the "Purple Cow" --
I'm sorry, now, I wrote it!
But I can tell you anyhow,
I'll kill you if you quote it!
```

Figure 11.16
Contents of *output.txt*

```
File appended successfully
```

Figure 11.17
Console Output from Example 11.10

writing to it. If the file *output.txt* exists, we will start writing at the end of its current contents, whereas if the file does not exist, it will be created.

In this program, we append four additional lines to the file (lines 21–29).

Assuming that before this program is executed, the file *output.txt* contains the poem shown in Figure 11.14, then after this program is executed, the file *output.txt* will contain the text shown in Figure 11.16, and the output to the console is that shown in Figure 11.17.

COMMON ERROR TRAP

Opening a file for writing will cause the existing file data to be deleted. If you intend to add new data to a file while maintaining the original contents, open the file for appending.

11.4 Reading Structured Text Files

Sometimes a text file is organized so that each line represents data related to a particular record or object. For instance, an airline company could have data stored in a file where each line represents a flight segment, with the following comma-separated data:

- flight number
- origin airport
- destination airport
- number of passengers
- average ticket price

Such a file could contain the following data:

```
AA123,BWI,SFO,235,239.5
AA200,BOS,JFK,150,89.3
AA900,LAX,CHI,201,201.8
...
```

As we read the file, we should **parse** each line, that is, separate the line into the individual pieces of data (flight number, origin airport, etc.) called **tokens**. In this case, the comma is the **delimiter**, that is, a comma separates one token from the next. We will store the tokens from each line into a corresponding *FlightRecord* object.

The *StringTokenizer* class, in the *java.util* package, is designed to parse *Strings*, that is, to separate *Strings* into tokens.

11.4.1 Parsing a *String* Using *StringTokenizer*

Two constructors of the class *StringTokenizer* are shown in Table 11.7.

As you can see, the default delimiters are the whitespace characters. To parse a *String* like *AA123,BWI,SFO,235,239.5,* we instantiate our *StringTokenizer* object with two arguments; the second argument indicates that the delimiter is a comma.

Some useful methods of the *StringTokenizer* class are shown in Table 11.8.

Example 11.11 shows how the *StringTokenizer* class can be used in a Java program.

TABLE 11.7 *StringTokenizer* Constructors

StringTokenizer Constructor Summary
Constructor name and argument list
`StringTokenizer( String str )`
constructs a *StringTokenizer* object for the specified *String* using space, tab, carriage return, newline, and form feed as the default delimiters
`StringTokenizer( String str, String delim )`
constructs a *StringTokenizer* object for the specified *String* using *delim* as the delimiters

TABLE 11.8 *StringTokenizer* Methods

Useful *StringTokenizer* Methods	
Return value	**Method name and argument List**
int	countTokens( )
	returns the number of unretrieved tokens in this object; the count is decremented as tokens are retrieved
String	nextToken( )
	returns the next token
boolean	hasMoreTokens( )
	returns *true* if more tokens are available to be retrieved; returns *false*, otherwise

```
1 /* Demonstrating the StringTokenizer class
2    Anderson, Franceschi
3 */
4
5 import java.util.StringTokenizer;
6
7 public class UsingStringTokenizer
8 {
9   public static void main( String [ ] args )
10   {
11    String flightRecord1 = "AA123,BWI,SFO,235,239.5";
12    StringTokenizer stfr1 = new StringTokenizer( flightRecord1, "," );
13                                      // the delimiter is a comma
14
15    while ( stfr1.hasMoreTokens( ) )
16      System.out.println( stfr1.nextToken( ) );
17   }
18 }
```

EXAMPLE 11.11 Demonstrating the *StringTokenizer* Class

Line 5 imports the *StringTokenizer* class.

The *flightRecord1 String* variable is declared and initialized at line 11. At line 12, the *StringTokenizer* object *stfr1* is instantiated using the constructor with two arguments: the first argument, *flightRecord1*, is the *String* that we want to tokenize, and the second argument, a *String* containing just a comma, is the delimiter.

Lines 15 and 16 loop through all the tokens of *stfr1* and process them; here, we simply echo them to the console.

The *hasMoreTokens* method, called at line 15, returns *true* if the object *stfr1* has more tokens to be retrieved. If so, we execute the body of the *while* loop. The *nextToken* method, called at line 16, does several things. First, it returns the next token as a *String*. Second, it decrements the number of tokens left to be retrieved. Eventually, when all tokens have been retrieved, the *hasMoreTokens* method returns *false*, which causes us to exit the *while* loop.

When the program in Example 11.11 runs, it will produce the output shown in Figure 11.18.

You may wonder why we didn't use a *for* loop and the *countTokens* method, as in the following:

```
for ( int i = 0; i < stfr1.countTokens( ); i++ ) // incorrect!
   System.out.println( stfr1.nextToken( ) );
```

This code won't work because the return value of *countTokens* is the number of tokens **remaining to be retrieved**. The body of the loop retrieves one token, so each time we evaluate the loop condition by calling *countTokens*, the count of tokens is 1 fewer. The result is that we retrieve only half of the tokens.

COMMON ERROR TRAP

Using a *for* loop and the *countTokens* method in the loop condition will process only half of the tokens because *countTokens* returns a smaller number at each iteration.

We could use a *for* loop, however, if we capture the token count before the loop begins and use that value in our loop condition. Thus, the code that follows could be used instead of the *while* loop in Example 11.11.

REFERENCE POINT

You can read more about the *StringTokenizer* class on Sun Microsystems' Java website: *www.java.sun.com*.

```
int numberOfTokens = stfr1.countTokens( );

for ( int i = 0; i < numberOfTokens; i++ )
   System.out.println( stfr1.nextToken( ) );
```

Figure 11.18

Output from Example 11.11

```
AA123
BWI
SFO
235
239.5
```

11.4.2 Reading Structured Data Using *StringTokenizer*

Now we are ready to put the previous two ideas together: Let's say that we have a file named *flights.txt* containing many flight records, and we want to read the data into variables. Again, suppose that the file is in the same format as the *flightRecord1 String* in Section 11.4.1; that is, it looks like the following:

```
AA123,BWI,SFO,235,239.5
AA200,BOS,JFK,150,89.3
AA900,LAX,CHI,201,201.8
...
```

where each line represents a flight segment with the following comma-separated data: flight number, origin airport, destination airport, number of passengers, and average ticket price.

First, we will build a class called *FlightRecord*, encapsulating a flight record as reflected by the data in the file. Each line read from the file will be parsed and used to instantiate a *FlightRecord* object. Since we do not know how many lines (i.e., how many flight records) are in the file, we will place all the flight records into an *ArrayList* object as opposed to a fixed-length array.

Our simplified *FlightRecord* class is shown in Example 11.12. It has only a constructor (lines 17–35) and the *toString* method (lines 37–49).

```
 1 /* The FlightRecord class
 2    Anderson, Franceschi
 3 */
 4
 5 import java.text.DecimalFormat;
 6
 7 public class FlightRecord
 8 {
 9   public static final DecimalFormat MONEY
10                        = new DecimalFormat( "$###.00" );
11   private String flightNumber;     // ex. = AA123
12   private String origin;           // origin airport; ex. = BWI
13   private String destination;      // destination airport; ex. = SFO
14   private int numPassengers;       // number of passengers
15   private double avgTicketPrice;   // average ticket price
16
17   /** Constructor
18   *  @param  startFlightNumber   flight number
19   *  @param  startOrigin         origin airport
20   *  @param  startDestination    destination airport
```

```
   *  @param  startNumPassengers  number of passengers
   *  @param  startAvgTicketPrice average ticket price
   */
  public FlightRecord( String startFlightNumber,
                       String startOrigin,
                       String startDestination,
                       int startNumPassengers,
                       double startAvgTicketPrice )
  {
    flightNumber = startFlightNumber;
    origin = startOrigin;
    destination = startDestination;
    numPassengers = startNumPassengers;
    avgTicketPrice = startAvgTicketPrice;
  }

  /** toString
  * @return flight number, origin, destination,
  *         number of passengers, and average ticket price
  */
  public String toString( )
  {
    return "Flight " + flightNumber
           + ": from " + origin
           + " to " + destination
           + "\n\t" + numPassengers + " passengers"
           + "; average ticket price: "
           + MONEY.format( avgTicketPrice );
  }
  // accessors, mutators, and other methods ...
}
```

EXAMPLE 11.12 The *FlightRecord* Class

Example 11.13 shows our client class, which will read the file, *flights.txt*, parse each line using *StringTokenizer*, then instantiate a *FlightRecord* object and add it to the *ArrayList* named *listFlightRecords.*

```
/* Reading structured data from a text file
   Anderson, Franceschi
*/

import java.io.File;
import java.io.FileNotFoundException;
```

```
import java.io.IOException;
import java.util.StringTokenizer;
import java.util.Scanner;
import java.util.ArrayList;

public class ReadFlights
{
  public static void main( String [ ] args )
  {
   // instantiate ArrayList to hold FlightRecord objects
   ArrayList<FlightRecord> listFlightRecords =
                      new ArrayList<FlightRecord>( );

   try
   {
        Scanner file = new Scanner( new File( "flights.txt" ) );

        while ( file.hasNext( ) ) // test for the end of the file
        {
            // read a line
            String stringRead = file.nextLine( );

             // process the line read
            StringTokenizer st = new
                    StringTokenizer( stringRead, "," );
            String flightNumber = st.nextToken( );
            String origin = st.nextToken( );
            String destination = st.nextToken( );

            try
            {
               int numPassengers =
                   Integer.parseInt( st.nextToken( ) );
               double avgTicketPrice =
                   Double.parseDouble( st.nextToken( ) );

               FlightRecord frTemp = new FlightRecord(
                                      flightNumber, origin, destination,
                                      numPassengers, avgTicketPrice );

               // add FlightRecord obj to listFlightRecords
               listFlightRecords.add( frTemp );
            }

           catch ( NumberFormatException nfe )
```

```
52          {
53               System.out.println( "Error in flight record: "
54                                                + stringRead
55                                                + "; record ignored" );
56          }
57      }
58
59      // release resources associated with flights.txt
60      file.close( );
61    }
62
63    catch ( FileNotFoundException fnfe )
64    {
65      System.out.println( "Unable to find flights.txt" );
66    }
67
68    catch ( IOException ioe )
69    {
70      ioe.printStackTrace( );
71    }
72
73    // print the FlightRecords read
74    for ( FlightRecord flight : listFlightRecords )
75        System.out.println( flight );
76  }
77 }
```

EXAMPLE 11.13 Demonstrating How to Read Structured Data from a File

Lines 5–10 import the classes needed for input and exception handling, as well as *StringTokenizer* and *ArrayList.* The *FlightRecord* class is also used in this program, but is assumed to be in the same directory as the *ReadFlights* class.

This example is similar to Example 11. 8 in that we instantiate *a Scanner* object (line 22), use the *nextLine* method to read a line at a time (line 27), and handle both *FileNotFoundException* (lines 63–66) and *IOException* (lines 68–71). The difference is that instead of just printing each line of text that we read from the file, we parse that line using *StringTokenizer* and pass the data we extracted as our arguments to the *FlightRecord* constructor to instantiate a *FlightRecord* object (lines 43–45). One intermediate step is to

```
AA123,BWI,SFO,235,239.5
AA200,BOS,JFK,150,89.3
AA900,LAX,CHI,201,201.8
```

Figure 11.19
Contents of *flights.txt*

```
Flight AA123: from BWI to SFO
        235 passengers; average ticket price: $239.50
Flight AA200: from BOS to JFK
        150 passengers; average ticket price: $89.30
Flight AA900: from LAX to CHI
        201 passengers; average ticket price: $201.80
```

Figure 11.20
Output from *ReadFlights.java*

convert the *String* tokens representing the number of passengers and average ticket price to an *int* and *double*, respectively. We catch any *NumberFormatException* that might occur during the conversion (lines 51–56). If an exception does occur, we print an error message and skip the record with the invalid data.

The *FlightRecord* object is then added to the *ArrayList listFlightRecords* at lines 47–48. The *ArrayList listFlightRecords* is declared and instantiated at lines 16–18, before the *try* block so that *listFlightRecords* is available for printing the *FlightRecord* objects at lines 73–75, after we finish reading the file. If the *flights.txt* file contains the data shown in Figure 11.19, the program will produce the output shown in Figure 11.20.

CODE IN ACTION

On the CD-ROM included with this book, you will find a Flash movie with a step-by-step illustration of reading from a text file. Click on the link for Chapter 11 to start the movie.

Skill Practice
with these end-of-chapter questions

11.10.1 Multiple Choice Exercises

Questions 5, 6, 7, 8, 9, 10

11.10.2 Reading and Understanding Code

Questions 12, 13, 14, 15, 16, 17, 18, 19, 20, 21

11.10.3 Fill In the Code

Questions 27, 28, 29, 30, 31, 32

11.10.4 Identifying Errors in Code

Questions 34, 35, 36

11.10.5 Debugging Area

Questions 37, 38, 39, 40, 41, 42

11.10.6 Write a Short Program

Questions 43, 44, 45, 46, 47, 48, 49, 50, 51

11.5 Programming Activity 1: Reading from a Structured Text File

In this activity, you will read from a text file using an end-of-file controlled *while* loop performing this activity:

> Read a text file containing transaction items for a bank account. Loop through all the transaction items and calculate the new balance of the bank account. Assume that we do not know the number of transaction items, i.e., lines, in the file.

The framework will display the current transaction and current balance so that you can check the correctness of your code as the program executes.

For example, Figure 11.21 demonstrates the animation: We are currently scanning a check for the amount of $200.00. The original balance was $0.00 and the new balance is –$200.00. Ideally, this is not your bank account.

Instructions

In the Chapter 11 directory on the CD-ROM accompanying this book, you will find the Programming Activity 1 directory. Copy the contents of the directory onto a directory on your disk.

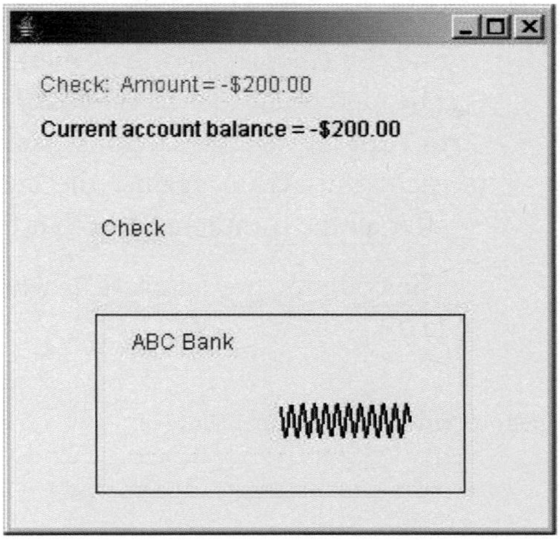

Figure 11.21
Animation Showing a $200 Check and the New Balance

```
Check # 13 : -200.00
Check # 14 : -100.00
Withdrawal June 12 : -200.00
Withdrawal June 17 : -400.00
Withdrawal June 23 : -100.00
Deposit : 4000.00
Deposit : 100.00
Something else : -1000.00
Check # 16 : -500.00
Check # 15 : -100.00
```

Figure 11.22
Contents of the *transactions.txt* File

- Open the file "*transactions.txt*" with a text editor. You will see that each line contains a transaction name and transaction amount separated by a colon, as shown in Figure 11.22.
- Note that the transaction amounts are positive or negative. For instance,
  - A check or a withdrawal has a negative amount.
  - A deposit has a positive amount.
  - An unknown transaction has either a positive or negative amount.

- Now open the *Accounting.java* file. Search for five stars (*****) to find the *balanceCheckBook* method where you will add your code. The method header has already been coded for you. Write the code to read all the transactions from the file *transactions.txt*, process each transaction against the account, and calculate the balance after all the transactions in that file have been processed.

  The code for the *balanceCheckBook* method is shown in Example 11.14.

```
public void balanceCheckBook( )
{
  // ***** Write the body of this method *****
  //
  //  Using a while loop, read the file transactions.txt
  // The file transactions.txt contains money
  // transactions between you and your bank
  //
  //  You will need to call the method animate inside
  //  the body of the loop reading the file contents
  //
  // The animate method takes 3 arguments:
  //    a String, representing the type of transaction
  //    a double, representing the transaction money amount
  //    a double, representing the new checkbook balance
  // So if these 3 variables are:
  //     transactionName, currentAmount, and balance,
  //  then the call to animate will be:
  //
  //  animate( transactionName, currentAmount, balance );
  //
  // You should make that call in the body of your while
  // loop, after you have updated the checkbook balance
  //


  //
  // end of student code
  //
}
```

EXAMPLE 11.14 ***balanceCheckBook* Method in *Accounting.java***

- Begin with a checkbook balance of 0.00.
- To process the transactions, you will need to read one line at a time from the *transactions.txt* file and parse the *String* that you retrieve. You can use the *StringTokenizer* class for this. The delimiter will be a colon. Then process the transaction; you do not need to check the type of transaction. Just add the amount of the transaction to the checkbook balance. Adding a negative transaction amount will decrease the balance, as expected. Be sure to use *try/catch* blocks where appropriate.
- After you have processed each transaction, call the *animate* method. This method belongs to the *Accounting* class, so you will call *animate* without using an object reference. The API of the *animate* method is the following:

```
public void animate( String currentTransaction,
                     double currentAmount,
                     double currentBalance )
```

  As you can see, the *animate* method takes three arguments: *currentTransaction* is the transaction name ("*Deposit*" for example), *currentAmount* is the amount of the transaction (*-45.00*, for example), and *currentBalance* is the current balance of the checkbook. Assuming that you have a *String* variable called *transactionName*, a *double* variable called *amount*, and another *double* called *balance*, a call to *animate* will look like the following:

```
animate( transactionName, amount, balance );
```

- When you call *animate*, the window will display the current transaction graphically. It will also display the transaction amount (red if negative, blue if positive), and the current checkbook balance (in black). By adding the previous checkbook balance to the current transaction amount, you will be able to compute in your head what the current checkbook balance should be and determine if your program is working correctly.
- When you reach the end of the file, print the final balance.

To test your code, compile and run the *Accounting* application.

If you have time . . .

- Modify the file *transactions.txt* by deleting or adding transactions manually with a text editor. Run the program again and check that your code still gives the correct result.

- Using a text editor, modify the file *transactions.txt* by entering a positive amount to all transactions. Change the *balanceCheckBook* method so that it determines which transactions are positive and which are negative. Run the program again and check that your code still gives the correct result.

Troubleshooting

If your method implementation does not animate or animates incorrectly, check these items:

- Verify that you coded the priming read correctly.
- Verify that you coded the call to *animate* at the proper time.
- Verify that you coded the condition for exiting the loop correctly.
- Verify that you coded the body of the loop correctly.

DISCUSSION QUESTIONS ?

1. What exceptions can occur during this program?
2. Explain why we use the *StringTokenizer* class.

11.6 Writing and Appending to Structured Text Files

Earlier in this chapter, we learned how to write character data or *Strings* to text files. But very often, our data will be other data types, such as integers, *doubles*, *booleans*, or even objects. In this section, we will demonstrate writing primitive data types to a structured text file.

FileOutputStream, a subclass of the *OutputStream* class, is designed to write a stream of bytes to a file. It has several constructors, one of which takes a filename and a mode as its two arguments. The *boolean mode* variable specifies whether we are writing (*false*) or appending (*true*) to the file.

The *PrintWriter* class is designed for converting basic data types to characters and writing them to a text file. The *PrintWriter* class provides *print* and *println* methods for all primitive data types, as well as for *Strings* and objects. The *print* method writes the argument value to the file, whereas the *println* method writes the argument value to the file followed by a *newline* character. The constructors and method APIs are shown in Table 11.9.

Example 11.15 shows how the *PrintWriter* class can be used to write *Strings* and primitive data types to a text file named *grade.txt*.

TABLE 11.9 Useful Classes, Constructors, and Methods for Writing to a Structured Text File

Classes, Constructors, and Methods for Writing to a Structured Text File		
Class	**Constructors**	**Exceptions Thrown**
`FileOutputStream`	`FileOutputStream( String filename, boolean mode )` constructs a *FileOutputStream* object from a *String* representing the name of a file; if *mode* is *false*, we will write to the file; if *mode* is *true*, we will append to the file	`FileNotFoundException`
`PrintWriter`	`PrintWriter( OutputStream os )` constructs a *PrintWriter* object from the *OutputStream* object	None
	Method APIs	

`PrintWriter`	`void print( int i )`
	`void print( double d )`
	`void print( char c )`
	`void print( boolean b )`
	`...`
	`void println( int i )`
	`void println( double d )`
	`...`
	writes the argument to a text file
		None

`PrintWriter`	`void close( )` releases the resources associated with the *PrintWriter* object	None

```
/* Demonstrating how to write basic data types to a text file
   Anderson, Franceschi
*/

import java.io.FileOutputStream;
import java.io.PrintWriter;
import java.io.FileNotFoundException;

public class WriteGradeFile
{
  public static void main( String [ ] args )
  {
    try
```

```
14     {
15       FileOutputStream fos = new FileOutputStream
16                              ( "grade.txt", false );
17       // false means we will be writing to grade.txt,
18       // rather than appending to it
19
20       PrintWriter pw = new PrintWriter( fos );
21
22       // write data to the file
23       pw.print( "Grade: " );
24       pw.println( 95 );
25       pw.print( "Letter grade: " );
26       pw.println( 'A');
27       pw.print( "Current GPA: " );
28       pw.println( 3.68 );
29       pw.print( "Successful student: " );
30       pw.println( true );
31
32       // release the resources associated with grade.txt
33       pw.close( );
34     }
35
36     catch ( FileNotFoundException fnfe )
37     {
38       System.out.println( "Unable to find grade.txt" );
39     }
40   }
41 }
```

EXAMPLE 11.15 Writing Primitive Data Types to a Text File

Lines 15–16 instantiate a *FileOutputStream* object to write to the file "*grade.txt.*" The *FileOutputStream* constructor throws a *FileNotFoundException*. Our code catches that exception at lines 36–39. This is the only *catch* block because the methods of the *PrintWriter* class do not throw exceptions.

Line 20 instantiates a *PrintWriter* object, which we will use to write to the file. At lines 22 to 30, using the *PrintWriter* object *pw*, we call the methods *print* and *println*, passing various *String* and primitive data types arguments (*int*, *char*, *double*, and *boolean*) to be written to the file. When we want a *newline* character appended to the output, we call *println*, rather than *print*.

```
Grade: 95
Letter grade: A
Current GPA: 3.68
Successful student: true
```

Figure 11.23
Contents of the *grade.txt* File

After this program is executed, the file *grade.txt* will contain the data shown in Figure 11.23.

CODE IN ACTION

On the CD-ROM included with this book, you will find a Flash movie with a step-by-step illustration of reading from and writing to a text file. Click on the link for Chapter 11 to start the movie.

11.7 Reading and Writing Objects to a File

Throughout this book, we have emphasized the benefits of object-oriented programming. Just as we can write text and primitive data types to a file and subsequently read them from the file, we can also write objects to a file and subsequently read them as objects. This is convenient for two reasons:

- We can write these objects directly to a file without having to convert the objects to primitive data types or *Strings*.
- We can read the objects directly from a file, without having to read *Strings* and convert these *Strings* to primitive data types in order to instantiate objects.

To read objects from a file, the contents of the file must have been written as objects. So our first order of business should be to learn how to write objects to a file.

11.7.1 Writing Objects to Files

The *ObjectOutputStream* class, coupled with the *FileOutputStream* class, provides the functionality to write objects to a file. We are familiar with the *FileOutputStream* class, which we used in the last section to write structured data to a text file.

The *ObjectOutputStream* class, which is a subclass of *OutputStream*, provides a convenient way to write objects to a file. Its *writeObject* method takes one argument—the object to be written.

The classes, constructors, and methods we will use are shown in Table 11.10.

We will use the *FlightRecord* class developed earlier in the chapter. However, in order for an object to be written to a file (and later to be read using the *ObjectInputStream* class), that object must implement the *Serializable* interface. When an object implements the *Serializable* interface, its state can be converted to a byte stream to be written to a file, such that this byte stream can be converted back into a copy of the object when read from the file. Therefore, our modified *FlightRecord2* class will implement *Serializable*, which is in the *java.io* package.

The *Serializable* interface has no methods to implement. As a result, the only things we have to worry about when writing a class implementing *Serializable* are the following:

- the *import* statement
- the class header showing the class *implements Serializable*

TABLE 11.10 Useful Classes, Constructors, and Methods for Writing Objects to a File

Classes, Constructors, and Methods for Writing Objects to a File		
Class	**Constructor**	**Exceptions Thrown**
`FileOutputStream`	`FileOutputStream( String filename, boolean mode )` constructs a *FileOutputStream* object from a *String* representing the name of a file; if *mode* is *false*, we will write to the file; if *mode* is *true*, we will append to the file	`FileNotFoundException`
`ObjectOutputStream`	`ObjectOutputStream( OutputStream out )` creates an *ObjectOutputStream* that writes to the *OutputStream out*	`IOException`
	Method API	
`ObjectOutputStream`	`void writeObject( Object o )` writes the object argument to a file. That object must be an instance of a class that implements the *Serializable* interface. Otherwise, a run-time exception will be generated	`IOException`

Example 11.16 shows the *FlightRecord2* class. This class is identical to the *FlightRecord* class except that it *imports Serializable* (line 5) and *implements* the *Serializable* interface (line 8).

```
 1 /* The FlightRecord2 class
 2    Anderson, Franceschi
 3 */
 4
 5 import java.io.Serializable;
 6 import java.text.DecimalFormat;
 7
 8 public class FlightRecord2 implements Serializable
 9 {
10   public static final DecimalFormat MONEY
11                         = new DecimalFormat( "$###.00" );
12   private String flightNumber;     // ex. = AA123
13   private String origin;           // origin airport; ex. = BWI
14   private String destination;      // destination airport; ex. = SFO
15   private int numPassengers;       // number of passengers
16   private double avgTicketPrice;   // average ticket price
17
18   /** Constructor
19   *  @param  startFlightNumber   flight number
20   *  @param  startOrigin         origin airport
21   *  @param  startDestination    destination airport
22   *  @param  startNumPassengers  number of passengers
23   *  @param  startAvgTicketPrice average ticket price
24   */
25   public FlightRecord2( String startFlightNumber,
26                         String startOrigin,
27                         String startDestination,
28                         int startNumPassengers,
29                         double startAvgTicketPrice )
30   {
31     flightNumber = startFlightNumber;
32     origin = startOrigin;
33     destination = startDestination;
34     numPassengers = startNumPassengers;
35     avgTicketPrice = startAvgTicketPrice;
36   }
37
38   /** toString
39   * @return flight number, origin, destination,
```

```
  *         number of passengers, and average ticket price
  */
  public String toString( )
  {
    return "Flight " + flightNumber
           + ": from " + origin
           + " to " + destination
           + "\n\t" + numPassengers + " passengers"
           + "; average ticket price: "
           + MONEY.format( avgTicketPrice );
  }
  // accessors, mutators, and other methods ...
}
```

EXAMPLE 11.16 The *FlightRecord2* Class

Example 11.17 shows how the *FileOutputStream* and *ObjectOutputStream* classes can be used in a Java program to write *FlightRecord2* objects to a file named *objects.*

```
/* Demonstrating how to write objects to a file
   Anderson, Franceschi
*/

import java.io.FileOutputStream;
import java.io.ObjectOutputStream;
import java.io.FileNotFoundException;
import java.io.IOException;

public class WritingObjects
{
  public static void main( String [ ] args )
  {
   // instantiate the objects
   FlightRecord2 fr1 = new FlightRecord2( "AA31", "BWI", "SFO",
                                          200, 235.9 );
   FlightRecord2 fr2 = new FlightRecord2( "CO25", "LAX", "JFK",
                                          225, 419.9 );
   FlightRecord2 fr3 = new FlightRecord2( "US57", "IAD", "DEN",
                                          175, 179.5 );

   try
```

```
23     {
24      FileOutputStream fos = new FileOutputStream
25                                   ( "objects", false );
26              // false means we will write to objects
27
28      ObjectOutputStream oos = new ObjectOutputStream( fos );
29
30      // write the objects to the file
31      oos.writeObject( fr1 );
32      oos.writeObject( fr2 );
33      oos.writeObject( fr3 );
34
35      // release resources associated with the objects file
36      oos.close( );
37     }
38
39     catch ( FileNotFoundException fnfe )
40     {
41       System.out.println( "Unable to write to objects" );
42     }
43
44     catch ( IOException ioe )
45     {
46       ioe.printStackTrace( );
47     }
48   }
49 }
```

EXAMPLE 11.17 Writing Objects to a File

Lines 14–20 declare and instantiate three *FlightRecord2* objects that we will write to the *objects* file.

Lines 24 and 25 instantiate a *FileOutputStream* object for writing to the *objects* file, then line 28 instantiates an *ObjectOutputStream* object, which we will use to write the *FlightRecord2* objects to the file.

At lines 30–33, using the *ObjectOutputStream* object *oos*, we call the *writeObject* method, passing the three *FlightRecord2* objects we instantiated. The *writeObject* method takes a *Serializable* object as its parameter, here a *FlightRecord2* object, and writes it to the file in such a way that the stream of bytes can be read using the *readObject* method from the *ObjectInputStream* class. Both the *ObjectOutputStream* constructor and the *writeObject* method can throw an *IOException*, which will be caught at line 44.

After this program is executed, the *objects* file will contain a representation of the three *FlightRecord2* objects.

One more note about writing objects to files: A file containing objects can be quite large. Not only does the object data get written to the file, but also the name of the class, a description of each data field, and other information needed to reconstruct the objects when the file is subsequently read.

The *writeObject* method, however, does not write any *static* class variables to the file. Thus, you may consider declaring any constants as *static*, if appropriate. For example, the object file we create in Example 11.17 by writing three *FlightRecord* objects is 241 bytes long. If we had not declared the constant *DecimalFormat* object *MONEY* as *static* in the *FlightRecord2* class, the size of the object file would be 1,945 bytes!

Similarly, the *writeObject* method does not write to the file any instance variable that is declared to be *transient*. Thus, you can also save space in the file by declaring an instance variable as *transient*. An instance variable is a good candidate to be declared *transient* if you can easily reproduce its value, or if the variable has a value of 0 at the time the file is created. For example, suppose our *FlightRecord* had an additional instance variable named *totalRevenue*, which stored a value we calculated by multiplying *avgTicketPrice* by *numPassengers*. Because we can easily recalculate the value for *totalRevenue*, we can declare it as *transient*; then, that instance variable will not be written to the object file.

SOFTWARE ENGINEERING TIP

To save disk space when writing to an object file, declare the class data as *static* or *transient* where appropriate.

You declare an instance variable as *transient* by inserting the keyword *transient* between the access modifier and the data type of the instance variable, as in the following syntax:

```
accessModifier transient dataType instanceVariableName
```

Thus, the following declaration would declare the *totalRevenue* instance variable as *transient*:

```
private transient double totalRevenue;
```

11.7.2 Reading Objects from Files

Reading objects from a file somewhat parallels writing objects to a file.

The class *ObjectInputStream*, a subclass of *InputStream*, coupled with *FileInputStream*, provides the functionality we need. We are already familiar with the *FileInputStream* class.

ObjectInputStream is designed to read objects from a file. The *readObject* method, which does not take any arguments, reads the next object from the file and returns it. Because the *readObject* method returns a generic *Object*, we must type cast the returned object to the appropriate class. When the end of the file is reached, the *readObject* method throws an *EOFException*. This is in contrast to the *Scanner* class, which provides the *hasNext* method to test whether the end of the file has been reached.

The classes, constructors, and methods discussed previously are shown in Table11.11.

TABLE 11.11 Useful Classes, Constructors, and Methods for Reading Objects from a File

Classes, Constructors, and Methods for Reading Objects from a File		
Class	**Constructors**	**Exceptions Thrown**
`FileInputStream`	`FileInputStream( String filename )` constructs a *FileInputStream* object from a *String* representing the name of a file	`FileNotFoundException`
`ObjectInputStream`	`ObjectInputStream( InputStream in )` constructs an *ObjectInputStream* from the *InputStream in*	`IOException`
	Method API	
`ObjectInputStream`	`Object readObject( )` reads the next object and returns it. The object must be an instance of a class that implements the *Serializable* interface. When the end of the file is reached, an *EOFException* is thrown	`IOException`, `ClassNotFoundException`, `EOFException`

Example 11.18 shows how these *FileInputStream* and *ObjectInputStream* classes can be used in a Java program to read objects from a file. We assume that the file *objects* contains *FlightRecord2* objects, as written in the previous section.

```
/* Demonstrating how to read objects from a file
   Anderson, Franceschi
*/

import java.io.FileInputStream;
import java.io.ObjectInputStream;
import java.io.FileNotFoundException;
import java.io.EOFException;
import java.io.IOException;

public class ReadingObjects
{
  public static void main( String [ ] args )
  {
   try
   {
     FileInputStream fis = new FileInputStream( "objects " );
     ObjectInputStream ois = new ObjectInputStream( fis );

     try
     {
       while ( true )
       {
         // read object, type cast returned object to FlightRecord
         FlightRecord2 temp = ( FlightRecord2 ) ois.readObject( );

         // print the FlightRecord2 object read
         System.out.println( temp );
       }
     } // end inner try block

     catch ( EOFException eofe )
     {
      System.out.println( "End of the file reached" );
     }

     catch ( ClassNotFoundException cnfe )
     {
      System.out.println( cnfe.getMessage( ) );
```

```
40      }
41
42      finally
43      {
44       System.out.println( "Closing file" );
45       ois.close( );
46      }
47    } // end outer try block
48
49    catch ( FileNotFoundException fnfe )
50    {
51       System.out.println( "Unable to find objects" );
52    }
53
54    catch ( IOException ioe )
55    {
56        ioe.printStackTrace( );
57    }
58  }
59 }
```

EXAMPLE 11.18 Reading Objects from a File

Lines 5 through 9 import the needed classes from the *java.io* package. The *ClassNotFoundException* class is part of the *java.lang* package and does not need to be imported.

Line 17 associates a *FileInputStream* object with the *objects* file, and line 18 instantiates an *ObjectInputStream* object for reading the objects from the file.

The *while* loop, from lines 22 to 29, reads and prints each object in the file. We will continue reading until the *readObject* method throws an *EOFException*, which will transfer control to the *catch* block (lines 32–35). Thus, our condition for the *while* loop is

```
while ( true )
```

In that *catch* block, we print a message that the end of the file was detected. Given this *while* loop construction, we do not need a priming read. Inside the *while* loop, we read an object, then print it. When the end of the file is detected, the output statement (line 28) will not be executed.

On line 25, we read an object from the file and assign it to the *FlightRecord2* object reference *temp*. Because the *readObject* method returns an *Object*, we need to type cast the return value to a *FlightRecord2* object. The *readObject* method can also throw a *ClassNotFoundException* or an *IOException*, which will be caught at lines 37 or 54, respectively.

Because an *EOFException* will occur when the end of the file is reached, the *EOFException catch* block will always execute in a normal program run. Thus, any code following the *while* loop in the *try* block will not execute. In order to be able to close the *objects* file, we need to use nested *try/catch* blocks. The inner *try* block (lines 20–30) encloses the *while* loop; its associated *catch* blocks handle the *EOFException* and *ClassNotFoundException*. The outer *try* block (lines 15–47) encloses the instantiations of the *FileInputStream* and *ObjectInputStream* objects, the inner *try* block, and the *finally* block where we close the file (line 45). We can close the file in the *finally* block because the *ois* object reference, declared in the outer *try* block, is visible (that is, in scope) inside the *finally* block.

The *catch* blocks following the outer *try* block handle any *FileNotFoundException* and any other *IOExceptions* that occur in the inner or outer *try* blocks.

It is important to place the *catch* clause with the *EOFException* ahead of the *catch* clause with the *IOException*; otherwise, the *EOFException catch* block will never be reached because *EOFException* is a subclass of *IOException*, and therefore will match an *IOException catch* block.

Figure 11.24 shows the console output when this program is executed. Note that after we read the last object in the file and we try to read another

Figure 11.24
Output from Example 11.18

```
Flight AA31: from BWI to SFO
    200 passengers; average ticket price: $235.90
Flight CO25: from LAX to JFK
    225 passengers; average ticket price: $419.90
Flight US57: from IAD to DEN
    175 passengers; average ticket price: $179.50
End of the file reached
Closing file
```

object, the code executes the *catch* block for the *EOFException*, then the *finally* block.

Skill Practice
with these end-of-chapter questions

11.10.1 Multiple Choice Exercises
Question 11

11.10.2 Reading and Understanding Code
Questions 22, 23

11.10.3 Fill In the Code
Questions 30, 31, 32, 33

11.10.6 Write a Short Program
Question 50

11.10.8 Technical Writing
Question 63

11.8 Programming Activity 2: Reading Objects from a File

In this activity, you will read objects from a file and perform this activity:

> Read an object file containing bank account transaction objects. Loop through all the objects and calculate the new balance of the bank account. Assume that we do not know the number of transaction items, that is, objects, in the file.

Notice that this activity is identical to Programming Activity 1, except that the transactions you will read are stored in the file as objects.

The framework will display the current transaction and current balance so that you can check the correctness of your code as the program executes.

For example, Figure 11.25 demonstrates the animation: We are currently scanning a check transaction for the amount of $500.00. The original balance was $0.00 and the new balance is now –$500.00.

Task Instructions: Reading from the transactions.obj File

In the Chapter 11 directory on the CD -ROM accompanying this book, you will find a Programming Activity 2 directory. Copy the contents of the directory onto a directory on your disk.

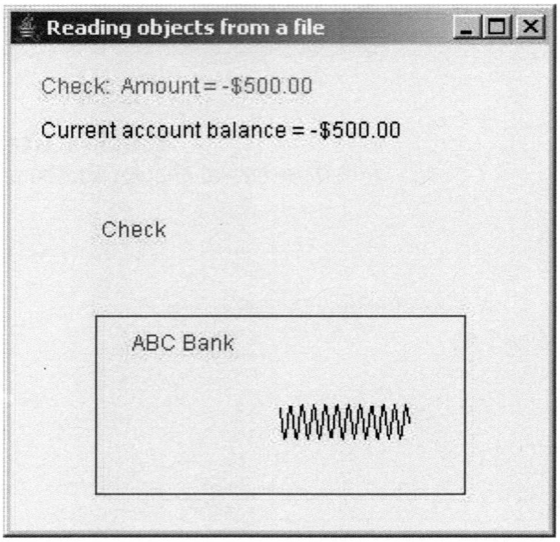

Figure 11.25
Animation of a $500 Check and the New Balance

- Open the *Accounting.java* file. Search for five stars (*****) to find the *balanceCheckBook* method where you will add your code. The method header has been coded for you. Write the code to read the transactions from the *transactions.obj* file, and calculate the balance after all the transactions in that file have been executed. This program first writes *Transaction* objects to the file *transactions.obj*; that code is provided. You need to code the body of the *balanceCheckBook* method in order to read that file. Example 11.19 shows the student code section of the *Accounting.java* file.

```
public void balanceCheckBook( )
{
//
// ***** Student writes the body of this method *****
//
// Using a while loop, read the file transactions.obj
// The file transactions.obj contains transaction objects
//
//  You will need to call the animate method inside
//  the body of the loop that reads the objects
//
// The animate method takes 2 arguments:
//    a Transaction object, representing the transaction
//    a double, representing the new checkbook balance
//  So if these two variables are transaction and balance,
//   then the call to animate will be:
```

```
//
//    animate( transaction, balance );
//
//  You should make that call in the body of your while
//  loop, after you have updated the checkbook balance
//



//
//  end of student code
//
}
```

EXAMPLE 11.19 The *balanceCheckBook* Method

- Begin with a checkbook balance of 0.00.
- To process the transactions, you will need to read one *Transaction* object at a time from the *transactions.obj* file; you will retrieve the transaction amount using the *getAmount* method of the *Transaction* class. The API for that method is:

```
public double getAmount( )
```

- Then process the transaction; you do not need to check the type of transaction. Just add the amount to the checkbook balance.
- After you have processed each transaction, call the *animate* method. This method belongs to the *Accounting* class, so you will call *animate* without using an object reference. The API of the *animate* method is the following:

```
public void animate( Transaction currentTransaction,
                     double currentBalance )
```

As you can see, the *animate* method takes two arguments:

- *currentTransaction* is the current *Transaction* object
- *currentBalance* is the current balance of the checkbook

Assuming that you have a *Transaction* object reference called *transactionObject* and a *double* called *balance*, a call to *animate* will look like the following:

```
animate( transactionObject, balance );
```

When you call *animate*, the window will display the current transaction graphically. It will also display the transaction amount (red if negative, blue if positive) and the current checkbook balance (in black). By adding the previous checkbook balance to the current transaction amount, you will be able to compute the current checkbook balance and check that your program is correct.

- Stop reading from the file when you reach the end of the file. You will need to set up a *catch* block to handle the *EOFException* that occurs when the end of the file is reached.
- Display the ending balance in a dialog box.

To test your code, compile and run the *Accounting.java* application.

If you have time . . .

- Modify the *main* method of the *Accounting* class, adding another transaction. Run the program again and verify that your code still yields the correct result. To add another transaction, you could, for instance, write this code:

```
Withdrawal w2 = new Withdrawal( -200.00 );
transactionList.add( w2 );
```

You can add a transaction of type *Check*, *Withdrawal*, *Deposit*, or *UnknownTransaction* (all of which are subclasses of the *abstract* class *Transaction*).

Troubleshooting

If your method implementation does not animate or animates incorrectly, check these items:

- Verify that you have coded the call to *animate* at the proper time.
- Verify that you have coded the condition for exiting the loop correctly.
- Verify that you have coded the body of the loop correctly.

DISCUSSION QUESTIONS ?

1. Explain why we cannot simply read the *transactions.obj* file as a text file.
2. Explain why we need to type cast each object that we read from the file.

11.9 Chapter Summary

CHAPTER SUMMARY

- Java provides exception classes so that unexpected, illegal operations at run time can be trapped and handled. This provides the programmer with a tool to keep the program running instead of terminating.
- When calling a constructor or method that *throws* a checked exception, you must use *try* and *catch* blocks; otherwise, the code will not compile.
- For calls to a constructor or method that *throws* an unchecked exception, *try* and *catch* blocks are optional. If *try* and *catch* blocks are not used, the exception will be caught at run time by the Java Virtual Machine.
- When a *try* block assigns a value to a variable and that variable is used after the *try/catch* block, the variable must be initialized before the *try* block is entered.
- A variable defined inside a *try* block is local to that block.
- To define your own exception, create a class that extends an existing exception class. This class will consist of a constructor that accepts a message and passes the message to the superclass constructor.
- The method that will generate the exception includes the *throws* clause in the method header. If the invalid condition is detected, the method *throws* a new object of the user-defined exception type, passing the appropriate message to the constructor.
- The *java.io* package contains classes for input and output operations.
- In order to read from a file, that file must exist; otherwise, a *FileNotFoundException* will be thrown.
- When we open a file for writing, the file is created if it does not exist. If the file already exists, the contents of the file are deleted.
- When we open a file for appending, the file is created if it does not exist. If the file already exists, we start writing at the end of the file.
- The *FileWriter* and *BufferedWriter* classes provide functionality to write to a text file.

- The *StringTokenizer* class in the *java.util* package is helpful in parsing a *String* consisting of fields separated by one or more delimiters.
- The *FileOutputStream* and *PrintWriter* classes provide functionality to write primitive data types to a text file.
- Objects can be written to a file; they must be instantiated from a class that *implements* the *Serializable* interface.
- The *Serializable* interface has no methods; therefore, no additional methods need to be implemented in a class that *implements* the *Serializable* interface.
- The *FileOutputStream* and *ObjectOutputStream* classes provide functionality to write objects to a file.
- To avoid writing class data to a file of objects, declare the data as *static* or *transient*, where appropriate.
- The *FileInputStream* and *ObjectInputStream* classes provide the functionality to read objects from a file.
- The *readObject* method returns the object read as an *Object* class reference. That object reference must be type cast to the appropriate class.

11.10 Exercises, Problems, and Projects

11.10.1 Multiple Choice Exercises

1. Why are exceptions useful?
   - ❑ They can replace selection statements, thus saving CPU time.
   - ❑ Exceptions enable programmers to attempt to recover from illegal situations and continue running the program.
2. Some methods that *throw* an exception require *try* and *catch* blocks, while some do not.
   - ❑ True
   - ❑ False
3. What keyword is found in the header of a method that could detect an error and generate an appropriate exception?
   - ❑ *throw*
   - ❑ *throws*

- ❑ *exception*
- ❑ *exceptions*

4. When coding a *try* and *catch* block, it is mandatory to code a *finally* block.
   - ❑ True
   - ❑ False
5. Most input and output related classes can be found in the package
   - ❑ *java.file*
   - ❑ *java.inputoutput*
   - ❑ *java.io*
   - ❑ *java.readwrite*
6. If we open a file for reading and the file does not exist,
   - ❑ there is a compiler error.
   - ❑ an exception is thrown.
   - ❑ the file will be created automatically.
7. When we open a file for writing, then
   - ❑ we will be adding data at the end of the file.
   - ❑ the contents of the file, if any, will be deleted.
   - ❑ there is a run-time error if the file does not exist.
8. When we open a file for appending, then
   - ❑ we will be adding data at the end of the file.
   - ❑ the contents of the file, if any, will be deleted.
   - ❑ there is a run-time error if the file does not exist.
9. In the following code located inside a *try* block:

```
Scanner file = new Scanner(
                 new File( "data.txt" ) );
```

   - ❑ the code will not compile.
   - ❑ the argument to the *Scanner* constructor is an anonymous object.
   - ❑ there will be a run-time error, even if the file *data.txt* exists.

10. The *StringTokenizer* class is useful to parse strings. In what package is the *StringTokenizer* class?
    - ❑ *java.io*
    - ❑ *java.util*
    - ❑ *java.string*
11. Which interface must be implemented by a class whose objects will be written to a file directly?
    - ❑ none
    - ❑ *Serializable*
    - ❑ *IO*
    - ❑ *Object*

11.10.2 Reading and Understanding Code

12. Assuming the file *words.txt* holds the following data:

    CS1 Java Illuminated

    what is the output of this code sequence:

    a. if the file is found?

    b. if the file is not found?

```
try
{
  Scanner file = new Scanner( new File( "words.txt" ) );

  String result = "";

  while ( file.hasNext( ) )
  {
    String s = file.next( );

    result += s;
    result += " AND ";
  }
  System.out.println( "result is " + result );
  file.close( );

}
catch ( FileNotFoundException fnfe )
```

```
{
   System.out.println( "Unable to find words.txt" );
}
catch ( IOException ioe )
{
  ioe.printStackTrace( );
}
```

13. What is the output of this code sequence?

```
StringTokenizer st = new StringTokenizer( "A B C D" );

while ( st.hasMoreTokens( ) )
   System.out.print( st.nextToken( ) );
```

14. What is the output of this code sequence?

```
StringTokenizer st = new StringTokenizer( "AA:BB:CC", ":" );

while ( st.hasMoreTokens( ) )
   System.out.println( st.nextToken( ) );
```

15. What is the output of this code sequence?

```
StringTokenizer st = new StringTokenizer( "A B C D" );
String result = "";

while ( st.hasMoreTokens( ) )
{
   result += st.nextToken( );
}
System.out.println( result );
```

For Questions 16, 17, 18, and 19, you should assume that the file *data.txt* contains the following text:

```
A
B
C
A
B
A
```

16. What is the output of this code sequence?

```
try
{
 Scanner file = new Scanner( new File( "data.txt" ) );

 String result = "";
```

```
  while ( file.hasNext( ) )
  {
    String s = file.nextLine( );
    result += s;
  }

  System.out.println( "result is " + result );
  file.close( );
}

catch ( IOException ioe )
{
  ioe.printStackTrace( );
}
```

17. What is the output of this code sequence?

```
try
{
  Scanner file = new Scanner( new File( "data.txt" ) );

  int n = 0;
  while ( file.hasNext( ) )
  {
    String s = file.nextLine( );

    if ( s.equals( "A" ) )
         n++;
  }

  System.out.println( "The value of n is " + n );
  file.close( );
}
catch ( IOException ioe )
{
  ioe.printStackTrace( );
}
```

18. What is the output of this code sequence?

```
try
{
  Scanner file = new Scanner( new File( "data.txt" ) );
```

```
  while ( file.hasNext( ) )
  {
    String s = file.nextLine( );

    if ( s.equals( "A" ) )
         System.out.println( "Excellent" );
    else if ( s.equals( "B" ) )
         System.out.println( "Good" );
    else
         System.out.println( "Try to do better" );
  }
  file.close( );
}
catch ( IOException ioe )
{
  ioe.printStackTrace( );
}
```

19. What is the output of this code sequence?

```
try
{
 Scanner file = new Scanner( new File( "data.txt" ) );

 String s = " ";
 while ( file.hasNext( ) )
 {
   s = file.nextLine( );
 }

 if (  s.equals( "A" ) )
   System.out.println( "Nice finish" );

 file.close( );
}
catch ( IOException ioe )
{
  ioe.printStackTrace( );
}
```

20. The file *data.txt* contains the following text:

```
CS1
```

What does the file *data.txt* contain after this code sequence is executed?

```
try
{
 FileWriter fw = new FileWriter( "data.txt", true );
 BufferedWriter bw = new BufferedWriter( fw );

 bw.write( "Java Illuminated" );
 bw.newLine( );

 bw.close( );
}
catch ( IOException ioe )
{
  ioe.printStackTrace( );
}
```

21. What does the file *data.txt* contain after this code sequence is executed?

```
try
{
 FileWriter fw = new FileWriter( "data.txt", false );
 BufferedWriter bw = new BufferedWriter( fw );

 String s = "ABCDEFGH";
 String temp = "";

 for ( int i = 0; i < s.length( ); i++ )
 {
   if ( i % 2 == 0 )
      bw.write( s.charAt(i) );
 }
 bw.newLine( );
 bw.close( );
}

catch ( IOException ioe )
{
  ioe.printStackTrace( );
}
```

22. The file *data.txt* contains the following text:

```
CS1
```

What does the file contain after the following code sequence is executed?

```
try
{
 FileOutputStream fos = new FileOutputStream( "data.txt", true );
 PrintWriter pw = new PrintWriter( fos );

 for ( int i = 0; i < 5; i++ )
    pw.println( i );

 pw.close( );
}
catch ( IOException ioe )
{
  ioe.printStackTrace( );
}
```

23. What does the file *data.txt* contain after the following code sequence is executed?

```
try
{
 FileOutputStream fos = new FileOutputStream( "data.txt", false );
 PrintWriter pw = new PrintWriter( fos );

 int s = 0;
 for ( int i = 0; i < 5; i++ )
 {
   s += i;
 }
 pw.print( "The result is " );
 pw.print( s );
 pw.close( );
}
catch ( IOException ioe )
{
  ioe.printStackTrace( );
}
```

11.10.3 Fill in the Code

24. This code segment reads a file named *data.txt* that contains one data item per line, and outputs only the data items that are integers. Hint: You may need to use nested *try* and *catch* blocks.

```
String s = "";
int n = 0;
try
{
   Scanner file = new Scanner( new File( "data.txt" ) );
   while ( file.hasNext( ) )
   {
      s = file.nextLine( );
      // your code goes here

   }
}
catch ( IOException ioe )
{
  ioe.printStackTrace( );
}
```

25. This code retrieves the "*C*" in the string "*ABC$D*" using *StringTokenizer* and outputs it:

```
StringTokenizer st = new StringTokenizer( "A$B$C$D", "$" );
String s = "";
// your code goes here

System.out.println( s );
```

For Questions 29, 30, 31, and 32, you should assume that the file *data.txt* contains the following:

```
Java
Illuminated:
Programming
Is Not A
Spectator
Sport
```

26. This code sequence reads the first two lines of the file *data.txt* and outputs them to the console.

```
try
{
  Scanner file = new Scanner( new File( "data.txt" ) );
  // your code goes here
```

27. This code sequence reads the file *data.txt* and outputs its contents to the console.

```
try
{
  Scanner file = new Scanner( new File( "data.txt" ) );

  String result = "";
  // your code goes here

}
catch ( IOException ioe )
{
  ioe.printStackTrace( );
}
```

28. This code sequence reads the file *data.txt*, concatenates all the lines with a space between them, and outputs them as:

```
Java Illuminated: Programming Is Not A Spectator Sport
```

```
try
{
  Scanner file = new Scanner( new File( "data.txt" ) );

  String result = "";
  // your code goes here

}
catch ( IOException ioe )
{
  ioe.printStackTrace( );
}
```

29. This code sequence reads the file *data.txt* and outputs only the lines that contain the *String* "*Sp*". Assume that we do not know the contents of the file before reading it.
For the current example, the output will be:

```
Spectator
Sport
```

```
try
{
  Scanner file = new Scanner( new File( "data.txt" ) );

  String result = "";
  // your code goes here
```

```
}
catch ( IOException ioe )
{
  ioe.printStackTrace( );
}
```

30. This code sequence loops through the array *grades* and writes all its elements into the file *data.txt*, one per line:

```
int [ ] grades = { 98, 76, 82, 90, 100, 75 };
try
{
  FileOutputStream fos = new FileOutputStream( "data.txt", false );
  // your code goes here

}
// and your code continues here
```

31. This code sequence loops through the array *grades*, calculates the average, and writes the average into the file *data.txt*:

```
int [ ] grades = { 98, 76, 82, 90, 100, 75 };
double average = 0.0;
for ( int i = 0; i < grades.length; i++ )
{
  // some of your code goes here

}
// and more code goes here

try
{
  FileOutputStream fos = new FileOutputStream( "data.txt", false );
  PrintWriter pw = new PrintWriter( fos );
  // and more code goes here

}
catch ( IOException ioe )
{
  ioe.printStackTrace( );
}
```

32. This code sequence writes the values of the variables *i* and *d* to the file *data.txt*, one line at a time.

```
int i = 45;
double d = 6.7;
try
```

```
{
  FileOutputStream fos = new FileOutputStream( "data.txt", false );
  PrintWriter pw = new PrintWriter( fos );
  // your code goes here

}
catch ( IOException ioe )
{
  ioe.printStackTrace( );
}
```

33. This code sequence appends the value of the variable *f* to the file *data.txt*:

```
float f = 13.5f;
try
{
  // your code goes here
```

11.10.4 Identifying Errors in Code

34. Where is the error in this code sequence?

```
StringTokenizer st = new StringTokenizer( "1 2 3" );
int i = st.nextToken( );
```

35. Where is the error in this code sequence?

```
try
{
  Scanner file = new Scanner( new File( "data.txt" ) );
  String s = file.nextLine( );
}
catch ( ArithmeticException ae )
{
  System.out.println( ae.getMessage( ) );
}
```

36. Where is the error in this code sequence?

```
try
{
  Scanner file = new Scanner( new File( "data.txt" ) );
  file.write( "Hello" );
}
```

```
catch ( IOException ioe )
{
  ioe.printStackTrace( );
}
```

11.10.5 Debugging Area—Using Messages from the Java Compiler and Java JVM

37. You coded the following in the class *Test.java*:

```
import java.io.IOException;
import java.io.File;
import java.util.Scanner;

public class Test
{
  public static void main( String [ ] args )
  {
      try    // line 9
      {
             Scanner file = new Scanner( new File( "data.txt" ) );

             String stringRead = file.nextLine( );
             System.out.println( stringRead );
      }
  }
}
```

At compile time, you get the following error:

```
Test.java:9: 'try' without 'catch' or 'finally'
   try
   ^
1 error
```

Explain what the problem is and how to fix it.

38. You coded the following in the class *Test.java*:

```
import java.io.IOException;
import java.io.File;
import java.util.Scanner;
public class Test
{
  public static void main( String [ ] args )
  {
      try
      {
       Scanner file = new Scanner( new File( "data.txt" ) );
```

```
         String stringRead = file.nextLine( );
      }
      catch ( IOException ioe )
      {
         ioe.printStackTrace( );
      }
      System.out.println( "string read: " + stringRead );
      // line above is 19
   }
}
```

At compile time, you get the following error:

```
Test.java:19: cannot find symbol
symbol  : variable stringRead
location: class Test
   System.out.println( "string read: " + stringRead );
                                          ^
1 error
```

Explain what the problem is and how to fix it.

39. You coded the following in the class *Test.java*:

```
import java.io.IOException;
import java.io.File;
import java.util.Scanner;

public class Test
{
  public static void main( String [ ] args )
  {
        String stringRead;
        try
        {
              Scanner file = new Scanner( new File( "data.txt" ) );

              stringRead = file.nextLine( );
        }
        catch ( IOException ioe )
        {
              ioe.printStackTrace( );
        }
        System.out.println( "string read: " + stringRead );
        // line above is line 21
  }
}
```

At compile time, you get the following error:

```
Test.java:21: variable stringRead might not have been initialized
System.out.println( "string read: " + stringRead );
                                      ^
1 error
```

Explain what the problem is and how to fix it.

40. You coded the following in the class *Test.java*:

```
String s = "A,B,C,D,E,F";
StringTokenizer st = new StringTokenizer( s, "," );

for ( int i = 0; i < st.countTokens( ); i++ )
     System.out.print( st.nextToken( ) + ":" );
```

The code compiles and runs, but the result is

```
A:B:C:
```

You expected

```
A:B:C:D:E:F:
```

Explain what the problem is and how to fix it.

41. In order to read from the file *data.txt*, you coded the following in the *Test.java* class:

```
try
{
  Scanner file = new Scanner( new File( "datatxt" ) );

  String s = file.nextLine( );
  System.out.println( "Line read is " + s );
}
catch ( IOException ioe )
{
  System.out.println( ioe.getMessage( ) );
}
```

The code compiles and runs, but here is the output:

```
datatxt (The system cannot find the file specified)
```

42. You coded the following in the class *Test.java*:

```
BufferedWriter bw = new BufferedWriter( "data.txt" );
...
```

At compile time, you get the following error:

```
Test.java:12: cannot find symbol
symbol  : constructor BufferedWriter (java.lang.String)
location: class java.io.BufferedWriter
      BufferedWriter bw = new BufferedWriter( "data.txt" );
                          ^
1 error
```

Explain what the problem is and how to fix it.

11.10.6 Write a Short Program

43. Write a program that reads a file and writes a copy of the file to another file with line numbers inserted.

44. In Internet programming, programmers receive parameters via a query string, which looks like a *String* with fields separated by the "&" character. Each field typically has a metadata part and a data part separated by the equal sign. An example of a query string is:

    ```
    first=Mike&last=Jones&id=mike1&password=hello
    ```

    Using *StringTokenizer* at least once, parse a query string and output each field on a different line after replacing the equal sign with a colon followed by a space. For example, for the preceding sample query string, the output should be:

    ```
    first: Mike
    last: Jones
    id: mike1
    password: hello
    ```

45. Write a program that reads a file that contains only one line; output all the characters, one character per line.

46. Write a program that reads a file and counts how many lines it contains.

47. Write a program that reads a text file that contains a grade (for instance, 87) on each line. Calculate and print the average of the grades.

48. Write a program that reads a text file and outputs every line of the file separated by a blank line.

49. An HTML file starts with <HTML> and ends with </HTML>. Write a program that reads a file and checks whether that is true.

50. Often websites display the visitor count ("You are visitor number 5246"). Write a program that reads a file that holds the visitor count, outputs it, and updates the file, incrementing the visitor count by 1.

51. Often on websites, the beginning of an article is displayed followed by the word *more* and several dots (as in *more*...). Write a program that reads the first two lines of a file, and displays them inside an applet, adding the word *more* in blue followed by three dots.

11.10.7 Programming Projects

52. Design your own *MyStringTokenizer* class that implements a method *myNextToken* as follows: When two delimiters are next to each other in the *String*, there is a token between them (this is different from the *StringTokenizer* class). For instance, if the *String* is "A,B,C,,,D" and the delimiter is a comma, you should consider that there are six tokens, with the fourth and fifth tokens being empty *Strings*. Test your class with a client program.

53. We are interested in checking the number of times a given word (for example, the word *secret*) appears in a file. You should assume that lines do not wrap, that is, a line does not continue on the next line. Warning: You could have letters arranged like *secsecret*. Design a class that encapsulates that idea. Test it with a client program.

54. Design a class that checks if the contents of two text files are identical and, if not, determines how many lines are different. Lines are different if they differ in one or more characters. Test your class with a client program.

55. Design a class that encapsulates the contents of a text file. Include the following methods in your class: *numberOfLinesInFile*, *longestLineInFile* (the line number of the line containing the maximum number of characters), *shortestLineInFile*, and *averageNumberOfCharactersPerLine*. Test your class with a client program.

56. The most common characters in an HTML file are < and >. Every < must be followed eventually by a > character before the next < character is found. There should be an equal number of both in the file. Design a class that encapsulates that idea. Test your class with a client program.

57. A file contains web addresses, one on each line. Design a class that encapsulates the concept of counting the number of college addresses (contains *.edu*), government addresses (contains *.gov*), business addresses (contains *.com*), organization addresses (contains *.org*), or other addresses. Test your class with a client program.

58. In cryptograms, each character is encoded into another. If the text is long enough, one can, as a strategy, use the frequency of occurrence of each character. The most frequently occurring character will likely be the code for an *e*, because *e* is the most frequently used letter of the English alphabet. Design a class that attempts to determine the relative frequency of each letter by reading a file and keeping track of the number of times each of the 26 English alphabet characters appears. Also provide methods, such as *highestFrequencyCharacter* and *lowestFrequencyCharacter*. Test your class with a client program.

59. Design a class that calculates statistics on data in a file. We expect the file to contain grades represented by integer values, one per line. If you encounter a value that is not an integer, you should throw an exception, print a message to the console, skip that value, and continue processing. Store the grades that you read in an *ArrayList* so that all the grades are available for retrieval. You should also have, as a minimum, methods that return the grade average, the highest grade, the lowest grade, and ones that return all the grades as an array of letter grades. Test your class with a client class.

60. Write a class encapsulating the concept of a home, assuming that it has the following attributes: the number of rooms, the square footage, and whether it has a basement. Write a client program that creates five *Home* objects, writes them to a file as objects, then reads them from the file as objects, outputs a description of each object using the *toString* method (which the *Home* class should override), and outputs the number of *Home* objects. When reading the objects, you should assume that you do not know the number of objects in the file.

61. Write a class named *CarPlate* encapsulating the concept of a car license plate, assuming that it has the following attributes: the plate number, the state, and its color. Write a client program that creates three *CarPlate* objects, writes them to a file as objects, then reads them from the file as objects, outputs a description of each of the objects using the *toString* method (which the *CarPlate* class should

override), and outputs the number of objects. When reading the objects, you should assume that you do not know the number of objects in the file.

11.10.8 Technical Writing

62. Are exceptions a good thing or a bad thing? Argue both sides.
63. With respect to writing objects to and reading objects from a file, discuss the importance of documenting your code well.

11.10.9 Group Project (for Groups of 2, 3, or More Students)

64. A friend of yours owns two houses at Football City, the site of the next Super Bowl. Your friend wants to rent those two houses for the Friday, Saturday, and Sunday of the Super Bowl weekend. House #1 has 3BR (3 bedrooms), 3BA (3 baths), and house #2 has 1BR, 1BA.

    For this project, concurrency is not an issue; you should assume that two customers will never access your system at exactly the same time. You should also assume that the management-side software and the customer-side software will never run at the same time. We can assume that we run the management-side software first, then the customer-side software.

    This friend has asked you to build a file-based reservation system enabling the following:

    A. Management-side software:

       Your friend controls the rental price and may change it every day. He/she sends you a change file every day; this file may be empty, in which case there are no pricing changes. If the file is not empty, pricing has changed (for one or more houses, or for one or more days). You are in charge of this project, and therefore, you are in charge of specifying the file format; however, this must be a simple text file because your friend is not a computer person.

       You do not have to simulate the act of sending the file by your friend; you should assume that the file is a text file in your directory and that you only need to read the data.

       Your management-side software needs to read this file and update a different file, with which you control the reservation system. You can create your own design for the structure of that file. Of course, prices for existing reservations cannot be changed.

Finally, your management-side software should write to a file the status of the reservations; that is, which house is rented to whom, when, and for what price.

B. Customer-side software:

The customer-side software allows a customer to make a reservation. You should prompt the customer for a possible reservation, offering whatever house is available, when, and at what price. Do not offer a customer a house that is already rented.

In this simple version, a customer makes and pays for the reservation at the same time. Also, a reservation cannot be cancelled. When a reservation is made, the customer-side software automatically updates the file controlling the reservations.

CHAPTER 12

Graphical User Interfaces

CHAPTER CONTENTS

Introduction

Many applications we use every day have a graphical user interface, or GUI (pronounced goo-ey), which allows us to control the operation of the program visually. For example, web browsers, such as Microsoft Internet Explorer, provide menus, buttons, drop-down lists, and other visual input and output devices to allow the user to communicate with the program through mouse clicks, mouse movements, and by typing text into boxes.

GUIs enable the user to select the next function to be performed, to enter data, and to set program preferences, such as colors or fonts. GUIs also make a program easier to use because a GUI is a familiar interface to users. If you design your program's GUI well, users can quickly learn to operate your program, in many cases, without consulting documentation or requiring extensive training.

Java is very rich in GUI classes. In this chapter, we will present some of those classes, along with the main concepts associated with developing a GUI application.

12.1 GUI Applications Using *JFrame*

The first step in developing a GUI application is to create a window. We've opened graphical windows in our applets, but so far, we have not displayed a window in our applications. Instead, we've communicated with users through the Java console and dialog boxes. We will use the *JFrame* class in the *javax.swing* package to create a window for our GUI applications. The inheritance hierarchy for the *JFrame* class is shown in Figure 12.1.

REFERENCE POINT

Inheritance, including which class members are inherited, is discussed in Chapter 10.

Inheriting directly from *Object* is the *Component* class, which represents a graphical object that can be displayed. Inheriting from the *Component* class is the *Container* class, which, as its name indicates, can hold other objects. This is good because we will want to add GUI components to our window. The *Window* class, which inherits from the *Container* class, can be used to create a basic window. The *Frame* class, which inherits from the *Window* class, adds a title bar and a border to the window. The title bar contains icons that allow the user to minimize, maximize, resize, and close the window. This is the type of window we are accustomed to seeing.

We need to step down one more level of inheritance, however, to the *JFrame* class before we are ready to create our GUI application. A *JFrame* object is a *swing* component. Thus, the *JFrame* class provides the functionality of *Frame*, as well as support for the *swing* architecture. We'll explain more about the *swing* components later in this chapter. For now, Figure 12.1 shows us that a *JFrame* object is a *Component*, a *Container*, a *Window*, and a *Frame* by inheritance, so we can use a *JFrame* object to display a window that will hold our GUI components, and thus present our GUI to the user. Our typical GUI application class will be a subclass of *JFrame*, inheriting its functionality as a window and a container. Thus, the class header for our GUI applications will follow this pattern:

```
public class ClassName extends JFrame
```

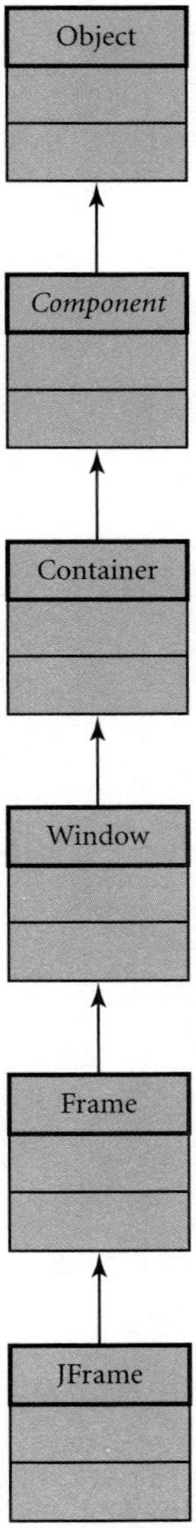

Figure 12.1
Inheritance Hierarchy for *JFrame*

Table 12.1 shows two constructors and some important methods of the *JFrame* class, some of which are inherited from its superclasses. Because our GUI applications extend the *JFrame* class, our applications inherit these methods also.

Example 12.1 shows a shell GUI application class. This class demonstrates the general format for building GUI applications, but has no components.

```
/*  A Shell GUI Application
    Anderson, Franceschi
*/

import javax.swing.JFrame;
import java.awt.Container;
// other import statements here as needed

public class ShellGUIApplication extends JFrame
{
  private Container contents;
  // declare other instance variables

  // constructor
  public ShellGUIApplication( )
  {
    // call JFrame constructor with title bar text
    super( "A Shell GUI Application" );

```

TABLE 12.1 *JFrame* Constructors and Methods

Useful Constructors and Methods of the *JFrame* Class	
Class	**Constructor**
JFrame	JFrame( ) constructs a *JFrame* object, initially invisible, with no text in the title bar
JFrame	JFrame(String titleBarText) constructs a *JFrame* object, initially invisible, with *titleBarText* displayed in the window's title bar
Methods	
Return value	**Method name and argument list**
Container	getContentPane( ) returns the content pane object for this window
void	setDefaultCloseOperation(int operation) sets the default operation when the user closes this window, that is, when the user clicks on the X icon in the top-right corner of the window
void	setSize(int width, int height) sizes the window to the specified *width* and *height* in pixels
void	setVisible(boolean mode) displays this window if *mode* is *true*; hides the window if *mode* is *false*

```
    // get container for components
    contents = getContentPane( );

    // set the layout manager

    // instantiate GUI components and other instance variables

    // add GUI components to the content pane

```

```
29       // set original size of window
30       setSize( 300, 200 );
31
32       // make window visible
33       setVisible( true );
34    }
35
36    public static void main( String [ ] args )
37    {
38      ShellGUIApplication basicGui = new ShellGUIApplication( );
39      basicGui.setDefaultCloseOperation( JFrame.EXIT_ON_CLOSE );
40    }
41 }
```

EXAMPLE 12.1 A Shell GUI Application Using *JFrame*

We have defined one instance variable, *contents*, which is a *Container* object reference (line 11). Our subsequent GUI applications will define instance variables for the components to be placed in the window, as well as instance variables to hold the data of the application as primitive data types or objects.

The *main* method is coded at lines 36–40. We start by instantiating an object of this application class (line 38), which invokes the constructor (lines 14–34).

At line 39, we call the *setDefaultCloseOperation* method. The *EXIT_ON_CLOSE* argument is a useful *static* constant of the *JFrame* class, which specifies that the GUI application should terminate when the user closes the window.

A constructor in a GUI application has several tasks to perform:

- Call the constructor of the *JFrame* superclass.
- Get an object reference to the content pane container. We will add our GUI components to the content pane.
- Set the layout manager. Layout managers arrange the GUI components in the window.
- Instantiate each component.
- Add each component to the content pane.
- Set the size of the window.
- Display the window.

In our constructor, at line 18, we call the *JFrame* constructor, passing as an argument, a *String* representing the text that we want to be displayed in the title bar of the window. As in any subclass, this must be the first statement in the constructor.

At line 21, we call the *getContentPane* method, inherited from the *JFrame* class, and assign its return value to *contents*. The *getContentPane* method returns a *Container* object reference; subsequent applications will add our GUI components to this container.

Although this shell application does not have any GUI components, we have inserted comments to indicate where the component-related operations should be performed. Later in this chapter, we show you how to perform these actions.

COMMON ERROR TRAP

Be sure to call the *setSize* method to set the initial dimensions of the window and call the *setVisible* method to display the window and its contents. Omitting the call to the *setSize* method will create a default *JFrame* consisting of a title bar only, although it will be resizable by the user. If you omit the call to the *setVisible* method, the window will not open when the application begins.

We then set the initial size of the window to a width of 300 pixels and a height of 200 pixels by calling the *setSize* method (line 30). Finally, we call the *setVisible* method (line 33) so that the window will be displayed when the constructor finishes executing. Calling the *setSize* and *setVisible* methods is not required, but if you omit either method call, you will get unfavorable results. If you omit the call to *setSize*, the window will consist of just the title bar. If you omit the call to *setVisible*, the window will not be displayed when the application begins.

The window generated by running Example 12.1 is shown in Figure 12.2. Note the text in the title bar, which was set by calling the *JFrame* constructor. When you run the program, try minimizing, maximizing, moving, resizing, and closing the window.

We have opened a window successfully, but an empty window is not very impressive. In the next section, we will show you how to start adding GUI components to the window.

Figure 12.2
The Window Generated by Example 12.1

12.2 GUI Components

We have already said that a **component** is an object having a graphical representation. Labels, text fields, buttons, radio buttons, checkboxes, and drop-down lists are examples of components. A component performs at least one of these functions:

- displays information
- collects data from the user
- allows the user to initiate program functions

Java provides an extensive set of classes that can be used to add a GUI to your applications. Table 12.2 lists some GUI components and the Java classes that encapsulate them. All classes listed in Table 12.2 belong to the *javax.swing* package.

Java supports two implementations of GUI components: AWT (Abstract Window Toolkit) and *swing*.

The AWT components are the original implementation of Java components and hand off some of the display and behavior of the component to the native windowing system. In other words, on a PC, AWT components,

TABLE 12.2 Selected GUI Components and Java Classes

Component	Purpose	Java Class
Label	Displays an image or read-only text. Labels are often paired with text fields and are used to identify the contents of the text field.	*JLabel*
Text field	A single-line text box for displaying information and accepting user input.	*JTextField*
Text area	Multiple-line text field for data entry or display.	*JTextArea*
Password field	Single-line text field for accepting passwords without displaying the characters typed.	*JPasswordField*
Button	Command button that the user clicks to signal that an operation should be performed.	*JButton*
Radio button	Toggle button that the user clicks to select one option in the group. Clicking on a radio button deselects any previously selected option.	*JRadioButton*
Checkbox	Toggle button that the user clicks to select 0, 1, or more options in a group.	*JCheckBox*
List	List of items that the user clicks to select one or more items.	*JList*
Drop-down list	Drop-down list of items that the user clicks to select one item.	*JComboBox*

such as buttons and frames, are rendered by the Windows windowing system; on a Macintosh computer, AWT components are rendered by the MacOS windowing system; on a Unix computer, AWT components are rendered by the X-Window system. As a result, the AWT GUI components automatically take on the appearance and behavior (commonly called the **look and feel**) of the windowing system on which the application is running. One disadvantage of AWT components, however, is that because of the inconsistencies in the look and feel among the various windowing systems, an application may behave slightly differently from one platform to another. Because AWT components rely on the native windowing system, they are often called **heavyweight** components.

The *swing* components are the second generation of GUI components, developed entirely in Java to provide a consistent look and feel from platform to platform. As such, they are often referred to as **lightweight** components. Some of the benefits of *swing* components are:

- Applications run consistently across platforms, which makes maintenance easier.
- The *swing* architecture has its roots in the model-view-controller paradigm, which facilitates programming:
  - the model represents the data for the application
  - the view is the visual representation of that data
  - the controller takes user input on the view and updates the model accordingly
- The *swing* components can be rendered in multiple windowing system styles, so your application can take on the look and feel of the platform on which it is running, if desired.

Given the advantages of *swing* over AWT, we will build our GUI applications using *swing* components exclusively. You can recognize a *swing* component because its class name begins with *J*. Thus, *JFrame* is a *swing* component. *Swing* components are found in the *javax.swing* package.

A summary of the inheritance hierarchy for selected *swing* components is shown in Figure 12.3. *JComponent* is the base class for all swing components, except for top-level containers such as *JFrame*. Notice that the *JFrame* class does not inherit from the *JComponent* class. However, the *JFrame* class and the *JComponents* shown in Table 12.2 do share some common superclasses: *Component* and *Container*. Thus, the *JComponents* are

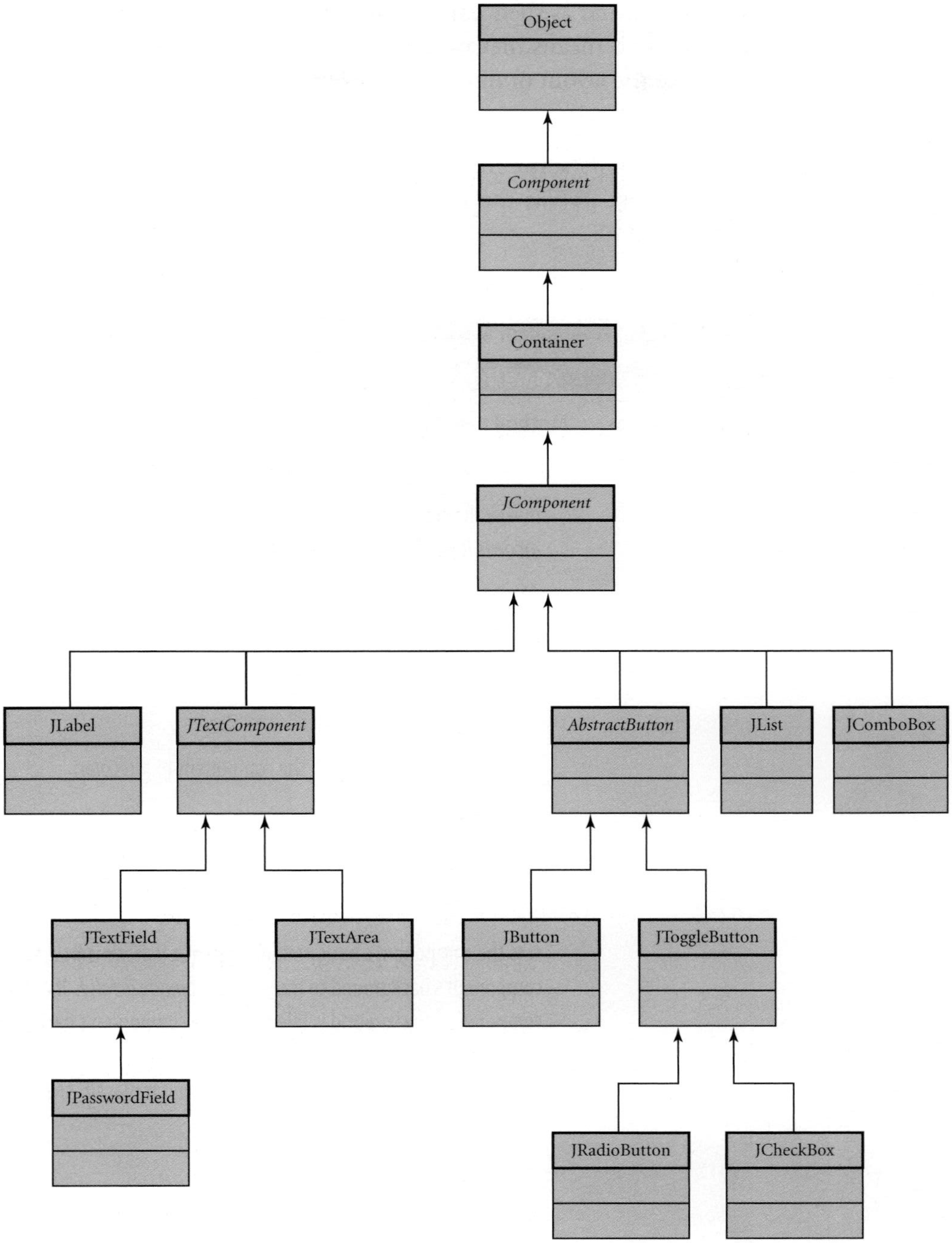

Figure 12.3
The Inheritance Hierarchy for Some GUI Classes

Containers, and as such, can contain other *JComponents* or other *Container* objects. This means that we can nest GUI components, which will help us organize the layout of our windows. We will show you how to do that later in the chapter.

Table 12.3 lists some important methods of *JComponent*. Because these methods are *public*, the GUI components shown in Figure 12.3 inherit these methods.

TABLE 12.3 *JComponent* Methods

Some Useful Methods of the *JComponent* Class	
Return value	**Method name and argument list**
`void`	`setVisible( boolean mode )`
	makes the component visible if *mode* is *true*; hides the component if *mode* is *false*. The default is visible.
`void`	`setToolTipText( String toolTip )`
	sets the tool tip text to *toolTip*. When the mouse lingers over the component, the tool tip text will be displayed.
`void`	`setForeground( Color foreColor )`
	sets the foreground color of the component to *foreColor*.
`void`	`setBackground( Color backColor )`
	sets the background color of the component to *backColor*.
`void`	`setOpaque( boolean mode )`
	sets the component's background to opaque if *mode* is *true*; sets the component's background to transparent if *mode* is *false*. If opaque, the component's background is filled with the component's background color; if transparent, the component's background is filled with the background color of the container on which it is placed. The default is transparent.
`void`	`setEnabled( boolean mode )`
	enables the component if *mode* is *true*; disables the component if *mode* is *false*. An enabled component can respond to user input.

12.3 A Simple Component: *JLabel*

Now it's time to place a component into the window. We will start with a simple component, a label, encapsulated by the *JLabel* class. A user does not interact with a label; the label just displays some information, such as a title, an identifier for another component, or an image.

Example 12.2 creates a window containing two labels, one that displays text and one that displays an image. Figure 12.4 shows the window when the application is run.

```
/*  Using JLabels to display text and images
    Anderson, Franceschi
*/

import java.awt.Container;
import javax.swing.JFrame;
import javax.swing.ImageIcon;
import javax.swing.JLabel;
import java.awt.FlowLayout;
import java.awt.Color;

public class Dinner extends JFrame
{
  private Container contents;
  private JLabel labelText;
  private JLabel labelImage;

  // Constructor
  public Dinner( )
  {
    super( "What's for dinner?" );       // call JFrame constructor

    contents = getContentPane( );        // get content pane

    contents.setLayout( new FlowLayout( ) ); // set layout manager

    // use the JLabel constructor with a String argument
    labelText = new JLabel( "Sushi tonight?" );

    // set label properties
    labelText.setForeground( Color.WHITE );
    labelText.setBackground( Color.BLUE );
    labelText.setOpaque( true );
```

```
    // use the JLabel constructor with an ImageIcon argument
    labelImage = new JLabel( new ImageIcon( "sushi.jpg" ) );

    // set tool tip text
    labelImage.setToolTipText( "photo of sushi" );

    // add the two labels to the content pane
    contents.add( labelText );
    contents.add( labelImage );

    setSize( 300, 200 );
    setVisible( true );
  }

  public static void main( String [ ] args )
  {
    Dinner dinner = new Dinner( );
    dinner.setDefaultCloseOperation( JFrame.EXIT_ON_CLOSE );
  }
}
```

EXAMPLE 12.2 A Simple GUI Component: *JLabel*

Java provides classes to help us organize window contents. These classes are called layout managers. They implement the *LayoutManager* interface and determine the size and position of the components within a container. We will use the simple *FlowLayout* layout manager for the next few examples; later in the chapter, we will look into two other, more sophisticated layout managers: *BorderLayout* and *GridLayout.*

The *FlowLayout* layout manager arranges components in rows from left to right in the order in which the components are added to the container.

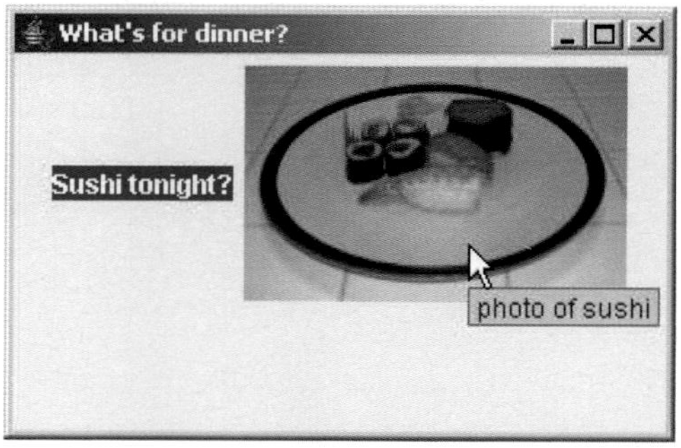

Figure 12.4
Running Example 12.2

Whenever a newly added component does not fit into the current row, the *FlowLayout* layout manager starts a new row. With *FlowLayout*, if the user resizes the window, the components may be rearranged into fewer or more rows. We will use the default constructor of the *FlowLayout* class, which centers the components within each row.

To add components to a window, we use two methods of the *Container* class, shown in Table 12.4, to set the layout manager and add components to the window. Remember that we obtain the content pane of the *JFrame* window as a *Container* object. We call these methods using the content pane object reference.

In Example 12.2, we declare two *JLabel* instance variables at lines 15–16. At line 25, we set *FlowLayout* as the layout manager.

Next, we instantiate our *JLabel* objects. Table 12.5 shows several constructors of the *JLabel* class.

The *SwingConstants* interface, which is implemented by many *JComponents* that display text, such as labels, text fields, and buttons, provides a collection of *static int* constants that can be used for positioning and orientation of the text within a component.

REFERENCE POINT

More information about the *SwingConstants* interface can be found on the Sun Microsystems website: www.java.sun.com.

The first *JLabel* object reference, *labelText*, is instantiated at line 28, using the constructor with a *String* argument.

The second *JLabel* object reference, *labelImage*, is instantiated at line 36, using the constructor that takes an *Icon* argument. The *ImageIcon* class

TABLE 12.4 Useful Methods of the *Container* Class

Useful Methods of the *Container* Class	
Return value	**Method name and argument list**
`void`	`setLayout( LayoutManager mgr )` sets the layout manager of the window to *mgr*
`Component`	`add( Component component )` adds the *component* to the container, using the rules of the layout manager. Returns the argument.
`void`	`removeAll( )` removes all components from the window

TABLE 12.5 Constructors of the *JLabel* Class

Useful Constructors of the *JLabel* Class	
Class	**Constructor**
`JLabel`	`JLabel( String text )` creates a *JLabel* object that displays the specified *text*
`JLabel`	`JLabel( String text, int alignment )` creates a *JLabel* object that displays the specified *text*. The *alignment* argument specifies the alignment of the text within the label component. The *alignment* value can be any of the following *static int* constants from the *SwingConstants* interface: LEFT, CENTER, RIGHT, LEADING, or TRAILING. By default, the label text is left-adjusted.
`JLabel`	`JLabel( Icon image )` creates a *JLabel* object that displays the *image*.

COMMON ERROR TRAP

As for any object reference, it is mandatory to instantiate a component before using it. Forgetting to instantiate a component before adding it to the content pane will result in a *NullPointerException* at run time.

COMMON ERROR TRAP

Be sure to place the call to the *setVisible* method after adding all the components to the window. If you add components to the window after calling *setVisible*, those components will not be visible until the window is repainted.

encapsulates an image and implements the *Icon* interface, so an *IconImage* object can be used wherever an *Icon* argument is required. One of the *ImageIcon* constructors takes as a *String* argument the filename where the image is stored. Its API is:

```
public ImageIcon( String filename )
```

Lines 31–33 call the *setForeground*, *setBackground*, and *setOpaque* methods inherited from the *JComponent* class to set some properties of *labelText*. On line 39, we set up a tool tip that will pop up the message "photo of sushi" when the user pauses the mouse pointer over the image. You can see this tool tip displayed in Figure 12.4.

In lines 42–43, we add the two labels to the window. Because we are using the *FlowLayout* layout manager, the labels appear in the order we added them to the component, first *labelText*, then *labelImage*, centered left to right in the window. If the user resizes the window to be about the same width as the *JLabel labelText*, the layout manager will arrange the display so that the image appears under the text (as a second row).

Note that the last statement of the constructor (line 46) is a call to the *setVisible* method to make the window visible. A common error is to call the *setVisible* method earlier in the constructor, then add more components to the window. If you do this, however, the components added after the call to the *setVisible* method will not display until the window is repainted, for example, as a result of the user resizing the window.

Skill Practice
with these end-of-chapter questions

12.18.1 Multiple Choice Exercises
Questions 1, 2, 3, 4

12.18.2 Reading and Understanding Code
Question 18

12.18.3 Fill In the Code
Question 27

12.18.4 Identifying Errors in Code
Question 42

12.18.5 Debugging Area
Questions 46, 47

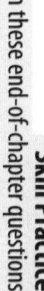

12.4 Event Handling

Now we know how to open a window in an application, and we know how to display labels and images. But the user can't interact with our application yet, except to display a tool tip. We need to add some interactive GUI components, like buttons or text fields or lists. By interacting with these components the user will control which operations of the program will take place, and in what order.

GUI programming uses an **event-driven model** of programming, as opposed to the procedural model of programming we have been using thus far. By that, we mean that by using a GUI, we put the user in interactive control. For example, we might display some text fields, a few buttons, and a selectable list of items. Then our program will "sit back" and wait for the user to do something. When the user enters data into a text field, presses a button, or selects an item from the list, our program will respond, perform the function that the user has requested, then sit back again and wait for the user to do something else. These user actions generate **events**. Thus, the processing of our program will consist of responding to events caused by the user interacting with GUI components.

When the user interacts with a GUI component, the component **fires an event**. Java provides interfaces, classes, and methods to handle these events. Using these Java tools, we can register our application's interest in being notified when an event occurs for a particular component, and we can specify the code we want to be executed when that event occurs.

To allow a user to interact with our application through a GUI component, we need to perform the following functions:

1. write an event handler class (called a **listener**)
2. instantiate an object of that class
3. register that listener on one or more components

A typical event handler class *implements* a listener interface. The listener interfaces, which inherit from the *EventListener* interface, are supplied in the *java.awt.event* and *javax.swing.event* packages. A listener interface specifies one or more *abstract* methods that an event handler class needs to implement. The listener methods receive as a parameter an event object, which represents the event that was fired.

An application can instantiate multiple event handlers, and a single event handler can be the listener for multiple components.

Event classes are subclasses of the *EventObject* class, as shown in Figure 12.5, and are in the *java.awt.event* and *javax.swing.event* packages. From the *EventObject* class, the event classes inherit the *getSource* method, which returns the object reference of the component that fired the event. Its API is shown in Table 12.6.

Thus, with some simple *if/else* statements, an event handler that is registered as the listener for more than one component can identify which of the components fired the event and decide on the appropriate action.

The types of listeners that we can register on a component depend on the types of events that the component fires. Table 12.7 shows some user activities that generate events, the type of event object created, and the appropriate listener interface for the event handler to implement. Some of these components can fire other events, as well.

To add event handling to our *ShellGUIApplication* class, we will follow the following pattern. The code we need to add is shown in bold.

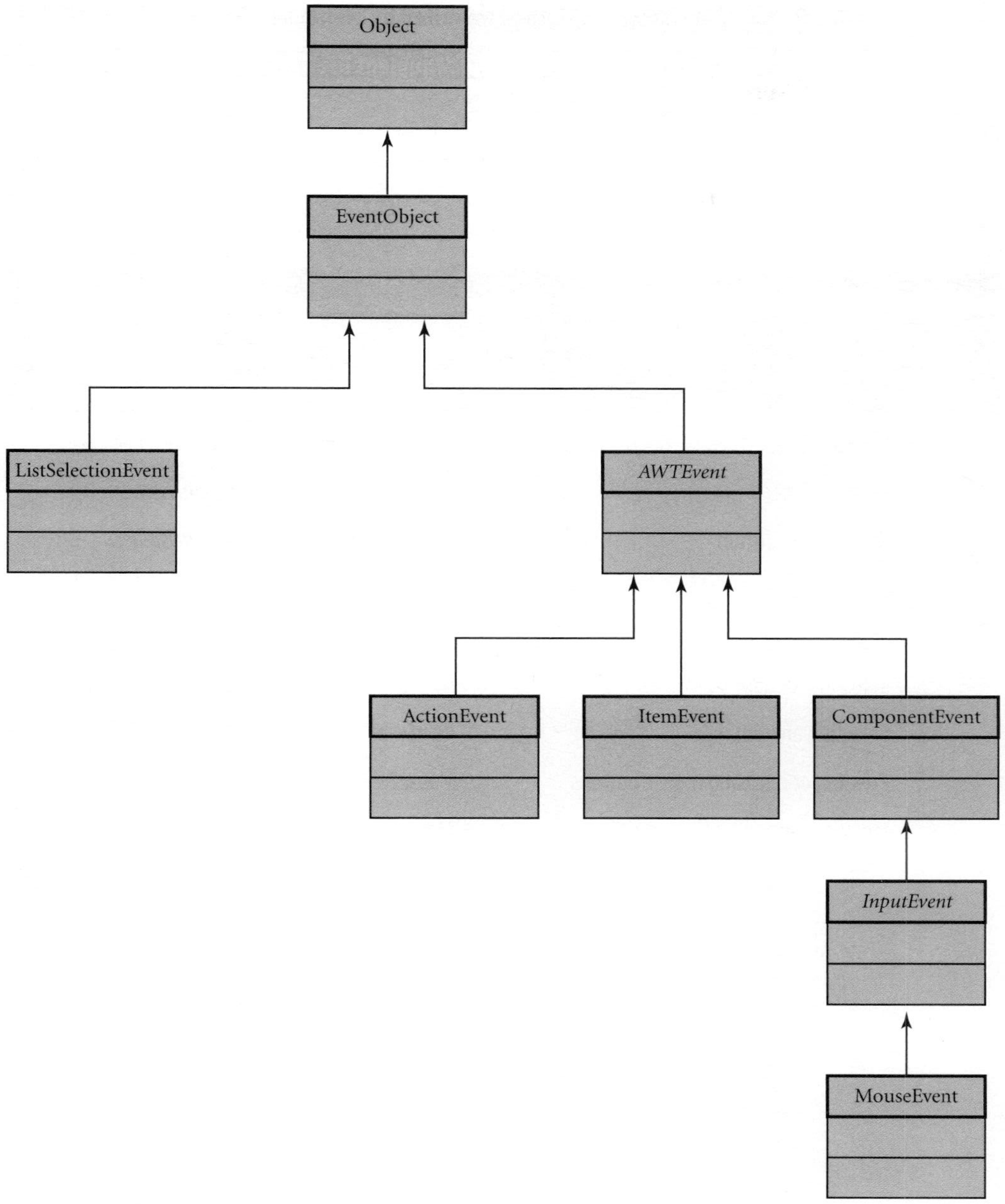

Figure 12.5
Event Class Hierarchy

TABLE 12.6 The *getSource* Method Inherited by Event Classes

Return value	Method name and argument list
`Object`	`getSource( )` returns the object reference of the component that fired the event

TABLE 12.7 Component Events and Listeners

JComponent	User Interaction That Generates an Event	The Event Object Created	Listener Interface the Event Handler Should Implement
JTextField	Pressing Enter	*ActionEvent*	*ActionListener*
JTextArea	Pressing Enter	*ActionEvent*	*ActionListener*
JButton	Pressing the button	*ActionEvent*	*ActionListener*
JRadioButton	Selecting a radio button	*ItemEvent*	*ItemListener*
JCheckBox	Selecting or deselecting a checkbox	*ItemEvent*	*ItemListener*
JList	Selecting an item	*ListSelectionEvent*	*ListSelectionListener*
JComboBox	Selecting an item	*ItemEvent*	*ItemListener*
Any component	Pressing or releasing mouse buttons	*MouseEvent*	*MouseListener*
Any component	Moving or dragging the mouse	*MouseEvent*	*MouseMotionListener*

```
// import statements as needed

public class ClassName1 extends JFrame
{
  // declare components and other instance variables

  // constructor
  public ClassName1( )
  {
     // call JFrame constructor
     // get content pane
     // set the layout manager
     // instantiate components and other instance variables
     // add components to the content pane
     // declare and instantiate event handler objects
```

```
        // register event handlers on components

        // set window size
        // make window visible
    }

    // private event handler class
    private class EventHandlerName implements ListenerName
    {
       // implement the methods of the listener interface
       // to process the events
    }

    public static void main( String [ ] args )
    {
       // instantiate application object
    }
}
```

Although we can define an event handler class as *public* in its own source file, we usually declare an event handler as a ***private* inner class** within the GUI application class. A *private* inner class is defined within the *public* class and has access to all the members of the *public* class. Thus, declaring our event handler as a *private* inner class simplifies our code by giving the event handler direct access to our application's GUI components.

In the constructor, we instantiate an object of our event handler class. Then we register that event handler on a component by calling an *add. . . Listener* method. Table 12.8 shows a few of these methods. We call the *add...Listener* method using the object reference of the component on which we want to register the listener and passing as an argument the event handler object we instantiated.

TABLE 12.8 Some *add...Listener* Methods

***add. . . Listener* Method APIs**
`void addActionListener( ActionListener handler )`
`void addItemListener( ItemListener handler )`
`void addListSelectionListener( ListSelectionListener handler )`
`void addMouseListener( MouseListener handler )`
`void addMouseMotionListener( MouseMotionListener handler )`

12.5 Text Fields

Now we are ready for our first GUI program with user interaction. For this first example, we will build a GUI that takes an ID and a password from a user. If the ID is "open" and the password is "sesame", we display "Welcome!" Otherwise, we display "Sorry: wrong login".

We will use a *JTextField* for the ID and a *JPasswordField* for the password. For confidentiality of passwords, the *JPasswordField* does not display the characters typed by the user. Instead, as each character is typed, the *JPasswordField* displays an echo character. The default echo character is *, but we can specify a different character, if desired. We will also use a *JTextArea* to display a legal warning to potential hackers. Both *JTextField* and *JTextArea* are direct subclasses of *JTextComponent*, which encapsulates text entry from the user. *JTextField* displays a single-line field and *JTextArea* displays a multiline field.

Table 12.9 lists some useful constructors and methods of these text classes.

TABLE 12.9 Constructors and Methods of *JTextField, JTextArea,* and *JPasswordField*

Useful Constructors and Methods of the *JTextField, JTextArea,* and *JPasswordField* Classes	
Constructors	
Class	**Constructor**
`JTextField`	`JTextField( String text, int numColumns )` constructs a text field initially filled with *text*, with the specified number of columns
`JTextField`	`JTextField( int numberColumns )` constructs an empty text field with the specified number of columns
`JTextArea`	`JTextArea( String text )` constructs a text area initially filled with *text*
`JTextArea`	`JTextArea( int numRows, int numColumns )` constructs an empty text area with the number of rows and columns specified by *numRows* and *numColumns*
`JTextArea`	`JTextArea( String text, int numRows, int numColumns )` constructs a text area initially filled with *text*, and with the number of rows and columns specified by *numRows* and *numColumns*
`JPasswordField`	`JPasswordField( int numberColumns )` constructs an empty password field with the specified number of columns

TABLE 12.9 (continued)

Methods Common to *JTextField, JTextArea,* and *JPasswordField* Classes	
Return value	**Method name and argument list**
`void`	`setEditable( boolean mode )` sets the properties of the text component as editable or noneditable, depending on whether *mode* is *true* or *false*. The default is editable.
`void`	`setText( String newText )` sets the text of the text component to *newText*.
`String`	`getText( )` returns the text contained in the text component.

Additional Methods of the *JPasswordField* Class	
Return value	**Method name and argument list**
`void`	`setEchoChar( char c )` sets the echo character of the password field to *c*.
`char [ ]`	`getPassword( )` returns the text entered in this password field as an array of *chars*. Note: This method is preferred over the *getText* method for getting the password typed by the user.

Example 12.3 implements our login application, and Figure 12.6 shows the application in action.

```
/* Using JTextFields, JTextArea, and JPasswordField
   Anderson, Franceschi
*/

import javax.swing.JFrame;
import javax.swing.JLabel;
import javax.swing.JTextField;
import javax.swing.JPasswordField;
import javax.swing.JTextArea;
import java.awt.Container;
import java.awt.FlowLayout;
import java.awt.Color;
import java.awt.event.ActionListener;
import java.awt.event.ActionEvent;

```

```
public class Login extends JFrame
{
 private Container contents;
 private JLabel idLabel, passwordLabel, message;
 private JTextField id;
 private JPasswordField password;
 private JTextArea legal;

 // Constructor
 public Login( )
 {
  super( "Login Screen" );
  contents = getContentPane( );
  contents.setLayout( new FlowLayout( ) );

  idLabel = new JLabel( "Enter id" ); // label for ID
  id = new JTextField( "", 12 );      // instantiate ID text field

  passwordLabel = new JLabel( "Enter password" ); // password label
  password = new JPasswordField( 8 ); // instantiate password field
  password.setEchoChar( '?' );        // set echo character to '?'

  message = new JLabel( "Log in above" );  // label to hold messages

  // instantiate JTextArea with legal warning
  legal = new JTextArea( "Warning: Any attempt to illegally\n"
           + "log in to this server is punishable by law.\n"
           + "This corporation will not tolerate hacking,\n"
           + "virus attacks, or other malicious acts." );
  legal.setEditable( false );        // disable typing in this field

  // add all components to the window
  contents.add( idLabel );
  contents.add( id );
  contents.add( passwordLabel );
  contents.add( password );
  contents.add( message );
  contents.add( legal );

  // instantiate event handler for the text fields
  TextFieldHandler tfh = new TextFieldHandler( );

  // add event handler as listener for ID and password fields
  id.addActionListener( tfh );
```

```
60   password.addActionListener( tfh );
61
62   setSize( 250, 200 );
63   setVisible( true );
64  }
65
66  // private inner class event handler
67  private class TextFieldHandler implements ActionListener
68  {
69   public void actionPerformed( ActionEvent e )
70   {
71    if ( id.getText( ).equals( "open" )
72     && ( new String( password.getPassword( ) ) ).equals( "sesame" ) )
73    {
74     message.setForeground( Color.BLACK );
75     message.setText( "Welcome!" );
76    }
77    else
78    {
79     message.setForeground( Color.RED );
80     message.setText( "Sorry: wrong login" );
81    }
82   }
83  }
84
85  public static void main( String [ ] args )
86  {
87   Login login = new Login( );
88   login.setDefaultCloseOperation( JFrame.EXIT_ON_CLOSE );
89  }
90 }
```

EXAMPLE 12.3 The *Login* Class

Lines 5–14 import the various classes that we use in this program. Line 16 declares the class, which we name *Login*, as a subclass of *JFrame.*

We declare our instance variables at lines 18–22. In addition to our three components: the *JTextField id*, the *JPasswordField password*, and the *JTextArea legal*, we also have three *JLabel* components: *idLabel*, *passwordLabel*, and *message.* The *idLabel* and *passwordLabel* components provide descriptions for the corresponding text fields. We will use the *message* label to display feedback to the user on whether the login was successful.

Figure 12.6
Running Example 12.3

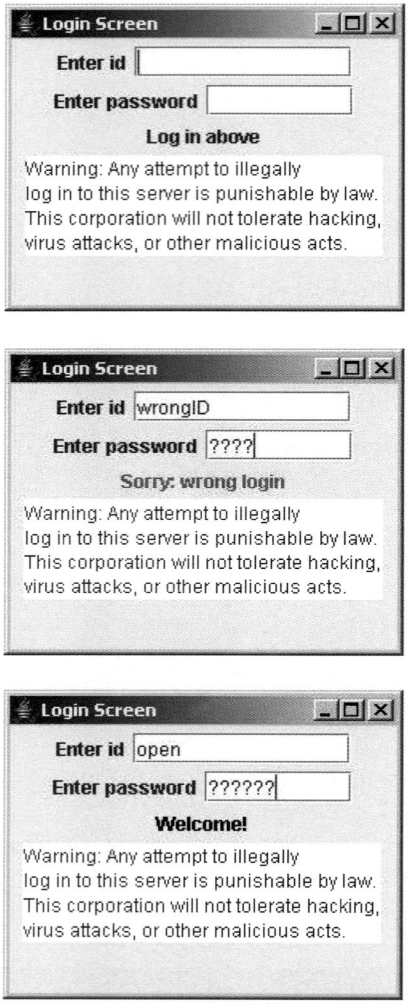

At line 32, we instantiate the *JTextField id* using the constructor that takes an initial value and the size of the text field. The initial value is blank, and we want the text field to accommodate 12 characters. At line 35, we instantiate the *JPasswordField password* and set its length to 8 characters. At line 36, we call the *setEchoChar* method to reset the echo character from its default of * to ?. Thus, when the user types characters into the password field, a ? will be displayed for each character typed.

At lines 40–44, we instantiate the *JTextArea legal.* By default, a user can enter data into a text area. However, since we are using this text area only to display a legal warning, we turn off the ability of the user to type into the text area by calling the *setEditable* method with the argument *false* (line 45).

At lines 47–53, we add all the components to the content pane. As Figure 12.6 shows, the components will be displayed in the window in the order we added them to the container.

After the window is displayed, our application will wait for the user to interact with the components. When the user enters a value into either the *id* or the *password* field, we want to check whether the values the user entered are correct. This will be the job of the event handler for those fields.

Pressing the *Enter* key in a text field generates an *ActionEvent*; therefore, at lines 66–83, we coded our event handler as the *private* inner class, *TextFieldHandler*, which *implements* the *ActionListener* interface. As shown in Table 12.10, the *ActionListener* interface has only one *abstract* method, *actionPerformed*, which receives an *ActionEvent* parameter.

Be sure that you code the *actionPerformed* method correctly, as shown in Table 12.10. Failure to code the header properly causes a compiler error. For example, misspelling the method name generates the following compiler error:

```
Login.TextFieldHandler is not abstract and does not override abstract
method actionPerformed(java.awt.event.ActionEvent) in
java.awt.event.ActionListener
private class TextFieldHandler implements ActionListener
        ^
1 error
```

COMMON ERROR TRAP

Be sure that the header of the *actionPerformed* method is coded correctly. Otherwise, your method will not override the *abstract actionPerformed* method, as required by the *ActionListener* interface.

In the constructor, we declare and instantiate a *TextFieldHandler* object reference, *tfh* (line 55–56). Then at lines 58–60, we register *tfh* as the listener on the *id* and *password* components. When either *id* or *password* is in focus (that is, if the mouse was last clicked on the component) and the user

TABLE 12.10 *ActionListener* Method API

`public void actionPerformed( ActionEvent event )`
An event handler that implements the *ActionListener* interface writes code in this method to respond to the *ActionEvent* fired by any registered components.

presses the *Enter* key, the component that is in focus will fire an action event and our *actionPerformed* method will be executed.

We implement the *actionPerformed* method at lines 69–82. Because we defined this event handler as a *private* inner class, the *actionPerformed* method can directly access the *id* and *password* fields. At lines 71–72, we test if the ID and password entered by the user are correct.

As shown in Table 12.9, the *getPassword* method of the *JPasswordField* class returns an array of *chars*. At line 72, to convert that array of *chars* to a *String*, we use a constructor of the *String* class with the following API, which takes an array of *chars* as an argument:

```
public String( char [ ] charArray )
```

If the user has typed correct values into both the *id* and *password* fields, our event handler sets the foreground color to black and sets the text of *message* to "Welcome!" (lines 74–75). If either the id or the password is incorrect, we set the foreground color to red and set the text of *message* to "Sorry: wrong login" (lines 79–80).

COMMON ERROR TRAP

If you do not register a listener on a component, the component will not fire an event. Thus, the event handler will not execute when the user interacts with the component.

Note that we did not register our event handler for the *JTextArea*. We have disabled typing into that field, so the user cannot enter new text into that field. Also, if we did not register a listener on the *id* and *password* components, the user could still type characters into these two fields and press the *Enter* key, but no events would fire, and therefore, our application would not respond to the user's actions.

Figure 12.6 shows the application when the window first opens, after the user enters incorrect login values, and after the user enters correct login values. We suggest you become familiar with this application. First run the application as it is written. Then, delete either line 59 or 60, which registers the listeners on the components, and test the application again. Finally, change the echo character and test the application again.

12.6 Command Buttons

Handling an event associated with a button follows the same pattern as Example 12.3. We instantiate an event handler and add that event handler as a listener for the button. Clicking on a button generates an *ActionEvent*, so our listener needs to implement the *ActionListener* interface.

In Example 12.4, we present the user with a text field and two command buttons. The user enters a number into the text field, then presses one of the two buttons. When the user clicks on the first button, we square the number; when the user clicks on the second button, we cube the number. We then display the result using a label component. To determine whether to square or cube the number, our event handler will need to identify which button was clicked by calling the *getSource* method of the *ActionEvent* class, as described in Table 12.6.

This example will demonstrate the following:

- how to handle an event originating from a button
- how to determine which component fired the event

```
/* Simple Math Operations Using JButtons
   Anderson, Franceschi
*/

import javax.swing.*;
import java.awt.*;
import java.awt.event.*;

public class SimpleMath extends JFrame
{
 private Container contents;
 private JLabel operandLabel, resultLabel, result;
 private JTextField operand;
 private JButton square, cube;

 public SimpleMath( )
 {
  super( "Simple Math" );
  contents = getContentPane( );
  contents.setLayout( new FlowLayout( ) );

  operandLabel = new JLabel( "Enter a number" ); // text field label
  operand = new JTextField( 5 ); // text field is 5 characters wide

  // instantiate buttons
  square = new JButton( "Square" );
  cube = new JButton( "Cube" );

  resultLabel = new JLabel( "Result:" ); // label for result
  result = new JLabel( "???" );          // label to hold result

  // add components to the window
```

```
  contents.add( operandLabel );
  contents.add( operand );
  contents.add( square );
  contents.add( cube );
  contents.add( resultLabel );
  contents.add( result );

  // instantiate our event handler
  ButtonHandler bh = new ButtonHandler( );

  // add event handler as listener for both buttons
  square.addActionListener( bh );
  cube.addActionListener( bh );

  setSize( 175, 150 );
  setVisible( true );
 }

 // private inner class event handler
 private class ButtonHandler implements ActionListener
 {
  // implement actionPerformed method
  public void actionPerformed( ActionEvent ae )
  {
   try
   {
    double op = Double.parseDouble( operand.getText( ) );

    // identify which button was pressed
    if ( ae.getSource( ) == square )
      result.setText( ( new Double( op * op ) ).toString( ) );
    else if ( ae.getSource( ) == cube )
      result.setText( ( new Double( op * op * op ) ).toString( ) );
   }
   catch ( NumberFormatException e )
   {
    operandLabel.setText( "Enter a number" );
    operand.setText( "" );
    result.setText( "???" );
   }
  }
 }

 public static void main( String [ ] args )
 {
```

```
78   SimpleMath sm = new SimpleMath( );
79   sm.setDefaultCloseOperation( JFrame.EXIT_ON_CLOSE );
80  }
81 }
```

EXAMPLE 12.4 Simple Math using *JButton*

As you have seen in the previous examples, GUI applications use a number of Java classes. For Example 12.4, as well as the remaining examples in this chapter, we will use the bulk *import* statement, which replaces the individual class names with the wildcard character (*). Its syntax is:

```
import packageName.*;
```

In this way, we write only one *import* statement per package (lines 5–7).

Notice that the *java.awt.event* package is different from the *java.awt* package. You might assume that importing *java.awt.** also imports the classes in the *java.awt.event* package. That is not the case, however; we need to import both packages.

COMMON ERROR TRAP

The *java.awt.event* package is not imported with the *java.awt* package. Include *import* statements for both the *java.awt* and the *java.awt.event* packages.

At lines 51–74, we define our event handler, *ButtonHandler*, as a *private* inner class. Because clicking a button fires an *ActionEvent*, our event handler implements the *ActionListener* interface. Thus, we provide our code to handle the event in the *actionPerformed* method. Line 59 retrieves the data the user typed into the text field and attempts to convert the text to a *double*. Because the *parseDouble* method will *throw* a *NumberFormatException* if the user enters a value that cannot be converted to a *double*, we perform the conversion inside a *try* block.

The *if* statement at line 62 calls the *getSource* method using the *ActionEvent* object reference to test if the component that fired the event is the *square* button. If so, we set the text of the *result* label to the square of the number entered.

If the *square* button did not fire the event, we test if the source of the event was the *cube* button (line 64). If so, we set the text of the *result* label to the cube of the number entered. Actually, the test in line 64 is not necessary, because we registered our event handler as the listener for only two buttons. So if the source isn't the *square* button, then the *cube* button must have fired the event. However, in order to improve readability and maintenance, it is good practice to check the source of the event specifically, in particular if additional buttons or components will be added to the application later.

SOFTWARE ENGINEERING TIP

Verify the source component before processing the event.

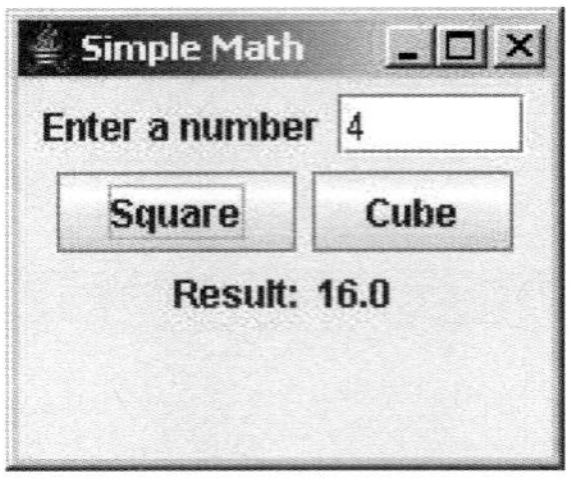

Figure 12.7
Running Example 12.4

In the constructor, at lines 40–41, we declare and instantiate the *ButtonHandler* event handler, *bh*. At lines 43–45, we call the *addActionListener* method to register the handler on our two buttons.

The output of this example is shown in Figure 12.7. When you run this example, try entering a valid number into the text field, and press each button. Then try to enter text that cannot be converted to a number. Also, try deleting either statement that registers the event listener on the buttons (line 44 or 45), and run the application again.

12.7 Radio Buttons and Checkboxes

If you have ever completed a survey on the web, you are probably acquainted with radio buttons and checkboxes.

Radio buttons prompt the user to select one of several mutually exclusive options. Clicking on any radio button deselects any previously selected option. Thus, in a group of radio buttons, a user can select only one option at a time.

Checkboxes are often associated with the instruction "check all that apply"; that is, the user is asked to select 0, 1, or more options. A checkbox is a toggle button in that if the option is not currently selected, clicking on a checkbox selects the option, and if the option is currently selected, clicking on the checkbox deselects the option.

The *JRadioButton* and *JCheckBox* classes, which belong to the *javax.swing* package, encapsulate the concepts of radio buttons and checkboxes, respectively. We will present two similar examples in order to illustrate how to use these classes and how they differ. Both examples allow the user to select the background color for a label component. We display three color options: red, green, and blue. Using radio buttons, only one option can be selected at a time. Thus, by clicking on a radio button, the user will cause the background of the label to be displayed in one of three colors. Using checkboxes, the user can select any combination of the three color options, so the label color can be set to any of eight possible combinations. Table 12.11 lists all these combinations.

Table 12.12 shows several constructors of the *JRadioButton, ButtonGroup,* and *JCheckBox* classes.

TABLE 12.11 Selecting Colors Using Radio Buttons vs. Checkboxes

Using Radio Buttons
(1 selection possible at a time)

red	green	blue	Resulting Color
◉	○	○	red
○	◉	○	green
○	○	◉	blue

Using Checkboxes
(0 to 3 selections possible at a time)

red	green	blue	Resulting Color
☐	☐	☐	black
☑	☐	☐	red
☐	☑	☐	green
☐	☐	☑	blue
☑	☑	☐	yellow
☑	☐	☑	purple
☐	☑	☑	blue-green
☑	☑	☑	white

TABLE 12.12 Useful Constructors of the *JRadioButton*, *ButtonGroup*, and *JCheckBox* Classes

Class	Constructor
`JRadioButton`	`JRadioButton( String buttonLabel )` constructs a radio button labeled *buttonLabel*. By default, the radio button is initially deselected.
`JRadioButton`	`JRadioButton( String buttonLabel, boolean selected )` constructs a radio button labeled *buttonLabel*. If *selected* is *true*, the button is initially selected; if *selected* is *false*, the button is deselected.
`ButtonGroup`	`ButtonGroup( )` constructs a button group. Adding buttons to this group makes the buttons mutually exclusive.
`JCheckBox`	`JCheckBox( String checkBoxLabel )` constructs a checkbox labeled *checkBoxLabel*. By default, the checkbox is initially deselected.
`JCheckBox`	`JCheckBox( String checkBoxLabel, boolean selected )` constructs a checkbox labeled *checkBoxLabel*. If *selected* is *true*, the checkbox is initially selected; if *selected* is *false*, the checkbox is initially deselected.

Selecting or deselecting radio buttons and checkboxes fires an *ItemEvent*. To receive this event, our event handler needs to implement the *ItemListener* interface, which has only one method, shown in Table 12.13.

Note that selecting a radio button fires both an *ItemEvent* and an *ActionEvent*, so an alternative for radio buttons is to register a handler that implements the *ActionListener* interface. We have chosen to use an *ItemListener* for both radio buttons and checkboxes to demonstrate the similarities and differences between the two components.

TABLE 12.13 *ItemListener* Method API

`public void itemStateChanged( ItemEvent event )`

An event handler that implements the *ItemListener* interface writes code in this method to respond to the *ItemEvent* fired by any registered components.

Example 12.5 shows the color selection application using radio buttons.

```
/* Select a Color using JRadioButtons
   Anderson, Franceschi
*/

import javax.swing.*;
import java.awt.*;
import java.awt.event.*;

public class ChangingColors extends JFrame
{
 private Container contents;
 private JRadioButton red, green, blue;
 private ButtonGroup colorGroup;
 private JLabel label;
 private Color selectedColor = Color.RED;

 public ChangingColors( )
 {
  super( "Selecting a color" );
  contents = getContentPane( );
  contents.setLayout( new FlowLayout( ) );

  red = new JRadioButton( "red", true );
  green = new JRadioButton( "green" );
  blue = new JRadioButton( "blue" );

  label = new JLabel( "Watch my background" );
  label.setForeground( Color.GRAY );
  label.setOpaque( true );
  label.setBackground( selectedColor );

  contents.add( red );
  contents.add( green );
  contents.add( blue );
  contents.add( label );

  // create button group
  colorGroup = new ButtonGroup( );
  colorGroup.add( red );
  colorGroup.add( green );
```

```
41    colorGroup.add( blue );
42
43    // create RadioButtonHandler event handler
44    // and register it on the radio buttons
45    RadioButtonHandler rbh = new RadioButtonHandler( );
46    red.addItemListener( rbh );
47    green.addItemListener( rbh );
48    blue.addItemListener( rbh );
49
50    setSize( 225, 200 );
51    setVisible( true );
52  }
53
54  private class RadioButtonHandler implements ItemListener
55  {
56    public void itemStateChanged( ItemEvent ie )
57    {
58     if ( ie.getSource( ) == red )
59        selectedColor = Color.RED;
60     else if ( ie.getSource( ) == green )
61        selectedColor = Color.GREEN;
62     else if ( ie.getSource( ) == blue )
63        selectedColor = Color.BLUE;
64
65     label.setBackground( selectedColor );
66    }
67  }
68
69  public static void main( String [ ] args )
70  {
71    ChangingColors cc = new ChangingColors( );
72    cc.setDefaultCloseOperation( JFrame.EXIT_ON_CLOSE );
73  }
74 }
```

EXAMPLE 12.5 Selecting Colors Using *JRadioButtons*

The various instance variables are declared at lines 11–15. The instance variable *selectedColor*, which is initialized to red, will store the choice of the user and will be used to set the background of the *JLabel* component *label*. The three radio buttons and *label* are instantiated at lines 23–27. At line 23, we use a *JRadioButton* constructor with two arguments to instantiate the radio button *red*. The first argument is the title of the radio button; the second argument, *true*, specifies that *red* is selected. Thus, when the window appears, the

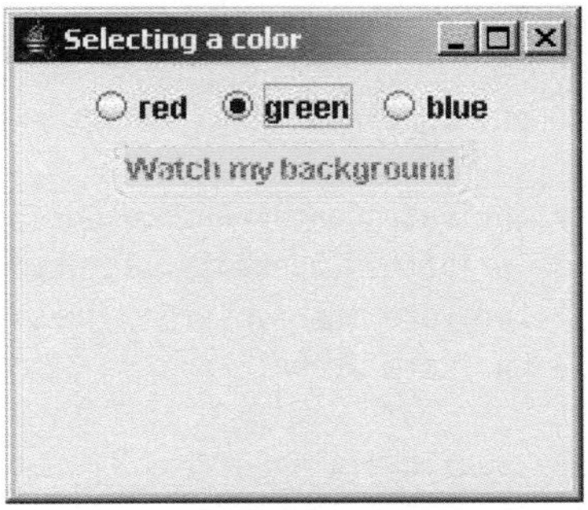

Figure 12.8
Running Example 12.5

red radio button will be selected. In order to reflect the effect of the selected radio button, we set the background color of the label to red at line 30.

At lines 24 and 25, *green* and *blue* are instantiated using the *JRadioButton* constructor with only a *String* argument, specifying the radio button titles. The four components are added to the content pane at lines 32–35.

At lines 37–41, we instantiate a *ButtonGroup* object, then add the *red*, *green*, and *blue* radio buttons to *colorGroup* so that they will be mutually exclusive selections.

At lines 43–48, we instantiate our event handler, *RadioButtonHandler rbh*, and call the *addItemListener* method to register the listener *rbh* on the three radio buttons.

At lines 54–67, the *private* class *RadioButtonHandler implements* the *ItemListener* interface. The only method of *ItemListener*, *itemStateChanged*, is overriden at lines 56–66. Inside *itemStateChanged*, we use an *if/else* statement to determine which radio button was selected in order to set *selectedColor* to the appropriate color.

Figure 12.8 shows a run of the example after the user has clicked on the *green* radio button. Try running the example and clicking on each radio button. Try modifying the code: for example, delete the lines adding the radio buttons to the button group, then compile and run the program again.

COMMON ERROR TRAP

Forgetting to make *JRadioButtons* part of the same *ButtonGroup* makes them independent and not mutually exclusive.

Example 12.6 shows the color selection application using checkboxes.

```
/*  Using JCheckBoxes
    Anderson, Franceschi
*/

import javax.swing.*;
import java.awt.*;
```

```java
import java.awt.event.*;

public class MixingColors extends JFrame
{
  private Container contents;
  private JCheckBox red, green, blue;
  private int redValue, greenValue, blueValue;
  private JLabel label;

  public MixingColors( )
  {
    super( "Selecting a color" );
    contents = getContentPane( );
    contents.setLayout( new FlowLayout( ) );

    red = new JCheckBox( "red" );
    green = new JCheckBox( "green" );
    blue = new JCheckBox( "blue" );

    label = new JLabel( "Watch my background" );
    label.setOpaque( true );
    label.setForeground( Color.GRAY );
    label.setBackground( new Color ( 0, 0, 0 ) );

    contents.add( red );
    contents.add( green );
    contents.add( blue );
    contents.add( label );

    // create CheckBoxHandler event handler
    // and register it on the checkboxes
    CheckBoxHandler cbh = new CheckBoxHandler( );
    red.addItemListener( cbh );
    green.addItemListener( cbh );
    blue.addItemListener( cbh );

    setSize( 225, 200 );
    setVisible( true );
  }

  private class CheckBoxHandler implements ItemListener
  {
    public void itemStateChanged( ItemEvent ie )
    {
      if ( ie.getSource( ) == red )
```

```
52    {
53     if ( ie.getStateChange( ) == ItemEvent.SELECTED )
54       redValue = 255;
55     else
56       redValue = 0;
57    }
58    else if ( ie.getSource( ) == green )
59    {
60     if ( ie.getStateChange( ) == ItemEvent.SELECTED )
61       greenValue = 255;
62     else
63       greenValue = 0;
64    }
65    else if ( ie.getSource( ) == blue )
66    {
67     if ( ie.getStateChange( ) == ItemEvent.SELECTED )
68       blueValue = 255;
69     else
70       blueValue = 0;
71    }
72
73    label.setBackground(
74         new Color( redValue, greenValue, blueValue ) );
75   }
76  }
77
78  public static void main( String [ ] args )
79  {
80   MixingColors mc = new MixingColors( );
81   mc.setDefaultCloseOperation( JFrame.EXIT_ON_CLOSE );
82  }
83 }
```

EXAMPLE 12.6 Using *JCheckBoxes*

The various instance variables are declared at lines 11–14. The instance variables *redValue*, *greenValue*, and *blueValue* will store the red, green, and blue intensity values, depending on which checkboxes the user selects. These values will be used to set the background color of the *JLabel* component *label*.

The three checkboxes and *label* are instantiated at lines 22–26. We use a *JCheckBox* constructor with a *String* argument that specifies the checkbox titles. The four components are added to the content pane at lines 31–34.

TABLE 12.14 A Useful Method of the *ItemEvent* Class

Return value	Method name and argument list
`int`	`getStateChange( )` returns the state of the checkbox. If the checkbox is selected, the value *SELECTED* is returned; if the checkbox is deselected, the value *DESELECTED* is returned, where *SELECTED* and *DESELECTED* are *static int* constants of the *ItemEvent* class.

At lines 36–41, we instantiate the *CheckBoxHandler* event handler and register the *cbh* listener on the three checkboxes by calling the *addItemListener* method for each checkbox.

At lines 47–76, we define the *private* inner class, *CheckBoxHandler*, which *implements* the *ItemListener* interface. The only method of *ItemListener*, *itemStateChanged*, is overriden at lines 49–75. Inside *itemStateChanged*, we first use an *if/else* statement to determine which checkbox fired the event. We then use a nested *if/else* statement to determine if that checkbox has just been selected. The *getStateChange* method in the *ItemEvent* class returns this information. Its API is shown in Table 12.14. The *ItemEvent* class provides the *static int* constants *SELECTED* and *DESELECTED* for convenience in coding this method call. Every click on our checkboxes will fire an event, so calling the *getStateChange* method helps us to distinguish between the event fired when the user selects a checkbox from the event fired when the user deselects a checkbox.

If the source checkbox was selected, we set the corresponding color value to 255 (lines 54, 61, and 68). If the source checkbox was deselected, we set the corresponding color value to 0 (lines 56, 63, and 70). For example, if the *red* checkbox is the source of the event, then we check whether the *red* checkbox was selected. If so, we set *redValue* to 255. Otherwise, the *red* checkbox must have been deselected, so we set *redValue* to 0.

At lines 73–74, we set the background color of *label* to a color we instantiate using the values of *redValue*, *greenValue*, and *blueValue* for the color's respective intensities of red, green, and blue.

Figure 12.9 shows a run of the example after the user has selected the red and green checkboxes.

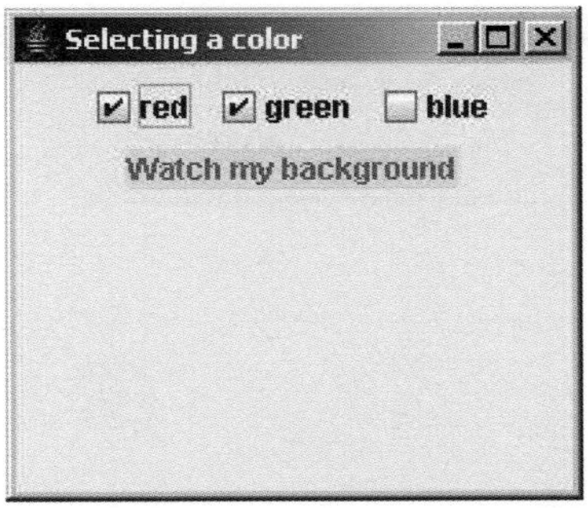

Figure 12.9
Running Example 12.6

12.8 Programming Activity 1: Working with Buttons

In this activity, you will work with two *JButtons* that control one electrical switch. Specifically, you will write the code to perform the following operations:

1. If the user clicks on the "OPEN" button, open the switch.
2. If the user clicks on the "CLOSE" button, close the switch.

The framework for this Programming Activity will animate your code so that you can check its accuracy. Figures 12.10 and 12.11 show the application after the user has clicked on the button labeled "OPEN" and the button labeled "CLOSE", respectively.

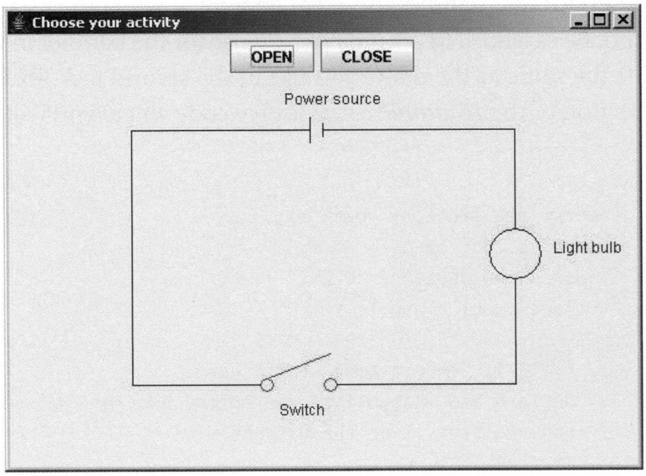

Figure 12.10
User Clicked on "OPEN"

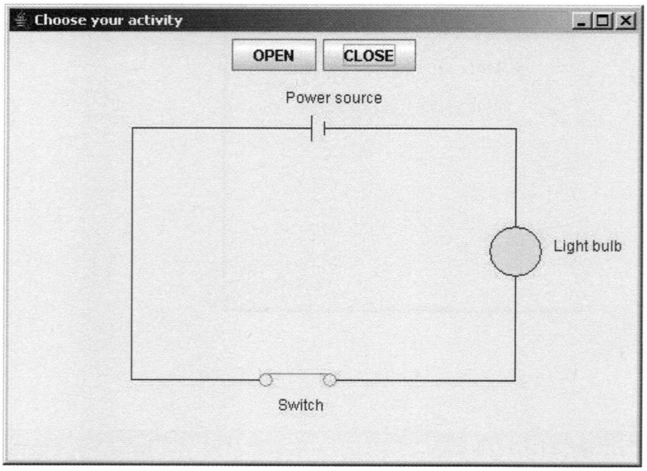

Figure 12.11
User Clicked on "CLOSE"

Instructions

In the Chapter 12 Programming Activity 1 directory on the CD-ROM accompanying this book, you will find the source files needed to complete this activity. Copy all the files to a directory on your computer. Note that all files should be in the same directory.

Open the *JButtonPractice.java* source file. Searching for five stars (*****) in the source code will position you to the first code section and then to the second location where you will add your code. In task 1, you will fill in the code to instantiate a button handler and register the handler on the appropriate components. In task 2, you will code the *private* class implementing the listener interface that handles the event generated when the user clicks on either button. Be careful: The class name you use for the handler in the first task needs to be the same as the name you use in the second task. Example 12.7 shows the section of the *JButtonPractice* source code where you will add your code.

```
...
open = new JButton( "OPEN" );
contents.add( open );
close = new JButton( "CLOSE" );
contents.add( close );

// ***** 1. Student code starts here
// declare and instantiate the button handler
// and register it on the buttons
```

```
      // end of task 1

     setSize( 500, 375 );
     setVisible( true );
  }

  // ***** 2. Student code restarts here
  // Code a private class to implement the correct Listener
  // and its required method
  // To open the switch, call the open method with the statement
  //   open( );
  // To close the switch, call the close method with the statement
  //   close( );
  // The last statement of the method should be
  //   animate( );


  // end of task 2
```

EXAMPLE 12.7 Location of Student Code in *JButtonPractice.java*

The framework will animate your code so that you can watch your code work. For this to happen, be sure that you call the *animate* method.

To test your code, compile and run the *JButtonPractice.java* file, then click on each button.

Troubleshooting

If your method implementation does not animate, check these tips:

- Verify that the last statement in your method inside the *private* class is:

  `animate( );`

- Verify that your listener is registered on the components.
- Verify that you have identified the origin of the event correctly.

? DISCUSSION QUESTIONS

1. Explain why the *getSource* method is useful here.
2. Could you implement the preceding with *JRadioButtons* instead of *JButtons*? What interface would you implement? What would be the method of the interface that you would need to override? What type of event would you handle?

12.9 Lists

In GUIs, often users are asked to select one or more items in a list. Sometimes all items in the list are displayed by default, and sometimes clicking a button displays the items in a scrollable window. Java provides the *JList* class for the former and the *JComboBox* class for the latter.

The *JList* class encapsulates a list in which the user can select one or more items. An item is selected by clicking on it. A range of items can be selected by clicking on the first item in the range, then holding down the *Shift* key while selecting the last item in the range. You can add an item to a selected group of items by holding down the control (*CTRL*) key while clicking on that item.

When the user clicks on one or more items in a list, the *JList* component fires a *ListSelectionEvent*. Our event handler for a *JList* will implement the *ListSelectionListener* interface, which has only one method, *valueChanged*, with the API shown in Table 12.15.

Table 12.16 shows some useful constructors and methods of the *JList* class.

Example 12.8 shows how to use the *JList* class. In this application, we allow the user to choose from a list of countries. We then display a typical food from the country selected.

We construct our *JList* (line 31) by providing an array of *Strings*, *countryList*, which holds the names of the countries to be displayed in the list. When the user selects a country from the list, we display the food image in a *JLabel* component, named *foodImage*, which we instantiate at line 32.

SOFTWARE ENGINEERING TIP

Arrange items in lists in a logical order so that the user can find the desired item quickly.

Notice that our list of countries is arranged alphabetically to simplify finding a desired country. In this case, we have only five countries; however, with a longer list, the alphabetical ordering would make it easy for the user to find a particular item in the list. Another option is to display the most likely choice first, then display the remaining items in alphabetical order.

TABLE 12.15 *ListSelectionListener* Method API

```
public void valueChanged( ListSelectionEvent e )
```

An event handler that implements the *ListSelectionListener* interface writes code in this method to respond to the *ListSelectionEvent* fired by any registered components.

TABLE 12.16 Useful Methods of the *JList* Class

Useful Constructors and Methods of the *JList* Class	
Constructor	
Class	**Constructor**
`JList`	`JList( Object [ ] arrayName )` constructs a new *JList* component initially filled with the objects in *arrayName*. Often, the objects are *Strings*.
Methods	
Return value	**Method name and argument list**
`void`	`setSelectionMode( int selectionMode )` sets the number of selections that can be made at one time. The following *static int* constants of the *ListSelectionModel* interface can be used to set the selection mode: SINGLE_SELECTION–one selection allowed SINGLE_INTERVAL_SELECTION–multiple contiguous items can be selected MULTIPLE_INTERVAL_SELECTION—multiple contiguous intervals can be selected (This is the default.)
`int`	`getSelectedIndex( )` returns the index of the selected item. The index of the first item in the list is 0.
`void`	`setSelectedIndex( int index )` selects the item at *index*. The index of the first item in the list is 0.

For example, if most users reside in the United States, you could list "USA" first in the list, with the remaining countries alphabetized starting in the second position of the list.

We declare and instantiate the instance variable, *foods*, as an array of *ImageIcons* (lines 17–22). The *foods* array stores images of the food samplings in the same order as the countries in our list. We initialize the *foodImage* label to the first element of *foods* array (line 32). Thus, when we first display the window, the label will show the food sampling from France, which is the first country in the list. In order to match the displayed food sampling with

Figure 12.12
Running Example 12.8

the list selection, we programmatically select the first item of the *countries* list (line 36), using the method *setSelectedIndex* of the *JList* class.

For this application, we will allow the user to select only one country at a time, so we set the selection mode of the list to single selection at line 35 using the *setSelectionMode* method of the *JList* class. The argument passed to the method, *SINGLE_SELECTION*, is a *static int* constant of the *ListSelectionModel* interface.

At lines 50–56, we define our event handler as the *private* inner class, *ListHandler*, which implements the *ListSelectionListener* interface. The only method of *ListSelectionListener*, *valueChanged*, is overriden at lines 52–55. We set up the appropriate food icon to display by calling the *getSelectedIndex* method of the *JList* class. This method returns the index of the item selected by the user. Because we have set up the *foods* array in the same order as the *countries* array, we can use the return value from the *getSelectedIndex* method as the index into the *foods* array to retrieve the corresponding food image for the country selected. In this way, we pass the corresponding array element of *foods* to the *setIcon* method of *JLabel* so that the *foodImage* label will display the appropriate food sampling. Figure 12.12 shows this example running after the user has clicked on "Greece".

```
 1 /* Using JList to show a sampling of international foods
 2     Anderson, Franceschi
 3 */
 4
 5 import javax.swing.*;
 6 import java.awt.*;
 7 import javax.swing.event.*;
 8
 9 public class FoodSamplings extends JFrame
10 {
11  private Container contents;
12  private JList countries;
```

```
private JLabel foodImage;

private String [ ] countryList =
           { "France", "Greece", "Italy", "Japan", "USA" };
private ImageIcon [ ] foods =
           {  new ImageIcon( "cheese.jpg" ),
              new ImageIcon( "fetaSalad.jpg" ),
              new ImageIcon( "pizza.jpg" ),
              new ImageIcon( "sushi.jpg" ),
              new ImageIcon( "hamburger.jpg" ) };

public FoodSamplings( )
{
 super( "Food samplings of various countries" );
 contents = getContentPane( );
 contents.setLayout( new FlowLayout( ) );

 // instantiate the components
 countries = new JList( countryList );
 foodImage = new JLabel( foods[0] );

 // allow single selections only
 countries.setSelectionMode( ListSelectionModel.SINGLE_SELECTION );
 countries.setSelectedIndex( 0 );

 // add components to the content pane
 contents.add( countries );
 contents.add( foodImage );

 // set up event handler
 ListHandler lslh = new ListHandler( );
 countries.addListSelectionListener( lslh );

 setSize( 350, 150 );
 setVisible( true );
}

private class ListHandler implements ListSelectionListener
{
 public void valueChanged( ListSelectionEvent lse )
 {
  foodImage.setIcon( foods[countries.getSelectedIndex( )] );
 }
}
```

```
public static void main( String args[ ] )
{
 FoodSamplings fs = new FoodSamplings( );
 fs.setDefaultCloseOperation( JFrame.EXIT_ON_CLOSE );
}
}
```

EXAMPLE 12.8 Using *JList* to Display Food Samplings

12.10 Combo Boxes

A *JComboBox* implements a drop-down list. When the combo box appears, one item is displayed, along with a button showing a down arrow. When the user presses on the button, the combo box "drops" open and displays a list of items, with a scroll bar for viewing more items. The user can select only one item from the list.

When the user selects an item, the list closes and the selected item is the one item displayed. A *JComboBox* fires an *ItemEvent*, so the event handler must implement the *ItemListener* interface, and thus, provide the *itemStateChanged* method.

Table 12.17 shows the APIs for a constructor and some useful methods of the *JComboBox* class. The constructor is similar to the *JList* constructor in that it takes an array of objects. The *JComboBox* class also provides the *getSelectedIndex* method, so that the event handler can determine which item the user has selected, and the *setSelectedIndex* method, which typically is used to initialize the default item displayed when the list appears. The *setMaximumRowCount* method allows us to specify how many items to display when the combo box opens. The user can use the scroll bar to move through all the items in the list.

To illustrate a combo box, we will display five possible destinations for a spring break vacation: Cancun, Colorado, Jamaica, Orlando, and Pinehurst. When the user selects a destination, information about that destination will be displayed in a text area.

The information about our vacation specials is stored in the file *specials.txt.* Each line in the file represents a vacation destination, the sponsoring organization, a brief description, and a price.

The contents of the *specials.txt* file is shown in Figure 12.13.

TABLE 12.17 Useful Constructors and Methods of the *JComboBox* Class

Useful Constructors and Methods of the *JComboBox* Class	
Constructor	
Class	**Constructor**
JComboBox	JComboBox(Object [ ] arrayName) constructs a new *JComboBox* component initially filled with the objects in *arrayName*. Often, the objects are *Strings*.
Methods	
Return value	**Method name and argument list**
void	setSelectedIndex(int index) sets the item at *index* as selected. The index of the first item in the list is 0.
int	getSelectedIndex( ) returns the index of the selected item. The index of the first item in the list is 0.
void	setMaximumRowCount(int size) sets the number of rows that will be visible at one time to *size*.

```
Cancun,Club Med,all inclusive,1230
Colorado,Club Med,all inclusive,780
Jamaica,Extreme Vacations,all inclusive,1150
Orlando,Disney Vacations,unlimited pass to DisneyWorld,800
Pinehurst,Golf Concepts,unlimited golf,900
```

Figure 12.13
Contents of the *specials.txt* File

We will first create a *Vacation* class to encapsulate the information about each vacation destination. Then we will create a *VacationList* class that reads vacation information from a text file and creates an *ArrayList* of *Vacation* objects. Finally, our application will retrieve data from a *VacationList* object to create the items for our *JComboBox* dynamically.

For simplicity, in our *Vacation* class (Example 12.9), we have coded only an overloaded constructor (lines 17–32), the accessor method for the *location* instance variable (lines 34–40), and the *toString* method (lines 42–51).

```
1 /* Vacation class
2    Anderson, Franceschi
3 */
4
5 import java.text.DecimalFormat;
6
7 public class Vacation
8 {
9  public final DecimalFormat MONEY
10                    = new DecimalFormat( "$#,##0.00" );
11
12  private String location;
13  private String organization;
14  private String description;
15  private double price;
16
17  /** Constructor
18  *  @param  startLocation       location
19  *  @param  startOrganization   organization
20  *  @param  startDescription    description
21  *  @param  startPrice          price
22  */
23  public Vacation( String startLocation,
24                   String startOrganization,
25                   String startDescription,
26                   double startPrice )
27  {
28   location = startLocation;
29   organization = startOrganization;
30   description = startDescription;
31   price = startPrice;
32  }
33
34  /** getLocation
35  *  @return location
36  */
37  public String getLocation( )
38  {
```

```
   return location;
  }

  /** toString
  *  @return location, organization, description, and price
  */
  public String toString( )
  {
   return "Location: " + location + "\n"
         + "Organization: " + organization + "\n"
         + "Description: " + description + "\n"
         + "Price: " + MONEY.format( price );
  }
}
```

EXAMPLE 12.9 The *Vacation* Class

Our next step is to create the *VacationList* class, shown in Example 12.10, which we will use to read vacation information from a file and build a list of *Vacation* objects. We assume that we do not know how many records are in the file; thus, we will choose an *ArrayList* rather than an array to store the *Vacation* objects.

Again, for simplicity, we have coded just an overloaded constructor (lines 12–56), the *getLocationList* method (lines 58–67), and the *getDescription* method (lines 69–76). The only instance variable, *vacationList*, is an *ArrayList* of *Vacation* objects. The overloaded constructor takes one argument, the name of the file that contains the data.

At lines 23–45, the *while* loop reads each line of the file, creates a *Vacation* object, and adds the object to the *ArrayList*. The *getLocationList* method returns a *String* array of the *location* for each *Vacation* object. We will call this method in our GUI application to create the items for our *JComboBox*. The *getDescription* method returns the *String* representation of the *Vacation* object stored at a given index of *vacationList*. Our GUI application will call this method to display information about the vacation destination that the user has selected from the *JComboBox*.

REFERENCE POINT

The *ArrayList* class is explained in Chapter 9. *I/O* classes and the *StringTokenizer* class are discussed in Chapter 11.

```
1 /* VacationList class
2    Anderson, Franceschi
3 */
4
```

```
import java.util.*;
import java.io.*;

public class VacationList
{
 private ArrayList<Vacation> vacationList;

 /** Constructor
 *  @param  fileName  the name of the file containing the data
 */
 public VacationList( String fileName )
 {
  vacationList = new ArrayList<Vacation>( );
  try
  {
   File file = new File( fileName );
   Scanner br = new Scanner( file );

   while ( br.hasNext( ) )
   {
    String record = br.nextLine( );
    // extract the fields from the records
    StringTokenizer st = new StringTokenizer( record, "," );
    String loc = st.nextToken( );
    String org = st.nextToken( );
    String desc = st.nextToken( );

    try
    {
     double pr = Double.parseDouble( st.nextToken( ) );

     Vacation vacationTemp = new Vacation( loc, org, desc, pr );
     vacationList.add( vacationTemp );
    }
    catch ( NumberFormatException nfe )
    {
     System.out.println( "Error in vacation record: "
                         + record + "; record ignored" );
    }

   }
   br.close( );
  }
```

```
  catch ( FileNotFoundException fnfe )
  {
   System.out.println( "Unable to find " + fileName );
  }
  catch ( IOException ioe )
  {
   ioe.printStackTrace( );
  }
 }

 /** getLocationList
 *  @return array of locations
 */
 public String [ ] getLocationList( )
 {
  String [ ] temp = new String[vacationList.size( )];
  for ( int i = 0; i < vacationList.size( ); i++ )
         temp[i] = ( vacationList.get( i ) ).getLocation( );
  return temp;
 }

 /** getDescription
 *  @param  index     index of vacation in vacationList
 *  @return description of vacation at index
 */
 public String getDescription( int index )
 {
  return ( ( vacationList.get( index ) ).toString( ) );
 }
}
```

EXAMPLE 12.10 The *VacationList* Class

We are now ready to code a GUI application, shown in Example 12.11.

The instance variable, *vacations*, a *VacationList* object reference, will store an *ArrayList* of vacation information. We instantiate *vacations* (line 20) by passing the filename that the *main* method passed to the constructor (line 53). For simplicity in execution of the application, we have hard-coded the filename. However, we could have accepted the filename as a command-line argument to the application or we could have prompted the user for the filename.

REFERENCE POINT

Retrieving command-line arguments is discussed in Chapter 8.

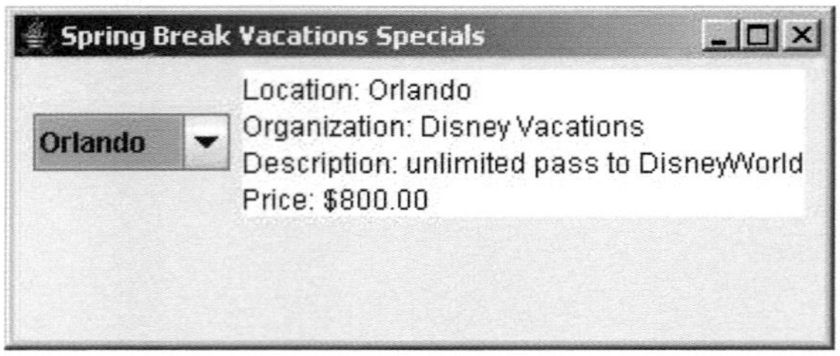

Figure 12.14
Running Example 12.11

We then instantiate our *JComboBox* (line 26) by passing to the constructor the array of locations returned by the *getLocationList* method of the *VacationList* class.

At line 27, we call the *setMaximumRowCount* method of the *JComboBox* class with an argument of *4* to set the maximum number of items that the user will see when the combo box opens.

We use a *JTextArea* component, named *summary*, to display the vacation descriptions, because the descriptions are of variable length. At line 28, we instantiate the *JTextArea*, with the initial value being the description of the first *Vacation* object in *vacations*. We retrieve the first description by calling the *getDescription* method of the *VacationList* class with an index of 0. By default, a *JComboBox* displays the first item in the list, so in this way, we will match the description with the first item displayed.

At lines 42–49, we define the *ItemListenerHandler* event handler. At line 46, we call the *getSelectedIndex* method of the *JComboBox* class to determine which item the user has selected. Using that returned index, we call the *getDescription* method of the *VacationList* class to set the text of the *JTextArea* to the description matching the selected item.

Figure 12.14 shows a run of the application, after the user has clicked on "*Orlando*" inside the combo box. Try running the example, then modify the number of visible rows by changing the argument of the *setMaximumRowCount* method, and run the example again.

```
1 /* Using a JComboBox to display dynamic data
2    Anderson, Franceschi
3 */
4
5 import javax.swing.*;
6 import java.awt.*;
7 import java.awt.event.*;
```

```
public class VacationSpecials extends JFrame
{
 private VacationList vacations;

 private Container contents;
 private JComboBox places;
 private JTextArea summary;

 public VacationSpecials( String fileName )
 {
  super( "Spring Break Vacations Specials" );
  vacations = new VacationList( fileName );

  contents = getContentPane( );
  contents.setLayout( new FlowLayout( ) );

  // instantiate components
  places = new JComboBox( vacations.getLocationList( ) );
  places.setMaximumRowCount( 4 );
  summary = new JTextArea( vacations.getDescription( 0 ) );

  // add components to content pane
  contents.add( places );
  contents.add( summary );

  // set up event handler
  ItemListenerHandler ilh = new ItemListenerHandler( );
  places.addItemListener( ilh );

  setSize( 350, 150 );
  setVisible( true );
 }

 private class ItemListenerHandler implements ItemListener
 {
  public void itemStateChanged( ItemEvent ie )
  {
   int index = places.getSelectedIndex( );
   summary.setText( vacations.getDescription( index ) );
  }
 }

 public static void main( String [ ] args )
 {
```

```
  VacationSpecials vs = new VacationSpecials( "specials.txt" );
  vs.setDefaultCloseOperation( JFrame.EXIT_ON_CLOSE );
 }
}
```

EXAMPLE 12.11 The *VacationSpecials* class

Skill Practice
with these end-of-chapter questions

12.18.1 Multiple Choice Exercises

Questions 5, 6, 7, 8

12.18.2 Reading and Understanding Code

Questions 16, 19, 20, 21, 22, 23, 24, 25, 26

12.18.3 Fill In the Code

Questions 28, 29, 31, 32

12.18.4 Identifying Errors in Code

Questions 43, 44, 45

12.18.5 Debugging Area

Questions 49, 50

12.18.6 Write a Short Program

Questions 51, 52, 53, 54, 55, 56, 57

CODE IN ACTION

On the CD-ROM included with this book, you will find a Flash movie with a step-by-step illustration of working with GUI components. Click on the link for Chapter 12 to start the movie.

12.11 Adapter Classes

We have learned that events are associated with event listener interfaces, and that we implement at least one interface in order to process an event. So far, we have used the *ActionListener*, *ItemListener*, and *ListSelection-*

Listener interfaces, each of which has only one method. For mouse events, there are two listeners: the *MouseListener* and the *MouseMotionListener*. The *MouseListener* interface specifies five methods to implement and the *MouseMotionListener* interface specifies two methods to implement. If we want to use *MouseListener* but need only one of its five methods to process a *MouseEvent*, we still have to implement the other four methods as "do-nothing" methods with empty method bodies. For convenience, Java provides **adapter classes**, each of which *implements* an interface and provides an empty body for each of the interface's methods. For mouse events, the adapter classes are *MouseAdapter* and the *MouseMotionAdapter*. Thus, instead of implementing an interface, we can extend the appropriate adapter class and override only the method or methods we need. For example, if we want to process a *MouseEvent* using only one method of the five in the *MouseListener* interface, we can simply extend the *MouseAdapter* class and override that one method. We will do that in our next example.

SOFTWARE ENGINEERING TIP

When you need to implement only a few methods of a listener interface having more than one method, consider extending the corresponding adapter class instead.

12.12 Mouse Movements

A truly interactive application allows the user to point and click using the mouse. Any mouse activity (clicking, moving, or dragging) by the user generates a *MouseEvent*. When any mouse activity occurs, we will be interested in determining where on the window the user clicked, moved, or dragged the mouse. To determine the (x, y) coordinate of the mouse event, we can call two methods of the *MouseEvent* class, *getX* and *getY*, which are described in Table 12.18.

Depending on the type of mouse activity, our application will implement either a *MouseListener* interface or a *MouseMotionListener* interface. As

TABLE 12.18 Useful Methods of the *MouseEvent* Class

Return value	Method name and argument list
`int`	`getX( )` returns the *x* value of the (x, y) coordinate of the mouse activity
`int`	`getY( )` returns the *y* value of the (x, y) coordinate of the mouse activity

TABLE 12.19 Methods of the *MouseListener* Interface

MouseListener Interface Method APIs
`public void mousePressed( MouseEvent e )`
called when the mouse button is pressed
`public void mouseReleased( MouseEvent e )`
called when the mouse button is released after being pressed
`public void mouseClicked( MouseEvent e )`
called when the mouse button is pressed and released
`public void mouseEntered( MouseEvent e )`
called when the mouse enters the registered component
`public void mouseExited( MouseEvent e )`
called when the mouse exits the registered component

mentioned, both of the listener interfaces have been implemented as adapter classes that we can extend. The *MouseListener* interface includes the five *abstract* methods described in Table 12.19.

To illustrate how to use the *MouseAdapter* class, we will build a simple submarine hunt game. A submarine is hidden somewhere in the window, and the user will try to sink the submarine by clicking the mouse at various locations in the window, simulating the dropping of a depth charge. Each time the user clicks the mouse, we will indicate how close that click is to the submarine. If the user clicks too far from the submarine, we will display "In the water" in the title bar and draw a blue circle where the mouse was clicked. If the user clicks close to the submarine, we will display "Close ..." in the title bar. Finally, if the submarine is hit, we will change the title bar to "Sunk!", display the submarine, and remove the listener so that the game ends.

Before designing the GUI class, we first code a class to encapsulate the functionality of the submarine hunt game; this class (Example 12.12) enables us to create a game of a given size, enable play, and enforce the rules of the game.

The instance variable, *status* (line 17), a *String*, stores the state of the last shot fired to the submarine. We also define a *boolean* flag variable, *hit*, which is initially *false* (lines 18 and 33). Thus, we will change *hit* to *true* when the user successfully hits the submarine.

In the constructor, we randomly generate the (*x*, *y*) coordinate for the center of the submarine and store the generated values in the *xCtr* and *yCtr* instance variables (lines 29–32).

The *play* method (lines 60–80) processes a play from the user, setting the value of *status* to either "Sunk!", "Close…", or "In the water" based on the *x* and *y* coordinate of the shot fired by the user. "Sunk!" means the submarine has been hit, "Close..." means that our shot was within two lengths of the center of the submarine, and "In the water" means that our shot was more than two lengths away. If the submarine was hit, we set the value of *hit* to *true* (line 71).

In the *draw* method (lines 82–110), we test the value of *status*. If *status* is equal to "Sunk!", the submarine has been hit so we draw a red depth charge and the sunken submarine (lines 91–102), revealing its location. If *status* is equal to "In the water", we draw a filled blue circle (lines 106–107) at the location of the shot fired. If *status* is equal to "Close…", we do not draw anything so that we do not give too big of a hint to the player.

```
 1 /* SubHunt class
 2    Anderson, Franceschi
 3 */
 4
 5 import java.awt.Graphics;
 6 import java.awt.Color;
 7 import java.util.Random;
 8
 9 public class SubHunt
10 {
11  public static int DEFAULT_GAME_SIZE = 300;
12  public static int SIDE = 28; // size of submarine
13
14  private int gameSize;
15  private int xCtr;     // x coordinate of center of submarine
16  private int yCtr;     // y coordinate of center of submarine
17  private String status = "";
18  private boolean hit;
```

```
/** Constructor
*  @param  newGameSize         gameSize
*/
public SubHunt( int newGameSize )
{
 if ( newGameSize > SIDE )
  gameSize = newGameSize;
 else
  gameSize = DEFAULT_GAME_SIZE;
 // generate submarine center
 Random random = new Random( );
 xCtr = SIDE / 2 + random.nextInt( gameSize - SIDE );
 yCtr = SIDE / 2 + random.nextInt( gameSize - SIDE );
 hit = false;
}

/** getStatus
*  @return status
*/
public String getStatus( )
{
 return status;
}

/** getGameSize
*  @return gameSize
*/
public int getGameSize( )
{
 return gameSize;
}

/** isHit
*  @return hit
*/
public boolean isHit( )
{
 return hit;
}

/** play
*  @param  x the x coordinate of the play
*  @param  y the y coordinate of the play
```

```
*/
public void play( int x, int y )
{
  // is click within the submarine?
  if ( Math.abs( x - xCtr ) < SIDE / 2
      && Math.abs( y - yCtr ) < SIDE / 2 )
  {
    status = "Sunk!";
    hit = true;
  }
  // is click close?
  else if ( Math.abs( x - xCtr ) < 2 * SIDE
            && Math.abs( y - yCtr ) < 2 * SIDE )
    status = "Close ...";
  // click is too far from submarine
  else
    status = "In the water";
}

/** draw
*  @param  g a Graphics object
*  @param  x the x coordinate of the play
*  @param  y the y coordinate of the play
*/
public void draw( Graphics g, int x, int y )
{
 if ( status.equals( "Sunk!" ) )
 {
  // draw sunken submarine
  g.setColor( Color.BLACK );
  g.fillRoundRect( xCtr - SIDE/2, yCtr - SIDE/2, SIDE/2, SIDE,
                   15, 15 );
  g.fillRoundRect( xCtr - SIDE/4, yCtr - SIDE/3, SIDE/2, SIDE/2,
                   7 , 7 );
  g.drawLine( xCtr + SIDE/4, yCtr - SIDE/12,
                   xCtr + SIDE/2, yCtr - SIDE/12 );

  // draw red depth charge
  g.setColor( Color.RED );
  g.fillOval( x - SIDE/4, y - SIDE/4, SIDE/2, SIDE/2 );
 }
 else if ( status.equals( "In the water" ) ) // draw blue circle
 {
  g.setColor( Color.BLUE );
  g.fillOval( x - SIDE/2, y - SIDE/2, SIDE, SIDE );
```

```
  }
  // else Close ... , do not draw
 }
}
```

EXAMPLE 12.12 The *SubHunt* Class

Example 12.13 shows the GUI client class that enables a user to play the submarine hunting game.

In this game, the only mouse action we care about is a click; therefore, we are interested in only one method of the *MouseListener* interface: *mouseClicked*. To simplify our code, we can extend the *MouseAdapter* class, which provides implementations for the five *MouseListener* methods, so our event handler needs to override only the *mouseClicked* method.

At lines 11–16, we declare our instance variables. The *ints x* and *y* represent the *x* and *y* coordinate where the player clicked the mouse. The *SubHunt* instance variable *sub* represents the submarine hunting game that we will display inside the window. When the user plays, we will use the *sub* reference to call the various methods of the *SubHunt* class to enable play and enforce the rules of the game. We will use *gameStarted* in the *paint* method. Before the game starts *gameStarted* is *false*, and becomes *true* (line 48) when the window opens.

In this example, we have set up the listener reference, *mh*, as an instance variable (line 16) rather than defining the reference as a local variable to the constructor, as we have done in previous examples. We define *mh* as an instance variable because when the submarine is hit, the event handler needs to access that listener to turn it off. The event handler is instantiated at line 24.

In this application, we want the listener to handle mouse clicks anywhere in the window, so we register the *mouseListener* on our window (*JFrame*) component, which is the *SubHuntClient* object. Thus, we do not use an object reference to call the *addMouseListener* method, and line 25 is equivalent to:

```
this.addMouseListener( mh );
```

The constructor also instantiates *sub*.

At lines 31–41, we define our mouse event handler, *MouseHandler*, as extending *MouseAdapter*. Inside the method *mouseClicked*, overridden at lines 33–40, we call the *MouseEvent* methods *getX* and *getY* to get the (x, y)

coordinate where the mouse was clicked. Then we call the *play* method of *SubHunt* with *sub* (line 37) to process the play. Next, we update the title of the window by getting the updated status and display that status in the window title bar by calling the *setTitle* method (line 38). Finally, we call the *repaint* method (line 39). The *repaint* method is inherited from the *Component* class and has the API shown in Table 12.20. A call to *repaint* forces a call to the *paint* method, which our application cannot call directly. The *paint* method (lines 43–53) updates the drawing in the window. Because we want to preserve any previously drawn blue circles, rather than clear the window and redraw every time, we set *gameStarted* to *true* the first time *paint* is called (lines 45–49). In this way, we call *super.paint(g)* only when the window opens, before the first shot is fired. A subsequent call to *super.paint()* would erase the contents of the window, and we would lose all the previously drawn blue circles.

Then we draw the result of the last shot fired (line 50) by calling the *draw* method from *SubHunt* with *sub*, passing the *Graphics* object *g* and the mouse position. Finally, if the submarine has been hit, we remove *mh* as a listener to this object (line 52) by calling the *removeMouseListener* method, inherited from the *Component* class.

Figure 12.15 shows a run of this game. At this point, the user has sunk the submarine.

```
 1 /* Using MouseListener
 2    Anderson, Franceschi
 3 */
 4
 5 import javax.swing.*;
 6 import java.awt.*;
 7 import java.awt.event.*;
 8
 9 public class SubHuntClient extends JFrame
10 {
11  private int x;      // current x mouse position
12  private int y;      // current y mouse position
13  private SubHunt sub;    // submarine
14  private boolean gameStarted = false;
15
16  private MouseHandler mh; // mouse event handler
17
```

```
public SubHuntClient( )
{
 super( "Click in the window to sink the sub" );

 sub = new SubHunt( SubHunt.DEFAULT_GAME_SIZE );
 // instantiate event handler and register listener on window
 mh = new MouseHandler( );
 addMouseListener( mh );

 setSize( sub.getGameSize( ), sub.getGameSize( ) );
 setVisible( true );
}

private class MouseHandler extends MouseAdapter
{
 public void mouseClicked( MouseEvent me )
 {
  x = me.getX( );
  y = me.getY( );
  sub.play( x, y );
  setTitle( sub.getStatus( ) );
  repaint( );
 }
}

public void paint( Graphics g )
{
 if ( !gameStarted )
 {
  super.paint( g );
  gameStarted = true;
 }
 sub.draw( g, x, y );
 if ( sub.isHit( ) )
  removeMouseListener( mh );
}

public static void main( String [ ] args )
{
 SubHuntClient subH = new SubHuntClient( );
 subH.setDefaultCloseOperation( JFrame.EXIT_ON_CLOSE );
}
}
```

EXAMPLE 12.13 A Simple Game Using a *MouseListener*

The second interface related to mouse events is *MouseMotionListener*, which has two methods, *mouseMoved* and *mouseDragged*, shown in Table 12.21. Dragging the mouse is defined as the user moving the mouse with the mouse button pressed, but not released.

TABLE 12.20 The *repaint* Method API in the *Component* Class

Return value	Method name and argument list
`void`	`repaint( )` automatically forces a call to the *paint* method

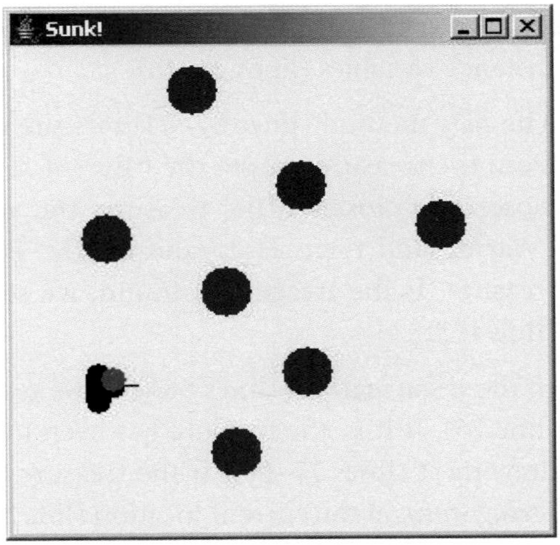

Figure 12.15
A Run of Example 12.13

TABLE 12.21 *MouseMotionListener* Interface Method APIs

MouseMotionListener Interface Method APIs
`public void mouseMoved( MouseEvent e )` called when the mouse is moved onto a component
`public void mouseDragged( MouseEvent e )` called when the mouse button is pressed on a component and the mouse is dragged

In order to illustrate how to use the *MouseMotionListener* interface with a *MouseEvent* class, we will build a simple treasure hunt game that is similar to the submarine hunt game. A treasure is hidden somewhere in the window, and the user will try to find it, not by clicking the mouse button, but by moving the mouse inside the window. Depending on how close the mouse is to the treasure, we will display a message at the mouse location so that the user can find the treasure and win the game.

Again, we first code a class to encapsulate the functionality of the treasure hunt game (Example 12.14).

The *status* (line 17) instance variable, a *String*, stores the state of the player's position compared to the location of the treasure. We also define a *boolean* flag variable, *gameOver*, which is initially *false* (line 18); when the user finds the treasure, we will change it to *true*.

In the constructor, we randomly generate the (*x*, *y*) coordinate for the center of the treasure and store the generated values in the *xCtr* and *yCtr* instance variables (lines 24–26).

The *play* method (lines 37–64) sets the value of *status*. If the player is far from the treasure, we set the value of *status* to "Cold." As the user moves closer and closer to the treasure, the value becomes "Lukewarm," then "Warm," and then "Hot," and finally "Found" when the player finds the treasure. If the treasure is found, we set the value of *gameOver* to *true* (line 47).

In the *draw* method (lines 66–84), we test if the value of *status* is "Found" (line 75). If it is, the treasure has been found and we reveal its location by drawing it (lines 77–80). If the treasure has not been found, we draw the *String status* at the current location (line 83), determined by the parameters *x* and *y* sent to the *draw* method.

```
1 /* TreasureHunt class
2    Anderson, Franceschi
3 */
4
5 import java.awt.*;
6 import java.util.Random;
7
8 public class TreasureHunt
9 {
10  public static int GAME_SIZE = 300; // side of window
11  public static int SIDE = 40; // side of treasure
```

```

private int xCtr;  // x coordinate of center of treasure
private int yCtr;  // y coordinate of center of treasure
private int x;     // current x mouse position
private int y;     // current y mouse position
private String status = ""; // message
private boolean gameOver = false;

/** Constructor
*/
public TreasureHunt( )
{
 Random random = new Random( );
 xCtr = SIDE / 2 + random.nextInt( GAME_SIZE - SIDE );
 yCtr = SIDE / 2 + random.nextInt( GAME_SIZE - SIDE );
}

/** isGameOver
*  @return gameOver
*/
public boolean isGameOver( )
{
 return gameOver;
}

/** play
*  @param  x the x coordinate of the play
*  @param  y the y coordinate of the play
*/
public void play( int x, int y )
{
 // is mouse within treasure?
 if ( Math.abs( x - xCtr ) < SIDE / 2
      && Math.abs( y - yCtr ) < SIDE / 2 )
 {
     gameOver = true;
     status = "Found";
 }
 // is mouse within half-length of the treasure?
 else if ( Math.abs( x - xCtr ) < ( 1.5 * SIDE )
           && Math.abs( y - yCtr ) < ( 1.5 * SIDE ) )
      status = "Hot";
 // is mouse within 1 length of the treasure?
 else if ( Math.abs( x - xCtr ) < ( 2 * SIDE )
           && Math.abs( y - yCtr ) < ( 2 * SIDE ) )
      status = "Warm";
```

```
  // is mouse within 2 lengths of the treasure?
  else if ( Math.abs( x - xCtr ) < ( 3 * SIDE )
            && Math.abs( y - yCtr ) < ( 3 * SIDE ) )
       status = "Lukewarm";
  else // mouse is not near treasure
       status = "Cold";
 }

 /** draw
 *  @param  g a Graphics object
 *  @param  x the x coordinate of the play
 *  @param  y the y coordinate of the play
 */
 public void draw( Graphics g, int x, int y )
 {
  g.setColor( Color.BLUE );

  if ( status.equals( "Found" ) ) // if found, draw treasure
  {
   g.setColor( Color.RED );
   g.fillRect( xCtr - SIDE / 2, yCtr - SIDE / 2, SIDE, SIDE );
   g.setColor( Color.GREEN );
   g.drawString( "$$$", xCtr - SIDE / 4, yCtr );
  }
  else
   g.drawString( status, x, y );   // display current status
 }
}
```

EXAMPLE 12.14 The *TreasureHunt* Class

Example 12.15 shows the GUI client class, which enables a user to play the treasure hunt game.

In this application, instead of coding the event handler as a *private* inner class, we define our application class as implementing the *MouseMotionListener* interface. As a result, our application is a listener, and we register the listener on itself.

Thus, in our class definition, we include the clause *implements MouseMotionListener* (lines 9–10).

Again, the instance variables *x* and *y* (lines 12–13) will store the current location of the mouse. The *TreasureHunt* instance variable *hunt* represents the treasure hunting game that we will display inside the window.

```
/* A Treasure Hunt using MouseMotionListener
   Anderson, Franceschi
*/

import javax.swing.*;
import java.awt.*;
import java.awt.event.*;

public class TreasureHuntClient extends JFrame
                             implements MouseMotionListener
{
 private int x;      // current x mouse position
 private int y;      // current y mouse position
 private TreasureHunt hunt;

 public TreasureHuntClient( )
 {
  super( "Move the mouse to find the treasure" );

  hunt = new TreasureHunt( );
  // application registers on itself
  // since it is a MouseMotionListener itself
  addMouseMotionListener( this );

  setSize( hunt.GAME_SIZE, hunt.GAME_SIZE );
  setVisible( true );
 }

 public void mouseDragged( MouseEvent me )
 { } // we do not want to process mouse drag events

 public void mouseMoved( MouseEvent me )
 {
  // get location of mouse
  x = me.getX( );
  y = me.getY( );
  hunt.play( x, y );
  repaint( );
 }

 public void paint( Graphics g )
 {
  super.paint( g );
```

```
    hunt.draw( g, x, y );
    if ( hunt.isGameOver( ) )
     removeMouseMotionListener( this );
  }

  public static void main( String [ ] args )
  {
    TreasureHuntClient th_gui = new TreasureHuntClient( );
    th_gui.setDefaultCloseOperation( JFrame.EXIT_ON_CLOSE );
  }
}
```

EXAMPLE 12.15 A Simple Game Using *MouseMotionListener*

Figure 12.16
The User Is Getting Close to the Treasure

Figure 12.17
The User Has Found the Treasure

At lines 21–23, we register this *TreasureHunt* object on itself as a *MouseMotionListener*. In this game, the only event we want to handle is the user moving the mouse. Because *TreasureHuntClient* implements the *MouseMotionListener* interface, however, we must implement both the *mouseMoved* and the *mouseDragged* methods. We are interested in the *mouseMoved* method only; thus, we implement *mouseDragged* with an empty body (lines 29–30). Note that we could not use the *MouseMotionAdapter* class because our application (which is the listener) already extends the *JFrame* class. Remember that a class can extend only one class, but can implement multiple interfaces.

The *mouseMoved* method is implemented at lines 32–39. At lines 34–36, we assign the (*x*, *y*) coordinate of the mouse position to the instance variables *x* and *y*, using the *getX* and *getY* methods of the *MouseEvent* class. Then we call the *play* method of *TreasureHunt* with *hunt* (line 37) to process the play, and call the *repaint* method (line 38) to update the window.

We begin the *paint* method (lines 41–47) with a call to the *paint* method of the *JFrame* superclass to clear the contents of the window. Then we draw the result of the current move (line 44) by calling the *draw* method from *TreasureHunt* with *hunt*, passing the *Graphics* object *g* and the mouse location. Finally, if the game is over (i.e., the treasure has been found), we remove this object, the current *JFrame*, as a listener (line 46) by calling the *removeMouseMotionListener* method.

Figures 12.16 and 12.17 show the program running. In Figure 12.16, the user is getting close to the treasure, and in Figure 12.17, the user has found the treasure.

12.13 Layout Managers: *GridLayout*

We have been using the *FlowLayout* layout manager because it is the easiest to use. The *FlowLayout* layout manager adds new components from left to right, creating as many rows as needed. A problem, however, is that if the user resizes the window, the components are rearranged to fit the new window size. Typically, GUIs can be quite complex and use many components, all of which need to be organized so that the user interface is effective and easy to use even if the user resizes the window. Two useful layout managers that give us more control over the organization of components within a window are the *GridLayout* and the *BorderLayout*.

Regardless of the layout manager used, the constructor of our application will still perform the following setup operations:

- declare and instantiate the layout manager
- use the *setLayout* method of the *Container* class to set the layout manager of the content pane of the *JFrame*
- instantiate components
- add components to the content pane using one of the *add* methods of the *Container* class

The *GridLayout* organizes the container as a grid. We can visualize the layout as a table made up of equally sized cells in rows and columns. Each cell can contain one component. The first component added to the container is placed in the first column of the first row; the second component is placed in the second column of the first row, and so on. When all the cells in a row are filled, the next component added is placed in the first cell of the next row.

Table 12.22 shows two constructors of the *GridLayout* class.

Example 12.16 shows how to use a *GridLayout* to display a chessboard. A two-dimensional array of *JButtons*, named *squares* (line 13), will make up the chessboard. A two-dimensional array of *Strings*, named *names*, will hold the position of each square (lines 14–22). The position of a square is composed of a letter representing the row (a–h) and a number representing

TABLE 12.22 *GridLayout* Constructors

Constructors	
Class	**Constructor**
`GridLayout`	`GridLayout( int numberOfRows, int numberOfColumns )` creates a grid layout with the number of rows and columns specified by the arguments.
`GridLayout`	`GridLayout( int numberOfRows, int numberOfColumns, int hGap, int vGap )` creates a grid layout with the specified number of rows and columns and with a horizontal gap of *hGap* pixels between columns and a vertical gap of *vGap* pixels between rows. Horizontal gaps are also placed at the left and right edges, and vertical gaps are placed at the top and bottom edges.

the column (1–8). When the user clicks on a button of the chessboard, we will set the text of that button to display its position on the board, retrieving the name from the array *names*.

```
/* Using GridLayout to organize our window
   Anderson, Franceschi
*/

import javax.swing.*;
import java.awt.*;
import java.awt.event.*;

public class ChessBoard extends JFrame
{
 public static final int SIDE = 8;
 private Container contents;
 private JButton [ ][ ] squares;
 private String [ ][ ] names =
  { { "a1","a2","a3","a4","a5","a6", "a7", "a8" },
    { "b1","b2","b3","b4","b5","b6", "b7", "b8" },
    { "c1","c2","c3","c4","c5","c6", "c7", "c8" },
    { "d1","d2","d3","d4","d5","d6", "d7", "d8" },
    { "e1","e2","e3","e4","e5","e6", "e7", "e8" },
    { "f1","f2","f3","f4","f5","f6", "f7", "f8" },
    { "g1","g2","g3","g4","g5","g6", "g7", "g8" },
    { "h1","h2","h3","h4","h5","h6", "h7", "h8" } };

 public ChessBoard( )
 {
  super( "Click a square to reveal its position" );
  contents = getContentPane( );

  // set layout to an 8-by-8 Grid
  contents.setLayout( new GridLayout( SIDE, SIDE ) );

  squares = new JButton[SIDE][SIDE];

  ButtonHandler bh = new ButtonHandler( );

  for ( int i = 0; i < names.length; i++ )
  {
   for ( int j = 0; j < SIDE; j++ )
   {
    // instantiate JButton array
    squares[i][j] = new JButton( );

    // make every other square red
    if ( ( i + j ) % 2 == 0 )
      squares[i][j].setBackground( Color.RED );
```

```
46
47     // add the JButton
48     contents.add( squares[i][j] );
49
50     // register listener on button
51     squares[i][j].addActionListener( bh );
52    }
53   }
54
55   setSize( 400, 400 );
56   setVisible( true );
57  }
58
59  private class ButtonHandler implements ActionListener
60  {
61   public void actionPerformed( ActionEvent ae )
62   {
63     for ( int i = 0; i < SIDE; i++ )
64     {
65       for ( int j = 0; j < SIDE; j++ )
66       {
67         if ( ae.getSource( ) == squares[i][j] )
68         {
69           squares[i][j].setText( names[i][j] );
70           return;
71         }
72       }
73     }
74   }
75  }
76
77  public static void main( String [ ] args )
78  {
79    ChessBoard myGame = new ChessBoard( );
80    myGame.setDefaultCloseOperation( JFrame.EXIT_ON_CLOSE );
81  }
82 }
```

EXAMPLE 12.16 Using *GridLayout* to Display a Chessboard

At line 30, we instantiate a *GridLayout* anonymous object using the constructor with two arguments representing the number of rows and columns in the grid, here *SIDE* and *SIDE*. The constant *SIDE* is declared at line 11 and has the value 8. Still at line 30, we pass the *GridLayout* anonymous object as the argument of the *setLayout* method. Thus, components

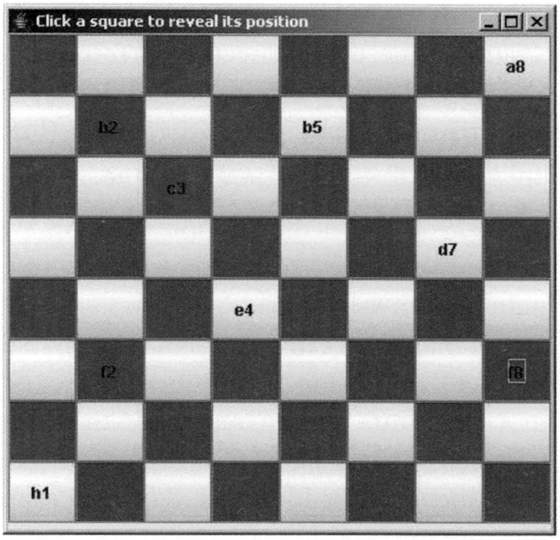

Figure 12.18
Running Example 12.16

will be added cell by cell to an 8-by-8 grid, with each row being filled before starting the next row.

At line 34, we declare and instantiate the listener *bh*, a *ButtonHandler* object reference. Since we are interested in events related to buttons, our *ButtonHandler private* inner class *implements* the *ActionListener* interface and overrides the *actionPerformed* method.

At line 32, we instantiate the two-dimensional array *squares*. Because we have a two-dimensional array of *JButtons*, we use nested *for* loops at lines 36–53 to instantiate the *JButtons*, add them to the content pane, and register the listener on all of the buttons. Inside the inner loop, the value of the expression $(i + j)$ will alternate between an even and odd number. Accordingly, at lines 43–45, we set the background of every other button to red.

In the *actionPerformed* method, we use nested *for* loops at lines 63–73 to identify the source of the event; that is, which button the user clicked. When a button is clicked, the condition of the *if* statement at line 67 will evaluate to *true* when the *i* and *j* indices are such that *squares[i][j]* is the button that was clicked. We then set the text of that button to its board position (line 69), using the corresponding element in the two-dimensional array *names*. Having found the source of the event, we then exit the event handler via the *return* statement (line 70) to interrupt the *for* loops, and thus to avoid unnecessary processing.

Figure 12.18 shows the example running. When you run this program, click on various squares; resize the window, and check that the layout manager maintains an 8-by-8 grid.
Layout managers can be set dynamically, based on user input. For example, the user could enter the number of rows or columns of the grid. Or based on user input, we can rearrange the components using another layout manager, such as *FlowLayout*. The user could also instruct us to remove components and add others. Our next example, the Tile Puzzle game, will illustrate some of these capabilities.

In the Tile Puzzle game, eight tiles displaying the digits 1 through 8 are scrambled on a 3-by-3 grid, leaving one cell empty. Any tile adjacent to the empty cell can be moved to the empty cell by clicking on the numbered tile. The goal is to rearrange the tiles so that the numbers are in the correct order, as shown in Figure 12.19.

The Tile Puzzle game can also be played on a 4-by-4, a 5-by-5, and more generally, an n-by-n grid. Example 12.18 will set up a 3-by-3 grid for the

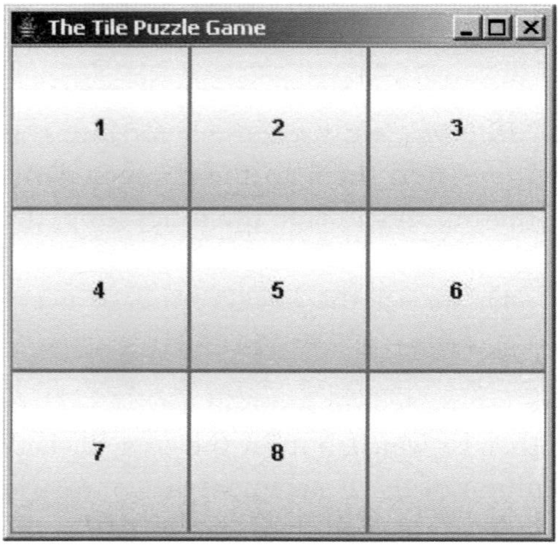

Figure 12.19
The Winning Position of a 3-by-3 Tile Puzzle Game

first game, then will randomly select a 3-by-3, a 4-by-4, a 5-by-5, or a 6-by-6 grid for subsequent games. Once you understand this example, you can modify it to allow the user to specify the size of the grid.

Before designing the GUI class, we first code a class to encapsulate the functionality of the tile puzzle game; this class (Example 12.17) handles the creation of a game of a given size, enables play, and enforces the rules of the game.

The instance variable *tiles* (line 7), a two-dimensional array of *Strings*, stores the state of the puzzle. Each element of *tiles* will be a cell in the puzzle grid. The instance variable *side*, declared at line 8, represents the size of the grid. The instance variables *emptyRow* and *emptyCol*, declared at lines 9–10, identify the empty cell in the puzzle grid.

The constructor (lines 12–18) calls the *setUpGame* method (lines 20-44), passing the size of the grid (*newSide*) as an argument. We also call the *setUpGame* method before starting each new game in the GUI class.

Inside the *setUpGame* method, we assign *newSide* to *side*. Rather than randomly generating each tile label, which would complicate this example, we assign the labels to the tiles in descending order using nested *for* loops (lines 33–41). We set the empty cell to the last cell in the grid at lines 42–43.

The *tryToPlay* method (lines 71–89) first checks if the play is legal by calling the *possibleToPlay* method (line 77). If the *possibleToPlay* method returns *true*, we proceed with the play and return *true*, otherwise we return *false*. Playing means swapping the values of the empty cell (*emptyRow*, *emptyCol*) and the cell that was just played, represented by the two parameters of *tryToPlay*, *row*, and *col*.

The *possibleToPlay* method is coded at lines 91–101. If the play is legal, that is, if the tile played is within one cell of the empty cell, the method returns *true*; otherwise, the method returns *false*.

The *won* method (lines 103–119) checks if the tiles are in order. If the user has won the game, the *won* method returns *true*; otherwise, the method returns *false*.

Figure 12.20 shows the game in progress.

```
/* TilePuzzle class
*  Anderson, Franceschi
*/

public class TilePuzzle
{
 private String [ ][ ] tiles;
 private int side; // grid size
 private int emptyRow;
 private int emptyCol;

 /** constructor
 *  @param  newSide  grid size
 */
 public TilePuzzle( int newSide )
 {
  setUpGame( newSide );
 }

 /** setUpGame
 *  @param  newSide   grid size
 */
 public void setUpGame( int newSide )
 {
    if ( newSide < 1 )
      side = 3;
    else
      side = newSide;
    emptyRow = side - 1;
    emptyCol = side - 1;
    tiles = new String[side][side];

  // initialize tiles
  for ( int i = 0; i < side; i++ )
  {
   for ( int j = 0; j < side; j++ )
   {
     tiles[i][j] = String.valueOf( ( side * side )
                        - ( side * i + j + 1 ) );
   }
  }
  // set empty cell label to blank
  tiles[side - 1][side - 1] = "";
 }

 /** getSide
 *  @return side
```

```
*/
public int getSide( )
{
  return side;
}

/** getTiles
*  @return a copy of tiles
*/
public String [ ][ ]  getTiles( )
{
 String[ ][ ] copyOfTiles = new String[side][side] ;

 for ( int i = 0; i < side; i++ )
 {
  for ( int j = 0; j < side; j++ )
  {
    copyOfTiles[i][j] = tiles[i][j];
  }
 }
 return copyOfTiles;
}

/** tryToPlay
*  enable play if play is legal
*  @return true if the play is legal, false otherwise
*/
public boolean tryToPlay( int row, int col )
{
 if ( possibleToPlay( row, col ) )
 {
  // play: switch empty String and tile label at row, col
  tiles[emptyRow][emptyCol] = tiles[row][col];
  tiles[row][col] =  "";
  // update emptyRow and emptyCol
  emptyRow = row;
  emptyCol = col;
  return true;
 }
 else
  return false;
}

/** possibleToPlay
*  @return true if the play is legal, false otherwise
*/
```

```
public boolean possibleToPlay( int row, int col )
{
 if ( ( col == emptyCol && Math.abs( row - emptyRow ) == 1 )
        || ( row == emptyRow && Math.abs( col - emptyCol ) == 1 ) )
   return true;
 else
   return false;
}

/** won
*  @return true if the tiles are all at the right place, false otherwise
*/
public boolean won( )
{
 for ( int i = 0; i < side ; i++ )
 {
  for ( int j = 0; j < side; j++ )
  {
    if ( !( tiles[i][j].equals(
                      String.valueOf( i * side + j + 1 ) ) )
                      && ( i != side - 1 || j != side - 1 )  )
       return false;
  }
 }
 return true;
}
}
```

EXAMPLE 12.17 *TilePuzzle* Class

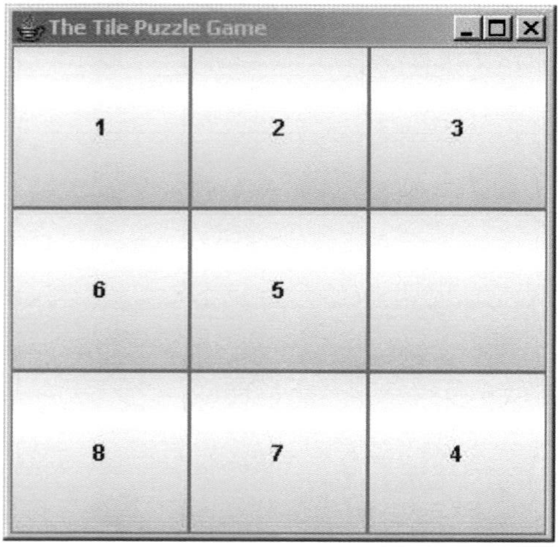

Figure 12.20
Running Example 12.18

Example 12.18 shows the GUI client class that enables a user to play the tile puzzle game.

Each cell of the grid is a button. At line 14, we declare a two-dimensional array of *JButtons* named *squares*. Each element of *squares* will be a cell in the game grid. The *TilePuzzle* instance variable *game*, declared at line 15, represents the tile puzzle game that we will display inside the window. When the user plays, we will call the various methods of the *TilePuzzle* class to enforce the rules of the game.

The constructor (lines 17–22) instantiates *game* and calls the *setUpGameGUI* method. We also call the *setUpGameGUI* method (lines 24–44) before starting each new game.

Inside the *setUpGameGUI* method, we remove all the components from the content pane by calling the *removeAll* method of the *Container* class (line 27) and set the layout manager (line 28) as a *GridLayout* with a grid size equal to the *side* instance variable of *game*. We instantiate the *squares* array and our event handler at lines 30 and 32. After that, we use nested *for* loops (lines 34–44) to instantiate each button, add it to the container, and register the event handler. The *squares* array parallels the *tiles* array of the *TilePuzzle* class; the *squares* buttons are labeled with the values of *tiles*.

Inside the *private* class *ButtonHandler* (lines 71–88), the *actionPerformed* method identifies the button that was clicked and calls the *tryToPlay* method at line 81 with the row and column arguments corresponding to the button that originated the event. If the play is legal, the *tryToPlay* method returns *true* and we update the puzzle grid by calling the *update* method at line 82.

Inside the *update* method (lines 50–69), we first update the *squares* button array (lines 52–58). We then test if this move solved the puzzle by calling the *won* method (line 60) with our instance variable *game*. If the *won* method returns *true*, we congratulate the user by popping up a dialog box at lines 62–63.

We then randomly generate a grid size between 3 and 6 (lines 64–65) for the next game and call the *setUpGame* method with *game* at line 66 and the *setUpGameGUI* method to begin the game with the new grid size at line 67.

```
1 /** Using GridLayout dynamically
2 *  Anderson, Franceschi
3 */
4
```

```
import javax.swing.*;
import java.awt.*;
import java.awt.event.*;
import java.util.Random;

public class TilePuzzleClient extends JFrame
{
 private Container contents;

 private JButton [ ][ ] squares;
 private TilePuzzle game; // the tile puzzle game

 public TilePuzzleClient( int newSide )
 {
  super( "The Tile Puzzle Game" );
  game = new TilePuzzle( newSide );
  setUpGameGUI( );
 }

 private void setUpGameGUI( )
 {
  contents = getContentPane( );
  contents.removeAll( ); // remove all components
  contents.setLayout( new GridLayout( game.getSide( ),
      game.getSide( ) ) );
  squares = new JButton[game.getSide( )][game.getSide( )];

  ButtonHandler bh = new ButtonHandler( );

  // for each button: instantiate button with appropriate button label,
  // add to container, and register listener
  for ( int i = 0; i < game.getSide( ); i++ )
  {
   for ( int j = 0; j < game.getSide( ); j++ )
   {
     squares[i][j] = new JButton( game.getTiles( ) [i][j] );
     contents.add( squares[i][j] );
     squares[i][j].addActionListener( bh );
   }
  }

  setSize( 300, 300 );
  setVisible( true );
 }

 private void update( int row, int col )
 {
```

```
  for ( int i = 0; i < game.getSide( ); i++ )
  {
   for ( int j = 0; j < game.getSide( ); j++ )
   {
     squares[i][j].setText( game.getTiles( ) [i][j] );
   }
  }

  if ( game.won( ) )
  {
    JOptionPane.showMessageDialog( TilePuzzleClient.this,
             "Congratulations! You won!\nSetting up new game" );
    Random random = new Random( );
    int sideOfPuzzle = 3 + random.nextInt( 4 );
    game.setUpGame( sideOfPuzzle );
    setUpGameGUI( );
  }
 }

 private class ButtonHandler implements ActionListener
 {
  public void actionPerformed( ActionEvent ae )
  {
   for ( int i = 0; i < game.getSide( );  i++ )
   {
    for ( int j = 0; j < game.getSide( ); j++ )
    {
      if ( ae.getSource( ) == squares[i][j] )
      {
        if ( game.tryToPlay( i, j ) )
           update( i, j );
        return;
      }
    }
   }
  }
 }

 public static void main( String [ ] args )
 {
  TilePuzzleClient myGame = new TilePuzzleClient(  3  );
  myGame.setDefaultCloseOperation( JFrame.EXIT_ON_CLOSE );
 }
}
```

EXAMPLE 12.18 Setting *GridLayout* Dynamically in the Tile Puzzle Game

12.14 Layout Managers: *BorderLayout*

A *BorderLayout* organizes a container into five areas: north, south, west, east, and center, with each area holding at most one component. Thus, for each area, you can add one component or no component. The size of each area expands or contracts depending on the size of the component in that area, the sizes of the components in the other areas, and whether the other areas contain a component. Figure 12.21 shows the areas in a sample border layout.

In contrast to the *FlowLayout* and *GridLayout* layout managers, the order in which we add components to a *BorderLayout* is not important. We use a second argument in the *add* method to specify the area in which to place the component. This *add* method of the *Container* class has the API shown in Table 12.23.

Figure 12.21
***BorderLayout* Areas**

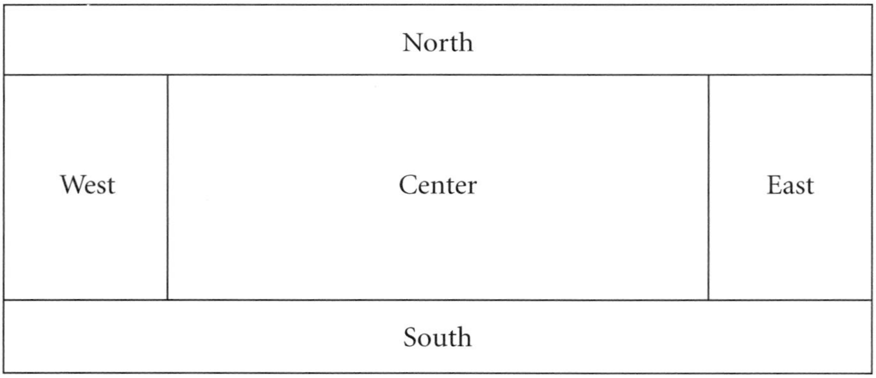

TABLE 12.23 The *Container add* Method for Using a *BorderLayout*

Return value	Method name and argument list
`void`	`add( Component c, Object borderlayoutArea )` adds the component *c* to the container. The area defined by *borderlayoutArea* can be specified using any of the following *static String* constants in the *BorderLayout* class: *NORTH, SOUTH, EAST, WEST, CENTER*.

TABLE 12.24 *BorderLayout* Constructors

Constructors	
Class	**Constructor**
`BorderLayout`	`BorderLayout( )` creates a new border layout with no gaps between components.
`BorderLayout`	`BorderLayout( int hGap, int vGap )` creates a border layout with a horizontal gap of *hGap* pixels between components and a vertical gap of *vGap* pixels between components. Unlike *GridLayout*, horizontal gaps are not placed at the left and right edges, and vertical gaps are not placed at the top and bottom edges.

Two *BorderLayout* constructors are shown in Table 12.24. The *BorderLayout* is the default layout for a *JFrame* class, so if we want to use a border layout for our GUI application, we do not need to instantiate a new layout manager.

Example 12.20 uses a *BorderLayout* to illustrate bidding order in the card game of Bridge. There are four players: North, East, South, and West. Players take turns bidding in clockwise order, starting with the dealer. In this example, we assume the player sitting in the North position is the dealer, so North will bid first. A bid consists of a level and a suit, with the lowest bid being 1 Club and the highest bid being 7 No trump. Each new bid must be higher than the previous bid, that is, a new bid must name a higher-ranked suit at the same level, or any suit at a higher level. Suits are ranked in the following ascending order: Clubs, Diamonds, Hearts, Spades, and No trump. Thus, if the current bid is 3 Hearts, the next possible bids are, in order, 3 Spades, 3 No trump, 4 Clubs, 4 Diamonds, 4 Hearts, and so on. We will use a window managed by a *BorderLayout* manager to simulate sequential bids by our four Bridge players. At any point, a player can "pass" or "double" the previous bid, but for simplicity and to illustrate bidding order only, we do not take these bids into account.

Example 12.19 shows the class encapsulating the functionality of Bridge bidding.

The *String* arrays *suitNames* and *players*, the *int* instance variables *dealer*, *bidder*, *level*, and *suit*, declared and initialized at lines 7–17, will help us keep track of the bidding and enforce the bidding order. The *bidder* instance variable represents the next bidder: its value is used as an index into the *players* array to represent North, East, South, and West, respectively. Similarly, *suit* will be used as an index into the *suitNames* array. The *level* instance variable will store a value between 1 and 7, which are the valid levels of bidding in Bridge. The first legal bid in Bridge is 1 Club so we have initialized *level* to 1 and *suit* to 0.

The method *getPlayer* (lines 32–39), given a parameter representing an index, returns the corresponding player, *getBidder* (lines 41–47) returns the current bidder, and *isBiddingAllowed* (lines 49–55) returns *true* if the bidding level is between 1 and 7 and *false* if it is not.

The method *nextBid* (lines 57–81) returns the current bid and sets up the next bid. After checking that the bidding can continue (line 63), we define the current bid at lines 65–69, and we set up the values for the next bid (lines 71–75). We increment *bidder*, using the modulus operator to cycle through the valid indexes of the *players* array. We also increment *suit*, cycling through the possible indexes for the *suitNames* array. Whenever the next suit index is 0, we increment *level*.

```
1 /** BridgeBidding class
2 *    Anderson, Franceschi
3 */
4
5 public class BridgeBidding
6 {
7   private String [ ] suitNames =
8    { "Club", "Diamond", "Heart", "Spade", "No trump" };
9   private String [ ] players =
10   { "North", "East", "South", "West" };
11  // next bidder
12  private int bidder;           // the next bidder
13  private int dealer;           // the dealer
14
15  // bidding will open at 1 Club
16  private int level = 1;              // current level
17  private int suit = 0;               // index of current suit
18
19  /** Constructor
```

```
* @param newDealer  dealer
*/
public BridgeBidding( int newDealer )
{
 if ( newDealer >= 0 && newDealer < players.length )
  dealer = newDealer;
 else
  dealer = 0;
 players[dealer] += " - Dealer";
 bidder = dealer;
}

/** getPlayer
* @param player  the index of the player
* @return a String, the name of the player
*/
public String getPlayer( int player )
{
 return players[player];
}

/** getBidder
* @return bidder
*/
public int getBidder( )
{
 return bidder;
}

/** isBiddingAllowed
* @return true if level is strictly less than 8, false otherwise
*/
public boolean isBiddingAllowed( )
{
 return ( level >= 1 && level <= 7 );
}

/** nextBid
* Returns current bid and sets up next bid
* @return a String, the current bid
*/
public String nextBid( )
{
 if ( isBiddingAllowed( ) )
 {
```

```
    String currentBid = level + " " + suitNames[suit];

    // add an "s" if level > 1 and suit is not No trump
    if ( level > 1 && suit != suitNames.length - 1 )
     currentBid += "s";

    // set up next bid
    bidder = ( bidder + 1 ) % players.length;
    suit = ( suit + 1 ) % suitNames.length;
    if ( suit == 0 )
     level++;

    return currentBid;
   }
   else
    return "Pass";
  }
}
```

EXAMPLE 12.19 *BridgeBidding* Class

In Example 12.20, we declare four buttons representing the players (line 12); we will place one button each in the north, east, south, and west areas of the border layout. We use the label *bid*, declared at line 13, to display the current bid in the center area. The *BridgeBidding* instance variable *bidding*, declared at line 15, represents the bidding sequence that we will display inside the window.

At line 23, we set the layout of the content pane to be a *BorderLayout.* Note that this statement is optional, because *BorderLayout* is the default layout manager for a subclass of the *JFrame* class.

When instantiating *bid* at lines 31–32, we use an overloaded *JLabel* constructor. We use the *static int* constant *CENTER* of the *SwingConstants* interface to center the text of the label within the component. By default, the text for a *JLabel* is left-aligned. Because the text on a *JButton* is centered by default, we can simply use the constructor with one argument when we instantiate the *JButtons* for the players.

We add the four buttons and the label to the content pane in the appropriate areas at lines 34–39. The order in which we add the components is not important because we specify a border layout area as the second argument of the *add* method.

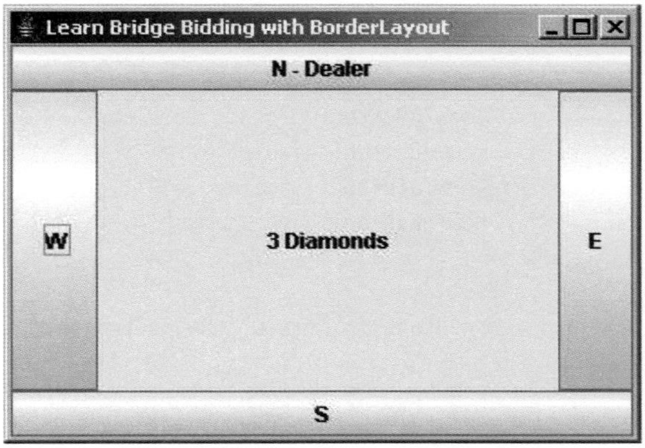

Figure 12.22
Running Example 12.20

In our *ButtonHandler* event handler (lines 51–69), the *actionPerformed* method first determines the button that fired the event, translating the source button to an integer value between 0 and 3. That value is assigned to the local variable *source*. We want to allow only bids that are legal and only from the player whose turn it is. If *source* is the bidder and bidding is allowed (lines 65–66), we display a new bid (line 67); otherwise, we do not.

Figure 12.22 shows the Bridge bidding example running.

```
1 /** Using BorderLayout to display Bridge bidding
2 *   Anderson, Franceschi
3 */
4
5 import javax.swing.*;
6 import java.awt.*;
7 import java.awt.event.*;
8
9 public class BridgeBiddingClient extends JFrame
10 {
11  private Container contents;
12  private JButton north, east, south, west;
13  private JLabel bid;
14
15  private BridgeBidding bidding;
16
17  public BridgeBiddingClient( )
18  {
19   super( "Learn Bridge Bidding with BorderLayout" );
20   bidding = new BridgeBidding( 0 );
21
22   contents = getContentPane( );
```

```
contents.setLayout( new BorderLayout( ) );  // optional

// instantiate button objects
north = new JButton( bidding.getPlayer( 0 ) );
east = new JButton( bidding.getPlayer( 1 ) );
south = new JButton( bidding.getPlayer( 2 ) );
west = new JButton( bidding.getPlayer( 3 ) );

// instantiate JLabel
bid = new JLabel( "No bid", SwingConstants.CENTER );

// order of adding components not important
contents.add( north, BorderLayout.NORTH );
contents.add( east, BorderLayout.EAST );
contents.add( south, BorderLayout.SOUTH );
contents.add( west, BorderLayout.WEST );
contents.add( bid, BorderLayout.CENTER );

ButtonHandler bh = new ButtonHandler( );
north.addActionListener( bh );
east.addActionListener( bh );
south.addActionListener( bh );
west.addActionListener( bh );

setSize( 350, 250 );
setVisible( true );
}

private class ButtonHandler implements ActionListener
{
 public void actionPerformed( ActionEvent ae )
 {
  int source = 0;
  if ( ae.getSource( ) == north )
    source = 0;
  else if ( ae.getSource( ) == east )
    source = 1;
  else if ( ae.getSource( ) == south )
    source = 2;
  else if ( ae.getSource( ) == west )
    source = 3;

  if ( source == bidding.getBidder( )
             && bidding.isBiddingAllowed( ) )
   bid.setText( bidding.nextBid( ) ); // set label to current bid
```

```
  }
 }

 public static void main( String [ ] args )
 {
  BridgeBiddingClient bbGui = new BridgeBiddingClient( );
  bbGui.setDefaultCloseOperation( JFrame.EXIT_ON_CLOSE );
 }
}
```

EXAMPLE 12.20 Using *BorderLayout* to Illustrate Bridge Bidding Order

12.15 Using Panels to Nest Components

Components can be nested. Indeed, since the *JComponent* class is a subclass of the *Container* class, a *JComponent* object is a *Container* object as well. As such, it can contain other components. We can use this feature to achieve more precise layouts.

The *JPanel* class is a general-purpose container, or a **panel**, and is typically used to hold other components. When nesting components, we usually place several components into a panel, and place the panel into the content pane of the current *JFrame*. Each panel has its own layout manager, which can vary from panel to panel, and the content pane for the *JFrame* application has its own layout manager, which can be different from any of the panels. We can even have multiple levels of nesting, as needed.

Figure 12.23 shows a window that uses multiple panels, along with the underlying layout of the window.

The content pane of the window is using a *GridLayout* with one row and two columns. In the first column, we have defined a panel managed by a *GridLayout* having five rows and one column. We placed five buttons into the panel, then placed the panel into the first column of the content pane grid. In the second column, we have defined a panel managed by a *BorderLayout*. We put five components into the panel and added the panel as the second column of the content pane grid. Thus, we have two panels, each of which has a different layout manager, and these two panels are added to the content pane, which is itself managed by a *GridLayout*.

In a Bridge game, depending on the bidding, one of the four players will be the "dummy" and will not participate in the play for the current hand. We

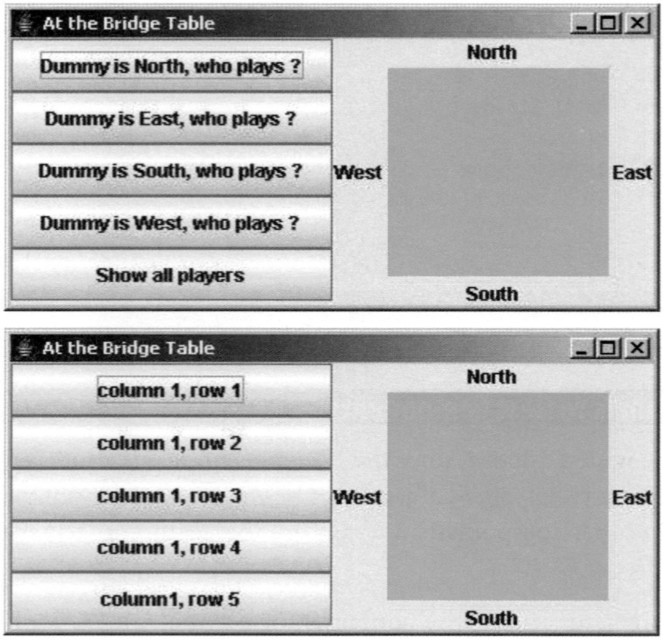

Figure 12.23
Sample Window and Underlying Layout

illustrate this concept in Example 12.21. The panel in column two of the content pane grid uses a *BorderLayout* layout manager to show four players around the Bridge table. The panel in column one of the content pane grid uses a *GridLayout* to provide five buttons.

If the user clicks on one of the first four buttons, we make the corresponding player disappear from the Bridge table (in column 2). If the user clicks the fifth button, we make all players visible. Thus, the actions we want to perform are different depending on whether the user clicks on one of the first four buttons or the "Show all players" button. So it makes sense to write two event handlers: one that listens to the first four buttons, and a second event handler that listens to the fifth button only.

In Example 12.21, we first define the layout manager for our content pane to be a *GridLayout* with one row and two columns (line 34). Then we set up the panel for the first column at lines 37–38, by instantiating the *JPanel* named *questionPanel* and setting the layout manager as a *GridLayout* with five rows and one column. At lines 40–48, we instantiate the event handler for the question buttons, instantiate the buttons, register the listener on the buttons, and add the buttons to the *questionPanel* in rows 1–4.

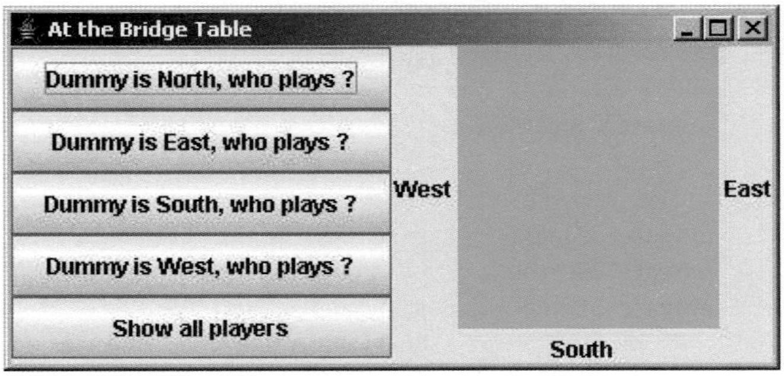

Figure 12.24
User Clicked Top Button

In lines 50–54, we set up the fifth row in this grid by instantiating the *reset* button, instantiating our separate listener for this button, and adding the button in the fifth row.

In lines 56–73, we set up column two, by instantiating the *JPanel gamePanel* and setting its layout to a *BorderLayout* with horizontal and vertical gaps of 3 pixels between elements. At lines 69–73, we add one component to each area of the *BorderLayout*, representing the four players and the Bridge table.

Finally, we add the two panels to the content pane of the application window at lines 75–77.

The *QuestionButtonHandler* event handler (lines 83–96) checks which question button was clicked and sets the visibility of the appropriate label in the *gamePanel* to *false*. The other three labels are made visible, in case they were hidden as a result of a previous button click.

The second event handler, *ResetButtonHandler* (lines 98–106), does not need to check the source of the event because the listener is registered only on the *reset* button component. Its job is to make every player's button visible.

When the application begins, we display the window shown in Figure 12.23. Figure 12.24 shows the window after the user has clicked on the top button ("Dummy is North, who plays?").

```
1  /** Nesting components using layout managers
2  *   Anderson, Franceschi
3  */
4
5  import javax.swing.*;
6  import java.awt.*;
7  import java.awt.event.*;
```

```java

public class BridgeRules extends JFrame
{
 private Container contents;

 // 1st row, column 1
 private JPanel questionPanel;
 private JButton [ ] questionButtons;
 private String [ ] questionNames = {
            "Dummy is North, who plays ?",
            "Dummy is East, who plays ?",
            "Dummy is South, who plays ?",
            "Dummy is West, who plays ?" };

 private JButton reset;

 // 1st row, column 2
 private JPanel gamePanel;
 private JLabel gameTable;
 private JLabel [ ] gameLabels;

 public BridgeRules( )
 {
  super( "At the Bridge Table" );

  contents = getContentPane( );
  contents.setLayout( new GridLayout( 1, 2 ) );

  // 1st row, col 1: question buttons and reset button
  questionPanel = new JPanel( );
  questionPanel.setLayout( new GridLayout( 5, 1 ) );

  QuestionButtonHandler qbh = new QuestionButtonHandler( );
  questionButtons = new JButton[questionNames.length];

  for ( int i = 0; i < questionNames.length; i ++ )
  {
     questionButtons[i] = new JButton( questionNames[i] );
     questionButtons[i].addActionListener( qbh );
     questionPanel.add( questionButtons[i] );
  }

  reset = new JButton( "Show all players" );
  ResetButtonHandler rbh = new ResetButtonHandler( );
```

```
        reset.addActionListener( rbh );

        questionPanel.add( reset );

        // 1st row, column 2: gamePanel contains the players and table
        gamePanel = new JPanel( );
        gamePanel.setLayout( new BorderLayout( 3, 3 ) );
        gameLabels = new JLabel[4];
        gameLabels[0] = new JLabel( "North", SwingConstants.CENTER );
        gameLabels[1] = new JLabel( "East", SwingConstants.CENTER );
        gameLabels[2] = new JLabel( "South", SwingConstants.CENTER );
        gameLabels[3] = new JLabel( "West", SwingConstants.CENTER );

        gameTable = new JLabel( );
        gameTable.setBackground( Color.GREEN );
        gameTable.setOpaque( true );

        gamePanel.add( gameLabels[0], BorderLayout.NORTH );
        gamePanel.add( gameLabels[1], BorderLayout.EAST );
        gamePanel.add( gameLabels[2], BorderLayout.SOUTH );
        gamePanel.add( gameLabels[3], BorderLayout.WEST );
        gamePanel.add( gameTable, BorderLayout.CENTER );

        // add panels to content pane
        contents.add( questionPanel );
        contents.add( gamePanel );

        setSize( 410, 200 );
        setVisible( true );
    }

    private class QuestionButtonHandler
                               implements ActionListener
    {
        public void actionPerformed( ActionEvent ae )
        {
            for ( int i = 0; i < questionButtons.length; i++ )
            {
                if ( ae.getSource( ) == questionButtons[i] )
                    gameLabels[i].setVisible( false );
                else
                    gameLabels[i].setVisible( true );
            }
        }
    }
```

```

private class ResetButtonHandler
                             implements ActionListener
{
  public void actionPerformed( ActionEvent ae )
  {
     for ( int i = 0; i < gameLabels.length; i++ )
       gameLabels[i].setVisible( true );
  }
}

public static void main( String [ ] args )
{
  BridgeRules myNestedLayout = new BridgeRules( );
  myNestedLayout.setDefaultCloseOperation( JFrame.EXIT_ON_CLOSE );
}
}
```

EXAMPLE 12.21 More Bridge Rules with Nested Components

Skill Practice
with these end-of-chapter questions

12.18.1 Multiple Choice Exercises

Questions 9, 10, 11, 12, 13, 14, 15

12.18.2 Reading and Understanding Code

Question 17

12.18.3 Fill In the Code

Questions 30, 33, 34, 35, 36, 37, 38, 39, 40, 41

12.18.5 Debugging Area

Question 48

12.18.6 Write a Short Program

Questions 58, 59, 60, 61, 62

12.18.8 Technical Writing

Question 73

CODE IN ACTION

On the CD-ROM included with this book, you will find a Flash movie with a step-by-step illustration of working with layout managers. Click on the link for Chapter 12 to start the movie.

12.16 Programming Activity 2: Working with Layout Managers

In this Programming Activity, you will complete the implementation of a version of the Tile Puzzle game (Examples 12.17 and 12.18) using a more complex GUI. As it stands, the application compiles and runs, but is missing a lot of code. Figure 12.25 shows the window that will open when you run the application without adding your code.

Once you have completed the five tasks of this Programming Activity, you should see the window in Figure 12.26 when you run your program and click on the "3-by-3" button.

When you click on one of the buttons labeled "3-by-3", "4-by-4", or "5-by-5", the tile puzzle will reset to a grid of that size.

In addition to the *TilePuzzle* class, we provide you with a prewritten *Game* class, which encapsulates a Tile Puzzle game in a panel. We have implemented the *Game* class as a *JPanel* component, so you can add it to your window as you would any other panel. It has two important methods,

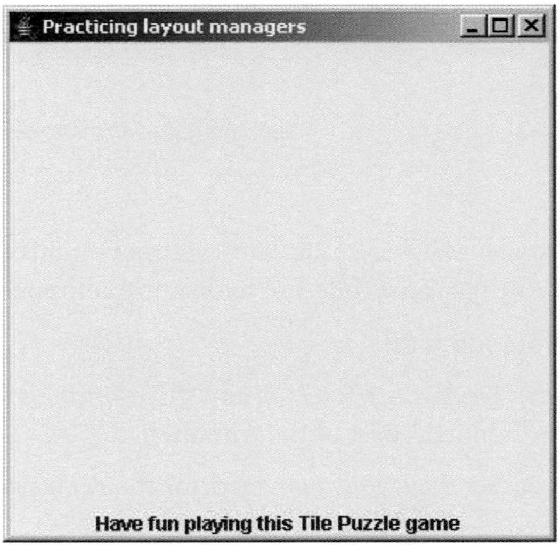

Figure 12.25
The Starting Window When Running the Prewritten Code

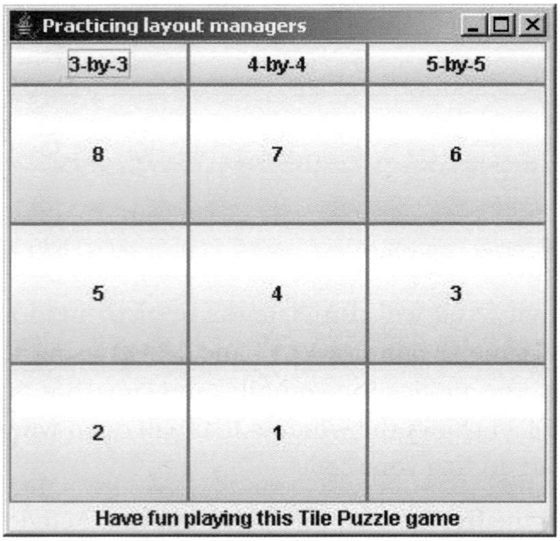

Figure 12.26
The Starting Window When the Activity Is Completed

TABLE 12.25 The *Game* Class API

Game Class API	
Constructor	
Class	**Constructor**
`Game`	`Game( int nSides )` instantiates a tile puzzle as an *nSides*-by-*nSides* grid
Method	
Return value	**Method name and argument list**
`void`	`setUpGame( int nSides )` resets the grid as an *nSides*-by-*nSides* grid

shown in Table 12.25. Thus, your job in this Programming Activity is not to write the game code, but to organize components in a window.

Your job is to:

1. Declare a *JPanel top* and three *JButtons* that will be added to the "north" part of the window.
2. Set the layout managers for the *game* panel and the *top* panel.

3. Add the *top* and the *game* panels.
4. Code an appropriate *private* listener class.
5. Instantiate the listener and register it on the appropriate components.

Instructions

Copy the source files in the Programming Activity 2 directory for this chapter to a directory on your computer.

1. Write the code to declare the needed instance variables. Load the *NestedLayoutPractice.java* source file and search for five asterisks in a row (*****). This will position you to the instance variables declaration.

```
// ***** Task 1: declare a JPanel named top
// also declare three JButton instance variables
// that will be added to the JPanel top
// these buttons will determine the grid size of the game:
//  3-by-3, 4-by-4, or 5-by-5

// task 1 ends here
```

2. Next, write the code to set the layout manager of the window and add the component *game* in the center of the window. In the *NestedLayoutPractice.java* source file, search again for five asterisks in a row (*****). This will position you inside the constructor.

```
// ***** Task 2: student code starts here
// instantiate the BorderLayout manager bl

// set the layout manager of the content pane contents to bl

game = new Game( 3 );  // instantiating the Game object
// add game to the center of the content pane

// task 2 ends here
```

3. Next, write the code to instantiate the *JPanel top* component, set its layout, instantiate the buttons from task 1, add them to *top*, and finally add *top* as the north component for our overall window. In the

NestedLayoutPractice.java source file, search again for five asterisks in a row (*****). This will position you inside the constructor.

```
// ***** Task 3: Student code restarts here

// instantiate the JPanel component named top

// set the layout of top to a 1-by-3 grid

// instantiate the JButtons that determine the grid size

// add the buttons to JPanel top

// add JPanel top to the content pane as its north component

// task 3 ends here
```

4. Next, write the code for the *private* inner class that implements the appropriate listener. In the *NestedLayoutPractice.java* source file, search again for five asterisks in a row (*****). This will position you between the constructor and the *main* method.

```
// ***** Task 4: Student code restarts here
// create a private inner class that implements ActionListener
// your method should identify which of the 3 buttons was the
//   source of the event.
// depending on which button was pressed,
//   call the setUpGame method of the Game class
//   with arguments 3, 4, or 5
// the API of that method is:
//   public void setUpGame( int nSides )

// task 4 ends here
```

5. Next, write the code to declare and instantiate a listener, and register it on the appropriate components. In the *NestedLayoutPractice.java* source file, search again for five asterisks in a row (*****). This will position you inside the constructor.

```
// ***** Task 5: Student code restarts here
// Note: search for and complete Task 4 before performing this task
// declare and instantiate an ActionListener
```

```
// register the listener on the 3 buttons
//   that you declared in Task 1

// task 5 ends here
```

After completing each task, compile your code.

When you have finished writing all the code, compile the source code and run the *NestedLayoutPractice* application. Try clicking on the three buttons that you added.

DISCUSSION QUESTIONS

1. Identify the various layout managers you used and the panels they manage.
2. Explain why the East and West areas do not show up on the window.

12.17 Chapter Summary

CHAPTER SUMMARY

- A graphical user interface allows the user to interact with an application through mouse clicks, mouse movements, the keyboard, and visual input components.
- The *JFrame* class provides the capabilities for creating a window that will hold GUI components.
- A constructor in a GUI application should call the constructor of the *JFrame* superclass, get an object reference to the content pane, set the layout manager, instantiate each component and add it to the window, set the size of the window, and make the window visible.
- A component is an object having a graphical representation and that displays information, collects data from the user, or allows the user to initiate program functions.
- Java provides a set of GUI components in the *javax.swing* package.
- A *JLabel* component can display text or an image.
- The *FlowLayout* layout manager arranges components in rows from left to right, starting a new row whenever a newly added component does not fit into the current row. If the window is resized, the components are rearranged.

CHAPTER SUMMARY

- Event-driven programming consists of setting up interactive components and event handlers and responding to events generated by user interaction with the components.
- To allow a user to interact with a component, we need to instantiate an object of that class, write an event handler class (called a listener), instantiate an object of the event handler class, and register that listener on the component.
- Event handlers implement a listener interface in the *java.awt.event* or the *javax.swing.event* package. The listener methods receive as a parameter an event object, which encapsulates information about the user interaction. The *getSource* method can be called to determine which component fired the event.
- Event handlers usually are instantiated as *private* inner classes so the handler will have access to the components of the application.
- A *JTextField* component displays a text field for user input. A *JPasswordField* component accepts user input without echoing the characters typed. A *JTextArea* component displays a multiple-line text input area. Events fired by these three components generate an *ActionEvent* object and require an *ActionListener* to handle the event.
- A *JButton* component implements a command button used for initiating operations. Clicking on a *JButton* component generates an *ActionEvent* object and requires an *ActionListener* to handle the event.
- *JRadioButton* components allow the user to select one of several mutually exclusive options. Clicking on any radio button deselects any previously selected option. *JRadioButton* components need to be added to a *ButtonGroup*, which manages the mutual exclusivity of the buttons. *JCheckBox* components are toggle buttons; successive clicks on a *JCheckBox* component alternately select and deselect that option. Events fired by these components generate an *ItemEvent* object and use an *ItemListener* to handle the event.
- The *JList* class encapsulates a list from which the user can select one or multiple items. Selecting an item from a *JList* component generates a *ListSelectionEvent* object and requires a *ListSelectionListener* to handle the event.

- A *JComboBox* implements a drop-down list. The user can select only one item from the list. A *JComboBox* fires an *ItemEvent*, so the event handler must implement the *ItemListener* interface.
- Adapter classes, which *implement* an interface and provide empty bodies for each method, are useful when only one of multiple component actions is processed.
- *MouseAdapter* and *MouseMotionAdapter* are adapter classes for the *MouseListener* and *MouseMotionListener* interfaces, respectively.
- The *GridLayout* layout manager arranges components into equally sized cells in rows and columns.
- A *BorderLayout* layout manager, which is the default layout manager for the *JFrame* class, organizes a container into five areas: north, south, west, east, and center, with each area holding at most one component. The size of each area expands or contracts depending on the size of the component in that area, the sizes of the components in the other areas, and whether the other areas contain a component.
- A *JPanel* component can be used as a general-purpose container. To create a complex arrangement of GUI components, we place several components into a panel and place the panel into the content pane of the current *JFrame*. Each panel and the content pane has its own layout manager.

12.18 Exercises, Problems, and Projects

12.18.1 Multiple Choice Exercises

1. An example of a GUI component class is
   - ❑ *ActionEvent*
   - ❑ *actionPerformed*
   - ❑ *JTextField*
   - ❑ *ActionListener*
2. What are the primary uses of GUI components? (Check all that apply.)
   - ❑ to display information
   - ❑ to facilitate the coding of methods

- ❑ to let the user control the program
- ❑ to collect information from the user

3. In what package do you find the *JButton*, *JTextField*, and *JComboBox* classes?
   - ❑ *javax.swing*
   - ❑ *java.swing*
   - ❑ *javax.awt*
   - ❑ *java.awt*
   - ❑ *java.io*
4. Components can be hidden.
   - ❑ true
   - ❑ false
5. In order to process an event when the user clicks on a button, what should the programmer do? (Check all that apply.)
   - ❑ Code a class that implements the *ActionListener* interface.
   - ❑ Declare and instantiate an object reference (a listener) of the class above.
   - ❑ Call the *actionPerformed* method.
   - ❑ Register the listener on the button.
6. Assuming everything has been coded correctly, what happens when the user clicks a button?
   - ❑ The *actionPerformed* method executes.
   - ❑ The *JButton* constructor executes.
   - ❑ The *main* method executes.
7. If you visit Sun Microsystems' Java website (*www.java.sun.com*) and look at the *KeyListener* interface, you will find that it has three methods: *keyPressed*, *keyTyped*, and *keyReleased*. We want to build a class that implements *KeyListener*. Which one of the three methods should we implement?
   - ❑ *keyPressed* only
   - ❑ *keyReleased* only

- ❑ *keyTyped* only
- ❑ All three methods

8. You are designing a GUI with three buttons; a different action will be taken depending on which button the user clicks. You want to code only one *private* class implementing the *ActionListener* interface. Inside the *actionPerformed* method, which method do you call to determine which button was clicked?
   - ❑ *getButton*
   - ❑ *getSource*
   - ❑ *getOrigin*
9. A class extending the *JFrame* class can also implement a listener interface.
   - ❑ true
   - ❑ false
10. *NewLayout* is a layout manager.
    - ❑ true
    - ❑ false
11. In the following code:

    ```
    GridLayout gl = new GridLayout( 6, 4 );
    ```

    what do the arguments 6 and 4 specify?
    - ❑ 6 refers to the number of columns and 4 to the number of rows.
    - ❑ 4 refers to the number of columns and 6 to the number of rows.
    - ❑ There will be 6 components organized in 4 different areas.
    - ❑ There will be 4 components organized in 6 different areas.
12. What is the maximum number of components that a *BorderLayout* can manage?
    - ❑ 2
    - ❑ 3
    - ❑ 4
    - ❑ 5
    - ❑ 6

13. In the following code:

```
BorderLayout bl = new BorderLayout( 7, 3 );
```

what do the arguments 7 and 3 represent?

- ❑ the horizontal and vertical gaps between the five areas of the component
- ❑ the vertical and horizontal gaps between the five areas of the component
- ❑ the number of rows and columns in the component
- ❑ the number of columns and rows in the component

14. In the following code:

```
contents.add( button, BorderLayout.NORTH );
```

what is the data type of the second argument?

- ❑ *int*
- ❑ *String*
- ❑ *BorderLayout*
- ❑ *NORTH*

15. Components can be nested.

- ❑ true
- ❑ false

12.18.2 Reading and Understanding Code

For Questions 16 to 21, consider the following code:

```
import javax.swing.*;
import java.awt.*;
import java.awt.event.*;

public class Game extends JFrame
{
 private JButton b1, b2, b3, b4;
 private Container contents;
 public Game( )
 {
```

```
  super( "Play this game" );
  contents = getContentPane( );
  contents.setLayout( new GridLayout( 2, 2 ) );
  b1 = new JButton( "Button 1" );
  b2 = new JButton( "Button 2" );
  b3 = new JButton( "Button 3" );
  b4 = new JButton( "Button 4" );
  contents.add( b1 );
  contents.add( b2 );
  contents.add( b3 );

  MyHandler mh = new MyHandler( );
  b1.addActionListener( mh );
  b2.addActionListener( mh );

  setSize( 400, 400 );
  setVisible( true );
 }

 private class MyHandler implements ActionListener
 {
  public void actionPerformed( ActionEvent ae )
  {
   System.out.println( "Hello" );
   if ( ae.getSource( ) == b2 )
      System.out.println( "Hello again" );
  }
 }
 public static void main( String [ ] args )
 {
  Game g = new Game( );
  g.setDefaultCloseOperation( JFrame.EXIT_ON_CLOSE );
 }
}
```

16. How many buttons will be displayed in the window?
17. How are the buttons organized in the window?
18. What is the text in the title bar of the window?
19. What happens when the user clicks on the button that says "Button 1"?
20. What happens when the user clicks on the button that says "Button 2"?
21. What happens when the user clicks on the button that says "Button 3"?

For Questions 22 to 26, consider the following code:

```
import javax.swing.*;
import java.awt.*;
import java.awt.event.*;

public class Game extends JFrame
{
 private JCheckBox c1, c2, c3;
 private int value1, value2, value3;
 private Container contents;
 public Game( )
 {
  super( "Play this game" );
  contents = getContentPane( );
  contents.setLayout( new FlowLayout( ) );
  c1 = new JCheckBox( "Choice 1" );
  c2 = new JCheckBox( "Choice 2" );
  c3 = new JCheckBox( "Choice 3" );
  contents.add( c1 );
  contents.add( c2 );
  contents.add( c3 );
  MyHandler mh = new MyHandler( );
  c1.addItemListener( mh );
  c2.addItemListener( mh );
  c3.addItemListener( mh );

  setSize( 400, 400 );
  setVisible( true );
 }

 private class MyHandler implements ItemListener
 {
  public void itemStateChanged( ItemEvent ie )
  {
    if ( ie.getSource( ) == c1 )
    {
      if ( ie.getStateChange( ) == ItemEvent.SELECTED )
        value1 = 1;
      else
        value1 = 0;
    }
    else if ( ie.getSource( ) == c2 )
    {
```

```
        if ( ie.getStateChange( ) == ItemEvent.SELECTED )
          value2 = 2;
        else
          value2 = 0;
      }
      else if ( ie.getSource( ) == c3 )
      {
        if ( ie.getStateChange( ) == ItemEvent.SELECTED )
          value3 = 4;
        else
          value3 = 0;
      }
      System.out.println( ( value1 + value2 + value3 ) );
    }
  }
  public static void main( String [ ] args )
  {
    Game g = new Game( );
    g.setDefaultCloseOperation( JFrame.EXIT_ON_CLOSE );
  }
}
```

22. How many checkboxes will be displayed in the window?
23. How are the checkboxes organized in the window?
24. What happens when the user checks "Choice 3" only?
25. What happens when the user checks "Choice 1" and "Choice 3"?
26. What happens when the user checks all the checkboxes?

12.18.3 Fill In the Code

For Questions 27 to 31, consider the following class:

```
import javax.swing.*;
import java.awt.*;
import java.awt.event.*;

public class A extends JFrame
{
 private Container c;
 private JButton b;
 private JTextField tf;

}
```

27. Inside the constructor, this code assigns the content pane of the frame to the *Container c*:

```
// your code goes here
```

28. Inside the constructor, this code instantiates the button *b* with the text "Button":

```
// your code goes here
```

29. Inside the constructor, this code instantiates the text field *tf*; after instantiation, the text field should be emtpy, but have space for 10 characters:

```
// your code goes here
```

30. Inside the constructor, and assuming that *c* has been assigned the content pane, this code sets the layout manager of the content pane to a 2-by-1 grid layout manager:

```
// your code goes here
```

31. Inside the *actionPerformed* method of a *private* inner class implementing the *ActionListener* interface, this code changes the text of *tf* to "Button clicked" if the button *b* was clicked; otherwise, nothing happens:

```
public void actionPerformed( ActionEvent ae )
{
  // your code goes here

}
```

32. Inside the constructor, this code registers the listener *mh* on the button *b*:

```
// the MyHandler class is a private class implementing
//  ActionListener
MyHandler mh = new MyHandler( );
// your code goes here
```

For Questions 33 to 41, consider the following class:

```
import javax.swing.*;
import java.awt.*;

public class B extends JFrame
{
 private Container c;
 private JPanel p1;
```

```
   private JPanel p2;
   private JButton [ ] buttons;          // length 12
   private JTextField [ ] textfields;    // length 10
   private JLabel label1;
   private JLabel label2;

}
```

Also, assume that all the instance variables have been instantiated and you are coding inside the constructor.

33. This code sets the layout manager of the content pane to be a border layout manager.

```
// your code goes here
```

34. This code adds *label1* to the north area of the window.

```
// your code goes here
```

35. This code adds *label2* to the east area of the window.

```
// your code goes here
```

36. This code sets the layout manager of the panel *p1* to be a 3-by-4 grid layout manager.

```
// your code goes here
```

37. This code places all the buttons of the array buttons inside the panel *p1*.

```
// your code goes here
```

38. This code adds the panel *p1* in the center area of the window.

```
// your code goes here
```

39. This code sets the layout manager of the panel *p2* to a 5-by-2 grid with four pixels between cells, both horizontally and vertically.

```
// your code goes here
```

40. This code places all the text fields of the array *textfields* inside the panel *p2*.

```
// your code goes here
```

41. This code adds the panel *p2* in the west area of the window.

```
// your code goes here
```

12.18.4 Identifying Errors in Code

42. Where is the error in this code sequence?

```
import java.swing.*;

public class MyGame extends JFrame
{
  // some code here
}
```

43. Where is the error in this code sequence?

```
import javax.swing.*;
import java.awt.event.*;

public class MyGame extends JFrame
{
  // some code here
 private class MyHandler extends ActionListener
 {
  public void actionPerformed( ActionEvent ae )
  { }
 }
}
```

44. Where is the error in this code sequence?

```
import javax.swing.*;
import java.awt.event.*;

public class MyGame extends JFrame
{
 // some code here
 private class MyHandler implements ItemListener
 {
  public void actionPerformed( ActionEvent ae )
  { }
 }
}
```

45. Where is the error in this code sequence?

```
import javax.swing.*;
import java.awt.event.*;

public class MyGame extends JFrame
```

```
{
 // some code here
 private class MyHandler implements ItemListener
 {
  public void itemStateChanged( ActionEvent e )
  { }
 }
}
```

12.18.5 Debugging Area—Using Messages from the Java Compiler and Java JVM

46. You coded the following in the file *MyGame.java:*

```
import javax.swing.*;
import java.awt.*;
import java.awt.event.*;

public class MyGame extends JFrame
{
 private Container c;
 private JLabel l;

 public MyGame( )
 {
  super( "My Game" );
  c = getContentPane( );
  c.setLayout( new FlowLayout( ) );
  c.add( l );  // Line 15
 }

 public static void main( String [ ] args )
 {
  MyGame mg = new MyGame( ); // Line 20
 }
}
```

The code compiles, but at run time, you get the following output:

```
Exception in thread "main" java.lang.NullPointerException
        at java.awt.Container.addImpl(Container.java:1027)
        at java.awt.Container.add(Container.java:352)
        at MyGame.<init>(MyGame.java:15)
        at MyGame.main(MyGame.java:20)
```

Explain what the problem is and how to fix it.

47. You coded the following in the file *MyGame.java*

```
import javax.swing.*;

public class MyGame extends JFrame
{
    public MyGame( )
    {
     super( "My Game" );
     setSize( 400, 400 );
    }

    public static void main( String [ ] args )
    {
     MyGame mg = new MyGame( );
    }
}
```

The code compiles, but at run time, you cannot see the window and the code terminates.

Explain what the problem is and how to fix it.

48. You coded the following in the file *MyGame.java*

```
import javax.swing.*;
import java.awt.*;

public class MyGame extends JFrame
{
 private Container c;
 private JTextField tf;

 public MyGame( )
 {
  super( "My Game" );
  c = getContentPane( );
  tf = new JTextField( "Hello" );
  c.add( tf, NORTH );
  setSize( 400, 400 );
  setVisible( true );
 }

 public static void main( String [ ] args )
 {
  MyGame mg = new MyGame( );
 }
}
```

When you compile your code, you get the following error:

```
MyGame.java:14: cannot find symbol
symbol  : variable NORTH
location: class MyGame
  c.add( tf, NORTH );
             ^
1 error
```

Explain what the problem is and how to fix it.

49. You coded the following in the file *MyGame.java:*

```
import javax.swing.*;
import java.awt.*;

public class MyGame extends JFrame
{
    // Some code here
    private class MyHandler implements ActionListener
    {
     public void actionPerformed( ActionEvent ae )
     { }
    }
}
```

When you compile your code, you get the following error:

```
MyGame.java:7: cannot find symbol
symbol  : class ActionListener
location: class MyGame
    private class MyHandler implements ActionListener
                                       ^
MyGame.java:9: cannot find symbol  : class ActionEvent
location: class MyGame.MyHandler
     public void actionPerformed( ActionEvent ae )
                                  ^
2 errors
```

Explain what the problem is and how to fix it.

50. You coded the following in the *MyGame.java* file:

```
import javax.swing.*;
import java.awt.*;
import java.awt.event.*;
```

```
public class MyGame extends JFrame
{
 private JButton b;
 private JTextField tf;
 private Container contents;
 public MyGame( )
 {
  super( "Play this game" );
  contents = getContentPane( );
  contents.setLayout( new GridLayout( 1, 2 ) );
  b = new JButton( "Click here" );
  tf = new JTextField( "Hello" );
  contents.add( b );
  contents.add( tf );
  setSize( 400, 400 );
  setVisible( true );
 }

 private class MyHandler implements ActionListener
 {
  public void actionPerformed( ActionEvent ae )
  {
   tf.setText( "Hi" );
  }
 }
 public static void main( String [ ] args )
 {
   MyGame g = new MyGame( );
   g.setDefaultCloseOperation( JFrame.EXIT_ON_CLOSE );
 }
}
```

The code compiles and runs. However, when you click the button, the text in the text field does not change.

Explain what the problem is and how to fix it.

12.18.6 Write a Short Program

51. Write a program that displays a text field and two buttons labeled “upper case” and “lower case”. When the user clicks on the upper case button, the text changes to upper case; when the user clicks on the lower case button, the text changes to lower case.

52. Write a program with two radio buttons and a text field. When the user clicks on one radio button, the text changes to lower case; when the user clicks on the other radio button, the text changes to upper case.

53. Write a program with two checkboxes and a text field. When no checkbox is selected, no text shows in the text field. When only the first checkbox is selected, the word "hello" shows in lower case. When only the second checkbox is selected, the word "HELLO" shows in upper case. When both checkboxes are selected, the word "HeLlO" shows (lower and upper case letters alternate).

54. Write a program with three radio buttons and a circle. (You can choose whether you draw the circle or if the circle is a label image.) When the user clicks on the first radio button, the circle becomes red. When the user clicks on the second radio button, the circle turns orange. When the user clicks on the third radio button, the circle becomes blue.

55. Write a program with three checkboxes and a circle drawn in black. Like the checkbox example in the chapter, each checkbox represents a color (red, blue, or green). Depending on the checkboxes selected, compute the resulting color as follows. If a checkbox is selected, assign the value 255 to the amount of the corresponding color. If a checkbox is not selected, assign 0 to the amount of the corresponding color. For example, if the checkboxes representing the colors red and blue are selected, the resulting color should be *Color(255, 0, 255)*. Color the circle appropriately.

56. Write a program that simulates a guessing game in a GUI program. Ask the user for a number between 1 and 6 in a text field, then roll a die randomly and tell the user if he or she won. Write the program in such a way that any invalid user input (i.e., not an integer between 1 and 6) is rejected and the user is asked again for input.

57. Write a program that simulates a guessing game in a GUI program. Generate a random number between 1 and 100; that number is hidden from the user. Ask the user for a number between 1 and 100 in a text field, then tell the user whether the number is too high, too low,

or the correct number. Let the user continue guessing until he or she guesses the correct number.

58. Write a program that displays a 5-by-5 grid of buttons, each with a different button label. When the user clicks on a button, its text is changed to "Visible".

59. Write a program that displays a 4-by-6 grid of buttons, each with some unique text. One button is the "winning" button, which your program determines randomly, inside the constructor. When the user clicks on a button, its text is changed to "No" if the button clicked is not the winning button, or to "Won" if the button clicked is the winning button.

60. Same as Exercise 59 with the following additions: Keep track of how many times the user clicks on buttons. If the user has not won after five clicks, the text on the last button clicked should be changed to "Lost". Once the user has lost or won, you should disable the game, that is, the buttons no longer respond to clicks from the user.

61. Write a program that displays in the title of the window the position of the mouse as the user moves the mouse around the window.

62. Write a program that draws a small circle that follows the mouse as the user moves the mouse around the window.

12.18.7 Programming Projects

63. Write a GUI-based tic-tac-toe game for two players.

64. Write a GUI-based program that analyzes a word. The user will type the word in a text field. Provide buttons for the following:

    - ❑ One button, when clicked, displays the length of the word.
    - ❑ Another button, when clicked, displays the number of vowels in the word.
    - ❑ Another button, when clicked, displays the number of upper case letters in the word.

    For this, you should design and code a separate (non-GUI) class encapsulating a word and its analysis, then instantiate an object of that class inside your GUI class and call the various methods as needed.

65. Write a GUI-based program that analyzes a soccer game. The user will type the names of two teams and the score of the game in four text fields. You should add appropriate labels and create buttons for the following:

    - ❑ One button, when clicked, displays which team won the game.
    - ❑ Another button, when clicked, displays the game score.
    - ❑ Another button, when clicked, displays by how many goals the winning team won.

    For this, you should design and code a separate (non-GUI) class encapsulating a soccer game, then instantiate an object of that class inside your GUI class and call the various methods as needed.

66. Write a GUI-based program that analyzes a round of golf. You will retrieve the data for 18 holes from a text file. On each line in the file will be the par for that hole (3, 4, or 5) and your score for that hole. Your program should read the file and display a combo box listing the 18 holes. When the user selects a hole, the score for that hole should be displayed in a label. Provide buttons for the following:

    - ❑ One button, when clicked, displays whether your overall score was over par, under par, or par.
    - ❑ Another button, when clicked, displays the number of holes for which you made par.
    - ❑ Another button, when clicked, displays how many birdies you scored (a birdie on a hole is 1 under par).

    For this, you should design and code a separate (non-GUI) class encapsulating the analysis, then instantiate an object of that class inside your GUI class and call the various methods as needed.

67. Write a GUI-based program that analyzes statistics for tennis players. You will retrieve the data from a text file. On each line in the file will be the name of a player, the player's number of wins for the year, and the player's number of losses for the year. Your program should read the file and display the list of players. When the user selects a player, the winning percentage of the player should be displayed in a label. Provide buttons for the scenarios that follow.

- ❑ One button, when clicked, displays which player had the most wins for the year.
- ❑ Another button, when clicked, displays which player had the highest winning percentage for the year.
- ❑ Another button, when clicked, displays how many players had a winning record for the year.

For this, you should design and code a separate (non-GUI) class encapsulating the tennis statistics analysis, then instantiate an object of that class inside your GUI class and call the various methods as needed.

68. Write a GUI-based program that simulates the selection of a basketball team. You will retrieve the data from a text file containing 10 lines. On each line will be the name of a player. Your program needs to read the file and display 10 checkboxes representing the 10 players. A text area will display the team, made up of the players being selected. A basketball team has five players. Your program should not allow the user to change his or her selection after the team has five players. Every time the user checks or unchecks a checkbox, the team in the text area should be updated accordingly. Provide buttons for the following:

- ❑ One button, when clicked, displays how many players are currently on the team.
- ❑ Another button, when clicked, displays how many players remain unselected.

For this, you should design and code a separate (non-GUI) class encapsulating the player selection process, then instantiate an object of that class inside your GUI class and call the various methods as needed.

69. Write a GUI-based program that analyzes a simplified pick of the NBA (National Basketball Association) draft. You will retrieve the data from a text file containing 10 lines. On each line will be the name of a player, the player's height, and the player's position on the court, each field separated by a space. Your program should read the file and display 10 radio buttons representing the 10 players. A text area will

display the information on the player corresponding to the radio button just selected. Every time the user clicks on a radio button, the information in the text area should be updated accordingly. Provide buttons for the following:

- ❑ One button, when clicked, displays how many centers are available in the draft.
- ❑ Another button, when clicked, displays the name of the tallest player in the draft.

For this, you should design and code a separate (non-GUI) class encapsulating the set of players available for the draft, then instantiate an object of that class inside your GUI class and call the various methods as needed.

70. Write a GUI-based program that displays a team on a soccer field. You will retrieve the data from a text file containing 11 lines. Each line will contain the name of a player. Your program should read the file and display the following window when it starts (you can assume that the players in the file are not in any particular order). Each cell is a button; when the user clicks on a button, the button replaces its text with the name of the player.

Left wing (11)	Striker (9)		Right wing (7)
Left midfielder (6)	Midfielder (10)		Right midfielder (8)
Left defender (3)	Stopper (4)	Sweeper (5)	Right defender (2)
	Goalie (1)		

71. Write a GUI-based program that displays a Monopoly® game. Add labels for the four train stations. Add buttons for all the Chance cells and set the text of these to a question mark. When the user clicks on one of the buttons, set its text to a message of your choice, chosen randomly from four messages.

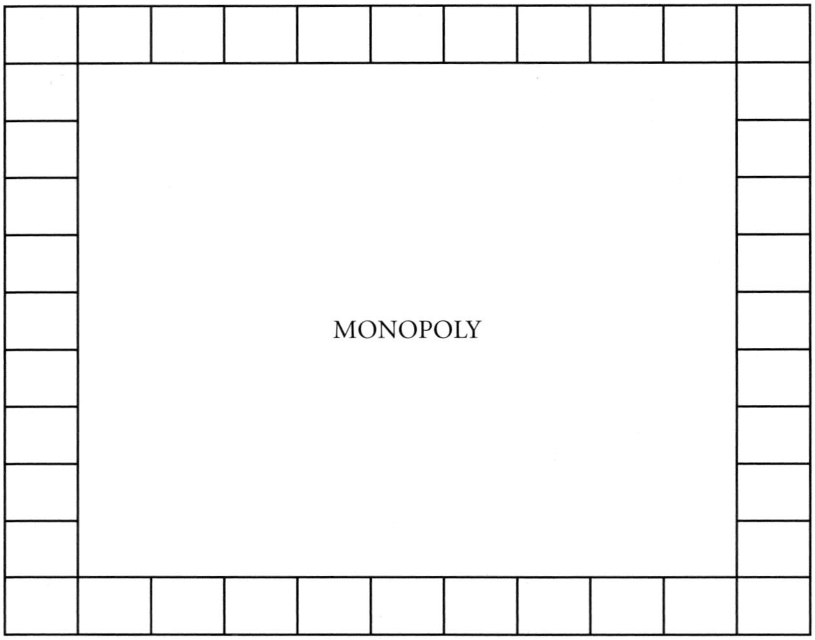

72. Write a GUI-based, simple drawing program. This program should have two buttons: one allowing the user to draw a rectangle, the other allowing the user to draw an oval. The user draws either a rectangle or an oval by pressing the mouse, dragging it, and releasing it. The top-left (x, y) coordinate of the rectangle (or enclosing rectangle for the oval) is where the user pressed the mouse button; the bottom-right point of the rectangle (or enclosing rectangle for the oval) drawn is where the user released the mouse button.You will need to organize the window in two areas: one for the buttons, one for drawing.

12.18.8 Technical Writing

73. You are writing a program that you expect to be used by many users, all with a different computer system. Would you use layout managers or would you hard code the position of components inside your GUI? Discuss.

12.18.9 Group Project (for a group of 1, 2, or 3 students)

74. Design and code a program that simulates an auction. You should consider the following:

    A file contains a list of items to be auctioned. You can decide on the format of this file and its contents. For example, the file could look like this:

    Oldsmobile, oldsmobile.gif, 100
    World Cup soccer ticket, soccerTickets.gif, 50
    Trip for 2 to Rome, trip.gif, 100

    In the preceding file sample, each line represents an item as follows: the first field is the item's description, the second field is the name of a file containing an image of the item, and the third field is the minimum bid. You can assume that each item's description is unique.

    Items are offered via an online-like auction. (You do not need to include any network programming; your program is a single-computer program.) Users of the program can choose which item to bid on from a list or a combo box. Along with displaying the description of the item, your program should show a picture of the item and the current highest bid (at the beginning, the current highest bid is the minimum bid). Users bid on an item by selecting the item, typing their name (you can assume that all users have a different name), and entering a price for the item. Your program should remember the highest bidder and the highest bid for each item by writing the information to a file. Furthermore, each time a bid is made, the item's highest bid, displayed on the screen, should be updated if necessary.

CHAPTER 13

Recursion

CHAPTER CONTENTS

Introduction

Small problems are easier to solve than big ones, with or without the help of a computer. For example, it is easy to see that 14 is a multiple of 7, but determining if 12,348 is a multiple of 7 requires some thinking ... or a well-programmed computer.

If we knew that 12,341 is a multiple of 7, then it would be easy to determine that 12,348 is also a multiple of 7, because 12,348 is simply 12,341 + 7. But then, it is not that easy to determine that 12,341 is a multiple of 7. But again, if we knew that 12,334 is a multiple of 7, then it would be easy to determine that 12,341 is also a multiple of 7, because 12,341 is simply 12,334 + 7. Well, if we keep subtracting 7 from the current number, eventually, either we will arrive at 0, which means that 12,348 is a multiple of 7, or we will arrive at a number less than 7 but not 0, which means that 12,348 is not a multiple of 7. Thus, we have reduced a large problem to a small problem that is easy to solve.

The idea of **recursion** is to reduce the size of a problem at each step so that we eventually arrive at a very small, easy-to-solve problem. That easy-to-solve problem is called the **base case**. The formula that reduces the size of the problem is called the **general case**. The general case takes us from solving a bigger problem to solving a smaller problem.

A method that uses recursion calls itself. In other words, in the body of a **recursive method**, there is a call to the method itself. The arguments passed are smaller in value (that is, they get us closer to the base case) than the original arguments. The recursive method will keep calling itself with arguments that are smaller and smaller in value, until eventually we reach the base case.

Any problem that can be solved recursively can also be solved using a loop, or iteration. Often, however, a recursive solution to a problem provides simpler, more elegant, and more compact code than its iterative counterpart.

13.1 Simple Recursion: Identifying the General and Base Cases

When designing a recursive solution for a problem, we need to do two things:

- define the base case
- define the rule for the general case

For example, if we want to print "Hello World" 100 times, we can do the following:

- print "Hello World" once
- print "Hello World" 99 times

Note that we do two things: first, we print "Hello World" once, which is easy to do. Then we reduce the size of the remaining problem to printing "Hello World" 99 times. In order to print "Hello World" 99 times, we print "Hello World" once, then we print "Hello World" 98 times. Continuing the same approach, to print "Hello World" 98 times, we print "Hello World" once, then we print "Hello World" 97 times, and so on. Eventually, we will reach a point where we print "Hello World" once, then print "Hello World" 0 times. Printing "Hello World" 0 times is an easy-to-solve problem; we simply do nothing. That is our base case for this problem.

Thus, our general approach to printing "Hello World" *n* times (where *n* is greater than 0) is to print "Hello World" once, and then print "Hello World" $n - 1$ times. As we reduce the number of times we print "Hello World," we will eventually reach 0, the base case. This condition is easy to detect. Thus, we can solve the large problem by reducing the problem to smaller and smaller problems until we find a problem that we know how to solve.

The following pseudocode illustrates the approach for our recursive method.

```
void printHelloWorldNTimes ( int  n )
{
  if ( n is greater than 0 )
  {
     print "Hello World"
     printHelloWorldNTimes( n – 1 )
  }
  // else do nothing
}
```

When *n* is greater than 0, we will execute the body of the *if* statement, printing "Hello World" once, then printing it $n - 1$ times. This is the general case for this problem. We can see that we are going from a problem of size *n* (print "Hello World" *n* times) to a problem of size $(n - 1)$ (print "Hello World" $n - 1$ times).

When n is 0 (or less), we do nothing, that is, the call to *printHelloWorldNTimes* with an argument of 0 does not generate any action. This is the base case, and this is when the recursive calls will end.

Example 13.1 shows this method.

```
1  /* Printing Hello World n times using recursion
2     Anderson, Franceschi
3  */
4
5  public class RecursiveHelloWorld
6  {
7    public static void main( String [ ] args )
8    {
9       // print "Hello World" 5 times using our recursive method
10      printHelloWorldNTimes( 5 );
11   }
12
13   // the recursive method
14   public static void printHelloWorldNTimes( int n )
15   {
16    if ( n > 0 )
17    {
18     // print "Hello World" once
19     System.out.println( "Hello World" );
20
21     // now print "Hello World" ( n - 1 ) times
22     printHelloWorldNTimes( n - 1 );
23     }
24     // if n is 0 or less, do nothing
25    }
26 }
```

EXAMPLE 13.1 Recursively Printing "Hello World" *n* Times

SOFTWARE ENGINEERING TIP

If the method does nothing in the base case, it is important to document that fact to show when the recursive calls will end.

We coded the *printHelloWorldNTimes* method from line 13 to line 25. That method prints "Hello World" n times, where n is an *int*, the only parameter of the method. We test at line 16 for the general case: n is greater than 0. There is no *else* clause: if n is 0 or less, we have reached the base case and the method does nothing.

The code for the general case is executed at lines 18–22. At line 19, we print "Hello World" once. At line 22, we make a recursive call to the *printHelloWorldNTimes* method in order to print "Hello World" $(n - 1)$ times. The method calls itself, but with an argument that is 1 less than the original argument n.

```
Hello World
Hello World
Hello World
Hello World
Hello World
```

Figure 13.1
Output of Example 13.1

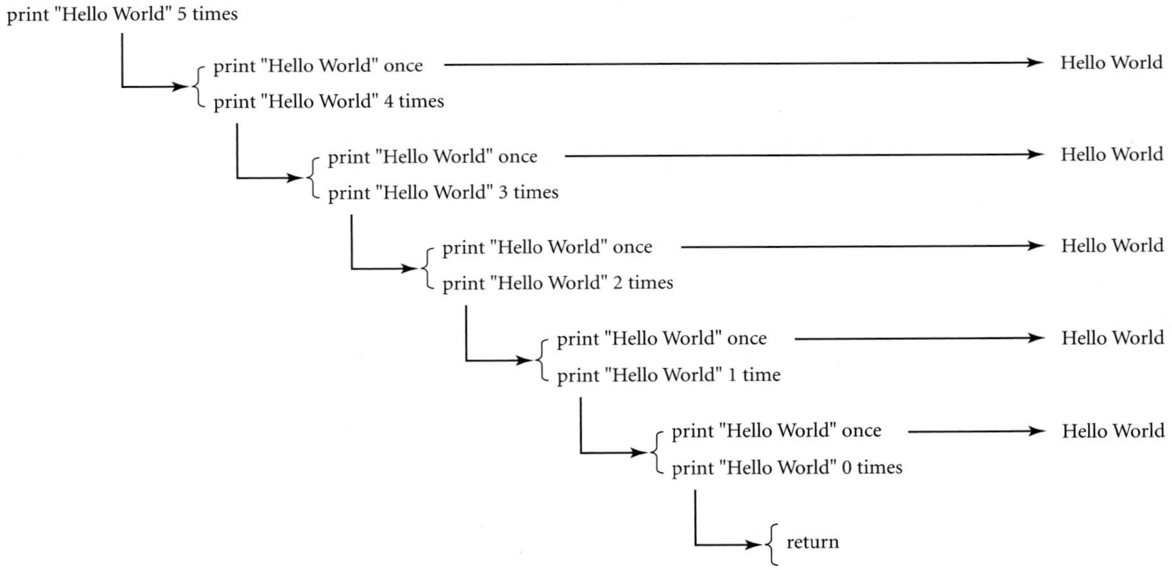

Figure 13.2
Recursive Method Calls

On line 10, we call the *printHelloWorldNTimes* method, passing the argument 5. Because *main* is *static*, it can call only *static* methods; therefore, we need to define our *printHelloWorldNTimes* method as *static*. In general, recursive methods can be defined as *static* or non-*static*.

Figure 13.1 shows the output of Example 13.1. As you can see, "Hello World" is indeed printed five times. Figure 13.2 illustrates how the recursive calls are executed and the output resulting from the calls.

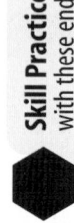

Skill Practice
with these end-of-chapter questions

13.10.1 Multiple Choice Exercises

Questions 1,3,4,5

13.10.2 Reading and Understanding Code

Questions 16,17,18,19

13.10.6 Write a Short Program

Questions 39,40,41,44

13.2 Recursion with a Return Value

In the preceding example, we coded a very simple method. Now let's look at some examples that are a little more complex, with recursive methods that return a value.

In a value-returning method the *return* statement can include a call to another value-returning method, as in:

```
public static int multiplyAbsoluteValueBy3( int n )
{
   return ( 3 * Math.abs( n ) );
}
```

In this case, the *multiplyAbsoluteValueBy3* method cannot return its value until the *abs* method returns a value, allowing the expression in the *return* statement to be fully evaluated.

The same principle applies to a value-returning method that is recursive. The return value of the recursive method often consists of an expression that includes a call to the method itself.

Thus, in the general case of the method, we could see code like:

```
return ( expression including a recursive call to the method );
```

Each execution of the recursive method must wait to return its value until its recursive call to the method returns a value. When the base case is reached, the method simply returns a value without making another recursive call. At that point, the method that invoked the method with the base case argument receives its return value, which allows that method to return a value to its caller, and so on, until the method is able to return a value to the initial caller. In this way, the return values unravel up to the initial caller.

To see how this works, let's look at an example of a recursive method that returns a value.

13.2.1 Computing the Factorial of a Number

We will define a recursive method to compute and return the factorial of a positive integer.

The factorial of a positive number is defined as follows:

$$\text{factorial}(n) = n! = n * (n - 1) * (n - 2) * (n - 3) * \ldots * 4 * 3 * 2 * 1$$

The factorial of a negative number is not defined. The factorial of 0, by convention is 1.

$$\text{factorial}(0) = 0! = 1$$

Let's define the base case and the general case for computing the factorial of a number.

In order to define the rule for the general case, we need to find a relationship between the problem at hand (computing the factorial of a number n), and a smaller, similar problem, involving, for example $(n - 1)$, $(n - 2)$, or other smaller values of n. So, here we will try to establish a relationship between factorial(n) and factorial($n - 1$), factorial($n - 2$), and so on.

Let's first examine what the value of factorial($n - 1$) is. Applying the preceding formula, we get:

$$\text{factorial}(n - 1) = (n - 1)! = (n - 1) * (n - 2) * (n - 3) * \ldots * 4 * 3 * 2 * 1$$

As we can see from the preceding formulas, there is a very simple relationship between factorial(n) and factorial($n - 1$):

$$\text{factorial}(n) = n * \text{factorial}(n - 1)$$

This is the relationship we will use for the formulation of the general case.

Using this formula, at each step we reduce the size of the problem (measured by the value of the input n) from n to $(n - 1)$. In order to compute factorial(n), we will call the factorial method with the argument $(n - 1)$ and multiply the returned value by n. The call to the factorial method with the argument ($n - 1$) will generate a recursive call to the factorial method with argument ($n - 2$), until eventually we generate a recursive call to the factorial method with the argument 0. We know how to compute factorial (0): by convention, it is 1. That is our base case and we have reached it. We will return 1, which will allow the unraveling of the recursive method calls until we solve the original problem, factorial(n).

Example 13.2 shows the code for calculating a factorial recursively. In order to keep things simple, we will also return 1 if the argument sent to the method is negative. However, we are careful in documenting our method to emphasize that the argument should be greater than or equal to 0. If we do not want to return anything when a negative argument is passed to the method, we would need to throw an exception, because the method is a value-returning method.

Here is how our *factorial(int n)* method will work;

- Base case: if n is negative or 0, the method returns 1
- General case: if n is greater than 0, the method returns n * *factorial(n – 1)*

```
/* Computing the factorial of a number using recursion
   Anderson, Franceschi
*/

public class RecursiveFactorial
{
  public static void main( String [ ] args )
  {
    // compute factorial of 5 and output it
    System.out.println( "Factorial ( 5 ) is "
                        + factorial( 5 ) );
  }

  /** recursive factorial method
  *   @param    n  a positive integer
  *   @return      the factorial of n
  */
  public static int factorial( int n )
  {
    if ( n <= 0 )     // base case
      return 1;
```

```
22      else               // general case
23        return ( n * factorial ( n - 1 ) );
24    }
25 }
```

EXAMPLE 13.2 Computing a Factorial Using Recursion

At lines 10–11, we make the initial call to the *factorial* method and print the result. We simply compute the factorial of 5. You can modify the example to prompt the user for another value.

We coded the *factorial* method at lines 14–24. The *factorial* method takes an *int* parameter named *n*, and returns the factorial of *n* as an *int*. At line 20, we test if *n* is less than or equal to 0. If that is true, we have reached the base case, and the *factorial* method returns 1. If *n* is greater than 0, the code skips to line 23, where we have coded the general case. We make a recursive call to the *factorial* method with an argument of $(n - 1)$. The value returned by that recursive call is then multiplied by *n* and the result is returned.

Figure 13.3 shows the output of Example 13.2.

We can verify that factorial(5) is 120. Indeed,

$$5\,! = 5 * 4 * 3 * 2 * 1 = 120$$

To illustrate how the recursive method calls return their values, let's modify Example 3.2 to include some output statements inside the *factorial* method. In this way, we can trace the recursive calls.

We want to trace the following:

- each call to the *factorial* method and its argument
- the detection of the base case and the value returned at that point
- the expression that evaluates to the return value

Example 13.3 is similar to Example 13.2, except that its *factorial* method includes the trace features described previously.

```
Factorial ( 5 ) is 120
```

Figure 13.3
Output of Example 13.2

The *factorial* method is coded at lines 14–34. At line 20, we output a message indicating that the method has been called, along with the parameter value. When the base case is detected, we output a message indicating that the method has reached the base case and report its return value (lines 23–24). For the general case, we output the expression that will be returned by the method (lines 30–31). Figure 13.4 shows the output of Example 13.3. We can see the recursive calls to the *factorial* method with the value of the argument being reduced by 1 until the base case, 0, is reached. At that point, each recursively called method, in turn, returns a value to its caller, until the initial invocation of the method returns the value 120.

```
1 /* Computing the factorial of a number using recursion
2    Anderson, Franceschi
3 */
4
5 public class RecursiveFactorialWithTrace
6 {
7   public static void main( String [ ] args )
8   {
9     // compute factorial of 5 and output it
10    System.out.println( "\nFactorial( 5 ) is "
11                        + factorial( 5 ) );
12  }
13
14  /** recursive factorial method
15  *   @param    n  a positive integer
16  *   @return   the factorial of n
17  */
18  public static int factorial( int n )
19  {
20    System.out.println( "factorial( " + n + " ) called" );
21    if ( n == 0 )     // base case
22    {
23      System.out.println( "\nBase case detected" );
24      System.out.println( "factorial( " + n + " ) returning 1\n" );
25      return 1;
26    }
27    else              // general case
28    {
29      int factorialNMinus1 = factorial( n - 1 );
30      System.out.println( "factorial( " + n + " ) returning "
31                          + n + " * " + factorialNMinus1 );
32      return ( n * factorialNMinus1 );
33    }
```

```
  }
}
```

EXAMPLE 13.3 Tracing the Recursive Calls of the *Factorial* Method

```
factorial( 5 ) called
factorial( 4 ) called
factorial( 3 ) called
factorial( 2 ) called
factorial( 1 ) called
factorial( 0 ) called

Base case detected
factorial( 0 ) returning 1

factorial( 1 ) returning 1 * 1
factorial( 2 ) returning 2 * 1
factorial( 3 ) returning 3 * 2
factorial( 4 ) returning 4 * 6
factorial( 5 ) returning 5 * 24

Factorial( 5 ) is 120
```

Figure 13.4
Output of Example 13.3

Identifying the base case is critical. When a method is called, the JVM stores the method's arguments and the caller's return address on a **stack**. When the method returns to the caller, the JVM removes the data for that method call from the stack. If a recursive method never reaches a base case, the method continues calling itself indefinitely, causing the JVM to continue placing values on the stack until memory for the stack is full. At this time, the JVM generates a *StackOverflowError*, which terminates the program.

REFERENCE POINT

We discuss stacks in Chapter 14.

For example, if we did not code the base case in our *factorial* method, the method would look like the following:

```
public static int factorial( int n )
{
   // n must be a positive integer
   return ( n * factorial ( n - 1 ) );
}
```

When the method is called, the recursive calls keep being made because the base case is never reached. This eventually generates a *StackOverflowError*.

COMMON ERROR TRAP

Failure to code the base case will result in a run-time error.

```
Exception in thread "main" java.lang.StackOverflowError
   at RecursiveFactorial.factorial(RecursiveFactorial.java:23)
   at RecursiveFactorial.factorial(RecursiveFactorial.java:23)
   at RecursiveFactorial.factorial(RecursiveFactorial.java:23)
   at RecursiveFactorial.factorial(RecursiveFactorial.java:23)
```

Figure 13.5
A Run of Example 13.2 if the Base Case Is Not Coded

Figure 13.5 shows a run of Example 13.2 (the *RecursiveFactorial* class) with lines 20 to 22 commented out.

CODE IN ACTION

On the CD-ROM included with this book, you will find a Flash movie with a step-by-step illustration of recursion. Click on the link for Chapter 13 to start the movie.

13.2.2 Computing the Greatest Common Divisor

A common algebra problem is to calculate the greatest common divisor, or **gcd**, of two positive integers. The gcd is the greatest positive integer that divides evenly into both numbers.

For example, consider 50 and 20. We can figure in our head that 5 divides evenly into both numbers, but so does 10. Since we can't find a number greater than 10 that divides evenly into both numbers, 10 is the gcd of 50 and 20.

It is easy to guess the gcd of two small numbers, but it is more difficult to guess the gcd of two large numbers, such as 123,450 and 60,378. The following Euclidian algorithm finds the gcd of two positive integers a and b. This algorithm derives from the fact that the gcd of two integers a and b (with $a > b$) is the same as the gcd of b and the remainder of a / b.

```
Step 1:
  r0 = a % b
  if ( r0 is equal to 0 )
      gcd ( a, b ) = b
      stop
  else
      go to step 2

Step 2:
  repeat step 1 with b and r0, instead of a and b.
```

Let's run the algorithm on our first example, 50 and 20. We substitute 50 for *a* and 20 for *b*.

```
Step 1:
   r0 = 50 % 20 = 10
   is 10 equal to 0 ?  no, go to Step 2.

Step 2:
   r0 = 20 / 10  = 0
   is 0 equal to 0 ?
      yes. gcd( 50, 20 ) = 10
      stop
```

Therefore, the gcd of 50 and 20 is 10.

Let's now run the algorithm on our second example, 123,450 and 60,378.

The remainder of 123,450 divided by 60,378 is 2,694.

2694 is not equal to 0

so we take the remainder of 60,378 divided by 2,694, which is 1,110

1,110 is not equal to 0

so we take the remainder of 2,694 divided by 1,110, which is 474

474 is not equal to 0

so we take the remainder of 1,110 divided by 474, which is 162

162 is not equal to 0

so we take the remainder of 474 divided by 162, which is 150

150 is not equal to 0

so we take the remainder of 162 divided by 150, which is 12

12 is not equal to 0

so we take the remainder of 150 divided by 12, which is 6

6 is not equal to 0

so we take the remainder of 12 divided by 6, which is 0

0 is equal to 0

so the gcd of 123, 450 and 60,378 is 6

Let's go back to our algorithm and look at Step 1 as a method taking two parameters, *a* and *b*. Step 2 is a method call to Step 1 with two different parameters, *b* and *r*0. It is very simple to calculate *r*0, since *r*0 is the remainder of the division of *a* by *b*. Using the modulus operator, *r*0 is *a* % *b*. Therefore, this algorithm can easily be coded as a recursive method.

Let's call the two parameters of the method, *dividend* and *divisor*, in that order.

When the remainder of the division of *dividend* by *divisor* is 0, we have reached the base case and the method returns *divisor*. The general case is when the remainder of the division of *dividend* by *divisor* is not 0. The method then calls itself with *divisor* and the remainder of the division of *dividend* by *divisor*.

Example 13.4 shows the code for the recursive implementation of the greatest common divisor solution.

```
/* Computing the greatest common divisor using recursion
   Anderson, Franceschi
*/

public class RecursiveGCD
{
  public static void main( String [ ] args )
  {
    // compute and output gcd of 123450 and 60378
    System.out.println( "The GCD of " + 123450 + " and "
                        + 60378 + " is " + gcd( 123450, 60378 ) );
  }

  /** recursive gcd method
  *   @param    dividend  the first strictly positive integer
  *   @param    divisor   the second strictly positive integer
  *   @return             the gcd of dividend and divisor
  */
  public static int gcd( int dividend, int divisor )
  {
    if ( dividend % divisor == 0 )      // base case
      return divisor;
    else                                // general case
      return ( gcd ( divisor, dividend % divisor ) );
  }
}
```

EXAMPLE 13.4 Computing the GCD of Two Integers Using Recursion

Figure 13.6
Output of Example 13.4

```
The GCD of 123450 and 60378 is 6
```

We make the call to the *gcd* method at lines 10–11 with arguments 123450 and 60378 and output the result.

The *gcd* method is coded from lines 14–25. The method header shows that the *gcd* method takes two *int* parameters named *dividend* and *divisor*, and returns an *int*, the greatest common divisor of *dividend* and *divisor*. At line 21, we check for the base case by testing if the remainder of the integer division of *dividend* by *divisor* is 0. If so, the *gcd* method returns *divisor* without making another recursive call.

If the remainder is not 0, we are in the general case, so we make a recursive call at line 24 with the arguments *divisor* and the remainder of the division (*dividend % divisor*). We return the value returned by that call.

Figure 13.6 shows the output of Example 13.4.

As we did with the recursive *factorial* method, let's modify Example 13.4 to include some output statements inside the *gcd* method in order to trace the recursive calls.

The *gcd* method in Example 13.5, (lines 14–39), is the same as the *gcd* method in Example 13.4, except that each time the method is called, we print the parameter values and result of the modulus operation (lines 21–23) to verify that the method is correctly detecting the general and base cases. We also print a message when the base case is reached (lines 27–28). At lines 34–36, we output the value returned by the method in the general case.

Figure 13.7 shows the output of Example 13.5. We can see the recursive calls all the way to the base case, and the return value from each recursive call. As we can see, the return value stays the same throughout the process. Such a recursive method is called **tail recursive**.

```
 1 /* Computing the greatest common divisor using recursion
 2    Anderson, Franceschi
 3 */
 4
 5 public class RecursiveGCDWithTrace
 6 {
 7   public static void main( String [ ] args )
 8   {
 9     // compute gcd of 123450 and 60378 and output it
10     System.out.println( "\nThe GCD of " + 123450 + " and "
11                          + 60378 + " is " + gcd( 123450, 60378 ) );
12   }
13
14   /** recursive gcd method with trace
15    *   @param    dividend   the first strictly positive integer
```

```
 *   @param    divisor    the second strictly positive integer
 *   @return              the gcd of dividend and divisor
 */
public static int gcd( int dividend, int divisor )
{
  System.out.print( "gcd( " + dividend + ", " + divisor + " )" );
  System.out.println( "   " + dividend + " % " + divisor + " = "
                      + ( dividend % divisor ) );

  if ( dividend % divisor == 0 )  // base case
  {
    System.out.println( "\nbase case reached, returning "
                        + divisor + "\n" );
    return divisor;
  }
  else                    // general case
  {
    int temp = gcd( divisor, dividend % divisor );
    System.out.println( "gcd( " + divisor + ", "
                        + ( dividend % divisor )
                        + " ) returning " + temp );
    return ( temp );
  }
}
}
```

EXAMPLE 13.5 Tracing the Recursive Calls of the *gcd* Method

Figure 13.7
Output of Example 13.5

```
gcd( 123450, 60378 )   123450 % 60378 = 2694
gcd( 60378, 2694 )   60378 % 2694 = 1110
gcd( 2694, 1110 )   2694 % 1110 = 474
gcd( 1110, 474 )   1110 % 474 = 162
gcd( 474, 162 )   474 % 162 = 150
gcd( 162, 150 )   162 % 150 = 12
gcd( 150, 12 )   150 % 12 = 6
gcd( 12, 6 )   12 % 6 = 0

base case reached, returning 6

gcd( 12, 6 ) returning 6
gcd( 150, 12 ) returning 6
gcd( 162, 150 ) returning 6
gcd( 474, 162 ) returning 6
gcd( 1110, 474 ) returning 6
gcd( 2694, 1110 ) returning 6
gcd( 60378, 2694 ) returning 6

The GCD of 123450 and 60378 is 6
```

CODE IN ACTION

On the CD-ROM included with this book, you will find a Flash movie with a step-by-step illustration of various recursive methods. Click on the link for Chapter 13 to start the movie.

13.3 Recursion with Two Base Cases

Recursive formulations can be more complex than the examples we have discussed. The general case can involve more than one recursive call, with different arguments. This, in turn, means that we can have more than one base case.

Suppose we are playing a networked video game online. There are n players who would like to play. Unfortunately, that game can be played with only p players. We will make the assumption that p is an integer between 0 and n (for instance, n could be 100 and p could be 8). Otherwise, we simply cannot play the game.

Our problem is to determine how many different ways we can choose p players from among n players. We will call that number *Combinations*(n, p).

The math formula for *Combinations*(n, p) is:

$$\text{Combinations}(n, p) = n! \,/\, ((n - p)! * p!)$$

Our goal here is to come up with a recursive solution to the problem and thus to code *Combinations*(n, p) recursively.

There are some obvious cases to consider. If we have the same number of players as the number who can play the game, then p equals n, and we pick all the players. There is only one way to do that, so *Combinations*(n, n) = 1.

If the game requires no players, then p equals 0, and we do not pick any players. Again, there is only one way to do that so *Combinations*(n, 0) = 1.

But what is the answer in the general case where the value of *Combinations* (n, p) may not be so obvious?

One way to look at that problem is as follows:

Among these n potential players, let's focus on one player in particular. We will call that player Louis. We can either pick Louis or not pick Louis. Therefore, the total number of possibilities of picking p players among n potential players is equal to the sum of the following two numbers:

- the number of possibilites of picking p players, including picking Louis, among n
- the number of possibilities of picking p players, without picking Louis, among n

If we pick Louis, then we will have to choose $(p - 1)$ more players. But we cannot pick Louis again, so there are only $(n - 1)$ potential players left. The number of such possibilities is *Combinations*$(n-1, p-1)$.

If we do not pick Louis, then we still have to choose p players. But since we are not picking Louis, there are only $(n - 1)$ potential players left. The number of such possibilities is *Combinations*$(n-1, p)$.

Therefore, we can write the following recursive formula:

```
Combinations( n, p ) = Combinations( n – 1, p – 1 )
                       + Combinations( n – 1, p )
```

If we look at the two terms on the right side of the preceding formula, we can see that:

- In the first term, both parameters, n and p, have been decreased by 1.
- In the second term, one parameter, n, has been decreased by 1, while p is unchanged.

Therefore, solving the problem of computing *Combinations*(n, p) using this formula translates into solving two similar, but smaller, problems. That is our general case.

Our next concern is to decide what the base case or cases are. In other words, as we apply the preceding formula repeatedly, when will we reach an easy-to-solve problem? Since we have two recursive terms on the right side of the formula, we will have two base cases.

Let's look at the first term, *Combinations*$(n - 1, p - 1)$. We can see that both n and p decrease by 1 at the same time. When we start, p is greater than or equal to 0 and less than or equal to n. Therefore, as we keep applying the formula and concentrate on the first term, we can see that p will eventually reach 0, and that p will reach 0 before n does. As discussed earlier, *Combinations*$(n, 0) = 1$, because there is only one way to pick 0 players from a set of n players—do not pick any. This is one base case.

Let's now look at the second term, *Combinations*$(n - 1, p)$. We can see that n decreases by 1 while p is unchanged. We know that p must be less than or equal to n (we cannot pick more than n players among n players). As n decreases and p does not, n will eventually reach p. As discussed earlier, *Combinations*$(n, n) = 1$, because there is only one way to pick n players among n players—pick them all. This is our other base case.

Example 13.6 shows the code for this example.

```
/* Computing the number of combinations
   of picking p objects among n, using recursion
   Anderson, Franceschi
*/

public class RecursiveCombinations
{
  public static void main( String [ ] args )
  {
    // compute and output number of combinations
    System.out.println( "C( 5, 2 ) = "
                          + combinations( 5, 2 ) );
  }

  /** recursive combinations method
  *   @param    n a positive number
  *   @param    p a positive number, less than or equal to n
  *   @return   the number of combinations of choosing p among n
  */
  public static int combinations( int n, int p )
  {
    if ( p == 0 )           // base case # 1
      return 1;
    else if ( n == p )      // base case # 2
      return 1;
    else                    // general case
```

```
27         return ( combinations( n - 1, p - 1 )
28                  + combinations( n - 1, p ) );
29     }
30 }
```

EXAMPLE 13.6 Computing Combinations Recursively

In this example, we use the *combinations* method to compute the number of ways of picking 2 players among 5.

We call the *combinations* method with arguments, 5 and 2, and output the returned value at lines 11–12.

The *combinations* method is coded at lines 15–29. The method header, at line 20, shows that the *combinations* method takes two *int* parameters, the number of players (n) and the number of players to select (p). The return value, an *int*, is the number of combinations of picking p players among n.

At line 22, we test for the first base case ($p == 0$). If *true*, we return 1. If p is not equal to 0, we test for the second base case (n is equal to p). If that is *true*, we return 1. If p is not equal to 0 and n is not equal to p, then we are in the general case and the code skips to lines 27–28. We make two recursive calls to the *combinations* method. The first recursive call is with arguments $n - 1$ and $p - 1$. The second recursive call is with arguments $n - 1$ and p. We add the values returned by these two recursive calls and return the result.

The output of Example 13.6 is shown in Figure 13.8.

We can verify that our algorithm is correct. As discussed earlier,

$$\text{Combinations}(n, p) = n! \,/\, (\,(\,n - p\,)! * p!\,)$$

Thus,

$$\text{Combinations}(\,5, 2\,) = 5! \,/\, (\,3! * 2!\,) = 10$$

Those of us with a mathematics background can verify that

```
Combinations( n, p ) = Combinations( n – 1, p – 1 ) +
                       Combinations( n – 1, p )
```

Figure 13.8
Output of Example 13.6

```
C( 5, 2 ) = 10
```

that is,

```
n! / ( ( n – p )! * p! ) = ( n – 1 )! / ( ( n – p )! * ( p – 1 )! )
                          + ( n – 1 )! / ( ( n – 1 – p )! * p! )
```

What happens if we code for only one base case when there are two or more base cases?

When the method is called, the recursive calls will continue to be made, because the missing base cases will never be detected. This will eventually generate a *StackOverflowError*.

COMMON ERROR TRAP

There can be more than one base case. Failing to take into account all base cases can result in a *StackOverflowError* at run time.

13.4 Programming Activity 1: Checking for a Palindrome

In this activity, you will work with recursion to perform this function:

Code a recursive method to determine if a *String* is a palindrome.

A palindrome is a word, phrase, or sentence that is symmetrical, that is, it is spelled the same forward and backward. Examples are "otto," "mom," "madam," and "able was I ere I saw elba."

How can we determine, using recursion, whether a *String* is a palindrome?

If the *String* has two or more characters, we can check if the first and last characters are identical. If they are not identical, then the *String* is not a palindrome. That is a base case.

If the first and last characters are identical, then we need to check if the substring comprised of all the characters between the first and last characters is a palindrome. That is the general case.

If the *String* is a palindrome, each recursive call will reduce the size of the argument, that is, the number of characters in the argument *String*, by 2. Eventually, the recursive calls will result in a *String* argument consisting of 0 or 1 character. Both are trivial palindromes. That is our second base case. Note that we will reach this base case only if the *String* is a palindrome. Indeed, if the *String* is not a palindrome, the recursive calls will detect the first base case as soon as the first and last characters of the *String* argument are different, and the recursive method will return *false*.

For example, to check if "madam" is a palindrome, we take the steps that follow.

Here is the original *String*:

m	a	d	a	m

We compare the first and last characters.

m	a	d	a	m

They are equal, so we now check the substring comprised of the characters between the first and last characters. Again, we compare the first and last characters of this substring.

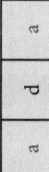

a	d	a

They are equal, so we now check the substring comprised of the characters between the first and last characters.

d

There is only one character in this substring, so we have reached our second base case. The *String* "madam" is a palindrome.

Let's now check if "modem" is a palindrome.

Here is the original *String*:

m	o	d	e	m

We compare the first and last characters.

m	o	d	e	m

They are equal, so we now check the substring comprised of the characters between the first and last characters. Again, we check the first and last characters.

o	d	e

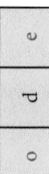

They are not equal, so we have reached the first base case. The *String* "modem" is not a palindrome.

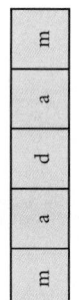

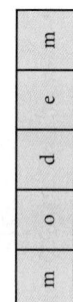

Instructions

In the Chapter 13 Programming Activity 1 directory on the CD-ROM accompanying this book, you will find the source files needed to complete this activity. Copy all of the files to a directory on your computer. Note that all files should be in the same directory.

Open the *PalindromeClient.java* source file. Searching for five stars (*****) in the source code will position you to the location where you will add your code. In this task, you will fill in the code inside the *recursivePalindrome* method to determine if a *String* representing a word or a sentence is a palindrome. The method returns *true* if the *String* is a palindrome, *false* if the *String* is not a palindrome. Example 13.7 shows the section of the *PalindromeClient* source code where you will add your code.

```
public boolean recursivePalindrome( String pal )
{
  // ***** Student writes the body of this method *****

  // Using recursion, determine if a String representing
  // a word or a sentence is a palindrome
  // If it is, return true, otherwise return false

  // We call the animate method inside the body of this method
  // The call to animate is already coded below

  animate( pal );

  //
  // Student code starts here
  //

  return true; // replace this dummy return statement

  //
  // End of student code - PA 1
  //
}
```

EXAMPLE 13.7 Location of Student Code in *PalindromeClient*

The framework will animate your code so that you get some feedback on the correctness of your code. It will display the argument *String* passed to the recursive method at each recursive call of that method. Your result will be displayed in red and the correct result will be displayed in green.

To test your code, compile and run the application; when the program begins, a dialog box will prompt you for a word or a sentence, as shown in Figure 13.9.

Click "Cancel" to exit the program; click "OK" to continue and animate your code.

If you enter an empty *String* or a *String* with more than 26 characters, the program will prompt you for another *String*. This part is already coded for you.

Figure 13.10 shows the output if you enter "able was I ere I saw elba". We can see the argument *String* of our recursive method shrinking by two characters at each recursive call until we reach a base case.

If you insert an extra "h" into the preceding phrase, and enter "able was I here I saw elba", which is not a palindrome, the final result of your anima-

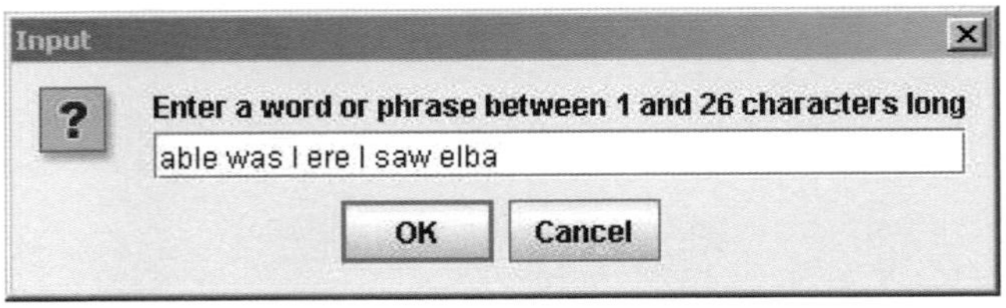

Figure 13.9
Opening Dialog Box

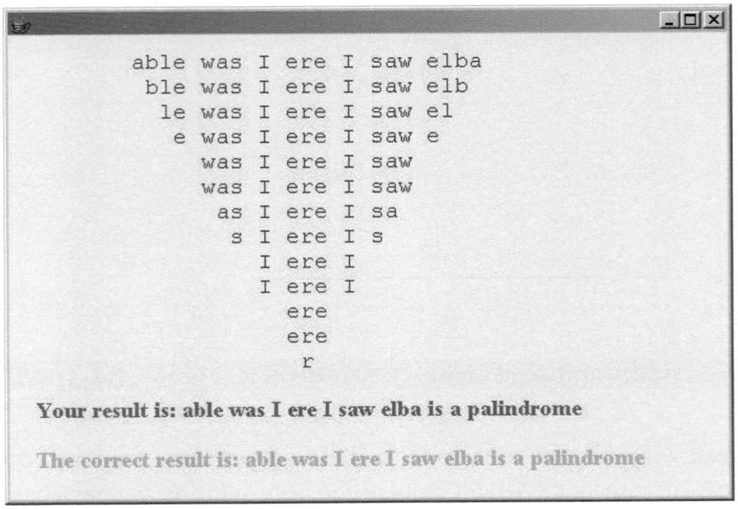

Figure 13.10
Sample Final Screen for Programming Activity 1

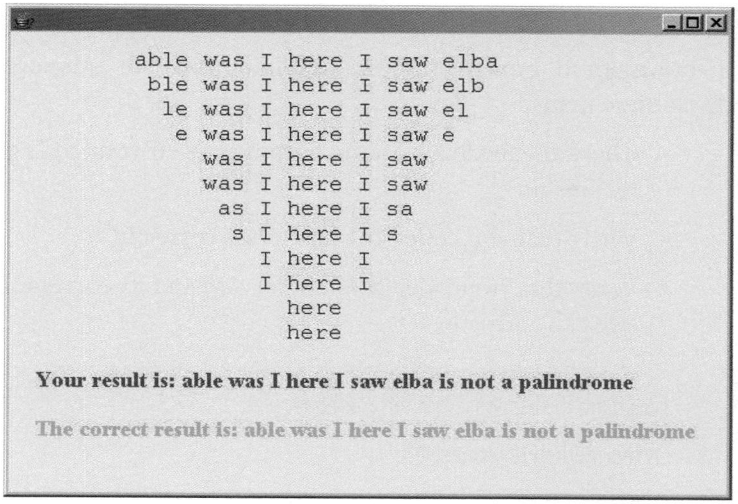
able was I here I saw elba
ble was I here I saw elb
le was I here I saw el
e was I here I saw e
was I here I saw
was I here I saw
as I here I sa
s I here I s
I here I
I here I
here
here
Your result is: able was I here I saw elba is not a palindrome
The correct result is: able was I here I saw elba is not a palindrome

Figure 13.11
Sample Final Screen for Programming Activity 1

tion is shown in Figure 13.11. When the argument *String* of our recursive method become "here", the recursive calls stop and the method returns *false.*

Task Instructions

Inside the method *recursivePalindrome* of class *PalindromeClient,* write the code to solve the palindrome problem:

- The *recursivePalindrome* method header has already been coded for you. Write the code to check if the parameter of the method, *pal,* is a palindrome. Return *true* if it is, *false* if it is not. Your method should be recursive, that is, it should call itself. We have provided a dummy *return* statement so that the code will compile. You should replace the dummy statement with your appropriate *return* statement.
- Be sure your code ignores case differences; that is, Otto and Racecar are indeed palindromes.
- The call to the *animate* method has already been written for you. It should be the first statement in the body of the method and is simply:

```
animate( pal );
```

Troubleshooting

If your method implementation does not animate or animates incorrectly, check these items:

- Check the feedback on the output to see if your code gives the correct result.
- Verify that you coded the base cases correctly.
- Verify that you coded the general case and its corresponding recursive call correctly.

DISCUSSION QUESTIONS ?

1. What are the base cases for this method?
2. Is this method tail recursive?
3. What happens if you do not code one of the base cases?

13.5 Binary Search Revisited: A Recursive Solution

In Chapter 8, we presented a binary search algorithm to search a sorted array for a given value. That algorithm was iterative, using a *while* loop.

Let's look at how we can define a recursive solution to this problem. We will assume that the array is sorted in ascending order.

Again, we need to define the base cases and the general case, and the general case must reduce the size of the problem.

When searching for a value in an array, we have two possible outcomes:

- We find the value and return its array index.
- We do not find the value and return −1.

Overall, our strategy is similar to the iterative solution. First, we will look at the middle element of the array. If the value of the middle element is the value we are looking for, we will return its index. That is our first base case.

If the value of the middle element is greater than the value we are looking for, then the value we are looking for cannot be found in elements with array indexes higher than the index of the middle element. Therefore, we will continue our search in the lower half of the array only. We will do that by making a recursive call to our search method, specifying the lower half of the original array as the subarray to search.

Similarly, if the value of the middle element is lower than the value we are looking for, then the value we are looking for cannot be found in elements with array indexes lower than the index of the middle element. Therefore, we will continue our search in the upper half of the array only. We will do that by making a recursive call to our search method, specifying the upper half of the original array as the subarray to search. That is our formulation for the general case.

As we continue searching, the size of the subarray that we search will shrink with every recursive call. Indeed, every recursive call cuts the size of the subarray we search in half. In this recursive algorithm, not only does the size of the problem decrease with each recursive call, but it also decreases by a large amount.

If the value we are looking for is not in the array, the part of the array that we are searching will continue shrinking until it is empty. At that point, we know that we will not find our value in the array. We have reached our other base case, and we return –1.

Example 13.8 shows the code for a recursive binary search.

```
/* Searching a sorted array using recursion
   Anderson, Franceschi
*/

import java.util.Scanner;

public class RecursiveBinarySearch
{
  public static void main( String [ ] args )
  {
    // define an array sorted in ascending order
    int [ ] numbers = { 3, 6, 7, 8, 12, 15, 22, 36, 45,
                        48, 51, 53, 64, 69, 72, 89, 95 };

    Scanner scan = new Scanner( System.in );
    System.out.print( "Enter a value to search for > " );
    int value = scan.nextInt( );

    int index = recursiveBinarySearch
                ( numbers, value, 0, numbers.length - 1 );
    if ( index != -1 )
      System.out.println( value + " found at index " + index );
```

```
23     else
24       System.out.println( value + " not found" );
25   }
26
27   /** recursiveBinarySearch method
28   *   @param    arr   the array sorted in ascending order
29   *   @param    key   the value to search for in the subarray
30   *   @param    start the subarray's first index
31   *   @param    end   the subarray's last index
32   *   @return   the array index at which key was found,
33   *             or -1 if key was not found
34   */
35   public static int recursiveBinarySearch
36                ( int [ ] arr, int key, int start, int end )
37   {
38     if ( start <= end )
39     {
40       // look at the middle element of the subarray
41       int middle = ( start + end ) / 2;
42
43       if ( arr[middle] == key )     // found key, base case
44         return middle;
45       else if ( arr[middle] > key ) // look lower
46         return recursiveBinarySearch( arr, key, start, middle - 1 );
47       else                          // look higher
48         return recursiveBinarySearch( arr, key, middle + 1, end );
49     }
50     else                            // key not found, base case
51       return -1;
52   }
53 }
```

EXAMPLE 13.8 Searching an Array Sorted in Ascending Order

We coded the *recursiveBinarySearch* method at lines 27–52. That method takes four parameters: *arr*, the array we are searching, *key*, the value we are searching for; and *start* and *end*, which represent, respectively, the first and last index of the subarray of *arr* that we should search.

At line 38, we test if the subarray we are searching contains at least one element. If it does not, we have reached a base case and we know that we will not find *key*. Thus, we return −1 in the *else* clause at line 51. If the subarray has at least one element, we assign the index of the middle element of the subarray to *middle* at line 41. We then compare the array element at index *middle* to *key* at line 43. If they are equal, we have reached the other base case (we have found *key*) so we return *middle* at line 44.

If the array element at index *middle* is greater than *key*, we call the *recursiveBinarySearch* method with the subarray consisting of all elements with values lower than *middle* (from *start* to *middle* − 1) at line 46. If the array element at index *middle* is smaller than *key*, then we call the *recursiveBinarySearch* method with the subarray consisting of all elements with values higher than *middle* (from *middle* + 1 to *end*) at line 48. In both cases, whatever is returned by the recursive call is returned by the method.

REFERENCE POINT

Various algorithms for sorting an array are discussed in detail in Chapter 8, as is searching a sorted array using an iterative binary search algorithm.

In *main*, we begin by instantiating our array to search. Note that the values are in ascending order (lines 12–13). We then prompt the user for the search key and make the call to the recursive binary search method, passing the entire array as the subarray to search (lines 19–20). We output the result of our search at lines 21–24.

Figure 13.12 shows the output from Example 13.8 when the key value is found, and when the key value is not found.

Let's run the preceding example on the value 7 in order to illustrate the various recursive calls and the case where the value is found.

Here is the array *numbers*, sorted in ascending order.

Value	3	6	7	8	12	15	22	36	45	48	51	53	64	69	72	89	95
Index	0	1	2	3	4	5	6	7	8	9	10	11	12	13	14	15	16

```
Enter a value to search for > 7
7 found at index 2
```

```
Enter a value to search for > 34
34 not found
```

Figure 13.12
Two Runs of Example 13.8

We calculate the index *middle* by adding the indexes *start* and *end*, then dividing by 2. Thus, when the *recursiveBinarySearch* method is first called, *middle* is 8.

The element at index 8 (45) is greater than 7, so we call the *recursiveBinarySearch* method, searching the left subarray, highlighted here.

Value	3	6	7	8	12	15	22	36	45	48	51	53	64	69	72	89	95
Index	0	1	2	3	4	5	6	7	8	9	10	11	12	13	14	15	16

The index *middle* is now calculated to be 3 ((0 + 7)/2).

The element at index 3 (8) is greater than 7, so we call the *recursiveBinarySearch* method, searching the left subarray, highlighted here.

Value	3	6	7	8	12	15	22	36	45	48	51	53	64	69	72	89	95
Index	0	1	2	3	4	5	6	7	8	9	10	11	12	13	14	15	16

The index *middle* is now calculated to be 1 ((0 + 2)/2).

The element at index 1 (6) is smaller than 7, so we call the *recursiveBinarySearch* method, searching the right subarray, highlighted here.

Value	3	6	7	8	12	15	22	36	45	48	51	53	64	69	72	89	95

Index	0	1	2	3	4	5	6	7	8	9	10	11	12	13	14	15	16

The index *middle* is now calculated to be 2 ((2 + 2)/2).

The element at index 2 (7), is equal to 7. We have found the value and return its index, 2.

Let's now run the preceding example on the value 34 in order to illustrate the various recursive calls and the base case when the value is not found.

Here is the array *numbers* again:

Value	3	6	7	8	12	15	22	36	45	48	51	53	64	69	72	89	95
Index	0	1	2	3	4	5	6	7	8	9	10	11	12	13	14	15	16

The index *middle* when the *recursiveBinarySearch* method is first called is 8 ((0 + 16)/2).

The element at index 8 (45) is greater than 34, so we call the *recursiveBinarySearch* method, searching the left subarray highlighted here.

Value	3	6	7	8	12	15	22	36	45	48	51	53	64	69	72	89	95
Index	0	1	2	3	4	5	6	7	8	9	10	11	12	13	14	15	16

The index *middle* is now calculated to be 3 ((0 + 7)/2).

The element at index 3 (8) is smaller than 34, so we call the *recursiveBinarySearch* method, searching the right subarray, highlighted here.

Value	3	6	7	8	12	15	22	36	45	48	51	53	64	69	72	89	95
Index	0	1	2	3	4	5	6	7	8	9	10	11	12	13	14	15	16

The index *middle* is now calculated to be 5 ((4 + 7)/2).

The element at index 5 (15) is smaller than 34, so we call the *recursiveBinarySearch* method, searching the right subarray, highlighted here.

Value	3	6	7	8	12	15	22	36	45	48	51	53	64	69	72	89	95
Index	0	1	2	3	4	5	6	7	8	9	10	11	12	13	14	15	16

The index *middle* is now calculated to be 6 ((6 + 7)/2).

The element at index 6 (22) is smaller than 34, so we call the *recursiveBinarySearch* method, searching the right subarray, highlighted here.

Value	3	6	7	8	12	15	22	36	45	48	51	53	64	69	72	89	95
Index	0	1	2	3	4	5	6	7	8	9	10	11	12	13	14	15	16

The index *middle* is now calculated to be 7 ((7 + 7)/2).

The element at index 7 (36) is larger than 34, so we call the *recursiveBinarySearch* method, searching the left subarray. However, that left subarray is empty. We have not found 34, so we return −1.

Skill Practice
with these end-of-chapter questions

13.10.1 Multiple Choice Exercises
Questions 2, 6, 7, 8

13.10.2 Reading and Understanding Code
Questions 9, 10, 11, 12, 13, 14, 15, 20, 21, 22, 23

13.10.3 Fill In the Code
Questions 24, 25, 26, 27, 28

13.10.4 Identifying Errors in Code
Questions 29, 30, 31, 32

13.10.5 Debugging Area
Questions 33, 34, 35, 36, 37, 38

13.10.6 Write a Short Program
Questions 42, 43, 45, 46, 47

13.10.8 Technical Writing
Question 63

13.6 Programming Activity 2: The Towers of Hanoi

A well-known problem that lends itself to an elegant recursive formulation is the Towers of Hanoi. Here it is:

- There are three towers, which we can represent as the source tower, the temporary tower, and the destination tower.
- We have a stack of *n* disks piled on the source tower; all the disks have a different diameter. The largest disk is at the bottom and the smallest disk is at the top.

- The goal is to transfer all the disks, one at a time, to the destination tower using all three towers for help. No larger disk can be placed on top of a smaller one.

The recursive solution to the problem for the general case ($n >= 1$) is as follows:

1. Transfer the top ($n - 1$) disks from the source tower to the temporary tower.
2. Transfer the one remaining disk (the largest) from the source tower to the destination tower.
3. Transfer the ($n - 1$) disks from the the temporary tower to the destination tower.

The base case, when $n = 0$ (there are 0 disks to transfer), is to do nothing.

The first and third operations are simply recursive calls using a smaller number of disks ($n - 1$) than the original problem.

In the case of $n = 5$, Figures 13.13–13.16 illustrate the recursive solution and formulation. In the figures, the left, middle, and right towers represent the source, temporary, and destination towers, respectively.

In this activity, you will work with recursion to perform the following function:

Code a recursive method to solve the Towers of Hanoi problem

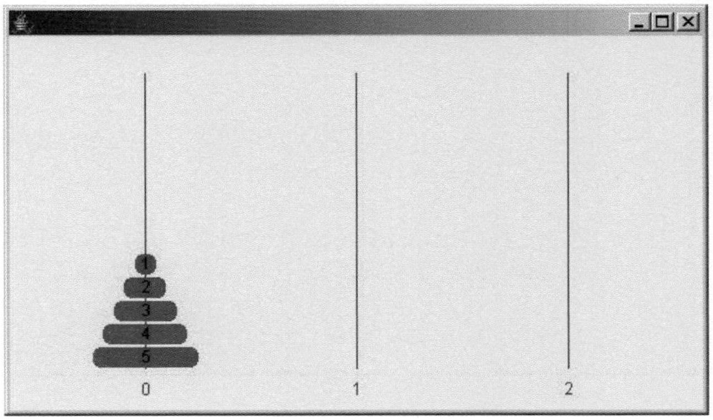

Figure 13.13
Starting Position With Five Disks

Figure 13.14
Position After Step 1

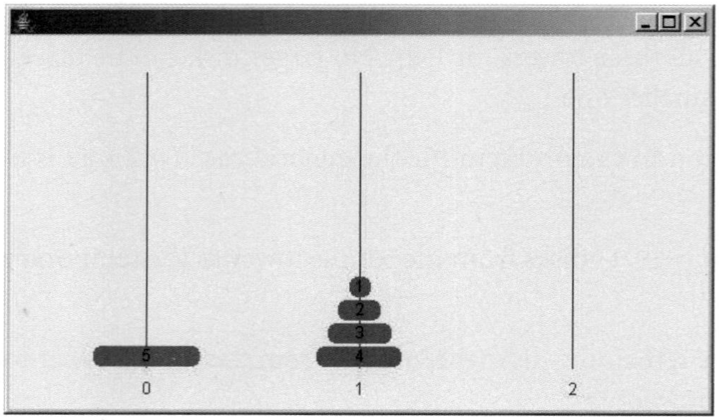

Figure 13.15
Position After Step 2

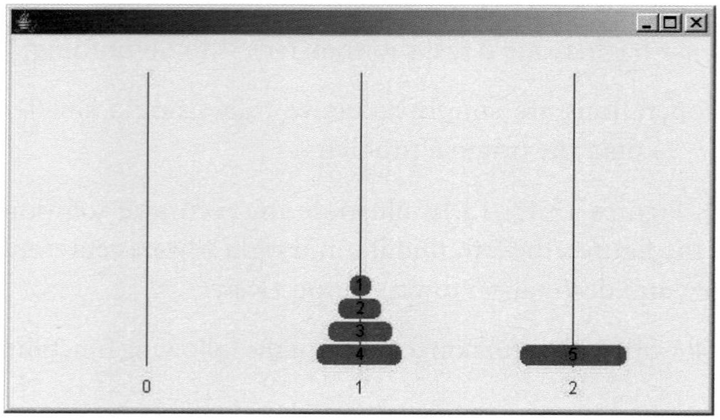

Figure 13.16
Position After Step 3

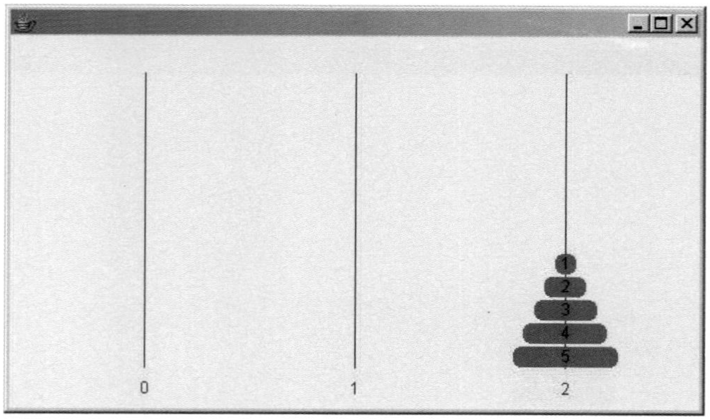

Instructions

In the Chapter 13 Programming Activity 2 directory on the CD-ROM accompanying this book, you will find the source files needed to complete this activity. Copy all of the files to a directory on your computer. Note that all files should be in the same directory.

Open the *HanoiClient.java* source file. Searching for five stars (*****) in the source code will position you to the code section where you will add your code. In this task, you will fill in the code inside the *recursiveTOfH* method to solve the Towers of Hanoi problem. Example 13.9 shows the section of the *HanoiClient* source code where you will add your code.

```
public void recursiveTOfH( int numDisks, int fromTower,
                           int toTower, int useTower )
{
   // ***** Student writes the body of this method *****
   //
   // Using recursion, transfer numDisks disks from the tower
   // fromTower to the tower toTower using the tower
   // useTower

   // The disks are numbered as follows: if we started with n disks,
   //   the disk at the top is disk # 1
   //   and the disk at the bottom is disk # n

   // We call the moveDisk method inside the body of this method

   // The moveDisk method moves one disk and takes 3 arguments:
   //   an int, representing the disk number to be moved
   //   an int, representing the tower to move the disk from
   //   an int, representing the tower to move the disk to

   // So if these three variables are:
   //   diskNumber, fromTower, and toTower
   //   then the call to moveDisks will be:

   //   moveDisk( diskNumber, fromTower, toTower );

   if ( numDisks > 0 )
   {
```

```
    // Student code starts here
    // 1. Move ( numDisks - 1 ) disks from fromTower
    //    to useTower using toTower

    // 2. Move one disk from fromTower to toTower
    //    Print a message to the screen, then
    //    call moveDisk in order to animate.

    // 3. Move ( numDisks - 1 ) disks from useTower to toTower
    //    using fromTower

  }

  // Base case:  0 disks to move ==> do nothing

  //
  // end of student code
  //
}
```

EXAMPLE 13.9 Location of Student Code in *HanoiClient*

The framework will animate your code so that you get some feedback on the correctness of your code. It will display the disks being moved from one tower to another until the whole set of disks has been moved from the left tower to the right tower. Code to enforce the rules has already been written.

To test your code, compile and run the application; when the program begins, a dialog box will prompt you for the number of disks as shown in Figure 13.17.

Click “Cancel” to exit the program; click “OK” to continue and animate your code.

If you enter an integer less than 1 or greater than 9, the program will use a default value of 4. If you enter 5, as shown in Figure 13.17, the first screen will be as shown in Figure 13.13. An intermediate position is shown in Figure 13.18.

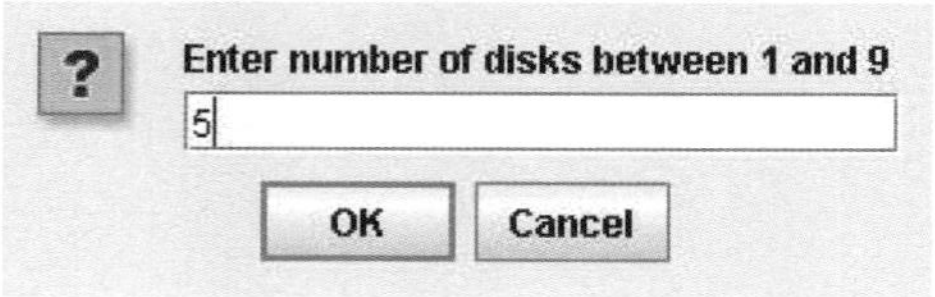

Figure 13.17
Opening Dialog Box

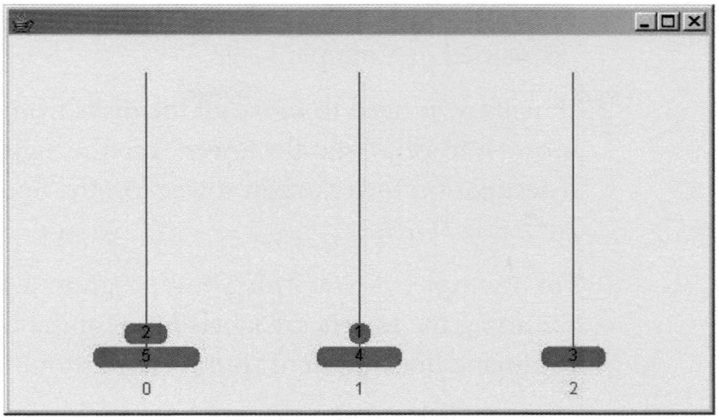

Figure 13.18
An Intermediate Position in the Animation

Task Instructions

- In the file *HanoiClient.java*, the *recursiveTOfH* method header is:

```
public void recursiveTOfH( int numDisks, int fromTower,
                           int toTower, int useTower )
```

  This method takes four parameters: *numDisks*, representing the number of disks to be moved, and 3 *ints* representing the tower to move the disks from, the tower to move the disks to, and the tower to use to accomplish that task of moving *numDisks* disks from tower *fromTower* to tower *toTower*. For instance, with five disks, our method call in the *main* method is:

```
recursiveTOfH( 5, 0, 2, 1 );
```

  The preceding method call is interpreted as: move 5 disks from tower 0 to tower 2, using tower 1 as a temporary holding tower.

- Your code goes in three places, all of them inside the *if* statement.

  1. First, you need to move all the disks except the bottom one from the *fromTower* (source tower, "left tower" on the figures) to the *useTower* (temporary tower, "middle tower" on the figures) using the *toTower* ("destination tower, right tower" on the figures). You do this by calling *recursiveTOfH* with the appropriate arguments.
  2. Then, you need to move the bottom disk from the *fromTower* (source tower, "left tower" on the figures) to the *toTower* (destination tower, "right tower" on the figures). To track your progress, output the move to the command line ("Move disk *x* from tower *y* to tower *z*"). You also need to call the *moveDisk*

method so that the code animates. The API of *moveDisk* is explained in Example 13.9.

3. Finally, you need to move all the disks from the *useTower* (temporary tower, "middle tower" on the figures) to the *toTower* (destination tower, "right tower" on the figures). Again, you call *recursiveTOfH*.

For example, if you run your program with three disks, and assuming the towers are labeled 0, 1, and 2 from left to right, the command line output of your method should read something like:

```
Move disk 1 from tower 0 to tower 2
Move disk 2 from tower 0 to tower 1
Move disk 1 from tower 2 to tower 1
Move disk 3 from tower 0 to tower 2
Move disk 1 from tower 1 to tower 0
Move disk 2 from tower 1 to tower 2
Move disk 1 from tower 0 to tower 2
```

Troubleshooting

If your method implementation does not animate or animates incorrectly, check these items:

- Check the feedback on the output to see if your code violates the rules.
- Verify that you coded the first recursive call correctly.
- Verify that you coded the second recursive call correctly.

DISCUSSION QUESTIONS ?

1. What is the base case for the method?
2. As the number of disks increases, what happens to the time it takes for the method to run?

13.7 Animation Using Recursion

Sometimes, we want to animate an object on the screen by moving the object from one location to another. We could do this using a *for* loop by changing the starting *x* value of the object until we reach the destination location. A recursive solution to the same problem is to move the object one pixel, then move the object the rest of the distance.

Let's revisit the *Astronaut* class from Chapter 7. We will code one additional method in the *Astronaut* class: a recursive method that will move the astronaut from left to right a certain number of pixels. The number of pixels between the starting point and the end point, or distance to move, is a parameter of the method.

In the general case, when the distance is greater than or equal to 1, we draw the astronaut, move the *x* coordinate of the astronaut by 1 pixel to the right, and call the recursive method with the distance argument reduced by 1. Since the distance argument is reduced by 1, we are reducing the size of the problem.

As the distance argument decreases at every step, it will eventually reach 0. That is the base case. Thus, if the distance is negative or equal to 0, then we will not move the astronaut and the method does nothing.

The pseudocode for the general case, when the argument passed to the method is positive, is as follows:

```
draw the astronaut
erase the astronaut
increment sX, the starting x coordinate of the astronaut, by 1
call animateAstronautRecursive with the distance argument
   decreased by 1
```

Since the *draw* method is already coded, we use it to draw the astronaut each time our recursive method is called. Our recursive method is named *animateAstronautRecursive*. In Example 13.10, that method is coded at lines 17–35. The constructors and other methods of the *Astronaut* class are identical to those in Chapter 7.

Our *animateAstronautRecursive* method takes three parameters:

- *distance*, an *int*, the distance to move the astronaut
- *g*, a *Graphics* object reference, which represents the graphics context of the window
- *background*, a *Color* object reference, the background color of the window

At line 25, we test for the base case. If the distance is less than or equal to 0, we do nothing. Otherwise, we execute lines 27–32.

We first call the *draw* method to draw the astronaut, then pause for 100 milliseconds (1/10 of a second). At lines 29–30, we set the current color to the background color passed to the method, then erase the astronaut by filling a rectangle enclosing the astronaut with the background color. At line 31, we increment *sX* by 1. The next time we draw the astronaut—if we draw it—will be at a position one pixel to the right of the previous position. We make the recursive call to *animateAstronautRecursive* at line 32 with the distance decremented by 1.

```
 1 /* An Astronaut Class
 2    Anderson, Franceschi
 3 */
 4
 5 import java.awt.Graphics;
 6 import java.awt.Color;
 7
 8 public class Astronaut
 9 {
10   // the starting (x,y) coordinate for the Astronaut
11   private int sX;
12   private int sY;
13   private double scale; // scaling factor, 1.0 is full size
14
15   // constructors and other methods, including draw, per Chapter 7
16
17   /** recursive horizontal animation method
18   *   @param    distance     the distance of the animation
19   *   @param    g            the Graphics context object
20   *   @param    background   the background color of the animation
21   */
22   public void animateAstronautRecursive
23                ( int distance, Graphics g, Color background )
24   {
25     if ( distance > 0 )
26     {
27       draw( g );
28       Pause.wait( 0.1 );
29       g.setColor( background );
30       g.fillRect( sX, sY, 270, 290 );
31       sX = sX + 1;
32       animateAstronautRecursive( distance - 1, g, background );
33     }
34     // if distance <= 0 do nothing
35   }
36 }
```

EXAMPLE 13.10 The *Astronaut* Class

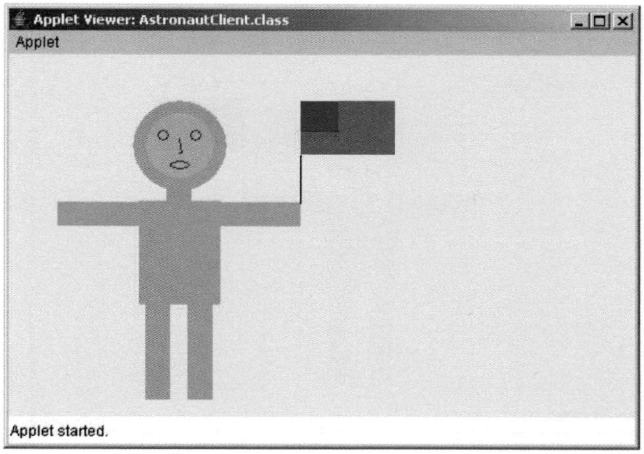

Figure 13.19
The Start of the Animation in Example 13.11

Now, we can create the applet class, which will be the *Astronaut* client. The applet has three instance variables: *contents*, a *Container* object reference; *astro*, an *Astronaut* object reference; and *width*, an *int*, which is the distance to move the astronaut. *Contents* represents the content pane of the applet. We will animate the astronaut horizontally over *width* number of pixels. To keep the example simple, we have initialized *width* to 100.

We call the *animateAstronautRecursive* method of the *Astronaut* class in the applet's *paint* method at lines 26–28. We want the background color of the animation to be the background color of the applet. Thus, the third argument passed to the *animateAstronautRecursive* method is the return value from *contents.getBackground( )*.

The method draws the astronaut, erases it, draws it again, erases it again, . . . so the last step is to erase it. We call the *draw* method at line 29 so that the astronaut displays in the applet window after the animation finishes.

Example 13.11 shows the *AstronautClient* applet class. Its output is shown in Figures 13.19 and 13.20.

```
1 /* Astronaut client
2    Anderson, Franceschi
3 */
4
5 import javax.swing.JApplet;
6 import java.awt.Graphics;
7 import java.awt.Container;
8
9 public class AstronautClient extends JApplet
```

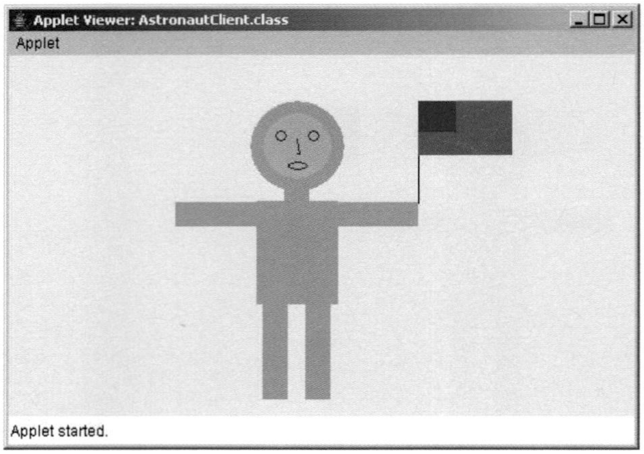

Figure 13.20
The End of the Animation from Example 13.11

```
{
  private Container contents;
  private Astronaut astro;
  private int width = 100; // width of the horizontal animation

  public void init( )
  {
    // instantiate the Astronaut object
    astro = new Astronaut( 0, 0, 1.0 );
    contents = getContentPane( );
    contents.setSize( 500, 300 );
  }

  public void paint( Graphics g )
  {
    super.paint( g );
    // animate the astronaut over the current background
    astro.animateAstronautRecursive
                  ( width, g, contents.getBackground( ) );
    astro.draw( g );
  }
}
```

EXAMPLE 13.11 The *AstronautClient* Applet

13.8 Recursion Versus Iteration

Recursion and iteration are different approaches to solving a problem.

- A recursive function is implemented using decision constructs (e.g., *if/else* statements) and repeatedly calls itself.

- An iterative function is implemented with looping constructs (e.g., *while* or *for* statements) and repeatedly executes the loop.

Most programmers would not use recursion to print "Hello World" n times; they would simply use the following *for* loop:

```
for ( int i = 0; i < n; i++ )
     System.out.println( "Hello World" );
```

Similarly, a factorial method can easily be coded using iteration.

However, other problems, such as the Towers of Hanoi and the binary search, are more easily coded using recursion rather than iteration.

Often, the recursive solution to a problem is more elegant and easier to understand than an equivalent iterative solution. The main difficulty in coding a recursive method is the problem-solving part. The implementation, using Java or any other programming language, is easier than the equivalent code that uses iteration.

Another consideration when deciding to use recursion or iteration is the efficiency of the method at execution time. This is called the running time of the method, and is often measured in order of magnitude as a function of the size of the input.

For instance, for the Hello World example, the input is n. Using iteration, we will execute the loop n times, and the test condition of the *for* statement will be executed $(n + 1)$ times. When the running time of a method can be expressed as n multiplied by a constant value $(n \times c)$, we say that the order of magnitude of its running time is n; we say it is "big-Oh" of n or $O(n)$.

Using recursion, and considering Example 13.1, the *printHelloWorldNTimes* method will call itself n times before reaching the base case $(n = 0)$, for which the method does nothing. At each recursive call, the method performs a small and finite number of operations: it tests for n being greater than 0, and then prints "Hello World" once before calling itself; so it performs two operations before calling itself. Since it calls itself n times overall, the approximate running time of the method is $2 * n$, and therefore the order of magnitude of its running time is also $O(n)$ (orders of magnitude ignore constant factors).

So in this case, the running times of iteration and recursion are of the same order of magnitude. However, the overhead associated with all the recursive method calls will add to the running time. That will make recursion slower than iteration, which is often the case.

SOFTWARE ENGINEERING TIP

Readability and maintenance are important considerations when coding a method. If running times are equivalent and a recursion implementation is easier to understand than the equivalent iteration implementation, choose recursion over iteration, otherwise, iteration is generally preferred.

13.9 Chapter Summary

CHAPTER SUMMARY

- The idea of recursion is to convert or reduce a bigger problem to a smaller, similar problem. The relationship between the bigger problem and the smaller problem is called the general case.
- By reducing the size of a problem to a smaller problem recursively, we eventually arrive at a small problem that is easy to solve. That small problem is called the base case.
- Solving a problem using recursion typically involves coding a recursive method.
- A recursive method
  - can be a *static* method or an instance method,
  - can take 0, 1, or more parameters,
  - and can be a *void* or a value-returning method.
- A recursive method calls itself.
- Problem solving using recursion involves two steps: generating a recursive formulation of the problem for the general case, and solving the base case(s).
- There can be one or more base cases.
- Most base cases are simple, but some can be more complex.
- Most general cases are simple, but some can be more complex.
- A recursive method calls itself repeatedly until a base case is reached.
- A recursive method typically includes an *if/else* statement that tests for the base case.
- If the recursive method does not test for the base case, calling the method will typically result in a stack overflow run-time error.
- Recursion is typically an alternative to iteration. The coding of a recursive method is typically compact and elegant. However, a recursive method may not be as efficient as its iterative equivalent.

13.10 Exercises, Problems, and Projects

13.10.1 Multiple Choice Exercises

1. A recursive method
   - ❑ is always a *static* method
   - ❑ is never a *static* method
   - ❑ may or may not be *static*
2. A recursive method
   - ❑ is always a method with a *void* return value
   - ❑ is always a value-returning method
   - ❑ can be either of the above
3. When formulating a recursive solution, what should you consider?
   - ❑ base cases and general case
   - ❑ base cases only
   - ❑ general case only
4. A recursive method
   - ❑ is a method containing a loop
   - ❑ calls itself
   - ❑ is part of the *java.recursion* package
5. When coding a class that includes a recursive method, we need to import the *java.recursion* package.
   - ❑ true
   - ❑ false
6. If the base case of a recursive method is not taken into account when coding the method, the likely outcome is
   - ❑ a compiler error
   - ❑ a run-time error
   - ❑ no error

7. If there are several base cases in a recursive method, omitting the code for one of them will result in

   ❑ a compiler error

   ❑ a run-time error

   ❑ no error

8. If a recursive method makes a recursive call with the same argument that it was passed, the likely outcome is

   ❑ a compiler error

   ❑ a run-time error

   ❑ no error

13.10.2 Reading and Understanding Code

For Questions 9 to 11, consider the following method:

```
public static int foo1( int n )
{
 if ( n == 0 )
   return 0;
 else if ( n > 0 )
   return foo1( n - 1 );
 else
   return foo1( n + 1 );
}
```

9. What is the value of *i* after the following code is executed?

```
int i = foo1( 0 );
```

10. What is the value of *i* after the following code is executed?

```
int i = foo1( 4 );
```

11. What does the *foo1* method do?

For Questions 12 to 15, consider the following method:

```
public static int foo2( int n )
{
 // n is guaranteed to be >= 0
 if ( n < 10 )
   return n;
 else
   return foo2( n - 10 );
}
```

12. What is the value of *i* after the following code is executed?

```
int i = foo2( 7 );
```

13. What is the value of *i* after the following code is executed?

```
int i = foo2( 13 );
```

14. What is the value of *i* after the following code is executed?

```
int i = foo2( 65 );
```

15. What does the *foo2* method return when the argument is a positive integer?

For Questions 16 to 19, consider the following method:

```
public static void foo3( String s )
{
 if ( s.length( ) > 0 )
 {
   System.out.print( s.charAt( s.length( ) – 1 ) );
   foo3( s.substring( 0, s.length( ) – 1 ) );
 }
}
```

16. What is the output of the following code?

```
foo3( "" );
```

17. What is the output of the following code?

```
foo3( "Hi" );
```

18. What is the output of the following code?

```
foo3( "Hello" );
```

19. What does the *foo3* method do?

For Questions 20 to 23, consider the following method:

```
public static int foo4( int n, int p )
{
  // p is guaranteed to be >= 0
  if ( p == 0 )
   return 1;
  else
   return ( n * foo4( n, p – 1 ) );
}
```

20. What is the value of *i* after the following code is executed?

```
int i = foo4( 6, 0 );
```

21. What is the value of *i* after the following code is executed?

```
int i = foo4( 5, 1 );
```

22. What is the value of *i* after the following code is executed?

```
int i = foo4( 4, 3 );
```

23. What does the *foo4* method return as a function of its two parameters, *n* and *p*?

13.10.3 Fill In the Code

24. This recursive method returns the number of times a given character is found in a *String*:

```
public static int foo( String s, char c )
{
  if ( s.length( ) == 0 )
    return 0;
  else
  {
    // your code goes here

  }
}
```

25. This recursive method returns "even" if the length of a given *String* is even, and "odd" if the length of the *String* is odd.

```
public static String foo( String s )
{
  if ( s.length( ) == 0 )
      return "even";
  else if ( s.length( ) == 1 )
      return "odd";
  else
       // your code goes here
}
```

26. This recursive method returns the sum of all the integers from 0 to a given number.

```
public static int foo( int n )
{
  // n is guaranteed to be >= 0
  if ( n == 0 )
      return 0;
  else
```

```
  {
     // your code goes here

  }
}
```

27. This recursive method returns *true* if its *String* parameter contains the characters *A* and *B* in consecutive locations; otherwise, it returns *false*.

```
public static boolean foo( String s )
{
  if (      )              // base case # 1

  else if (       )        // base case # 2

  else                     // general case
    return foo( s.substring( 1, s.length( ) ) );
}
```

28. This recursive method squares a number until the result is greater than or equal to 1000, then returns the result. For instance, *foo(10)* returns 10000, *foo(6)* returns 1296, and *foo(1233)* returns 1233.

```
public static int foo( int n )
{
  // n is guaranteed to be greater than 1
  if ( n >= 1000 )              // base case

  else                          // general case

}
```

13.10.4 Identifying Errors in Code

29. You coded the following in the file *Test.java*. Where is the error?

```
int p = foo( 4 );
// more code here

public static int foo( int n )
{
 int p = foo( n – 1 );
 if ( n == 0 )
   return 1;
 else
   return ( n * p );
}
```

30. You coded the following method. Where is the error?

```
public static double foo( int n )
{
 if ( n == 0 )
   return 1.0;
 else if ( n < 0 )
   return foo( n - 1 );
 else
   return foo( n + 1 );
}
```

31. You coded the following method. Where is the error?

```
public static boolean foo( int n )
{
 // n is guaranteed to be >= 0
 if ( n == 0 )
   return true;
 else
   foo( n - 1 );
}
```

32. You coded the following method. Where is the error?

```
public static boolean foo( int n )
{
 // n is guaranteed to be >= 0
 if ( n == 0 )
   return true;
 else
   return foo( n );
}
```

13.10.5 Debugging Area—Using Messages from the Java Compiler and Java JVM

33. You coded the following in the file *Test.java*:

```
System.out.println( foo( 5 ) );
// more code here

public static int foo( int n )
{
 return ( n * foo( n - 1 ) );  // line 15
}
```

The code compiles, but when it runs, you get the following output:

```
Exception in thread "main" java.lang.StackOverflowError
at Test.foo(Test.java:15)
at Test.foo(Test.java:15)
at Test.foo(Test.java:15)
....
```

Explain what the problem is and how to fix it.

34. You coded the following in the file *Test.java*:

```
System.out.println( foo( 5 ) );
// more code here

public static int foo( int n )
{
 if ( n == 0 )
   return foo( 0 );  // line 15
 else
   return ( n * foo( n – 1 ) );
}
```

The code compiles, but when it runs, you get the following output:

```
Exception in thread "main" java.lang.StackOverflowError
at Test.foo(Test.java:15)
at Test.foo(Test.java:15)
at Test.foo(Test.java:15)
....
```

Explain what the problem is and how to fix it.

35. You coded the following in the file *Test.java*:

```
System.out.println( foo( 5 ) );
// more code here

public static int foo( int n )       // line 9
{
 if ( n == 0 )
   return 1;
 else
   System.out.println( n * foo( n - 1 ) );
}        // line 15
```

At compile time, you get the following error:

```
Test.java:15: missing return statement
}
^
1 error
```

Explain what the problem is and how to fix it.

36. You coded the following in the file *Test.java*:

```
System.out.println( foo( 5 ) );
// more code here

public static int foo( int n )
{
 if ( n == 0 )
   return 1;
 else
   return ( foo( n ) * ( n - 1 ) );
}
```

The code compiles, but when it runs, you get the following message, repeated many times, before finally stopping.

```
Exception in thread "main" java.lang.StackOverflowError
      at Test.foo(Test.java:15)
      at Test.foo(Test.java:15)
      at Test.foo(Test.java:15)
```

Explain what the problem is and how to fix it.

37. You coded the following in the file *Test.java*:

```
System.out.println( foo( "Hello" ) ); // line 6
// more code here

public static int foo( String s )    // line 9
{
 if ( s.length( ) == 0 )
   return 0;
 else
   return ( 1 +
     foo( s.substring( 0, s.length( ) - 2 ) ) ); // line 15
}
```

The code compiles, but when it runs, you get the following output:

```
Exception in thread "main" java.lang.StringIndexOutOfBoundsException:
String index out of range: -1
at java.lang.String.substring(String.java:1938)
        at Test.foo(Test.java:14)
        at Test.foo(Test.java:14)
        at Test.foo(Test.java:14)
        at Test.main(Test.java:6)
```

Explain what the problem is and how it happens.

38. You coded the following in the file *Test.java:*

```
System.out.println( foo( "Hello" ) ) ; // line 6
// more code here

public static int foo( String s )     // line 9
{
 if ( s.length( ) == 0 )              // line 11
   return 0;
 else
 {
    String temp = null;
    if ( s.length( ) > 1 )
         temp = s.substring( 0, s.length( ) – 1) ;
    return ( 1 + foo( temp ) ) ;      // line 18
 }
}
```

The code compiles, but when it runs, you get the following output:

```
Exception in thread "main" java.lang.NullPointerException
        at Test.foo(Test.java:11)
        at Test.foo(Test.java:18)
        at Test.foo(Test.java:18)
        at Test.foo(Test.java:18)
        at Test.foo(Test.java:18)
        at Test.foo(Test.java:18)
        at Test.main(Test.java:6)
```

Explain what the problem is and how to fix it.

13.10.6 Write a Short Program

39. Using recursion, write a program that takes a word as an input and outputs that word backward.

40. Using recursion, write a program that keeps prompting the user for a word containing a $ character. As soon as the user inputs a word containing the $ character, you should output that word and your program will terminate.
41. Using recursion, write a program that takes a word as an input and outputs that word with all characters separated by a space.
42. Using recursion, write a program that takes a word as an input and outputs the number of times the letter *a* is found in that word.
43. Using recursion, write a program that takes an integer value as an input and outputs the Fibonacci value for that number. The Fibonacci value of a number is defined as follows:

```
Fib( 1 ) = 1
Fib( 2 ) = 1
Fib( n ) = Fib ( n – 1 ) + Fib( n – 2 ) for n >= 3
```

44. Using recursion, write a program that takes a positive number as an input and keeps dividing that number by 3 until the result is less than 1, at which time output that result.
45. Using recursion, write a program that takes 10 numbers as inputs and outputs the minimum of these numbers.
46. Using recursion, write a program that takes 10 words representing Internet addresses as inputs and outputs the number of words containing .edu.
47. Rewrite Example 13.8, *RecursiveBinarySearch*, using an array sorted in descending order.

13.10.7 Programming Projects

48. Write a class with just one instance variable, a *String* representing a binary number. Write a recursive method taking only one parameter that converts that binary number to its decimal equivalent. Your program should include a client class to test your class.
49. Write a class with just one instance variable, an *int*. Your constructor should take an *int* as its only parameter. Write a recursive method that checks if that *int* is a multiple of 5. Your program should include a client class to test your class.

50. Write a class with just one instance variable, a *String* representing some HTML code. Your constructor should take a file name as its only parameter (you will need to make up some sample HTML files to test your program). Write a recursive method returning the number of occurrences of a specified character in the HTML *String*. Your program should include a client class to test your class. In particular, call the recursive method to check whether the sample files contain an equal number of < and > characters.

51. Write a class with just one instance variable, a *String* representing a password. Write a recursive method to check if the password contains at least one character that is a digit (0 to 9). Your program should include a client class to test your class.

52. Write a class with two instance variables, representing the same password. Write a recursive method that checks if both passwords are equal. Your program should include a client class to test your class.

53. Write a class with two instance variables, representing an old password and a new password. Write a recursive method that returns the number of places where the two passwords have different characters. The passwords can have different lengths. Write another, non-recursive method returning whether the two passwords are sufficiently different. The method takes an *int* parameter indicating the minimum number of differences that qualify the passwords as being sufficiently different. Your program should include a client class to test your class.

54. Write a class with just one instance variable, an integer array. Your constructor should take an integer array as its only parameter. Write a recursive method that returns the sum of all elements in the array. Your program should include a client class to test your class.

55. Write a class with just one instance variable, an integer array. Your constructor should take an integer array as its only parameter. Write a recursive method that returns the maximum value of all the elements in the array. Your program should include a client class to test your class.

56. Write a class with the functionality of checking a list of names to determine whether the same name is present in two consecutive locations; you can assume that the list contains fewer than 100 names. The method solving that problem should be recursive. Your program should include a client class to test your class.

57. A professor has a policy to give at least one A in his or her class. Write a class that encapsulates that idea, including a recursive method checking for at least one A in a set of grades. You can assume that there are 30 students. Your program should include a client class to test your class.

58. Write a class with just one instance variable, an array representing grades between 0 and 100. You can assume that there are 15 grades. Your constructor should take an array as its only parameter. Write a recursive method that returns the average of all grades. Your program should include a client class to test your class.

59. Write a class with just one instance variable, an *int*. Your constructor should take an *int* as its only parameter. Write a recursive method that converts that *int* to a *String* representing that number in binary. Your program should include a client class to test your class.

60. Write a class potentially representing a *String* of binary digits (0s and 1s). Your constructor should take a *String* as its only parameter (that *String* may contain only 0s and 1s, or it may not). Write a recursive method that checks whether that *String* contains 0s and 1s only. Write another recursive method that converts that *String* to its decimal equivalent. Your method should be different from the one in Exercise 48: it should take two parameters, the *String* representing the binary number, and an *int* representing an exponent. Your program should include a client class to test your class.

61. Write a class with an *int* array as its only instance variable. Write a recursive method that uses the following recursive strategy in order to sort the array:

    - ❑ Sort the left half of the array (this is a recursive call).
    - ❑ Sort the right half of the array (this is another recursive call).
    - ❑ Merge the two sorted halves of the array so that the array is sorted (there is no recursive call here).

62. Write an applet that shows a very small circle growing from small to large and then shrinking to its original size. Your applet should allow the user to input the minimum radius and the maximum radius (and also check that the minimum radius is smaller than the maximum

radius). The expansion and contraction of the circle should be performed by two recursive methods.

13.10.8 Technical Writing

63. Think of an example of a problem, different from the chapter problems, which can be solved by an iterative formulation and a recursive formulation. Discuss which one you would prefer to code and why.

13.10.9 Group Projects (for a group of 1, 2, or 3 students)

64. Consider a rectangular grid of integers. We are interested in computing recursively the largest sum of any path from a top position to a bottom position. A valid path is defined as follows:

    - ❑ It should start at a number in the top row and end at a number in the bottom row.
    - ❑ It should include a number in every row.
    - ❑ From row i to row $(i + 1)$, a valid path can be created:
        - down vertically (in the same column)
        - down diagonally one column to the left (if possible)
        - down diagonally one column to the right (if possible)

    For instance, let's assume we have the following rectangle of numbers:

2	5	17	12	3
15	8	4	11	10
9	18	6	20	16
14	13	12	1	7

Note: Your program should accept any positive number at any spot within the rectangle.

Examples of valid paths are:

$2 \rightarrow 8 \rightarrow 18 \rightarrow 14$

$17 \rightarrow 4 \rightarrow 18 \rightarrow 14$

$5 \rightarrow 4 \rightarrow 20 \rightarrow 12$

In this example, the path generating the largest sum is:

$17 \rightarrow 11 \rightarrow 20 \rightarrow 12$ for a total of $17 + 11 + 20 + 12 = 60$

Your program should accept from the user a rectangle of integers; to keep it simple, you can limit the size of the rectangle to a maximum of 10 columns by 20 rows. Your program should, recursively, compute and output the path that generates the largest sum.

65. Write a class with an *int* array as its only instance variable. Write a recursive method that uses the following Merge Sort algorithm in order to sort the array.

- ❑ If the array has only 1 element, then the array is already sorted and there is nothing to do; otherwise:
  - Sort the left half of the array by calling the method (this is a recursive call)
  - Sort the right half of the array by calling the method (this is another recursive call)
  - Merge the two sorted half-arrays into one so that the resulting array is sorted

Because of the recursive nature of this method, you need to think about what parameters that method should have, in addition to the array itself. In fact, at each recursive call, the method sorts a sub-array of the original array; so your parameters should define a sub-array within the original array.

To merge the two sorted half-arrays into one resulting sorted array, you can loop through both half-arrays and compare each pair of elements, and place the smaller of the two in the resulting array. The following is an example of what an array would look like before and after the various steps of the algorithm:

The unsorted array, before applying the algorithm:

Value	78	12	37	25	24	20	55	9
Index	0	1	2	3	4	5	6	7

The array, after the first recursive call. The left half-array, from index 0 to index 3, is sorted.

Value	12	25	37	78	24	20	55	9
Index	0	1	2	3	4	5	6	7

The array, after the second recursive call and before the merging step. The left half-array, from index 0 to index 3, and the right half-array, from index 4 to index 7, are sorted.

Value	12	25	37	78	9	20	24	55
Index	0	1	2	3	4	5	6	7

The array after the merge step, the array is now sorted.

Value	9	12	20	24	25	37	55	78
Index	0	1	2	3	4	5	6	7

Here is an example of what the array and resulting array would look like during the merge step: The elements 9, 12, and 20 have been processed and placed at their correct place in the resulting array. We are now processing 25 from the left half-array and 24 from the right half-array. Note that during the merge step, we need a separate array to store the sorted elements.

The array:

Value	12	25	37	78	9	20	24	55
Index	0	1	2	3	4	5	6	7

The resulting array:

Value	9	12	20					
Index	0	1	2	3	4	5	6	7

For tracing purposes, add a statement as you enter the method to output that the method is called; include the starting and ending indexes delimiting the sub-array on which the method is called. Also, add a counter to track how many times the method is called as the recursive calls unfold. In your client program, use arrays with 4, 8, 16, 32, and 64 elements. How many recursive calls are made in each case? More generally, if the array contains 2^n elements, how many recursive calls are made?

CHAPTER 14

An Introduction to Data Structures

CHAPTER CONTENTS

Introduction

As our programs execute, we often need a means to organize data in memory. In Chapters 8 and 9, we used arrays as a convenient method to store multiple variables of the same data type. In Chapter 9, we also introduced the *ArrayList* as an array that dynamically expands, as needed.

In fact, arrays and *ArrayLists* are just two examples of **data structures**, which are methodologies a program uses to store its data in memory.

An *ArrayList* dynamically adjusts its size by increasing its capacity by approximately 50% whenever it runs out of space. If an *ArrayList*'s current capacity is 640 objects, and it is full (that is, it holds 640 objects), adding one more object will cause its capacity to increase to 961 objects. If that 641st object is the last object added to the *ArrayList*, then memory space for 320 elements will have been allocated, but not used. Obviously, this is not an efficient use of memory space.

However, *ArrayLists* are useful in some situations, such as reading data from a file, where we don't know in advance how many items we will need to store in memory. Once the data is read, we know that the size of the *ArrayList* will not change further, so we can trim the capacity of the *ArrayList* to its current size using the *trimToSize* method, thus releasing the unused memory.

In other situations, however, the number of data items may dynamically increase or decrease as the program executes. For these cases, we need a data structure that efficiently grows and shrinks as items are added and removed.

A new data structure that we will illustrate in this chapter is the **linked list**, which can expand (or shrink) one object at a time, keeping the size of the list to a minimum at all times. An advantage, then, of linked lists is that they do not consume unnecessary memory.

14.1 Linked Lists

14.1.1 Linked-List Concepts and Structure

A **linked list** can be thought of as a chain of linked nodes.

A **node** is an object with two attributes:

- data—The data can be a primitive data type (for example, an *int*), or it can be a reference to an object of a specified class.

- the location of the next node in the chain—We say that a node "**points to**," or "**refers to**" the next node.

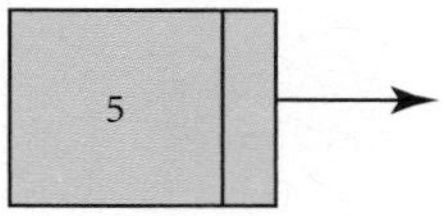

Figure 14.1
A node

Figure 14.1 shows how we can visualize a node containing the integer value 5. The arrow points to the next node in the list.

In the last node of the list, the location of the next node contains the value *null*, to indicate that there are no more nodes in the list.

Figure 14.2 illustrates a linked list of four video game players. The object data stored at each node has the following attributes: the player's ID, the player's name, and the name of the player's favorite game.

From the standpoint of program design, this linked list can be implemented using three classes:

- a *Player* class, encapsulating a player
- a *PlayerNode* class, encapsulating a node
- a *PlayerLinkedList* class, encapsulating the linked list.

In the *Player* class, we will have three instance variables:

- an *int* storing the user ID of the player
- a *String* storing the name of the player
- a *String* storing the name of the player's favorite game.

Often, a node class is designed in a general manner to store a generic *Object*. Implementing a list of generic *Objects* has the advantage of reusability; indeed, we could instantiate the list with any type of *Object* we want. In this chapter, we will first implement a linked list of the primitive type, *int*, then a linked list of *Player* objects, and then a linked list of generic *Objects*.

In the *IntegerNode* class, we have two instance variables:

- an *int*
- an *IntegerNode* object reference, representing the next node.

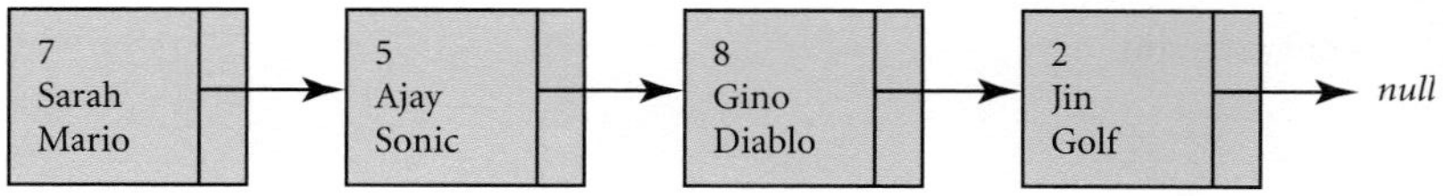

Figure 14.2
A Linked List

Thus, the *IntegerNode* class is defined using an object reference of its own type. Indeed, one of its instance variables is an *IntegerNode* object reference.

We define our two instance variables using the following statements:

```
private int data;
private IntegerNode next;
```

Based on this definition of the *IntegerNode* class, we need only one instance variable in the linked-list class, a reference to the first node, which we call the **head** of the linked list. Indeed, the first node will give us access to the second node, which in turn will give us access to the third node, and so on, until we reach the last node. We will know when we have reached the end of the linked list, because the reference to the next *IntegerNode* will have the value *null.*

SOFTWARE ENGINEERING TIP

Include an instance variable in the linked-list class to store the number of items in the list for quick and direct access to that information as needed.

Often, linked-list classes have another instance variable that holds the number of items in the linked list. Although the number of items can be calculated by looping through and counting all the nodes in the linked list, it is convenient to store the number of items as an instance variable. So our *IntegerLinkedList* class, encapsulating the linked list, will have two instance variables:

- an *IntegerNode* object reference, named *head*, representing the first node of the linked list
- an *int*, named *numberOfItems*, representing the number of items in the linked list.

14.1.2 Linked-List Basics

Example 14.1 shows our *IntegerNode* class:

```
/* The IntegerNode class
   Anderson, Franceschi
*/

public class IntegerNode
{
  private int data;
```

```
private IntegerNode next;

/** default constructor
*   sets data to 0, and next to null
*/
public IntegerNode( )
{
  data = 0;
  next = null;
}

/** overloaded constructor
*   @param newData data value
*/
public IntegerNode( int  newData )
{
  setData( newData );
  next = null;
}

/** accessor for data
*   @return    the value of the node
*/
public int getData( )
{
  return data;
}

/** accessor for next
*   @return   the reference to the next node
*/
public IntegerNode getNext( )
{
  return next;
}

/** mutator for data
*   @param    newData   the new value for the node
*/
public void setData( int newData )
{
  data = newData;
```

```
50   }
51
52   /** mutator for next
53   *   @param   nd   the new value for next
54   */
55   public void setNext( IntegerNode  nd )
56   {
57     next = nd;
58   }
59 }
```

EXAMPLE 14.1 The *IntegerNode* Class

The code for this class is straightforward. We code two constructors at lines 10 to 26. Both of these constructors set the value of *next* to *null*. This will be the desired action when a node is created. However, to allow a client (which will be the linked-list class) to reset the value of *next* as the list expands and shrinks, we provide the *setNext* method.

14.1.3 Methods of a Linked List

For our class encapsulating a linked list, we need to consider the following issues:

- We do not want client programs to change the head node of our list. Thus, we will not provide an accessor or a mutator for the head node.
- Client programs should not be able to change the number of items in the list. Only the methods of the class should update the number of items as we insert or delete items in the list. Thus, we will provide an accessor for the number of items in the list so that the client can view the number of items, but no mutator.

With a linked list, there is some basic functionality that we need to provide, such as

- insert an item
- delete an item
- list, in order, all the items in the list, and return that list as a *String*.

Table 14.1 shows the APIs of the *insert*, *delete*, and *toString* methods.

In our linked list of *ints*, we do not store the *ints* in any predetermined order. Thus, there are only two logical places to insert a node: at the

TABLE 14.1 ***IntegerLinkedList* Methods**

Methods of the *IntegerLinkedList* Class	
Return value	**Method name and argument list**
`void`	`insert( int value )` inserts *value* at the beginning of the list
`boolean`	`delete( int value )` removes the first item on the list that is equal to *value* and returns *true*. If there is no such item on the list, the method returns *false*.
`String`	`toString( )` returns a *String* representation of the list

beginning and at the end of the list. Inserting at the end will consume CPU time, since we will have to loop through all nodes in the list to find the end. So we have decided to insert at the beginning of the linked list because it is easier and faster. Since it will always be possible to insert a new node at the beginning of a list, our *insert* method has a *void* return value.

Other options for implementing a linked list include providing methods to insert at the end of the list, or at a specified position in the list, or at a position before or after a node containing a specified value or object.

When inserting a new *int*, our *insert* method performs the following steps:

1. Instantiate a new node containing the *int* to be inserted.
2. Attach that node at the beginning of the list, that is, make that node point to the previous head node. If the list originally was empty and the previous head node has the value *null*, then the *next* field of the new node is given the value *null*.
3. Indicate that the new node is now the head of the list, that is, make *head* point to the new node.
4. Increase the number of items in the list by 1.

Figures 14.3a to 14.3d illustrate the first three steps.

There are many alternatives for deleting an item from a linked list. We can delete the first element or the last item, or delete an item based on specified

Figure 14.3a
Inserting: Our Original Linked List

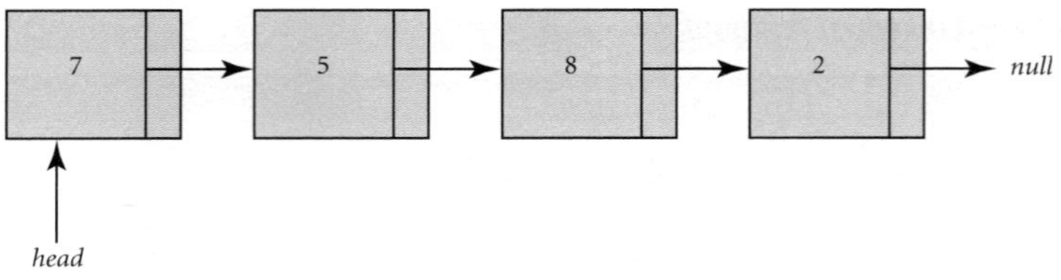

Figure 14.3b
Step 1: The New Node is Instantiated

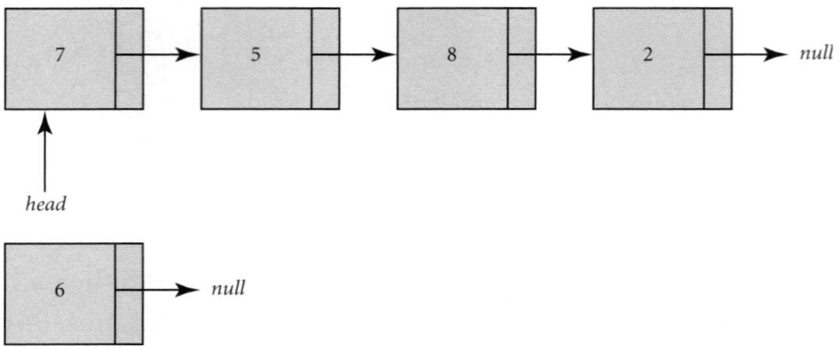

Figure 14.3c
Step 2: The New Node Has Been Attached to the Beginning of the List

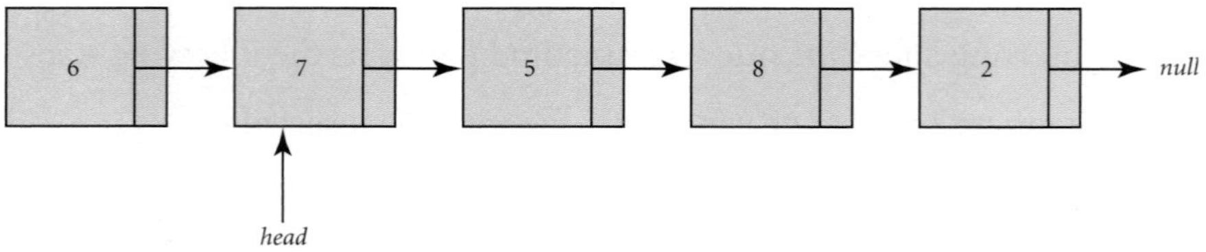

Figure 14.3d
Step 3: *head* Now Points to the New Node

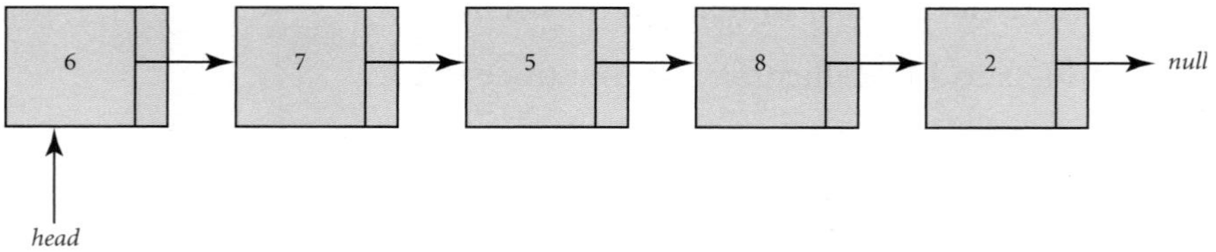

criteria. Such criteria can be the value of the item, or it can be the position of an item in the list. We will implement one *delete* method only: one that deletes an item based on its value.

In order to delete an item, we will traverse the list searching for an item whose value matches a specified value passed as the argument of the *delete* method. **Traversing** a list means looping through the nodes in the list, one after the other, starting at the first node. If we find such an item, we will remove it from the list and return *true*. If we do not find the item, we will return *false*.

There are three possible outcomes when searching for such an item:

1. Such an item can be found and is located somewhere after the head node.
2. Such an item can be found and is located at the head node. Special care must be taken here. There will be a change in the head node of the list and our code will need to handle that.
3. Such an item cannot be found. In this case, no deletion can take place, and we will return *false*.

In the first case, when the node to delete is located after the first node in the list, we need to connect the node before the deleted node (the "previous" node) to the node after the deleted node. To do this, we replace the previous node's *next* field with the *next* field of the deleted node. Thus, as we traverse the list, we need to keep track of the previous node, as well as the current node. To do this, we maintain two node references, *previous* and *current*.

Once we have located the node to delete and it is not the first node of the list, we perform the following steps:

1. Set the *next* field in the *previous* node to the *next* field in the node to be deleted (*current*).
2. Decrease the number of items in the list by 1.

The *current* node becomes unreachable and is therefore a candidate for garbage collection.

Figures 14.4a and 14.4b illustrate deleting a node with the value 8, which is located somewhere in the middle of the list.

Figure 14.4a
The List Before Deleting the Item Whose Value is 8

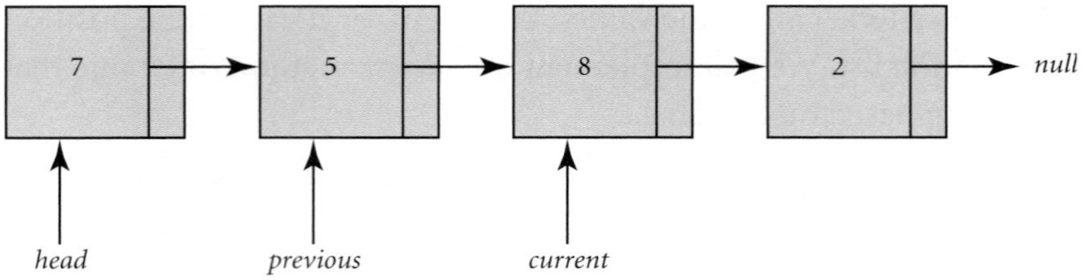

Figure 14.4b
The *previous* Node is Connected to the Node After *current*, Deleting the Item Whose Value is 8

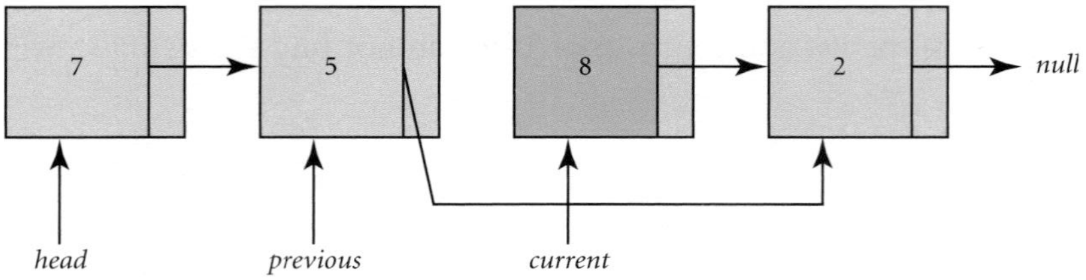

When the node to delete is the head node, we need to make the node pointed to by the deleted node the new *head* of the list. Thus, we perform the following steps:

1. Assign the *next* field of the *current* node to *head.*
2. Decrease the number of items in the list by 1.

Figures 14.5a and 14.5b illustrate deleting the first node in the list.

Figure 14.5a
Before Deleting the Item whose Value is 7

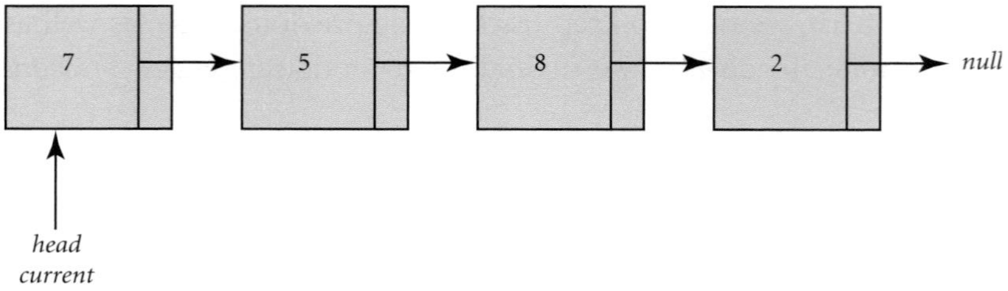

Figure 14.5b
After Updating *head*, the First Node in the List is Deleted

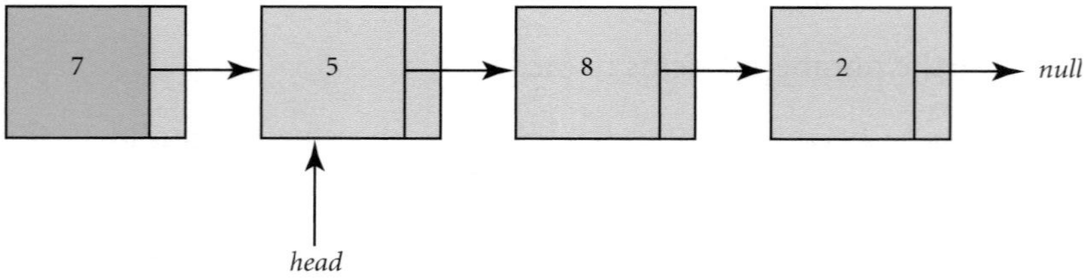

Example 14.2 shows our *IntegerLinkedList* class.

```
/* The IntegerLinkedList class
   Anderson, Franceschi
*/

public class IntegerLinkedList
{
  private IntegerNode head;
  private int numberOfItems;

  /** default constructor
  *   constructs an empty list
  */
  public IntegerLinkedList( )
  {
    head = null;
    numberOfItems = 0;
  }

  /** accessor for numberOfItems
  *   @return   numberOfItmes
  */
  public int getNumberOfItems( )
  {
    return numberOfItems;
  }

  /** insert method
  *   @param    value  data to  insert
  *    inserts node at head
  */
  public void insert( int value )
  {
    IntegerNode nd = new IntegerNode( value );
    nd.setNext( head );
    head = nd;
    numberOfItems++;
  }

  /** delete method
  *   @param    value   the value to delete
  *   @return   true if value was deleted from the list, false otherwise
```

```
  */
  public boolean delete( int value )
  {
    IntegerNode current = head;
    IntegerNode previous = null;
    while ( current != null
           && current.getData( ) != value )
    {
      previous = current;
      current = current.getNext( );
    }

    if ( current == null ) // not found
        return false;
    else
    {
      if ( current == head )
        head = head.getNext( );  // delete head
      else
        previous.setNext( current.getNext( ) );

      numberOfItems--;
      return  true;
    }
  }

  /** toString
  *   @return    values in list separated by a space
  */
  public String toString( )
  {
    String listString = "";
    IntegerNode current = head;
    for ( int i = 0; i < numberOfItems; i++ )
    {
      listString += current.getData( ) + "  ";
      current = current.getNext( );
    }
    return listString;
  }
}
```

EXAMPLE 14.2 The *IntegerLinkedList* Class

The default constructor (lines 10–17) initializes the *head* and *numberOfItems* instance variables to *null* and 0, respectively. The *insert* method, coded from lines 27 to 37, inserts a node containing its parameter *value* at the beginning of the list. At line 33, we create a new node *nd* with the data *value.* At line 34, we connect *nd* to the first node in the list by setting its *next* field to the current head of the list. At line 35, we assign the new node *nd*, to *head*, making it the first node in the linked list. Figures 14.3a to 14.3d illustrate the impact on the list of lines 33–35. At line 36, we increment *numberOfItems* to reflect the addition of a node to the list.

The *delete* method, coded from lines 39 to 66, returns *true* if the deletion is successful and *false* if the deletion is not successful.

Using a *while* loop at lines 47–52, we walk through, or traverse, the list searching for a node containing *value*, our *delete* method's parameter. At lines 45 and 46, we declare and initialize two *IntegerNode* references, which we will use to track the current and previous nodes as we traverse the list. Because each node points only to the next node in the list, we can traverse the list in a forward direction only. Once we have reached a node, we do not have a way to backtrack to the previous node. Thus, as we traverse the list, we must remember the previous node because we will need to change the value of its next node. We update *previous* and *current* at lines 50–51 by assigning *current* to *previous*, then moving *current* to the next node in the list by calling the *getNext* method.

Once we find *value*, we will connect *previous* to the *IntegerNode* after *current.* If we have reached the end of the list, that is, *current* is *null* (line 47), or if we have found *value* (line 48), we are ready to either return *false* or delete the node by updating the links in our list. At that point, we exit the *while* loop and skip to line 54.

Note that the order of the expressions in the *while* loop condition is critical. Expressions in a compound condition are evaluated left to right, so (*current != null*) is evaluated first. If this expression is *false* (that is, *current* is *null*), then the whole *while* loop condition cannot evaluate to *true*, so the second expression is not evaluated. This is important because the second expression uses *current* to call the *getData* method. If *current* is *null*, the evaluation of the second expression would generate a *NullPointerException.* In this way, we are taking advantage of Java's short-circuit evaluation of logical AND operations.

If we reversed the order of the expressions in the *while* loop condition, as shown here,

```
// incorrect ordering of expressions!
while ( current.getData( ) != value
        && current != null )
```

reaching the end of the list would always generate a *NullPointerException.*

REFERENCE POINT

Short-circuit evaluation of logical expressions is discussed in Chapter 5.

At line 54, we test whether *current* is *null*, because a *null* value indicates that we exited the *while* loop because the list is empty or we reached the end of the list without finding *value.* Either way, the deletion is unsuccessful and we return *false* at line 55.

COMMON ERROR TRAP

When traversing a list, always test if a node reference is *null* before calling a method using that reference. Failure to do so might result in a *NullPointerException* at run time. More generally, when coding a linked-list method, always pay attention to the possibility of an object reference being *null* before using that reference to call a method.

If *current* is not *null*, we have found *value.* We update the list and return *true* at lines 58–64. If *current* is the head node, we found *value* at the beginning of the list, so we need to update the *head* instance variable. In this case, we assign the node after *head* to *head* at line 59. Note that if there was only one element in the list before the deletion, *head* becomes *null* (at this point the list will be empty). Figures 14.5a and 14.5b show the impact of executing line 59 on the list (before and after).

If *current* is not the head node, we skip to line 61 where we set the node pointed to by *previous* to be the node after *current.* At this point, *current* is no longer part of the linked list.

At line 63, we decrement *numberOfItems*, to reflect one fewer item in the list. Finally, at line 64, we return *true.* Figures 14.4a and 14.4b show the impact of executing line 61 on the list (before and after).

SOFTWARE ENGINEERING TIP

There are many ways to code the deletion of a node in the list. Try to write code that is easy to read and maintain.

Our last method, *toString*, is at lines 68–81. Our *toString* method traverses the list and returns a *String* containing the data from each item in the list. A *toString* method traversing the list is especially useful at the debugging stage, when we want to verify that we have properly added or deleted an element. We can test our code by calling *toString* before and after such operations.

14.1.4 Testing a Linked-List Class

Like any class that we design, we want to test the class before using it in a program. In particular, we should test two important methods: *insert* and *delete.* Furthermore, we want to test all possible scenarios.

Considering our *insert* method, which always inserts at the head of the list, we want to test a minimum of two situations:

- inserting into an empty list
- inserting into a nonempty list.

As we will see later in the chapter, there are other types of linked lists and their *insert* methods may require more test cases than the ones previously mentioned.

After each insertion, we can use the *toString* method to verify that the items were inserted correctly.

For the *delete* method, we should test the following scenarios:

- attempting to delete from an empty list
- deleting an item in the middle of the list
- deleting an item stored in the head node
- deleting an item stored in the last node in the list
- attempting to delete an item not in the list.

After each deletion, we can use the *toString* method to check that the items were deleted correctly.

Example 14.3 shows a client program that tests the *IntegerLinkedList* class.

```
/* The IntegerLinkedListTest class
   Anderson, Franceschi
*/

public class IntegerLinkedListTest
{
  public static void main( String [ ] args )
  {
    // construct empty IntegerLinkedList
    IntegerLinkedList numbers = new IntegerLinkedList( );
    System.out.println( "Number of items in the list: "
     + numbers.getNumberOfItems( ) + "\n" + numbers.toString( ) );

    numbers.insert( 7 );  // insert in empty list
    System.out.println( "Number of items in the list: "
     + numbers.getNumberOfItems( ) + "\n" + numbers.toString( ) );
```

```
17
18     numbers.insert( 2 );  // insert in list with one item
19     System.out.println( "Number of items in the list: "
20      + numbers.getNumberOfItems( ) + "\n" + numbers.toString( ) );
21
22     numbers.insert( 5 );  // insert in list with two items
23     System.out.println( "Number of items in the list: "
24      + numbers.getNumberOfItems( ) + "\n" + numbers.toString( ) );
25
26     if ( ! numbers.delete( 8 ) )     // unsuccessful - not in list
27         System.out.println( "8 could not be deleted:" );
28
29     if ( numbers.delete( 2 ) )       // successful
30         System.out.println( "2 was successfully deleted:" );
31     System.out.println( "Number of items in the list: "
32        + numbers.getNumberOfItems( ) + "\n" + numbers.toString( ) );
33
34     if ( numbers.delete( 7 ) )       // successful
35         System.out.println( "7 was successfully deleted:" );
36     System.out.println( "Number of items in the list: "
37        + numbers.getNumberOfItems( ) + "\n" + numbers.toString( ) );
38
39     if ( numbers.delete( 5 ) )       // successful
40         System.out.println( "5 was successfully deleted:" );
41     System.out.println( "Number of items in the list: "
42        + numbers.getNumberOfItems( ) + "\n" + numbers.toString( ) );
43
44     if ( ! numbers.delete( 8 ) )     // unsuccessful - empty list
45         System.out.println( "8 could not be deleted:" );
46     System.out.println( "Number of items in the list: "
47        + numbers.getNumberOfItems( ) + "\n" + numbers.toString( ) );
48   }
49 }
```

EXAMPLE 14.3 The *IntegerLinkedListTest Class*

In this example, we instantiate the *IntegerLinkedList numbers* object at line 10, then traverse the empty list at lines 11–12.

We successively insert 7, 2, and 5 and traverse *numbers* after each insertion at lines 14–24.

```
Number of items in the list: 0

Number of items in the list: 1
7
Number of items in the list: 2
2  7
Number of items in the list: 3
5  2  7
8 could not be deleted:
2 was successfully deleted:
Number of items in the list: 2
5  7
7 was successfully deleted:
Number of items in the list: 1
5
5 was successfully deleted:
Number of items in the list: 0

8 could not be deleted:
Number of items in the list: 0
```

Figure 14.6
Output of Example 14.3

After that, we test our *delete* method. At line 26, we attempt to delete the value 8; we know this will fail, as the output in Figure 14.6 shows.

We then delete in the middle of the list at line 29, at the end of the list at line 34, and at the beginning of the list (actually the only item left at that point) at line 39. Another attempt to delete is made at line 44, but at that time the list is empty, which causes us to execute line 45, as shown in Figure 14.6.

SOFTWARE ENGINEERING TIP

Testing all the methods in a linked list is critical to avoid errors at run time. Try to test all possible scenarios of all methods.

CODE IN ACTION

In the CD-ROM included in this book, you will find a Flash movie with a step-by-step illustration of Linked List methods. Click on the link for Chapter 14 to start the movie.

14.2 Linked Lists of Objects

Our next step is to design and code a linked list of objects, for example *Player* objects, described earlier in the chapter.

Since each node in our list will store a *Player* reference, we start by defining our *Player* class, shown in Example 14.4.

```
/* The Player Class
   Anderson, Franceschi
*/

public class Player
{
  private int id;
  private String name;
  private String game;

  /** constructor
  * @param i   id
  * @param n  name
  * @param g  game
  */
  public Player( int i, String n, String g )
  {
     id = i;
     name = n;
     game = g;
  }

  /** copy constructor
  * @param p  Player object
  * copies into this object all instance variables of p
  */
  public Player( Player  p )  // copy constructor
  {
     id = p.id;
     name = p.name;
     game = p.game;
  }

  /** accessor for id
  * @return   id
  */
```

```
public int getID( )
{
   return id;
}

/** accessor for name
* @return name
*/
public String getName( )
{
   return name;
}

/** accessor for game
* @return game
*/
public String getGame( )
{
   return game;
}

/** mutator for Id
* @param i  new value for id
*/
public void setID( int i )
{
  id = i;
}

/** mutator for name
* @param n  new value for name
*/
public void setName( String n )
{
   name = n;
}

/** mutator for game
* @param g  new value for game
*/
public void setGame( String g )
{
   game = g;
}

```

```
82  /** equals method
83  *  @param p reference to object to compare to this
84  *  @return  true if p is Player object
85  *   and all instance variables equal this, false otherwise
86  */
87  public boolean equals(  Object p )
88  {
89    if (  ! ( p instanceof  Player ) )
90         return false;
91    else
92    {
93         Player  objPlayer = ( Player ) p;
94         return ( id == objPlayer.id && name.equals( objPlayer.name )
95              && game.equals( objPlayer.game ) );
96    }
97  }
98
99  /** toString method
100 *  @return  String representation of Player object
101 */
102 public String toString( )
103 {
104    return ( "id: " + id + "\tname: "
105             + name + "\tgame: " + game );
106 }
107 }
```

EXAMPLE 14.4 The *Player* Class

The code for this class is straightforward. We declared the three instance variables, along with an overloaded constructor, accessors and mutators, and the standard *equals* and *toString* methods. We have added a **copy constructor** at lines 23–32; that constructor takes a *Player* object parameter and copies all its instance variables into the object that it constructs. Such a copy constructor is very convenient and useful when coding a method that returns a *Player* object, when we want to return a copy of that object without breaking encapsulation.

Example 14.5 shows our *PlayerNode* class:

```
/* The PlayerNode class
   Anderson, Franceschi
*/

```

```
public class PlayerNode
{
  private Player player;
  private PlayerNode next;
  /** default constructor
  *  initializes player and next references to null
  */
  public PlayerNode( )
  {
    player = null;
    next = null;
  }

  /**  overloaded constructor
  *  @param  p
  *  initializes player reference to p
  */
  public PlayerNode( Player p )
  {
    setPlayer( p );
    next = null;
  }

  /**  accessor for player
  *  @return copy of player
  */
  public Player getPlayer( )
  {
    return new Player( player);
  }

  /**  accessor for next
  *  @return next
  */
  public PlayerNode getNext( )
  {
    return next;
  }

  /**  mutator for player
  *  @param p  new Player reference
  */
  public void setPlayer( Player p )
  {
    player = new Player( p );
```

```
50   }
51
52   /**  mutator for next
53   *  @param pn reference to new PlayerNode
54   */
55   public void setNext( PlayerNode pn )
56   {
57     next = pn;
58   }
59 }
```

EXAMPLE 14.5 The *PlayerNode* Class

The code for this class is similar to the code of the *IntegerNode* class. The overloaded constructor allows the client to set the *Player* object, while the default constructor sets the reference for the *Player* object to *null.* Our *getPlayer* method (lines 28–34) and *setPlayer* method (lines 44–50) use the copy constructor of the *Player* class.

14.2.1 A Linked-List Shell

For our class encapsulating a linked list of *Player* objects, we need to consider the following issues:

- We anticipate having many linked-list classes. Therefore, it makes sense to set up a linked-list superclass from which our more specialized linked-list classes will inherit.
- We provide some basic utility methods, but we omit methods to insert or delete nodes in the list, because those methods will have different names and implementations, depending on the functionality of a given subclass.
- We do not intend to instantiate objects from our superclass; thus, we declare our superclass *abstract.*

Example 14.6 shows our *abstract ShellLinkedList* class. This class defines methods that will be common to all subclasses. For example, in addition to the default constructor and the accessor for the number of items in the list, we provide a method to determine whether the list is empty and a *toString* method that can be used to print each node in the list. We declare both instance variables as *protected* so that our linked-list subclasses inherit the head and number of items in the list.

Table 14.2 shows the APIs of *ShellLinkedList* constructor and methods.

TABLE 14.2 *ShellLinkedList* Constructor and Methods

Constructor and Methods of the *abstract ShellLinkedList* Class	
Class	**Constructor and argument list**
`ShellLinkedList`	`ShellLinkedList( )` constructs an empty list
Return value	**Method name and argument list**
`int`	`getNumberOfItems( )` returns the number of items in the list
`boolean`	`isEmpty( )` returns *true* if the list contains 0 items, *false* otherwise
`String`	`toString( )` returns the contents of every node in the list

```
/* The ShellLinkedList class
   Anderson, Franceschi
*/

public abstract class ShellLinkedList
{
  protected PlayerNode head;
  protected int numberOfItems;

  /**  constructor
  *  sets head to null and numberOfitems to 0
  */
  public ShellLinkedList( )
  {
    head = null;
    numberOfItems = 0;
  }

  /**  accessor  for numberOfitems
  *  @return    numberOfitems
  */
  public int getNumberOfItems( )
  {
```

```
24     return numberOfItems;
25   }
26
27   /**  isEmpty
28   *  @return    true if no items in list; false otherwise
29   */
30   public boolean isEmpty( )
31   {
32     return ( numberOfItems == 0 );
33   }
34
35   /**  toString
36   *  @return the contents of the list
37   */
38   public String toString( )
39   {
40     String listString = "";
41     PlayerNode current = head;
42     for ( int i = 0; i < numberOfItems; i++ )
43     {
44       listString += current.getPlayer( ).toString( ) + "\n";
45       current = current.getNext( );
46     }
47     return listString;
48   }
49 }
```

EXAMPLE 14.6 The *ShellLinkedList* Class

We coded the method *isEmpty* at lines 27 to 33. It returns *true* if the list is empty, *false* otherwise.

The *toString* method, at lines 35–48, is similar to the *toString* method of the *IntegerLinkedList* class.

14.2.2 Generating an Exception

Now that we have a shell class for a linked list, we want to add some methods to perform operations on the linked list, such as inserting or deleting elements.

An issue may arise with the return value of the *delete* method. When deleting a node, we want to return the item that we are deleting. Indeed, we want to be able to delete a node based on the value of one or more of the fields of the object stored at that node, that is, the value of one or more of the

SOFTWARE ENGINEERING TIP

Do not include a mutator method for the number of items. Only the linked-list class should alter the number of items as items are inserted or deleted. Including a mutator method for the number of items could allow the client to corrupt its value.

SOFTWARE ENGINEERING TIP

Do not provide an accessor or mutator for the head node instance variable of the linked list. This will protect the head node from being accessed or changed outside the class.

SOFTWARE ENGINEERING TIP

Choose names for instance variables and methods that illustrate their function within the data structure. Your class will be easier for others and yourself to understand at maintenance time. Provide a *toString* method that traverses the list. This is helpful in testing the other methods of the class. In particular, traversing the list after calling the insert or delete methods can verify that an item was correctly added or removed.

instance variables of the *Player* class. For example, if the client wants to delete the first *Player* on the list with an ID of 5, we would then return that *Player* object to the client. If the list is empty or we cannot find a *Player* with ID 5, we do not want to return *null* because the client likely will attempt to use the returned object reference. A solution to this problem is to *throw* an exception when we are unable to delete the requested node. To do this, we will create our own exception class, *DataStructureException*, which we will use throughout this chapter.

It is good practice to define your own exception class as a subclass of the *Exception* class. This way, your class inherits the existing functionality of the *Exception* class, which simplifies coding the new class: you need to code only the constructor.

Example 14.7 shows our *DataStructureException* class, which *extends* the *Exception* class.

```
1 /* The DataStructureException Class
2    Anderson, Franceschi
3 */
4
5 public class DataStructureException extends Exception
6 {
7   /** constructor
8   * @param s error message
9   */
10  public DataStructureException( String s )
11  {
12     super( s );
13  }
14 }
```

EXAMPLE 14.7 The *DataStructureException* Class

The constructor for the class is coded at lines 7 to 13; it simply takes a *String* parameter and passes it to the superclass constructor. When one of our methods detects an error situation, such as an attempt to delete from an empty list, we will *throw* the exception using a statement like the following:

```
throw new DataStructureException( "Some error message here" );
```

The message we pass to the constructor will identify the type of error we detected.

The header of any method that *throws* the *DataStructureException* will add a *throws* clause, as in the following template:

```
accessModifier dataType methodName( parameter list )
                                throws DataStructureException
```

REFERENCE POINT

Exceptions are discussed extensively in Chapter 11.

Now we are ready to expand our shell linked-list class with more meaningful methods.

14.2.3 Other Methods of a Linked List

In addition to our *insert* and *delete* methods, we will also provide the functionality to retrieve, or **peek** at, the contents of a node, without deleting it.

Table 14.3 shows the APIs of the *insert*, *delete*, and *peek* methods.

Again, we will insert at the beginning of the list and our *insert* method has a *void* return value; our insert method works in the same manner as the insert method for a list of *ints*.

Our *delete* method will also delete a node based on a specific criteria. With our list of *ints*, the criterium was simply the value of an item; here, the criterium can be the value of one (or several) instance variables of an item. We will implement one *delete* method only: one that deletes an item based on a specified value of its *id* field. The implementation of a *delete* method that deletes an item based on a specified value of its *name* or *game* field is similar.

TABLE 14.3 *PlayerLinkedList* Methods

Methods of the *PlayerLinkedList* Class	
Return value	**Method name and argument list**
`void`	`insert( Player p )` inserts *Player p* at the beginning of the list
`Player`	`delete( int searchID )` returns and removes the first *Player* in the list with an ID equal to *searchID*. If there is no such *Player* in the list, the method throws a *Data StructureException*
`Player`	`peek( int searchID )` returns a copy of the first *Player* on the list whose ID is equal to *searchID.* If there is no such *Player* in the list, the method throws a *DataStructureException*

If we find such an item, we will remove it from the list and return a reference to that item. When deleting from a list of *ints*, it made sense to return a *boolean* value rather than the value of the item because we already knew the value of the item since it was passed as a parameter to the method. Here, we delete a node based on the value of the *id* field of an object, so we do not know the values of the other fields of that object. Thus, it makes sense to return an object reference rather than just *true* or *false*. If the item cannot be found, we will *throw* a *DataStructureException*.

Otherwise, the mechanics of deleting a node within the list, whether that node is the *head* node or is in the middle of the list, are exactly the same as with our linked list of *ints*.

REFERENCE POINT

Inheritance is discussed extensively in Chapter 10.

Example 14.8 shows our *PlayerLinkedList* class. This class *extends* and inherits the functionality of our *ShellLinkedList* class; thus *head* and *numberOfItems* are inherited instance variables.

```
/* The PlayerLinkedList class
   Anderson, Franceschi
*/

public class PlayerLinkedList extends ShellLinkedList
{

  /** default constructor
  *   calls constructor of ShellLinkedList class
  */
  public PlayerLinkedList( )
  {
    super( );
  }

  /** insert method
  *   @param    p   Player object to insert
  */
  public void insert( Player p )
  {
    // insert as head
    PlayerNode pn = new PlayerNode( new Player(  p ) );
    pn.setNext( head );
    head = pn;
```

```
    numberOfItems++;
  }

  /** delete method
  *   @param    searchID   id of Player to delete
  *   @return   the Player deleted
  */
  public Player delete( int searchID )
                             throws DataStructureException
  {
    PlayerNode current = head;
    PlayerNode previous = null;
    while ( current != null
            && current.getPlayer( ).getID( ) != searchID )
    {
      previous = current;
      current = current.getNext( );
    }

    if ( current == null ) // not found
        throw new DataStructureException( searchID
                  + " not found: cannot be deleted" );
    else
    {
      if ( current == head )
        head = head.getNext( );  // delete head
      else
        previous.setNext( current.getNext( ) );

      numberOfItems--;
      return current.getPlayer( );
    }
  }

  /** peek method
  *   @param    searchID   id of Player to search for
  *   @return   a copy of the Player found
  */
  public Player peek( int searchID )
                 throws DataStructureException
  {
    PlayerNode current = head;
    while ( current != null
            && current.getPlayer( ).getID( ) != searchID )
    {
```

```
70       current = current.getNext( );
71     }
72
73     if ( current == null ) // not found
74         throw new DataStructureException( searchID
75                       + " not found: cannot be deleted" );
76     else
77     {
78       return current.getPlayer( );
79     }
80   }
81 }
```

EXAMPLE 14.8 The *PlayerLinkedList* Class

The default constructor (lines 8–14) calls the constructor of the superclass to initialize the *head* and *numberOfItems* instance variables. The *insert* method, coded from lines 16 to 26, is similar to our *insert* method for a linked list of *ints*, except that it inserts a *Player* object instead of an *int*. When we insert a *Player*, there is already a *Player* object reference created in another class (where the *main* method is, for example), and we are careful to insert a copy of that *Player* object in our list by using the copy constructor of the *Player* class at line 23.

The *delete* method, coded from lines 28 to 57, returns the *Player* deleted if the deletion was successful and *throws* a *DataStructureException* if the deletion was not successful.

The *while* loop at lines 37–42 is very similar to the *delete* method for our linked list of *ints*. We first traverse the list searching for a node containing a *Player* object whose *id* has the same value as *searchID*, our *delete* method's parameter.

Once we find a *Player* whose *id* field matches *searchID*, we will connect *previous* to the *PlayerNode* after *current*. If we have reached the end of the list, that is, *current* is *null* (line 37), or if we have found a *Player* whose *id* value is *searchID* (line 38), we are ready to either *throw* an exception or delete the node by updating the links in our list. At that point, we exit the *while* loop and skip to line 44.

At line 44, we test whether *current* is *null*, because a *null* value indicates that we exited the *while* loop because the list is empty or we reached the end of the list (without finding a *Player* whose id is *searchID*). If the deletion is unsuccessful, we *throw* a *DataStructureException* with an appropriate message at lines 45–46.

If *current* is not *null*, that means that we have found a *Player* whose *id* is *searchID*. We update the list and return the deleted *Player* at lines 49–55.

The *peek* method is coded at lines 59–80. We traverse the list in the same way as the *delete* method, except that because we will not delete a node, we do not need to mark the node before *current*.

If we do not find a node containing a *Player* whose id is *searchID*, we *throw* an exception at lines 74–75. If we find one, we return a copy of the *Player* object contained in that node at line 78 so that we do not break encapsulation of our linked list.

SOFTWARE ENGINEERING TIP

Take care to avoid compromising the encapsulation of your linked list. Do not return an object reference to an item still on the list. Return a reference to a copy of that item.

14.2.4 Testing a Linked-List Class

Again, we want to test the class before using it in a program, and we want to test all possible scenarios, similarly to what we did with our linked list of *ints*.

After each insertion and deletion, we will use the *toString* method to verify that the items were inserted and deleted correctly.

Example 14.9 shows a client program that tests the *PlayerLinkedList* class.

```
/* The PlayerLinkedListTest class
   Anderson, Franceschi
*/

public class PlayerLinkedListTest
{
  public static void main( String [ ] args )
  {
    Player p1 = new Player( 7,"Sarah","Mario" );
    Player p2 = new Player( 2,"Jin","Golf" );
    Player p3 = new Player( 5,"Ajay","Sonic" );

    // construct empty PlayerLinkedList
    PlayerLinkedList players = new PlayerLinkedList( );
    System.out.println( "Number of items in the list: "
     + players.getNumberOfItems( ) + "\n" + players.toString( ) );

    players.insert( p1 );  // insert in empty list
    System.out.println( "Number of items in the list: "
     + players.getNumberOfItems( ) + "\n" + players.toString( ) );

    players.insert( p2 );  // insert in list of one item
    System.out.println( "Number of items in the list: "
```

```
      + players.getNumberOfItems( ) + "\n" + players.toString( ) );

     players.insert( p3 ); // insert in list of two items
     System.out.println( "Number of items in the list: "
      + players.getNumberOfItems( ) + "\n" + players.toString( ) );

     Player temp;     // will be assigned the deleted item

     try
     {
       temp = players.delete( 8 );      // unsuccessful
       System.out.println( "Player deleted: " + temp );
     }
     catch ( DataStructureException dse1 )
     {
       System.out.println( dse1.getMessage( ) + "\n" );
     }

     try
     {
       temp = players.peek( 2 );        // test peek
       System.out.println( "Player retrieved: " + temp );
       System.out.println( "Number of items in the list: "
        + players.getNumberOfItems( ) + "\n" + players.toString( ) );

       temp = players.delete( 2 );      // delete in the middle
       System.out.println( "Player deleted: " + temp );
       System.out.println( "Number of items in the list: "
        + players.getNumberOfItems( ) + "\n" + players.toString( ) );

       temp = players.delete( 7 );      // delete the last item
       System.out.println( "Player deleted: " + temp );
       System.out.println( "Number of items in the list: "
        + players.getNumberOfItems( ) + "\n" + players.toString( ) );

       temp = players.delete( 5 );      // delete the first item
       System.out.println( "Player deleted: " + temp );
       System.out.println( "Number of items in the list: "
        + players.getNumberOfItems( ) + "\n" + players.toString( ) );

       temp = players.delete( 7 );      // delete from empty list
       System.out.println( "Player deleted: " + temp );
       System.out.println( "Number of items in the list: "
```

```
67        + players.getNumberOfItems( ) + "\n" + players.toString( ) );
68      }
69      catch ( DataStructureException dse2 )
70      {
71        System.out.println( dse2.getMessage( ) );
72      }
73    }
74 }
```

EXAMPLE 14.9 The *PlayerLinkedListTest* Class

In this example, we instantiate three *Player* object references *p1, p2,* and *p3* at lines 9, 10, and 11. We instantiate the *PlayerLinkedList players* object reference at line 14, then traverse the empty list *players* at lines 15–16.

We successively insert *p1, p2,* and *p3* and traverse *players* after each insertion at lines 18–28.

After that, we test our *delete* method. Because our *delete* method *throws* a *DataStructureException,* we need to use *try* and *catch* blocks when calling that method.

At line 34, we attempt to delete an item in the list whose *id* is 8; we know this will fail, and as the output shows in Figure 14.7, we execute the *catch* block at lines 37–40.

In the next *try* block, at line 44, we call the *peek* method to see if there is a *Player* whose *id* is 2. We traverse the list at lines 46–47 to verify that the list has not been modified by the call to *peek.*

We then delete in the middle of the list at line 49, at the end of the list at line 54, and at the beginning of the list (actually the only item left at that point) at line 59. Another attempt to delete is made at line 64, but at that time the list is empty. This causes us to execute the second *catch* block at lines 69–72, as shown in Figure 14.7.

```
Number of items in the list: 0

Number of items in the list: 1
id: 7    name: Sarah    game: Mario

Number of items in the list: 2
id: 2    name: Jin      game: Golf
id: 7    name: Sarah    game: Mario

Number of items in the list: 3
id: 5    name: Ajay     game: Sonic
id: 2    name: Jin      game: Golf
id: 7    name: Sarah    game: Mario

8 not found: cannot be deleted

Player retrieved: id: 2 name: Jin      game: Golf
Number of items in the list: 3
id: 5    name: Ajay     game: Sonic
id: 2    name: Jin      game: Golf
id: 7    name: Sarah    game: Mario

Player deleted: id: 2   name: Jin      game: Golf
Number of items in the list: 2
id: 5    name: Ajay     game: Sonic
id: 7    name: Sarah    game: Mario

Player deleted: id: 7   name: Sarah    game: Mario
Number of items in the list: 1
id: 5    name: Ajay     game: Sonic

Player deleted: id: 5   name: Ajay     game: Sonic
Number of items in the list: 0

7 not found: cannot be deleted
```

Figure 14.7
Output of Example 14.9

Skill Practice
with these end-of-chapter questions

14.14.2 Reading and Understanding Code

Questions 14, 15, 16, 17, 18, 19, 20, 21

14.14.3 Fill In the Code

Questions 22, 23, 24, 25, 26, 27, 28, 29, 30, 31, 32

14.14.4 Identifying Errors in Code

Questions 33, 34

14.14.5 Debugging Area—Using Messages from the Java Compiler and Java JVM

Questions 39, 40, 41, 42

14.14.6 Write a Short Program

Questions 43, 44, 45, 46, 48, 50

14.14.8 Technical Writing

Question 72

14.3 Implementing a Stack Using a Linked List

Imagine a group of college students on a spring break, sharing an apartment. After they eat, they typically pile up the dirty dishes in the kitchen sink. Another meal is consumed, and more dirty dishes are piled on top of the existing ones. At the top of the pile is the dirty dish that was placed there last. Soon the students run out of clean dishes, and somebody will have to start cleaning them. He or she will start by cleaning the dish at the top of the pile, that is, the last dish placed on the pile. That approach is called **last in**, **first out**, or **LIFO**.

A **stack** is a linear data structure that organizes items in a last in, first out manner. Figure 14.8 shows a stack of trays. The tray at the top of the stack was put on the stack last, but will be taken off the stack first.

A stack can be represented by a linked list. In a linked list representing a stack:

- we insert, or **push**, at the beginning of the list
- we delete, or **pop**, the item at the beginning of the list

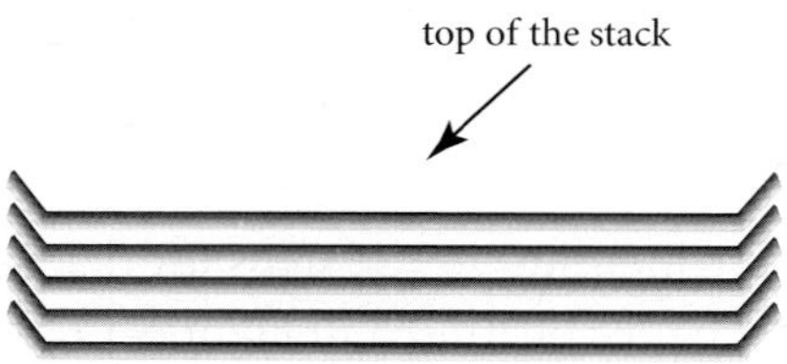

Figure 14.8
A Stack of Trays

Since we insert and delete at the beginning of the list, the item deleted is the last one that was inserted, reflecting the LIFO pattern.

Table 14.4 shows the APIs of the *push*, *pop*, and *peek* methods.

The *push* method is identical to the insert method of the *PlayerLinkedList* class discussed earlier, and is illustrated in Figures 14.3a to 14.3d.

The *pop* method is different from the *delete* method we coded earlier in our *PlayerLinkedList* class. In a stack, we always delete the first item in the list. Therefore, in a linked list implementing a stack, we do not delete an item based on the value of one of its instance variables. The *pop* method for our

TABLE 14.4 *PlayerStackLinkedList* Methods

Methods of the *PlayerStackLinkedList* Class	
Return value	**Method name and argument list**
`void`	`push( Player p )` inserts *Player p* at the top of the stack
`Player`	`pop( )` returns and removes the first *Player* of the list. If the list is empty, the method throws a *DataStructureException*.
`Player`	`peek( )` returns a copy of the first *Player* on the list without deleting it. If the list is empty, the method throws a *DataStructureException*.

stack returns a *Player* object, the one stored at the head of the linked list. If our stack is empty, our *pop* method will *throw* a *DataStructureException* in order to avoid returning a *null* object reference.

The steps required to pop the first item are identical to the steps for deleting the first node in the *PlayerLinkedList*. That is illustrated in Figures 14.5a and 14.5b.

Example 14.10 shows our *PlayerStackLinkedList* class. This class also *extends* and inherits the functionality of our *ShellLinkedList* class.

```
/* The PlayerStackLinkedList class
   Anderson, Franceschi
*/

public class PlayerStackLinkedList extends ShellLinkedList
{
  // head and numberOfItems are inherited instance variables

  public PlayerStackLinkedList( )
  {
    super( );
  }

  /** push method
  *   @param    p   Player object to insert
  */
  public void push( Player p )
  {
    PlayerNode pn = new PlayerNode( new Player(  p ) );
    pn.setNext( head );
    head = pn;
    numberOfItems++;
  }

  /** pop method
  *   @return   the Player object deleted
  */
  public Player pop( ) throws DataStructureException
  {
    if ( isEmpty( ) )
        throw new DataStructureException
                   ( "empty stack: cannot be popped" );
```

```
33     else
34     {
35       Player deleted = head.getPlayer( );
36       head = head.getNext( );
37       numberOfItems--;
38       return deleted;
39     }
40   }
41
42   /** peek method
43   *   @return   the Player object retrieved
44   */
45   public Player peek( ) throws DataStructureException
46   {
47     if ( isEmpty( ) )
48         throw new DataStructureException
49                    ( "empty stack: cannot peek" );
50     else
51     {
52         return head.getPlayer( );
53     }
54   }
55 }
```

EXAMPLE 14.10 The *PlayerStackLinkedList* Class

The *push* method, coded from lines 14 to 23, is identical to the *insert* method in the *PlayerLinkedList* class (Example 14.8).

In the *pop* method (lines 25–40), we first test if the stack is empty at line 30. If it is empty, we *throw* a *DataStructureException* with the appropriate argument at lines 31–32. If the stack is not empty, we delete the first item in the stack and return it. We call the *getPlayer* method from the *PlayerNode* class to get the *Player* stored at the head of the stack, and assign it to the *Player* reference *deleted* (line 35). The *deleted* reference is then returned at line 38. At lines 36 and 37, we perform the bookkeeping on the stack to reflect the deletion. We update *head* at line 36 and decrement *numberOfItems* at line 37.

The *peek* method is coded at lines 42–54. If the list is empty, we *throw* an exception at lines 48–49. If the list is not empty, we return a copy of the *Player* at the head of the list at line 52.

COMMON ERROR TRAP

When deleting a node from a linked list representing a stack, always check if the linked list is empty. Not doing so results in a *NullPointerException* at run time.

Like our previous linked list implementation, it is very important to test if the stack is empty before trying to delete a node; failure to do so will generate a *NullPointerException* at run time.

A similar program to Example 14.9 can be coded to test all possible scenarios when using the methods of the *PlayerStackLinkedList* class. This is proposed in the short program section of the exercises.

14.4 Implementing a Queue Using a Linked List

Imagine a line of people at an automated teller machine, or ATM, waiting to withdraw cash. The person at the front of the line is using the ATM. When a new customer arrives, the customer goes to the back of the line. As customers use the ATM, they exit the line, and the next customer moves to the front of the line. Thus, customers use the ATM in the order of their arrival times. We call this pattern "**first in**, **first out**," or **FIFO**.

A queue is a linear data structure that organizes items in a first in, first out manner.

Figure 14.9 shows a queue of people at an ATM. The person at the front of the queue arrived first and will use the ATM first. The person at the back arrived last and will use the ATM last. The next person to arrive will stand after the person currently at the back of the queue. That newly arrived person will become the new back of the line.

A queue can be represented by a linked list by providing the following operations:

- we insert, or **enqueue**, an item at the end of the list
- we delete, or **dequeue**, the item at the beginning of the list
- we *peek* at the item at the beginning of the list

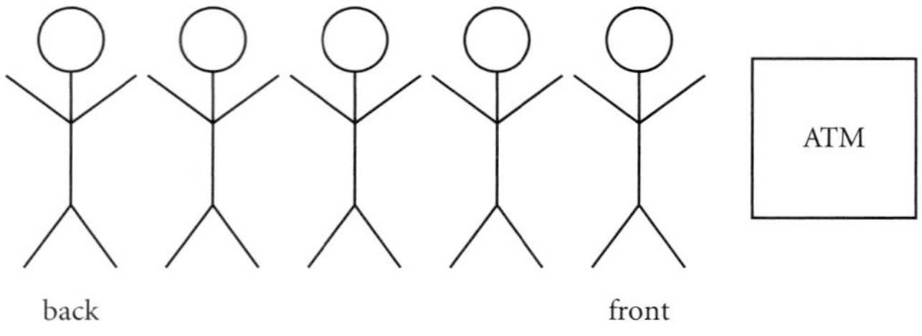

Figure 14.9
A Queue of People Waiting at the ATM

Table 14.5 shows the APIs of the *enqueue*, *dequeue*, and *peek* methods.

We can implement a queue using a linked list; however, we will make an important change. Because a queue inserts items at the end of the list, we will add an instance variable that represents the last node of the linked list. We call this the **tail reference**.

This way we will have direct access to the last node, without having to traverse the list. We will call that instance variable representing the last node in the list *tail*.

When inserting a new *Player*, our *insert* method will perform the following operations:

1. Instantiate a new node containing the *Player* to be inserted,
2. Attach that new node at the end of the list, i.e., make the last node in the list, *tail*, point to that new node,
3. Mark the new node so that it is the last node of the list, i.e., assign that node to *tail*,
4. Increase the number of items by 1.

TABLE 14.5 *PlayerQueueLinkedList* Methods

Methods of the *PlayerQueueLinkedList* Class	
Return value	**Method name and argument list**
`void`	`enqueue( Player p )` inserts *Player p* at the end of the list
`Player`	`dequeue( )` returns and removes the first *Player* from the list. If the list is empty, the method throws a *DataStructureException*.
`Player`	`peek( )` returns a copy of the first *Player* on the list, but does not delete the *Player*. If the list is empty, the method throws a *DataStructureException*.

Figures 14.10a to 14.10d illustrate the *enqueue* operation.

The *dequeue* method is identical to the *pop* method of a linked list implementing a stack.

Example 14.11 shows our *PlayerQueueLinkedList* class. This class also *extends* and inherits the functionality of our *ShellLinkedList* class.

Figure 14.10a
Inserting: Our Original Queue

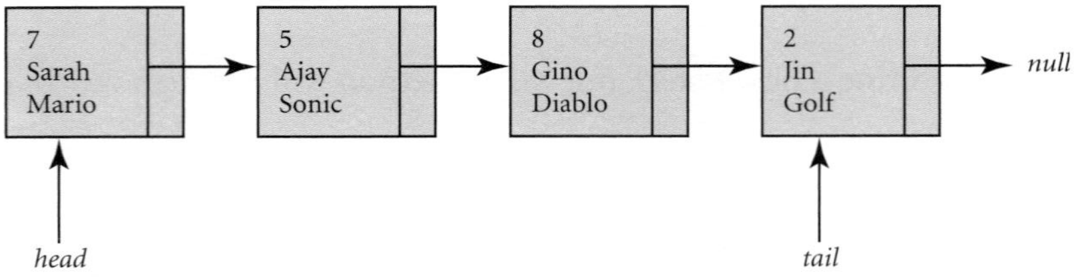

Figure 14.10b
Inserting: Our Queue and the New Node

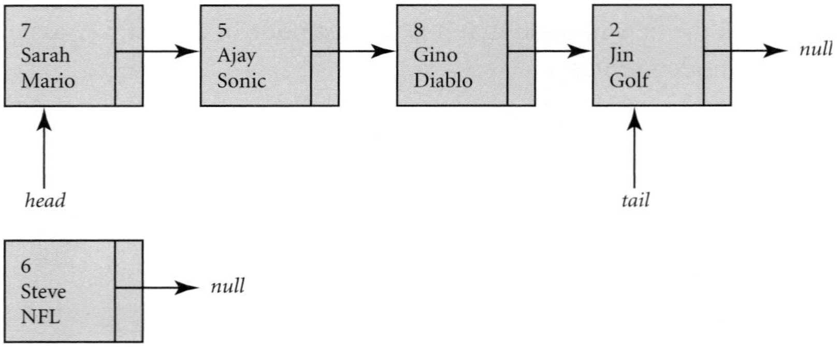

Figure 14.10c
Inserting: The New Node Has Been Attached at the End of the Queue

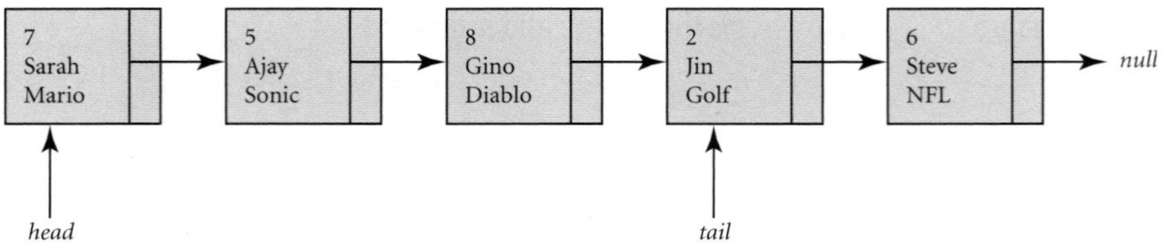

Figure 14.10d
Inserting: *tail* Has Been Updated

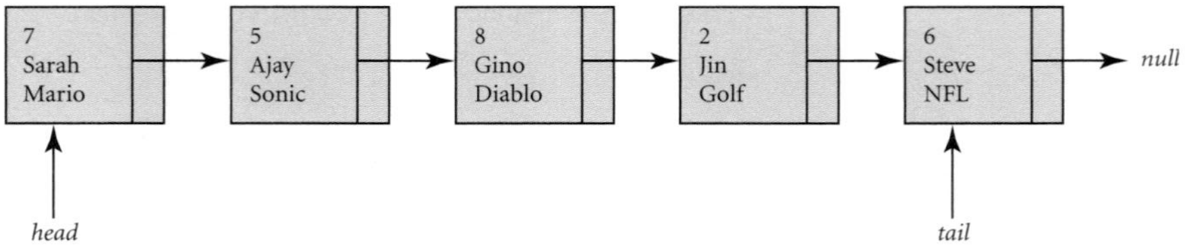

```java
/* The PlayerQueueLinkedList class
   Anderson, Franceschi
*/

public class PlayerQueueLinkedList extends ShellLinkedList
{
  // head and numberOfItems are inherited instance variables
  private PlayerNode tail;  // last node

  public PlayerQueueLinkedList( )
  {
    super( );
    tail = null;
  }

  /** enqueue method
  *   @param    p   Player object to insert
  */
  public void enqueue( Player p )
  {
    // insert as tail
    PlayerNode pn = new PlayerNode( new Player(  p ) );
    if ( isEmpty( ) )
    {
      tail = pn;
      head = pn;
    }
    else
    {
      tail.setNext( pn );
      tail = pn;
    }
    numberOfItems++;
  }

  /** dequeue method
  *   @return    p   the Player object deleted
  */
  public Player dequeue( ) throws DataStructureException
  {
    if ( isEmpty( ) )
        throw new DataStructureException
          ( "empty queue: cannot dequeue" );
```

```
44     else
45     {
46       Player deleted = head.getPlayer( );
47       head = head.getNext( );
48       numberOfItems--;
49       return deleted;
50     }
51   }
52
53   /** peek method
54   *   @return    p   the Player object retrieved
55   */
56   public Player peek( ) throws DataStructureException
57   {
58     if ( isEmpty( ) )
59         throw new DataStructureException
60            ( "empty queue: cannot peek" );
61     else
62     {
63         return head.getPlayer( );
64     }
65   }
66 }
```

EXAMPLE 14.11 The *PlayerQueueLinkedList* Class

The constructor, from lines 10 to 14, calls the constructor of the superclass, and because it constructs an empty list, sets *tail* to *null.* The *dequeue* and *peek* methods are identical to the *pop* and *peek* methods of our *PlayerStackLinkedList* class, except for the message passed to the *DataStructureException* constructor.

The *enqueue* method, which we coded at lines 16–34, inserts an item at the end of the list. We first instantiate a *PlayerNode* object reference named *pn* at line 22, using the parameter *Player p* of the *enqueue* method.

Because we insert at the end of the list, we must properly handle the case when the queue is empty, in which case *tail* is *null.* We test if the queue is empty at line 23. If it is, we assign *pn* to *head* and *tail* at lines 25 and 26. After we execute these two lines, the queue contains one element, and that element is both the first and last item in the queue.

If the list is not empty, control skips to line 30, where we attach *pn* at the end of the list by setting the *next* instance variable of *tail* to *pn*. We then assign *pn* to *tail* in order to reflect that *pn* is now the last node of the list. Finally, and in all cases (empty list or not), we increment *numberOfItems* by 1 at line 33.

Figures 14.10a to 14.10d show the impact on the list of executing lines 22, 30, and 31 step by step.

It is important to test if a queue is empty when coding the *enqueue* method. Indeed, if the queue is empty, then both *head* and *tail* are *null*. The code

```
tail.setNext( pn )
```

at line 30 would, in this case, generate a *NullPointerException*.

A similar program to Example 14.9 can be coded to test all possible scenarios when using the methods of the *PlayerQueueLinkedList* class. This is proposed in the short program section of the exercises.

COMMON ERROR TRAP

Before inserting or deleting an item in a linked list representing a queue, always check if the linked list is empty. Not doing so results in a *NullPointerException* at run time.

Skill Practice
with these end-of-chapter questions

14.14.1 Multiple Choice
Questions 2, 3, 4, 5, 6, 7

14.14.6 Write a Short Program
Questions 52, 53

14.14.8 Technical Writing
Question 73

14.5 Array Representation of Stacks

Earlier in this chapter, we discussed how a stack can be represented by a linked list. Since a stack is a last in, first out data structure, we coded the *push* (insert) and *pop* (delete) methods of the linked list to insert or delete at the beginning of the list. Linked lists offer the advantage of being expandable one object at a time, so we do not have to worry about running out of capacity.

However, if we know in advance that the number of objects on a stack will always be less than some maximum number, we can represent the stack using an array, which is easier to implement.

Table 14.6 shows the APIs of the *push*, *pop*, and *peek* methods for a stack implemented using an array.

To match the LIFO functionality of a stack, we instantiate the array with the maximum number of elements. We add items to the stack starting at index 0, storing the items in adjacent locations in the array. To keep track of the array index of the last element inserted, we maintain an index **top**, short for "top of the stack." We always remove (*pop*) the item at the top of the stack.

To push an item onto the stack, we increment the value of *top* by 1 and store the element at the new *top* index. To pop an item from the stack, we return the item at index *top* and decrement the value of *top* by 1.

Figure 14.11a shows how we can visualize a stack of *Players*. Figure 14.11b and 14.11c show the stack after pushing a *Player* (*6, Steve, NFL*) and then popping one element. Figure 14.11c shows that the array element at index 3

TABLE 14.6 *ArrayStack* Methods

Methods of the *ArrayStack* Class	
Return value	**Method name and argument list**
`boolean`	`push( Player p )` inserts *Player p* at the top of the stack, if the stack is not full. Returns *true* if the insertion was successful (that is, if the stack was not full before insertion); *false* otherwise.
`Player`	`pop( )` removes and returns the *Player* at the top of the stack, if the stack is not empty. If the stack is empty, the method throws a *DataStructureException*.
`Player`	`peek( )` returns a copy of the *Player* at the top of the stack if the stack is not empty. If the stack is empty, the method throws a *DataStructureException*.

	index	*Player* object
top	2	(8, Gino, Diablo)
	1	(7, Sarah, Mario)
	0	(2, Jin, Golf)

Figure 14.11a
Our Original Stack

	index	*Player* object
top	3	(6, Steve, NFL)
	2	(8, Gino, Diablo)
	1	(7, Sarah, Mario)
	0	(2, Jin, Golf)

Figure 14.11b
Our Stack After Inserting Player (6, Steve, NFL)

	index	*Player* object
	3	(6, Steve, NFL)
top	2	(8, Gino, Diablo)
	1	(7, Sarah, Mario)
	0	(2, Jin, Golf)

Figure 14.11c
Our Stack After Popping Once

is still *Player (6, Steve, NFL)*, but that is irrelevant. Since *top* has the value 2, the element at index 3 is not on the stack. When the next item is pushed onto the stack, we will reuse that element.

One disadvantage of implementing a stack with an array is that the array has a fixed size, and it is possible that the array can be filled completely with elements of the stack. Thus, our *push* method needs to test if the array is full before pushing an element onto the stack. Similarly, our *pop* method needs to test if the array is empty before popping an element from the stack.

Example 14.12 shows our *ArrayStack* class.

```
/* The ArrayStack class
   Anderson, Franceschi
*/

public class ArrayStack
{
  private static final int STACK_SIZE = 100; // maximum array size
  private Player [ ] stack;              // array of Player objects
  private int top;             // last used index; top of the stack

  public ArrayStack( )
  {
    stack = new Player [STACK_SIZE];
    top = -1; // stack is empty
  }

  /** push method
  *   @param    p   Player object to insert
  *   @return   true if insertion was successful false otherwise
  */
  public boolean push( Player p )
  {
    if ( !isFull( ) ) // is there room to insert?
    {
      stack[++top] = new Player( p ) ;
      return true;
    }
    else
      return false;
  }

  /** pop method
  *   @return   the Player deleted
  */
  public Player pop( ) throws DataStructureException
  {
    if ( !isEmpty( ) ) // is there an item to delete?
      return ( stack[top--] );
    else
      throw new DataStructureException
                  ( "Stack empty: cannot pop" );
  }
```

```
43
44   /** peek method
45   *   @return   the Player at the top of the stack
46   */
47   public Player peek( ) throws DataStructureException
48   {
49     if ( !isEmpty( ) ) // stack is not empty
50       return new Player( stack[top] );
51     else
52       throw new DataStructureException
53                 ( "Stack empty: cannot peek" );
54   }
55
56   /** isEmpty method
57   *   @return   true if stack is empty, false otherwise
58   */
59   public boolean isEmpty( )
60   {
61     return ( top == -1 );
62   }
63
64   /** isFull method
65   *   @return   true if stack is full, false otherwise
66   */
67   public boolean isFull( )
68   {
69     return ( top == ( STACK_SIZE - 1 ) );
70   }
71
72   public String toString( )
73   {
74     String stackString = "";
75     for ( int i = top; i >= 0; i-- )
76       stackString += ( i + ": " + stack[i] + "\n" );
77     return stackString;
78   }
79 }
```

EXAMPLE 14.12 The *ArrayStack* Class

We declare *STACK_SIZE*, *stack*, and *top*, our three fields at lines 7–9.

Stack is an array of *Players*. *STACK_SIZE* is the size of the array *stack*. *Top* represents the index of the element of the array *stack* that is at the top of the stack. The value of *top* will vary from *–1* (when the stack is empty) to *STACK_SIZE – 1* (when the stack is full).

In the default constructor, coded at lines 11–15, we instantiate *stack* and then set *top* to −1, which indicates that the stack is empty. When a client program pushes the first *Player* onto the stack, *top* will be incremented, so that the top of the stack will be the array element at index 0.

We coded the *push* method at lines 17–30. The *push* method returns *true* (line 26) if the stack is not full before we insert, and *false* (line 29) if it is, in which case we cannot insert. We test if the stack is not full at line 23. If it is not full, we use the prefix auto-increment operator to combine two operations at line 25: first increment *top* by 1, then assign a copy of *p*, the *Player* parameter of the *push* method, to the element at index *top*.

We coded the *pop* method at lines 32–42. The *pop* method attempts to delete and return a *Player* object from the top of the stack. The method *throws* a *DataStructureException* at lines 40–41 if the stack is empty, in which case we cannot pop. If it is not empty, we use the postfix auto-decrement operator to combine two operations at line 38: first return the *Player* stored at index *top* in the array *stack*, then decrement *top* by 1.

COMMON ERROR TRAP

Do not confuse the top of the stack with the last index in the array. Array elements with an index higher than *top* are not on the stack.

We have also coded a few other methods in this class. The *peek* method, at lines 44–54, is similar to *pop*, except that it does not delete from the stack and it returns a copy of the element at the top of the stack, rather than the element itself, preserving encapsulation. The *isEmpty* and *isFull* methods are coded at lines 56–62 and 64–70, respectively. And the *toString* method, coded at lines 72–78, returns a *String* representation of the contents of the stack. Note that in that method, we loop from *top* to 0, not from *STACK_SIZE – 1* to 0.

As before, a program similar to Example 14.9 can be coded to test all possible scenarios on the methods of the *ArrayStack* class. This is proposed in the short program section of the exercises.

14.6 Programming Activity 1: Writing Methods for a Stack Class

In this activity, you will work with a stack represented by an array, performing this activity:

Code the *push* and *pop* methods to insert onto and delete from a stack represented by an array of *ints*.

The framework will animate your code to give you feedback on the correctness of your code. It will display the state of the stack at all times. The result of your operation will be displayed, reflecting the value returned by your *push* or *pop* method. The items in the stack will be displayed in black while the array elements that are not part of the stack will be displayed in red.

Instructions

Copy the contents of the Programming Activity 1 folder for this chapter on the CD-ROM accompanying this book onto a directory on your computer. Open the *StackArray.java* source file. Searching for five stars (*****) in the source code will position you to the code section where you will add your code.

In this task, you will fill in the code inside the methods *push* and *pop* to insert onto and delete from a stack. Example 14.13 shows the section of the *StackArray* source code where you will add your code. This example is different from the one in the chapter. The stack is an array of *ints*, not *Players*. The *isFull* and *isEmpty* methods have not been provided; you can code them or not, depending on how you want to implement the *push* and *pop* methods.

```
/** push method
*   @param    value  value to be pushed onto the stack
*   @return   true if successful, false if unsuccessful
*/
public boolean push( int value )
{
 // ***** 1. Student code starts here *****
 // stack is an int array instance variable representing
 // the array that stores our stack

 // top is an instance variable representing
 // the index of the top of the stack

 // CAPACITY is a static constant representing
 // the size of the array stack


 // The push method adds the argument value
 // to the top of the stack, if it is possible
 // code the push method here
```

```
  // end of student code, part 1
 }

 /** pop method
 *   @return   the value of the top element of the stack, if
 *             successful
 */
 public int pop( ) throws DataStructureException
 {
  // ***** 2. Student code restarts here *****
  // stack is an int array instance variable representing
  // the array that stores our stack

  // top is an instance variable representing
  // the index of the top of the stack

  // CAPACITY is a static constant representing
  // the size of the array stack

  // The pop method deletes the element
  // at the top of the stack, if it is possible
  // code the pop method here


  // end of student code, part 2
 }
```

Example 14.13 Location of Student Code in *StackArray* Class

To test your code, compile and run the application; the class *StackPractice* contains the *main* method. When the program begins, a window will display the state of the stack, along with two buttons labeled "push" and "pop," as shown in Figure 14.12.

Click on the "push" button to insert onto the stack. Click on the "pop" button to delete from the stack. Close the window to exit the program.

If you successively push 34, 56, 12, and 98 onto the stack, then pop once, the window will look like the one shown in Figure 14.13.

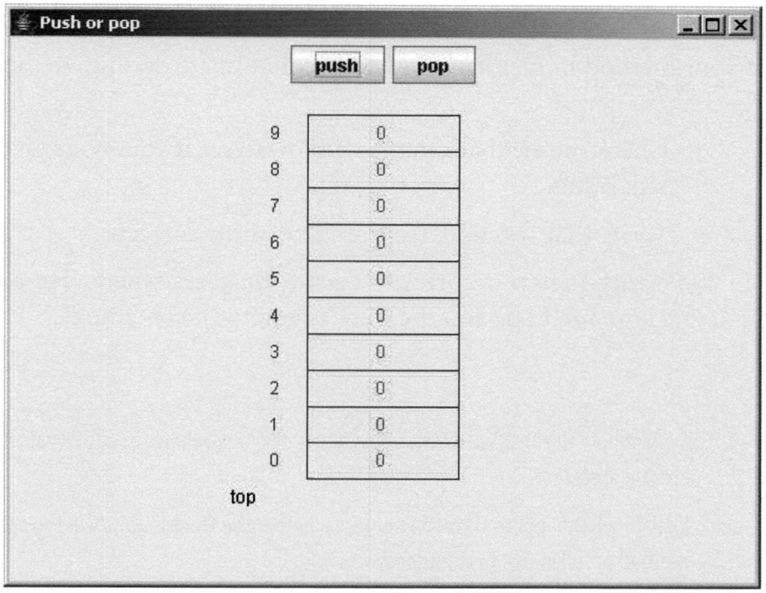

Figure 14.12
Opening Window

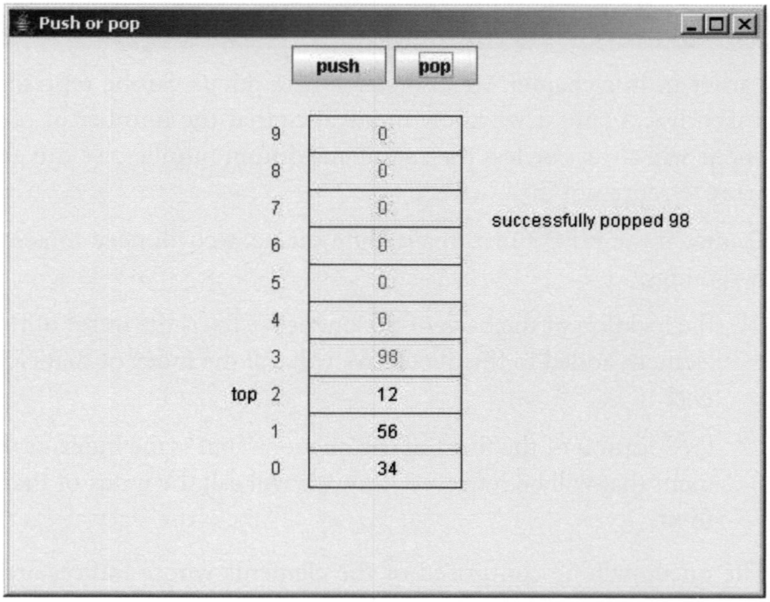

Figure 14.13
Sample Window After Performing Some Stack Operations

Troubleshooting

If your method implementation does not animate or animates incorrectly, check these items:

- Check the feedback in the window to see if your code gives the correct result.
- Verify that you updated the value of *top* correctly.
- Verify that you correctly coded the cases where the stack is full (*push* method) and the stack is empty (*pop* method).

DISCUSSION QUESTIONS ?

1. Explain how the array elements above the index *top* can have assigned values, but are still irrelevant.
2. Explain what happens if you do not test whether the stack is empty in the *pop* method or full in the *push* method.

14.7 Array Representation of Queues

Earlier in this chapter, we also saw how a queue can be represented by a linked list. Again, if we know in advance that the number of objects in a queue will always be less than some maximum number, we can also use an array to represent the queue.

To match the FIFO functionality of a queue, we will need to keep track of two things:

1. the location of the back of the queue—This is the index of the last element added to the queue. We will call the index of that element *back*.
2. the location of the front of the queue—That is the index of the element that will be retrieved next. We will call the index of that element *front*.

The queue will be comprised of the elements whose indices are between *back* and *front*, inclusive.

To dequeue, or delete from the queue, we will return the item at index *front* and increase the value of *front* by one. To enqueue, or insert an element in the queue, we will increment the value of *back* by one, and insert the element at the array index *back*.

There is one important problem in representing a queue with a standard array: the number of available elements for the queue in the array will shrink over time as we enqueue and dequeue, since enqueueing and dequeueing both advance their indexes toward the end of the array.

To illustrate this point, let's consider a queue represented by an array of eight elements. We start by enqueueing five players in this order: (*5, Ajay, Sonic*), (*2, Jin, Golf*), (*7, Sarah, Mario*), (*8, Gino, Diablo*), and (*6, Steve, NFL*). Since (*5, Ajay, Sonic*) was the first to be inserted in the queue, that *Player* is now at the front of the queue. (*6, Steve, NFL*), inserted last, is at the back of the queue. Thus, (*5, Ajay, Sonic*) will be stored at index 0 and (*6, Steve, NFL*) will be stored at index 4, as shown in Figure 14.14a. Suppose now that we dequeue once. *Front* now has the value 1, as shown in Figure 14.14b. The array element at index 0 is no longer in the queue and its value is irrelevant. Since we insert at the back, the array element at index 0 can no longer be used for the queue. If we dequeue again, *front* will have the value 2, and we will no longer be able to use the array element at index 1. As we keep enqueueing and dequeueing, the values of *back* and *front* keep increasing and we have less and less usable space in the array. Indeed, when *back* reaches 7, we will no longer be able to enqueue at all.

SOFTWARE ENGINEERING TIP

When implementing a queue as an array, think of it as a circular array.

There is a solution to this problem: it is to deal with the array as if it were circular. After *back* reaches the last index of the array, we start enqueueing again at index 0. Thus, in a circular array, the next index after the last array index is 0. Let's say that at one point the *back* marker reaches 7 and the *front* marker is at 5. When we enqueue a new object, we will store that object at index 0, which is the "next" index after 7 if we imagine that the array is circular. This way, our useful array capacity never shrinks and is always 8.

How do we know that we have reached the last array index and that the next index should be 0? We simply add 1 to the value of *back*, and then take that number modulo the size of the array, which we call QUEUE_SIZE.

Figure 14.14a
Our Queue After Enqueueing the First Five Elements

	index	*Player* object
	7	
	6	
	5	
back	4	(6, Steve, NFL)
	3	(8, Gino, Diablo)
	2	(7, Sarah, Mario)
	1	(2, Jin, Golf)
front	0	(5, Ajay, Sonic)

Figure 14.14b
Our Queue After Dequeueing Once

	index	*Player* object
	7	
	6	
	5	
back	4	(6, Steve, NFL)
	3	(8, Gino, Diablo)
	2	(7, Sarah, Mario)
front	1	(2, Jin, Golf)
	0	(5, Ajay, Sonic)

Table 14.7 shows the APIs of the *enqueue* and *dequeue* methods.

Figure 14.15 illustrates a sequence of insertions and deletions in a queue of *Players* implemented as a circular array. When we begin, the queue is empty. The value of *front* is 0 and the value of *back* is *QUEUE_SIZE – 1*. When we enqueue the first item, that element is placed at index

```
( back + 1 ) % QUEUE_SIZE
```

which is now 0, and *back* will be given the value 0. If we enqueue again, the new element will be placed at index 1 and *back* will be given the value 1. If we enqueue two more items, they will be placed at indexes 2 and 3, respectively, and back will be given the value 3. If we then dequeue, we will return the item at index 0, and *front* will become 1. If we dequeue again, we will return the item at index 1, and *front* will become 2.

TABLE 14.7 *ArrayQueue* Methods

Methods of the *ArrayQueue* Class	
Return value	**Method name and argument list**
`boolean`	`enqueue( Player p )` inserts *Player p* at the back of the queue if the queue is not full. Returns *true* if the insertion was successful (queue was not full), *false* otherwise.
`Player`	`dequeue( )` returns and removes the *Player* at the front of the queue. If the queue is empty, the method throws a *DataStructureException*.
`Player`	`peek( )` returns a copy of the *Player* at the front of the queue. If the queue is empty, the method throws a *DataStructureException*.

When we enqueue, we first need to check if the queue is full. When the queue is full, the relationship between *back* and *front* is:

```
( back + 1 – front ) % QUEUE_SIZE == 0
```

For example, in a full queue with 8 elements, the values of *front* and *back* could be 0 and 7, respectively, or they could be 5 and 4 or any other pair of values for which the expression above is *true*.

When we dequeue, we first need to check if the queue is empty. When the queue is empty, the relationship between *front* and *back* is the same as when the queue is full:

```
( back + 1 – front ) % QUEUE_SIZE == 0
```

Indeed, when there is only one item in the queue, *back* and *front* have the same index value. When we dequeue that last item from the queue, *front* will increase by 1 modulo *QUEUE_SIZE*, resulting in the preceding relationship between *front* and *back*. Figure 14.16 shows an example of an empty queue and a full queue.

COMMON ERROR TRAP

Do not confuse array indexes 0 and *QUEUE_SIZE – 1* with front and back. In a queue represented by a circular array, the indexes 0 and *QUEUE_SIZE – 1* are irrelevant.

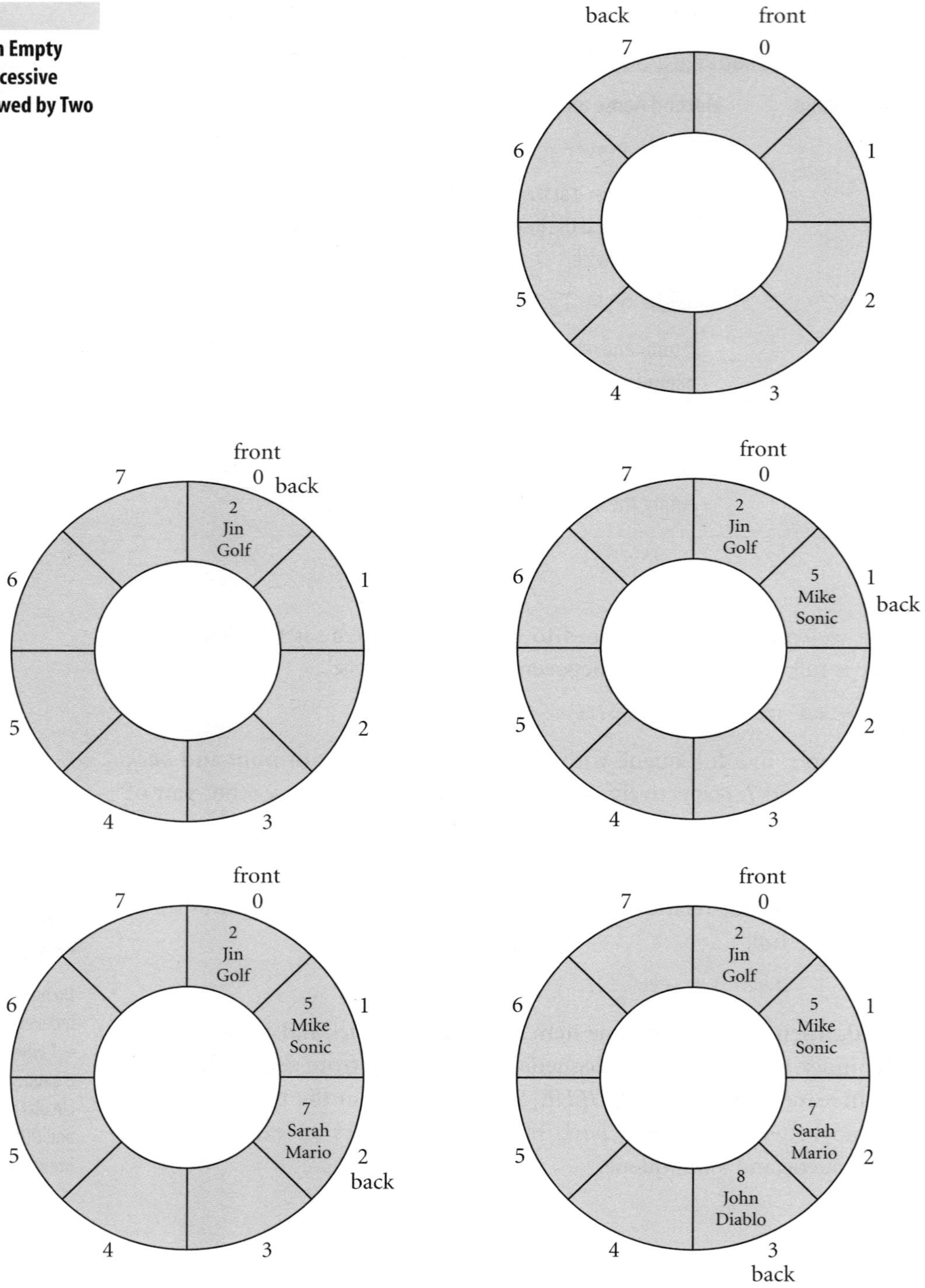

Figure 14.15
Starting with an Empty Queue, Four Successive Insertions Followed by Two Deletions

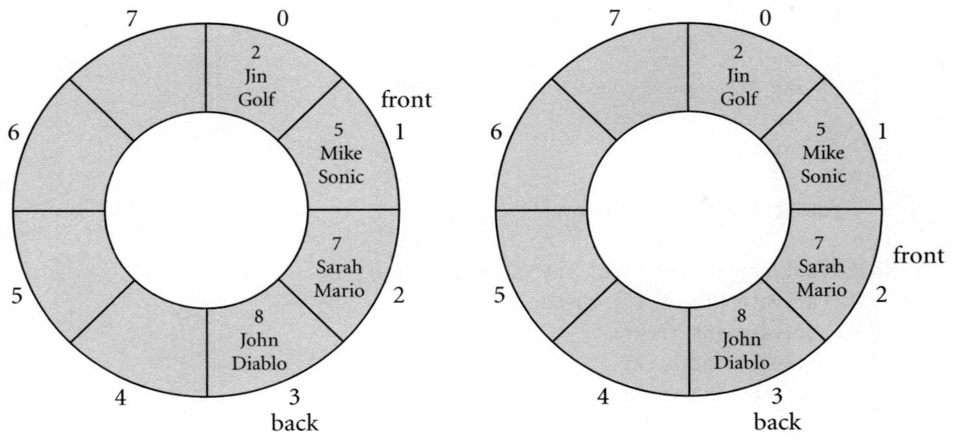

Figure 14.15
(continued)

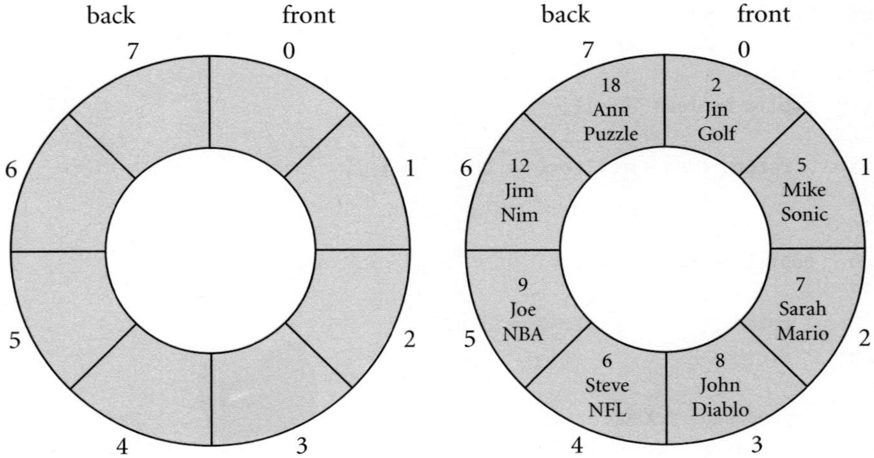

Figure 14.16
An Empty Queue and a Full Queue.

So, how do we know if the queue is full or empty? In order to distinguish a full queue from an empty queue, we must add another instance variable to our class. We will keep track of the number of elements in the queue: if the number of elements is 0, then the queue is empty; if the number of elements is equal to the size of the array, then the queue is full.

Example 14.14 shows our *ArrayQueue* class.

```
/* The ArrayQueue class
   Anderson, Franceschi
*/

public class ArrayQueue
{
  private static final int QUEUE_SIZE = 8;
  private Player [ ] queue;
  private int front;
  private int back;
  private int numberOfItems;

  public ArrayQueue( )
  {
    queue = new Player[QUEUE_SIZE];
    front = 0;
    back = QUEUE_SIZE - 1;
    numberOfItems = 0;
  }

  public boolean isFull( )
  {
    return ( numberOfItems == QUEUE_SIZE );
  }

  public boolean isEmpty( )
  {
    return ( numberOfItems == 0 );
  }

  /** enqueue method
  *   @param    p   the Player to insert
  *   @return   true if list is not full, false otherwise
  */
  public boolean enqueue( Player newPlayer )
  {
    if ( !isFull( ) )
    {
      queue[( back + 1 ) % QUEUE_SIZE] = newPlayer;
      back = ( back + 1 ) % QUEUE_SIZE;
```

```
      numberOfItems++;
      return true;
    }
    else
      return false;
  }

  /** dequeue method
  *   @return    the Player deleted
  */
  public Player dequeue( ) throws DataStructureException
  {
    if ( !isEmpty( ) )
    {
      front = ( front + 1 ) % QUEUE_SIZE;
      numberOfItems--;
      return queue[( QUEUE_SIZE + front - 1 ) % QUEUE_SIZE];
    }
    else
      throw new DataStructureException
                  ( "Queue empty: cannot dequeue" );
  }

  /** toString method
  *   @return   a front-to-back String representation of the queue
  */
  public String toString( )
  {
    String queueString = "";
    if ( !isEmpty( ) )
    {
      if ( back >= front )
      {
        for ( int i = front; i <= back; i++ )
          queueString += queue[i].toString( ) + "\n";
      }
      else
      {
        for ( int i = front; i < QUEUE_SIZE; i++ )
          queueString += queue[i].toString( ) + "\n";
        for ( int i = 0; i <= back; i++ )
          queueString += queue[i].toString( ) + "\n";
```

```
83         }
84      }
85      return queueString;
86   }
87 }
```

EXAMPLE 14.14 The *ArrayQueue* Class

In the constructor, coded at lines 13–19, we instantiate the array *queue*, set *front* to 0, *back* to *QUEUE_SIZE – 1*, and *numberOfItems* to 0. When the first element is inserted in the queue, *back* will be increased by 1 modulo *QUEUE_SIZE* and its value will become 0.

The *isFull* and *isEmpty* methods, coded at lines 21–24 and 26–29, enable a client program to check if the queue is full or empty before enqueueing or dequeueing a *Player.* Our *enqueue, dequeue,* and *toString* methods also call these methods.

In the *enqueue* method, coded at lines 31–46, we attempt to insert a *Player* into the queue. The *enqueue* method returns *false* if the queue is full (line 45) to indicate that we cannot insert. If the queue is not full, we place the *Player* at the back of the queue, update *back* accordingly, increment the number of items, and return *true* (lines 39–42).

In the *dequeue* method, coded at lines 48–62, we attempt to delete and return a *Player* from the front of the queue. The method *throws* a *Data StructureException* at lines 60–61 if the queue is empty, in which case there are no *Players* to delete. If the queue is not empty, we update *front*, decrement the number of items, and return the *Player* that was at the front of the queue (lines 55–57).

We could also code a *peek* method. It would be similar to the *peek* method we coded for the *StackArray* class, except that *top* would be replaced by *front.* Coding the *peek* method is included as an exercise at the end of the chapter.

The *toString* method, coded at lines 64–86, is more complex than the *toString* methods we have written so far. If the queue is not empty (line 70), we want to loop from *front* to *back* in order to build the *String* representation of the queue. With a circular queue, however, *back* is not always greater than *front.* Thus, we need to check where *back* is located in relation to *front.*

If *back* is greater than or equal to *front*, we use a single *for* loop at lines 74–75 to loop from *front* to *back* as we build our *String* representation of the queue. If *back* is less than *front*, however, we need to use two *for* loops: one to loop from *front* to the last array index, *QUEUE_SIZE – 1* (lines 79–80), and one to loop from 0 to *back* (lines 81–82).

As before, a very similar program to Example 14.9 can be coded to test all possible scenarios on the methods of the *ArrayQueue* class. This is proposed in the short program section of the exercises.

As we have demonstrated, a stack or queue can be implemented using either an array or a linked list. Each implementation has advantages and disadvantages. Arrays are easier to code and every item in the stack or queue can be accessed directly through its index. Linked lists are easily expanded one item at a time. To expand an array, we would need to instantiate a new, larger array and copy the elements of the existing stack or queue to the new array, which is quite tedious.

Table 14.8 summarizes these tradeoffs.

TABLE 14.8 Array Versus Linked List Implementation of a Stack or a Queue

	Array	Linked List
Easily expanded	No	Yes
Direct access to every item	Yes	No
Easy to code	Yes	No

14.8 Sorted Linked Lists

Let's go back to our linked list of video game players. If we want to display that list on a website so that all the players can see it, we might want to display the list in ascending (or descending) order by *id* number, or in alphabetical order by name or game. If we store the items in the list in sorted order, we can display the list by simply calling the *toString* method.

The items can be sorted based on the values of one of their instance variables. Often, but not always, a class is designed so that one of the instance variables uniquely identifies an object: that instance variable is called a **key**. For the *Player* class, it is reasonable to assign a different *id* value to every *Player* object, and designate the *id* instance variable as the key.

A linked list that stores its nodes in ascending order (or descending order) according to a key value is called a **sorted linked list**. Without loss of generality, we will consider a linked list sorted in ascending order.

Table 14.9 shows the APIs of the *insert*, *delete*, and *peek* methods for a sorted linked list. The only difference in this API from that of our unsorted list is that the location for inserting an element is dependent on the key value, rather than always inserting at the beginning of the list.

By default, an empty list is sorted, so a newly instantiated list is sorted. As we add elements, we need to maintain the sorted order of the list. Thus, the *insert* method must locate the proper position for inserting each element so that the inserted element's *id* is greater than the *id* of the previous element (if any) and less than or equal to the *id* of the next element (if any). We will find that proper place by traversing the list, comparing the value of the *id* of the new *Player* with the values of the *id*s of the *Players* stored at the various nodes in the list.

If the value of the item to insert will place it at the beginning of the list, then we will insert it in the same manner as we did in our earlier examples.

TABLE 14.9 *PlayerSortedLinkedList* Methods

Methods of the *PlayerSortedLinkedList* Class	
Return value	**Method name and argument list**
`void`	`insert( Player p )` inserts *Player p* in a location that keeps the list sorted in ascending order
`Player`	`delete( int searchID )` returns and removes the first *Player* of the list with an *id* equal to *searchID*. If there is no such *Player* on the list, the method throws a *DataStructureException*.

When inserting a new *Player* in the middle or at the end of the list, our *insert* method will do the following:

1. Instantiate a new node containing the *Player* to be inserted.
2. Traverse the list to identify the location to insert the new node. We will call the node before the insertion point *previous*, and the node after the insertion point *current*.
3. Attach the new node to *current*, that is, make the new node point to *current*.
4. Attach *previous* to the new node, that is, make *previous* point to the new node.
5. Increase the number of items in the list by 1.

Figures 14.17a to 14.17d illustrate inserting a node somewhere in the middle of the sorted list.

The insertion code corresponding to Figures 14.17c and 14.17d is shown in Example 14.15 at lines 38–39.

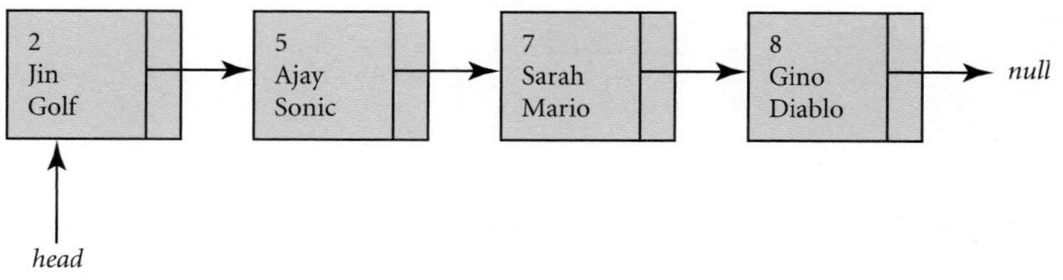

Figure 14.17a
Our Original Sorted List Before Inserting *Player* (*6, Steve, NFL*)

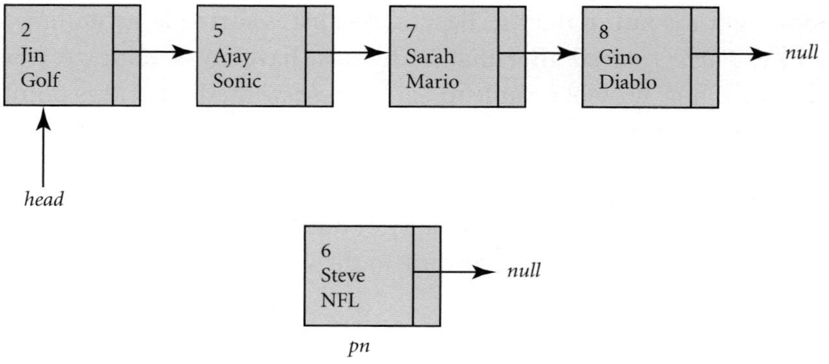

Figure 14.17b
Step 1: Instantiate the New Node

Figure 14.17c
Steps 2 and 3: Insert Occurs between *previous* and *current*. Attach the New Node to *current*.

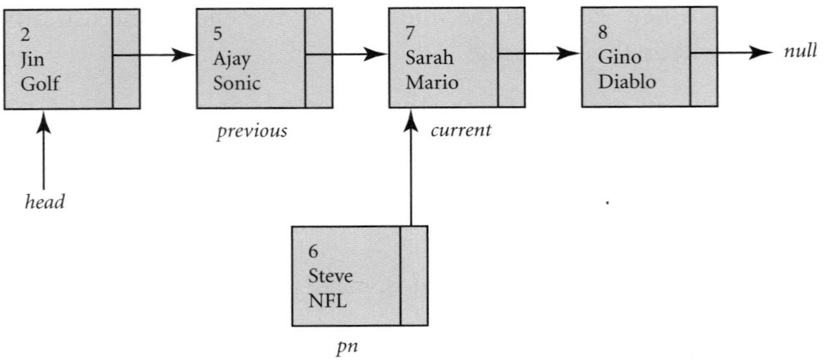

Figure 14.17d
Step 4: Attach *previous* to the New Node.

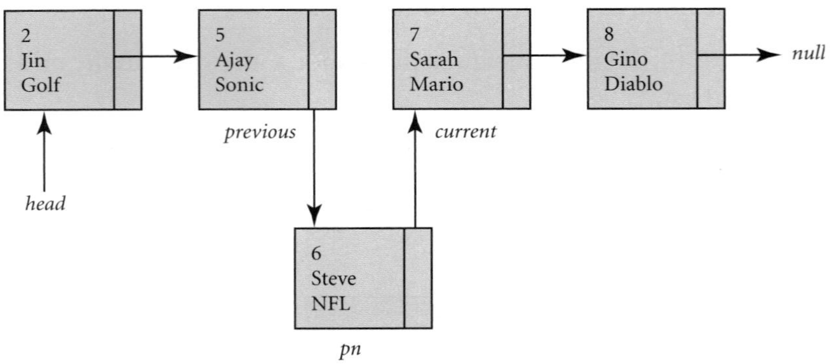

Keeping the list in sorted order also impacts our *delete* method. If the item we are looking for is not in the list, we may be able to determine that fact without traversing the entire list. As soon as we visit an item with a value greater than the key value, we know that the item we are looking for is not in the list. Because the list is sorted in ascending order, all the *Players* stored after that node must have an *id* value greater than the key. Thus, we will be able to exit our *delete* method at this point, saving CPU time.

Example 14.15 shows our *PlayerSortedLinkedList* class. This class also *extends* and inherits the functionality of our *ShellLinkedList* class. The list is sorted in ascending order according to the value of each *Player*'s *id*.

```
/* The PlayerSortedLinkedList class
   Anderson, Franceschi
*/

public class PlayerSortedLinkedList extends ShellLinkedList
{
  // head and numberOfItems are inherited instance variables

  public PlayerSortedLinkedList( )
  {
    super( );
  }

  /** insert method
  *   @param    p   Player object to insert
  */
  public void insert( Player p )
  {
    PlayerNode pn = new PlayerNode( new Player( p ) );

    // we will insert after previous and before current
    PlayerNode current = head;
    PlayerNode previous = null;
    while ( current != null
           && ( current.getPlayer( ) ).getID( ) < p.getID( ) )
    {
      previous = current;
      current = current.getNext( );
    }

    if ( previous == null ) // insert as head
    {
      pn.setNext( head );
      head = pn;
    }
    else
    {
      pn.setNext( current );
      previous.setNext( pn );
```

```
40     }
41     numberOfItems++;
42   }
43
44   /** delete method
45   *   @param    searchID   id of Player to delete
46   *   @return   the Player deleted
47   */
48   public Player delete( int searchID )
49                         throws DataStructureException
50   {
51     PlayerNode current = head;
52     PlayerNode previous = null;
53     while ( current != null
54             && current.getPlayer( ).getID( ) != searchID )
55     {
56       if ( ( current.getPlayer( ) ).getID( ) > searchID )
57            throw new DataStructureException
58                ( searchID + " not found: cannot be deleted" );
59       previous = current;
60       current = current.getNext( );
61     }
62
63     if ( current == null ) // not found
64            throw new DataStructureException
65                ( searchID + " not found: cannot be deleted" );
66     else        // searchID found at Player at node current
67     {
68       if ( current == head )
69            head = head.getNext( );  // delete head
70       else
71            previous.setNext( current.getNext( ) );
72
73       numberOfItems--;
74       return current.getPlayer( );
75     }
76   }
77 }
```

EXAMPLE 14.15 The *PlayerSortedLinkedList* Class

The *insert* method, which we coded at lines 14 to 42, inserts a node containing a copy of its *Player* parameter *p*. Line 19 declares and instantiates a *PlayerNode* object, called *pn*, which we will insert in the linked list. To get ready to search for the insertion point for the new *Player*, we declare two *PlayerNode* object references, *current* and *previous*, at lines 22–23, and assign them *head* and *null*. We use *current* to traverse the list, going just past the point of insertion, and we use *previous* to track the node just before *current*. We will insert *pn* between *previous* and *current*. From lines 24 to 29, we use a *while* loop to traverse the list. We construct our *while* loop condition so that we will exit the loop if the list is empty or if we have reached the end of the list (we test if *current* is *null* at line 24), or if we are visiting a node containing a *Player* whose *id* is larger than or equal to the *id* value of *p*, the *Player* parameter of the *insert* method (line 25).

As mentioned earlier, there are two different cases for insertion: either we insert at the beginning of the list, or we insert in the middle or at the end of the list. At line 31 we test if *previous* is *null*, in which case we never entered the *while* loop because the list is empty or because the head node contains a *Player* whose *id* value is greater than *p*'s *id*. Either way, we insert at the beginning of the list at lines 33 and 34.

If *previous* is not *null*, we will insert in the middle of the list or at the end of the list. To insert the node *pn* between *previous* and *current*, we connect *pn* to *current* at line 38, and *previous* to *pn* at line 39. Figures 14.17a to 14.17d show the step-by-step impact of lines 19, 38, and 39 on the sorted linked list.

The *delete* method (lines 44–76) is very similar to the *delete* method of the *PlayerLinkedList* class. The only difference is at lines 56–58. We first test at line 56 if the *id* of the *Player* at *current* is greater than *searchID*. If that is *true*, we have no chance of finding a *Player* object with an *id* of *searchID* since the list is sorted in ascending order. Therefore, we *throw* a *DataStructureException* with an appropriate message, and we exit the method.

Let's test our *PlayerSortedLinkedList* class. In order to keep things simple, we will test the *insert* method only, because the *delete* method is, as discussed, almost identical to the *delete* method of the *PlayerLinkedList* class.

We want to test the following cases:

- insert in an empty list
- insert at the beginning of the list
- insert in the middle of the list
- insert at the end of the list.

We traverse the list after each insertion to check that the *Player* was inserted at the correct location in the sorted linked list.

Example 14.16 shows how to use the *PlayerSortedLinkedListTest* class and how to test its methods.

```
/* The PlayerSortedLinkedListTest class
   Anderson, Franceschi
*/

public class PlayerSortedLinkedListTest
{
  public static void main( String [ ] args )
  {
    Player p1 = new Player( 7,"Sarah","Mario" );
    Player p2 = new Player( 2,"Jin","Golf" );
    Player p3 = new Player( 5,"Ajay","Sonic" );
    Player p4 = new Player( 8,"Gino","Diablo" );

    // construct empty PlayerSortedLinkedList
    PlayerSortedLinkedList players =
                  new PlayerSortedLinkedList( );

    System.out.println( "Number of items in the list: "
       + players.getNumberOfItems( ) + "\n" + players.toString( ) );

    System.out.println( "inserting " + p1 );
    players.insert( p1 );     // insert in empty list
    System.out.println( "Number of items in the list: "
       + players.getNumberOfItems( ) + "\n" + players.toString( ) );

    System.out.println( "inserting " + p2 );
    players.insert( p2 );     // insert at the beginning of the list
    System.out.println( "Number of items in the list: "
       + players.getNumberOfItems( ) + "\n" + players.toString( ) );

    System.out.println( "inserting " + p3 );
    players.insert( p3 );     // insert in the middle of the list
    System.out.println( "Number of items in the list: "
       + players.getNumberOfItems( ) + "\n" + players.toString( ) );

    System.out.println( "inserting " + p4 );
    players.insert( p4 );    // insert at the end of the list
    System.out.println( "Number of items in the list: "
```

```
39         + players.getNumberOfItems( ) + "\n" + players.toString( ) );
40   }
41 }
```

EXAMPLE 14.16 The *PlayerSortedLinkedListTest* Class

In Example 14.16, we instantiate our usual four *Player* objects *p1*, *p2*, *p3*, and *p4* at lines 9–12. We chose the *id* values so that our four test cases will be covered when we successively insert the *Player* objects. We instantiate the *PlayerSortedLinkedList players* object at lines 14–16.

We first traverse the empty list at lines 18–19. Then, we successively insert *p1*, *p2*, *p3*, and *p4*, traversing the list after each insertion (lines 21–39). Figure 14.18

```
Number of items in the list: 0

inserting id: 7        name: Sarah   game: Mario
Number of items in the list: 1
id: 7    name: Sarah   game: Mario

inserting id: 2        name: Jin     game: Golf
Number of items in the list: 2
id: 2    name: Jin     game: Golf
id: 7    name: Sarah   game: Mario

inserting id: 5        name: Ajay    game: Sonic
Number of items in the list: 3
id: 2    name: Jin     game: Golf
id: 5    name: Ajay    game: Sonic
id: 7    name: Sarah   game: Mario

inserting id: 8        name: Gino    game: Diablo
Number of items in the list: 4
id: 2    name: Jin     game: Golf
id: 5    name: Ajay    game: Sonic
id: 7    name: Sarah   game: Mario
id: 8    name: Gino    game: Diablo
```

Figure 14.18
Output of Example 14.16

shows the output of Example 14.16. As we can see, *players* remains sorted in ascending order after each insertion.

CODE IN ACTION

In the CD-ROM included in this book, you will find a Flash movie with a step-by-step illustration of sorted linked list methods. Click on the link to Chapter 14 to start the movie.

14.9 Programming Activity 2: Writing *Insert* and *Delete* Methods for a Sorted Linked List

In this activity, you will work with a sorted linked list of integers, performing the following activity:

Code the *insert* and *delete* methods to insert and delete nodes in a sorted linked list of *ints.*

The framework will animate your code to give you feedback on the correctness of your code. It will display the state of the sorted linked list at all times.

Instructions

Copy the contents of the Programming Activity 2 folder for this chapter on the CD-ROM accompanying this book onto a directory on your computer. Open the *LinkList.java* source file. Searching for five stars (*****) in the source code will position you to the code section where you will add your code.

In this task, you will fill in the code inside the *insert* and *delete* methods for a sorted linked list of integers. Example 14.17 shows the section of the *LinkList* source code where you will add your code. This example is different from the one presented earlier in the chapter. The linked list is an array of *ints*, not *Players.* The *delete* method returns a *boolean* value to indicate whether the deletion was successful. Since the client has already provided the *int* value to delete, there is no reason to return the value to the client.

You can first code the *insert* method and run the application. Once the *insert* method works properly, you can code the *delete* method and run the application again. We have provided a dummy *return* statement in the *delete* method so that the *LinkList.java* file will compile if only the *insert* method is coded. When you write the *delete* method, modify the dummy *return* statement to return the appropriate value.

```
public void insert( int i )
{
  // ***** Student writes the body of this method *****

  // code the insert method of a linked list of ints
  // the int to insert in the linked list is i

  // we call the animate method inside the body of this method
  // as you traverse the list looking for the place to insert,
  // call animate as follows:

  //    animate( head, current );
  // where    head is the instance variable head of the linked list
  //          current is the node that you are visiting

  // you can start coding now

  // in order to improve the animation (this is optional):
  // just before inserting, i.e., connecting the nodes,
  // make the call

  //    animate( head, previous, Visualizer.ACTION_INSERT_AFTER );

  // where    head is the instance variable head of the linked list
  //          previous is the node (not null) after which to insert

  // if you are inserting at the beginning of the list,
  // just before inserting, make the call

  //    animate( head, head, Visualizer.ACTION_INSERT_BEFORE );

  // where    head is the instance variable head of the linked list

  //
  // Student code starts here
  //
```

```
  //
  // End of student code, part 1
  //

  // call animate again with one argument, head,
  // to show the status of the list
     animate( head );
}


public boolean delete( int i )
{
  // ***** Student writes the body of this method *****

  // code the delete method of a linked list of ints
  // the int to delete in the linked list is i
  // if deletion is successful, return true
  // otherwise, return false

  // we call the animate method inside the body of this method
  // as you traverse the list looking for the node to delete,
  // call animate as follows:

  //    animate( head, current );

  // where    head is the instance variable head of the linked list
  //          current is the node that you are visiting

  // you can start coding now

  // in order to improve the animation (this is optional):
  // just before deleting, i.e., connecting the nodes,
  // make the call

  //    animate( head, current, Visualizer.ACTION_DELETE );

  // where    head is the instance variable head of the linked list
  //          current is the node that you are deleting

  //
  // Student code starts here
  //

  // call animate again to show the status of the list
  // if returning true
     animate( head ); //  draw the list
```

```
        return true;  //  replace this return statement
    //
    // End of student code, part 2
    //
  }
```

EXAMPLE 14.17 Location of Student Code in *LinkList*

When coding the *insert* and *delete* methods, you will need to use constructors and methods of the *Node* class. The API of the *Node* class is shown in Table 14.10.

TABLE 14.10 API of the *Node* class

Constructors and Methods of the *Node* Class	
	Constructors
Class	**Constructor and argument list**
`Node`	`Node( int i )` constructs a new *Node* object whose *data* instance variable is *i*. The *Node* points to the value *null*.
`Node`	`Node( int i, Node next )` constructs a new *Node* object whose *data* instance variable is *i*. The *Node* points to *next*.
	Methods
Return value	**Method name and argument list**
`void`	`setNext( Node next )` sets the *Node* object reference pointed to by this *Node* to *next*.
`void`	`setData( int i )` sets the *data* instance variable to *i*.
`Node`	`getNext( )` returns an object reference to the *Node* pointed to by this *Node*.
`int`	`getData( )` returns the *data* stored in this *Node*.

Figure 14.19
Opening Window

To test your code, compile and run the *LinkedListPractice.java* file, which contains the *main* method. When the program begins, a window will display the state of the linked list (the list is empty when we start), along with various buttons labeled "insert," "delete," "traverse," "count," and "clear," as shown in Figure 14.19.

To insert or delete a value, type the integer into the text field labeled "Node Data," then click on the "insert" or "delete" button. The application only accepts integers greater than or equal to 0 and less than or equal to 9999; it will not let you enter characters that are not digits. The main panel will visually represent the sorted linked list. The text area at the bottom will give you feedback on your operations. Close the window to exit the program.

Figure 14.20 shows the application after successively inserting 45, 67, and 78, traversing the list, then deleting 67. The ground symbol on the second node indicates a *null* value for the *next* instance variable.

Troubleshooting

If your method implementation does not animate or animates incorrectly, check these items:

- Check the feedback in the window to see if your code gives the correct result.

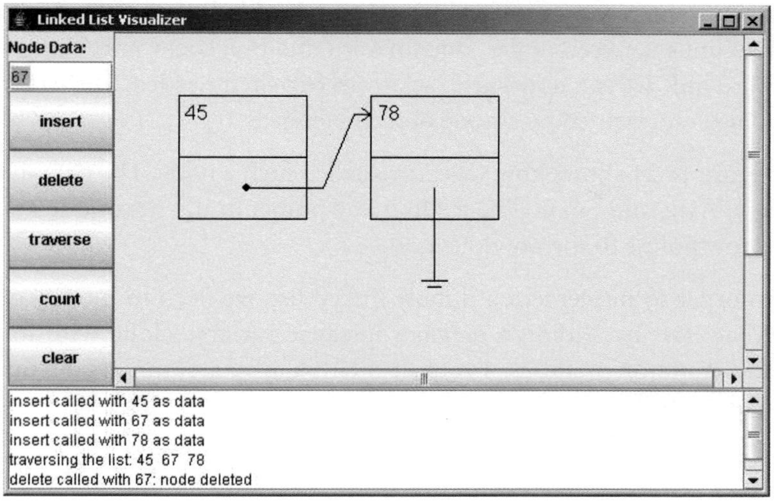

Figure 14.20
Sample Window after Performing Some Operations.

- Verify that you correctly call *animate* inside the two methods (you may need to call *animate* more than once).
- Verify that you correctly coded both cases of the *insert* method: insert at the beginning and insert in the middle of the list.
- Verify that you correctly coded all the cases of the *delete* method: fail to delete, delete at the beginning, and delete in the middle or at the end of the list.

? DISCUSSION QUESTIONS

1. Explain why it is important to update *head* when inserting at the beginning of a list.
2. Explain the difference between deleting in a nonsorted list and deleting in a sorted list.

14.10 Doubly Linked Lists

So far, when traversing a linked list and looking for a node containing a particular value, we have used two nodes, which we called *previous* and *current*. We kept track of the *previous* node because we had no way to go backward in the list from the *current* node.

This problem can be solved by using a **doubly linked list**, which provides two links between nodes, one forward and one backward. Using the backward link, we can now backtrack from *current* if needed. The backward link is also represented by a node object reference.

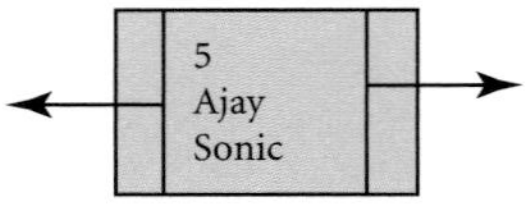

Figure 14.21
A Node with Two Links

Figure 14.21 shows how we can visualize such a node. The data in the node is *5*, *Ajay*, and *Sonic*. The right arrow points to the next node and the left arrow points to the previous node.

In order to implement a doubly linked list, we need to modify our *Player Node* class by adding a *previous* instance variable along with its accessor and mutator methods. Example 14.18 shows a summary of our revised *PlayerNode* class.

```
/* The PlayerNode class
   Anderson, Franceschi
*/

public class PlayerNode
{
  private Player player;        // the player at that node
  private PlayerNode next;      // the next PlayerNode
  private PlayerNode previous;  // the previous PlayerNode

 // constructors
 // accessors are getPlayer, getNext, getPrevious
 // mutators are setPlayer, setNext, setPrevious
}
```

EXAMPLE 14.18 Summary of the *PlayerNode* Class for a Doubly Linked List

When inserting a node, we need to reset both forward and backward links, i.e., the *next* and *previous* instance variables. Suppose, for example, that we insert a node containing *Player p* before a node named *current.* We will illustrate only the general case, when *current* is in the middle or at the end of the doubly linked list, that is, *current* is neither *head* nor *null.*

The steps we need to perform are the following:

1. Instantiate the new node.

2. Attach the new node to *current* by setting its *next* field to *current.*

3. Attach the node before *current* to the new node by setting its *next* field to the new node.
4. Set *previous* in the new node to point to the node before *current*.
5. Set *previous* in *current* to point to the new node.
6. Add 1 to the number of items in the list.

Steps 2 and 3 set the forward links and Steps 4 and 5 set the backward links.

Figures 14.22a to 14.22f provide a step-by-step illustration of the steps for inserting a node in the middle of a doubly linked list. Note that we no longer need to keep a *previous* object reference, because we can get the location of the previous node from the *current* node.

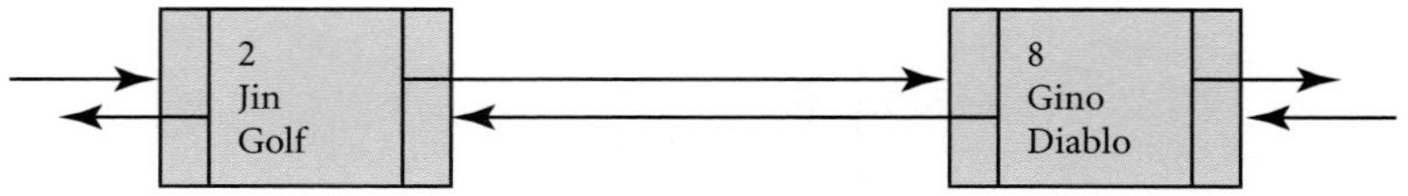

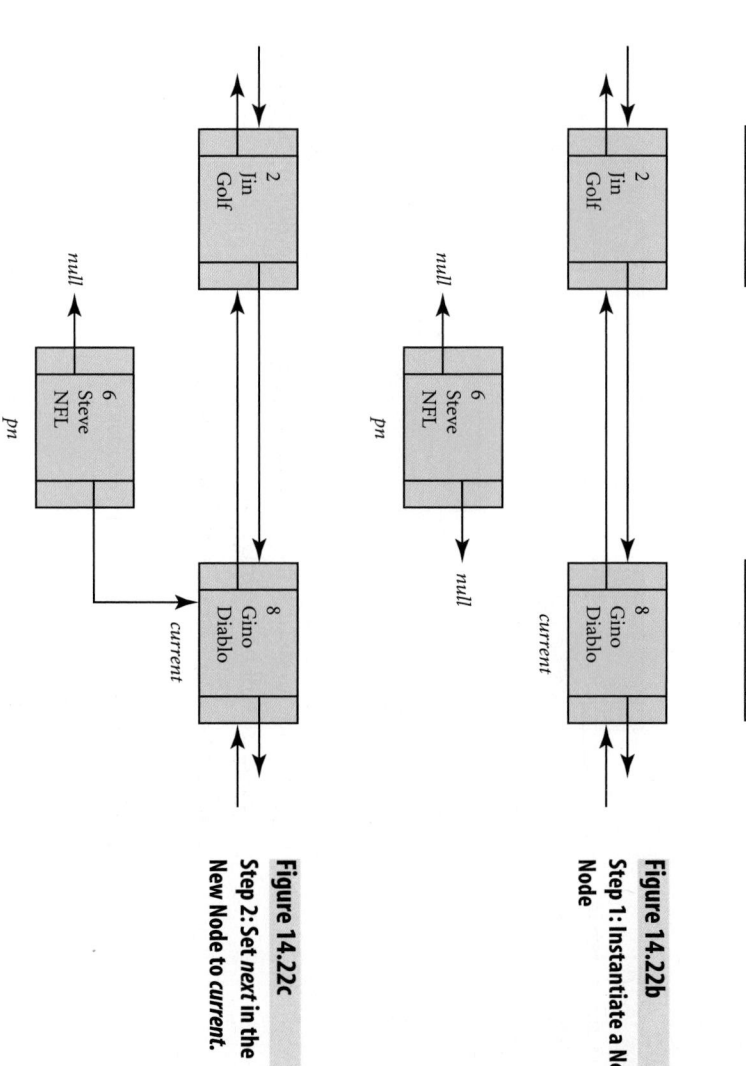

Figure 14.22a
Our Original Doubly Linked List

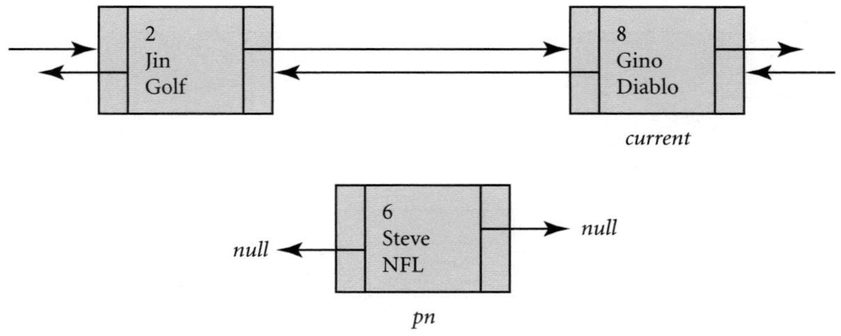

Figure 14.22b
Step 1: Instantiate a New Node

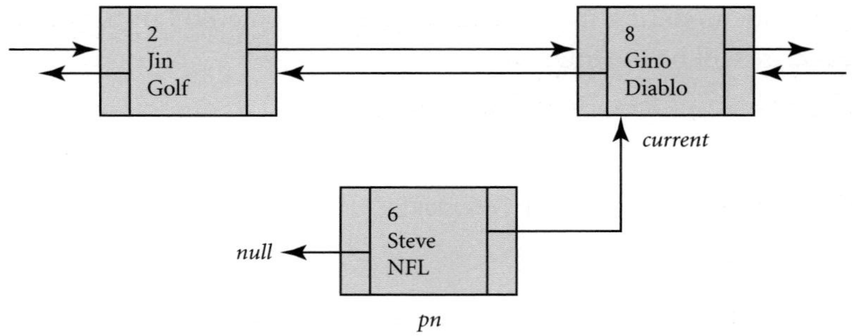

Figure 14.22c
Step 2: Set *next* in the New Node to *current*.

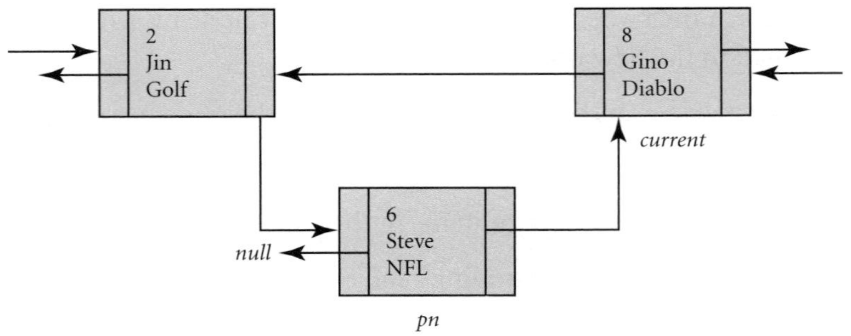

Figure 14.22d
Step 3: Set *next* in the Node Before *current* to the New Node

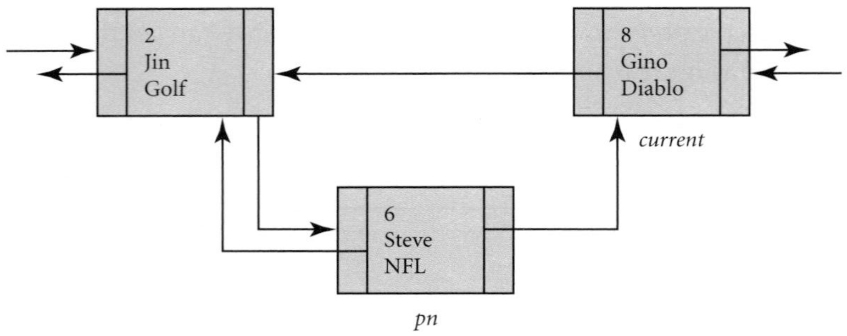

Figure 14.22e
Step 4: Set *previous* in the New Node to the Node Before *current*

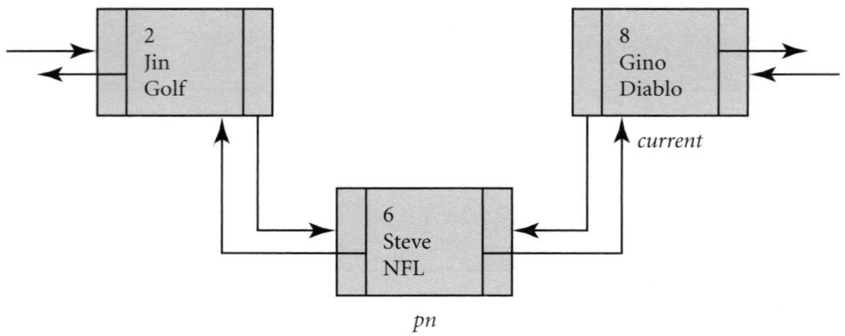

Figure 14.22f
Step 5. Set *previous* in *current* to the New Node

Our code updating the links inside the *insert* method of the doubly linked list class will be the following:

```
PlayerNode pn = new PlayerNode( new Player( p ) );    // Step 1
pn.setNext( current );                                // Step 2
( current.getPrevious( ) ).setNext( pn );             // Step 3
pn.setPrevious( current.getPrevious( ) );             // Step 4
current.setPrevious( pn );                            // Step 5
numberOfItems++;                                      // Step 6
```

The order in which these statements are executed is important. Indeed, if Step 5 were executed immediately after Step 1, we would overwrite the reference to the previous node. Then we could not access the node before *current*, and we would be unable to properly reset the links between the nodes.

Note that if *current* is either *head* (insert at the beginning) or *null* (insert at the end), the preceding code needs to be modified; that is proposed in the group project.

When deleting a node, we also need to reset all the appropriate forward and backward links. Suppose, for example, that we delete a node named *current*. We will illustrate only the general case, when *current* is in the middle of the doubly linked list. In this case, *current* is neither the *head* nor the last node in the list (since we are deleting *current*, we are assuming that *current* is not *null*), that is, there is a node after *current* in the list.

To delete a node, *current*, from the middle of a doubly linked list, we need to perform the following steps.

1. Set *next* in the node before *current* to the node after *current*.
2. Set *previous* in the node after *current* to the node before *current*.
3. Decrease the number of items by 1

Figures 14.23a to 14.23c give a step-by-step illustration of deleting a node.

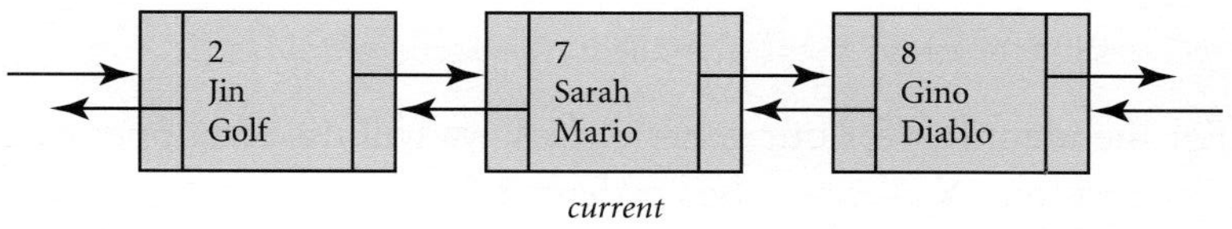

Figure 14.23a
Our Original Linked List

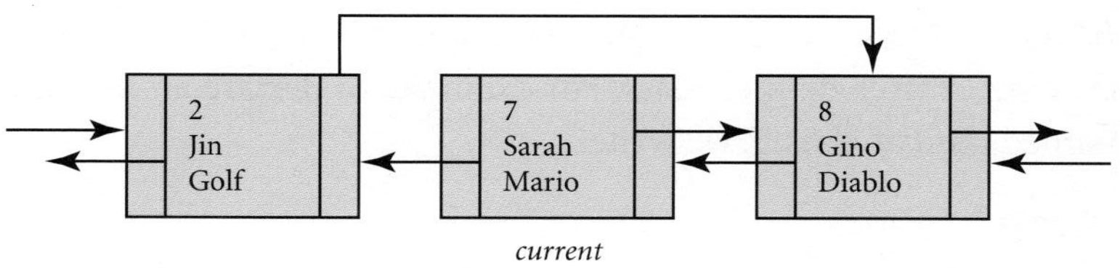

Figure 14.23b
Step 1: Set *next* in the Node Before *current* to the Node After *current*

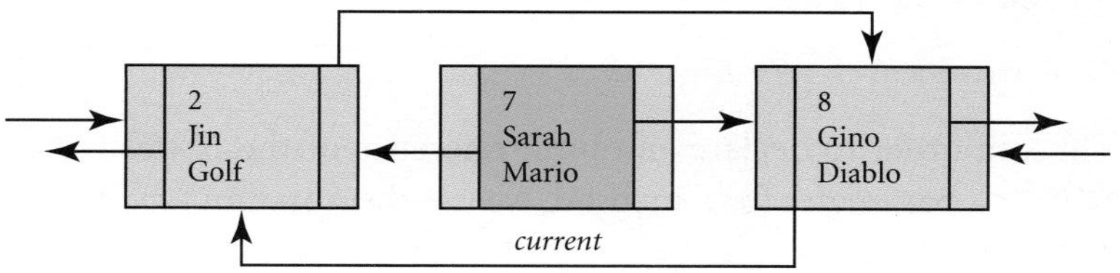

Figure 14.23c
Step 2: Set *previous* in the Node After *current* to the Node Before *current*

Our code updating the links inside the *delete* method of the doubly linked list class is:

```
( current.getPrevious( ) ).setNext( current.getNext( ) );          // Step 1

( current.getNext( ) ).setPrevious( current.getPrevious( ) );   // Step 2

numberOfItems--;                                                   // Step 3
```

Again, note that if *current* is either *head* or the last node in the list, the previous code would need to be modified; that is also proposed in the group project at the end of the chapter, which builds a sorted, doubly linked list.

14.11 Linked Lists Using Generic Types

In Chapter 9, we introduced the concept of generics and how to use existing Java classes that implement generic types, specifically the *ArrayList* class. User-defined classes can also implement generic types. In this section, we will build a linked list class that implements generic types, so that the client can specify the class type of the data stored in our linked list. In a linked list, the data of the item is stored in the node; thus, the data in our *Node* class will be a generic object.

The basic syntax for the header of a class that implements generics is:

```
AccessModifier class className<IdentifierForGenericClass>
```

For the identifier for our generic class, we will use the upper case letter *T*. Thus, for our *Node* class, the header will be:

```
public class Node<T>
```

Inside the class, we can then use that identifier, here *T*, as we would use an existing or user-defined class. For example, to declare an instance variable named *data* of class *T*, we write:

```
private T data;
```

In order to use an object reference of a class implementing generics, we use the following syntax:

```
ClassName<IdentifierForGenericClass>
```

Thus, in order to declare an object reference of the *Node* class as a return type or a parameter for a method, we use the notation *Node<T>*.

Example 14.19 shows our *Node<T>* class.

```
/** The Node class
*   Anderson, Franceschi
*/

public class Node<T>
{
  private T data;
  private Node<T> next;

  /** default constructor
  *  sets data and next to null
  */
  public Node( )
  {
    data = null;
    next = null;
  }

  /**  constructor
  *   @param item reference to data item
  *  sets next to null
  */
  public Node( T item )
  {
    setData( item );
    next = null;
  }

  /**  accessor for data
  *   @return reference to data item
  */
  public T getData( )
  {
    return data;
  }

  /**  accessor for next
  *   @return next
  */
  public Node<T> getNext( )
  {
```

```
    return next;
  }

  /**  mutator for data
  *   @param reference to data item
  */
  public void setData( T item  )
  {
    data = item;
  }

  /**  mutator for next
  *   @param reference to next Node
  */
  public void setNext( Node<T> nd )
  {
    next = nd;
  }
}
```

EXAMPLE 14.19 The *Node* Class Using Generics

Example 14.20 shows our *ShellLinkedList<T>* class.

```
/* The ShellLinkedList class
   Anderson, Franceschi
*/

public abstract class ShellLinkedList<T>
{
  protected Node<T> head;
  protected int numberOfItems;

  /**  constructor
  *   sets head to null and numberOfItems to 0
  */
  public ShellLinkedList( )
  {
    head = null;
    numberOfItems = 0;
  }

```

```
  /**  accessor for numberOfItems
  *   @return  numberOfItems
  */
  public int getNumberOfItems( )
  {
    return numberOfItems;
  }

  /**  isEmpty method
  *   @return  true if no items in list; false otherwise
  */
  public boolean isEmpty( )
  {
    return ( numberOfItems == 0 );
  }

  /**  toString method
  *   @return  all items in the list
  */
  public String toString( )
  {
    String listString = "";
    Node<T> current = head;
    for ( int i = 0; i < numberOfItems; i++ )
    {
      listString += current.getData( ).toString( ) + "\n";
      current = current.getNext( );
    }
    return listString;
  }
}
```

EXAMPLE 14.20 The *ShellLinkedList* Class Using Generics

Our *GenericLinkedList* class, shown in Example 14.21, implements the same methods as our *PlayerLinkedList* from earlier in the chapter. The only differences in the code are the class header and the declaration of the instance variable *head*.

```
/* The GenericLinkedList class
   Anderson, Franceschi
*/

```

```
public class GenericLinkedList<T> extends ShellLinkedList<T>
{
  // head and numberOfItems are inherited instance variables

  /**  constructor
  *   calls constructor of ShellLinkedList
  */
  public GenericLinkedList( )
  {
    super( );
  }

  /** insert method
  *   @param    item   T object to insert
  */
  public void insert( T item )
  {
    // insert as head
    Node<T> nd = new Node<T>( item );
    nd.setNext( head );
    head = nd;
    numberOfItems++;
  }

  /** delete method
  *   @param    item   T object to delete
  *   @return   true if the deletion was successful, false otherwise
  */
  public boolean delete( T item )
  {
    Node<T> current = head;
    Node<T> previous = null;
    while ( current != null
            && ! (  item.equals ( current.getData(  )  )  )  )
    {
      previous = current;
      current = current.getNext( );
    }

    if ( current == null ) // not found
        return false;
    else
    {
      if ( current == head )
```

```
49           head = head.getNext( );  // delete head
50         else
51           previous.setNext( current.getNext( ) );
52
53         numberOfItems--;
54         return true;
55       }
56     }
57 }
```

EXAMPLE 14.21 The *GenericLinkedList* Class with Generics

Our *GenericLinkedList* class, shown in Example 14.21, implements the same methods as our *PlayerLinkedList*

The *insert* method, coded at lines 17–27, is very similar to the insert method of the *PlayerLinkedList* class. Instead of a *Player* reference, its parameter *item* is a *T* reference, where *T* is a generic class. It also inserts *item* at the beginning of the list. At line 20, we declare and instantiate a *Node<T>* object reference, which is then connected to the list. The rest of the *insert* method is identical to the code in our *insert* method of a non-generic linked list class.

REFERENCE POINT

Declaring and instantiating objects of a class implementing generics is discussed in Chapter 9.

Because we do not know in advance what type of object our class will be instantiated with, we implemented our *delete* method differently. We cannot delete an item based on the value of one of its fields because we do not know what the fields of that item are, since that item is a generic object. Thus, the parameter of our *delete* method is a generic object of the same type as the items in the list. There is no need to return an item if we find it and can delete it because we already have that item as the parameter of the method. For that reason, our *delete* method returns a *boolean* value: *true* if we were able to delete the parameter item, *false* otherwise. In order to compare *item* with the items in the list, we call the *equals* method at line 38, inherited by any class from the *Object* class, and which will need to be overwritten in the class the client specifies as the type for the linked list.

Now that we have defined and implemented our linked class storing generic objects, how do we use it in a client class? We use the same syntax as we would using an existing Java class implementing generics, as we learned in Chapter 9. In fact, in the *GenericLinkedList* class, we used the *Node* class, which implements generics.

Example 14.22 shows a client class using the *GenericLinkedList* class.

```
/* The LinkedListTest class
   Anderson, Franceschi
*/

public class LinkedListTest
{
  public static void main( String [ ] args )
  {
    Player p1 = new Player( 7,"Sarah","Mario" );
    Player p2 = new Player( 2,"Jin","Golf" );
    Player p3 = new Player( 5,"Ajay","Sonic" );

    // construct empty LinkedList of Player objects
    GenericLinkedList<Player> players = new GenericLinkedList<Player>( );
    System.out.println( "Number of items in the list: "
     + players.getNumberOfItems( ) + "\n" + players.toString( ) );

    players.insert( p1 );  // insert in empty list
    System.out.println( "Number of items in the list: "
     + players.getNumberOfItems( ) + "\n" + players.toString( ) );

    players.insert( p2 );  // insert in list of one item
    System.out.println( "Number of items in the list: "
     + players.getNumberOfItems( ) + "\n" + players.toString( ) );

    players.insert( p3 );  // insert in list of two items
    System.out.println( "Number of items in the list: "
     + players.getNumberOfItems( ) + "\n" + players.toString( ) );

    if (  players.delete(  p2 ) )      // delete in the middle
        System.out.println( "Player successfully deleted: "  );
    System.out.println( "Number of items in the list: "
      + players.getNumberOfItems( ) + "\n" + players.toString( ) );

    if (  players.delete(  p3 ) )      // delete at the beginning
       System.out.println( "Player successfully deleted: "  );
    System.out.println( "Number of items in the list: "
      + players.getNumberOfItems( ) + "\n" + players.toString( ) );
  }
}
```

EXAMPLE 14.22 *The LinkedListTest* Class

```
Number of items in the list: 0

Number of items in the list: 1
id: 7    name: Sarah    game: Mario

Number of items in the list: 2
id: 2    name: Jin      game: Golf
id: 7    name: Sarah    game: Mario

Number of items in the list: 3
id: 5    name: Ajay     game: Sonic
id: 2    name: Jin      game: Golf
id: 7    name: Sarah    game: Mario

Player succesfully deleted:
Number of items in the list: 2
id: 5    name: Ajay     game: Sonic
id: 7    name: Sarah    game: Mario

Player succesfully deleted:
Number of items in the list: 1
id: 7    name: Sarah    game: Mario
```

Figure 14.24
Output of Example 14.22

The only statement that is specific to the generic character of the *GenericLinkedList* is at line 14 when we declare and instantiate an object reference of *GenericLinkedList.* If we wanted to declare and instantiate a list containing *Integer* objects, we would have written:

```
GenericLinkedList<Integer> numbers = new GenericLinkedList<Integer>( );
```

Figure 14.24 shows the output of Example 14.22.

14.12 Recursively Defined Linked Lists

A linked list can be defined recursively. A recursively defined linked list is made up of two items:

- *first*, an item, which is the first item in the linked list
- *rest*, a linked list, which consists of the rest of the linked list.

REFERENCE POINT

Recursion is discussed extensively in Chapter 13.

Figure 14.25 shows a representation of a recursively defined linked list.

In our recursively defined linked list, we have two instance variables: the item *first* and the linked list *rest*. Because we can access the rest of the list through the *rest* instance variable, we do not need a node class.

In designing our class encapsulating a recursive linked list of generic objects, we will limit ourselves to an unsorted linked list. We will insert at the beginning of the list. When we delete, we will attempt to delete and return an object that matches a parameter object. When we cannot delete, we will return *false*.

Table 14.11 shows the APIs of the *insert* and *delete* methods.

After we insert, *first* will hold the item inserted, and *rest* will hold the original list. Figures 14.26a and 14.26b show a recursively defined linked list before and after inserting a *Player* named *p*. In the figures, *p1* represents the

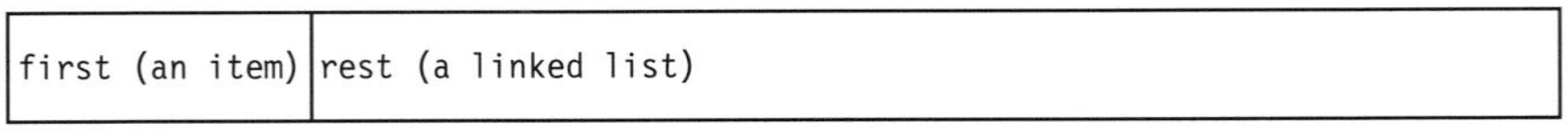

Figure 14.25
A Recursively Defined Linked List

TABLE 14.11 *RecursiveLinkedList* Methods

Methods of the *RecursiveLinkedList* Class	
Return value	**Method name and argument list**
`void`	`insert( T item )` inserts *item* at the beginning of the list.
`boolean`	`delete( T item)` removes the first object of the list that matches *item* and returns *true*. If there is no such object in the list, the method returns *false*.

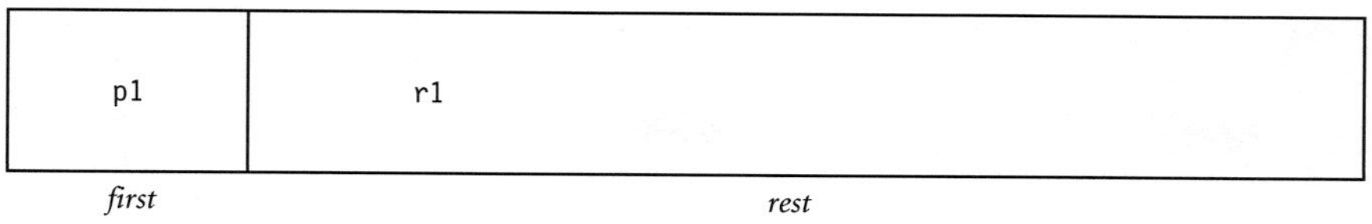

Figure 14.26a
The List Before Inserting *Player p*

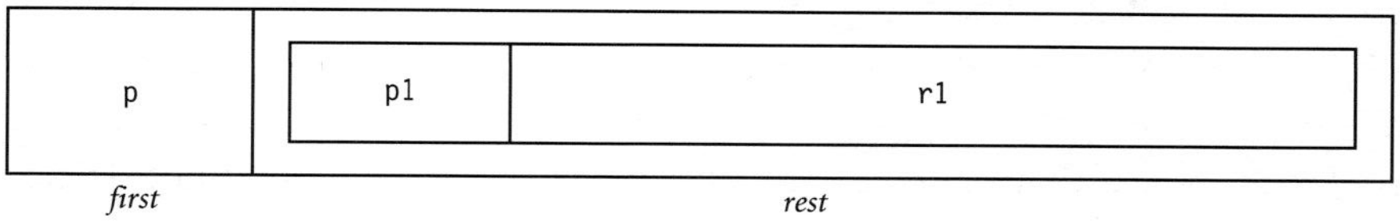

Figure 14.26b
The List After Inserting *Player p*

current first item, and *r1* represents the rest of the list before the insertion. The *insert* method is not recursive.

The *delete* method is recursive. We have three base cases:

- The list is empty.
- The element to delete is the first item of the list.
- The element to delete is not the first item of the list and the rest of the list is empty.

In the general case, we try to delete the element from the rest of the list.

If the list is empty (the first base case), we will return *false*. If the list is not empty, we will look at *first* and check to see if it matches the parameter *item*. If it does (the second base case), we will delete *first*, and *rest* will become our list. If it does not, then we will attempt to delete inside *rest*. If *rest* is *null*, we cannot delete (the third base case) and we will return *false*. If *rest* is not *null*, we will make a recursive call to the *delete* method with *rest* (the general case).

More generally, we want to do the following:

- If the list is empty (base case #1), the method returns.
- Process *first*, that is, the first element in the list (base case #2); the method may or may not return at that point.
- If *rest* is *null*, that is, the list has only 1 item, (base case #3), the method returns.
- If *rest* is not *null*, make a recursive call on *rest*.

Example 14.23 shows our *RecursiveLinkedList* class. Because of its recursive design, the *RecursiveLinkedList* class does not extend the *ShellLinkedList* class.

```
/* The RecursiveLinkedList class
   Anderson, Franceschi
*/

public class RecursiveLinkedList<T>
{
  private T first;
  private RecursiveLinkedList<T> rest;

  public RecursiveLinkedList( )
  {
    first = null;
    rest = null;
  }

  /** insert method
  *   @param    item object to insert at beginning of list
  */
  public void insert( T item )
  {
    if ( isEmpty( ) )    // is list empty?
      first = item;
    else
    {
      RecursiveLinkedList<T> tempList =
                 new RecursiveLinkedList<T>( );
      tempList.first = first;
      tempList.rest = rest;
      first = item;
      rest = tempList;
    }
  }

  /** delete method
  *   @param    item   the T object to delete
  *   @return   true if item is deleted, false otherwise
  */
  public boolean delete( T item )
  {
    if ( isEmpty( ) )                    // is list empty?
      return false;
```

```
42     else if ( first.equals( item ) )  // found it
43     {
44        T temp = first;
45        if ( rest == null )
46          first = null;
47        else        // rest not null
48        {
49          first = rest.first;
50          rest = rest.rest;
51        }
52        return true;
53     }
54     else if ( rest == null )
55        return false;
56     else                                  // try to delete in rest
57        return rest.delete( item );
58   }
59
60   public boolean isEmpty( )
61   {
62     return ( first == null );
63   }
64
65   public String toString( )
66   {
67     String listString = "";
68     if ( first != null )
69     {
70        listString = first.toString( ) + "\n";
71        if ( rest != null )
72          listString += rest.toString( );
73     }
74     return listString;
75   }
76 }
```

EXAMPLE 14.23 The *RecursiveLinkedList* Class

We declare the two instance variables at lines 7–8: *first* represents the first *T* object in the list, and *rest* represents the rest of the list, which is a *RecursiveLinkedList* object reference itself. We coded the default constructor, which constructs an empty list, at lines 10–14.

We coded the *insert* method at lines 16–32. After insertion, *first* will be the method's *T* parameter *item*, and *rest* will be the list before we inserted *item*.

We begin by testing if the list is empty by calling the *isEmpty* method (defined at lines 60 to 63), which returns *true* if *first* is *null*. If the list is empty, we assign *item* to *first* at line 22. If *first* is not *null*, we copy the current list into a new list at lines 25–28. We instantiate a temporary list, *tempList*. We then assign *first* to the *first* instance variable of *tempList* and *rest* to the *rest* instance variable of *tempList*. At that point, we have copied the current list into *tempList*. Now we can insert the new item into the first position (line 29) and make *tempList* the rest of the list (line 30).

The recursive *delete* method (lines 34–58) takes the *T* parameter *item*. If the list is empty (line 40), we return *false*. If the list is not empty, then *first* is not *null*, and we can call the *equals* method on *first*. More generally, when processing a recursively designed list, not testing for all the base case conditions could result in a *NullPointerException*.

If the list is not empty and *first* is equal to *item* (line 42), we do the necessary bookkeeping on the list to delete the first element at lines 44–51 before returning *true* at line 52. In order to delete the first element of the list, we need to update *first* and *rest*. *First* will be assigned the first element of *rest*. However, *rest* could be *null*, in which case *rest* does not have a first element. Thus, we test if *rest* is *null* at line 45. If it is, the list is now empty, so we assign *null* to *first* at line 46. If *rest* is not *null*, we assign the first element of *rest* to *first* at line 49, and we assign the rest of *rest* to *rest* at line 50.

Figures 14.27a to 14.27c show the list before deleting *Player p*, after line 49 is executed, and after line 50 is executed, when *Player p* has been deleted from the list.

Finally, if the list is not *null* and the *first* is not equal to *item*, we skip to line 54, where we test if *rest* is *null*. If it is, we cannot delete and return *false*. If *rest* is not *null*, we make the recursive call to try to delete from *rest* at line 57.

Figure 14.27a
The List Before Deleting *Player p*

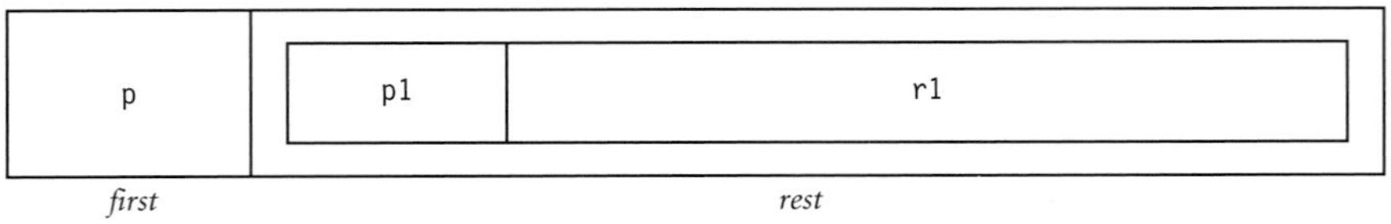

Figure 14.27b
The List After *first* is Assigned *first* of *rest*

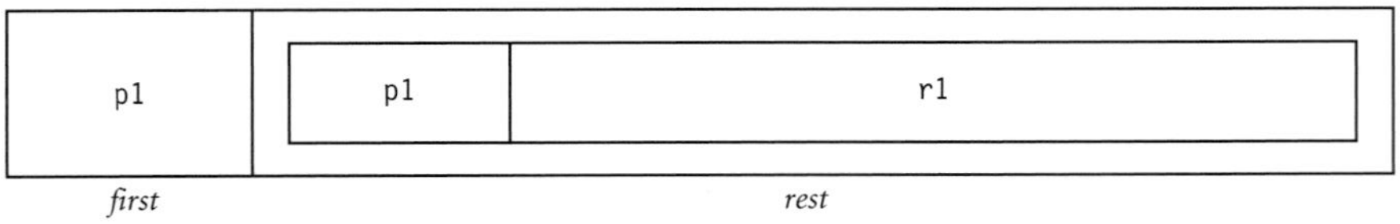

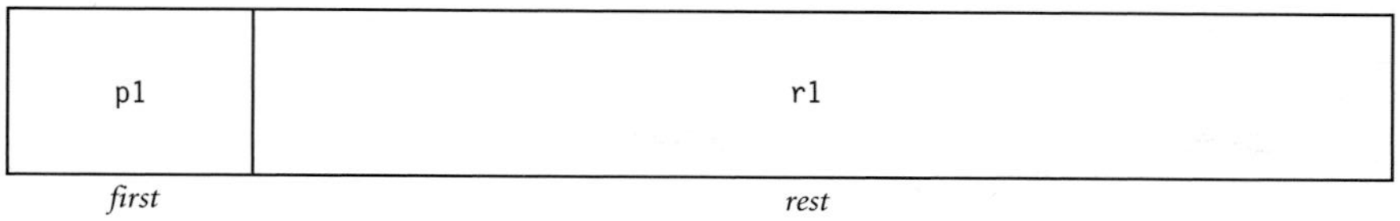

Figure 14.27c
The List After *rest* of *rest* is Assigned to *rest*. *Player p* Has Been Deleted.

We coded our *toString* method at lines 65–75. This method is also recursive. If the list is empty, it returns the empty *String*. If the list is not empty, we assign the contents of *first* to the temporary variable *listString* at line 70. Note that the class the client specifies as the type of the *RecursiveLinkedList* will need to provide an overridding *toString* method. We then need to traverse *rest* in order to add its contents to *listString*. But *rest* could be *null*, in which case we are finished traversing the list. So if *rest* is not *null* (line 71), we traverse *rest* at line 72 by making the recursive call:

```
rest.toString( )
```

That recursive call returns a *String* representing the contents of *rest*; we concatenate that *String* to *listString* at line 72 before returning *listString* at line 74.

Example 14.24 shows how to use our *RecursiveLinkedList* class in a client program.

```
/* The RecursiveLinkedListTest class
   Anderson, Franceschi
*/

public class RecursiveLinkedListTest
{
  public static void main( String [ ] args )
  {
    Player p1 = new Player( 7,"Sarah","Mario" );
    Player p2 = new Player( 2,"Jin","Golf" );
    Player p3 = new Player( 5,"Ajay","Sonic" );

    RecursiveLinkedList<Player> players =
                new RecursiveLinkedList<Player>( );
    System.out.println( "The list is\n"
        + ( players.isEmpty( ) ? "empty\n" : players.toString( ) ) );

    players.insert( p1 );
    System.out.println( "Inserting " + p1 );
    System.out.println( "The list is\n"
        + ( players.isEmpty( ) ? "empty\n" : players.toString( ) ) );

```

```
23     players.insert( p2 );
24     System.out.println( "Inserting " + p2 );
25     System.out.println( "The list is\n"
26         + ( players.isEmpty( ) ? "empty\n" : players.toString( ) ) );
27
28     players.insert( p3 );
29     System.out.println( "Inserting " + p3 );
30     System.out.println( "The list is\n"
31         + ( players.isEmpty( ) ? "empty\n" : players.toString( ) ) );
32
33     if ( players.delete( p2 ) )  // delete in middle of list
34       System.out.println( "Player deleted: " + p2 );
35     System.out.println( "The list is\n"
36       + ( players.isEmpty( ) ? "empty\n" : players.toString( ) ) );
37
38     if ( players.delete( p1 ) )  // delete at end of the list
39       System.out.println( "Player deleted: " + p1 );
40     System.out.println( "The list is\n"
41       + ( players.isEmpty( ) ? "empty\n" : players.toString( ) ) );
42
43     if ( players.delete( p1 ) )  // attempt to delete will fail
44       System.out.println( "Player deleted: " + p1 );
45     System.out.println( "The list is\n"
46       + ( players.isEmpty( ) ? "empty\n" : players.toString( ) ) );
47
48     if ( players.delete( p3 ) )  // delete only Player In list
49       System.out.println( "\nPlayer deleted: " + p3 );
50     System.out.println( "The list is\n"
51       + ( players.isEmpty( ) ? "empty\n" : players.toString( ) ) );
52
53     if ( players.delete( p3 ) )  // try to delete from empty list
54       System.out.println( "\nPlayer deleted: " + p3 );
55     System.out.println( "The list is\n"
56       + ( players.isEmpty( ) ? "empty\n" : players.toString( ) ) );
57   }
58 }
```

EXAMPLE 14.24 The *RecursiveLinkedListTest* Class

COMMON ERROR TRAP

When processing a recursively defined list, not testing for all the base case conditions can eventually result in a *NullPointerException* at run time.

In Example 14.24, we again instantiate our usual three *Player* object references *p1*, *p2*, and *p3* at lines 9–11. We instantiate the *RecursiveLinkedList* *players* at lines 13–14. This example tests the following operations:

- inserting in an empty list (line 18)
- inserting in a list of one element (line 23)
- inserting in a list of two elements (line 28)

- deleting an element in the middle of the list (line 33)
- deleting an element at the end of the list (line 38)
- failing to delete from a non-empty list (line 43)
- deleting the only element in the list (line 48)
- failing to delete from an empty list (line 53)

Figure 14.28 shows the output of Example 14.24.

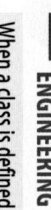

SOFTWARE ENGINEERING TIP

When a class is defined recursively, think in terms of implementing recursive methods.

```
The list is
empty

Inserting id: 7         name: Sarah  game: Mario
The list is
id: 7    name: Sarah    game: Mario

Inserting id: 2         name: Jin    game: Golf
The list is
id: 2    name: Jin      game: Golf
id: 7    name: Sarah    game: Mario

Inserting id: 5         name: Ajay   game: Sonic
The list is
id: 5    name: Ajay     game: Sonic
id: 2    name: Jin      game: Golf
id: 7    name: Sarah    game: Mario

Player deleted: id: 2   name: Jin    game: Golf
The list is
id: 5    name: Ajay     game: Sonic
id: 7    name: Sarah    game: Mario

Player deleted: id: 7   name: Sarah  game: Mario
The list is
id: 5    name: Ajay     game: Sonic

The list is
id: 5    name: Ajay     game: Sonic


Player deleted: id: 5   name: Ajay   game: Sonic
The list is
empty

The list is
empty
```

Figure 14.28
Output of Example 14.24

Skill Practice
with these end-of-chapter questions

14.14.1 Multiple Choice

Questions 1, 8, 9, 10, 11, 12, 13

14.14.4 Identifying Errors in Code

Questions 35, 36, 37, 38

14.14.6 Write a Short Program

Questions 47, 49, 51, 54, 55, 56, 57, 58

14.14.8 Technical Writing

Question 72

CHAPTER SUMMARY

14.13 Chapter Summary

- A data structure is a mechanism for organizing the data a program stores in memory.
- A linked list is a data structure consisting of nodes linked together like a chain.
- Typical instance variables for a node are an object reference to the data stored at the node, and a node reference, which points to the next node in the list.
- Because each node has a reference to the next node as an instance variable, a linked list needs only one instance variable, its first node, which is usually called *head*. Often, for convenience, we also include an instance variable representing the number of items in the list.
- A linked list can be expanded one node at a time, therefore optimizing memory use.
- A stack is a data structure organized as Last In, First Out.
- A queue is a data structure organized as First In, First Out.
- A linked list can be used to represent a stack. In that case, we push onto the stack by inserting an item at the beginning of the list. We pop by deleting the first item of the list.

- A linked list can also be used to represent a queue. In that case, we enqueue by inserting at the end of the list. We dequeue by deleting the first item of the list. Because we insert at the end of the list, it is useful to have an instance variable representing the last node in the list, often called *tail.*
- A stack can also be represented by an array, if we know in advance the maximum number of items that will be stored on the stack at one time. An instance variable called *top* represents the index of the last array element pushed onto the stack. We pop, or delete, that element, unless the stack is empty. We push, or insert, onto the stack a new element at index (*top* + *1*), unless the stack is full.
- A queue can also be represented by an array, if we know in advance the maximum number of items that will be stored in the queue at one time. A circular array is usually implemented for the queue. Two instance variables called *front* and *back* represent the indexes of the first and last element inserted in the queue. We dequeue, or delete, the element at index *front* unless the queue is empty. We enqueue, or insert, a new element at index (*back* + *1% QUEUE_SIZE*), unless the queue is full.
- In a class encapsulating a data structure, a method returning an object can *throw* an exception if we cannot return or cannot find the object. Indeed, when the object we are looking for is not found, it is preferable to *throw* an exception than to return *null.*
- A linked list can be sorted in ascending or descending order. One of the instance variables of the list objects is used as the key to sort the list elements. The *insert* method finds the appropriate location to insert an item so that the list remains sorted.
- A variation of the linked list includes a doubly linked list. In this case, each node contains three instance variables: an object representing the data, a node reference representing the next node, and another node reference representing the previous node. The latter enables us to backtrack in the list, if we need to, whereas in a singly linked list, we can traverse the list in a forward direction only. However, implementing such a list is more difficult; each method, in particular *insert* and *delete,* involves more operations to maintain these double links between nodes.

- Linked lists can implement generic types; when such a linked list is instantiated, the client specifies the class of the items for the list.
- Linked lists can also be recursively defined. A recursively defined linked list is made up of two elements: *first*, which is the first item in the linked list, and *rest*, a linked list that consists of the rest of the linked list.

14.14 Exercises, Problems, and Projects

14.14.1 Multiple Choice Exercises

1. What is an advantage of linked lists over arrays?
   - ❑ Linked lists are easily expanded.
   - ❑ Linked lists are limited in size.
   - ❑ Linked lists can store objects, whereas arrays are limited to primitive data types.
2. How is a stack organized?
   - ❑ FIFO
   - ❑ LIFO
   - ❑ Items are sorted in ascending order.
   - ❑ Items are sorted in descending order.
3. How is a queue organized?
   - ❑ FIFO
   - ❑ LIFO
   - ❑ Items are sorted in ascending order.
   - ❑ Items are sorted in descending order.
4. The following linked list represents a stack. If we pop once from the stack, what item is popped?

   (7, Ajay, NFL) → *(3, Sarah, Mario)* → *(9, Jin, Golf)* →
   head

   (5, Joe, Sonic) → *null*
   - ❑ *(7, Ajay, NFL)*
   - ❑ *(3, Sarah, Mario)*

- ❑ (*9, Jin, Golf*)
- ❑ (*5, Joe, Sonic*)

5. The linked list that follows represents a stack. After we push the player (*5, Joe, Sonic*) onto the stack, what are the first and last items on the stack?

   (*7, Ajay, NFL*) → (*3, Sarah, Mario*) → (*9, Jin, Golf*) → *null*

   head

   - ❑ (*7, Ajay, NFL*) and (*9, Jin, Golf*)
   - ❑ (*5, Joe, Sonic*) and (*9, Jin, Golf*)
   - ❑ (*3, Sarah, Mario*) and (*5, Joe, Sonic*)
   - ❑ (*7, Ajay, NFL*) and (*5, Joe, Sonic*)

6. The linked list that follows represents a queue. If we dequeue once, what item is dequeued?

   (*7, Ajay, NFL*) → (*3, Sarah, Mario*) → (*9, Jin, Golf*) →

   head

   (*5, Joe, Sonic*) → *null*

   tail

   - ❑ (*7, Ajay, NFL*)
   - ❑ (*3, Sarah, Mario*)
   - ❑ (*9, Jin, Golf*)
   - ❑ (*5, Joe, Sonic*)

7. The linked list that follows represents a queue. After we enqueue the player (*5, Joe, Sonic*), what are now the first and last items on the queue?

   (*7, Ajay, NFL*) → (*3, Sarah, Mario*) → (*9, Jin, Golf*) → *null*

   head *tail*

   - ❑ (*7, Ajay, NFL*) and (*9, Jin, Golf*)
   - ❑ (*5, Joe, Sonic*) and (9, Jin, Golf)
   - ❑ (*3, Sarah, Mario*) and (*5, Joe, Sonic*)
   - ❑ (*7, Ajay, NFL*) and (*5, Joe, Sonic*)

8. The diagram that follows shows the current state of a stack represented by an array of 50 integers. After pushing 36 and 62 onto the stack and then popping once, what will be the value of *top*, and what element will be stored at index *top*?

Index	Item stored
47 (top)	28
46	98
..	..
3	17
2	12
1	20
0	45

- ❑ *top* is 47 and the element at index *top* is 28
- ❑ *top* is 49 and the element at index *top* is 62
- ❑ *top* is 48 and the element at index *top* is 36
- ❑ *top* is 49 and the element at index *top* is 20

9. The diagram that follows shows the current state of a stack represented by an array of 50 integers. After pushing 36, 88, and 62 onto the stack and popping three times from the stack, what will be the value of *top* and what element will be stored at index *top*?

Index	Item stored
47 (top)	28
46	98
..	..
3	17
2	12
1	20
0	45

- ❑ *top* is 49 and the element at index *top* is 62
- ❑ *top* is 47 and the element at index *top* is 28

- ❑ *top* is 46 and the element at index *top* is 98
- ❑ *top* is 50 and the element at index *top* is 17

10. The diagram that follows shows the current state of a queue represented by a circular array of 8 integers. After enqueuing 36 and 62, and dequeuing once, what are the values of *front* and *back*, and what elements are stored at indexes *front* and *back*?

Index	Item stored
7	
6 (back)	28
5	97
4	25
3	54
2 (front)	12
1	
0	

- ❑ *front* = 0, stores 62; *back* = 5, stores 97
- ❑ *front* = 3, stores 54; *back* = 0, stores 62
- ❑ *front* = 3, stores 54; *back* = 8, stores 62
- ❑ *front* = 1, stores 36; *back* = 6, stores 28

11. The diagram that follows shows the current state of a queue represented by a circular array of 8 integers. After enqueuing 36, 100, 83, 77, and 62, what are the values of *front* and *back*, and what elements are stored at indexes *front* and *back*?

Index	Item stored
7	
6 (back)	28
5	97
4	25
3	54
2 (front)	12
1	
0	

- ❑ *front* = 2, stores 12; *back* = 11, stores 62
- ❑ *front* = 2, stores 12; *back* = 3, stores 62
- ❑ *front* = 3, stores 62; *back* = 6, stores 28
- ❑ *front* = 2, stores 12; *back* = 1, stores 83

12. The diagram that follows shows the current state of a queue represented by a circular array of 8 integers. After dequeuing 5 times, what are the values of *front* and *back*, and what elements are stored at indexes *front* and *back*?

Index	**Item stored**
7	
6 (back)	28
5	97
4	25
3	54
2 (front)	12
1	
0	

- ❑ *front* = 7; *back* = 6; the queue is empty
- ❑ *front* = 2; *back* = 1; the queue is empty
- ❑ *front* = 2; *back* = 6; the queue is empty

13. The diagram that follows shows the current state of a queue represented by a circular array of 8 integers. After dequeuing 8 times, what are the values of *front* and *back*, and what elements are stored at indexes *front* and *back*?

Index	**Item stored**
7	
6 (back)	28
5	97
4	25
3	54
2 (front)	12
1	
0	

- ❑ *front* = 7; *back* = 6; the queue is empty
- ❑ *front* = 2; *back* = 1; the queue is empty
- ❑ *front* = 2; *back* = 6; the queue is empty
- ❑ *front* = 6; *back* = 2; the queue is empty

14.14.2 Reading and Understanding Code

For Questions 14 to 21, consider the following classes from this chapter: *Player*, *PlayerNode*, and *PlayerLinkedList*.

14. What does this method of the *PlayerLinkedList* class do?

```
public void foo1( Player p, Player q )
{
 insert( p );
 insert( q );
}
```

15. What does this method of the *PlayerLinkedList* class do?

```
public int foo2( )
{
 PlayerNode nd = head;
 int i = 0;
 while ( nd != null )
 {
  i++;
  nd = nd.getNext( );
 }
 return i;
}
```

16. What does this method of the *PlayerLinkedList* class do?

```
public boolean foo3( )
{
 if ( numberOfItems > 0 )
 {
   head = null;
   numberOfItems = 0;
   return true;
 }
 else
   return false;
}
```

17. What does this method of the *PlayerLinkedList* class do?

```
public int foo4( )
{
 PlayerNode nd = head;
 int i = 0;
 while ( nd != null )
 {
  if ( nd.getPlayer( ).getGame( ).equals( "Sonic" ) )
      i++;
  nd = nd.getNext( );
 }
 return i;
}
```

18. What does this method of the *PlayerLinkedList* class do?

```
public boolean foo5( int i )
{
 PlayerNode nd = head;

 while ( nd != null )
 {
  if ( nd.getPlayer( ).getID( ) == i )
      return true;
  nd = nd.getNext( );
 }
 return false;
}
```

19. What does this method of the *PlayerLinkedList* class do?

```
public void foo6( )
{
 PlayerNode nd = head;
 while ( nd != null )
 {
   if ( nd.getPlayer( ).getGame( ).equals( "Diablo" ) )
     System.out.println( nd.getPlayer( ).toString( ) );
   nd = nd.getNext( );
 }
}
```

20. What does this method of the *PlayerLinkedList* class do?

```
public void foo7( Player p )
{
 if ( numberOfItems == 0 )
   System.out.println( "Do nothing" );
```

```
  else
  {
    PlayerNode pn = new PlayerNode( p );
    pn.setNext( head.getNext( ) );
    head.setNext( pn );
    numberOfItems++;
  }
}
```

21. What does this method of the *PlayerLinkedList* class do?

```
public boolean foo8( )
{
 if ( numberOfItems <= 2 )
   return false;
 else
 {
   head.setNext( ( head.getNext( ) ).getNext( ) );
   numberOfItems--;
   return true;
 }
}
```

14.14.3 Fill In the Code

22. Consider the following state of a linked list of *Player* items.

    → (*7, Ajay, NFL*) → (*3, Sarah, Mario*) → (*9, Jin, Golf*) →
    previous

    (*5, Joe, Sonic*) →

    As indicated, *previous* is the *PlayerNode* whose player is (*7, Ajay, NFL*)

    Write the code to modify the list so that (*9, Jin, Golf*) has been deleted.

    → (*7, Ajay, NFL*) → (*3, Sarah, Mario*) → (*5, Joe, Sonic*) →

    ```
    // your code goes here
    ```

23. Consider the following state of a linked list of *Player* items.

    → (*7, Ajay, NFL*) → (*3, Sarah, Mario*) → (*9, Jin, Golf*) →
    previous

    (*5, Joe, Sonic*) →

    As indicated, *previous* is the *PlayerNode* whose player is (*7, Ajay, NFL*)

Write the code to modify the list so that the two items in the middle have been deleted.

→ (*7, Ajay, NFL*) → (*5, Joe, Sonic*) →

```
// your code goes here
```

24. Consider the following state of a linked list of *Player* items.

→ (*7, Ajay, NFL*) → (*3, Sarah, Mario*) → (*9, Jin, Golf*) →
    previous   *current*

(*5, Joe, Sonic*) →

As indicated, *previous* is the *PlayerNode* whose player is (*7, Ajay, NFL*) and *current* is the *PlayerNode* whose player is (*3, Sarah, Mario*). Write the code to modify the list so that the two nodes in the middle have been swapped as shown here. (You need to swap the actual nodes, rather than modify their respective data.)

→ (*7, Ajay, NFL*) → (*9, Jin, Golf*) → (*3, Sarah, Mario*) →

(*5, Joe, Sonic*) →

```
// your code goes here
```

For Questions 25 to 28, consider the *LLNode* class that follows, representing a node with a *char* instance variable, representing a grade (A, B, C, D, or F):

```
public class LLNode
{
   private char grade;
   private LLNode next;

   // constructors and methods here
}
```

25. Code the overloaded constructor with one parameter, a *char*.

```
// your code goes here
```

26. Code the overloaded constructor with two parameters.

```
// your code goes here
```

27. Code the accessors for the class.

```
// your code goes here
```

28. Code the mutators for the class.

```
// your code goes here
```

For Questions 29 to 31, consider the following *DifferentLinkedList* class, using the *LLNode* class from Questions 25 to 28 (assume that the *LLNode* class has all appropriate accessors, mutators, and other methods).

```
public class DifferentLinkedList
{
  private LLNode head;
  // there is no instance variable for
  // the number of items in the list

  // constructors and methods here
}
```

29. Code a method that returns *true* if the list is empty; *false* otherwise.

```
// your code goes here
```

30. Code a method that returns *true* if the list contains at least one item; *false* otherwise.

```
// your code goes here
```

31. Code a method that returns the number of items in the list.

```
// your code goes here
```

32. Consider a method of class *PlayerLinkedList* with the following header:

```
public Player retrieveMe( int index )
```

Write a few statements showing how you would call that method from a client program.

```
// your code goes here
```

14.14.4 Identifying Errors in Code

33. What would happen if you execute the following code just before traversing a linked list?

```
head.setNext( head );
```

34. Suppose we have coded the following method in the *PlayerLinkedList* class. Where is the error?

```
public int getHeadID( )
{
  return head.getID( );
}
```

35. Suppose we modify the code of the *push* method in the *StackArray* class as follows (that is, without incrementing *top*). What type of problem could that method create?

```
public boolean push( Player p )
{
  if ( !isFull( ) ) // is there room to insert?
  {
    stack[top] = p;
    return true;
  }
  else
   return false;
}
```

36. Suppose we modify the code of the *pop* method in the *StackArray* class as follows (that is, without decrementing *top*). What type of problem could that method create?

```
public Player pop( ) throws DataStructureException
{
  if ( !isEmpty( ) ) // is there an item to delete?
    return ( stack[top] );
  else
    throw new DataStructureException
                ( "Stack empty: cannot pop" );
}
```

37. Suppose we modify the code of the *enqueue* method in the *Queue-Array* class as follows (that is, without incrementing the number of items). What type of problem could that method create?

```
public boolean enqueue( Player newPlayer )
{
  if ( !isFull( ) )
  {
    queue[( back + 1 ) % QUEUE_SIZE] = newPlayer;
    back = ( back + 1 ) % QUEUE_SIZE;
    return true;
  }
  else
    return false;
}
```

38. Suppose we modify the code of the *dequeue* method in the *Queue-Array* class as follows (that is, with a change in the expression computing the index in the *return* statement). Where is the error?

```
public Player dequeue( ) throws DataStructureException
{
  if ( !isEmpty( ) )
  {
    front  = ( front + 1 ) % QUEUE_SIZE;
    numberOfItems--;
    return queue[(front - 1 ) % QUEUE_SIZE];
  }
  else
    throw new DataStructureException
                ( "Queue empty: cannot dequeue" );
}
```

14.14.5 Debugging Area—Using Messages from the Java Compiler and Java JVM

39. You coded the following inside the *main* method of the *Test* class, using the *Player* and *PlayerNode* classes.

```
PlayerNode pn = new PlayerNode( );
Player p = pn.getPlayer( );
p.setID( 10 );          // line 10
```

The code compiles, but at run time you get a *NullPointerException* at line 10.

```
Exception in thread "main" java.lang.NullPointerException
 at Player.<init>(Player.java:29)
 at PlayerNode.getPlayer(PlayerNode.java:33)
   at Test.main(Test.java:10)
```

Explain what the problem is and how to fix it.

40. You coded the following in the *main* method of the *Test* class, using the *Player* and *PlayerLinkedList* classes.

```
Player p = new Player( 5,"Ajay","Mario" );
PlayerLinkedList pll = new PlayerLinkedList( );
pll.insert( p );
PlayerNode temp = pll.getHead( );          // line 10
System.out.println( " head is " + temp.toString( ) );
```

At compile time, you get the following error:

```
Test.java:10: cannot find symbol
symbol  : method getHead ()
location: class PlayerLinkedList
  PlayerNode temp = pll.getHead( );          // line 10
                       ^
1 error
```

EXERCISES, PROBLEMS, AND PROJECTS

Explain what the problem is and how to fix it.

41. You coded the following in the *main* method of the *Test* class, using the *Player* and *PlayerLinkedList* classes.

```
Player p = new Player( 5,"Ajay","Mario" );
PlayerLinkedList pll = new PlayerLinkedList( );
pll.insert( p );
if ( pll.delete( 5 ) )       // line 10
     System.out.println( "Successful deletion" );
```

At compile time, you get the following error:

```
Test.java:10: incompatible types
found   : Player
required: boolean
  if ( pll.delete( 5 ) )  // line 10
                 ^
1 error
```

Explain what the problem is and how to fix it.

42. You coded the following inside the *foo* method of the *PlayerLinkedList* class.

```
PlayerNode current = head;   // line 9
while ( current.getPlayer( ).getID( ) != 99 )
     current = current.getNext( );
// more code here but no problem
```

The code compiles, but at run time you get a *NullPointerException* at line 10.

```
Exception in thread "main" java.lang.NullPointerException
        at PlayerLinkedList.foo(PlayerLinkedList.java:10)
        at Test.main(Test.java:24)
```

What would be a possible scenario that may have caused this error? Explain how to fix this problem.

14.14.6 Write a Short Program

43. Modify the *PlayerLinkedList* class to include one more method: that method inserts a new player in the third position of the list, *head* being the first position. If the list is empty, the method will insert the new player as the head of the list. Be sure to test your method with the appropriate client code.

44. Modify the *PlayerLinkedList* class to include one more method: that method inserts a new player in the next-to-last position of the list. If the list is empty, the method will insert the new player as the head of the list. Be sure to test your method with the appropriate client code.

45. Modify the *PlayerLinkedList* class to include one more method: that method inserts a new player in the last position of the list. For this, you cannot use the *tail* instance variable. Be sure to test your method with the appropriate client code.

46. Modify the *PlayerLinkedList* class to include one more method: that method deletes the second node of the list, if there is one. Be sure to test your method with the appropriate client code.

47. Modify the *GenericLinkedList* class to include one more method: that method inserts a new item at a given position (a parameter of the method). If the list is empty, the method will insert the new item as the head of the list. If the value of the parameter is greater than the number of items in the list, then the method inserts at the end of the list. You should consider that *head* is at position 1 in the list. Be sure to test your method with the appropriate client code.

48. Modify the *GenericLinkedList* class to include one more method: that method deletes an item at a given position (a parameter of the method). If the value of the parameter is greater than the number of elements in the list, then no item is deleted and an exception is thrown. Your method should return the item deleted, if any. You should consider that the first node is at position 1 in the list. Be sure to test your method with the appropriate client code.

49. Modify the *PlayerLinkedList* class to include one more method: that method takes a parameter that represents a game. The method inserts a new player at a position just after the first *Player* of the list with a *game* instance variable equal to that game. If there is no such node, then your method should insert at the end of the list. Be sure to test your method with the appropriate client code.

50. Modify the *PlayerLinkedList* class to include one more method: a traversal that outputs the players in the list until we reach a player with a given *id*; that player's data should not be output. Be sure to test your method with the appropriate client code.

51. Modify the *GenericLinkedList* class to include one more method: a method that returns the *n*th item on the list (*n* is a parameter of the method). If there is no *n*th item on the list, the method should *throw* an exception. Test your method with a client that traverses the list by requesting each item in position order.

52. Modify the *PlayerStackLinkedList* class to include one more method: a method that returns the ID of the last player on the stack. Be sure to test your method with the appropriate client code.

53. Modify the *PlayerQueueLinkedList* class to include one more method: a method that outputs every other player in the queue, that is, it outputs the first player, skips the second, outputs the third player, skips the fourth, and so on. Be sure to test your method with the appropriate client code.

54. Modify the *RecursiveLinkedList* class to include one more method: one that inserts at the end of the list. Be sure to test your method with the appropriate client code.

55. Modify the *RecursiveLinkedList* class to include one more method: one that deletes at the end of the list. Be sure to test your method with the appropriate client code.

56. Modify the *RecursiveLinkedList* class to include one more method: one that deletes at the beginning of the list. Be sure to test your method with the appropriate client code.

57. Code a class encapsulating a stack of *doubles* using an array of 10 elements. Be sure to test your methods with the appropriate client code.

58. Code a class encapsulating a queue of *chars* using a circular array of 10 elements. Be sure to test your methods with the appropriate client code.

14.14.7 Programming Projects

59. Modify the *PlayerLinkedList* to include two more methods: one that returns the *Player* with the minimum *id*, and one that returns all the games played by players with a given *id*. You also need to include the appropriate client code to test your classes.

60. Modify the *PlayerLinkedList* to include two more methods: one that returns the *Player* with the first name in alphabetical order, and one that returns all of the *ids* of the players playing a given game. You also need to include the appropriate client code to test your classes.

61. Code a class encapsulating a singly linked list of website objects. A website has two attributes: a URL address (a *String*, you do not need to use the existing URL Java class) and ten or fewer keywords describing the topic of the website. In addition to *insert*, *delete*, *peek*, and *toString*, add one more method: a method that, based on a keyword, returns all URL addresses in the list containing that keyword. Your *delete* method should delete an item based on the value of its URL. You also need to include the appropriate client code to test your classes.

62. Code a class encapsulating a singly linked list of football teams. A football team has three attributes: its nickname, its number of wins, and its number of losses (assume there are no tied games). In addition to *insert*, *delete*, *peek*, and *toString*, add two more methods: a method that returns the nicknames of the teams with the most wins, and another method that returns the five best teams based on winning percentages (if multiple teams have the same winning percentage, you can return the first five such teams in the list). You also need to include the appropriate client code to test your classes.

63. Code a class encapsulating a singly linked list of HTML tags. We will define a valid HTML tag as a string of characters starting with < and ending with >. In addition to *insert*, *delete*, *peek*, and *toString*, add two more methods: a method that returns *true* or *false*, checking if the list contains valid HTML tags only (as previously defined), and another that counts how many items in the list contain the slash (/) character in them. You also need to include the appropriate client code to test your classes.

64. Code a class encapsulating a singly linked list of stocks. A stock is defined by the following attributes: its ticker symbol (a short word, for instance AMD), its price (for example 54.35), and the company's earnings per share (for example 3.25). In addition to *insert*, *delete*, *peek*, and *toString*, add two more methods: a method that returns the

list of all the tickers for the penny stocks (a penny stock is a stock whose price is $1.00 or less), and another method that, given a number representing a price earnings ratio (the price earnings ratio of a stock, also known as P/E ratio, is the price of the stock divided by the earnings per share), returns all the tickers with a price earnings ratio less than or equal to that number. You also need to include the appropriate client code to test your classes.

65. Code a class encapsulating a singly linked list of books. A book is defined by the following attributes: its title, its author, its price, and how many are in stock. In addition to *insert*, *delete*, *peek*, and *toString*, add two more methods: a method that, based on a word, returns all the book titles in the list containing that word, and another returning the list of book titles that are out of stock, i.e., there are quantity 0 in stock. You also need to include the appropriate client code to test your classes.

66. Code a class encapsulating a stack of clothes using an array. A clothing item has the following attributes: its name, its color, and whether it can be washed at high temperature. We will limit our stack to 100 clothing items. In addition to *push*, *pop*, *peek*, and *toString*, add two more methods: a method that returns all the clothing items of a given color, and another method that returns how many clothing items in the stack can be washed at high temperature. You also need to include the appropriate client code to test your classes.

67. Code a class encapsulating a queue of foods using a circular array. A food has the following attributes: its name, the number of calories per serving, and the number of servings per container. We will limit our queue to 100 foods. In addition to *enqueue*, *dequeue*, *peek*, and *toString*, add two more methods: a method that returns the average calories per serving of all the foods in the queue, and another method that returns the food item with the highest "total calories" (i.e., calories per serving times number of servings). You also need to include the appropriate client code to test your classes.

68. Code a class encapsulating a sorted linked list of *Auto* objects (you can use the *Auto* class from Chapter 7). Your list should be sorted in ascending order using the model as the key. In addition to *insert*, *delete*, *peek*, and *toString*, add two more methods: a method that

returns all the *Auto* objects in the list that have a number of miles greater than a given number, and another method that returns all the *Auto* objects in the list that are located after a given model name. You also need to include the appropriate client code to test your classes.

69. Code a class encapsulating a sorted linked list of *Auto* objects (you can use the *Auto* class from Chapter 7). Your list should be sorted in descending order using *gallonsOfGas* as the key. In addition to *insert, delete, peek,* and *toString,* add two more methods: a method that returns the average value of *gallonsOfGas* of all the *Autos* in the list, and another method that returns all the *Autos* in the list that have a *gallonsOfGas* value less than a certain number. You also need to include the appropriate client code to test your classes.
70. Code a stack class using a generic type; the stack should be represented by an array. You should include *push, pop* and *toString* methods. You also need to include the appropriate client code to test your class. In the client class, you should declare and instantiate stacks using at least two different class types.
71. Code a queue class using generics; the queue should be represented by a circular array. You should include *enqueue, dequeue,* and *toString* methods. You also need to include the appropriate client code to test your class. In the client class, you should declare and instantiate queues using at least two different class types.

14.14.8 Technical Writing

72. In this chapter, we coded a linked list class with just two instance variables: the head node and the number of items in the list. We also said that we did not really need the number of items in the list. Explain how we can traverse the whole list if the class has only one instance variable, *head.*
73. Consider the *PlayerQueueLinkedList* class presented in this chapter, which includes an instance variable called *tail,* in addition to *head.* We want to make the list circular, that is, *tail* "points to" *head.* If you made the method call *tail.getNext( ),* it would return *head.* Describe why and how you would need to modify the *toString* method of the class (assume you do not know the number of items in the list).

14.14.9 Group Project (for a group of 1, 2, or 3 students)

74. Code a doubly linked, sorted list (in ascending order). Each item of the list will just store an *int*.

    You need to code three classes: *Node*, *SortedList*, and *GroupProject*

    The *Node* class has three instance variables, all *private*:

    - ❑ an *int*, representing the value stored inside the *Node*
    - ❑ a *Node* (*next*)
    - ❑ another *Node* (*previous*)

    The methods to code are: constructor (at least one), accessors, mutators.

    The *SortedList* class is a doubly linked list, sorted in ascending order.

    It has two instance variables, both private:

    - ❑ an *int*, representing the number of items in the list
    - ❑ a *Node*, representing the head node in the list

    The methods to code are:

    - ❑ *insert*: this method takes one parameter, an *int*; it has a *void* return value.
    - ❑ *delete*: this method takes one parameter, an *int*; it returns a *boolean* value. If we were successful in deleting the item (i.e., the value of the parameter was found in the list), then we return *true*; if we were not successful, then we want to output a message that the value was not found, and therefore, not deleted, and return *false*.
    - ❑ *toString*: this method takes no parameters and returns a *String* representation of the list.
    - ❑ constructor (at least one), and accessors and mutators as appropriate.

    All methods should keep the list sorted in ascending order.

The *GroupProject* class contains the *main* method; it should do the following:

- ❑ create a *SortedList* object reference
- ❑ insert successively the values 25, 17, 12, 21, 78, and 47 in the sorted list
- ❑ output the contents of the sorted list using the *toString* method
- ❑ delete from the sorted list the value 30, using the *delete* method (obviously, 30 will not be found)
- ❑ output the contents of the sorted list using the *toString* method
- ❑ delete from the sorted list the value 21, using the *delete* method
- ❑ output the contents of the sorted list using the *toString* method

Your *insert* and *delete* methods should work properly in all possible scenarios: inserting in an empty list, inserting at the beginning of a list, inserting in the middle of a list, inserting at the end of a list, deleting from an empty list (cannot delete), deleting an item not in the list (cannot delete), deleting the first item in a list, deleting in the middle of a list, deleting the last item in a list.

CHAPTER 15

Running Time Analysis

CHAPTER CONTENTS

Introduction

Today's Internet websites have millions of users. With the success of Web 2.0 Internet sites, the databases storing data on the web servers have grown in size dramatically, both to accommodate the growing number of users and the growing volume of data that is posted by these users.

Scientific applications have also experienced a data explosion. Sensors used in these scientific applications, such as meteorology or fluid mechanics, are becoming more precise at the same time they are getting cheaper. More and more sensors are being used, and application programs have to manage more and more data.

Programs that handle and manipulate this ever-increasing amount of data need to use algorithms that are well-designed and efficient so that they minimize waiting time for users. Two programs that solve the same problem by using two different algorithms can result in two completely different levels of performance—everything else, (in particular the hardware platform), being equal. For example, two search engines performing the same search could run at two different speeds: one could return results in tenths of a second while the other could take several seconds to return results.

Most programmers tend to disregard speed and space (memory utilization) issues when writing code. They rely on increasing hardware performance to solve speed problems and the decreasing cost of memory to solve space problems. However, with the data explosion and the resulting data processing issues that we are experiencing today across many industries, designing efficient algorithms has become more and more important. In this chapter, we will focus on algorithms' speed performance rather than space utilization.

When we measure the performance of an algorithm, we use the expression **running time**. We cannot predict a single, precise running time for many algorithms, because the amount of processing depends in large part on the number of inputs and the values of those inputs. So we express the running time of an algorithm as a mathematical function of its inputs. This allows us to compare the relative performance of multiple algorithms. For example, the running time for computing the factorial of an integer varies according to the value for which we are computing the factorial. Factorials of larger numbers require more processing to compute than factorials of smaller numbers. If we can express the running time of multiple algorithms that compute a factorial as a function of their input, then we can compare the relative efficiency of each algorithm. In other cases, such as sorting an array of integers, the running time depends on the number of array elements. Similarly, if we express the running time as a function of the number of elements in the array, we can compare the relative efficiency of multiple sorting algorithms.

The input value or number of inputs for an algorithm represent the size of the problem for which we are trying to compute the running time. We will call that number ***n***. We are interested in relative time, independently of the hardware platform used, not absolute time. Furthermore, we are typically interested in the order of magnitude of the algorithm, rather than a precise mathematical expression as a function of n. Indeed, if n is very large (for example, 1 million or more), performance does not vary noticeably if the algorithm takes n steps or $n + 17$ steps to complete.

However, if an algorithm has a running time expressed as n^2, then the number of inputs has a big impact on performance. For example, we can predict that 10 inputs will require the execution of 100 statements and 1,000 inputs will require the execution of 1 million statements.

The objectives of this chapter are:

- To be able to evaluate the running time of a given algorithm through various methods.
- To understand that how we code an algorithm directly impacts its running time.

15.1 Orders of Magnitude and Big-Oh Notation

Table 15.1 shows examples of various orders of magnitude for an algorithm as a function of the number of inputs n, along with the corresponding number of statement executions for different values of n.

Let's look at an example to see how you can use these values. Sequential Search has a running time of n, and Binary Search has a running time of *log n*. Thus, if we are searching an array of 1 million users for a particular user name, a Sequential Search will take, on average, the execution of an order of 1 million statements, while a Binary Search will require the execution of

TABLE 15.1 Comparisons of Various Functions Representing Running Times

Order of Magnitude	Number of Statements Executed			
	$n = 10$	$n = 20$	$n = 1,000$	$n = 1$ million
$\log n$	2.23	3.23	Approx. 10	Approx. 20
n	10	20	1000	10^6
$n \log n$	22.3	64.6	Approx. 10,000	Approx. 20 * 10^6
n^2	100	400	10^6	10^{12}
n^3	1,000	8,000	10^9	10^{18}
2^n	1,024	Approx. 10^6	Approx. 10^{300}	Approx. 10^{300000}

REFERENCE POINT

Sequential Search and Binary Search are explained in Chapter 8.

only 20 statements. Remember, however, that for a Binary Search to work, the array must already be sorted. Later in this chapter, we will discuss how to compute these running times.

As you can see from the table, algorithms that have a running time where n is the exponent of the function, such as 2^n, take a very large number of statement executions and are very slow; they should be used only if no better algorithm can be found.

Running times of algorithms are often represented using the **Big-Oh** or the **Big-Theta** notation, as in $O(n)$ or $\Theta(n^2)$, for example. The mathematical definition of Big-Theta is as follows:

A function $f(n)$ is Big-Theta of another function $g(n)$, or $\Theta(g(n))$, if and only if:

1. $f(n)$ is **Big-Omega** of $g(n)$, or $\Omega(g(n))$, i.e., there exist two positive constants, $n1$ and $c1$, such that for any $n >= n1, f(n) >= c1 * g(n)$

   In other words, for n sufficiently big, $g(n)$ is a lower bound of $f(n)$; that is, $g(n)$ is smaller than $f(n)$, if we ignore the constants.

and

2. $f(n)$ is Big-Oh of $g(n)$, or $O(g(n))$, i.e., there exist two positive constants, $n2$ and $c2$, such that for any $n >= n2, f(n) <= c2 * g(n)$.

   In other words, for n sufficiently big $g(n)$ is an upper bound of $f(n)$; that is, $g(n)$ is bigger than $f(n)$, if we ignore the constants.

It has become common in the industry to say Big-Oh instead of Big-Theta. Indeed, we are really interested in an upper bound running time (Big-Oh), and as tight an upper bound as possible (Big-Theta).

Although the preceding definition may sound a bit complex, when trying to estimate the Big-Oh of a particular function representing a running time, the following rules can be used:

- Keep only the dominant term, i.e., the term that grows the fastest as n grows.
- Ignore the coefficient of the dominant term.

Table 15.2 shows a few examples illustrating these rules.

As an example, we will show that the function $f(n) = 3 * n^2 + 6 * n + 12$ is $\Theta\ (n^2)$.

First we show that $f(n)$ is $\Omega(n^2)$:

For $n >= 0$,

$f(n) = 3 * n^2 + 6 * n + 12 >= 3 * n^2$

So if we choose $n1 = 0$ and $c1 = 3$, we just proved by definition that $f(n)$ is $\Omega\ (n^2)$.

Now we show that the same function $f(n)$ is $O(n^2)$.

For $n >= 1$, we can rewrite $f(n)$ as

$f(n) = n^2 * (3 + 6 / n + 12 / n^2)$

TABLE 15.2 Examples of Functions Representing Running Times and Their Respective Big-Oh

$f(n)$	Dominant Term	Big-Oh
$2 * n + 19$	$2 * n$	$O(n)$
$3 * n^2 + 6 * n + 12$	$3 * n^2$	$O(n^2)$
$n^3 + 9 * n^2 + 5 * n + 2$	n^3	$O(n^3)$
$3 * 2^n + 5 * n^3 + 3 * n + 7$	$3 * 2^n$	$O(2^n)$
$n + 7 * \log n$	n	$O(n)$
$2 * n * \log n + 8 * n + \log n + 8$	$2 * n * \log n$	$O(n * \log n)$
$3 * \log n + 35$	$3 * \log n$	$O(\log n)$

For $n >= 6$, we have

$6 / n <= 1$ and $12 / n^2 < 1$

therefore,

$f(n) <= n^2 * (3 + 1 + 1) = 5 * n^2$

So if we choose $n2 = 6$ and $c2 = 5$, we just proved by definition that $f(n)$ is $O(n^2)$.

Since $f(n)$ is both Big-Omega (n^2) and Big-Oh(n^2), then $f(n)$ is Big-Theta(n^2).

To show that a polynomial function is Big-Oh of its most dominant term, we simply factor by the most dominant term as follows:

For $n > 0$,

$f(n) = a_p\, n^p + a_{p-1}\, n^{p-1} + \ldots + a_2\, n^2 + a_1\, n + a_0$ where a_p is strictly positive

$f(n) = a_p\, n^p\, (1 + (a_{p-1} / a_p)\, 1 / n + \ldots + (a_2 / a_p)\, 1 / n^{p-2} + (a_1 / a_p)\, 1 / n^{p-1} + (a_p / a_0)\, 1 / n^p)$

$f(n) <= a_p\, n^p\, (1 + |(a_{p-1} / a_p)|\, 1 / n + \ldots + |(a_2 / a_p)|\, 1 / n^{p-2} + |(a_1 / a_p)|\, 1 / n^{p-1} + |(a_p / a_0)|\, 1 / n^p)$

All a_i's are constants; let M be the maximum of all $|(a_i / a_p)|$.

Thus,

$f(n) <= a_p\, n^p\, (1 + M\, 1 / n + \ldots + M\, 1 / n^{p-2} + M\, 1 / n^{p-1} + M\, 1 / n^p)$

$f(n) <= a_p\, n^p\, (1 + M\, (1 / n + \ldots + 1 / n^{p-2} + 1 / n^{p-1} + 1 / n^p))$

$f(n) <= a_p\, n^p\, (1 + M\, (-1 + 1 + 1 / n + \ldots + 1 / n^{p-2} + 1 / n^{p-1} + 1 / n^p))$

since we know mathematically that

$1 + a + a^2 + \ldots + a^p = \Sigma\, a^i$ from $i = 0$ to p is equal to $(1 - a^{p+1}) / (1 - a)$ for a different from 1.

Using $a = 1/n$, we get

$f(n) <= a_p\, n^p\, (1 + M\, (-1 + (1 - 1 / n^{p+1}) / (1 - 1 / n)))$

$f(n) <= a_p\, n^p\, (1 + M\, (-1 + (1 - 1 / n^{p+1}) * (n / (n - 1))))$

Thus,

$f(n) <= a_p\, n^p\, (1 + M\, (-1 + (n / (n - 1))))$

$f(n) <= a_p\, n^p\, (1 + M\, ((-n + 1 + n) / (n - 1)))$

$f(n) <= a_p\, n^p\, (1 + M\, (1 / (n - 1)))$

Thus,

$f(n) <= a_p\, n^p\, (1 + M)$ for $n >= 2$

choosing $n_0 = 2$ and $c_0 = a_p\ (1 + M)$.

For $n >= n_0$, we have

$f(n) <= c_0\ n^p$

and therefore,

$f(n)$ is $O(n^p)$, i.e., $f(n)$ is Big-Oh of its most dominant term.

15.2 Running Time Analysis of Algorithms: Counting Statements

One simple method to analyze the running time of a code sequence or a method is simply to count the number of times each statement is executed and to calculate a total count of statement executions.

Example 15.1 is a method that calculates the total value of all the elements of an array of size n and returns the sum.

```
public static int addElements( int [ ] arr )
{
  int sum = 0;              // ( 1 )
  int i = 0;                // ( 2 )
  while ( i < arr.length )  // ( 3 )
  {
     sum += arr[i];         // ( 4 )
     i++;                   // ( 5 )
  }
  return sum;               // ( 6 )
}
```

EXAMPLE 15.1 A Single Loop

Let's count how many times each statement is executed.

Assuming the array has n elements, we can develop the following analysis:

Statement	# Times Executed
(1)	1
(2)	1
(3)	$n+1$
(4)	n
(5)	n
(6)	1

Note that the loop condition, $i < arr.length$, is executed one more time than each statement of the loop body: when i is equal to *arr.length*, we evaluate the loop condition, but we exit the loop and thus do not execute the two statements in the loop body. Thus, the total number of statements executed, $T(n)$, is equal to:

$$
\begin{aligned}
T(n) &= 1 + 1 + (n + 1) + n + n + 1 \\
&= 3n + 4 \\
&= O(n)
\end{aligned}
$$

So we can say that the running time of the *addElements* method is O(n). Note that in the end, we do not need an exact count of the statements executed, since we are really interested in the Big-Oh running time of the function.

REFERENCE POINT

Multidimensional arrays are explained in Chapter 9.

Example 15.2 is a method that determines the maximum value in a two-dimensional array of *ints*.

```
public static int calculateMaximum( int [ ][ ] arr )
{
  int maximum  = arr[0][0];                      // ( 1 )
  for ( int i = 0; i < arr.length; i++ )         // ( 2 )
  {
   for ( int j = 0; j < arr[i].length; j++ )     // ( 3 )
   {
    if ( maximum < arr[i][j] )                   // ( 4 )
         maximum  = arr[i][j];                   // ( 5 )
   }
  }
  return maximum;                                // ( 6 )
}
```

EXAMPLE 15.2 A Double Loop

Let's count how many times each statement is executed. Assuming the array has n rows and each row has n columns, we can develop the following analysis:

Statement	# Times Executed
(1)	1
(2)	$1 + (n + 1) + n = 2 * n + 2$
(3)	$n * (1 + (n + 1) + n) = 2 * n^2 + 2 * n$
(4)	$n * n = n^2$
(5)	between 0 and $n * n$
(6)	1

Statement (2) actually contains three statements: *int* $i = 0$ is executed 1 time, $i < arr.length$ is executed $(n + 1)$ times as i goes from 0 to n; and i++ is executed n times as i is incremented n times.

In evaluating the number of times statements (3), (4), and (5) will be executed, we first note that we will enter the outer loop n times. Statement (3) also contains three statements: *int* $j = 0$ is executed each time we enter the outer loop, or n times; $j < arr.length$[i] is executed $(n + 1)$ times each time we enter the outer loop, or $n * (n + 1)$ times, as j goes from 0 to n; and j++ is executed n times each time we enter the outer loop, or $n * n$ times.

Since we enter the outer loop n times and for each outer loop iteration, we enter the inner loop n times, statement (4) will be executed $n * n$ times. As for statement (5), it will be executed once each time the Boolean expression *maximum* < *arr*[i][j] evaluates to *true*. We cannot tell how many times that will happen, but we can tell that it will happen no more than $n * n$ times. We will call this unknown value x.

Thus, the total number of statements executed, $T(n)$, is equal to:

$$T(n) = 1 + (2 * n + 2) + (2 * n^2 + 2 * n) + (n^2) + x + 1$$
$$= 3 * n^2 + 4 * n + 2 + x$$

with $x <= n * n$

Furthermore, since the value of x is between 0 and n^2,

$$3 * n^2 + 4 * n + 2 <= T(n) <= 3 * n^2 + 4 * n + 2 + n^2$$

$$3 * n^2 + 4 * n + 2 <= T(n) <= 4 * n^2 + 4 * n + 2$$

since $T(n)$ has both lower and upper bounds that are $O(n^2)$, $T(n)$ is $O(n^2)$.

For our third example, let's compute the running time of a Sequential Search, implemented by the code shown in Example 15.3.

REFERENCE POINT

Sequential Search is explained in Chapter 8.

```
public int sequentialSearch( int [ ] array, int key )
{
  for ( int i = 0; i < array.length; i++ )     // ( 1 )
    if ( array[ i ] == key )                  // ( 2 )
      return i;                               // ( 3 )
  return -1;                                  // ( 4 )
}
```

EXAMPLE 15.3 Sequential Search Algorithm

Let's count how many times each statement is executed. Assuming the array has n elements, we can develop the following analysis:

Statement	# Times Executed
(1)	$1 + (\text{between } 1 \text{ and } (n + 1)) + (\text{between } 0 \text{ and } n)$
(2)	between 1 and n
(3)	0 or 1
(4)	1 or 0

Thus, if $T(n)$ represents the total number of statements executed, we can say that

$$1 + (1) + (0) + 1 + 1 <= T(n) <= 1 + (n + 1) + n + n + 1$$

$$4 <= T(n) <= 3n + 3$$

$T(n) <= 3n + 3$ shows that $T(n)$ is $O(n)$.

However, we cannot really tell, from the coding of the function, how many statements will be executed as a function of n. In these situations, it is interesting to consider three running times:

- the worst-case running time
- the best-case running time
- the average-case running time.

In the worst case, where the search key is not found in the array or it is found in the last element, $T(n) = 3n + 3$, and therefore $T(n)$ is $O(n)$, as mentioned earlier.

In the best case, the element we are looking for is at index 0 of the array and only four statements will be executed, independently of the value of n. Thus, the best-case running time is $O(1)$ since we do not take the multiplying constant into consideration when we compute a Big-Oh.

In the average case, we find the element we are looking for in the middle of the array, and the value of $T(n)$ will be

$$\begin{aligned} T(n) &= 1 + (n + 1)/2 + n/2 + n/2 + 1 \\ &= 3n/2 + 2\tfrac{1}{2} \\ &= O(n) \end{aligned}$$

15.3 Running Time Analysis of Algorithms and Impact of Coding: Evaluating Recursive Methods

In this section, we will learn how to compute the running time of a recursive method. We will also look at how coding a method has a direct impact on its running time.

Consider coding a recursive method that takes one parameter, n, and returns 2^n. There are several ways to code that method, and we will consider two of them here so that we can assess which algorithm is more efficient.

REFERENCE POINT

Recursion is explained in Chapter 13.

Our first method, *powerOf2A*, is designed using these two facts:

- when $n = 0$, $2^0 = 1$. This is our base case.
- $2^n = 2 * 2^{n-1}$. This is our general case.

This first problem formulation results in the method shown in Example 15.4.

```
public static int powerOf2A( int n ) // n >= 0
{
   if ( n == 0 )
      return 1;
   else
      return 2 * powerOf2A( n - 1 );
}
```

EXAMPLE 15.4 First Recursive Formulation of 2^n

Our second method, *powerOf2B*, is designed using these two facts:

- when $n = 0$, $2^0 = 1$. This is our base case,
- $2^n = 2^{n-1} + 2^{n-1}$. This is our general case.

This second problem formulation results in the method shown in Example 15.5.

```
public static int powerOf2B( int n ) // n >= 0
{
   if ( n == 0 )
      return 1;
   else
      return powerOf2B( n - 1 ) + powerOf2B( n - 1 );
}
```

EXAMPLE 15.5 Second Recursive Formulation of 2^n

Let's compute the running time of *powerOf2A* as a function of the input n; we will call it $T1(n)$.

In the base case (n is equal to 0), *powerOf2A* makes only one comparison and returns 1. Thus,

$$T1(0) = 1$$

Generally, since it takes $T1(n)$ to compute and return *powerOf2A*(n), then it takes $T1(n-1)$ to compute and return *powerOf2A*($n-1$).

Thus, in the general case, the comparison in the *if* statement will cost us 1 instruction; computing and returning *powerOf2A*($n-1$) will cost us $T1(n-1)$; and multiplying that result by 2 will cost us 1 instruction. Thus, the total time $T1(n)$ can be expressed as follows:

$$\begin{aligned} T1(n) &= 1 + T1(n-1) + 1 \\ &= T1(n-1) + 2 \quad \text{// Equation 15.1} \end{aligned}$$

The preceding equation, which we will call Equation 15.1, is called a recurrence relation between $T1(n)$ and $T1(n-1)$ because $T1(n)$ is expressed as a function of $T1(n-1)$.

From there, we can use a number of techniques to compute the value of $T1(n)$ as a function of n.

Handwaving Method

This method is called handwaving because it is more an estimation method, rather than a method based on strict mathematics.

From the preceding recurrence relation, we can say that it costs us two instructions to go down one step (from n to $n-1$). Therefore, to go down n steps will cost us $2 * n$ instructions. We then add one instruction for $T(0)$, and get:

$$T1(n) = 2 * n + 1$$

Iterative Method

This method involves iterating several times, starting with the recurrence relation until we can identify a pattern. In general, we can say that

$$T1(x) = T1(x-1) + 2, \text{ where } x \text{ is some integer} \quad \text{// Equation 15.2}$$

We call this Equation 15.2, which is the same as Equation 15.1, except that x has been substituted for n.

We now want to express $T(n)$ as a function of $T(n-2)$; thus, we want to replace $T(n-1)$ in Equation 15.1 by an expression using $T(n-2)$.

Substituting $n-1$ for x in Equation 15.2, we get

$$T1(n-1) = T1(n-2) + 2$$

Plugging in the value of $T1(n-1)$ into Equation 15.1, we get

$$T1(n) = T1(n-2) + 2 + 2$$

$$= T1(n-2) + 2 * 2 \quad \text{// Equation 15.3}$$

Note that in Equation 15.3, we do not simplify $2 * 2$. In this way, we are trying to let a pattern develop so we can easily identify it.

SOFTWARE ENGINEERING TIP

When trying to develop and identify a pattern using iteration, do not precisely compute all the terms. Instead, leave them as patterns.

Using $x = n-2$ in Equation 15.2, we get

$$T1(n-2) = T1(n-3) + 2$$

Plugging in the value of $T1(n-2)$ into Equation 15.3, we get

$$T1(n) = T1(n-3) + 2 + 2 * 2$$

$$= T1(n-3) + 2 * 3 \quad \text{// Equation 15.4}$$

Using $x = n-3$ in Equation 15.2, we get

$$T1(n-3) = T1(n-4) + 2$$

Plugging in the value of $T1(n-3)$ into Equation 15.4, we get

$$T1(n) = T1(n-4) + 2 + 2 * 3$$

$$= T1(n-4) + 2 * 4$$

Now we can see the pattern as follows:

$T1(n) = T1(n-k) + 2 * k$, where k is an integer between 1 and n // Equation 15.5

Plugging in $k = n$ in Equation 15.5, we get

$$T1(n) = T1(0) + 2 * n = 1 + 2 * n = 2 * n + 1$$

Proof by Induction Method

If we can guess the value of $T1(n)$ as a function of n, then we can use a proof by induction in order to prove that our guess is correct. We can use the preceding iteration method to come up with a guess for $T1(n)$.

Generally, a proof by induction works as follows:

- Verify that our statement (equation in this case) is true for a base case.
- Assume that out statement is true up to n.
- Prove that it is true for $n + 1$.

Let's go through the induction steps with our guess that $T1(n) = 2 * n + 1$, which we may have generated from our iterative or handwaving method.

Step 1: Verify that the value that our guess gives to $T1(0)$ is correct.

$$\begin{aligned} T1(0) &= 2 * 0 + 1 \\ &= 1 \end{aligned}$$

Thus, our guess is correct for $T1(0)$.

Step 2: Assume that $T1(n) = 2 * n + 1$

Step 3: Prove that $T1(n + 1) = 2 * (n + 1) + 1$

Plugging in $x = n + 1$ in Equation 15.2, we get

$$T1(n + 1) = T1(n) + 2$$

Then, using our assumption and replacing $T1(n)$ by $2 * n + 1$, we get

$$\begin{aligned} T1(n + 1) &= 2 * n + 1 + 2 \\ &= 2 * n + 2 + 1 \\ &= 2 * (n + 1) + 1 \end{aligned}$$

Thus, we just proved, by induction, that our guess $T1(n) = 2 * n + 1$ is correct.

Other Methods

Another method is to use the Master Theorem, but that is beyond the scope of this book.

So the running time of *powerOf2A*(n) is $2 * n + 1$, or $O(n)$.

Let's now compute the running time of *powerOf2B* as a function of the input n. We will call it $T2(n)$.

In the base case (n is equal to 0), *powerOf2B* takes only one comparison to return 1. Thus,

$$T2(0) = 1$$

Generally, since it takes $T2(n)$ to compute and return *powerOf2B*(n), then it takes $T2(n-1)$ to compute and return *powerOf2B*($n-1$). Thus, in the general case, the comparison in the *if* statement will cost us one instruction; computing and returning *powerOf2B*($n-1$) will cost us $T2(n-1)$; doing it a second time will cost us another $T2(n-1)$; and adding the two and returning the sum as the result will cost us one instruction. Thus, the total time $T2(n)$ can be expressed as follows:

$$T2(n) = 1 + T2(n-1) + T2(n-1) + 1$$

$$= 2 * T2(n-1) + 2 \qquad \text{// Equation 15.6}$$

From there, we will use the iteration method in order to compute the value of $T2(n)$ as a function of n.

Substituting x for n, we can rewrite Equation 15.6 as follows:

$$T2(x) = 2 * T2(x-1) + 2 \quad \text{// Equation 15.7}$$

Using $x = n - 1$ in Equation 15.7, we get

$$T2(n-1) = 2 * T2(n-2) + 2$$

Plugging in the value of $T2(n-1)$ into Equation 15.6, we get

$$T2(n) = 2 * (2 * T2(n-2) + 2) + 2$$

$$= 2^2 * T2(n-2) + 2^2 + 2 \qquad \text{// Equation 15.8}$$

Again, we leave $2^2 + 2$ as an expression to try to let a pattern develop.

Using $x = n - 2$ in Equation 15.7, we get

$$T2(n-2) = 2 * T2(n-3) + 2$$

Plugging in the value of $T2(n-2)$ into Equation 15.8, we get

$$T2(n) = 2^2 * (2 * T2(n-3) + 2) + 2^2 + 2$$

$$= 2^3 * T2(n-3) + 2^3 + 2^2 + 2 \qquad \text{// Equation 15.9}$$

Using $x = n - 3$ in Equation 15.7, we get

$$T2(n-3) = 2 * T2(n-4) + 2$$

Plugging in the value of $T2(n-3)$ into Equation 15.9, we get

$$T2(n) = 2^3 * (2 * T2(n-4) + 2) + 2^3 + 2^2 + 2$$

$$= 2^4 * T2(n-4) + 2^4 + 2^3 + 2^2 + 2 \qquad \text{// Equation 15.10}$$

Now we can see the pattern as follows:

$$T2(n) = 2^k * T2(n-k) + 2^k + 2^{k-1} + \ldots + 2^2 + 2,$$

where k is an integer between 1 and n // Equation 15.11

Noting that

$$\begin{aligned} 2^k + 2^{k-1} + \ldots + 2^2 + 2 &= -1 + 2^k + 2^{k-1} + \ldots + 2^2 + 2 + 1 \\ &= -1 + (2^{k+1} - 1) / (2 - 1) \\ &= 2^{k+1} - 2 \end{aligned}$$

Equation 15.11 becomes

$T2(n) = 2^k * T2(n-k) + 2^{k+1} - 2$, where k is an integer between 1 and n // Equation 15.12

Plugging in $k = n$ in Equation 15.12 in order to reach the base case of $T2(0)$, we get

$$\begin{aligned} T2(n) &= 2^n * T2(0) + 2^{n+1} - 2 \\ &= 2^n * 1 + 2^{n+1} - 2 \\ &= 2^n + 2^{n+1} - 2 \\ &= 2^n (1 + 2) - 2 \\ &= 3 * 2^n - 2 \\ &= O(2^n) \end{aligned}$$

Thus, *powerOf2A* runs in $O(n)$ while *powerOf2B* runs in $O(2^n)$, although they perform the same function.

As a result, computing 2^{20} using *powerOf2A* will cost 20 statement executions while computing 2^{20} using *powerOf2B* will cost 1 million statement executions.

This simple example shows that how we code a method can have a significant impact on its running time.

15.4 Programming Activity: Tracking How Many Statements Are Executed by a Method

REFERENCE POINT

Selection Sort is explained in Chapter 8.

In this activity, you will work with a variable-size integer array. Specifically, you will perform the following operations:

1. Write code to keep track of the number of statement executions during a selection sort.
2. Run a simulation to compute the number of statements executed as a function of the number of elements in the array.

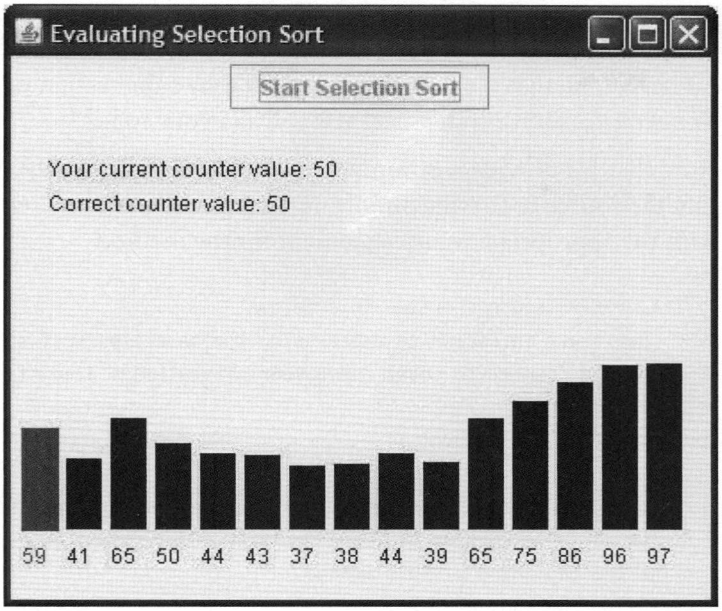

Figure 15.1
Animation of the Programming Activity

3. Estimate the running time of Selection Sort as a function of *n*, the number of elements in the array being sorted.

The framework for this Programming Activity will animate your algorithm so that you can perform a simulation on the number of statement executions inside the *selectionSort* method compared to the number of elements in the array that is sorted. For example, Figure 15.1 shows the current number of statement executions for an array of 15 elements.

At this point, the application has executed 50 statements.

Instructions

In the Chapter 15 Programming Activity directory on the CD-ROM accompanying this book, you will find the source files needed to complete this activity. Copy all the files to a directory on your computer. Note that all files should be in the same directory.

Open the *RunningTimePractice.java* source file. Searching for five stars (*****) in the source code will position you at the sample method where you will add your code. In this task, you will fill in the code for the *selectionSort* method in order to keep track of the number of statement executions needed to sort an array using the Selection Sort algorithm. You should not instantiate the array; we have done that for you. Example 15.6 shows the section of the *Running-TimePractice* source code where you will add your code.

Note that we provide a dummy *return* statement (*return* 0;). We do this so that the source code will compile. Just replace the dummy *return* statement with the appropriate *return* statement for the method.

```
// 1. *****  student writes this method
/**  Sorts arr in ascending order using the selection sort algorithm
*    Adds a counter to count the number of statement executions
*/
public int selectionSort( )
{
 // Note:  To count the number of statement executions, use a counter
 // The variable counter has been declared and initialized for you
 // at the beginning of this method
 // Inside the body of the inner loop, increment the counter
 // Replace the return statement so that this method returns the value of
 // the counter. To slow down or accelerate the animation, modify the
 // argument of Pause.wait in the animate method
 int counter = 0;
 int temp, indexOfMax;
 for ( int i = 0; i < size; i++ )
 {
   // find index of largest value in the subarray
   indexOfMax = 0;
   animate( i, 0, counter );
   for ( int j = 1; j < arr.length – i; j++ )
   {

    if ( arr[j] > arr[indexOfMax] )
     indexOfMax = j;
    animate( i, j, counter );
   }
   // swap arr[indexOfMax] and arr[arr.length - i]
   temp = arr[indexOfMax];
```

```
      arr[indexOfMax] = arr[arr.length - i - 1];
      arr[arr.length - i - 1] = temp;
    }
    return 0;
  } // end of selectionSort
```

EXAMPLE 15.6 Location of Student Code in RunningTimePractice

Our framework will animate your algorithm so that you can watch your code work. If you want to accelerate or slow down the animation, modify the argument of *Pause.wait* in the *animate* method.

To test your code, compile and run the *RunningTimePractice* source code. When the program begins, you will be prompted for the number of elements in the array. Because the values of the array are randomly generated, the values will be different each time the program runs.

Troubleshooting

If the animation is incorrect, and you think your method does return a correct value for the counter, verify that you correctly incremented the counter inside the inner loop.

In order to derive a closed-end expression for the number of statement executions as a function of the size of the array, follow these tips:

- If n is the size of the array, compare n, n^2, n^3, n^4, ..., 2^n, to the value of the counter
- When doing the preceding, divide n, n^2, n^3, n^4, ..., 2^n by the number of statements executed

? DISCUSSION QUESTIONS

1. What is the value of the counter with the following array sizes: 5, 10, 15, 20, 25?
2. In relation to *n*, the size of the array, what is the value of the counter?
3. What is the running time of Selection Sort in Big-Oh notation?
4. If the array is already sorted in either the correct or opposite order, does that make a difference in the number of statement executions? What can you say about the worst-case and best-case running times?

15.5 Running Time Analysis of Searching and Sorting Algorithms

In studying the running time of various searching and sorting algorithms, we will look at the following scenarios:

- best case
- worst case
- average case

Some methods have a very efficient running time. We mentioned earlier that the running time of Binary Search was log *n*. Thus, searching a sorted array of 1 billion items using Binary Search will only take 30 statement executions since log (1 billion) is approximately 30.

Example 15.7 shows the code of the recursive binary search method introduced in Chapter 13.

```
public static int recursiveBinarySearch
                ( int [ ] arr, int key, int start, int end )
{
  if ( start <= end )
  {
    // look at the middle element of the subarray
    int middle = ( start + end ) / 2;

    if ( arr[middle] == key )     // found key, base case
      return middle;
    else if ( arr[middle] > key ) // look lower
      return recursiveBinarySearch( arr, key, start, middle - 1 );
    else                          // look higher
      return recursiveBinarySearch( arr, key, middle + 1, end );
  }
  else                            // key not found, base case
    return -1;
}
```

EXAMPLE 15.7 Recursive Binary Search

In the best-case scenario, we will find the search value exactly in the middle of the array, at the array index we check first. Thus, the best-case running time of Binary Search is $O(1)$. In the worst-case scenario, we will not find the search value in the array. Let's compute the running time of the worst-case scenario.

In the general case, the comparison of the first *if* statement will cost us one instruction; the assignment statement will cost us two instructions; the comparison in the second *if* statement will cost us one instruction; the comparison in the *else/if* statement will also cost us one instruction, computing and returning *recursiveBinarySearch(arr, key, start, middle* – 1) or *recursiveBinarySearch(arr, key, middle* + 1, *end*) will cost us $T(n/2 - 1)$ or $T(n/2)$ instructions. Note that only one recursive call will be made. Thus, the total time $T(n)$ can be expressed as follows:

$$\begin{aligned} T(n) &= 1 + 2 + 1 + 1 + T(n / 2) \\ &= T(n / 2) + 5 \qquad \text{// Equation 15.13} \end{aligned}$$

In the base case (n is equal to 1), *recursiveBinarySearch* makes only the first comparison, one addition, one division, the second comparison, and then returns the index of the found element or –1. Thus,

$$T(1) = 5.$$

From there, we will use the iteration method in order to compute the value of $T2(n)$ as a function of n.

Substituting x for n, we can rewrite Equation 15.13 as follows:

$$T(x) = T(x / 2) + 5 \qquad \text{// Equation 15.14}$$

Using $x = n / 2$ in Equation 15.14, we get

$$\begin{aligned} T(n / 2) &= T((n / 2) / 2) + 5 \\ &= T(n / 2^2) + 5 \end{aligned}$$

Plugging in the value of $T(n / 2)$ into Equation 15.13, we get

$$\begin{aligned} T(n) &= (T(n / 2^2) + 5) + 5 \\ &= T(n / 2^2) + 5 * 2 \qquad \text{// Equation 15.15} \end{aligned}$$

Using $x = n / 2^2$ in Equation 15.14, we get

$$\begin{aligned} T(n / 2^2) &= T((n / 2^2) / 2) + 5 \\ &= T(n / 2^3) + 5 \end{aligned}$$

Plugging in the value of $T(n / 2^2)$ into Equation 15.15, we get

$$\begin{aligned} T(n) &= (T(n / 2^3) + 5) + 5 * 2 \\ &= T(n / 2^3) + 5 * 3 \qquad \text{// Equation 15.16} \end{aligned}$$

Using $x = n / 2^3$ in Equation 15.14, we get

$$\begin{aligned} T(n / 2^3) &= T((n / 2^3) / 2) + 5 \\ &= T(n / 2^4) + 5 \end{aligned}$$

Plugging in the value of $T(n / 2^3)$ into Equation 15.16, we get

$$T(n) = (T(n / 2^4) + 5) + 5 * 3$$
$$= T(n / 2^4) + 5 * 4 \quad \text{// Equation 15.17}$$

Now we can see the pattern as follows:

$$T(n) = T(n / 2^k) + 5 * k,$$
$$\text{where } k \text{ is an integer between 1 and } n \quad \text{// Equation 15.18}$$

We now want to choose k such that $n / 2^k$ is equal to 1 in order to reach our base case. If $n / 2^k = 1$, then $n = 2^k$ and taking the log of each side:

$$\begin{aligned} \log n &= \log 2^k \\ &= k \log 2 \\ &= k * 1 \\ &= k \end{aligned}$$

Plugging in $k = \log n$ in Equation 15.18, we get

$$\begin{aligned} T(n) &= T(1) + 5 * \log n \\ &= 2 + 5 * \log n \\ &= O(\log n) \end{aligned}$$

Thus, Binary Search is $O(\log n)$ in the worst case. Note that the value of the original constant, here 5, does not impact the order of magnitude of the running time.

REFERENCE POINT

Insertion Sort is explained in Chapter 8.

In the average case, we will find the search value after performing half the number of comparisons as in the worst-case scenario. Thus, the average running time of binary search is also $O(\log n)$.

Now, let's calculate the running time of Insertion Sort as a function of n, the number of elements in the array. From Chapter 8, the code of the Insertion Sort method is shown in Example 15.8.

```
/**  Performs an Insertion Sort on an integer array
*    @param array   array to sort
*/
public static void insertionSort( int [ ] array )
{
  int j, temp;

  for ( int i = 0; i < array.length; i++ )
  {
```

```
        j = i;
        temp = array[i];

        while ( j != 0 && array[j - 1] > temp )
        {
            array[j] = array[j - 1];
            j--;
        }

        array[j] = temp;
    }
}
```

EXAMPLE 15.8 Insertion Sort

The *for* loop header will execute $n + 1$ times. We will execute the body of the *for* loop n times.

In the best case, the array is already sorted. In this case, the *while* loop condition will always evaluate to *false*, and we will never execute the *while* loop body. So inside the *for* loop, the three statements and the loop condition will each execute once for each iteration of the *for* loop, thus executing a total of $4 * n$ times. Therefore, the best-case running time is $O(n)$.

In the worst case, the array is sorted in the opposite order. In this case, the *while* loop condition will always be *true* for its first evaluation, and we will enter the *while* loop every time we iterate the *for* loop. Thus, the two statements inside the *while* loop will each execute $(1 + 2 + 3 + 4 + \ldots (n - 1))$ times. Since $(1 + 2 + 3 + 4 + \ldots + (n - 1)) = n * (n - 1) / 2$, the worst-case running time of insertion sort is $O(n^2)$.

In the average case, we will enter the *while* loop half the times we try. The average case is still $O(n^2)$.

Bubble Sort, presented in Programming Activity 2 of Chapter 8, like Insertion Sort, is implemented with a double loop and also is $O(n^2)$.

Merge Sort and Quick Sort are two sorting algorithms implemented recursively.

The pseudocode for Merge Sort, which is the subject of the Group Project of Chapter 13, is as follows:

- If the array has only one element, it is already sorted, thus do nothing; otherwise:
  - Merge sort the left half of the array
  - Merge sort the right half of the array
  - Merge the two sorted half-arrays into one in a sorted manner

The last operation involves looping through all the elements of the two half-arrays; it takes $O(n)$; thus, we can derive the following recursive formulation for its running time of Merge Sort:

$$\begin{aligned} T(n) &= T(n/2) + T(n/2) + n \\ &= 2\,T(n/2) + n \end{aligned}$$

Using derivation, we get:

$$\begin{aligned} T(n) &= 2\,T(n/2) + n \\ &= 2\,(2\,T(n/2^2) + n/2) + n \\ &= 2^2\,T(n/2^2) + 2n \end{aligned}$$

Continuing to iterate,

$$\begin{aligned} T(n) &= 2^2\,T(n/2^2) + 2n \\ &= 2^2\,(2\,T(n/2^3) + n/2^2) + 2n \\ &= 2^3\,T(n/2^3) + 3n \\ T(n) &= 2^3\,T(n/2^3) + 3n \\ &= 2^3\,(2\,T(n/2^3) + n/2^3) + 3n \\ &= 2^4\,T(n/2^4) + 4n \end{aligned}$$

Thus, we identify the general pattern

$$T(n) = 2^k\,T(n/2^k) + kn$$

Choosing k so that $n/2^k = 1$ in order to reach the base case, i.e., $n = 2^k$, $k = \log n$, we get

$$\begin{aligned} T(n) &= n\,T(1) + n \log n \\ &= O(n \log n) \end{aligned}$$

So Merge Sort is $O(n \log n)$, better than Insertion Sort, Bubble Sort, and Selection Sort. It is the same for best-case, worst-case, and average-case scenarios.

The analysis of the running time of Quick Sort is the subject of the Group Project for this chapter.

CODE IN ACTION

On the CD-ROM included with this book, you will find a Flash movie with a step-by-step illustration of how to compute running times for various methods. Click on the link for Chapter 15 to start the movie.

Skill Practice
with these end-of-chapter questions

15.7.1 Multiple Choice Exercises

Questions 1, 2, 3, 4, 5, 6, 7, 8, 9, 10

15.7.2 Compute the Running Time of a Method

Questions 11, 12, 13, 14, 15, 16, 17, 18

15.7.4 Technical Writing

Question 27

15.6 Chapter Summary

SUMMARY

- The running time of an algorithm is expressed as a function of its inputs or its number of inputs.
- Orders of magnitude are, in increasing order of execution time: constant, log, polynomial, and exponential. Exponential running times are undesirable.
- Big-Oh notation is the industry standard notation for running times.
- Considering a mathematical function that represents a running time of an algorithm, that function is Big-Oh of its most dominant term.
- The coding of a method directly impacts its running time.

15.7 Exercises, Problems, and Projects

15.7.1 Multiple Choice Exercises

1. What is the Big-Oh of this function:

   $T(n) = n^2 - 2n + 99$

   - ❑ $O(n^2)$
   - ❑ $O(99)$
   - ❑ $O(n)$
   - ❑ $O(1)$

2. What is the Big-Oh of this function:

   $T(n) = n^3 + 10n^2 + 20n + 30$

   - ❑ $O(n^3)$
   - ❑ $O(n^2)$
   - ❑ $O(n)$
   - ❑ $O(1)$

3. What is the Big-Oh of this function:

   $T(n) = n^2 + n * \log n + 12n + 5$

   - ❑ $O(n * \log n)$
   - ❑ $O(n^2)$
   - ❑ $OO(n)$
   - ❑ $O(1)$

4. We have the following recurrence relation representing the running time of a function; what is the running time of that function?

   $T(n) = T(n - 1) + 1$

   - ❑ $O(2^n)$
   - ❑ $O(n * \log n)$
   - ❑ $O(n^2)$
   - ❑ $O(n)$

5. Which of these running times is the worst?

- ❑ $O(n^5)$
- ❑ $O(2^n)$
- ❑ $O(n * \log n)$
- ❑ $O(n)$

6. Look at the following method

```
public static int foo1( int n )
{
  if ( n > 1 )
      return ( 2 * foo1( n / 4 ) );
  else
      return 1;
}
```

What recurrence formulation best illustrates the running time of the preceding method?

- ❑ $T(n) = T(n * 4) + 3$
- ❑ $T(n) = T(n / 4) + 3$
- ❑ $T(n) = T(n - 4) + 3$
- ❑ $T(n) = T(n + 4) + 3$

7. What is $\Sigma\ i$ for $i = 1$ to n equal to ?

- ❑ n^2
- ❑ $n * (n + 1) / 2$
- ❑ $2n$
- ❑ n

8. What is $\Sigma\ 1$ for $i = 1$ to n equal to ?

- ❑ n^2
- ❑ n
- ❑ $n * (n + 1) / 2$
- ❑ i

9. What is the running time of the *foo2* method?

```
public static void foo2( int n )
{
  for ( int i = n; i > 0; i– )
  {
   for ( int j = 0; j < n; j++ )
     System.out.println( "Hello" );
  }
}
```

- ❑ $O(n^4)$
- ❑ $O(n^3)$
- ❑ $O(n^2)$
- ❑ $O(n)$

10. What is the running time of the *foo3* method?

```
public static void foo3( int n )
{
  for ( int i = 0; i < n; i++ )
  {
   for ( int j = 0; j < i; j++ )
     System.out.println( "Hello" );
  }
}
```

- ❑ $O(n^4)$
- ❑ $O(n^3)$
- ❑ $O(n^2)$
- ❑ $O(n)$

15.7.2 Compute the Running Time of a Method

11. What is the running time of the *foo4* method (assume that the parameter *arr* is a two-dimensional array of *n* rows and *n* columns)?

```
public static void foo4( int [ ][ ] arr )
{
  for ( int i = 0; i < arr.length; i++ )
  {
   for ( int j = arr[i].length - 1; j >= 0; j++ )
     System.out.println( "Hello world" );
  }
}
```

12. What is the running time of the *foo5* method (assume that the parameter *arr* is a three-dimensional array where each dimension has exactly *n* elements)?

```
public static void foo5( int [ ][ ][ ] arr )
{
  for ( int i = 0; i < arr.length; i++ )
  {
   for ( int j = 0; j < arr[i].length; j++ )
   {
    for ( int k = 0; k < arr[i][j].length; k++ )
     System.out.println( "Hello world" );
   }
  }
}
```

13. What is the running time of the *foo6* method?

```
public static void foo6( int n )
{
  if ( n <= 0 )
     System.out.println( "Hello world" );
  else
     foo6( n - 1 );
}
```

14. What is the running time of the *foo7* method?

```
public static int foo7( int n )
{
  // n is guaranteed to be >= 0
  if ( n == 0 )
      return 0;
  else
      return ( n + foo7( n - 1 ) );
}
```

15. What is the running time of the *foo8* method?

```
public static int foo8( int n )
{
  // n is guaranteed to be >= 1
  if ( n == 1 || n == 2 )
      return 1;
  else
      return ( foo8( n - 1 ) + foo8( n - 2 ) );
}
```

Hint: Note that $T(n-2) <= T(n-1)$.

16. What is the running time of the *foo9* method?

```
public static void foo9( int n )
{
  // n is guaranteed to be >= 0
  if ( n == 0 )
     System.out.println( "done" );
  else
     foo9( n / 2 );
}
```

17. What is the running time of the *foo10* method as a function of n and p?

```
public static void foo10( int n, int p )
{
  // n and p are guaranteed to be >= 1
  if ( p >= n )
     System.out.println( "done" );
  else
     foo10( n, 2 * p );
}
```

18. What is the running time of the *foo11* method?

```
public static void foo11( int n )
{
  // n is guaranteed to be >= 0
  if ( n == 0 )
      return 0;
  else
      return ( 5 + 2 * foo11( n - 1 ) );
}
```

15.7.3 Programming Projects

19. Write a program that includes a method taking a single-dimensional array of *ints* as its only parameter, and returning the average of all the elements of the array. Add the necessary code to count how many statements are executed in the innermost loop. Run several simulations depending on the number of elements in the parameter integer array. What is the running time of that method as a function of the number of elements of the parameter array?

20. Write a program that includes a method converting a two-dimensional array of *ints* to a two-dimensional array of *boolean* values; if the integer value is greater than or equal to 0, then the corresponding *boolean* value is *true*, otherwise it is *false*. Add the necessary code to count how many statements are executed in the innermost loop. Run several simulations depending on the number of rows and columns in the argument integer array. What is the running time of that method as a function of the number of rows and columns of the parameter array? (You should assume that each row has the same number of columns.)

21. Write a program that includes a method computing the largest element of a given column (represented by a parameter of the method) of a two-dimensional array of *ints*. Add the necessary code to count how many statements are executed in the innermost loop. Run several simulations depending on the number of rows and columns in the parameter integer array, as well as the index of the column for which the method calculates the largest element. Does the running time of the method depend on the column index? the number of rows? the number of columns? What is the running time of that method as a function of the number of rows and columns of the parameter array and the column index? (You should assume that each row has the same number of columns.)

22. Write a program that includes a method taking a two-dimensional array of *ints* as its only parameter, and returning a single dimensional array of *ints* such that each element of the returned array is the sum of the corresponding row in the parameter array. Add the necessary code to count how many statements are executed in the innermost loop. Run several simulations depending on the number of rows and columns in the parameter integer array. What is the running time of that method as a function of the number of rows and columns of the parameter array? (You should assume that each row has the same number of columns.)

23. Write a program that implements a recursive Binary Search and add the necessary code to count how many times *binarySearchRecursive* is being called. Run several simulations on arrays of 32, 64, and 128 elements. How many times is the method called in the best-case scenario and worst-case scenario? Does that match our analysis in the chapter?

24. Write a program that implements the recursive method to compute the factorial of a number from Chapter 13 and add the necessary code to count how many times the method is being called. Run several simulations depending on the value of *n*. How many times is the method called? What is the running time of this method?

25. Write a program that includes a method converting a *String* of 0s and 1s to its equivalent decimal number and add the necessary code to count how many times the method is being called. Run several simulations depending on the length of the input *String*. How many times is the method called? What is the running time of that method?

26. Write a program that includes a method converting a decimal number to its equivalent binary number represented by a *String* of 0s and 1s and add the necessary code to count how many times the method is being called. Run several simulations depending on the decimal number. How many times is the method called? What is the running time of that method?

15.7.4 Technical Writing

27. Explain why it is important to consider running time when coding algorithms. Use an example to illustrate your point. Your example, web-based or not, should deal with a lot of data.

15.7.5 Group Project (for a group of 1, 2, or 3 students)

28. Write a class with an *int* array as its only instance variable. Write a recursive method that uses the Quick Sort algorithm in order to sort the array. (Quick Sort is explained below.) You will then add the appropriate code and perform the appropriate simulations to evaluate the running time of the method as a function of the number of elements in the array.

    Here is how Quick Sort works:

    - ❑ Partition the array so that all the elements to the left of a certain index are smaller than the element at that index and all the elements to the right of that index are greater than or equal to the element at that index. You should code a separate method to partition the array. (See explanation that follows.)

- ❑ Sort the left part of the array using Quick Sort (this is a recursive call).
- ❑ Sort the right part of the array using Quick Sort (this is another recursive call).

To partition the array elements in the manner previously explained, you should code another method (this one nonrecursive) as explained as follows:

- ❑ Choose an element of the array (for example, the first element). We call this element **pivot**.
- ❑ This method partitions the array elements so that all the elements left of pivot are less than pivot, and all the element right of pivot are greater than or equal to pivot.
- ❑ This method returns an *int* representing the array index of pivot (after the elements have been partitioned in the order described previously).
- ❑ In order to rearrange the array elements as previously described, implement the following pseudocode:

The following is pseudocode to partition a subarray whose lower index is *low* and higher index is *high*.

```
Assign element at index low to pivot
Initialize j to low
Loop from (low + 1) to high with variable i
   If (array element at index i is smaller than pivot)
       Increase j by 1
       Swap array elements at indexes i and j
Swap array elements at index low and j
Return j
```

Using a counter, keep track of the number of statement executions performed when using Quick Sort to sort an array of n elements. In particular, you should run simulation runs on these two situations:

- ❑ The array is not sorted
- ❑ The array is pre-sorted in the correct order

You should perform a mathematical analysis of the running time of Quick Sort in the average case based on its recursive formulation (using iteration, as we did in the chapter examples).

APPENDIX A

Java Reserved Words and Keywords

These words have contextual meaning for the Java language and cannot be used as identifiers.

abstract	default	goto	package	synchronized
assert	do	if	private	this
boolean	double	implements	protected	throw
break	else	import	public	throws
byte	enum	instanceof	return	transient
case	extends	int	short	true
catch	false	interface	static	try
char	final	long	strictfp	void
class	finally	native	super	volatile
const	float	new	switch	while
continue	for	null		

The words *true*, *false*, and *null* are literals. The remainder of the words are Java keywords, although *const* and *goto* are not currently used in the Java language.

APPENDIX B

Operator Precedence

These rules of operator precedence are followed when expressions are evaluated. Operators in a higher level in the hierarchy—defined by their row position in the table—are evaluated before operators in a lower level. Thus, an expression in parentheses is evaluated before a shortcut postincrement is performed, and so on with the operators in each level. When two or more operators on the same level appear in an expression, the evaluation of the expression follows the corresponding rule for same-statement evaluation shown in the second column.

<table>
<tr><th>Operators</th><th>Order of Same-Statement Evaluation</th><th>Operation</th></tr>
<tr><td>( )</td><td>left to right</td><td>parentheses for explicit grouping</td></tr>
<tr><td>++ − −</td><td>right to left</td><td>shortcut postincrement and postdecrement</td></tr>
<tr><td>++ − − !</td><td>right to left</td><td>shortcut preincrement and predecrement, logical unary NOT</td></tr>
<tr><td>* / %</td><td>left to right</td><td>multiplication, division, modulus</td></tr>
<tr><td>+ -</td><td>left to right</td><td>addition or String concatenation, subtraction</td></tr>
<tr><td>< <= > >=
instanceof</td><td>left to right</td><td>relational operators: less than, less than or equal to, greater than, greater than or equal to; instanceof</td></tr>
<tr><td>== !=</td><td>left to right</td><td>equality operators: equal to and not equal to</td></tr>
<tr><td>&&</td><td>left to right</td><td>logical AND</td></tr>
<tr><td>||</td><td>left to right</td><td>logical OR</td></tr>
<tr><td>?:</td><td>left to right</td><td>conditional operator</td></tr>
<tr><td>= += -= *= /= %=</td><td>right to left</td><td>assignment operator and shortcut assignment operators</td></tr>
</table>

APPENDIX C

The Unicode Character Set

Java characters are encoded using the Unicode Character Set, which is designed to support international alphabets, punctuation, and mathematical and technical symbols. Each character is stored as 16 bits, so as many as 65,536 characters are supported.

The American Standard Code for Information Interchange (ASCII) character set is supported by the first 128 Unicode characters from 0000 to 007F, which are called the controls and Basic Latin characters, as shown on the next page.

Any character from the Unicode set can be specified as a *char* literal in a Java program by using the following syntax: '\uNNNN' where NNNN are the four hexadecimal digits that specify the Unicode encoding for the character.

For more information on the Unicode character set, visit the Unicode Consortium's website: *www.unicode.org*.

Controls and Basic Latin Characters

	000	001	002	003	004	005	006	007
0	NUL 0000	DLE 0010	SP 0020	0 0030	@ 0040	P 0050	` 0060	p 0070
1	SOH 0001	DC1 0011	! 0021	1 0031	A 0041	Q 0051	a 0061	q 0071
2	STX 0002	DC2 0012	" 0022	2 0032	B 0042	R 0052	b 0062	r 0072
3	ETX 0003	DC3 0013	# 0023	3 0033	C 0043	S 0053	c 0063	s 0073
4	EOT 0004	DC4 0014	$ 0024	4 0034	D 0044	T 0054	d 0064	t 0074
5	ENQ 0005	NAK 0015	% 0025	5 0035	E 0045	U 0055	e 0065	u 0075
6	ACK 0006	SYN 0016	& 0026	6 0036	F 0046	V 0056	f 0066	v 0076
7	BEL 0007	ETB 0017	' 0027	7 0037	G 0047	W 0057	g 0067	w 0077
8	BS 0008	CAN 0018	(0028	8 0038	H 0048	X 0058	h 0068	x 0078
9	HT 0009	EM 0019	) 0029	9 0039	I 0049	Y 0059	i 0069	y 0079
A	LF 000A	SUB 001A	* 002A	: 003A	J 004A	Z 005A	j 006A	z 007A
B	VT 000B	ESC 001B	+ 002B	; 003B	K 004B	[005B	k 006B	{ 007B
C	FF 000C	FS 001C	, 002C	< 003C	L 004C	\ 005C	l 006C	| 007C
D	CR 000D	GS 001D	- 002D	= 003D	M 004D	] 005D	m 006D	} 007D
E	SO 000E	RS 001E	. 002E	> 003E	N 004E	^ 005E	n 006E	~ 007E
F	SI 000F	US 001F	/ 002F	? 003F	O 004F	_ 005F	o 006F	DEL 007F

APPENDIX D

Representing Negative Integers

The industry standard method for representing negative integers is called **two's complement**. Here is how it works:

For an integer represented using 16 bits, the leftmost bit is reserved for the sign bit. If the sign bit is 0, then the integer is positive; if the sign bit is 1, then the integer is negative.

For example, let's consider two numbers, one positive and one negative.

0000 0101 0111 1001 is a positive integer, which we call a.

1111 1111 1101 1010 is a negative integer, which we will call b.

Using the methodology presented in Chapter 1 for converting a binary number to a decimal number, we can convert the binary number, a, to its decimal equivalent. Hence, the value of a is calculated as follows:

$$\begin{aligned} a &= 2^{10} + 2^{8} + 2^{6} + 2^{5} + 2^{4} + 2^{3} + 2^{0} \\ &= 1{,}024 + 256 + 64 + 32 + 16 + 8 + 1 \\ &= 1{,}401 \end{aligned}$$

In contrast, b, the negative number, is represented in binary using the two's complement method. The leftmost bit, which is the sign bit, is a 1, indicating that b is negative. To calculate the value of a negative number, we first calculate its two's complement. The two's complement of any binary number is another binary number, which when added to the original number, will yield a sum consisting of all 0s and a carry bit of 1 at the end.

To calculate the two's complement of a binary number, *n*, subtract *n* from 2^d, where *d* is the number of binary digits in *n*. The following formula summarizes that rule:

```
Two's complement of n = 2^d – n
```

Knowing that $2^d - 1$ is always a binary number containing all 1s, we can simplify our calculations by first subtracting 1 from 2^d, then adding a 1 at the end.

```
Two's complement of n = 2^d – 1 – n + 1
```

So to calculate the two's complement of *b*, which has 16 digits, we subtract *b* from a binary number consisting of 16 1s, then add 1, as shown here.

```
              2^d – 1  1111 1111 1111 1111
                  – b  1111 1111 1101 1010
                       0000 0000 0010 0101
                  + 1  ___________________1
two's complement of b  0000 0000 0010 0110
```

Thus, the two's complement of *b*, which we will call *c*, is 0000 0000 0010 0110.

Another, simpler, way to calculate a two's complement is to invert each bit, then add 1. Inverting bits means to change all 0s to 1s and to change all 1s to 0s. Using this method, we get:

```
          b  1111 1111 1101 1010

b inverted  0000 0000 0010 0101
       + 1  ___________________1
         c  0000 0000 0010 0110
```

We can verify that the two's complement of *b* is correct by calculating the sum of *b* and *c*.

```
    b    1111 1111 1101 1010
    c    0000 0000 0010 0110
b + c  1 0000 0000 0000 0000
```

Converting *c* to decimal will give us the value of our original number *b*, which, as we remember, is negative. We have:

```
b =  – (  2^5 + 2^2 + 2^1 )
  =  – (  32 +  4  + 2 )
  =  –38
```

Because a leftmost bit of 0 indicates that the number is positive, using 16 bits, the largest positive number (we will call it *max*) that we can represent is:

```
0111 1111 1111 1111
```

$max = (2^{14} + 2^{13} + 2^{12} + 2^{11} + 2^{10} + 2^{9} + 2^{8} + 2^{7} + 2^{6} + 2^{5} + 2^{4} + 2^{3} + 2^{2} + 2^{1} + 2^{0})$

This is equivalent to $2^{15} - 1$, which is 32,768 − 1, or 32,767.

Using 16 bits, then, the smallest negative number (we will call it *min*) that we can represent is:

```
1000 0000 0000 0000
```

The two's complement of *min* is *min* itself. If we invert the bits and add 1, we get the same value we started with:

```
           min       1000 0000 0000 0000

  min inverted       0111 1111 1111 1111
           + 1                         1
                     -------------------
two's complement     1000 0000 0000 0000
```

and therefore *min* is -2^{15} or −32,768.

Thus, using 16 bits, we can represent integers between −32,768 and 32,767.

APPENDIX E

Representing Floating-Point Numbers

IEEE 754, a specification accepted worldwide and used by the Java language, defines how to represent floating-point numbers in binary numbers. Single-precision floating-point numbers use 32 bits of memory, and double-precision floating-point numbers use 64 bits.

Here is how single- and double-precision floating-point numbers are represented:

Single precision (32 bits)

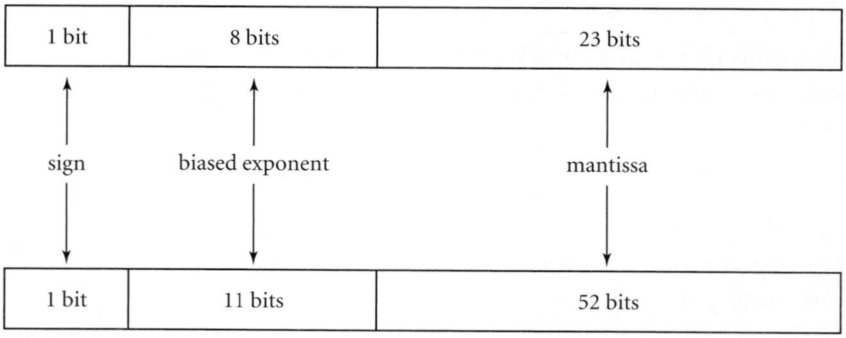

Double precision (64 bits)

The leftmost bit stores the sign of the floating-point number; a 0 indicates a positive number, while a 1 indicates a negative number.

To represent the exponent of the number, which can be positive or negative, each representation stores a positive, biased exponent, calculated by adding a fixed bias, or scaling factor, to the real exponent of the number.

The purpose of the bias is to be able to represent both extremely large and extremely small numbers. The bias is equal to

$$2^{(\text{\# of bits of the biased exponent} - 1)} - 1.$$

Thus, for single precision, the bias is

$$2^{(8-1)} - 1 = 2^7 - 1 = 127.$$

In single-precision, the 8-bit biased exponent can store 256 positive values (0 to 255). Thus, with a bias of 127, we can represent floating-point numbers with real exponents from −127 to 128, as shown here:

Real exponent	−127	−126	...	0	...	127	128
+ Bias	127	127	...	127	...	127	127
Biased exponent	0	1	...	127	...	254	255

Conversely, to find the real exponent from the biased exponent, we subtract the bias. For example, if the biased exponent is 150, then the real exponent is 150 − 127, which is 23. Similarly, if the biased exponent is 3, the actual exponent is 3 − 127, which is −124.

For double precision, the bias is

$$2^{(11-1)} - 1 = 2^{10} - 1 = 1023.$$

A floating-point number is considered to be in the form:

$$(-1)^{\text{sign}} * (1 + \text{significand}) * 2^{(\text{biased exponent} - \text{bias})}$$

By definition, the significand is of the form 0 followed by a dot followed by a string of 0s and 1s, for example, 0.1101. That string of 0s and 1s is known as the mantissa.

For example, if the significand is 0.1101, then the mantissa is 110100...0

As an example, let's convert a single-precision binary number to a decimal floating-point number. We will convert the following single-precision IEEE 754 floating-point number:

0	10000111	11010000....0

The leftmost digit, 0, tells us that the number is positive. The biased exponent is 10000111, which converted to decimal, is:

$$\begin{aligned} &= 2^7 + 2^2 + 2^1 + 2^0 \\ &= 128 + 4 + 2 + 1 \\ &= 135 \end{aligned}$$

The bias for single-precision floating-point numbers is 127, so the number is

$$= (-1)^0 * (1 + .1101) * 2^{(135 - 127)}$$
$$= 1.1101 * 2^8$$
$$= 1\ 1101\ 0000$$

In decimal, the number is:

$$= 2^8 + 2^7 + 2^6 + 2^4$$
$$= 256 + 128 + 64 + 16$$
$$= 464$$

Given that .1 is $1/2^1$ or $1/2$ in decimal, and .01 is $1/2^2$ or $1/4$, and .0001 is $1/2^4$ or $1/16$ in decimal, we also could have calculated the number using this method:

$$= 1.1101 * 2^8$$
$$= (1 + 1 * 1/2^1 + 1 * 1/2^2 + 0 * 1/2^3 + 1 * 1/2^4) * 2^8$$
$$= (1 + 1/2 + 1/4 + 1/16) * 2^8$$
$$= (1 + 1/2 + 1/4 + 1/16) * 256$$
$$= 464$$

Now, let's convert a decimal floating-point number into single-precision, binary format. Here, we will convert the number −5.375, which we'll call *y*. First we convert the whole number portion (5) to binary, getting 101.

$$5 = 101$$

Then we convert the fractional part to binary:

$$.375 = .25 + .125$$
$$= 1/4 + 1/8$$
$$= 1/2^2 + 1/2^3$$
$$= 0 * 1/2^1 + 1 * 1/2^2 + 1 * 1/2^3$$

Thus, .375 as represented in binary is .011.

Therefore, *y* can be represented in binary as:

$$y = -\ 101.011$$
$$= -1.01011 * 2^2$$

We now can deduce the sign, the biased exponent, and the mantissa. The sign is 1 because the number is negative. The significand is 1.01011, and therefore the mantissa is 01011000…00. The exponent is 2, so the biased exponent is 129 (2 plus the bias for single-precision numbers, which is 127).

$$\text{Biased exponent} = 2 + 127$$
$$= 129$$

Converting 129 to binary, we get:

$$129 = 1000\ 0001$$

Therefore, the IEEE 754 single-precision value of the number *y* is

1	10000001	010110000...0

APPENDIX F

Java Classes APIs

In this appendix, we have compiled the APIs for the Java classes and interfaces used in this book. There are more methods and constructors for the classes presented here, and there are many more classes in the Java class library. We invite you to explore the Java APIs at www.java.sun.com.

ActionEvent

Package: java.awt.event

Description: Contains information relating to the action event fired by a component. This event is passed to any *ActionListener* registered on the component.

A Useful Method of the *ActionEvent* Class

Return value	Method name and argument list
`Object`	`getSource( )` returns the object reference of the component that fired the event. This method is inherited from the *EventObject* class.

ActionListener Interface

Package: java.awt.event

Description: Interface implemented by a class that will handle *ActionEvents* fired by a user interface component.

Interface Method to be Implemented

`public void actionPerformed( ActionEvent event )`

An event handler that implements the *ActionListener* interface provides code in this method to respond to the *ActionEvent* fired by any registered components.

ArrayList

Package: java.util

Description: implements a dynamically resizable array of object references

Constructors

`ArrayList<E>( )`

constructs an *ArrayList* object of data type *E* with an initial capacity of 10

`ArrayList<E>( int initialCapacity )`

constructs an *ArrayList* object of data type *E* with the specified initial capacity. Throws an *IllegalArgumentException*

Useful Methods of the *ArrayList* Class (*E* represents the data type of the *ArrayList*.)

Return value	Method name and argument list
`boolean`	`add( E element )`
	appends the specified *element* to the end of the list. Returns *true.*
`void`	`clear( )`
	removes all the elements from the list
`E`	`get( int index )`
	returns the element at the specified *index* position; the element is not removed from the list.

Return value	Method name and argument list
`E`	`remove( int index )` returns and removes the element at the specified *index* position
`E`	`set( int index, E newElement )` returns the element at the specified *index* position and replaces that element with *newElement*.
`int`	`size( )` returns the number of elements in the list
`void`	`trimToSize( )` sets the capacity to the list's current size

BigDecimal

Package: java.math

Description: provides methods that perform addition, subtraction, multiplication, and division so that the results are exact, without the rounding errors caused by floating-point operations.

Constructor

`BigDecimal( String num )`

creates a *BigDecimal* object equivalent to the decimal number *num* expressed as a *String*. Throws a *NumberFormatException*.

Useful Methods of the *BigDecimal* Class

Return value	Method name and argument list
`BigDecimal`	`add( BigDecimal num )` returns a *BigDecimal* object equal to the current *BigDecimal* object plus *num*
`BigDecimal`	`subtract( BigDecimal num )` returns a *BigDecimal* object equal to the current *BigDecimal* object minus *num*
`BigDecimal`	`multiply( BigDecimal num )` returns a *BigDecimal* object equal to the current *BigDecimal* object times *num*

`BigDecimal` `divide( BigDecimal num )`

returns a *BigDecimal* object equal to the current *BigDecimal* object divided by *num*. Throws an *ArithmeticException*.

`int` `compareTo( BigDecimal num )`

returns 0 if the current *BigDecimal* object is equal to *num*; -1 if the current *BigDecimal* object is less than *num*; and 1 if the current *BigDecimal* object is greater than *num*.

BorderLayout

Package: java.awt

Description: a layout manager that arranges user interface components into five areas: NORTH, SOUTH, EAST, WEST, and CENTER. Each area can hold, at most, one component.

Constructors

`BorderLayout( )`

creates a border layout with no gaps between components

`BorderLayout( int hGap, int vGap )`

creates a border layout with a horizontal gap of *hGap* pixels between components and a vertical gap of *vGap* pixels between components. Unlike *GridLayout*, horizontal gaps are not placed at the left and right edges, nor are vertical gaps placed at the top and bottom edges.

BufferedWriter

Package: java.io

Description: writes text to a character output stream, using buffering for efficiency

Constructor

`BufferedWriter( Writer w )`

constructs a *BufferedWriter* object from a *Writer* object

Useful Methods of the *BufferedWriter* Class	
Return value	**Method name and argument list**
`void`	`close( )` releases the resources associated with the *BufferedWriter* object. Throws an *IOException*.
`void`	`newLine( )` writes a line separator. Throws an *IOException*.
`void`	`write( String s )` writes a *String* to the current *OutputStream* object. This method is inherited from the *Writer class*. Throws an *IOException*.

ButtonGroup

Package: javax.swing

Description: creates a mutually exclusive group of buttons

Constructor
`ButtonGroup( )` constructs a button group. Adding buttons to a *ButtonGroup* makes the buttons in the group mutually exclusive.

A Useful Method of the *ButtonGroup* Class	
Return value	**Method name and argument list**
`void`	`add( AbstractButton button )` adds the *button* to the button group. The argument can be an object of the *JButton*, *JRadioButton*, or *JCheckBox* class because these are subclasses of the *AbstractButton* class.

Color

Package: java.awt

Description: creates colors to be used in producing graphical output

Constructor
`Color( int red, int green, int blue )` instantiates a *Color* object with the combined color intensities of *red*, *green*, and *blue*. Each color intensity can range from 0 to 255.

Predefined *Color* Constants

Color Constant	Red	Green	Blue
`Color.BLACK`	0	0	0
`Color.BLUE`	0	0	255
`Color.CYAN`	0	255	255
`Color.DARK_GRAY`	64	64	64
`Color.GRAY`	128	128	128
`Color.GREEN`	0	255	0
`Color.LIGHT_GRAY`	192	192	192
`Color.MAGENTA`	255	0	255
`Color.ORANGE`	255	200	0
`Color.PINK`	255	175	175
`Color.RED`	255	0	0
`Color.WHITE`	255	255	255
`Color.YELLOW`	255	255	0

Container

Package: java.awt

Description: a user interface component that can contain other components. *JComponent* is a subclass of *Container*; thus, all *JComponents* inherit these methods.

Useful Methods of the *Container* Class

Return value	Method name and argument list
`Component`	`add( Component component )`
	adds the *component* to the container, using the rules of the layout manager. Returns *component*.
`void`	`removeAll( )`
	removes all components from the container
`void`	`setLayout( LayoutManager mgr )`
	sets the layout manager of the container to *mgr*

DecimalFormat

Package: java.text

Description: provides methods for formatting numbers for output

Constructor

`DecimalFormat( String pattern )`

instantiates a *DecimalFormat* object with the output *pattern* specified in the argument

A Useful Method of the *DecimalFormat* Class

Return value	Method name and argument list
`String`	`format( double number )`
	returns a *String* representation of *number* formatted according to the *DecimalFormat* pattern used to instantiate the object. This method is inherited from the *NumberFormat* class.

Commonly Used Pattern Symbols for a *DecimalFormat* Object

Symbol	Meaning
0	Required digit. If the value for the digit in this position is 0, insert a zero.
#	Digit. Don't insert a character if the digit is 0.
.	Decimal point
,	Comma separator
%	Multiply by 100 and display a percentage sign

Double

Package: java.lang

Description: wrapper class that creates an equivalent object from a *double* variable and provides methods for converting a *String* to a *double* primitive type and a *Double* object.

Constructor

`Double( double d )`

instantiates a *Double* object with a *double* instance variable having the same value as *d*.

Useful Methods of the *Double* Wrapper Class

Return value	Method name and argument list
`double`	`parseDouble( String s )`
	static method that converts the *String s* to a *double* and returns that value. Throws a *NumberFormatException*.
`Double`	`valueOf( String s )`
	static method that converts the *String s* to a *Double* object and returns that object. Throws a *NumberFormatException*.

Enum

Package: java.lang

Description: provides for creation of enumerated types

Useful Methods for *enum* Objects

Return value	Method name and argument list
`int`	`compareTo( Enum eObj )`
	compares two *enum* objects and returns a negative number if *this* object is less than the argument, a positive number if *this* object is greater than the argument, and 0 if the two objects are equal.
`boolean`	`equals( Object eObj )`
	returns *true* if *this* object is equal to the argument *eObj*; returns *false* otherwise.
`int`	`ordinal( )`
	returns the numeric value of the *enum* object. By default, the value of the first object in the list is 0, the value of the second object is 1, and so on.
`String`	`toString( )`
	returns the name of the *enum* constant
`Enum`	`valueOf( String enumName )`
	static method that returns the *enum* object whose name is the same as the *String* argument *enumName*.

Exception

Package: java.lang

Description: the superclass for all predefined Java exceptions. All subclasses of the *Exception* class inherit these *public* methods.

Useful Methods of *Exception* Classes	
Return value	**Method name and argument list**
`String`	`getMessage( )`
	returns a message indicating the cause of the exception. This method is inherited from the *Throwable* class.
`void`	`printStackTrace( )`
	prints the line number of the code that caused the exception, along with the sequence of method calls leading up to the exception
`String`	`toString( )`
	returns a *String* containing the exception class name and a message indicating the cause of the exception

File

Package: java.io

Description: represents platform-independent file names

Constructor

`File( String pathname )`

constructs a *File* object with the *pathname* file name so that the file name is platform-independent.

FileOutputStream

Package: java.io

Description: writes bytes to a file

Constructor

`FileOutputStream( String filename, boolean mode )`

constructs a *FileOutputStream* object from a *String* representing the name of a file; if mode is *false*, we will write to the file; if *mode* is *true*, we will append to the file. Throws a *FileNotFoundException*.

FileWriter

Package: java.io

Description: writes characters to a text file

Constructor	
`FileWriter( String fileName, boolean mode )`	constructs a *FileWriter* object from a *String* representing the name of a file; if *mode* is *false*, we will write to the file; if it is *true*, we will append to the file. Throws an *IOException*.

FlowLayout

Package: java.awt

Description: layout manager that arranges components left to right, starting a new row when a newly added component does not fit on the current row

Constructor	
`FlowLayout( )`	creates a flow layout with components centered.

Graphics

Package: java.awt

Description: represents the current graphical context, including the component on which drawing will take place and the current color.

Useful Methods of the *Graphics* Class

Return value	Method name and argument list
`void`	`clearRect( int x, int y, int width, int height )`
	draws a solid rectangle in the current background color with its top left corner at (*x*, *y*), with the specified *width* and *height* in pixels.
`void`	`drawLine( int xStart, int yStart, int xEnd, int yEnd )`
	draws a line starting at (*xStart*, *yStart*) and ending at (*xEnd*, *yEnd*)

`void` `drawOval( int x, int y, int width, int height )`

draws the outline of an oval inside an invisible rectangle with the specified *width* and *height* in pixels. The top left corner of the rectangle is (*x*, *y*).

`void` `drawRect( int x, int y, int width, int height )`

draws the outline of a rectangle with its top left corner at (*x*, *y*), with the specified *width* and *height* in pixels.

`void` `drawPolygon( Polygon p )`

draws the outline of *Polygon p*.

`void` `drawString( String s, int x, int y )`

displays the *String s*. If you were to draw an invisible rectangle around the first letter of the *String*, (*x*, *y*) would be the lower left corner of that rectangle.

`void` `fillOval( int x, int y, int width, int height )`

draws a solid oval inside an invisible rectangle with the specified *width* and *height* in pixels. The top left corner of the rectangle is (*x*, *y*).

`void` `fillRect( int x, int y, int width, int height )`

draws a solid rectangle with its top left corner at (*x*, *y*), with the specified *width* and *height* in pixels.

`void` `fillPolygon( Polygon p )`

draws the *Polygon p* and fills its area with the current color.

`void` `setColor( Color c )`

sets the current foreground color to the *Color* specified by *c*.

GridLayout

Package: java.awt

Description: a layout manager that arranges components in a grid with a fixed number of rows and columns

Constructors

`GridLayout( int numberOfRows, int numberOfColumns )`

creates a grid layout with the number of rows and columns specified by the arguments.

```
GridLayout( int numberOfRows, int numberOfColumns,
            int hGap, int vGap )
```

creates a grid layout with the specified number of rows and columns and with a horizontal gap of *hGap* pixels between columns and a vertical gap of *vGap* pixels between rows. Horizontal gaps are also placed at the left and right edges, and vertical gaps are placed at the top and bottom edges.

Integer

Package: java.lang

Description: wrapper class that creates an equivalent object for an *int* variable and provides methods for converting a *String* to an *int* primitive type and an *Integer* object

Constructor

`Integer( int i )`

instantiates an *Integer* object with an *int* instance variable having the same value as *i*.

Useful Methods of the *Integer* Wrapper Class

Return value	Method name and argument list
`int`	`parseInt( String s )`
	static method that converts the *String s* to an *int* and returns that value. Throws a *NumberFormatException*.
`Integer`	`valueOf( String s )`
	static method that converts the *String s* to an *Integer* object and returns that object. Throws a *NumberFormatException*.

ItemEvent

Package: java.awt.event

Description: contains information relating to the item event fired by a component. This event is passed to any *ItemListener* registered on the component.

Useful Methods of the *ItemEvent* Class

Return value	Method name and argument list
`Object`	`getSource( )` returns the object reference of the component that fired the event. This method is inherited from the *EventObject* class.
`int`	`getStateChange( )` If the item is selected, the value *SELECTED* is returned; if the item is deselected, the value *DESELECTED* is returned, where *SELECTED* and *DESELECTED* are *static int* constants of the *ItemEvent* class.

ItemListener Interface

Package: java.awt.event

Description: interface implemented by a class that will handle *ItemEvents* fired by a user interface component

Interface Method to be Implemented

`public void itemStateChanged( ItemEvent event )`

An event handler that implements the *ItemListener* interface writes code in this method to respond to the *ItemEvent* fired by any registered components.

JButton

Package: javax.swing

Description: a command button user interface component. When a user presses the button, an *ActionEvent* is fired.

Constructor

`JButton( String buttonLabel )`

constructs a command button labeled *buttonLabel*

A Useful Method of the *JButton* Class	
Return value	**Method name and argument list**
`void`	`addActionListener( ActionListener handler )`
	registers an event handler for *ActionEvents* on this button. This method is inherited from the *AbstractButton* class.

JCheckBox

Package: javax.swing

Description: a checkbox user interface component. When a user clicks the checkbox, its state alternates between selected and not selected. Each click fires an *ItemEvent.*

Constructors
`JCheckBox( String checkBoxLabel )`
constructs a checkbox labeled *checkBoxLabel*. By default, the checkbox is initially deselected.
`JCheckBox( String checkBoxLabel, boolean selected )`
constructs a checkbox labeled *checkBoxLabel*. If *selected* is *true*, the checkbox is initially selected; if *selected* is *false*, the checkbox is initially deselected.

Useful Methods of the *JCheckBox* Class	
Return value	**Method name and argument list**
`void`	`addItemListener( ItemListener handler )`
	registers an event handler for *ItemEvents* on this checkbox. This method is inherited from the *AbstractButton* class.
`boolean`	`isSelected( )`
	returns *true* if the checkbox is selected; *false* otherwise. This method is inherited from the *AbstractButton* class.
`void`	`setSelected( boolean state )`
	selects the checkbox if *state* is *true;* deselects the checkbox if *state* is *false*. This method is inherited from the *AbstractButton* class.

JComboBox

Package: javax.swing

Description: a drop-down list user interface component. When a user selects an item from the list, an *ItemEvent* is fired.

Constructor

`JComboBox( Object [ ] arrayName )`

constructs a new *JComboBox* component initially filled with the objects in *arrayName*. Often, the objects are *Strings*.

Useful Methods of the *JComboBox* Class

Return value	Method name and argument list
`void`	`addItemListener( ItemListener handler )` registers an event handler for *ItemEvents* on this combo box.
`int`	`getSelectedIndex( )` returns the index of the selected item. The index of the first item in the list is 0.
`void`	`setMaximumRowCount( int size )` sets the number of rows that will be visible at one time. If the list has more items than the maximum number visible at one time, scrollbars are added.
`void`	`setSelectedIndex( int index )` sets the item at *index* as selected. The index of the first item in the list is 0.

JComponent

Package: javax.swing

Description: The superclass for Swing user interface components, except for top-level components, such as *JFrame* and *JApplet*. Subclasses include *JButton, JCheckBox, JRadioButton, JList, JTextField, JTextArea, JPasswordField, JComboBox, JPanel*, and others, which inherit these *public* methods.

Useful Methods of the *JComponent* Class	
Return value	**Method name and argument list**
`void`	`addMouseListener( MouseListener handler )` registers a *MouseListener* object on the component. This method is inherited from the *Component* class.
`void`	`addMouseMotionListener( MouseMotionListener handler )` registers a *MouseMotionListener* object on the component. This method is inherited from the *Component* class.
`void`	`repaint( )` automatically forces a call to the *paint* method. This method is inherited from the *Component* class.
`void`	`setBackground( Color backColor )` sets the background color of the component to *backColor.*
`void`	`setEnabled( boolean mode )` enables the component if *mode* is *true*, disables the component if *mode* is *false.* An enabled component can respond to user interaction.
`void`	`setForeground( Color foreColor )` sets the foreground color of the component to *foreColor*.
`void`	`setOpaque( boolean mode )` sets the component's background to opaque if *mode* is *true;* sets the component's background to transparent if *mode* is *false*. If opaque, the component's background is filled with the component's background color; if transparent, the component's background is filled with the background color of the container on which it is placed. The default is transparent.
`void`	`setToolTipText( String toolTip )` sets the tool tip text to *toolTip*. When the mouse lingers over the component, the tool tip text will be displayed.
`void`	`setVisible( boolean mode )` makes the component visible if *mode* is *true;* hides the component if mode is *false*. The default is visible.

JFrame

Package: javax.swing

Description: a window user interface component

Constructors

`JFrame( )`

constructs a *JFrame* object, initially invisible, with no text in the title bar.

`JFrame( String titleBarText )`

constructs a *JFrame* object, initially invisible, with *titleBarText* displayed on the window's title bar.

Useful Methods of the *JFrame* Class

Return value	Method name and argument list
`Container`	`getContentPane( )` returns the content pane object for this window.
`void`	`setDefaultCloseOperation( int operation )` sets the default operation when the user closes this window, that is, when the user clicks on the X icon in the top-right corner of the window.
`void`	`setSize( int width, int height )` sizes the window to the specified *width* and *height* in pixels. This method is inherited from the *Component* class.
`void`	`setVisible( boolean mode )` displays this window if *mode* is *true*; hides the window if *mode* is *false*. This method is inherited from the *Component* class.

JLabel

Package: javax.swing

Description: a user interface component that displays text or an image. A *JLabel* does not fire any events.

Constructors

`JLabel( String text )`

creates a *JLabel* object that displays the specified *text*.

`JLabel( String text, int alignment )`

creates a *JLabel* object that displays the specified *text*. The *alignment* argument specifies the alignment of the text within the label component. The *alignment* value can be any of the following *static int* constants of the *SwingConstants* interface: LEFT, CENTER, RIGHT, LEADING, or TRAILING. By default, the label text is left-adjusted.

`JLabel( Icon image )`

creates a *JLabel* object that displays the *image*.

Useful Methods of the *JLabel* Class

Return value	Method name and argument list
`void`	`setIcon( Icon newIcon )` sets the *Icon* to be displayed in the label as *newIcon*.
`void`	`setText( String newText )` sets the text to be displayed in the label as *newText*.

JList

Package: javax.swing

Description: A list user interface component. When a user selects one or more items from the list, an *ItemEvent* is fired.

Constructor

`JList( Object [ ] arrayName )`

constructs a new *JList* component initially filled with the objects in *arrayName*. Often, the objects are *Strings*.

Useful Methods of the *JList* Class

Return value	Method name and argument list
`void`	`addListSelectionListener( ListSelectionListener handler )` registers an event handler for *ItemEvents* fired by this list.
`int`	`getSelectedIndex( )` returns the index of the selected item. The index of the first item in the list is 0.
`void`	`setSelectedIndex( int index )` selects the item at *index*. The index of the first item in the list is 0.
`void`	`setSelectionMode( int selectionMode )` sets the number of selections that can be made at one time. The following *static int* constants of the *ListSelectionModel* interface can be used to set the selection mode: SINGLE_SELECTION—one selection allowed SINGLE_INTERVAL_SELECTION—multiple contiguous items can be selected MULTIPLE_INTERVAL_SELECTION—multiple contiguous intervals can be selected (This is the default.)

JOptionPane

Package: javax.swing

Description: pops up an input or output dialog box

Useful Methods of the *JOptionPane* Class

Return value	Method name and argument list
`String`	`showInputDialog( Component parent, Object prompt )` *static* method that pops up an input dialog box, where *prompt* asks the user for input. Returns the characters typed by the user as a *String*.
`void`	`showMessageDialog( Component parent, Object message )` *static* method that pops up an output dialog box with *message* displayed. The *message* argument is usually a *String*.

JPasswordField

Package: javax.swing

Description: A single-line text field user interface component that allows users to enter text, such as a password, without the text being displayed. When a user presses the *Enter* key with the cursor in the field, an *ActionEvent* is fired.

Constructor	
`JPasswordField( int numberColumns )`	constructs an empty password field with the specified number of columns.

Useful Methods of the *JPasswordField* Class

Return value	Method name and argument list
`void`	`addActionListener( ActionListener handler )` registers an event handler for this password field. This method is inherited from the *JTextField* class.
`char [ ]`	`getPassword( )` returns the text entered in this password field as an array of *char*s.
`void`	`setEchoChar( char c )` sets the echo character of the password field to *c*.
`void`	`setEditable( boolean mode )` sets the properties of the password field as editable or non-editable, depending on whether *mode* is *true* or *false*. The default is editable. This method is inherited from the *JTextComponent* class.
`void`	`setText( String newText )` sets the text of the password field to *newText*. This method is inherited from the *JTextComponent* class.

JRadioButton

Package: javax.swing

Description: a radio button user interface component. When a user presses the button, other radio buttons in the *ButtonGroup* are deselected and an *ItemEvent* is fired.

Constructors

`JRadioButton( String buttonLabel )`

constructs a radio button labeled *buttonLabel*. By default, the radio button is initially deselected.

`JRadioButton( String buttonLabel, boolean selected )`

constructs a radio button labeled *buttonLabel*. If *selected* is *true*, the button is initially selected; if *selected* is *false*, the button is deselected.

Useful Methods of the *JRadioButton* Class

Return value	Method name and argument list
`void`	`addItemListener( ItemListener handler )` registers an event handler for *ItemEvents* for this radio button. This method is inherited from the *AbstractButton* class.
`boolean`	`isSelected( )` returns *true* if the radio button is selected; *false* otherwise. This method is inherited from the *AbstractButton* class.
`void`	`setSelected( boolean state )` selects the radio button if *state* is *true*; deselects the radio button if *state* is *false*. This method is inherited from the *AbstractButton* class.

JTextArea

Package: javax.swing

Description: a multi-line text field user interface component. When a user presses the *Enter* key with the cursor in the field, an *ActionEvent* is fired.

Constructors

`JTextArea( String text )`

constructs a text area initially filled with *text*.

`JTextArea( int numRows, int numColumns )`

constructs an empty text area with the number of rows and columns specified by *numRows* and *numColumns*.

`JTextArea( String text, int numRows, int numColumns )`

constructs a text area initially filled with *text*, and with the number of rows and columns specified by *numRows* and *numColumns*.

Useful Methods of the *JTextArea* Class	
Return value	**Method name and argument list**
`String`	`getText( )`
	returns the text contained in the text area. This method is inherited from the *JTextComponent* class.
`void`	`setEditable( boolean mode )`
	sets the properties of the text area as editable or non-editable, depending on whether *mode* is *true* or *false*. The default is editable. This method is inherited from the *JTextComponent* class.
`void`	`setText( String newText )`
	sets the text of the text area to *newText*. This method is inherited from the *JTextComponent* class.

JTextField

Package: javax.swing

Description: a single-line text field user interface component. When a user presses the *Enter* key with the cursor in the field, an *ActionEvent* is fired.

Constructors

`JTextField( String text, int numColumns )`

constructs a new text field initially filled with *text*, with the specified number of columns

`JTextField( int numberColumns )`

constructs an empty text field with the specified number of columns.

Useful Methods of the *JTextField* Class	
Return value	**Method name and argument list**
`void`	`addActionListener( ActionListener handler )`
	registers an event handler for *ActionEvents* fired by this text field.

`String` `getText( )`

returns the text contained in the text field. This method is inherited from the *JTextComponent* class.

`void` `setEditable( boolean mode )`

sets the properties of the text field as editable or non-editable, depending on whether *mode* is *true* or *false*. The default is editable. This method is inherited from the *JTextComponent* class.

`void` `setText( String newText )`

sets the text of the text field to *newText*. This method is inherited from the *JTextComponent* class.

ListSelectionListener Interface

Package: javax.swing.event

Description: interface implemented by a class that will handle *ListSelectionEvents* fired by a user interface component, such as a *JList*.

Interface Method to be Implemented

`public void valueChanged( ListSelectionEvent e )`

An event handler that implements the *ListSelectionListener* interface writes code in this method to respond to the *ListSelectionEvent* fired by any registered components.

Math

Package: java.lang

Description: provides methods for performing common mathematical computations. All methods are *static*.

Predefined *static* Constants

	Data type	Description
E	double	the base of the natural logarithm. Approximate value is 2.78
PI	double	pi, the ratio of the circumference of a circle to its diameter. Approximate value is 3.14.

Math Class Method Summary Note: All methods are *static.*	
Return value	**Method name and argument list**
`dataTypeOfArg`	`abs( arg )` returns the absolute value of the argument *arg*, which can be a *double*, *float*, *int,* or *long.*
`double`	`log( double a )` returns the natural logarithm (in base e) of its argument. For example, log(1) returns 0 and log(*Math.E*) returns 1.
`dataTypeOfArgs`	`max( argA, argB )` returns the larger of the two arguments. The arguments can be *doubles*, *floats*, *ints*, or *longs*.
`dataTypeOfArgs`	`min( argA, argB )` returns the smaller of the two arguments. The arguments can be *doubles*, *floats*, *ints*, or *longs*.
`double`	`pow( double base, double exp )` returns the value of *base* raised to the *exp* power
`int`	`round( float a )` returns the closest integer to its argument, *a*.
`double`	`sqrt( double a )` returns the positive square root of *a*.

MouseEvent

Package: java.awt.event

Description: object containing information relating to a mouse event generated by the user moving or dragging the mouse or clicking its buttons on a component. This event is passed to any *MouseListener* or *MouseMotion-Listener* registered on the component.

Useful Methods of the *MouseEvent* Class

Return value	Method name and argument list
`int`	`getX( )` returns the *x* value of the (*x*, *y*) coordinate of the mouse activity.
`int`	`getY( )` returns the *y* value of the (*x*, *y*) coordinate of the mouse activity.

MouseListener Interface

Package: java.awt.event

Description: interface implemented by a class that will handle *MouseEvents* (press, release, click, enter, exit).

Interface Methods to be Implemented

`public void mouseClicked( MouseEvent e )`

called when the mouse button is pressed and released on a registered component.

`public void mouseEntered( MouseEvent e )`

called when the mouse enters a registered component.

`public void mouseExited( MouseEvent e )`

called when the mouse exits a registered component.

`public void mousePressed( MouseEvent e )`

called when the mouse button is pressed on a registered component.

`public void mouseReleased( MouseEvent e )`

called when the mouse is released after being pressed on a registered component.

MouseMotionListener Interface

Package: java.awt.event

Description: Interface implemented by a class that will handle *MouseEvents* (move, drag).

Interface Methods to be Implemented

`public void mouseDragged( MouseEvent e )`

called when the mouse is dragged after its button is pressed on a registered component.

`public void mouseMoved( MouseEvent e )`

called when the mouse is moved onto a registered component.

NumberFormat

Package: java.text

Description: provides methods for formatting numbers in currency, percent, and other formats. There are no constructors for this class.

Useful Methods of the *NumberFormat* Class

Return value	Method name and argument list
`String`	`format( double number )` returns a *String* representation of *number* formatted according to the *NumberFormat* object reference used to call the method.
`NumberFormat`	`getCurrencyInstance( )` *static* method that creates a format for printing money.
`NumberFormat`	`getPercentInstance( )` *static* method that creates a format for printing a percentage.

ObjectInputStream

Package: java.io

Description: Reads serialized objects from a file.

Constructor

`ObjectInputStream( InputStream in )`

constructs an *ObjectInputStream* from the *InputStream in*.Throws an *IOException*.

A Useful Method of the *ObjectInputStream* Class

Return value	Method name and argument list
`Object`	`readObject( )`
	reads the next object and returns it. The object read must be an instance of a class that implements the *Serializable* interface. When the end of the file is reached, an *EOFException* is thrown. Also throws an *IOException* and *ClassNotFoundException*.

ObjectOutputStream

Package: java.io

Description: writes objects in a serialized format to a file

Constructor

`ObjectOutputStream( OutputStream out )`

creates an *ObjectOutputStream* that writes to the *OutputStream* *out*. Throws an *IOException*.

A Useful Method of the *ObjectOutputStream* Class

Return value	Method name and argument list
`void`	`writeObject( Object obj )`
	writes the object *obj* to a file. That object must be an instance of a class that implements the *Serializable* interface. Throws an *InvalidClassException*, *NotSerializableException*, and *IOException*.

Polygon

Package: java.awt

Description: encapsulates a polygon represented by a set of (x, y) coordinates that are the vertices of a polygon.

Constructor

`Polygon( )`

creates an empty *Polygon*.

A Useful Method of the *Polygon* Class

Return value	Method name and argument list
`void`	`addPoint( int x, int y )`
	appends the coordinate to the polygon.

PrintWriter

Package: java.io

Description: writes primitive data types and *Strings* to a text file

Constructor	
`PrintWriter( OutputStream os )`	constructs a *PrintWriter* object from the *OutputStream* object.

Useful Methods of the *PrintWriter* class

Return value	Method name and argument list
`void`	`close( )` releases the resources associated with the *PrintWriter* object.
`void`	`print( boolean b )` prints the *boolean b* to the *OutputStream*.
`void`	`print( char c )` prints the character *c* to the *OutputStream*.
`void`	`print( double d )` prints the *double d* to the *OutputStream*.
`void`	`print( int i )` prints the *int i* to the *OutputStream*.
`void`	`print( String s )` prints the *String s* to the *OutputStream*.
`void`	`println( boolean b )` prints the *boolean b* to the *OutputStream* and appends a newline.
`void`	`println( char c )` prints the character *c* to the *OutputStream* and appends a newline.
`void`	`println( double d )` prints the *double d* to the *OutputStream* and appends a newline.
`void`	`println( int i )` prints the *int i* to the *OutputStream* and appends a newline.

`void` `println( String s )`

prints the *String s* to the *OutputStream* and appends a newline.

Random

Package: java.util

Description: Generates random numbers

Constructor

`Random( )`

creates a random number generator.

A Useful Method of the *Random* Class

Return value	Method name and argument list
`int`	`nextInt ( int number )` returns a random number ranging from 0 up to, but not including, *number* in uniform distribution.

Scanner

Package: java.util

Description: provides support for reading from an input stream or file

Constructors

`Scanner( InputStream source )`

creates a *Scanner* object for reading from *source.* If *source* is *System.in*, this instantiates a *Scanner* object for reading from the Java console.

`Scanner( File source )`

creates a *Scanner* object for reading from a file. (See the *File* class.) Throws a *FileNotFoundException*.

Selected Methods of the *Scanner* Class

Return value	Method name and argument list
`void`	`close( )` releases resources associated with an open input stream.

`boolean` `hasNext( )`

returns *true* if there is another token in the input stream; *false*, otherwise.

`boolean` `hasNextBoolean( )`

returns *true* if the next token in the input stream can be read as a *boolean*; *false*, otherwise.

`boolean` `hasNextByte( )`

returns *true* if the next token in the input stream can be read as a *byte*; *false*, otherwise.

`boolean` `hasNextDouble( )`

returns *true* if the next token in the input stream can be read as a *double*; *false*, otherwise.

`boolean` `hasNextFloat( )`

returns *true* if the next token in the input stream can be read as a *float*; *false*, otherwise.

`boolean` `hasNextInt( )`

returns *true* if the next token in the input stream can be read as an *int*; *false*, otherwise.

`boolean` `hasNextLong( )`

returns *true* if the next token in the input stream can be read as a *long*; *false*, otherwise.

`boolean` `hasNextShort( )`

returns *true* if the next token can be read as a *short*; *false*, otherwise.

`String` `next( )`

returns the next token in the input stream as a *String*.

`boolean` `nextBoolean( )`

returns the next input token as a *boolean*. Throws an *InputMismatchException*.

`byte` `nextByte( )`

returns the next input token as a *byte*. Throws an *InputMismatchException*.

`double` `nextDouble( )`

returns the next input token as a *double*. Throws an *InputMismatchException*.

`float` `nextFloat( )`

returns the next input token as a *float*. Throws an *InputMismatchException*.

`int` `nextInt( )`

returns the next input token as an *int*. Throws an *InputMismatchException*.

`String` `nextLine( )`

returns the remainder of the input line as a *String*.

`long` `nextLong( )`

returns the next input token as a *long*. Throws an *InputMismatchException*.

`short` `nextShort( )`

returns the next input token as a *short*. Throws an *InputMismatchException*.

String

Package: java.lang

Description: provides support for storing, searching, and manipulating sequences of characters

Constructors

`String( String str )`

creates a *String* object with the value of *str*, which can be a *String* object or a *String* literal.

`String( )`

creates an empty *String* object.

`String( char [ ] charArray )`

creates a *String* object containing the characters in the *char* array *charArray*.

Methods	
Return value	**Method name and argument list**
`char`	`charAt( int index )` returns the character at the position specified by *index*. The first index is 0.
`int`	`compareTo( String str )` compares the value of the two *Strings*. If the *String* object is less than the argument, a negative integer is returned. If the *String* object is greater than the *String* argument, a positive number is returned; if the two *Strings* are equal, a 0 is returned.
`boolean`	`equals( Object str )` compares the value of two *Strings*. Returns *true* if *str* is a *String,* is not *null,* and is equal to the *String* object; *false* otherwise.
`boolean`	`equalsIgnoreCase( String str )` compares the value of two *Strings,* treating upper- and lowercase characters as equal. Returns *true* if the *Strings* are equal; *false* otherwise.
`int`	`indexOf( char searchChar )` returns the index of the first occurrence of *searchChar* in the *String.* Returns –1 if not found.
`int`	`indexOf( String substring )` returns the index of the first occurrence of *substring* in the *String.* Returns –1 if not found.
`int`	`length( )` returns the number of characters in the *String*.
`String`	`substring( int startIndex, int endIndex )` returns a substring of the *String* object beginning at the character at index *startIndex* and ending at the character at index (*endIndex – 1*)
`String`	`toLowerCase( )` converts all letters in the *String* to lowercase
`String`	`toUpperCase( )` converts all letters in the *String* to uppercase

StringTokenizer

Package: java.util

Description: parses a *String* into tokens using specified delimiters

Constructors	
`StringTokenizer( String str )`	constructs a *StringTokenizer* object for the specified *String* using space, tab, carriage return, newline, and form feed as the default delimiters.
`StringTokenizer( String str, String delim )`	constructs a *StringTokenizer* object for the specified *String* using *delim* as the delimiters.

Useful Methods of the *StringTokenizer* Class

Return value	Method name and argument list
`int`	`countTokens( )` returns the number of unretrieved tokens in this object; the count is decremented as tokens are retrieved.
`boolean`	`hasMoreTokens( )` returns *true* if more tokens are available to be retrieved; returns *false* otherwise.
`String`	`nextToken( )` returns the next token.

System

Package: java.lang

System.out

The *out* class constant of the *System* class is a *PrintStream* object, which represents the standard system output device. The following *PrintStream* methods can be called using the object reference **System.out** in order to print to the Java console.

Methods	
Return value	**Method name and argument list**
`void`	`print( argument )`
	prints *argument* to the standard output device. The argument is usually any primitive data type or a *String* object.
`void`	`println( argument )`
	prints *argument* to the standard output device, then prints a newline character. The argument is usually any primitive data type or a *String* object.

APPENDIX G

Solutions to Selected Exercises

1.7 Exercises, Problems, and Projects

1.7.1 Multiple Choice Exercises:

1. Java

4. servers

7. is a multiple of 4

10. C

13. *javac Hello.java*

1.7.2 Converting Numbers

16. 11000011100

19. 0x15

1.7.3 General Questions

22. 750 millions

25. red = 51; green = 171; blue = 18

28. *javac*

2.7 Exercises, Problems, and Projects

2.7.1 Multiple Choice Exercises

1. `int a;`

2.7.2 Reading and Understanding Code

4. 12.5
7. 2.0
10. 4
13. 5
16. 2.4
19. 5
22. 0

2.7.3 Fill In the Code

25.
```
boolean a;
a = false;
```

28.
```
float avg = (float) ( a + b ) / 2;
System.out.println( "The average is " + avg );
```

31. `a *= 3;`

2.7.4 Identifying Errors in Code

34. cannot assign a *double* to a *float* variable (possible loss of precision)
37. there should not be a space between – and =

2.7.5 Debugging Area—Using Messages from the Java Compiler and Java JVM

40. cannot assign a *double* to an *int* variable (possible loss of precision). Change to:
```
int a = 26;
```

43. =+ is different from += (shortcut operator). Here, *a* is assigned the value + 3. To add 3 to *a*, change the second statement to:
```
a += 3;
```

3.19 Exercises, Problems, and Projects

3.19.1 Multiple Choice Exercises

1. `import`

4. `new`

7. it is a class method

10. `double`

13. `Math.E;`

3.19.2 Reading and Understanding Code

16. hello

19. 3.141592653589793

22. 8

3.19.3 Fill In the Code

25. `System.out.println( s.length( ) );`

28.
```
System.out.print( "Welcome" );
System.out.print( "to" );
System.out.print( "Java" );
System.out.print( "Illuminated\n" );
```

31.
```
// code below assumes we have imported Scanner
Scanner scan = new Scanner( System.in );
System.out.print( "Enter two integers > " );
int i = scan.nextInt( );
int j = scan.nextInt( );
int min = Math.min( i, j );
System.out.println( "min of " + i + " and " + j + " is " + min );
```

34.
```
// code below assumes we have imported Scanner
Scanner scan = new Scanner( System.in );
System.out.print( "Enter a double > " );
double number = scan.nextDouble( );
double square = Math.pow( number, 2 );
System.out.println( number + " square = " + square );
```

3.19.4 Identifying Errors in Code

37. The Java compiler does not recognize system. It should be *System*, not system.

40. The *round* method of the *Math* class returns a *long*; a *long* cannot be assigned to a *short* variable due to a potential loss of precision.

43. The *char* 'H' cannot be assigned to the *String s*. The two data types are not compatible.

3.19.5 Debugging Area—Using Messages from the Java Compiler and Java JVM

46. Java is case sensitive. The *Math* class needs to be spelled with an upper case M.

49. In the output statement, we are just printing the value of *grade* without any formatting. To format *grade* as a percentage, the output statement should be:

```
System.out.println( "Your grade is " + percent.format( grade ) );
```

4.7 Exercises, Problems, and Projects

4.7.1 Multiple Choice Exercises

1. `java.awt`

4. true

7. the (x, y) coordinate of the upper-left corner of the rectangle we are drawing

10. 256

4.7.2 Reading and Understanding Code

13. 250 pixels

4.7.3 Fill In the Code

16. `g.setColor( Color.RED );`

19. `g.fillRect( 50, 30, 50, 270 );`

4.7.4 Identifying Errors in Code

22. There should be double quotes around the literal *Find a bug*, not single quotes. Single quotes are used for a *char*, not a *String*.

25. There is no *public color* instance variable in the *Graphics* class. The *setColor* mutator method should be used to set the color of the *Graphics* object.

4.7.5 Debugging Area—Using Messages from the Java Compiler and Java JVM

28. We are trying to override the *paint* method, which is an instance method. The header of *paint* should therefore not include the keyword *static*.

5.14 Exercises, Problems, and Projects

5.14.1 Multiple Choice Exercises

1.

❑ `a < b`	`true`
❑ `a != b`	`true`
❑ `a == 4`	`false`
❑ `( b – a ) <= 1`	`false`
❑ `Math.abs( a – b ) >= 2`	`true`
❑ `( b % 2 == 1 )`	`true`
❑ `b <= 5`	`true`

4. yes

7.

❑ `a < b || b < 10`	no
❑ `a != b && b < 10`	yes
❑ `a == 4 || b < 10`	yes
❑ `a > b && b < 10`	no

5.14.2 Reading and Understanding Code

10. *true*

13. 27 is divisible by 3
    End of sequence

16. Hello 3
    Hello 4
    Done

19. Number 3
    Number 4
    Other number

5.14.3 Fill In the Code

22.
```
if ( a )
  a = false;
else
  a = true;
```

25.
```
if ( b % c == 0 )
  a = true;
else
  a = false;
```

28.
```
if ( a && b > 10 )
  c++;
```

5.14.4 Identifying Errors in Code

31. The *&&* operator cannot be applied to two *int* operands (*a1* and *a2*).

34. We need a set of parentheses around *b1*.

37. There is no error.

5.14.5 Debugging Area—Using Messages from the Java Compiler and Java JVM

40. The expression `a = 31` evaluates to an *int*, 31. The *if* condition requires a *boolean* expression. To fix the problem, replace `a = 31` by `a == 31`.

6.14 Exercises, Problems, and Projects

6.14.1 Multiple Choice Exercises

1. the code runs forever

4. true

6.14.2 Reading and Understanding Code

7. Enter an int > 3
   Enter an int > 5
   Hello
   Enter an int > –1
   Hello

10. 8 and 42

13. 3

16. 40 and 60

19. 3
    3
    3
    3
    4

6.14.3 Fill In the Code

22.
```
System.out.print( "Enter an integer > " );
int value = scan.nextInt( );
while ( value != 20 )
{
  if ( value >= start )
    System.out.println( value );
  System.out.print( "Enter an integer > " );
  value = scan.nextInt( );
}
```

25.
```
Scanner scan = new Scanner( System.in );
word = scan.next( );
while ( ! word.equals( "end" ) )
{
  // and your code goes here
  sentence += word;
  word = scan.next( );
}
```

28.
```
Scanner scan = new Scanner( System.in );
int sum = 0;
System.out.println( "Enter an integer > " );
int value = scan.nextInt( );
while ( value != 0 && value != 100 )
```

```
{
  sum += value;
  System.out.println( "Enter an integer > " );
  value = scan.nextInt( );
}
System.out.println( "sum is " + sum );
```

6.14.4 Identifying Errors in Code

31. The variable *num* needs to be initialized after it is declared.

34. The loop is infinite. *Number* is always different from 5 or different from 7. The logical OR (||) should be changed to a logical AND (&&).

6.14.5 Debugging Area—Using Messages from the Java Compiler and Java JVM

37. It is an infinite loop; *i* should be incremented, not decremented, inside the body of the *while* loop so that the loop eventually terminates.

40. In the *for* loop header, the loop initialization statement, the loop condition, and the loop update statement should be separated by semicolons (;), not commas(,).

7.18 Exercises, Problems, and Projects

7.18.1 Multiple Choice Exercises

1. The convention is to start with an uppercase letter.

4. true

7. can be basic data types, existing Java types, or user-defined types (from user-defined classes).

10. one parameter, of the same type as the corresponding field.

13. These fields do not need to be passed as parameters to the methods because the class methods have direct access to them.

16. All of the above.

7.18.2 Reading and Understanding Code

19. *double*

22. an instance method (keyword *static* not used)

25.
```
public static void foo3( double d );
```

7.18.3 Fill In the Code

28.
```
private int grade;
private char letterGrade;
```

31.
```
public TelevisionChannel( String newName, int newNumber,
                          boolean newCable )
{
  name = newName;
  number  = newNumber;
  cable = newCable;
}
```

34.
```
public String toString( )
{
  return ( "name: " + name + "\tnumber: "
           + number + "\tcable: " + cable );
}
```

37.
```
public String typeOfChannel( )
{
  if ( cable )
    return "cable";
  else
    return "network";
}
```

7.18.4 Identifying Errors in Code

40. The *toString* method needs to return a *String*, not output data.

43. The method header is incorrect; it should be

```
public double calcTax( )
```

46. There are two errors: The assignment operator = should not be used when declaring an *enum* set. And the *enum* constant objects should not be *String* literals but identifiers.

7.18.5 Debugging Area—Using Messages from the Java Compiler and Java JVM

49. The compiler understands that *Grade* is a method since its header says it returns a *char*. It looks as if it is intended to be a constructor so the keyword *char* should be deleted from the constructor header.

52. The constructor assigns the parameter *letterGrade* to itself, therefore not changing the value of the instance variable *letterGrade*, which by default is the space character. The constructor could be recoded as follows:

```
public Grade( char newLetterGrade )
{
  letterGrade = newLetterGrade;
}
```

8.10 Exercises, Problems, and Projects

8.10.1 Multiple Choice Exercises:

1. `int [ ] a;` and `int a[ ];`
4. `0`
7. `a.length`
10. false

8.10.2 Reading and Understanding Code

13. 48.3
16. 12
    48
    65
19. 14
22. It counts how many elements in the argument array have the value 5.
25. It returns an array of *Strings* identical to the argument array except that the *Strings* are all in lower case.

8.10.3 Fill In the Code

28.
```
if ( a[i] > 20 )
  System.out.println( a[i] );
```

31.
```
System.out.println( "a[" + i + "] = " + a[i] );
```

34.
```
if ( a.length < 2 )
  return false;
else if ( a[0].equals( a[1] ) )
  return true;
else
  return false;
```

8.10.4 Identifying Errors in Code

37. Index –1 is out of bounds; the statement `System.out.println( a[-1] );` will generate a run-time exception.

40. When declaring an array, the square brackets should be empty. Replace `a[3]` by `a[ ]`.

43. Although the code compiles, it outputs the hash code of the array *a*. To output the elements of the array, we need to loop through the array elements and output them one by one.

8.10.5 Debugging Area—Using Messages from the Java Compiler and Java JVM

46. Index `a.length` is out of bounds; when *i* is equal to `a.length`, the expression `a[i]` will generate a run-time exception. Replace `<=` with `<` in the loop condition.

9.10 Exercises, Problems, and Projects

9.10.1 Multiple Choice Exercises

1. `int[ ][ ] a`; and `int a[ ][ ]`;

4. *false*

7. a[2].length

10. true

13. *java.util*

9.10.2 Reading and Understanding Code

16. 3

19. Munich
    Stuttgart
    Berlin
    Bonn

22. Munich
    Berlin
    Ottawa

25. It counts and returns the number of elements in the argument array *a*

28. It returns an *int* array of the same length as the length of the array argument *a*. Each element of the returned array stores the number of columns of the corresponding row in the array argument *a*.

31. 7 (at index 0) 45 (at index 1) 21 (at index 2)

9.10.3 Fill In the Code

34.
```
System.out.println( geo[0][5] );
```

37.
```
for ( int i = 0; i < geo.length; i++ )
{
  for ( int j = 0; j < geo[i].length; j++ )
       System.out.println( geo[i][j] );
}
```

40.
```
int count = 0;
for ( int j = 0; j < a[1].length; j++ )
{
  if ( a[1][j] == 6 )
        count++;
}
System.out.println( "# of 6s in the 2nd row: " + count );
```

43. This method returns the product of all the elements in an array.

```
public static int foo( int [ ][ ] a )
{
  int product = 1;
  for ( int i = 0; i < a.length; i++ )
  {
    for ( int j = 0; j < a[i].length; j++ )
    {
      product *= a[i][j];
    }
  }
  return product;
}
```

46.
```
System.out.println( languages.size( ) );
```

49.
```
for ( String s : languages )
{
  if ( s.charAt( 0 ) == 'P' )
    System.out.println( s );
}
```

9.10.4 Identifying Errors in Code

52. array dimension missing in `new double [ ][10]`

    Example of correct code: `double [ ][ ] a = new double [4][10];`

55. Cannot declare an *ArrayList* of a basic data type; the type needs to be a class (for example: *Double*)

58. Correct syntax is `variable = expression`; Because `a.size( )` is not a variable, we cannot assign a value to it.

9.10.5 Debugging Area—Using Messages from the Java Compiler and Java JVM

61. Other than `a[0][0]`, the first row is not taken into account because *i* is initialized to 1 in the outer loop. It should be `int i = 0;` not `int i = 1;`

64. Index 3 is out of bounds. There are only 3 elements in *a*; the last index is 2.

67. Because *ArrayList* elements begin at index 0, the statement

    ```
    a.set( 1, 'J' );
    ```

    sets the value of the second element of the *ArrayList*. To set the value of the first element, use this statement:

    ```
    a.set( 0, 'J' );
    ```

10.10 Exercises, Problems, and Projects

10.10.1 Multiple Choice Exercises:

1. a class inheriting from another class.
4. *protected* and *public* instance variables and methods.
7. You cannot instantiate an object from an *abstract* class.
10. The class must be declared *abstract*.

10.10.2 Reading and Understanding Code

13. *B* inherits from *A: name, price, foo2, foo3*

    C inherits from *B: name, price, foo1, foo2, foo3*

16. ```
    A( ) called
    B( ) called
    B version of foo1( ) called
    ```
    ```

19.
```
A( ) called
B( ) called
C( ) called
```

10.10.3 Fill In the Code

22.
```
private char middle;
public G( String f, String n, char m )
{
  super( f, n );
  middle = m;
}
```

25.
```
public class K extends F implements I
```

10.10.4 Identifying Errors in Code

28. There is no error. `new D( )` returns a *D* object reference. *D* inherits from *C*, therefore a *D* object reference "is a" *C* object reference. Thus, it can be assigned to *c2*.

31. The *foo* method does not have a method body; it must be declared *abstract*. The *K* class must be declared *abstract* as well.

10.10.5 Debugging Area—Using Messages from the Java Compiler and Java JVM

34. The instance variable *n* of class *M* is private, and is not inherited by *P*. Therefore, it is not visible inside class *P*.

11.10 Exercises, Problems, and Projects

11.10.1 Multiple Choice Exercises

1. exceptions enable programmers to attempt to recover from illegal situations and continue running the program.

4. false

7. the contents of the file, if any, will be deleted.

10. *java.util*

11.10.2 Reading and Understanding Code

13. ABCD

16. result is ABCABA

19. Nice finish

22. 0
    1
    2
    3
    4

11.10.3 Fill In the Code

25.
```
while ( st.hasMoreTokens( ) )
{
  s = st.nextToken( );

  if ( s.equals( "C" ) )
    break;
}
```

28.
```
String s = file.nextLine( );
while ( s != null )
{
  result += s + " ";
  s = file.nextLine( );
}
System.out.println( result );
```

31.
```
average += grades[i];
...
average /= grades.length;
...
pw.print( average );
pw.close( );
```

11.10.4 Identifying Errors in Code

34. the *nextToken* method returns a *String*; the return value cannot be assigned to an *int* variable.

11.10.5 Debugging Area—Using Messages from the Java Compiler and Java JVM

37. the *catch* block is missing; you need to add it after the *try* block as follows:

```
catch ( IOException ioe )
{
  ioe.printStackTrace( );
}
```

40. At each iteration, the number of tokens left in *st* is 1 less than at the previous iteration. Therefore, the *countTokens* method returns successively 6, 5, 4, 3 whereas the value of *i* is successively 0, 1, 2, and 3, at which time the *for* loop terminates. To fix the problem, assign the value of the number of tokens in *st* to a variable, and use that variable in your *for* loop header as follows:

```
int numberOfTokens = st.countTokens( );
for ( int i = 0; i < numberOfTokens; i++ )
```

12.18 Exercises, Problems, and Projects

12.18.1 Multiple Choice Exercises

1. *JTextField*

4. true

7. All three of them

10. false

13. the horizontal and vertical gaps between the 5 areas of the component

12.18.2 Reading and Understanding Code

16. 3

19. "Hello" is output to the console

22. 3

25. 5 is output to the console

12.18.3 Fill In the Code

28.
```
b = new JButton( "Button" );
```

31.
```
public void actionPerformed( ActionEvent ae )
{
  if ( ae.getSource( ) == b )
    tf.setText( "Button clicked" );
}
```

34.
```
c.add( label1, BorderLayout.NORTH );
```

37.
```
for ( int i = 0; i < buttons.length; i++ )
  p1.add( buttons[i] );
```

40.
```
for ( int i = 0; i < textfields.length; i++ )
  p2.add( textfields[i] );
```

12.18.4 Identifying Errors in Code

43. *ActionListener* is an interface; it can be implemented but not extended

12.18.5 Debugging Area—Using Messages from the Java Compiler and Java JVM

46. We are trying to add the label *l* to the content pane before *l* has been instantiated. To fix the problem, instantiate *l* before line 15 as follows:

```
l = new Jlabel( "Hello" );
```

49. *ActionListener* and *ActionEvent* need to be imported. To fix the problem, add the following *import* statement:

```
import java.awt.event.*;
```

13.10 Exercises, Problems, and Projects

13.10.1 Multiple Choice Exercises

1. may or may not be *static*
4. calls itself
7. a run-time error

13.10.2 Reading and Understanding Code

10. 0
13. 3
16. There is no output
19. *foo3* outputs the argument *String* in reverse
22. 64

13.10.3 Fill In the Code

25.
```
return foo( s.substring( 2, s.length( ) ) );
```

28.
```
if ( n >= 1000 )      // base case
  return n;
else                  // general case
  return foo( n * n );
```

13.10.4 Identifying Errors in Code

31. In the *else* clause, the *return* keyword is missing.

13.10.5 Debugging Area—Using Messages from the Java Compiler and Java JVM

34. The base case is not coded properly; it needs to return a value, not make another recursive call. Instead of *return foo(0);*, you can code *return 1;*

37. In the general case, the method makes the recursive call with the original *String* less the last two characters as the argument. Therefore, there should be two base cases: when the *String* has 0 characters (empty *String*) and when the *String* has one character. Assuming this method counts the number of characters in the *String* argument, we can add the following code after the first base case:

```
else if ( s.length( ) == 1 )
  return 1;
```

14.14 Exercises, Problems, and Projects

14.14.1 Multiple Choice Exercises

1. Linked lists are easily expanded.
4. (*7, Ajay, NFL*)
7. (*7, Ajay, NFL*) and (*5, Joe, Sonic*)
10. *front* = 3, stores 54; *back* = 0, stores 62
13. *front* = 7; *back* = 6; the list is empty

14.14.2 Reading and Understanding Code

16. If the list is not empty, it resets it to empty and returns *true*. Otherwise, it returns *false*.
19. It outputs all the *Player* objects in the list whose *game* field is *Diablo*.

14.14.3 Fill In the Code

22.
```
previous.getNext( ).setNext(
                    previous.getNext( ).getNext( ).getNext( ) );
```

25.
```
public LLNode( char newGrade )
{
  grade = newGrade;
  next = null;
}
```

28.
```
public void setGrade( char newGrade )
{
  grade = newGrade;
}
public void setNext( LLNode newNext )
{
  next = newNext;
}
```

31.
```
public int numberOfItems( )
{
  int count = 0;
  LLNode current = head;
  while ( current != null )
  {
    count++;
    current = current.getNext( );
  }
  return count;
}
```

14.14.4 Identifying Errors in Code

34. The *getID* method belongs to the *Player* class and cannot be called using *head*, a *PlayerNode* object reference.

37. The number of items in the queue would never increase and we would always be able to insert into that queue, eventually overwriting items that are in the queue. This is a logic error. Furthermore, the queue would always be considered empty since the number of items always has the value 0. We would never be able to delete an item from the queue.

14.14.5 Debugging Area—Using Messages from the Java Compiler and Java JVM

40. There is no *getHead* method in the *PlayerLinkedList* class. In order to get a copy of the *Player* object stored at the first node of the list, we can code a method returning the *Player*.

15.7 Exercises, Problems, and Projects

15.7.1 Multiple Choice Exercises

1. $O(n^2)$
4. $O(n)$
7. $n * (n + 1) / 2$
10. $O(n^2)$

15.7.2 Compute the Running Time of a Method

13. $O(n)$
16. $O(\log n)$.

Index

L

O